A-Z DEVON

CONTENTS

Key to Map Pages	2-5
Large Scale Exeter City Centre	6-7
Large Scale Plymouth City Centre	8-9
Map Pages	10-159
Road M (Refere	176
Index t	238
Index to	240

GW00672242

REFERENCE

Motorway	**M5**
Primary Route	**A30**
A Road	**A3052**
B Road	**B3212**
Dual Carriageway	
One-way Street Traffic flow on A Roads is also indicated by a heavy line on the driver's left	
Road Under Construction Opening dates are correct at the time of publication	
Proposed Road	
Restricted Access	
Pedestrianized Road	
Track / Footpath	
Residential Walkway	
Railway	Station Heritage Station Level Crossing Tunnel
Tramway	Stop
Built-up Area	MARSH RD.
Beach	
Local Authority Boundary	
National Park Boundary	
Posttown Boundary	
Postcode Boundary (within Posttown)	
Map Continuation	**20** Large Scale Centres **8** Road Map Pages **160**

Airport	
Car Park (Selected)	P
Church or Chapel	†
City Wall (Large Scale only)	
Cycleway (Selected)	
Fire Station	■
Hospital	H
House Numbers A & B Roads only	13 8
Information Centre	i
National Grid Reference	³25
Park & Ride	Honiton Road **P+R**
Police Station	▲
Post Office	★
Safety Camera with Speed Limit Fixed cameras and long term road works cameras. Symbols do not indicate camera direction.	(30)
Toilet: without facilities for the Disabled with facilities for the Disabled	▽ ▽
Viewpoint	
Educational Establishment	
Hospital or Healthcare Building	
Industrial Building	
Leisure or Recreational Facility	
Place of Interest	
Public Building	
Shopping Centre or Market	
Other Selected Buildings	

SCALE

Map Pages 10-159	Map Pages 6-9 & 124 (inset)
1:16,896 3¾ inches (9.52 cm) to 1 mile 5.9cm to 1km	1:8,448 7½ inches (19.05 cm) to 1 mile 11.8cm to 1km
0 ¼ ½ Mile	0 ⅛ ¼ Mile
0 250 500 750 Metres	0 100 200 300 400 Metres

Copyright of Geographers' A-Z Map Company Limited

Fairfield Road, Borough Green, Sevenoaks, Kent TN15 8PP
Telephone: 01732 781000 (Enquiries & Trade Sales)
01732 783422 (Retail Sales)
www.az.co.uk
Copyright © Geographers' A-Z Map Co. Ltd.
Edition 3 2012

Ordnance Survey® This product includes mapping data licensed from Ordnance Survey® with the permission of the Controller of Her Majesty's Stationery Office.

© Crown Copyright 2012. All rights reserved. Licence number 100017302

Safety camera information supplied by www.PocketGPSWorld.com
Speed Camera Location Database Copyright 2012 © PocketGPSWorld.com

Every possible care has been taken to ensure that, to the best of our knowledge, the information contained in this atlas is accurate at the date of publication. However, we cannot warrant that our work is entirely error free and whilst we would be grateful to learn of any inaccuracies, we do not accept any responsibility for loss or damage resulting from reliance on information contained in this publication.

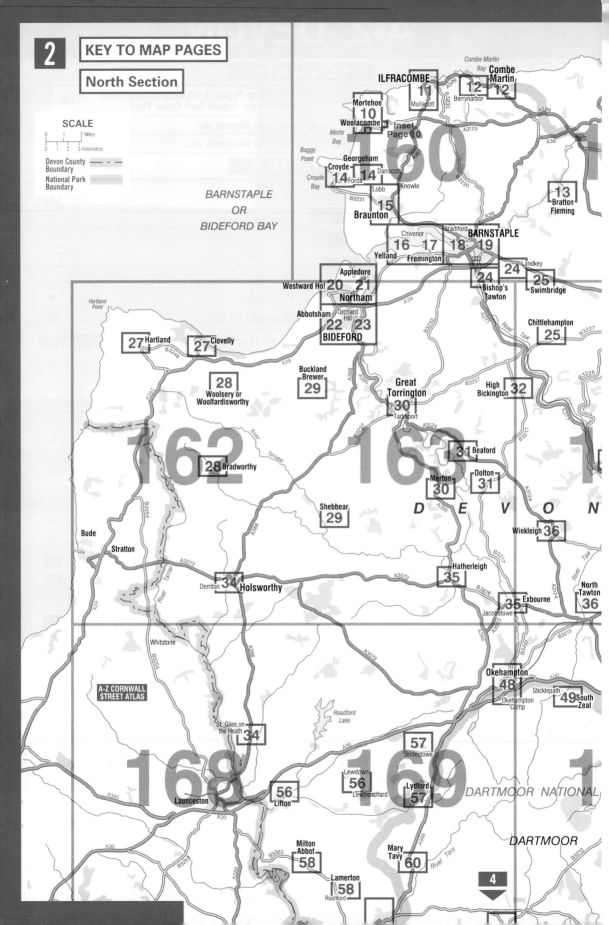

2

KEY TO MAP PAGES

North Section

SCALE

0   1   2 Miles
0   1   2   3 Kilometres

– – – Devon County Boundary

National Park Boundary

BARNSTAPLE
OR
BIDEFORD BAY

ILFRACOMBE **11**

Combe Martin Bay

Combe Martin **12**

12 Berrynarbor

Mullacott

Mortehoe **10**

Woolacombe **10**

Morte Bay

Inset Page 10

A3123

13 Bratton Fleming

Baggy Point

Georgeham

Croyde **14** **14** Darracott

14 Forda

Croyde Bay

Lobb Knowle

15 Braunton

B3231

Chivenor Bradiford

16 **17** **18** **19** BARNSTAPLE

Yelland Fremington

24 **24** Landkey

Appledore

Westward Ho! **20** **21**

Northam

24 Bishop's Tawton

25 Swimbridge

Hartland Point

Abbotsham Orchard Hill

22 **23**

BIDEFORD

Chittlehampton

25

27 Hartland

B3248

27 Clovelly

Buckland Brewer

29

Great Torrington

30

Taddiport

High Bickington **32**

28

Woolsery or Woolfardisworthy

31 Beaford

28 Bradworthy

Merton

30

Dolton

31

D E V O N

Bude

Shebbear

29

Winkleigh **36**

Stratton

Hatherleigh

35

Derriton **34** Holsworthy

North Tawton

36

35 Exbourne

Jacobstowe

Whitstone

Okehampton

48

Sticklepath

49 South Zeal

Okehampton Camp

St. Giles on the Heath **34**

Roadford Lake

57 Bridestowe

168

Lewdown

56

Lewtrenchard

Lydford

57

DARTMOOR NATIONAL

Launceston

56 Lifton

A-Z CORNWALL STREET ATLAS

DARTMOOR

Milton Abbot

58

Mary Tavy **60**

River Tavy

Lamerton

58

Rushford

4

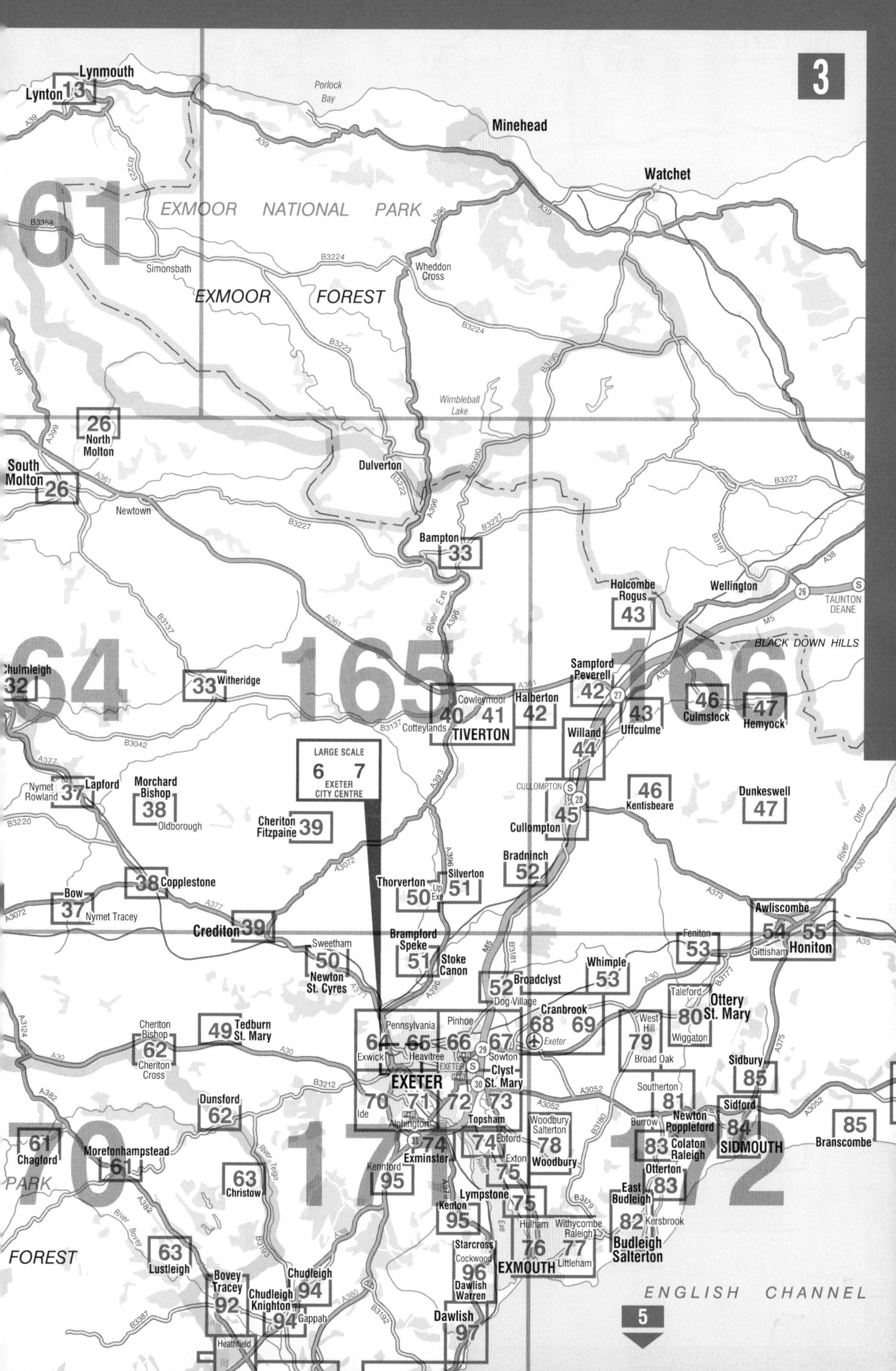

Lynmouth
Lynton
Porlock Bay
Minehead
Watchet
EXMOOR NATIONAL PARK
Simonsbath
Wheddon Cross
EXMOOR FOREST
Wimbleball Lake
North Molton
South Molton
Dulverton
Newtown
Bampton
Holcombe Rogus
Wellington
TAUNTON DEANE
BLACK DOWN HILLS
Chulmleigh
Witheridge
Sampford Peverell
Cowleymoor
Halberton
Cotteylands
TIVERTON
Willand
Uffculme
Culmstock
Hemyock
LARGE SCALE
EXETER CITY CENTRE
Kentisbeare
Dunkeswell
Nymet Rowland
Lapford
Morchard Bishop
Oldborough
Cheriton Fitzpaine
Cullompton
Bradninch
Copplestone
Thorverton
Up Exe
Silverton
Bow
Nymet Tracey
Crediton
Sweetham
Newton St. Cyres
Brampford Speke
Stoke Canon
Broadclyst
Whimple
Feniton
Awliscombe
Gittisham
Honiton
Dog Village
Cranbrook
Talefond
Ottery St. Mary
West Hill
Wiggaton
Cheriton Bishop
Cheriton Cross
Tedburn St. Mary
Pennsylvania
Pinhoe
Exwick
Heavitree
Sowton
Exeter
Clyst St. Mary
EXETER
Broad Oak
Sidbury
Southerton
Dunsford
Ide
Alphington
Topsham
Woodbury Salterton
Burrow
Newton Poppleford
Sidford
Branscombe
Chagford
Moretonhampstead
Exminster
Ebford
Colaton Raleigh
SIDMOUTH
PARK
Kenford
Christow
Exton
Woodbury
Otterton
Lympstone
East Budleigh
Kenton
Hulham
Withycombe Raleigh
Kersbrook
FOREST
Lustleigh
Starcross
Cockwood
EXMOUTH
Littleham
Budleigh Salterton
Bovey Tracey
Chudleigh
Chudleigh Knighton
Dawlish Warren
ENGLISH CHANNEL
Dawlish
Gappah
Heathfield
River Exe
River Teign
River Bovey
River Otter

5

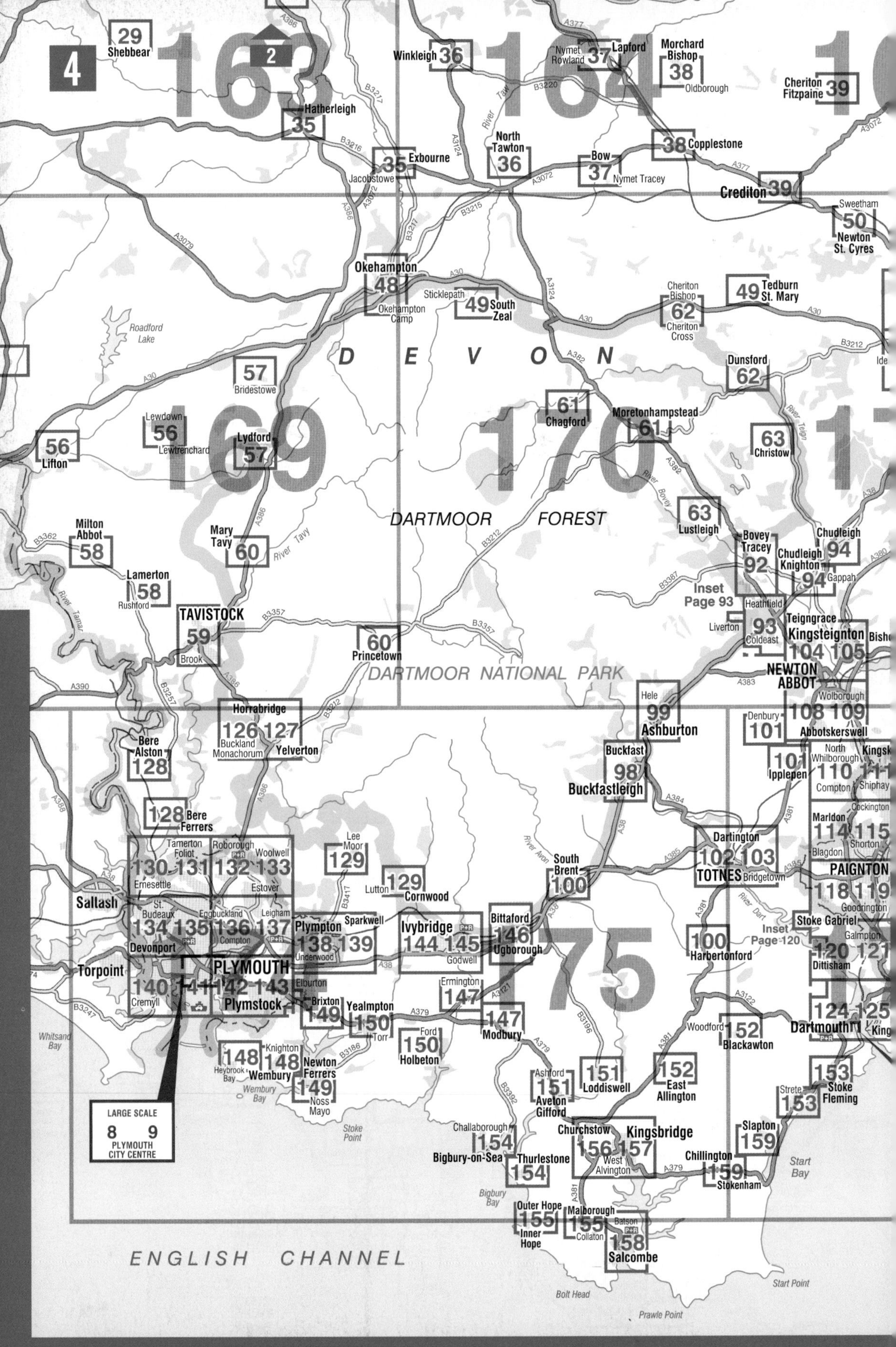

4

29 Shebbear

163

2

35 Hatherleigh

Winkleigh **36**

164

Nymet Rowland **37** Lapford

Morchard Bishop **38** Oldborough

Cheriton Fitzpaine **39**

16

35 Exbourne
Jacobstowe

North Tawton **36**

Bow **37** Nymet Tracey

38 Copplestone

A377

169

Okehampton **48**
Okehampton Camp

Sticklepath

49 South Zeal

Crediton **39**

Sweetham

50 Newton St. Cyres

D E V O N

57 Bridestowe

Cheriton Bishop **62** Cheriton Cross

49 Tedburn St. Mary

Dunsford **62**

Ide

56 Lewdown Lewtrenchard

57 Lydford

61 Chagford

Moretonhampstead **61**

Christow **63**

56 Lifton

Mary Tavy **60**
River Tavy

D A R T M O O R   F O R E S T

Lustleigh **63**

Bovey Tracey **92**

Chudleigh **94**
Chudleigh Knighton **94** Gappah

Milton Abbot **58**

Lamerton **58** Rushford

169

170

17

Inset Page 93

Heathfield

Teigngrace **93** Coldeast

Kingsteignton **104 105** Bishe

TAVISTOCK 59 Brook

60 Princetown

NEWTON ABBOT

Wolborough

Denbury **101**

108 109

D A R T M O O R   N A T I O N A L   P A R K

Hele

99 Ashburton

Horrabridge **126 127**
Buckland Monachorum Yelverton

Buckfast **98**

Buckfastleigh

Abbotskerswell

101 Ipplepen

North Whilborough **110 111** Kingsk
Compton Shiphay

Bere Alston **128**

128 Bere Ferrers

Lee Moor **129**

Marldon **114 115** Shorton
Blagdon

Cockington

PAIGNTON

Tamerton Foliot **130 131** Roborough **132 133** Woolwell
Ernesettle Estover

Lutton **129** Cornwood

South Brent **100**

Dartington **102 103** Bridgetown

TOTNES

118 119 Goodrington

Stoke Gabriel
Galmpton

Saltash

St. Budeaux **134 135** Eggbuckland **136 137** Leigham
Compton

Plympton 138 139 Sparkwell

Ivybridge 144 145 Godwell

Bittaford **146** Ugborough

100 Harbertonford

Inset Page 120

120 121 Dittisham

Torpoint

Devonport

PLYMOUTH

140 141 142 143 Plymstock

Elburton

Brixton **149**

Yealmpton **150** Torr

Ford

Ermington **147**

147 Modbury

Woodford **152** Blackawton

124 125 King

Dartmouth

Cremyll

Knighton **148 148** Newton Ferrers

Heybrook Bay Wembury

150 Holbeton

151 Loddiswell

152 East Allington

Strete **153** Stoke Fleming

153

149 Noss Mayo

Ashford **151** Aveton Gifford

Churchstow

156 157 West Alvington

Kingsbridge

Chillington

Slapton **159**

LARGE SCALE
8 9
PLYMOUTH CITY CENTRE

Challaborough **154**
Bigbury-on-Sea

Thurlestone **154**

159 Stokenham

Start Bay

Bigbury Bay

Outer Hope **155** Malborough **155** Batson Collaton

Inner Hope

158 Salcombe

Start Point

E N G L I S H   C H A N N E L

Bolt Head

Prawle Point

175

Roadford Lake

Whitsand Bay

Wembury Bay

Stoke Point

River Tamar

River Taw

River Teign

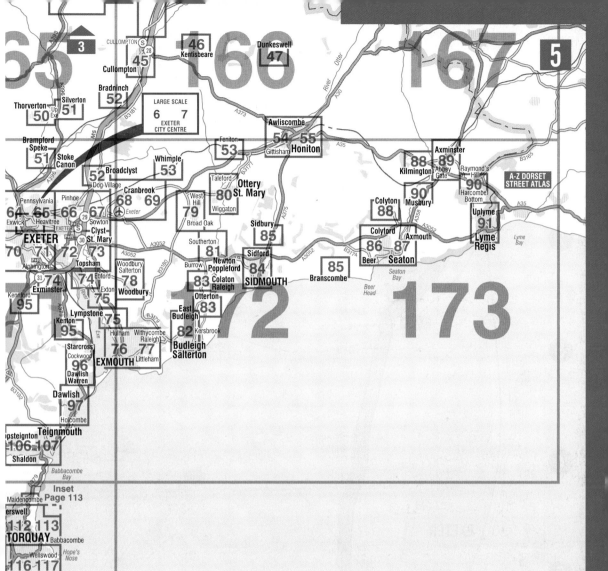

65

3

166

167

CULLOMPTON S
46 Kentisbeare
45 Cullompton
Dunkeswell 47

Bradninch
52 Silverton
51
Thorverton
50 Up Exe
A373
Awliscombe
54 55
Honiton
Gittisham

A-Z DORSET
STREET ATLAS

Brampford
Speke 51
Stoke Canon
Feniton
53
Axminster
88 89 Abbey
Kilmington Gate
Raymond's
Hill

Broadclyst
52 Dog Village
Whimple
53
Taleford
West Hill
80 Ottery St. Mary
Wiggaton
Harcombe
Bottom
Uplyme
91
Lyme Regis

Pennsylvania
Pinhoe
64 65 66 67 68 69 Cranbrook
Exwick Heavitree Sowton
79 Broad Oak
Colyton
88
Musbury
90
Colyford
86 87
Seaton
A3052

EXETER Clyst St. Mary
Sidbury
85
Southerton
81
Colyford
Axmouth
Lyme Bay

70 71 72 73
Topsham
Alphington Ebford
Woodbury Salterton
78 Woodbury
Burrow
Newton Poppleford
83 Colaton Raleigh
Sidford
84
SIDMOUTH
Beer
85
Branscombe
Seaton Bay
173

74 74 Exton
Exminster
95
Lympstone Kenton
95
Otterton
83
East Budleigh
82 Kersbrook
Budleigh Salterton
Beer Head

172

Withycombe Raleigh
76 77 Littleham
EXMOUTH

Starcross Cockwood
96 Dawlish Warren

Dawlish
97
Holcombe

Teignmouth
106 107
Shaldon

Babbacombe Bay

Inset
Page 113

112 113 Babbacombe
TORQUAY
Wellswood Hope's Nose
116 117

Tor Bay

ENGLISH CHANNEL

BRIXHAM
122 123 Berry Head
Hillhead

Inset
Page 123

Inset
Page 124
LARGE SCALE
DARTMOUTH CENTRE

LARGE SCALE
6 7
EXETER CITY CENTRE

KEY TO MAP PAGES

South Section

SCALE
0   1   2 Miles
0   1   2   3 Kilometres
Devon County Boundary
National Park Boundary

6
A
B
C
D
E
1
2
3
4
5
6
7
64
70
EXETER
EX4
EXETER ST. DAVID'S
EXETER CENTRAL
St. David's
St. Thomas
Exe Island
Mount Dinham
Friars Green
Haven Banks
Exe View Cottages
Station
Rec. Grd.
Old Bakery Cl.
Waggoners Wy.
Cowley Bridge Road
Red Cow Village
Taddyforde Ct.
Taddyforde Est.
New North Road
Streatham Rise
Streatham Dr.
Prince of Wales Rd.
Playground
Thornton
Horseguards
The Quadrangle
Highcross Rd.
Hillside
Hoopern Mews
Hoopern Valley
Taddiforde Brook
Northfield
Elmbrook
Brookfield M.
Univ. of Exeter
B3183
Velwell Road
Howell Road
Linden Vale
Castle Mount
Reservoir (covered)
Dane's Road
King Stephen Cl.
Addington Ct.
Montague Rl.
Prison La.
HMP Exeter
Blackall Road
Elm Grove Road
Bury Meadow
Woodbine T.
Hele Road
Clock Tower
Exeter College (Hele Road Cen.)
Attwill's Almshouses
Eldertree Gs.
St. Clements La.
Telford Rd.
Clayton Rd.
Isambard Pde.
Kingdom M.
Wessex Estate
Bonhay Road
Brunel Cl.
Tavistock Rd.
Play. Fld.
Play. Area
Looe Road
Point Exe.
Walnut Gs.
Montpelier Ct.
Queens Terrace
Bystock Ter.
Bystock Cl.
Church Path
Silver Ter.
Little Silver
Warehouse
Depot
Peep Lane
Shirehampton House
Belvedere Court
Richmond Road
Richmond Court
St. Michael's M.
Jubilee Court
Exeter College
Victoria Yd.
St. Wilfrid's Sch.
Sta. Yd.
Queen Street
Constantine Ho.
Marcus Ho.
Julius Ho.
Augustus Ho.
Inland Revenue
Longbrook
Northernhay Gdns.
Statue
War Mem.
Exeter Castle
Exeter Phoenix
Mus. & Art Gall.
Library
Castle St.
Bailey
Northernhay Pl.
Northernhay Sq.
Harlequins Shop. Cen.
Maddocks Row
Paul Street
Musgrave Row
Queen St.
Bradninch Pl.
Gandy St.
Market Sq.
Pancras Sq.
Guildhall
Guildhall Shopping Centre
Goldsmith St.
High Street
Catherine St.
Martins La.
Cathedral Yard
St. Johns Pl.
Princesshay
Bedford St.
Friary
Chapel
Liby.
Exeter Cathedral
The Cloisters
The Close
Deanery Pl.
Bear St.
Palace Gate
Exeter Cathedral School
Kalendarhay La.
South Street
City Bank
Broadgate
Cath. Yd.
War Meml.
Waterbeer St.
North St.
Mecca Bingo
Synagogue Pl.
St. Mary's Arches
Mary Arches St.
Mitre La.
The Catacombs
Cemetery
Burial Grd.
Bartholomew St. West
Bartholomew St. East
St. Olaves M.
Carpenter Cl.
The Mint
Priory Gs.
St. Olaves Cl.
Pickwick Arc.
Exeter Corn Exch.
St. Nicholas Priory
Tuckers Hall
Homecourt Ho.
Friernhay Ct.
Friernhay St.
All Hallows Ct.
Cin.
McCoys Arc.
Fore Street
King St.
John St.
Smythen St.
City Arc.
King St. Bus. Pk.
Market St.
George St.
Guinea St.
Stepcote Hill
West St. Mews
St. Mary Steps
Preston Street
Rack St.
Rack La.
Grendon Bldgs.
Wheatley Ct.
Mermaid Ct.
Mermaid Yd.
Tunworth Ct.
Coombe St.
James Ct.
Gatier La.
Spacex Gall.
Art Ho.
Western Wy.
Western Way
Magdalen
Holloway
Lower Coombe St.
Sub.
Southgate
Friars Ga.
Friars Wk.
St. Peters M.
Cygnet New Theatre
Water Gate
Quay Gate
Colleton
Lucky Lane
Riverside Ct.
King's Wharf
Quay Steps
Quay La.
Cricklepit
Commercial Road
Exbridge House
Exeter Foyer
Quay Hill
Quay Bri.
Quay Ho. Visitor Cen.
Weavers Ct.
Carders Ct.
Dyers Ct.
Gabriel Ct.
Fullers Ct.
Shearman Ct.
Serge Ct.
Teazle Ct.
Cricklepit Bridge
Butt's Foot Ferry
Crescent
Clipper Quay
Canal Basin
Waterside
Piazza Terracina
Terracina Ct.
Haven Banks Outdoor Education Centre
The Coolings
Exeter Tenpin
Haven Banks Retail Park
Haven Rd.
Diamond Rd.
Stream Ct.
Coney Ct.
Flowers Hay Ct.
Water Lane
Hampden Pl.
Sydney Pl.
Williams Av.
Homeclyst Ho.
Iris Av.
Painters Ct.
Greenford Villas
Chamberlain Rd.
Haven Cl.
Chandlers Wk.
Monitor Cl.
Maritime Ct.
Compass Quay
Michael Browning Way
City Industrial Estate
Colleton
Barbican Steps
Barbican Ct.
West View Ter.
Eagle Cottages
Powhay Mills
Higher Leat
St. Edmonds Ct.
Tudor Ct.
Tudor St.
Fitness First Health Club Exeter
Bonhay
River Exe
Frog St.
Trumans Ct.
Edmund St.
New Bridge St.
Renslade Ho.
Eagle Yd.
Mission Ct.
Rackclose La.
West St.
Exe Bri. Nth.
Exe Bri. Sth.
Alphington St.
Alphington Road
A377
Weir
Millers Crossing
Blackaller Weir
Dinham Road
Dinham Crescent
Dinham Mews
Lower North Street
Iron Bridge
Bridge Ct.
Bell Court
Napier Ter.
Exe Street
Haldon Road
Henrietta Pl.
Mt. Dinham Ct.
Comm. Cen.
Nth. Bri. Pl.
St. Davids Ter.
Rockside Villas
Fountain Ct.
Sch.
Flood Relief Channel
Playing Fields
Club
Sports Ground
Changing Rooms
Flowerpot
Factory
Western Road
Lynwood Av.
Emmanuel Rd.
Emmanuel Ct.
Flowerpot La.
Hayes Barton Ct.
Victoria Ct.
Okehampton Road
Okehampton St.
Okehampton Pl.
Landscore Rd.
Manor Rd.
Montgomery Prim. School
Cambridge St.
Cornwall St.
Redvers Rd.
Brunswick St.
Buller Rd.
Albion St.
Oakfield St.
Clarence Rd.
Cleveland St.
Clinton St.
Nelson Rd.
Drakes Rd.
Rugby Rd.
Maple Road
Lawrence Av.
St. Thomas Pleasure Grounds
Playgrd.
Pool
Park Vw.
Prospect Pl.
Carousel Ct.
Fishers
St. Thomas Shopping Centre
Cowick Street
St. Thomas Ct.
The Arches
Exebridge Retail Park
Riverside Leisure Centre
Gervase Av.
Shooting Marsh Stile
Great Shilhay
Ashmore Ct.
Swan Yd.
Club Wks.
B3212
Church Lane
Union St.
Cecil Rd.
Oxford Rd.
Beaufort Road
Church Rd.
Buller Ct.
Francis Cl.
Wardrew Rd.
Cowick St.
Old Vicarage Rd.
Chieftain Way
Coles M.
Sanford Rd.
Prim. Sch.
School Rd.
Adelaide Ct.
Queen's Rd.
Sydney Rd.
Regent St.
Ferndale Rd.
Powderham Rd.
West Exe Children's Centre
Churchill Road
Barton Rd.
Brewers Ct.
Willeys Av.
Scafords Rd.
Levers
John St.
Felixwell Ct.
Kingfisher

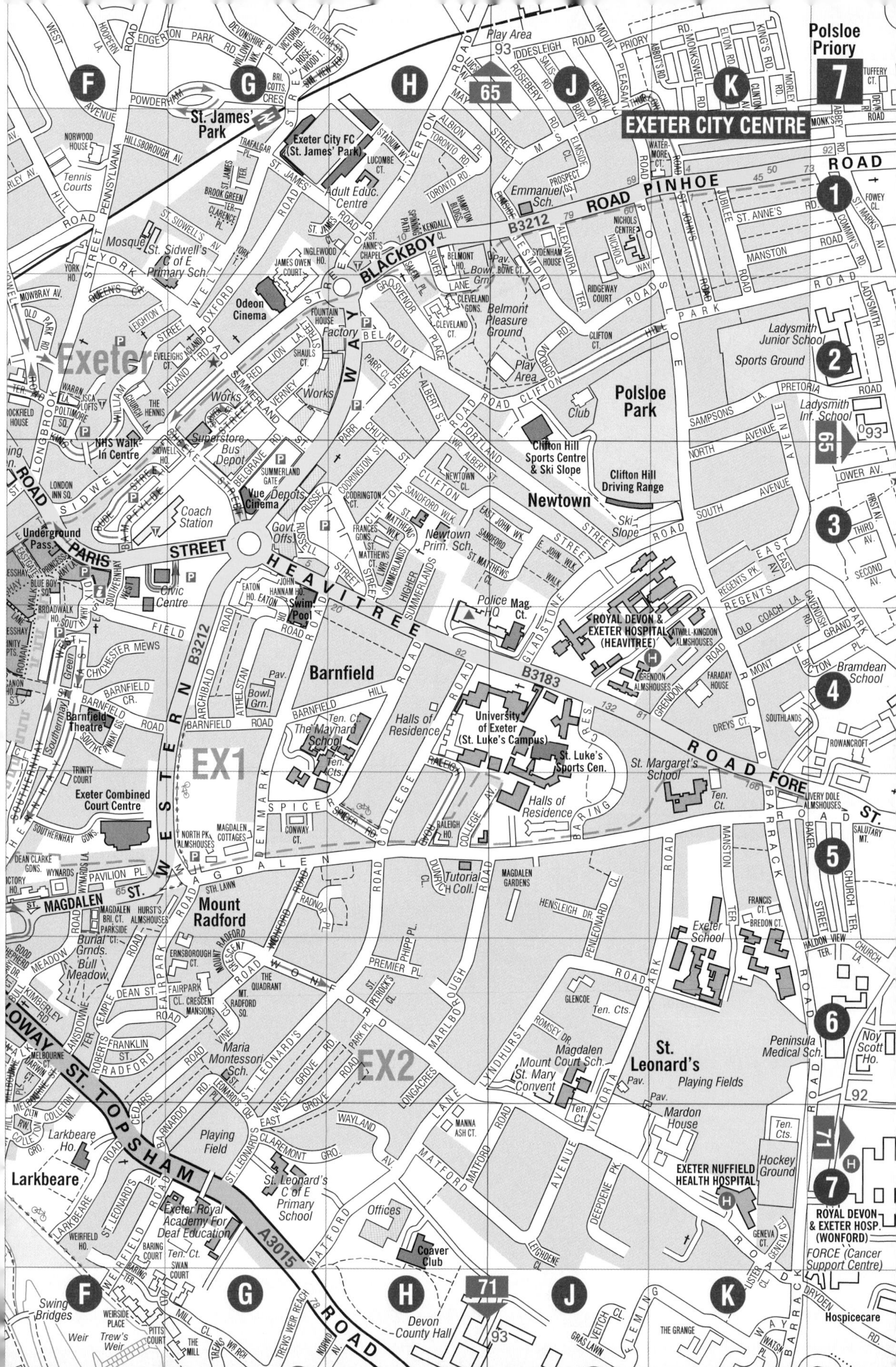

Polsloe Priory
7
EXETER CITY CENTRE
65
71
93
92
F
G
H
J
K
1
2
3
4
5
6
7
St. James' Park
Exeter City FC (St. James' Park)
Adult Educ. Centre
Mosque
St. Sidwell's C of E Primary Sch.
Odeon Cinema
Emmanuel Sch.
Exeter
Belmont Pleasure Ground
Polsloe Park
Clifton Hill Sports Centre & Ski Slope
Clifton Hill Driving Range
Newtown
Newtown Prim. Sch.
Ladysmith Junior School
Sports Ground
Ladysmith Inf. School
NHS Walk-In Centre
Superstore
Bus Depot
Vue Cinema
Depots
Coach Station
Underground Pass.
Civic Centre
Govt. Offs.
Swim Pool
Police HQ
Mag. Ct.
ROYAL DEVON & EXETER HOSPITAL (HEAVITREE)
Barnfield
Barnfield Theatre
Exeter Combined Court Centre
EX1
The Maynard School
Halls of Residence
University of Exeter (St. Luke's Campus)
St. Luke's Sports Cen.
St. Margaret's School
Bramdean School
Mount Radford
Maria Montessori Sch.
EX2
Exeter School
St. Leonard's
Playing Fields
Magdalen Mount Court Sch.
St. Mary Convent
Mardon House
Peninsula Medical Sch.
Noy Scott Ho.
Hockey Ground
EXETER NUFFIELD HEALTH HOSPITAL
ROYAL DEVON & EXETER HOSP. (WONFORD)
FORCE (Cancer Support Centre)
Hospicecare
Larkbeare
Playing Field
St. Leonard's C of E Primary School
Exeter Royal Academy For Deaf Education
Offices
Coaver Club
Devon County Hall
Swing Bridges
Weir
Trew's Weir
HEAVITREE ROAD
BLACKBOY ROAD
PINHOE ROAD
PARIS STREET
WESTERN WAY
MAGDALEN ROAD
TOPSHAM ROAD
FORE ST.
B3212
B3183
A3015

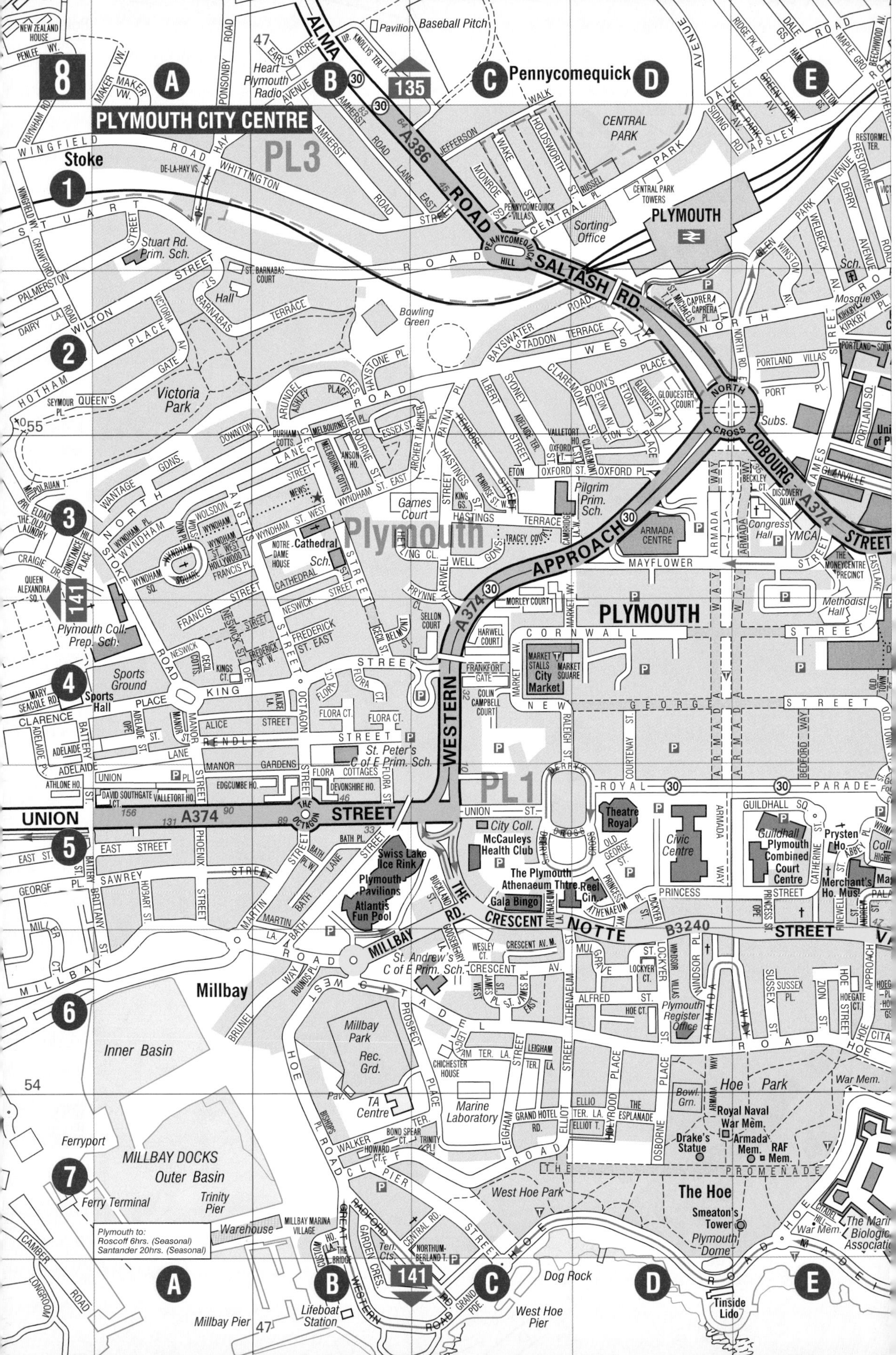

8
PLYMOUTH CITY CENTRE
PL3
PL1
Stoke
Pennycomequick
CENTRAL PARK
Plymouth
PLYMOUTH
PLYMOUTH
Millbay
MILLBAY DOCKS
Outer Basin
Inner Basin
Ferryport
Ferry Terminal
Trinity Pier
Warehouse
MILLBAY MARINA VILLAGE
Millbay Pier
Lifeboat Station
Plymouth to:
Roscoff 6hrs. (Seasonal)
Santander 20hrs. (Seasonal)
The Hoe
Hoe Park
West Hoe Park
West Hoe Pier
Dog Rock
Tinside Lido
Smeaton's Tower
Plymouth Dome
Royal Naval War Mem.
Drake's Statue
Armada Mem.
RAF Mem.
War Mem.
The Marine Biological Association
Marine Laboratory
Millbay Park Rec. Grd.
TA Centre
Victoria Park
Sports Ground
Sports Hall
Plymouth Coll. Prep. Sch.
Stuart Rd. Prim. Sch.
Cathedral
Cathedral Sch.
Games Court
Pilgrim Prim. Sch.
ARMADA CENTRE
Congress Hall
YMCA
Sorting Office
Bowling Green
Baseball Pitch
Pavilion
Heart Plymouth Radio
City Market
MARKET STALLS
MARKET SQUARE
St. Peter's C of E Prim. Sch.
St. Andrew's C of E Prim. Sch.
Swiss Lake Ice Rink
Plymouth Pavilions
Atlantis Fun Pool
City Coll.
McCauleys Health Club
The Plymouth Athenaeum Thtre.
Reel Cin.
Gala Bingo
Theatre Royal
Civic Centre
Guildhall
Plymouth Combined Court Centre
Prysten Ho.
Merchant's Ho. Mus.
Plymouth Register Office
Methodist Hall
THE MONEYCENTRE PRECINCT
Mosque
Subs.
UNION STREET
WESTERN APPROACH
SALTASH RD.
ALMA ROAD
NOTTE STREET
ROYAL PARADE
NEW GEORGE STREET
CORNWALL STREET
MAYFLOWER STREET
ARMADA WAY
COBOURG STREET
NORTH CROSS
THE CRESCENT
MILLBAY RD.
CITADEL ROAD
HOE ROAD
MADEIRA ROAD
GRAND PDE.
WESTERN ROAD
NORTH ROAD WEST
CENTRAL PARK AVENUE
A386
A374
B3240
135
141
A B C D E
1 2 3 4 5 6 7
47
54
55

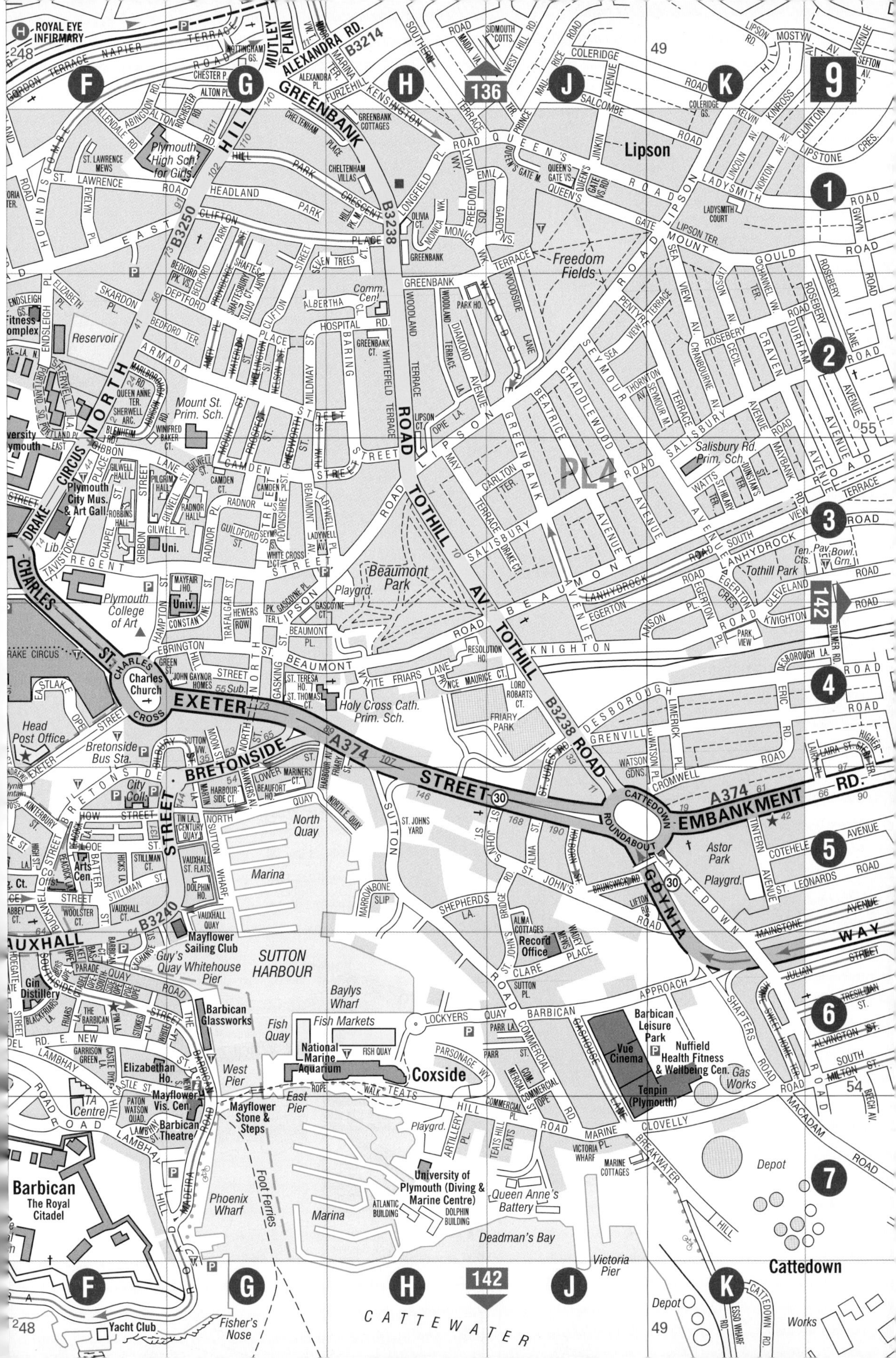

9
136
142
142
F
G
H
J
K
1
2
3
4
5
6
7
48
49
54
55
PL4
ROYAL EYE INFIRMARY
NAPIER TERRACE
GORDON TERRACE
MUTLEY PLAIN
ALEXANDRA RD.
B3214
GREENBANK
Plymouth High Sch. for Girls
NORTH HILL
B3250
CLIFTON PLACE
HEADLAND PARK
ST. LAWRENCE ROAD
HOUNDISCOMBE RD.
TORTHILL ROAD
B3238
LONGFIELD PL.
QUEEN'S ROAD
Lipson
LIPSON ROAD
MOUNT GOULD ROAD
Freedom Fields
LADYSMITH ROAD
LADYSMITH COURT
SALISBURY ROAD
Salisbury Rd. Prim. Sch.
GREENBANK AVENUE
BEAUMONT ROAD
Beaumont Park
Tothill Park
KNIGHTON ROAD
LANHYDROCK ROAD
DESBOROUGH ROAD
GRENVILLE ROAD
CROMWELL ROAD
EMBANKMENT RD.
A374
CATTEDOWN ROUNDABOUT
GDYNIA WAY
Astor Park
CATTEDOWN ROAD
Reservoir
Mount St. Prim. Sch.
ARMADA WAY
HOSPITAL RD.
Comm. Cen.
Plymouth City Mus. & Art Gall.
DRAKE CIRCUS
Uni.
Univ.
Plymouth College of Art
CHARLES ST.
Charles Church
CHARLES CROSS
EXETER STREET
BRETONSIDE
Bretonside Bus Sta.
Head Post Office
Holy Cross Cath. Prim. Sch.
FRIARY PARK
North Quay
Marina
SUTTON HARBOUR
SUTTON ROAD
ST. JOHNS YARD
City Coll.
Arts Cen.
B3240
VAUXHALL
Mayflower Sailing Club
Guy's Quay Whitehouse Pier
Gin Distillery
Barbican Glassworks
Baylys Wharf
Fish Quay
Fish Markets
National Marine Aquarium
Coxside
Record Office
CLARE PLACE
BARBICAN APPROACH
Barbican Leisure Park
Vue Cinema
Nuffield Health Fitness & Wellbeing Cen.
Tenpin (Plymouth)
Gas Works
Elizabethan Ho.
West Pier
Mayflower Vis. Cen.
Barbican Theatre
Mayflower Stone & Steps
East Pier
TA Centre
LAMBHAY HILL
MADEIRA ROAD
Barbican
The Royal Citadel
Phoenix Wharf
Foot Ferries
University of Plymouth (Diving & Marine Centre)
Queen Anne's Battery
Deadman's Bay
Victoria Pier
Depot
Cattedown
Works
Yacht Club
Fisher's Nose
CATTEWATER
MACADAM ROAD
BREAKWATER HILL
ESSO WHARF RD.

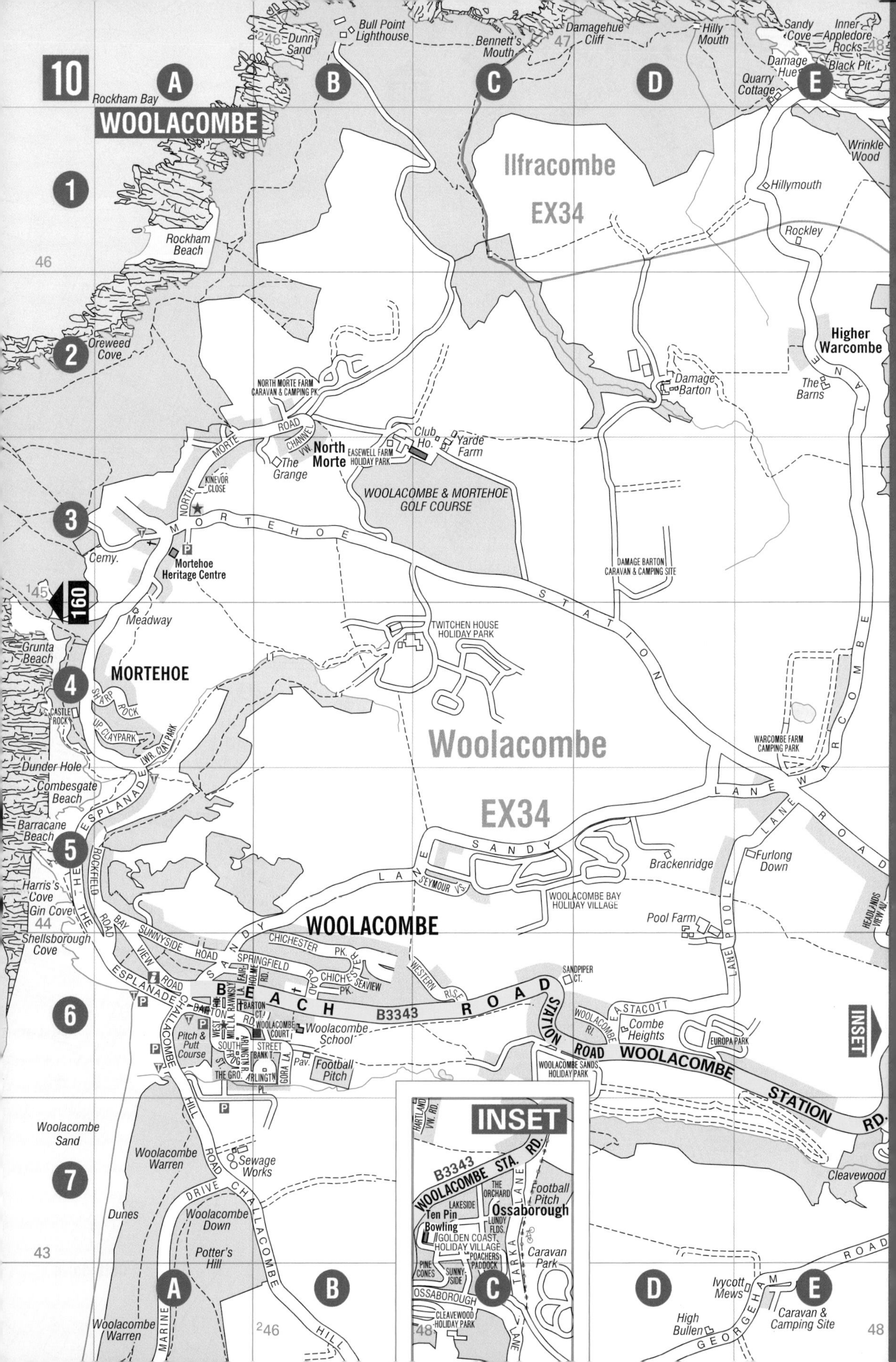
WOOLACOMBE
Rockham Bay
Bull Point Lighthouse
Dunn Sand
Bennett's Mouth
Damagehue Cliff
Hilly Mouth
Sandy Cove
Inner Appledore Rocks
Damage Hue
Black Pit
Quarry Cottage
Wrinkle Wood
Ilfracombe
EX34
Hillymouth
Rockley
Rockham Beach
Oreweed Cove
Higher Warcombe
Damage Barton
The Barns
NORTH MORTE FARM CARAVAN & CAMPING PK.
North Morte
Club Ho.
Yarde Farm
EASEWELL FARM HOLIDAY PARK
The Grange
KINEVOR CLOSE
WOOLACOMBE & MORTEHOE GOLF COURSE
MORTEHOE
Cemy.
Mortehoe Heritage Centre
DAMAGE BARTON CARAVAN & CAMPING SITE
STATION
160
Meadway
TWITCHEN HOUSE HOLIDAY PARK
Grunta Beach
MORTEHOE
CASTLE ROCK
SHARP ROCK
UP. CLAYPARK
LWR. CLAY PARK
Woolacombe
WARCOMBE FARM CAMPING PARK
Dunder Hole
Combesgate Beach
EX34
Barracane Beach
THE ESPLANADE
SANDY LANE
Brackenridge
Furlong Down
Harris's Cove
Gin Cove
Shellsborough Cove
SEYMOUR VS.
WOOLACOMBE BAY HOLIDAY VILLAGE
WOOLACOMBE
Pool Farm
HEADLANDS VIEW AV.
ROCKFIELD ROAD
BAY VIEW ROAD
SUNNYSIDE ROAD
CHICHESTER PK.
SPRINGFIELD ROAD
WESTERN RISE
SEAVIEW
SANDPIPER CT.
POOLE LANE
ESPLANADE
BEACH
B3343
ROAD
STATION ROAD
WOOLACOMBE RI.
EASTACOTT
Combe Heights
INSET
BARTON
BARTON CT.
Woolacombe School
WOOLACOMBE COURT
EUROPA PARK
Pitch & Putt Course
SOUTH ST.
BANK T.
GORA LA.
Pav.
Football Pitch
THE GRO.
ARLINGTN PL.
WOOLACOMBE SANDS HOLIDAY PARK
WOOLACOMBE STATION RD.
CHALLACOMBE HILL
Woolacombe Sand
Woolacombe Warren
Sewage Works
INSET
HARTLAND VW. RD.
B3343
WOOLACOMBE STA. RD.
THE ORCHARD
Football Pitch
LAKESIDE
Ten Pin Bowling
Ossaborough
LUNDY FLDS.
GOLDEN COAST HOLIDAY VILLAGE
TARKA LANE
POACHERS PADDOCK
Caravan Park
PINE CONES
SUNNYSIDE
OSSABOROUGH
CLEAVEWOOD HOLIDAY PARK
Cleavewood
DRIVE CHALLACOMBE
Dunes
Woolacombe Down
Potter's Hill
Ivycott Mews
Caravan & Camping Site
High Bullen
GEORGEHAM ROAD
MARINE
Woolacombe Warren
HILL

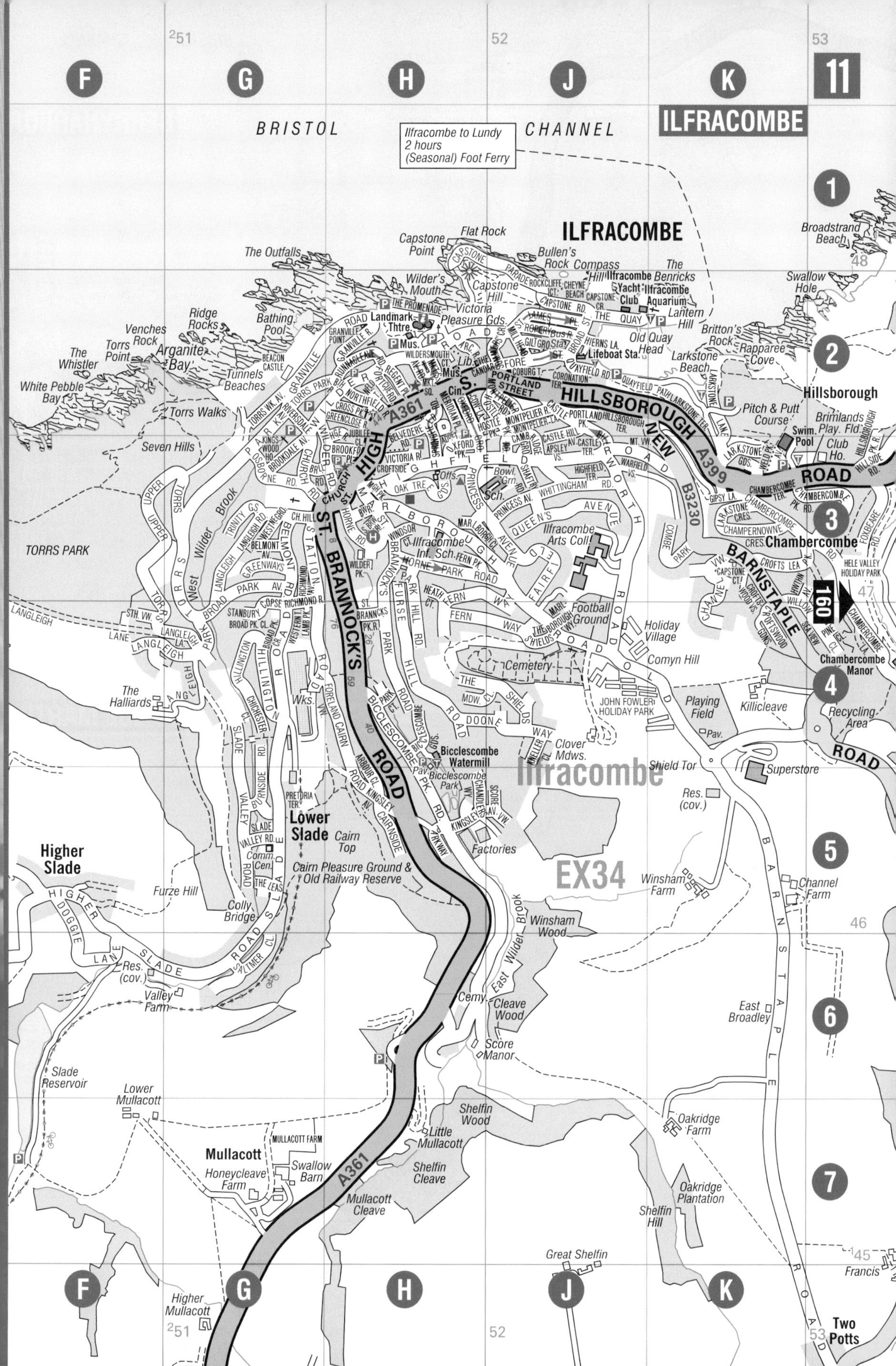
F
G
H
J
K
51
52
53
BRISTOL CHANNEL
Ilfracombe to Lundy
2 hours
(Seasonal) Foot Ferry
ILFRACOMBE
Capstone Point
Flat Rock
The Outfalls
Bullen's Rock
Compass Hill
The Benricks
Ilfracombe Yacht Club
Ilfracombe Aquarium
Lantern Hill
Wilder's Mouth
Capstone Hill
Victoria Pleasure Gds.
Landmark Thtre.
Mus.
Bathing Pool
Ridge Rocks
Venches Rock
Torrs Point
Arganite Bay
The Whistler
White Pebble Bay
Tunnels Beaches
Torrs Walks
Seven Hills
TORRS PARK
Old Quay Head
Lifeboat Sta.
Britton's Rock
Rapparee Cove
Larkstone Beach
Broadstrand Beach
Swallow Hole
Hillsborough
Pitch & Putt Course
Brimlands Play. Fld.
Swim. Pool
Club Ho.
HILLSBOROUGH ROAD
NEW ROAD
A399
B3230
A361
HIGH ST.
PORTLAND STREET
ST. BRANNOCK'S ROAD
Chambercombe
HELE VALLEY HOLIDAY PARK
160
BARNSTAPLE ROAD
Chambercombe Manor
Ilfracombe Arts Coll.
Ilfracombe Inf. Sch.
Football Ground
Holiday Village
Comyn Hill
Cemetery
JOHN FOWLER HOLIDAY PARK
Playing Field
Killicleave
Recycling Area
Superstore
Shield Tor
Res. (cov.)
Clover Mdws.
Bicclescombe Watermill
Bicclescombe Park
Factories
Ilfracombe
EX34
Winsham Farm
Channel Farm
Winsham Wood
Lower Slade
Cairn Top
Cairn Pleasure Ground & Old Railway Reserve
Wks.
The Halliards
Higher Slade
Furze Hill
Colly Bridge
HIGHER DOGGIE LANE
SLADE ROAD
Valley Farm
Cemy.
Cleave Wood
Score Manor
East Wilder Brook
West Wilder Brook
East Broadley
Slade Reservoir
Lower Mullacott
Mullacott
MULLACOTT FARM
Honeycleave Farm
Swallow Barn
Little Mullacott
Shelfin Wood
Shelfin Cleave
Mullacott Cleave
Oakridge Farm
Oakridge Plantation
Shelfin Hill
Great Shelfin
Higher Mullacott
Francis
Two Potts
1
2
3
4
5
6
7
48
47
46
45

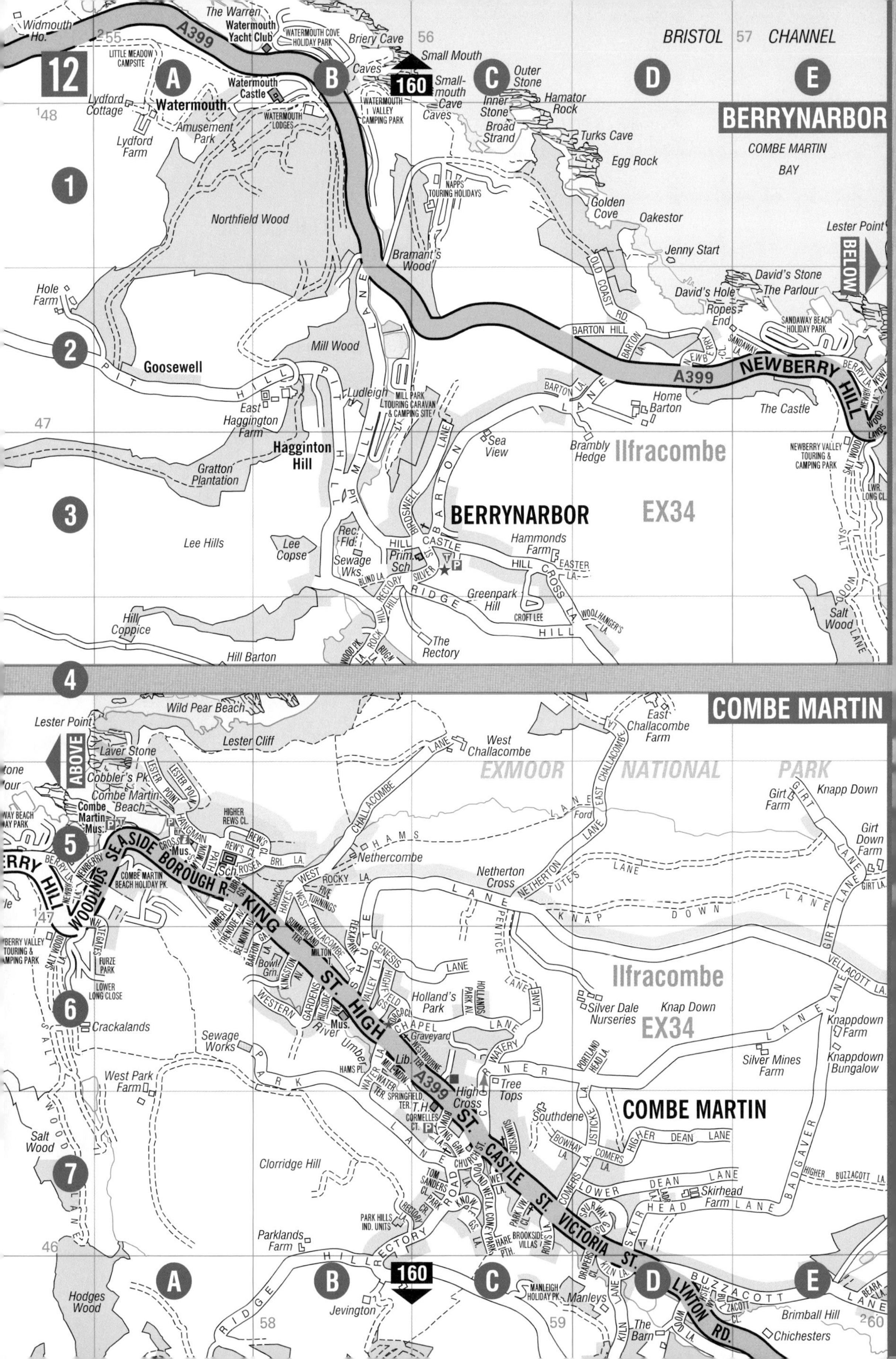
12
BERRYNARBOR
COMBE MARTIN
BRISTOL CHANNEL
COMBE MARTIN BAY
A
B
C
D
E
1
2
3
4
5
6
7
160
A399
Widmouth Ho.
The Warren
Watermouth Yacht Club
WATERMOUTH COVE HOLIDAY PARK
LITTLE MEADOW CAMPSITE
Watermouth Castle
Watermouth
Lydford Cottage
Lydford Farm
WATERMOUTH LODGES
Amusement Park
Briery Cave
Small Mouth
Caves
Small-mouth Cave
Caves
WATERMOUTH VALLEY CAMPING PARK
Outer Stone
Inner Stone
Hamator Rock
Broad Strand
Turks Cave
Egg Rock
NAPPS TOURING HOLIDAYS
Northfield Wood
Golden Cove
Oakestor
Lester Point
Jenny Start
BELOW
Bramant's Wood
OLD COAST RD
David's Stone
David's Hole
The Parlour
Ropes End
SANDAWAY BEACH HOLIDAY PARK
Hole Farm
Goosewell
Mill Wood
BARTON HILL
BARTON LA.
NEWBERRY CL.
SANDAWAY
NEWBERRY HILL
BERRY LA.
WOODLANDS
Ludleigh
MILL PARK TOURING CARAVAN & CAMPING SITE
PIT HILL
East Haggington Farm
Haggington Hill
BARTON LANE
Home Barton
The Castle
Sea View
Brambly Hedge
Ilfracombe
NEWBERRY VALLEY TOURING & CAMPING PARK
SALT WOOD LA.
LWR. LONG CL.
Gratton Plantation
BIRDSWELL LA.
ST. BARTON
EX34
Lee Hills
Lee Copse
Rec. Fld.
Sewage Wks.
Prim. Sch
CASTLE HILL
Hammonds Farm
EASTER LA.
CROSS LA.
BLIND LA.
RECTORY HILL
SILVER
RIDGE
Greenpark Hill
CROFT LEE
WOOLHANGER'S LA.
SALT WOOD LANE
Salt Wood
Hill Coppice
Hill Barton
The Rectory
ROCK HILL
Wild Pear Beach
Lester Point
Lester Cliff
ABOVE
Laver Stone
Cobbler's Pk.
LESTER POINT
LESTER POINT
Combe Martin Beach
Combe Martin Mus.
HANGMAN PATH
HIGHER REWS CL.
REW'S CL.
Mus.
Sch.
ROSEA
BRI. LA.
West Challacombe
East Challacombe Farm
EXMOOR NATIONAL PARK
CHALLACOMBE LANE
EAST CHALLACOMBE LA.
Ford
Girt Farm
Knapp Down
Girt Down Farm
SEASIDE HILL
BOROUGH R.
KING ST.
HIGH ST.
COMBE MARTIN BEACH HOLIDAY PK.
HAMS
Nethercombe
ROCKY LA.
WEST CHALLACOMBE
FIVE TURNINGS
Netherton Cross
NETHERTON LANE
TUTE'S LANE
KNAP DOWN LANE
GIRT LANE
GIRT LA.
VELLACOTT LA.
FURZE PARK
LOWER LONG CLOSE
SALT WOOD LA.
Bowl Grn.
KINGSTON AV.
SUMMERLAND TER.
MILTON
SHUTE
VALLEY LA.
GENESIS
LANE
Holland's Park
HOLLANDS PARK AV.
PENTICE LANE
WESTERN GARDENS
Crackalands
Silver Dale Nurseries
Knap Down
Knappdown Farm
Knappdown Bungalow
Silver Mines Farm
Sewage Works
River Umber
Mus.
CHAPEL LANE
Graveyard
WATERY LANE
PORTLAND HEAD LA.
CORNER LANE
West Park Farm
HAMS PL.
PARK LANE
Lib.
WESTBOURNE TER.
High Cross
Tree Tops
T.H.
CORMELLES CT.
SPRINGFIELD TER.
Southdene
COMBE MARTIN
Salt Wood
Clorridge Hill
CASTLE ST.
VICTORIA ST.
BOWHAY LA.
COMERS LA.
HIGHER DEAN LANE
BADGAVER LANE
HIGHER BUZZACOTT LA.
LOWER DEAN LANE
Skirhead Farm
HEAD LANE
CHURCH ST.
TOM SANDERS CL.
ROAD
RECTORY ROAD
KNOWLE GS.
PARK HILLS IND. UNITS
PARK VW. CL.
BROOKSIDE VILLAS
WET LA.
ROWS LA.
Parklands Farm
RIDGE HILL
RECTORY
MANLEIGH HOLIDAY PK.
Manleys
DRAPERS CL.
KILN LANE
LYNTON RD.
BUZZACOTT LANE
Brimball Hill
Chichesters
Hodges Wood
Jevington
The Barn
55
56
57
48
47
46
58
59
60

BRISTOL CHANNEL

71 272 73

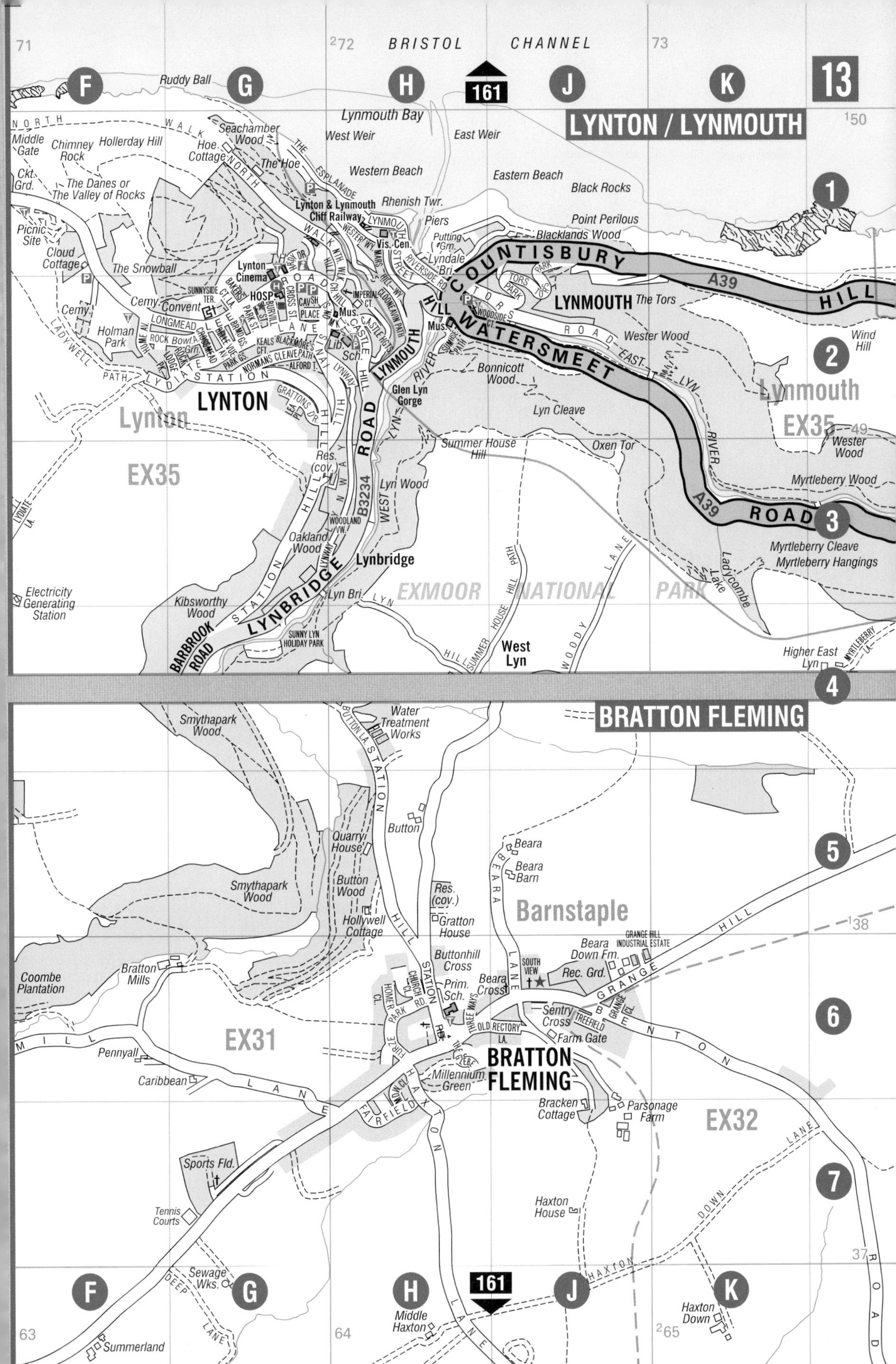

LYNTON / LYNMOUTH

Ruddy Ball
Lynmouth Bay
West Weir
East Weir
161
NORTH WALK
Middle Gate
Chimney Rock
Hollerday Hill
Hoe Cottage
Seachamber Wood
THE ESPLANADE
Western Beach
Eastern Beach
Black Rocks
1
Ckt. Grd.
The Danes or The Valley of Rocks
The Hoe
Lynmouth & Lynton Cliff Railway
Rhenish Twr.
Point Perilous
Blacklands Wood
COUNTISBURY HILL
A39
Picnic Site
Cloud Cottage
The Snowball
Lynton Cinema
NORTH WALK NTH WALK WESTER WAY
Vis. Cen.
Piers
Putting Grn.
Lyndale Bri.
TORS PARK
WATERSMEET
LYNMOUTH
The Tors
Wind Hill
2
Cemy.
Convent
HOSP
P P P
Mus.
Lib.
Wester Wood
Lynmouth
EX35
49
Wester Wood
Holman Park
LONGMEAD
ROCK
Bowl.
KEALS
BLACKMORES
NORMANS CLEAVE PATH
ALFORD T.
Glen Lyn Gorge
Bonnicott Wood
RIVER EAST LYN
RIVER LYN
Myrtleberry Wood
3
LADYWELL PATH
LYDIATE LA.
Lynton
EX35
B3234
Res. (cov.)
Lyn Wood
Summer House Hill
Lyn Cleave
Oxen Tor
Lacycombe Lake
Myrtleberry Cleave
Myrtleberry Hangings
Electricity Generating Station
Kibsworthy Wood
Oakland Wood
WOODLAND VW.
WEST HILL
Lynbridge
Lyn Bri.
RIVER LYN
SUMMER HOUSE HILL PATH
WOODY LANE
West Lyn
Higher East Lyn
MYRTLEBERRY
4
BARBROOK ROAD
LYNBRIDGE
STATION ROAD
SUNNY LYN HOLIDAY PARK
EXMOOR NATIONAL PARK

Smythapark Wood
Water Treatment Works
STATION LANE
BUTTON LA.
Quarry House
Button
Beara
BEARA LANE
Beara Barn
5
138
Smythapark Wood
Button Wood
Res. (cov.)
Gratton House
Barnstaple
Beara Down Fm.
GRANGE HILL INDUSTRIAL ESTATE
Rec. Grd.
GRANGE HILL
6
Coombe Plantation
Bratton Mills
MILL LANE
HILL
Hollywell Cottage
Buttonhill Cross
CHURCH
Prim. Sch.
HOMER WAY
PARK RD.
Beara Cross
SOUTH VIEW
Sentry Cross
Farm Gate
TREEFIELD
GRANGE CL.
BRENTON LANE
EX31
Pennyall
Caribbean
FAIRFIELD
THREE WAYS
OLD RECTORY LA.
BRATTON FLEMING
Millennium Green
Bracken Cottage
Parsonage Farm
EX32
7
HAXTON
Sports Fld.
DEEP LANE
Tennis Courts
Sewage Wks.
Haxton House
HAXTON DOWN LANE
DOWN ROAD
37
Summerland
Middle Haxton
Haxton Down
63 64 265

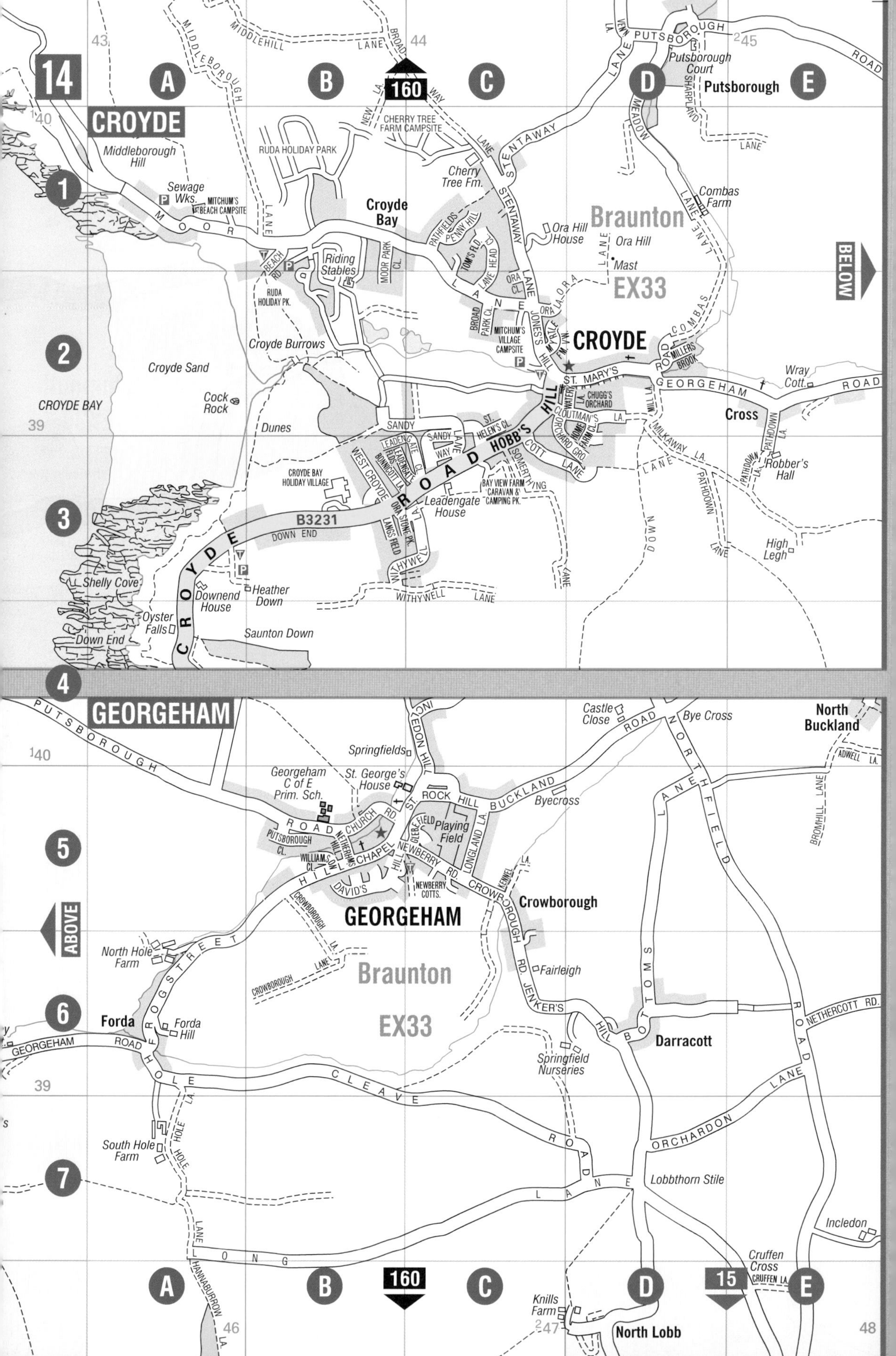
CROYDE
GEORGEHAM
Middleborough Hill
Sewage Wks.
MITCHUM'S BEACH CAMPSITE
RUDA HOLIDAY PARK
CHERRY TREE FARM CAMPSITE
Cherry Tree Fm.
Croyde Bay
Riding Stables
RUDA HOLIDAY PK.
Croyde Burrows
Croyde Sand
CROYDE BAY
Cock Rock
Dunes
CROYDE BAY HOLIDAY VILLAGE
Leadengate House
BAY VIEW FARM CARAVAN & CAMPING PK.
MITCHUM'S VILLAGE CAMPSITE
CROYDE
Braunton
EX33
Ora Hill House
Ora Hill
Mast
Putsborough Court
Putsborough
Combas Farm
Wray Cott.
Cross
Robber's Hall
High Legh
Shelly Cove
Downend House
Heather Down
Oyster Falls
Down End
Saunton Down
B3231
MOOR LANE
CROYDE ROAD
HOBB'S HILL
ST. MARY'S ROAD
GEORGEHAM ROAD
STENTAWAY LANE
Springfields
Georgeham C of E Prim. Sch.
St. George's House
Playing Field
Byecross
Castle Close
Bye Cross
North Buckland
Crowborough
North Hole Farm
Forda
Forda Hill
Fairleigh
Darracott
Springfield Nurseries
South Hole Farm
Lobbthorn Stile
Incledon
Cruffen Cross
Knills Farm
North Lobb
PUTSBOROUGH ROAD
CLEAVE ROAD
LONG LANE
ORCHARDON LANE
NETHERCOTT RD.
NORTHFIELD ROAD
BOTTOMS LANE
FROGSTREET
HOLE LA.
HANNABURROW LA.
BELOW
ABOVE
160
15

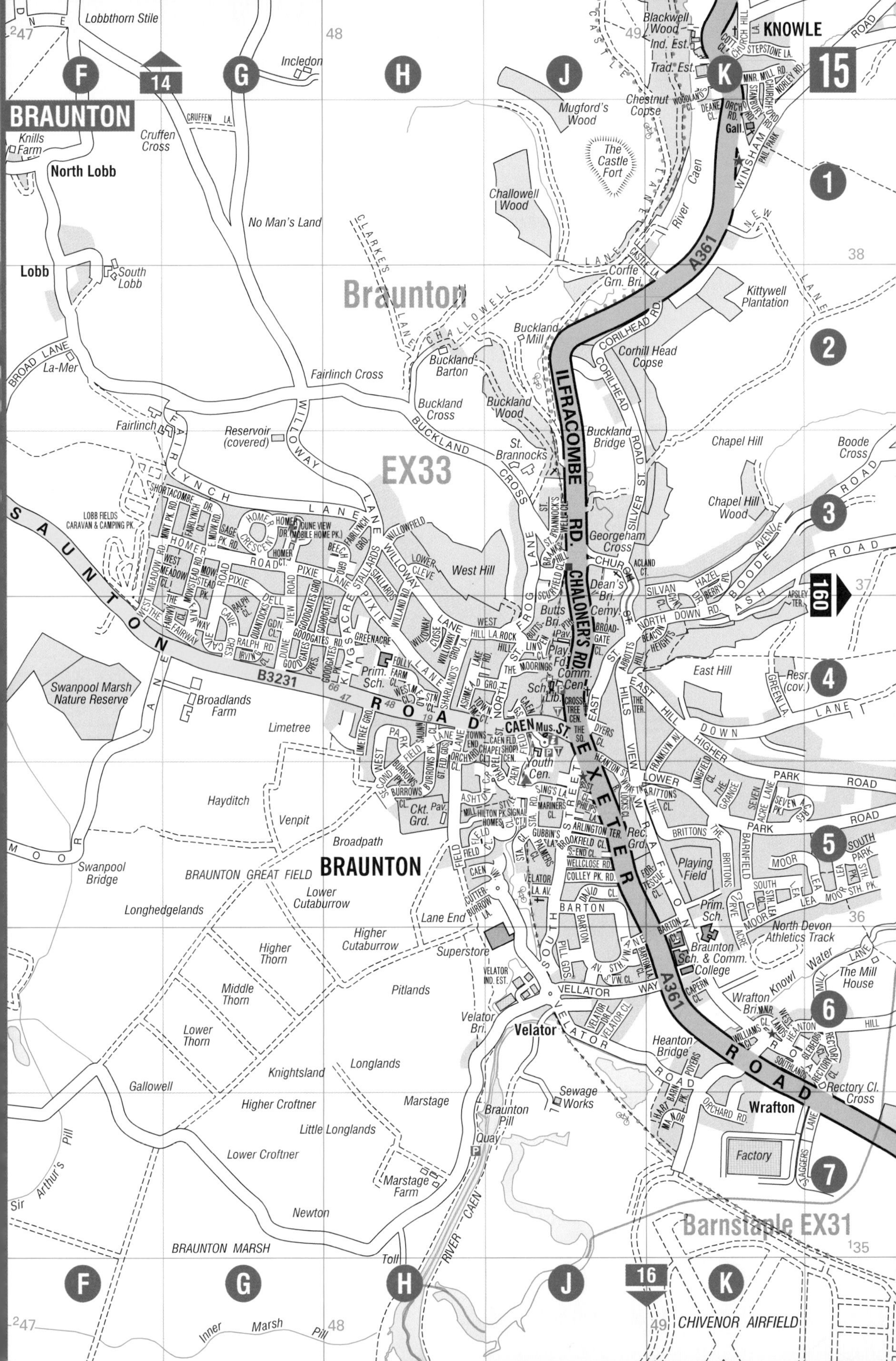

BRAUNTON
Lobbthorn Stile
Incledon
KNOWLE
Blackwell Wood
Ind. Est.
Trad. Est.
Knills Farm
North Lobb
Cruffen Cross
Mugford's Wood
Chestnut Copse
The Castle Fort
Challowell Wood
No Man's Land
Lobb
South Lobb
Braunton
Corffe Grn. Bri.
Kittywell Plantation
Buckland Mill
Buckland Barton
Corhill Head Copse
La-Mer
Fairlinch Cross
Buckland Cross
Buckland Wood
Fairlinch
Reservoir (covered)
St. Brannocks
Buckland Bridge
Chapel Hill
Boode Cross
EX33
Chapel Hill Wood
LOBB FIELDS CARAVAN & CAMPING PK.
West Hill
Georgeham Cross
ILFRACOMBE RD.
CHALONER'S RD.
SAUNTON ROAD
B3231
A361
Swanpool Marsh Nature Reserve
Broadlands Farm
Prim. Sch.
East Hill
Resr. (cov.)
Limetree
Youth Cen.
Haydith
Venpit
Broadpath
Ckt. Grd.
Rec. Grd.
Playing Field
BRAUNTON GREAT FIELD
BRAUNTON
Swanpool Bridge
Lower Cutaburrow
Longhedgelands
Lane End
Higher Cutaburrow
North Devon Athletics Track
Higher Thorn
Superstore
Braunton Sch. & Comm. College
The Mill House
Middle Thorn
Pitlands
Wrafton Bri.
Lower Thorn
Velator Bri.
Velator
Heanton Bridge
Knightsland
Longlands
Gallowell
Sewage Works
Rectory Cl. Cross
Higher Croftner
Marstage
Braunton Pill
Wrafton
Little Longlands
Quay
Factory
Lower Croftner
Marstage Farm
Newton
Barnstaple EX31
BRAUNTON MARSH
Toll
RIVER CAEN
Inner Marsh Pill
CHIVENOR AIRFIELD
Sir Arthur's Pill
14
16
160

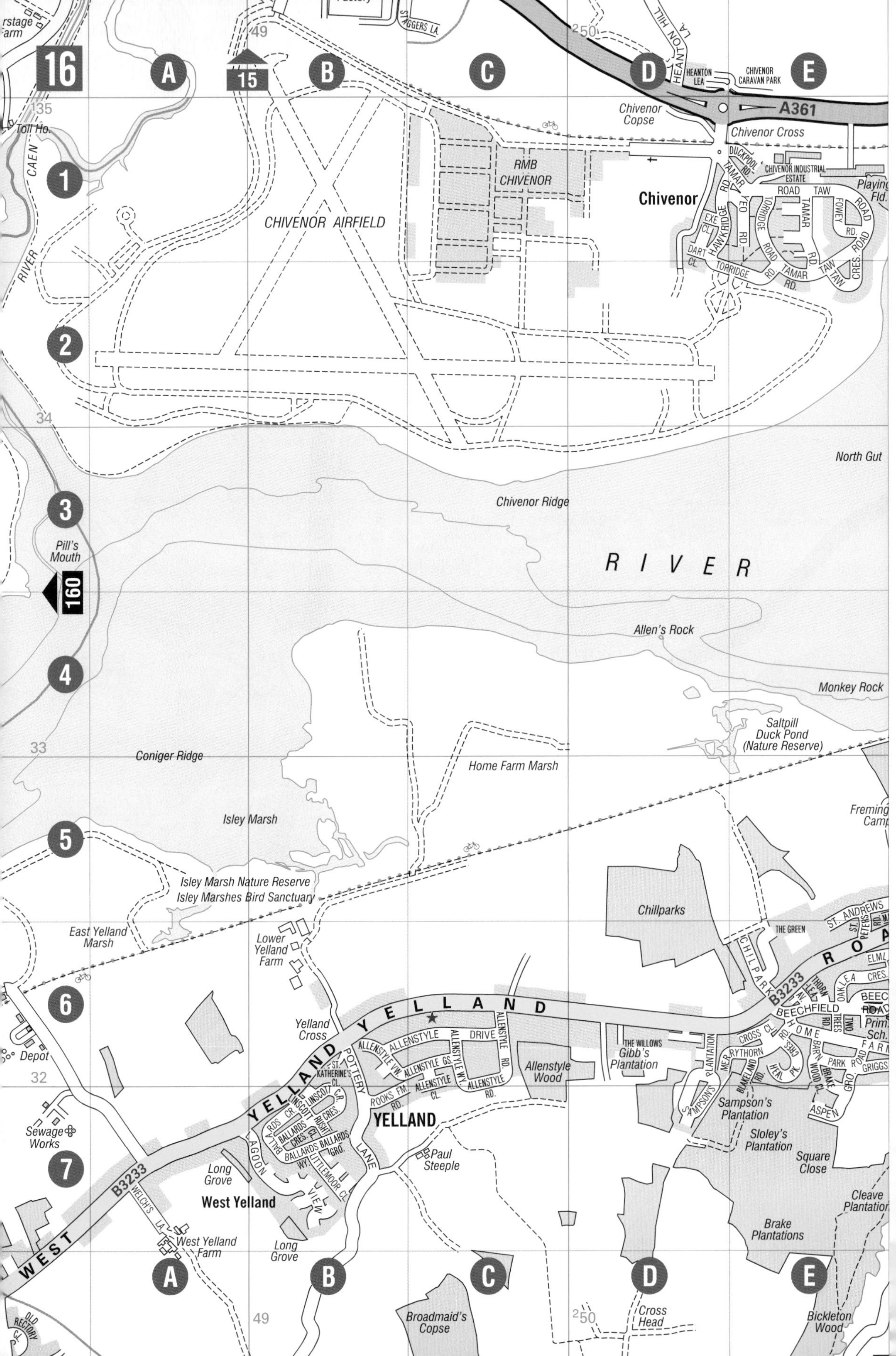

A
B
C
D
E
15
1
2
3
4
5
6
7
160
CHIVENOR AIRFIELD
RMB CHIVENOR
Chivenor
Chivenor Copse
Chivenor Cross
A361
HEANTON LEA
CHIVENOR CARAVAN PARK
HEANTON LA
CHIVENOR INDUSTRIAL ESTATE
Toll Ho.
CAEN
RIVER
Chivenor Ridge
RIVER
North Gut
Pill's Mouth
Allen's Rock
Monkey Rock
Saltpill Duck Pond (Nature Reserve)
Coniger Ridge
Home Farm Marsh
Isley Marsh
Isley Marsh Nature Reserve
Isley Marshes Bird Sanctuary
East Yelland Marsh
Lower Yelland Farm
Chillparks
Yelland Cross
YELLAND
YELLAND
West Yelland
Long Grove
Depot
Sewage Works
B3233
WEST
West Yelland Farm
Paul Steeple
Broadmaid's Copse
Cross Head
Allenstyle Wood
Gibb's Plantation
Sampson's Plantation
Sloley's Plantation
Square Close
Brake Plantations
Cleave Plantation
Bickleton Wood
THE GREEN
THE WILLOWS

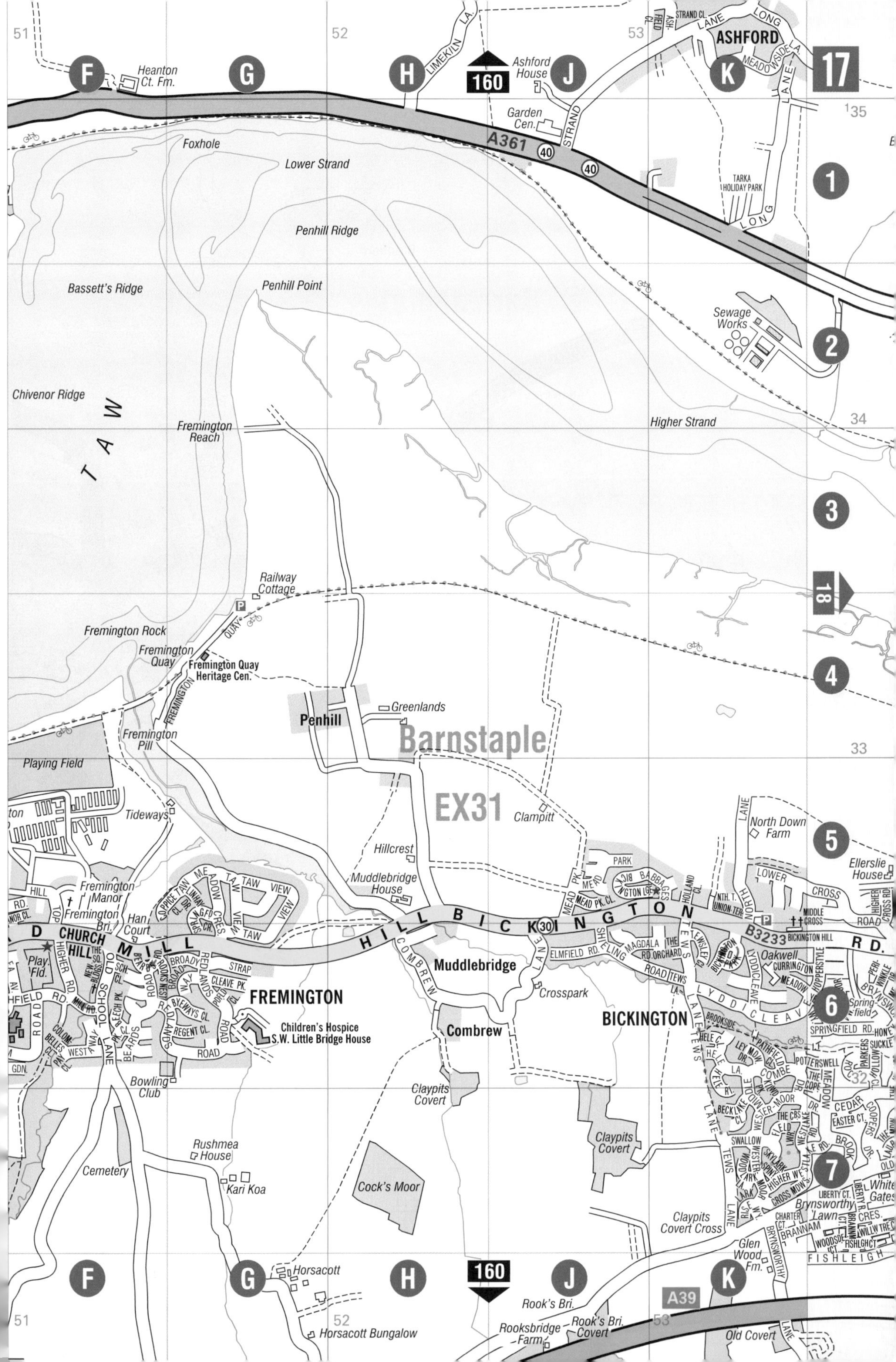

17
160
18
ASHFORD
Ashford House
Garden Cen.
Heanton Ct. Fm.
A361
Foxhole
Lower Strand
Penhill Ridge
Penhill Point
Bassett's Ridge
Chivenor Ridge
TAW
Fremington Reach
Higher Strand
Sewage Works
TARKA HOLIDAY PARK
Railway Cottage
Fremington Rock
Fremington Quay
Fremington Quay Heritage Cen.
Greenlands
Penhill
Barnstaple
EX31
Fremington Pill
Playing Field
Tideways
Clampitt
North Down Farm
Ellerslie House
Hillcrest
Muddlebridge House
Fremington Manor
Han Court
Muddlebridge
Combrew
Crosspark
FREMINGTON
Children's Hospice S.W. Little Bridge House
BICKINGTON
Oakwell
B3233
BICKINGTON HILL
Bowling Club
Claypits Covert
Rushmea House
Kari Koa
Cemetery
Cock's Moor
Claypits Covert Cross
Brynsworthy Lawn
Glen Wood Fm.
Horsacott
Horsacott Bungalow
Rook's Bri.
Rooksbridge Farm
Rook's Bri. Covert
A39
Old Covert

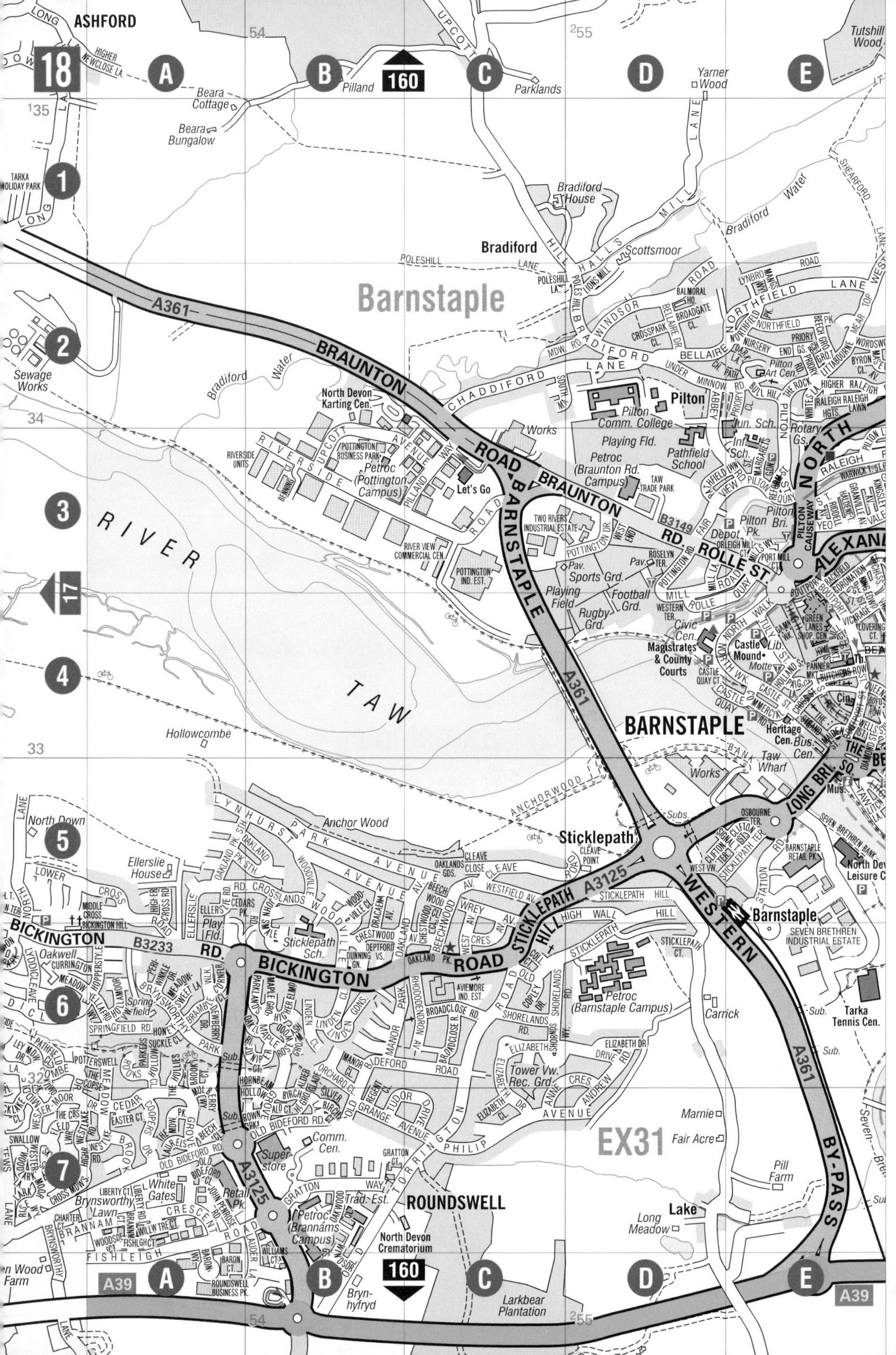

18
160
17
ASHFORD
Pilland
Parklands
Beara Cottage
Beara Bungalow
Yarner Wood
Tutshill Wood
TARKA HOLIDAY PARK
Bradiford House
Bradiford
Scottsmoor
Barnstaple
A361
BRAUNTON ROAD
Sewage Works
Bradiford Water
North Devon Karting Cen.
POTTINGTON BUSINESS PARK
Petroc (Pottington Campus)
RIVERSIDE UNITS
Let's Go
RIVER VIEW COMMERCIAL CEN.
POTTINGTON IND. EST.
TWO RIVERS INDUSTRIAL ESTATE
TAW TRADE PARK
Pilton
Pilton Comm. College
Playing Fld.
Pathfield School
Petroc (Braunton Rd. Campus)
Sports Grd.
Playing Field
Football Grd.
Rugby Grd.
Pilton Art Cen.
Pilton Pk.
Pilton Bri.
Depot
ROLLE ST.
Civic Cen.
Magistrates & County Courts
Castle Mound
Motte
GREEN LANES SHOP. CEN.
PANNIER MKT.
Heritage Cen.
Bus Cen.
BARNSTAPLE
Taw Wharf
Works
LONG BRI.
Mus.
RIVER TAW
Hollowcombe
Anchor Wood
Sticklepath
North Down
Ellerslie House
BICKINGTON RD.
B3233
BICKINGTON ROAD
Sticklepath Sch.
AVIEMORE IND. EST.
Petroc (Barnstaple Campus)
Carrick
STICKLEPATH HILL
A3125
WESTERN
Barnstaple
SEVEN BRETHREN INDUSTRIAL ESTATE
BARNSTAPLE RETAIL PK.
North Devon Leisure C.
Tarka Tennis Cen.
Tower Vw. Rec. Grd.
EX31
Marnie
Fair Acre
Pill Farm
Lake
Long Meadow
Comm. Cen.
Superstore
Retail Pk.
Trad. Est.
Petroc (Brannams Campus)
ROUNDSWELL
North Devon Crematorium
White Gates
Brynsworthy Lawn
ROUNDSWELL BUSINESS PK.
Bryn-hyfryd
Larkbear Plantation
A39
A361 BY-PASS
Wood Farm

Playford Mill
Shirwell Cross
SHIRWELL RD.
Fort
Roborough Plantation
160
ROAD
F
G
H
J
K
Coxleigh Barton
Trayne Farm
Roborough
NORTH ROAD
HOUSE
LANE
1
2
3
4
5
6
7
ROBOROUGH
Nursery
SMOKY
RALEIGH PARK
Kingdon's Gdns.
NORTH DEVON DISTRICT HOSPITAL
Mill Leat
Stoneyard Wood
Stoneyard Plantation
Old Mill Leat
RALEIGH
Pav.
Playing Field
RIVER YEO
Ash Plantation
Goodleigh Cross
A39
HIGHER RALEIGH RD.
Frankmarsh Wood
Stoneyard Farm
WEIRSIDE WY.
LONG MEADOW DR.
SILVERWOOD HEIGHTS
Spts. Grd.
HEPPENSTALL RD.
LETHABY ROAD
CHURCHILL RD.
BELMONT
DERBY ROAD
FRANKMARSH PK.
Prim. Sch.
Cemetery
GORWELL
KINGS RD.
JEWELL CRES.
CONCORDE DRIVE
Gorwell House
MARTIN
VALLEY CLOSE
ROAD
Wellclose
Waytown Cottage
Lilly
BEAR STREET
GOODLEIGH
Crookmans Corner
CHANTER'S Sch.
Fort Hill
WALTON WAY
ELGAR CL.
Maidenford
Res. (cov.)
EX32
SOWDEN
Westacott Heights
Bus Sta.
TA Cen.
BARBICAN LANE
VICTORIA RD.
EASTERN AVENUE
Forches Cross Prim. Sch.
Westacott
ORCHARD PL.
Depot
Depots
WILKEY CL.
BARTON
Comm. Cen.
Rec. Grd.
Westacott Grange
Black Rock Pit
Rock Pk.
NEWPORT
HOLLOWTREE RD.
Ind. Est.
Superstores
Newport
Comm. Cen.
Superstores
Funder Zone
WHIDDON VALLEY IND. EST.
WHIDDON DRIVE
WESTACOTT
A361
Bowl. Grn.
Pav.
Ten. Cts.
Pitch & Putt
Bus Depot
Play. Fld.
Jungleland Garden Cen.
Sch.
Sch. Cl.
The Park Comm. Sch.
All Weather Pitch
PORTMORE GOLF COURSE
Rock Pk. Sprts. Gd.
Sports Grd.
Barnstaple P+R
B3138
SOUTH ST.
Spts. Fld.
A39
Club House
Driving Range
Sub Sta.
Rumsam
Whiddon
Pill Ho.
Greendale Farm
PILL LANE
ROAD
BISHOP'S TAWTON RD.
KING'S RIVER VW.
Rose-hill
LANDKEY
MOUNTVIEW HOME PARK
24
Woodstrait
North Devon Hospice
A377
Cradlemans Cross
VENN ROAD
56
57
58
135
34
33
32

160
ROYAL NORTH DEVON GOLF COURSE
BARNSTAPLE OR BIDEFORD BAY
Burrows Centre
Sandymere
NORTHAM BURROWS COUNTRY PARK
Pebble Ridge
Bideford
EX39
ROYAL NORTH DEVON GOLF COURSE
Pimpley Bridge
SANDYMERE ROAD
Sandymere Spts. Cen.
Club House
Underborough
LINKS ROAD
Woodbine Cottage
ATLANTIC WAY
NELSON RD.
STANWELL HILL
WESTWARD HO!
Kipling Tors
Putting Grn.
Ckt. Grd.
GOLDEN BAY HOLIDAY VILLAGE
BEACHSIDE HOLIDAY PK.
BRADDICKS HOLIDAY CEN.
CENTURY DRIVE
BAY VIEW ROAD
Buckleigh
BUCKLEIGH
CORNBOROUGH
PUSEHILL
Pusehill
The Old Granary
South Pusehill
West Pusehill
Lake Farm Ho.
Orchard
Foxwold
SILFORD CROSS
RALEIGH
Silford Farm
Silford Cottages
Stoneleigh
Daddon Hill Farm
DADDON HILL
Gresham Court
Lenwood
Muddix Farm
Lenwood Country Club
Tennis Cts.
Club House
Fordlands
Fordlands Farm
Port Hill
HEYWOOD ROAD
A386
A39
B3236
163
22
Woodville
LAKENHAM HILL
Inf. Sch.
Jun. Sch.
Liby.

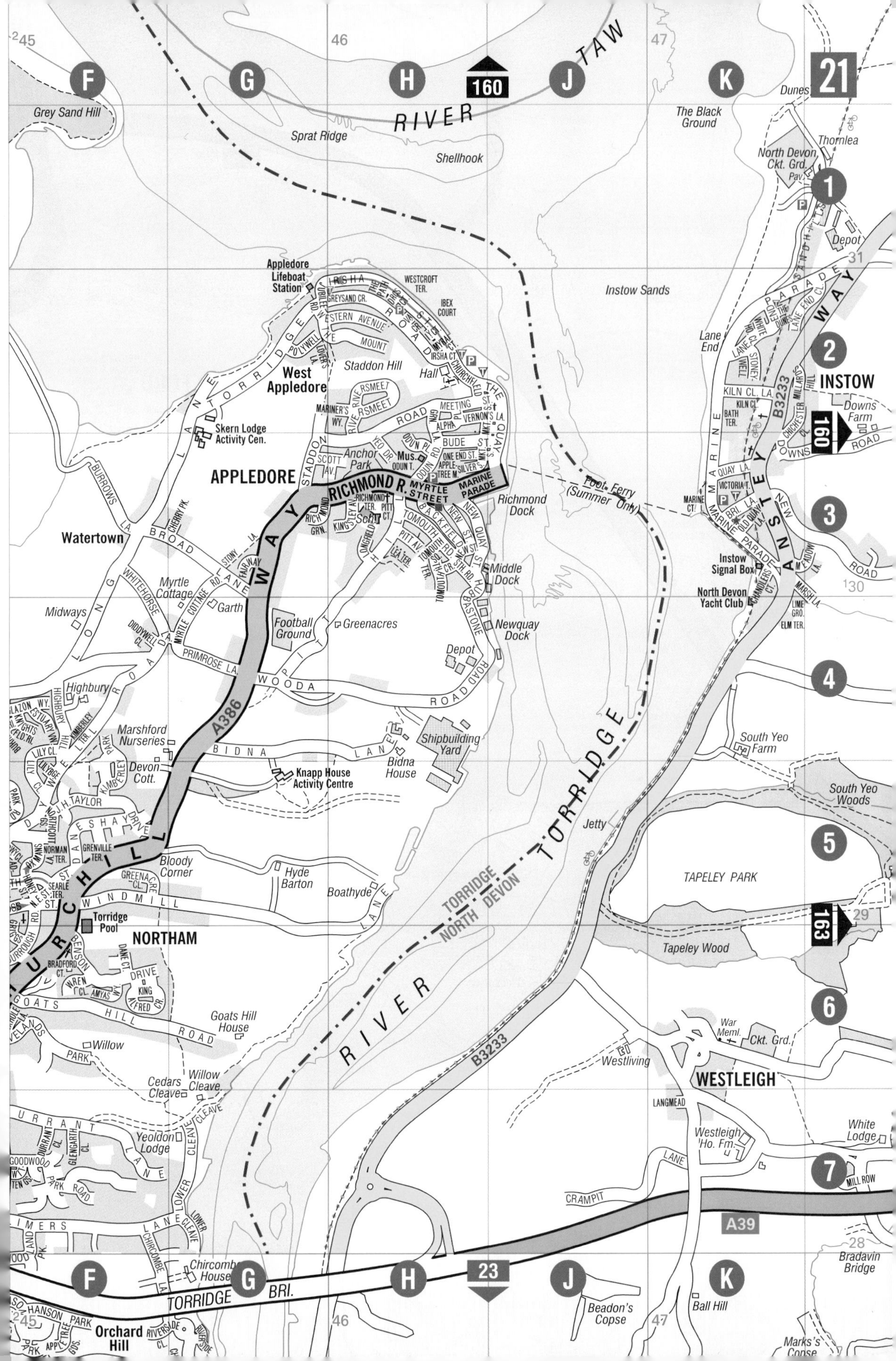
RIVER TAW
160
Grey Sand Hill
Sprat Ridge
Shellhook
The Black Ground
Dunes
Thornlea
North Devon Ckt. Grd.
Instow Sands
Appledore Lifeboat Station
West Appledore
Staddon Hill
APPLEDORE
Skern Lodge Activity Cen.
Anchor Park
RICHMOND R.
MYRTLE STREET
MARINE PARADE
Richmond Dock
Foot Ferry (Summer Only)
INSTOW
Downs Farm
Lane End
Instow Signal Box
North Devon Yacht Club
Watertown
Midways
Myrtle Cottage
Garth
Football Ground
Greenacres
Middle Dock
Newquay Dock
Depot
WOODA ROAD
Highbury
Marshford Nurseries
Devon Cott.
Knapp House Activity Centre
Bidna House
Shipbuilding Yard
South Yeo Farm
South Yeo Woods
RIVER TORRIDGE
Jetty
TAPELEY PARK
Tapeley Wood
163
Bloody Corner
Hyde Barton
Boathyde
Torridge Pool
NORTHAM
TORRIDGE
NORTH DEVON
Goats Hill House
Willow
Westliving
WESTLEIGH
War Meml.
Ckt. Grd.
Cedars Cleave
Willow Cleave
Yeoldon Lodge
Westleigh Ho. Fm.
White Lodge
MILL ROW
CRAMPIT LANE
A39
A386
B3233
Bradavin Bridge
Chircombe House
TORRIDGE BRI.
23
Beadon's Copse
Ball Hill
Orchard Hill
Marks's Copse

Bideford
EX39
BIDEFORD
Abbotsham
Higher Winsford
Rickard's Down
Bowden Green
Upcott
Edgehill Theatre
Kingsley School
Bideford College
BIDEFORD COMM. HOSP.
Atlantis Adventure Pk.
ATLANTIC VILLAGE
Ultimate Adventure Cen.
The Big Sheep
A39
B3236
BUCKLEIGH RD.
CLOVELLY ROAD
ABBOTSHAM ROAD
NORTHDOWN
Turner's Wood
Godborough Castle (remains of)
Kenwith Valley Nature Reserve
Badgershill Wood
Moreton Park
Moreton Woods
Playing Fields
Bowood Plantations
Nine Acre Plantation
Upcott Wood
Jennetts Reservoir
Alverdiscott Plantation
Littleham Wood
20
163
30

TORRIDGE BRIDGE
A39
A386
B3233
Orchard Hill
Southcott
Southcott Marsh
Pillhead Marsh
Pillhead Ho.
Pillhead Farm
Pillhead Copse
Pillhead Bri.
Beadon's Copse
Ball Hill
Marks's Copse
Colley Moor Plantation
Council Offices
Cattle Market
King George V Playing Fields
Rugby Football Ground
Victoria Park
Burton Art Gallery & Museum
Bideford to Lundy 2hrs. (Seasonal) Foot Ferry
Bideford Quay Fountain
Clarence Wharf
Queens' Wharf
Bideford Long Bri.
East-the-Water
Cemetery
Superstore
Goodleigh Cottage
Leopards Lea
Cleave Wood
Broomhayes School
Warmington Hill
Warmington
Port Farm
Bideford Business Park
Bay View
Bybury
Tennacott Farm
Tennacott Wood
The Old Keeper's Cottage
Beara
Beara Wood
Addlehole Wood
Community Centre
Wooder Wharf
Depot
Mallacleave
Picnic Site
Lodge Plantation
Hallsannery Field Cen.
Hallsannery Farm
Hallsannery
Pillmouth
RIVER TORRIDGE
RIVER YEO
NEW ROAD
THE QUAY
BARNSTAPLE ST.
MANTEO WAY
GAMMATON ROAD
ALVERDISCOTT ROAD
TENNACOTT LANE
21
163

163

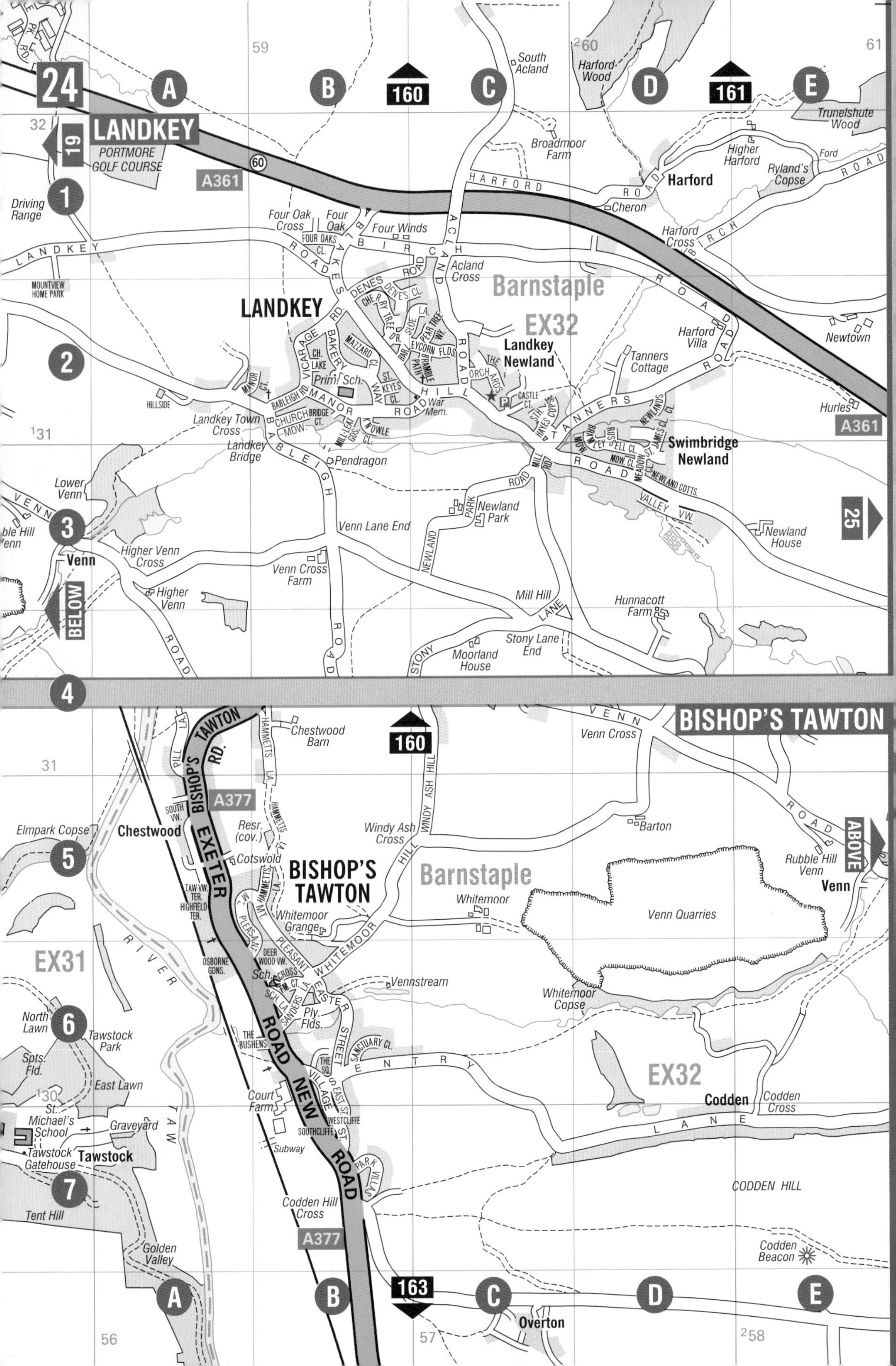
24
LANDKEY
PORTMORE GOLF COURSE
A361
Driving Range
LANDKEY
Barnstaple
EX32
Landkey Newland
Swimbridge Newland
Harford
Four Oak Cross
Four Oak
Four Winds
Acland Cross
South Acland
Harford Wood
Broadmoor Farm
Higher Harford
Ryland's Copse
Trunelshute Wood
Cheron
Harford Cross
Harford Villa
Tanners Cottage
Newtown
Hurles
Landkey Town Cross
Landkey Bridge
Pendragon
Lower Venn
Venn
Higher Venn Cross
Higher Venn
Venn Lane End
Venn Cross Farm
Newland Park
Newland House
Mill Hill
Hunnacott Farm
Stony Lane End
Moorland House
BISHOP'S TAWTON
Chestwood Barn
Venn Cross
Elmpark Copse
Chestwood
Windy Ash Cross
Barton
Rubble Hill Venn
Venn
Barnstaple
Whitemoor
Venn Quarries
Whitemoor Grange
Vennstream
Whitemoor Copse
EX31
North Lawn
Tawstock Park
East Lawn
St. Michael's School
Graveyard
Tawstock Gatehouse
Tawstock
Tent Hill
Golden Valley
Court Farm
Subway
Codden Hill Cross
A377
EX32
Codden
Codden Cross
CODDEN HILL
Codden Beacon
Overton
160
161
163
25
19
ABOVE
BELOW

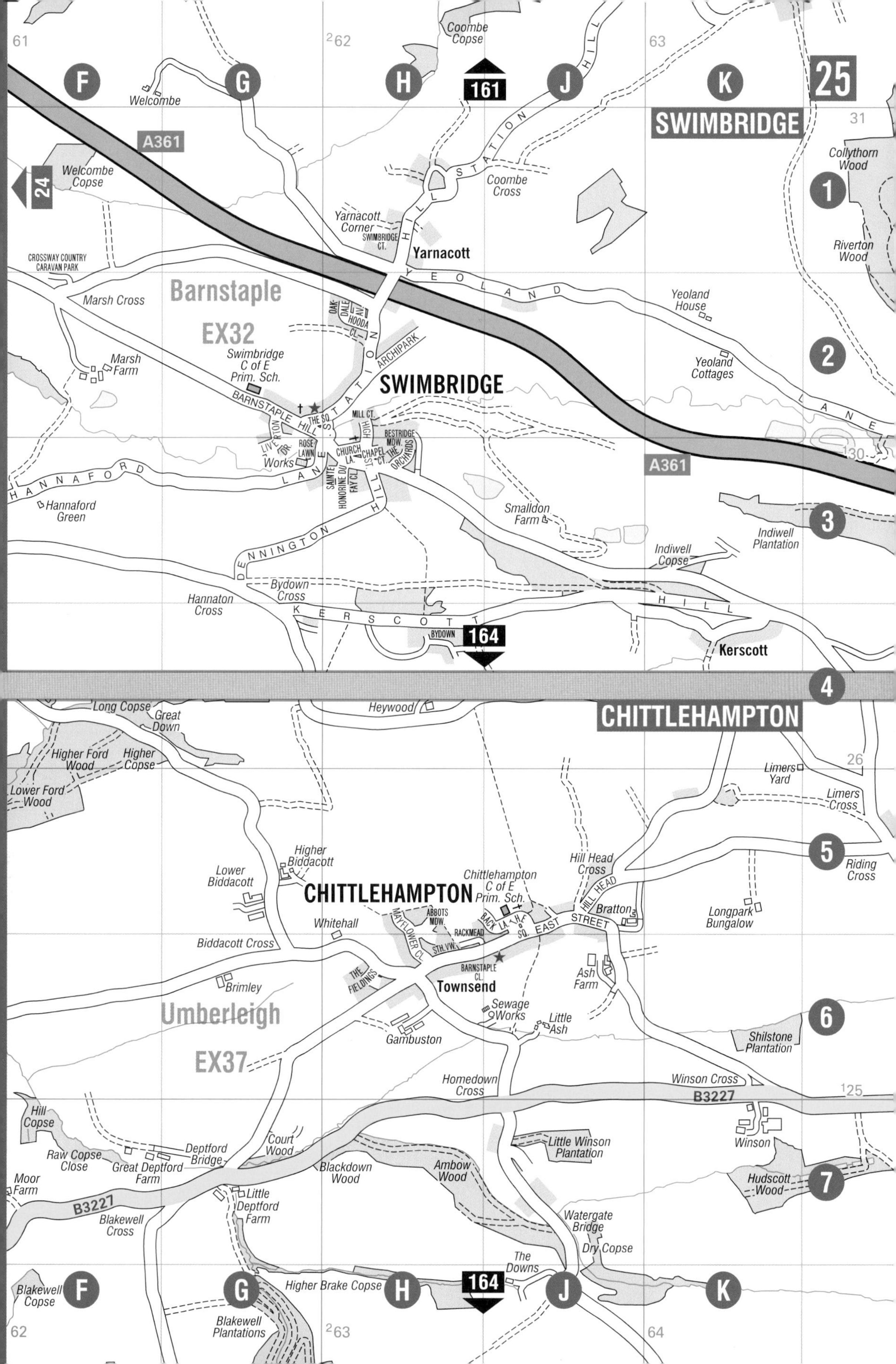

61   62   63

Welcombe

A361

24

Welcombe Copse

CROSSWAY COUNTRY CARAVAN PARK

Marsh Cross

Barnstaple

EX32

Marsh Farm

HANNAFORD

Hannaford Green

Swimbridge C of E Prim. Sch.

BARNSTAPLE HILL

LIVERTON

OAK DALE AV. HOODA CL.

STATION

ARCHIPARK

Yarnacott Corner

SWIMBRIDGE CT.

Yarnacott

YEOLAND

Coombe Copse

Coombe Cross

STATION HILL

Yeoland House

Yeoland Cottages

Collythorn Wood

1

Riverton Wood

2

THE SQ.

ROSE LAWN

CHURCH LA.

CHAPEL CT.

SAINTE HONORINE DU FAY CT.

MILL CT.

BESTRIDGE MDW.

THE ORCHARDS

SWIMBRIDGE

Works

DENNINGTON LANE

KERSCOTT

Bydown Cross

Hannaton Cross

BYDOWN 164

Smalldon Farm

Indiwell Copse

HILL

A361

130

Indiwell Plantation

3

Kerscott

4

Long Copse

Great Down

Heywood

26

Higher Ford Wood

Higher Copse

Lower Ford Wood

Lower Biddacott

Higher Biddacott

Whitehall

CHITTLEHAMPTON

Biddacott Cross

Umberleigh

EX37

Brimley

THE FIELDINGS

MAYFLOWER CL.

STH. VW.

ABBOTS MDW.

RACKMEAD

BACK LA.

SQ.

Chittlehampton C of E Prim. Sch.

EAST STREET

Hill Head Cross

HILL HEAD

Bratton Street

Limers Yard

Limers Cross

Riding Cross

5

Longpark Bungalow

BARNSTAPLE CL.

Townsend

Gambuston

Sewage Works

Ash Farm

Little Ash

Homedown Cross

Winson Cross

B3227

Shilstone Plantation

6

Winson

125

Hill Copse

Raw Copse Close

Moor Farm

B3227

Blakewell Cross

Deptford Bridge

Great Deptford Farm

Court Wood

Little Deptford Farm

Blackdown Wood

Ambow Wood

Little Winson Plantation

Watergate Bridge

The Downs

Dry Copse

Hudscott Wood

7

Blakewell Copse

Blakewell Plantations

Higher Brake Copse

164

62   63   64

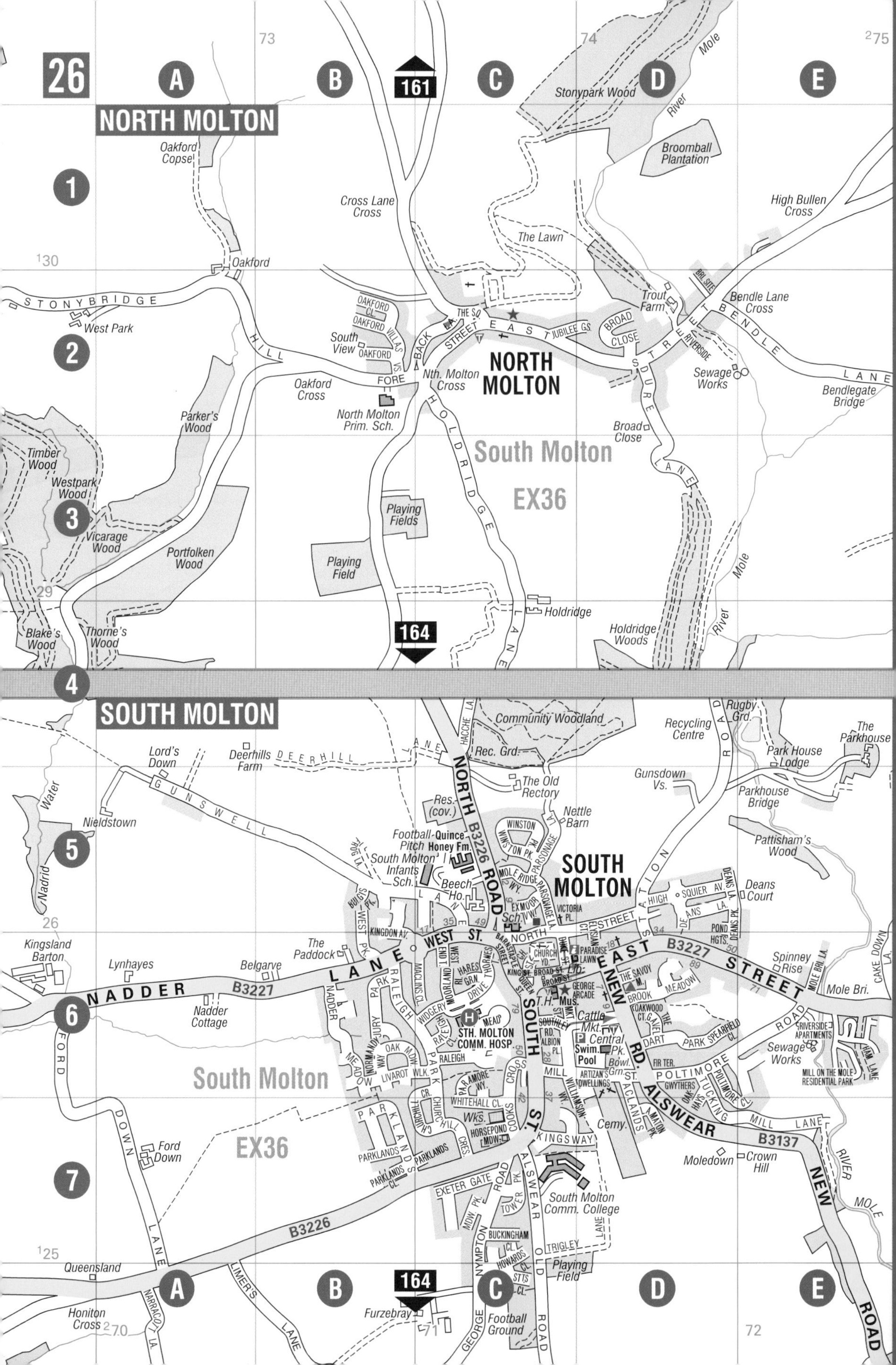
NORTH MOLTON
SOUTH MOLTON
161
164
164
Oakford Copse
Stonypark Wood
Broomball Plantation
River Mole
Cross Lane Cross
High Bullen Cross
The Lawn
Oakford
STONYBRIDGE HILL
West Park
Trout Farm
Bendle Lane Cross
BENDLE LANE
South View
OAKFORD CL.
OAKFORD VILLAS
OAKFORD VS.
BACK
THE SQ.
EAST STREET
JUBILEE GS.
BROAD CLOSE
RIVERSIDE
BRL SITE
Sewage Works
Bendlegate Bridge
FORE
Oakford Cross
Nth. Molton Cross
North Molton Prim. Sch.
NORTH MOLTON
SOURE LANE
Broad Close
HOLDRIDGE LANE
Parker's Wood
Timber Wood
Westpark Wood
Vicarage Wood
Portfolken Wood
South Molton
EX36
Playing Fields
Playing Field
Holdridge
Holdridge Woods
Blake's Wood
Thorne's Wood
Community Woodland
Rec. Grd.
HACCHE LA.
HACCHE LANE
Rugby Grd.
Recycling Centre
STATION ROAD
The Parkhouse
Park House Lodge
Parkhouse Bridge
Gunsdown Vs.
Lord's Down
Deerhills Farm
DEERHILL LANE
GUNSWELL
The Old Rectory
Nettle Barn
Water
Nieldstown
Nadrid
Res. (cov.)
Football Pitch
Quince Honey Fm.
South Molton Infants Sch.
Beech Ho.
NORTH ROAD B3226
WINSTON PK.
PARSONAGE LA.
MOLE RIDGE WY.
EXMOOR VW.
SOUTH MOLTON
Pattisham's Wood
Deans Court
SQUIER AV.
DEANS LA.
DEANS PK.
POND HGTS.
HIGH
FROG LA.
BOUCHS
WEST PK.
KINGDON AV.
WEST ST.
NORTH
VICTORIA PL.
STREET
EAST STREET B3227
Spinney Rise
MOLE BRI. LA.
CAKE DOWN LA.
Mole Bri.
Kingsland Barton
Lynhayes
The Paddock
Belgarve
LANE
NADDER B3227
Nadder Cottage
CHURCH YD.
PARADISE LAWN
ELYSIAN CT.
BARNSTAPLE STREET
QUEEN ST.
KING ST.
BROAD ST.
GEORGE ARCADE
T.H. Mus.
NEW RD.
THE SAVOY
BROOK
MEADOW
OAKWOOD CT.
GANEL
DART
PARK
SPEARFIELD CL.
ROAD
RIVERSIDE APARTMENTS
Sewage Works
FARM LANE
MILL ON THE MOLE RESIDENTIAL PARK
NADDER MEADOW
JURY PARK
RALEIGH
MACLINS CL.
WEST END
MOORLAND
HARES GRN.
THORNES DRIVE
WIDGERY
RALEIGH CL.
STH. MOLTON COMM. HOSP.
MEAD
SOUTH ST.
SOUTHLEY RD.
ALBION PL.
Cattle Mkt.
Central Pk.
Swim. Pool
Bowl. Grn.
FIR TER.
POLTIMORE
ST. ACLANDS
ALSWEAR
GWYTHERS
TUCKING
MILL LANE
B3137
NORMANDY WAY
OAK MDW.
LIVAROT WLK.
RALEIGH PARK
PARAMORE WY.
CROSS
MILL
ARTIZAN'S DWELLINGS
WILLIAMSON WY.
Cemy.
Ford
South Molton
EX36
DOWN LANE
Ford Down
PARKLANDS
CHURCHILL CR.
CHURCH HILL CRES.
WHITEHALL CL.
Wks.
COOKS
HORSEPOND MDW.
KINGSWAY
Moledown
Crown Hill
RIVER MOLE
NEW ROAD
PARKLANDS CL.
EXETER GATE
NYMPTON ROAD
TOWER PK.
MDW. PK.
ALSWEAR OLD ROAD
South Molton Comm. College
B3226
BUCKINGHAM CL.
HOWARDS CL.
STTS CL.
TRIGLEY
LANE
Playing Field
Queensland
LIMER'S LANE
NARRACOTT LA.
Honiton Cross
Furzebray
GEORGE
Football Ground
A
B
C
D
E
1
2
3
4
5
6
7
73
74
75
130
29
26
125
70
71
72

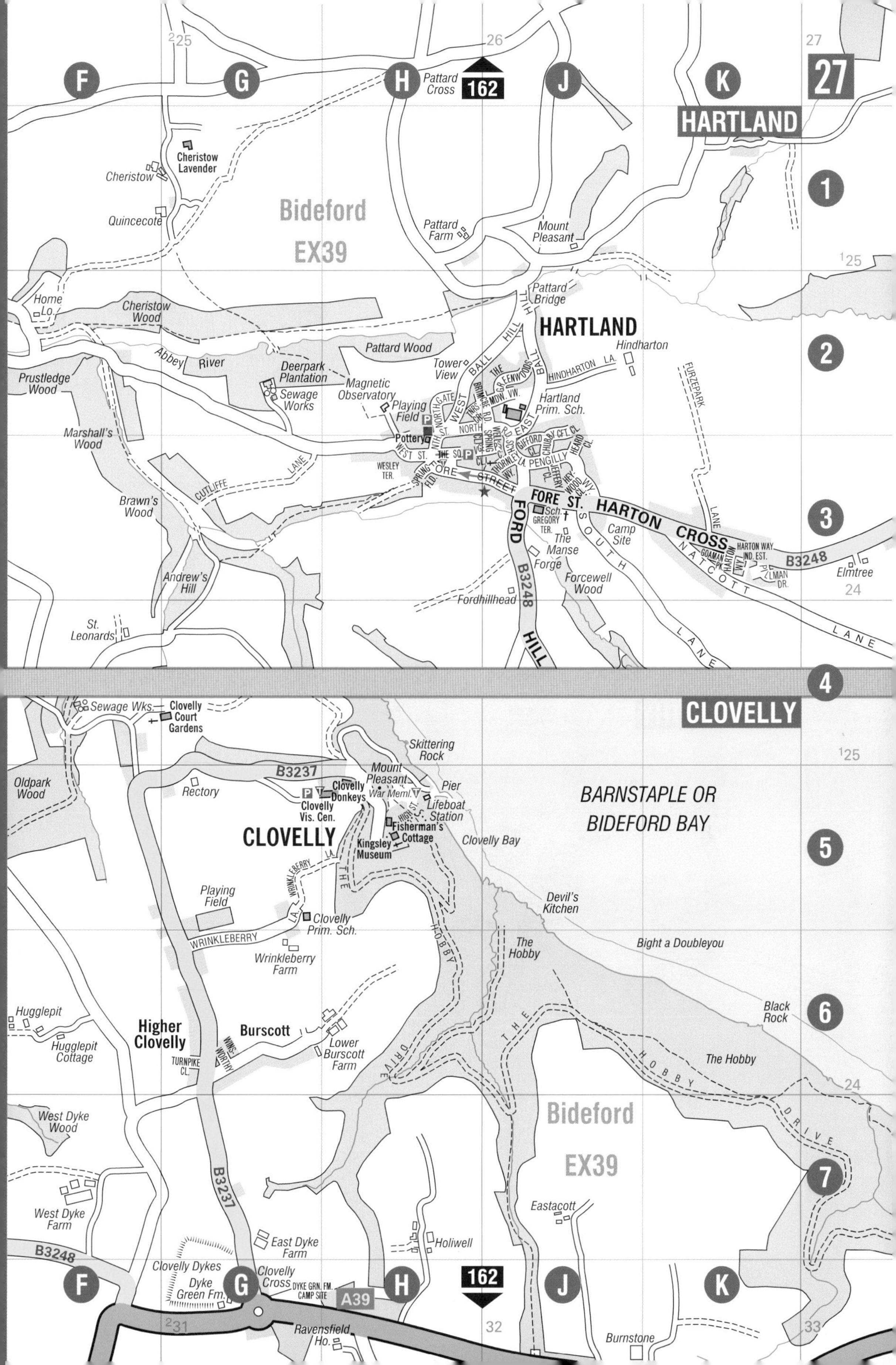

Map Labels — Hartland (top)

225 26 27
1 125

Cheristow Lavender
Cheristow
Quincecote
Home Lo
Bideford EX39
Pattard Cross
Pattard Farm
Mount Pleasant
Pattard Bridge
HARTLAND
Hindharton
Hindharton La.
Furzepark

Cheristow Wood
Abbey River
Pattard Wood
Deerpark Plantation
Sewage Works
Magnetic Observatory
Tower View
Prustledge Wood
Marshall's Wood
Playing Field
Pottery
Hartland Prim. Sch.
Gifford Cft. Cl.
Pengilly

Brawn's Wood
CUTLIFFE
WEST ST.
WESLEY TER.
SPRINGFORD
FLORE STREET
THORNLEY WY.
WOOD WY.
HEARD CL.

Andrew's Hill
FORD HILL
B3248
Sch.
GREGORY TER.
The Manse Forge
FORE ST.
HARTON CROSS
NATCOTT
Camp Site
GOAMAN PK.
HARTON IND. EST.
HARTON WAY
B3248
Elmtree

St. Leonards
Fordhillhead
Forcewell Wood
PITMAN DR.
NATCOTT LANE
LANE
24

Map Labels — Clovelly (bottom)

Sewage Wks.
Clovelly Court Gardens
Oldpark Wood
Rectory
B3237
Clovelly Donkeys
Clovelly Vis. Cen.
P
CLOVELLY
Kingsley Museum
Skittering Rock
Mount Pleasant
War Meml.
Pier
Lifeboat Station
Fisherman's Cottage
Clovelly Bay

BARNSTAPLE OR BIDEFORD BAY
125

5

Playing Field
WRINKLEBERRY LA.
Clovelly Prim. Sch.
WRINKLEBERRY
Wrinkleberry Farm
THE HOBBY DRIVE
Devil's Kitchen
The Hobby
Bight a Doubleyou

Hugglepit
Hugglepit Cottage
Higher Clovelly
Burscott
TURNPIKE CL.
KINGS WORTHY
Lower Burscott Farm
Black Rock
The Hobby
6

West Dyke Wood
B3237
Bideford EX39
THE HOBBY DRIVE
24

West Dyke Farm
B3248
Clovelly Dykes
Dyke Green Fm.
East Dyke Farm
Clovelly Cross
DYKE GRN. FM. CAMP SITE
Eastacott
Holiwell
7

A39
162
Ravensfield Ho.
Burnstone
231 32 233

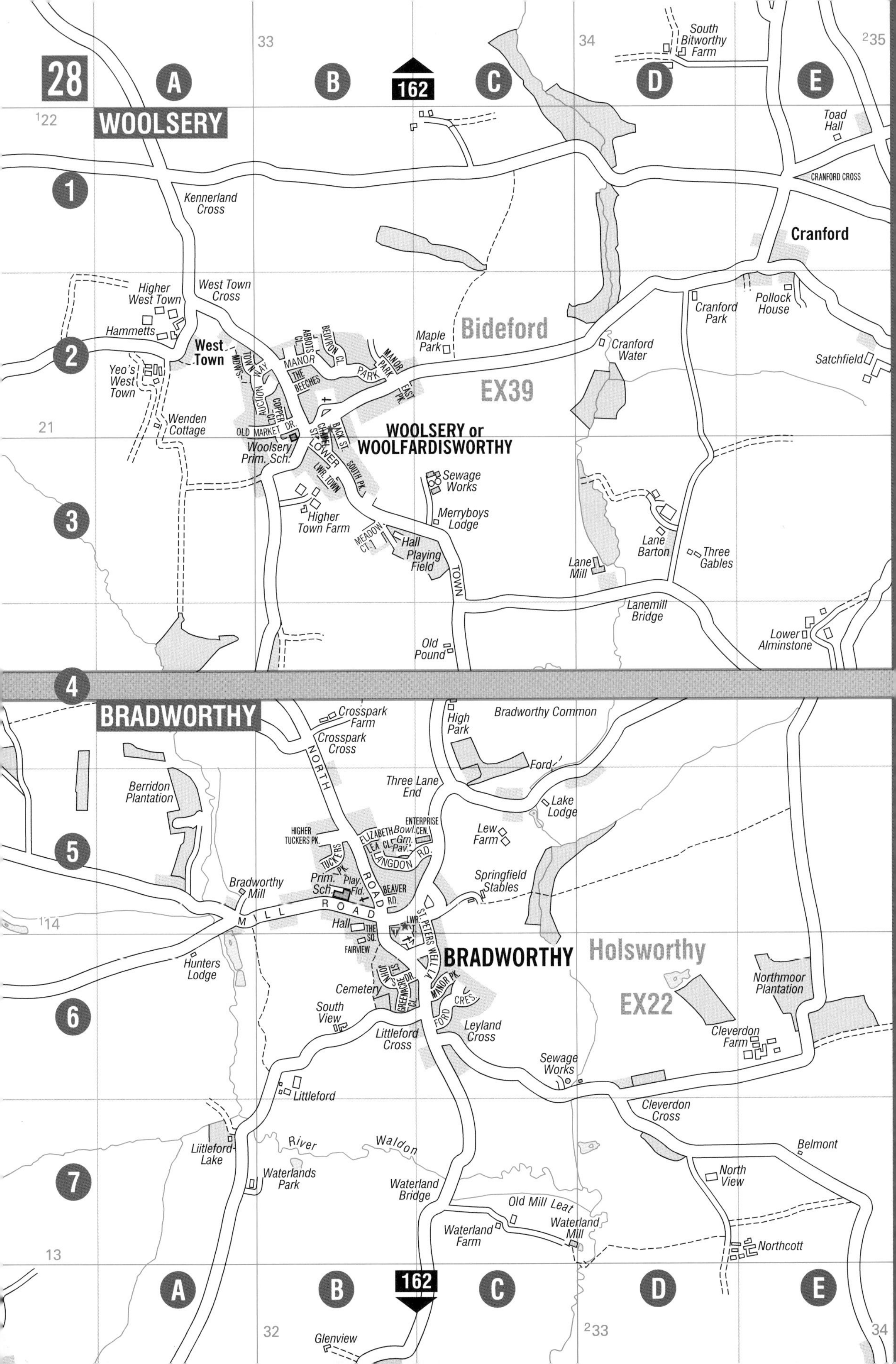
WOOLSERY
162
South Bitworthy Farm
Toad Hall
CRANFORD CROSS
Kennerland Cross
Cranford
Higher West Town
West Town Cross
Hammetts
West Town
Yeo's West Town
Wenden Cottage
Bideford
Maple Park
Cranford Water
Cranford Park
Pollock House
Satchfield
EX39
WOOLSERY or WOOLFARDISWORTHY
Woolsery Prim. Sch.
OLD MARKET DR.
Sewage Works
Merryboys Lodge
Higher Town Farm
Hall
Playing Field
Lane Barton
Three Gables
Lane Mill
Lanemill Bridge
Old Pound
Lower Alminstone
BRADWORTHY
Crosspark Farm
Crosspark Cross
High Park
Bradworthy Common
Ford
Berridon Plantation
Three Lane End
Lake Lodge
Lew Farm
HIGHER TUCKERS PK.
ENTERPRISE CEN.
Bradworthy Mill
Springfield Stables
MILL ROAD
Hall
FAIRVIEW
BRADWORTHY
Holsworthy
Hunters Lodge
Cemetery
Northmoor Plantation
EX22
South View
Littleford Cross
Leyland Cross
Cleverdon Farm
Sewage Works
Littleford
Cleverdon Cross
River Waldon
Belmont
Liitleford Lake
Waterlands Park
Waterland Bridge
North View
Old Mill Leat
Waterland Mill
Waterland Farm
Northcott
162
Glenview

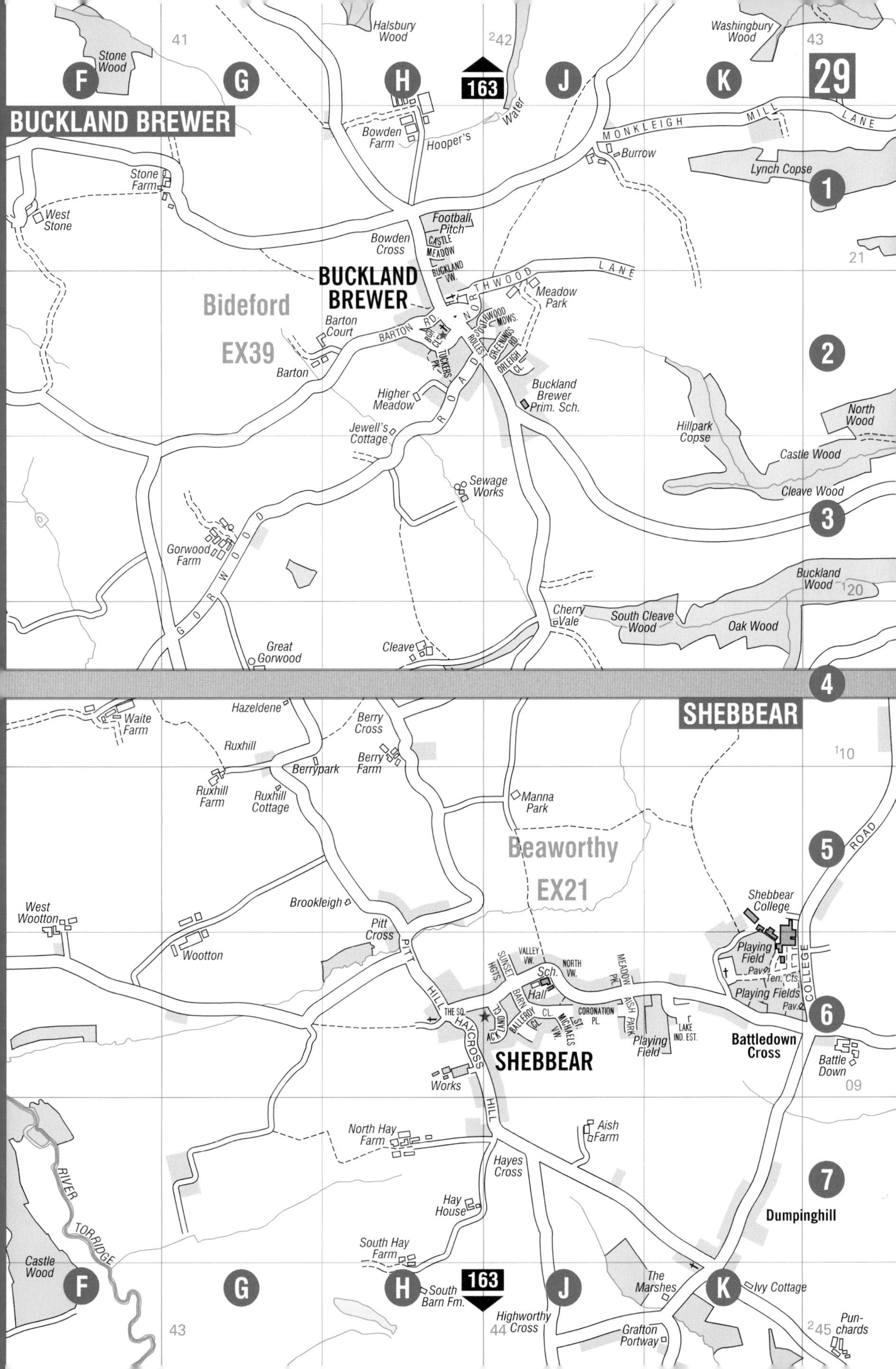
BUCKLAND BREWER
SHEBBEAR
BUCKLAND BREWER
SHEBBEAR
Bideford
EX39
Beaworthy
EX21
163
163
Stone Wood
Halsbury Wood
Washingbury Wood
Bowden Farm
Hooper's Water
Monkleigh Mill Lane
Burrow
Lynch Copse
Stone Farm
West Stone
Football Pitch
Bowden Cross
Castle Meadow
Buckland Vw.
Northwood Lane
Meadow Park
Barton Court
Barton Rd.
Barton
Southwood Mdws.
Greenings Rd.
Orleigh Cl.
Tuckers Pk.
Rolles Road
Higher Meadow
Buckland Brewer Prim. Sch.
Hillpark Copse
North Wood
Castle Wood
Cleave Wood
Jewell's Cottage
Sewage Works
Gorwood Farm
Gorwood Road
Buckland Wood
South Cleave Wood
Oak Wood
Cherry Vale
Great Gorwood
Cleave
Hazeldene
Waite Farm
Berry Cross
Ruxhill
Berry Farm
Berrypark
Ruxhill Farm
Ruxhill Cottage
Manna Park
College Road
West Wootton
Brookleigh
Shebbear College
Pitt Cross
Playing Field
Wootton
Pitt Hill
Sunset Hgts.
Valley Vw.
North Vw.
Sch.
Hall
Meadow Pk.
Ten. Cts.
Pav.
Playing Fields
The Sq.
Haycross Hill
Barn Cl.
Ballerdy Cl.
Coronation Pl.
St. Michaels Vw.
Ash Park
Lake Ind. Est.
Playing Field
Battledown Cross
Battle Down
Works
North Hay Farm
Aish Farm
Hayes Cross
River Torridge
Hay House
Dumpinghill
South Hay Farm
The Marshes
Castle Wood
South Barn Fm.
Ivy Cottage
Highworthy Cross
Grafton Portway
Pun-chards
F G H J K
1 2 3 4 5 6 7
41 242 43 21 120 110 09 43 44 245

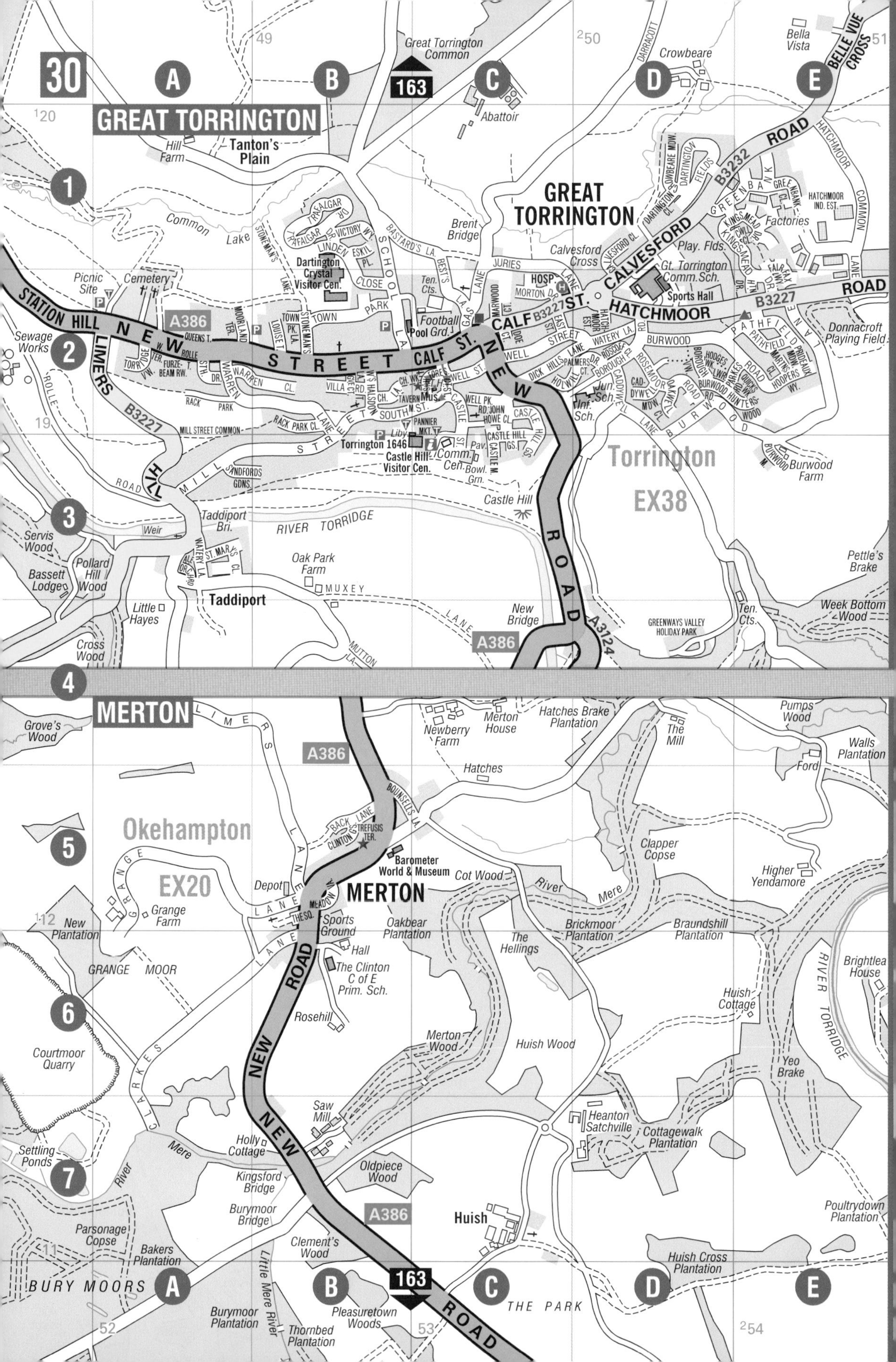
GREAT TORRINGTON
Great Torrington Common
163
Tanton's Plain
Hill Farm
Abattoir
Crowbeare
Bella Vista
BELLE VUE CROSS
GREAT TORRINGTON
Common
Lake
Brent Bridge
Calvesford Cross
CALVESFORD
HATCHMOOR ROAD
Gt. Torrington Comm.Sch.
Sports Hall
Play. Flds.
Factories
HATCHMOOR IND. EST.
Dartington Crystal Visitor Cen.
Picnic Site
Cemetery
Sewage Works
STATION HILL
NEW STREET
CALF ST.
A386
B3227
Football Pool Grd.
Ten. Cts.
Donnacroft Playing Field
Mus.
Torrington 1646
Castle Hill Visitor Cen.
Comm. Cen.
Bowl. Grn.
Castle Hill
Inf. Sch.
Jun. Sch.
Torrington
EX38
Burwood Farm
RIVER TORRIDGE
Taddiport Bri.
Weir
Servis Wood
Pollard Hill Wood
Bassett Lodge
Taddiport
Oak Park Farm
MUXEY LANE
Little Hayes
Cross Wood
New Bridge
A3124
NEW ROAD
Pettle's Brake
Week Bottom Wood
GREENWAYS VALLEY HOLIDAY PARK
MERTON
Grove's Wood
Newberry Farm
Merton House
Hatches Brake Plantation
The Mill
Pumps Wood
Walls Plantation
Ford
Hatches
Okehampton
EX20
Barometer World & Museum
MERTON
Cot Wood
Clapper Copse
Higher Yendamore
Depot
Grange Farm
New Plantation
Sports Ground
Hall
The Clinton C of E Prim. Sch.
Oakbear Plantation
River Mere
Brickmoor Plantation
Braundshill Plantation
The Hellings
GRANGE MOOR
Rosehill
Huish Wood
Huish Cottage
Brightlea House
Courtmoor Quarry
Merton Wood
Yeo Brake
Saw Mill
Holly Cottage
Heanton Satchville
Cottagewalk Plantation
Settling Ponds
Kingsford Bridge
Oldpiece Wood
Burymoor Bridge
Huish
Parsonage Copse
Bakers Plantation
Clement's Wood
Poultrydown Plantation
Huish Cross Plantation
BURY MOORS
Little Mere River
Burymoor Plantation
Thornbed Plantation
Pleasuretown Woods
THE PARK
163

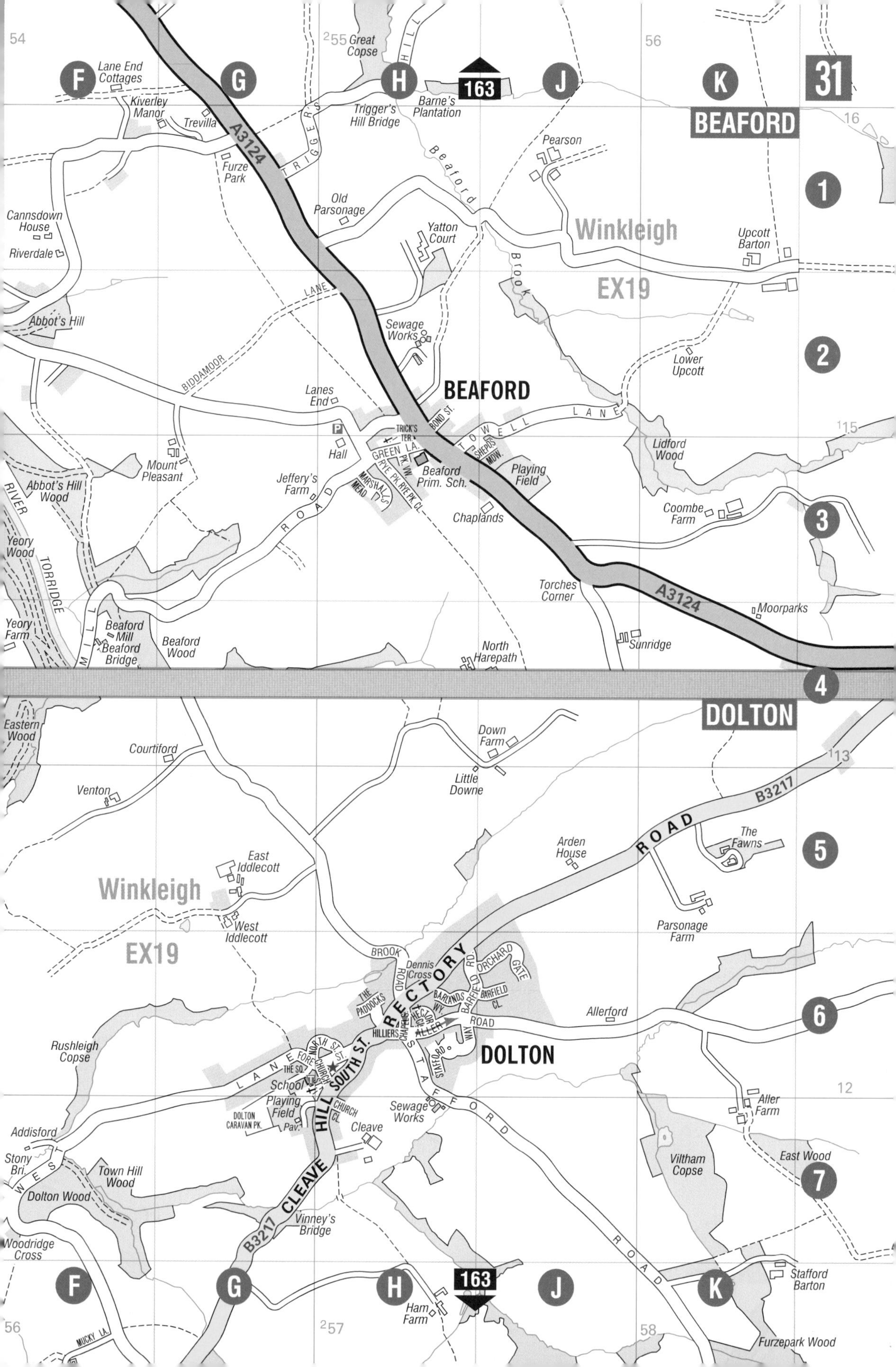

BEAFORD
DOLTON
Winkleigh
EX19
A3124
B3217
Great Copse
Lane End Cottages
Kiverley Manor
Trevilla
Trigger's Hill Bridge
Barne's Plantation
Pearson
Furze Park
Old Parsonage
Yatton Court
Cannsdown House
Riverdale
Upcott Barton
Abbot's Hill
Sewage Works
Lower Upcott
Lanes End
Hall
Mount Pleasant
Abbot's Hill Wood
Jeffery's Farm
Beaford Prim. Sch.
Playing Field
Lidford Wood
Coombe Farm
Chaplands
Yeory Wood
River Torridge
Torches Corner
Moorparks
Yeory Farm
Beaford Mill
Beaford Bridge
Beaford Wood
North Harepath
Sunridge
Eastern Wood
Courtiford
Down Farm
Little Downe
Venton
East Iddlecott
Arden House
The Fawns
West Iddlecott
Parsonage Farm
Dennis Cross
Allerford
Rushleigh Copse
School
Playing Field
Dolton Caravan Pk.
Sewage Works
Cleave
Aller Farm
Addisford
Stony Bri.
Town Hill Wood
Dolton Wood
Vinney's Bridge
Viltham Copse
East Wood
Woodridge Cross
Ham Farm
Stafford Barton
Furzepark Wood
Mucky La.
163

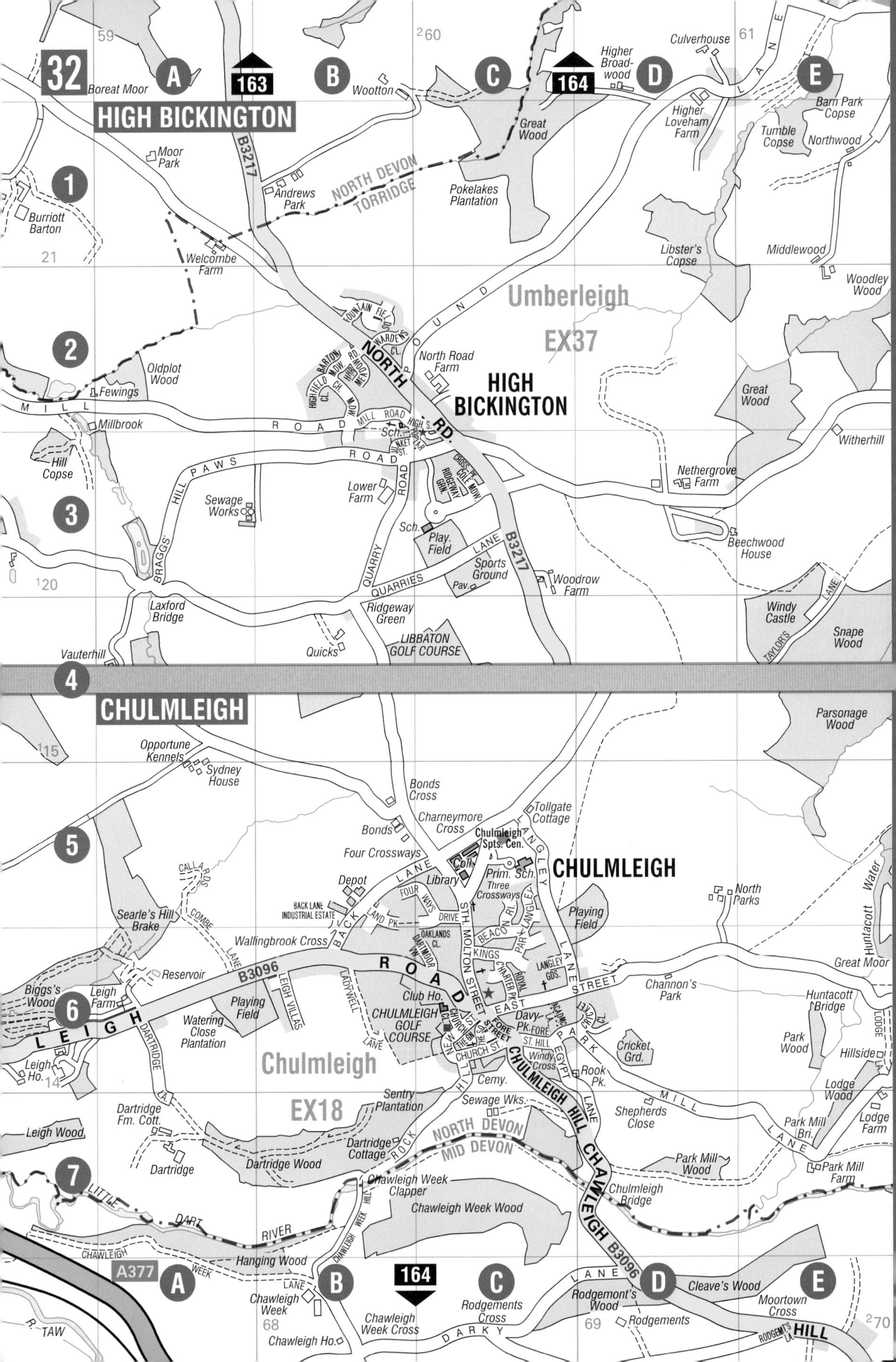
HIGH BICKINGTON
163
164
Boreat Moor
Moor Park
Burriott Barton
Andrews Park
Welcombe Farm
Wootton
Great Wood
Pokelakes Plantation
Higher Broad-wood
Culverhouse
Higher Loveham Farm
Barn Park Copse
Tumble Copse
Northwood
Libster's Copse
Middlewood
Woodley Wood
Umberleigh
EX37
NORTH DEVON
TORRIDGE
North Road Farm
HIGH BICKINGTON
Oldplot Wood
Fewings
Millbrook
Hill Copse
Sewage Works
Lower Farm
Play. Field
Sports Ground
Woodrow Farm
Nethergrove Farm
Witherhill
Great Wood
Beechwood House
Windy Castle
Snape Wood
Laxford Bridge
Ridgeway Green
Quicks
LIBBATON GOLF COURSE
Vauterhill
B3217
NORTH RD.
MILL ROAD
HILL PAWS ROAD
QUARRIES LANE
QUARRY ROAD
BRAGGS'
POUND
TAYLOR'S LANE
CHULMLEIGH
Opportune Kennels
Sydney House
Bonds Cross
Charneymore Cross
Bonds
Four Crossways
Tollgate Cottage
Chulmleigh Spts. Cen.
Coll.
Library
Prim. Sch.
Three Crossways
CHULMLEIGH
Depot
BACK LANE INDUSTRIAL ESTATE
Searle's Hill Brake
Wallingbrook Cross
Reservoir
Biggs's Wood
Leigh Farm
Playing Field
Watering Close Plantation
Club Ho.
CHULMLEIGH GOLF COURSE
Chulmleigh
EX18
Leigh Ho.
Dartridge Fm. Cott.
Dartridge
Leigh Wood
Sentry Plantation
Dartridge Cottage
Dartridge Wood
Cemy.
Sewage Wks.
NORTH DEVON
MID DEVON
Chawleigh Week Clapper
Chawleigh Week Wood
Hanging Wood
Chulmleigh Bridge
Playing Field
Channon's Park
North Parks
Parsonage Wood
Great Moor
Huntacott Water
Huntacott Bridge
Park Wood
Hillside
Cricket Grd.
Rook Pk.
Shepherds Close
Lodge Wood
Lodge Farm
Park Mill Bri.
Park Mill Wood
Park Mill Farm
Chawleigh Week
Chawleigh Ho.
Chawleigh Week Cross
Rodgements Cross
Rodgemont's Wood
Rodgements
Cleave's Wood
Moortown Cross
A377
R. TAW
LITTLE DART RIVER
B3096
LEIGH ROAD
CHULMLEIGH HILL
CHAWLEIGH
DARKY LANE
HILL
EAST STREET
FORE STREET
STH. MOLTON STREET
LANGLEY LANE
MILL LANE
PARK
EGYPT LANE
BACK LANE

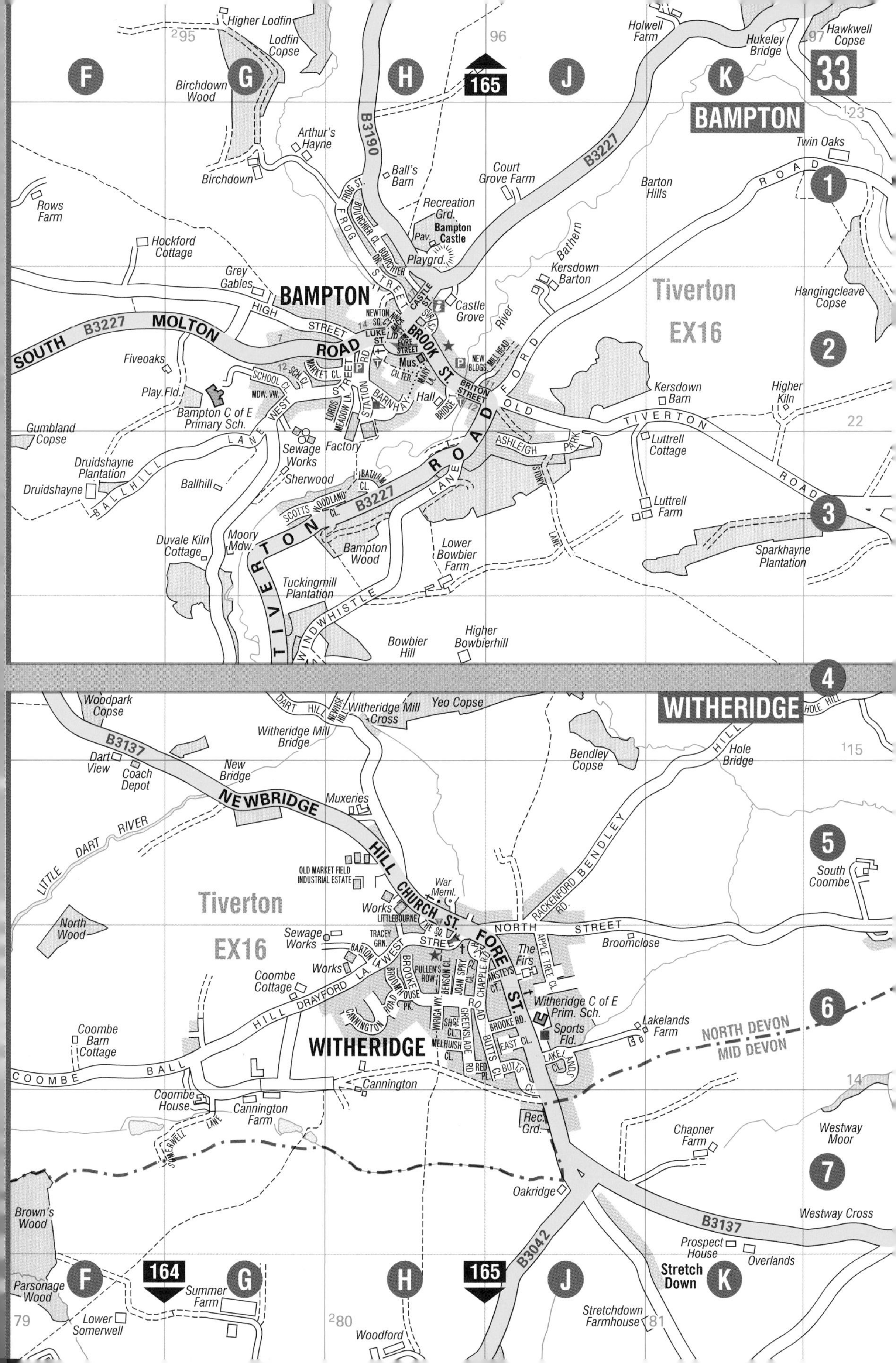
BAMPTON
WITHERIDGE
Tiverton
EX16
Higher Lodfin
Lodfin Copse
Birchdown Wood
Arthur's Hayne
Birchdown
Rows Farm
Hockford Cottage
Grey Gables
Ball's Barn
Recreation Grd.
Bampton Castle
Court Grove Farm
Holwell Farm
Hukeley Bridge
Hawkwell Copse
Twin Oaks
Barton Hills
Kersdown Barton
Hangingcleave Copse
Castle Grove
Fiveoaks
Play.Fld.
Bampton C of E Primary Sch.
Gumbland Copse
Druidshayne Plantation
Druidshayne
Ballhill
Sewage Works
Sherwood
Factory
Kersdown Barn
Higher Kiln
Luttrell Cottage
Luttrell Farm
Sparkhayne Plantation
Duvale Kiln Cottage
Moory Mdw.
Bampton Wood
Lower Bowbier Farm
Tuckingmill Plantation
Bowbier Hill
Higher Bowbierhill
Woodpark Copse
Witheridge Mill Cross
Yeo Copse
Witheridge Mill Bridge
Dart View
Coach Depot
New Bridge
Bendley Copse
Hole Bridge
Muxeries
LITTLE DART RIVER
OLD MARKET FIELD INDUSTRIAL ESTATE
War Meml.
South Coombe
North Wood
Works
Sewage Works
Broomclose
The Firs
Coombe Cottage
Witheridge C of E Prim. Sch.
Sports Fld.
Lakelands Farm
NORTH DEVON
MID DEVON
Coombe Barn Cottage
Cannington
Coombe House
Cannington Farm
Rec. Grd.
Chapner Farm
Westway Moor
Oakridge
Westway Cross
Brown's Wood
Prospect House
Overlands
Stretch Down
Parsonage Wood
Summer Farm
Lower Somerwell
Woodford
Stretchdown Farmhouse
SOUTH MOLTON ROAD
HIGH STREET
TIVERTON ROAD
OLD TIVERTON ROAD
NEWBRIDGE HILL
CHURCH ST.
FORE ST.
NORTH STREET
BENDLEY HILL
HILL DRAYFORD LA.
COOMBE BALL
B3227
B3190
B3137
B3042
165
164

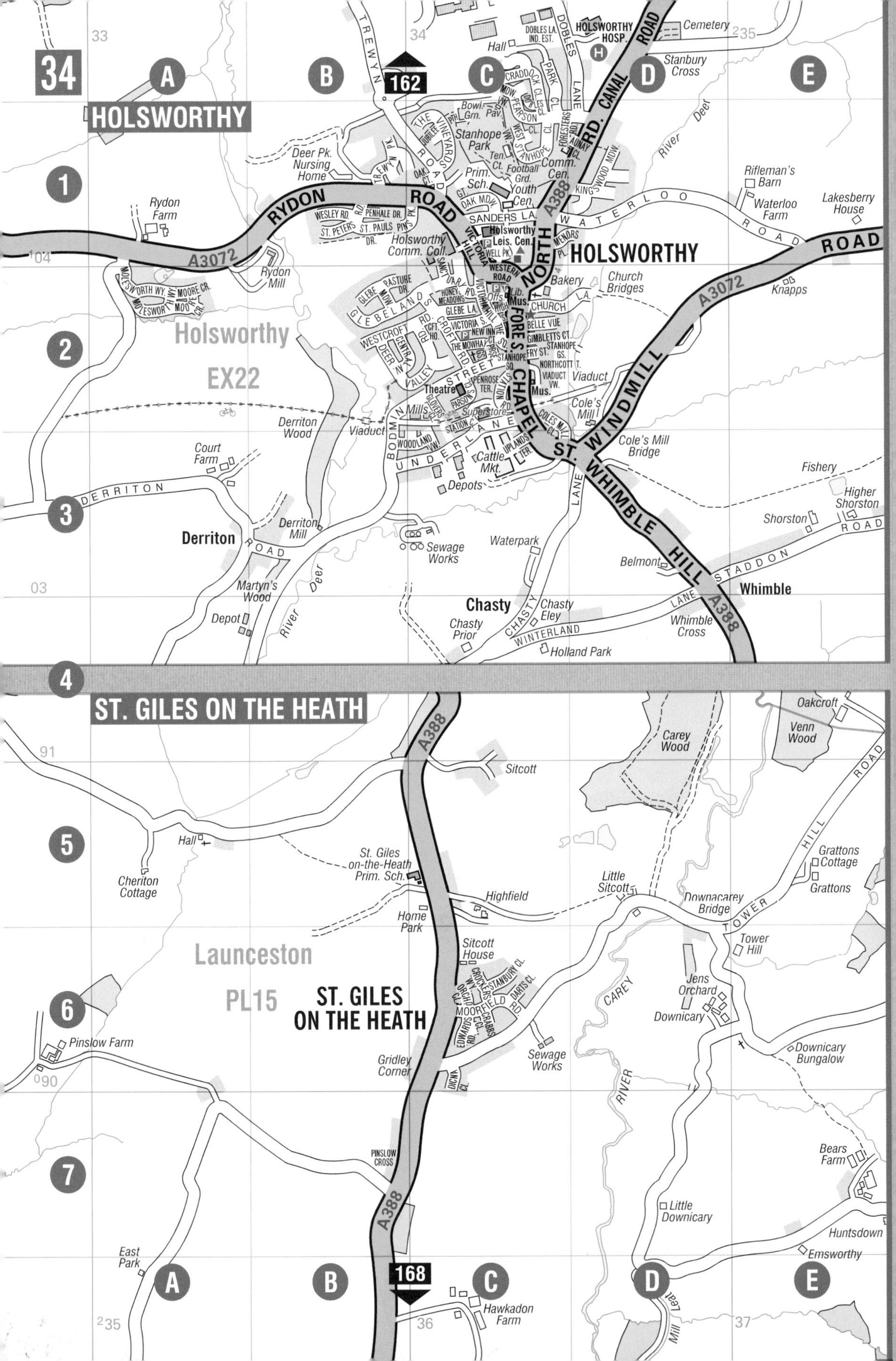

HOLSWORTHY
ST. GILES ON THE HEATH
162
168
A
B
C
D
E
1
2
3
4
5
6
7
Holsworthy
EX22
Launceston
PL15
RYDON ROAD
A3072
A388
NORTH RD.
CANAL ROAD
WATERLOO ROAD
ST. WHIMBLE HILL
WINDMILL
CHAPEL
FORE S
DERRITON ROAD
STADDON ROAD
WINTERLAND LANE
CHASTY LANE
TOWER HILL ROAD
Rydon Farm
Rydon Mill
Deer Pk. Nursing Home
Stanhope Park
Prim. Sch.
Youth Cen.
Comm. Cen.
Holsworthy Leis. Cen.
Holsworthy Comm. Coll.
HOLSWORTHY HOSP.
Cemetery
Stanbury Cross
Rifleman's Barn
Waterloo Farm
Lakesberry House
Knapps
Bakery
Church Bridges
Viaduct
Cole's Mill
Cole's Mill Bridge
Theatre
Superstore
Cattle Mkt.
Depots
Derriton Wood
Derriton Mill
Derriton
Court Farm
Martyn's Wood
Depot
River Deer
Sewage Works
Waterpark
Chasty
Chasty Prior
Chasty Eley
Holland Park
Belmont
Whimble
Whimble Cross
Fishery
Higher Shorston
Shorston
Oakcroft
Venn Wood
Carey Wood
Sitcott
Hall
Cheriton Cottage
St. Giles on-the-Heath Prim. Sch.
Highfield
Home Park
Little Sitcott
Downacarey Bridge
Grattons Cottage
Grattons
Tower Hill
Sitcott House
ST. GILES ON THE HEATH
Jens Orchard
Downicary
Downicary Bungalow
Sewage Works
Gridley Corner
Pinslow Farm
PINSLOW CROSS
RIVER CAREY
Bears Farm
Little Downicary
Huntsdown
Emsworthy
East Park
Hawkadon Farm
Mill Leat

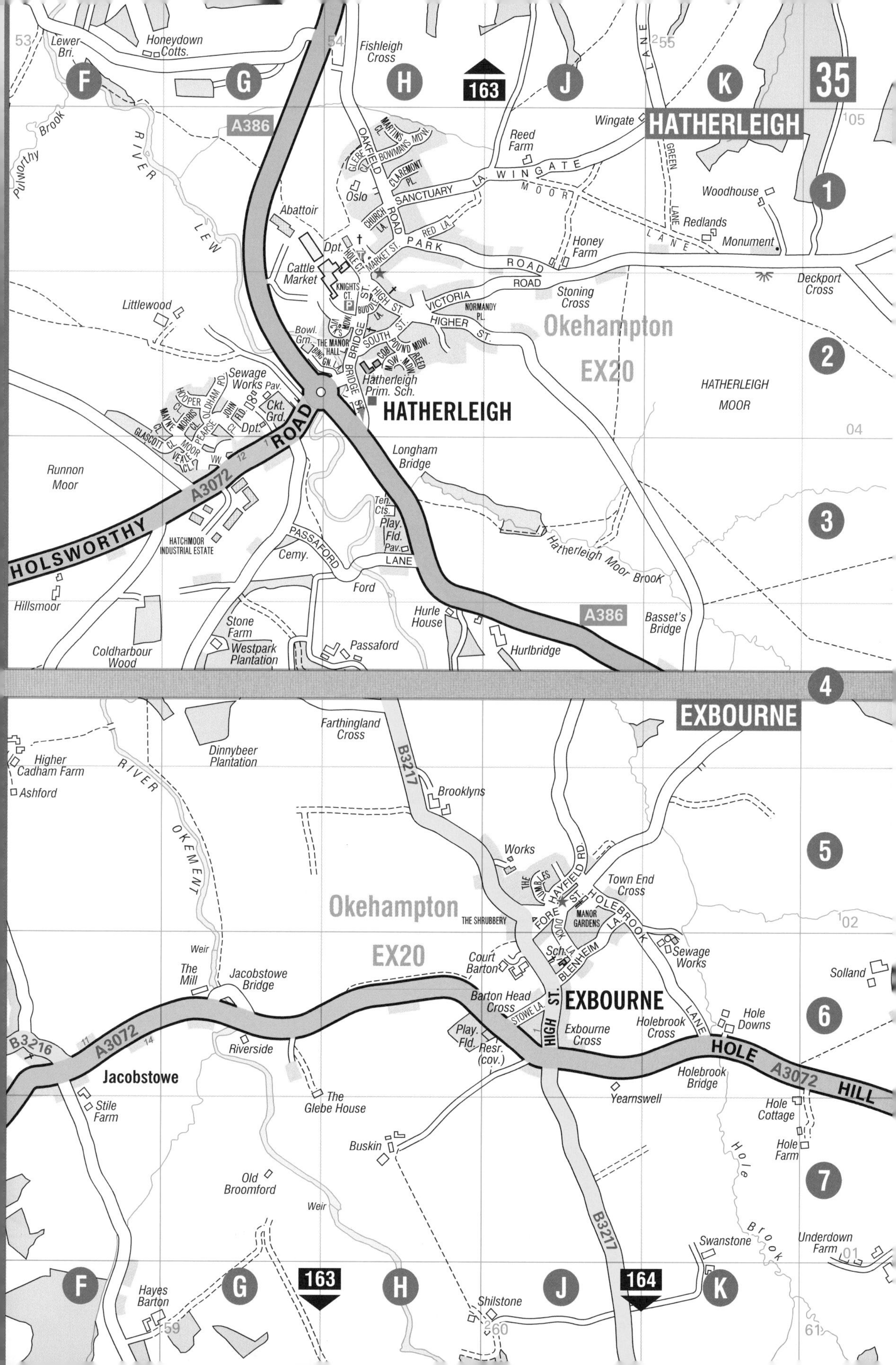

HATHERLEIGH
EXBOURNE
163
164
Okehampton
EX20
HATHERLEIGH
EXBOURNE
Jacobstowe
A386
A3072
B3217
B3216
HOLSWORTHY ROAD
HOLE HILL
Lewer Bri.
Honeydown Cotts.
Fishleigh Cross
Wingate
Reed Farm
Woodhouse
Redlands
Monument
Honey Farm
Deckport Cross
Stoning Cross
HATHERLEIGH MOOR
Pulworthy Brook
RIVER LEW
Abattoir
Oslo
Cattle Market
Littlewood
Sewage Works
Ckt. Grd.
Hatherleigh Prim. Sch.
Longham Bridge
Runnon Moor
HATCHMOOR INDUSTRIAL ESTATE
Cemy.
Play. Fld.
Ford
Hurle House
Hatherleigh Moor Brook
Basset's Bridge
Hillsmoor
Stone Farm
Westpark Plantation
Passaford
Hurlbridge
Coldharbour Wood
Farthingland Cross
Higher Cadham Farm
Ashford
Dinnybeer Plantation
RIVER OKEMENT
Brooklyns
Works
Town End Cross
THE SHRUBBERY
MANOR GARDENS
Sewage Works
Court Barton
Barton Head Cross
Exbourne Cross
Holebrook Cross
Solland
Hole Downs
Weir
The Mill
Jacobstowe Bridge
Riverside
Stile Farm
The Glebe House
Buskin
Yearnswell
Holebrook Bridge
Hole Cottage
Hole Farm
Hole Brook
Old Broomford
Weir
Swanstone
Underdown Farm
Hayes Barton
Shilstone

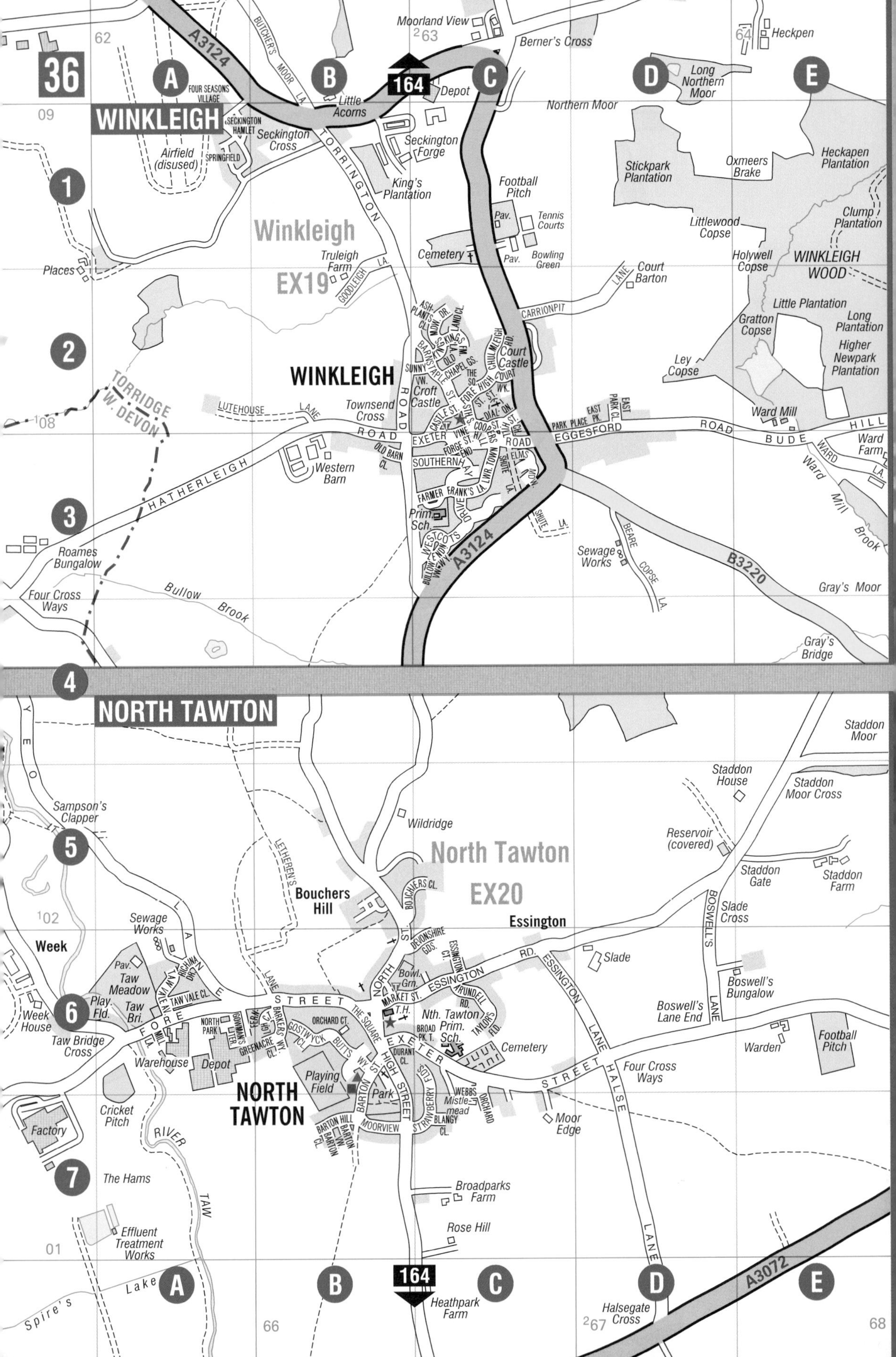
WINKLEIGH
NORTH TAWTON
164
A3124
Moorland View
Berner's Cross
Heckpen
Long Northern Moor
Little Acorns
Depot
Northern Moor
Four Seasons Village
Seckington Hamlet
Seckington Cross
Springfield
Airfield (disused)
Seckington Forge
King's Plantation
Stickpark Plantation
Oxmeers Brake
Heckapen Plantation
Football Pitch
Tennis Courts
Bowling Green
Cemetery
Winkleigh
EX19
Truleigh Farm
Places
Littlewood Copse
Clump Plantation
Holywell Copse
WINKLEIGH WOOD
Court Barton
Little Plantation
Gratton Copse
Long Plantation
Higher Newpark Plantation
Ley Copse
Court Castle
Croft Castle
Townsend Cross
TORRIDGE
W. DEVON
Lutehouse Lane
Hatherleigh Road
Exeter Road
Eggesford Road
Bude Road
Ward Mill
Ward Farm
Ward Mill Brook
Western Barn
Prim. Sch.
Roames Bungalow
Four Cross Ways
Bullow Brook
Sewage Works
Beare Copse La.
B3220
Gray's Moor
Gray's Bridge
Staddon Moor
Staddon House
Staddon Moor Cross
Sampson's Clapper
Wildridge
North Tawton
EX20
Reservoir (covered)
Staddon Gate
Staddon Farm
Bouchers Hill
Essington
Slade Cross
Week
Slade
Boswell's Bungalow
Boswell's Lane End
Taw Meadow
Taw Bri.
Play. Fld.
Week House
Taw Bridge Cross
Fore Street
Nth. Tawton Prim. Sch.
Cemetery
Warden
Football Pitch
Four Cross Ways
Warehouse
Depot
Playing Field
Park
Moor Edge
Factory
Cricket Pitch
River Taw
The Hams
Broadparks Farm
Rose Hill
Effluent Treatment Works
Lake
Spire's
Heathpark Farm
Halsegate Cross
A3072

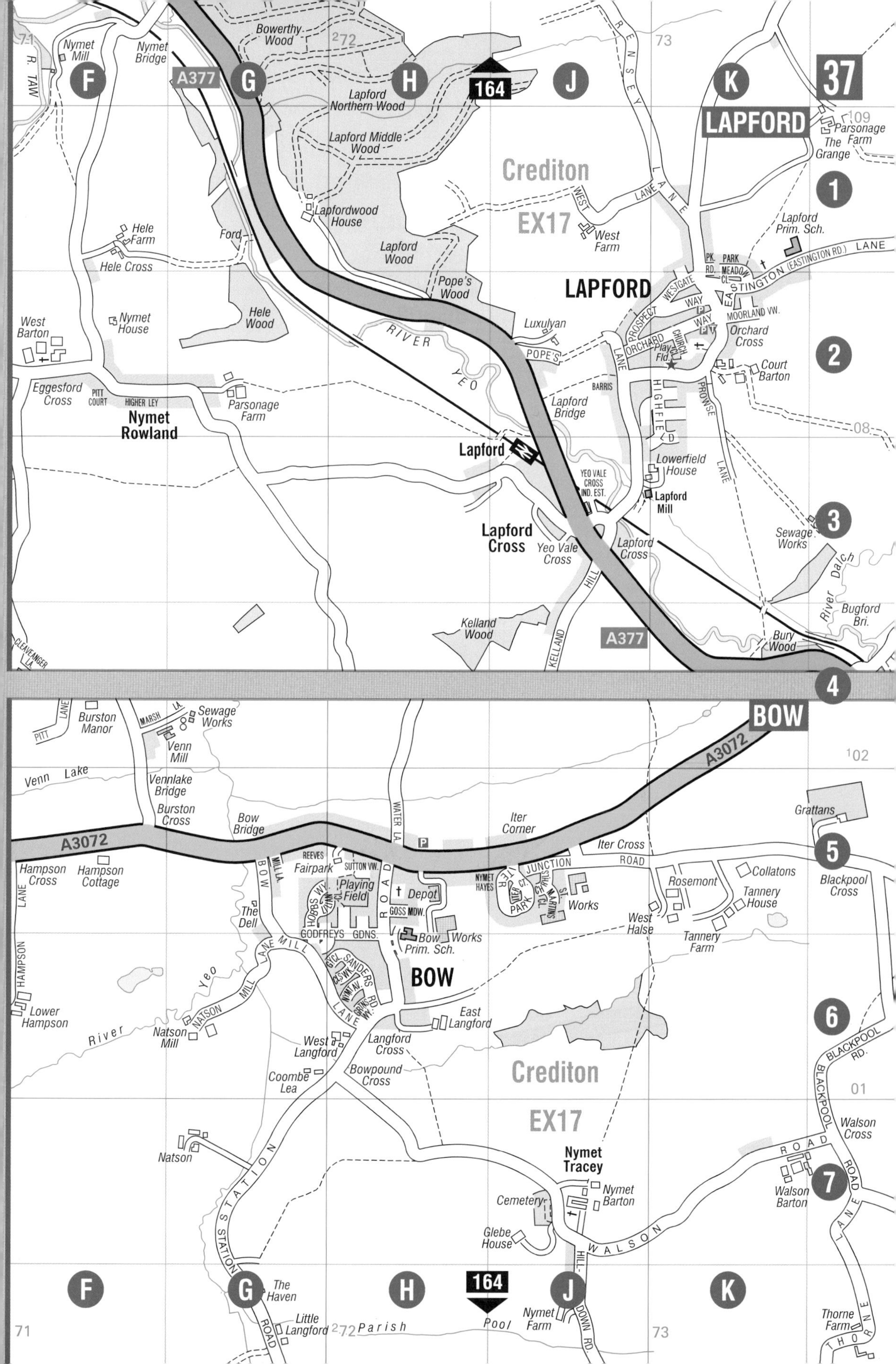

F | **G** | **H** | 164 | **J** | **K** | **37**

R. TAW

Nymet Mill

Nymet Bridge

A377

Bowerthy Wood

272

Parsonage Farm

109

The Grange

Lapford Northern Wood

1

Lapford Middle Wood

Crediton

EX17

WEST LANE

CHURCH LANE

Lapford Prim. Sch.

Hele Farm

Ford

Lapfordwood House

West Farm

PK. PARK RD. PARK MEAD CL.

Hele Cross

Lapford Wood

EASTINGTON (EASTINGTON RD.) LANE

Nymet House

Pope's Wood

WESTGATE WAY

MOORLAND VW.

LAPFORD

2

West Barton

RIVER YEO

Luxulyan

PROSPECT LANE

ORCHARD LANE

PLAY FLD.

EA. WAY

Orchard Cross

POPE'S

Playing Fld.

HIGHFIELD

PROWSE LANE

Court Barton

Eggesford Cross

PITT COURT

HIGHER LEY

Parsonage Farm

Lapford Bridge

BARRIS

08

Nymet Rowland

Lapford Bridge

Lapford

Lowerfield House

3

Yeo Vale Cross IND. EST.

Lapford Mill

Sewage Works

Lapford Cross

Yeo Vale Cross

Lapford Cross

River Dalch

Bugford Bri.

CLEVEANGER LA.

KELLAND HILL

Kelland Wood

A377

Bury Wood

4

BOW

A3072

Burston Manor

MARSH LA.

Sewage Works

PITT

LANE

Venn Mill

102

Venn Lake

Vennlake Bridge

WATER LA.

Iter Corner

Grattans

Burston Cross

Bow Bridge

A3072

BOW

P

Iter Cross ROAD

5

Hampson Cross

Hampson Cottage

REEVES

Fairpark

SUTTON VW.

NYMET HAYES

ITER CT. JUNCTION PARK

Rosemont

Collatons

Blackpool Cross

HAMPSON LANE

The Dell

MILL LA.

Playing Field

GOSS MDW.

Depot

ST. MARTINS

Works

Tannery House

GODFREYS

GDNS.

BOW Works Prim. Sch.

West Halse

Tannery Farm

6

Lower Hampson

River Yeo

Natson Mill

West Langford

East Langford

Langford Cross

Crediton

BLACKPOOL RD.

01

Natson

STATION

Coombe Lea

Bowpound Cross

EX17

Walson Cross

Walson Barton

7

Nymet Tracey

Cemetery

Nymet Barton

Glebe House

WALSON HILL

DOWN RD.

THORNE LANE

F | **G** | **H** | 164 | **J** | **K**

71

The Haven

STATION ROAD

Little Langford

272 Parish

Pool

Nymet Farm

73

Thorne Farm

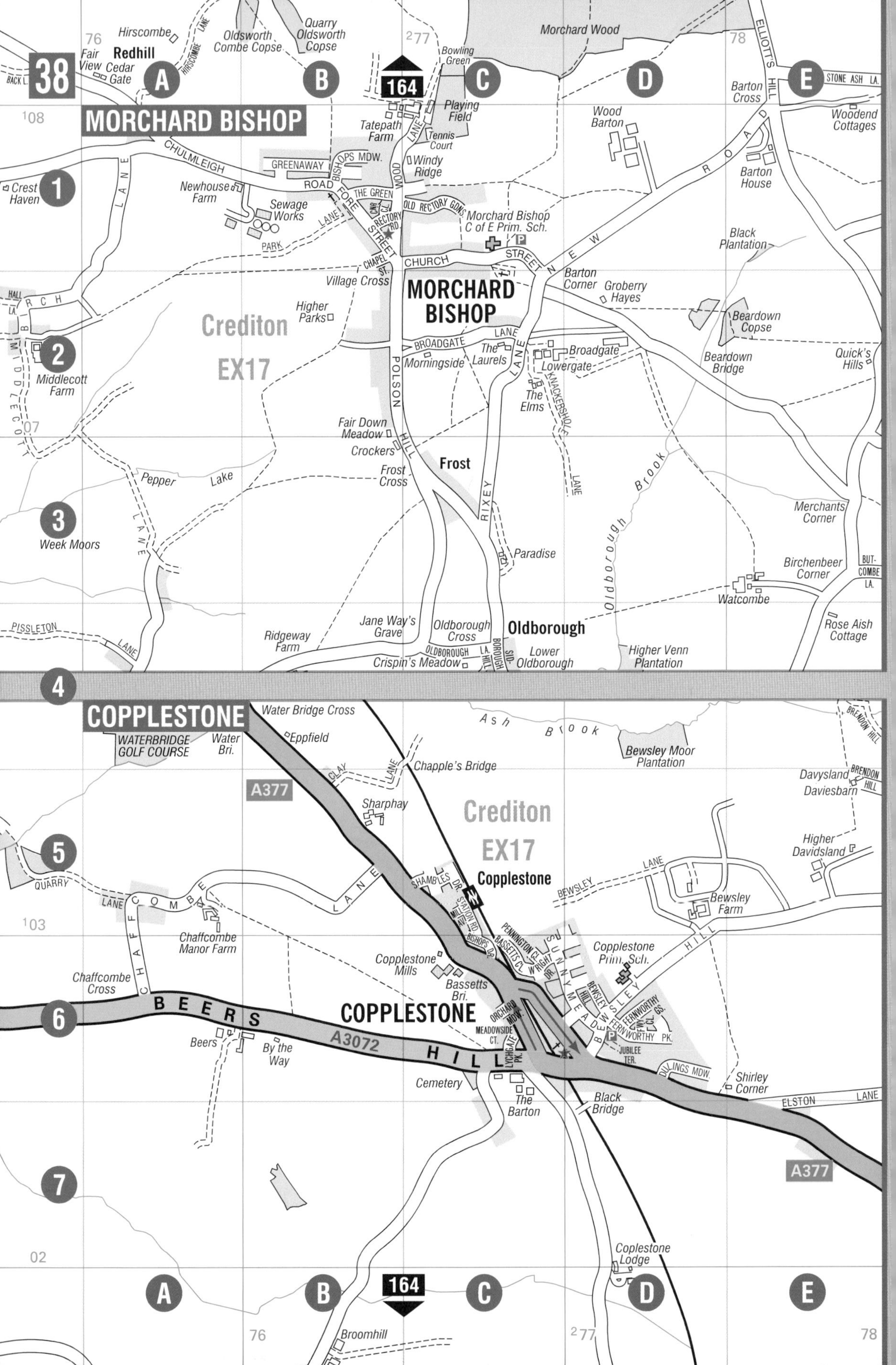
MORCHARD BISHOP
Redhill
Hirscombe
Fair View
Cedar Gate
Oldsworth Combe Copse
Quarry
Oldsworth Copse
Bowling Green
Morchard Wood
Elliott's Hill
Stone Ash La.
164
Barton Cross
Woodend Cottages
Wood Barton
Playing Field
Tatepath Farm
Tennis Court
Windy Ridge
Chulmleigh Road
Greenaway
Bishops Mdw.
Wood Lane
Barton House
Crest Haven
Newhouse Farm
Sewage Works
The Green
Old Rectory Gdns
Morchard Bishop C of E Prim. Sch.
Black Plantation
Fore Street
Park Lane
Chapel St.
Church Street
New Road
Village Cross
Barton Corner
Groberry Hayes
MORCHARD BISHOP
Higher Parks
Birch Hall La.
Beardown Copse
Crediton
EX17
Broadgate Lane
The Laurels
Broadgate
Lowergate
Morningside
Beardown Bridge
Quick's Hills
Middlecott Farm
Middlecott
Polson Hill
The Elms
Knackershole Lane
Fair Down Meadow
Crockers
Frost
Frost Cross
Pepper Lake
Oldborough Brook
Merchants Corner
Week Moors
Rixey Lane
Paradise
Birchenbeer Corner
Butcombe La.
Watcombe
Pissleton Lane
Jane Way's Grave
Oldborough Cross
Oldborough
Rose Aish Cottage
Ridgeway Farm
Oldborough La.
Borough Hill
Lower Oldborough
Higher Venn Plantation
Crispin's Meadow
COPPLESTONE
Water Bridge Cross
Waterbridge Golf Course
Water Bri.
Eppfield
Ash Brook
Brendon Hill
Bewsley Moor Plantation
Clay Lane
Chapple's Bridge
A377
Davysland
Daviesbarn
Sharphay
Crediton
EX17
Higher Davidsland
Quarry Lane
Chaffcombe Lane
Copplestone
Bewsley Lane
Bewsley Farm
Shambles Dr.
Station Rd
Mill Av.
Bishops Dr.
Pennington Cl.
Bassetts Cl.
Wright Dr.
Sunnymead
Bewsley Hill
Copplestone Prim. Sch.
Chaffcombe Manor Farm
Copplestone Mills
Bassetts Bri.
Chaffcombe Cross
Beers Hill
COPPLESTONE
Orchard Mdw.
Meadowside Ct.
Fernworthy
Fernworthy Pk.
Jubilee Ter.
Dillings Mdw.
Beers
By the Way
A3072
Lychgate Pk.
Cemetery
The Barton
Black Bridge
Shirley Corner
Elston Lane
Coplestone Lodge
Broomhill

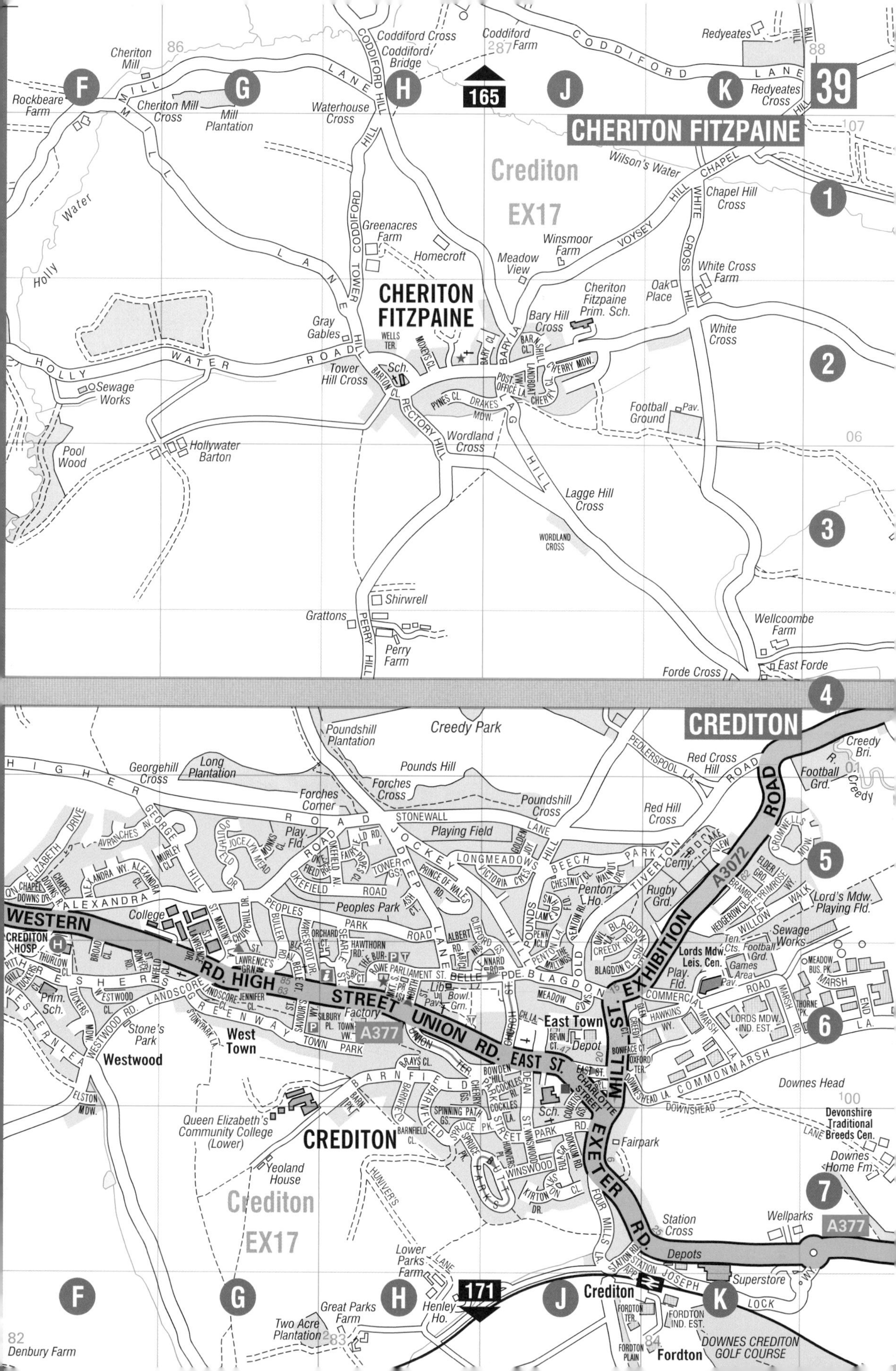
CHERITON FITZPAINE
Crediton
EX17
CHERITON FITZPAINE
Cheriton Mill
Rockbeare Farm
Cheriton Mill Cross
Mill Plantation
Coddiford Cross
Coddiford Bridge
Coddiford Farm
Waterhouse Cross
Redyeates
Redyeates Cross
CODDIFORD LANE
MILL LANE
CODDIFORD HILL
Wilson's Water
Chapel Hill Cross
CHAPEL HILL
VOYSEY HILL
WHITE CROSS HILL
Holly Water
Greenacres Farm
Homecroft
Meadow View
Winsmoor Farm
White Cross Farm
Oak Place
Cheriton Fitzpaine Prim. Sch.
Bary Hill Cross
White Cross
Gray Gables
TOWER HILL
HOLLY WATER ROAD
Tower Hill Cross
Sch.
Sewage Works
Hollywater Barton
Pool Wood
RECTORY HILL
Wordland Cross
LAGG HILL
Football Ground
Pav.
Lagge Hill Cross
WORDLAND CROSS
Shirwell
Grattons
PERRY HILL
Perry Farm
Wellcoombe Farm
Forde Cross
East Forde
165
1
2
3
4
F
G
H
J
K
CREDITON
Creedy Park
Poundshill Plantation
Creedy Bri.
Football Grd.
R. Creedy
Red Cross Hill
PEDLERSPOOL LA.
Pounds Hill
Long Plantation
Georgehill Cross
HIGHER ROAD
Forches Cross
Forches Corner
Poundshill Cross
Red Hill Cross
STONEWALL LANE
Playing Field
Play. Fld.
JOCKEY HILL
LONGMEADOWS
BEECH PARK
TIVERTON RD.
Cemy.
A3072
ROAD
Rugby Grd.
Penton Ho.
EXHIBITION
Lord's Mdw. Playing Fld.
Sewage Works
Peoples Park
PEOPLES PARK ROAD
ALEXANDRA RD.
WESTERN RD.
HIGH STREET
UNION RD.
EAST ST.
MILL ST.
College
CREDITON HOSP.
Prim. Sch.
Lords Mdw. Leis. Cen.
Play. Fld.
Games Area
Pav.
COMMERCIAL RD.
LORDS MDW. IND. EST.
MARSH
MEADOW BUS. PK.
Factory
A377
East Town
Depot
Stone's Park
West Town
Westwood
GREENWAY
TOWN PARK
BARNFIELD
COMMONMARSH
Downes Head
DOWNSHEAD LANE
Devonshire Traditional Breeds Cen.
Downes Home Fm.
Queen Elizabeth's Community College (Lower)
CREDITON
Yeoland House
Fairpark
EXETER RD.
Sch.
Crediton
EX17
Station Cross
Wellparks
A377
Depots
Lower Parks Farm
Great Parks Farm
Two Acre Plantation
Henley Ho.
171
Crediton
Superstore
FORDTON TER.
FORDTON IND. EST.
Fordton
DOWNES CREDITON GOLF COURSE
Denbury Farm
5
6
7
F
G
H
J
K

Cotleigh Cleave
Brookvale
Worth Ho.
Bolham House
Prim. Sch.
Bolham
Sports Grd.
Pav.
Knightshayes Lodge
Knightshayes Plantation
KNIGHTSHAYES PARK
LONG LANE
Warren Cross
Kensington Ct.
Worth Park Farm
Velvains
Rix Cottages
Works
A361
Exe Vale
Swinesbridge
Lower Farleigh
Higher Farleigh
Farleigh House
Worth Lodge
RACKENFORD RD.
Petroc (Tiverton Campus)
Cricket Pitch
Playing Field
Hockey Grd.
Exe Valley Leisure Cen.
Tiverton Cemetery
Prescott
Prescott Cottages
Lower Prescott
Tiverton High Sch.
Playing Field
Rugby Football Grd.
TIVERTON & DIST. HOSPITAL
Tiverton Town FC (Ladysmead)
Youth Cen.
People's Park
Trad. Est.
Factory
Tiverton Castle
HILL LEAT RD.
KENNEDY WAY
LONGDRAG
B3137
A3126
165
Highfield Vineyards
Ditchetts
Highfield
St. Johns RC Prim. Sch.
Hensleigh Cottage
Wynardsmead Cottages
Cotteylands
Ashley Park Farm
Whitcombe
Hillcroft
Rec. Grd.
Play. Fld.
Depot
Sch.
Lib.
T.H.
Cin.
Mus.
Superstore
Council Offs.
Sports Ground
Football Grd.
Works
Vis. Cen.
Training Ship Hermes
GREAT WESTERN WAY
A396
Shrinkhills
Deyman's Hill House
Tumbling Fields
TIVERTON
Lit. Silver Bri.
High Mount
Horn Hill
Ragged Cottage
Mogridge Farm
Cranmore Cottage
Cranmore Castle Fort
Collipriest Dairy
Carriage House
Park Wood
Castlebarn
Howden Court
Higher Howden Farm
Garden Copse
South Hill Plantation
Ashley
Collipriest
Garden Cott.
Wood Close
Patcott Wood
Whitehall Farm
Lower Collipriest Farm
The Guoil
Holwell Combe
Lodge Hill Farm
Hills-borough
EXETER RD.
RIVER EXE

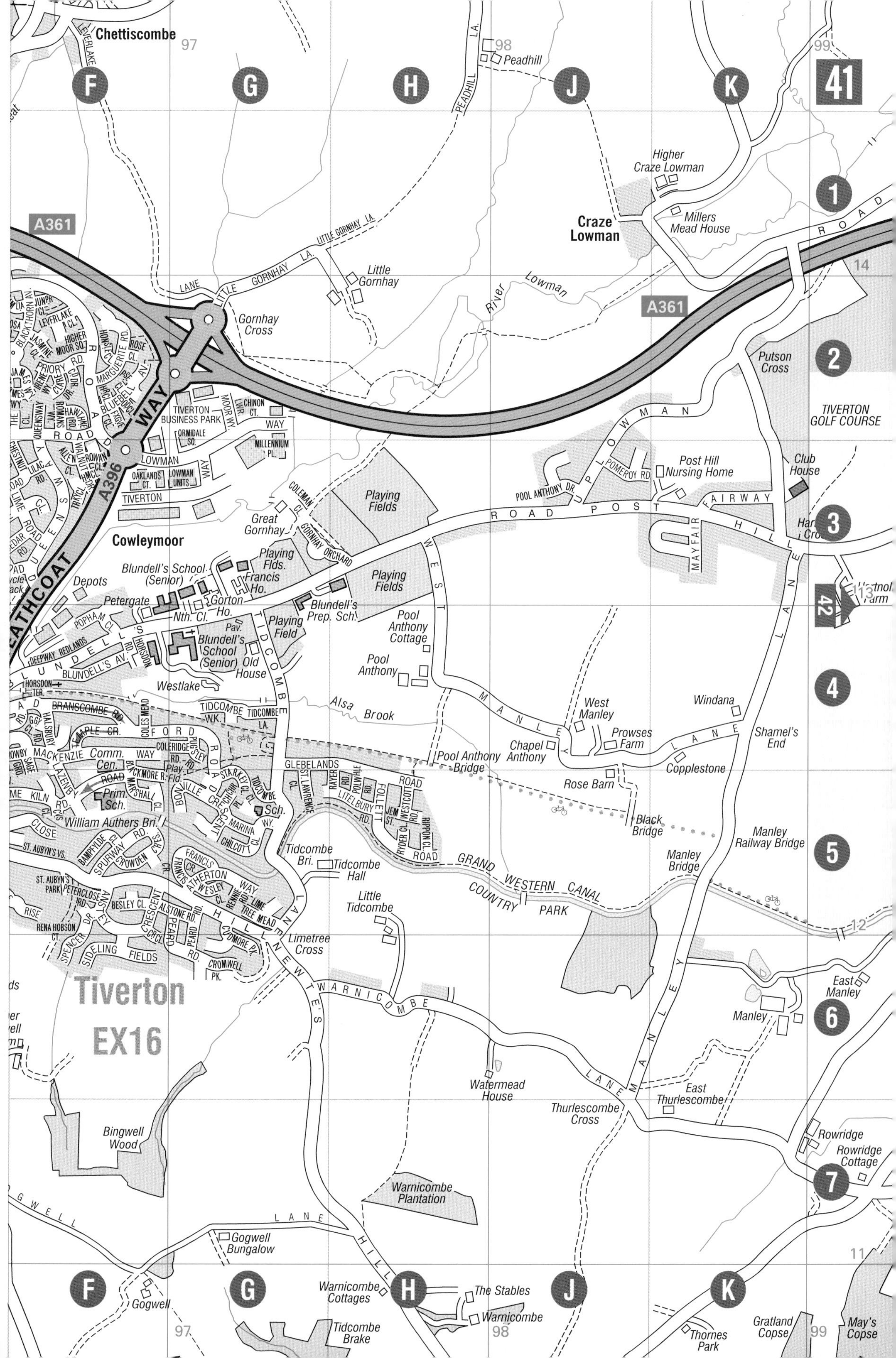

Chettiscombe
LEVERLAKE
97
98
99
F
G
H
J
K
PEADHILL LA.
Peadhill
Higher
Craze Lowman
Craze
Lowman
Millers
Mead House
A361
LITTLE GORNHAY LA.
LANE
LITTLE GORNHAY LA.
Little
Gornhay
Gornhay
Cross
River Lowman
ROAD
14
Putson
Cross
TIVERTON
GOLF COURSE
TIVERTON
BUSINESS PARK
MOOR WY.
CHINON CT.
WAY
ORMIDALE SQ.
MILLENNIUM PL.
LOWMAN
OAKLANDS CT.
LOWMAN UNITS
TIVERTON
A396
WAY
HEATHCOAT
LOWMAN
POMEROY RD.
Post Hill
Nursing Home
Club
House
POOL ANTHONY DR.
ROAD
POST
HILL
FAIRWAY
MAYFAIR
COLEMAN CL.
Great
Gornhay
GORNHAY ORCHARD
Playing
Fields
Cowleymoor
Blundell's School
(Senior)
Playing
Flds.
Francis
Ho.
Depots
Petergate
Gorton
Ho.
Nth. Cl.
Blundell's
Prep. Sch.
Playing
Field
WEST
Pool
Anthony
Cottage
Pool
Anthony
POPHAM CL.
BLUNDELL'S
DEEPWAY
REDLANDS
BLUNDELL'S AV.
Pav.
Blundell's
School
(Senior)
Old
House
Westlake
TIDCOMBE
HORSDON TER.
BRANSCOMBE RD.
TEMPLE CR.
COLES MEAD
TIDCOMBE WK.
TIDCOMBE LA.
Alsa Brook
MANLEY
West
Manley
Windana
Shamel's
End
Prowses
Farm
Chapel
Anthony
LANE
Pool Anthony
Bridge
Copplestone
Rose Barn
Comm.
Cen.
FORD
ROAD
COLERIDGE
MACKENZIE WAY
GLEBELANDS
ST. LAWRENCE CL.
RAYER RD.
POLWHELE RD.
FOLLETT RD.
ROAD
LITELBURY RD.
WESTCOTT RD.
RIPPON CL.
RYDER CL.
JEM ST.
Prim.
Sch.
Sch.
KILN
CLOSE
William Authers Bri.
ST. AUBYN'S VS.
BAMPFYLDE CL.
SPURWAY
CROWDEN CRES.
CHILCOTT CL.
MARINA
Black
Bridge
Manley
Railway Bridge
Manley
Bridge
Tidcombe
Bri.
Tidcombe
Hall
GRAND WESTERN CANAL
COUNTRY PARK
ATHERTON
FRANCIS CR.
WESLEY CL.
RENNIE
LIME
TREE MEAD
WAY
ST. AUBYN'S PARK
PETERCLOSE RD.
BESLEY CL.
ALSTONE RD.
PEARD RD.
CUDMORE PK.
CRESCENT
RISE
RENA HOBSON CT.
SPENCER DR.
SIDELING FIELDS
CROMWELL PK.
Limetree
Cross
Little
Tidcombe
12
NEWTE'S
WARNICOMBE
LANE
MANLEY
East
Manley
Manley
Tiverton
EX16
Watermead
House
Thurlescombe
Cross
East
Thurlescombe
Rowridge
Rowridge
Cottage
Bingwell
Wood
Warnicombe
Plantation
GOGWELL
LANE
HILL
Gogwell
Bungalow
11
Gogwell
Warnicombe
Cottages
The Stables
Warnicombe
Tidcombe
Brake
Thornes
Park
Gratland
Copse
May's
Copse
1
2
3
4
5
6
7
42
13

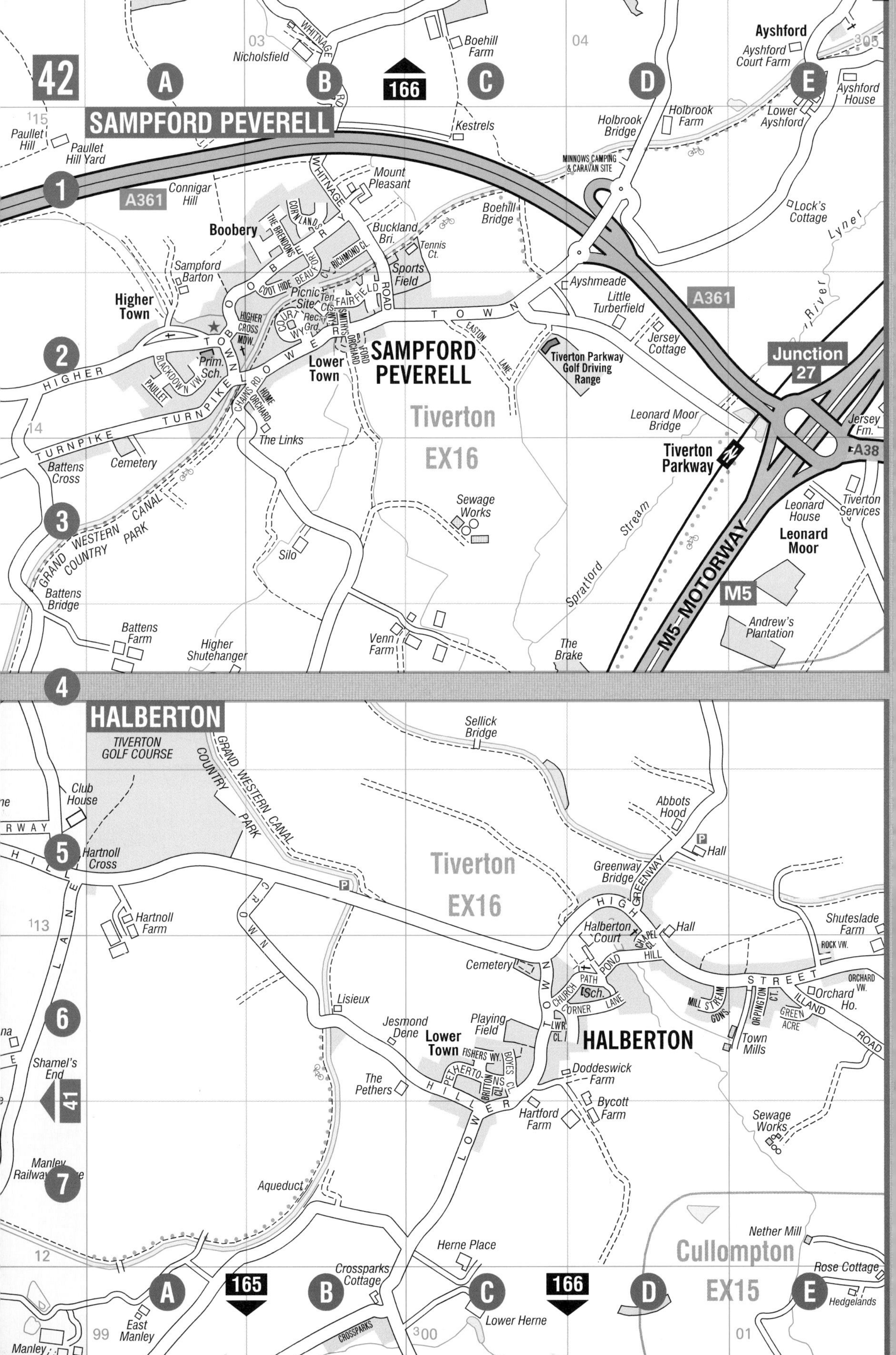
SAMPFORD PEVERELL
HALBERTON
Nicholsfield
Boehill Farm
Ayshford
Ayshford Court Farm
Ayshford House
Lower Ayshford
Holbrook Bridge
Holbrook Farm
Kestrels
Paullet Hill
Paullet Hill Yard
Connigar Hill
A361
Mount Pleasant
Boobery
Buckland Bri.
Tennis Ct.
Sports Field
Sampford Barton
Higher Town
Boehill Bridge
Lock's Cottage
Ayshmeade
Little Turberfield
Jersey Cottage
Tiverton Parkway Golf Driving Range
Junction 27
Lower Town
Tiverton
EX16
Leonard Moor Bridge
Tiverton Parkway
Jersey Fm.
A38
Battens Cross
Cemetery
The Links
Sewage Works
Leonard House
Tiverton Services
Leonard Moor
GRAND WESTERN CANAL COUNTRY PARK
Silo
Spratford Stream
M5 MOTORWAY
M5
Andrew's Plantation
Battens Bridge
Battens Farm
Higher Shutehanger
Venn Farm
The Brake
TIVERTON GOLF COURSE
Sellick Bridge
Club House
Abbots Hood
Hall
Hartnoll Cross
Greenway Bridge
Hartnoll Farm
Halberton Court
Shuteslade Farm
Cemetery
Orchard Ho.
Lisieux
Jesmond Dene
Playing Field
Town Mills
The Pethers
Doddeswick Farm
Bycott Farm
Hartford Farm
Sewage Works
Shamel's End
Aqueduct
Nether Mill
Herne Place
Cullompton
EX15
Crossparks Cottage
Rose Cottage
Hedgelands
East Manley
Lower Herne
Manley
166
165
41

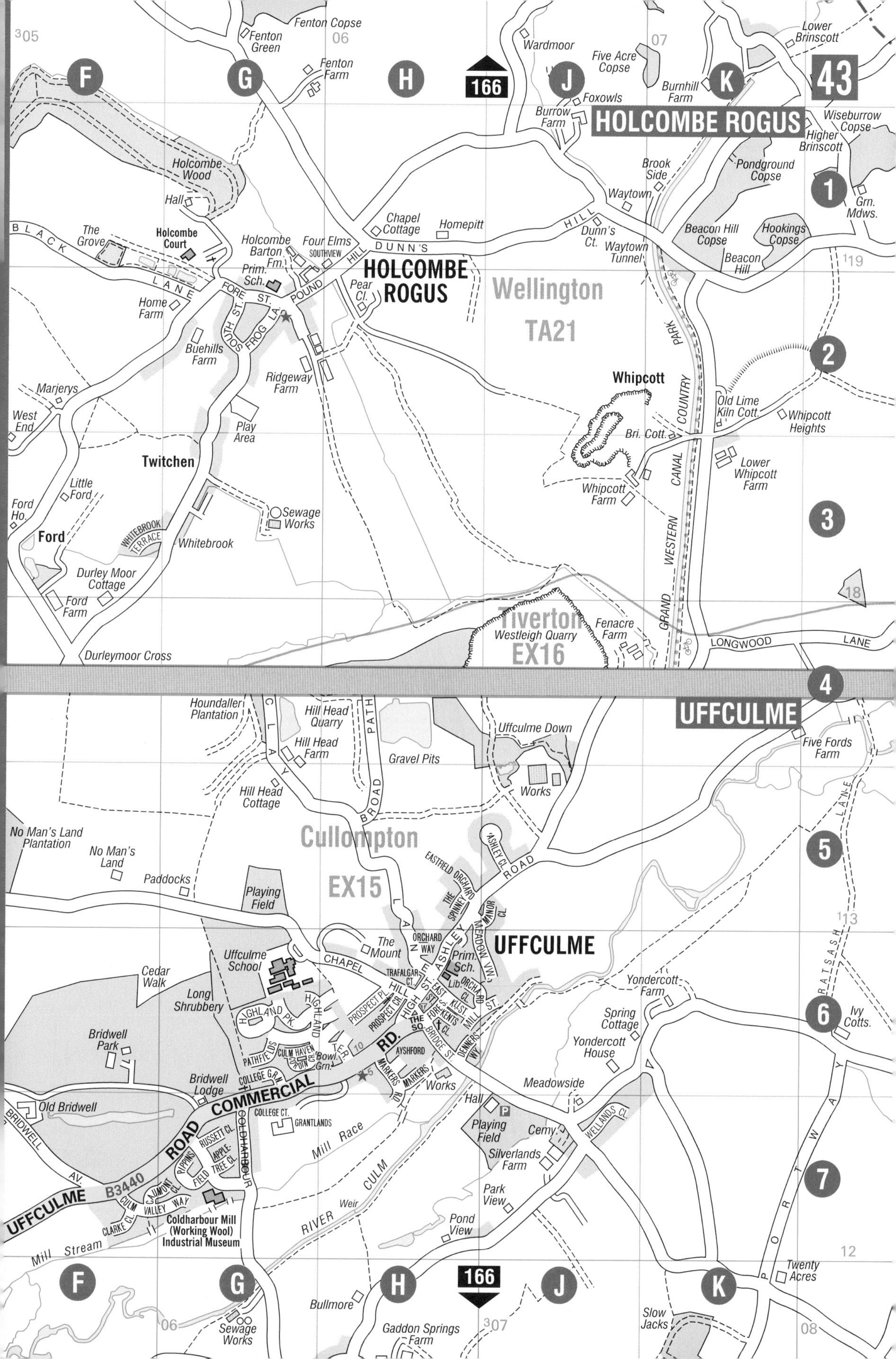
43
HOLCOMBE ROGUS
UFFCULME
166
Fenton Copse
Fenton Green
Fenton Farm
Wardmoor
Five Acre Copse
Lower Brinscott
Burnhill Farm
Foxowls
Burrow Farm
Wiseburrow Copse
Higher Brinscott
Pondground Copse
Brook Side
Waytown
Grn. Mdws.
Holcombe Wood
Hall
Chapel Cottage
Homepitt
Dunn's Hill
Dunn's Ct.
Waytown Tunnel
Beacon Hill Copse
Hookings Copse
Beacon Hill
Black Lane
The Grove
Holcombe Court
Holcombe Barton Fm.
Four Elms
Southview
Prim. Sch.
Home Farm
Fore St.
South St.
Frog La.
Pound
Pear Cl.
HOLCOMBE ROGUS
Wellington
TA21
Buehills Farm
Ridgeway Farm
Whipcott
Old Lime Kiln Cott.
Whipcott Heights
Bri. Cott.
Lower Whipcott Farm
Whipcott Farm
Grand Western Canal Country Park
Marjerys
West End
Play Area
Twitchen
Little Ford
Ford Ho.
Ford
Whitebrook Terrace
Whitebrook
Sewage Works
Durley Moor Cottage
Ford Farm
Durleymoor Cross
Tiverton
Westleigh Quarry
EX16
Fenacre Farm
Longwood Lane
Houndaller Plantation
Clay Lane
Hill Head Quarry
Hill Head Farm
Path
Gravel Pits
Uffculme Down
Works
Five Fords Farm
Hill Head Cottage
Broad Road
No Man's Land Plantation
No Man's Land
Paddocks
Cullompton
EX15
Ashley Cl.
Ashley Road
Eastfield
Orchard
The Spinney
Manor Cl.
Ratsash Lane
Playing Field
The Mount
Orchard Way
Meadow Vw.
UFFCULME
Uffculme School
Chapel Hill
Trafalgar Ct.
Prim. Sch.
Lib.
Orchard Cl.
Cedar Walk
Long Shrubbery
Highland Pk.
Highland Ter.
Prospect Pl.
Prospect Cr.
High St.
East St.
Forest Cl.
Kents Cl.
Mill St.
The Sq.
Bridge St.
Denners Wy.
Yondercott Farm
Spring Cottage
Yondercott House
Ivy Cotts.
Bridwell Park
Pathfields
Culm Haven
Coombe Ct.
Bowl. Grn.
Ayshford
Markers Rd.
Works
Meadowside
Bridwell Lodge
College Grn.
Commercial Road
Old Bridwell
College Ct.
Grantlands
Coldharbour
Hall
Playing Field
Cemy.
Wellands Cl.
Bridwell Av.
Russett Cl.
Pippins Field
Apple Tree Cl.
Mill Race
River Culm
Silverlands Farm
Park View
Portway
Uffculme B3440
Culm Valley Way
Caumont Cl.
Clarke Cl.
Coldharbour Mill (Working Wool) Industrial Museum
Weir
Pond View
Mill Stream
Bullmore
Twenty Acres
Slow Jacks
Gaddon Springs Farm
Sewage Works
F G H J K
1 2 3 4 5 6 7
305 06 07 307 08
119 18 113 12

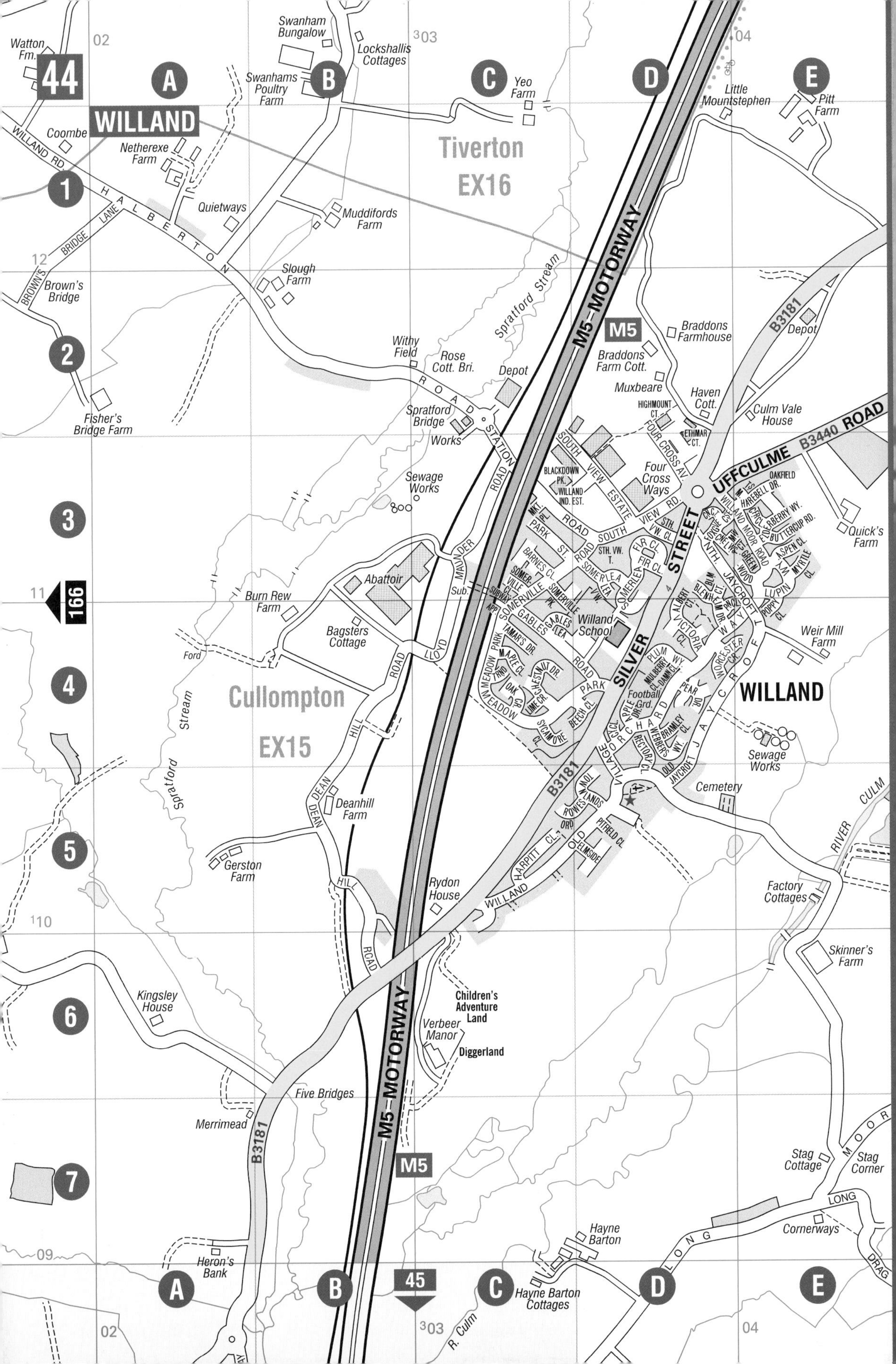
WILLAND
Watton Fm.
Coombe
Netherexe Farm
Quietways
Swanham Bungalow
Swanhams Poultry Farm
Lockshallis Cottages
Yeo Farm
Little Mountstephen
Pitt Farm
Tiverton
EX16
Muddifords Farm
Slough Farm
WILLAND RD.
HALBERTON
BROWN'S BRIDGE LANE
Brown's Bridge
Fisher's Bridge Farm
Withy Field
Rose Cott. Bri.
Spratford Stream
Depot
Spratford Bridge
Works
Sewage Works
STATION ROAD
M5
M5-MOTORWAY
Braddons Farmhouse
Braddons Farm Cott.
Muxbeare
Haven Cott.
Culm Vale House
B3181
B3440
UFFCULME ROAD
Four Cross Ways
SOUTH VIEW ESTATE
FOUR CROSS AV.
SILVER STREET
Abattoir
Burn Rew Farm
Bagsters Cottage
MAUNDER
LLOYD ROAD
HILL
Sub.
Willand School
Football Grd.
Quick's Farm
Weir Mill Farm
WILLAND
JAYCROFT
Sewage Works
Cemetery
Cullompton
EX15
Spratford Stream
Ford
DEAN HILL ROAD
Deanhill Farm
Gerston Farm
Rydon House
WILLAND
Factory Cottages
RIVER CULM
Skinner's Farm
Children's Adventure Land
Verbeer Manor
Diggerland
Kingsley House
Five Bridges
Merrimead
Stag Cottage
Stag Corner
MOOR
LONG
LONG DRAG
Cornerways
Hayne Barton
Hayne Barton Cottages
Heron's Bank
R. Culm
02
303
04
12
11
110
09
166
45
A
B
C
D
E
1
2
3
4
5
6
7

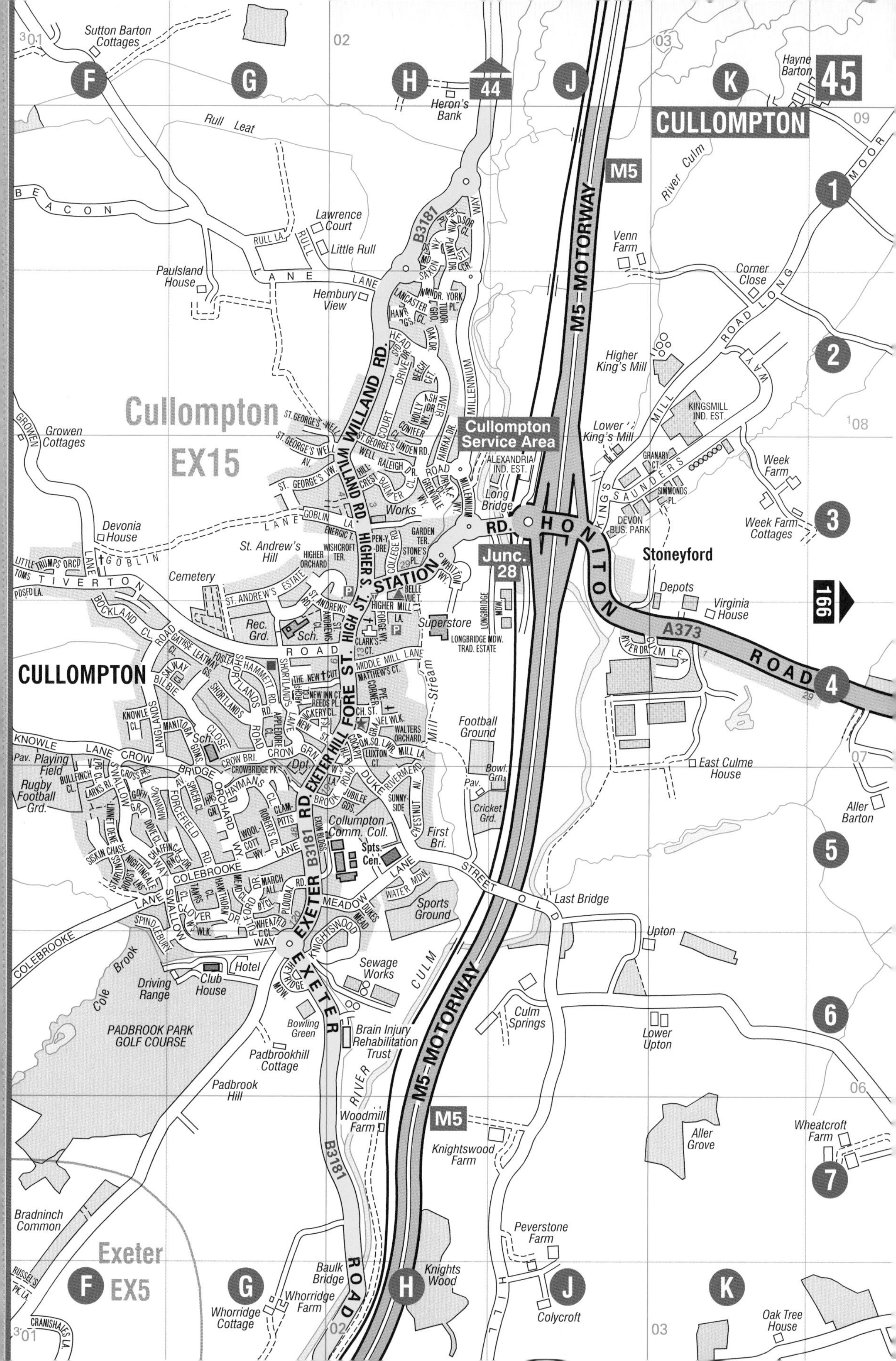

45
CULLOMPTON
Cullompton
EX15
Exeter
EX5
44
166
Junc. 28
Cullompton Service Area
M5-MOTORWAY
M5
A373
B3181
HONITON RD.
Sutton Barton Cottages
Heron's Bank
Hayne Barton
Rull Leat
BEACON LANE
River Culm
Lawrence Court
Little Rull
Paulsland House
Hembury View
Venn Farm
Corner Close
LONG ROAD
Higher King's Mill
KINGSMILL IND. EST.
Lower King's Mill
Growen Cottages
WILLAND RD.
MILLENNIUM WAY
ALEXANDRIA IND. EST.
Long Bridge
SAUNDERS WAY
DEVON BUS. PARK
Week Farm
Week Farm Cottages
Stoneyford
Devonia House
GOBLIN LANE
St. Andrew's Hill
TIVERTON ROAD
Cemetery
HIGHER ST.
HIGH ST.
STATION RD.
Superstore
LONGBRIDGE MDW. TRAD. ESTATE
Depots
Virginia House
Rec. Grd.
Sch.
FORE ST.
Mill Stream
Football Ground
East Culme House
CULLOMPTON
KNOWLE LANE
CROW BRIDGE
Playing Field
Rugby Football Grd.
EXETER HILL
Collumpton Comm. Coll.
Spts. Cen.
First Bri.
Bowl. Grn.
Pav.
Cricket Grd.
Aller Barton
OLD STREET
Last Bridge
COLEBROOKE LANE
Sports Ground
Upton
Cole Brook
Driving Range
Club House
Hotel
Sewage Works
CULM
PADBROOK PARK GOLF COURSE
Bowling Green
Brain Injury Rehabilitation Trust
Culm Springs
Lower Upton
Padbrookhill Cottage
Padbrook Hill
RIVER
Woodmill Farm
Knightswood Farm
Aller Grove
Wheatcroft Farm
Bradninch Common
EXETER ROAD
Peverstone Farm
Baulk Bridge
Knights Wood
Whorridge Farm
Whorridge Cottage
Colycroft
Oak Tree House

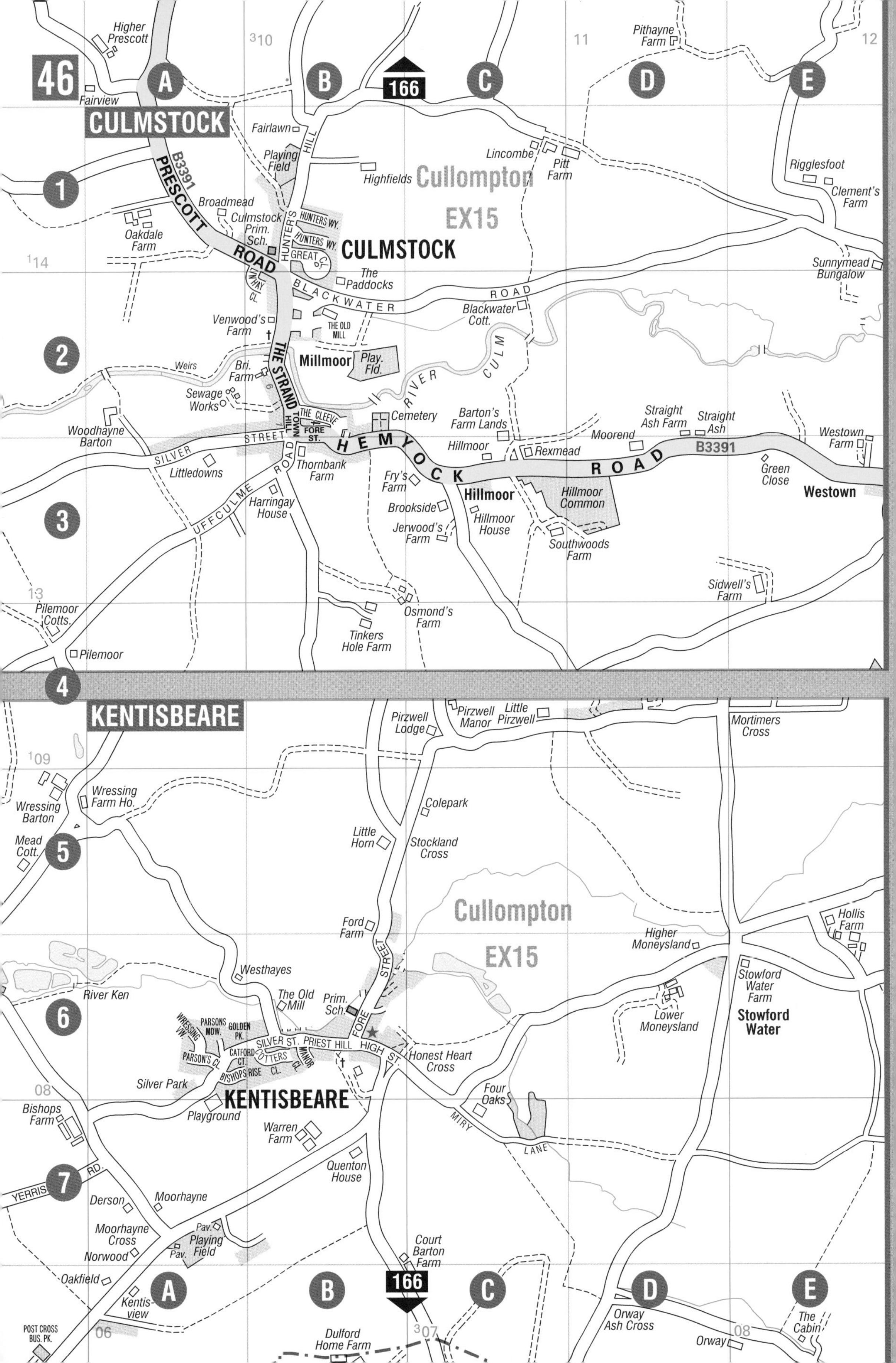
CULMSTOCK
Higher Prescott
Fairview
Fairlawn
Playing Field
Highfields
Cullompton
EX15
Lincombe
Pitt Farm
Pithayne Farm
Rigglesfoot
Clement's Farm
Broadmead
Culmstock Prim. Sch.
Oakdale Farm
HUNTERS WY.
GREAT CL.
The Paddocks
PRESCOTT ROAD
B3391
BLACKWATER ROAD
Blackwater Cott.
Sunnymead Bungalow
Venwood's Farm
THE OLD MILL
Millmoor
Play. Fld.
Weirs
Bri. Farm
THE STRAND
Sewage Works
RIVER CULM
Woodhayne Barton
THE CLEEVE
TOWN HILL
FORE ST.
Cemetery
Barton's Farm Lands
Straight Ash Farm
Straight Ash
Westown Farm
SILVER STREET
Littledowns
Thornbank Farm
HEMYOCK ROAD
Hillmoor
Rexmead
Moorend
Green Close
Westown
UFFCULME ROAD
Harringay House
Fry's Farm
Brookside
Jerwood's Farm
Hillmoor House
Hillmoor Common
Southwoods Farm
Sidwell's Farm
Pilemoor Cotts.
Pilemoor
Osmond's Farm
Tinkers Hole Farm
166
KENTISBEARE
Pirzwell Lodge
Pirzwell Manor
Little Pirzwell
Mortimers Cross
Wressing Barton
Wressing Farm Ho.
Colepark
Mead Cott.
Little Horn
Stockland Cross
Ford Farm
Higher Moneysland
Hollis Farm
Westhayes
FORE STREET
River Ken
The Old Mill
Prim. Sch.
Stowford Water Farm
Lower Moneysland
Stowford Water
WRESSING VW.
PARSONS MDW.
GOLDEN PK.
SILVER ST.
PRIEST HILL
HIGH ST.
Honest Heart Cross
PARSON'S CL.
CATFORD CT.
COTTERS CL.
MANOR CL.
BISHOPS RISE
Silver Park
Four Oaks
Bishops Farm
Playground
Warren Farm
MIRY LANE
Quenton House
YERRIS RD.
Derson
Moorhayne
Moorhayne Cross
Norwood
Pav.
Playing Field
Court Barton Farm
Oakfield
Kentisview
Orway Ash Cross
Orway
The Cabin
POST CROSS BUS. PK.
Dulford Home Farm

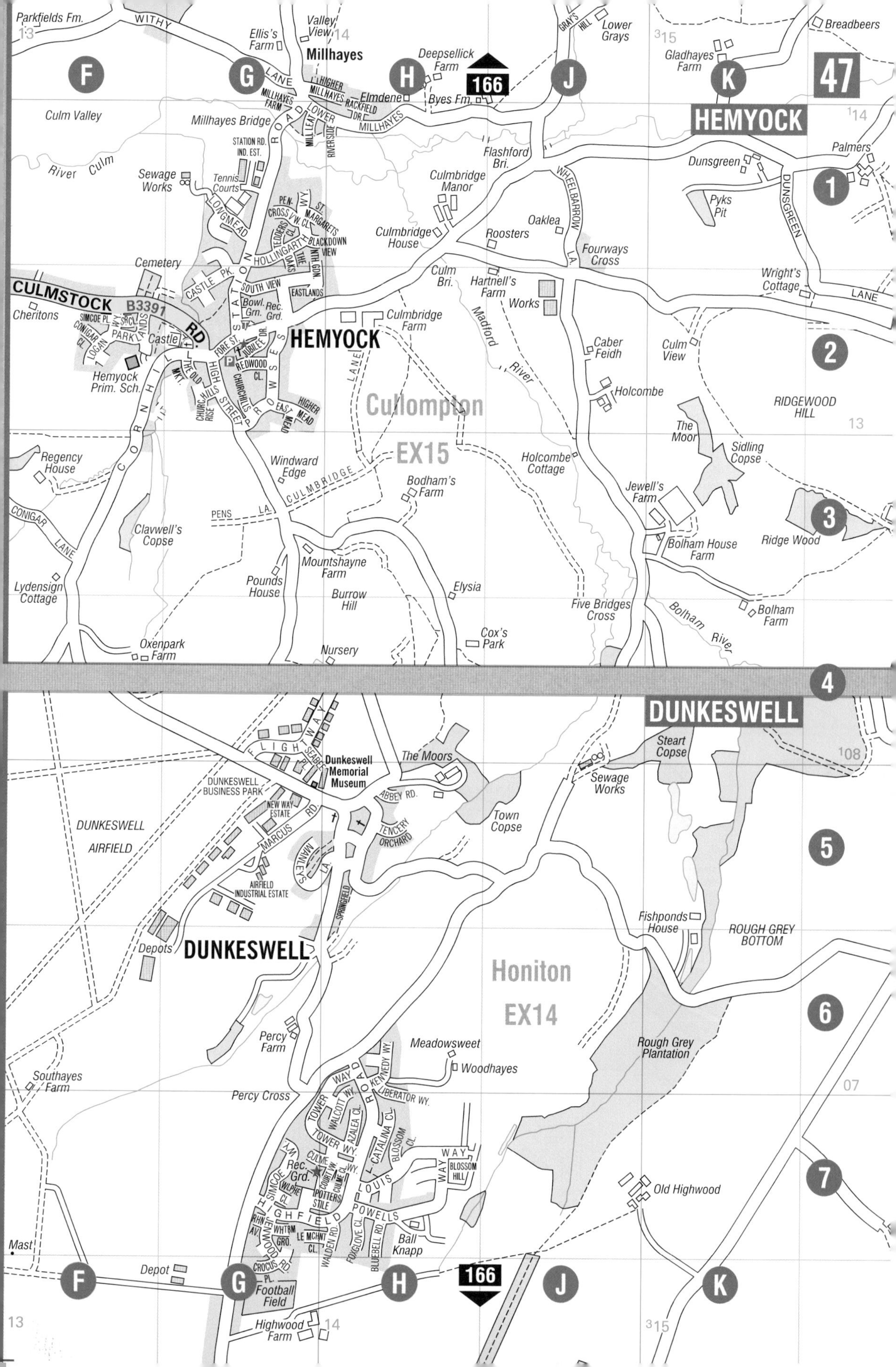
47
166
HEMYOCK
Millhayes
Culm Valley
River Culm
Millhayes Bridge
Sewage Works
Tennis Courts
Cemetery
CULMSTOCK RD.
B3391
Cheritons
Castle
Hemyock Prim. Sch.
HEMYOCK
Culmbridge Manor
Culmbridge House
Culmbridge Farm
Flashford Bri.
Culm Bri.
Roosters
Oaklea
Hartnell's Farm
Works
Fourways Cross
Dunsgreen
Pyks Pit
Palmers
Wright's Cottage
Gladhayes Farm
Breadbeers
Lower Grays
Deepsellick Farm
Byes Fm.
Elmdene
Ellis's Farm
Valley View
Parkfields Fm.
Caber Feidh
Holcombe
Culm View
RIDGEWOOD HILL
The Moor
Sidling Copse
Jewell's Farm
Bolham House Farm
Ridge Wood
Bolham Farm
Bolham River
Five Bridges Cross
Holcombe Cottage
Madford River
Cullompton
EX15
Bodham's Farm
Windward Edge
Regency House
Clavwell's Copse
Lydensign Cottage
Mountshayne Farm
Pounds House
Burrow Hill
Elysia
Cox's Park
Nursery
Oxenpark Farm
DUNKESWELL
Steart Copse
Sewage Works
The Moors
Town Copse
Dunkeswell Memorial Museum
DUNKESWELL BUSINESS PARK
DUNKESWELL AIRFIELD
AIRFIELD INDUSTRIAL ESTATE
Depots
DUNKESWELL
Fishponds House
ROUGH GREY BOTTOM
Honiton
EX14
Rough Grey Plantation
Percy Farm
Percy Cross
Meadowsweet
Woodhayes
Southayes Farm
Old Highwood
Rec. Grd.
Ball Knapp
Mast
Depot
Football Field
Highwood Farm
166

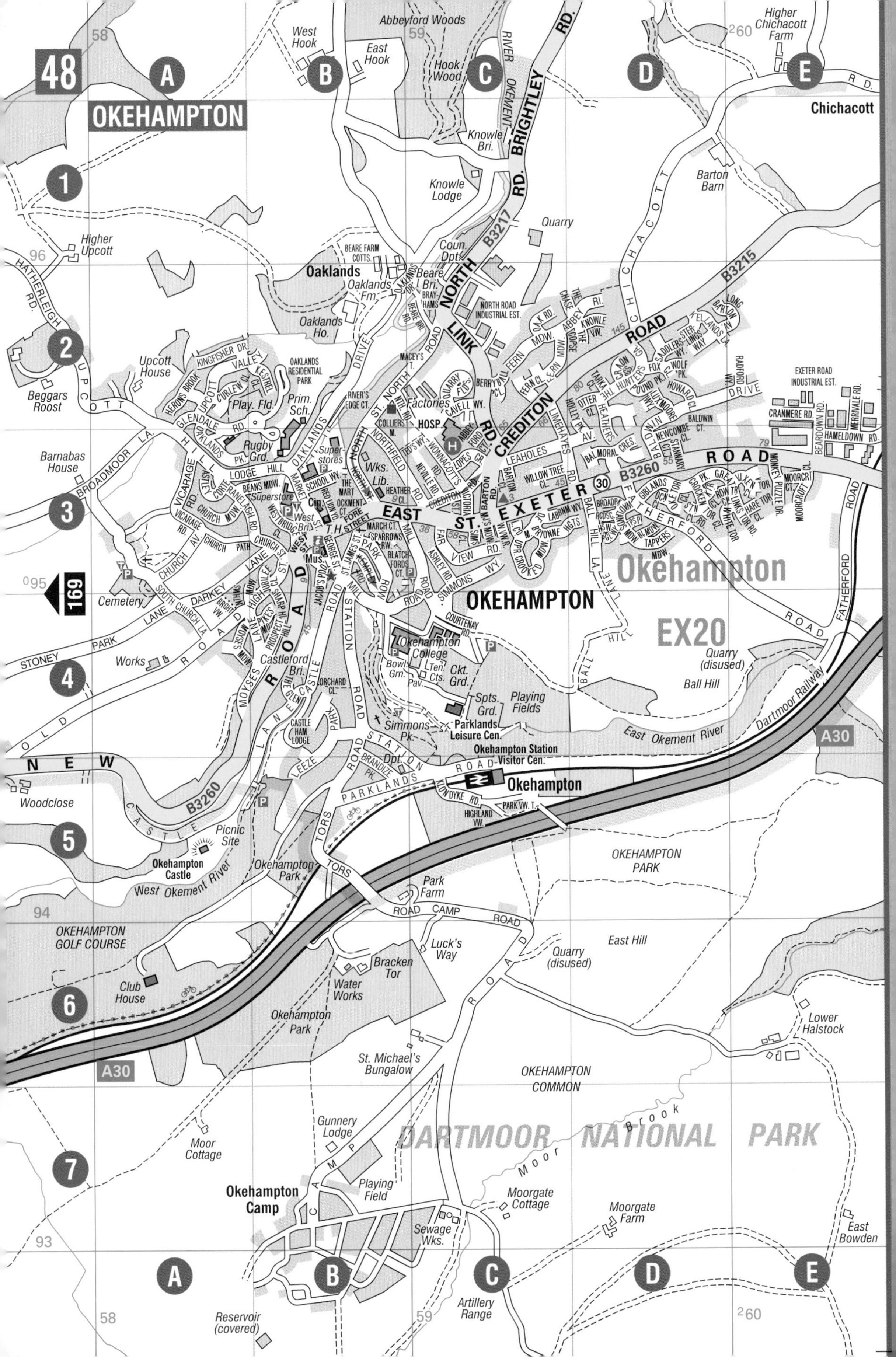
OKEHAMPTON
Okehampton
EX20
Chichacott
Oaklands
Okehampton Station Visitor Cen.
Okehampton Castle
OKEHAMPTON GOLF COURSE
OKEHAMPTON PARK
OKEHAMPTON COMMON
DARTMOOR NATIONAL PARK
Okehampton Camp
East Okement River
West Okement River
Dartmoor Railway
A30
B3260
B3215
B3217
169

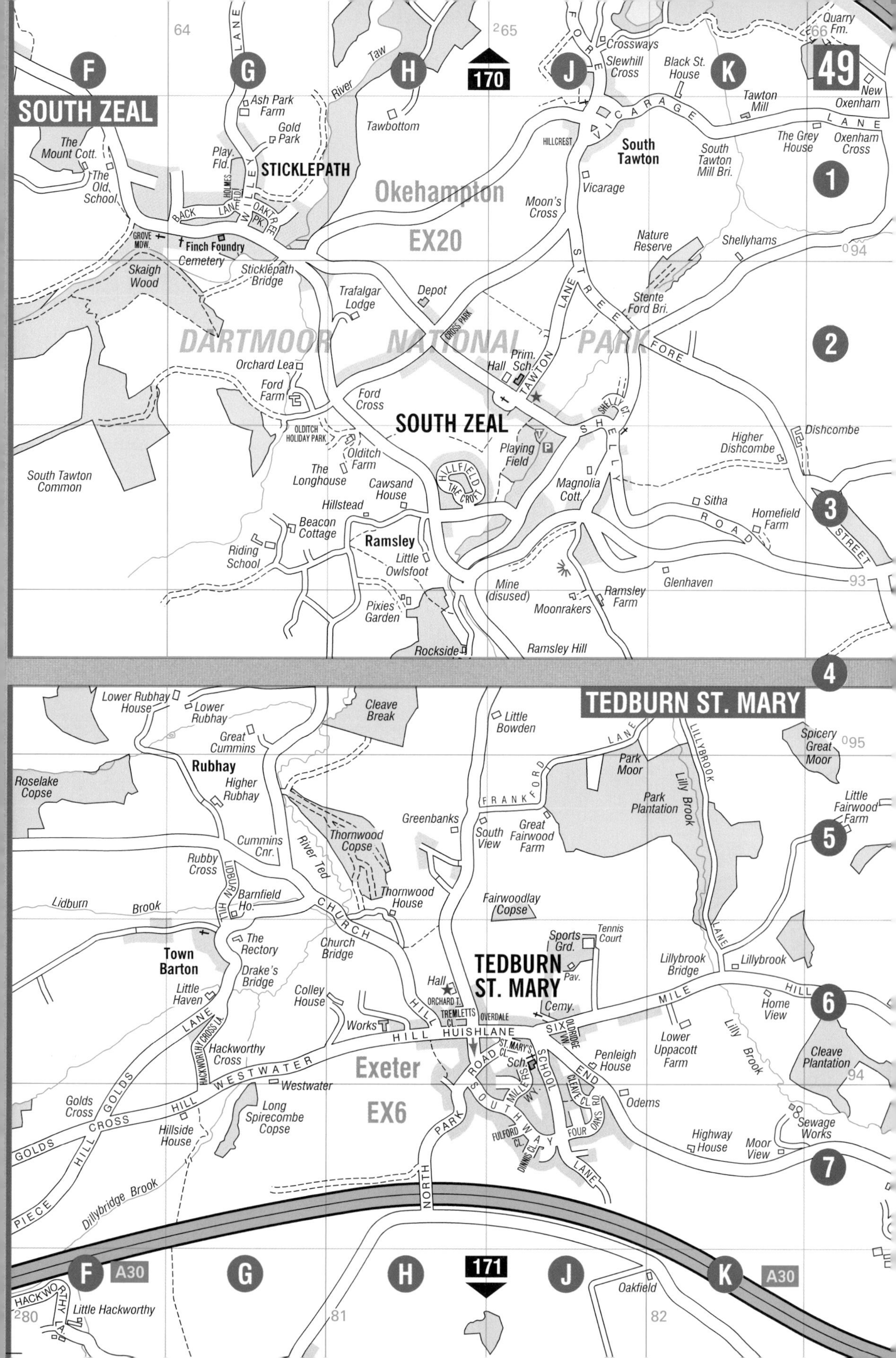

SOUTH ZEAL
170
F
G
H
J
K
Quarry Fm.
Crossways
Slewhill Cross
Black St. House
Tawton Mill
New Oxenham
The Grey House
Oxenham Cross
South Tawton
South Tawton Mill Bri.
Ash Park Farm
Gold Park
Tawbottom
River Taw
STICKLEPATH
Okehampton
EX20
The Mount Cott.
The Old School
Play. Fld.
Vicarage
Moon's Cross
Nature Reserve
Shellyhams
Finch Foundry
Cemetery
Skaigh Wood
Sticklepath Bridge
Trafalgar Lodge
Depot
Stente Ford Bri.
DARTMOOR NATIONAL PARK
Orchard Lea
Ford Farm
Ford Cross
Hall
Prim. Sch.
SOUTH ZEAL
Playing Field
Higher Dishcombe
Dishcombe
Olditch Holiday Park
Olditch Farm
The Longhouse
Cawsand House
Magnolia Cott.
Sitha
Homefield Farm
South Tawton Common
Hillstead
Beacon Cottage
Ramsley
Little Owlsfoot
Riding School
Mine (disused)
Ramsley Farm
Moonrakers
Glenhaven
Pixies Garden
Rockside
Ramsley Hill
TEDBURN ST. MARY
Lower Rubhay House
Lower Rubhay
Cleave Break
Little Bowden
Great Cummins
Rubhay
Higher Rubhay
Roselake Copse
Park Moor
Park Plantation
Lilly Brook
Spicery Great Moor
Little Fairwood Farm
Greenbanks
South View
Great Fairwood Farm
Thornwood Copse
River Ted
Cummins Cnr.
Rubby Cross
Lidburn Brook
Barnfield Ho.
Thornwood House
Fairwoodlay Copse
Sports Grd.
Tennis Court
Town Barton
The Rectory
Church Bridge
Drake's Bridge
TEDBURN ST. MARY
Lillybrook Bridge
Lillybrook
Little Haven
Colley House
Hall
Pav.
Cemy.
Home View
Cleave Plantation
Works
Hackworthy Cross
Exeter
EX6
Penleigh House
Lower Uppacott Farm
Westwater
Odems
Golds Cross
Long Spirecombe Copse
Hillside House
Highway House
Moor View
Sewage Works
Dillybridge Brook
A30
171
Oakfield
Little Hackworthy

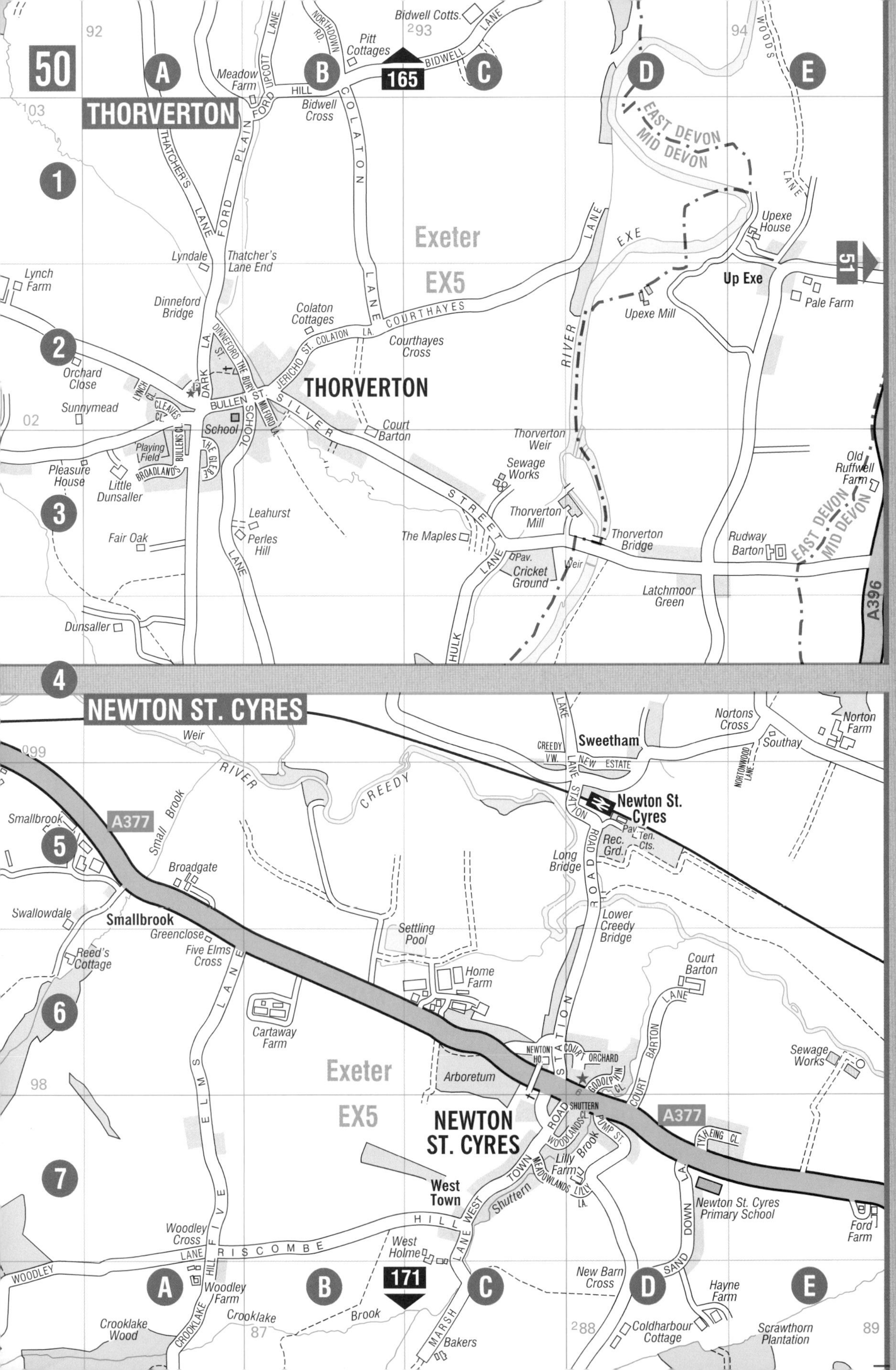
THORVERTON
NEWTON ST. CYRES
165
171
51
Exeter
EX5
Thatcher's Lane End
Dinneford Bridge
Colaton Cottages
Courthayes Cross
Court Barton
Thorverton Weir
Sewage Works
Thorverton Mill
Thorverton Bridge
The Maples
Cricket Ground
Latchmoor Green
Rudway Barton
Old Ruffwell Farm
Up Exe
Upexe House
Upexe Mill
Pale Farm
EAST DEVON
MID DEVON
RIVER EXE
Bidwell Cotts.
Pitt Cottages
Bidwell Cross
Meadow Farm
Lyndale
Lynch Farm
Orchard Close
Sunnymead
Pleasure House
Little Dunsaller
Playing Field
School
Leahurst
Perles Hill
Fair Oak
Dunsaller
A396
Sweetham
Newton St. Cyres
Nortons Cross
Norton Farm
Southay
Long Bridge
Lower Creedy Bridge
Rec. Grd.
Settling Pool
Home Farm
Cartaway Farm
Arboretum
Court Barton
Sewage Works
Smallbrook
Swallowdale
Broadgate
Greenclose
Five Elms Cross
Reed's Cottage
A377
RIVER CREEDY
Weir
West Town
West Holme
Woodley Cross
Woodley Farm
Crooklake Wood
Crooklake
Bakers
New Barn Cross
Coldharbour Cottage
Hayne Farm
Scrawthorn Plantation
Newton St. Cyres Primary School
Ford Farm
Lilly Farm
Shuttern Brook

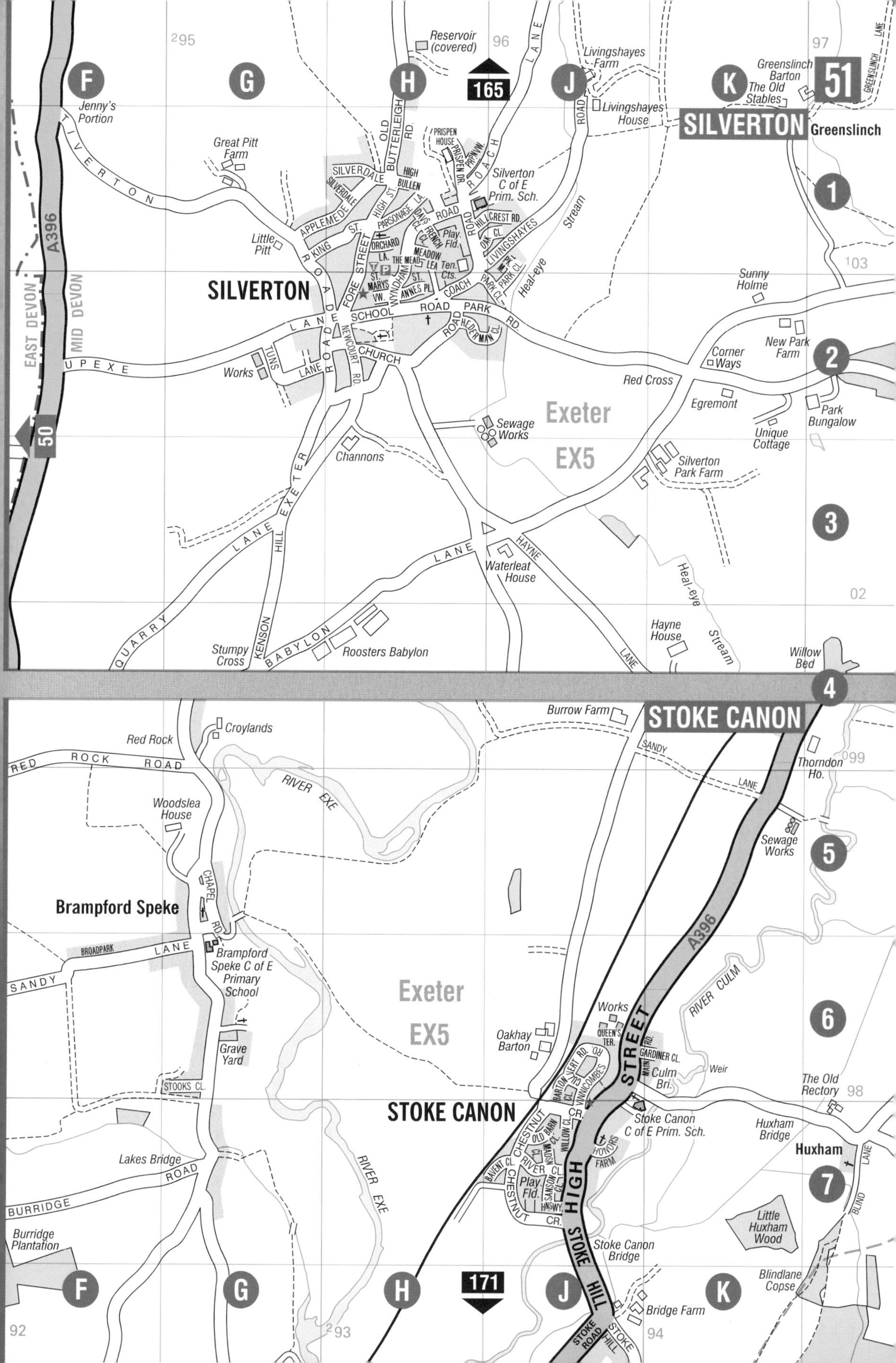
SILVERTON
Greenslinch
Silverton
Exeter
EX5
Stoke Canon
STOKE CANON
Brampford Speke
Huxham
Jenny's Portion
Great Pitt Farm
Little Pitt
Reservoir (covered)
Livingshayes Farm
Livingshayes House
Greenslinch Barton
The Old Stables
Silverton C of E Prim. Sch.
Sunny Holme
New Park Farm
Corner Ways
Red Cross
Egremont
Park Bungalow
Unique Cottage
Silverton Park Farm
Sewage Works
Channons
Works
Waterleat House
Hayne House
Stumpy Cross
Roosters Babylon
Willow Bed
Heal-eye Stream
Burrow Farm
Croylands
Red Rock
Woodslea House
Thorndon Ho.
Brampford Speke C of E Primary School
Grave Yard
Oakhay Barton
Culm Bri.
Weir
The Old Rectory
Stoke Canon C of E Prim. Sch.
Huxham Bridge
Little Huxham Wood
Stoke Canon Bridge
Bridge Farm
Blindlane Copse
Lakes Bridge
Burridge Plantation
River Exe
River Culm
A396
EAST DEVON
MID DEVON
165
171
50

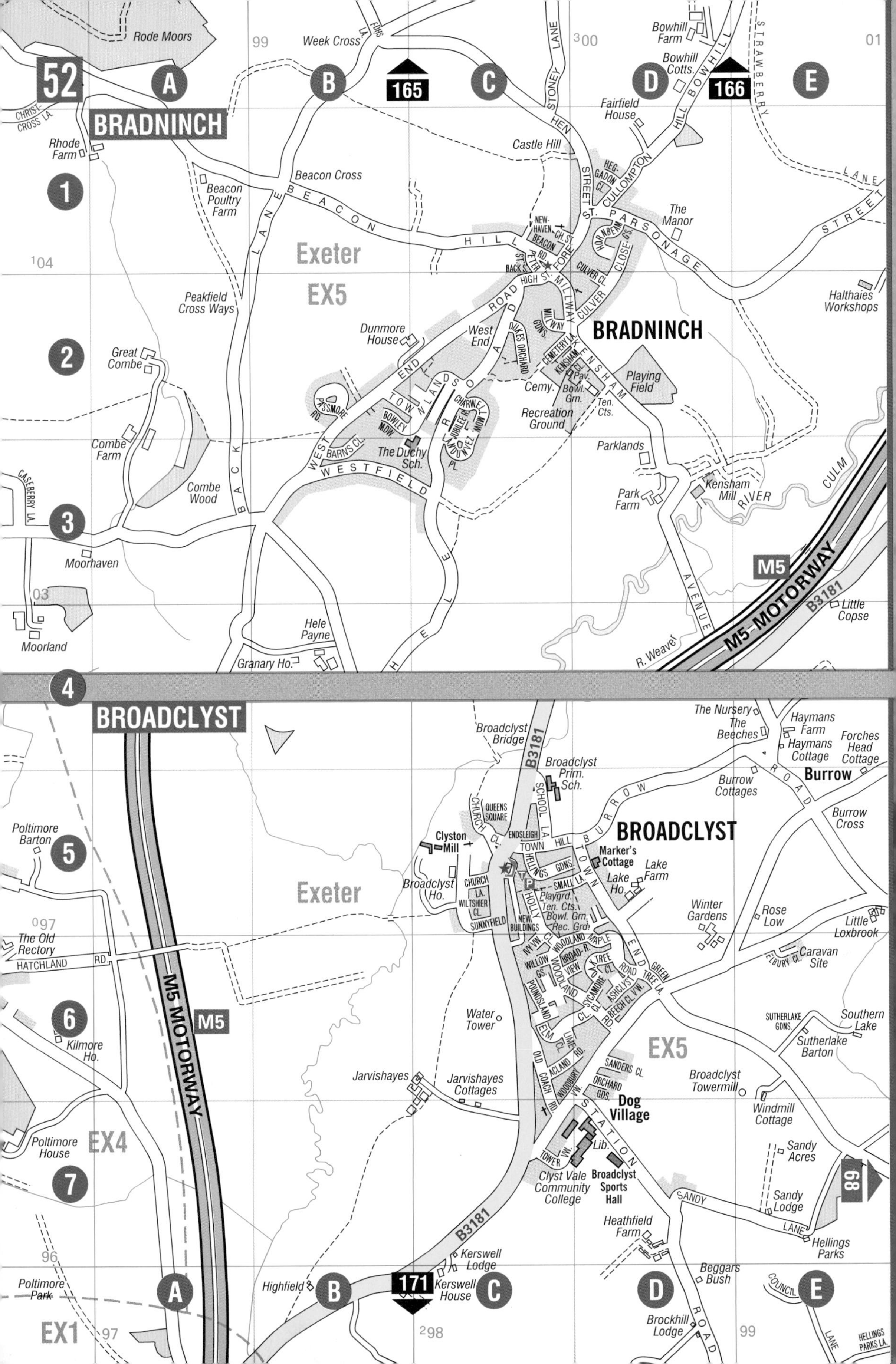
BRADNINCH
Rode Moors
Week Cross
165
166
Bowhill Farm
Bowhill Cotts.
Fairfield House
Castle Hill
Rhode Farm
Beacon Cross
Beacon Poultry Farm
The Manor
Exeter
EX5
Peakfield Cross Ways
Dunmore House
West End
BRADNINCH
Playing Field
Halthaies Workshops
Great Combe
Cemy.
Recreation Ground
Combe Farm
The Duchy Sch.
Parklands
Combe Wood
Park Farm
Kensham Mill
RIVER CULM
Moorhaven
M5
M5 MOTORWAY
B3181
Little Copse
Moorland
Hele Payne
Granary Ho.
R. Weaver
BROADCLYST
The Nursery
The Beeches
Haymans Farm
Haymans Cottage
Forches Head Cottage
Broadclyst Bridge
Broadclyst Prim. Sch.
Burrow Cottages
Burrow
Burrow Cross
Poltimore Barton
Clyston Mill
BROADCLYST
Marker's Cottage
Lake Farm
Lake Ho.
Broadclyst Ho.
Exeter
Winter Gardens
Rose Low
Little Loxbrook
The Old Rectory
Caravan Site
Water Tower
Southern Lake
Kilmore Ho.
Sutherlake Barton
EX5
Jarvishayes
Jarvishayes Cottages
Broadclyst Towermill
Windmill Cottage
Dog Village
Poltimore House
EX4
Sandy Acres
Clyst Vale Community College
Broadclyst Sports Hall
Sandy Lodge
Heathfield Farm
Hellings Parks
Kerswell Lodge
Beggars Bush
Poltimore Park
Highfield
171
Kerswell House
Brockhill Lodge
EX1
68

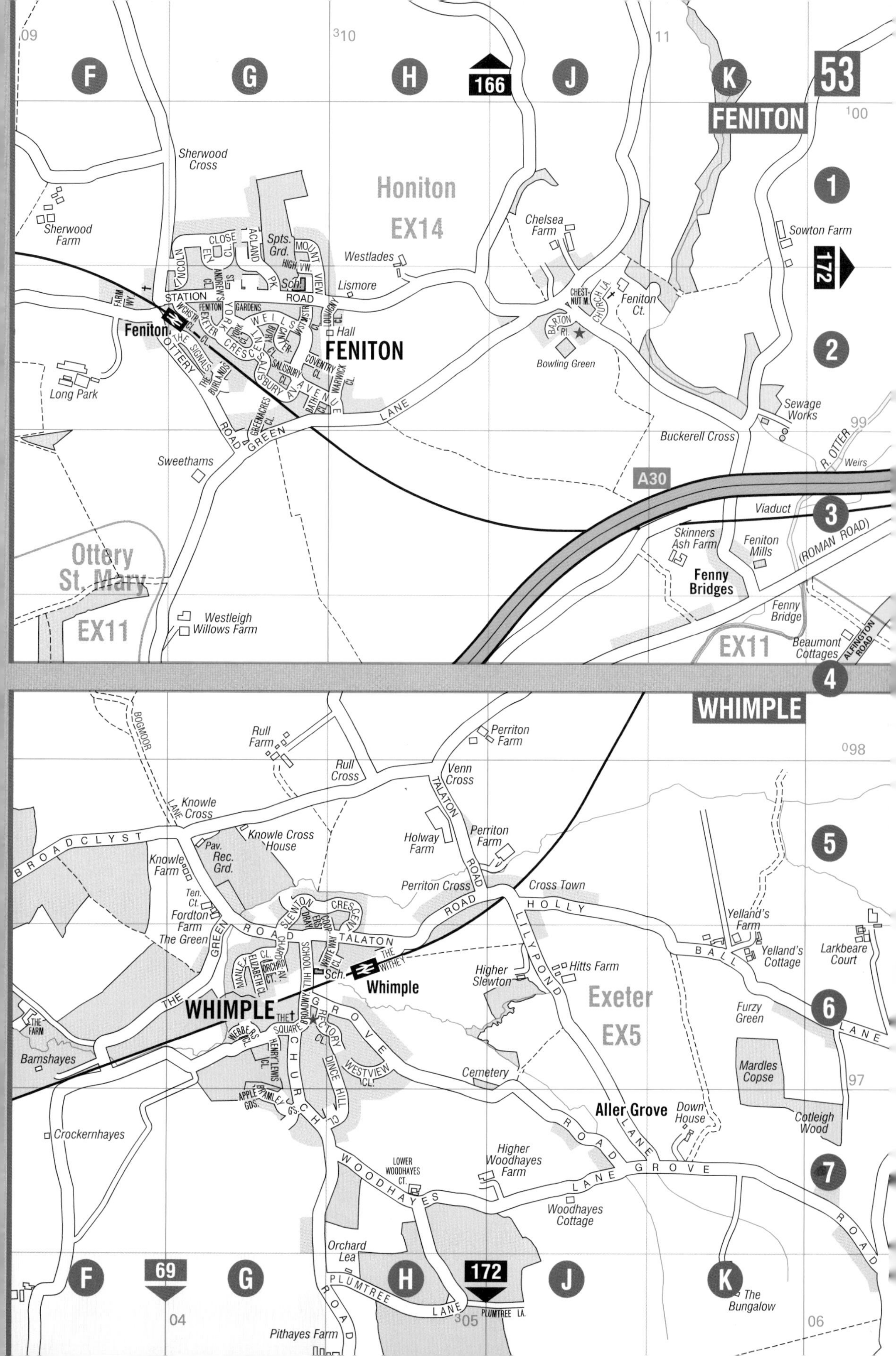
FENITON
Sherwood Cross
Sherwood Farm
Honiton
EX14
Chelsea Farm
Sowton Farm
Westlades
Lismore
Feniton Ct.
Feniton
FENITON
Hall
Bowling Green
Long Park
Sewage Works
Buckerell Cross
Sweethams
R. OTTER
Weirs
A30
Viaduct
Skinners Ash Farm
Feniton Mills
(ROMAN ROAD)
Fenny Bridges
Fenny Bridge
Ottery St. Mary
EX11
Westleigh Willows Farm
Beaumont Cottages
ALFINGTON ROAD
WHIMPLE
Rull Farm
Perriton Farm
Rull Cross
Venn Cross
Knowle Cross
Knowle Cross House
Holway Farm
Perriton Farm
BROADCLYST
Knowle Farm
Pav.
Rec. Grd.
Ten. Ct.
Fordton Farm
The Green
Perriton Cross
Cross Town
HOLLY BALL LANE
Yelland's Farm
Yelland's Cottage
Larkbeare Court
Higher Slewton
Hitts Farm
Whimple
WHIMPLE
Exeter
EX5
Furzy Green
Barnshayes
Mardles Copse
Cemetery
Crockernhayes
Aller Grove
Down House
Cotleigh Wood
Higher Woodhayes Farm
LOWER WOODHAYES CT.
WOODHAYES LANE
GROVE ROAD
Woodhayes Cottage
Orchard Lea
PLUMTREE LANE
PLUMTREE LA.
The Bungalow
Pithayes Farm
166
172
69
172

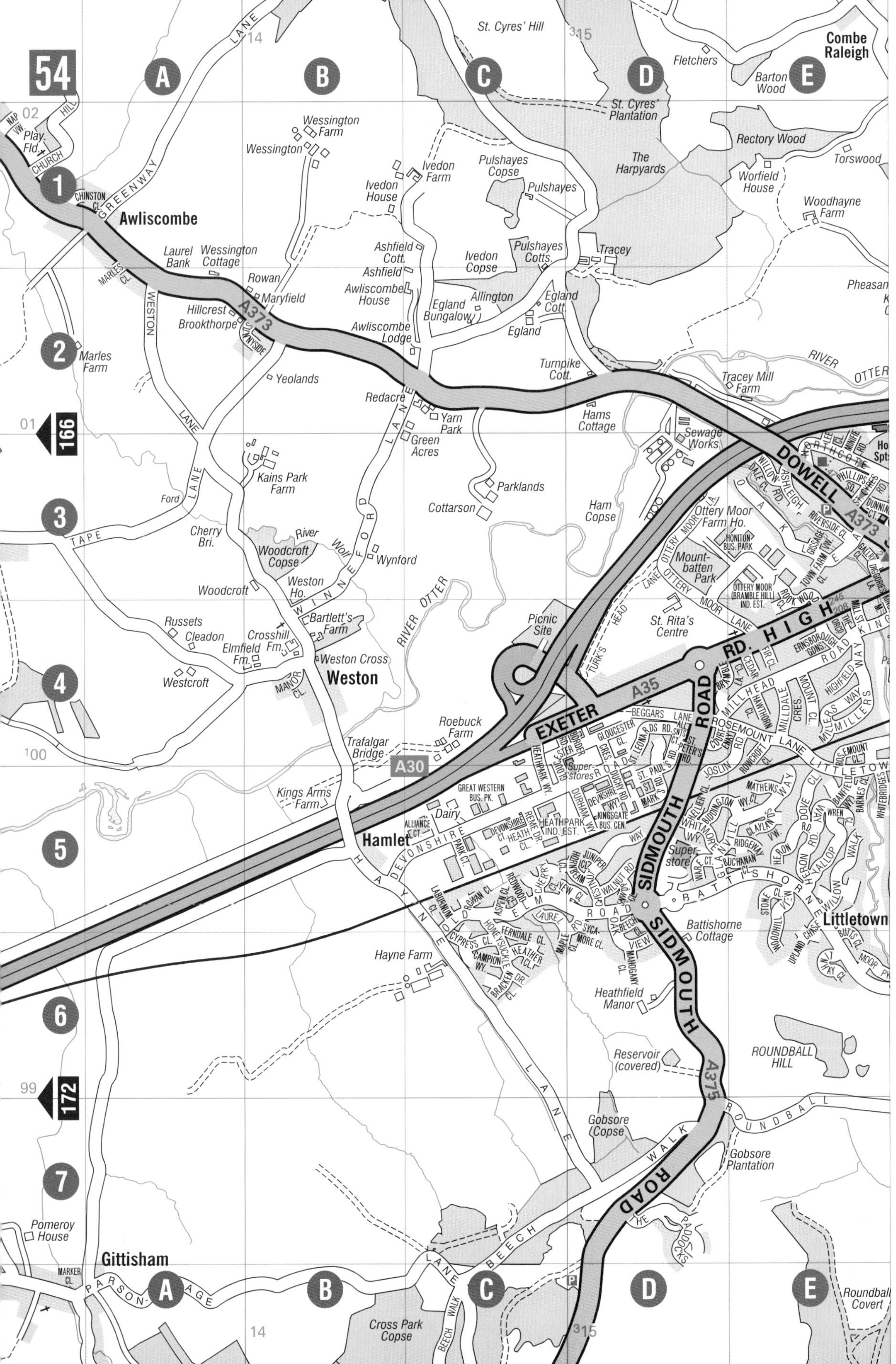
A
B
C
D
E
1
2
3
4
5
6
7
14
315
02
01
100
99
166
172
St. Cyres' Hill
Fletchers
Combe Raleigh
Barton Wood
St. Cyres' Plantation
Rectory Wood
Torswood
The Harpyards
Wessington Farm
Wessington
Ivedon Farm
Ivedon House
Pulshayes Copse
Pulshayes
Worfield House
Woodhayne Farm
Play. Fld.
NAP VW.
HILL
CHURCH
CHINSTON CL.
GREENWAY
LANE
Awliscombe
Laurel Bank
Wessington Cottage
MARLES CL.
Rowan
Maryfield
Hillcrest
Brookthorpe
SUNNYSIDE
A373
Ashfield Cott.
Ashfield
Awliscombe House
Ivedon Copse
Pulshayes Cotts.
Tracey
Allington
Egland Bungalow
Egland Cott.
Egland
Awliscombe Lodge
Pheasan
WESTON
Marles Farm
Yeolands
Turnpike Cott.
RIVER OTTER
Tracey Mill Farm
Redacre
Yarn Park
Hams Cottage
Green Acres
Sewage Works
DOWELL
Kains Park Farm
Parklands
Cottarson
Ham Copse
Ford
Cherry Bri.
TAPE
River Wolf
Woodcroft Copse
Wynford
WINNEFORD
Weston Ho.
Woodcroft
Ottery Moor Farm Ho.
HONITON BUS. PARK
Mount-batten Park
OTTERY MOOR LA.
OTTERY MOOR LANE
OTTERY MOOR (BRAMBLE HILL) IND. EST.
Bartlett's Farm
Russets
Cleadon
Crosshill Fm.
Elmfield Fm.
Weston Cross
Weston
Westcroft
MANOR CL.
Picnic Site
St. Rita's Centre
TURK'S HEAD LANE
HIGH
A35
EXETER RD.
Roebuck Farm
Trafalgar Bridge
A30
BEGGARS LANE
GLOUCESTER CL.
Super-stores
GREAT WESTERN BUS. PK.
HEATHPARK WY.
Kings Arms Farm
Dairy
ALLIANCE CT.
Hamlet
DEVONSHIRE
PARK CT.
HEATHPARK IND. EST.
KINGSGATE BUS. CEN.
SIDMOUTH ROAD
ROSEMOUNT LANE
MILLHEAD
LITTLETOWN
Super-store
BATTISHORNE
Battishorne Cottage
Littletown
HAYNE LANE
Hayne Farm
Heathfield Manor
ROUNDBALL HILL
Reservoir (covered)
A375
ROUNDBALL
Gobsore Copse
WALK
Gobsore Plantation
Pomeroy House
Gittisham
MARKER CL.
PARSONAGE
BEECH LANE
BEECH WALK
PADDOCKS
Roundball Covert
Cross Park Copse

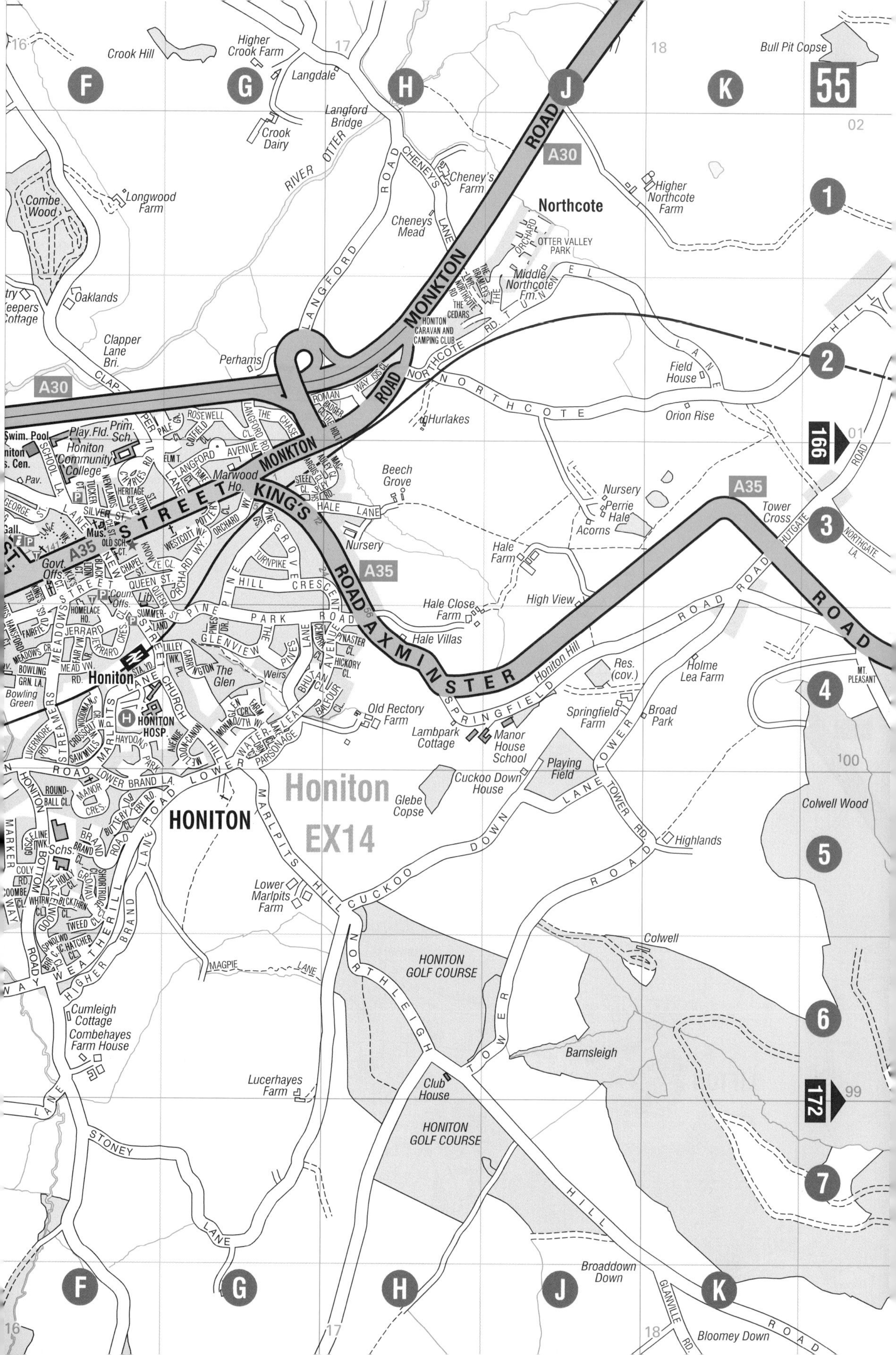

Crook Hill
Higher Crook Farm
Langdale
Langford Bridge
Crook Dairy
Bull Pit Copse
Longwood Farm
Combe Wood
Oaklands
Clapper Lane Bri.
Perhams
Cheney's Farm
Cheneys Mead
Northcote
Higher Northcote Farm
OTTER VALLEY PARK
Middle Northcote Fm.
HONITON CARAVAN AND CAMPING CLUB
Field House
Orion Rise
Hurlakes
Beech Grove
Nursery
Perrie Hale
Acorns
Hale Farm
Tower Cross
Hale Close Farm
High View
Hale Villas
Holme Lea Farm
Res. (cov.)
Springfield Farm
Broad Park
Old Rectory Farm
Lambpark Cottage
Manor House School
Playing Field
Cuckoo Down House
Glebe Copse
Honiton
EX14
HONITON
Highlands
Colwell Wood
Lower Marlpits Farm
Colwell
HONITON GOLF COURSE
Barnsleigh
Club House
Lucerhayes Farm
Cumleigh Cottage
Combehayes Farm House
Broaddown Down
Bloomey Down
MONKTON ROAD
KING'S ROAD
AXMINSTER ROAD
A30
A35
RIVER OTTER
NORTHCOTE LANE
HALE LANE
PINE PARK ROAD
SPRINGFIELD ROAD
TOWER ROAD
CUCKOO DOWN LANE
NORTHLEIGH HILL
MARLPITS HILL
STONEY LANE
MAGPIE LANE
GLANVILLE RD.
HONITON HOSP.
Honiton Community College
Prim. Sch.
Play. Fld.
Marwood Ho.
Mus.
Govt. Offs.
Coun. Offs.
Lib.
The Glen
Bowling Green
Schs.
MT. PLEASANT
166
172

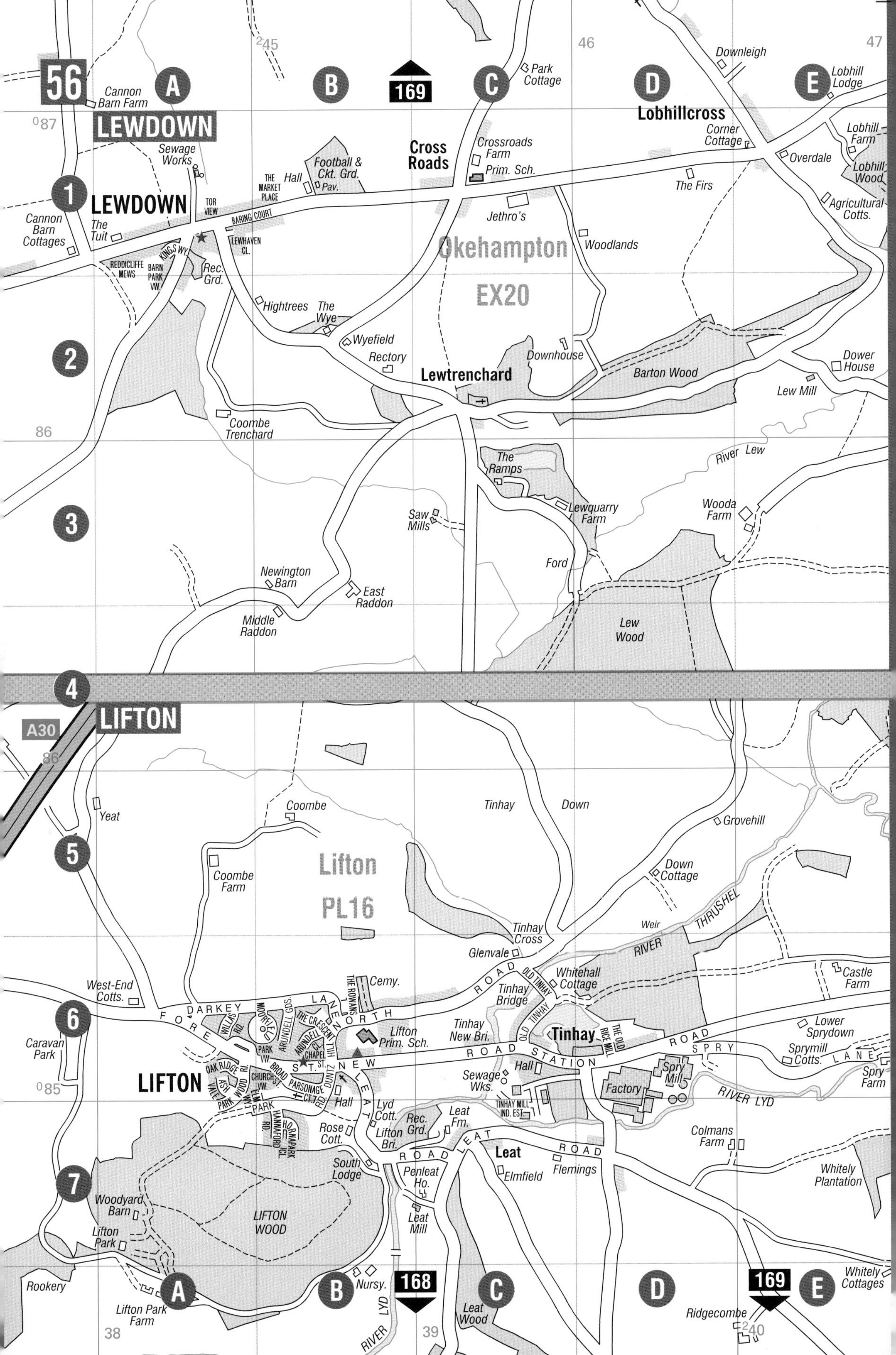

56

⁰87

LEWDOWN

Ⓐ   Ⓑ   ▲ **169**   Ⓒ   Ⓓ   Ⓔ

²45   46   47

Cannon Barn Farm

Downleigh

Lobhill Lodge

1

LEWDOWN

Cannon Barn Cottages

The Tuit

REDDICLIFFE MEWS

Sewage Works

THE MARKET PLACE

Hall

Football & Ckt. Grd.

Pav.

BARING COURT

LEWHAVEN CL.

TOR VIEW

KING'S WY.

BARN PARK VW.

Rec. Grd.

Cross Roads

Crossroads Farm

Prim. Sch.

Park Cottage

Lobhillcross

Corner Cottage

Overdale

Lobhill Farm

Lobhill Wood

The Firs

Agricultural Cotts.

2

Hightrees

The Wye

Wyefield

Rectory

Jethro's

Okehampton

EX20

Woodlands

Downhouse

Lewtrenchard

Barton Wood

Lew Mill

Dower House

3

Coombe Trenchard

The Ramps

Saw Mills

Newington Barn

Middle Raddon

East Raddon

Lewquarry Farm

Ford

River Lew

Wooda Farm

Lew Wood

4

LIFTON

A30

⁸6

Ⓐ   Ⓑ   ▼ **168**   Ⓒ   Ⓓ   ▼ **169**   Ⓔ

5

Yeat

Coombe

Coombe Farm

Lifton
PL16

Tinhay Down

Down

Grovehill

Down Cottage

6

West-End Cotts.

Caravan Park

⁰85

LIFTON

FORE

DARKEY LANE

WILLAS

MOOR

ARUNDELL

SCHOOL

THE CRESCENT

LANE NORTH

THE ROWANS

Cemy.

Lifton Prim. Sch.

PARK VW.

OAK RIDGE RD.

VALE

PARK

BROAD WOOD

PARSONAGE CL.

RD.

Hall

CHURCH

CL.

HAMMACRD.

THORNPARK CL.

Rose Cott.

Lyd Cott.

Lifton Bri.

Rec. Grd.

Leat Fm.

Tinhay Cross

Glenvale

ROAD

Tinhay Bridge

Tinhay New Bri.

Sewage Wks.

NEW LEAT

STATION ROAD

OLD TINHAY

Whitehall Cottage

Tinhay

Hall

Tinhay Mill Ind. Est.

Leat

Elmfield

Flemings

RIVER THRUSHEL

Weir

RIVER

Castle Farm

Lower Sprydown

Sprymill Cotts.

Spry Mill

THE OLD RICE MILL

ROAD

SPRY LANE

Factory

ROAD

RIVER LYD

Spry Farm

Colmans Farm

Whitely Plantation

7

Woodyard Barn

Lifton Park

Rookery

LIFTON WOOD

South Lodge

Penleat Ho.

Leat Mill

Leat Wood

Ridgecombe

Whitely Cottages

Lifton Park Farm

RIVER LYD

38   39   ²40

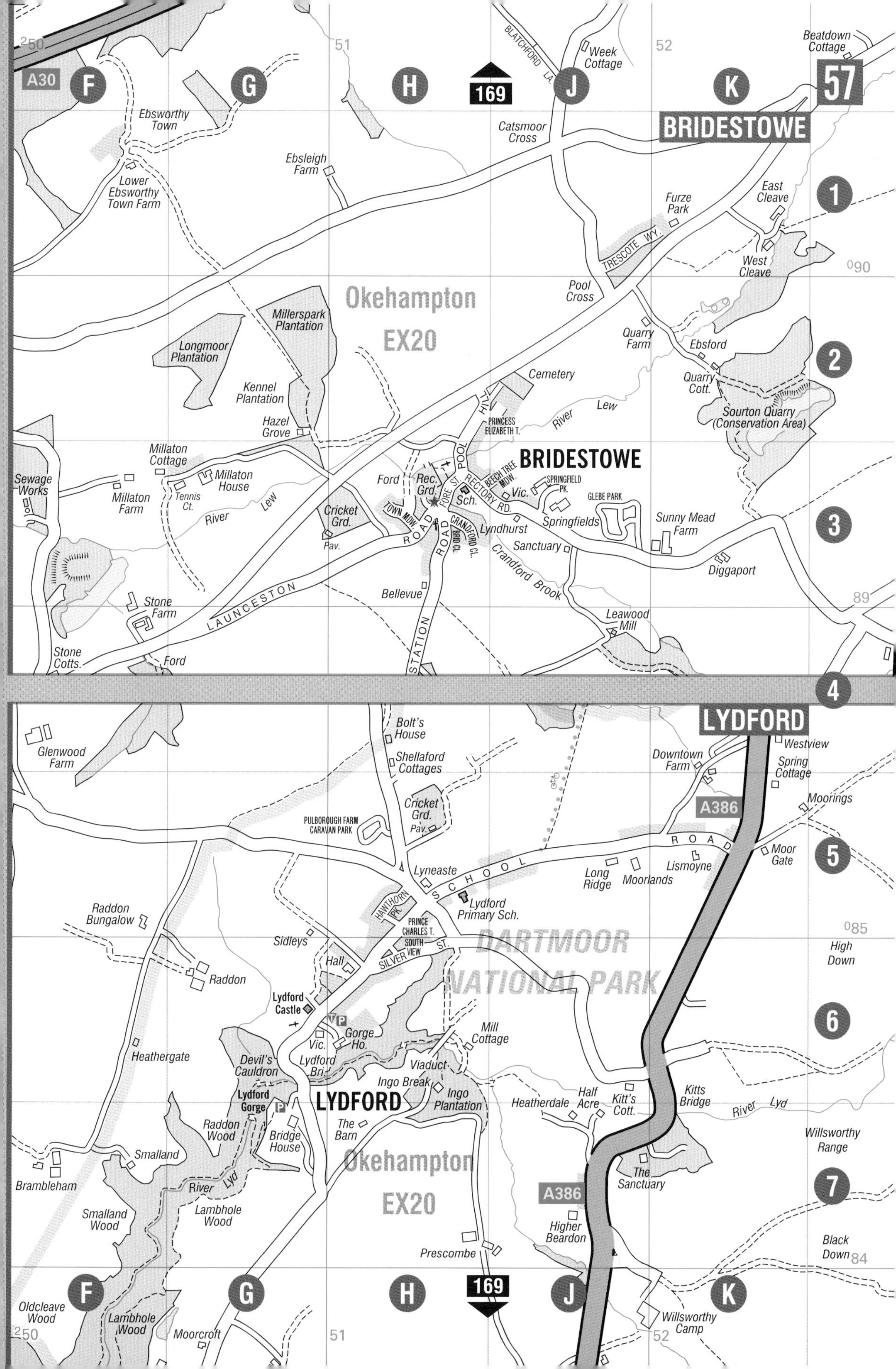
BRIDESTOWE
LYDFORD
A30
A386
169
Okehampton
EX20
DARTMOOR
NATIONAL PARK
BRIDESTOWE
LYDFORD
Ebsworthy Town
Lower Ebsworthy Town Farm
Ebsleigh Farm
Catsmoor Cross
Week Cottage
Beatdown Cottage
Furze Park
East Cleave
West Cleave
Pool Cross
Quarry Farm
Ebsford
Quarry Cott.
Sourton Quarry (Conservation Area)
Millerspark Plantation
Longmoor Plantation
Kennel Plantation
Hazel Grove
Millaton Cottage
Millaton House
Millaton Farm
Sewage Works
Tennis Ct.
River Lew
Cricket Grd.
Pav.
Cemetery
Rec. Grd.
Sch.
Vic.
Lyndhurst
Sanctuary
Springfields
Sunny Mead Farm
Diggaport
Crandford Brook
Bellevue
Leawood Mill
Stone Farm
Stone Cotts.
Ford
Glenwood Farm
Bolt's House
Shellaford Cottages
Downtown Farm
Westview
Spring Cottage
Moorings
Moor Gate
Pulborough Farm Caravan Park
Lyneaste
Long Ridge
Moorlands
Lismoyne
Lydford Primary Sch.
Raddon Bungalow
Raddon
Sidleys
Hall
Lydford Castle
Heathergate
Devil's Cauldron
Lydford Gorge
Gorge Ho.
Lydford Bri.
Mill Cottage
Viaduct
Ingo Break
Ingo Plantation
Heatherdale
Half Acre
Kitt's Cott.
Kitts Bridge
River Lyd
High Down
Willsworthy Range
Raddon Wood
Bridge House
The Barn
Smalland
Brambleham
Smalland Wood
Lambhole Wood
The Sanctuary
Higher Beardon
Prescombe
Black Down
Oldcleave Wood
Moorcroft
Willsworthy Camp

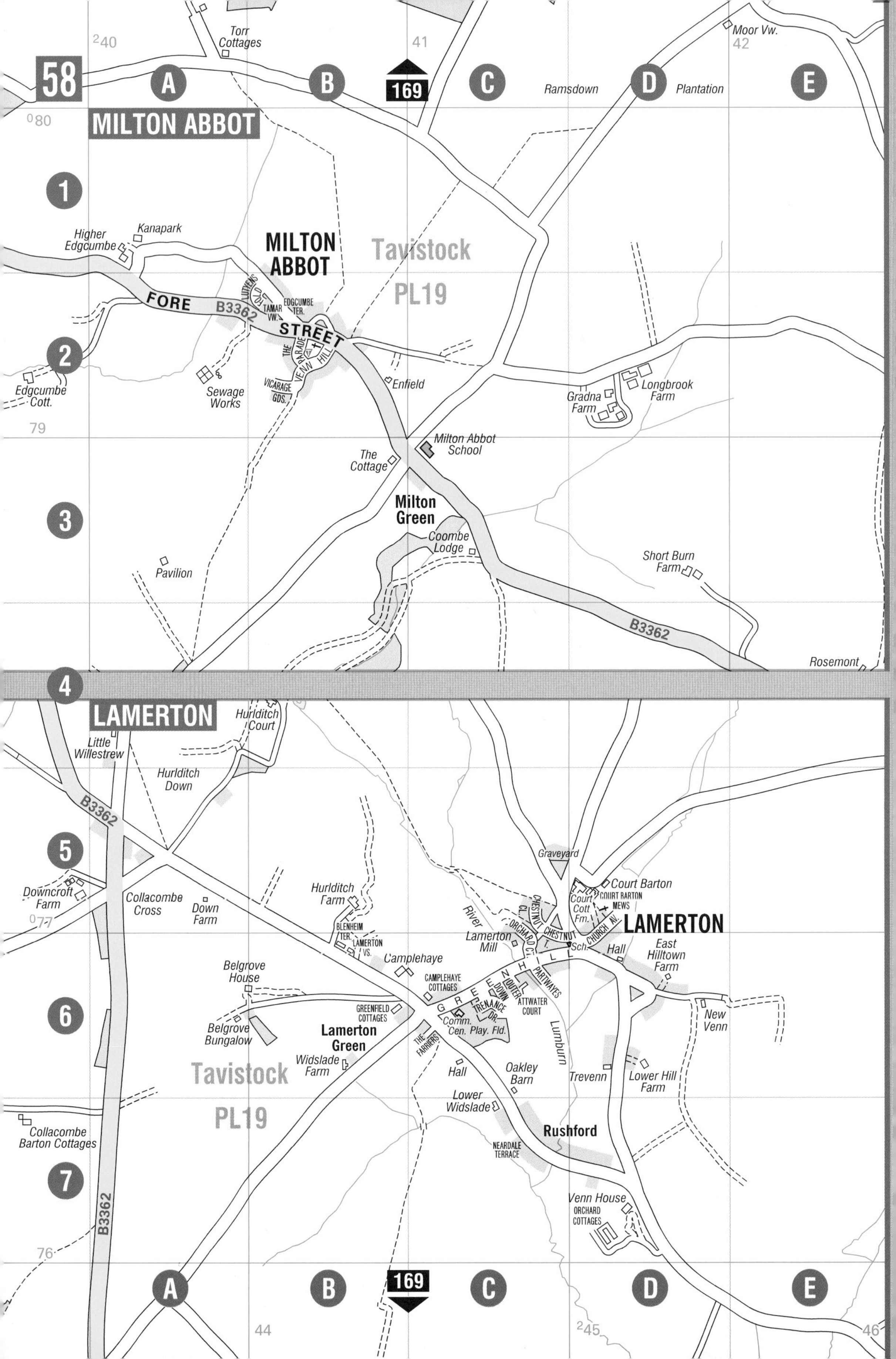

240   41   42

080

Moor Vw.

Torr Cottages

Ramsdown   Plantation

1

Higher Edgcumbe   Kanapark

MILTON ABBOT

Tavistock PL19

FORE   B3362   STREET

LUTYENS WK.
TAMAR VW.
EDGCUMBE TER.
THE VEW
NEW HILL
VICARAGE GDS.

Enfield

Gradna Farm   Longbrook Farm

2

Edgcumbe Cott.

Sewage Works

79

The Cottage

Milton Abbot School

Milton Green

3

Pavilion

Coombe Lodge

Short Burn Farm

B3362

Rosemont

4

LAMERTON

Hurlditch Court

Little Willestrew

Hurlditch Down

Graveyard

Court Barton
COURT BARTON MEWS
Court Cott Fm.

LAMERTON

5

Downcroft Farm

077

Collacombe Cross

Down Farm

Hurlditch Farm

BLENHEIM TER.
LAMERTON VS.

CHESTNUT
ORCHARD CT.
CHESTNUT
Sch.

River

Lamerton Mill

Hall

East Hilltown Farm

B3362

Belgrove House

Camplehaye

Camplehaye Cottages

GREEN HILL
OUTER DOWN
INNER DOWN
TRENANCE DR.
CARTWAYS

New Venn

6

Belgrove Bungalow

GREENFIELD COTTAGES

Lamerton Green

Widslade Farm

THE FARRIERS

Comm. Cen. Play. Fld.

ATTWATER COURT

Lumburn

Trevenn

Lower Hill Farm

Tavistock PL19

Hall

Lower Widslade

Oakley Barn

Collacombe Barton Cottages

Rushford

7

NEARDALE TERRACE

Venn House
ORCHARD COTTAGES

B3362

76

A   B   169   C   D   E

44   245   46

TAVISTOCK
Tavistock
PL19
TAVISTOCK
Grammerby Wood
Wilminstone Farm
North Park Bungalows
Hurdwick
Hurdwick House
Kennels
Kestrel
Sandy Park House
Exeter Lane Bri.
Boarding Ho.
Kelly College
Sports Grd.
Play. Fld.
Lower Rowden Wood
Longstone
Churchpark Cottages
Strawberry Cottage
Downhouse Farm
Alvina
Freedom Villas
Launceston New Road Bridge
Crease Lane Bridge
Meadow End
Trehurst
Res. (cov.)
Council Offs.
Ruswyn
Lodge Wood
St. Peter's C of E Junior School
Club Ho.
Meadowlands Leisure Pool
The Meadows Pleasure Ground
Drake Mem.
Tavistock College
Sports Cen.
Games Court
Playing Fields
Football Ground
New Cemetery
Brook Mill
Brook
Super-store
Tanglewood
Brook Farm
Caravan & Camp Site
East Crowndale
Crowndale Villas
Crowndale Farm
Canal (disused)
Rixhill
The Bungalow
High Winds
Hillside Cott.
Sewage Works
Crowndale Wood
Anderton
Anderton Cottage
Whitchurch
The Chantry
Whitchurch Ho.
Whitchurch Primary School
Trevaunance
Cricket Ground
TAVISTOCK GOLF COURSE
PLYMOUTH ROAD INDUSTRIAL ESTATE
PIXON TRADING CENTRE
WESTBRIDGE IND. EST.
CRELAKE IND. EST.
Rifle Range
WILMINSTONE IND. EST.
A386
A390
B3357
CALLINGTON ROAD
PLYMOUTH ROAD
PARKWOOD ROAD
DOLVIN RD.
MOUNT TAVY ROAD
KILWORTHY ROAD
EXETER ROAD
MILL HILL LANE
CREASE LANE
WHITCHURCH ROAD
DOWN ROAD
CROWNDALE
RIVER TAVY
Tiddy Brook
169

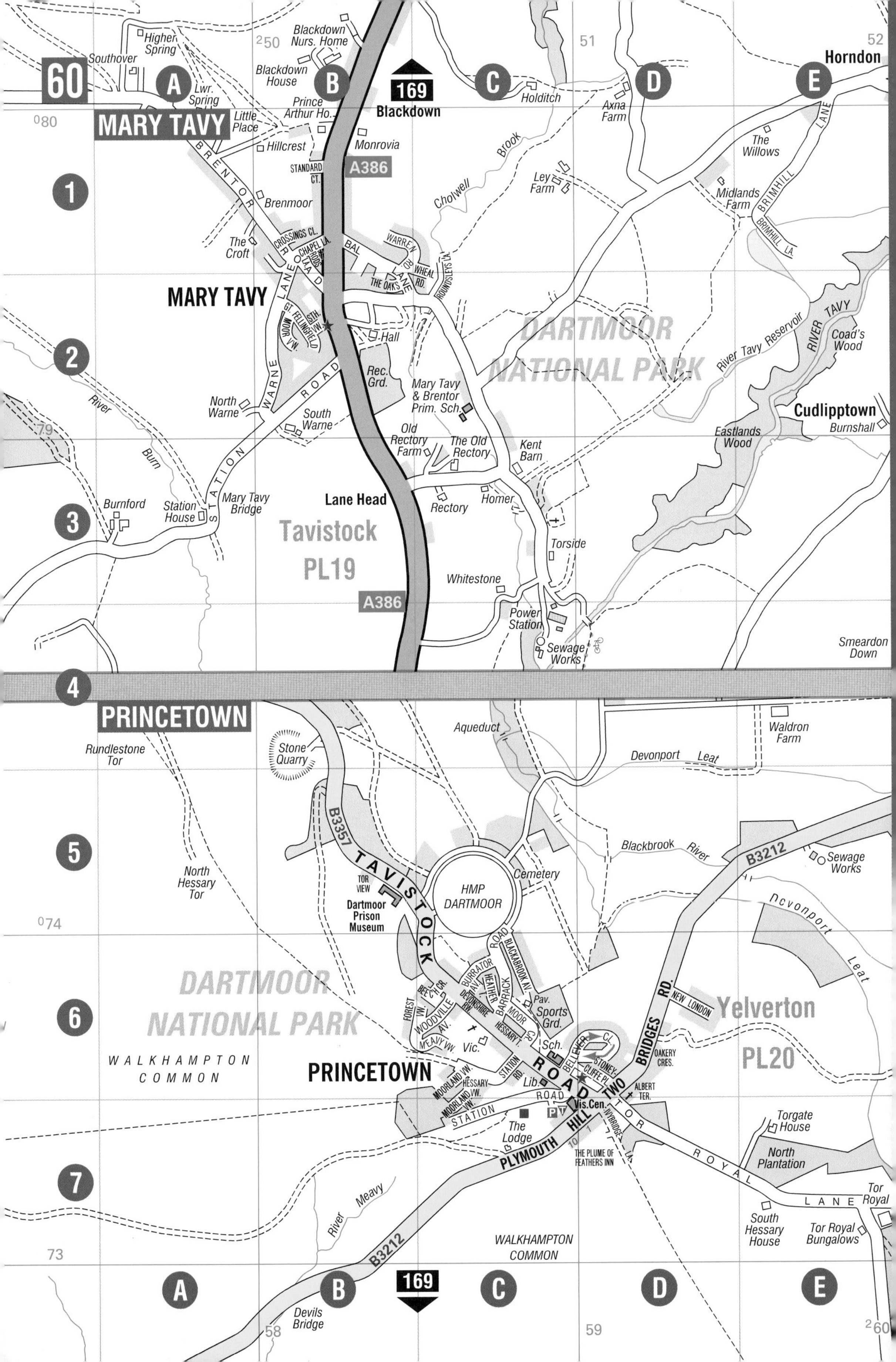
MARY TAVY
PRINCETOWN
169
Blackdown
169
Higher Spring
Southover
Lwr. Spring
Little Place
Blackdown Nurs. Home
Blackdown House
Prince Arthur Ho.
Holditch
Axna Farm
Horndon
Hillcrest
Monrovia
A386
Chotwell Brook
Ley Farm
The Willows
Midlands Farm
Brimhill Lane
Brenmoor
The Croft
Mary Tavy
Dartmoor National Park
River Tavy Reservoir
River Tavy
Coad's Wood
Hall
Rec. Grd.
Mary Tavy & Brentor Prim. Sch.
North Warne
South Warne
Cudlipptown
Burnshall
Eastlands Wood
River Burn
Old Rectory Farm
The Old Rectory
Kent Barn
Burnford
Station House
Mary Tavy Bridge
Lane Head
Rectory
Homer
Tavistock PL19
Torside
Whitestone
Power Station
Sewage Works
Smeardon Down
Rundlestone Tor
Stone Quarry
Aqueduct
Waldron Farm
Devonport Leat
Blackbrook River
B3357
Tavistock Road
B3212
Sewage Works
North Hessary Tor
Tor View
Dartmoor Prison Museum
HMP Dartmoor
Cemetery
Dartmoor National Park
Walkhampton Common
Yelverton PL20
Pav. Sports Grd.
Sch.
Vic.
Lib.
Vis.Cen.
The Lodge
Plymouth Hill
Two Bridges Rd.
Tor Royal Lane
The Plume of Feathers Inn
Torgate House
North Plantation
Tor Royal
South Hessary House
Tor Royal Bungalows
River Meavy
Walkhampton Common
Devils Bridge

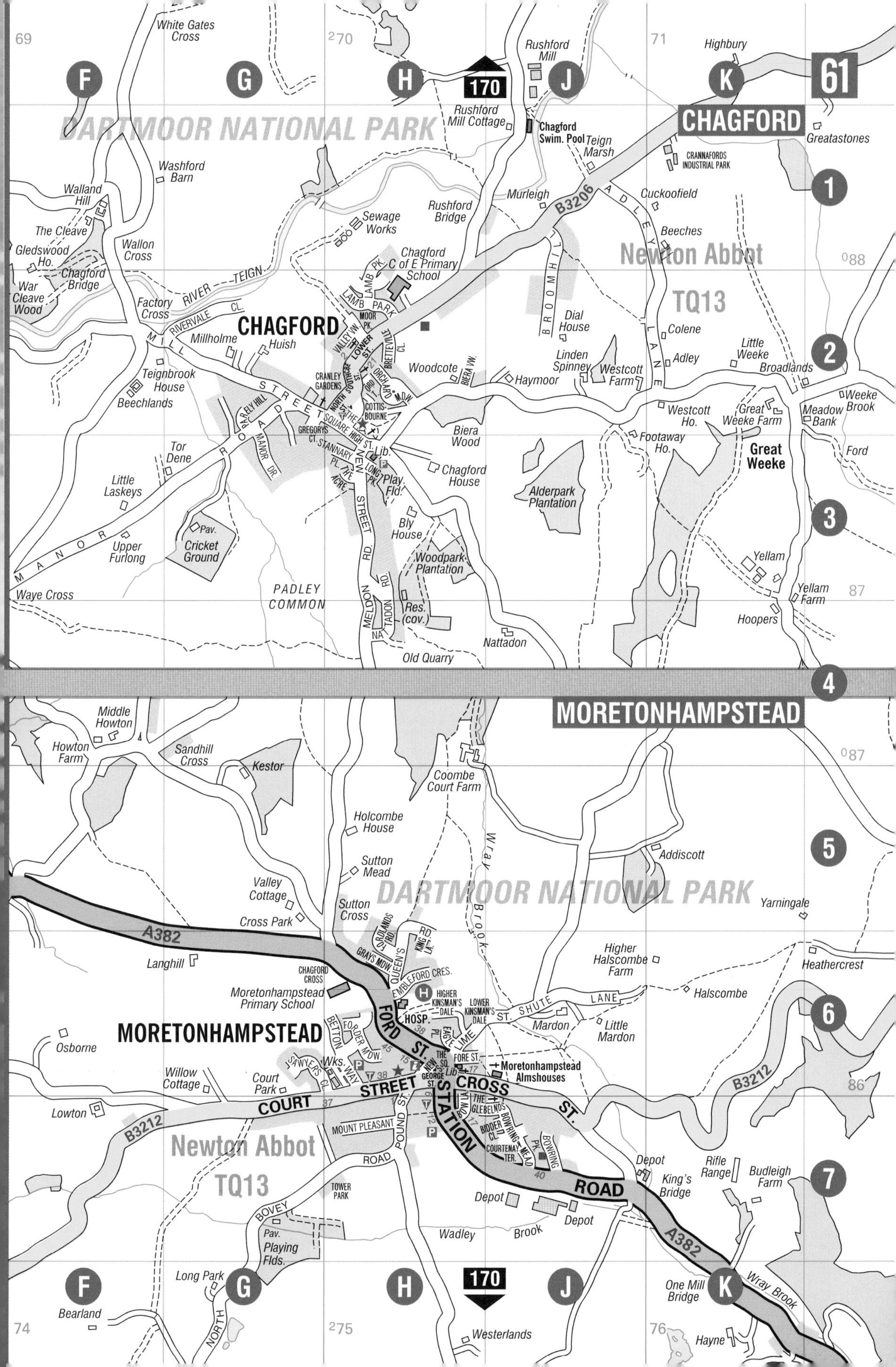
CHAGFORD
MORETONHAMPSTEAD
DARTMOOR NATIONAL PARK
Newton Abbot
TQ13
White Gates Cross
Rushford Mill
Highbury
Rushford Mill Cottage
Chagford Swim. Pool
Teign Marsh
Greatastones
CRANNAFORDS INDUSTRIAL PARK
Washford Barn
Walland Hill
Murleigh
Cuckoofield
The Cleave
Sewage Works
Rushford Bridge
Beeches
Gledswood Ho.
Wallon Cross
Chagford Bridge
Chagford C of E Primary School
War Cleave Wood
RIVER TEIGN
Factory Cross
RIVERVALE CL.
Millholme
Huish
Dial House
Colene
Adley
Little Weeke
Broadlands
Teignbrook House
Beechlands
Woodcote
Haymoor
Linden Spinney
Westcott Farm
Weeke Brook
Meadow Bank
Westcott Ho.
Great Weeke Farm
Great Weeke
Ford
Footaway Ho.
Tor Dene
Biera Wood
Chagford House
Little Laskeys
Play. Fld.
Alderpark Plantation
Bly House
Upper Furlong
Cricket Ground
Woodpark Plantation
Yellam
Yellam Farm
Waye Cross
PADLEY COMMON
Res. (cov.)
Hoopers
Nattadon
Old Quarry
MANOR ROAD
MILL STREET
B3206
ADLEY LANE
BROOMHILL
Middle Howton
Howton Farm
Sandhill Cross
Kestor
Coombe Court Farm
Holcombe House
Addiscott
Sutton Mead
Valley Cottage
Sutton Cross
Cross Park
Yarningale
Wray Brook
Higher Halscombe Farm
Heathercrest
Langhill
CHAGFORD CROSS
Moretonhampstead Primary School
Halscombe
HOSP.
Mardon
Little Mardon
Osborne
Moretonhampstead Almshouses
Willow Cottage
Court Park
Lowton
COURT STREET
CROSS ST.
STATION ROAD
FORD ST.
SHUTE LANE
MOUNT PLEASANT
POUND ST.
TOWER PARK
BOVEY ROAD
Depot
King's Bridge
Rifle Range
Budleigh Farm
Playing Flds.
Wadley Brook
Long Park
One Mill Bridge
Bearland
Westerlands
Hayne
B3212
A382
170
69
270
71
088
87
087
86
74
275
76
F
G
H
J
K
1
2
3
4
5
6
7

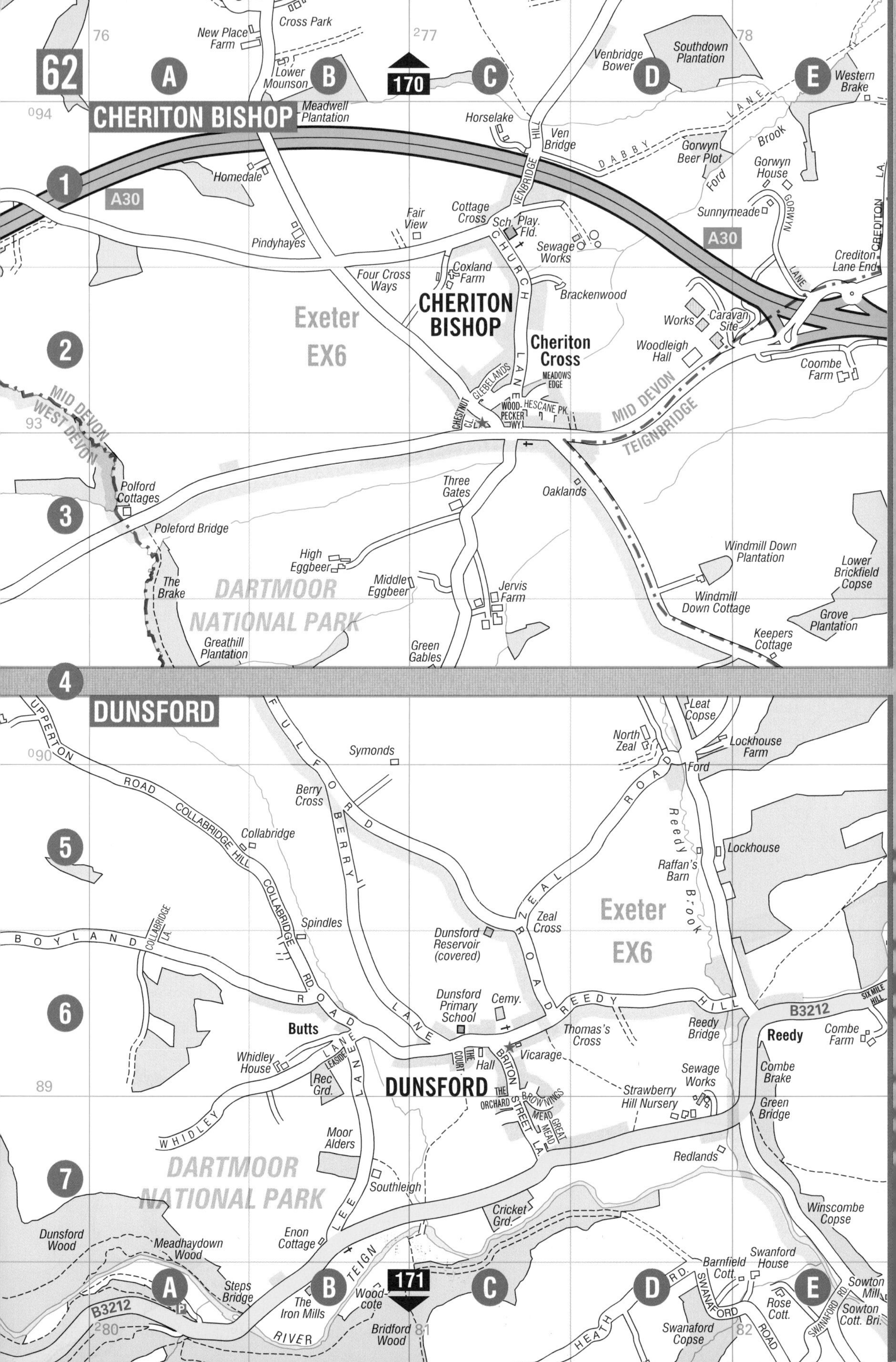
CHERITON BISHOP
DUNSFORD
170
171
New Place Farm
Cross Park
Lower Mounson
Meadwell Plantation
Horselake
Ven Bridge
Venbridge Bower
Southdown Plantation
Western Brake
Homedale
A30
Pindyhayes
Fair View
Cottage Cross
Sch. Play. Fld.
Sewage Works
Four Cross Ways
Coxland Farm
Brackenwood
CHERITON BISHOP
Cheriton Cross
Exeter EX6
Gorwyn Beer Plot
Gorwyn House
Sunnymeade
Crediton Lane End
Works
Caravan Site
Woodleigh Hall
Coombe Farm
MID DEVON
WEST DEVON
TEIGNBRIDGE
Polford Cottages
Poleford Bridge
Three Gates
Oaklands
High Eggbeer
Middle Eggbeer
Jervis Farm
The Brake
DARTMOOR NATIONAL PARK
Greathill Plantation
Green Gables
Windmill Down Plantation
Windmill Down Cottage
Lower Brickfield Copse
Grove Plantation
Keepers Cottage
Leat Copse
North Zeal
Lockhouse Farm
Ford
Symonds
Berry Cross
Collabridge
Reedy Brook
Raffan's Barn
Lockhouse
Spindles
Zeal Cross
Dunsford Reservoir (covered)
Exeter EX6
Dunsford Primary School
Cemy.
Butts
Whidley House
Rec Grd.
Hall
Vicarage
Thomas's Cross
Reedy Bridge
Reedy
Combe Farm
Combe Brake
Green Bridge
Sewage Works
Strawberry Hill Nursery
DUNSFORD
Moor Alders
Redlands
Southleigh
Cricket Grd.
Winscombe Copse
Dunsford Wood
Meadhaydown Wood
Enon Cottage
Steps Bridge
The Iron Mills
Woodcote
Bridford Wood
Barnfield Cott.
Swanford House
Rose Cott.
Swanaford Copse
Sowton Mill
Sowton Cott. Bri.
B3212
RIVER TEIGN

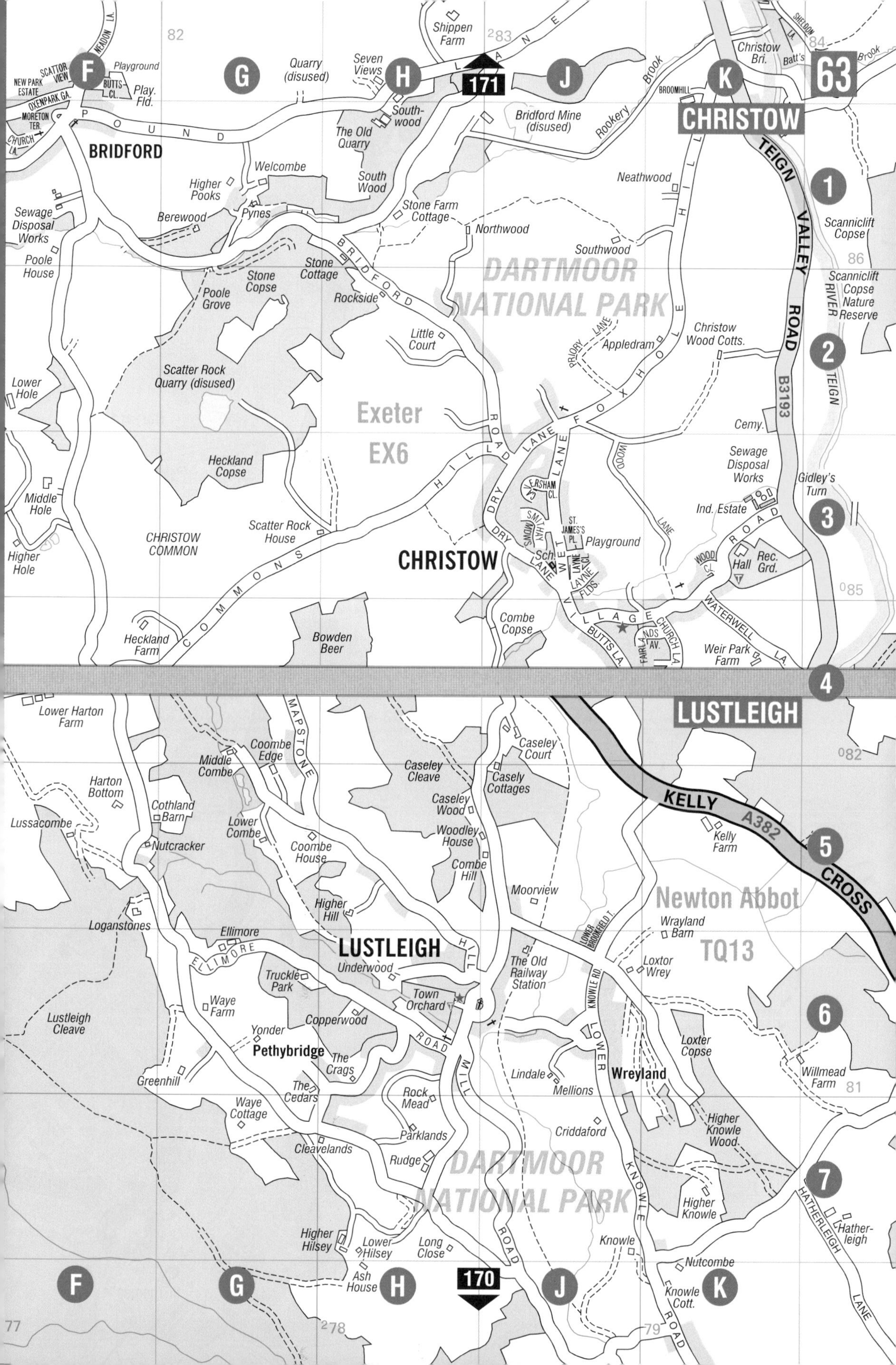
63
171
170
CHRISTOW
LUSTLEIGH
BRIDFORD
CHRISTOW
LUSTLEIGH
DARTMOOR NATIONAL PARK
Exeter EX6
Newton Abbot TQ13
TEIGN VALLEY ROAD
B3193
KELLY CROSS
A382
Shippen Farm
Quarry (disused)
Seven Views
Southwood
The Old Quarry
South Wood
Bridford Mine (disused)
Christow Bri.
Neathwood
Scanniclift Copse
Scanniclift Copse Nature Reserve
Welcombe
Higher Pooks
Pynes
Berewood
Sewage Disposal Works
Poole House
Stone Farm Cottage
Northwood
Southwood
Poole Grove
Stone Copse
Stone Cottage
Rockside
Little Court
Appledram
Christow Wood Cotts.
Scatter Rock Quarry (disused)
Heckland Copse
Scatter Rock House
CHRISTOW COMMON
Lower Hole
Middle Hole
Higher Hole
Heckland Farm
Bowden Beer
Combe Copse
Cemy.
Sewage Disposal Works
Gidley's Turn
Ind. Estate
Rec. Grd.
Hall
Playground
Weir Park Farm
Lower Harton Farm
Harton Bottom
Lussacombe
Cothland Barn
Nutcracker
Middle Combe
Coombe Edge
Lower Combe
Coombe House
Caseley Cleave
Caseley Court
Casely Cottages
Caseley Wood
Woodley House
Combe Hill
Moorview
Kelly Farm
Wrayland Barn
Loxtor Wrey
Loganstones
Higher Hill
Ellimore
Underwood
Truckle Park
Town Orchard
The Old Railway Station
Waye Farm
Copperwood
Yonder
Pethybridge
The Crags
Lustleigh Cleave
Greenhill
The Cedars
Rock Mead
Parklands
Waye Cottage
Cleavelands
Rudge
Lindale
Mellions
Wreyland
Loxter Copse
Willmead Farm
Criddaford
Higher Knowle Wood
Higher Knowle
Hather-leigh
Higher Hilsey
Lower Hilsey
Long Close
Ash House
Knowle
Nutcombe
Knowle Cott.

Cowley
Sewage Works
Cowley Bri. Junction
Barton Place Wood
Hill Close Copse
Lower Plantation
Higher Park Plantation
EX5
Hidden Valley
Cowley Bridge
Barton Place
Barton Place Farm
Bellenden
Bellevue Farm
Cottage Farm
Belle Vue Valley Equestrian Centre
EAST DEVON
EXETER
Exwick Weir
Thomas Hall
Sundown Gardens
Argyll Gdns.
EXWICK WOOD
Exwick Barton
Creedy
The Cottage
The Oaks
Exeter
Duryard
Three Corner Copse
The Knap
Ash Plot
Bolsters Wood
Playing Fld.
Tennis & Cricket Centre
UNIVERSITY OF EXETER (STREATHAM CAMPUS)
Streatham Sports Park
Amory Building
Northcott Theatre
Hamlyns Farm
Exwick Mills
EX4
Reed Hall
Great Hall
Queen's Bldg.
Museum
EXETER TEIGNBRIDGE
Exwick
St.David's
Exeter St. David's
Artwell Farm
The Haven Orchard
Cleve Cottage
Exwick Heights Prim. Sch.
Playing Field
Exwick Play. Flds.
Exeter College
HMP EXETER
Clock Tower
Exeter Central
Whitestone Cross
Barley Wood
Lugg's Fm.
Foxhayes
St. Thomas Cemetery
Sports Ground
Playing Fields
EXETER
Flowerpot
Reservoir (covered)
Redhills
Mount Dinham
Millers Crossing
Exe Island
Upper Old Wheatley Farm
Burnets Brakes
Eastdown Plantation
Friars Green
St.Thomas
Leisure Cen.
Wheatley
A377
A396
B3183

171
70
9

171
Stoke Woods
Pennsylvania Road
Five Oaks
Rixlade Cott.
Rixlade
Goffin's Farm
Fairy Dell
Lower Rollestone
The Cottage
Reservoir (covered)
Moongate
Panorama
Pennsylvania Picnic Site
Rolleston House
Rollestone Barton
Lower Covert
Great Hill
Compass Cottage
Play Area
The Grange
The Old Barn
Higher Duryard
Stoke Valley
Mary Pole Head
Res. (covered)
Higher Hoopern Farm
Higher Hoopern Ho.
Botanic Gardens
Hoopern House
Pennsylvania
Weirs
XFi Building
Mincinglake Bridge
Mincinglake Valley Park
Stoke Hill Junior Sch.
Stoke Hill
Prince Charles Road
Coal Distribution Centre
Exmouth Junction
Superstore
Polsloe Bridge
Polsloe Priory
St. James'
Devon County Cricket Grd.
St. James' Pk.
Exeter City F.C.
Black Boy Rd.
Pinhoe Road
B3212
Polsloe Park
Clifton Hill Sports Cen. & Ski Slope
Newtown
Ladysmith Jun. Sch.
Sports Grd.
Exeter Cemetery
Chapels
War Mem.
Cycle Training Area
Hamlin Lane Playing Fields
Honeylands Cen.
Whipton Road
Beacon Lane
Celia Cres.
Chancellor's Way
Iolanthe Dr.
Summer Lane
Sidwell St.
Paris St.
Heavitree Road
B3183
Western Way
Royal Devon & Exeter Hosp. (Heavitree)
University of Exeter
St. Luke's Spts. Cen.
Barnfield
Leisure Cen.
Civic Cen.
Coach Sta.
Cath.
The Cloisters
Castle
Arts Cen.
Fore Street
EX1
EX2
Heavitree Pleasure Ground
Heavitree
Whipton Lane
East Wonford Hill
Mt. Radford
Magdalen Road
Topsham Road
Holloway Street
Larkbeare
Exeter School
St. Leonard's
Royal Devon & Exeter Hospital (Wonford)
Wonford
Nuffield Health Hosp.
Force (Cancer Supp. Cen.)
Wonford Ho. Hosp.
Playing Flds.
Football Grd.
Acad. for Deaf Educ.
Coaver
Wood-water Bri.
Woodwater
71
7
66
92
93
94
95
F
G
H
J
K
1
2
3
4
5
6
7

66
171
65
72
Cheynegate Cott.
Ashford Copse
Park Farm
Reservoir (covered)
Hilltop
Beacon Down
Beacon Down Lodge
Ash Copse
Old Park
Twin Gables
Beacon Hill
Beaconhill Cottage
Beacon Rise
Church Lawn
EAST DEVON
EXETER
Cheynegate
Church Cross
Beacon House
War Mem.
Pinhill View
Riding School
Home Farm
PINHOE
Peterhayes
Pinbrook Mount
Clay Pit
Jones Pyne
EX4
Pincourt Farm
Works
Sch.
Play. Fld.
Lib.
Hall
EXHIBITION FIELDS
Eastern Field
Roman Ho.
St.James School
Sports Grd.
Exeter Arena Athletics Stadium
Bowl. Grn.
Grandstand
Isca Bowls & Bridge Cen.
Chancel Bri.
Pinhoe
Play.Fld.
Willowbrook School
Playing Field
Play. Flds.
Little Pilton
Children's Reception Home
Pilton Ho.
Whipton
Superstore
Monkerton
Exeter
Quarry House
Games Cts.
Higher Furlong
Nursery
St. Luke's Science & Sports Coll.
Playing Fields
Junction 29
Comm. Cen.
Honeylands Cen. Sch.
Inf. Sch.
Jun. Sch.
EXETER COMMUNITY HOSPITAL
Ellen Tinkham School
Rock Gardens
Cycle Training Area
Hamlin Lane Playing Fields
EX1
EXETER BUSINESS PARK
Hill Barton Farm
Meteorological Office
Upper Moor Plantation
Honiton Road
Caravan Site
Heavitree
Education Centres
Prim. Sch.
THE OMEGA CENTRE
SOWTON INDUSTRIAL ESTATE
THE ALPHA CENTRE
M5
MOTORWAY
KESTREL BUSINESS PARK
Police Training College
Football Grd.
EX2
Southam
St. Peter's C of E School
Devon & Cornwall Constabulary HQ
Middle Moor Sports Ground
Exeter Coll.
Walter Daw Prim. Schl
Peninsula Ho.
Wood-water Bri.
Sowton P+R
DCC
B3181
B3212
B3183
A3015
HONITON ROAD
PINHOE ROAD
WHIPTON VILLAGE RD.
BARTON ROAD
HILL BARTON ROAD
SUMMER LANE
BEACON LANE
HARRINGTON LANE
CUMBERLAND WAY
HOLLOW LANE
MOOR LANE
WONFORD HILL
SIDMOUTH RD.
RYDON LANE
EAST WONFORD HILL

67
171
68
171
73
EX5
West Clyst
Moonhill Copse
Mosshayne
West Clyst Farm
West Clyst Cottage
WEST CLYST BARNYARD
Kerswell Barton
Brockhill
Merrie Brocke
Wishford Farm
HELLINGS
PARKS LA.
COUNCIL LANE
WISH MEADOW LANE
STATION
LODGE TRADING ESTATE
HUNGRY FOX ESTATE
Bridge Cottages
Railway Terrace
Broadclyst Station
Shermoor Farm
ALEXANDRA TER.
CLYST AV.
COTTERELL RD.
Clystlands
ROAD
CLYST VALLEY
M5 MOTORWAY
M5
B3181
HILL
MOSSHAYNE LANE
Mosshayne Cottage
Mosshayne Cottages
Brook
Pin
Roblynn's Hideaway
Ash Bungalow
Sewage Works
LANGATON LANE
The Linhays
MILL LANE
Carrow Mill
HONITON ROAD
Coach Bridge
Hayes Farm
Hayes House
Clyst Honiton Picnic Site
WATERSLADE LA.
Clyst Honiton
CLYST HONITON BY-PASS
B3174
SHIP LA.
ST. MICHAELS HILL
ST. MICHAELS CL.
CHURCH SIDE
CLYSTSIDE
Clyst Honiton C of E Prim. Sch.
Play. Fld.
Home Farm
Pound Corner
B3184
A30
Sunnymead
Highstone
The Lilacs
Lower Stone
BLACKHORSE LANE
Blackhorse
ENDSLEIGH CRES.
Clyst Honiton Bridge
Redhayes Lodge
Taylor's Brake
SOWTON LANE
Sowton Brake
Star Dairy
Weir
RIVER CLYST
War Mem.
Venn's Farm
Sowton
Sowton Barton
Marlborough Cottages
Marlborough Cross
Marlborough Farm
Dymond's Farm
Dymond's Bridge
Lower Holbrook Cottages
Wroford Manor
Holbrook Bridge
Oakview
Fawns Cottages
Alder Croft
Oliver's Cottages
Holbrook Farm
Higher Holbrook Farm
Bishop's Court
Home Covert
BISHOP'S COURT LA.
BISHOP'S CT. RD.
Depot
F
G
H
J
K
1
2
3
4
5
6
7
97
98
99
95
94
93
92

Southern Lake
Sutherlake Barton
Paynes Farm
A
B
C
D
E
172
Vinnacombes
SAUNDERCROFT RD.
Clystia
52
Heath-beam Cottage
Ballamount
Wind Whistle
Hellings Parks
Crannaford Cottage
Crannaford House
Godfrey's Farm
Elbury Farm
COUNCIL LA.
HELLINGS PARK LA.
Tillhouse Farm
Weir
Stillwoods Farm
LODGE TRADING ESTATE
CRANBROOK
LONDON
Jack-in-the-Green
Higher Lodge
Rockbeare Court Farm
Sunnyhayes
Little Hayes
Green Acres
Blue Hayes Farm
Blue Hayes
Railway Terrace
Broadclyst Station
BLUEHAYES
Rockbeare Bridge
CHERRY TREE CL.
VALLEY VW.
STONEY
LANE
PARSONS
Rockbeare Prim. Sch.
Sch.
COPSECLOSE
ROAD
South Whimple Farm
Exeter
EX5
Clystlands
COTTERELL RD.
STATION
ROAD
B3174
HONITON
Works
Coppice Farm
Coach Bridge
Treasbeare Farm
Sewage Works
67
EXETER INTERNATIONAL AIRPORT
Terminal
Pound Corner
B3184
A30
HARRIER COURT
Depot
EXETER AIRPORT INDUSTRIAL ESTATE
EXETER AIRPORT BUSINESS PK.
MERLIN BUS. PK.
SKYWAYS BUS. PK.
Training Centre
Fair Oak Fm.
FAIR OAK CT.
LANCASTER CT.
SILVERDOWN OFFICE PK.
NEWBERY COMMERCIAL CEN.
Southwood Cross
MARWOOD
Wares Farm
Deer Copse
300
01
96
95
94
93
1
2
3
4
5
6
7

02 03 04

SOUTHBROOK

Lower Southbrook

Southbrook House

Higher Southbrook

LANE

Farlands

The Nursery

Higher Cobden

Lower Cobden

Middle Cobden

Little Cobden

Orchard Lea

PLUMTREE LA.

CHURCH ROAD

Pithayes Farm

1

96

Hand and Pen

ROMAN ROAD

ROAD LONDON ROAD

B3174

Grange Lodge

GRIBBLE LANE

Bodley Bridge

HAND AND PEN COTTAGES

2

Strete Ralegh Farm

Madges Cross

Strete Farm

Strete House

LANE

TURKEY LANE

3

95

ROCKBEARE

GREENACRE VW.

BIRCHBRIDGE VW.

THE SQ.

BIRCH END

HAZE GRD.

THE VILLAGE

Football Ground

LOWBROOK

SILVER LANE

The Grange

GRANGE COTTS.

REWE LANE

GRIBBLE LANE

Crosspark

Homefield

Tanner's Farmhouse

Carradale Farm

A30

TURKEY LANE

4

The Old Rectory

Lions Farm

Lawns Cottage

Ford Farm

Manor Cross

Higher Upcott

The Croft

Little Upcott

Lower Upcott

Allercombe

ALLERCOMBE LA.

PALMER'S LA.

5

Woodhouse Farm

Silverdale

SILVER LANE

RAG LANE

Rockbeare Manor

Higher Marsh Farm

MARSH GREEN LA.

MARSH GREEN HILL

94

Higher Southwood Farm

Home Covert

Lower Southwood

Westcott Ho.

RAG LANE

Little Westcott Farm

WESTCOTT LANE

Marsh Green Farm

HOUNDBEARE LANE

Cotties Farm

Manor Farm

Marsh Green

Lower Marsh

MARSH

6

Great Houndbeare Farm

LANE

7

A30

Great Covert

The Park

MILE LANE

QUARTER

New Ford Farm

WITHY BED LA.

Withy Bed Copse

93

Roundbeare

Beautiport Farm

02 03 04

Rill Copse

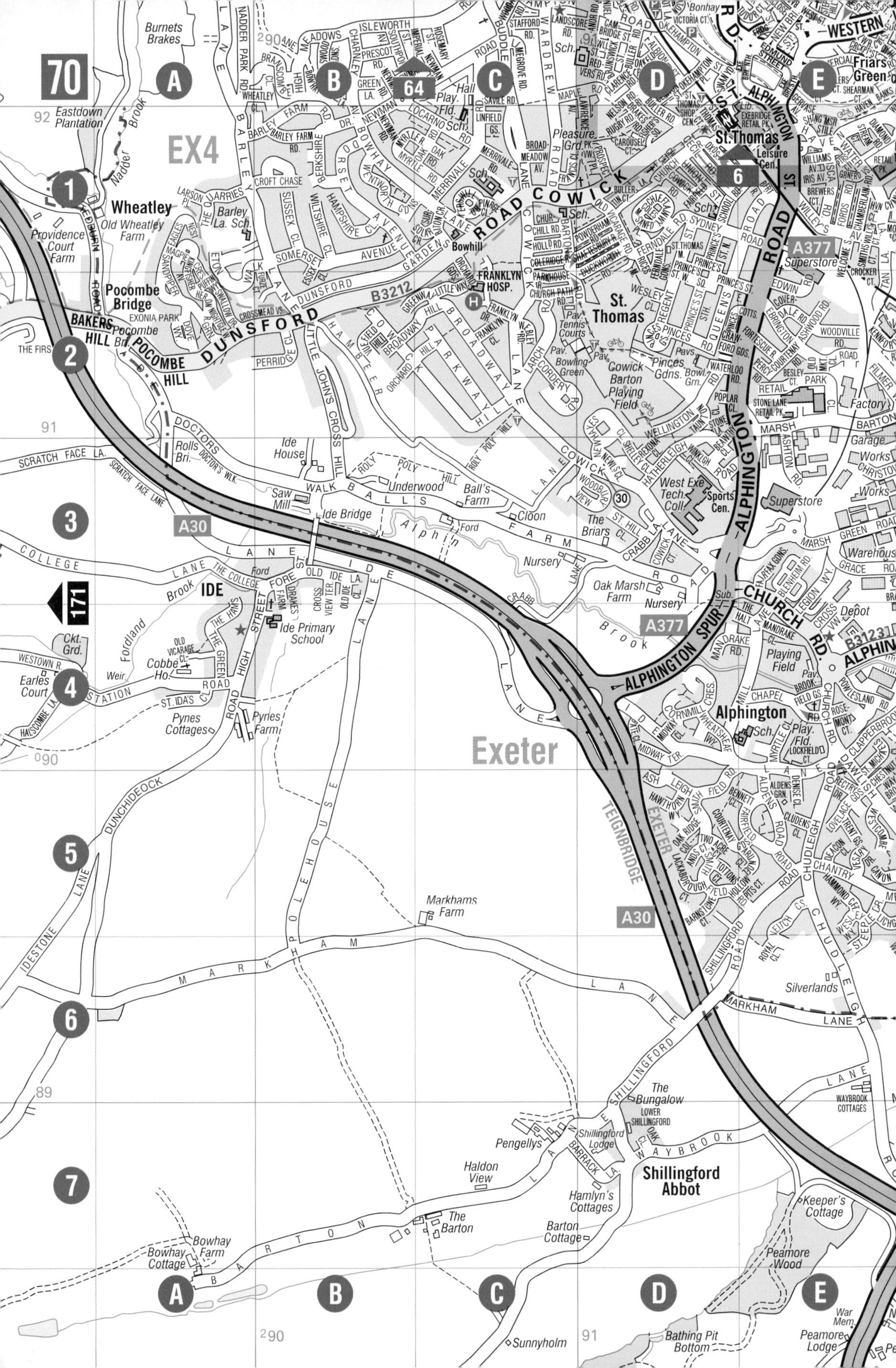

Mt. Radford
WONFORD HILL
65
7
72
74
St. Leonard's
EXETER NUFFIELD HOSP.
ROYAL DEVON & EXETER HOSPITAL (Wonford)
NHS Walk-in Cen.
Wonford
WONFORD HO. HOSP.
FORCE (Cancer Supp. Cen.
Hospiscare
The Cedars
St.Loye's
Exeter School
Football Grd.
Larkbeare
Haven Banks
Gas Works
Coaver Club
Devon Co.Hall
Acad. for Deaf Educ.
TOPSHAM ROAD
A3015
EXETER
Flood Channel
Bramham's Farm Playing Field
St. James's Weir
Salmon Pool
Duck's Marsh
Mill Race
University of Plymouth (Exeter Campus)
Isca College of Media Arts
Wyvern Barracks
TA Centre
Wynstream Sch.
The Chestnut Cen.
Super-store
Wonford Sports Cen.
Mushroom Farm
Nurseries
LUDWELL LANE
LUDWELL VALLEY PARK
Playing Fields
Southbrook College
Millbrook Cottage
Sports Ground
Exeter & Devon Crematorium
Northbrook Park
Northbrook Golf Course
Club Ho.
Salmonpool Bridge
Incinerator
Grace Road Playing Field
Marsh Barton
MARSH BARTON TRADING ESTATE
BROOK RD.
HENNOCK ROAD CENTRAL
RIVER EXE
RIVER EXE COUNTRY PARK
EXETER CANAL
Alphin Brook
Cycle Track
Higher Wear
King George V Playing Field
Countess Wear
Youth Hostel
Countess Wear Bri.
Lower Wear
EX2
Cemetery
BAD HOMBURG WAY
B3123
THE MATFORD CENTRE (Exeter Livestock Centre)
Retail Park
MARSH BARTON TRAD. EST.
Knowle Hill
Matford P+R
Matford
Matford Brook Cottages
Matford Barton
Matford Mill
Matford Bridge
Matfield
Cotfield
DAWLISH ROAD
Grassmead
BRIDGE ROAD
A379
Matford Park Farm
Matford Home Farm
Depot
RIVERSIDE VALLEY PARK
Highfield Bungalow
Enfield Bungalow
Wracombe Farm
EX6
SANNERVILLE WY.
Trood House
A30
Church Path Hill Plantation
Kiln Close Plantation
M5
M5 MOTORWAY
Exminster Ho.
Milbury Barton
Pond House
Fish Pond

72
A
B
C
D
E
1
2
3
4
5
6
7
66
71
74
E. WONFORD HILL
HONITON ROAD
QUARRY LANE
WOODWATER LANE
PLUMTREE DR.
Walter Daw Prim. Sch.
Wood-water Bri.
St.Loye's
LANSDOWNE
RIFFORD RD.
LUDWELL LANE
Super-store
Wonford Sports Cen.
Mushroom Farm
Nurseries
Play. Fld.
St. Peter's C of E School
Peninsula Ho.
Southam
SIDMOUTH RD.
RYDON PARK
Devon & Cornwall Constabulary HQ
Middle Moor
Sports Ground
SOWTON INDUSTRIAL ESTATE
MALLARD RD.
KESTREL WY.
KESTREL BUSINESS PARK
HEARTS OF OAK
Exeter Coll.
Exeter Service Area
FALCON ROAD
Sowton P+R
DCC
MOOR LANE
Digby & Sowton
BISHOPS CT. IND. EST.
Clyst Heathfield Plantation
Hotel
Bishops Court Sand Quarry
APPLE LANE
Digby P+R (for Royal Devon & Exeter Hospital at Wonford, only)
Prim. Sch.
RUSSELL WALK
DIGBY DRIVE
RYDON LA. RETAIL PK.
A3015
A379
RUSSELL WAY
M5
Sandy Gate
Junction 30
Sandy Park Conference Centre
Sandy Park
Exeter Chiefs RUFC (Sandy Park Stadium)
Sandygate
THE SILVERS
Pynes Hill
PYNES HILL BUSINESS PARK
LUDWELL VALLEY PARK
Playing Field
Southbrook College
Woodwater Park
Superstore
EX2
Beech Cottage
NEWCOURT
St. Bridget Nurseries
Primrose Orchard
Bricknells Cottage
RYDON LANE
OLD RYDON LANE
West of England Sch. & College for Young People with Little or No Sight
Vic.
Weir View
Wynards Cottages
Lavender Lodge
Builder's Yard
RIVER CLYST
TOPSHAM ROAD
RYDON ROAD
EXETER GOLF COURSE
Exeter & District Community Health Service NHS Trust HQ
M5 MOTORWAY
EXETER
EAST DEVON
Newcourt Barton
Cott's Cottage
Cott's Farm
King George V
Playing
Pav.
90
91
92
95
96
89
Countess Wear
Club Ho.
Linkways
Exeter
Youth Hostel
DAWLISH RD.
BRI.
LOWER WEAR RD.
Sch.
Playing Field
Lower Wear
GLASSHOUSE LA.
NEWPORT ROAD
Seabrook House
Newport Lodge
Football Grd.
Tumbling Hills
Gdn. Cen.
THE WALLED GARDEN
NEWPORT PARK
RIVER EXE
EXE VALLEY PARK
Sewage Works
Nurseries
Sainthill Nurseries
Broom Park Nurseries
Five Acres
Highfield Farm
CLYST ROAD
Old Sludge Beds Nature Reserve
The Retreat
EXETER
TEIGNBRIDGE
WESSEX CLOSE
RETREAT DRIVE
RIVERSIDE RD.
Club
Playing Field
Water Tower
Cemetery
EX6
Exe Reed Beds Nature Reserve
SANNERVILLE WY.
MILBURY LANE
Milbury Barton
Exeter Canal
TOPSHAM
Playing Field
Sch.
Lib.
Swim. Pool
Topsham

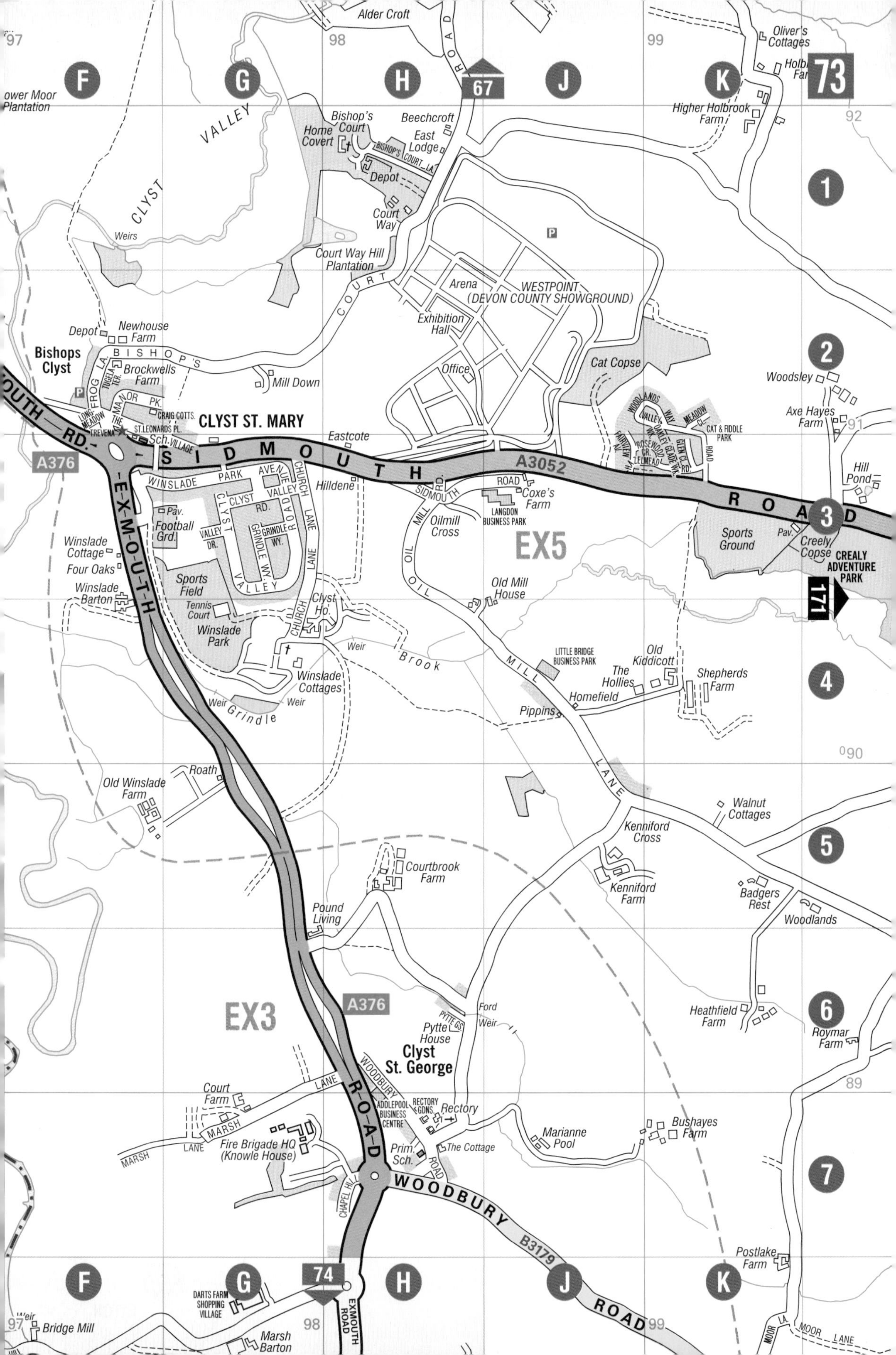

Alder Croft
Oliver's Cottages
Higher Holbrook Farm
Bishop's Court
Home Covert
Beechcroft
East Lodge
Depot
Court Way
Court Way Hill Plantation
CLYST VALLEY
Weirs
WESTPOINT (DEVON COUNTY SHOWGROUND)
Arena
Exhibition Hall
Office
Cat Copse
Depot
Newhouse Farm
Bishops Clyst
Brockwells Farm
Mill Down
CLYST ST. MARY
Eastcote
SIDMOUTH ROAD
A3052
A376
EXMOUTH RD.
Woodsley
Axe Hayes Farm
Hill Pond
Hilldene
Coxe's Farm
LANGDON BUSINESS PARK
Oilmill Cross
EX5
Sports Ground
Creely Copse
CREALY ADVENTURE PARK
171
Winslade Cottage
Four Oaks
Winslade Barton
Football Grd.
Sports Field
Tennis Court
Winslade Park
Clyst Ho.
Old Mill House
LITTLE BRIDGE BUSINESS PARK
Old Kiddicott
The Hollies
Shepherds Farm
Homefield
Pippins
Winslade Cottages
Weir
Brook
Grindle
Roath
Old Winslade Farm
Walnut Cottages
Kenniford Cross
Kenniford Farm
Courtbrook Farm
Badgers Rest
Woodlands
Pound Living
EX3
A376
Ford
Weir
Pytte House
Clyst St. George
Heathfield Farm
Roymar Farm
Court Farm
Rectory
Marianne Pool
Bushayes Farm
Fire Brigade HQ (Knowle House)
ADDLEPOOL BUSINESS CENTRE
Prim. Sch.
The Cottage
WOODBURY ROAD
B3179
Postlake Farm
74
DARTS FARM SHOPPING VILLAGE
Bridge Mill
Marsh Barton
EXMOUTH ROAD
MOOR LANE
MARSH LANE

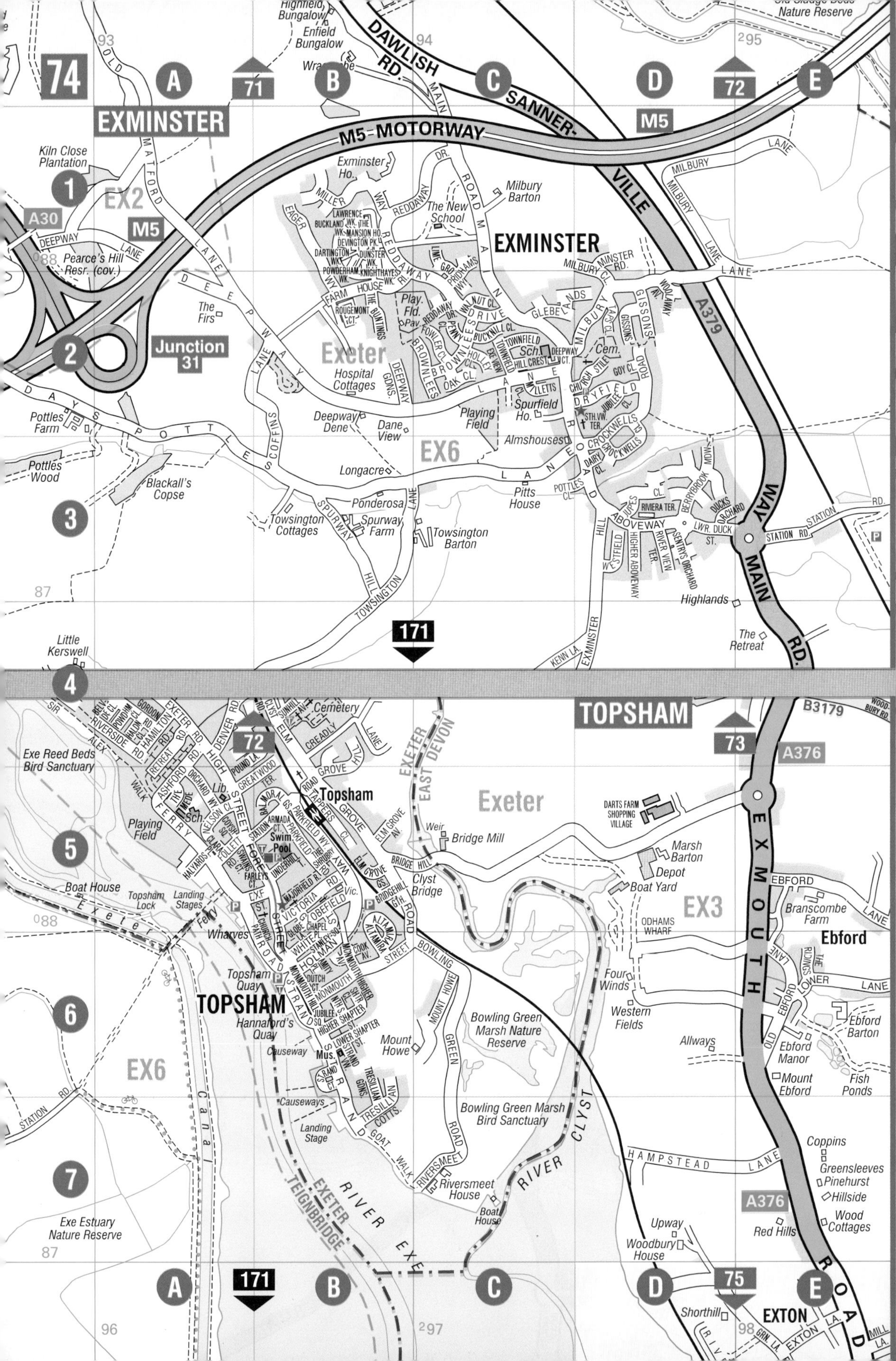
EXMINSTER
M5-MOTORWAY
DAWLISH RD.
SANNERVILLE WAY
A379
Kiln Close Plantation
EX2
A30
M5
Pearce's Hill Resr. (cov.)
Junction 31
The Firs
Exminster Ho.
Milbury Barton
The New School
EXMINSTER
Exeter
Hospital Cottages
Play. Fld.
Playing Field
Spurfield Ho.
Almshouses
Deepway Dene
Dane View
EX6
Longacre
Pottles Farm
Pottles Wood
Blackall's Copse
Ponderosa
Spurway Farm
Towsington Cottages
Towsington Barton
Pitts House
Highlands
The Retreat
Little Kerswell
171
TOPSHAM
B3179
A376
Exe Reed Beds Bird Sanctuary
Playing Field
Cemetery
Topsham
Swim Pool
Exeter
DARTS FARM SHOPPING VILLAGE
Bridge Mill
Clyst Bridge
Marsh Barton
Depot
Boat Yard
EX3
ODHAMS WHARF
Boat House
Topsham Lock
Landing Stages
Ferry
Wharves
Topsham Quay
TOPSHAM
Hannaford's Quay
Causeway
Mus.
Mount Howe
Bowling Green Marsh Nature Reserve
Bowling Green Marsh Bird Sanctuary
Four Winds
Western Fields
Allways
EXMOUTH ROAD
Ebford
Branscombe Farm
Ebford Manor
Ebford Barton
Mount Ebford
Fish Ponds
Coppins
Greensleeves
Pinehurst
Hillside
Wood Cottages
Red Hills
EX6
Canal
Exe Estuary Nature Reserve
Causeways
Landing Stage
RIVER EXE
RIVER CLYST
EXETER TEIGNBRIDGE
Riversmeet House
Boat House
HAMPSTEAD LANE
Upway
Woodbury House
Shorthill
EXTON
75
72
73
71

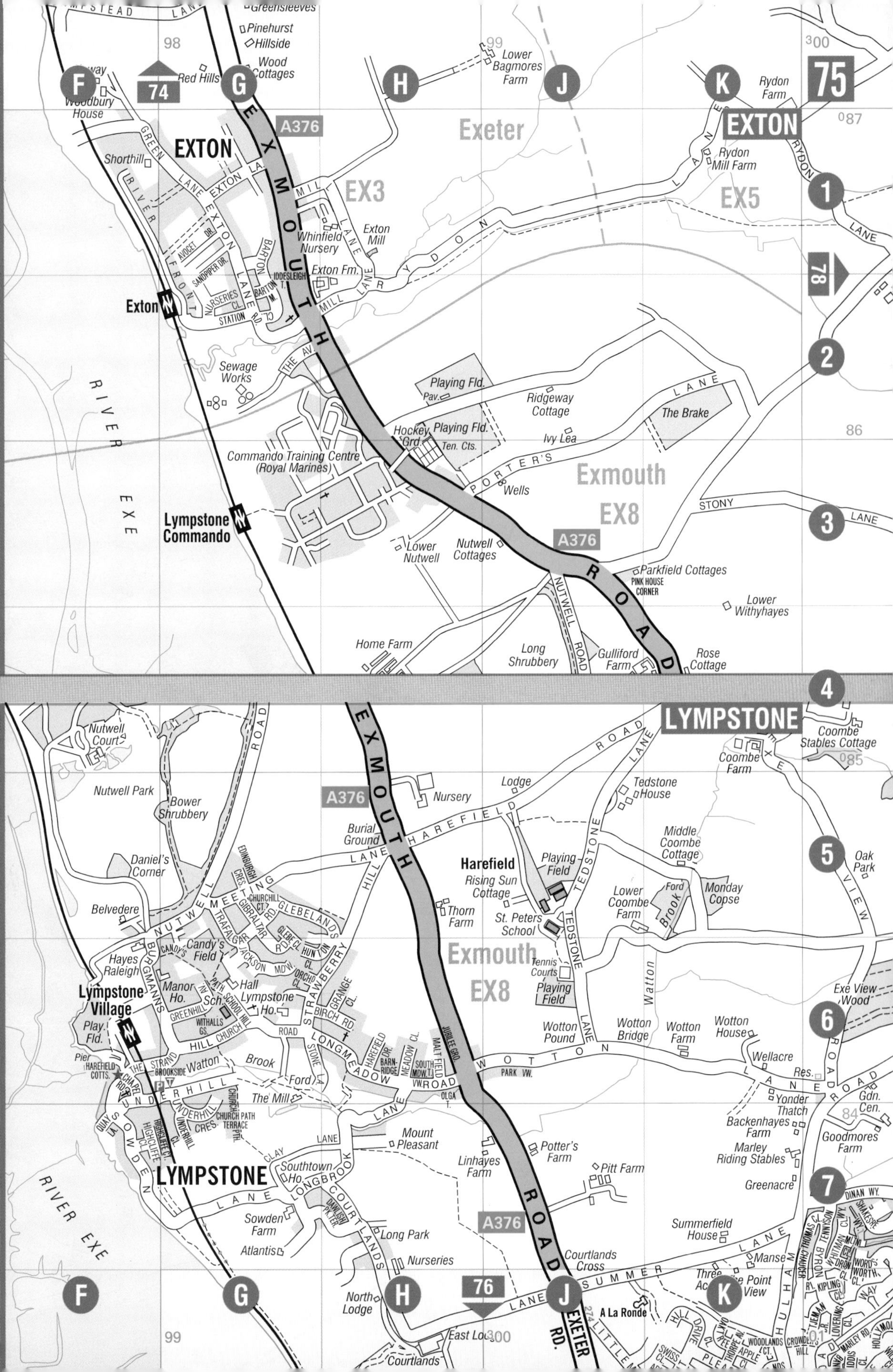
75
EXTON
Exeter
EX3
EX5
Exmouth
EX8
LYMPSTONE
Lympstone Village
Lympstone Commando
Exton
Harefield
RIVER EXE
EXMOUTH ROAD
A376
74
76
78

75
171
EXMOUTH
Hulham
RIVER EXE
EXETER ROAD
MARINE WAY
A376
Cockle Sand
Kings Lake
Shelly Bank
Little Bull Hill
Point Lake
The Point
Exmouth Rugby Football Club
Imperial Rd. Athletics Track
Exmouth Town FC
Exe Sailing Club
Exmouth Quay
Pier
Exmouth Bus Sta.
Exmouth Sports Centre
Leisure Cen.
Theatre
Elizabeth Hall
Beach Gardens
Exmouth Pav.
Exmouth Lifeboat Station
The Great Exmouth 00 Model Railway
Cricket Ground
The Maer
Maer Bridge
Conger Rocks
Foot Ferry (Summer Only)
EAST DEVON
TEIGNBRIDGE
Dawlish
Exe Estuary Local Nature Reserve
EX7
East Devon Tennis Centre
Exmouth Community College (Green Close)
Phear Park
Miniature Golf Course
Raleigh Park
Warren View Sports Grd.
King George's Field
Football Grd.
Lower Halsdon Farm
Higher Halsdown Farm
West Lodge
East Lodge
Courtlands
North Lodge
Nurseries
Sowden Farm
Courtlands Cross
Summerfield House
Three Acres
The Point in View
Manse
Greenacre
Pitt Farm
A La Ronde
C of E Prim. Sch.
Marpool Prim. Sch.
HOSP.
Hotel
Playing Field
SUMMER LANE
LITTLEMEAD LANE
SALTERTON RD.
ST. ROLLE RD.
DOUGLAS AVENUE
QUEEN'S DRIVE
ESPLANADE
WITHYCOMBE ROAD
MARPOOL HILL
ASHLEIGH ROAD
A B C D E
1 2 3 4 5 6 7

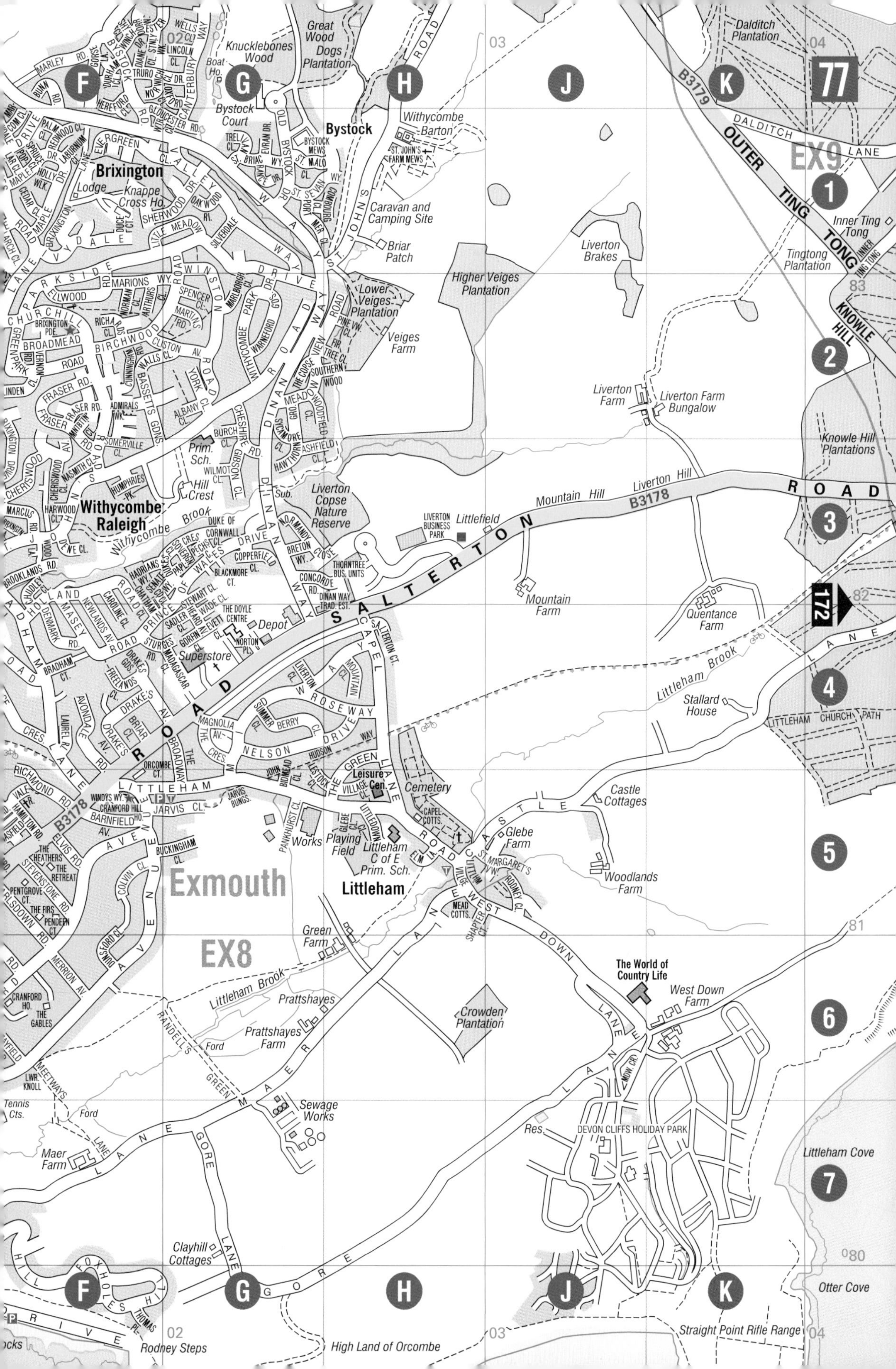
Brixington
Bystock
Withycombe Raleigh
Exmouth
EX8
EX9
Littleham
Bystock Court
Knucklebones Wood
Great Wood Dogs Plantation
Withycombe Barton
Caravan and Camping Site
Briar Patch
Lower Veiges Plantation
Veiges Farm
Higher Veiges Plantation
Liverton Brakes
Dalditch Plantation
Inner Ting Tong
Tingtong Plantation
Knowle Hill Plantations
Liverton Farm
Liverton Farm Bungalow
Liverton Copse Nature Reserve
Littlefield
Mountain Farm
Quentance Farm
Stallard House
Littleham Brook
Castle Cottages
Glebe Farm
Woodlands Farm
Cemetery
Playing Field
Littleham C of E Prim. Sch.
Works
Depot
Superstore
Prim. Sch.
Hill Crest
Leisure Cen.
The World of Country Life
West Down Farm
Crowden Plantation
Green Farm
Prattshayes
Prattshayes Farm
Sewage Works
Maer Farm
Clayhill Cottages
DEVON CLIFFS HOLIDAY PARK
Littleham Cove
Otter Cove
Straight Point Rifle Range
High Land of Orcombe
Rodney Steps
Tennis Cts.
B3178
B3179
SALTERTON ROAD
OUTER TING TONG
172

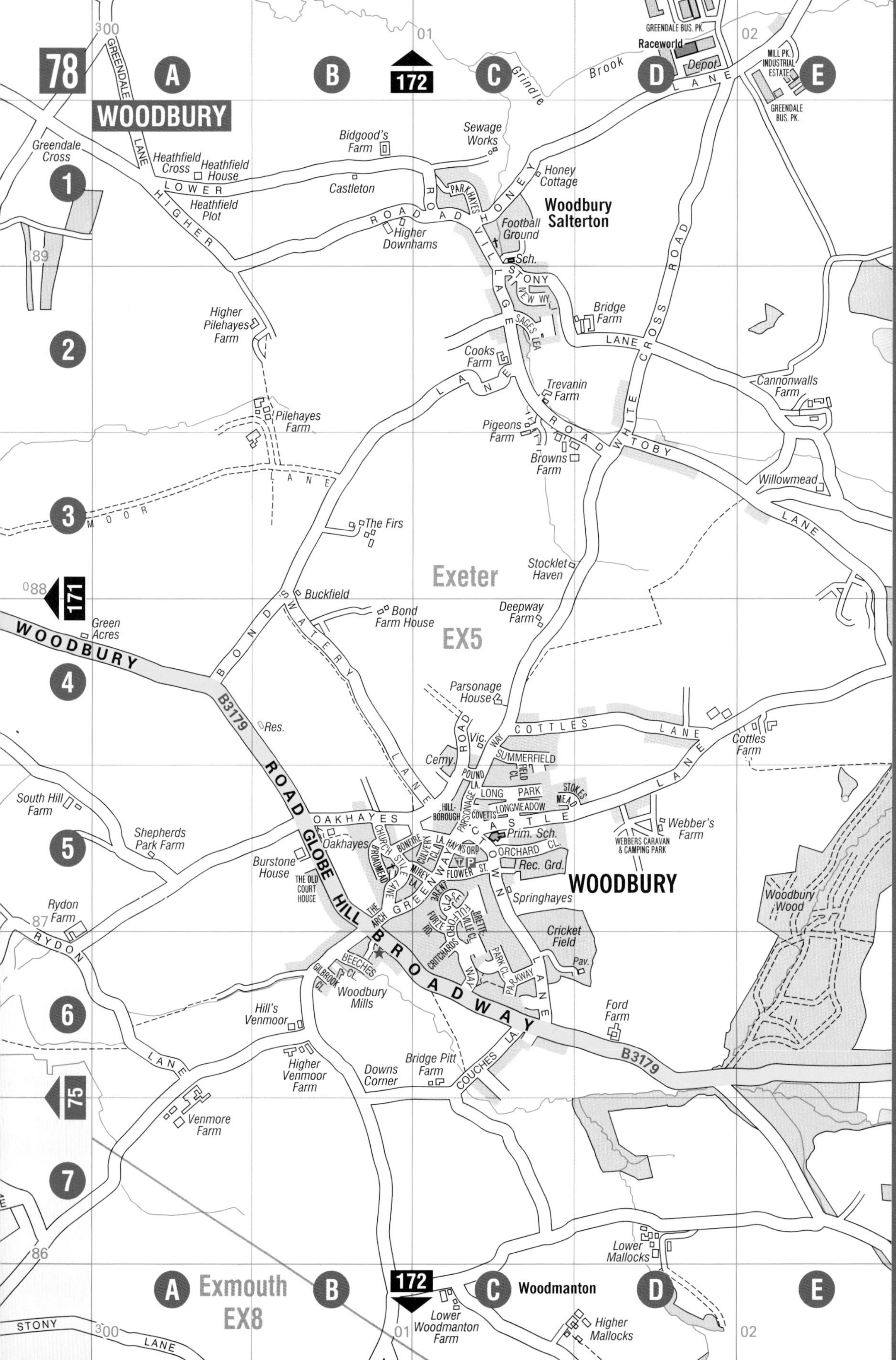
WOODBURY
A
B
C
D
E
172
171
75
Greendale Cross
Heathfield Cross
Heathfield House
Heathfield Plot
Bidgood's Farm
Castleton
Sewage Works
Higher Downhams
Honey Cottage
Woodbury Salterton
Football Ground
Sch.
Bridge Farm
Higher Pilehayes Farm
Pilehayes Farm
Cooks Farm
Trevanin Farm
Pigeons Farm
Browns Farm
Cannonwalls Farm
Willowmead
The Firs
Stocklet Haven
Exeter
EX5
Buckfield
Bond Farm House
Deepway Farm
Green Acres
Parsonage House
Res.
Vic.
Cemy.
Cottles Farm
South Hill Farm
Shepherds Park Farm
Oakhayes
Burstone House
THE OLD COURT HOUSE
Prim. Sch.
Rec. Grd.
WOODBURY
Springhayes
Webber's Farm
WEBBERS CARAVAN & CAMPING PARK
Woodbury Wood
Cricket Field
Pav.
Rydon Farm
Woodbury Mills
Hill's Venmoor
Ford Farm
Higher Venmoor Farm
Downs Corner
Bridge Pitt Farm
Venmore Farm
Lower Mallocks
Woodmanton
Lower Woodmanton Farm
Higher Mallocks
Exmouth
EX8
Raceworld
Depot
GREENDALE BUS. PK.
MILL PK. INDUSTRIAL ESTATE
Grindle Brook
B3179
WOODBURY ROAD
GLOBE HILL
BROADWAY
LOWER ROAD
HIGHER LANE
GREENDALE LANE
VILLAGE ROAD
HONEY LANE
STONY LANE
WHITE CROSS ROAD
TOBY LANE
MOOR LANE
BOND LANE
SWATERY LANE
COTTLES LANE
CASTLE LANE
TOWN LANE
OAKHAYES
RYDON LANE
COUCHES LA.
STONY LANE
PARKHAYES
NEW WY.
SAGES LEA
SUMMERFIELD
FIELD CL.
POUND LA.
LONG PARK
STOKES MEAD
LONGMEADOW
HILLBOROUGH
COVETTS
PARSONAGE WAY
CHURCH STILE LANE
BROADMEAD
BONFIRE LA.
CULVERY CL.
MIREY LA.
HAYNSORD
ORCHARD CL.
FLOWER ST.
GREENWAY
THE ARCH
BRENT CL.
FULFORD WAY
FURZE RD.
CRITCHARDS
BRETTEVILLE CL.
PARK CL.
PARKWAY
BEECHES CL.
GILBROOK CL.

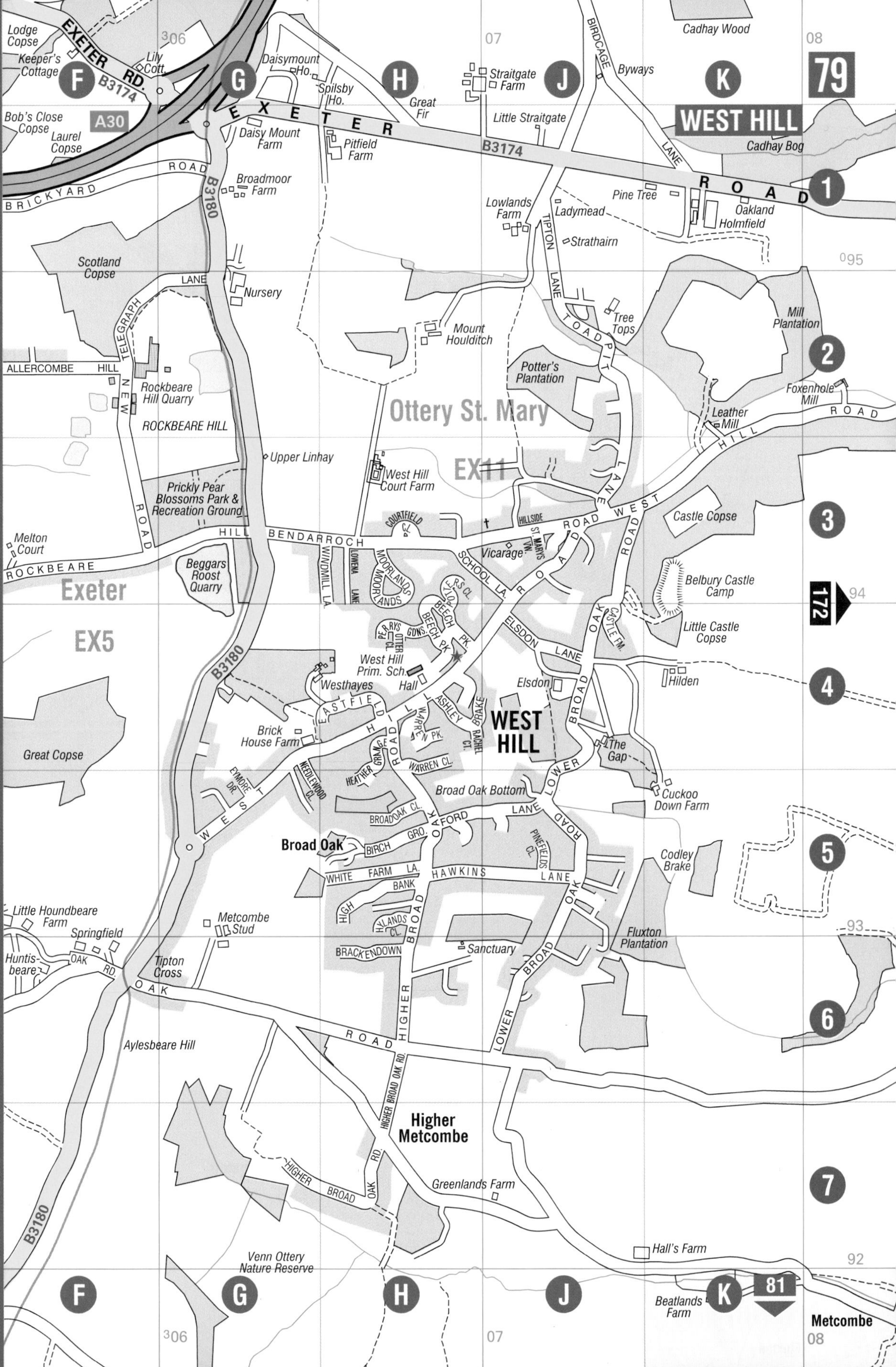

Grid references along top and bottom: F, G, H, J, K

Grid numbers: 306, 07, 08

79 — WEST HILL

Place names and labels visible on the map:

- Lodge Copse
- Keeper's Cottage
- Bob's Close Copse
- Laurel Copse
- EXETER RD B3174
- Lily Cott
- A30
- Daisymount Ho.
- Spilsby Ho.
- Daisy Mount Farm
- Pitfield Farm
- Great Fir
- Straitgate Farm
- Little Straitgate
- Byways
- Cadhay Wood
- Cadhay Bog
- B3174
- ROAD
- Broadmoor Farm
- B3180
- Lowlands Farm
- Ladymead
- Tipton Lane
- Pine Tree
- Oakland
- Holmfield
- Strathairn
- Mill Plantation
- Foxenhole Mill
- Scotland Copse
- TELEGRAPH LANE
- Nursery
- Mount Houlditch
- Tree Tops
- Potter's Plantation
- Leather Mill
- TOAD PIT LANE
- HILL ROAD
- ALLERCOMBE HILL
- NEW ROAD
- Rockbeare Hill Quarry
- ROCKBEARE HILL
- Upper Linhay
- Ottery St. Mary
- EX11
- Castle Copse
- 172
- Melton Court
- ROCKBEARE
- Exeter EX5
- Prickly Pear Blossoms Park & Recreation Ground
- HILL
- BENDARROCH ROAD
- West Hill Court Farm
- COURTFIELD
- St. Mary's
- HILLSIDE
- WEST ROAD
- Vicarage
- Belbury Castle Camp
- Little Castle Copse
- Beggars Roost Quarry
- WINDMILL LA.
- LOWENA
- MOORLANDS
- SCHOOL LA.
- ELSDON LANE
- CASTLE FM.
- Hilden
- B3180
- PERRYS ORCHARD
- BEECH
- GDNS.
- BEECH PK.
- Westhayes
- West Hill Prim. Sch.
- Hall
- WARREN PK.
- RACHEL CT.
- BROAD OAK ROAD
- Elsdon
- The Gap
- Cuckoo Down Farm
- Brick House Farm
- EASTFIELD ROAD
- HEATHER GRANGE
- ASHLEY CT.
- WEST HILL
- GRANGE
- BRAKE
- LOWER LANE
- Great Copse
- EYMORE DR.
- NEEDLEWOOD CL.
- HEATHER
- WARREN CL.
- Broad Oak Bottom
- Codley Brake
- Little Houndbeare Farm
- Springfield
- Huntisbeare
- OAK RD.
- Metcombe Stud
- Broad Oak
- BIRCH GRO.
- WHITE FARM LA.
- BANK
- HAWKINS
- PINEFIELDS CL.
- BROAD OAK CL.
- OXFORD
- BROAD OAK LANE
- Fluxton Plantation
- Tipton Cross
- OAK ROAD
- HIGH
- HIGHLANDS
- BRACKENDOWN
- Sanctuary
- LOWER BROAD OAK ROAD
- Aylesbeare Hill
- HIGHER BROAD OAK ROAD
- Higher Metcombe
- HIGHER BROAD OAK RD.
- Greenlands Farm
- Venn Ottery Nature Reserve
- Hall's Farm
- Beatlands Farm
- 81
- Metcombe

Grid numbers (right side): 08, 095, 94, 93, 92
Grid numbers/rows: 1, 2, 3, 4, 5, 6, 7
Bottom grid numbers: 306, 07, 08

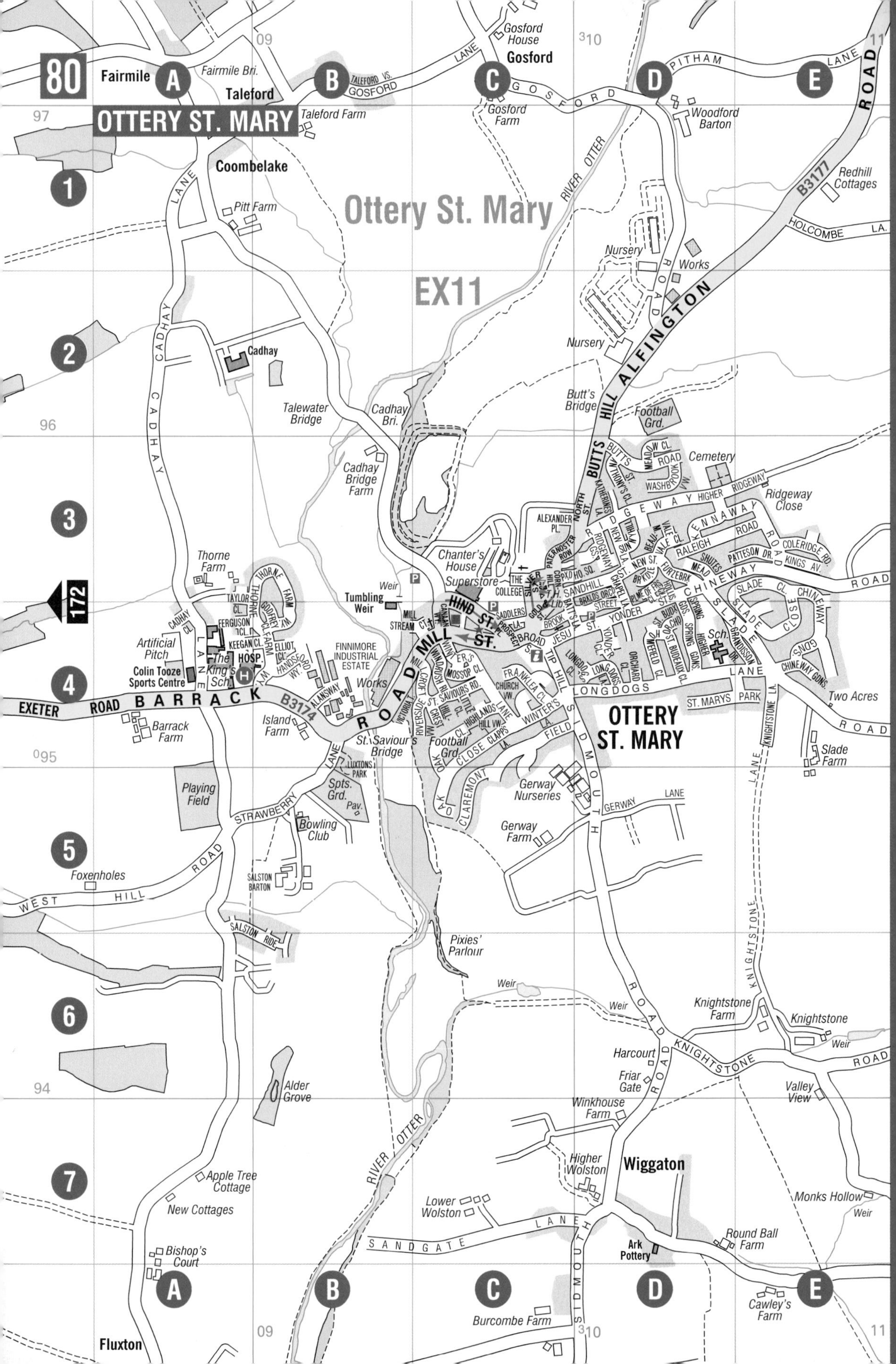

OTTERY ST. MARY
Ottery St. Mary
EX11
OTTERY ST. MARY
Fairmile
Fairmile Bri.
Taleford
Taleford Farm
Coombelake
Pitt Farm
Gosford House
Gosford
Gosford Farm
Woodford Barton
Redhill Cottages
Cadhay
Talewater Bridge
Cadhay Bri.
Cadhay Bridge Farm
Nursery
Works
Butt's Bridge
Football Grd.
Cemetery
Ridgeway Close
Chanter's House
Superstore
Tumbling Weir
Thorne Farm
Artificial Pitch
Colin Tooze Sports Centre
The King's Sch.
HOSP.
FINNIMORE INDUSTRIAL ESTATE
Barrack Farm
Island Farm
St. Saviour's Bridge
Football Grd.
Gerway Nurseries
Gerway Farm
Playing Field
Spts. Grd.
Bowling Club
Foxenholes
SALSTON BARTON
Two Acres
Slade Farm
Pixies' Parlour
Alder Grove
Knightstone Farm
Knightstone
Harcourt
Friar Gate
Valley View
Winkhouse Farm
Higher Wolston
Wiggaton
Lower Wolston
Apple Tree Cottage
New Cottages
Bishop's Court
Monks Hollow
Round Ball Farm
Ark Pottery
Burcombe Farm
Cawley's Farm
Fluxton
EXETER ROAD
BARRACK ROAD
B3174
MILL ROAD
CADHAY LANE
STRAWBERRY LANE
WEST HILL ROAD
SALSTON RIDE
RIVER OTTER
GOSFORD ROAD
PITHAM LANE
B3177
HOLCOMBE LA.
BUTTS HILL
ALFINGTON ROAD
SIDMOUTH ROAD
KNIGHTSTONE ROAD
KNIGHTSTONE LANE
SANDGATE LANE
GERWAY LANE
LONGDOGS LANE
CHINEWAY ROAD
HIND ST.
BROAD ST.
YONDER ST.
ST. MARYS PARK
172
09
310
11
97
96
95
94
A
B
C
D
E
1
2
3
4
5
6
7

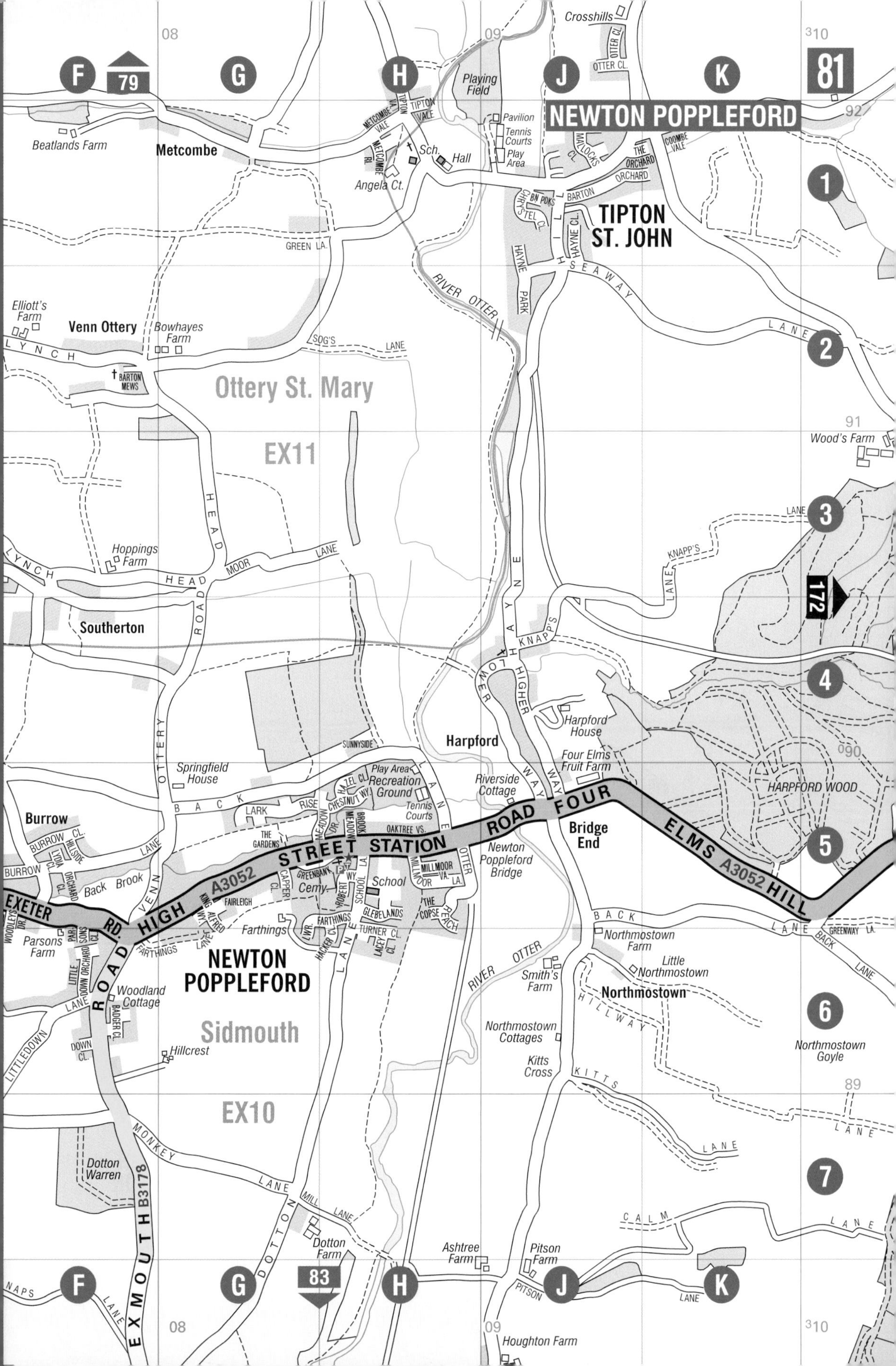
NEWTON POPPLEFORD
TIPTON ST. JOHN
Metcombe
Beatlands Farm
Crosshills
Playing Field
Pavilion
Tennis Courts
Play Area
Sch.
Hall
Angela Ct.
Venn Ottery
Elliott's Farm
Bowhayes Farm
Ottery St. Mary
EX11
Hoppings Farm
Southerton
Springfield House
Burrow
Harpford
Harpford House
Four Elms Fruit Farm
Riverside Cottage
HARPFORD WOOD
Bridge End
Newton Poppleford Bridge
Recreation Ground
Play Area
Tennis Courts
School
Cemy.
Farthings
Parsons Farm
Woodland Cottage
NEWTON POPPLEFORD
Sidmouth
EX10
Hillcrest
Dotton Warren
Dotton Farm
Ashtree Farm
Pitson Farm
Houghton Farm
Northmostown Farm
Little Northmostown
Northmostown
Smith's Farm
Northmostown Cottages
Kitts Cross
Northmostown Goyle
Wood's Farm
RIVER OTTER
STATION ROAD
FOUR ELMS HILL
A3052
HIGH STREET
EXETER RD.
EXMOUTH ROAD B3178
MONKEY LANE
DOTTON LANE
MILL LANE
SEAWAY LANE
KNAPP'S LANE
HAYNE LANE
BACK LANE
HEAD MOOR LANE
HEAD ROAD
OTTERY LANE
VENN LANE
LYNCH
SOG'S LANE
GREEN LA.
CALM LANE
PITSON LANE
KITTS LANE
HILLWAY
GREENWAY LA.
LITTLEDOWN LANE
NAPS LANE
79
83
172
08
09
310
92
91
90
89
F G H J K
1 2 3 4 5 6 7

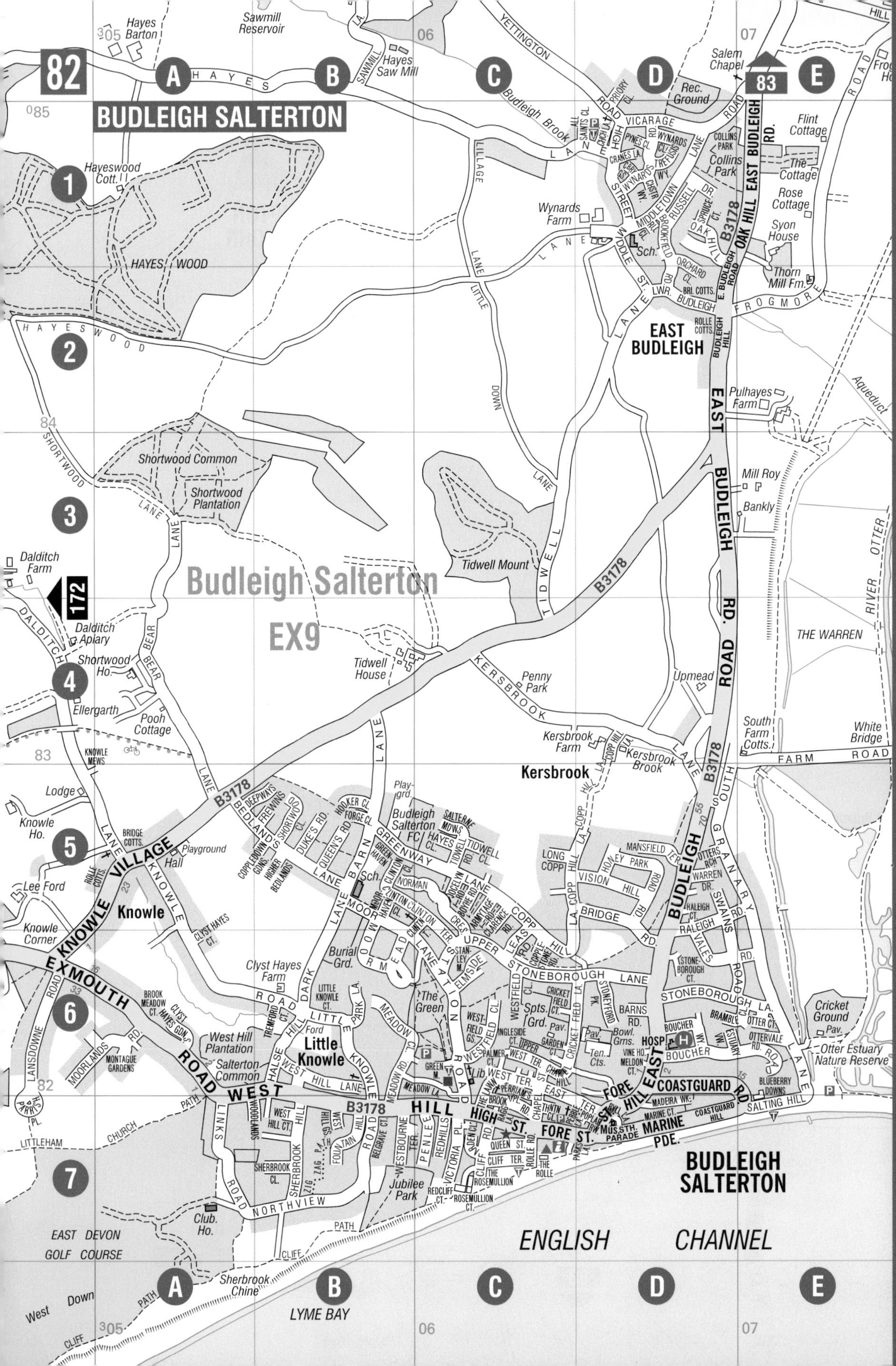
BUDLEIGH SALTERTON
Budleigh Salterton
EX9
EAST BUDLEIGH
Kersbrook
Knowle
Little Knowle
BUDLEIGH SALTERTON
ENGLISH CHANNEL
LYME BAY
EAST DEVON GOLF COURSE
HAYES WOOD
Hayes Barton
Sawmill Reservoir
Hayes Saw Mill
Hayeswood Cott.
Shortwood Common
Shortwood Plantation
Tidwell Mount
Tidwell House
Penny Park
Dalditch Farm
Dalditch Apiary
Shortwood Ho.
Ellergarth
Pooh Cottage
Lodge
Knowle Ho.
Lee Ford
Knowle Corner
Clyst Hayes Farm
West Hill Plantation
Salterton Common
Club. Ho.
Sherbrook Chine
West Down
Jubilee Park
The Green
Spts. Grd.
Burial Grd.
Budleigh Salterton FC
Playground
Hall
Wynards Farm
Rec. Ground
Salem Chapel
Collins Park
Flint Cottage
The Cottage
Rose Cottage
Syon House
Thorn Mill Fm.
Pulhayes Farm
Mill Roy
Bankly
Upmead
Kersbrook Farm
Kersbrook Brook
South Farm Cotts.
White Bridge
THE WARREN
RIVER OTTER
Aqueduct
Cricket Ground
Otter Estuary Nature Reserve
Budleigh Brook
HAYES
HAYESWOOD
SHORTWOOD LANE
DALDITCH
BEAR LANE
KNOWLE MEWS
BRIDGE COTTS.
ROLLE COTTS.
KNOWLE VILLAGE
EXMOUTH ROAD
WEST HILL
LANSDOWNE ROAD
PARRISH PL.
LITTLEHAM
CHURCH PATH
LINKS ROAD
NORTHVIEW ROAD
CLIFF PATH
B3178
YETTINGTON
SAWMILL LA.
LILLAGE LANE
LITTLE DOWN LANE
TIDWELL LANE
KERSBROOK LANE
EAST BUDLEIGH ROAD
OAK HILL
FROGMORE ROAD
FARM ROAD
VICARAGE ROAD
HIGH STREET
MIDDLE ST.
LWR. BUDLEIGH
MIDDLETOWN LANE
RUSSELL DR.
BROOKFIELD RD.
ORCHARD CL.
BRI. COTTS.
ROLLE COTTS.
SPRUCE CT.
OAK HILL
WYNARDS CL.
WYNARDS WY.
PYNES CL.
CRANES LA.
ALL SAINTS CL.
PRIORY CL.
CHURCH LA.
Sch.
BEDLANDS LA.
DEEPWAYS
FREWINS
SHORTWOOD CL.
HIGHER BEDLANDS
COPPLEDOWN GDNS.
DUKE'S RD.
QUEEN'S RD.
HOOKER CL.
FORGE CL.
BARN LANE
GREENWAY
SALTERNE MDWS.
HAYES CL.
TIDWELL RD.
TIDWELL CL.
GREENHAVEN
CLINTON CL.
NORMAN CL.
JOCELYN RD.
BOYNE RD.
ARMYTAGE RD.
CLARENCE RD.
CLINTON TER.
CLINTON CRES.
STANLEY M.
ELMSIDE
UPPER STONEBOROUGH LANE
MOORMEAD
DARK LANE
LITTLE KNOWLE
LITTLE KNOWLE CT.
PARK LA.
KNOWLE
MEADOW RD.
MEADOW CL.
CLYST HAYES CT.
CLYST HAYES GDNS.
BROOK MEADOW CT.
MOORLANDS
MONTAGUE GARDENS
TREMFORD CT.
HALSE HILL
WEST HILL LANE
WEST HILL CT.
WOODLANDS
SHERBROOK HILL
SHERBROOK CL.
ZIG ZAG PATH
HILLSIDE
FOUNTAIN HILL
BELGRAVE CT.
WESTBOURNE TER.
PENLEE
REDHILLS
VICTORIA PL.
STATION ROAD
WESTFIELD CL.
WESTFIELD GS.
LEAS RD.
COPPLESTONE RD.
COPP HILL LANE
LONG COPP
VISION HILL ROAD
HONEY PARK ROAD
MANSFIELD TER.
BRIDGE RD.
CRICKET FIELD LA.
CRICKET FIELD CT.
STONEYFORD PK.
INGLESIDE CT.
UPPER WEST TER.
WEST TER.
GARDEN CT.
PALMER CT.
PERRIAM'S PL.
CHAPEL ST.
EAST TER.
THE LAWN
BROOK RD.
HIGH ST.
FORE ST.
QUEEN ST.
CLIFF TER.
ROLLE RD.
THE ROLLE
THE ROSEMULLION
ROSEMULLION CT.
REDCLIFF CT.
CLIFF RD.
DEN CL.
MEADOW LA.
GREEN M.
Lib.
Pav.
Bowl. Grns.
Ten. Cts.
BARNS RD.
STONEBOROUGH LA.
STONEBOROUGH CT.
BOUCHER WY.
BOUCHER
HOSP
VINE HO.
MELDON CT.
EAST HILL
FORE ST. HILL
COASTGUARD RD.
COASTGUARD HILL
MADEIRA WK.
MARINE CT.
MARINE PDE.
STH. PARADE
Mus.
OTTERS REACH
WARREN DR.
RALEIGH CT.
RALEIGH RD.
SWAINS RD.
VALES ROAD
GRANARY LANE
BRAMBLE LA.
OTTER CT.
OTTERVALE RD.
ESTUARY VW.
BLUEBERRY DOWNS
SALTING HILL
SOUTH FARM ROAD
BUDLEIGH
83
172
A B C D E
1 2 3 4 5 6 7
305 06 07
085 84 83 82

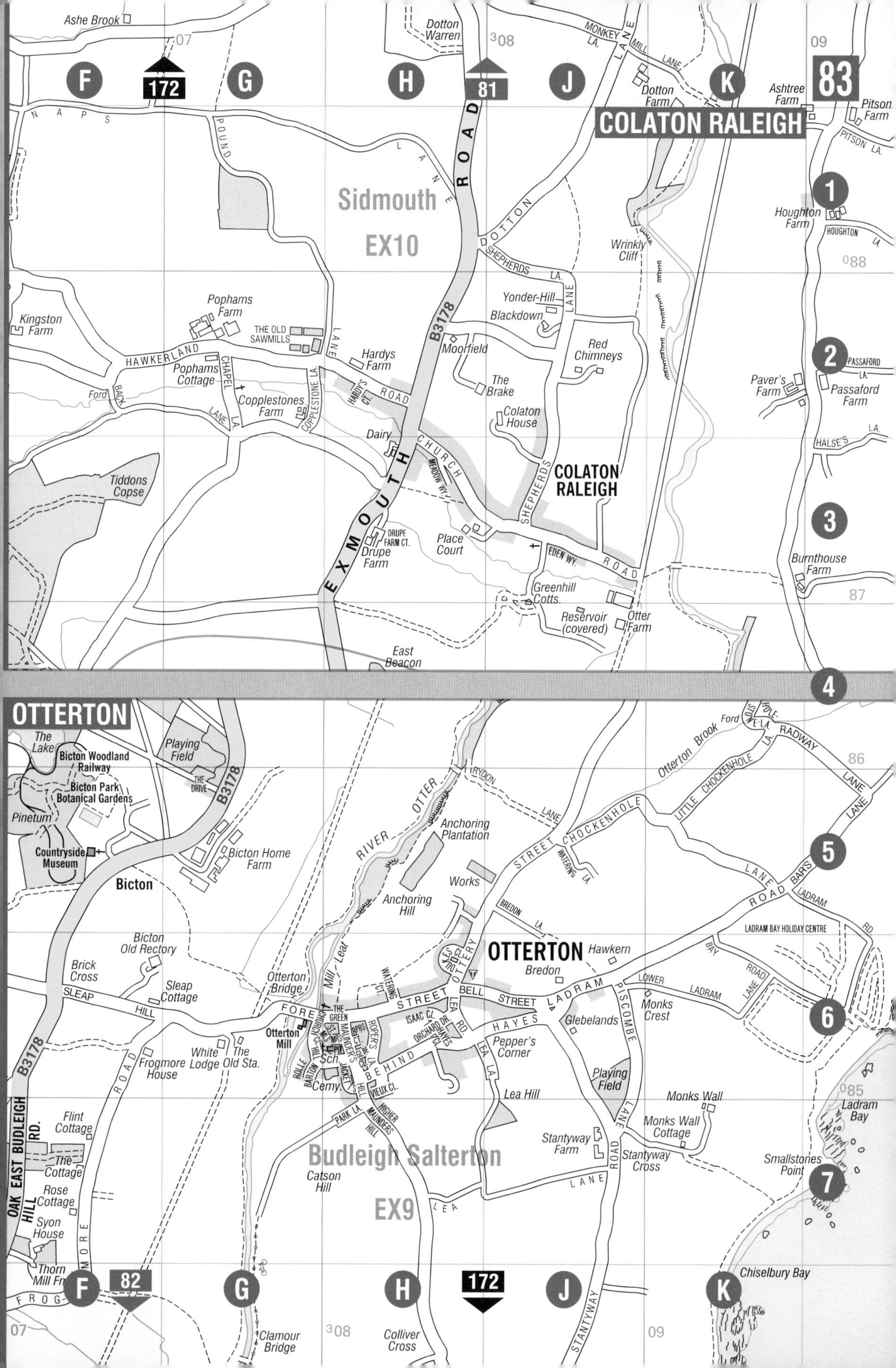
COLATON RALEIGH
Sidmouth
EX10
Ashe Brook
Dotton Warren
Dotton Farm
Ashtree Farm
Pitson Farm
PITSON LA.
MONKEY LA.
MILL LANE
NAPS LANE
POUND LANE
EXMOUTH ROAD
B3178
DOTTON LANE
SHEPHERDS LA.
Houghton Farm
HOUGHTON LA.
Wrinkly Cliff
Yonder-Hill
Blackdown
Kingston Farm
Pophams Farm
THE OLD SAWMILLS
HAWKERLAND ROAD
Hardys Farm
Moorfield
Red Chimneys
PASSAFORD LA.
Paver's Farm
Passaford Farm
Pophams Cottage
CHAPEL LA.
Copplestones Farm
COPPLESTONE LA.
HARDY'S CT.
The Brake
Colaton House
Ford
BACK LANE
Dairy
CHURCH ROAD
MEADOW WY.
HALSE'S LA.
Tiddons Copse
COLATON RALEIGH
SHEPHERDS LANE
DRUPE FARM CT.
Drupe Farm
Place Court
EDEN WY.
Burnthouse Farm
Greenhill Cotts.
Reservoir (covered)
Otter Farm
East Beacon
OTTERTON
The Lake
Bicton Woodland Railway
Bicton Park Botanical Gardens
Pinetum
Playing Field
THE DRIVE
Countryside Museum
Bicton Home Farm
Bicton
RIVER OTTER
IRYDON LANE
Anchoring Plantation
Works
Anchoring Hill
Otterton Brook
Ford
HOLE LA.
RADWAY LANE
LITTLE CHOCKENHOLE LA.
CHOCKENHOLE LANE
STREET
WATERING LA.
BARS LANE
ROAD
LADRAM RD
LADRAM BAY HOLIDAY CENTRE
BREDON LA.
Bicton Old Rectory
Brick Cross
Sleap Cottage
SLEAP HILL
Otterton Bridge
Mill Leat
WATERING CT.
OTTERY ST.
OTTERTON
Hawkern
Bredon
BAY ROAD
LOWER LADRAM LANE
Monks Crest
FORE STREET
BELL STREET
LADRAM
PISCOMBE LANE
THE GREEN
Otterton Mill
MAUNDERS
ROPER'S LA.
ISAAC CL.
ORCHARD DR.
HAYES
LEA RD
Glebelands
Pepper's Corner
White Lodge
The Old Sta.
Frogmore House
ROAD
BEHIND HAYES
Sch.
Cemy.
ROLLE BARTON
JACKETT'S HILL
VIEUX CL.
LEA LA.
Lea Hill
Playing Field
Monks Wall
Ladram Bay
PARK LA.
HIGHER MAUNDERS HILL
Flint Cottage
The Cottage
OAK HILL
EAST BUDLEIGH RD.
B3178
Budleigh Salterton
Catson Hill
Stantyway Farm
Monks Wall Cottage
Stantyway Cross
LANE
Smallstones Point
Rose Cottage
Syon House
EX9
LEA
MORE
Thorn Mill Fm
Chiselbury Bay
FROG
STANTYWAY
Clamour Bridge
Colliver Cross
F G H J K
1 2 3 4 5 6 7
07 308 09 088 87 86 085

172
81
82
172

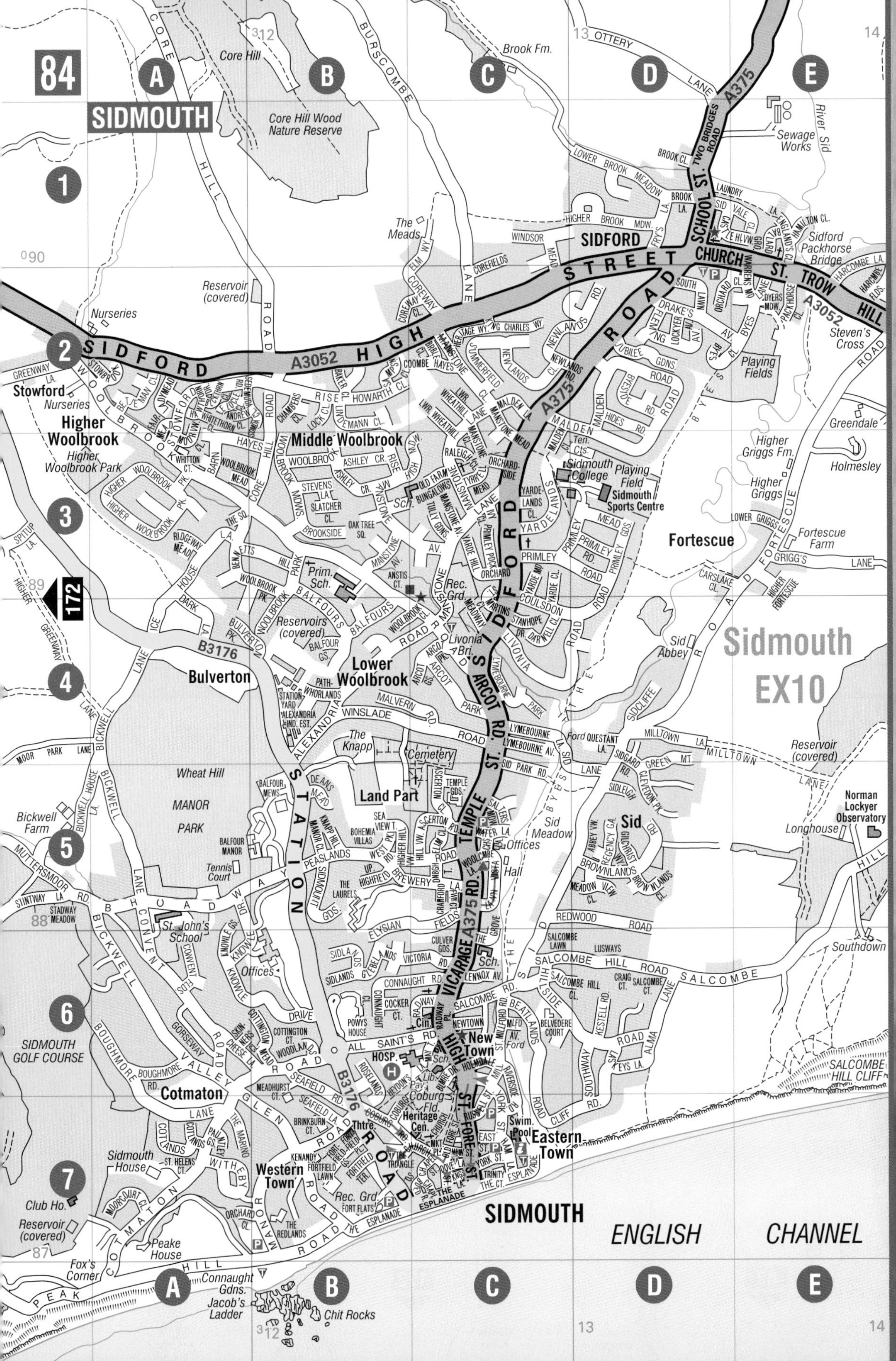
84
SIDMOUTH
A
B
C
D
E
1
2
3
4
5
6
7
Core Hill
Core Hill Wood Nature Reserve
Brook Fm.
Sewage Works
River Sid
SIDFORD
Sidford Packhorse Bridge
Steven's Cross
Playing Fields
Stowford
Nurseries
Higher Woolbrook
Higher Woolbrook Park
Middle Woolbrook
Lower Woolbrook
Bulverton
Sidmouth College
Sidmouth Sports Centre
Playing Field
Fortescue
Fortescue Farm
Higher Griggs Fm.
Higher Griggs
Greendale
Holmesley
Sid Abbey
Sidmouth EX10
172
The Meads
Reservoir (covered)
Reservoirs (covered)
Prim. Sch.
Rec. Grd.
Livonia Bri.
The Knapp
Cemetery
Land Part
Wheat Hill
MANOR PARK
Bickwell Farm
Tennis Court
St. John's School
Offices
Sid Meadow
Sid
Norman Lockyer Observatory
Longhouse
Southdown
SALCOMBE HILL CLIFF
SIDMOUTH GOLF COURSE
Cotmaton
Sidmouth House
Club Ho.
Peake House
Fox's Corner
Connaught Gdns.
Jacob's Ladder
Chit Rocks
Western Town
Eastern Town
New Town
HOSP.
Coburg Fld.
Heritage Cen.
Thtre.
Swim. Pool
Rec. Grd.
SIDMOUTH
ENGLISH
CHANNEL
A3052
A375
B3176
SIDFORD HIGH STREET
STREET
CHURCH ST.
TROW HILL
SIDFORD ROAD
TEMPLE ST.
ARCOT RD.
VICARAGE RD.
HIGH ST.
STATION ROAD
SALCOMBE HILL ROAD
SALCOMBE ROAD
REDWOOD ROAD
MILLTOWN LANE
WINSLADE ROAD
PEAK HILL
THE ESPLANADE
OTTERY LANE
BURSCOMBE LANE
CORE HILL ROAD
WOOLBROOK ROAD
MANSTONE LANE
BYES LANE
SID LANE
BICKWELL LANE
MUTTERSMOOR RD.
MANOR ROAD
COTMATON ROAD
GLEN ROAD
SEAFIELD RD.
ALL SAINT'S RD.
BROADWAY
CONVENT RD.
CLIFF RD.
SOUTHWAY
12
13
14
90
89
88
87

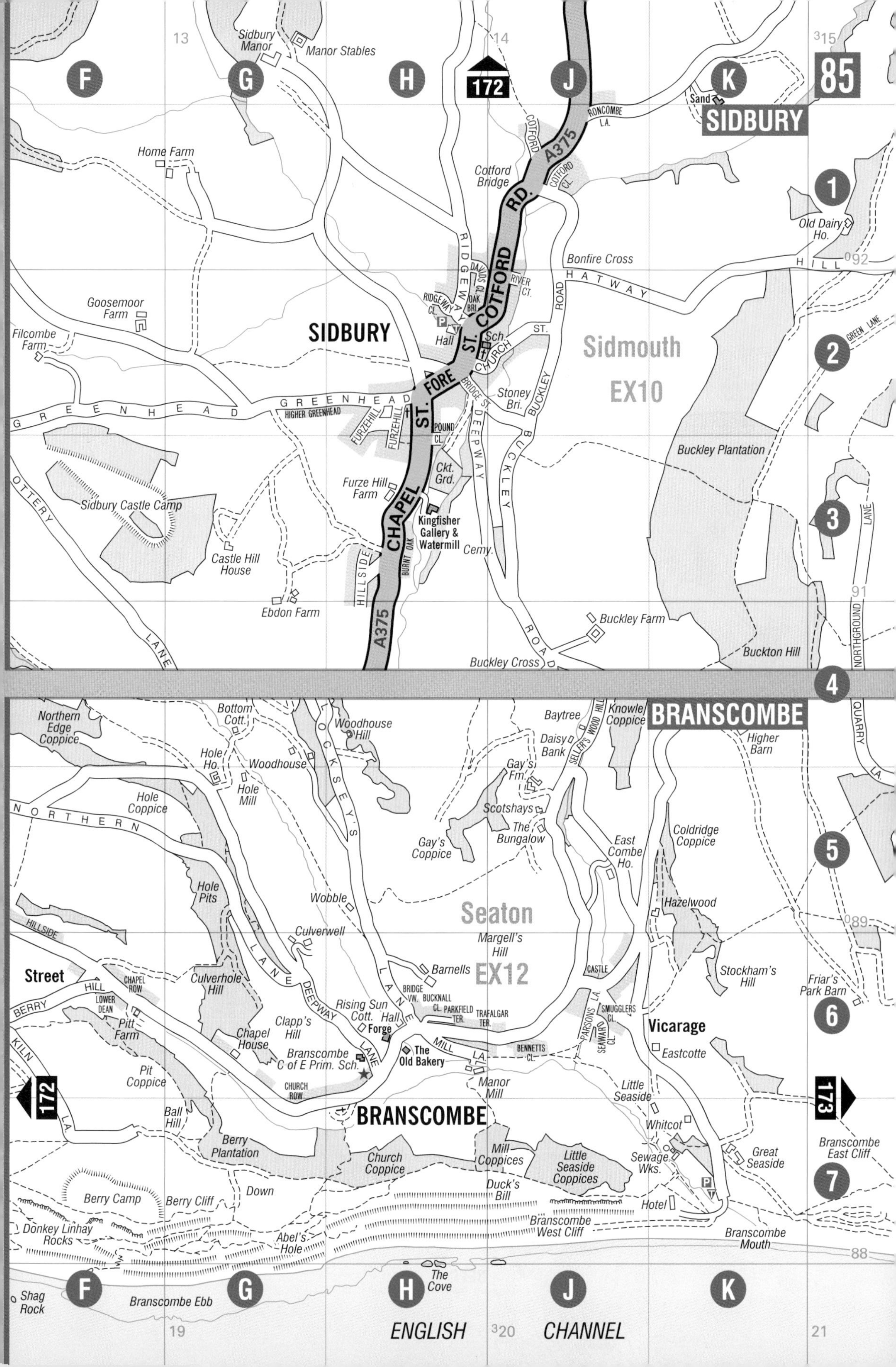

SIDBURY

F G H 172 J K

1

2

3

4

Sidbury Manor
Manor Stables
Home Farm
Cotford Bridge
RONCOMBE LA.
Sand
Old Dairy Ho.
COTFORD RD.
A375
GREEN LANE
Bonfire Cross
Cotford
Goosemoor Farm
RIVER CT.
HATWAY
ROAD
Filcombe Farm
RIDGEWAY CL.
OAK BRI.
DAVIDS BRI.
SIDBURY
Hall
Sch.
CHURCH ST.
Stoney Brn.
BUCKLEY
Sidmouth EX10
Buckley Plantation
GREENHEAD
HIGHER GREENHEAD
FURZEHILL
FURZEHILL
POUND CL.
BRIDGE ST.
STEEPWAY
NORTHGROUND LANE
OTTERY
Sidbury Castle Camp
FORE ST.
CHAPEL ST.
Furze Hill Farm
Ckt. Grd.
Kingfisher Gallery & Watermill
Cemy.
Castle Hill House
BURNT OAK
HILLSIDE
Ebdon Farm
A375
ROAD
Buckley Farm
Buckton Hill
Buckley Cross

F G H J K

BRANSCOMBE

5

6

7

Northern Edge Coppice
Bottom Cott.
Woodhouse Hill
Baytree
Knowle Coppice
QUARRY LA.
Hole Ho.
Woodhouse
Daisy Bank
SELLERS WOOD HILL
Higher Barn
Hole Coppice
Hole Mill
COCKSEYS
Gay's Fm.
NORTHERN
Scotshays
Coldridge Coppice
Gay's Coppice
The Bungalow
East Combe Ho.
Hazelwood
Hole Pits
Wobble
Seaton
Margell's Hill
CASTLE
Stockham's Hill
Friar's Park Barn
HILLSIDE
Culverwell
LANE
EX12
Street
BERRY HILL
CHAPEL ROW
LOWER DEAN
Culverhole Hill
DEEPWAY LANE
Barnells
BRIDGE VW.
BUCKNALL CL.
PARKFIELD TER.
TRAFALGAR TER.
PARSONS LA.
SMUGGLERS LA.
SEAWARD
Vicarage
Eastcotte
KILN LA.
172
Pitt Farm
Clapp's Hill
Chapel House
Rising Sun Cott.
Hall
Forge
MILL LA.
BENNETTS CL.
173
Pit Coppice
Branscombe C of E Prim. Sch.
CHURCH ROW
The Old Bakery
Manor Mill
Little Seaside
Whitcot
Branscombe East Cliff
Ball Hill
Berry Plantation
BRANSCOMBE
Church Coppice
Mill Coppices
Duck's Bill
Little Seaside Coppices
Sewage Wks.
Great Seaside
Berry Camp
Berry Cliff
Down
Branscombe West Cliff
Hotel
Branscombe Mouth
Donkey Linhay Rocks
Abel's Hole
Shag Rock
Branscombe Ebb
The Cove

F G H J K

ENGLISH CHANNEL

19 20 21

86
Morganhayes Covert
22
23
24
A
B
C
D
E
1
2
3
4
5
6
7
92
91
90
89
173
Whitwell Fm.
Quest
Whitwell
Colyton Sports Cen.
Playing Field
Colyton Grammar Sch.
Stafford La.
Lane
Little Owls
Gully Shoot Cross
Holyford
The Oaks
Bakery
Horriford Farm
Holyford Cottage
Leacroft Farm
Leacroft Touring Park
Pratt's Hill
Bridewell Coppice
Holyford Woods Local Nature Reserve
Holyford Bottom
Holyford Coppice
Seaton Down
Seaton Down Coppice
Stafford Bridge
St. Nicholas House
Harepath Fm.
Peacehaven
Rolle Ct.
Ashdown Farm
Reservoir (covered)
A3052
Harepath
Hill
Appletree
Uppacott
Barnards Mead
Barnards
Manor Farm
Chalet Park
Motel
Gatcombe Ash
Gatcombe Lane
Picnic Site
Seaton
EX12
Manor Farm Caravan Site
Resr (cov.)
Seaton Down Hill
B3172
Gatcombe Farm
Gatcombe Coppice
Couchill Coppice
Couchill Farm
Res. (cov.)
Foxenholes
Whispering Firs
Couchill Common
Couchill
Hollyhead Road
Hollyhead Cross
B3174
Stovar Long Lane
Football Grd.
Bovey Lane
Reservoir (covered)
Youth Hostel
Paizen Lane
Townsend Lane
Quarry Lane
New Road
Causeway
Barline
Prim. Sch.
Beer Heights Light Railway
Pecorama
Mare Lane
Underleys
West Underleys
Park
Cemetery
Clapp's La.
Southdown Rd.
Common Hill
Beer
Coastguard Sta.
South Down Cotts.
Beer Head Caravan Park
Little Common
Fathoms
The Bluff
Briarclyst
White Cliff
Art Gall.
Jubilee Meml. Grd.
Beer Roads
Beer Road
Beer Hill
Beer Hill Cott.
Lew Hollow
Seaton Hole
Old Beer Road
Bunts Lane
Durley Road
West Acres
Highcliffe Cl.
Miniature Golf Course
West Walk
Castle Hill
Seafield Gds.
Seaton Down Rd.
Queen St.
Liby.
Townsend Rd.
Marlpit Lane
Churston Rise
Upper Churston Ri.
Honey Ditches Dr.
Seaton Down Cl.
Tracey's Av.
Lydgates
Homer La.
Newlands Park
Valley Rd.
Harepath Lane
Elizabeth Way
Play. Fld.
Prim. Sch.
Hosp.
Roman Way
Wychall Pk.
Axeview Rd.
Elmfield Rd.
Scalwell Lane
Scalwell Mead
Thornfield Cl.
Poplar Tree
Drovers Way
Burnham
Barnards Hill Lane
Couchill La.
Couchill Dr.
Merrow Down Dr.
Fremington Rd.
Marlpit Cl.
Greenway
Wessiters
Sunset Ho.
Westcliffe Ter.
Sands Court

COLYFORD
Colyton
Colyford Common
Local Nature
Reserve
EX24
Colyford
Motoring
Memories
Motor
Museum
BOSHILL
A3052
Boshill Cross
Boshill House
Boshill Court
Axe View
Crabhayne Farm
Axe Bridge
Hope Pool
Hedge Corner
Boshill Wood
Stedcombe Lodge
Stedcombe House
Stedcombe Farm
Stedcombe Cott.
Keepers Cottage
Stedcombe Wood
Axe Marsh
Seaton Tramway
Safford Barton House
Shiloh
Whispering
Stafford Brook
Cemetery
Hawkesdown Hill
Camp Wood Hill Fort
The Old Vicarage
AXMOUTH
Axe Farm
Camping Site
Sewage Wks.
Picnic Site
Hall
Millmead
Haven Farm
Stepps Cross
Higher Barn
Coombe Ter.
Coombe Orchard
Higher Axmouth
The Forge
Shearing Ground Coppice
Two Acre Coppice
Parsonage Barn
The Batch
Bindon
The Bungalow
Sewage Works
Football Grd.
Seaton Marshes
Local Nature
Reserve
SEATON
Seaton Tramway
Depot
Haven Cliff Plantation
Old Coastguard Station
Club House
AXE CLIFF
GOLF COURSE
Haven Higher Barn
Haven Cliff House
Harbour Cotts.
Axmouth Bri.
Axe Yacht Club
Haven Cliff
Bindon Cliffs
Sparrowbush Ledge
Seaton Beach
SEATON BAY
RIVER AXE
AXMOUTH ROAD
B3172
CHURCH ST.
HIGHER LANE
BUSHES LA.
GREEN LA.
BARN CLOSE LANE
STONY CLOSE LA.
STEPPS LANE
SQUIRE'S LA.
HARBOUR RD.
THE UNDERFLEET
SWAN HILL ROAD
Superstore
Seaton
H.Mus.
173
325
26
27
92
91
090
89

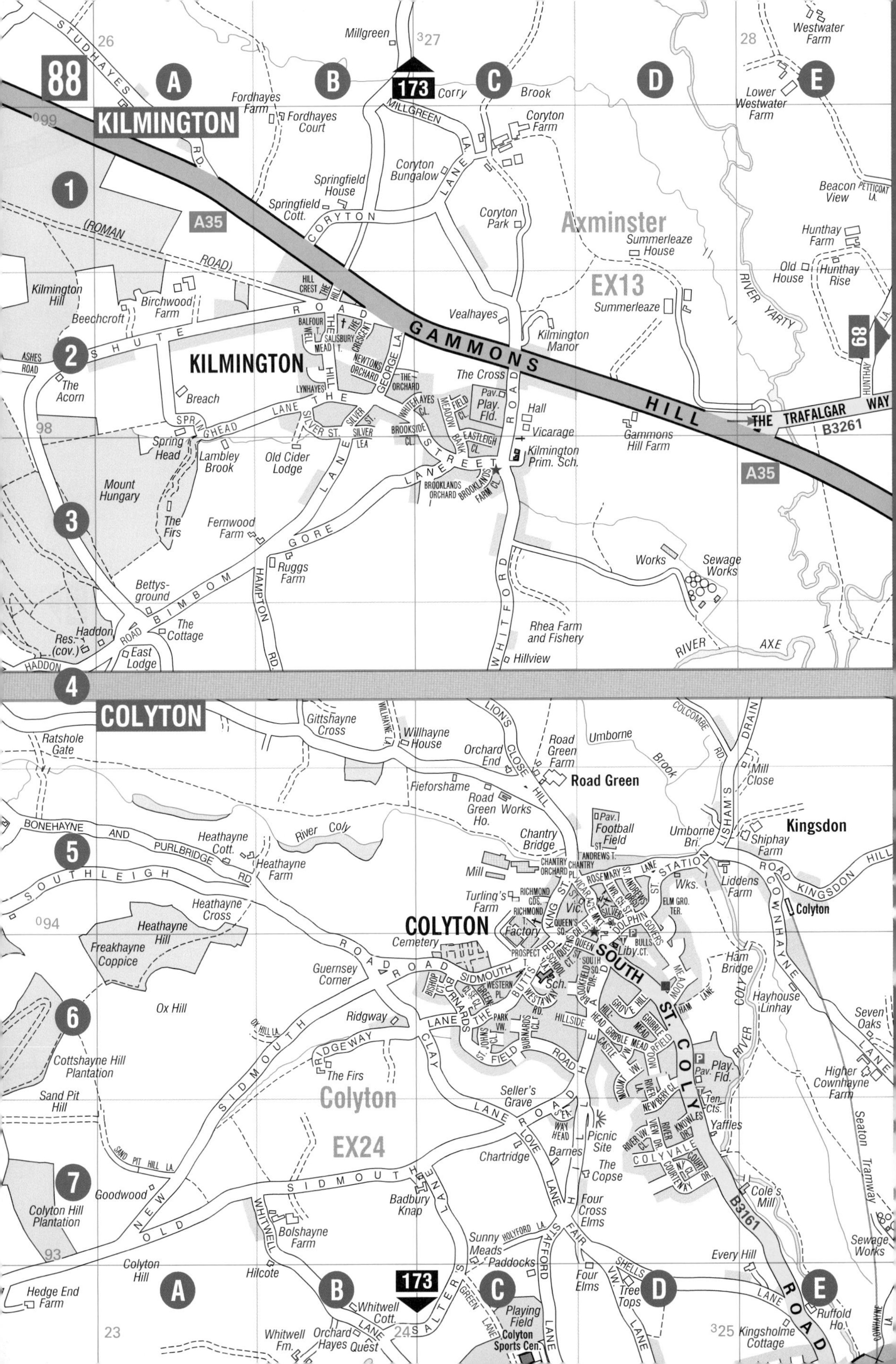
KILMINGTON
COLYTON
173
89
A35
B3261
B3161
Axminster
EX13
Colyton
EX24
GAMMONS HILL
THE TRAFALGAR WAY
Kilmington Hill
Birchwood Farm
Beechcroft
The Acorn
Breach
Spring Head
Lambley Brook
Mount Hungary
The Firs
Fernwood Farm
Ruggs Farm
Bettysground
The Cottage
East Lodge
Haddon
Res. (cov.)
Fordhayes Farm
Fordhayes Court
Springfield House
Springfield Cott.
Coryton Bungalow
Coryton Farm
Coryton Park
Millgreen
Corry Brook
Vealhayes
Kilmington Manor
The Cross
Hall
Vicarage
Kilmington Prim. Sch.
Old Cider Lodge
Summerleaze House
Summerleaze
Gammons Hill Farm
Westwater Farm
Lower Westwater Farm
Beacon View
Hunthay Farm
Old House
Hunthay Rise
Works
Sewage Works
Rhea Farm and Fishery
Hillview
RIVER AXE
RIVER YARTY
Ratshole Gate
Gittshayne Cross
Willhayne House
Orchard End
Road Green Farm
Road Green
Umborne
Fieforshame
Road Green Ho.
Works
Chantry Bridge
Football Field
Umborne Bri.
Mill Close
Kingsdon
Shiphay Farm
Liddens Farm
Heathayne Cott.
Heathayne Farm
Heathayne Cross
Heathayne Hill
Freakhayne Coppice
River Coly
Mill
Turling's Farm
Cemetery
Factory
Vic.
Liby.
Sch.
Guernsey Corner
Ridgway
Ox Hill
Cottshayne Hill Plantation
Sand Pit Hill
Goodwood
Colyton Hill Plantation
Colyton Hill
Hedge End Farm
The Firs
Seller's Grave
Picnic Site
The Copse
Barnes
Chartridge
Badbury Knap
Bolshayne Farm
Four Cross Elms
Sunny Meads
Paddocks
Four Elms
Tree Tops
Hilcote
Whitwell Cott.
Whitwell Fm.
Orchard Hayes Quest
Playing Field
Colyton Sports Cen.
Ham Bridge
Hayhouse Linhay
Seven Oaks
Higher Cownhayne Farm
Seaton Tramway
Yaffles
Cole's Mill
Sewage Works
Every Hill
Ruffold Ho.
Kingsholme Cottage
Colyton
Play. Fld.
Ten. Cts.

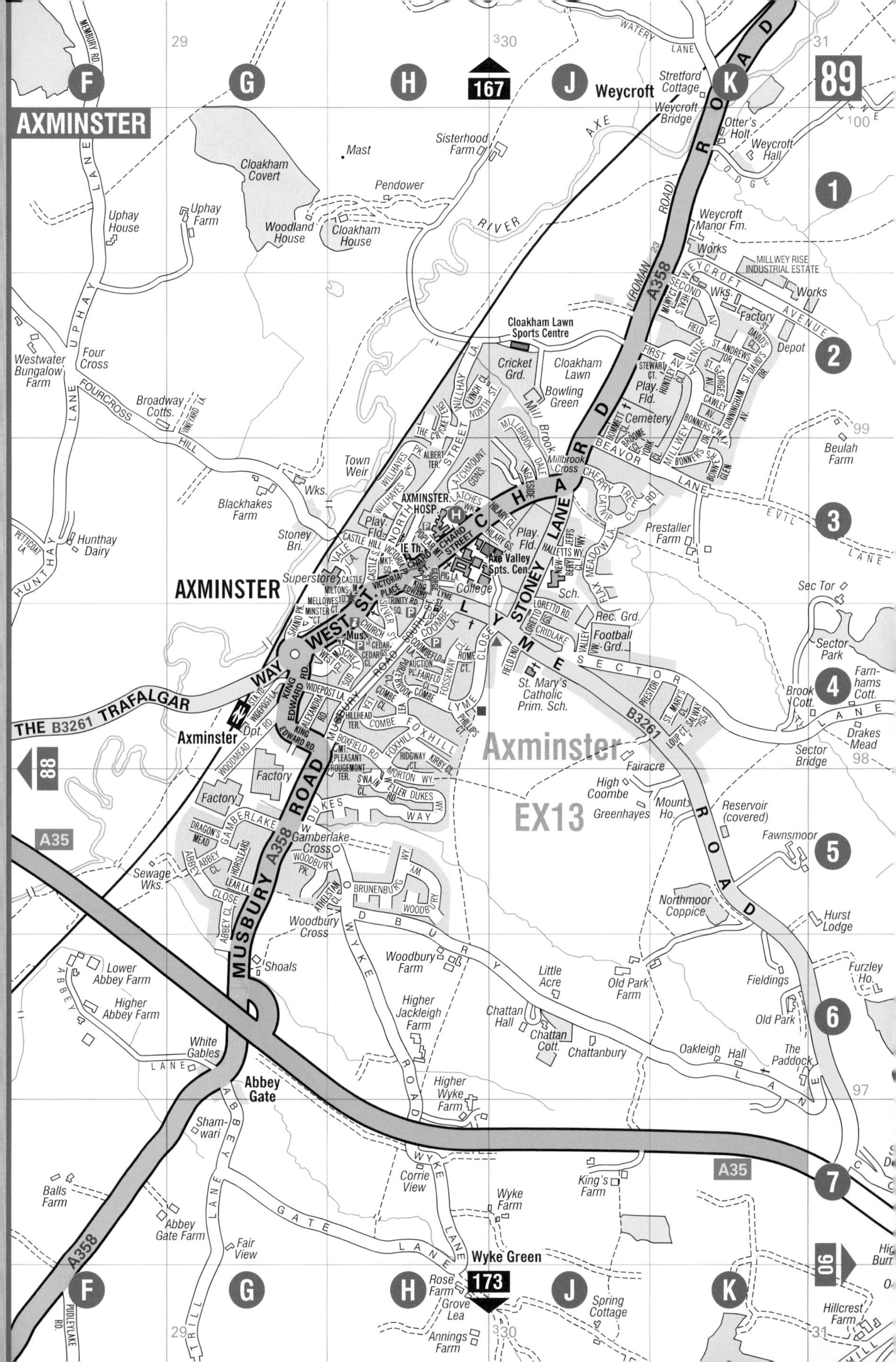
AXMINSTER
F
G
H
J
K
167
173
88
90
Weycroft
Stretford Cottage
Weycroft Bridge
Otter's Holt
Weycroft Hall
Sisterhood Farm
Mast
Cloakham Covert
Pendower
Woodland House
Cloakham House
Uphay House
Uphay Farm
Weycroft Manor Fm.
Works
MILLWEY RISE INDUSTRIAL ESTATE
Cloakham Lawn Sports Centre
Cricket Grd.
Cloakham Lawn
Bowling Green
Four Cross
Westwater Bungalow Farm
Broadway Cotts.
Town Weir
Blackhakes Farm
Hunthay Dairy
Stoney Bri.
AXMINSTER HOSP.
Axe Valley Spts. Cen.
Superstore
College
Millbrook Cross
Cemetery
Play. Fld.
Beulah Farm
Prestaller Farm
Sec Tor
Sector Park
Rec. Grd.
Football Grd.
St. Mary's Catholic Prim. Sch.
Axminster
EX13
Fairacre
High Coombe
Greenhayes
Mounts Ho.
Reservoir (covered)
Brook Cott.
Farnhams Cott.
Drakes Mead
Sector Bridge
Fawnsmoor
Factory
Gamberlake Cross
Sewage Wks.
Woodbury Cross
Shoals
Northmoor Coppice
Hurst Lodge
Lower Abbey Farm
Higher Abbey Farm
Woodbury Farm
Little Acre
Old Park Farm
Fieldings
Furzley Ho.
Old Park
Higher Jackleigh Farm
Chattan Hall
Chattan Cott.
Chattanbury
Oakleigh Hall
The Paddock
White Gables
Abbey Gate
Higher Wyke Farm
Shamwari
Corrie View
King's Farm
Balls Farm
Abbey Gate Farm
Wyke Farm
Fair View
Wyke Green
Rose Farm
Grove Lea
Annings Farm
Spring Cottage
Hillcrest Farm
A358
A35
B3261
THE B3261 TRAFALGAR WAY
MUSBURY ROAD
CHARD ROAD
LYME ROAD
STONEY LANE
WEST ST.
SECTOR LANE
WOODBURY LANE
WYKE ROAD
ABBEY GATE LANE
WEYCROFT AVENUE
BEAVOR LANE
EVIL LANE
FOURCROSS HILL
UPHAY LANE
HUNTHAY LANE
WATERY LANE
LODGE LANE
RIVER AXE
(ROMAN ROAD)
TRILL LANE

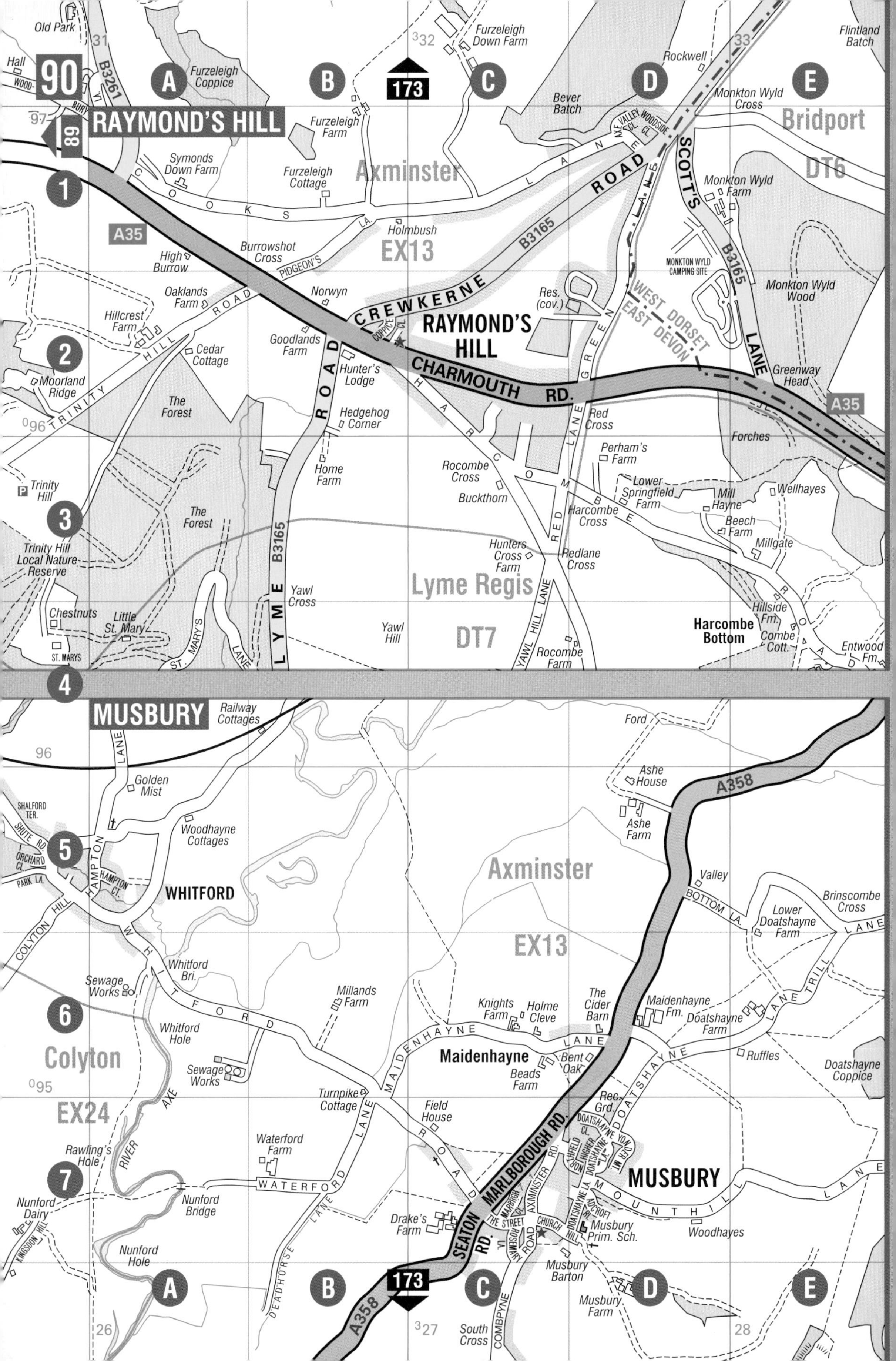
RAYMOND'S HILL
89
173
A
B
C
D
E
1
2
3
4
5
6
7
Old Park
Hall
Furzeleigh Coppice
Furzeleigh Down Farm
Rockwell
Flintland Batch
Bever Batch
Monkton Wyld Cross
Bridport
DT6
Furzeleigh Farm
Symonds Down Farm
Furzeleigh Cottage
Axminster
CROOKS LANE
ROAD
SCOTT'S
Monkton Wyld Farm
A35
Holmbush
EX13
B3165
MONKTON WYLD CAMPING SITE
High Burrow
Burrowshot Cross
PIDGEON'S LA.
Oaklands Farm
Norwyn
CREWKERNE
Res. (cov.)
WEST DORSET
EAST DEVON
Monkton Wyld Wood
Hillcrest Farm
Goodlands Farm
RAYMOND'S HILL
LANE
Cedar Cottage
Hunter's Lodge
CHARMOUTH RD.
Greenway Head
Moorland Ridge
TRINITY HILL ROAD
The Forest
Hedgehog Corner
Red Cross
Forches
Perham's Farm
Rocombe Cross
Home Farm
Lower Springfield Farm
Mill Hayne
Wellhayes
Trinity Hill
Buckthorn
Harcombe Cross
Beech Farm
The Forest
Millgate
Trinity Hill Local Nature Reserve
Hunters Cross Farm
Redlane Cross
Lyme Regis
Yawl Cross
Chestnuts
Little St. Mary
Yawl Hill
DT7
Hillside Fm.
Harcombe Bottom
Combe Cott.
Entwood Fm.
ST. MARYS
ST. MARY'S LANE
LYME ROAD
YAWL HILL LANE
Rocombe Farm
MUSBURY
Railway Cottages
Ford
96
Golden Mist
Ashe House
A358
Ashe Farm
SHALFORD TER.
SHUTE RD.
ORCHARD CL.
PARK LA.
HAMPTON
HAMPTON CT.
Woodhayne Cottages
WHITFORD
Axminster
Valley
BOTTOM LA.
Brinscombe Cross
Lower Doatshayne Farm
COLYTON HILL
EX13
Whitford Bri.
Sewage Works
Millands Farm
Knights Farm
Holme Cleve
The Cider Barn
Maidenhayne Fm.
Doatshayne Farm
Whitford Hole
WHITFORD ROAD
MAIDENHAYNE LANE
Maidenhayne
Bent Oak
Ruffles
Doatshayne Coppice
Colyton
Sewage Works
Beads Farm
095
Turnpike Cottage
Field House
Rec. Grd.
EX24
Waterford Farm
MARLBOROUGH RD.
Rawling's Hole
RIVER AXE
MUSBURY
WATERFORD LANE
MOUNT HILL LANE
Nunford Dairy
Nunford Bridge
Drake's Farm
Musbury Prim. Sch.
Woodhayes
KINGSDON HILL
Nunford Hole
SEATON RD.
AXMINSTER RD.
Mushbury Barton
DEADHORSE LANE
Musbury Farm
26
327
South Cross
COMBPYNE
28

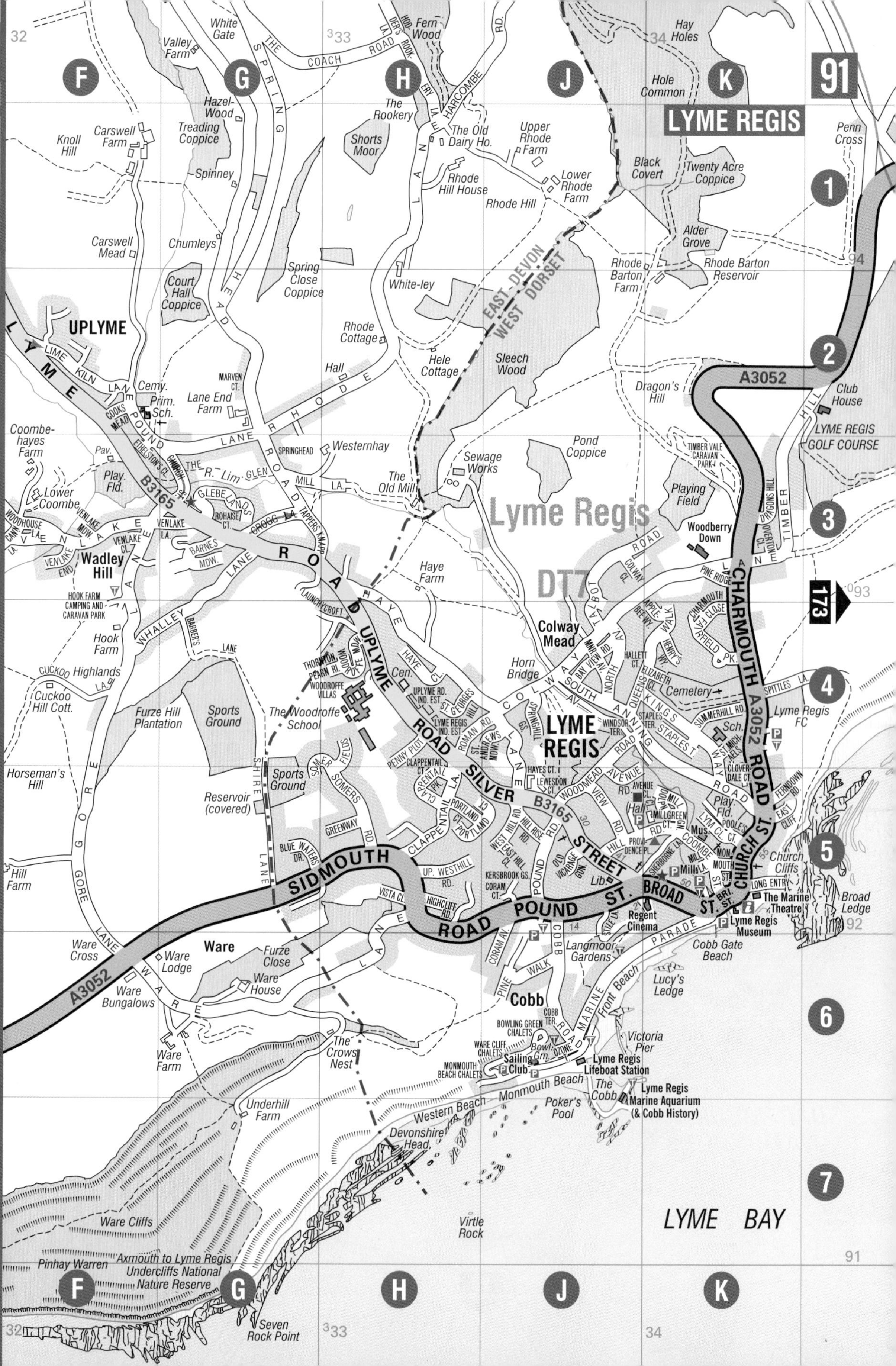
LYME REGIS
Lyme Regis
DT7
UPLYME
LYME REGIS
Wadley Hill
Colway Mead
Ware
Cobb
LYME BAY
A3052
B3165
SIDMOUTH ROAD
POUND ST.
BROAD ST.
SILVER STREET
UPLYME ROAD
CHARMOUTH ROAD
LYME ROAD
RHODE LANE
COACH ROAD
SPRINGHEAD ROAD
EAST DEVON
WEST DORSET
Valley Farm
White Gate
Fern Wood
Hay Holes
Hole Common
Carswell Farm
Knoll Hill
Hazel-Wood
Treading Coppice
Shorts Moor
The Rookery
The Old Dairy Ho.
Upper Rhode Farm
Black Covert
Twenty Acre Coppice
Penn Cross
Spinney
Rhode Hill House
Lower Rhode Farm
Rhode Hill
Alder Grove
Carswell Mead
Chumleys
Spring Close Coppice
White-ley
Rhode Barton Farm
Rhode Barton Reservoir
Court Hall Coppice
Rhode Cottage
Hele Cottage
Sleech Wood
Dragon's Hill
Club House
Hall
Lane End Farm
Prim. Sch.
Cemy.
Coombe-hayes Farm
Westernhay
Pond Coppice
LYME REGIS GOLF COURSE
Sewage Works
The Old Mill
Play. Fld.
Lower Coombe
Playing Field
Woodberry Down
Haye Farm
Hook Farm Camping and Caravan Park
Hook Farm
Horn Bridge
Highlands
Cuckoo Hill Cott.
Furze Hill Plantation
Sports Ground
The Woodroffe School
Cemetery
Lyme Regis FC
Horseman's Hill
Reservoir (covered)
Hill Farm
Regent Cinema
Lib.
Mus.
Church Cliffs
The Marine Theatre
Broad Ledge
Lyme Regis Museum
Cobb Gate Beach
Ware Cross
Ware Lodge
Furze Close
Ware House
Ware Bungalows
Langmoor Gardens
Lucy's Ledge
Front Beach
Victoria Pier
Ware Farm
The Crows Nest
Sailing Club
Lyme Regis Lifeboat Station
The Cobb
Lyme Regis Marine Aquarium (& Cobb History)
Monmouth Beach
Western Beach
Poker's Pool
Underhill Farm
Devonshire Head
Virtle Rock
Ware Cliffs
Pinhay Warren
Axmouth to Lyme Regis Undercliffs National Nature Reserve
Seven Rock Point
Bowling Green Chalets
Ware Cliff Chalets
Monmouth Beach Chalets
Timber Vale Caravan Park
Parade
Marine Parade

173

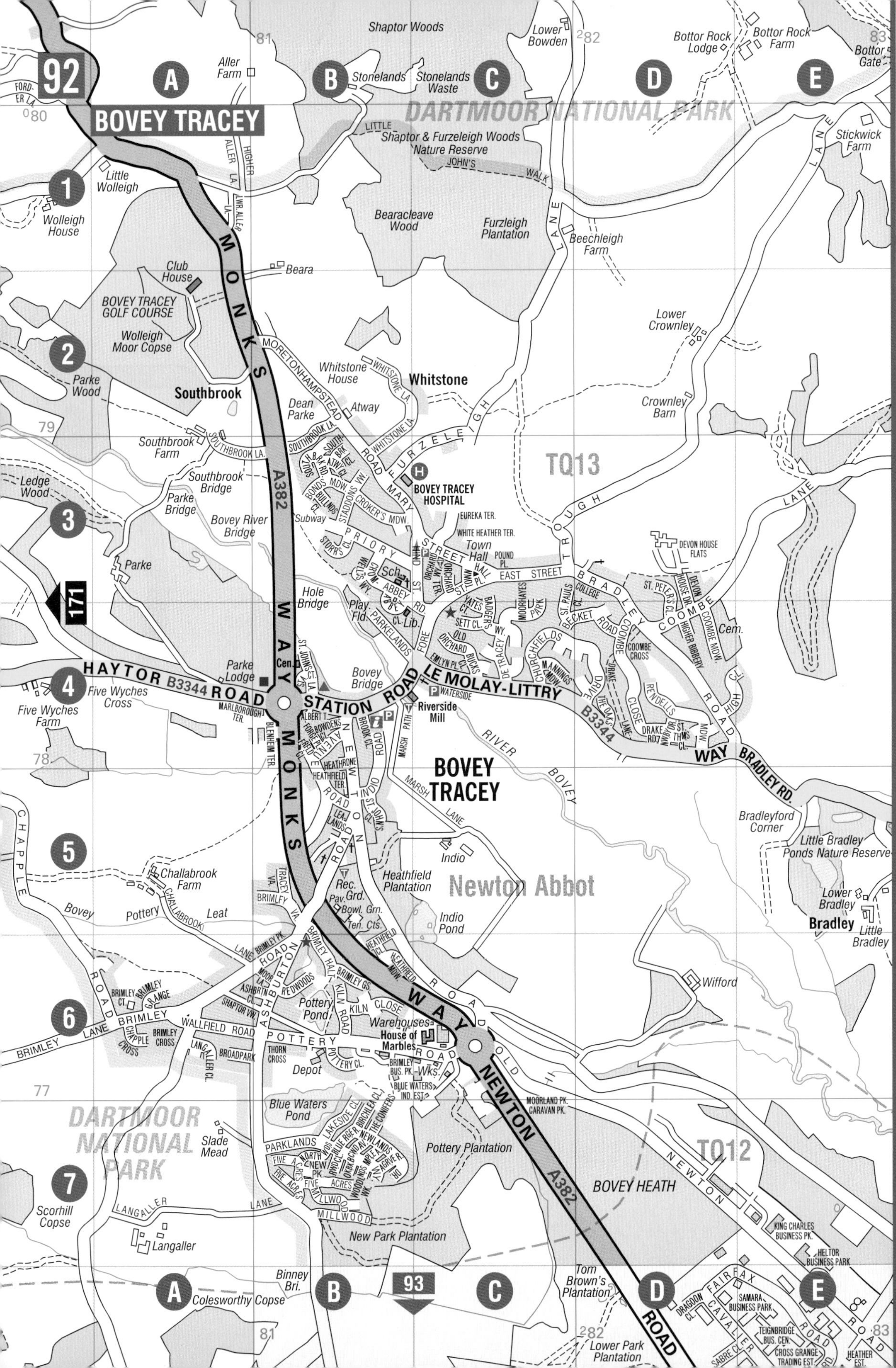
BOVEY TRACEY
DARTMOOR NATIONAL PARK
Shaptor Woods
Aller Farm
Stonelands
Stonelands Waste
Lower Bowden
Bottor Rock Lodge
Bottor Rock Farm
Bottor Gate
Shaptor & Furzeleigh Woods Nature Reserve
LITTLE JOHN'S WALK
Stickwick Farm
Little Wolleigh
Wolleigh House
Bearacleave Wood
Furzleigh Plantation
Beechleigh Farm
Beara
Club House
BOVEY TRACEY GOLF COURSE
Wolleigh Moor Copse
Lower Crownley
Crownley Barn
Parke Wood
Southbrook
Whitstone House
Whitstone
Dean Parke
Atway
MONKS WAY
A382
MORETONHAMPSTEAD ROAD
FURZELEIGH
Southbrook Farm
SOUTHBROOK LA.
Southbrook Bridge
Ledge Wood
Parke Bridge
Bovey River Bridge
BOVEY TRACEY HOSPITAL
TQ13
TROUGH LANE
EUREKA TER.
WHITE HEATHER TER.
Town Hall
POUND PL.
EAST STREET
DEVON HOUSE FLATS
Parke
PRIORY
Sch.
Hole Bridge
Play. Fld.
PARKELANDS
Lib.
FORE
BRADLEY
COOMBE
Cem.
171
HAYTOR ROAD B3344
Parke Lodge
Cen.
Five Wyches Cross
Five Wyches Farm
STATION ROAD
LE MOLAY-LITTRY WAY
Bovey Bridge
Riverside Mill
WATERSIDE
B3344
BRADLEY RD.
RIVER BOVEY
BOVEY TRACEY
MARSH LANE
NEWTON ROAD
Bradleyford Corner
Little Bradley Ponds Nature Reserve
Indio
Heathfield Plantation
Newton Abbot
Challabrook Farm
Rec. Grd.
Indio Pond
Lower Bradley
Bradley
Little Bradley
Bovey Pottery Leat
CHALLABROOK LANE
CHAPPLE ROAD
BRIMLEY LANE
WALLFIELD ROAD
ASHBURTON ROAD
KILN CLOSE
Pottery Pond
Warehouses
House of Marbles
Wifford
POTTERY ROAD
Depot
Wks.
BLUE WATERS IND. EST.
MOORLAND PK. CARAVAN PK.
OLD NEWTON ROAD
Blue Waters Pond
Slade Mead
Pottery Plantation
TQ12
BOVEY HEATH
Scorhill Copse
LANGALLER LANE
Langaller
MILLWOOD
New Park Plantation
KING CHARLES BUSINESS PK.
HELTOR BUSINESS PARK
Binney Bri.
Colesworthy Copse
93
Tom Brown's Plantation
FAIRFAX
SAMARA BUSINESS PARK
TEIGNBRIDGE BUS. CEN.
CROSS GRANGE TRADING EST.
HEATHER EST.
Lower Park Plantation
NEWTON ROAD

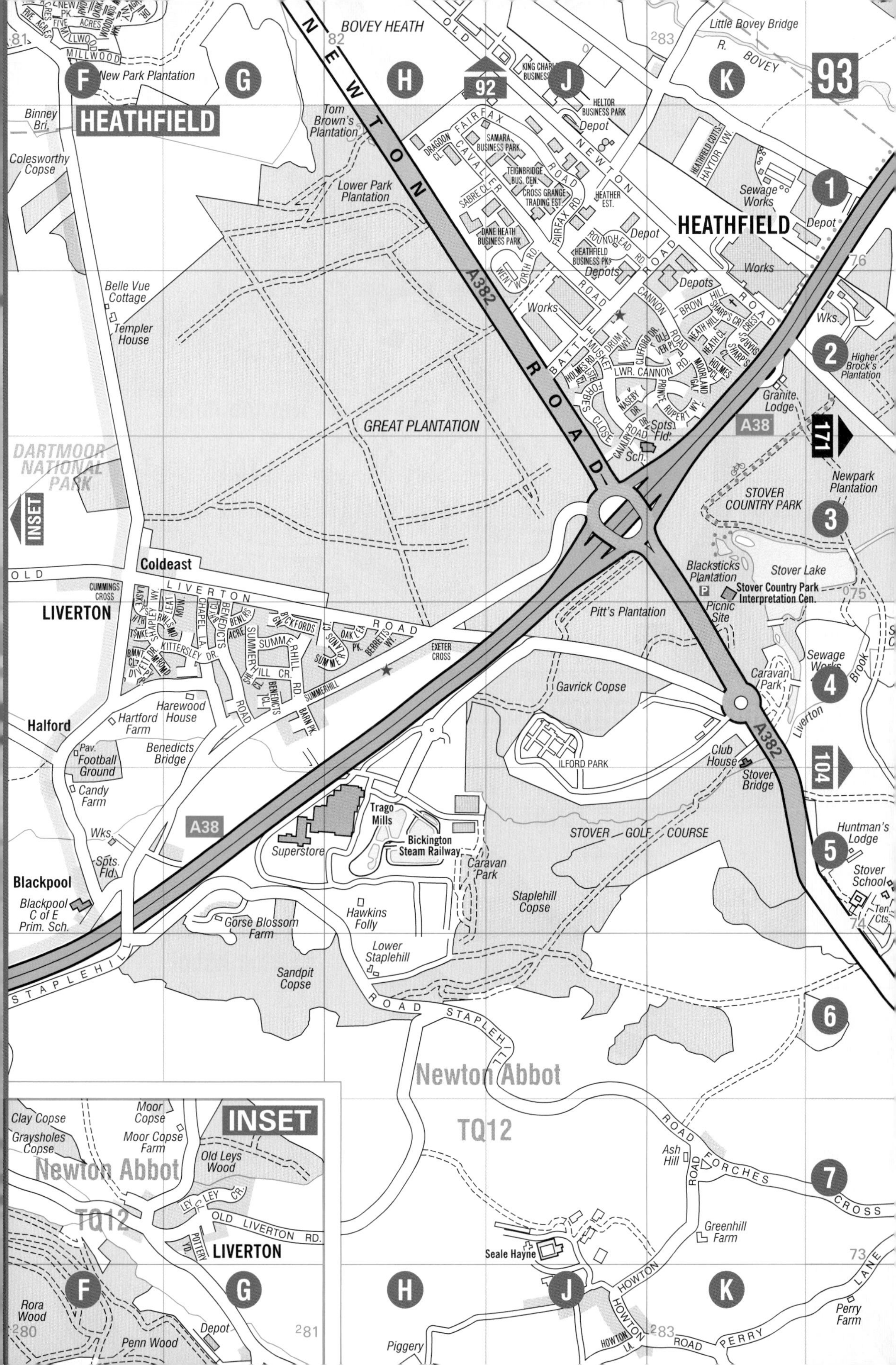

93
HEATHFIELD
BOVEY HEATH
Little Bovey Bridge
R. BOVEY
New Park Plantation
Binney Bri.
Colesworthy Copse
Tom Brown's Plantation
Lower Park Plantation
NEWTON ROAD
A382
GREAT PLANTATION
Belle Vue Cottage
Templer House
DARTMOOR NATIONAL PARK
INSET
Coldeast
LIVERTON
OLD LIVERTON ROAD
CUMMINGS CROSS
EXETER CROSS
Halford
Hartford Farm
Harewood House
Benedicts Bridge
Football Ground
Candy Farm
Blackpool
Blackpool C of E Prim. Sch.
A38
Trago Mills
Superstore
Bickington Steam Railway
Caravan Park
Gorse Blossom Farm
Hawkins Folly
Lower Staplehill
Sandpit Copse
STAPLEHILL ROAD
Newton Abbot
TQ12
Staplehill Copse
STOVER GOLF COURSE
ILFORD PARK
Gavrick Copse
Pitt's Plantation
Blacksticks Plantation
Stover Country Park Interpretation Cen.
Picnic Site
Stover Lake
STOVER COUNTRY PARK
Newpark Plantation
Granite Lodge
Higher Brock's Plantation
Sewage Works
Depot
Works
Club House
Stover Bridge
Huntman's Lodge
Stover School
Ash Hill
FORCHES CROSS ROAD
Greenhill Farm
Seale Hayne
HOWTON ROAD
HOWTON LA.
PERRY ROAD
PERRY LANE
Perry Farm
Piggery
Clay Copse
Graysholes Copse
Moor Copse
Moor Copse Farm
Old Leys Wood
LEY CR.
POTTERY YD.
Rora Wood
Penn Wood
Depot
92
171
104

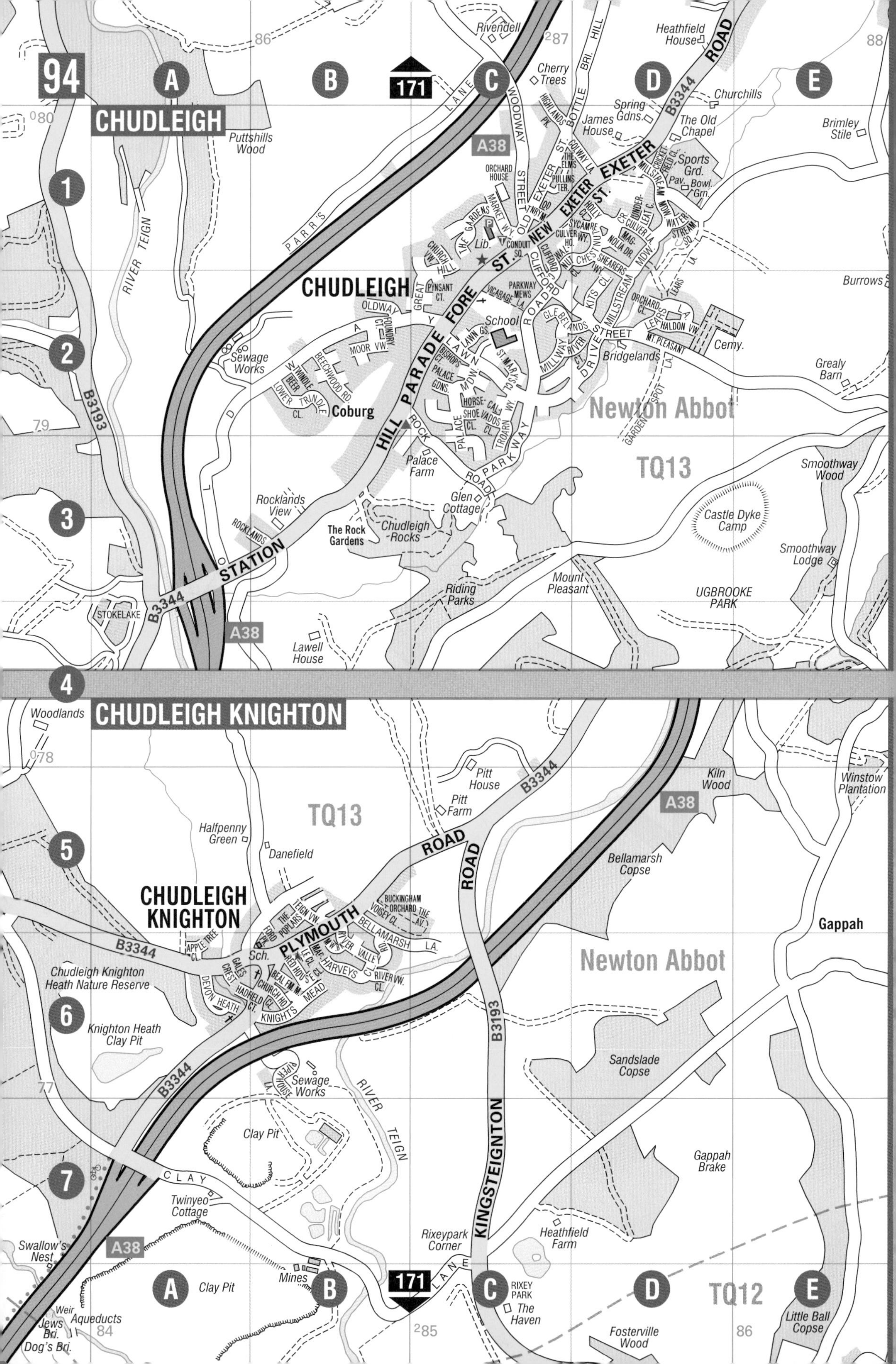
CHUDLEIGH
CHUDLEIGH KNIGHTON
171
A
B
C
D
E
1
2
3
4
5
6
7
86
287
88
080
79
078
77
84
285
86
Rivendell
Heathfield House
Cherry Trees
Churchills
Spring Gdns.
James House
The Old Chapel
Brimley Stile
Sports Grd.
Pav.
Bowl. Grn.
Puttshills Wood
A38
RIVER TEIGN
PARR'S LANE
WOODWAY STREET
BOTTLE BRI. HILL
B3344
EXETER ROAD
NEW EXETER ST.
OLD EXETER ST.
ORCHARD HOUSE
MARKET WY.
THE GARDENS
Lib.
CONDUIT SQ.
FORE ST.
CHURCH HILL
CHURCH VW.
CHUDLEIGH
GREAT PYNSANT CT.
VICARAGE LA.
PARKWAY MEWS
CLIFFORD ROAD
Burrows
OLDWAY
FOUNDRY CT.
MOOR VW.
School
LAWN GS.
ST. MARY'S CL.
GLEBELANDS
MILLWAY
RIVER DRIVE
MILLSTREAM MDW.
KITS CL.
SHEARERS WY.
ORCHARD CL.
HALDON VW.
LEARS LA.
MT. PLEASANT
STREET
Cemy.
Bridgelands
Grealy Barn
Sewage Works
WINDLE
BEER
LOWER TRINDLE CL.
TRINDLE
BEECHWOOD RD
Coburg
HILL PARADE
BISHOPS CT.
PALACE GDNS.
PALACE MDW.
HORSESHOE CL.
CAVALDOS CL.
TROARN WY.
PARKWAY
ROCK ROAD
Newton Abbot
SPOT LA.
GARDEN
TQ13
Palace Farm
Glen Cottage
Smoothway Wood
Rocklands View
ROCKLANDS
STATION
The Rock Gardens
Chudleigh Rocks
Castle Dyke Camp
Smoothway Lodge
Riding Parks
Mount Pleasant
UGBROOKE PARK
STOKELAKE
Lawell House
Woodlands
Pitt House
Pitt Farm
Kiln Wood
Winstow Plantation
TQ13
Halfpenny Green
Danefield
ROAD
Bellamarsh Copse
CHUDLEIGH KNIGHTON
BUCKINGHAM ORCHARD
THE AV.
VOISEY CL.
TEIGN VW.
THE POPLARS
PLYMOUTH
BELLAMARSH LA.
VALLEY RD.
Gappah
B3344
APPLE TREE CL.
Sch.
GALES CREST
RED HOUSE CL.
HARVEYS
RIVER VW. CL.
Newton Abbot
Chudleigh Knighton Heath Nature Reserve
DEVON HEATH
HADFIELD CT.
CHURCH HO.
KNIGHTS MEAD
Knighton Heath Clay Pit
B3193
Sewage Works
RIPPER HOUSE LA.
Sandslade Copse
Clay Pit
RIVER TEIGN
KINGSTEIGNTON
CLAY LANE
Gappah Brake
Twinyeo Cottage
Heathfield Farm
Swallow's Nest
Rixeypark Corner
Mines
Clay Pit
RIXEY PARK
The Haven
TQ12
Little Ball Copse
Weir
Aqueducts
Jews Bri.
Dog's Bri.
Fosterville Wood

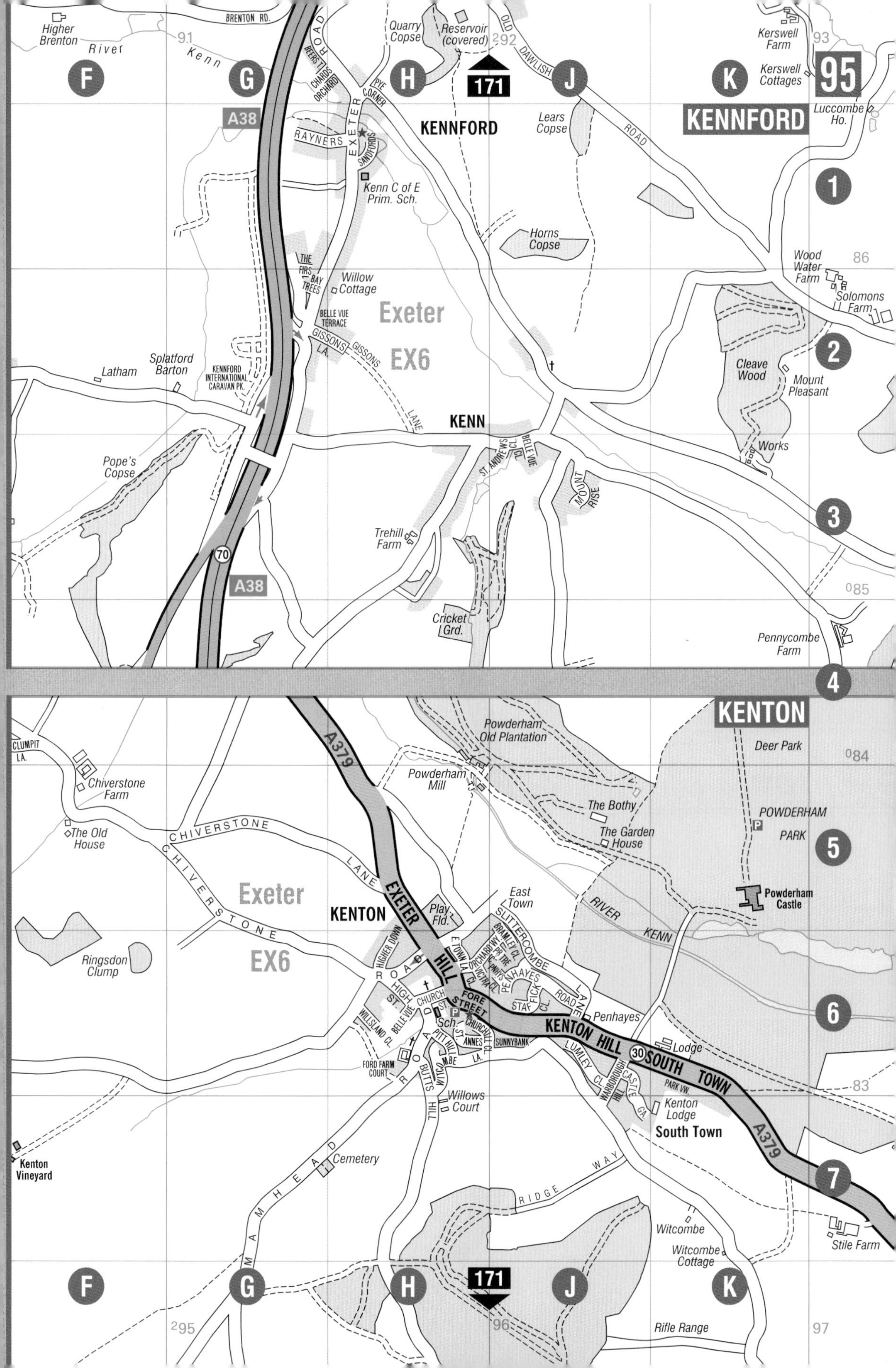

BRENTON RD.
Higher Brenton
River Kenn
ROAD
BEERS
CHARDS ORCHARD
PYE CORNER
Quarry Copse
Reservoir (covered)
171
OLD DAWLISH ROAD
Kerswell Farm
Kerswell Cottages
KENNFORD
Luccombe Ho.
A38
RAYNERS
EXETER
SANDFORDS
Kenn C of E Prim. Sch.
Lears Copse
Horns Copse
THE FIRS
BAY TREES
Willow Cottage
BELLE VUE TERRACE
Exeter
EX6
Wood Water Farm
Solomons Farm
GISSONS LA.
GISSONS LANE
Cleave Wood
Mount Pleasant
Latham
Splatford Barton
KENNFORD INTERNATIONAL CARAVAN PK.
KENN
ST. ANDREWS CL.
BELLE VUE CL.
Works
Pope's Copse
MOUNT RISE
Trehill Farm
70
A38
Cricket Grd.
Pennycombe Farm
KENTON
Powderham Old Plantation
Deer Park
CLUMPIT LA.
A379
Powderham Mill
Chiverstone Farm
The Bothy
POWDERHAM PARK
The Old House
CHIVERSTONE LANE
The Garden House
Exeter
EXETER HILL
East Town
Powderham Castle
KENTON
Play. Fld.
RIVER KENN
Ringsdon Clump
EX6
HIGHER DOWN
SLITTERCOMBE LANE
BRAMLEY CL.
ORCHARD WY.
E. TOWN LA.
PENHAYES RD.
ROAD
HIGH ST.
CHURCH ST.
FORE STREET
VICTORIA CL.
PENHAYES CL.
STAFFICK CL.
Penhayes
WILLSLAND CL.
BELLE VUE
Sch.
CHURCHILL CL.
ST. ANNES
SUNNYBANK
KENTON HILL
30
SOUTH TOWN
Lodge
PITT HILL
LUMLEY CL.
WARBOROUGH HILL
CASTLE GA.
PARK VW.
FORD FARM COURT
BUTTS HILL
WILLOWS LA.
Willows Court
Kenton Lodge
South Town
A379
Kenton Vineyard
MAMHEAD ROAD
Cemetery
RIDGE WAY
Witcombe
Witcombe Cottage
Stile Farm
171
Rifle Range
F G H J K
1 2 3 4 5 6 7
91 292 93 86 085 084 83 295 96 97

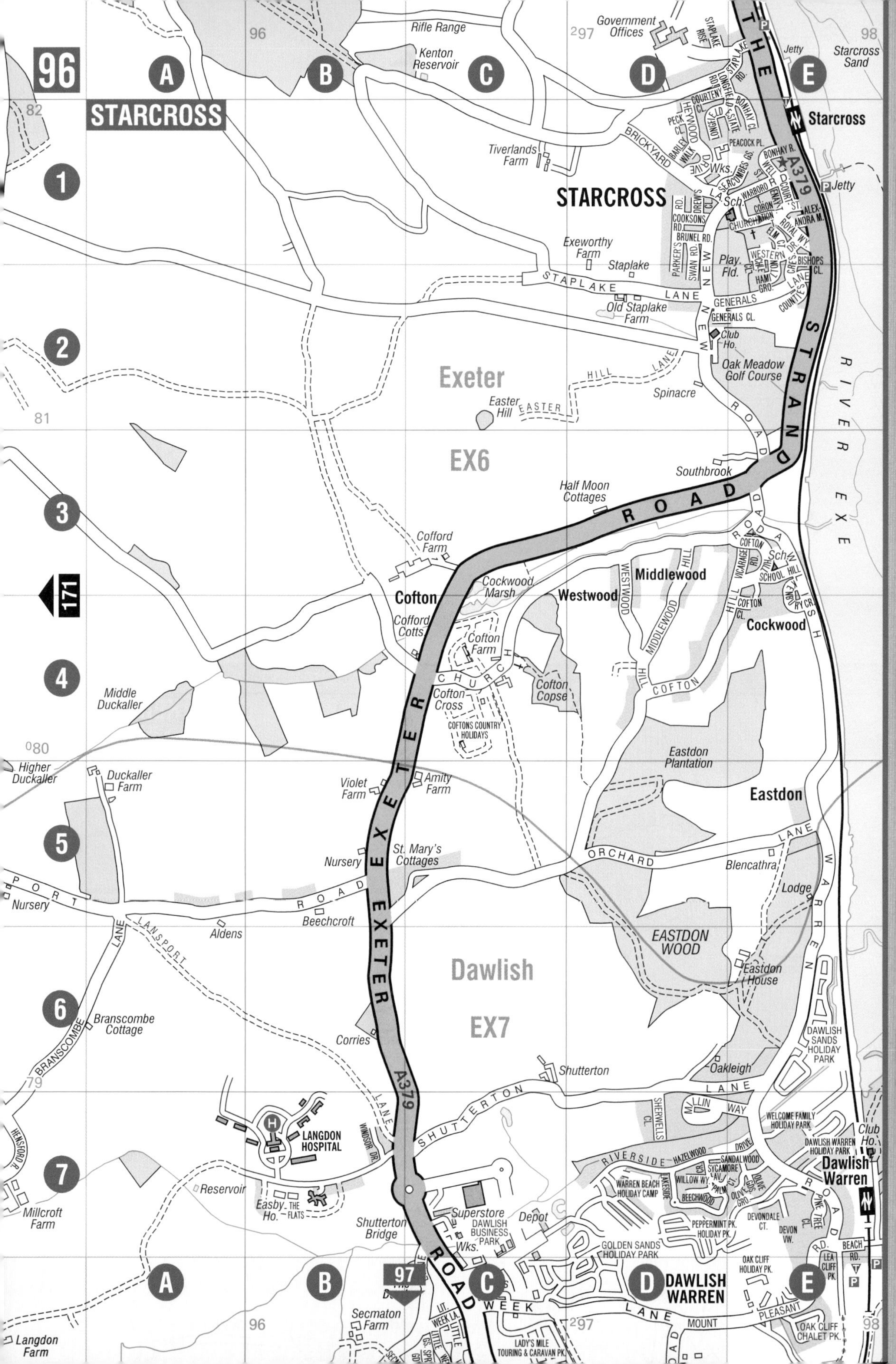
STARCROSS
Starcross
Starcross Sand
Jetty
Rifle Range
Kenton Reservoir
Government Offices
Tiverlands Farm
Exeworthy Farm
Staplake
Old Staplake Farm
Oak Meadow Golf Course
Spinacre
Exeter
EX6
Easter Hill
Southbrook
Half Moon Cottages
THE STRAND
ROAD
A379
RIVER EXE
Cofford Farm
Cofton
Cockwood Marsh
Westwood
Middlewood
Cockwood
Cofford Cotts.
Cofton Farm
Cofton Copse
Cofton Cross
COFTONS COUNTRY HOLIDAYS
Middle Duckaller
Higher Duckaller
Duckaller Farm
Violet Farm
Amity Farm
Eastdon Plantation
Eastdon
Nursery
St. Mary's Cottages
ORCHARD LANE
Blencathra
Lodge
PORT ROAD
LANSPORT LANE
Aldens
Beechcroft
EXETER ROAD
EASTDON WOOD
Eastdon House
Dawlish
EX7
Branscombe Cottage
Corries
Shutterton
DAWLISH SANDS HOLIDAY PARK
Oakleigh
SHUTTERTON LANE
LANGDON HOSPITAL
WINDSOR DR.
WELCOME FAMILY HOLIDAY PARK
DAWLISH WARREN HOLIDAY PARK
Club Ho.
Dawlish Warren
Reservoir
Millcroft Farm
Easby Ho.
THE FLATS
Shutterton Bridge
Superstore
DAWLISH BUSINESS PARK
Depot
Wks.
WARREN BEACH HOLIDAY CAMP
GOLDEN SANDS HOLIDAY PARK
PEPPERMINT PK. HOLIDAY PK.
OAK CLIFF HOLIDAY PK.
DEVONDALE CT.
DEVON VW.
LEA CLIFF PK.
DAWLISH WARREN
WEEK LANE
MOUNT PLEASANT
OAK CLIFF CHALET PK.
Secmaton Farm
Langdon Farm
LADY'S MILE TOURING & CARAVAN PK.
97
171

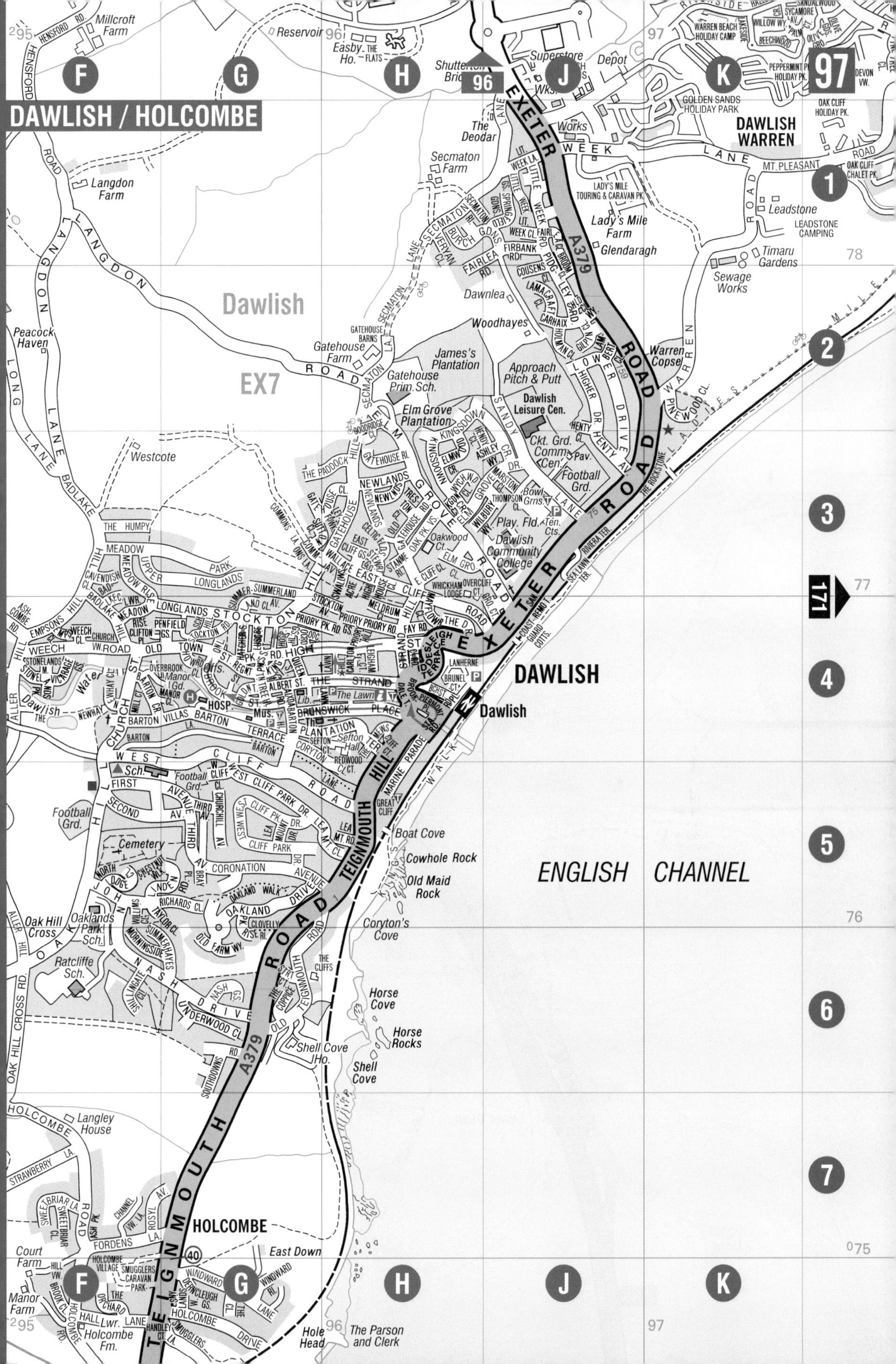
DAWLISH / HOLCOMBE
96
171
F
G
H
J
K
1
2
3
4
5
6
7
Millcroft Farm
Reservoir
Easby Ho.
Superstore
Depot
Works
The Deodar
Secmaton Farm
Langdon Farm
Lady's Mile Farm
Glendaragh
Leadstone
LEADSTONE CAMPING
Timaru Gardens
Sewage Works
DAWLISH WARREN
GOLDEN SANDS HOLIDAY PARK
WARREN BEACH HOLIDAY CAMP
PEPPERMINT PK. HOLIDAY PK.
OAK CLIFF HOLIDAY PK.
OAK CLIFF CHALET PK.
LADY'S MILE TOURING & CARAVAN PK.
Dawlish
EX7
Peacock Haven
Gatehouse Farm
Gatehouse Prim.Sch.
James's Plantation
Woodhayes
Dawnlea
Approach Pitch & Putt
Dawlish Leisure Cen.
Warren Copse
Elm Grove Plantation
Ckt. Grd. Comm. Cen.
Pav.
Football Grd.
Westcote
Play. Fld.
Ten. Cts.
Bowl. Grns.
Dawlish Community College
Oakwood Ct.
EXETER ROAD
A379
TEIGNMOUTH ROAD
DAWLISH
Dawlish
HOSP.
Mus.
Lib.
The Lawn
Sefton Hall
Sch.
Football Grd.
Cemetery
Oak Hill Cross
Oaklands Park Sch.
Ratcliffe Sch.
Boat Cove
Cowhole Rock
Old Maid Rock
Coryton's Cove
Horse Cove
Horse Rocks
Shell Cove Ho.
Shell Cove
ENGLISH CHANNEL
Langley House
HOLCOMBE
Court Farm
Manor Farm
Holcombe Fm.
East Down
Hole Head
The Parson and Clerk
78
77
76
75
95
96
97

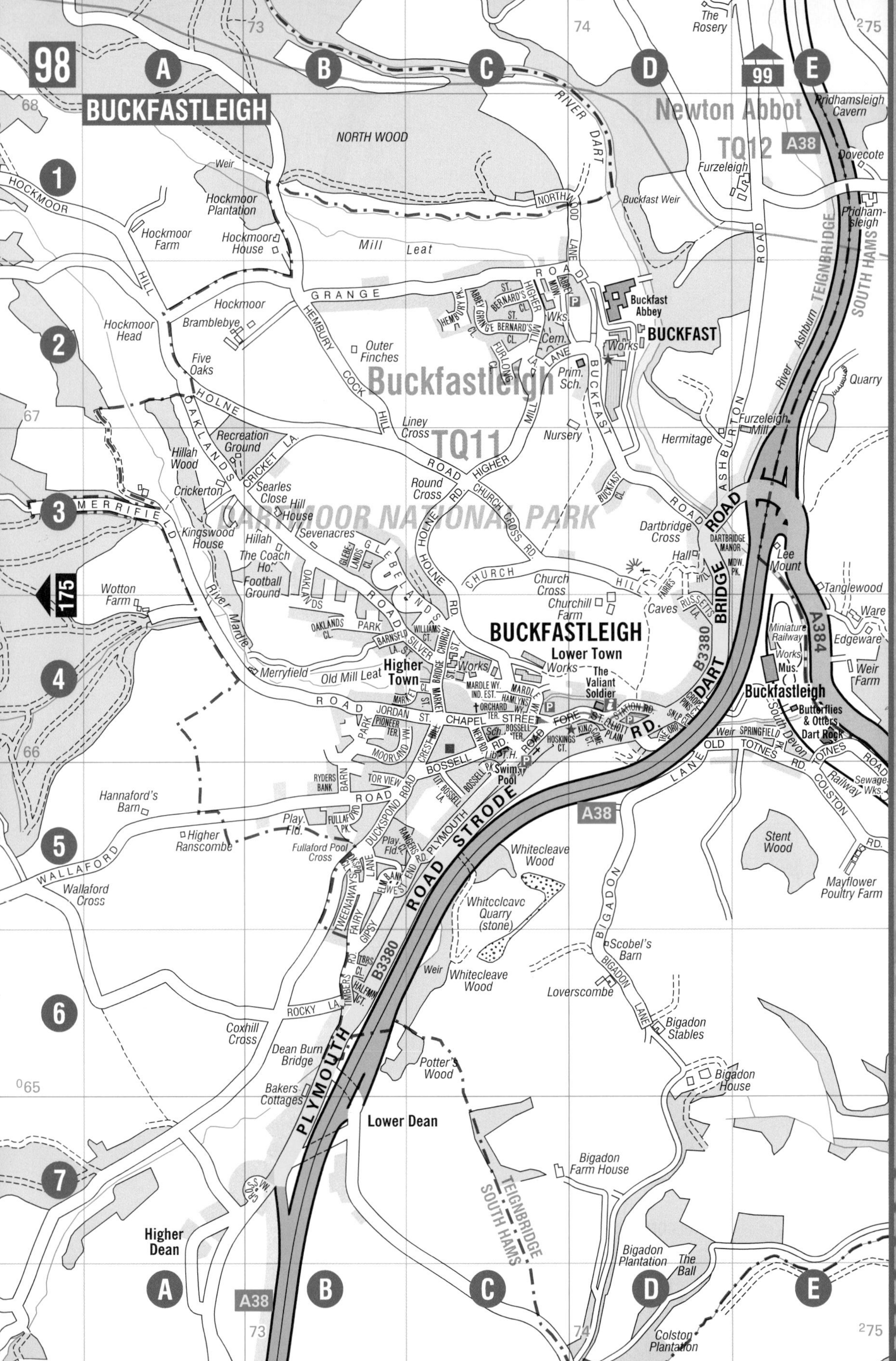
BUCKFASTLEIGH
Buckfastleigh
BUCKFASTLEIGH
Lower Town
Higher Town
BUCKFAST
Buckfast Abbey
DARTMOOR NATIONAL PARK
TQ11
TQ12
Newton Abbot
NORTH WOOD
Hockmoor Plantation
Hockmoor Farm
Hockmoor House
Hockmoor Head
Bramblebye
Five Oaks
Outer Finches
Liney Cross
Round Cross
Recreation Ground
Hillah Wood
Crickerton
Searles Close
Hill House
Sevenacres
Kingswood House
The Coach Ho.
Football Ground
Wotton Farm
Merryfield
Old Mill Leat
Mill Leat
Church Cross
Churchill Farm
Caves
Nursery
Hermitage
Dartbridge Cross
Lee Mount
Tanglewood
Edgeware
Weir Farm
Miniature Railway
Buckfastleigh
Butterflies & Otters
Dart Rock
South Devon Railway
Sewage Wks.
Stent Wood
Mayflower Poultry Farm
The Valiant Soldier
Swim. Pool
Hannaford's Barn
Higher Ranscombe
Wallaford Cross
Fullaford Pool Cross
Whitecleave Wood
Whitecleave Quarry (stone)
Scobel's Barn
Loverscombe
Bigadon Stables
Bigadon House
Bigadon Farm House
Bigadon Plantation
The Ball
Colston Plantation
Coxhill Cross
Dean Burn Bridge
Bakers Cottages
Potter's Wood
Lower Dean
Higher Dean
The Rosery
Pridhamsleigh Cavern
Dovecote
Furzeleigh
Buckfast Weir
Pridhamsleigh
Quarry
Furzeleigh Mill
TEIGNBRIDGE
SOUTH HAMS
A38
A384
B3380
PLYMOUTH ROAD
STRODE ROAD
DART BRIDGE ROAD
ASHBURTON ROAD
175
99

ASHBURTON
DARTMOOR NATIONAL PARK
Newton Abbot
TQ13
BORO WOOD
Whiddon Scrubbs
Woodencliff Wood
Place Wood
Place House (Sixth Form Centre)
Linhay Hill Quarry
Druid Cottage
Rewdown Cross
DRUID ROAD
Lurgecombe
Rewlea Cross
Oaklands
Wooda Wray
Cuddyford Cross
Longstone Cross
Tower Hill Farm
Tennis Courts
Lodge
Rockpark Cross
Rew
Cuddyford Bridge
Place Cross
Academy
Ashmoor Rec. Cen.
Football Ground
Cricket Ground
Brookland
Westabrook Farm
Pittmoor Mill
Rew Cross
Barnsey Bridge
Byland
Holne Turn
Hele
HEADBOROUGH ROAD
Great Bridge
Elmfield
HOSP.
EAST STREET
EASTERN
ASHBURTON ROAD
B3357 ROAD
BY-PASS
A38
Pigspark Cross
Trenavian
DOLBEARE
PITLEY ROAD
Pitley Cross
Pitley Farm
Dolbeare Farm
Higher Barn
Reservoir (covered)
Mus.
Sch.
Depot
WEST ST.
WESTERN RD.
BOWDEN HILL
WHISTLEY HILL
Waverley Hall
The Ferns
River
Castle Bridge
Sunnyfield
Chuley Bridge
CHULEY
Yolland Hill
Whistley Hill Cross
Dipwell
TEIGNBRIDGE
SOUTH HAMS
CABBAGE HILL
Gulwell
Chuley Cross
Neilgate Corner
Well Farm
Woodend
Priestaford
Halsworthy
Sladesdown
Furzeleigh
Lower Waye
170
175
98
F G H J K
1 2 3 4 5 6 7

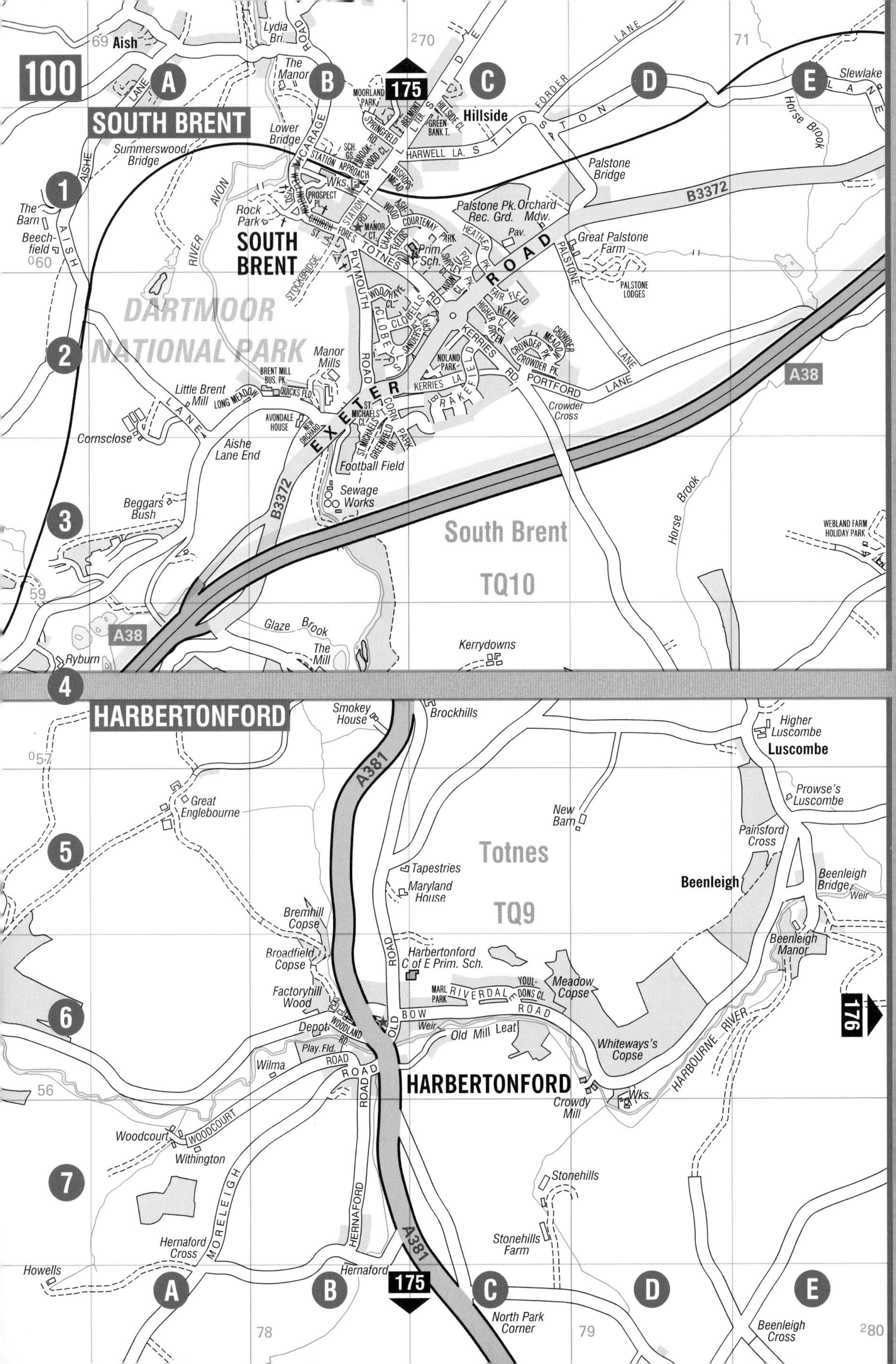
SOUTH BRENT
Aish
Lydia Bri.
The Manor
Lower Bridge
Summerswood Bridge
Hillside
Palstone Bridge
B3372
Slewlake Lane
Horse Brook
The Barn
Beechfield
Rock Park
SOUTH BRENT
DARTMOOR NATIONAL PARK
River Avon
Palstone Pk. Rec. Grd.
Orchard Mdw.
Great Palstone Farm
Palstone Lodges
Prim. Sch.
Manor Mills
Little Brent Mill
Brent Mill Bus. Pk.
Cornsclose
Aishe Lane End
Avondale House
Crowder Cross
A38
Football Field
Sewage Works
Beggars Bush
South Brent
TQ10
Webland Farm Holiday Park
Glaze Brook
The Mill
Kerrydowns
Ryburn
175
HARBERTONFORD
Smokey House
Brockhills
Higher Luscombe
Luscombe
Prowse's Luscombe
Great Englebourne
New Barn
A381
Painsford Cross
Totnes
TQ9
Tapestries
Maryland House
Beenleigh
Beenleigh Bridge
Bremhill Copse
Broadfield Copse
Beenleigh Manor
Harbertonford C of E Prim. Sch.
Factoryhill Wood
Meadow Copse
Riverdale
Old Mill Leat
Bow Road
Depot
Play. Fld.
Wilma
HARBERTONFORD
Whiteways's Copse
Crowdy Mill
Harbourne River
176
Woodcourt
Withington
Moreleigh Road
Hernaford Road
Stonehills
Stonehills Farm
Hernaford Cross
Hernaford
Howells
North Park Corner
Beenleigh Cross

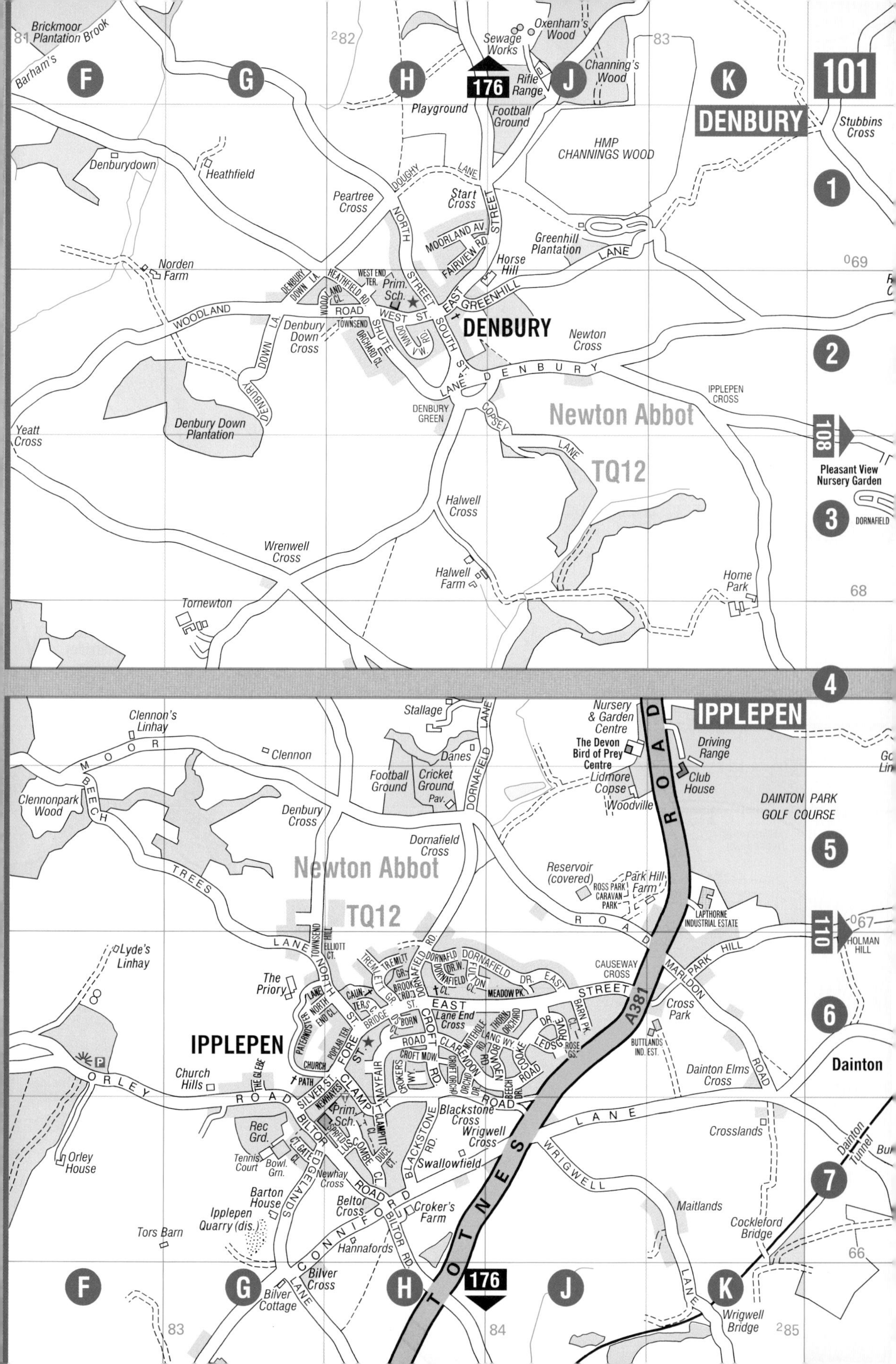
DENBURY
IPPLEPEN
Newton Abbot
TQ12
HMP CHANNINGS WOOD
Denbury Down Plantation
Dainton
DAINTON PARK GOLF COURSE
The Devon Bird of Prey Centre
Pleasant View Nursery Garden
A381
TOTNES ROAD
176
108
110

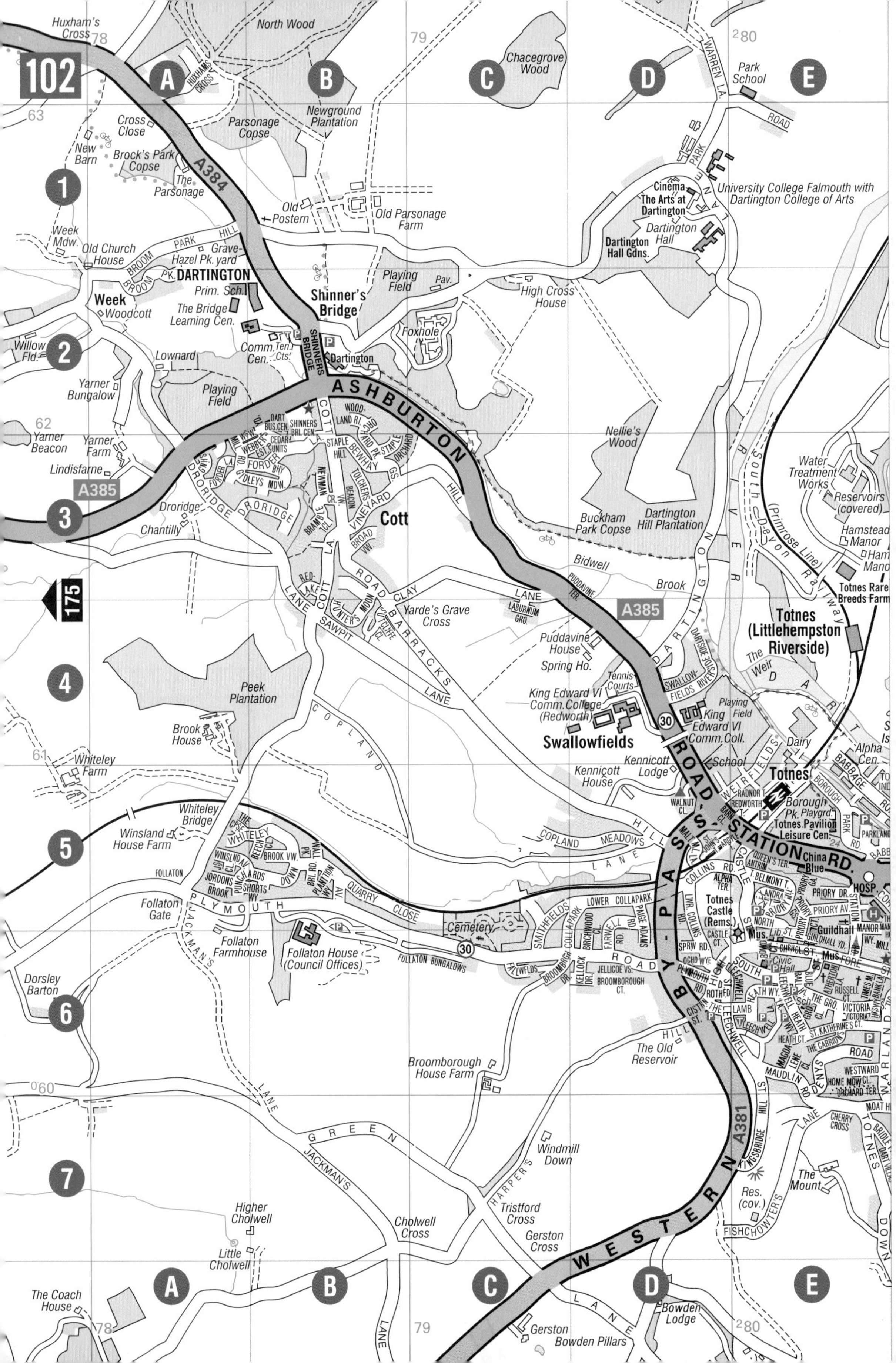
North Wood
Huxham's Cross
Chacegrove Wood
Park School
Newground Plantation
Parsonage Copse
Cross Close
New Barn
Brock's Park Copse
The Parsonage
A384
Old Postern
Old Parsonage Farm
Cinema
The Arts at Dartington
University College Falmouth with Dartington College of Arts
Dartington Hall
Dartington Hall Gdns.
Week Mdw.
Old Church House
Grave-yard
Hazel Pk.
DARTINGTON
Prim. Sch.
Week
Woodcott
Shinner's Bridge
Playing Field
High Cross House
Foxhole
The Bridge Learning Cen.
Willow Fld.
Lownard
Comm. Cen.
Dartington
ASHBURTON
Yarner Bungalow
Playing Field
Yarner Beacon
Yarner Farm
Nellie's Wood
Water Treatment Works
Reservoirs (covered)
Lindisfarne
A385
Droridge
Chantilly
Cott
Buckham Park Copse
Dartington Hill Plantation
Hamstead Manor
South Devon Railway (Primrose Line)
Totnes Rare Breeds Farm
Bidwell
Brook
175
Yarde's Grave Cross
Totnes (Littlehempston Riverside)
Puddavine House
Spring Ho.
The Weir
Peek Plantation
King Edward VI Comm.College (Redworth)
King Edward VI Comm.Coll.
Swallowfields
Brook House
Whiteley Farm
Dairy
Alpha Cen.
Kennicott House
Kennicott Lodge
School
Totnes
Whiteley Bridge
Winsland House Farm
Borough Pk.
Totnes Pavilion Leisure Cen.
China Blue
STATION RD.
BY-PASS
Follaton Gate
Cemetery
Totnes Castle (Rems.)
Mus.
Guildhall
Follaton Farmhouse
Follaton House (Council Offices)
Dorsley Barton
The Old Reservoir
Broomborough House Farm
Windmill Down
WESTERN BY-PASS
A381
The Mount
Res. (cov.)
Higher Cholwell
Cholwell Cross
Tristford Cross
Gerston Cross
Little Cholwell
The Coach House
Bowden Lodge
Gerston
Bowden Pillars

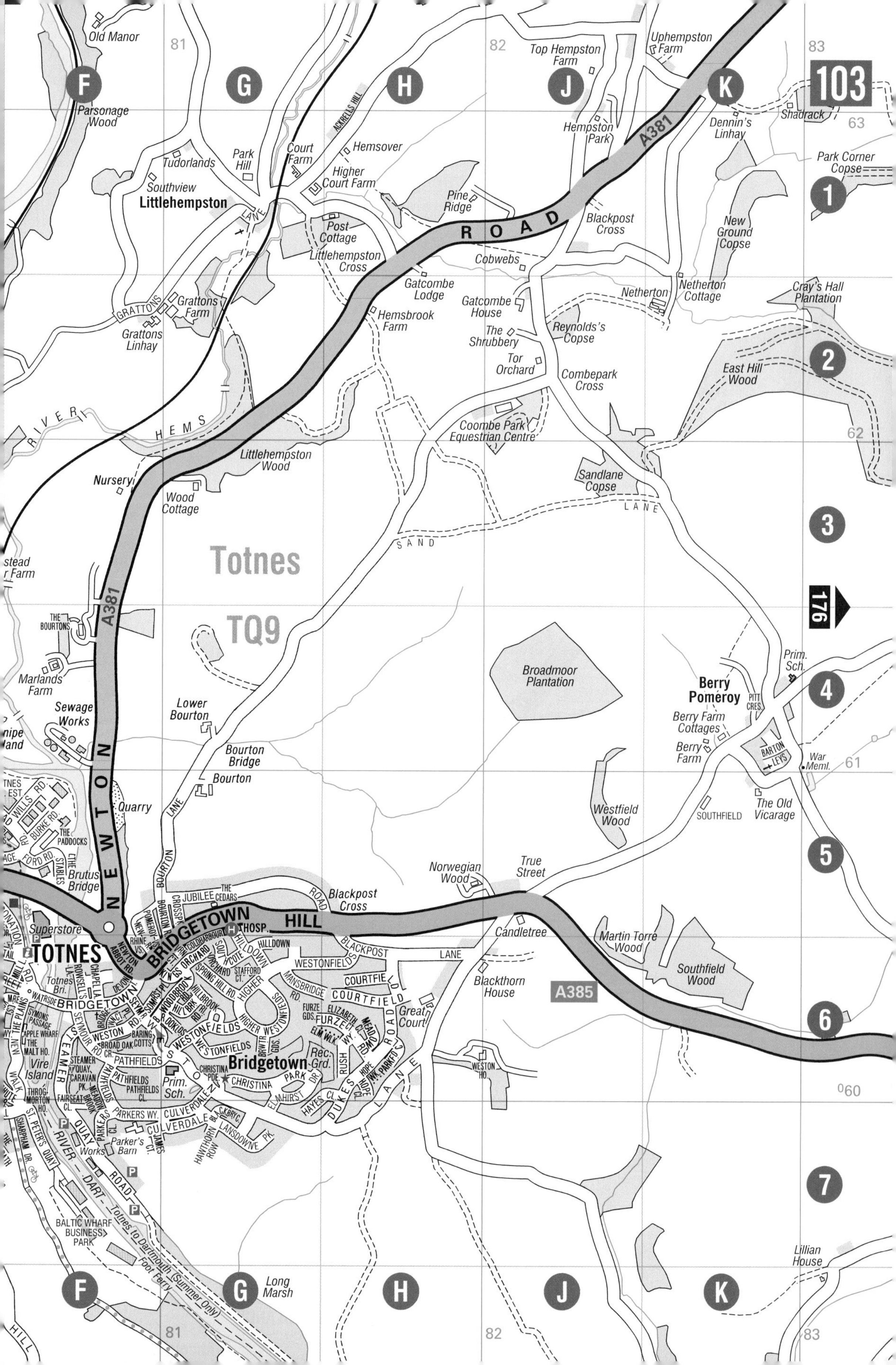
Old Manor
Parsonage Wood
Tudorlands
Park Hill
Southview
Littlehempston
Court Farm
Hemsover
Higher Court Farm
Post Cottage
Littlehempston Cross
Pine Ridge
Top Hempston Farm
Uphempston Farm
Hempston Park
A381
Shadrack
Dennin's Linhay
Park Corner Copse
New Ground Copse
Blackpost Cross
ROAD
Cobwebs
Gatcombe Lodge
Gatcombe House
Netherton
Netherton Cottage
Cray's Hall Plantation
Grattons Farm
Grattons Linhay
Hemsbrook Farm
The Shrubbery
Reynolds's Copse
Tor Orchard
Combepark Cross
East Hill Wood
RIVER HEMS
Coombe Park Equestrian Centre
Littlehempston Wood
Nursery
Wood Cottage
Sandlane Copse
SAND LANE
Totnes
TQ9
THE BOURTONS
Marlands Farm
Sewage Works
Broadmoor Plantation
Berry Pomeroy
Prim. Sch.
PITT CRES.
Berry Farm Cottages
Berry Farm
BARTON LEYS
War Meml.
The Old Vicarage
SOUTHFIELD
Lower Bourton
Bourton Bridge
Bourton
Quarry
Westfield Wood
NEWTON
Brutus Bridge
Norwegian Wood
True Street
Blackpost Cross
BRIDGETOWN HILL
Candletree
Martin Torre Wood
Southfield Wood
Superstore
TOTNES
Totnes Bri.
BRIDGETOWN
WESTONFIELDS
COURTFIELD
Great Court
Blackthorn House
A385
Bridgetown
Rec. Grd.
Prim. Sch.
Vire Island
WESTON HO.
STEAMER QUAY
RIVER DART
Totnes to Dartmouth (Summer Only) Foot Ferry
Parker's Barn
BALTIC WHARF BUSINESS PARK
Long Marsh
Lillian House
HILL

104
STOVER COUNTRY PARK
Newpark Plantation
Stover Lake
Lower Teigngrace Heathfield Plantation
Ventiford Cotts.
Summerlane Copse
Leygreen
PRESTON MANOR CLAY WORKS
PRESTON
Manor Farm
Higher Preston Cross
Manor Cottage
Burnells
Mortimer's Farm
Sampson's Farm
Lower Preston Cross
Clay Works
Stable Copse
Ventiford Brook
Sewage Works
Liverton Brook
Stover Bridge
Alderpark Copse
Ventiford Bridge
TEMPLER WY.
Goilmoors Plantation
New Orchard Copse
Huntman's Lodge
Stover School
Ten. Cts.
A382
93
Clay Works
Rectory
Locks Bridge
Hearders
TEIGNGRACE
SCHOOL RD.
SCHOOL COTTS.
Canal (disused)
RIVER TEIGN
Clay Pit
Lower Lodge
Twelve Oaks Farm
TWELVE OAKS FARM CARAVAN PARK
Butland's Plantation
Breakwater
Teign Bridge
Mount Pleasant
Forches Cross
GREYCOAT LANE
Newton Abbot
TQ12
Teignbridge Crossing
Clay Cellars
FORCHES CROSS
BOVEY TRACEY ROAD
Playing Field
Woodside
The Little House
Orchid Paradise
Burnham Nurseries
Playing Field
Teignbridge Gate
TEIGNBRIDGE ROAD
Blatchford
Blatchford Farm
Blatchford Brook
Segar's Plantation
Perry Farm
PERRY LANE
RINGSLADE
Clay Pit
Berry Knowles
Linden Lea
Sandford Orleigh Farm
HOWTON
171
Quarry (dis.)
Club House
Ringslade
Whitehill House
Bramble Ct. Barn
Lower Loady Farm
Higher Loady Park
EXETER RD.
ORLEIGH CROSS
WEST GOLDS WY.
NEWTON ABBOT COMM. HOSP.
HELE PARK GOLF COURSE
Club House
Highweek
Res. (cov.)
Gaze Hill
War Memorial
CHURCH
Mile End
MILE END ROAD
BELVEDERE RD.
GAZE HILL
WHITEHILL RD.
VILLAGE
PITT HILL ROAD
HIGHWEEK
SUNNYBANK
TRAFALGAR
JETTY MARSH
HAMILTON
ASHBURTON ROAD
A383
Hele Park
NORMAN CL.
APPLEGARTH
Castle Dyke
COOMBESHEAD
BLENHEIM
CHURCHILLS
FOXWELL
Prim. Sch.
Coombeshead College
SEYMOUR
KNOWLES HILL
LITTLEJOY ROAD
MOORSEND
CHERCOMBE
BURNLEY
BROAD RIDGE CL.
VALLEY
ROSEMARY AV.
ROBERTS WY.
GREENAWAY RD.
NEVILLE RD.
Sub.
Sch.
Newton Abbot Leis. Cen.
NETLEY RD.
Newton Abbot College
ABBOTSBURY
CHERCOMBE BRIDGE
Littlejoy Plantation
EMBLETT DR.
BARTON
OAK PARK
GLEBE CL.
BUSHELL RD.
Sch.
BROADLANDS
HALCYON
108
Prim. School Play. Fld.
MANOR
CORONATION
BRADLEY LANE
Abbotsbury
A B C D E
1 2 3 4 5 6 7
84
85
72
73
74
075

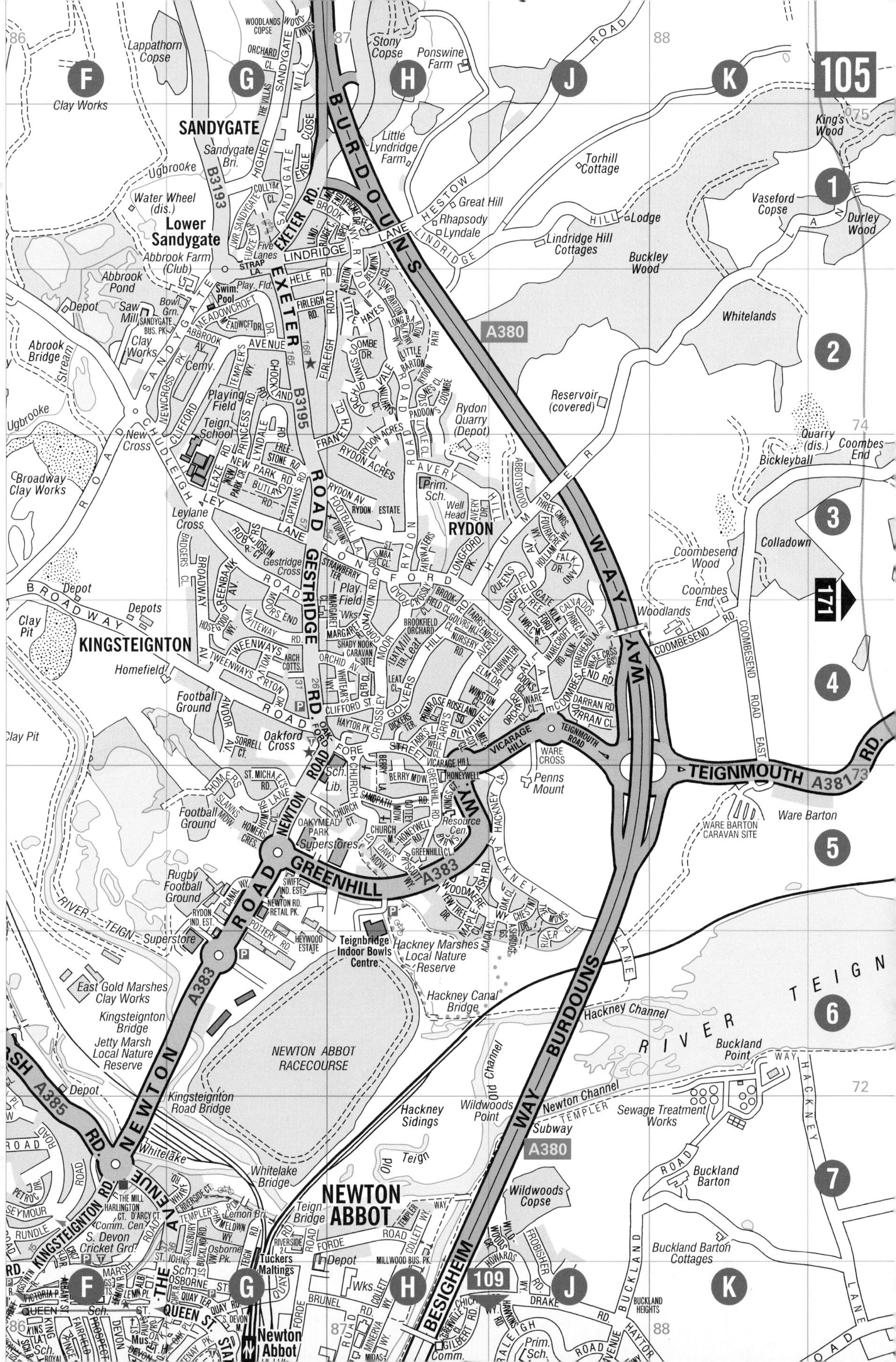
SANDYGATE
Lower Sandygate
KINGSTEIGNTON
RYDON
NEWTON ABBOT
NEWTON ABBOT RACECOURSE
RIVER TEIGN
BURDOUNS WAY
TEIGNMOUTH RD.
A380
A381
A383
A385
B3193
B3195
171
109

Humber
Higher Humber Farm
Westerland
Westerland Cottage
Humber Down
TEIGNMOUTH GOLF COURSE
Club House
Picnic Site
Rowden Copse
Res. (cov.)
Beacon Park Plantation
Ashwell House
Ashwell
Ashwell Croft
Rowden Cross
Higher Redway Farm
Cemy.
CLANAGE CROSS
The Bishops Palace (ruins)
Ashhill Farm
Higher Coombe Farm
WHIDBORNE MEWS
Ash Hill
Summerhill
Fairview
Teignmouth TQ14
Delamore
Orchard Nursery
Shute Farm
BISHOPSTEIGNTON
Prim. Sch.
Forder Cross
Lodge
High Winnard
Coles Barn House
NEWTON
A381
TEIGNMOUTH
ROAD
New Shute Farm
Nursery
BISHOPSTE
R I V E R
Gravel Point
Coombe Cellars
Hearn Field
Pav.
Elmfield
Holywell Cottages
Arch Brook Hill
Arch Brook Bridge
TEIGNFIELD CARAVAN SITE
DEVON VALLEY HOLIDAY VILLAGE
Little Saltings
Ringmore
Longmeadow Farm
Newton Abbot TQ12
Westborough
COMBEINTEIGNHEAD
Butts
Lang Barn Farm
Galmswell Farm
Charlecombe Hill Farm
Mill Bottom Plantation
Littlefield
Moorlands
Rushlands
Ringmore Heights

171

Dawlish
EX7
TEIGNMOUTH
SHALDON
Teignmouth
Coombe
Holcombe Covert
Venn Farm
Buddleford Villa
Buddleford
Buddleford Farm
Holcombe Down Cross
Higher Holcombe House
Higher Holcombe Farm
Middle Holcombe House
Court Farm
Manor Farm
Hazeldown School
Playing Fields
Resr. (cov.)
Comm. Cen.
Cemy.
Trinity School
Nursery Sch.
Higher Coombe Farm
Ford
Headway Cross
Play. Fld.
Prim. Sch.
Inverteign Prim. Sch.
Sports Field
Broadmeadow Sports Cen.
BROADMEADOW IND. EST.
HOSP.
Teignmouth Comm. Sch.
Playing Fields
Sprey Point
The Rowdens
Lido Pool
Teign Corinthian Yacht Club
Mus.
Milford Pk. Sports Grd.
Pav.
Bitton Ho.
Bitton Pk.
Works
Drawbridge
Western Quay
Eastern Quay
New Quay
The Salty
The Den
The Grand Pier
Lucette Lighthouse
The Point
Lifeboat Station
Spratt Sands
East Pole Sand
Foot Ferry
Quay
King George's Field
Ringmore Towers
Fonthill
Homeyards Gdns.
The Ness
Shaldon Wildlife Trust
COAST VIEW HOLIDAY PK.
Shaldon Approach Golf Course
Res. (cov.)
New Barn Farm
EXETER ROAD
B3192
A379
A381
TEIGNMOUTH ROAD
DAWLISH ROAD
HOLCOMBE ROAD
BITTON PARK RD.
HIGHER BROOK ST.
SHALDON BRI.
BRIDGE RD.
TORQUAY RD.
TORQUAY ROAD
HIGHER EXETER
SOUTH DEVON COAST PATH
PROMENADE
F G H J K
1 2 3 4 5 6 7
93 94 295
75 74 73 72

171

EAST OGWELL
BROADLANDS
WOLBOROUGH
ABBOTSKERSWELL
Abbotsbury
Two Mile Oak
Broadridge Wood
Chercombe Bridge
West Hill
Mill Copse
Foxley
Emblett Hill
Bradley Pit
Powsey Moor
Lang's Copse
Undercleave
East Hill
Ransley Quarry (dis.)
Moor View
Manor House
Milton Farm
Stubbins Cross
Swallowfield
Adam Shah
The Shrubbery
Ogwell Grange
Rectory
Rydon Brake
Rydon Ball Farm
New Park
Rydonball Plantation
Rydon Cross
Rydon Lodge
Moorview Farm
Devon Wildlife Centre & Hospital
Rydonball Cross
Higherdown Gardens
Abbotskerswell Cross
Oldbarn Cross
Conitor Copse
Higher Langford
Crystalwood
The Old Cider Works
The Mallands
Abbotshill Caravan Park
Spinner's Moon
Higher Lodge
Grange Park Caravan Park
Grange Quarry (dis.)
Grange Copse
Cricket Ground
Great Castors
Ruby Farm
Two Mile Oak Cross
Dornafield Farm
Home Park
Blackrock Copse
Country Touring Caravan Centre
Broomhill
Gulland Cross
Wolborough Barton
Bishop Dunstan School
Cemetery
Ogwell Cross
Brunel Lodge
Industrial Est.
Baker's Park
Tennis Courts
Nursery
Berry's Wood
Fort
Bradley
Mellon's Copse
Dagger's Copse
River Lemon
Sewage Works
Higher Tor Farm
Paddocks
Newton Abbot College
Newton Abbot Leis. Cen.
ASHBURTON RD.
A383
A381
A382
TOTNES ROAD
WOLBOROUGH ST.
DENBURY ROAD
OGWELL ROAD
WHIDDON
COACH RD.
104
171
176
101

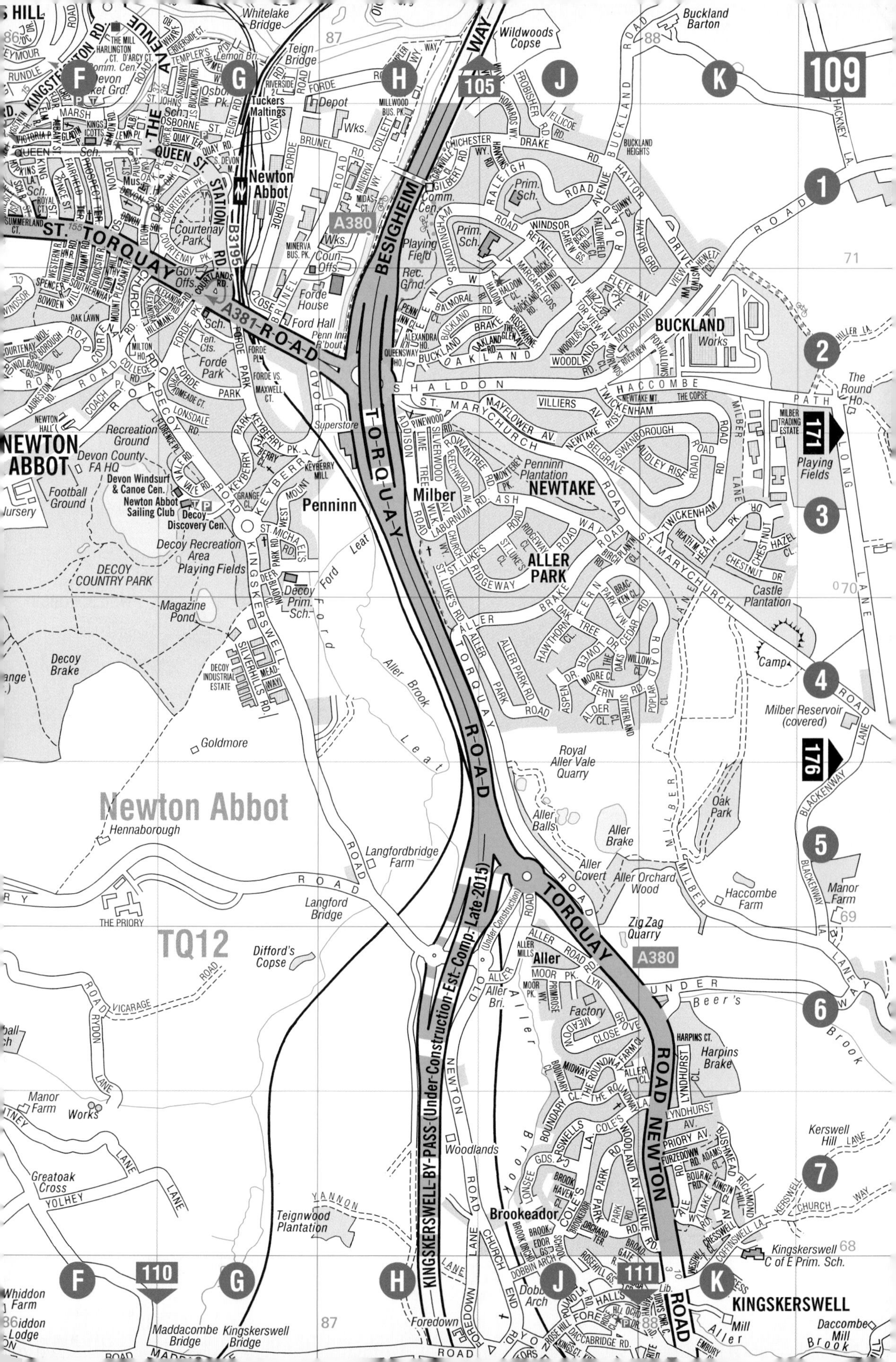

109
105
110
111
171
176
A380
A381
B3195
Newton Abbot
NEWTON ABBOT
TQ12
Whitelake Bridge
Teign Bridge
Wildwoods Copse
Buckland Barton
Tuckers Maltings
Depot
Wks.
Forde House
Ford Hall
Penn Inn R'bout
Superstore
Courtenay Park
Gov. Offs.
Recreation Ground
Devon County FA HQ
Football Ground
Devon Windsurf & Canoe Cen.
Newton Abbot Sailing Club
Decoy Discovery Cen.
Decoy Recreation Area Playing Fields
DECOY COUNTRY PARK
Magazine Pond
Decoy Brake
Decoy Prim. Sch.
DECOY INDUSTRIAL ESTATE
Goldmore
Hennaborough
THE PRIORY
Penninn
Milber
NEWTAKE
ALLER PARK
BUCKLAND
Works
Prim. Sch.
Playing Field
Rec. Grnd.
Comm. Cen.
Pennin Plantation
MILBER TRADING ESTATE
Playing Fields
The Round Ho.
Castle Plantation
Camp
Milber Reservoir (covered)
Royal Aller Vale Quarry
Aller Balls
Aller Brake
Aller Covert
Aller Orchard Wood
Oak Park
Haccombe Farm
Manor Farm
Zig Zag Quarry
Langfordbridge Farm
Langford Bridge
Difford's Copse
Aller
Aller Bri.
Factory
Harpins Brake
Kerswell Hill
Brookeador
Woodlands
Teignwood Plantation
Manor Farm
Works
Greatoak Cross
Whiddon Farm
Maddacombe Bridge
Kingskerswell Bridge
Foredown
Dobbin Arch
KINGSKERSWELL
Kingskerswell C of E Prim. Sch.
Mill
Daccombe Mill
TORQUAY ROAD
BESIGHEIM WAY
ST. MARYCHURCH ROAD
NEWTON ROAD
KINGSKERSWELL BY-PASS (Under Construction Est. Comp. Late 2015)
SHALDON ROAD
HACCOMBE PATH
QUEEN ST.
THE AVENUE
STATION RD.
KINGSTEIGNTON RD.
BUCKLAND ROAD
HAYTOR DRIVE
LONG LANE
MILBER LANE
KEYBERRY ROAD
KINGSKERSWELL ROAD
ALLER BRAKE ROAD
ALLER ROAD
OLD NEWTON ROAD
DECOY ROAD
RYDON LANE
YOLHEY LANE
CHURCH WAY
Aller Brook
Ford Leat
Beer's Brook
Aller Brook
F G H J K
1 2 3 4 5 6 7
86 87 88
68 69 70 71

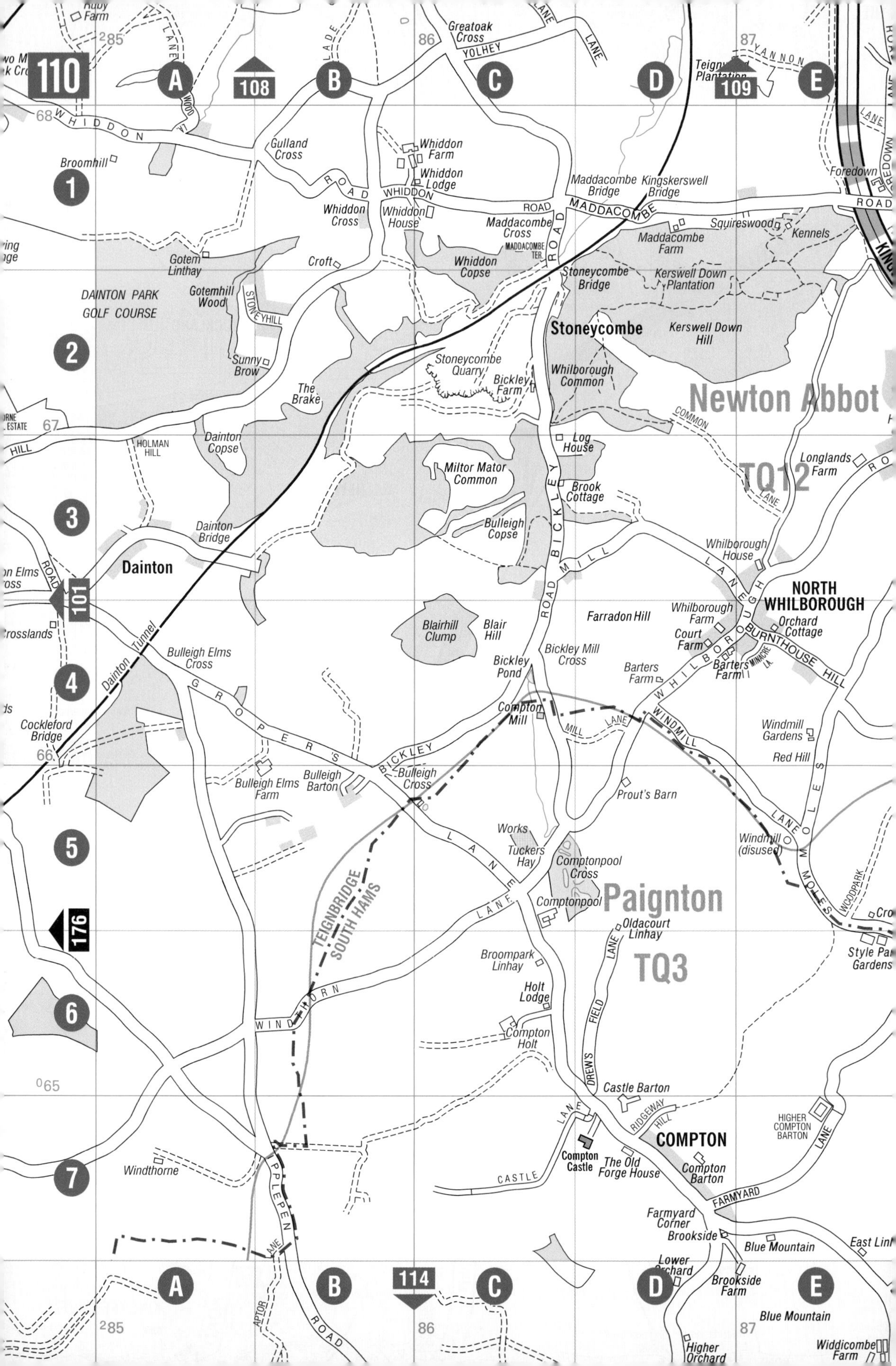

Dainton Park Golf Course
Dainton
Stoneycombe
Newton Abbot
North Whilborough
Paignton
Compton
TQ12
TQ3
Teignbridge
South Hams
Whiddon Farm
Whiddon Lodge
Whiddon House
Whiddon Cross
Gulland Cross
Greatoak Cross
Maddacombe Bridge
Kingskerswell Bridge
Maddacombe Cross
Maddacombe Farm
Squireswood
Kennels
Foredown
Teign Plantation
Broomhill
Gotem Linthay
Gotemhill Wood
Croft
Whiddon Copse
Stoneycombe Bridge
Kerswell Down Plantation
Kerswell Down Hill
Sunny Brow
The Brake
Stoneycombe Quarry
Bickley Farm
Whilborough Common
Dainton Copse
Log House
Miltor Mator Common
Brook Cottage
Longlands Farm
Dainton Bridge
Bulleigh Copse
Whilborough House
Farradon Hill
Whilborough Farm
Orchard Cottage
Court Farm
Blairhill Clump
Blair Hill
Bickley Pond
Bickley Mill Cross
Barters Farm
Crosslands
Bulleigh Elms Cross
Dainton Tunnel
Compton Mill
Windmill Gardens
Red Hill
Cockleford Bridge
Bulleigh Elms Farm
Bulleigh Barton
Bulleigh Cross
Prout's Barn
Works
Tuckers Hay
Comptonpool Cross
Comptonpool
Windmill (disused)
Oldacourt Linhay
Broompark Linhay
Style Park Gardens
Holt Lodge
Compton Holt
Castle Barton
Higher Compton Barton
Windthorne
Compton Castle
The Old Forge House
Compton Barton
Farmyard Corner
Brookside
Blue Mountain
East Linhay
Lower Orchard
Brookside Farm
Higher Orchard
Widdicombe Farm
Whiddon Road
Maddacombe Road
Yolhey Lane
Lade Lane
Wood Lane
Stoneyhill
Holman Hill
Common Lane
Bickley Road
Mill Lane
Groper's Lane
Bickley Lane
Burnthouse Hill
Whilborough Lane
Windmill Lane
Moles Lane
Minacre La.
Woodpark
Drew's Field Lane
Ridgeway Hill
Farmyard Lane
Castle Lane
Windthorn
Ipplepen Road
Aptor
Yannon
Maddacombe Ter.
108
109
101
176
114
A
B
C
D
E
1
2
3
4
5
6
7
285
86
87
68
67
66
65

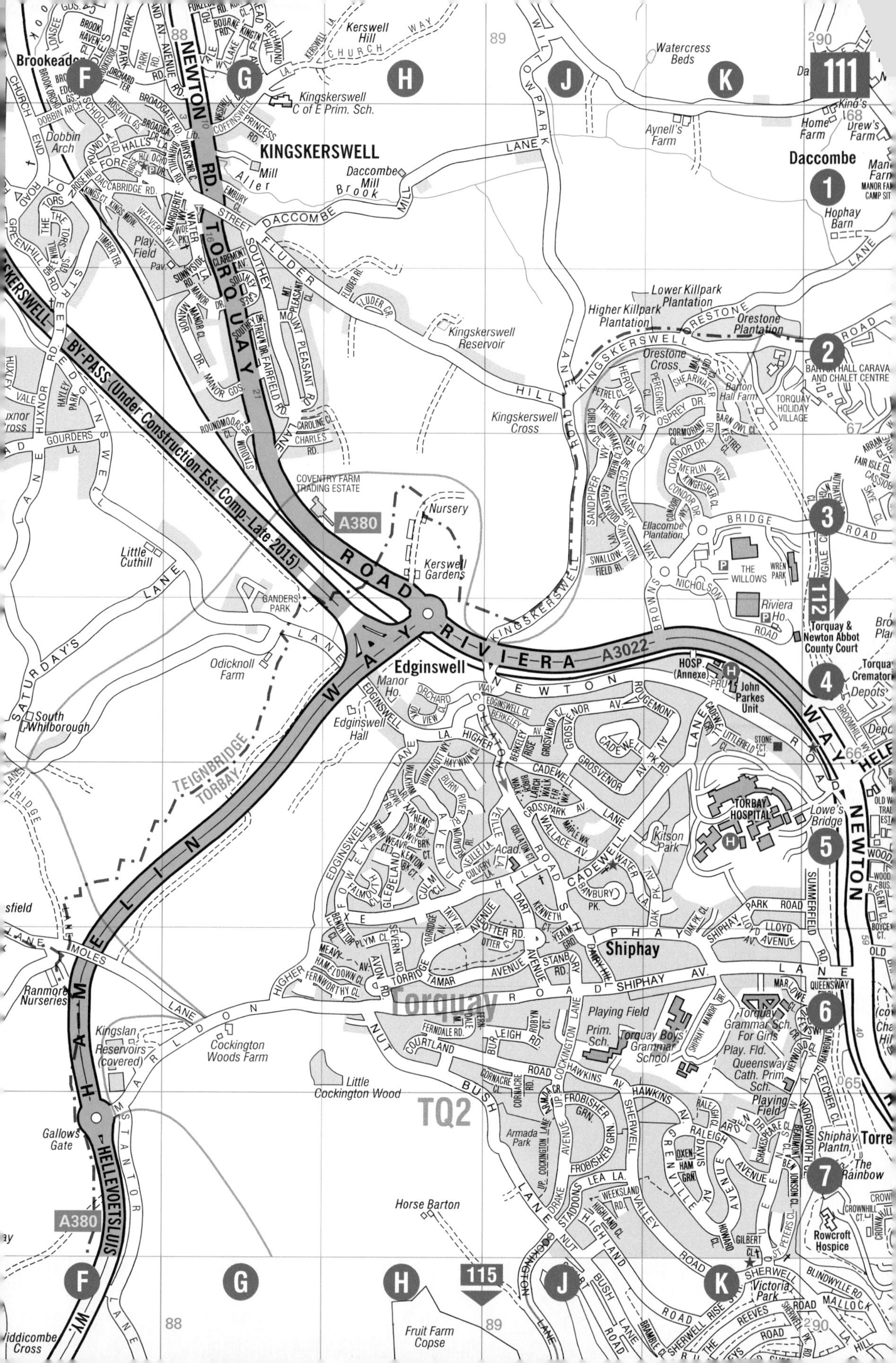
111
112
115
Brookeador
KINGSKERSWELL
Kingskerswell C of E Prim. Sch.
Kerswell Hill
Watercress Beds
Aynell's Farm
Home Farm
Drew's Farm
Daccombe
Hophay Barn
Dobbin Arch
Daccombe Mill
Aller Brook
Mill
Play Field
Lower Killpark Plantation
Higher Killpark Plantation
Orestone Plantation
Kingskerswell Reservoir
Orestone Cross
Barton Hall Farm
BARTON HALL CARAVAN AND CHALET CENTRE
TORQUAY HOLIDAY VILLAGE
Kingskerswell Cross
COVENTRY FARM TRADING ESTATE
Nursery
Kerswell Gardens
Ellacombe Plantation
THE WILLOWS
WREN PARK
Riviera Ho.
Torquay & Newton Abbot County Court
Little Cuthill
GANDERS PARK
Odicknoll Farm
South Whilborough
Edginswell
Manor Ho.
Edginswell Hall
HOSP. (Annexe)
John Parkes Unit
Torquay Crematorium
Depots
TORBAY HOSPITAL
Lowe's Bridge
Kitson Park
TEIGNBRIDGE
TORBAY
Acad.
Shiphay
Torquay
Playing Field
Prim. Sch.
Torquay Boys Grammar School
Torquay Grammar Sch. For Girls
Play. Fld.
Queensway Cath. Prim. Sch.
Playing Field
Shiphay Plantn
Torre
The Rainbow
Rowcroft Hospice
Ranmore Nurseries
Kingslan Reservoirs (covered)
Cockington Woods Farm
Little Cockington Wood
TQ2
Armada Park
Gallows Gate
Horse Barton
Victoria Park
Fruit Fruit Farm Copse
Widdicombe Cross
KINGSKERSWELL BY-PASS (Under Construction-Est. Comp.-Late 2015)
NEWTON RD.
TORQUAY ROAD
RIVIERA WAY A3022
HAMELIN WAY
HELLEVOETSLUIS WAY
NEWTON ROAD
A380
SHIPHAY LANE
SHIPHAY AV.
BARTON HILL
SHERWELL VALLEY ROAD
MOLES LANE
SATURDAY'S LANE
ORESTONE ROAD
KINGSKERSWELL HILL
NICHOLSON ROAD
BRIDGE ROAD
DACCOMBE MILL LANE
FLUDER HILL

112
INSET
Newton Abbot
TQ12
Daccombe
Daccombe Cross
The Old Barn
Home Farm
Drew's Farm
King's Well
Manor Farm
MANOR FARM CAMP SITE
Hophay Barn
Barton Cross
Chalfont
Daccombe Brake
Great Hill
Pinecott
Riding Sch.
Brunel Manor
Ashley Priors
Orestone House
Rock House
Cliffs
Giant Rock
Valley of Rocks
Watcombe Priors
Washington House
Watcombe Hall
Watcombe Woods Picnic Site
Watcombe
Mayfield Sch.
Watcombe Prim. Sch.
The Avenues
Orestone Plantation
TEIGNBRIDGE
TORBAY
KINGSKERSWELL RD.
Barton
BARTON HALL CARAVAN AND CHALET CENTRE
Barton Hall Farm
TORQUAY HOLIDAY VILLAGE
SUNCREST CARAVAN SITE
Mincent Hill
Playing Field
King George V Playing Field
TORQUAY GOLF COURSE
Quarry (dis.)
Petit Tor
TEIGNMOUTH ROAD
A379
ST. MARYCHURCH ROAD
THE WILLOWS
111
TQ2
Prim. School
Industrial Estate
Spts. Cen.
Lummaton Quarry (Limestone)
Combe Pafford
Playing Field
Broomhill Plantation
Depot
Wks.
Torquay & Newton Abbot County Court
Torquay Crematorium
Cemetery
Depots
Johns Parkes Unit
RIVIERA WAY
HELE ROAD
B3199
Hele Cross
Hele
Windmill Hill
Playing Field
Cemetery
BRIDGE RETAIL PARK
OLD WOODS TRADING ESTATE
BARTON ROAD IND. UNITS
WOODLAND BUS. PK.
TORBAY HOSPITAL
Lowe's Bridge
Torquay Comm. Coll.
Playing Fields
Playing Field
Daison Wood
Torquay
Cuthbert Mayne Sch.
St. Marychurch
Babbacombe Model Village
Babbacombe Cliff Railway
Club Ho.
Prim. Sch.
Academy
Cary Park
TQ1
NEWTON ROAD
A3022
Res. (covered)
Chapel Hill
Prim. Sch.
MT. STUART HOSP.
Stantaway Hill
Torquay Utd. FC (Plainmoor)
Swim. Pool
Plainmoor
Torre Grammar Sch. For Girls Play. Fld.
Queensway Cath. Prim.
Playing Field
Shiphay Plantn.
Torre
The Rainbow
Upton
Coach Sta.
Ellacombe
Rowcroft Hospice
TORQUAY
Upton Pk.
Victoria Park
116
Torre
Mem. Gs.
Lib. T.H.
Casino
Res. (cov.)
Warberry C. Prim. Sch.
A
B
C
D
E
1
2
3
4
5
6
7

MAIDENCOMBE **93** F

Shackley Bench

G

INSET

TQ12 **92**

H

GABWELL LA. GABWELL HILL MRTONS RD. STOKE HILL

Higher Gabwell Farm

J

ROAD

K

Torquay **113**

69

TEIGNBRIDGE TORBAY

Higher Gabwell

LONGPARK ROAD

A379

STEEP

TQ1

Ross Hill

1

Higher Shells

Maidencombe Cross

Mandhu

Windsong

Waverly

Solomon's Post

Maidencombe Farm

BRIM

P

Maidencombe Beach

SLADNOR PARK RD.

CADEORES DR.

Court Farm

HILLE

ROCK HOUSE LANE

MAIDENCOMBE

2

CLADDON LANE

TEIGNMOUTH RD.

Maidencombe Manor

Pinecott

Cliffside

Shackley Bench

068

nhills

Whitsand Beach

Watcombe Head

Watcombe Beach

Boat Ho.

Shag Cliff

3

Roundhouse Point

Petit Tor Beach

Petit Tor Downs

4

BABBACOMBE BAY

66

Oddicombe Beach

Blackball Rocks

5

The DOWNS

Half Tide Rock

Babbacombe Beach

Breakwater

Withy Point

BEDFORD RD.

SEFTON CL.

Theatre P

The Grove

Quarry (dis)

Gasking's Rock

Shelter Cove

Flagstaff Point

6

PERINVILLE

WALLS HILL RD.

BABBACOMBE

BABBACOMBE BUS. PK.

Walls Hill

WARWICK CL.

Works

Community Centre

Walls Hill

Quarry (disused)

LONG QUARRY POINT

065

Primary School

Play Fld.

Tennis Courts

Redgate Beach

7

A379

ANSTEYS

Devil's Point

Ansteys Cove

Warberry Copse

Asheldon Copse

Warberry Hill

COVE

Burial Ground

117

J

K

F

G

H

BISHOPS

Stoodley Knowle School

94

BLACK HEAD

Kent's Cavern

Wellswood

Playing Field

295

Windthorne
Compton Castle
The Old Forge House
Compton Barton
Farmyard Corner
Brookside
Blue Mountain
East Linh
Lower Orchard
Brookside Farm
Higher Orchard
Widdicombe Farm
Newton Abbot
TQ12
Stringland La.
Hulstercombe Linhay
Monkshaven
Aptor Cottages
Aptor
Lovelane Cotts.
Lovelane Farm
Church View Farm
Nellor Copse
Marldon House
Aptor Pool
Butterball Copse
Hopper Wood
Marldon Tor
Beech Glade
Plane Tor
Kiln Cross
Strainytor
Strainytor Copse
Totnes
TQ9
Loventor Copse
Burrow Orchard
Sunnylands
MARLDON
Marldon C of E Prim. Sch.
Farthing Cross
Hazelwood Farm
Hazel Wood
Hazelwood
Nursery
Five Lanes
Occombe House
Oak Valley Centre
Culvertor Wood
Westerland Green
Culvertor Farm
Culvertor House
Middle Westerland
Mid. Westerland Cross
Four Acres Roots
Lower Westerland Farm
Lit. Westerland
Windmill Hill
Reservoirs (covered)
A380
Paignton
Wildwoods Farm
Oakend
Oak End Wood
Wildwoods Plantation
The Beacon
South Hams
Torbay
The Old Farm House
TQ3
Widend Touring Park
Ash Plantation
Cruel Cross
Ramshill Cross
Rams Hill Copse
Nursery
Buttshill Copse
Higher Blagdon Cottages
King's Aish House
Smallcombe Cross
King's Aish Orchard
Comm. Cen.
Prim. Sch.
Higher Blagdon
Res. (cov.)
Middle Blagdon
Blagdon
Lower Blagdon Manor
Stone Hill
Comm. Cen.
Marldon Way
King's Ash Road
Totnes Road
Ramshill Lane
Widdicombe Lane
Higher Ramshill
Blagdon Road
Marldon Lane
Smallwell Lane
Farthing Lane
Moorview
Westerland Lane
Vicarage Hill
Five Lanes Road
Penpelep Lane
West Lane

110
176
118

F
G
H
J
K
111
119
116
88
89
290
A380
1
2
3
4
5
6
7
62
61
Horse Barton
Widdicombe Cross
Stanton
Stanton Cottages
Stanton Barton
Stanton Linhay
Fruit Farm Copse
Rosery Grange
Meadow Farm
Almhouses
Cockington Country Pk. Visitor Cen.
Cockington Court Craft Centre
Cockington Country Park
Church Wood
Cockington Forge
Cockington
Ridgefield
Chelston
Victoria Park
Torquay
TQ2
Warren Barn
Lanscombe
Lodge
Hellinghay Plantation
Thornhill Brake
Manscombe Plantation
Scadson Plantation
Petersfield
TOTNES ROAD
COCKINGTON LANE
Occombe Cross
Radio Transmitting Sta.
Three Burrows
East Down
Burrow Down
East Down Plantation
Round Down Wood
Browse's Brake
Hollicombe Lake
Round Hill
Ten Acre Brake
Livermead
Preston Prim. Sch.
Hollicombe
Depot
Round Hill
Oil Cove
TORBAY
Preston Park
Playing Field
Preston
Shorton
Shorton Manor
Shorton Woods
Shorton Farm
Res. (cov.)
Hollicombe Park
Hollicombe Beach
Chadwell Cen.
Resource Cen.
Hollicombe Head
TORBAY ROAD
A3022
B3201
B3060
Preston Sands
Comm. Cen.
Oldway Mansion
Oldway
Tennis Courts
Playing Field
Oldway Primary Sch.
Torbay Sch.
Parkfield
TOR BAY
REDCLIFFE COURT
Playing Field
Cemetery
War Mem.
Cemy.
Lib.
Victoria Park
Paignton Pier
PAIGNTON
The Green
Sands
HOSP.
SHOP. CEN.
ESPLANADE RD.
MARINE PARADE
MANOR RD.

112
115
A
B
C
D
E
1
2
3
4
5
6
7
290
91
92
64
63
62
61
Ellacombe
Rowcroft Hospice
Torre
Victoria Park
Chelston
Torre Abbey
Waves Leis. Pool
Riviera Intl. Cen.
Torre Abbey Meadows
Abbey Park
Spanish Barn
Torre Abbey Sands
TORQUAY
Princess Theatre
Princess Pier
Landing Stage
Harbreck Rock
Corbyn's Beach
Corbyn's Head
Thornhill Brake
Two Parks
Torquay
Livermead
Livermead Sands
LIVERMEAD HEAD
Oil Cove
Round Hill
Hollicombe Park
Chadwell Cen.
Resource Cen.
Hollicombe Head
Torquay to Brixham (Summer Only) Foot Ferry
South Pier
Slipway
Beacon Quay Slipway
Living Coasts
Haldon Pier
The Millstones
Beacon Cove
Prince of Wales Steps
Peaked Tor Cove
Old Harbour
The Pavilion
Stentiford Hill
Gala Bingo
Casino
Upton Pk.
Mus.
Torwood Gds.
Sports Cen.
Warberry C Prim. Sch.
Torquay
TORBAY ROAD
A3022 ROAD
AVENUE
THE KING'S DR.
A379
STRAND
TORWOOD STREET
TOR

F   G   H   113   J   K

94   295

Devil's Point

Ansteys Cove

Beach

Warberry Copse

Warberry Hill

THE ATRIUM

Wellswood

Burial Ground

BLACK HEAD

Stoodley Knowle School

Kent's Cavern & Visitor Centre

Playing Field

Brandy Cove

1

64

Hope Cove

2

HOPE'S NOSE

Lincombe Slopes

Manor Gardens

Kilmorie

MARINE

AVENUE

DRIVE

WHIDBORNE

THATCHER

Thatcher House

Compass Marine South Mount

3

Meadfoot Beach

Slipway

Thatcher Point

063

Thatcher Rock

4

5

62

6

B A Y

7

61

F   G   H   J   K

93   94   295

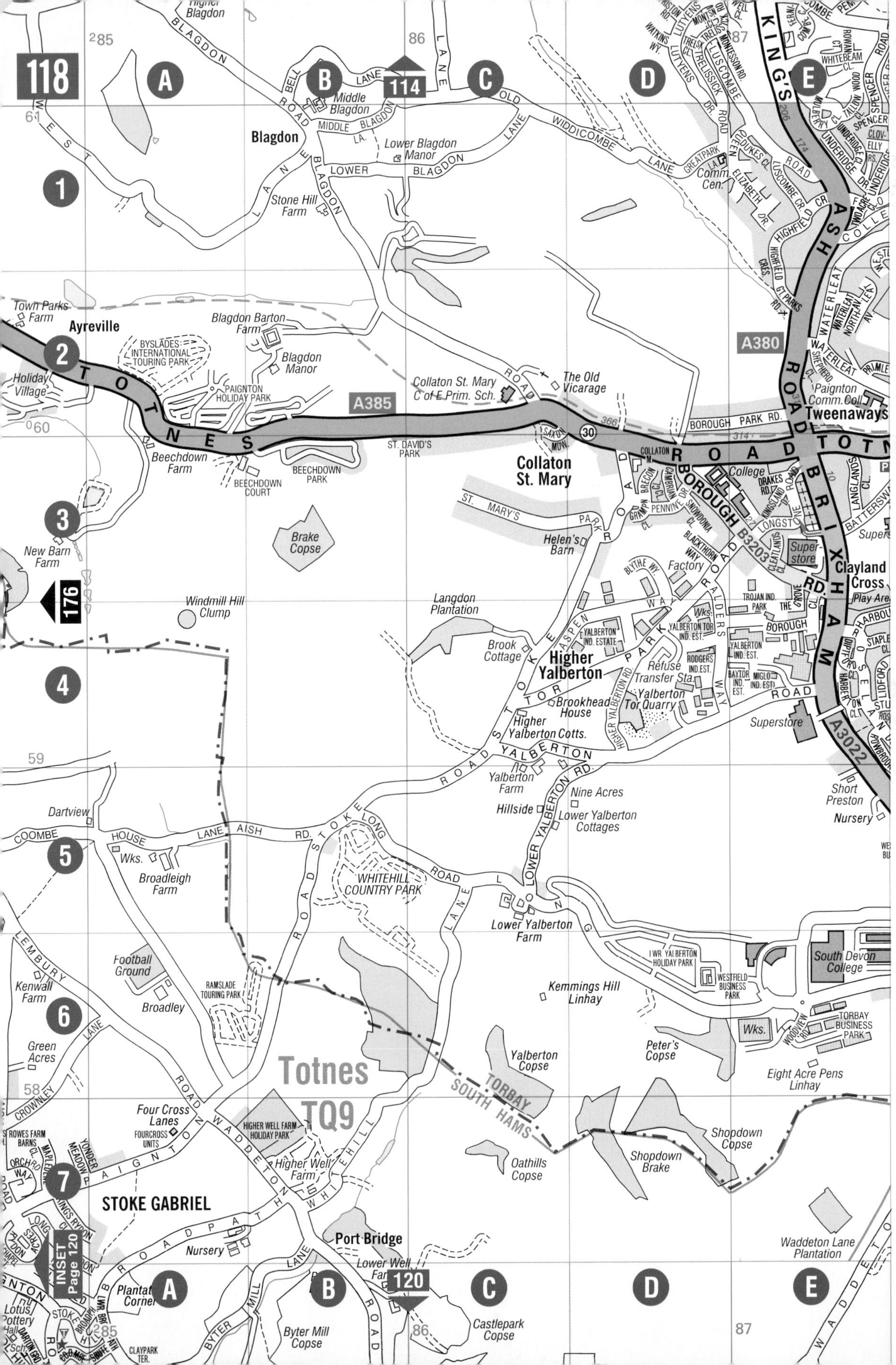
Higher Blagdon
Blagdon
Middle Blagdon
Lower Blagdon Manor
Stone Hill Farm
Town Parks Farm
Ayreville
Blagdon Barton Farm
BYSLADES INTERNATIONAL TOURING PARK
Blagdon Manor
PAIGNTON HOLIDAY PARK
Holiday Village
Collaton St. Mary C of E Prim. Sch.
The Old Vicarage
A385
A380
TOTNES ROAD
Beechdown Farm
BEECHDOWN COURT
BEECHDOWN PARK
ST. DAVID'S PARK
Collaton St. Mary
Tweenaways
Paignton Comm. Coll.
BOROUGH PARK RD.
College
B3203
KING'S ASH ROAD
BRIXHAM RD.
New Barn Farm
Brake Copse
Helen's Barn
Factory
Super-store
Clayland Cross
Windmill Hill Clump
Langdon Plantation
Brook Cottage
Higher Yalberton
YALBERTON IND. ESTATE
YALBERTON TOR IND. EST.
Refuse Transfer Sta.
Yalberton Tor Quarry
Brookhead House
Higher Yalberton Cotts.
TROJAN IND. PARK
RODGERS IND. EST.
BAYTOR IND. EST.
MIGLO IND. EST.
Superstore
A3022
Yalberton Farm
Nine Acres
Hillside
Lower Yalberton Cottages
Short Preston
Nursery
Dartview
COOMBE HOUSE LANE
AISH RD.
Wks.
Broadleigh Farm
WHITEHILL COUNTRY PARK
LONG ROAD
Lower Yalberton Farm
IWR YALBERTON HOLIDAY PARK
WESTFIELD BUSINESS PARK
South Devon College
Kemmings Hill Linhay
TORBAY BUSINESS PARK
Football Ground
Kenwall Farm
Broadley
RAMSLADE TOURING PARK
Green Acres
Yalberton Copse
Peter's Copse
Eight Acre Pens Linhay
Totnes TQ9
TORBAY
SOUTH HAMS
Four Cross Lanes
FOURCROSS UNITS
HIGHER WELL FARM HOLIDAY PARK
Higher Well Farm
Oathills Copse
Shopdown Brake
Shopdown Copse
STOKE GABRIEL
Port Bridge
Nursery
Lower Well Farm
Waddeton Lane Plantation
Plantation Corner
Byter Mill Copse
Castlepark Copse
Lotus Pottery
CLAYPARK TER.
INSET Page 120
114
120
176

F
G
H
J
K
115
121
1
2
3
4
5
6
7
PAIGNTON
Paignton
TOR BAY
TQ3
TQ4
Brixham
TQ5
GOODRINGTON
Goodrington
St. Michaels
Primley Cross
BROADSANDS
Paignton Pier
Paignton Harbour
Black Rock
Fairy Cove
Savage Hole
ROUNDHAM HEAD
Cliff Gardens
Goodrington Sands North
Middle Stone
Goodrington Sands South
Saltern Cove
Armchair Rock
Shell Cove
Crystal Cove
Broad Sands
Churston Point
Paignton Zoo
Botanic Nursery
Jungle Express
Quarry (dis.)
Clennon Hill
Playing Field
Sports Pitch
Sports Fields
Torbay Leisure Cen.
Quaywest Waterpark
Grand Prix Go Karts
The Seashore Cen.
Goodrington Park
Dartmouth Steam Railway
Sugar Loaf Hill & Saltern Cove Nature Reserve
Recreation Ground
Primley Wood
Primley House
Roselands Prim. Sch.
White Rock Prim. Sch.
Apollo Cinema
Victoria Park
Marl Pits
Works
DARTMOUTH ROAD
BRIXHAM ROAD
A3022
A379
B3201
TORBAY RD.
SANDS RD.
ESPLANADE
PENWILL WAY
GOODRINGTON ROAD
HOOKHILLS ROAD
GRANGE ROAD
ROSELANDS DRIVE
MARLDON RD.
HYDE RD.
TORQUAY RD.
CECIL RD.

120
STOKE GABRIEL
Port Bridge
118
Nursery
Plantation Corner
Pords Bridge
Lower Well Farm
Higher Well Farm
Oathills Copse
Totnes
Castlepark Copse
TQ9
Byter Mill Copse
Quarry Wood
Water Lane Plantation
Mill Pool
Byter Downe House
Waddeton Pool
South Downs Wood
Overcreek
WADDETON ROAD
Pool Plantation
East Farm
Waddeton Home farm
Waddeton Barton
Waddeton Court
Sandridge Bottom
Kennel Wood
Toms Plantation
East Wood
The Cliffs
Sandridge Boat House
Slate Wood
Slipways
Boat House
Quay
RIVER DART
Higher Gurrow Point
Gurrow Point House
Lower Gurrow Point
Flat Owers
INSET
STOKE GABRIEL
Totnes
Five-Knot Farm
Southlands Kennels
TQ9
Southlands Farm
Totnes to Dartmouth (Summer Only) Foot Ferry
Rivendale
East Cornworthy
Seagull House
DITTISHAM MILL CREEK
Dittisham Mill
176
DITTISHAM COURT
Football Pitch
Dittisham Sailing Club
DITTISHAM
Bramble Torre
Meadow Cottages
Pier
Foot Ferry
Greenway Quay
Ferry Cottage
Greenway
Hunterswood
Totnes to Greenway (Summer Only) Foot Ferry
Dartmouth
TQ6
Lower Dittisham
The Old Rectory
The River Farm
Binhay Copse
River Farm House
Greenway & Dittisham to Dartmouth (Summer Only) Foot Ferry
Anchor Stone
Cott Farm
River Farm Cottage
Bozomzeal Cross
Reservoir (covered)
Res. (cov.)
Hamblyn's Coombe
Waterfields Cottage
Bullcombe Copse
Foxhole Copse
Downton Wood
LORD'S WOOD
Little Coombe
Foxenhole
Fire Beacon Hill
124
Little Coombe Plantation

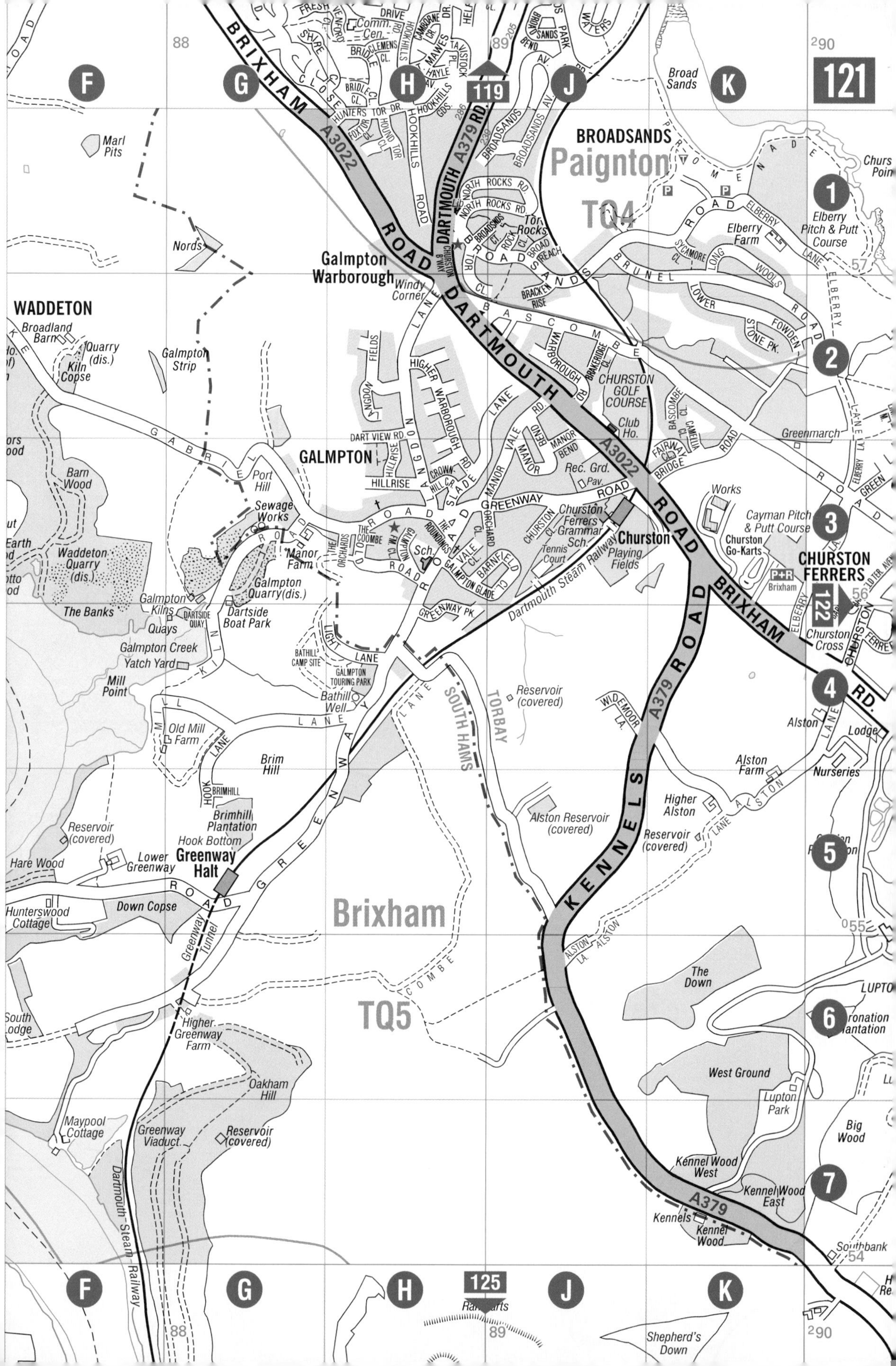
BROADSANDS
Paignton
TQ4
Broad Sands
Elberry Pitch & Putt Course
Elberry Farm
Churston Point
Galmpton Warborough
Windy Corner
WADDETON
Broadland Barn
Quarry (dis.)
Kiln Copse
Galmpton Strip
Marl Pits
Nords
GALMPTON
Port Hill
Sewage Works
Manor Farm
Barn Wood
Waddeton Quarry (dis.)
The Banks
Galmpton Kilns
Dartside Quay
Quays
Dartside Boat Park
Galmpton Quarry (dis.)
Galmpton Creek
Yatch Yard
Mill Point
Bathill Camp Site
Galmpton Touring Park
Bathill Well
Old Mill Farm
Brim Hill
Brimhill Plantation
Hook Bottom
Reservoir (covered)
Lower Greenway
Greenway Halt
Hare Wood
Hunterswood Cottage
Down Copse
Greenway Tunnel
South Lodge
Higher Greenway Farm
Oakham Hill
Maypool Cottage
Greenway Viaduct
Dartmouth Steam Railway
Brixham
TQ5
SOUTH HAMS
TORBAY
Alston Reservoir (covered)
Higher Alston
Alston Farm
Alston
Lodge
Nurseries
CHURSTON GOLF COURSE
Club Ho.
Rec. Grd.
Pav.
Churston Ferrers Grammar Sch.
Tennis Court
Churston
Playing Fields
Works
Cayman Pitch & Putt Course
Churston Go-Karts
P+R Brixham
CHURSTON FERRERS
Churston Cross
Greenmarch
The Down
West Ground
Lupton Park
Big Wood
Kennel Wood West
Kennel Wood East
Kennels
Kennel Wood
Southbank
Shepherd's Down
Ramparts
BRIXHAM ROAD
DARTMOUTH ROAD
A3022
A379
DARTMOUTH RD.
KENNELS ROAD
GREENWAY ROAD
GABRIEL
BASCOMBE ROAD
BROADSANDS ROAD
BROADSANDS AV.
BRUNEL ROAD
ELBERRY LANE
PROMENADE
119
122
125
F G H J K
1 2 3 4 5 6 7
88 89 290
57 56 55 54

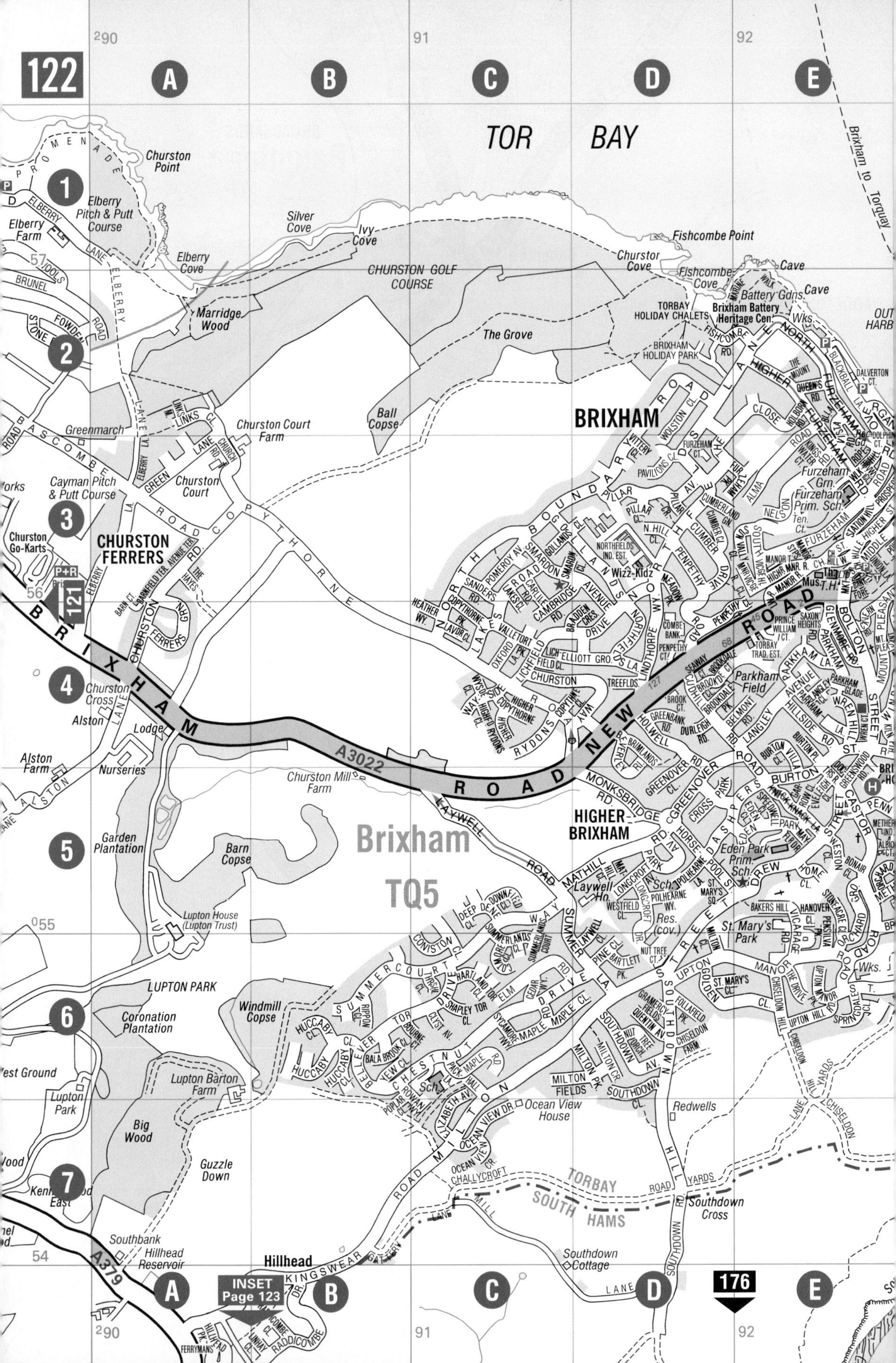
TOR BAY
Churston Point
Elberry Pitch & Putt Course
Elberry Farm
Silver Cove
Ivy Cove
Elberry Cove
Fishcombe Point
Churston Cove
Fishcombe Cove
Cave
Battery Gdns.
CHURSTON GOLF COURSE
Marridge Wood
The Grove
TORBAY HOLIDAY CHALETS
Brixham Battery Heritage Cen.
BRIXHAM HOLIDAY PARK
Brixham to Torquay
Ball Copse
BRIXHAM
Greenmarch
Churston Court Farm
Churston Court
Cayman Pitch & Putt Course
Churston Go-Karts
CHURSTON FERRERS
Churston Cross
Alston
Lodge
Alston Farm
Nurseries
Churston Mill Farm
A3022
BRIXHAM ROAD
NEW ROAD
Garden Plantation
Barn Copse
Brixham
TQ5
HIGHER BRIXHAM
Lupton House (Lupton Trust)
LUPTON PARK
Coronation Plantation
Windmill Copse
Lupton Barton Farm
Lupton Park
Big Wood
Guzzle Down
Ocean View House
Redwells
TORBAY
SOUTH HAMS
Southdown Cross
Southdown Cottage
Southbank
Hillhead Reservoir
Hillhead
A379
Wizz-Kidz
Parkham Field
Eden Park Prim. Sch.
St. Mary's Park
Laywell Ho.
Furzeham Grn.
Furzeham Prim. Sch.
Mus.
T.H.
290
91
92
57
56
055
54
INSET Page 123
121
176

Brixham Breakwater Lighthouse
THE BREAKWATER
Brixham Marina
Jetty
Torbay Lifeboat Station
Breakwater Beach
The Hard
Shoalstone Beach
Shoalstone Pool
Shoalstone Point
Coastguard Station
BERRY HEAD ROAD
VICTORIA RD.
Ash Hole Cavern
Berry Head Farm
Quay
Berry Head Quarry (dis.)
Berry Head Fortifications
Berry Head Lighthouse
BERRY HEAD
Beacon
Visitor Cen.
Old Redoubt
BERRY HEAD COUNTRY PARK
The Bungalow
Beacon
LOUVILLE CAMP
Old Redoubt
Picnic Site
Berry Head National Nature Reserve
Mew Stone
Cod Rock
LANDSCOVE HOLIDAY VILLAGE
Durl Head
Durl Rock
Kiln House
GILLARD ROAD
Football Ground
Pav.
Playing Field
Leisure Centre
Brixham College
Brixham C of E Prim. Sch.
Play. Fld.
Swim. Cen.
Astley Park
Pav.
New Fish Quay
New Pier
Outdoor Education Centre
HARBOUR
Golden Hind
Statue
Brixham Yacht Club
Foot Ferry (Summer Only)
HEATH RISE
MARINA DRIVE
WALL PARK ROAD
RANSCOMBE RD.
LOWER REA RD.
HIGHER RANSCOMBE
CENTRY RD.
BARN ROAD
DOUGLAS AV.
SEA LANE
MARINA RD.
MUDSTONE LANE
MEADOWS
HIGHER PENN
ST. MARY'S BAY HOLIDAY CENTRE
ST. MARY'S BAY
Mussel Rock
ENGLISH CHANNEL
Camping Site
SHARKHAM POINT CARAVAN PARK
SOUTH BAY HOLIDAY CAMP
Mine (dis.)
Berry Head National Nature Reserve
Shaft (dis.)
Mag Rock
Sharkham Point
INSET
A379
KINGSWEAR ROAD
Hillhead
RADDICOMBE DRIVE
Raddicombe Farm
PENHILL LA.
Pennhill Chase
Pennhill
BRIDGE RD.
SLAPPER'S HILL
B3205
HILLHEAD HOLIDAY PARK
Brixham TQ5
Dartmouth TQ6
Nethway Quarry (disused)
F
G
H
J
K
1
2
3
4
5
6
7
93
94
295
57
56
54
053
290
91

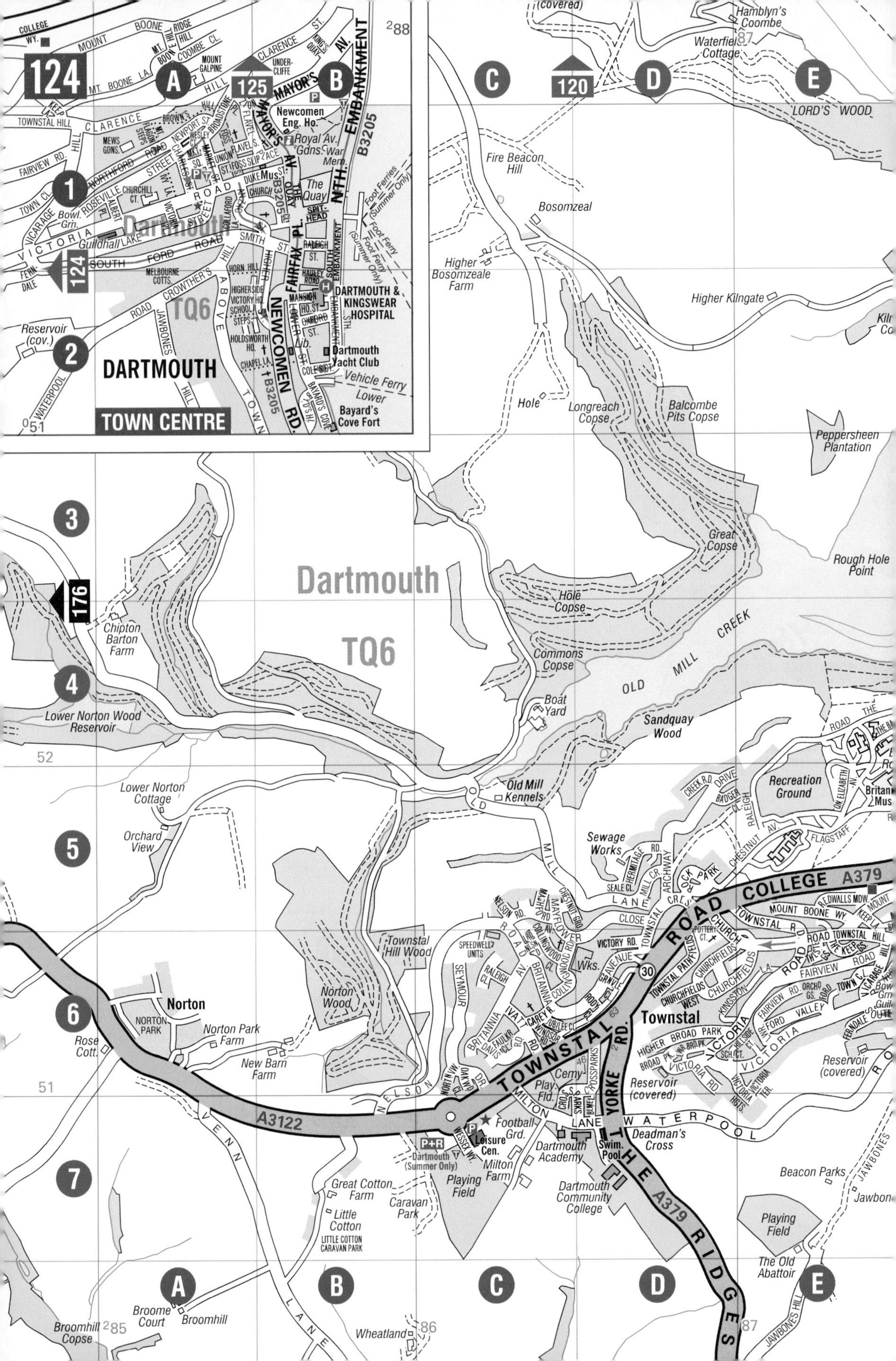

124
125
120
176
TOWN CENTRE
DARTMOUTH
Dartmouth
TQ6
MOUNT BOONE
BOONE RIDGE
MT. BOONE LA.
COLLEGE WY.
COOMBE CL.
MOUNT GALPINE
CLARENCE HILL
CLARENCE ST.
KING'S QUAY
UNDERCLIFFE
MAYOR'S AV.
NTH. EMBANKMENT
B3205
Newcomen Eng. Ho.
Royal Av. Gdns.
War Mem.
TOWNSTAL HILL
FAIRVIEW RD.
MEWS GDNS.
NORTHFORD ROAD
NEWPORT ST.
BROADSTONE
FLAVEL PLACE
MKT. SQ.
FOSS ST.
DUKE ST.
Mus.
The Quay
SPIT-HEAD
Foot Ferries (Summer Only)
Foot Ferry (Summer Only)
Foot Ferry
TOWN CL.
VICARAGE HILL
ROSEVILLE ST.
CHURCHILL CT.
ALBERT PL.
Bowl. Grn.
VICTORIA ROAD
Guildhall
LAKE
SOUTH FORD ROAD
SMITH ST.
FAIRFAX PL.
RALEIGH ST.
HAULEY ROAD
SOUTH EMBANKMENT
FERNDALE
MELBOURNE COTTS.
HORN HILL
HIGHERSIDE
VICTORY HO.
SCHOOL STEPS
HOLDSWORTH HO.
CHAPEL LA.
CROWTHER'S HILL
ABOVE TOWN
NEWCOMEN RD.
MANSION HO. ST.
OXFORD ST.
Lib.
DARTMOUTH & KINGSWEAR HOSPITAL
Dartmouth Yacht Club
COLE'S CT.
Vehicle Ferry
Lower Bayard's Cove Fort
BAYARD'S COVE
Reservoir (cov.)
WATERPOOL ROAD
JAWBONES HILL
Hamblyn's Coombe
Waterfield Cottage
LORD'S WOOD
Fire Beacon Hill
Bosomzeal
Higher Bosomzeale Farm
Higher Kilngate
Hole
Longreach Copse
Balcombe Pits Copse
Peppersheen Plantation
Great Copse
Rough Hole Point
Hole Copse
Chipton Barton Farm
Commons Copse
OLD MILL CREEK
Boat Yard
Sandquay Wood
Lower Norton Wood Reservoir
Lower Norton Cottage
Orchard View
Old Mill Kennels
OLD MILL LANE
Recreation Ground
Britannia Mus.
Sewage Works
HERMITAGE RD.
ARCHWAY DRIVE
CREEK RD.
BADGER CL.
RALEIGH
CHESTNUT AV.
FLAGSTAFF
COLLEGE ROAD
A379
REDWALLS MDW.
MOUNT BOONE WY.
TOWNSTAL RD.
TOWNSTAL HILL
CHURCH ROAD
CHURCHFIELDS
KINGSTON LA.
FAIRVIEW ROAD
Townstal Hill Wood
SPEEDWELL UNITS
SEYMOUR DR.
RALEIGH CL.
NELSON RD.
MAYFLOWER CL.
VICTORY RD.
AVENUE
Wks.
BRITANNIA AV.
Norton Wood
Norton
NORTON PARK
Norton Park Farm
Rose Cott.
New Barn Farm
Townstal
HIGHER BROAD PARK
VICTORIA RD
Reservoir (covered)
TOWNSTAL RD.
YORKE RD.
Cemy.
Play Fld.
MILTON LANE
WATERPOOL
Deadman's Cross
A3122
NELSON
Football Grd.
Leisure Cen.
P+R
Dartmouth (Summer Only)
Milton Farm
Dartmouth Academy
Swim. Pool
Dartmouth Community College
Beacon Parks
Jawbones
VENN LANE
Great Cotton Farm
Little Cotton
LITTLE COTTON CARAVAN PARK
Caravan Park
Playing Field
THE RIDGES
A379
Playing Field
The Old Abattoir
JAWBONES HILL
Broome Court
Broomhill
Broomhill Copse
Wheatland
A
B
C
D
E
1
2
3
4
5
6
7

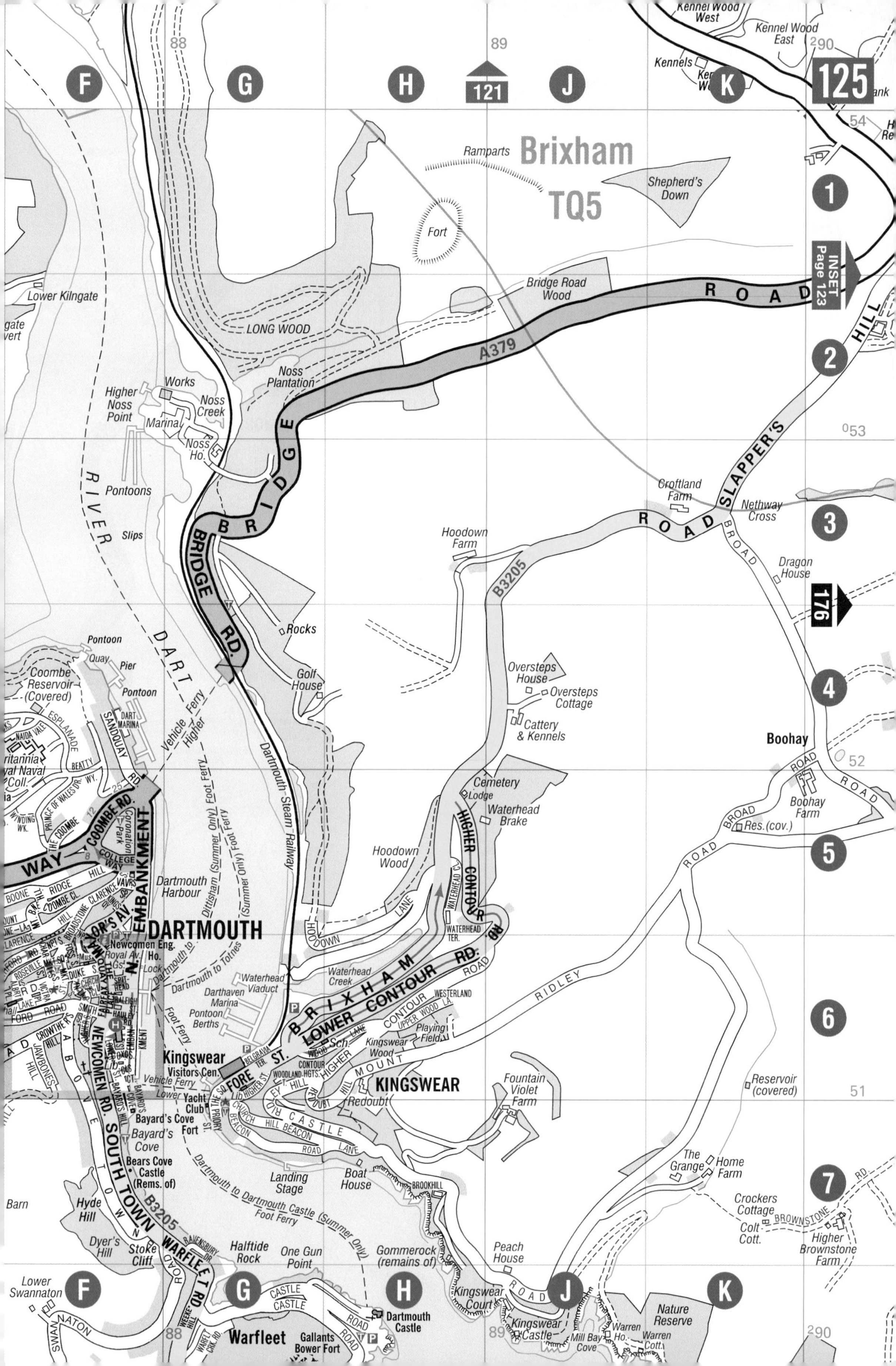

Brixham
TQ5

Ramparts

Shepherd's
Down

Fort

Bridge Road
Wood

ROAD

Lower Kilngate

gate
vert

LONG WOOD

Higher
Noss
Point

Works

Noss Creek

Marina

Noss
Plantation

A379

BRIDGE

Croftland
Farm

ROAD

SLAPPER'S

Nethway
Cross

BROAD

HILL

Dragon
House

176

INSET
Page 123

Noss
Ho.

Pontoons

RIVER

Slips

Hoodown
Farm

B3205

Oversteps
House

Oversteps
Cottage

Boohay

BROAD

ROAD

Cattery
& Kennels

ROAD

Boohay
Farm

Res. (cov.)

BRIDGE RD.

Pontoon

Coombe
Reservoir
(Covered)

Quay

Pier

Pontoon

DART MARINA

Rocks

Golf
House

DART

Cemetery
Lodge

Waterhead
Brake

NAIDA VALE

ESPLANADE

SANDQUAY

Vehicle Ferry

Higher
Foot Ferry

Britannia
yal Naval
Coll.
ia

THE PRINCE OF WALES RD.

Hoodown
Wood

HIGHER CONTOUR RD.

Ditcham (Summer Only) Foot Ferry

Dartmouth Steam Railway

Dartmouth to Totnes

WINDING WK.

The COOMBE

COOMBE RD.

Coronation
Park

College
Way

COOMBE CL.

WAY

VAVRS.

EMBANKMENT

Dartmouth
Harbour

HOODOWN LANE

WATERHEAD RD

HIGHER CONTOUR RD.

RIDLEY

Reservoir
(covered)

BOONE

COOMBE CL.

RIDGE

Newcomen Eng.
Ho.

DARTMOUTH

Dartmouth to Totnes

Lock

Waterhead
Creek

WATERHEAD
TER.

BRIXHAM

LOWER CONTOUR RD.

ROAD

CLARENCE

MOUNT

UPPER CONTOUR LA.

Darthaven
Marina

Pontoon
Berths

Playing
Field

Kingswear
Wood

MOUNT

MOUNT

Fountain
Violet
Farm

WESTERLAND

NEWCOMEN RD.

SOUTH TOWN

SWANNATON

HYDE RD.

Foot Ferry

Lower Yacht
Club

FORE ST.

BELGRAVE TER.

HIGHER ST.

Sch.

WOODLAND HGTS.

CONTOUR

HILL

Kingswear

Visitors Cen.

Vehicle Ferry

KINGSWEAR

Reservoir
(covered)

Bayard's
Cove
Fort

Bayard's
Cove

Bears Cove
Castle
(Rems. of)

THE PRIORY

CHURCH HILL

CASTLE HILL BEACON

REDOUBT

Redoubt

CASTLE ROAD

BEACON LANE

Fountain
Violet
Farm

The
Grange

Home
Farm

B3205

Barn

Hyde
Hill

Dyer's
Hill

Stoke
Cliff

RAVENSBURY
RD.

WARFLEET
ROAD

Landing
Stage

Boat
House

Dartmouth to Dartmouth Castle (Summer Only)
Foot Ferry

BROOKHILL

Crockers
Cottage

Colt
Cott.

BROWNSTONE

Higher
Brownstone
Farm

Lower
Swannaton

F

Warfleet

CASTLE ROAD

Halftide
Rock

One Gun
Point

Dartmouth
Castle

Gallants
Bower Fort

Gommerock
(remains of)

Kingswear
Court

Kingswear
Castle

Peach
House

Warren
Ho.

Mill Bay

Warren
Cott.

Nature
Reserve

ROAD

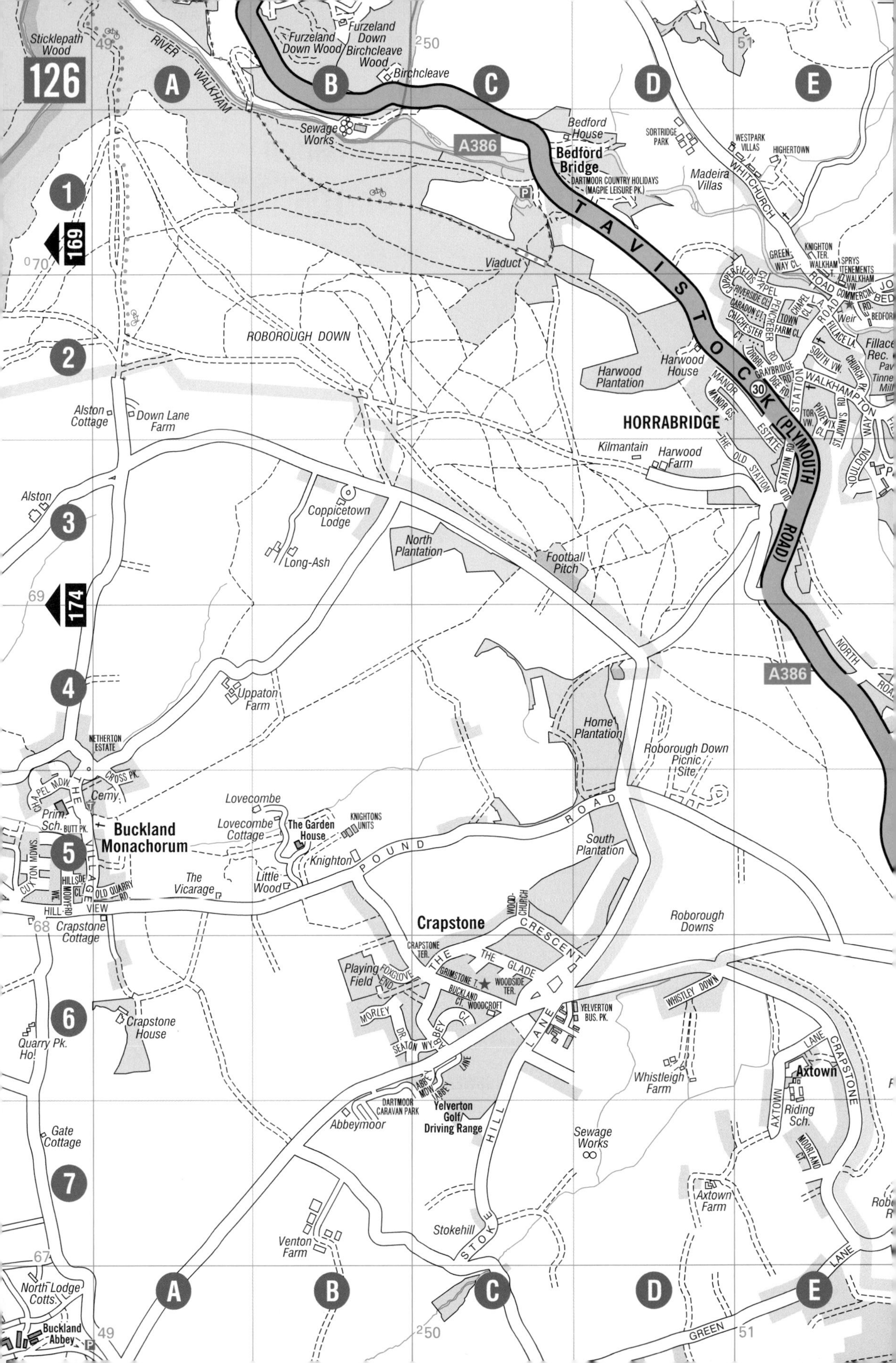
Sticklepath Wood
River Walkham
Furzeland Down Wood
Furzeland Down
Birchcleave Wood
Birchcleave
Sewage Works
A386
Bedford House
Bedford Bridge
Dartmoor Country Holidays (Magpie Leisure Pk.)
Tavistock (Plymouth) Road
Sortridge Park
Westpark Villas
Hightown
Madeira Villas
Whitchurch Road
Viaduct
Roborough Down
Harwood Plantation
Harwood House
HORRABRIDGE
Kilmantain
Harwood Farm
Alston Cottage
Down Lane Farm
Alston
Coppicetown Lodge
Long-Ash
North Plantation
Football Pitch
169
174
Uppaton Farm
Netherton Estate
Home Plantation
Roborough Down Picnic Site
Cross Pk.
Cemy.
Chapel Mdw.
Prim. Sch.
Butt Pk.
Buckland Monachorum
Lovecombe
Lovecombe Cottage
The Garden House
Knightons Units
Pound Road
Knighton
South Plantation
The Vicarage
Little Wood
Old Quarry Rd.
Village View
Crapstone Cottage
Crapstone
Wood-church
The Crescent
Crapstone Ter.
The Glade
Playing Field
Foxglove End
Grimstone T.
Woodside Ter.
Buckland Ct.
Woodcroft
Yelverton Bus. Pk.
Whistley Down
Roborough Downs
Crapstone House
Quarry Pk. Ho.
Morley Dr.
Seaton Wy.
Abbey Cl.
Abbey Mdw.
Abbey Lane
Dartmoor Caravan Park
Abbeymoor
Yelverton Golf/ Driving Range
Hill Lane
Whistleigh Farm
Axtown
Axtown Lane
Crapstone Lane
Riding Sch.
Moorland Ct.
Sewage Works
Gate Cottage
Axtown Farm
Venton Farm
Stokehill
Stoke Hill
North Lodge Cotts.
Buckland Abbey
Green Lane
Walkhampton Road
Station Road
Manor Estate
The Old Station
Fillace Rec.
Weir

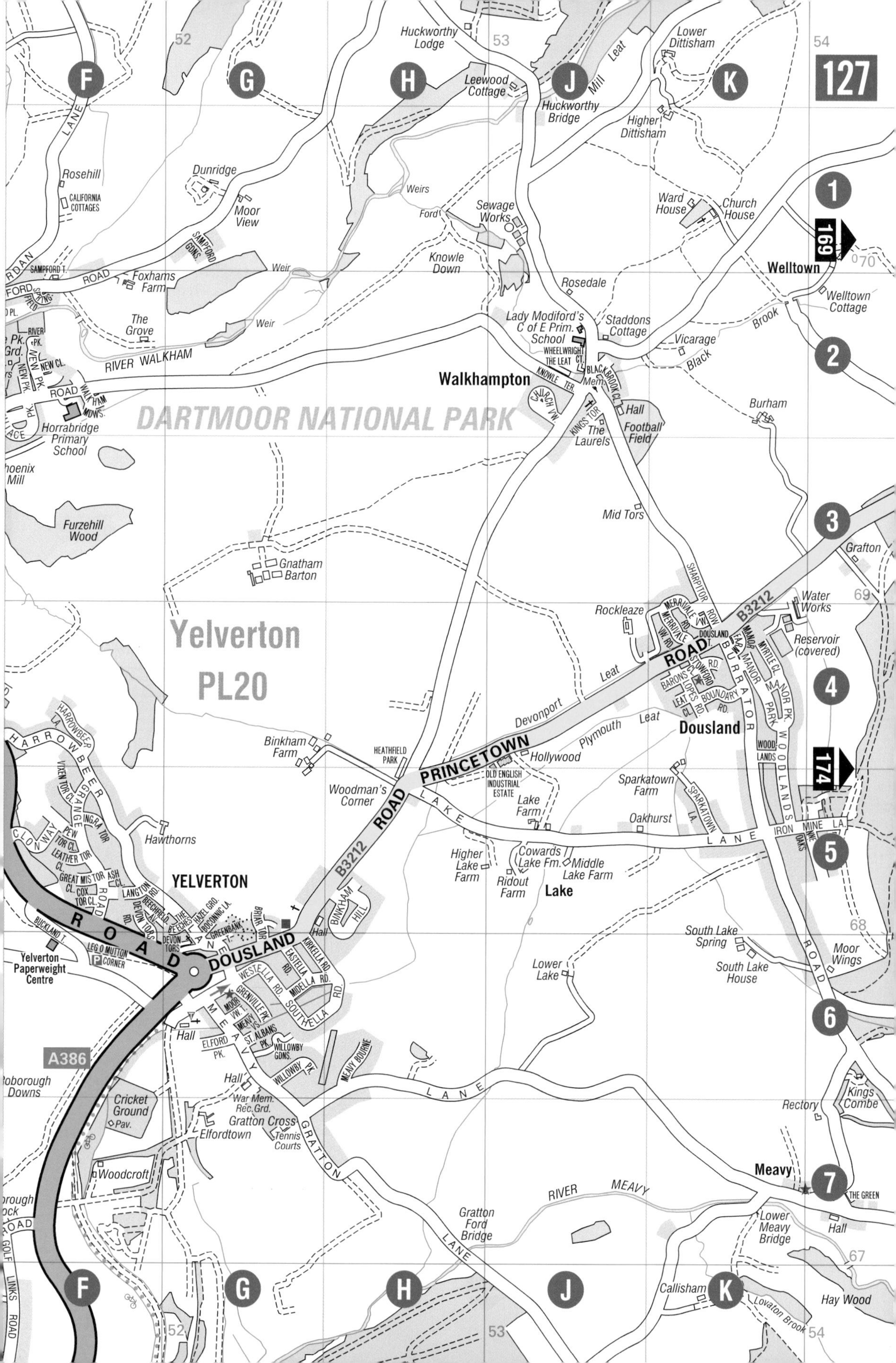
F
G
H
J
K
52
53
54
Huckworthy Lodge
Leewood Cottage
Huckworthy Bridge
Mill Leat
Lower Dittisham
Higher Dittisham
Rosehill
CALIFORNIA COTTAGES
Dunridge
Moor View
Weirs
Ford
Sewage Works
Ward House
Church House
169
Welltown
70
Welltown Cottage
SAMPFORD GDNS.
SAMPFORD T.
ROAD
Foxhams Farm
Weir
Knowle Down
Rosedale
The Grove
Weir
Lady Modiford's C of E Prim. School
Staddons Cottage
Vicarage
Black Brook
RIVER WALKHAM
WHEELWRIGHT CT.
THE LEAT
Walkhampton
KNOWLE TER.
BLACKBROOK CL.
Mem.
Burham
DARTMOOR NATIONAL PARK
CHURCH VW.
KINGS TOR
Hall
The Laurels
Football Field
Horrabridge Primary School
Furzehill Wood
Mid Tors
Gnatham Barton
Grafton
SHARPITOR ROW
Rockleaze
MERRIVALE VW.
MERRIVALE RD.
B3212
Water Works
69
Yelverton
PL20
DOUSLAND T.
Reservoir (covered)
ROAD
Leat
MANOR PK.
Devonport
BARONS CL.
STOWFORD RD.
BURRATOR
MYRTLE CL.
Dousland
BOUNDARY RD.
WOODLANDS
Binkham Farm
HEATHFIELD PARK
PRINCETOWN
Hollywood
Plymouth Leat
174
OLD ENGLISH INDUSTRIAL ESTATE
Sparkatown Farm
SPARKATOWN LA.
Woodman's Corner
ROAD
LAKE
Lake Farm
Oakhurst
IRON MINE LA.
Hawthorns
LANE
Higher Lake Farm
Cowards Lake Fm.
Middle Lake Farm
Ridout Farm
YELVERTON
Lake
B3212
BINKHAM HILL
68
ROAD
South Lake Spring
South Lake House
Moor Wings
Lower Lake
Yelverton Paperweight Centre
LEG O MUTTON CORNER
DOUSLAND
KIRKELLA RD.
EASTELLA RD.
MIDELLA RD.
SOUTHELLA RD.
WESTELLA RD.
GRENVILLE PK.
MEAVY
Hall
ELFORD PK.
ST. ALBANS PK.
WILLOWBY GDNS.
WILLOWBY PK.
MEAVY BOURNE
A386
Roborough Downs
Cricket Ground
Pav.
Hall
War Mem. Rec. Grd.
Gratton Cross
Tennis Courts
LANE
Elfordtown
GRATTON
Rectory
Kings Combe
Woodcroft
Meavy
RIVER MEAVY
THE GREEN
Gratton Ford Bridge
LANE
Lower Meavy Bridge
Hall
67
Callisham
Lovaton Brook
Hay Wood
GOLF LINKS ROAD
1
2
3
4
5
6
7

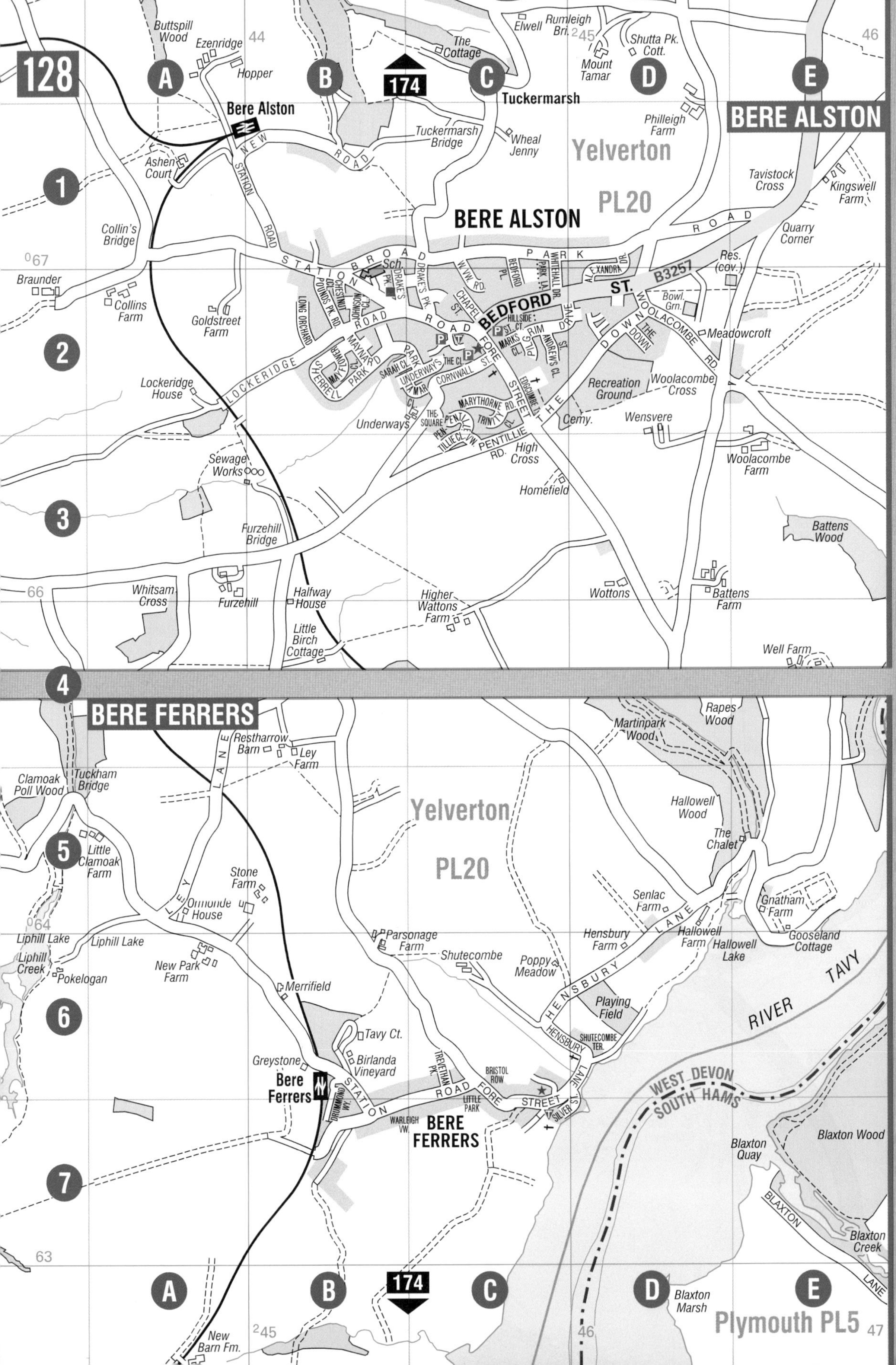
BERE ALSTON
Bere Alston
Buttspill Wood
Ezenridge
Hopper
The Cottage
174
Tuckermarsh
Elwell
Rumleigh Bri.
Mount Tamar
Shutta Pk. Cott.
Phillleigh Farm
Yelverton
PL20
Tuckermarsh Bridge
Wheal Jenny
Ashen Court
Tavistock Cross
Kingswell Farm
Quarry Corner
Collin's Bridge
Braunder
Collins Farm
Goldstreet Farm
Res. (cov.)
Bowl. Grn.
Meadowcroft
B3257
BEDFORD ST.
Lockeridge House
Recreation Ground
Woolacombe Cross
Cemy.
Wensvere
Underways
High Cross
Woolacombe Farm
Sewage Works
Homefield
Furzehill Bridge
Battens Wood
Whitsam Cross
Furzehill
Halfway House
Higher Wattons Farm
Wottons
Battens Farm
Little Birch Cottage
Well Farm
BERE FERRERS
Restharrow Barn
Ley Farm
Martinpark Wood
Rapes Wood
Clamoak Poll Wood
Tuckham Bridge
Hallowell Wood
The Chalet
Little Clamoak Farm
Stone Farm
Ormonde House
Senlac Farm
Gnatham Farm
Liphill Lake
Liphill Creek
Pokelogan
New Park Farm
Parsonage Farm
Shutecombe
Poppy Meadow
Hensbury Farm
Hallowell Farm
Hallowell Lake
Gooseland Cottage
Merrifield
Playing Field
RIVER TAVY
Tavy Ct.
Greystone
Birlanda Vineyard
Bere Ferrers
BERE FERRERS
WEST DEVON
SOUTH HAMS
Blaxton Quay
Blaxton Wood
Blaxton Creek
Blaxton Marsh
New Barn Fm.
Plymouth PL5

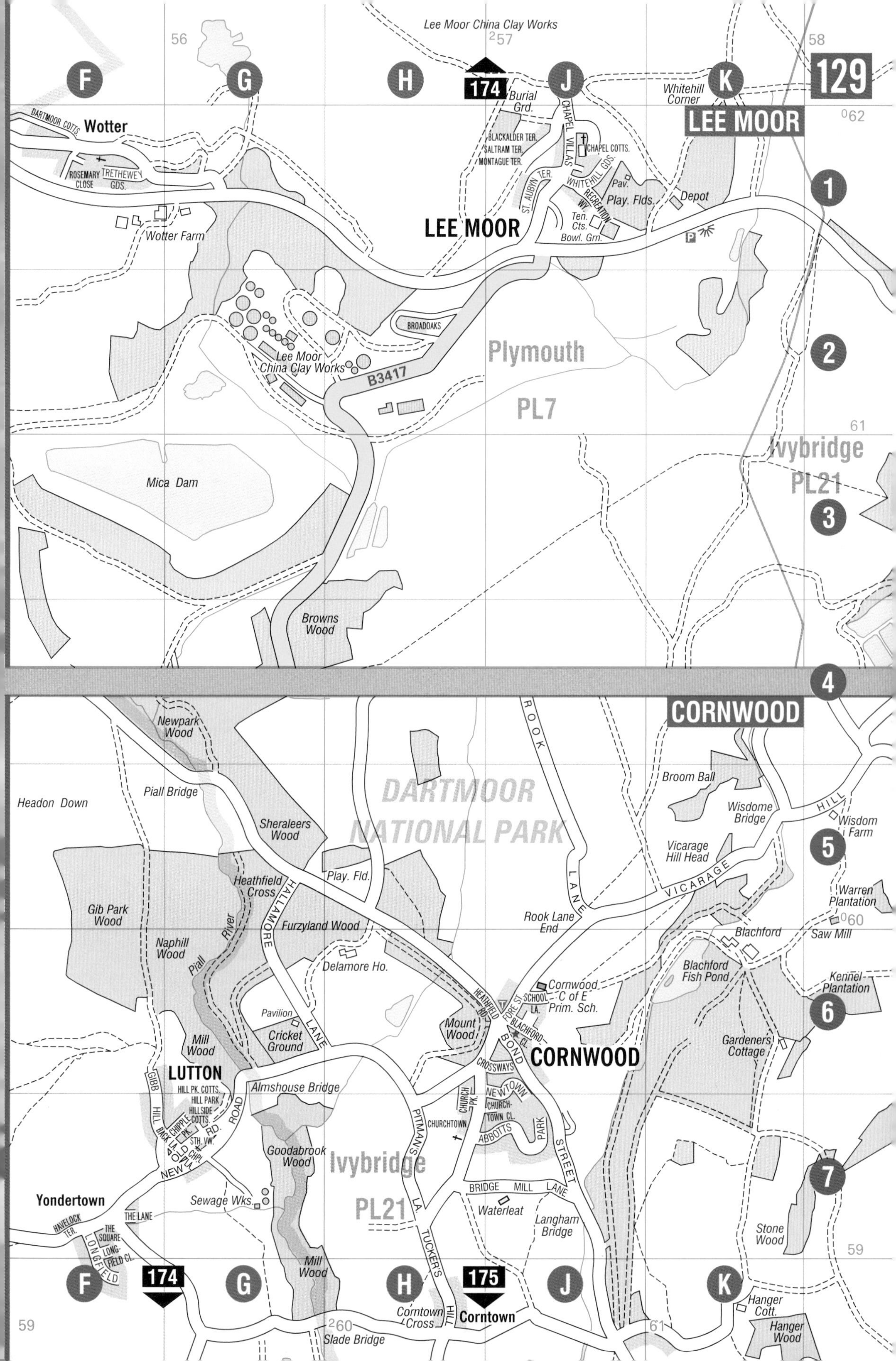
Lee Moor China Clay Works
LEE MOOR
Wotter
Dartmoor Cotts.
Rosemary Close
Trethewey Gds.
Wotter Farm
Burial Grd.
Blackalder Ter.
Saltram Ter.
Montague Ter.
Chapel Villas
Chapel Cotts.
St. Aubyn Ter.
Whitehill Gds.
Recreation Wy.
Pav.
Play. Flds.
Ten. Cts.
Bowl. Grn.
Depot
Whitehill Corner
Broadoaks
Lee Moor China Clay Works
B3417
Plymouth
PL7
Mica Dam
Browns Wood
Ivybridge
PL21
CORNWOOD
Newpark Wood
Piall Bridge
Headon Down
Sheraleers Wood
DARTMOOR NATIONAL PARK
Rook Lane
Broom Ball
Wisdome Bridge
Hill
Wisdom Farm
Vicarage Hill Head
Vicarage
Warren Plantation
Saw Mill
Gib Park Wood
Naphill Wood
Piall River
Heathfield Cross
Hallamore Lane
Play. Fld.
Furzyland Wood
Rook Lane End
Blachford
Blachford Fish Pond
Delamore Ho.
Cornwood C of E Prim. Sch.
Fore St.
School La.
Heathfield Rd.
Blachford Cl.
Kennel Plantation
Pavilion
Cricket Ground
Mount Wood
Mill Wood
Bond
Crossways
Gardeners Cottage
LUTTON
Gibb Hill
Hill Pk. Cotts.
Hill Park
Hillside Cotts.
Chipple Pk.
Back La.
Sth. Vw. Rd.
Old Chpl. Rd.
New Road
Almshouse Bridge
Church Pk.
Churchtown
Newtown
Churchtown Cl.
Abbotts Park
Pitman's La.
Goodabrook Wood
Ivybridge
PL21
Street
Yondertown
The Lane
Sewage Wks.
Bridge Mill Lane
Waterleat
Langham Bridge
Havelock Ter.
The Square
Longfield
Longfield Cl.
Tuckers Hill
Stone Wood
Mill Wood
Corntown Cross
Corntown
Slade Bridge
Hanger Cott.
Hanger Wood
174
175
F
G
H
J
K
1
2
3
4
5
6
7
56
57
58
62
61
60
59

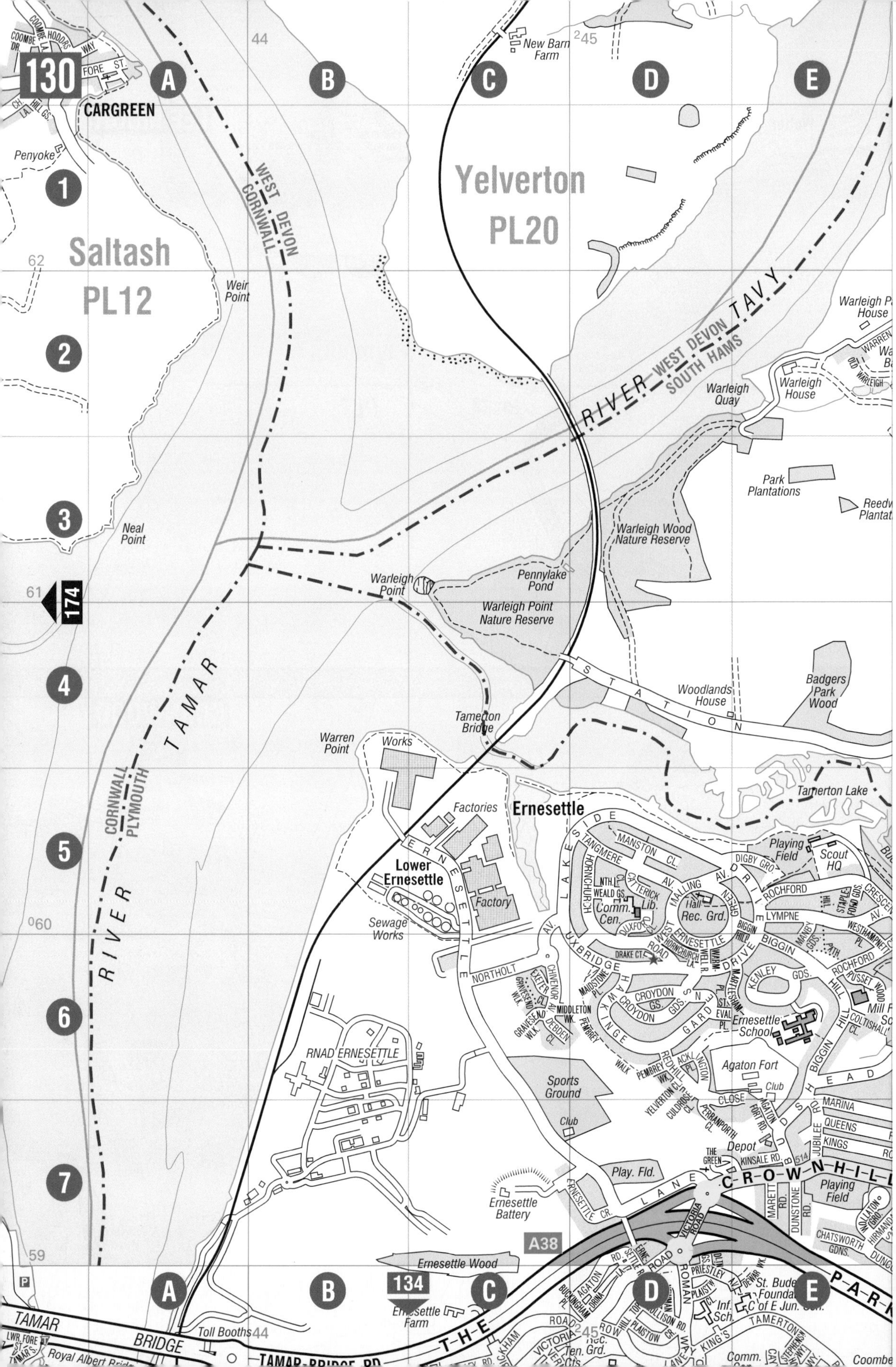

CARGREEN
Penyoke
Saltash
PL12
Yelverton
PL20
Weir Point
Neal Point
Warleigh Point
Warren Point
WEST DEVON
CORNWALL
RIVER TAMAR
CORNWALL
PLYMOUTH
RIVER TAVY
WEST DEVON
SOUTH HAMS
New Barn Farm
Warleigh House
Warleigh Quay
Park Plantations
Warleigh Wood Nature Reserve
Pennylake Pond
Warleigh Point Nature Reserve
Tamerton Bridge
STATION ROAD
Woodlands House
Badgers Park Wood
Works
Factories
Ernesettle
Lower Ernesettle
Factory
Sewage Works
Tamerton Lake
Playing Field
Scout HQ
RNAD ERNESETTLE
Sports Ground
Club
Agaton Fort
Ernesettle School
Depot
Play. Fld.
Ernesettle Battery
Ernesettle Wood
Ernesettle Farm
Toll Booths
TAMAR BRIDGE
Royal Albert Bridge
TAMAR BRIDGE RD
THE PARKWAY
CROWNHILL
A38
St. Budeaux Foundation C of E Jun. Sch.
Inf. Sch.
Ten. Grd.
Rec. Grd.
Comm. Cen.
Lib.
Hall
174
134

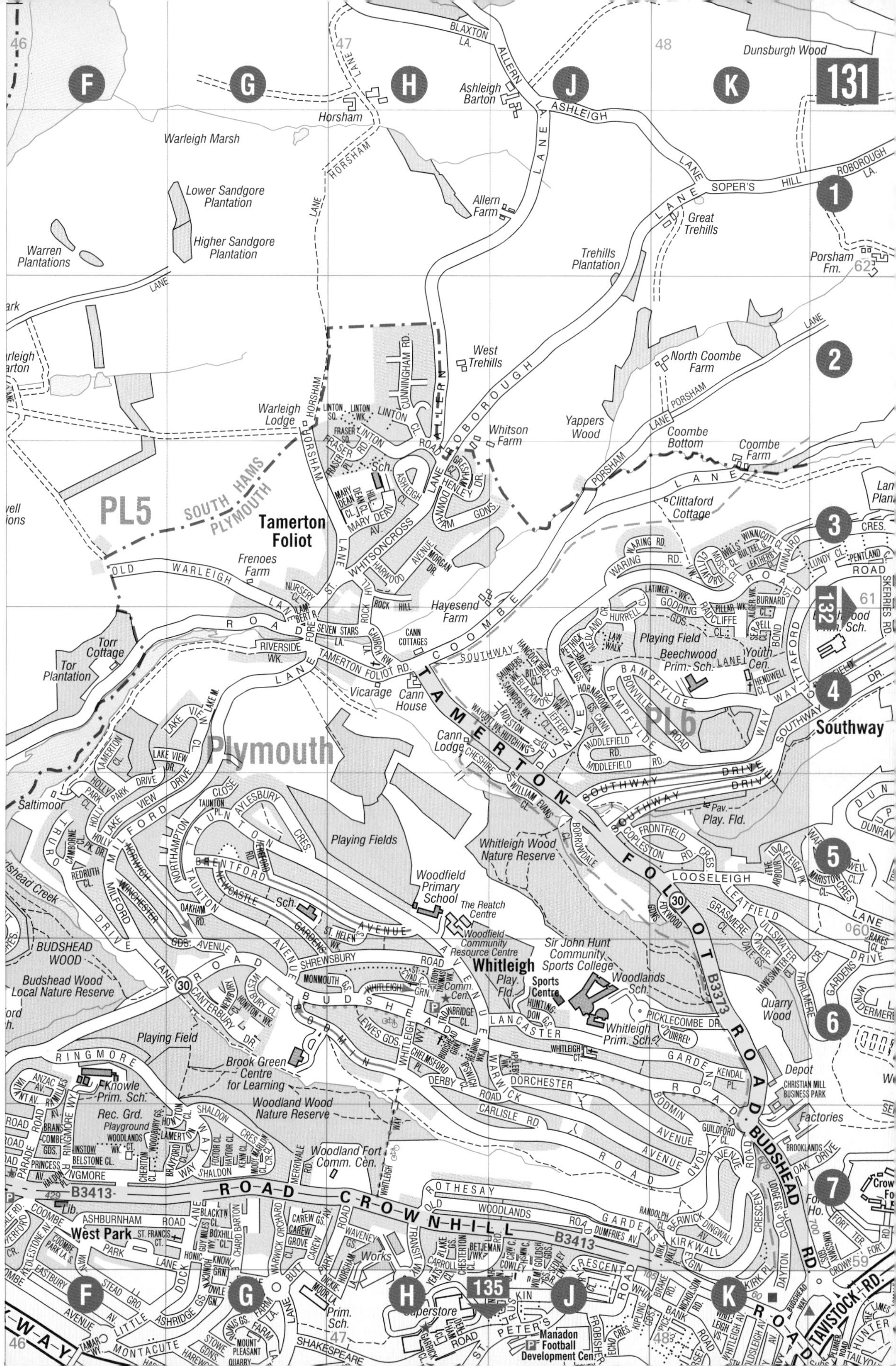

131
Dunsburgh Wood
Blaxton La.
Allern La.
Ashleigh Barton
Ashleigh Lane
Horsham
Horsham Lane
Warleigh Marsh
Lower Sandgore Plantation
Higher Sandgore Plantation
Warren Plantations
Allern Farm
Soper's Hill
Roborough La.
Great Trehills
Trehills Plantation
Porsham Fm.
West Trehills
North Coombe Farm
Porsham Lane
Yappers Wood
Coombe Bottom
Coombe Farm
Whitson Farm
Warleigh Lodge
Roborough Lane
Clittaford Cottage
PL5
South Hams
Plymouth
Tamerton Foliot
Frenoes Farm
Old Warleigh Lane
Hayesend Farm
Torr Cottage
Tor Plantation
Riverside Wk.
Coombe Lane
Cann Cottages
Vicarage
Cann House
Cann Lodge
Southway Lane
Tamerton Foliot Road
Beechwood Prim. Sch.
Playing Field
Youth Cen.
PL6
Southway
Southway Drive
Plymouth
Saltimoor
Playing Fields
Pav.
Play. Fld.
Whitleigh Wood Nature Reserve
Woodfield Primary School
The Reatch Centre
Woodfield Community Resource Centre
Whitleigh
Sir John Hunt Community Sports College
Sports Centre
Woodlands Sch.
Whitleigh Prim. Sch.
Budshead Creek
Budshead Wood
Budshead Wood Local Nature Reserve
Playing Field
Brook Green Centre for Learning
Woodland Wood Nature Reserve
Knowle Prim. Sch.
Rec. Grd.
Playground
Woodland Fort Comm. Cen.
Quarry Wood
Depot
Christian Mill Business Park
Factories
Budshead Road
B3373
B3413
Crownhill Road
West Park
Works
Superstore
Prim. Sch.
Manadon Football Development Cen.
Tavistock Rd.
135
132
F
G
H
J
K
1
2
3
4
5
6
7
46
47
48
59
60
61
62

Dunsburgh Wood
Dunsburgh Farm
Works
Playing Field
Depot
174
A386
Lower Leigh
Roborough
Porsham Plantation
Haxter Wood
SOUTH HAMS
PLYMOUTH
BELLIVER INDUSTRIAL ESTATE
Ten Acre Brake
Porsham Farm
PL5
PL6
Arnold's Hill Coppice
Porsham Coppice
Play. Field
Widewell Wood
Playground
Hursley Bungalows
Bickleigh Down
BICKLEIGH DOWN BUSINESS PARK
Woolwell
Superstore
Offices
Porsham Wood
Lidgate
Belliver Coppice
The Brake
Coombe Farm
Langley Plantation
Factory
Widewell Prim. Sch.
Widewell
Beechwood Prim. Sch.
Youth Cen.
Oakwood Prim. Sch.
Sports Grd.
George Junc.
Glenholt
Southway
Plymouth
MORGAN RD.
PLYMBRIDGE
B3432
Notre Dame RC Sch.
Play. Fld.
Playing Field
Games Courts
Island Farm
Student Village
Halls of Residence
The College of St. Mark & St. John (Marjon)
Sports Ground
Devonshire Health & Raquets Club
PLYMOUTH NUFFIELD HEALTH HOSP.
Marjon Sports & Leisure
Games Court
Kingdom Hall
Superstore
Rowans
Staff Accommodation
Derriford
Depot
CHRISTIAN MILL BUSINESS PARK
Factories
Water Works
Works
Windsor House
Reservoir (covered)
DERRIFORD HOSPITAL
GLENBOURNE UNIT
DERRIFORD BUSINESS PARK
Offices
Peninsula Medical School
Derriford Health & Leisure Centre
Plymouth Swallows Sch. of Gymnastics
TAMAR SCIENCE PARK
Prim. Sch.
Play. Fld.
Crownhill Fort
TA Centre
SEATON BUSINESS PARK
PLYMOUTH INTERNATIONAL BUSINESS PARK
NHS TREATMENT CEN.
Academy
Bircham Valley Local Nature Reserve
Fursdon
Smallack Farm
TAVISTOCK ROAD
136
Plymbridge Nursery Sch.
Play. Fld.
Sports

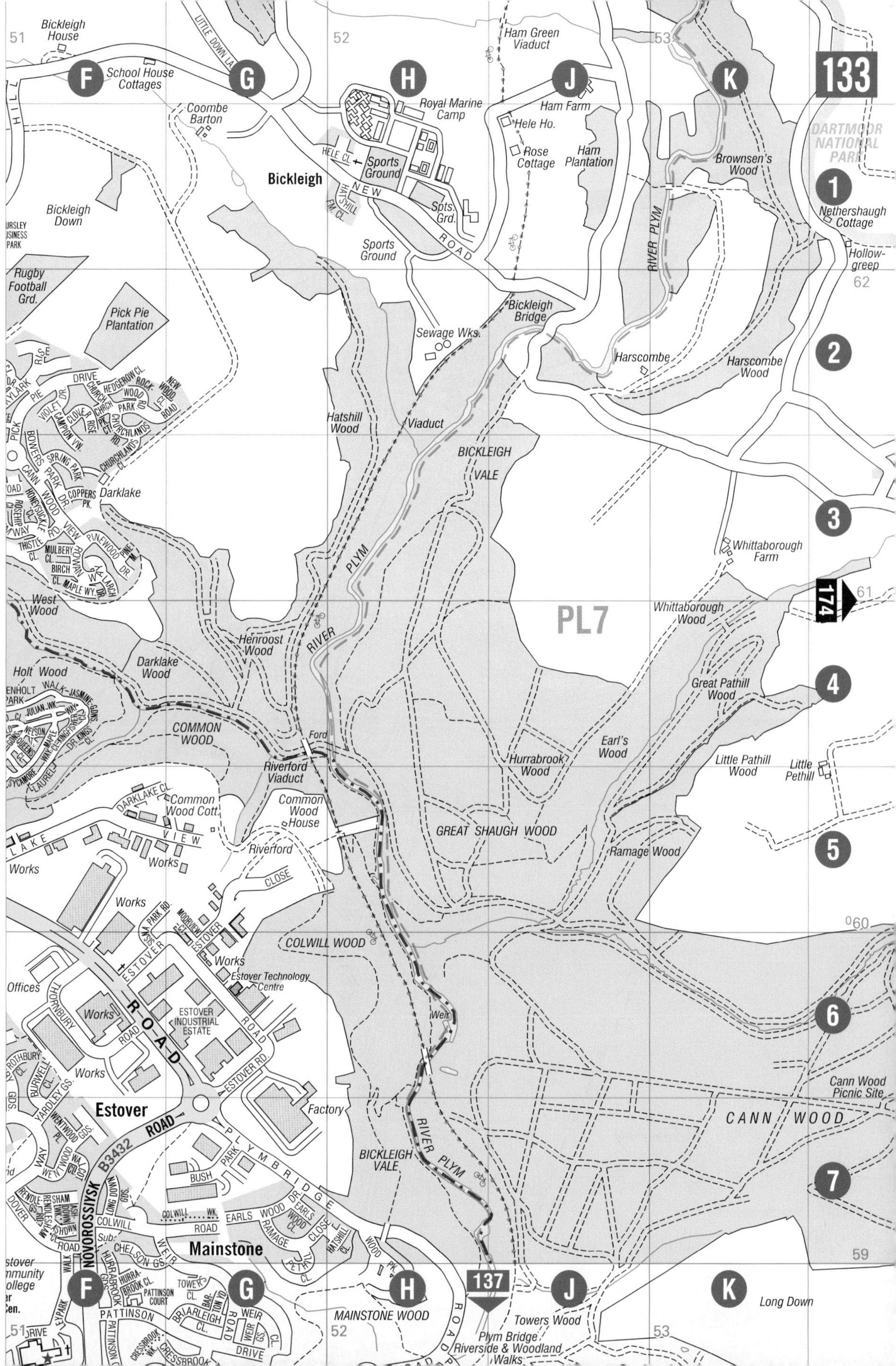
Bickleigh House
School House Cottages
Coombe Barton
Bickleigh Down
Rugby Football Grd.
Pick Pie Plantation
Ham Green Viaduct
Royal Marine Camp
Bickleigh
Sports Ground
Spts. Grd.
Ham Farm
Hele Ho.
Rose Cottage
Ham Plantation
Brownsen's Wood
RIVER PLYM
DARTMOOR NATIONAL PARK
Nethershaugh Cottage
Hollow-greep
Bickleigh Bridge
Sewage Wks.
Harscombe
Harscombe Wood
Hatshill Wood
Viaduct
BICKLEIGH VALE
Darklake
Whittaborough Farm
174
PL7
Whittaborough Wood
West Wood
Henroost Wood
Holt Wood
Darklake Wood
Great Pathill Wood
COMMON WOOD
Ford
Riverford Viaduct
Earl's Wood
Hurrabrook Wood
Little Pathill Wood
Little Pethill
Common Wood Cott.
Common Wood House
GREAT SHAUGH WOOD
Riverford
Ramage Wood
Works
COLWILL WOOD
Estover Technology Centre
Offices
ESTOVER INDUSTRIAL ESTATE
Weir
Factory
Estover
Cann Wood Picnic Site
CANN WOOD
BICKLEIGH VALE
Mainstone
137
Long Down
MAINSTONE WOOD
Towers Wood
Plym Bridge Riverside & Woodland Walks
NEW ROAD
ESTOVER ROAD
B3432
NOVOROSSIYSK ROAD
PLYMBRIDGE ROAD
COLWILL ROAD

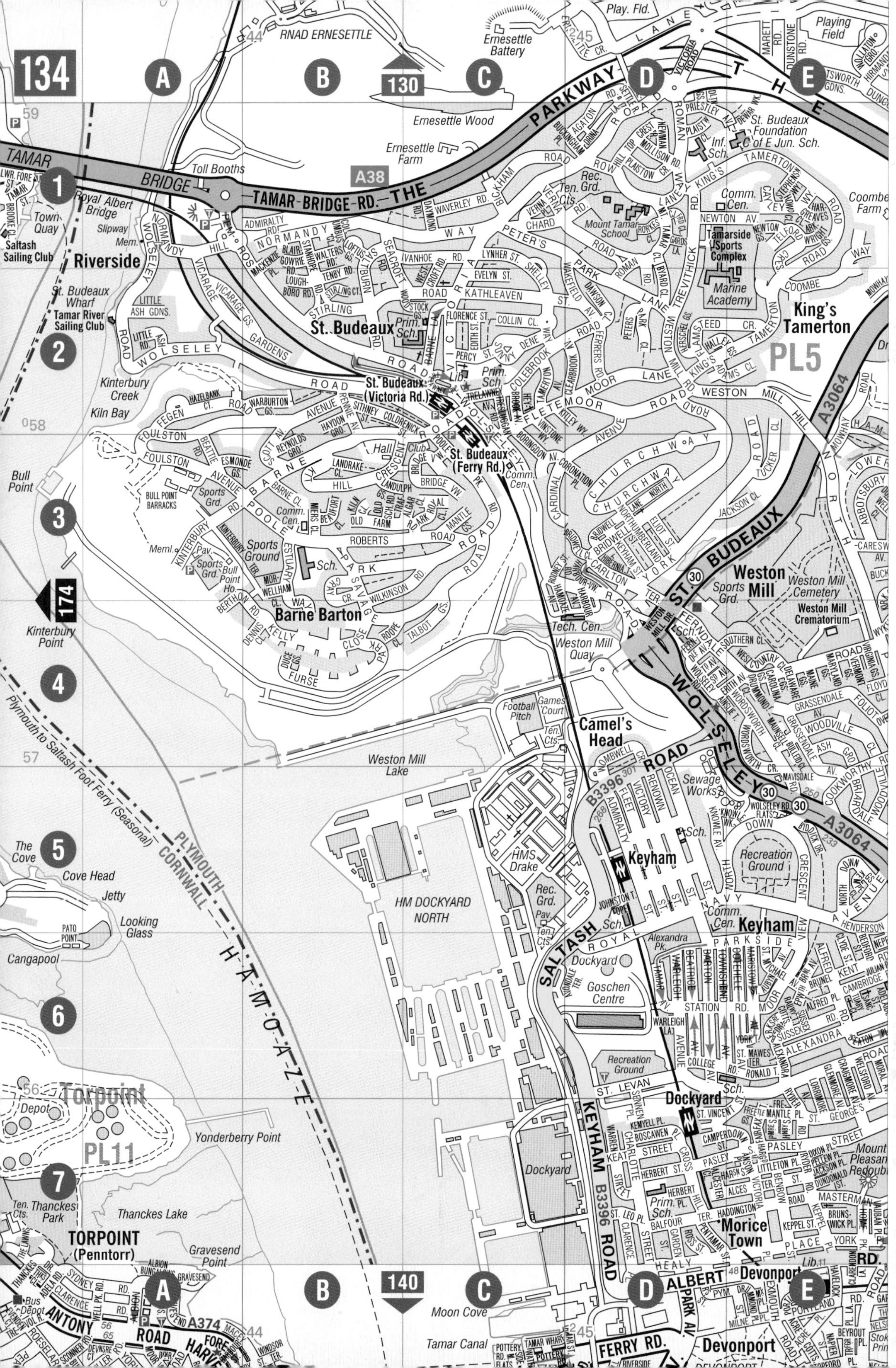
RNAD ERNESETTLE
130
Ernesettle Battery
Ernesettle Wood
Ernesettle Farm
Toll Booths
TAMAR BRIDGE
TAMAR-BRIDGE-RD. THE PARKWAY
A38
Royal Albert Bridge
Town Quay
Saltash Sailing Club
Riverside
St. Budeaux Wharf
Tamar River Sailing Club
Kinterbury Creek
Kiln Bay
St. Budeaux
St. Budeaux (Victoria Rd.)
St. Budeaux (Ferry Rd.)
Bull Point
BULL POINT BARRACKS
Sports Ground
174
Kinterbury Point
Barne Barton
Plymouth to Saltash Foot Ferry (Seasonal)
Weston Mill Lake
Weston Mill Quay
Tech. Cen.
Camel's Head
Football Pitch
HMS Drake
HM DOCKYARD NORTH
PLYMOUTH
CORNWALL
HAMOAZE
The Cove
Cove Head
Jetty
Looking Glass
Cangapool
Torpoint
PL11
Yonderberry Point
Thanckes Park
Thanckes Lake
TORPOINT (Penntorr)
Gravesend Point
140
Moon Cove
Tamar Canal
Mount Tamar School
Tamarside Sports Complex
Marine Academy
St. Budeaux Foundation C of E Jun. Sch.
King's Tamerton
PL5
Coombe Farm
A3064
ST BUDEAUX
Weston Mill
Weston Mill Cemetery
Weston Mill Crematorium
WOLSELEY ROAD
Sewage Works
Recreation Ground
Keyham
B3396
SALTASH ROAD
Dockyard
Goschen Centre
Dockyard
KEYHAM ROAD
Morice Town
Devonport
ALBERT ROAD
FERRY RD.
Mount Pleasant Redoubt
ANTONY ROAD
A374

CROWNHILL
Honicknowle
Manadon
Plymouth
Pennycross
Ham
North Prospect
Beacon Park
Peverell
Hartley
Mutley
Ford Park
Ford
Milehouse
PLYMOUTH
Pennycomequick
Stoke
PARKWAY
A38
A386
B3413
B3250
B3396
BY-PASS
TAVISTOCK ROAD
OUTLAND ROAD
ALMA ROAD
MANNAMEAD ROAD
MUTLEY PLAIN
ALEXANDRA RD.
MILEHOUSE RD.
Plymouth Argyle FC (Home Park)
Mayflower Leisure Centre
Central Park Leisure Pools
Plymouth Life Cen.
CENTRAL PARK
Pitch & Putt Golf Course
Manadon Football Development Cen.
All Saints C of E Academy
Burrington Industrial Estate
Walkham Business Park
Sports Ground
Playing Field
Ham Wood
Ham Brook
Manadon Wood
Blindman's Wood
Bladder Meadow
St. Boniface's RC Coll.
Stoke Damerel Comm. Coll.
City Business Park
Plymouth Coll.
Cemetery
Superstore
Supermarket
Scott Hosp.
Beacon Down Sports Ground
Pounds House
Bus Depot
Sports Cen.
Cricket Ground
Football Pitch
Bowling Greens
Putting Grn.
Baseball Pitch
Heart Plymouth Radio
Mutley Park
PL2
PL3
PL4
131
136
141
8
9
F
G
H
J
K
1
2
3
4
5
6
7
46
47
48

136
132
135
142
9
A
B
C
D
E
1
2
3
4
5
6
7
PL6
PL3
PL4
Crownhill Fort
Crownhill
Crownhill Fort Rd.
TA Centre
Seaton Business Park
Plymouth International Business Park
NHS Treatment Cen.
Derriford Health & Leisure Centre
Bircham Valley Local Nature Reserve
Fursdon
Higher Bircham Cottage
Poole Farm
Bircham Farm
Smallack Farm
Gov. Offs.
Fort Austin Avenue
B3413
Austin Avenue
Forder Valley
Novorossiysk Road
Bowden Battery
Garden Cen.
Widey Court Primary School
Courtlands School
Prim. Sch.
Brimble Park
Forder Valley Nature Reserve
Estover
Plymbridge Nursery Sch.
Eggbuckland Vale Prim. Sch.
Eggbuckland Community College
Activate Sports & Leisure
Hartley Vale
Eggbuckland
Austin Fort
The Parkway
A38
Tavistock Road
A386
Mannamead Road
B3250
Hartley
Hartley Park
Higher Compton
Playing Field
Mannamead Cen.
Efford Cemetery
Efford Crematorium
Bowling Green
Efford
High View Prim. Sch.
Mannamead
Broadcasting Ho.
Western College
Lower Compton Recreation Ground
Mutley Park
Mutley Plain
Lipson Vale
Old Laira Road
B3214
Laira
Laira Rail Depot
Lipson Comm. College
Lipson Sports Cen.
Play. Fld.
Rec. Grd.
Lipson
Alexandra Road
Embankment Road
A374
The Laira
Mount Gould Hospital
Mount Gould
Freedom Flds.
Point Quay
Boat Ho.
Military Road
Blandford Road
Efford Road
Higher Compton Road
Lower Compton Rd.
Eggbuckland Road
Delamere Road
Greystoke Avenue
Carradale Road
Michigan Way
Oregon Way
California Gdns.
Pathway
Manifold Gdns.
Fairview Avenue
Ashford Road
Seymour Avenue
Lipson Road
Beaumont Road
Gould Road

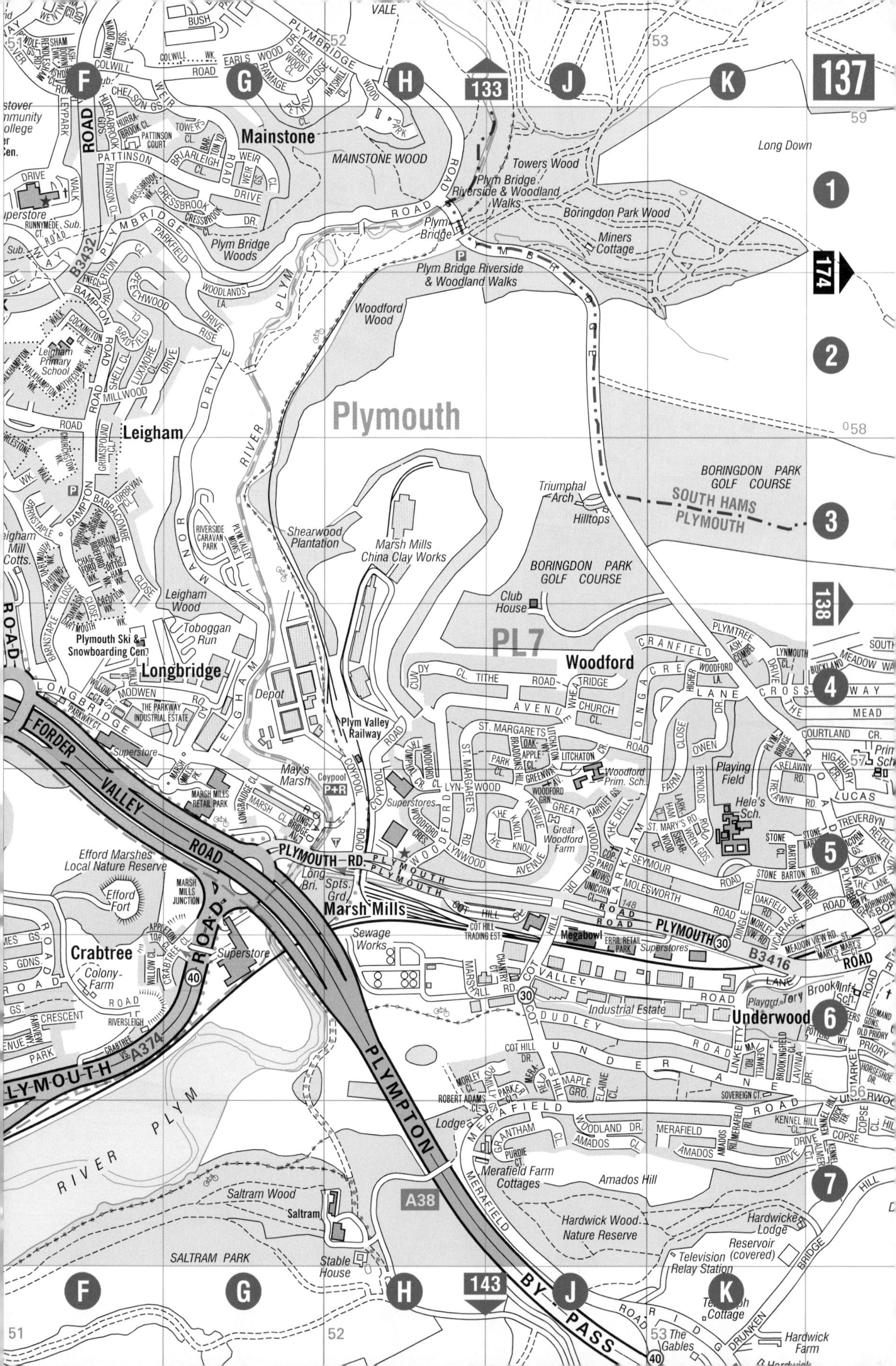
Mainstone
Mainstone Wood
Towers Wood
Plym Bridge Riverside & Woodland Walks
Boringdon Park Wood
Miners Cottage
Plym Bridge
Plym Bridge Woods
Long Down
Woodford Wood
Plymouth
Leigham
Leigham Primary School
Boringdon Park Golf Course
South Hams
Plymouth
Triumphal Arch
Hilltops
Shearwood Plantation
Marsh Mills China Clay Works
Riverside Caravan Park
Leigham Wood
Toboggan Run
Club House
PL7
Woodford
Plymouth Ski & Snowboarding Cen.
Longbridge
Depot
Plym Valley Railway
The Parkway Industrial Estate
Superstore
May's Marsh
Coypool
Superstores
Woodford Prim. Sch.
Playing Field
Hele's Sch.
Great Woodford Farm
Marsh Mills Retail Park
Efford Marshes Local Nature Reserve
Efford Fort
Marsh Mills Junction
Long Bri.
Spts. Grd.
Marsh Mills
Sewage Works
Cot Hill Trading Est.
Megabowl
Erril Retail Park
Crabtree
Colony Farm
Industrial Estate
Underwood
Forder Valley Road
Plymouth Road
Plympton By-Pass
River Plym
Saltram Wood
Saltram
Saltram Park
Stable House
A38
A374
B3416
B3432
Merafield Farm Cottages
Amados Hill
Hardwick Wood Nature Reserve
Hardwicke Lodge
Reservoir (covered)
Television Relay Station
Telegraph Cottage
The Gables
Hardwick Farm
Lodge
133
174
138
143
F G H J K
1 2 3 4 5 6 7
51 52 53
59 58 57 56

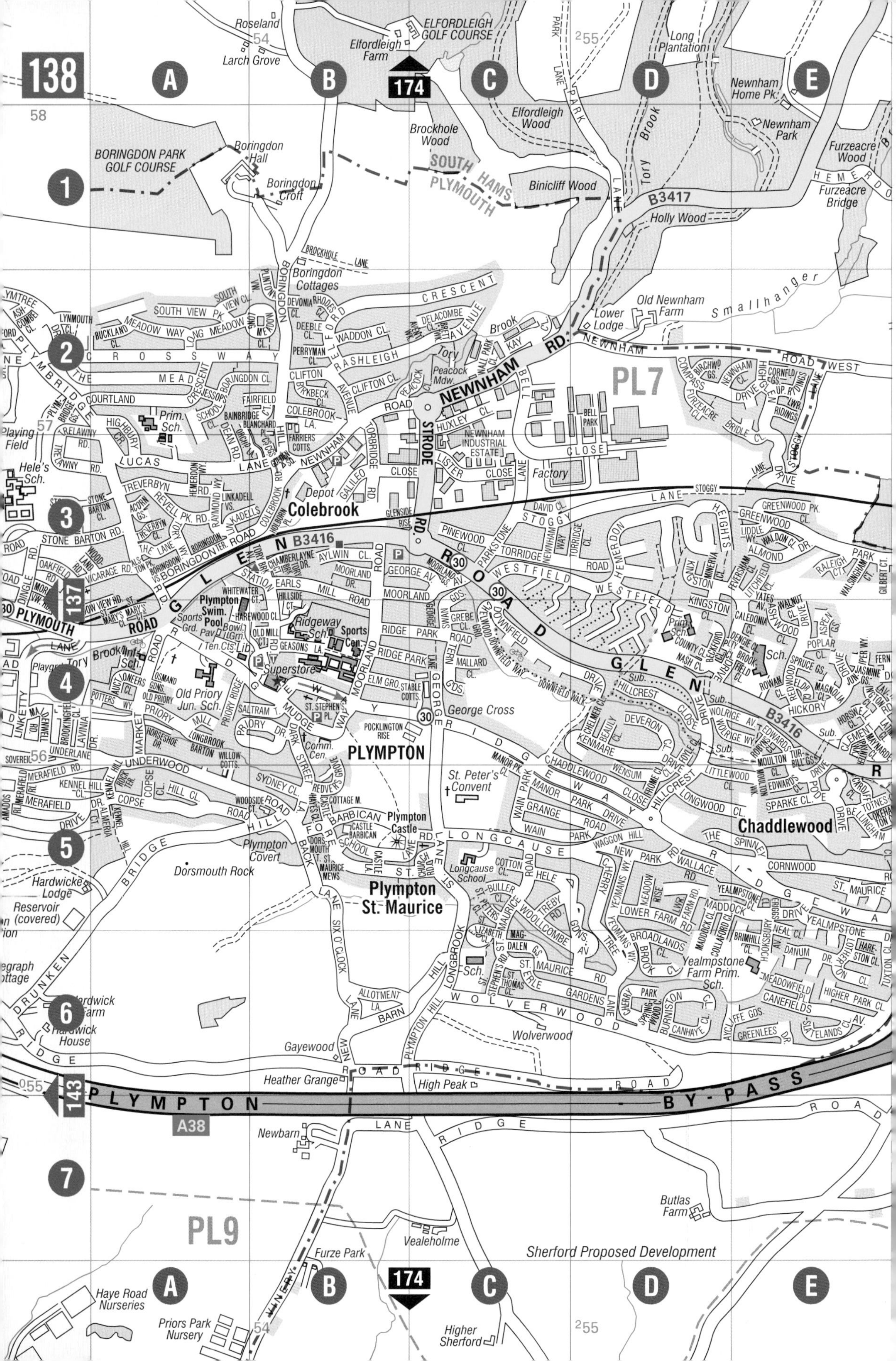
138
A
B
C
D
E
174
Roseland
Larch Grove
Elfordleigh Farm
ELFORDLEIGH GOLF COURSE
Long Plantation
Newnham Home Pk.
Newnham Park
Elfordleigh Wood
Brockhole Wood
Tory Brook
Furzeacre Wood
BORINGDON PARK GOLF COURSE
Boringdon Hall
Boringdon Croft
SOUTH HAMS
PLYMOUTH
Binicliff Wood
B3417
Holly Wood
Furzeacre Bridge
Boringdon Cottages
Smallhanger
Old Newnham Farm
Lower Lodge
NEWNHAM RD.
NEWNHAM ROAD WEST
PL7
Peacock Mdw.
NEWNHAM INDUSTRIAL ESTATE
Factory
Prim. Sch.
Playing Field
Hele's Sch.
Colebrook
Depot
B3416
GLEN ROAD
PLYMOUTH ROAD
137
Plympton Swim. Pool
Sports Grd.
Ridgeway Sch.
Sports Cen.
Superstore
Old Priory Jun. Sch.
Infs. Sch.
George Cross
PLYMPTON
St. Peter's Convent
Comm. Cen.
Plympton Castle
Plympton Covert
Dorsmouth Rock
Hardwicke Lodge
Reservoir (covered)
Plympton St. Maurice
Longcause School
Chaddlewood
Yealmpstone Farm Prim. Sch.
Sch.
Hardwick Farm
Hardwick House
Wolverwood
Gayewood
Heather Grange
High Peak
143
PLYMPTON BY-PASS
A38
Newbarn
Butlas Farm
PL9
Vealeholme
Furze Park
Sherford Proposed Development
Haye Road Nurseries
Priors Park Nursery
Higher Sherford
1
2
3
4
5
6
7
58
57
56
54
255

Plymouth
Hemerdon
Sparkwell
Langage
Smithaleigh
Blackpool
PL8
A38
B3416
SPARKWELL GOLF COURSE
Lobb Farm
Windwhistle Wood
Windwhistle Farm
Galva
Galvacot
Carthew House
Lowdamoor
Hemerdon Farm
Sterts Farm
Hemerdon Ball
Hemerdon Plantation
Hemerdon House
Beechwood Cross
Lodge
Sherwell
Graveyard
Hotel & Club Ho.
Welbeck Manor
Church Hall
Play. Fld.
Walks Coppice
Crownhill Plantation
Moll Tall's Cross
Walks Brake
Tin Wood
Crownhill Cottage
Beechwood
Six Acre Plantation
Parkside Farm
Sparkwell Bridge
Moor Bridge
Hemerdon Siding
Sheepland Plantation
Little Moor
Moor Cot
Langage Cross
Combe Cottage
Combe
Coombe Farm
Lower Langage
LANGAGE BUSINESS PARK
LANGAGE ENERGY CENTRE
LANGAGE INDUSTRIAL ESTATE
LANGAGE PARK
LANGAGE PK. OFFICE CAMPUS
CHADDLEWOOD DISTRICT CEN.
Chaddle Wood
Applethorn Slade
Ley
Voss
Ford Farm
Ford Cottages
SMITHALEIGH CARAVAN & CAMPING PARK
Collaford Wood
Collaford
Camping Site
Barn Park
Battisford
Wiverton House
Wiverton Acre
Tuxton Farm
Tuxton Wood
Choakford Lairage
Choakford Farm
Warren Wood
West Pitton
LEDGATE LANE
GALVA ROAD
PARK HILL
HOLLAND ROAD
KINGSWAY
SANDY ROAD
DEEP LANE
174

140
134
174
A
B
C
D
E
1
2
3
4
5
6
7
Thanckes Park
Thanckes Lake
Gravesend Point
Dockyard
KEYHAM RD.
Morice Town
Devonport
ALBERT RD.
B3396
PL2
Moon Cove
Tamar Canal
FERRY RD.
Torpoint Vehicle Ferry (Floating Bridges)
Rendel Park
ANTONY RD.
A374
HARVEY ST.
FERRY ST.
TORPOINT (Penntorr)
PL11
Torpoint Mosquito Sailing Club
Marina
HAMOAZE
Quay
Slipway
PARK AV.
A374
CHAPEL ST.
DEVONPORT PARK
Bowling Grn.
Tennis Courts
Hockey Pitches
Brickfields Recreation Grd.
Plymouth Albion RFC
Brickfields Stadium
Brickfields Sports Cen.
CUMBERLAND ROAD
HM DOCKYARD SOUTH
Cricket Ground
Scott Mem.
Admiralty Ho.
Mount Wise
Mount Wise Park
Mutton Cove Pier
Mount Wise Outdoor Pools
Mount Wise Hard
Pontoons
RIVER TAMAR
Cremyll to Plymouth Foot Ferry
The Narrows
Devil's Point
Shipyard
Cremyll
Works
B3247
The Avenue
Mount Edgcumbe Country Park Formal Gardens
Wilderness Point
Inswork Point
Torpoint
Southdown
Elm Park
Southdown Quay
Palmer Point
Ancarva Gwythvos
Palmer Rock
Empacombe
Garden Cottage
No.6 Redoubt
Mount Edgcumbe Farm
Barnpool Wood
Barn Pool
Sheep Park
Beech Wood
Cricket Grd.
Mount Edgcumbe House
Barrow Park
Lower Walk
Higher Walk
Dry Walk
Lower Deerhouse Plantation
MOUNT EDGCUMBE COUNTRY PARK
Amphitheatre Wood
Millbrook Lake
Nanny Parson's Grove
Harbour View Plantation
Drywalk Wood
Oak Plantation
Deer Park
Lady Emma's Cottage
PL10
Lower Anderton
Pigshill Wood
Wear Cottages
Wood Park Cottages
Woodpark
Crescent Plantation
Clarrick Woods
Grotton Plantation
Warren Plantation
Maker Lodge
Grave Yard
Redding Point Plantation
Inner Redding
Redoubt No.5
Picklecombe Seat
Red Seat
South Terrace
Friary Manor
44
45
53
54
55
52

PLYMOUTH
135
174
142
8
9
F
G
H
J
K
1
2
3
4
5
6
7
46
47
48
52
53
54
55
Stoke
Pennycomequick
Plymouth
The Millfields
Stonehouse
Millbay
Inner Basin
Outer Basin
Ferryport
Ferry Terminal
MILLBAY DOCKS
Millbay Pier
Trinity Pier
Stonehouse Barracks
Stonehouse Pool
Devonport High Sch. for Boys
Victoria Park
Millbay Park
Hoe Park
The Hoe
Drake's Statue
Smeaton's Tower
Plymouth Dome
Tinside Lido
Dog Rock
West Hoe Pier
Rusty Anchor
Lifeboat Station
Barbican
The Royal Citadel
Royal Corinthian Yacht Club
Fisher's Nose
Mayflower Stone & Steps
Coxside
Sutton Harbour
North Quay
Marina
Glassworks
Aquarium
Phoenix Wharf
Queen Anne's Battery
Landing Stage
Mount Batten Breakwater
Mount Batten Tower
Mount Batten Point
Batten Bay
Dunstone Point
JENNYCLIFF BAY
Eastern King Point
Western King Point
Firestone Bay
Drake's Island
The Bridge
THE SOUND
PLYMOUTH
CORNWALL
Plymouth to:
Roscoff 6hrs. (Seasonal)
Santander 20hrs. (Seasonal)
Plymouth to Saltash Foot Ferry (Seasonal)
Plymouth (Barbican) to Cawsand Foot Ferry (Seasonal)
Foot Ferry
UNION A374 ST.
EXETER A374 ST.
SALTASH RD.
WESTERN APPROACH
A386 RD.
NOTTE ST.
ROYAL PARADE
NEW GEORGE ST.
MAYFLOWER STREET
CORNWALL STREET
CHARLES STREET
COBOURG STREET
NORTH HILL
MADEIRA ROAD
HOE ROAD
CITADEL ROAD
GRAND PDE.
VAUXHALL
B3240
B3250
GREENBANK
ALEXANDRA
North Cross
Charles Cross
Stonehouse Bridge
Edgcumbe Street
Stoke Damerel Comm. Coll.
Baseball Pitch
Sports Cen.
Sports Hall
Cath.
City Mkt.
Thtre.
Civ. Cen.
Guildhall
Univ.
Mus.
Coll.
YMCA
Pct.
Theatre
Sutton Harbour Whitehouse Pier
Baylys Wharf
Fish Mkts.
Promenade
Warehouse
Millbay Marina Village

142
A
B
C
D
E
1
2
3
4
5
6
7
136
9
141
174
Lipson
Laira
Laira Rail Depot
Lipson Comm. Coll.
Lipson Sports Cen.
The Laira
Saltram Point
Boat Ho.
Point Quay
Mount Gould
Mount Gould Hospital
Freedom Flds.
Greenbank
Beaumont Park
St. Jude's
PL4
PLYMOUTH
Plymouth Yacht Haven
Plymouth
River Plym
Recycling Centre
Laira Bridge
Sugar Mill Business Park
Pomphlett Lake
Superstore
Faraday Mill Business Park
Waste Water Treatment Works
Cattedown
Coxside
North Quay
Sutton Harbour
Glassworks
Aquarium
Barbican Leis. Pk.
Mayflower Stone & Steps
Queen Anne's Battery
Deadman's Bay
Victoria Pier
Fisher's Nose
Foot Ferry
Corinthian Yacht Club
Esso Wharf
Cattedown Wharves
Cattewater
Turnchapel Wharves
Clovelly Bay
The Mount Batten Centre
Mount Batten Tower
Mount Batten Point
Mount Batten Breakwater
Hooelake Point
Turnchapel
Oreston
Breakwater Works
Hoe Lake
Radford Quarry
Radford Park
Radford Lake
Sewage Wks.
Hexton Quay
Hexton
Hooe
Fld. Study Centre
St. Luke's Hospice
Fort Stamford Country Club
Coastguard Lookout
Batten Bay
Dunstone Point
Rum Bay
Jennycliff Bay
Football Ground
Staddon Heights Golf Course
The White House
Staddon Fort
Club Ho.
Jennyscombe Wood
Brixtonhall Plantation
Barn Wood
Barn Farm
Radford House
Exeter St. A374
Embankment Rd.
Laira Bridge Rd.
Billacombe Rd.
Embankment A374
Alexandra Rd.
Gdynia Way

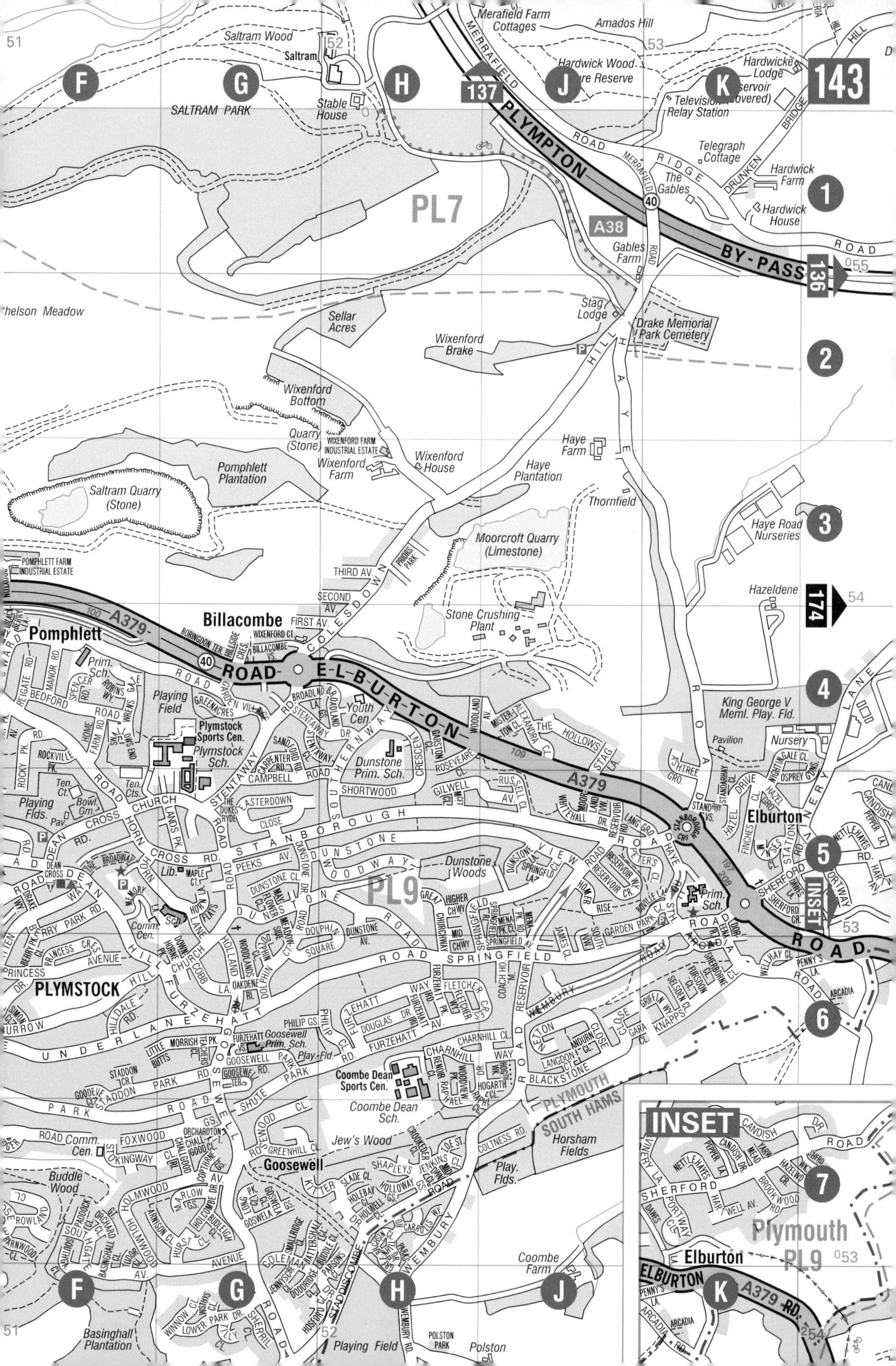

143
137
136
174
INSET
Saltram Wood
Saltram
SALTRAM PARK
Stable House
Merafield Farm Cottages
Amados Hill
Hardwick Wood
Hardwicke Lodge
Television Relay Station
Telegraph Cottage
Hardwick Farm
Hardwick House
The Gables
PLYMPTON BY-PASS
A38
PL7
Gables Farm
Stag Lodge
Drake Memorial Park Cemetery
Sellar Acres
Wixenford Brake
Wixenford Bottom
Quarry (Stone)
WIXENFORD FARM INDUSTRIAL ESTATE
Wixenford Farm
Wixenford House
Haye Farm
Haye Plantation
Thornfield
Pomphlett Plantation
Saltram Quarry (Stone)
Moorcroft Quarry (Limestone)
Haye Road Nurseries
Hazeldene
Stone Crushing Plant
POMPHLETT FARM INDUSTRIAL ESTATE
Billacombe
Pomphlett
A379
ELBURTON ROAD
King George V Meml. Play. Fld.
Pavilion
Nursery
Elburton
Playing Field
Plymstock Sports Cen.
Plymstock Sch.
Youth Cen.
Dunstone Prim. Sch.
Dunstone Woods
PL9
Prim. Sch.
PLYMSTOCK
Playing Flds.
Lib.
Comm. Cen.
Goosewell Prim. Sch.
Coombe Dean Sports Cen.
Coombe Dean Sch.
Jew's Wood
Goosewell
PLYMOUTH
SOUTH HAMS
Horsham Fields
Play. Flds.
Buddle Wood
Coombe Farm
Basinghall Plantation
Playing Field
Polston
POLSTON PARK
Plymouth PL9

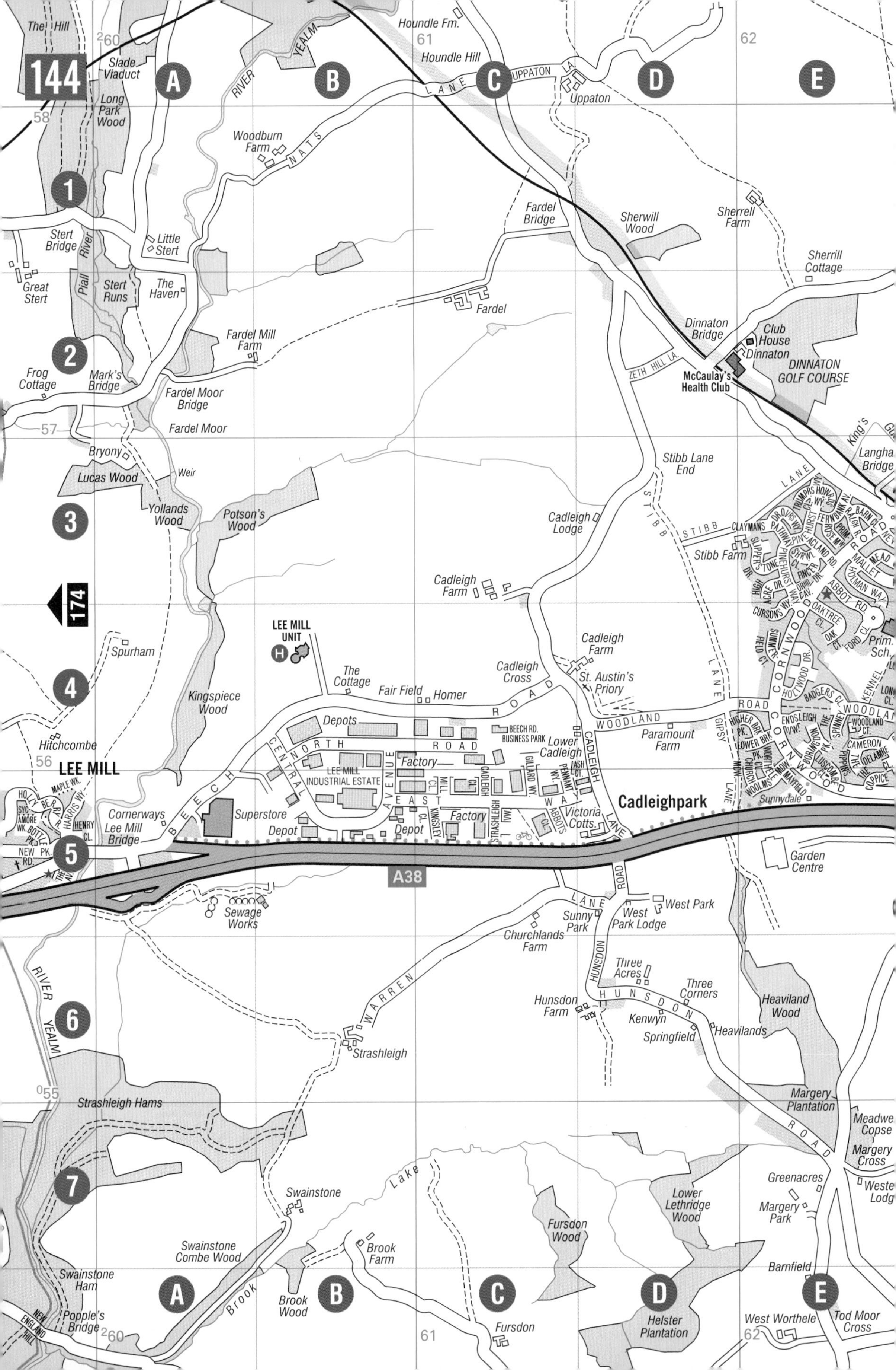
144
174
LEE MILL
LEE MILL UNIT
Cadleighpark
A38
The Hill
Slade Viaduct
Long Park Wood
Houndle Fm.
Houndle Hill
Uppaton
Woodburn Farm
Little Stert
Stert Bridge
Great Stert
Stert Runs
The Haven
Fardel Bridge
Sherwill Wood
Sherrell Farm
Sherrill Cottage
Fardel
Fardel Mill Farm
Frog Cottage
Mark's Bridge
Fardel Moor Bridge
Fardel Moor
Dinnaton Bridge
Club House
Dinnaton
DINNATON GOLF COURSE
McCaulay's Health Club
Bryony
Lucas Wood
Weir
Yollands Wood
Potson's Wood
Stibb Lane End
Cadleigh Lodge
Stibb Farm
Cadleigh Farm
Spurham
Kingspiece Wood
The Cottage
Fair Field
Homer
Cadleigh Cross
St. Austin's Priory
Hitchcombe
Depots
Factory
LEE MILL INDUSTRIAL ESTATE
BEECH RD. BUSINESS PARK
Lower Cadleigh
Paramount Farm
Superstore
Depot
Victoria Cotts.
Cornerways
Lee Mill Bridge
Sunnydale
Garden Centre
Sewage Works
Sunny Park
West Park
West Park Lodge
Churchlands Farm
Three Acres
Three Corners
Hunsdon Farm
Kenwyn
Springfield
Heavilands
Heaviland Wood
Strashleigh
Strashleigh Hams
Margery Plantation
Meadwe Copse
Margery Cross
Swainstone
Greenacres
Margery Park
Lower Lethridge Wood
Fursdon Wood
Swainstone Combe Wood
Brook Farm
Swainstone Ham
Brook Wood
Barnfield
Popple's Bridge
Fursdon
Helster Plantation
West Worthele
Tod Moor Cross
RIVER YEALM
Piall River
Lake
Brook
UPPATON LA.
NATS LANE
ZETH HILL LA.
STIBB LANE
WOODLAND ROAD
BEECH ROAD
NORTH ROAD
CENTRAL AVENUE
EAST WAY
CADLEIGH LANE
GIPSY LANE
CORNWOOD ROAD
HUNSDON ROAD
WARREN LANE
NEW ENGLAND HILL
King's
Langha Bridge
Prim. Sch.

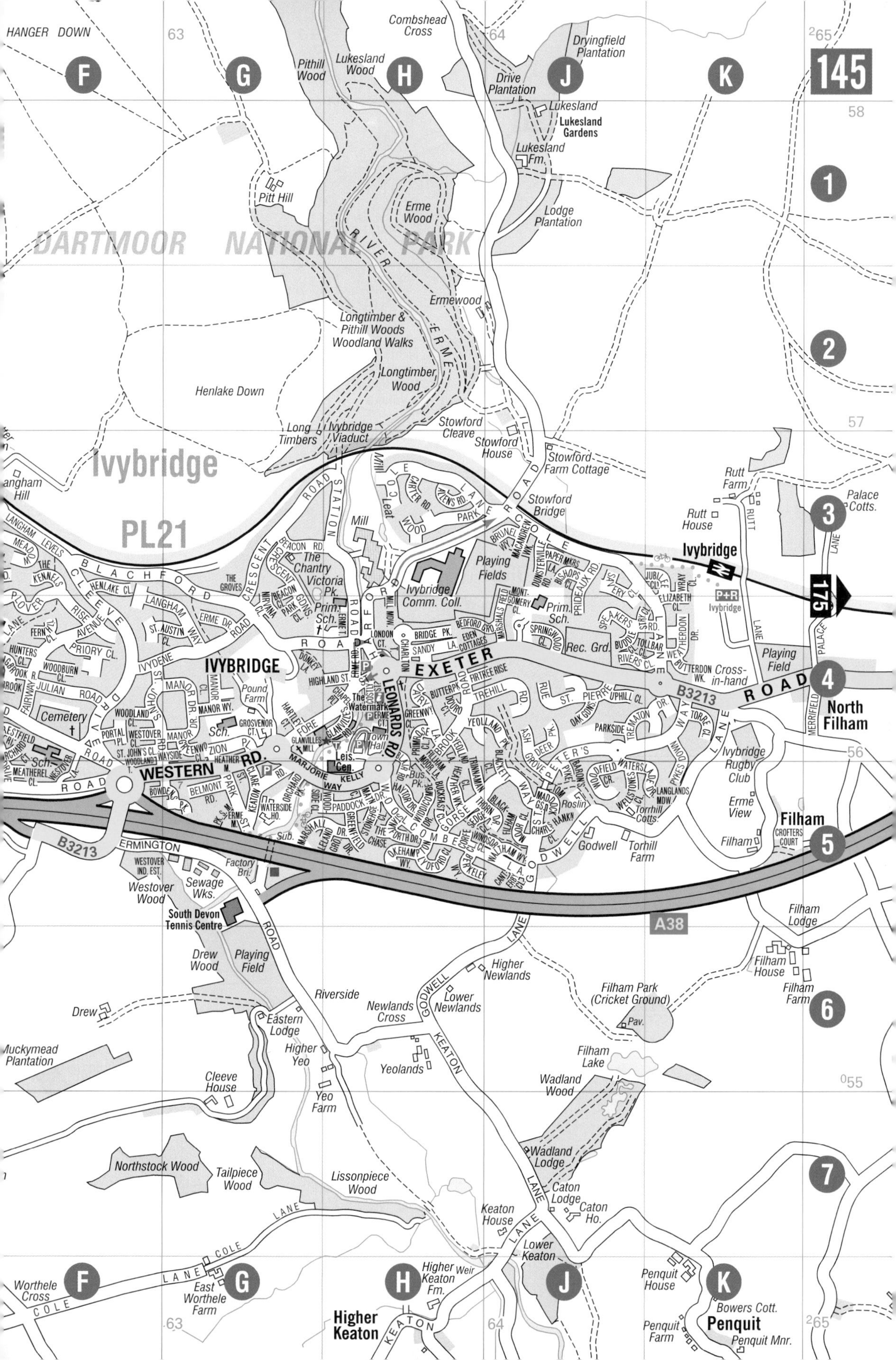

HANGER DOWN
Combshead Cross
Dryingfield Plantation
Pithill Wood
Lukesland Wood
Drive Plantation
Lukesland
Lukesland Gardens
Lukesland Fm.
Pitt Hill
Erme Wood
Lodge Plantation
DARTMOOR NATIONAL PARK
RIVER ERME
Ermewood
Longtimber & Pithill Woods Woodland Walks
Longtimber Wood
Henlake Down
Long Timbers
Ivybridge Viaduct
Stowford Cleave
Stowford House
Stowford Farm Cottage
Ivybridge
PL21
Stowford Bridge
Rutt Farm
Rutt House
Palace Cotts.
Ivybridge
The Chantry
Victoria Pk.
Mill
Ivybridge Comm. Coll.
Playing Fields
Prim. Sch.
Rec. Grd.
Playing Field
IVYBRIDGE
EXETER ROAD
B3213
North Filham
Cemetery
Sch.
WESTERN RD.
The Watermark
Town Hall
Leis. Cen.
Ivybridge Rugby Club
Erme View
Filham
Godwell
Torhill Farm
Roslin
Torrhill Cotts.
A38
Westover Ind. Est.
Westover Wood
Sewage Wks.
Factory Bri.
South Devon Tennis Centre
Drew Wood
Playing Field
Filham Lodge
Higher Newlands
Lower Newlands
Filham House
Filham Farm
Filham Park (Cricket Ground)
Drew
Riverside
Newlands Cross
Eastern Lodge
Muckymead Plantation
Higher Yeo
Yeolands
Filham Lake
Cleeve House
Yeo Farm
Wadland Wood
Northstock Wood
Tailpiece Wood
Lissonpiece Wood
Wadland Lodge
Caton Lodge
Caton Ho.
Keaton House
Lower Keaton
Higher Keaton Fm.
Weir
Penquit House
Worthele Cross
East Worthele Farm
Higher Keaton
Bowers Cott.
Penquit
Penquit Farm
Penquit Mnr.
COLE LANE
KEATON LANE
GODWELL LANE
175

BITTAFORD / UGBOROUGH

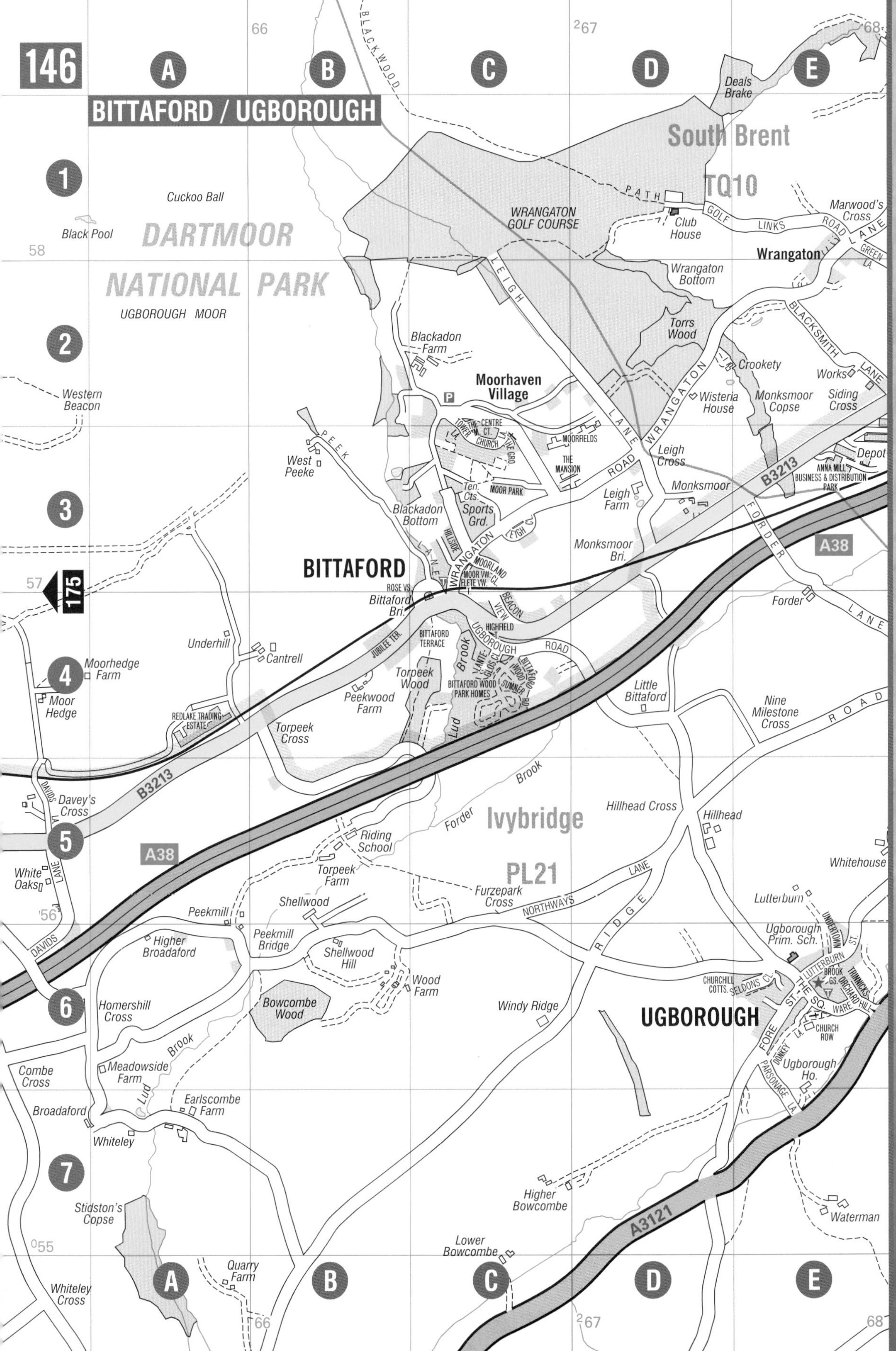

A
B
C
D
E
1
2
3
4
5
6
7
South Brent
TQ10
DARTMOOR
NATIONAL PARK
UGBOROUGH MOOR
Cuckoo Ball
Black Pool
Western Beacon
WRANGATON GOLF COURSE
Deals Brake
Club House
Marwood's Cross
Wrangaton
Wrangaton Bottom
Torrs Wood
Blackadon Farm
Moorhaven Village
Crookety
Works
Wisteria House
Monksmoor Copse
Siding Cross
West Peeke
Leigh Cross
Depot
ANNA MILL BUSINESS & DISTRIBUTION PARK
Monksmoor
Leigh Farm
Blackadon Bottom
Sports Grd.
Monksmoor Bri.
BITTAFORD
Bittaford Bri.
Forder
Underhill
Cantrell
Moorhedge Farm
Moor Hedge
REDLAKE TRADING ESTATE
Torpeek Wood
Peekwood Farm
Torpeek Cross
BITTAFORD WOOD PARK HOMES
Little Bittaford
Nine Milestone Cross
Davey's Cross
Ivybridge
Hillhead Cross
Hillhead
Riding School
White Oaks
A38
B3213
A3121
PL21
Torpeek Farm
Furzepark Cross
Whitehouse
Shellwood
Lutterburn
Peekmill
Higher Broadaford
Peekmill Bridge
Shellwood Hill
Ugborough Prim. Sch.
Wood Farm
Homershill Cross
Bowcombe Wood
Windy Ridge
UGBOROUGH
Ugborough Ho.
Combe Cross
Meadowside Farm
Earlscombe Farm
Broadaford
Whiteley
Higher Bowcombe
Waterman
Stidston's Copse
Lower Bowcombe
Quarry Farm
Whiteley Cross

175

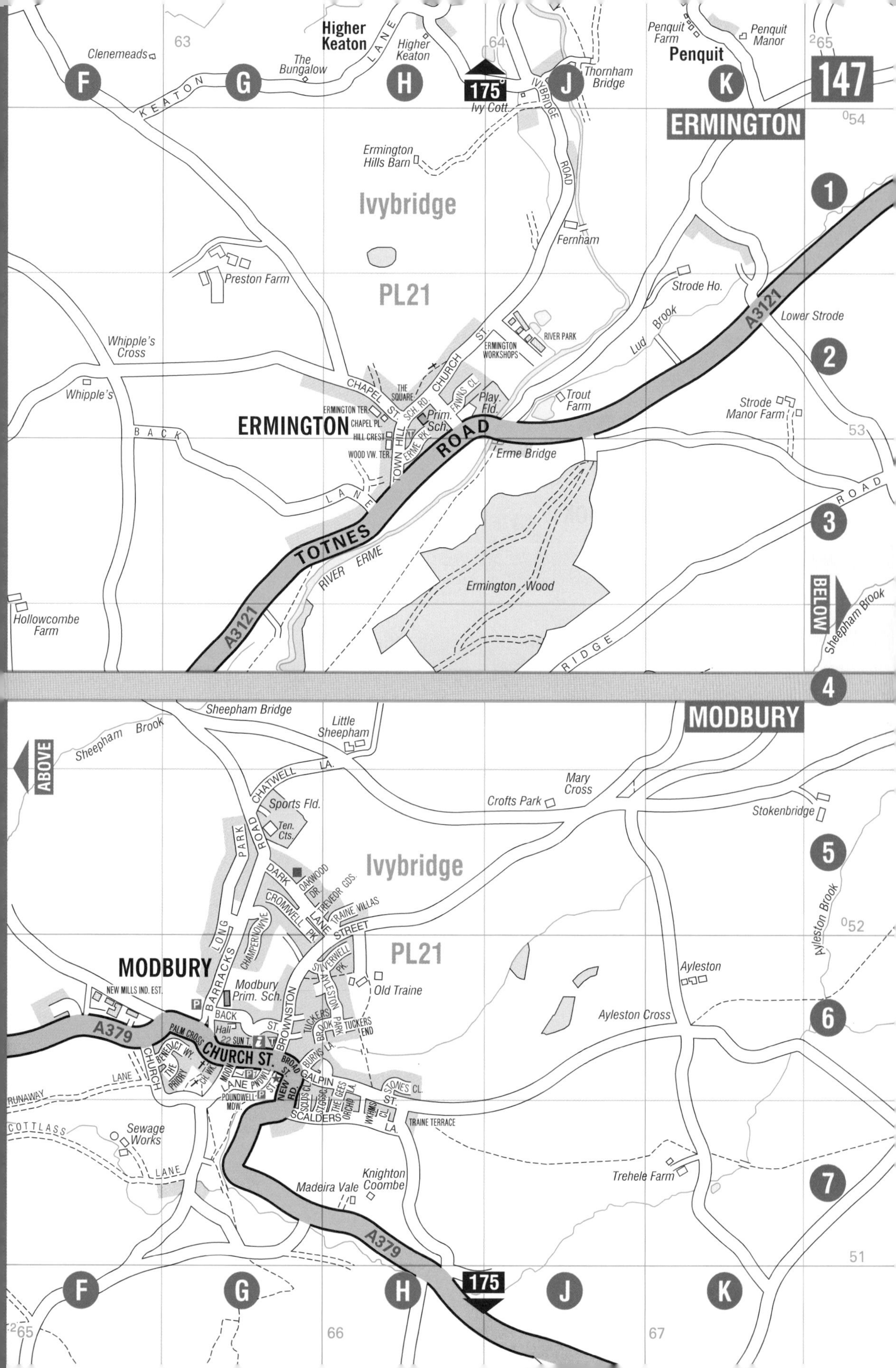
ERMINGTON
Higher Keaton
Clenemeads
The Bungalow
KEATON LANE
Ivy Cott.
Thornham Bridge
Penquit Farm
Penquit Manor
Penquit
IVYBRIDGE ROAD
Ermington Hills Barn
Ivybridge
Fernham
Preston Farm
PL21
Strode Ho.
Lower Strode
Lud Brook
RIVER PARK
ERMINGTON WORKSHOPS
Whipple's Cross
Whipple's
CHAPEL ST.
THE SQUARE
CHURCH ST.
FAWNS CL.
SCH. RD.
Play. Fld.
Prim. Sch.
ERMINGTON TER.
CHAPEL PL.
HILL CREST
WOOD VW. TER.
TOWN HILL
ERME PK.
Trout Farm
Strode Manor Farm
ERMINGTON
BACK LANE
TOTNES ROAD
A3121
Erme Bridge
ROAD
RIVER ERME
Ermington Wood
BELOW
Sheepham Brook
Hollowcombe Farm
RIDGE
MODBURY
Sheepham Bridge
Little Sheepham
ABOVE
CHATWELL LA.
Sports Fld.
Ten. Cts.
Mary Cross
Crofts Park
Stokenbridge
PARK ROAD
DARK LANE
OAKWOOD DR.
TREVEOR GDS.
TRAINE VILLAS
Ivybridge
CROMWELL PK.
STREET
CHAMPERNOWNE
LONG
BARRACKS
SILVERWELL PK.
AYLESTON PARK
PL21
Aylestone Brook
Ayleston
MODBURY
NEW MILLS IND. EST.
Modbury Prim. Sch.
Old Traine
Ayleston Cross
BACK ST.
BROWNSTON
TUCKERS BROOK
TUCKERS END
Hall
SUN T.
PALM CROSS
BENEDICT WY.
CHURCH ST.
A379
CHURCH LANE
THE PRIORY
CH. WK.
POUNDWELL
BROAD ST.
BURNS LA.
GALPIN ST.
STONES CL.
POUNDWELL MDW.
NEW RD.
SCALDERS LA.
ORCHID LA.
WYKEHAMS CL.
TRAINE TERRACE
RUNAWAY LANE
COTTLASS LANE
Sewage Works
Knighton Coombe
Madeira Vale
Trehele Farm
A379
175
F G H J K
1 2 3 4 5 6 7
63 64 65 66 67
54 53 52 51

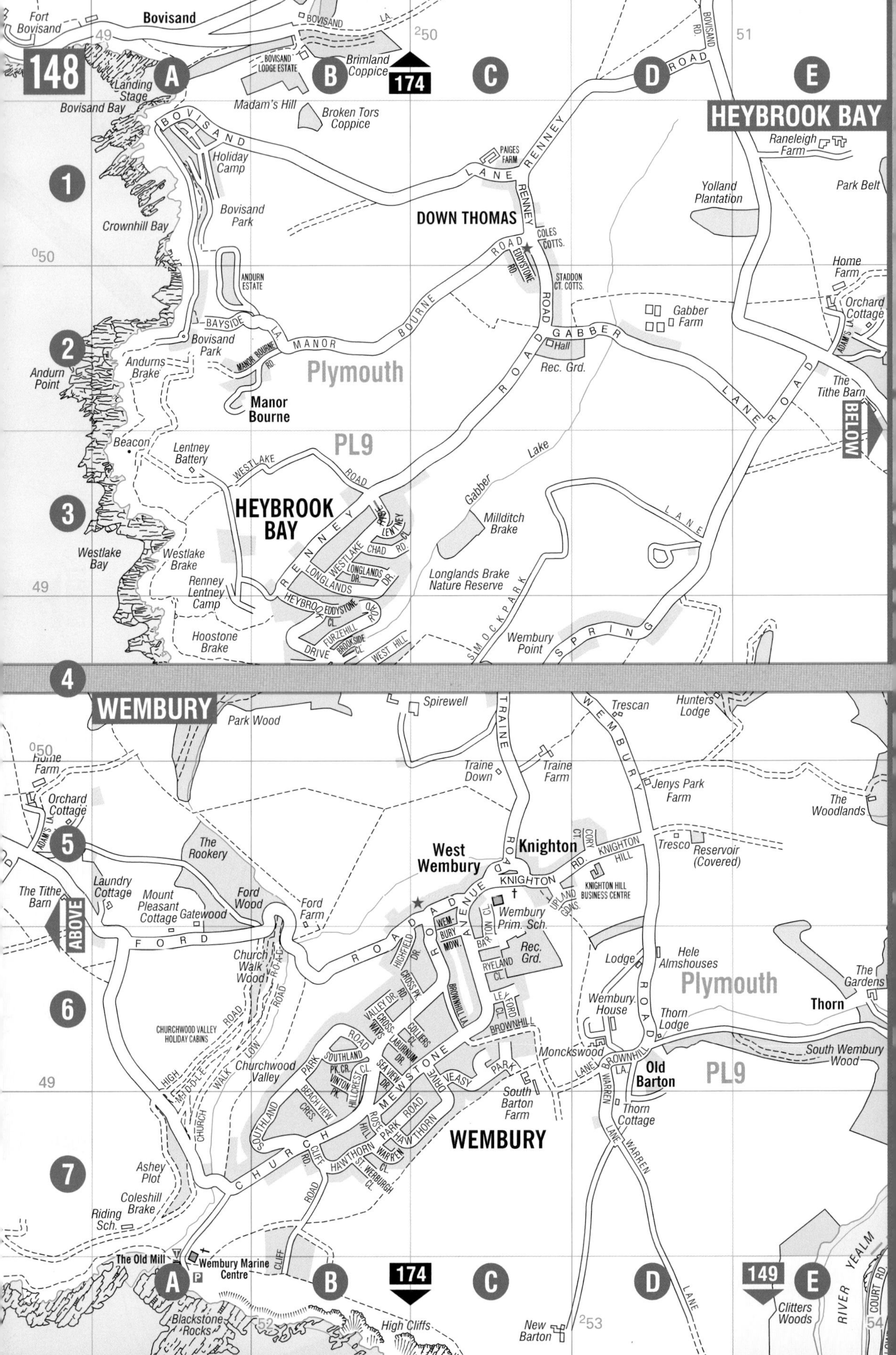

Bovisand

Fort Bovisand

Bovisand La.

BOVISAND RD.

A Landing Stage

Bovisand Bay

BOVISAND LODGE ESTATE

B Brimland Coppice

Madam's Hill

Broken Tors Coppice

174

C

RENNEY LANE

PAIGES FARM

D

BOVISAND RD.

E **HEYBROOK BAY**

Raneleigh Farm

1

Crownhill Bay

Holiday Camp

Bovisand Park

Bovisand Park

DOWN THOMAS

RENNEY ROAD

COLES COTTS.

EDDYSTONE RD.

STADDON CT. COTTS.

Yolland Plantation

Park Belt

Home Farm

Orchard Cottage

050

2

Andurn Point

ANDURN ESTATE

BAYSIDE LA.

MANOR BOURNE RD.

Andurns Brake

Bovisand Park

MANOR RD.

Plymouth

Gabber Farm

GABBER ROAD

Hall

Rec. Grd.

LANE ROAD

The Tithe Barn

BELOW

49

3

Beacon

Lentney Battery

Manor Bourne

PL9

WESTLAKE ROAD

HEYBROOK BAY

RENNEY ROAD

WESTLAKE RD.

LENTNEY RD.

CHAD RD.

LONGLANDS DR.

Gabber Lake

Millditch Brake

Longlands Brake Nature Reserve

SIMOCK PARK LANE

SPRING LANE

Westlake Bay

Westlake Brake

Renney Lentney Camp

HEYBRO. EDDYSTONE CL.

FURZEHILL CL.

BROOKSIDE CL.

WEST HILL

DRIVE

Hoostone Brake

Wembury Point

4

WEMBURY

Park Wood

Spirewell

TRAINE ROAD

Traine Down

Traine Farm

WEMBURY ROAD

Trescan

Jenys Park Farm

Hunters Lodge

The Woodlands

050

Home Farm

Orchard Cottage

ADAM'S LA.

5

The Tithe Barn

ABOVE

Laundry Cottage

The Rookery

Mount Pleasant Cottage

Gatewood

FORD ROAD

Ford Wood

Ford Farm

West Wembury

KNIGHTON ROAD

Knighton

CORY RD.

KNIGHTON HILL

KNIGHTON HILL BUSINESS CENTRE

Tresco

Reservoir (Covered)

6

Churchwood Valley Holiday Cabins

Church Walk Wood

LOW ROAD

HIGH ROAD

Churchwood Valley

FORD ROAD

KNIGHTON AVENUE

WEM- BURY MDW.

HIGHFIELD

CROSS PK.

BARTON CL.

Wembury Prim. Sch.

†

BROWNHILL

Rec. Grd.

RYELAND CL.

LET FORD CL.

Lodge

Wembury House

Thorn Lodge

Hele Almshouses

Plymouth

The Gardens

Thorn

49

7

MEDROSE LA.

SOUTHLAND PK. CR.

VINTON PK.

MILLCREST CL.

PARK ROAD

SOUTHLAND CRES.

BEACHVIEW

VALLEY DR.

CROSS WAYS

LABURNUM DR.

SEA VIEW DR.

MEWSTONE DRIVE

COLLIERS CL.

VEASY PARK

BROWNHILL

PARK ROAD

Monckswood

BROWNHILL LANE

WARREN LA.

Old Barton

PL9

South Wembury Wood

CHURCH ROAD

Ashey Plot

Coleshill Brake

Riding Sch.

HIGH ROAD

ROSE PK.

HAWTHORN WARREN

HILL

HAWTHORN

CLIFF ROAD

WERBURGH CL.

WEMBURY

South Barton Farm

WARREN LANE

Thorn Cottage

The Old Mill

A Wembury Marine Centre

CLIFF ROAD

B

174

C

New Barton

D

149

E

Clitters Woods

RIVER YEALM

COURT RD.

Blackstone Rocks

52

High Cliffs

053

54

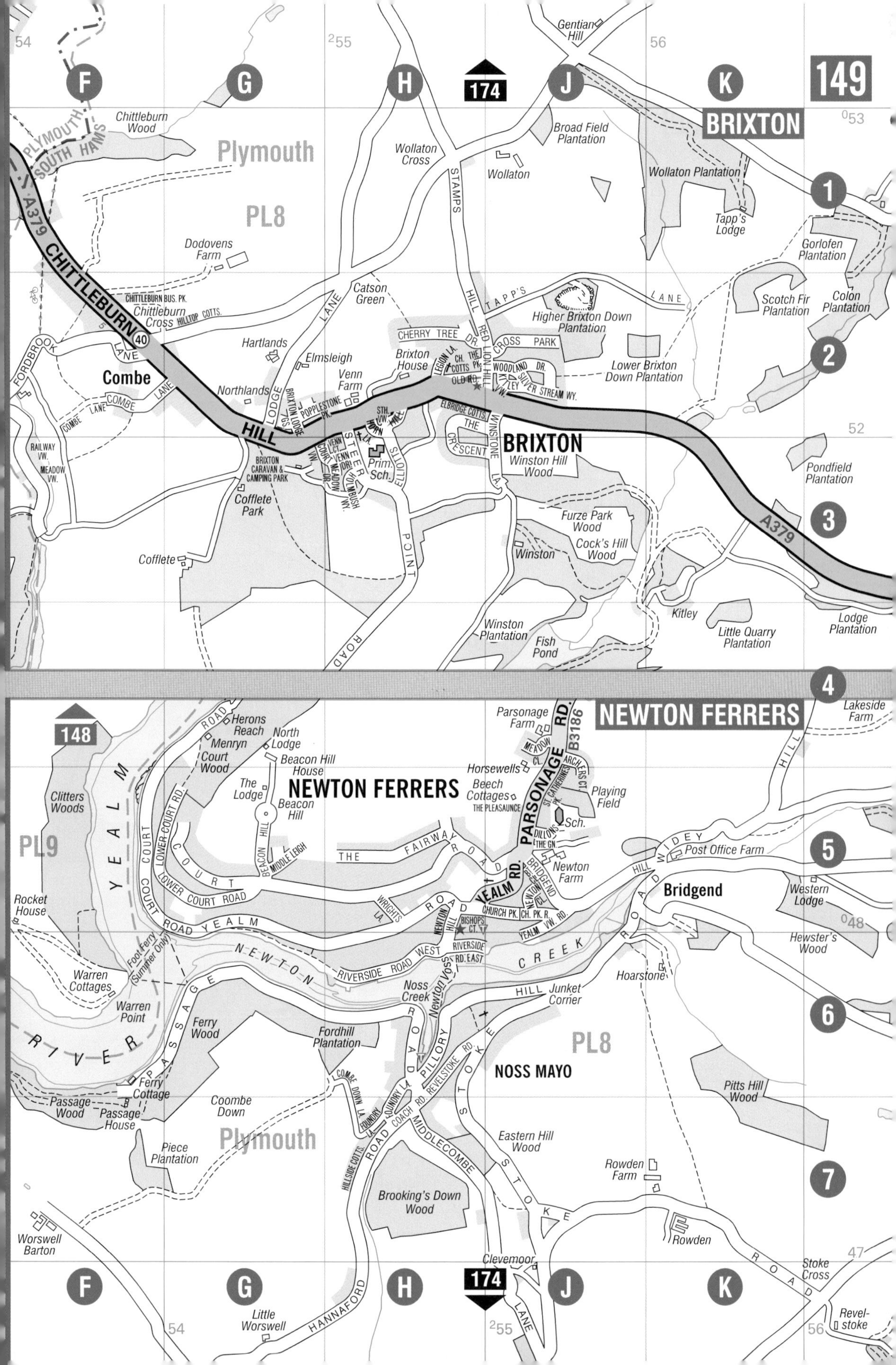

BRIXTON
NEWTON FERRERS
174
148
Plymouth
PL8
PL9
A379
CHITTLEBURN HILL
Chittleburn Wood
Dodovens Farm
Chittleburn Cross
Combe
Hartlands
Elmsleigh
Northlands
Catson Green
Wollaton Cross
Wollaton
Broad Field Plantation
Wollaton Plantation
Tapp's Lodge
Gorlofen Plantation
Scotch Fir Plantation
Colon Plantation
Higher Brixton Down Plantation
Lower Brixton Down Plantation
Brixton House
Venn Farm
Prim. Sch.
Winston Hill Wood
Pondfield Plantation
Furze Park Wood
Cock's Hill Wood
Winston
Cofflete Park
Cofflete
Kitley
Little Quarry Plantation
Lodge Plantation
Winston Plantation
Fish Pond
Gentian Hill
Lakeside Farm
Parsonage Farm
Herons Reach
North Lodge
Menryn
Court Wood
Beacon Hill House
The Lodge
Beacon Hill
Clitters Woods
Horsewells
Beech Cottages
Playing Field
Sch.
Post Office Farm
Newton Farm
Bridgend
Western Lodge
Hewster's Wood
Rocket House
Warren Cottages
Warren Point
Foot Ferry (Summer Only)
Noss Creek
Junket Corner
Hoarstone
Ferry Wood
Fordhill Plantation
NOSS MAYO
Ferry Cottage
Passage Wood
Passage House
Coombe Down
Piece Plantation
Pitts Hill Wood
Eastern Hill Wood
Rowden Farm
Brooking's Down Wood
Rowden
Worswell Barton
Clevemoor
Stoke Cross
Little Worswell
Revel-stoke
RIVER YEALM
NEWTON CREEK

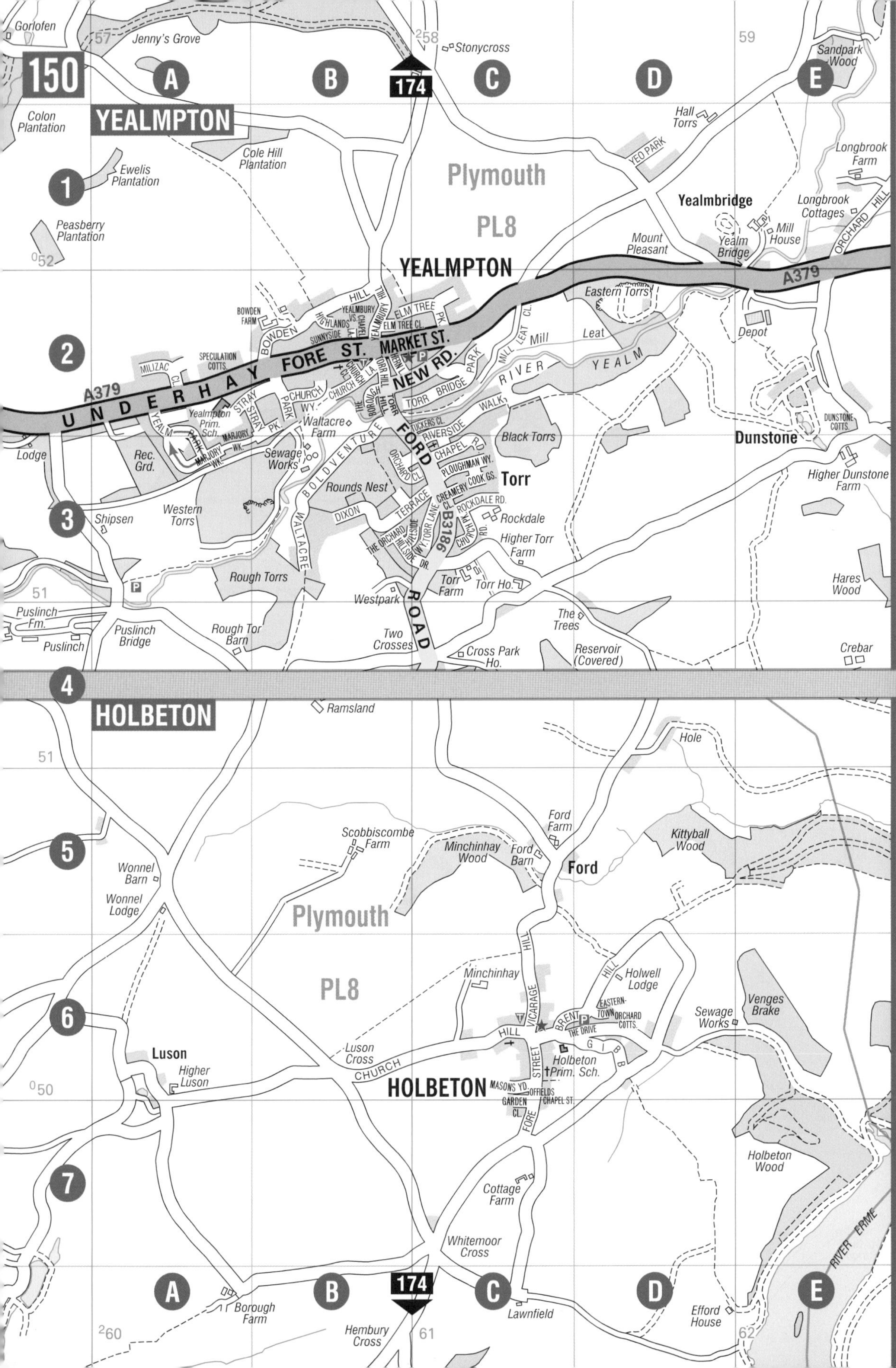
YEALMPTON
HOLBETON
Plymouth
PL8
YEALMPTON
HOLBETON
Yealmbridge
Dunstone
Torr
Ford
Luson
UNDERHAY
FORE ST.
MARKET ST.
NEW RD.
FORD ROAD
A379
B3186
Jenny's Grove
Gorlofen
Colon Plantation
Cole Hill Plantation
Ewelis Plantation
Peasberry Plantation
Stonycross
Hall Torrs
YEO PARK
Longbrook Farm
Longbrook Cottages
Mill House
Yealm Bridge
Mount Pleasant
Sandpark Wood
ORCHARD HILL
Eastern Torrs
Depot
Mill
Leat
RIVER YEALM
Black Torrs
Higher Dunstone Farm
Hares Wood
Crebar
Rockdale
Higher Torr Farm
Torr Farm
Torr Ho.
Westpark
Two Crosses
Cross Park Ho.
The Trees
Reservoir (Covered)
Rough Torrs
Rough Tor Barn
Rounds Nest
Western Torrs
Shipsen
Puslinch Fm.
Puslinch
Puslinch Bridge
Lodge
Rec. Grd.
Sewage Works
Waltacre Farm
Yealmpton Prim. Sch.
Ramsland
Hole
Ford Farm
Ford Barn
Kittyball Wood
Minchinhay Wood
Scobbiscombe Farm
Wonnel Barn
Wonnel Lodge
Minchinhay
Holwell Lodge
Sewage Works
Venges Brake
Holbeton Prim. Sch.
Luson Cross
Higher Luson
Cottage Farm
Whitemoor Cross
Holbeton Wood
RIVER ERME
Borough Farm
Hembury Cross
Lawnfield
Efford House
174
174

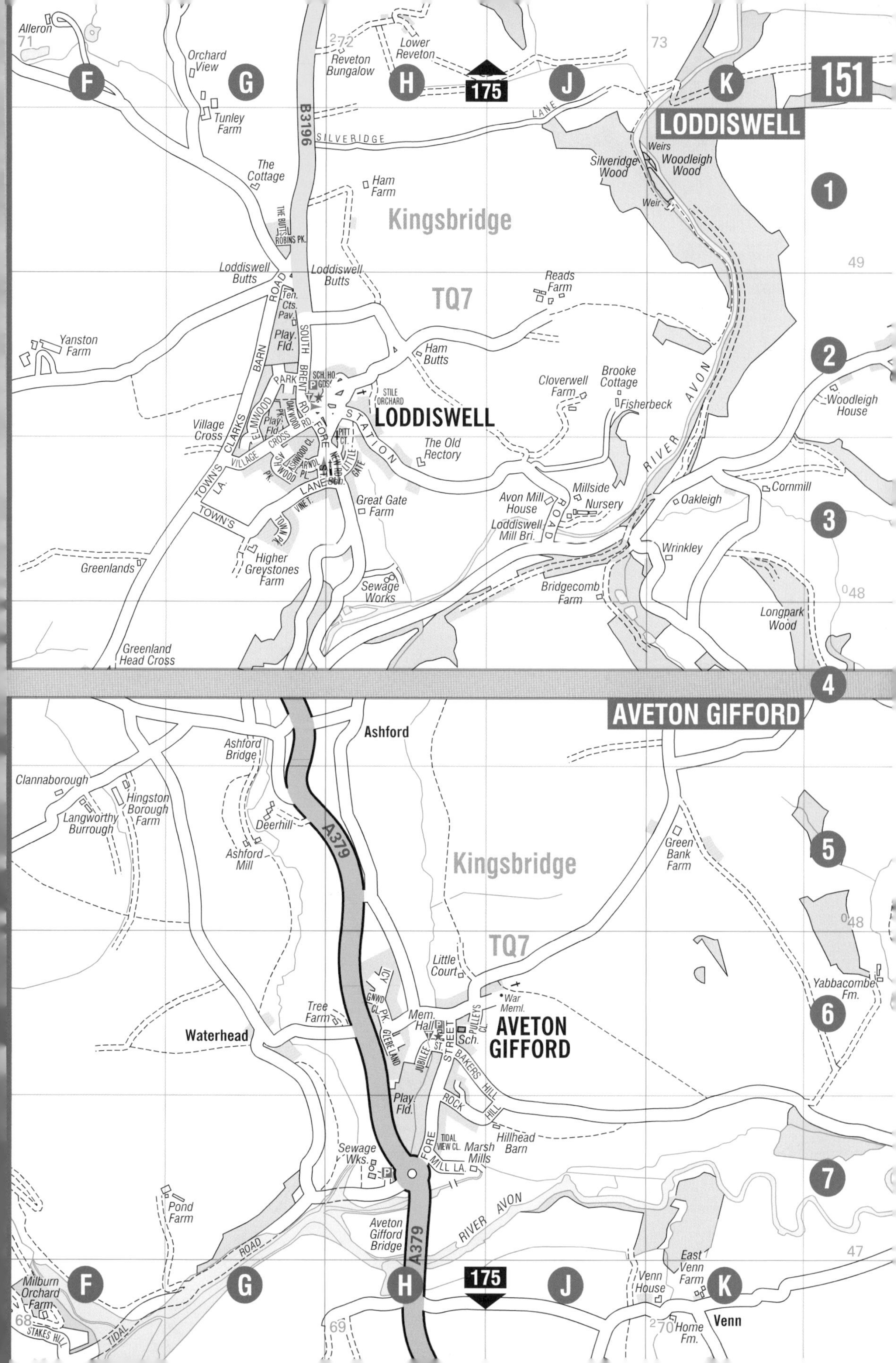

LODDISWELL
AVETON GIFFORD
175
Alleron
Orchard View
Tunley Farm
Reveton Bungalow
Lower Reveton
B3196
SILVERIDGE LANE
The Cottage
Ham Farm
Kingsbridge
THE BUTTS
ROBINS PK.
Silveridge Wood
Weirs
Woodleigh Wood
Weir
Loddiswell Butts
Loddiswell Butts
Reads Farm
TQ7
Yanston Farm
Ham Butts
Cloverwell Farm
Brooke Cottage
Fisherbeck
Woodleigh House
LODDISWELL
The Old Rectory
Village Cross
RIVER AVON
Great Gate Farm
Avon Mill House
Millside Nursery
Loddiswell Mill Bri.
Oakleigh
Cornmill
Wrinkley
Higher Greystones Farm
Greenlands
Sewage Works
Bridgecomb Farm
Longpark Wood
Greenland Head Cross
Ashford
Ashford Bridge
Clannaborough
Hingston Borough Farm
Langworthy Burrough
Deerhill
Ashford Mill
A379
Kingsbridge
Green Bank Farm
TQ7
Little Court
Yabbacombe Fm.
Tree Farm
Waterhead
Mem. Hall
War Meml.
AVETON GIFFORD
Hillhead Barn
Marsh Mills
Sewage Wks.
Pond Farm
RIVER AVON
Aveton Gifford Bridge
ROAD
TIDAL
STAKES HILL
Milburn Orchard Farm
Venn House
East Venn Farm
Home Fm.
Venn

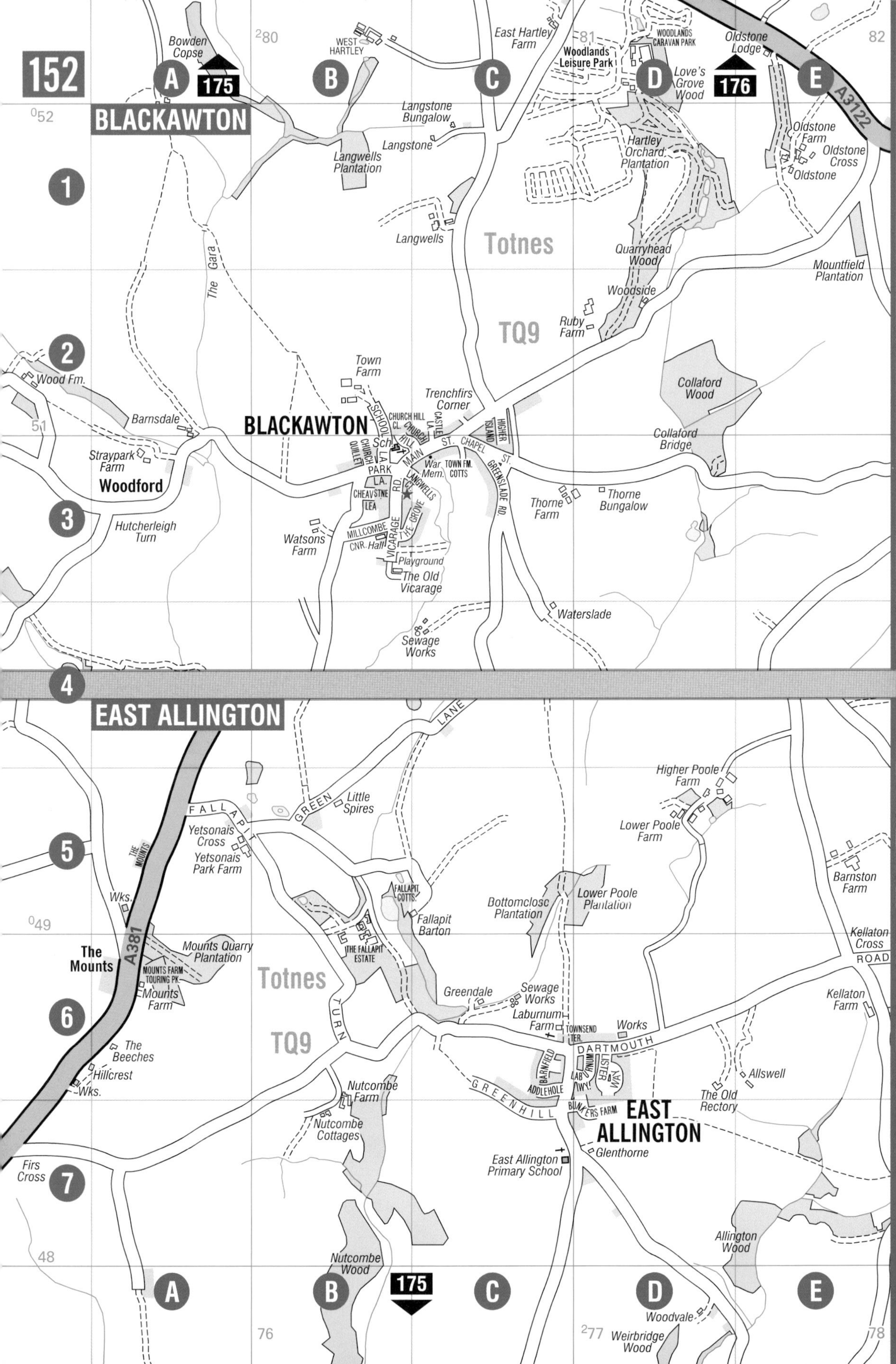
152
175
176
BLACKAWTON
EAST ALLINGTON
Bowden Copse
West Hartley
East Hartley Farm
Woodlands Leisure Park
Woodlands Caravan Park
Oldstone Lodge
Love's Grove Wood
A3122
Langstone Bungalow
Langstone
Langwells Plantation
Hartley Orchard Plantation
Oldstone Farm
Oldstone Cross
Oldstone
The Gara
Langwells
Totnes
Quarryhead Wood
Mountfield Plantation
Woodside
Ruby Farm
TQ9
Wood Fm.
Town Farm
Trenchfirs Corner
Collaford Wood
Barnsdale
Collaford Bridge
Straypark Farm
Woodford
Hutcherleigh Turn
Thorne Farm
Thorne Bungalow
Watsons Farm
Playground
The Old Vicarage
War Mem.
Waterslade
Sewage Works
Little Spires
Higher Poole Farm
Lower Poole Farm
Yetsonais Cross
Yetsonais Park Farm
Barnston Farm
Fallapit Cotts.
Fallapit Barton
Bottomclose Plantation
Lower Poole Plantation
Wks.
The Mounts
A381
Mounts Quarry Plantation
Mounts Farm Touring Pk.
Mounts Farm
The Fallapit Estate
Kellaton Cross
Kellaton Farm
Greendale
Sewage Works
Laburnum Farm
Townsend Ter.
Works
The Beeches
Hillcrest
Nutcombe Farm
Allswell
The Old Rectory
Nutcombe Cottages
East Allington Primary School
Glenthorne
Firs Cross
Allington Wood
Nutcombe Wood
Woodvale
Weirbridge Wood

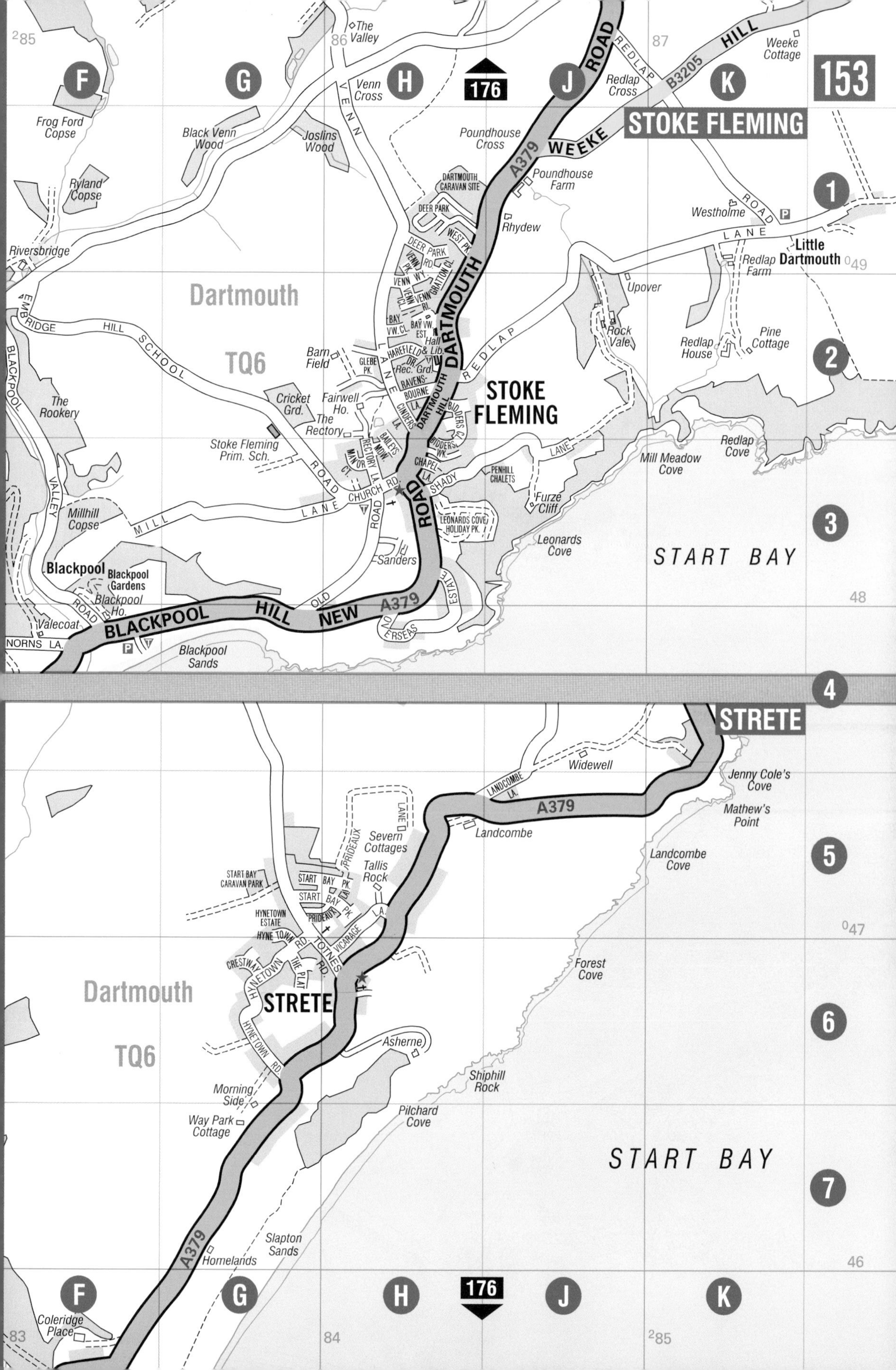

F · **G** · **H** · ▲ **176** · **J** · **K**

STOKE FLEMING

285 86 The Valley 87 Weeke Cottage

Frog Ford Copse

Black Venn Wood

Joslins Wood

Venn Cross

Poundhouse Cross

REDLAP

Redlap Cross

B3205

WEEKE HILL

1

Ryland Copse

Dartmouth Caravan Site

DEER PARK

Poundhouse Farm

A379

WEEKE ROAD

Westholme

Redlap Farm

Little Dartmouth

P

049

Riversbridge

DEER PARK

Rhydew

Upover

Redlap House

Pine Cottage

EMBRIDGE HILL

SCHOOL ROAD

Dartmouth

TQ6

VENN RD.

VENN WY.

VENN CLN. RI.

BAY.

VENN CL. EST.

BAY VW.

HAREFIELD

GLEBE PK.

BAY VW.

DR.

Hall

P & Lib.

Rec. Grd.

RAVENS:

DARTMOUTH

REDLAP

Rock Vale

Redlap Cove

2

The Rookery

Barn Field

Fairwell Ho.

The Rectory

Cricket Grd.

RECTORY LA.

BOURNE

CHAPEL

BUILDERS CT.

BIDDERS WK.

STOKE FLEMING

LANE

Mill Meadow Cove

48

Stoke Fleming Prim. Sch.

MILL LANE

CHURCH RD.

ROAD

SHADY

CHIVERS LA.

MANOR

PENHILL CHALETS

Furze Cliff

Leonards Cove

START BAY

3

Millhill Copse

VALLEY

Old Sanders

LEONARDS COVE HOLIDAY PK.

Blackpool

Blackpool Gardens

Blackpool Ho.

ROAD

BLACKPOOL HILL NEW ROAD

A379

NORNS LA.

Valecoat

P

Blackpool Sands

NO OVERSEAS ESTATE

4

STRETE

Widewell

LANDCOMBE LA.

A379

Jenny Cole's Cove

Mathew's Point

Severn Cottages

PRIDEAUX LANE

Tallis Rock

Landcombe

Landcombe Cove

5

START BAY CARAVAN PARK

START BAY PK.

START BAY PK.

PRIDEAUX LA.

047

HYNETOWN ESTATE

HYNE TOWN

HYNETOWN RD.

TOTNES RD.

VICARAGE

Dartmouth

TQ6

CRESTMAN

HYNETOWN RD.

THE PLAT

STRETE

Forest Cove

6

Asherne)

Shiphill Rock

Morning Side

Way Park Cottage

Pilchard Cove

START BAY

7

A379

Homelands

Slapton Sands

46

F · **G** · **H** · ▼ **176** · **J** · **K**

283

Coleridge Place

84 285

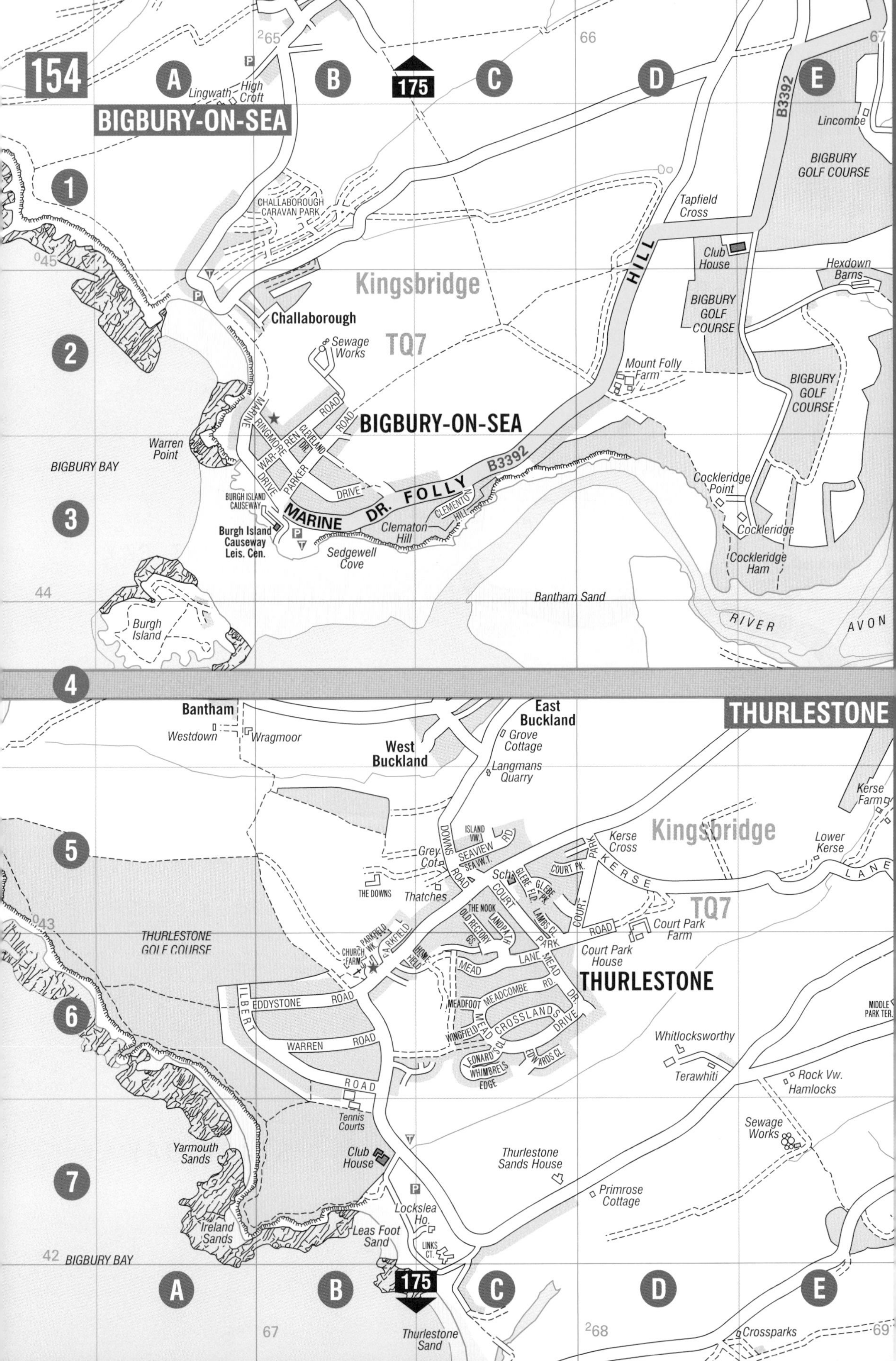

154
BIGBURY-ON-SEA
175
Lingwath
High Croft
CHALLABOROUGH CARAVAN PARK
Challaborough
Kingsbridge
TQ7
Sewage Works
BIGBURY-ON-SEA
MARINE DRIVE
RINGMORE DRIVE
WARREN DR.
CLEVELAND DR.
PARKER ROAD
MARINE DR. FOLLY HILL
B3392
CLEMENTON HILL
Clematon Hill
Sedgewell Cove
BURGH ISLAND CAUSEWAY
Burgh Island Causeway Leis. Cen.
Warren Point
BIGBURY BAY
Burgh Island
Bantham Sand
RIVER AVON
Tapfield Cross
Club House
BIGBURY GOLF COURSE
Lincombe
Hexdown Barns
Mount Folly Farm
Cockleridge Point
Cockleridge
Cockleridge Ham
THURLESTONE
Bantham
Westdown
Wragmoor
West Buckland
East Buckland
Grove Cottage
Langmans Quarry
Kerse Farm
Lower Kerse
Kerse Cross
KERSE LANE
Kingsbridge
TQ7
ISLAND VW.
SEAVIEW RD.
SEA VW. T.
DOWNS ROAD
Grey Cot
THE DOWNS
Thatches
Sch.
GLEBE FLD.
GLEBE PK.
COURT PK.
PARK
COURT ROAD
LAMBS CL.
COURT PARK
Court Park Farm
Court Park House
THE NOOK
OLD RECTORY GS.
LANDPATH
PARKFIELD WK.
PARKFIELD
CHURCH FARM
HOME FIELD
MEAD LANE
MEAD DR.
MEADCOMBE RD.
MEADFOOT
CROSSLANDS DRIVE
WINGFIELD
LEONARD'S CL.
EDWARDS CL.
WHIMBRELS EDGE
THURLESTONE
THURLESTONE GOLF COURSE
ILBERT
EDDYSTONE ROAD
WARREN ROAD
ROAD
Tennis Courts
Club House
Whitlocksworthy
Terawhiti
MIDDLE PARK TER.
Rock Vw.
Hamlocks
Sewage Works
Thurlestone Sands House
Primrose Cottage
Yarmouth Sands
Ireland Sands
Leas Foot Sand
Lockslea Ho.
LINKS CT.
BIGBURY BAY
Thurlestone Sand
Crossparks
A
B
C
D
E
1
2
3
4
5
6
7
265
66
67
268
69
045
44
043
42

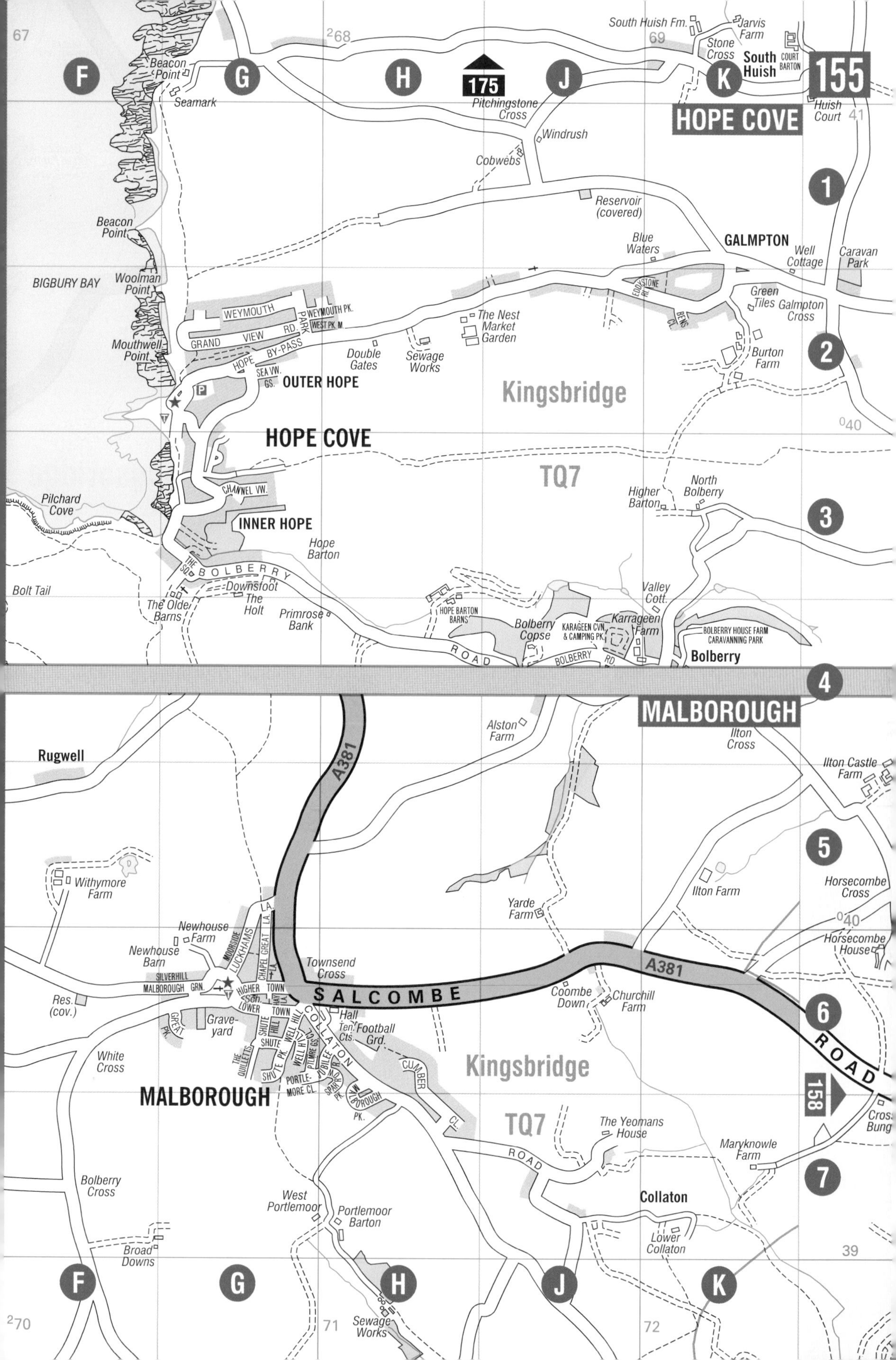
HOPE COVE
MALBOROUGH
175
158
South Huish Fm.
Jarvis Farm
Stone Cross
South Huish
COURT BARTON
Huish Court
Beacon Point
Seamark
Pitchingstone Cross
Windrush
Cobwebs
Reservoir (covered)
GALMPTON
Blue Waters
Well Cottage
Caravan Park
BIGBURY BAY
Woolman Point
WEYMOUTH PARK
GRAND VIEW RD.
WEYMOUTH PK.
WEST PK. M.
HOPE BY-PASS
EDDYSTONE RI.
BENS CL.
Green Tiles
Galmpton Cross
The Nest Market Garden
Burton Farm
Mouthwell Point
Double Gates
Sewage Works
SEA VW. GS.
OUTER HOPE
Kingsbridge
HOPE COVE
TQ7
CHANNEL VW.
North Bolberry
Higher Barton
Pilchard Cove
INNER HOPE
Hope Barton
THE SQ.
BOLBERRY
Bolt Tail
Downsfoot
The Holt
The Olde Barns
Primrose Bank
Valley Cott.
HOPE BARTON BARNS
Bolberry Copse
KARAGEEN CVN. & CAMPING PK.
Karrageen Farm
BOLBERRY HOUSE FARM CARAVANNING PARK
ROAD
BOLBERRY RD.
Bolberry
Alston Farm
Ilton Cross
Rugwell
A381
Ilton Castle Farm
Withymore Farm
Horsecombe Cross
Ilton Farm
Yarde Farm
Horsecombe House
Newhouse Farm
Newhouse Barn
MOORSIDE
LUCKHAMS
CHAPEL GREAT LA.
Townsend Cross
SILVERHILL
MALBOROUGH GRN.
HIGHER TOWN
LOWER TOWN
Res. (cov.)
SALCOMBE
ROAD
Coombe Down
Churchill Farm
Hall
Ten. Cts.
Football Grd.
GREAT PK.
Grave-yard
SHUTE HILL
WELL HILL
COLLATON
White Cross
THE QUILLETS
SHUTE PK.
PILMIRE GS.
JUBILEE
CUMBER CL.
Kingsbridge
MALBOROUGH
PORTLE-MORE CL.
SPARK PK.
TQ7
The Yeomans House
Maryknowle Farm
ROAD
Collaton
Bolberry Cross
West Portlemoor
Portlemoor Barton
Lower Collaton
Broad Downs
Sewage Works
F
G
H
J
K
1
2
3
4
5
6
7
67
268
69
41
040
39
270
71
72

Higher Nuckwell
71
72
A
B
C
D
E
PARKLAND CARAVAN & CAMPING SITE
46
Highwell
CHURCHSTOW
Higher Leigh Farm
A381
A379
Bantham Cross
Silvergates
BUTT PK.
West Gate
SCOTT'S CL.
GLEBELAND
Home Farm
A379
Coombe Royal Farm
1
Offields
SOUTH HAMS BUS. PK.
Polegate Cross
WOODLANDS CL.
WOODLANDS
WHITEHALL MANOR
PLYMOUTH
DARKY
A381
Pullyblanks Farm
Redford Cross
Poole
HART'S LA.
ELSTON PARK
Elston Farm
Whites Cottage
Norton
2
Elston Cross
Elston Cottages
A379
45
Kingsbridge
Huxton Fork
3
West Redford
Home Farm
Bowringsley Wood
The Grove
TQ7
175
Huxton Wood
East Redford
Bowringsley
Pier's Cottage
4
Huxton Cross
BOWRINGSLEY
Norden House
NORDEN
44
Butts Farm
TOWN PK.
A381
W. A
BALK WILL
Heddeswell Cross
Sch.
5
FERN BANK
TOWNSEND CL.
TOWNSEND R.
LWR. ST.
PHOENIX PL.
WEST ALVINGTON
Kingsbridge Comm. Col
Ckt. Grd.
Pav.
LONGFIELDS
A381
Heddeswell Farm
Coombe Lodge
Linham Barn
The Parlour
Weston
Preston Cross
Roke
Woodhouse Farm
6
Preston Farm
43
Yarnacombe Cross
The Old Granary
7
Oldaway Tongue
A381
Yarnacombe Farm
South Milton
Littlecombe Farm
72
Youngcombe

157
175
KINGSBRIDGE
Dodbrooke
West Charleton
Sigdon Orchard
Lower Sigdon
Coombe Farm
Reservoir (covered)
Res. (cov.)
Higher Centry
Centry
Hill Cross
Springhill
Play. Fld.
Pav.
Lower Slade Farm
Lower Coombe Royal
Coombe Croft
Croft Bungalow
King Cott.
Pennon
Crimps Cross
Bearscombe Cott.
Belle Cross Farm
Stable Cottage
South Falls
Bears-combe
Huxhams
Court Farm
Prim. Sch.
Washabrook Mill
Inish
Bowcombe
Depot
SOUTH HAMS HOSPITAL
Mus.
Duncombe Park
Bingo
Cine.
Resouce Cen.
Quayside Leisure Centre
Rec. Grd.
Rugby Football Ground
Duncombe
Duncombe Cross
Duncombe Court
High House Farm
Sandypark
Estuary View Farm
Bridge Ho.
New Bridge
April Cottage
Selworthy Ct.
Cemy.
The Grange
Leat Head
High House Point
Curch View
KINGSBRIDGE ESTUARY
Kingsbridge to Salcombe (Summer Only) Foot Ferry
Park Farm
Rivermead
Sewage Works
Sewage Wks.
Curlew Point
Sch.
Croft Farm
COOKWORTHY RD.
PROMENADE EMBANKMENT
A379
STENTIFORD HILL
WALLINGFORD ROAD
BELLE CROSS ROAD
SANDY LANE
BOWCOMBE ROAD
HIGH HOUSE LANE

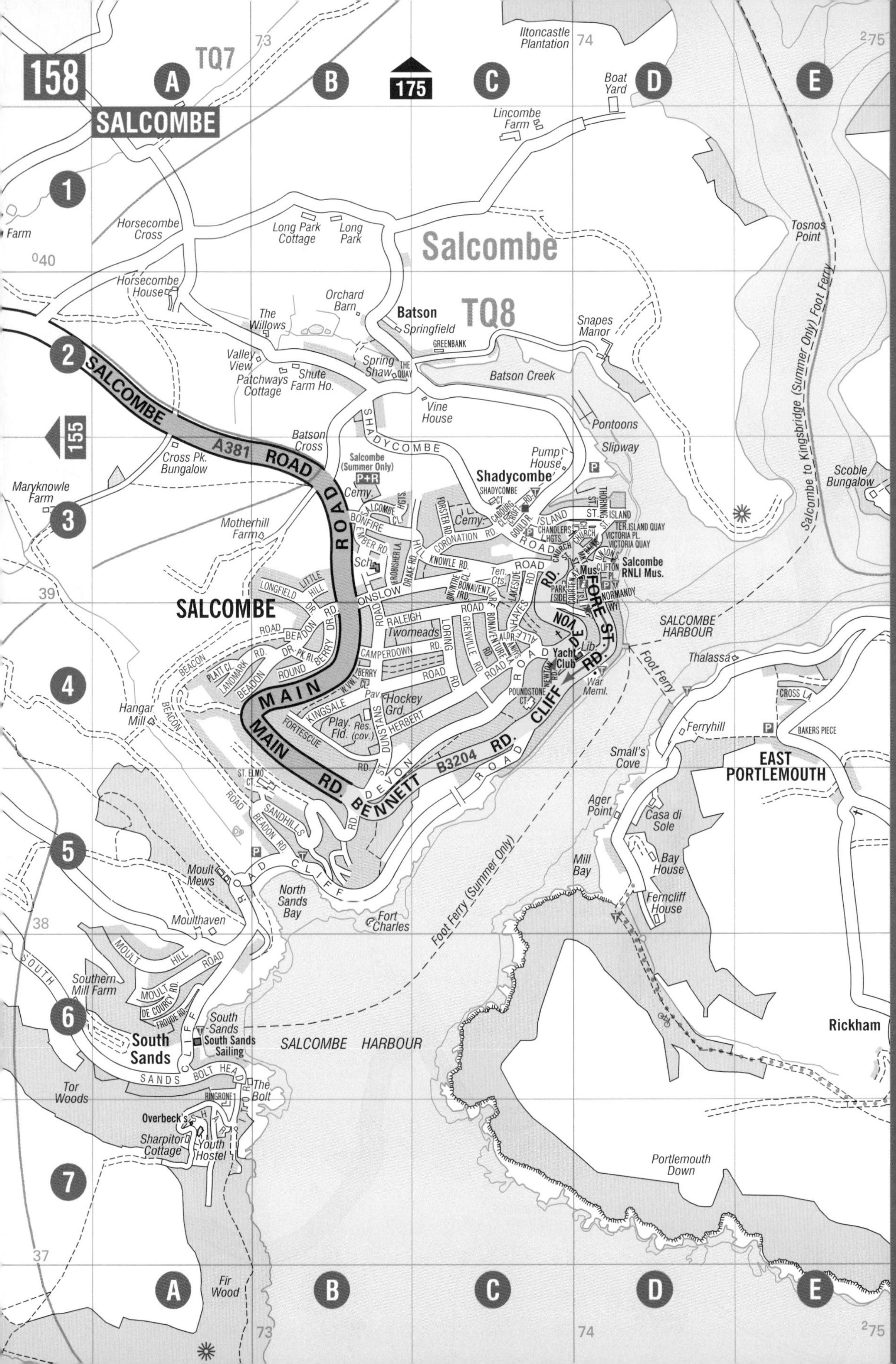
SALCOMBE
TQ7
TQ8
175
155
Salcombe
SALCOMBE
Iltoncastle Plantation
Boat Yard
Lincombe Farm
Horsecombe Cross
Long Park Cottage
Long Park
Horsecombe House
Orchard Barn
Batson
Springfield
GREENBANK
The Willows
Snapes Manor
Valley View
Patchways Cottage
Shute Farm Ho.
Spring Shaw
THE QUAY
Batson Creek
Vine House
Pontoons
Slipway
SALCOMBE ROAD
A381 ROAD
Cross Pk. Bungalow
Batson Cross
SHADYCOMBE
Salcombe (Summer Only)
P+R
Pump House
Shadycombe
Maryknowle Farm
Motherhill Farm
Cemy.
Sch.
Tosnos Point
Scoble Bungalow
Salcombe to Kingsbridge (Summer Only) Foot Ferry
CORONATION RD.
KNOWLE RD.
ISLAND
ISLAND QUAY
VICTORIA PL.
VICTORIA QUAY
Salcombe RNLI Mus.
Mus.
FORE ST.
LONGFIELD
LITTLE HILL
ONSLOW
RALEIGH
Twomeads
CAMPERDOWN RD.
Hockey Grd.
Play. Fld.
KINGSALE
FORTESCUE
HERBERT
DUNSTANS
MAIN RD.
BENNETT
B3204 RD.
DEVON
CLIFF RD.
Yacht Club
Lib.
War Meml.
POUNDSTONE CT.
SALCOMBE HARBOUR
Foot Ferry
Thalassa
CROSS LA.
Ferryhill
BAKERS PIECE
EAST PORTLEMOUTH
Small's Cove
Ager Point
Casa di Sole
Bay House
Mill Bay
Ferncliff House
Hangar Mill
ST. ELMO CT.
SANDHILLS
BEACON RD.
Moult Mews
North Sands Bay
Fort Charles
Foot Ferry (Summer Only)
Moulthaven
MOULT HILL ROAD
Southern Mill Farm
DE COURCY RD.
FROUDE RD.
South Sands
South Sands Sailing
SALCOMBE HARBOUR
SANDS BOLT HEAD
Tor Woods
The Bolt
RINGRONE
Overbeck's
Sharpitor Cottage
Youth Hostel
Rickham
Portlemouth Down
Fir Wood
Farm
A B C D E
1 2 3 4 5 6 7
73 74 75
40 39 38 37

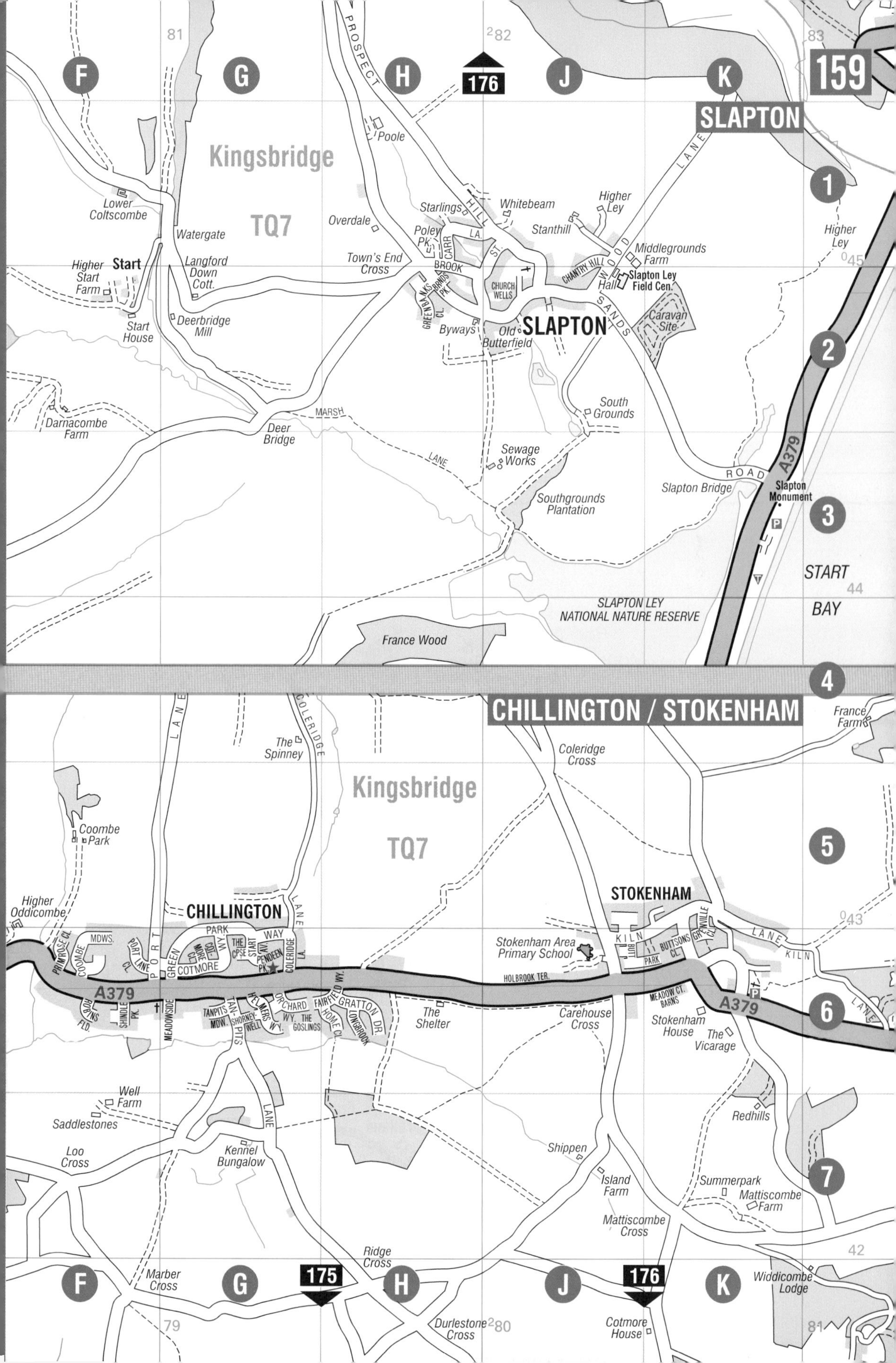

F **G** **H** 176 **J** **K**

81 282 83

Kingsbridge

TQ7

Poole

Lower Coltscombe

Watergate

Overdale

Higher Start Farm **Start**

Langford Down Cott.

Town's End Cross

Deerbridge Mill

Start House

Darnacombe Farm

Deer Bridge

MARSH

LANE

Starlings Whitebeam Higher Ley
Stanthill
Poley Pk. CARR LA.
HILL ST. Chantry Hill
BROOK
GREEN BANKS Middlegrounds Farm
CHURCH WELLS
Slapton Hall
Byways Old Butterfield **SLAPTON**
Slapton Ley Field Cen.

Higher Ley

045

Caravan Site

South Grounds

Sewage Works

Southgrounds Plantation

WOOD SANDS

ROAD

Slapton Bridge

Slapton Monument

P

A379

START 44

BAY

SLAPTON LEY NATIONAL NATURE RESERVE

France Wood

1

2

3

4

France Farm

The Spinney

Coleridge Cross

COLERIDGE

LANE

Kingsbridge

TQ7

Coombe Park

Higher Oddicombe

CHILLINGTON

PRIMROSE CL.
MDWS.
COOMBE CL.
PORT LANE
GREEN
PARK CL.
SHINDLE PK.
MEADOWSIDE
SPRINGS FLD.
TANPITS MDW.
CL. COTMORE
MORE WY.
THE CPSE.
PENDEEN WY.
START WY.
COLERIDGE LA.
SHORNEY WELL
TAN PITS
WEAVERS WY.
ORCHARD WY.
THE GOSLINGS
FAIRFIELD WY.
GRATTON DR.
HOME CL.
LONGBROOK

STOKENHAM

KILN PARK
BUTTSONS CL.
GRENVILLE CL.
LANE
KILN

Stokenham Area Primary School

HOLBROOK TER.

A379

The Shelter

Carehouse Cross

MEADOW CT. BARNS
Stokenham House
The Vicarage

Well Farm

Saddlestones

Loo Cross

Kennel Bungalow

LANE

Ridge Cross

The Goslings

Shippen

Island Farm

Mattiscombe Cross

Redhills

Summerpark
Mattiscombe Farm

Widdicombe Lodge

5

6

7

42

F Marber Cross **G** 175 **H** **J** 176 **K**

79 Durlestone Cross 280 Cotmore House 81

943

943

A
B
1
2
3
North West Point
LUNDY
Lundy Marine Conservation Zone
Lundy to:
Bideford 2hrs. (Seasonal)
Ilfracombe 2hrs. (Seasonal)
South West Point
Rat Island
Lundy lies 19 miles west of Morte Point
B R I S
Ilfracombe to Lundy 2hrs. (Seasonal)
Combe Martin Bay
ILFRACOMBE
Tunnels Beaches
Aquarium
A399
Hele
Lower Slade
Lee
Bull Point
Rockham Bay
Morte Point
Mortehoe
Heritage Centre
Higher Slade
Mullacott
Mill
Watermouth Castle
Chambercombe Manor
Berrynarbor
Pack o' Cards
Wildlife & Dinosaur Park
B3230
A361
A3123
B3343
Woolacombe
Trimstone
Cheglinch
Dean Cross
West Down
Berry Down Cross
Morte Bay
Baggy Point
Pickwell
North Buckland
Bittadon
Clifton
Churchill
Putsborough
Georgeham
Nethercott
Croyde Bay
Croyde
Forda
Darracott
Knowle
Winsham
Middle Marwood
Halsinger
Milltown
Muddiford
Lobb
B3231
Saunton
Marwood
Guineaford
Kingsheanton
Pippacott
Marwood Hill
Prixford
Broomhill Sculpture
BARNSTAPLE OR BIDEFORD BAY
Braunton
Heanton Punchardon
Ashford
DANGER AREA
Wrafton
TOLL
Chivenor
A361
Chivenor
River Taw
Bradiford
A39
R. Yeo
BARNSTAPLE
Bideford to Lundy 2hrs. (Seasonal)
Fremington Quay
Fremington
Bickington
Newport
Jungleland
A3125
Yelland
Lake
Landkey
Landkey Newland
Lifeboat Station
B3233
A39
Appledore
Maritime
Instow
Bickleton
Bishop's Tawton
Eastacombe
Westward Ho!
Northam
Signal Box
163
St. John's Chapel
Tawstock
A377
B3236
Westleigh
Holmacott
Buckleigh
A386
Horwood
A39
Lower Lovacott
Abbotsham
Orchard Hill
Newton Tracey
B3232
Harracott
Week
Big Sheep
East-the-Water
Woodtown
Hiscott
Ensis
Chapelton

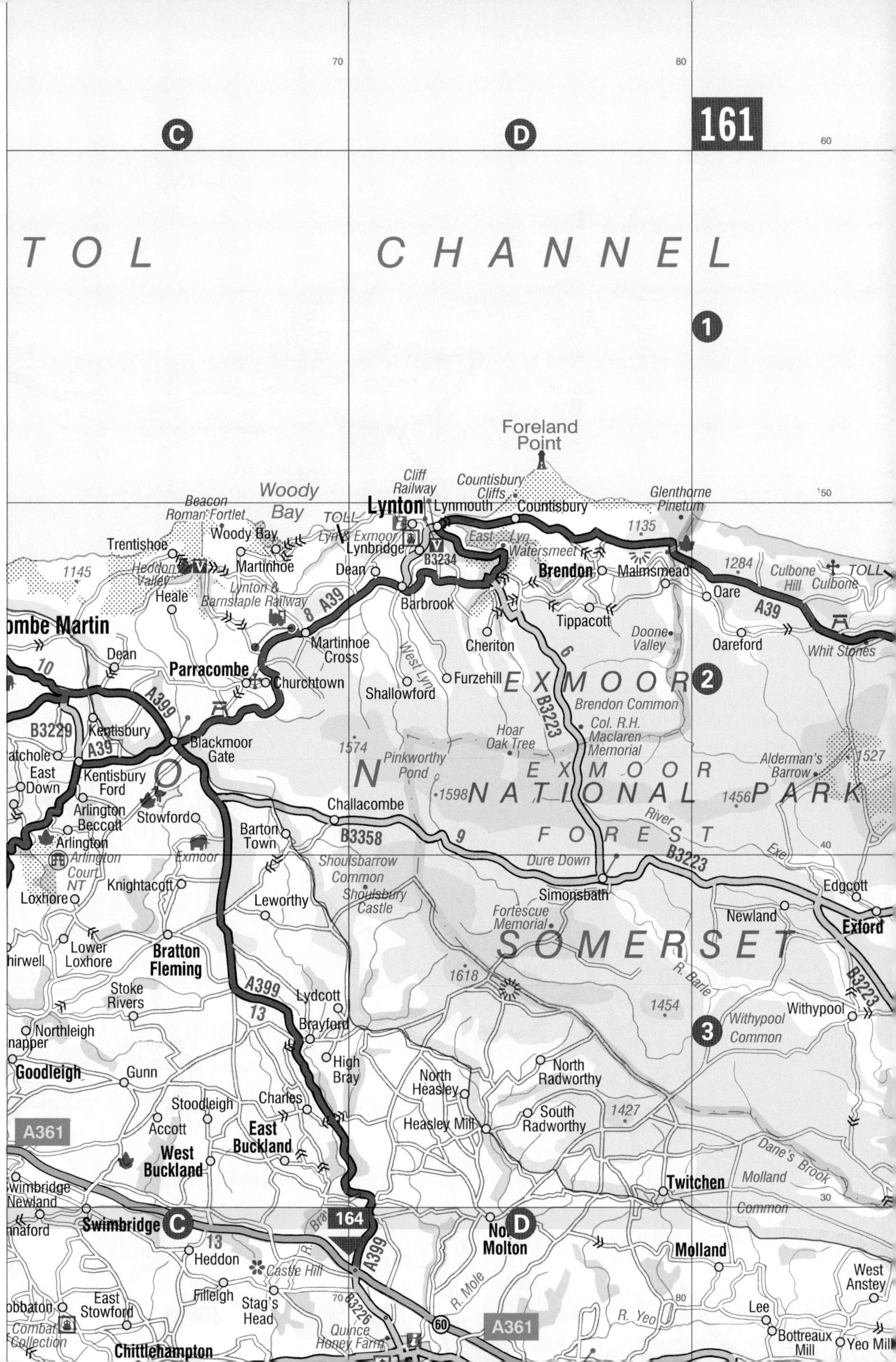

BRISTOL CHANNEL

Foreland
Point

Cliff
Railway
Countisbury
Cliffs
Glenthorne
Pinetum
150

Woody
Bay
Lynton Lynmouth Countisbury
Beacon
Roman Fortlet
TOLL
Lyn
1135
1284
Culbone TOLL
Trentishoe
Woody Bay
Exmoor
Lynbridge
East Lyn
Watersmeet
Malmsmead
Culbone
Hill
Culbone
1145
V
Martinhoe
Dean
B3234
V
Brendon
Oare
Whit Stones
Heale
Heddon
Valley
Barbrook
Tippacott
Oareford
A39
ombe Martin
Lynton &
Barnstaple Railway
8 A39
Martinhoe
Cross
Cheriton
Doone
Valley
2
Dean
Churchtown
Shallowford
Furzehill
Brendon Common
Alderman's
Barrow
1527
10
Parracombe
West Lyn
6
B3223
Col. R.H.
Maclaren
Memorial
B3229
Kentisbury
1574
Hoar
Oak Tree
EXMOOR
atcombe
A39
Blackmoor
Gate
Pinkworthy
Pond
1598
NATIONAL PARK
1456
East
Down
Kentisbury
Ford
Challacombe
FOREST
River
40
Arlington
Beccott
Stowford
Barton
Town
B3358
9
Dure Down
B3223
Exe
B3223
Edgcott
Arlington
Knightacott
Exmoor
Shoulsbarrow
Common
Shoulsbury
Castle
Simonsbath
Newland
Exford
Arlington
Court
NT
Fortescue
Memorial
SOMERSET
Loxhore
Leworthy
1618
1454
Withypool
Common
3
irwell
Lower
Loxhore
**Bratton
Fleming**
Lydcott
Withypool
Stoke
Rivers
A399
13
Brayford
1427
Dane's Brook
Northleigh
napper
High
Bray
North
Heasley
North
Radworthy
Molland
Common
Goodleigh
Gunn
Charles
Heasley Mill
South
Radworthy
A361
Stoodleigh
**East
Buckland**
Accott
**West
Buckland**
Twitchen
Molland
imbridge
Newland
164
Nor
Molton
Molland
West
Anstey
naford
Swimbridge
C
13
Bra
D
A399
Heddon
Castle Hill
R. Mole
Lee
Yeo Mill
bbaton
East
Stowford
Filleigh
Stag's
Head
B3226
30
60
A361
R. Yeo
Bottreaux
Mill
Combat
Collection
Chittlehampton
Quince
Honey Farm
70
80

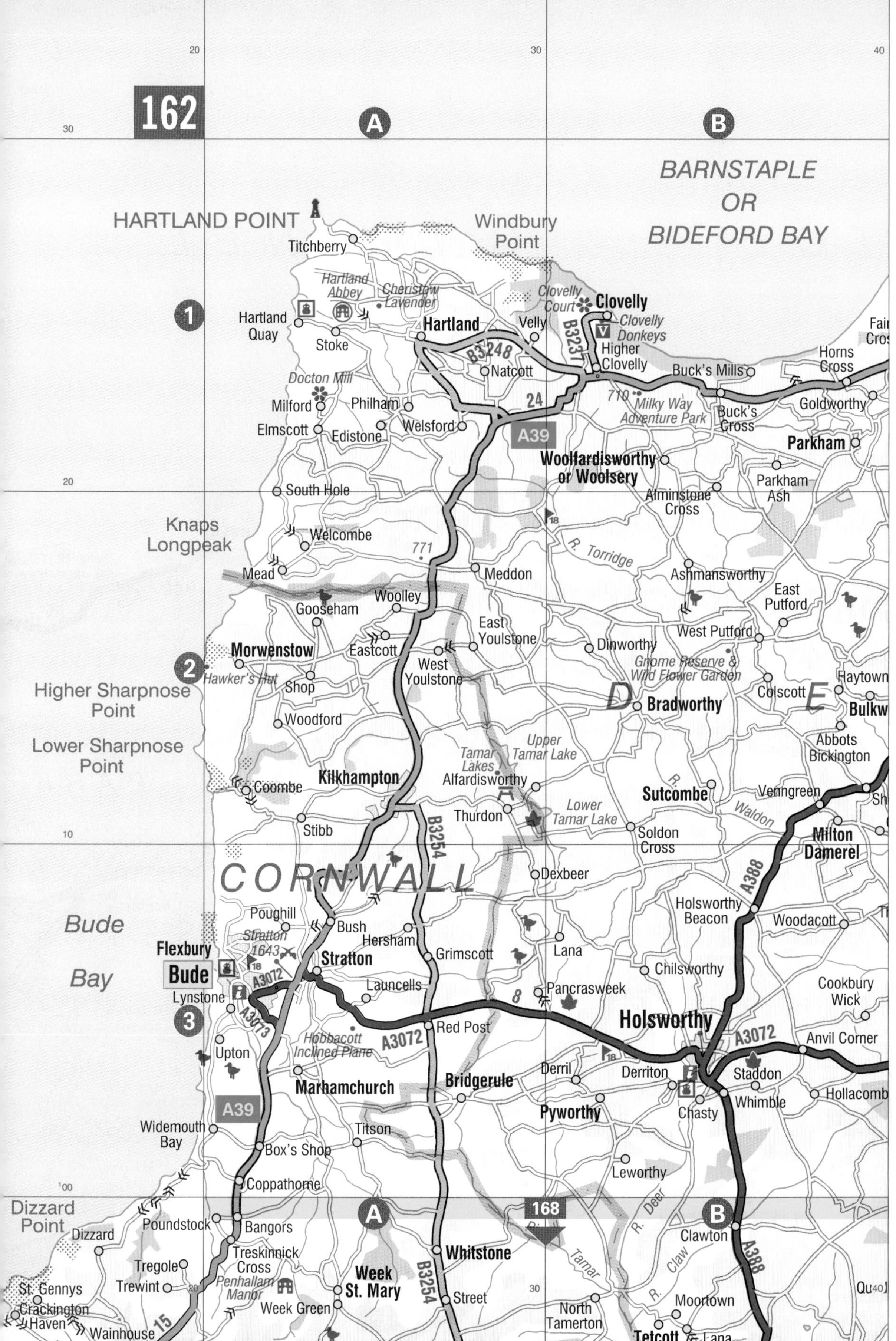

BARNSTAPLE
OR
BIDEFORD BAY

1

HARTLAND POINT
Titchberry
Windbury
Point

Hartland Abbey *Cheristow Lavender* Clovelly Court *Clovelly Donkeys* **Clovelly**

Hartland Quay Stoke **Hartland** Velly Higher Clovelly Buck's Mills Horns Cross Fair Cross

Docton Mill Natcott B3248 24 710 *Milky Way Adventure Park* Buck's Cross Goldworthy

Milford Philham Welsford A39 **Woolfardisworthy or Woolsery** **Parkham**

Elmscott Edistone Parkham Ash

South Hole Alminstone Cross

30

Knaps Longpeak Welcome 771 Meddon *R. Torridge* Ashmansworthy East Putford

Mead Woolley Gooseham West Putford

20

Morwenstow Eastcott East Youlstone Dinworthy *Gnome Reserve & Wild Flower Garden* Haytown

Higher Sharpnose Point *Hawker's Hut* Shop West Youlstone **D** **Bradworthy** Colscott **E** **Bulkw**

Lower Sharpnose Point Woodford Abbots Bickington

Coombe **Kilkhampton** *Tamar Lakes* Upper Tamar Lake Verngreen Sh

Stibb B3254 Alfardisworthy Lower Tamar Lake **Sutcombe** **Milton Damerel**

Thurdon Soldon Cross A388

10

C O R N W A L L Dexbeer Holsworthy Beacon Woodacott Ti

Poughill Bush Hersham Lana Chilsworthy Cookbury Wick

Bude *Stratton 1643* **Stratton** Grimscott

Flexbury **Bude** A3012 Launcells 8 Pancrasweek **Holsworthy** Anvil Corner

Bay Lynstone A3073 Derril Derriton Staddon Hollacomb

3 Upton *Hobbacott Inclined Plane* Red Post A3072 Whimble

Marhamchurch **Bridgerule** Derriton Chasty

Widemouth Bay Titson **Pyworthy** A3072

Box's Shop Leworthy

Coppathorne

00

Dizzard Point Dizzard Poundstock Bangors Ⓐ **168** Ⓑ Clawton A388

St. Gennys Tregole Trewint Treskinnick Cross *Penhallam Manor* **Week St. Mary** **Whitstone** B3254 Street North Tamerton Moortown Qu40

Crackington Haven Wainhouse Corner Jacobstow Week Green R. Deer R. Claw **Tetcott** Lana

15

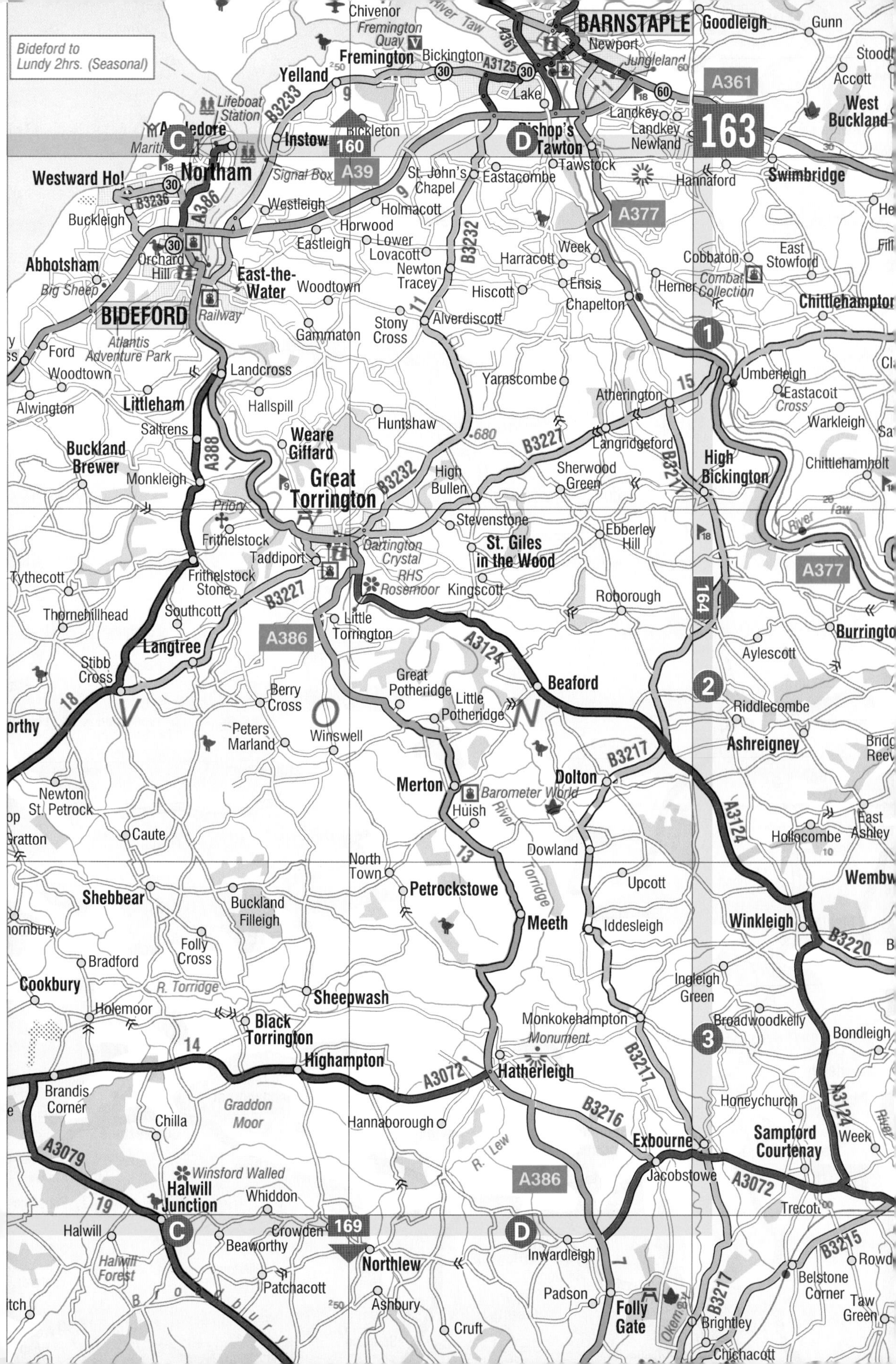

Bideford to Lundy 2hrs. (Seasonal)
BARNSTAPLE
Bideford
Great Torrington
Northam
Westward Ho!
Appledore
Instow
Fremington
Yelland
Chivenor
Bishop's Tawton
Swimbridge
West Buckland
Chittlehampton
Umberleigh
High Bickington
Beaford
Merton
Dolton
Petrockstowe
Meeth
Winkleigh
Shebbear
Sheepwash
Black Torrington
Highampton
Hatherleigh
Halwill Junction
Northlew
Exbourne
Sampford Courtenay
Folly Gate
Ashreigney
Langtree
Buckland Brewer
Littleham
Abbotsham
Weare Giffard
St. Giles in the Wood
Cookbury
163
160
164
169
A39
A361
A377
A386
A388
A3124
A3072
A3079
B3227
B3232
B3217
B3216
B3220
B3233
B3236
B3215

BARNSTAPLE
Newport
Jungleland
Goodleigh
Gunn
Stoodleigh
Accott
Charles
High Bray
North Heasley
Heasley Mill
North Radworthy
South Radworthy
1427
A361
164
Lake
Bishop's Tawton
Tawstock
Swimbridge Newland
Hannaford
Swimbridge
West Buckland
East Buckland
A
B
161
North Molton
A377
Heddon
Castle Hill
Filleigh
Stag's Head
A399
R. Bray
R. Mole
R. Yeo
Week
Harracott
Ensis
Chapelton
Cobbaton
Combat Collection
Herner
East Stowford
Chittlehampton
Quince Honey Farm
B3226
B3227
South Molton
Bish Mill
Newtown
1
Umberleigh
Eastacott Cross
Clapworthy
George Nympton
Bishop's Nympton
Ash Mill
Atherington
Langridgeford
B3217
Warkleigh
Satterleigh
Alswear
Mariansleigh
B3137
Rose Ash
Sherwood Green
High Bickington
Chittlehamholt
R. Mole
Romansleigh
Meshaw
Ebberley Hill
St. Giles the Wood
River Taw
King's Nympton
Venhay
Roborough
163
D
E
Burrington
Elstone
Week
Lutworthy
Aylescott
Beaford
2
A377
Chulmleigh
Riddlecombe
Ashreigney
Bridge Reeve
L. Dart River
Cheldon
East Worlington
West Worlington
Drayford
Chawleigh
Thelbridge Barton
B3096
B3042
Dolton
Barometer World
A3124
Eggesford
East Ashley
Hollocombe
Dowland
Filleigh
Torridge
Upcott
Wembworthy
Eastington
Meeth
Iddesleigh
Winkleigh
Eggesford
Lapford
Brownston
B3220
Brushford
Coldridge
Nymet Rowland
Lapford Cross
Morchard Bishop
Ingleigh Green
Oldborough
West Leigh
Weeke
Monkokehampton
Monument
Broadwoodkelly
3
Bondleigh
Lowton
East Leigh
Down St. Mary
A377
Hatherleigh
Honeychurch
Zeal Monachorum
A3072
Newbuildings
B3216
Exbourne
Sampford Courtenay
Week
River Taw
North Tawton
Burston
17
Copplestone
Elston
Jacobstowe
Bow
Coleford
Knowle
A386
Lew
Trecott
Nymet Tracey
Colebrooke
Penstone
170
Itton
Inwardleigh
B3215
Rowden
Hillerton
Yeoford
Padson
Belstone Corner
Taw Green
Heath Cross
Folly Gate
Okement
B3217
Brightley
Chichacott
A3124
Spreyton
Hittisleigh
Woodland Head

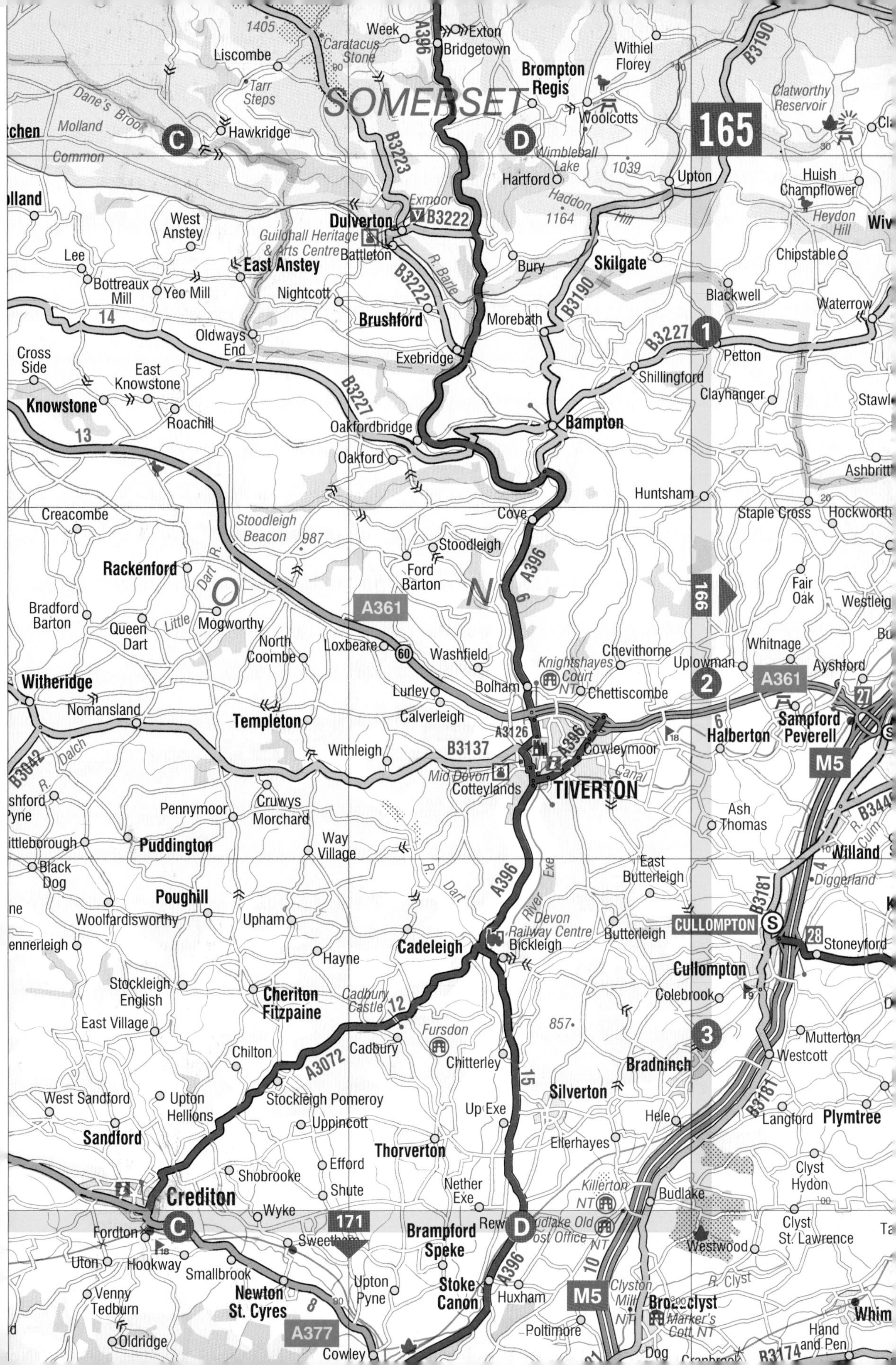
165
SOMERSET
1405
Caratacus Stone
Week
Exton
Bridgetown
A396
Withiel Florey
B3190
Brompton Regis
Woolcotts
Clatworthy Reservoir
Liscombe
Tarr Steps
Dane's Brook
Molland
Common
Hawkridge
C
D
Wimbleball Lake
1039
Hartford
Upton
Huish Champflower
Haddon Hill
1164
Heydon Hill
B3223
Exmoor
Dulverton
B3222
Guildhall Heritage & Arts Centre
Battleton
West Anstey
Lee
Bottreaux Mill
Yeo Mill
East Anstey
Nightcott
Brushford
R. Barle
Bury
Skilgate
Chipstable
Blackwell
Waterrow
14
Oldways End
Morebath
B3227
1
Petton
Shillingford
Exebridge
Cross Side
East Knowstone
Knowstone
Roachill
Oakfordbridge
Clayhanger
Bampton
13
Oakford
Huntsham
Ashbrittle
Creacombe
Stoodleigh Beacon
987
Cove
Staple Cross
Hockworthy
Stoodleigh
Ford Barton
Rackenford
Dart R.
Little
Mogworthy
A361
166
Fair Oak
Westleigh
Bradford Barton
Queen Dart
North Coombe
Loxbeare
60
Washfield
Knightshayes Court NT
Chevithorne
Uplowman
Whitnage
Ayshford
Witheridge
Nomansland
Templeton
Lurley
Calverleigh
Bolham
Chettiscombe
2
Sampford Peverell
27
M5
A3126
B3137
Withleigh
Cowleymoor
Halberton
6
18
B3042
Dalch
Mid Devon
Cotteylands
TIVERTON
Canal
Cruwys Morchard
Pennymoor
Ash Thomas
B3440
Puddington
Way Village
Black Dog
R. Dart
East Butterleigh
Willand
Diggerland
R. Culm
Poughill
A396
River Exe
Woolfardisworthy
Upham
Devon Railway Centre
Bickleigh
Butterleigh
CULLOMPTON
S
28
Stoneyford
B3181
Cadeleigh
Hayne
Cullompton
Stockleigh English
Cheriton Fitzpaine
Cadbury Castle
12
Colebrook
East Village
Fursdon
857
3
Mutterton
Chilton
Cadbury
A3072
Chitterley
Westcott
Bradninch
15
Silverton
West Sandford
Upton Hellions
Stockleigh Pomeroy
Up Exe
Hele
Langford
Plymtree
Sandford
Uppincott
Thorverton
Ellerhayes
Efford
Clyst Hydon
Shobrooke
Shute
Nether Exe
Killerton NT
Budlake
Crediton
Wyke
171
Brampford Speke
Rew
Budlake Old Post Office NT
Clyst St. Lawrence
Fordton
Sweetham
Westwood
Uton
Hookway
Smallbrook
Upton Pyne
Stoke Canon
Huxham
10
R. Clyst
Venny Tedburn
Newton St. Cyres
8
Clyston Mill NT
Broadclyst
Marker's Cott NT
Whimple
A377
Poltimore
Hand and Pen
Oldridge
Cowley
Dog
B3174

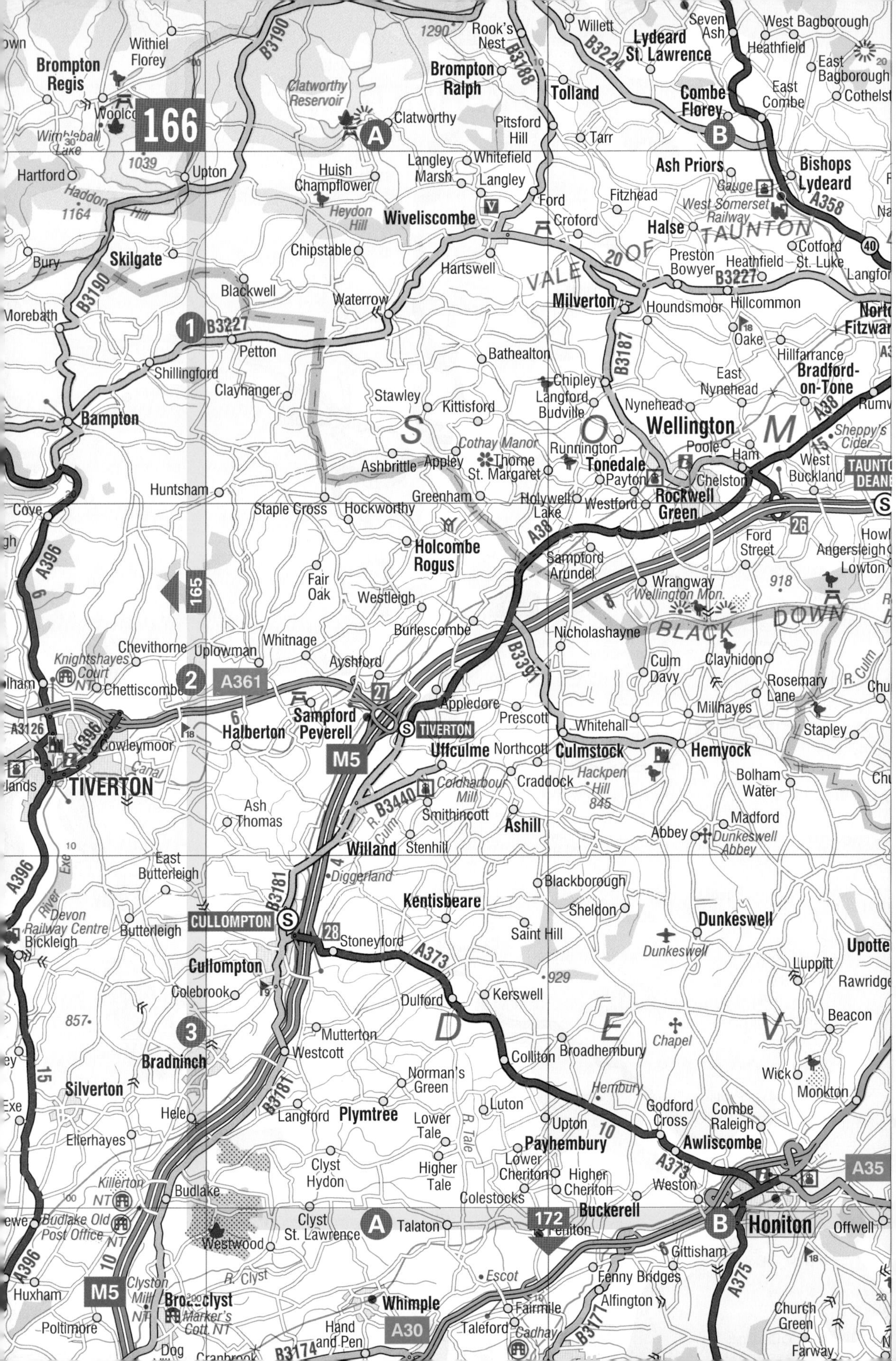
166
Brompton Regis
Withiel Florey
Wimbleball Lake
1039
B3190
1290
Rook's Nest
B3188
Clatworthy Reservoir
Clatworthy
A
Brompton Ralph
Willett
Lydeard St. Lawrence
B3224
Seven Ash
West Bagborough
Heathfield
East Bagborough
Cothelstone
East Combe
Tolland
Combe Florey
B
Pitsford Hill
Tarr
Hartford
Upton
Haddon Hill
1164
Huish Champflower
Langley Marsh
Whitefield
Langley
Ash Priors
Bishops Lydeard
Gauge
West Somerset Railway
A358
Fitzhead
Ford
Heydon Hill
Wiveliscombe
Croford
Halse
TAUNTON
Skilgate
Bury
Chipstable
Hartswell
VALE OF
Preston Bowyer
Heathfield
Cotford St. Luke
B3227
Langford
Blackwell
Waterrow
Milverton
Houndsmoor
Hillcommon
Norton Fitzwarren
Morebath
1
B3227
Petton
Shillingford
Clayhanger
Bathealton
Chipley
Langford Budville
B3187
Oake
Hillfarrance
East Nynehead
Bradford-on-Tone
Nynehead
Wellington
Stawley
Kittisford
Bampton
S
O
M
Cothay Manor
Runnington
Poole
Ham
Sheppy's Cider
West Buckland
Ashbrittle
Appley
Thorne St. Margaret
Tonedale
Payton
Rockwell Green
Chelston
TAUNTON DEANE
Huntsham
Greenham
Holywell Lake
Westford
Cove
Staple Cross
Hockworthy
A396
A38
26
Ford Street
Angersleigh
Lowton
Holcombe Rogus
Sampford Arundel
Wrangway
Wellington Mon.
918
165
Fair Oak
Westleigh
BLACK DOWN
Burlescombe
Nicholashayne
Whitnage
Chevithorne
Uplowman
Knightshayes Court NT
Chettiscombe
2
A361
Ayshford
27
Culm Davy
Clayhidon
Rosemary Lane
R. Culm
Appledore
Prescott
Millhayes
B3391
A3126
A396
Cowleymoor
Halberton
Sampford Peverell
TIVERTON
Whitehall
Stapley
Culmstock
Hemyock
TIVERTON
Uffculme
Northcott
M5
Canal
Coldharbour Mill
Craddock
Hackpen Hill
845
Bolham Water
B3440
Smithincott
Ash Thomas
Ashill
Madford
R. Culm
Abbey
Dunkeswell Abbey
Willand
Stenhill
East Butterleigh
Diggerland
Blackborough
A396
River Exe
B3181
Kentisbeare
Sheldon
Devon Railway Centre
Butterleigh
CULLOMPTON
Dunkeswell
Bickleigh
28
Stoneyford
Saint Hill
Dunkeswell
Upottery
A373
Luppitt
Rawridge
Cullompton
929
Colebrook
Kerswell
Dulford
857
Beacon
3
Mutterton
D
E
V
Chapel
Westcott
Colliton
Broadhembury
Bradninch
Norman's Green
Wick
Silverton
Hembury
Monkton
B3181
Hele
Langford
Plymtree
Lower Tale
Luton
Upton
Godford Cross
Combe Raleigh
R. Tale
Payhembury
Awliscombe
Ellerhayes
Clyst Hydon
Higher Tale
Lower Cheriton
Higher Cheriton
A373
Weston
A35
Killerton NT
Budlake
Colestocks
Budlake Old Post Office NT
Clyst St. Lawrence
A
Talaton
172
Feniton
Buckerell
B
Honiton
Offwell
Westwood
Gittisham
R. Clyst
Escot
Fenny Bridges
A396
Huxham
M5
Clyston Mill NT
Broadclyst
Marker's Cott. NT
Whimple
Alfington
A375
Church Green
Fairmile
B3177
Poltimore
Hand and Pen
A30
Taleford
Cadhay
B3174
Farway

TAUNTON

DORSET

Places and features

Courtway · Huntstile · North Petherton · Pumping Station · Middlezoy · Greylake · King's Sedge Moor · Henley · High Ham · King's Sedge Moor

NT · Fyne Court · Broomfield · Shearston · Thurloxton · Adsborough · North Newton · Maunsel Lock Canal Centre · Northmoor Green or Moorland · Thorngrove · Othery · Pathe · Low Ham · Pitney

Kingston St. Mary · Hestercombe · West Monkton · West Durston · Hedging · Bankland · King Alfred's Monument · Burrow Mump · NT · Burrowbridge · Bowdens · DANGER AREA · Wearne · Pict's Hill

Upper Cheddon · Cheddon Fitzpaine · Monkton Heathfield · Creech Heathfield · Charlton · East Lyng · West Lyng · Athelney · Stathe · Aller · Langport · B3153

Staplegrove · Bathpool · Durston · R. Tone · Meare Green · Willows & Wetlands NT · Woodhill · Oath · Wick · Portfield · Huish Episcopi · Pibsbury

Bishop's Hull · Lambrook · Creech St. Michael · Knapp · North Curry · Huntham · Stoke St. Gregory · Monument · Curry Rivel · Drayton · Priest's Ho. · Muchelney · Abbey · Muchelney Ham · Thorney

TAUNTON · Galmington · Henlade · Ruishton · Ham · Thornfalcon · Helland · West Sedge Moor · Swell · R. Isle · Midelney · Town Tree Nature

Trull · Haydon · Stoke St. Mary · Lillesdon · Newport · Wrantage · Meare Green · Curry Mallet · Fivehead · Isle Brewers · Hambridge · Lock-up · Kingsbury Episcopi · Coat

Staplehay · Shoreditch · Orchard Portman · Thurlbear · Slough Green · West Hatch · Hatch Beauchamp · Isle Abbotts · Stembridge Cider · West Lambrook · New Cross · East Lambrook · Manor

Pitminster · Fulwood · Corfe · Staple Fitzpaine · Bickenhall · Merryfield · Puckington · Westport · Barrington · Barrington Court NT · Shepton Beauchamp · Mid Lambrook · South Petherton

Sellick's Green · Blagdon Hill · Staple Hill · Curland · Curland Common · Windmill Hill · Ashill · Ilton · Ilford · Stocklinch · Hurcott · Moor · Over Stratton · Wigborough

Otterford · Blindmoor · Birchwood · Buckland St. Mary · Blackwater · Hare · Ham · Broadway · Horton Cross · Rapps · Whitelackington · Winterhay Green · Seavington St. Mary · Seavington St. Michael · Lopen · Merriott

Royston Water · Bishopswood · Newtown · Beetham · Street Ash · Horton · Donyatt · Ilminster · Allowenshay · Dinnington · Hinton St. George · Broadshard

Smeatharpe · Northay · Marsh · Combe St. Nicholas · Nimmer · Sea · Dowlish Wake · Kingstone · Perry's Cider · Chillington · Crewkerne

Newcott · Whitestaunton · Wadeford · Cuttiford's Door · Crimchard · Peasmarsh · Knowle St. Giles · Cricket Malherbie · Hornsbury · Chaffcombe · Cudworth · Roundham · Heritage Centre

Yarcombe · Warnbrook · Crawley · Chard · Street · Forton · Lydmarsh · Lakes & Gdns. · Cricket St. Thomas · Purtington · Hewish

Stockland · Burridge · Tatworth · Holy City · Whatley · Winsham · Wayford · Clapton · Seaborough

Millhayes · Chardstock · Birchill · South Chard · Perry Street · Forde Abbey · Bridge · Horn Ash · Laymore · Drimpton · Littlewindsor

Cotleigh · Ham · Heathstock · Membury · Castle · Alston · Churchill · Tytherleigh · Holditch · Chard Junction · Hewood · Blackdown · Greenham · Hursey · Broadwindsor

Wilmington · Turfmoor · South Common · Smallridge · Lower Holditch · Wadbrook · Thorncombe · Birdsmoorgate · Burstock · Pilsdon Pen · B3164

Widworthy · Dalwood · Loughwood Meeting House NT · Weycroft · Hawkchurch · Marshalsea · Bettiscombe · Pilsdon · Blackney · Monkwood · Bowood

Kilmington · Shute · Shute Barton NT · Axminster · Raymond's Hill · Blackpool Corner · Coney's Castle · Monkton Wyld · Marshwood · Lambert's Castle · Fishpond Bottom · South Bowood · Filford

Seaton Junction · Hampton · Abbey Gate · Whitchurch Canonicorum · Whitchurch · Broadoak · Salwayash · R. Char · Stoke Abbott

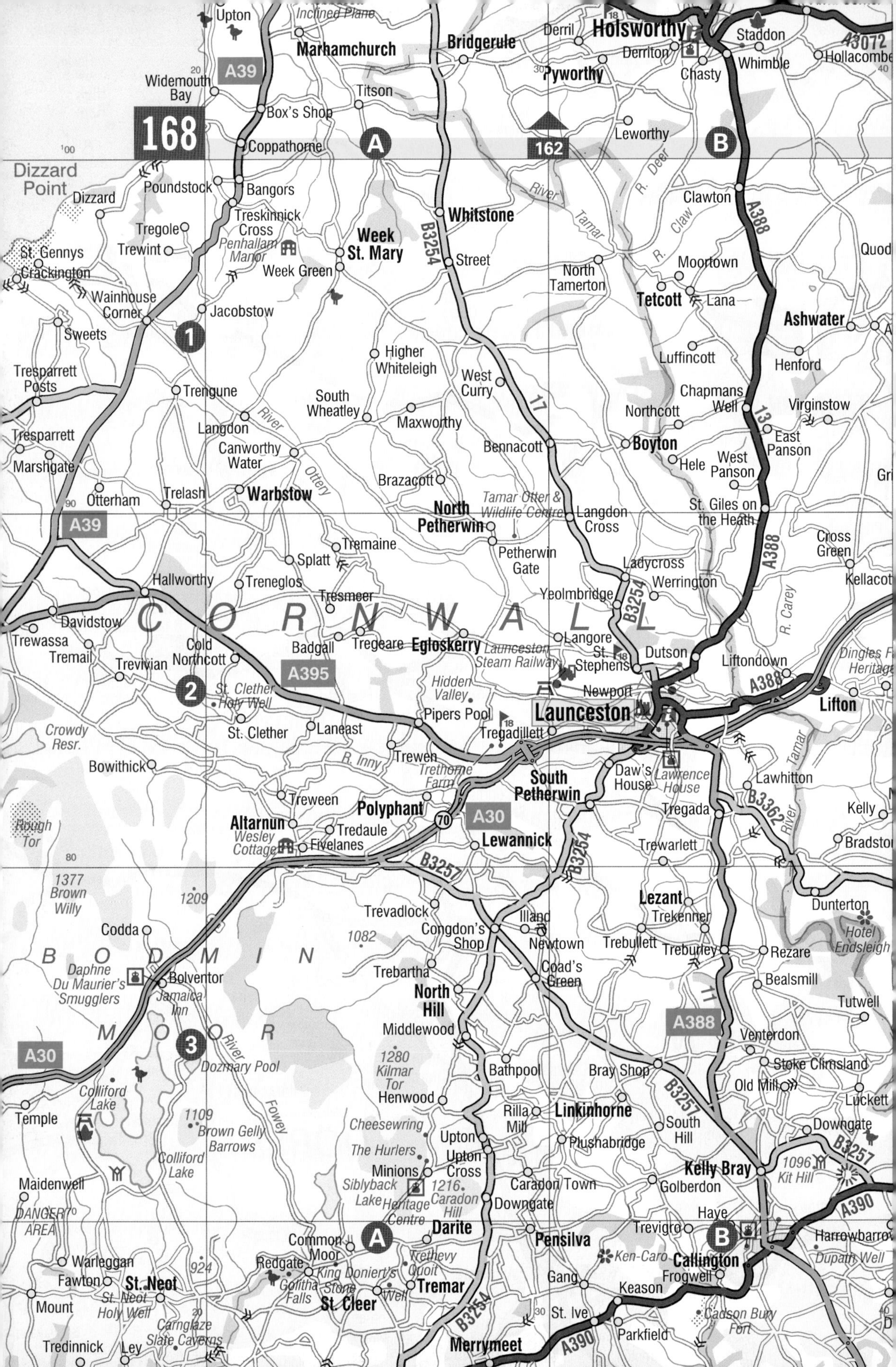

168
Upton
Marhamchurch
Bridgerule
Derril
Holsworthy
Staddon
A3072
Hollacombe
Whimble
Derriton
Pyworthy
Chasty
Widemouth Bay
A39
Titson
Box's Shop
Coppathorne
A
162
Leworthy
B
Dizzard Point
Dizzard
Poundstock
Bangors
Whitstone
Clawton
A388
Treskinnick Cross
Tregole
Trewint
Penhallam Manor
Week St. Mary
Week Green
Street
B3254
River Tamar
R. Deer
R. Claw
St. Gennys
Crackington
Wainhouse Corner
Jacobstow
North Tamerton
Moortown
Tetcott
Lana
Quod
Ashwater
Sweets
1
Higher Whiteleigh
West Curry
Luffincott
Henford
Tresparrett Posts
Trengune
South Wheatley
Maxworthy
Chapmans Well
Northcott
Virginstow
Langdon
River Ottery
Canworthy Water
Bennacott
Boyton
Hele
East Panson
West Panson
Tresparrett
Marshgate
Otterham
Trelash
Warbstow
Brazacott
Tamar Otter & Wildlife Centre
North Petherwin
Langdon Cross
St. Giles on the Heath
Tremaine
Petherwin Gate
Cross Green
Splatt
Ladycross
Werrington
Kellacott
Hallworthy
Treneglos
Tresmeer
Yeolmbridge
R. Carey
Davidstow
CORNWALL
Trewassa
Tremail
Cold Northcott
Badgall
Tregeare
Egloskerry
Launceston Steam Railway
Langore
St. Stephens
Dutson
Liftondown
Dingles Fairground Heritage
Trevivian
A395
2
St. Clether Holy Well
Hidden Valley
Newport
A388
Lifton
St. Clether
Laneast
Pipers Pool
Tregadillett
Launceston
Crowdy Resr.
Bowithick
R. Inny
Trewen
Trethorne Farm
South Petherwin
Daw's House
Lawrence House
Lawhitton
Tamar River
Treween
Polyphant
A30
Tregada
B3362
Kelly
Rough Tor
Altarnun
Wesley Cottage
Tredaule
Fivelanes
Lewannick
Trewarlett
Bradstone
B3257
1377 Brown Willy
1209
Trevadlock
Lezant
Trekenner
Dunterton
Codda
1082
Congdon's Shop
Illand
Newtown
Trebullett
Treburley
Rezare
Hotel Endsleigh
BODMIN MOOR
Daphne Du Maurier's Smugglers
Bolventor
Jamaica Inn
Trebartha
Coad's Green
Bealsmill
North Hill
Tutwell
A388
Middlewood
Venterdon
A30
3
River Fowey
Dozmary Pool
1280 Kilmar Tor
Bathpool
Bray Shop
Stoke Climsland
Colliford Lake
Henwood
Old Mill
Luckett
Temple
1109 Brown Gelly Barrows
Rilla Mill
Linkinhorne
South Hill
Cheesewring
Upton
Plushabridge
Downgate
Colliford Lake
The Hurlers
Upton Cross
Kelly Bray
1096 Kit Hill
Maidenwell
Minions
Siblyback Lake
Heritage Centre
1216 Caradon Hill
Caradon Town
Golberdon
DANGER AREA
Downgate
A390
Darite
Pensilva
Haye
Trevigro
B
Harrowbarrow
Common Moor
Trethevy Quoit
Ken-Caro
Callington
Dupath Well
Warleggan
924
Redgate
King Doniert's Stone
Golitha Falls
Tremar
Gang
Frogwell
Fawton
St. Neot
St. Neot Holy Well
St. Cleer
Keason
Mount
Carnglaze Slate Caverns
St. Ive
Cadson Bury Fort
Parkfield
Tredinnick
Ley
Merrymeet

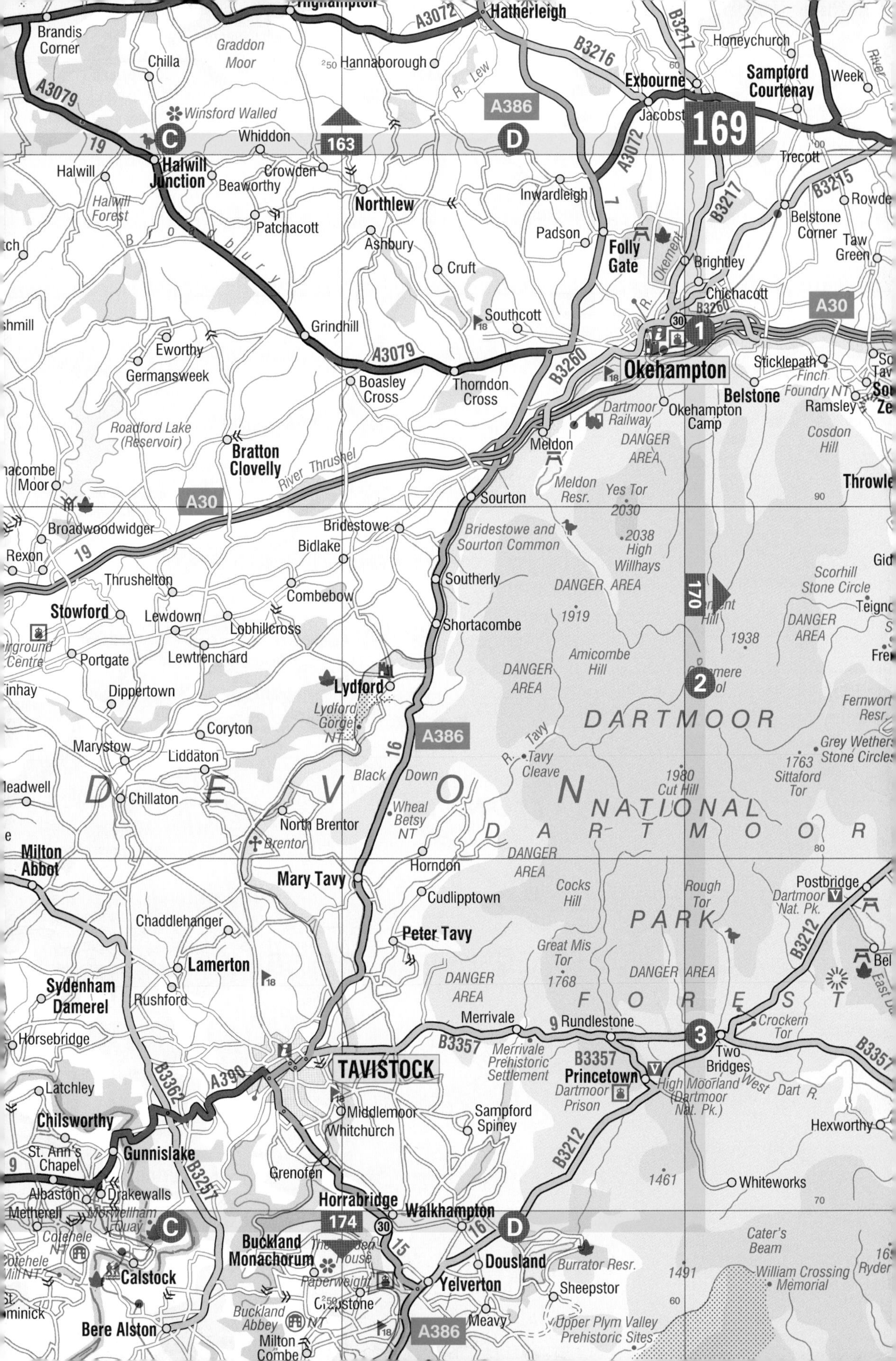

169
Hatherleigh
A3072
B3216
B3217
Honeychurch
Brandis Corner
Chilla
Graddon Moor
Hannaborough
Exbourne
Sampford Courtenay
Week
A3079
Winsford Walled
A386
Jacobstowe
163
Whiddon
C
D
Halwill
Halwill Junction
Beaworthy
Crowden
Northlew
Inwardleigh
Trecott
B3215
Rowden
Halwill Forest
Patchacott
Ashbury
Padson
Folly Gate
Belstone Corner
Taw Green
Brightley
Cruft
Chichacott
A30
Southcott
Okehampton
Grindhill
Eworthy
Germansweek
Boasley Cross
Thorndon Cross
B3260
Sticklepath
Finch Foundry NT
Belstone
Ramsley
Roadford Lake (Reservoir)
Dartmoor Railway
Okehampton Camp
Meldon
DANGER AREA
Cosdon Hill
Bratton Clovelly
River Thrushel
Meldon Resr.
Yes Tor 2030
Sourton
Broadwoodwidger
Bridestowe
Bridestowe and Sourton Common
2038 High Willhays
Rexon
Bidlake
Thrushelton
Southerly
Combebow
Stowford
Lewdown
Lobhillcross
170
Scorhill Stone Circle
Portgate
Lewtrenchard
Shortacombe
1919
1938
Amicombe Hill
Dippertown
Lydford
Lydford Gorge NT
Coryton
DARTMOOR
Fernworthy Resr.
Marystow
Liddaton
A386
R. Tavy
Tavy Cleave
Grey Wethers Stone Circles
1763 Sittaford Tor
Chillaton
DEVON
Black Down
1980 Cut Hill
NATIONAL
DARTMOOR
Wheal Betsy NT
North Brentor
Brentor
Milton Abbot
Horndon
Mary Tavy
Cocks Hill
Rough Tor
Postbridge
Dartmoor Nat. Pk.
Cudlipptown
PARK
Chaddlehanger
Peter Tavy
B3212
Lamerton
Great Mis Tor 1768
Sydenham Damerel
Rushford
FOREST
Merrivale
Rundlestone
Crockern Tor
Horsebridge
B3357
Merrivale Prehistoric Settlement
Princetown
Two Bridges
West Dart R.
TAVISTOCK
High Moorland (Dartmoor Nat. Pk.)
Dartmoor Prison
Latchley
B3362
A390
Middlemoor
Whitchurch
Sampford Spiney
Chilsworthy
Hexworthy
St. Ann's Chapel
Gunnislake
B3257
Grenofen
1461
Whiteworks
Albaston
Drakewalls
Metherell
Morwellham Quay
Horrabridge
Walkhampton
174
Cotehele NT
Buckland Monachorum
The Garden House
Dousland
Cater's Beam
Calstock
Cotehele Mill NT
Paperweight
Burrator Resr.
1491
William Crossing Memorial
Ryder
Yelverton
Sheepstor
St. Dominick
Crapstone
Buckland Abbey NT
Bere Alston
Meavy
Upper Plym Valley Prehistoric Sites
Milton Combe

170
Hatherleigh
Honeychurch
Exbourne
Sampford Courtenay
Week
North Tawton
Burston
Zeal Monachorum
St. Mary
Newbuildings
Copplestone
Elston
Coleford
Knowle
Bow
Nymet Tracey
Colebrooke
Penstone
A386
B3216
B3217
A3072
Trecott
164
Itton
Rowden
Belstone Corner
Taw Green
Inwardleigh
Padson
Folly Gate
Brightley
Chichacott
Heath Cross
Spreyton
Hillerton
Yeoford
Woodland Head
Hittisleigh Barton
Hittisleigh
B3215
A3124
A30
B3260
Southcott
Okehampton
Sticklepath
Finch Foundry NT
South Tawton
South Zeal
Belstone
Ramsley
Whiddon Down
Cheriton Bishop
Cheriton Cross
Crockernwell
Meldon
Dartmoor Railway
Okehampton Camp
DANGER AREA
Cosdon Hill
East Week
Spinster's Rock
Drewsteignton
Throwleigh
Stone Lane
Castle Drogo NT
Prestonbury Castle
Sourton
Meldon Resr.
Yes Tor 2030
2038 High Willhays
Bridestowe and Sourton Common
Wonson
A382
R. Teign
Easton
Cranbrook Castle
Gidleigh
Murchington
Scorhill Stone Circle
Chagford
B3206
Teigncombe
Okement Hill
169
Amicombe Hill
1919
1938
Shovel Down Stone Rows
Frenchbeer
Sloncombe
Middlecott
Moretonhampstead
Doccombe
B3212
Cranmere Pool
DARTMOOR
Fernworthy Resr.
Lettaford
Miniature Pony Centre
North Bovey
R. Bovey
R. Tavy
Tavy Cleave
Grey Wethers Stone Circles
1763 Sittaford Tor
1980 Cut Hill
NATIONAL
PARK
D
E
Lustleigh Cleave
Lustleigh
Wreyland
Manaton
Water
Grimspound
Hameldown Tor
Bowerman's Nose
Becky Falls
Cocks Hill
Rough Tor
Postbridge
Dartmoor Nat. Pk.
Hound Tor Medieval Village
Granite Tramway
Great Mis Tor 1768
Bellever
Church House NT
Bonehill
Haytor Rocks
Widecombe in the Moor
Haytor Vale
B3387
Brimley
Ilsington
Lewthorn Cross
FOREST
East Dart R.
Two Bridges
Crockern Tor
Higher Dunstone
1560 Rippon Tor
Merrivale
B3357
Rundlestone
Merrivale Prehistoric Settlement
Princetown
Dartmoor Prison
High Moorland (Dartmoor Nat. Pk.)
West Dart R.
Ponsworthy
Leusdon
Buckland in the Moor
Sigford
Ten Commandments Stone
A38
Dartmeet
Hexworthy
Poundsgate
Caton
Goodstone
Sampford Spiney
1461
Whiteworks
Venford Resr.
R. Dart
Ashburton
Hele
Holne
River Dart Adventures
A
B
175
Dousland
Burrator Resr.
Cater's Beam
1691 Ryder's Hill
Michelcombe
Hembury Castle
Scorriton
Combe
Woodland
Forder Green
Sheepstor
1491
William Crossing Memorial
Buckfast
Abbey
Upper Plym Valley Prehistoric Sites
Valiant Soldier
Hill House
Landscove
Buckfastleigh
Butterflies & Otters
Woolston

Chitterley
Bradninch
Silverton
M5
West Sandford
Upton Hellions
Stockleigh Pomeroy
Up Exe
Hele
Langford
Plymtree
A377
Sandford
A3072
Upp. cott
Thorverton
Ellerhayes
Efford
Shobrooke
Shute
165
Nether Exe
Killerton NT
Budla
171
Clyst Hydon
Crediton
C
D
Wyke
Rewe
Budlake Old Post Office NT
Clyst St. Lawrence
Tal
Fordton
Sweetham
Brampford Speke
Westwood
Uton
Hookway
Smallbrook
A396
10
Venny Tedburn
Newton St. Cyres
Upton Pyne
Stoke Canon
Huxham
Clyston Mill NT
R. Clyst
Broadclyst
Marker's Cott. NT
Whimp
8
Oldridge
Poltimore
Hand and Pen
Cowley
Dog Village
Cranbrook
B3174
B3181
Tedburn St. Mary
A377
30
Pennsylvania
Pinhoe
1
Rockbeare
A30
Allercombe
Pathfinder Village
Bill Douglas Centre
Whipton
Clyst Honiton
EXETER INTERNATIONAL
Exwick
B3212
29
Marsh Green
Whitestone
70
EXETER
Heavitree
Sowton
Wheatley
B3183
EXETER
B3184
Aylesbeare
B3180
A30
Longdown
St. Thomas
30
Clyst St. Mary
Farringdon
A3015
7
A3052
Culver
B3212
Ide
Alphington
Devon County Showground
Crealy
90
Lower Wear
3
40
B3123
Topsham
Clyst St. George
Woodbury Salterton
Hawkerl
B3180
Shillingford St. George
M5
Exminster
Woodbury
172
DANGER A
Dunchideock
31
Ebford
Topsham
Woodbury Castle
B3179
Bridford
Clapham
A379
Canal
Exton
Doddiscombsleigh
R. Kenn
Kennford
River
Bicton
Haldon Belvedere (Lawrence Castle)
Woodmanton
Kenn
Yettington
Christow
Higher Ashton
70
A376
2
Eas Budle
Bennah
Powderham
Exe
Lower Ashton
A la Ronde NT
Lympstone
B3179
Tottiford Resr.
Kenton
Bystock
Hulham
Knowle
A38
Devon & Exeter
South Town
Withycombe Raleigh
V
O
N
A380
Trusham
Starcross
B3178
5
Hennock
70
Littleham
B3193
Obelisk
Cockwood
EXMOUTH
World of Country Life
12
Heritage Centre
17
B3344
Waddon
16
Lifeboat Station
Chudleigh
Ashcombe
Coburg
Milton Hill
Bovey Tracey
Dawlish Warren
B3344
Ugbrooke
Chudleigh Knighton
Gappah
Luton
Ideford
5
Dawlish
A382
5
B3192
Little Haldon
Heathfield
Holcombe
3
Coldeast
Preston
Humber
A379
B3193
Sandygate
40
Teigngrace
Trago Mills
Bishopsteignton
Rural Life
30
South Knighton
Kingsteignton
B3195
Coombe
Teignmouth
Orchids
A381
Highweek
R. Teign
Bickington
A383
Newton Abbot
Ringmore
Wildlife Trust
A383
Shaldon
NEWTON ABBOT NT
Netherton
Combeinteignhead
30
Homeyards Botanical
Babbacombe
70
West Ogwell
East Ogwell
Wolborough
Stokeinteignhead
Plant World
Lower Gabwell
176
Higher Gabwell
A379
C
D
Abbotskerswell
Devon Wildlife Centre
Coffinswell
Bay
Denbury
Maidencombe
Two Mile Oak
Kingskerswell
30
Watcombe
Barton
Torbryan
Ipplepen
A3022
Model Village
A381
North Whilborough
Hele
St. Marychurch
Broadhempston

Bradninch
Silverton
M5
B3181
Langford
Plymtree
Norman's Green
Luton
Hembury
Upton
Godford Cross
Combe Raleigh
Wick
Monkton
A30
Exe
Hele
Ellerhayes
Lower Tale
Higher Tale
R. Tale
Payhembury
Awliscombe
172
Killerton NT
Clyst Hydon
A
Lower Cheriton
Higher Cheriton
Colestocks
166
Weston
B
A373
A35
Rewe
Budlake Old Post Office NT
Clyst St. Lawrence
Talaton
Buckerell
Feniton
Honiton
Offwell
A396
Westwood
Gittisham
R. Clyst
Escot
Fenny Bridges
A375
Huxham
Clyston Mill NT
Broadclyst
Marker's Cott. NT
Whimple
Fairmile
Alfington
Church Green
Poltimore
Hand and Pen
Taleford
Cadhay
B3177
Farway
Dog Village
Cranbrook
B3174
Ottery St. Mary
B3181
1
Pinhoe
Rockbeare
A30
West Hill
Allercombe
Tumbling Weir
Woodbridge
Whipton
Clyst Honiton
EXETER INTERNATIONAL
Marsh Green
Broad Oak
Wiggaton
Ark Pottery
Broad Down
B3212
29
Heavitree
Sowton
D
Fluxton
R. Otter
E
V
B3183
EXETER
Clyst St. Mary
B3184
Aylesbeare
B3180
Metcombe
Coombe
Sidbury
Sand
Blackbury
A3015
S
30
Farringdon
Venn Ottery
Southerton
Tipton St. John
Harpford
Harcombe
Devon County Showground
Crealy
A3052
Bowd
Sidford
A3052
Lower Wear
Topsham
Clyst St. George
Woodbury Salterton
B3180
Burrow
Newton Poppleford
B3176
Hawkerland
A375
Sid
Salcombe Regis
Weston
The Donkey Sanctuary
Branscombe
M5
Exminster
Topsham
Woodbury
DANGER AREA
B3178
Colaton Raleigh
SIDMOUTH
171
Canal
B3179
Woodbury Castle
Stowford
A379
Exton
Bicton Park
River Exe
Woodmanton
Yettington
Chapel
Otterton
Mill
2
A376
East Budleigh
Powderham
A la Ronde
B3179
Lympstone
Kenton
NT
Bystock
B3178
Kersbrook
Hulham
South Town
Withycombe Raleigh
Knowle
Starcross
Fairlynch
B3178
Littleham
Budleigh Salterton
Cockwood
EXMOUTH
World of Country Life
Lifeboat Station
Dawlish Warren
Dawlish
ENGLISH
Holcombe
A379
3
Teignmouth
Wildlife Trust
Shaldon
Homeyards Botanical
Babbacombe
Bay
A
B

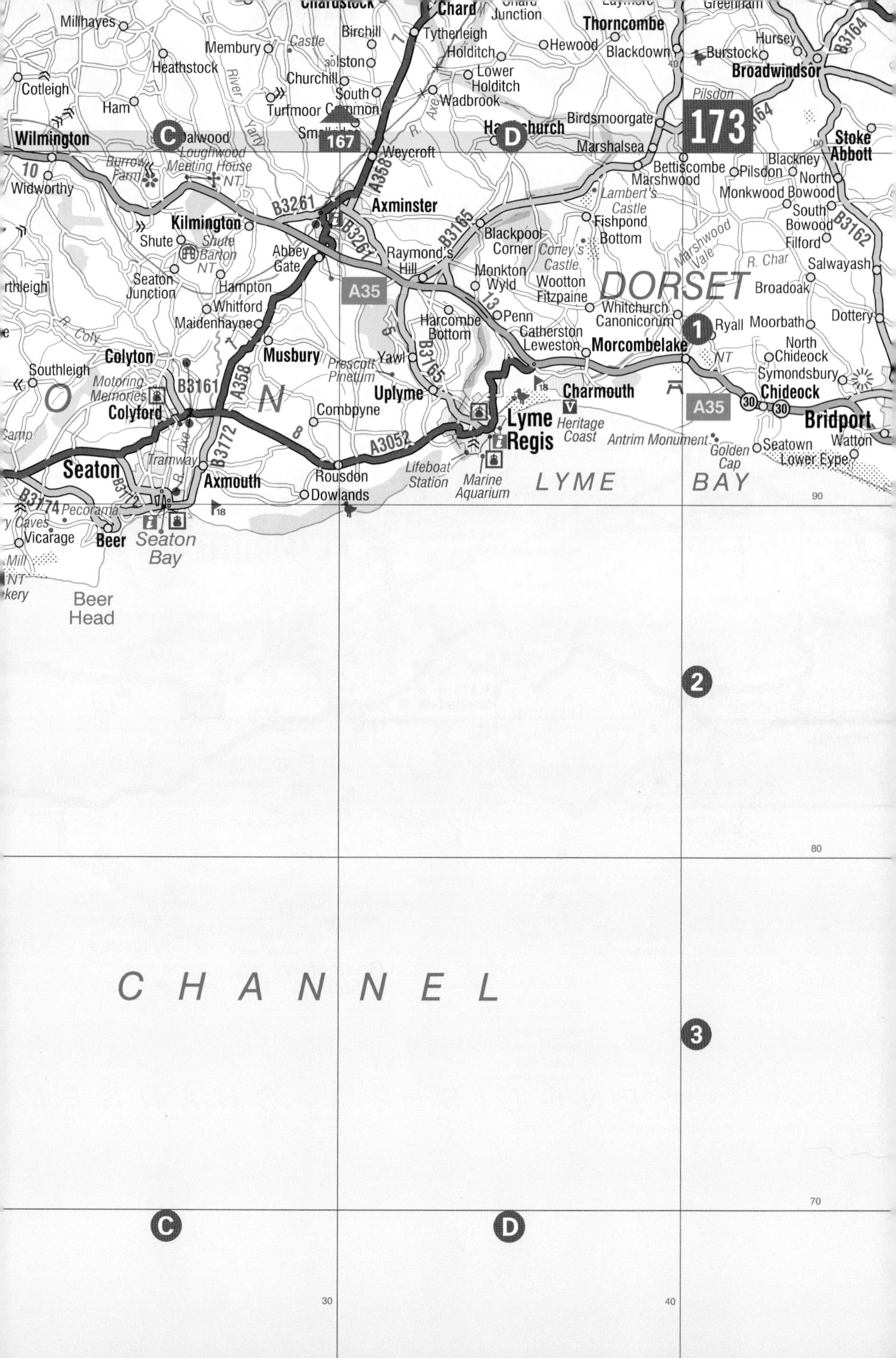
173
167
Chard
Tytherleigh
Thorncombe
Hewood
Blackdown
Burstock
Hursey
Broadwindsor
B3164
Millhayes
Membury
Castle
Birchill
Holditch
Lower Holditch
Heathstock
Churchill
South
Wadbrook
Cotleigh
Ham
Turfmoor Common
Smallridge
Pilsdon
Birdsmoorgate
Stoke Abbott
Wilmington
Dalwood
Hawkchurch
Marshalsea
Weycroft
Loughwood Meeting House NT
Burrow Farm
Widworthy
Bettiscombe
Marshwood
Pilsdon
Blackney
North Bowood
Monkwood
South Bowood
B3162
A358
Axminster
B3261
B3261
Kilmington
Shute
Shute Barton NT
Abbey Gate
Raymond's Hill
B3165
Blackpool Corner
Lambert's Castle
Fishpond Bottom
Coney's Castle
Marshwood Vale
Filford
R. Char
Salwayash
Seaton Junction
Hampton
Monkton Wyld
Wootton Fitzpaine
DORSET
Broadoak
A35
Whitford
Maidenhayne
Harcombe Bottom
Penn
Whitchurch Canonicorum
Ryall
Moorbath
Dottery
R. Coly
Catherston Leweston
Morcombelake
North Chideock
Southleigh
Colyton
Musbury
Prescott Pinetum
Yawl
B3165
NT
Symondsbury
Motoring Memories
B3161
Uplyme
Charmouth
Chideock
Colyford
Combpyne
A3052
Lyme Regis
Heritage Coast
Bridport
Seaton
Tramway
R. Axe
B3172
Axmouth
Rousdon
Dowlands
Lifeboat Station
Marine Aquarium
Antrim Monument
Golden Cap
Seatown
Watton
Lower Eype
LYME
BAY
B3174
Pecorama
Caves
Vicarage
Beer
Seaton Bay
Beer Head
CHANNEL
R. Yarty
R. Axe
C
D
1
2
3
30
40
70
80
90
100

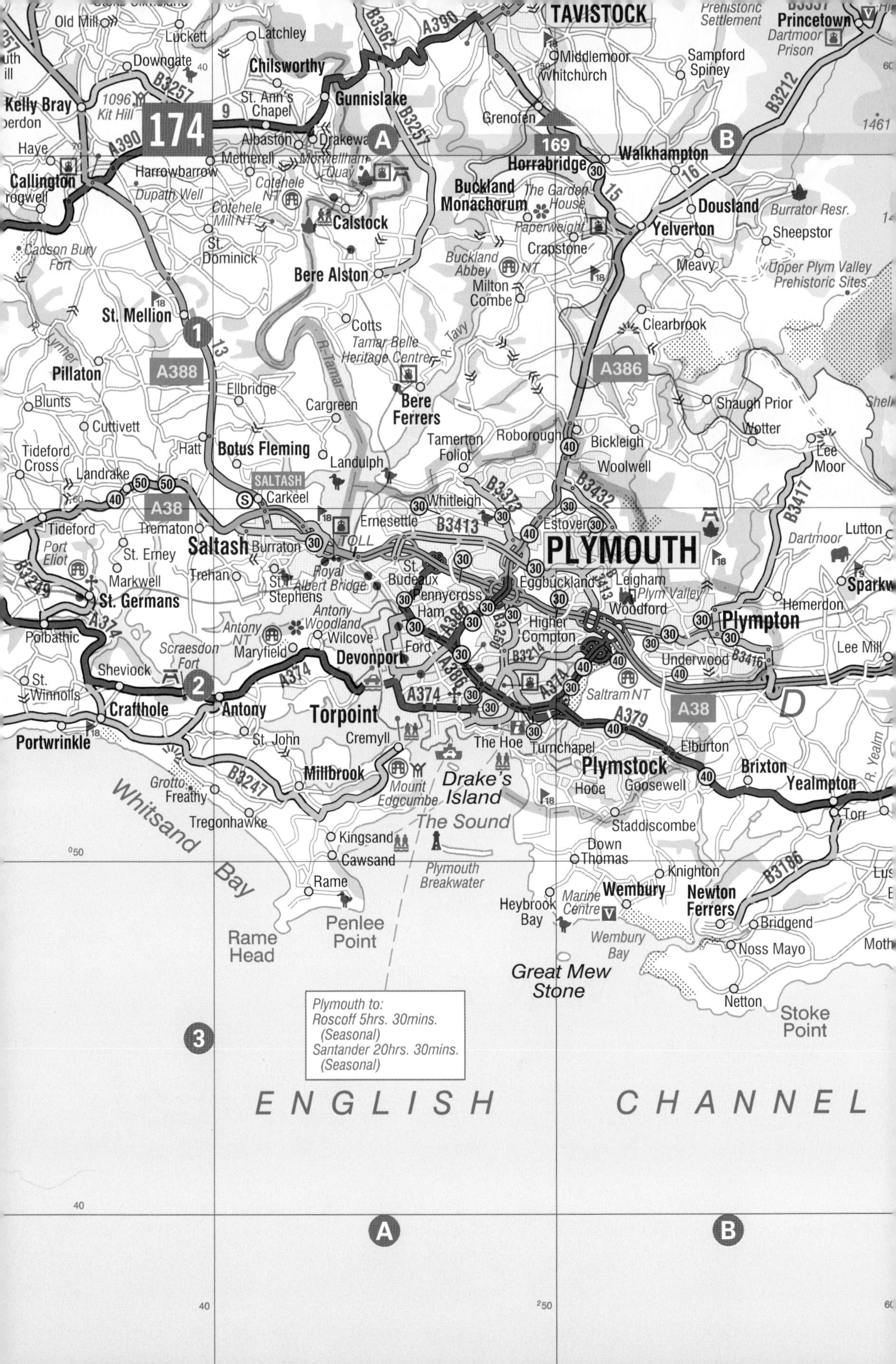

174
169
TAVISTOCK
PLYMOUTH
Princetown
Dartmoor Prison
Prehistoric Settlement
Old Mill
Luckett
Latchley
Downgate
Chilsworthy
Kelly Bray
1096 Kit Hill
St. Ann's Chapel
Gunnislake
Albaston
Drakewalls
Morwellham Quay
Haye
Callington
Metherell
Harrowbarrow
Dupath Well
Cotehele NT
Cotehele Mill NT
Calstock
St. Dominick
Cadson Bury Fort
Bere Alston
St. Mellion
Pillaton
R. Lynher
Cotts
Tamar Belle Heritage Centre
R. Tamar
R. Tavy
Ellbridge
Cargreen
Bere Ferrers
Blunts
Cuttivett
Tideford Cross
Hatt
Botus Fleming
Landulph
Tamerton Foliot
Roborough
Bickleigh
Woolwell
Landrake
SALTASH
Carkeel
Whitleigh
Ernesettle
Estover
Tideford
Trematon
Saltash
Burraton
TOLL
Port Eliot
St. Erney
Markwell
Trehan
St. Stephens
Royal Albert Bridge
St. Budeaux
Pennycross
Ham
Eggbuckland
Leigham
Plym Valley
Woodford
St. Germans
Antony Woodland
Antony NT
Wilcove
Maryfield
Higher Compton
Polbathic
Scraesdon Fort
Devonport
Ford
St. Winnolls
Sheviock
Crafthole
Antony
Torpoint
Portwrinkle
St. John
Cremyll
The Hoe
Turnchapel
Plymstock
Millbrook
Mount Edgcumbe
Drake's Island
Hooe
Goosewell
Grotto
Freathy
Tregonhawke
The Sound
Staddiscombe
Whitsand Bay
Kingsand
Cawsand
Down Thomas
Rame
Plymouth Breakwater
Rame Head
Penlee Point
Middlemoor
Whitchurch
Sampford Spiney
Grenofen
Horrabridge
Walkhampton
Buckland Monachorum
The Garden House
Paperweight
Dousland
Burrator Resr.
Yelverton
Sheepstor
Crapstone
Meavy
Buckland Abbey NT
Milton Combe
Upper Plym Valley Prehistoric Sites
Clearbrook
Shaugh Prior
Wotter
Lee Moor
Dartmoor
Lutton
Sparkwell
Hemerdon
Plympton
Lee Mill
Underwood
Saltram NT
Elburton
Brixton
Yealmpton
R. Yealm
Torr
Knighton
Wembury
Heybrook Bay
Marine Centre
Wembury Bay
Newton Ferrers
Bridgend
Noss Mayo
Great Mew Stone
Netton
Stoke Point
A390
A388
A38
A374
A386
A379
A386
B3257
B3362
B3212
B3249
B3247
B3413
B3373
B3432
B3417
B3416
B3250
B3214
B3186
Plymouth to:
Roscoff 5hrs. 30mins. (Seasonal)
Santander 20hrs. 30mins. (Seasonal)
ENGLISH CHANNEL
A
B
D
1
2
3

175
Ashburton
Buckfastleigh
Buckfast
Totnes
Ivybridge
South Brent
Modbury
Kingsbridge
Salcombe
Dartmeet
Poundsgate
Holne
Dartington
Harbertonford
Halwell
Blackawton
Aveton Gifford
Loddiswell
Churchstow
West Alvington
Malborough
Chillington
Stokenham
Slapton
Torcross
Ugborough
Bittaford
Cornwood
Diptford
Harberton
Ashprington
Cornworthy
Ipplepen
Broadhempston
Staverton
Kingston
Ringmore
Thurlestone
Outer Hope
Bigbury-on-Sea
Burgh Island
Bigbury Bay
Bolt Tail
Bolt Head
Start Bay
East Allington
Holbeton
NEWTON ABBOT
Kingsteignton
Bickington
A38
A385
A381
A379
A3121
A3122
A384
B3196
B3392
B3380
170
176

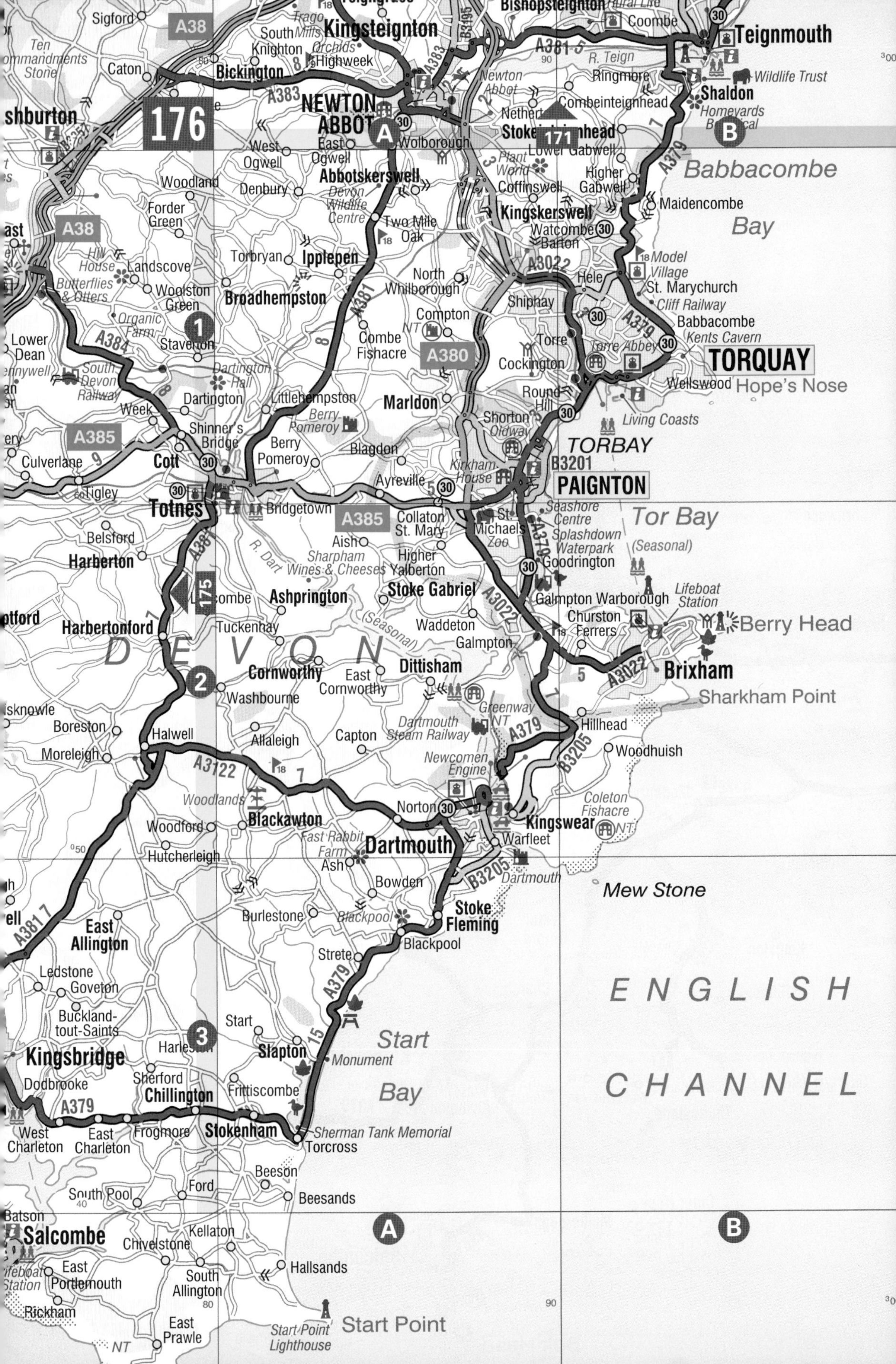

176
Teignmouth
Shaldon
Kingsteignton
Bishopsteignton
Newton Abbot
Ashburton
Bickington
Babbacombe Bay
Maidencombe
St. Marychurch
Babbacombe
TORQUAY
Hope's Nose
TORBAY
PAIGNTON
Tor Bay
Berry Head
Brixham
Sharkham Point
Totnes
Dartington
Ipplepen
Broadhempston
Abbotskerswell
Kingskerswell
Marldon
Cockington
Stoke Gabriel
Dittisham
Kingswear
Dartmouth
Mew Stone
Stoke Fleming
Blackpool
Strete
Start Bay
Slapton
Torcross
Beesands
Hallsands
Start Point
Kingsbridge
Salcombe
DEVON
ENGLISH CHANNEL
A38
A380
A381
A383
A385
A379
A3022
A3122
B3205
171
175

INDEX

Including Streets, Places & Areas, Industrial Estates, Selected Flats & Walkways, Service Areas, Stations and Selected Places of Interest.

HOW TO USE THIS INDEX

1. Each street name is followed by its Postcode District, then by its Locality abbreviation(s) and then by its map reference;
   e.g. **Aberdeen Av.** PL5: Plym . . . .1J **135** is in the PL5 Postcode District and the Plymouth Locality and is to be found in square 1J on page **135**. The page number is shown in bold type.

2. A strict alphabetical order is followed in which Av., Rd., St., etc. (though abbreviated) are read in full and as part of the street name;
   e.g. **Bow La.** appears after **Bowland Cl.** but before **Bowley Mdw.**

3. Streets and a selection of flats and walkways that cannot be shown on street map pages **10-159**, appear in the index with the thoroughfare to which they are connected shown in brackets; e.g. **Abbeyfield Ho.** TQ14: Teignm . . . . 4J **107** (off Heywoods Rd.)

4. Addresses that are in more than one part are referred to as not continuous.

5. Places and areas are shown in the index in BLUE TYPE and the map reference is to the actual map square in which the town centre or area is located and not to the place name shown on the map. Map references for entries that appear on street map pages **10-159** are shown first, with references to road map pages **160-176** shown in brackets;
   e.g. **ABBOTSKERSWELL** 6E **108** (1A **176**)

6. An example of a selected place of interest is **Allhallows Museum of Lace and Local Antiquities** 3F **55**

7. An example of a station is **Axminster Station (Rail)** . . . . 4G **89**, also included is **Park & Ride.**
   e.g. **Barnstaple (Park & Ride)** 7F **19**

8. Service Areas are shown in the index in BOLD CAPITAL TYPE; e.g. **CULLOMPTON SERVICE AREA** 3H **45**

9. Map references for entries that appear on large scale pages **6-9** & **124** are shown first, with small scale map references shown in brackets;
   e.g. **Alphington St.** EX2: Exe 6C **6** (7E **64**)

GENERAL ABBREVIATIONS

All. : Alley	**Ct.** : Court	**Info.** : Information	**Prom.** : Promenade
App. : Approach	**Cres.** : Crescent	**Intl.** : International	**Res.** : Residential
Arc. : Arcade	**Cft.** : Croft	**Junc.** : Junction	**Ri.** : Rise
Av. : Avenue	**Dr.** : Drive	**La.** : Lane	**Rd.** : Road
Bk. : Back	**E.** : East	**Lit.** : Little	**Rdbt.** : Roundabout
Bri. : Bridge	**Ent.** : Enterprise	**Lwr.** : Lower	**Shop.** : Shopping
B'way. : Broadway	**Est.** : Estate	**Mnr.** : Manor	**Sth.** : South
Bldg. : Building	**Fld.** : Field	**Mans.** : Mansions	**Sq.** : Square
Bldgs. : Buildings	**Flds.** : Fields	**Mkt.** : Market	**Sta.** : Station
Bungs. : Bungalows	**Gdn.** : Garden	**Mdw.** : Meadow	**St.** : Street
Bus. : Business	**Gdns.** : Gardens	**Mdws.** : Meadows	**Ter.** : Terrace
C'way. : Causeway	**Gth.** : Garth	**M.** : Mews	**Trad.** : Trading
Cen. : Centre	**Ga.** : Gate	**Mt.** : Mount	**Up.** : Upper
Chu. : Church	**Gt.** : Great	**Mus.** : Museum	**Va.** : Vale
Cir. : Circus	**Grn.** : Green	**Nth.** : North	**Vw.** : View
Cl. : Close	**Gro.** : Grove	**Pde.** : Parade	**Vs.** : Villas
Comn. : Common	**Hgts.** : Heights	**Pk.** : Park	**Vis.** : Visitors
Cnr. : Corner	**Ho.** : House	**Pas.** : Passage	**Wlk.** : Walk
Cott. : Cottage	**Ho's.** : Houses	**Pl.** : Place	**W.** : West
Cotts. : Cottages	**Ind.** : Industrial	**Pct.** : Precinct	**Yd.** : Yard

LOCALITY ABBREVIATIONS

Abb G : **Abbey Gate**	Bovis : **Bovisand**	Clyst M : **Clyst St Mary**	Dunst : **Dunstone**
A'sham : **Abbotsham**	Bow : **Bow**	Cockw : **Cockwood**	E All : **East Allington**
A'well : **Abbotskerswell**	Bradn : **Bradninch**	Coff : **Coffinswell**	E Bud : **East Budleigh**
Aish : **Aish**	Bradw : **Bradworthy**	Col R : **Colaton Raleigh**	E Ogw : **East Ogwell**
Alf : **Alfington**	Bram S : **Brampford Speke**	Cold : **Coldridge**	E Port : **East Portlemouth**
Alph : **Alphington**	Brans : **Branscombe**	Coll M : **Collaton St Mary**	E'don : **Eastdon**
Apple : **Appledore**	Brat F : **Bratton Fleming**	Colli : **Collipriest**	Ebf : **Ebford**
Ashb : **Ashburton**	Brau : **Braunton**	Colyf : **Colyford**	Elb : **Elburton**
Ashf : **Ashford**	Bride : **Bridestowe**	Colyt : **Colyton**	Erm : **Ermington**
Ashill : **Ashill**	Bridf : **Bridford**	C'head : **Combeinteignhead**	Exbo : **Exbourne**
Ashl : **Ashley**	Brixh : **Brixham**	Com M : **Combe Martin**	Exe : **Exeter**
Ash T : **Ash Thomas**	Brixt : **Brixton**	Com R : **Combe Raleigh**	Exmin : **Exminster**
Ave G : **Aveton Gifford**	Broadc : **Broadclyst**	Comp : **Compton**	Exmth : **Exmouth**
Avon : **Avonwick**	Broads : **Broadsands**	Coom : **Coombelake**	Exton : **Exton**
Awli : **Awliscombe**	Buck : **Buckfast**	Cop : **Copplestone**	Fen : **Feniton**
Axmin : **Axminster**	B'leigh : **Buckfastleigh**	Corn : **Cornwood**	Fil : **Filham**
Axmth : **Axmouth**	Buck B : **Buckland Brewer**	Cou W : **Countess Wear**	Forda : **Forda**
Ayle : **Aylesbeare**	Buck M : **Buckland Monachorum**	Cow : **Cowley**	Frem : **Fremington**
Bam : **Bampton**	Bud S : **Budleigh Salterton**	Crad : **Craddock**	Galm : **Galmpton**
Barn : **Barnstaple**	Burl : **Burlescombe**	Cranb : **Cranbrook**	Georgeh : **Georgeham**
Bat : **Batson**	Calv : **Calverleigh**	Cranf : **Cranford**	Gitt : **Gittisham**
Bea : **Beaford**	Car : **Cargreen**	C'stone : **Crapstone**	Good : **Goodrington**
Beer : **Beer**	Chag : **Chagford**	Cred : **Crediton**	Gos : **Gosford**
Bere A : **Bere Alston**	Chal : **Challaborough**	Crem : **Cremyll**	Gov : **Goveton**
Bere F : **Bere Ferrers**	Chaw : **Chawleigh**	Croy : **Croyde**	Gt T : **Great Torrington**
Berry : **Berrynarbor**	Cher B : **Cheriton Bishop**	Cull : **Cullompton**	Hacc : **Haccombe**
Berr P : **Berry Pomeroy**	Cher F : **Cheriton Fitzpaine**	Culm : **Culmstock**	Hal : **Halberton**
Bick'n : **Bickington**	Chet : **Chettiscombe**	Dacc : **Daccombe**	Harb : **Harberton**
Bickl : **Bickleigh**	Chev : **Chevithorne**	Darti : **Dartington**	H'ford : **Harbertonford**
Bic : **Bicton**	Chich : **Chichacott**	Dartm : **Dartmouth**	Harc : **Harcombe**
Bide : **Bideford**	Chil : **Chillington**	Daw : **Dawlish**	Harc B : **Harcombe Bottom**
Bigb : **Bigbury**	Chit : **Chittlehampton**	Daw W : **Dawlish Warren**	Harf : **Harford**
Bigb S : **Bigbury-on-Sea**	Chive : **Chivenor**	Den : **Denbury**	Harp : **Harpford**
Bish T : **Bishop's Tawton**	Chri : **Chrisrow**	Derr : **Derriton**	Hart : **Hartland**
Bi'ton : **Bishopsteignton**	Chud : **Chudleigh**	Dev : **Devonport**	Hath : **Hatherleigh**
Bitta : **Bittaford**	Chud K : **Chudleigh Knighton**	Ditt : **Dittisham**	Heat : **Heathfield**
Blacka : **Blackawton**	Chul : **Chulmleigh**	Dodd : **Doddiscombsleigh**	Heav : **Heavitree**
Blackp : **Blackpool**	Chur : **Churchstow**	Dol : **Dolton**	Hem : **Hemerdon**
Blag : **Blagdon**	Chur F : **Churston Ferrers**	Dous : **Dousland**	Hemy : **Hemyock**
Bolb : **Bolberry**	Clay : **Clayhidon**	Down T : **Down Thomas**	Hey B : **Heybrook Bay**
Bolh : **Bolham**	Clov : **Clovelly**	Drak : **Drakelands**	High B : **High Bickington**
Boo : **Boode**	Clyst H : **Clyst Honiton**	Dunk : **Dunkeswell**	High C : **Higher Clovelly**
Bov T : **Bovey Tracey**	Clyst G : **Clyst St George**	Dunsf : **Dunsford**	High M : **Higher Metcombe**

Abbeville Cl.—Albert Ter.

Hill : **Hillhead**
Holb : **Holbeton**
Holc : **Holcombe**
Holc R : **Holcombe Rogus**
Hols : **Holsworthy**
Hon : **Honiton**
Hooe : **Hooe**
Hope : **Hope**
Horn : **Horndon**
Horr : **Horrabridge**
Huish : **Huish**
Hux : **Huxham**
Ide : **Ide**
Ilfra : **Ilfracombe**
Ins : **Instow**
Ipp : **Ipplepen**
Ivy : **Ivybridge**
Kenn : **Kenn**
Kennf : **Kennford**
Kent : **Kentisbeare**
Kenton : **Kenton**
Kilm : **Kilmington**
Kingsb : **Kingsbridge**
Kingsk : **Kingskerswell**
Kingst : **Kingsteignton**
Kingsw : **Kingswear**
Know : **Knowle**
Lam : **Lamerton**
L'key : **Landkey**
Lap : **Lapford**
L Mill : **Lee Mill**
L Moor : **Lee Moor**
Lew : **Lewdown**
Lift : **Lifton**
L'ham : **Littleham**
L'ton : **Littlehempston**
Lit T : **Little Torrington**
Live : **Liverton**
Lobb : **Lobb**
Lodd : **Loddiswell**
Lwr D : **Lower Dean**
Lust : **Lustleigh**
Lutt : **Lutton**
Lyd : **Lydford**
Lym R : **Lyme Regis**
Lymp : **Lympstone**
Lynm : **Lynmouth**
Lynt : **Lynton**
Maid : **Maidencombe**
Malb : **Malborough**
Marl : **Marldon**
Mar B : **Marsh Barton**
Mar G : **Marsh Green**
Mary T : **Mary Tavy**
Matf : **Matford**
Meavy : **Meavy**
Mer : **Merton**
Metc : **Metcombe**
Mill : **Millbrook**
Mil A : **Milton Abbot**
Modb : **Modbury**
Monk : **Monkton**
Monk W : **Monkton Wyld**
Moor : **Moorhaven**
Morc : **Morchard Bishop**
More : **Moretonhampstead**
Mort : **Mortehoe**
Mus : **Musbury**
Nad : **Nadderwater**
Neth : **Netherton**
New A : **Newton Abbot**
New F : **Newton Ferrers**
New P : **Newton Poppleford**
New C : **Newton St Cyres**
N'ham : **Northam**
N Buck : **North Buckland**
N Mol : **North Molton**
N'town : **Northmostown**
N Taw : **North Tawton**
N Whil : **North Whilborough**
Norton : **Norton**
Noss M : **Noss Mayo**
Nym R : **Nymet Rowland**
Offw : **Offwell**
Oke : **Okehampton**
Ott'n : **Otterton**
Ott M : **Ottery St Mary**
Paig : **Paignton**
Pin : **Pinhoe**
Plym : **Plymouth**
Plymp : **Plympton**
Plyms : **Plymstock**
Polt : **Poltimore**
Pres : **Preston**
Prin : **Princetown**
Puts : **Putsborough**
Pyw : **Pyworthy**
Ray H : **Raymond's Hill**
Rewe : **Rewe**
Robo : **Roborough**
Rock : **Rockbeare**
Roun : **Roundswell**
St G : **St Giles on the Heath**
Salc : **Salcombe**
Salt : **Saltash**
Sam P : **Sampford Peverell**
San B : **Sandy Bay**
Saun : **Saunton**
Seat : **Seaton**
Shal : **Shaldon**
Sheb : **Shebbear**
Shil A : **Shillingford Abbot**
Shir : **Shirwell**
Shute : **Shute**
Sidb : **Sidbury**
Sidf : **Sidford**
Sidm : **Sidmouth**
Silv : **Silverton**
Slap : **Slapton**
Smal : **Smallridge**
Smit : **Smithaleigh**
Snap : **Snapper**
S Bre : **South Brent**
S'ton : **Southerton**
S Hui : **South Huish**
S Mil : **South Milton**
S Mol : **South Molton**
S Taw : **South Tawton**
S Zeal : **South Zeal**
Sow : **Sowton**
Spa : **Sparkwell**
Spri : **Spriddlestone**
Stad : **Staddiscombe**
Star : **Starcross**
Stic : **Sticklepath**
Sto C : **Stoke Canon**
Sto F : **Stoke Fleming**
Sto G : **Stoke Gabriel**
S'head : **Stokeinteignhead**
Stoke : **Stokenham**
Ston : **Stoneycombe**
Stow : **Stowford**
Strete : **Strete**
Stre R : **Strete Ralegh**
Swim : **Swimbridge**
Tale : **Taleford**
Tam F : **Tamerton Foliot**
Tavi : **Tavistock**
Taw : **Tawstock**
Ted M : **Tedburn St Mary**
Teigng : **Teigngrace**
Teignm : **Teignmouth**
Thor : **Thorverton**
Thur : **Thurlestone**
Tin : **Tinhay**
Tip J : **Tipton St John**
Tiv : **Tiverton**
Top : **Topsham**
Torp : **Torpoint**
Torq : **Torquay**
Torr : **Torr**
Tot : **Totnes**
Trew : **Trewetha**
Two O : **Two Mile Oak**
Two P : **Two Potts**
Uff : **Uffculme**
Ugb : **Ugborough**
Up E : **Up Exe**
U'man : **Uplowman**
Uply : **Uplyme**
Upp D : **Upper Dean**
Vela : **Velator**
Ven O : **Venn Ottery**
Wadd : **Waddeton**
Walk : **Walkhampton**
Ware : **Ware**
Wash : **Washfield**
Wem : **Wembury**
W Alv : **West Alvington**
W Cha : **West Charleton**
W Cly : **West Clyst**
W Hill : **West Hill**
Westl : **Westleigh**
Westo : **Weston**
West H : **Westward Ho!**
Wey : **Weycroft**
Whim : **Whimple**
Whip : **Whipton**
Whitc : **Whitchurch**
White : **Whitestone**
Whitf : **Whitford**
Wigg : **Wiggaton**
Wilc : **Wilcove**
Will : **Willand**
Wink : **Winkleigh**
Wins : **Winsham**
With : **Witheridge**
Won : **Wonford**
Wood : **Woodbury**
Wood S : **Woodbury Salterton**
Woolc : **Woolacombe**
Wools : **Woolsery**
Wors : **Worston**
Wot : **Wotter**
Wraf : **Wrafton**
Wran : **Wrangaton**
Wyke G : **Wyke Green**
Yeal : **Yealmpton**
Yell : **Yelland**
Yelv : **Yelverton**

A

Abbeville Cl. EX2: Exe . . . 2H **71**
ABBEY . . . **2B 166**
Abbey Cl. EX13: Axmin . . . 5G **89**
PL20: C'stone . . . 6C **126**
TQ13: Bov T . . . 4B **92**
TQ14: Teignm . . . 2J **107**
Abbey Ct. EX2: Sow . . . 7E **66**
PL1: Plym . . . 5F **9**
PL19: Tavi . . . 3J **59**
Abbey Cres. TQ2: Torq . . . 2C **116**
Abbeyfield TQ1: Torq . . . 5D **112**
Abbeyfield Ho. *TQ14: Teignm . . . 4J 107*
(off Heywoods Rd.)
Abbeyford Ct. EX20: Oke . . . 3C **48**
ABBEY GATE . . . **6G 89 (1C 173)**
Abbey Ga. La.
EX13: Abb G, Wyke G . . . 7G **89**
Abbey Grange Cl. TQ11: Buck . . . 2C **98**
Abbey La. EX13: Abb G . . . 6F **89**
PL20: C'stone . . . 6C **126**
Abbeymead M. PL19: Tavi . . . 4J **59**
Abbey Mdw. PL20: C'stone . . . 6C **126**
TQ11: Buck . . . 2C **98**
Abbey Park . . . **2B 116**
Abbey Pl. PL1: Plym . . . 5E **8** (3J **141**)
PL19: Tavi . . . 3H **59**
(Bannawell St.)
PL19: Tavi . . . 4J **59**
(Dolvin Rd.)
Abbey Ri. EX20: Oke . . . 2D **48**
PL19: Tavi . . . 4J **59**
Abbey Rd. EX4: Exe . . . 1K **7** (4J **65**)
EX14: Dunk . . . 5H **47**
EX31: Barn . . . 2D **18**
TQ2: Torq . . . 1C **116**
TQ13: Bov T . . . 3B **92**
Abbey Vw. EX10: Sidm . . . 5D **84**
Abbot Rd. PL21: Ivy . . . 3E **144**
ABBOTS BICKINGTON . . . **2B 162**
ABBOTSBURY . . . **1E 108**
Abbotsbury Rd. TQ12: New A . . . 7E **104**
Abbotsbury Way PL2: Plym . . . 3E **134**
Abbots Cl. EX39: Wools . . . 2B **28**
PL21: L Mill . . . 5C **144**
Abbots Dr. EX39: Bide . . . 5J **23**
Abbotsfield PL19: Tavi . . . 5F **59**
Abbotsfield Cl. PL19: Tavi . . . 5F **59**
Abbotsfield Cres. PL19: Tavi . . . 5F **59**
ABBOTSHAM . . . **4A 22 (1C 163)**
Abbotsham Rd.
EX39: A'sham, Bide . . . 3A **22**
Abbotshill Caravan Pk.
TQ12: A'well . . . 6D **108**
ABBOTSKERSWELL . . . **6E 108 (1A 176)**
Abbots Mdw. EX37: Chit . . . 5H **25**
Abbotsridge Dr. TQ12: E Ogw . . . 3C **108**
Abbots Rd. EX4: Exe . . . 1K **7** (4H **65**)
Abbotswood TQ12: E Ogw . . . 3C **108**
TQ12: Kingst . . . 3J **105**
Abbotts Hill EX33: Brau . . . 4J **15**
Abbotts Pk. PL21: Corn . . . 7J **129**
Abbotts Rd. PL3: Plym . . . 6K **135**
Abbrook Av. TQ12: Kingst . . . 2G **105**
Abelia Cl. TQ3: Paig . . . 6E **114**
Aberdeen Av. PL5: Plym . . . 1J **135**
Abingdon Rd. PL4: Plym . . . 1F **9**
Abney Cres. PL6: Plym . . . 4C **132**
Above Town
TQ6: Dartm . . . 2A **124** (6F **125**)
Aboveway EX6: Exmin . . . 3D **74**
Abyssinia Ct. *EX32: Barn . . . 6G 19*
(off Abyssinia Ter.)
Abyssinia Ter. EX32: Barn . . . 6G **19**
Acacia Cl. EX39: Bide . . . 4D **22**
TQ12: Kingst . . . 6H **105**
Academic La. EX18: Chul . . . 6C **32**
Acadia Rd. TQ1: Torq . . . 2G **117**
ACCOTT . . . **3C 161**
Ackland Cl. EX21: Sheb . . . 6J **29**
Acklington Pl. PL5: Plym . . . 6D **130**
Ackrells Hill TQ9: L'ton . . . 1H **103**
Acland Ct. EX33: Brau . . . 3J **15**
Acland Pk. EX14: Fen . . . 1G **53**
Acland Rd. EX4: Exe . . . 2G **7** (5G **65**)
EX5: Broadc . . . 6C **52**
EX32: L'key . . . 1C **24**
PL21: Ivy . . . 3E **144**
TQ8: Salc . . . 4C **158**
Aclands EX36: S Mol . . . 6D **26**
Acland Ter. EX4: Exe . . . 2G **7** (5F **65**)
Acland Way EX16: Tiv . . . 2A **40**
Acorn Gdns. PL7: Plymp . . . 3A **138**
Acre, The TQ13: Chag . . . 3H **61**
Acre Cotts. PL1: Dev . . . 1E **140**
Acre La. TQ1: Torq . . . 7G **113**
Acre Pl. PL1: Dev . . . 1E **140**
Activate Sports & Leisure . . . **3B 136**
Adams Cl. PL5: Plym . . . 2D **134**
Adam's La. PL9: Down T . . . 2E **148**
Adcroft Ri. EX13: Mus . . . 7D **90**
Addington Ct. EX4: Exe . . . 1E **6** (5F **65**)
Addison Cl. EX4: Exe . . . 6B **64**
Addison Rd. PL4: Plym . . . 2F **9** (1K **141**)
TQ4: Paig . . . 2G **119**
TQ12: New A . . . 2H **109**
Addlehole TQ9: E All . . . 6C **152**
Addlepool Bus. Cen.
EX3: Clyst G . . . 7H **73**
Adelaide Ct. EX2: Exe . . . 7B **6**
Adelaide La. PL1: Plym . . . 5A **8** (3G **141**)
Adelaide Pl. PL1: Plym . . . 4A **8** (2G **141**)
Adelaide St. PL1: Plym . . . 4A **8** (2G **141**)
PL2: Plym . . . 6E **134**
Adelaide St. Ope
PL1: Plym . . . 4A **8** (2G **141**)
Adelaide Ter. EX34: Ilfra . . . 3H **11**
PL1: Plym . . . 2C **8**
Adela Rd. PL11: Torp . . . 1A **140**
Adelphi La. TQ4: Paig . . . 2J **119**
Adelphi Mans. *TQ4: Paig . . . 2J 119*
(off Adelphi Rd.)
Adelphi Rd. TQ4: Paig . . . 1J **119**
Adley La. TQ13: Chag . . . 1J **61**
Admirals Ct. EX8: Exmth . . . 6C **76**
EX39: N'ham . . . 5E **20**
Admiral's Hard PL1: Plym . . . 4F **141**
Admirals Wlk. EX8: Exmth . . . 2F **77**
TQ14: Teignm . . . 1G **107**
Admiral Swimming Cen. . . . **4F 123**
Admiralty Cotts. PL1: Plym . . . 5F **141**
Admiralty Rd. PL1: Plym . . . 4F **141**
PL5: Plym . . . 1B **134**
Admiralty St. PL1: Plym . . . 4F **141**
PL2: Plym . . . 5D **134**
Admiralty St. La. W. PL1: Plym . . . 4F **141**
Admiral Vernon Ct. *EX2: Alph . . . 5E 70*
(off Chudleigh Rd.)
Adrian Cl. EX39: Bide . . . 1F **23**
ADSBOROUGH . . . **1C 167**
Adwell La. EX33: N Buck . . . 4E **14**
Agaton Fort Rd. PL5: Plym . . . 7E **130**
Agaton Rd. PL5: Plym . . . 1D **134**
Aidan Av. EX32: Barn . . . 7H **19**
Ailescombe Dr. TQ3: Paig . . . 1F **119**
Ailescombe Rd. TQ3: Paig . . . 1F **119**
Ainslie Ter. PL2: Plym . . . 4D **134**
Airborne Dr. PL6: Plym . . . 6C **132**
Aire Gdns. PL3: Plym . . . 6D **136**
Airfield Ind. Est. EX14: Dunk . . . 5G **47**
AISH
Buckfastleigh . . . **1A 100 (1C 175)**
Totnes . . . **2A 176**
Aish La. TQ10: Aish, S Bre . . . 1A **100**
Aish Pk. EX21: Sheb . . . 6J **29**
Aish Rd. TQ4: Paig . . . 5A **118**
TQ9: Sto G . . . 3B **120**
Alandale Cl. TQ14: Teignm . . . 3J **107**
Alandale Rd. TQ14: Teignm . . . 3J **107**
Alansway EX11: Ott M . . . 4B **80**
A La Ronde . . . **1C 76**
Albany Cl. EX8: Exmth . . . 2G **77**
Albany Ct. TQ3: Paig . . . 7H **115**
Albany Rd. TQ3: Pres . . . 5G **115**
Albany St. PL1: Dev . . . 2D **140**
TQ12: New A . . . 1F **109**
ALBASTON . . . **3C 169**
Albemarle Vs. PL1: Plym . . . 1E **140**
Alberta Ct. TQ14: Teignm . . . 4J **107**
Alberta Cres. EX4: Exe . . . 3J **65**
Albert Cl. EX17: Cred . . . 6H **39**
Albert Ct. *EX34: Ilfra . . . 2J 11*
(off Mill Head)
TQ1: Torq . . . 1D **116**
Albertha Cl. PL4: Plym . . . 2G **9** (1A **142**)
Albert La. EX32: Barn . . . 4F **19**
Albert Pl. EX8: Exmth . . . 6C **76**
EX39: Bide . . . 4E **22**
TQ6: Dartm . . . 1A **124** (6F **125**)
Albert Rd. EX17: Cred . . . 5H **39**
PL2: Dev . . . 1D **140**
TQ1: Torq . . . 1D **116**
Albert St. EX1: Exe . . . 2H **7** (5G **65**)
EX7: Daw . . . 4G **97**
Albert Ter. EX13: Axmin . . . 3H **89**
PL20: Prin . . . 6D **60**

Albert Ter.—Ashburton Cl.

Albert Ter. TQ12: New A . . . 1F 109
TQ13: Bov T . . . 4B 92
Albion Bungs. PL11: Torp . . . 1A 140
Albion Cl. EX12: Seat . . . 4D 86
Albion Ct. *EX8: Exmth . . . 6C 76*
(off Albion Pl.)
PL11: Torp . . . 1A 140
(off Gravesend Gdns.)
TQ5: Brixh . . . 5E 122
Albion Dr. PL2: Plym . . . 4G 135
Albion Gdns. TQ7: Kingsb . . . 3F 157
Albion Hill EX8: Exmth . . . 5D 76
TQ12: New A . . . 2F 109
Albion Pl. EX4: Exe . . . 1H 7 (5G 65)
EX8: Exmth . . . 5C 76
EX36: S Mol . . . 6C 26
Albion Rd. PL11: Torp . . . 1A 140
Albion St. EX4: Exe . . . 6A 6 (7D 64)
EX8: Exmth . . . 5C 76
TQ14: Shal . . . 6G 107
Albion Ter. *EX8: Exmth . . . 5C 76*
(off Henrietta Rd.)
Alcester Cl. PL2: Dev . . . 7D 134
Alcester St. PL2: Dev . . . 7E 134
Aldborough Ct. EX8: Exmth . . . 6E 76
Aldens Grn. EX2: Alph . . . 5E 70
Aldens Rd. EX2: Alph . . . 5E 70
Alden Wlk. PL6: Plym . . . 4C 136
Alder Cl. TQ12: New A . . . 4J 109
TQ14: Teignm . . . 3H 107
Alder Glade EX31: Roun . . . 6B 18
Alderney Rd. PL6: Plym . . . 3A 132
Alder Rd. PL19: Tavi . . . 6J 59
Aldersley Wlk. PL6: Plym . . . 3B 136
Alderson Dr. EX2: Sow . . . 7C 66
Alders Way TQ4: Paig . . . 4D 118
Aldrin Rd. EX4: Exe . . . 2G 65
Alexander Pl. EX11: Ott M . . . 3C 80
Alexander Wlk. EX2: Won . . . 7C 66
Alexandra Cinema, The
Scott Cinemas . . . 1E 108
Alexandra Cl. EX17: Cred . . . 5F 39
PL9: Elb . . . 4J 143
Alexandra Ct. EX32: Barn . . . 4F 19
Alexandra Dr. PL20: Bere A . . . 2D 128
Alexandra Ho. TQ12: New A . . . 2H 109
Alexandra La. TQ1: Torq . . . 1D 116
Alexandra M. EX6: Star . . . 1E 96
Alexandra Pl. PL4: Plym . . . 1G 9 (7K 135)
Alexandra Rd. EX7: Daw . . . 4G 97
EX13: Axmin . . . 4G 89
EX17: Cred . . . 5F 39
EX32: Barn . . . 3E 18
PL2: Plym . . . 6E 134
PL4: Plym . . . 1G 9 (7A 136)
PL6: Plym . . . 1A 136
(off Morshead Rd.)
TQ1: Torq . . . 7D 112
TQ12: New A . . . 2G 109
Alexandra Ter. EX4: Exe . . . 1J 7 (5H 65)
EX5: Broadc . . . 2K 67
EX6: Star . . . 1E 96
(off Royal Way)
EX8: Exmth . . . 6B 76
EX16: Tiv . . . 4B 40
(off John St.)
EX36: S Mol . . . 5C 26
(off North St.)
EX39: Bide . . . 2E 22
PL2: Plym . . . 6E 134
TQ9: Tot . . . 5E 102
TQ12: New A . . . 2F 109
TQ14: Teignm . . . 5H 107
Alexandra Way EX17: Cred . . . 5F 39
Alexandria Ind. Est. EX10: Sidm . . . 4B 84
EX15: Cull . . . 3J 45
Alexandria Rd. EX10: Sidm . . . 4B 84
ALFARDISWORTHY . . . 2A 162
ALFINGTON . . . 1B 172
Alfington Rd. EX11: Alf . . . 4K 53
EX11: Ott M . . . 2D 80
Alford Cl. EX1: Whip . . . 5B 66
Alford Cres. EX1: Whip . . . 5A 66
Alford Ter. EX35: Lynt . . . 2G 13
Alfranza Cl. EX1: Heav . . . 6A 66
Alfred Pl. PL2: Plym . . . 6E 134
Alfred Rd. PL2: Plym . . . 6E 134
Alfred St. PL1: Plym . . . 6D 8 (3J 141)
Alfriston Rd. TQ3: Paig . . . 7D 114
Alger Wlk. PL6: Plym . . . 4K 131
Alice La. PL1: Plym . . . 4B 8
Alice St. PL1: Plym . . . 4A 8 (2G 141)
Alice Templer Cl. EX2: Won . . . 2J 71
Alison Rd. TQ3: Pres . . . 5G 115
ALLALEIGH . . . 2A 176
Allen Bank EX32: Barn . . . 6F 19
Allenby Rd. PL2: Plym . . . 5F 135
Allen Cl. EX16: Tiv . . . 3F 41
Allendale Rd. PL4: Plym . . . 1F 9 (1K 141)
Allenhayes La. TQ8: Salc . . . 4C 158
Allenhayes Rd. TQ8: Salc . . . 4C 158
Allens Rd. PL21: Ivy . . . 3H 145
Allenstyle Cl. EX31: Yell . . . 6C 16
Allenstyle Dr. EX31: Yell . . . 6B 16
Allenstyle Gdns. EX31: Yell . . . 6C 16
Allenstyle Rd. EX31: Yell . . . 6C 16
Allenstyle Vw. EX31: Yell . . . 6B 16
Allenstyle Way EX31: Yell . . . 6C 16
ALLER
Kingskerswell . . . 6J 109
Othery . . . 1D 167
Aller Brake Rd. TQ12: New A . . . 4H 109
Aller Cl. TQ12: Kingsk . . . 6J 109
ALLERCOMBE . . . 5K 69 (1A 172)
Allercombe Hill EX5: Rock . . . 2F 79
Allercombe La. EX5: Rock . . . 5K 69
ALLER GROVE . . . 7J 53
Aller Hill EX7: Daw . . . 5F 97 & 4F 97
Aller Mills TQ12: Kingsk . . . 6J 109
Allern La. PL5: Tam F . . . 1J 131
ALLER PARK . . . 3J 109
Aller Pk. Rd. TQ12: New A . . . 4J 109
Aller Rd. EX19: Dol . . . 6H 31
TQ12: Kingsk . . . 6J 109
Allerton Wlk. PL6: Plym . . . 4C 136
Aller Va. Cl. EX2: Won . . . 1A 72
Alleyn Ct. EX12: Seat . . . 5D 86
Alleyn Gdns. PL3: Plym . . . 3K 135
Allhalland St. EX39: Bide . . . 3F 23
Allhallows Ct. EX4: Exe . . . 5C 6 (7E 64)
EX14: Hon . . . 3F 55
(off Northcote La.)
Allhallows Museum of
Lace & Local Antiquities . . . 3F 55
All Hallows Rd. TQ3: Pres . . . 4J 115
Alliance Ct. EX14: Hon . . . 5C 54
Allington Mead EX4: Exe . . . 2D 64
Allotment Gdns. TQ7: Kingsb . . . 3G 157
Allotment La. PL7: Plymp . . . 6B 138
ALLOWENSHAY . . . 2D 167
All Saints Cl. EX9: E Bud . . . 1D 82
All Saints Ct. EX14: Hon . . . 4D 54
All Saint's Rd. EX10: Sidm . . . 6B 84
TQ1: Torq . . . 7E 112
Alma Cotts. PL4: Plym . . . 5J 9 (3A 142)
Alma La. EX10: Sidm . . . 6D 84
Alma Pl. *EX2: Heav . . . 7J 65*
(off Sivell Pl.)
Alma Rd. PL3: Plym . . . 1B 8 (6G 135)
TQ5: Brixh . . . 3E 122
Alma Steps *TQ6: Kingsw . . . 7G 125*
(off Beacon Rd.)
Alma St. PL4: Plym . . . 5J 9 (3A 142)
Alma Villa Ri. EX5: Cranb . . . 4B 68
Almeria Ct. PL7: Plymp . . . 5A 138
ALMINSTONE CROSS . . . 1B 162
Almond Ct. EX31: Roun . . . 7B 18
Almond Dr. PL7: Plymp . . . 3E 138
Alpha Cen., The EX2: Sow . . . 7E 66
Alpha Pl. EX39: Apple . . . 2H 21
Alpha St. EX1: Heav . . . 6J 65
Alpha Ter. TQ9: Tot . . . 5D 102
Alphin Brook Ct. EX2: Mar B . . . 4F 71
Alphin Brook Rd. EX2: Mar B . . . 4E 70
ALPHINGTON . . . 4E 70 (1D 171)
Alphington Rd. EX2: Exe . . . 7C 6 (3E 70)
Alphington Spur EX2: Exe . . . 4D 70
Alphington St. EX2: Exe . . . 6C 6 (7E 64)
Alpine Rd. TQ1: Torq . . . 1D 116
Alsa Brook Mdw. EX16: Tiv . . . 2C 40
ALSTON . . . 3D 167
Alstone Rd. EX16: Tiv . . . 5F 41
Alston La. TQ5: Chur F . . . 6J 121
Alston Pk. PL7: Plymp . . . 3A 138
Alston Ter. EX8: Exmth . . . 6B 76
ALSWEAR . . . 1B 164
Alswear New Rd. EX36: S Mol . . . 7D 26
Alswear Old Rd. EX36: S Mol . . . 7C 26
Altamira EX3: Top . . . 5B 74
ALTARNUN . . . 2A 168
Alta Vista Cl. TQ14: Teignm . . . 2K 107
Alta Vista Rd. TQ4: Good . . . 3J 119
Alton Pl. PL4: Plym . . . 1G 9
Alton Rd. PL4: Plym . . . 1F 9
ALVERDISCOTT . . . 1D 163
Alverdiscott Rd. EX39: Bide . . . 4H 23
Alverdiscott Rd. Ind. Est.
EX39: Bide . . . 5J 23
Alver Grn. EX39: Bide . . . 4J 23
Alvington St. PL4: Plym . . . 6K 9 (3B 142)
Alvington Ter. *TQ7: Kingsb . . . 5F 157*
(off W. Alvington Hill)
ALWINGTON . . . 1C 163
Alwin Pk. PL6: Plym . . . 5B 132
Alwyns Cl. *TQ14: Teignm . . . 4J 107*
(off Lwr. Brimley Rd.)
Amacre Dr. PL9: Hooe . . . 6C 142
Amados Cl. PL7: Plymp . . . 7J 137
Amados Dr. PL7: Plymp . . . 7K 137
Amados Ri. PL7: Plymp . . . 7K 137
Ambassador Dr. EX1: Sow . . . 5D 66
Ambassador Ho. TQ4: Paig . . . 2J 119
Amersham Ct. *EX2: Won . . . 1K 71*
(off Wonford St.)
AMF Bowling
Torquay . . . 2E 116
Amherst Rd. PL3: Plym . . . 1B 8 (1H 141)
Amherst Rd. La. East
PL3: Plym . . . 1B 8 (7H 135)
Amity Pl. EX3: Top . . . 6B 74
PL4: Plym . . . 2G 9 (1K 141)
Amory Pl. *EX36: S Mol . . . 6C 26*
(off Cooks Cross)
Amory Rd. EX16: Tiv . . . 6C 40
Amyas Way EX39: N'ham . . . 6F 21
Amyatts Ter. *EX10: Sidm . . . 7C 84*
(off Church St.)
Anchorage, The *TQ4: Paig . . . 2J 119*
(off Belle Vue Rd.)
Anchorage Cl. TQ5: Brixh . . . 3G 123
Anchor Cen., The
TQ7: Kingsb . . . 4G 157
(off Bridge St.)
Anchorwood Bank EX31: Barn . . . 5C 18
Anderton Cl. PL19: Whitc . . . 7K 59
Anderton Ct. PL19: Whitc . . . 7K 59
Anderton La. PL19: Whitc . . . 7K 59
Andor Av. TQ12: Kingst . . . 4G 105
Andrea Ct. *TQ14: Teignm . . . 4H 107*
(off Yannon Dr.)
Andrew Cl. EX10: Sidm . . . 2A 84
Andrew Rd. EX31: Barn . . . 7D 18
Andrews Pk. TQ9: Sto G . . . 3B 120
Andurn Cl. PL9: Elb . . . 6J 143
Andurn Est. PL9: Down T . . . 2A 148
Angel Hill EX16: Tiv . . . 4C 40
Angel M. *EX14: Hon . . . 3F 55*
(off Silver St.)
Angel Ter. *EX16: Tiv . . . 4C 40*
(off Angel Hill)
ANGERSLEIGH . . . 2C 167
Anna Mill Business & Distribution Pk.
TQ10: Wran . . . 3E 146
Anne Cl. EX4: Exe . . . 3H 65
Anne Cres. EX31: Barn . . . 7C 18
Anning Rd. DT7: Lym R . . . 4J 91
Ann's Pl. PL3: Plym . . . 7F 135
Anson Ho. PL1: Plym . . . 3B 8
Anson Pl. PL2: Dev . . . 7E 134
PL4: Plym . . . 4K 9 (2B 142)
Anson Rd. EX8: Exmth . . . 2E 76
Anstey Cres. EX16: Tiv . . . 5F 41
Ansteys Cl. TQ1: Torq . . . 1G 117
Ansteys Ct. EX16: With . . . 6J 33
Anstey's Cove Rd. TQ1: Torq . . . 7G 113
Anstey Way EX39: Ins . . . 3K 21
Anstis Ct. EX10: Sidm . . . 3B 84
Anstis St. PL1: Plym . . . 3A 8 (2G 141)
Anthea Rd. TQ3: Pres . . . 5F 115
Anthony Pk. *PL19: Tavi . . . 3K 59*
(off Parkwood Rd.)
Anthony Rd. EX1: Heav . . . 6J 65
Antonine Cres. EX4: Exe . . . 6B 64
ANTONY . . . 2A 174
Antony Gdns. PL2: Plym . . . 3H 135
Antony Rd. PL11: Torp . . . 1A 140
Antrim Ter. TQ9: Tot . . . 5E 102
ANVIL CORNER . . . 3B 162
Anzac Av. PL5: Plym . . . 6F 131
Anzac St. TQ6: Dartm . . . 1A 124 (6F 125)
Apollo Cinema
Paignton . . . 1J 119
Applebee Way DT7: Lym R . . . 4K 91
Appleby Wlk. PL5: Plym . . . 6J 131
Apple Cl. EX8: Exmth . . . 1D 76
APPLEDORE
Bideford . . . 3H 21 (3A 160)
Tiverton . . . 2A 166
Appledore Cl. EX15: Cull . . . 4G 45
PL6: Plym . . . 4D 132
Appledore Lifeboat Station . . . 1G 21
Apple Dr. EX15: Will . . . 4D 44
Apple Farm Grange EX2: Sow . . . 2D 72
Applegarth Av. TQ12: New A . . . 6B 104
Applegarth Cl. TQ12: New A . . . 7B 104
Applehayes EX8: Exmth . . . 7E 76
Apple La. EX2: Sow . . . 2D 72
Applemede EX5: Silv . . . 1G 51
Apple Orchard EX38: Gt T . . . 3A 30
Appleton Tor Cl. PL3: Plym . . . 5F 137
Apple Tree Cl. EX16: With . . . 6J 33
TQ13: Chud K . . . 6A 94
Appletree Cl. EX15: Uff . . . 7G 43
EX32: Barn . . . 5J 19
(not continuous)
Appletree Gdns. EX39: N'ham . . . 1F 23
Appletree M. EX39: Apple . . . 3H 21
Apple Wharf TQ9: Tot . . . 6F 103
APPLEY . . . 1A 166
April Cl. EX8: Exmth . . . 1D 76
Apsley Ho. TQ1: Torq . . . 3E 116
Apsley Rd. PL4: Plym . . . 1E 8 (1J 141)
Apsley Ter. EX33: Brau . . . 3K 15
EX34: Ilfra . . . 3J 11
(off Highfield Rd.)
Apsley Vs. EX34: Ilfra . . . 3J 11
Apters Hill *TQ5: Brixh . . . 3E 122*
(off Middle St.)
Aptor La. TQ3: Marl . . . 2A 114
Arbour, The PL6: Plym . . . 5K 131
Arbour Cl. EX34: Ilfra . . . 4H 11
Arcade, The *EX20: Oke . . . 3B 48*
(off Fore St.)
Arcade Rd. EX34: Ilfra . . . 2H 11
Arcadia PL9: Elb . . . 6K 143
Arcadia Rd. PL9: Elb . . . 6K 143
Arch, The EX5: Wood . . . 5B 78
Arch Cotts. TQ12: Kingst . . . 4G 105
Archer Pl. PL1: Plym . . . 2C 8 (1H 141)
Archers Cl. EX15: Cull . . . 4G 45
Archers Ct. PL8: New F . . . 4J 149
Archer Ter. PL1: Plym . . . 3C 8 (2H 141)
Archery Cl. TQ7: Kingsb . . . 2F 157
Arches, The EX2: Exe . . . 7B 6
Archibald Rd. EX1: Exe . . . 4G 7 (6G 65)
Archipark EX32: Swim . . . 2H 25
Arch St. TQ14: Shal . . . 6G 107
Archway Av. PL4: Plym . . . 1C 142
Archway Dr. TQ6: Dartm . . . 5D 124
Arcot Gdns. EX10: Sidm . . . 4C 84
Arcot Pk. EX10: Sidm . . . 4C 84
Arcot Rd. EX10: Sidm . . . 4C 84
Arden Cl. EX9: Bud S . . . 7C 82
Arden Dr. TQ2: Torq . . . 7K 111
Arden Gro. PL2: Plym . . . 3H 135
Ardenney Ct. EX8: Exmth . . . 7E 76
Arena Pk. EX4: Whip . . . 3A 66
Argent Ct. *EX16: Tiv . . . 4D 40*
(off Bartows C'way.)
Argus Cl. EX14: Hon . . . 3G 55
Argyle Ter. TQ9: Tot . . . 5D 102
Argyll M. EX4: Exe . . . 3D 64
Argyll Rd. EX4: Exe . . . 2E 64
Arimoor Gdns. PL19: Tavi . . . 4K 59
Ark Pottery . . . 7D 80
Ark Royal Cl. PL5: Plym . . . 3C 134
Arkwright Gdns. PL5: Plym . . . 1E 134
Arley Cl. PL6: Plym . . . 4C 132
ARLINGTON . . . 2C 161
ARLINGTON BECCOTT . . . 2C 161
Arlington Court . . . 3C 161
Arlington Court Pk. . . . 3C 161
Arlington Pl. EX34: Woolc . . . 6B 10
Arlington Rd. EX34: Woolc . . . 6A 10
PL4: Plym . . . 7A 136
Arlington Ter. EX33: Brau . . . 5J 15
Armada Cen. PL1: Plym . . . 3D 8 (2J 141)
Armada Cl. EX12: Seat . . . 3E 86
Armada Ct. EX3: Top . . . 5B 74
PL19: Tavi . . . 5H 59
Armada Cres. TQ2: Torq . . . 7J 111
Armada Dr. TQ14: Teignm . . . 1G 107
Armada Memorial . . . 7E 8 (4J 141)
Armada St. PL4: Plym . . . 2F 9 (1K 141)
Armada Way EX39: West H . . . 6A 20
PL1: Plym . . . 7D 8 (3J 141)
(not continuous)
Armstrong Av. EX4: Exe . . . 2G 65
Armytage Rd. EX9: Bud S . . . 5C 82
Arnison Cl. PL9: Plyms . . . 7F 143
Arnold Cres. EX16: Tiv . . . 6B 40
Arnold's Point PL4: Plym . . . 1D 142
Arnside Cl. PL6: Plym . . . 7E 132
Arran Cl. TQ2: Torq . . . 3A 112
Arscott Gdns. PL9: Hooe . . . 7D 142
Arscott La. PL9: Hooe . . . 7D 142
Arthington TQ1: Torq . . . 6B 112
Art Ho. EX1: Exe . . . 5D 6
Arthurs Cl. EX8: Exmth . . . 2F 77
Arthurs Lea EX39: A'sham . . . 3A 22
Arthur's Rd. EX4: Whip . . . 3K 65
Arthur Ter. *PL11: Torp . . . 2A 140*
(off Bellevue Sq.)
Artillery Ct. EX2: Exe . . . 2H 71
Artillery Pl. PL4: Plym . . . 7H 9 (4A 142)
Artizan's Dwellings EX36: S Mol . . . 6D 26
Arts at Dartington, The . . . 1D 102
Arun Cl. PL3: Plym . . . 6D 136
Arundel Cl. EX2: Alph . . . 5E 70
Arundel Cres. PL1: Plym . . . 2B 8 (1H 141)
Arundell Cl. PL16: Lift . . . 6B 56
Arundell Gdns. PL16: Lift . . . 6B 56
Arundell Pl. TQ7: Lodd . . . 3G 151
Arundell Rd. EX20: N Taw . . . 6C 36
Arundel Ter. *PL2: Dev . . . 7E 134*
(off Victoria Pl.)
Ascension Way TQ2: Torq . . . 3B 112
Ascerton Cl. EX10: Sidm . . . 5C 84
Ascerton Rd. EX10: Sidm . . . 5C 84
ASH . . . 3A 176
ASHBRITTLE . . . 1A 166
Ashburn Cl. TQ13: Ashb . . . 4G 99
Ashburn Gdns. TQ13: Ashb . . . 3H 99
Ashburnham Rd. PL5: Plym . . . 7F 131
Ashburn Wlk. TQ4: Good . . . 7H 119
ASHBURTON . . . 4H 99 (1D 175)
Ashburton By-Pass TQ13: Ashb . . . 5G 99
Ashburton Cl. TQ13: Bov T . . . 6A 92

Ashburton Mus.—Bapton Cl.

Ashburton Mus. 4H 99
Ashburton Rd. TQ9: Darti, Tot 2B 102
TQ11: B'leigh 3D 98
TQ12: New A 6A 104
TQ13: Bov T 6B 92
Ashburton Swimming Pool 4H 99
(off Love La.)
ASHBURY 1D 169
Ash Cl. PL20: Yelv 5F 127
Ashclyst Forest 1A 172
Ashclyst Vw. EX5: Broadc 6D 52
ASHCOMBE 3D 171
Ashcombe Cl. PL7: Plymp 4K 137
Ashcombe Rd. EX7: Daw 4F 97
Ash Ct. EX17: Cred 5H 39
PL21: Ivy, L Mill 4D 144
Ashdown Cl. PL6: Plym 7F 133
Ashdown Wlk. PL6: Plym 7F 133
Ash Dr. EX15: Cull 2H 45
Asheldon Rd. TQ1: Torq 1G 117
Ashery Dr. PL9: Hooe 6D 142
Ashes Rd. EX13: Shute 2A 88
Ash Farm Cl. EX1: Pin 3E 66
Ashfield Cl. EX8: Exmth 3G 77
EX31: Ashf 1K 17
Ashfield Gdns. TQ2: Torq 2A 116
Ashfield Rd. TQ2: Torq 1A 116
Ashfield Ter. EX39: N'ham 5F 21
(off Diddywell Rd.)
ASHFORD
Barnstaple 1K 17 (3B 160)
Kingsbridge 4H 151 (3C 175)
Ashford Cl. PL3: Plym 7B 136
Ashford Cres. PL3: Plym 7B 136
Ashford Hill PL4: Plym 7B 136
Ashford Rd. EX3: Top 5A 74
PL4: Plym 7A 136
Ash Gro. EX8: Exmth 2D 76
EX12: Seat 2E 86
PL2: Plym 4E 134
PL21: Ivy 4J 145
Ashgrove Rd. TQ13: Bov T 7B 92
ASH HILL 3C 106
Ash Hill TQ14: Bi'ton 3C 106
Ash Hill Ct. EX12: Beer 7A 86
Ash Hill Rd. TQ1: Torq 7C 112
ASHILL
Ilminster 2D 167
Uffculme 2A 166
Ash Leigh EX2: Alph 5D 70
Ashleigh Cl. EX4: Exe 6C 64
PL5: Tam F 3H 131
TQ2: Torq 2B 112
TQ14: Teignm 2H 107
Ashleigh Ct. TQ1: Torq 3F 117
Ashleigh Cres. EX32: Barn 5G 19
Ashleigh Dr. TQ14: Teignm 2H 107
Ashleigh La. PL5: Tam F 1J 131
Ashleigh Mt. TQ14: Teignm 2H 107
Ashleigh Mt. Rd. EX4: Exe 6B 64
Ashleigh Pk. EX16: Bam 3J 33
TQ14: Teignm 2H 107
Ashleigh Ri. TQ14: Teignm 2H 107
Ashleigh Rd. EX8: Exmth 5D 76
EX14: Hon 3E 54
EX32: Barn 4F 19
TQ7: Kingsb 5E 156
Ashleigh Vs. TQ9: Tot 6D 102
(off Plymouth Rd.)
Ashleigh Way PL7: Plymp 5F 139
TQ14: Teignm 2H 107
ASHLEY 7B 40
Ashley Bk. La. EX16: Ashl 7B 40
Ashley Brake EX11: W Hill 4H 79
Ashley Cl. EX15: Uff 5J 43
Ashley Cres. EX10: Sidm 3B 84
Ashley Ho. EX8: Exmth 6D 76
Ashley Pl. PL1: Plym 2B 8
Ashley Priors La. TQ1: Torq 1E 112
Ashley Ri. EX16: Ashl 7B 40
Ashley Rd. EX15: Uff 6H 43
EX20: Oke 3C 48
Ashley Ter. EX34: Ilfra 3H 11
(off St Brannock's Pk. Rd.)
EX39: Bide 4E 22
(off Royston Rd.)
Ashley Way EX7: Daw 3J 97
ASHMANSWORTHY 2B 162
Ashmead Gro. EX33: Brau 4H 15
ASH MILL 1B 164
ASHMILL 1B 168
Ashmill Ct. TQ12: New A 7C 104
Ashmoor Recreation Cen. 2J 99
Ashmore Ct. EX2: Exe 7C 6
Ash Pk. EX7: Holc 7F 97
Ashplants Cl. EX19: Wink 2C 36
EX39: Bide 3C 22
ASHPRINGTON 2A 176
ASH PRIORS 1B 166
ASHREIGNEY 2A 164
Ashridge Gdns. PL5: Plym 1G 135
TQ12: Kingst 6J 105
Ash Rd. EX33: Brau 4K 15
TQ12: Kingst 5H 105
ASH THOMAS 2A 166
Ashton Cl. PL6: Plym 4D 132
Ashton Ct. TQ12: Kingst 2H 105
Ashton Cres. EX33: Brau 5H 15
Ashton Rd. EX2: Mar B 3E 70
Ashton Ter. TQ1: Torq 1G 117
Ashtree Cl. PL6: Plym 3E 132
Ashtree Gro. PL9: Elb 4K 143
Ash Va. PL16: Lift 6A 56
ASHWATER 1B 168
Ash Way TQ12: New A 3J 109
ASHWELL 2A 106
Ashwood TQ10: S Bre 1B 100
Ashwood Cl. PL7: Plymp 4E 138
TQ7: Lodd 3G 151
Ashwood Ct. TQ12: New A 2H 109
(off Marychurch Rd.)
Ashwood Pk. TQ7: Lodd 3G 151
Ashwood Pk. Rd. PL7: Plymp 3F 139
Ashwood Rd. EX2: Exe 2E 70
Aspen Cl. EX2: Won 1B 72
EX14: Hon 5C 54
EX15: Will 3E 44
PL19: Tavi 6J 59
Aspen Dr. TQ12: New A 4J 109
Aspen Gdns. PL7: Plymp 4E 138
Aspen Gro. EX31: Frem 7E 16
Aspen Way EX16: Tiv 1E 40
TQ4: Paig 4D 118
Astley Corte EX20: Oke 3A 48
Astor Dr. PL4: Plym 1D 142
Aswell Orchard TQ7: Lodd 3H 151
(off Little Gate)
ATHELNEY 1D 167
Athelstan Cl. EX13: Axmin 5G 89
Athelstan Rd. EX1: Exe 4G 7 (6G 65)
Athenaeum La.
PL1: Plym 5C 8 (3H 141)
Athenaeum Pl. PL1: Plym . . .5D 8 (3J 141)
Athenaeum St.
PL1: Plym 6C 8 (3H 141)
ATHERINGTON 1D 163
Atherton La. TQ9: Tot 6E 102
Atherton Pl. PL2: Dev 7D 134
(off Charlotte St.)
Atherton Way EX16: Tiv 5G 41
Athlone Ho. PL1: Plym 5A 8
Atkinson Cl. EX4: Whip 3K 65
Atlantic Bldg. PL4: Plym . . .7H 9 (4A 142)
Atlantic Ct. EX34: Ilfra 2H 11
(off Northfield Rd.)
Atlantic Village EX39: Bide 5B 22
Atlantic Way EX39: West H 5B 20
Atlantis Adventure Pk. 5A 22
Atlantis Fun Pool 5B 8
Atrium, The TQ1: Torq 1F 117
Attwater Ct. PL19: Lam 6C 58
Attwill's Almshouses
EX4: Exe 1B 6 (5D 64)
Attwood M. PL3: Plym 7G 135
Attwyll Av. EX2: Won 7K 65
Atway Cl. TQ13: Bov T 3B 92
Atwill-Kingdon Almshouses
EX1: Exe 4K 7
Auckland Rd. PL2: Plym 6F 135
Auctioneers Cl. PL7: Plymp 4A 138
Auction Pl. EX13: Axmin 4H 89
Auction Way EX39: Wools 2B 28
Audley Av. TQ2: Torq 5B 112
Audley Ri. TQ12: New A 3K 109
Augustine Cl. EX12: Seat 4D 86
Augustus Ho. EX4: Exe 2E 6 (5F 65)
Aunay Cl. EX22: Hols 1D 34
Austen Cl. EX4: Whip 4B 66
Austin Av. PL2: Plym 5F 135
Austin Cres. PL6: Plym 3D 136
Authers Hgts. EX16: Tiv 6B 40
Avalon Cl. EX4: Whip 2K 65
Aveland Rd. TQ1: Torq 6E 112
Avent Wlk. PL7: Plymp 2C 138
Avenue, The EX3: Exton 2G 75
EX12: Seat 5E 86
EX16: Tiv 5E 40
PL21: L Mill 5A 144
TQ12: New A 1F 109
TQ13: Chud K 5C 94
Avenue Ct. DT7: Lym R 5J 91
Avenue Mezidon-Canon
EX14: Hon 4G 55
Avenue Rd. DT7: Lym R 5J 91
EX34: Ilfra 2H 11
TQ2: Torq 7A 112
TQ12: Kingsk 7K 109
TQ13: Bov T 4B 92
Avenue Ter. TQ5: Chur F 3A 122
Avery Hill TQ12: Kingst 3H 105
AVETON GIFFORD 6H 151 (3C 175)
Aviemore Ind. Est. EX31: Barn 6C 18
Avoca Av. TQ1: Torq 7B 112
Avocet Dr. EX3: Exton 1G 75
Avocet Rd. EX2: Sow 6E 66
Avon Cl. PL3: Plym 5E 136
TQ10: S Bre 2C 100
Avondale Ho. TQ10: S Bre 2B 100
Avondale Rd. EX2: Won 7K 65
EX8: Exmth 4F 77
Avondale Ter. PL2: Plym 6D 134
Avon La. EX39: West H 5C 20
Avon Rd. EX39: Bide 4H 23
TQ2: Torq 6H 111
AVONWICK 2D 175
Avranches Av. EX17: Cred 5F 39
AWLISCOMBE 1A 54 (3B 166)
Axe Cliff Golf Course 5H 87
Axe Cl. PL3: Plym 5E 136
Axe Valley Caravan Pk.
EX12: Seat 4F 87
Axe Valley Cl. EX13: Ray H 1D 90
Axe Valley Heritage Mus. 5F 87
Axe Valley Sports Cen. 3J 89
Axeview Rd. EX12: Seat 3D 86
Axe Yacht Club 6G 87
AXMINSTER 3H 89 (1C 173)
Axminster Mus. 4H 89
Axminster Rd. EX13: Mus 7C 90
EX14: Hon 4H 55
Axminster Station (Rail) 4G 89
AXMOUTH 3H 87 (1C 173)
Axmouth Rd. EX12: Axmth 5G 87
Axmouth to Lyme Regis Undercliffs
National Nature Reserve 7F 91
AXTOWN 6E 126
Axtown La. PL20: Yelv 7E 126
Aycliffe Gdns. PL7: Plymp 6D 138
AYLESBEARE 1A 172
Aylesbury Cres. PL5: Plym 5G 131
AYLESCOTT 2A 164
Ayleston Pk. PL21: Modb 6H 147
Aylwin Cl. PL7: Plymp 3B 138
Ayres Cl. EX39: Bide 4H 23
AYREVILLE 2A 118 (1A 176)
Ayreville Rd. PL2: Plym 4G 135
Aysha Gdns. EX39: West H 5C 20
AYSHFORD 1E 42 (2A 166)
Ayshford EX15: Uff 6H 43
Azalea Cl. EX14: Dunk 7H 47
Azes La. EX32: Barn 4F 19

B

BABBACOMBE 6F 113 (1B 176)
Babbacombe Bus. Pk. TQ1: Torq . . .6F 113
(not continuous)
Babbacombe Cliff Railway 5E 112
Babbacombe Cl. PL6: Plym 3F 137
Babbacombe Corinthian Sailing Club
. . . . .5D 112
(off Fore St.)
Babbacombe Downs Rd.
TQ1: Torq 5E 112
Babbacombe Model Village 4E 112
Babbacombe Rd. TQ1: Torq 5E 112
Babbacombe Theatre 6F 113
Babbage Rd. TQ9: Tot 5E 102
Babbages EX31: Bick'n 5K 17
Babblebrook M. EX1: Pin 4E 66
Babeleigh Cl. EX39: Buck B 2H 29
Bableigh Rd. EX32: L'key 2B 24
Babylon La. EX5: Silv 4G 51
Backaborough La. EX39: Bide 4E 22
(off Capern Rd.)
Backfield EX39: Apple 3H 21
Back La. EX5: Bradn 3A 52
EX10: Col R 2F 83
EX10: New P 5G 81
EX10: N'town 5J 81
EX17: Morc 1A 38
EX18: Chul 6B 32
EX20: Mer 5B 30
EX20: Stic 1G 49
EX36: N Mol 2C 26
EX37: Chit 5J 25
PL6: Robo 1B 132
PL7: Plymp 5B 138
PL21: Erm 2F 147
PL21: Lutt 7G 129
Back La. Ind. Est. EX18: Chul 5B 32
Back Rd. TQ12: New A 1E 108
(not continuous)
Backs, The TQ6: Dartm 4E 124
Back St. EX5: Bradn 1C 52
EX16: Bam 2H 33
EX39: Wools 2B 28
PL21: Modb 6G 147
BADGALL 2A 168
Badgaver La. EX34: Com M 7E 12
Badger Cl. EX2: Won 7C 66
EX10: New P 6F 81
EX14: Hon 2H 55
TQ3: Pres 5F 115
TQ6: Dartm 5D 124
Badgers Cl. PL21: Ivy 4E 144
TQ7: Kingsb 5F 157
TQ12: Kingst 3G 105
Badgers Grn. TQ7: Kingsb 5F 157
Badgers Holt EX20: Oke 3A 48
(off Glendale Rd.)
Badgers Way TQ13: Bov T 4C 92
Badger Vw. PL9: Plyms 7F 143
Bad Homburg Way
EX2: Mar B, Matf 5G 71
Badlake Cl. EX7: Daw 3F 97
Badlake Hill EX7: Daw 3F 97
Badon Cl. EX4: Whip 2K 65
Baggy Point 2A 160
Bagshot Av. EX2: Exe 2G 71
Baileys Mdw. TQ6: Sto F 3H 153
Bailey St. EX4: Exe 3E 6 (6F 65)
Bainbridge Av. PL3: Plym 4A 136
Bainbridge Ct. PL7: Plymp 2A 138
Baker Cl. EX10: Sidm 2B 84
Bakers Cl. PL7: Plymp 4F 139
Bakers Ct. La. EX35: Lynt 2G 13
Bakers Hill EX2: Exe 2A 70
EX16: Tiv 4A 40
TQ5: Brixh 5E 122
TQ7: Ave G 6H 151
TQ12: New A 1E 108
Bakers M. EX15: Cull 4H 45
(off Fore St.)
Bakers Piece TQ8: E Port 4E 158
Bakers Pl. PL1: Dev 3E 140
Baker St. EX2: Won 5K 7 (7J 65)
Bakers Vw. TQ12: New A 1D 108
Bakery La. EX8: Exmth 5C 76
Bakery Way EX32: L'key 2B 24
Bala Brook Cl. TQ5: Brixh 6B 122
Baldwin Ct. EX20: Oke 2D 48
Baldwin Dr. EX20: Oke 3D 48
Balfour Cl. EX14: Hon 4H 55
Balfour Gdns. EX10: Sidm 4B 84
Balfour Mnr. EX10: Sidm 5A 84
Balfour Rd. EX10: Sidm 5B 84
Balfours EX10: Sidm 3B 84
Balfour Ter. EX13: Kilm 2B 88
PL2: Dev 7D 134
Balkwill Rd. TQ7: Kingsb 5E 156
Balland La. TQ13: Ashb 3J 99
Balland Pk. TQ13: Ashb 2J 99
Bal La. PL19: Mary T 1B 60
Ballard Gro. EX10: Sidf 1E 84
Ballards Cres. EX31: Yell 7B 16
Ballards Gro. EX31: Yell 7B 16
Ballards Way EX31: Yell 7B 16
Balleroy Cl. EX21: Sheb 6J 29
Ball Hill EX17: Cher F 1K 39
Ball Hill La. EX20: Oke 3D 48
Ballhill La. EX16: Bam 3F 33
Ball Mdw. EX20: Oke 3D 48
Ball's Farm Rd. EX2: Exe, Ide 3B 70
Balmoral Av. PL2: Plym 6E 134
Balmoral Cl. TQ12: New A 2H 109
Balmoral Cres. EX20: Oke 3D 48
Balmoral Gdns. EX3: Top 5B 74
Balmoral Ho. EX31: Barn 2D 18
Balmoral Ter. EX34: Ilfra 3H 11
(off St Brannock's Pk. Rd.)
Baltic Wharf Bus. Pk. TQ9: Tot 7F 103
Bampfylde Cl. EX16: Tiv 5F 41
Bampfylde La. EX1: Exe 3E 6
Bampfylde Rd. TQ2: Torq 1B 116
Bampfylde St. EX1: Exe 3F 7 (6F 65)
Bampfylde Way PL6: Plym 4J 131
BAMPTON 2H 33 (1D 165)
Bampton Castle 1H 33
Bampton Cl. TQ3: Marl 4D 114
Bampton Communication Mus. 2H 33
Bampton Rd. PL6: Plym 2F 137
Bampton St. EX16: Tiv 4D 40
Banbury Pk. TQ2: Torq 5J 111
Banfield Way EX14: Hon 5E 54
BANGORS 1A 168
Bank End EX39: Bide 1G 23
(off Chanters Rd.)
BANKLAND 1D 167
Bank La. TQ5: Brixh 3E 122
TQ9: Tot 6E 102
Banksia Cl. EX16: Tiv 1E 40
Bankside EX8: Exmth 1E 76
Bank St. TQ12: New A 1E 108
TQ14: Teignm 5J 107
Bank Ter. EX34: Woolc 6B 10
Bannawell St. PL19: Tavi 3H 59
Banner Ct. TQ3: Paig 1G 119
(off Winner St.)
BANTHAM 4A 154 (3C 175)
Baptist Chapel Ct. EX17: Cred 6H 39
(off High St.)
Baptist La. TQ7: Kingsb 4F 157
(off Fore St.)
TQ8: Salc 4C 158
(off Devon Rd.)
Bapton Cl. EX8: Exmth 2D 76

Bapton La.—Bear St.

Bapton La. EX8: Exmth ... 3D **76**
Barber's La. DT7: Uply ... 4G **91**
BARBICAN ... 7F **9** (3J **141**)
Barbican, The PL1: Plym ... 6F **9**
(New St.)
PL1: Plym ... 6G **9** (3K **141**)
(Quay Rd.)
Barbican App. PL4: Plym ... 6J **9** (3A **142**)
Barbican Cl. EX32: Barn ... 5F **19**
Barbican Ct. EX4: Exe ... 5B **6**
PL4: Plym ... 6F **9**
Barbican Glassworks ... 6G **9**
Barbican La. EX32: Barn ... 5G **19**
Barbican Leisure Pk. ... 6J **9** (3A **142**)
Barbican Pl. *EX32: Barn ... 5F 19*
(off Trinity St.)
Barbican Rd. EX32: Barn ... 5F **19**
PL7: Plymp ... 5B **138**
Barbican Steps EX4: Exe ... 4C **6** (6E **64**)
Barbican Ter. EX32: Barn ... 5F **19**
Barbican Theatre ... 7G **9** (4K **141**)
BARBROOK ... 2D **161**
Barbrook Rd. EX35: Lynt ... 4G **13**
Barbury Cres. PL6: Plym ... 2C **132**
Barchington Av. TQ2: Torq ... 2B **112**
Barcombe Hgts. TQ3: Pres ... 6G **115**
Barcombe La. TQ3: Pres ... 6H **115**
Barcombe M. TQ3: Pres ... 6H **115**
Barcombe Rd. TQ3: Pres ... 6G **115**
Barcote Wlk. PL6: Plym ... 2D **136**
Bardsey Cl. PL6: Plym ... 3B **132**
Barewell Cl. TQ1: Torq ... 5D **112**
Barewell Rd. TQ1: Torq ... 5D **112**
Barfield Cl. EX19: Dol ... 6J **31**
Barfield Rd. EX19: Dol ... 6H **31**
Baring Cotts. TQ9: Tot ... 6F **103**
Baring Ct. EX2: Exe ... 7F **7**
EX20: Lew ... 1A **56**
Baring Cres. EX1: Exe ... 5J **7** (6H **65**)
Baring St. PL4: Plym ... 2H **9** (1A **142**)
Baring Ter. EX2: Exe ... 7F **7** (1F **71**)
Barkers Way EX20: N Taw ... 6B **36**
Barlands Way EX19: Dol ... 6H **31**
Barle Cl. EX2: Sow ... 1C **72**
Barle Ct. EX16: Tiv ... 1E **40**
Barley Cl. EX15: Cull ... 5G **45**
Barleycorn *EX5: Cranb ... 3C 68*
(off Brooks Warren)
Barleycorn Flds. EX32: L'key ... 2B **24**
Barley Farm Rd. EX4: Exe ... 1B **70**
Barley La. EX4: Exe ... 6A **64**
Barley Mkt. St. PL19: Tavi ... 3J **59**
Barley Mt. EX4: Exe ... 7B **64**
Barley Wlk. EX6: Star ... 1D **96**
Barline EX12: Beer ... 7B **86**
Barlow Gdns. PL2: Plym ... 4G **135**
Barlow Rd. EX31: Barn ... 2F **19**
Barnardo Rd. EX2: Exe ... 7F **7** (1G **71**)
Barnards Farm EX12: Beer ... 7B **86**
Barnards Hill La. EX12: Seat ... 2D **86**
Barn Cinema ... 1D **102**
Barn Cl. EX21: Sheb ... 6J **29**
EX32: Barn ... 6H **19**
PL7: Plymp ... 5G **139**
PL21: Ivy ... 3E **144**
TQ9: Tot ... 5D **102**
Barn Cl. La. EX12: Axmth ... 5J **87**
Barn Ct. TQ5: Chur F ... 4A **122**
Barndale Cres. PL6: Plym ... 4C **132**
BARNE BARTON ... 3B **134**
Barne Cl. PL5: Plym ... 3B **134**
Barne La. PL5: Plym ... 2C **134**
Barne Rd. PL5: Plym ... 3B **134**
Barnes Cl. EX14: Hon ... 5E **54**
EX15: Will ... 3C **44**
Barnes Mdw. DT7: Uply ... 3G **91**
BARNFIELD ... 4G **7** (6G **65**)
Barnfield EX17: Cred ... 6H **39**
TQ9: E All ... 6C **152**
Barnfield Av. EX8: Exmth ... 5F **77**
Barnfield Cl. EX17: Cred ... 7H **39**
EX33: Brau ... 5K **15**
TQ5: Galm ... 3J **121**
Barnfield Cres. EX1: Exe ... 4F **7** (6F **65**)
Barnfield Dr. PL7: Plymp ... 4F **139**
Barnfield Hill EX1: Exe ... 4G **7** (6G **65**)
Barnfield Rd. EX1: Exe ... 4F **7** (6F **65**)
(not continuous)
TQ2: Torq ... 4K **115**
TQ3: Paig ... 7F **115**
TQ5: Brixh ... 5F **123**
Barnfield Ter. TQ5: Chur F ... 3A **122**
TQ12: A'well ... 6E **108**
Barnfield Theatre ... 4F **7** (6F **65**)
Barnfield Wlk. TQ7: Kingsb ... 3F **157**
Barnhay EX16: Bam ... 2H **33**
Barnhay, The TQ9: Sto G ... 4B **120**
Barn Hayes EX10: Sidm ... 3A **84**
Barnhill Rd. TQ12: Kingsk ... 1G **111**
Barnicott Cl. PL8: New F ... 5J **149**
Barningham Gdns. PL6: Plym ... 4B **132**
Barn La. EX9: Bud S ... 5B **82**
Barn Orchard EX5: Cranb ... 3B **68**
Barn Owl Cl. TQ2: Torq ... 2K **111**
Barn Pk. EX17: Cred ... 6H **39**
EX33: Wraf ... 7K **15**
TQ9: Sto G ... 3B **120**
TQ11: B'leigh ... 5B **98**
TQ12: Live ... 4G **93**
Barn Pk. Cl. TQ12: Ipp ... 6J **101**
Barnpark Cl. TQ14: Teignm ... 3J **107**
Barn Pk. Cotts. *PL9: Plyms ... 4E 142*
(off Millway Pl.)
Barn Pk. Rd. EX31: Frem ... 6E **16**
PL3: Plym ... 6J **135**
Barnpark Rd. TQ14: Teignm ... 4J **107**
Barnpark Ter. TQ14: Teignm ... 3J **107**
Barn Pk. Vw. EX20: Lew ... 1A **56**
Barnridge EX8: Lymp ... 6H **75**
Barn Rd. TQ4: Good ... 5J **119**
Barns Cl. EX5: Bradn ... 3B **52**
TQ12: Kingst ... 5H **105**
Barnsey Gdns. TQ13: Ashb ... 2G **99**
Barnsfield La. TQ11: B'leigh ... 4B **98**
Barnshill Cl. EX17: Cher F ... 2J **39**
Barnshill Ct. *EX17: Cher F ... 2J 39*
(off Barnshill Cl.)
Barnsley Cl. TQ14: Teignm ... 4J **107**
Barnsley Dr. TQ14: Teignm ... 4J **107**
Barns Pas. *EX34: Ilfra ... 3H 11*
(off High St.)
Barns Rd. EX9: Bud S ... 6D **82**
BARNSTAPLE ... 4E **18** (3B **160**)
Barnstaple (Park & Ride) ... 7F **19**
Barnstaple Castle Mound ... 4E **18**
Barnstaple Cl. EX37: Chit ... 6H **25**
PL6: Plym ... 3F **137**
Barnstaple Heritage Cen. ... 4E **18**
Barnstaple Hill EX32: Swim ... 2G **25**
Barnstaple Retail Pk. EX31: Barn ... 5E **18**
Barnstaple Station (Rail) ... 5E **18**
Barnstaple St. EX19: Wink ... 2C **36**
EX36: S Mol ... 6C **26**
EX39: Bide ... 4G **23**
Barnstaple Western By-Pass
EX31: Barn, Taw ... 3C **18**
Barnstone Ct. EX2: Alph ... 5D **70**
Barnwood Cl. PL9: Hooe ... 7F **143**
Barometer World & Museum ... 5B **30**
Baron Ct. EX31: Roun ... 7A **18**
Baron's Pyke PL21: Ivy ... 5J **145**
Barons Rd. PL20: Dous ... 4K **127**
Baron Way EX31: Roun ... 7A **18**
Barossa Pl. PL11: Torp ... 2A **140**
Barossa Rd. PL11: Torp ... 1A **140**
Barrack La. EX2: Shil A ... 7D **70**
Barrack Pl. PL1: Plym ... 3F **141**
Barrack Rd.
EX2: Exe, Won ... 5K **7** (7H **65**)
EX11: Ott M ... 4A **80**
PL20: Prin ... 6C **60**
Barracks Hill TQ9: Darti, Tot ... 4B **102**
Barracks Rd. PL21: Modb ... 6G **147**
Barrack St. PL1: Dev ... 2D **140**
Barradon Cl. TQ2: Torq ... 1C **112**
Barrie Gdns. PL5: Plym ... 2K **135**
BARRINGTON ... 2D **167**
Barrington Ho. *TQ1: Torq ... 1G 117*
(off Barrington Rd.)
Barrington Mead *EX10: Sidm ... 6C 84*
(off Salcombe Rd.)
Barrington Rd. TQ1: Torq ... 1G **117**
Barrington St. EX16: Tiv ... 4D **40**
Barris EX17: Lap ... 2J **37**
Barrowdale Cl. EX8: Exmth ... 1E **76**
Bar's La. EX9: Ott'n ... 5K **83**
Bartholomew Rd. PL2: Plym ... 6F **135**
Bartholomew St. E.
EX4: Exe ... 4C **6** (6E **64**)
Bartholomew St. W.
EX4: Exe ... 5C **6** (7E **64**)
Bartholomew Ter. EX4: Exe ... 5C **6**
BARTON ... 3B **112** (1B **176**)
Barton Acorn Youth Community & Sports Cen. ... 3C **112**
Barton Av. EX33: Brau ... 5J **15**
PL2: Plym ... 6D **134**
TQ3: Paig ... 1F **119**
Barton Cl. EX3: Exton ... 1G **75**
EX5: Sto C ... 6J **51**
EX10: Sidm ... 7B 84
(off The Triangle)
EX17: Cher F ... 2H **39**
EX20: N Taw ... 7B **36**
EX20: Oke ... 3C **48**
EX33: Brau ... 6K **15**
PL7: Plymp ... 4F **139**
PL9: Wem ... 6C **148**
TQ3: Paig ... 7F **115**
TQ7: Kingsb ... 5G **157**
Barton Ct. EX1: Whip ... 5B **66**
EX10: Sidm ... 7B 84
(off The Triangle)
EX34: Woolc ... 6A **10**
Barton Cres. EX7: Daw ... 4F **97**
TQ3: Paig ... 7F **115**
Barton Dr. TQ3: Paig ... 7F **115**
TQ12: New A ... 1C **108**
Barton Gdns. TQ3: Paig ... 7F **115**
Barton Ga. La. EX34: Com M ... 6A **12**
Barton Hall Caravan & Chalet Cen.
TQ2: Torq ... 2A **112**
Barton Hill EX7: Daw ... 4G **97**
EX20: N Taw ... 7B **36**
EX34: Berry ... 2D **12**
Barton Hill Rd. TQ2: Torq ... 4B **112**
Barton Hill Way TQ2: Torq ... 3A **112**
Barton La. EX2: Shil A ... 7B **70**
EX7: Daw ... 4F **97**
EX16: With ... 6H **33**
EX33: Brau ... 5J **15**
EX34: Berry ... 3C **12**
Barton La. Cl. EX33: Brau ... 6J **15**
Barton Leys TQ9: Berr P ... 4K **103**
Barton Lodge EX8: Exmth ... 6D **76**
Barton Mdw. Rd. EX37: High B ... 2B **32**
Barton M. EX3: Exton ... 2G **75**
EX11: Ven O ... 2F **81**
Barton Orchard EX10: Tip J ... 1J **81**
Barton Paddocks EX10: Tip J ... 1J **81**
Barton Ri. EX14: Fen ... 2J **53**
Barton Rd. EX2: Exe ... 7A **6** (1C **70**)
EX16: Tiv ... 2D **40**
EX20: Oke ... 3C **48**
EX32: Barn ... 5J **19**
EX34: Woolc ... 6A **10**
EX39: Buck B ... 2H **29**
PL9: Hooe ... 5C **142**
TQ1: Torq ... 6A **112**
TQ2: Torq ... 5A **112**
TQ3: Paig ... 7F **115**
Barton Rd. Ind. Units TQ2: Torq ... 5A **112**
Bartons, The *EX1: Heav ... 7A 66*
(off Honiton Rd.)
Barton St. EX20: N Taw ... 7B **36**
Barton Ter. EX7: Daw ... 4G **97**
Barton Tors EX39: Bide ... 4H **23**
BARTON TOWN ... 2C **161**
Barton Vw. EX20: N Taw ... 7B **36**
Barton Vs. EX7: Daw ... 4F **97**
Bartows C'way. EX16: Tiv ... 3D **40**
Barum Arc. EX32: Barn ... 4F **19**
Barum Cl. TQ3: Paig ... 7J **115**
Barum Ct. EX32: Barn ... 5F **19**
Barum Gate Bus. Pk. EX32: Barn ... 6J **19**
Bary Cl. EX17: Cher F ... 2J **39**
Bary La. EX17: Cher F ... 2J **39**
Bascombe Cl. TQ5: Chur F ... 2K **121**
Bascombe Rd. TQ5: Chur F ... 2J **121**
Basinghall Cl. PL9: Plyms ... 7F **143**
Basket Ope PL4: Plym ... 6F **9**
Bassett Cl. EX33: Brau ... 5J **15**
Bassetts Cl. EX17: Cop ... 6C **38**
EX39: N'ham ... 4E **20**
Bassetts Gdns. EX8: Exmth ... 2F **77**
Bastard's La. EX38: Gt T ... 1B **30**
Batavia Av. EX2: Cou W ... 4C **72**
Bate Cl. EX2: Alph ... 4D **70**
Bath Cl. EX14: Fen ... 2G **53**
Bath Ct. EX39: West H ... 5B **20**
BATHEALTON ... 1A **166**
Batherm Cl. EX16: Bam ... 3H **33**
Bathern Rd. EX2: Sow ... 1C **72**
Bath Hotel Rd. EX39: West H ... 5B **20**
Bathill Camp Site TQ5: Galm ... 4G **121**
Bath La. PL1: Plym ... 5B **8** (3H **141**)
TQ2: Torq ... 1B **116**
Bath Pl. EX34: Ilfra ... 2H **11**
PL1: Plym ... 5B **8**
Bath Pl. W. PL1: Plym ... 5B **8**
BATHPOOL
Linkhorne ... 3A **168**
Taunton ... 1C **167**
Bath Rd. EX8: Exmth ... 6C **76**
Bath St. PL1: Plym ... 6B **8** (3H **141**)
Bath Ter. EX39: Ins ... 2K **21**
TQ14: Teignm ... 5J **107**
BATSON ... 2B **158** (3D **175**)
Batson Gdns. TQ4: Paig ... 3G **119**
Battershall Cl. PL9: Plyms ... 7G **143**
Batter St. PL4: Plym ... 5F **9** (3K **141**)
Battersway Rd. TQ4: Paig ... 3E **118**
Battery Gdns. ... 2E **122**
Battery La. PL19: Tavi ... 5J **59**
Battery St. PL1: Plym ... 4A **8** (2G **141**)
(not continuous)
BATTISBOROUGH CROSS ... 3C **175**
Battishorne Way EX14: Hon ... 5D **54**
BATTLEDOWN CROSS ... 6K **29**
Battle Rd. TQ12: Heat ... 2J **93**
BATTLETON ... 1D **165**
Batt's La. EX11: Ott M ... 4C **80**
Bavent Cl. EX5: Sto C ... 7J **51**
Baxter Cl. EX2: Sow ... 2C **72**
Bayard's Cove
TQ6: Dartm ... 2B **124** (6F **125**)
Bayard's Cove Fort ... 2B **124** (7F **125**)
Bayards Cove Steps *TQ6: Dartm ... 2B 124*
(off Lower St.)
Bayard's Hill
TQ6: Dartm ... 2B **124** (6F **125**)
Bay Ct. EX12: Seat ... 6F **87**
Baydon Cl. PL6: Plym ... 2D **136**
Bayly's Rd. PL9: Plyms ... 5C **142**
Baymount Rd. TQ3: Paig ... 7G **115**
Bay Rd. EX9: Ott'n ... 6K **83**
Bayside La. PL9: Down T ... 2A **148**
Bayswater Rd. PL1: Plym ... 2C **8** (1H **141**)
Baythorpe Lodge *TQ2: Torq ... 4A 116*
(off Livermead Hill)
Baytor Ind. Est. TQ4: Paig ... 4E **118**
Baytree Cl. *PL6: Plym ... 4E 132*
(off Elm Rd.)
Baytree Gdns. PL2: Plym ... 4F **135**
Bay Trees EX6: Kennf ... 2G **95**
Bay Vw. TQ3: Pres ... 5K **115**
Bay Vw. Cl. TQ6: Sto F ... 2H **153**
Bay Vw. Ct. EX39: N'ham ... 6E **20**
Bay Vw. Dr. TQ14: Teignm ... 3J **107**
Bay Vw. Est. TQ6: Sto F ... 2H **153**
Bay Vw. Farm Caravan & Camping Pk.
EX33: Croy ... 3C **14**
Bay Vw. Rd. DT7: Lym R ... 4J **91**
EX34: Woolc ... 5A **10**
EX39: N'ham ... 6B **20**
Bay Vw. Steps *TQ5: Brixh ... 3F 123*
(off King St.)
Bazley Sq. EX1: Pin ... 4D **66**
Beach App. *TQ5: Brixh ... 3F 123*
(off Pump St.)
Beach Rd. EX7: Daw W ... 7E **96**
EX12: Seat ... 6F **87**
EX33: Croy ... 1B **14**
EX34: Woolc ... 6A **10**
EX39: West H ... 5C **20**
TQ1: Torq ... 6F **113**
TQ4: Paig ... 1J **119**
Beachside Holiday Pk.
EX39: West H ... 5A **20**
Beach St. EX7: Daw ... 4H **97**
Beach Vw. Cres. PL9: Wem ... 7B **148**
Beach Wlk. TQ4: Good ... 5J **119**
BEACON ... 3B **166**
Beacon, The EX8: Exmth ... 6C **76**
Beacon Av. EX4: Whip ... 4J **65**
Beacon Castle EX34: Ilfra ... 2G **11**
Beacon Cl. PL21: Ivy ... 3G **145**
Beacon Down Av. PL2: Plym ... 3G **135**
Beaconfield Rd. PL2: Plym ... 5G **135**
Beacon Heath EX4: Whip ... 3A **66**
Beacon Hgts. EX33: Brau ... 4K **15**
BEACON HILL ... 1B **66**
Beacon Hill EX5: Bradn ... 1B **52**
EX8: Exmth ... 6C **76**
PL8: New F ... 5G **149**
TQ1: Torq ... 3D **116**
Beacon La. EX4: Whip ... 3K **65**
EX15: Cull ... 1F **45**
TQ6: Kingsw ... 7G **125**
BEACON PARK ... 4G **135**
Beacon Pk. Rd. PL2: Plym ... 5F **135**
Beacon Pl. EX8: Exmth ... 6C **76**
Beacon Quay TQ1: Torq ... 3D **116**
Beacon Ri. EX18: Chul ... 6C **32**
Beacon Rd. EX5: Bradn ... 1C **52**
PL21: Ivy ... 3G **145**
TQ6: Kingsw ... 7G **125**
TQ8: Salc ... 4A **158**
Beacon Roman Fortlet ... 2C **161**
Beacon Ter. *TQ1: Torq ... 3D 116*
(off Beacon Hill)
Beacon Vw. PL21: Bitta ... 4C **146**
TQ9: Darti ... 3B **102**
Beadle Ct. PL19: Tavi ... 5H **59**
Beadon Dr. TQ8: Salc ... 4A **158**
Beadon Rd. TQ8: Salc ... 4B **158**
BEAFORD ... 3H **31** (2D **163**)
Beagle Rd. PL1: Dev ... 3E **140**
Beal Farm M. TQ13: Chud K ... 6B **94**
BEALSMILL ... 3B **168**
Beanhay Cl. TQ12: Live ... 4G **93**
Beans Mdw. EX20: Oke ... 3B **48**
Beara La. EX31: Brat F ... 5J **13**
EX34: Com M ... 7E **12**
Beardown Rd. EX20: Oke ... 3E **48**
Beards Rd. EX31: Frem ... 6F **17**
Beare Bri. Rd. EX20: Oke ... 2C **48**
Beare Cl. PL9: Hooe ... 7C **142**
Beare Copse La. EX19: Wink ... 3D **36**
Beare Farm Cotts. EX20: Oke ... 1B **48**
Bear La. EX9: Know ... 4A **82**
Bearne's La. *TQ12: New A ... 1E 108*
(off Bank St.)
Bears Cove Castle (remains of) ... 7F **125**
Bearsdown Cl. PL6: Plym ... 3D **136**
Bearsdown Rd. PL6: Plym ... 3D **136**
Bear St. EX1: Exe ... 5E **6** (7F **65**)
EX32: Barn ... 4E **18**

Beatlands Rd.—Biddick Dr.

Beatlands Rd. EX10: Sidm 6C **84**
Beatrice Av. PL2: Plym 6D **134**
PL4: Plym 2J **9** (1A **142**)
Beattie Rd. PL5: Plym 3A **134**
Beatty Cl. PL6: Plym 6B **132**
Beatty Way TQ6: Dartm 4F **125**
Beauchamp Cres. PL2: Plym 4H **135**
Beauchamp Rd. PL2: Plym 4H **135**
Beaudyn Wlk. PL6: Plym 4D **136**
Beaufort Cl. EX16: Sam P 2B **42**
PL5: Plym 3B **134**
Beaufort Ho. PL4: Plym 5G **9**
Beaufort Rd. EX2: Exe 7B **6** (1E **70**)
Beaufort Wlk. EX32: Barn 3G **19**
Beauly Cl. PL7: Plymp 4D **138**
Beaumaris Gdns. PL3: Plym 3A **136**
Beaumaris Rd. PL3: Plym 4A **136**
Beaumont Av. PL4: Plym 3G **9** (2K **141**)
Beaumont Cl. TQ2: Torq 7K **111**
TQ12: Live 4F **93**
Beaumont Lodge TQ3: Paig 7H **115**
Beaumont Park 3H **9** (2A **142**)
Beaumont Pl. PL4: Plym 4G **9** (2K **141**)
Beaumont Rd. PL4: Plym 4G **9** (2A **142**)
TQ12: New A 2F **109**
Beaumont St. PL2: Plym 6F **135**
Beauvale Cl. EX11: Ott M 3D **80**
Beaver Rd. EX22: Bradw 5B **28**
Beavers Brook Cl. TQ3: Pres 4H **115**
Beavor La. EX13: Axmin 3J **89**
BEAWORTHY 1C **169**
Beaworthy Cl. EX2: Exe 3D **70**
Becket Rd. TQ13: Bov T 4C **92**
Beckets Rd. TQ7: Kingsb 4G **157**
Beckford Cl. PL7: Plymp 4D **138**
Beckham Pl. PL3: Plym 5B **136**
Becklake Cl. EX31: Roun 7K **17**
Beckley Ct. PL1: Plym 3E **8** (2J **141**)
Beck's Sq. *EX16: Tiv 5C **40***
(off St George's Way)
Becky Falls 3B **170**
Bede Gdns. PL5: Plym 2H **135**
BEDFORD BRIDGE 1D **126**
Bedford Gro. PL21: Ivy 4H **145**
Bedford Pk. PL4: Plym 2G **9** (1K **141**)
*PL20: Bere A 2C **128***
(off Bedford St.)
Bedford Pk. Vs. PL4: Plym 1G **9** (1K **141**)
Bedford Pl. *PL19: Tavi 4J **59***
(off Plymouth Rd.)
PL20: Bere A 1C **128**
PL20: Horr 2E **126**
Bedford Rd. PL9: Plyms 4F **143**
PL20: Horr 2E **126**
TQ1: Torq 5F **113**
Bedford Row EX32: Barn 4E **18**
Bedford Sq. EX10: Sidm 7C **84**
PL19: Tavi 4J **59**
Bedford St. EX1: Exe 4E **6** (6F **65**)
*EX32: Barn 4F **19***
(off Buller Rd.)
PL2: Plym 6E **134**
PL20: Bere A 2C **128**
Bedford Ter. PL4: Plym 2F **9** (1K **141**)
Bedford Vs. PL19: Tavi 4H **59**
Bedford Way PL1: Plym 5E **8** (2J **141**)
Bedland's La. EX9: Bud S 5A **82**
Beech Av. EX4: Exe 3G **65**
PL4: Plym 6K **9** (4B **142**)
Beech Bank EX39: Bide 5C **22**
Beech Cl. EX5: Broadc 6D **52**
EX14: Hon 5D **54**
EX15: Will 4D **44**
EX31: Roun 7A **18**
PL19: Tavi 7J **59**
TQ9: Tot 5B **102**
Beech Ct. PL6: Plym 5E **132**
Beech Cres. PL20: Prin 6C **60**
Beech Cft. EX15: Cull 2H **45**
Beechcroft Rd. PL2: Plym 4G **135**
PL3: Plym 5B **136**
Beechdown Ct. TQ4: Coll M 3A **118**
Beechdown Pk. TQ4: Coll M 3B **118**
Beech Dr. TQ12: Ipp 6J **101**
Beeches, The EX39: Wools 2B **28**
PL20: Yelv 5G **127**
Beeches Cl. EX5: Wood 6B **78**
Beechfield Av. PL20: Yelv 5F **127**
TQ2: Torq 3A **112**
Beechfield Cl. *EX31: Frem 6E **16***
(off Thornlea Av.)
Beechfield Gro. PL3: Plym 5K **135**
Beechfield Pl. TQ2: Torq 3B **112**
Beechfield Rd. EX31: Frem 6E **16**
Beech Gro. EX31: Barn 2E **18**
EX33: Brau 3H **15**
Beech Gro. Ter. EX31: Barn 2E **18**
Beech Pk. EX11: W Hill 4H **79**
EX17: Cred 5J **39**
EX31: Frem 6F **17**
Beech Rd. EX16: Tiv 3E **40**
PL21: L Mill 5A **144**
Beech Rd. Bus. Pk. PL21: L Mill 4C **144**
Beech Tree Dr. EX16: Tiv 3B **40**
Beech Tree Mdw. EX20: Bride 3J **57**
Beech Trees La. TQ12: Ipp 5F **101**
Beech Wlk. EX14: Gitt, Hon 7C **54**
Beechway EX8: Exmth 4D **76**
Beechwood Av. EX31: Barn 6C **18**
PL4: Plym 1E **8** (7J **135**)
TQ12: New A 3H **109**
TQ13: Bov T 7B **92**
Beechwood Cl. EX31: Barn 5C **18**
Beechwood Ct. TQ14: Teignm 2F **107**
Beechwood Cres. EX7: Daw W 7D **96**
Beechwood Dr. TQ7: Kingsb 4G **157**
Beechwood Ri. PL6: Plym 2F **137**
Beechwood Rd. TQ13: Chud 2B **94**
Beechwood Ter. PL4: Plym 7J **135**
Beechwood Way PL7: Plymp 4G **139**
BEENLEIGH 5E **100**
BEER 7B **86** (2C **173**)
BEERCROCOMBE 1D **167**
Beer Head Caravan Pk.
EX12: Beer 7B **86**
Beer Heights Light Railway 7A **86**
Beer Hill EX12: Seat 6C **86**
Beer Quarry Caves 2C **173**
Beer Rd. EX12: Seat 6C **86**
Beers Hill EX17: Cop 6A **38**
Beers Ter. EX6: Kennf 1G **95**
BEESANDS 3A **176**
BEESON 3A **176**
Beeston Wlk. PL3: Plym 4D **136**
BEETHAM 2C **167**
Beggars La. EX14: Hon 4D **54**
Behind Hayes EX9: Ott'n 6H **83**
Belair Rd. PL2: Plym 4H **135**
Belair Vs. *PL2: Plym 4H **135***
(off Montpelier Rd.)
Belfield Av. TQ3: Marl 4D **114**
Belfield Cl. TQ3: Marl 3D **114**
Belfield Ri. TQ3: Marl 3D **114**
Belfield Rd. TQ3: Paig 7E **114**
Belfield Way TQ3: Marl 3D **114**
Belgrave Ct. EX9: Bud S 7B **82**
Belgrave La. PL4: Plym 7K **135**
Belgrave M. TQ2: Torq 1B **116**
Belgrave Rd. EX1: Exe 3G **7** (6G **65**)
PL4: Plym 7K **135**
TQ2: Torq 1B **116**
TQ12: New A 3J **109**
Belgrave Ter. TQ14: Teignm 4J **107**
Belgravia Ter. TQ6: Kingsw 6G **125**
Bellaire EX31: Barn 2D **18**
Bellaire Dr. EX31: Barn 2D **18**
Bellamarsh La.
TQ13: Chud K 5B **94**
Bellamy Cl. PL6: Plym 2B **136**
Bella Vista Rd. TQ5: Brixh 2E **122**
Bell Cl. PL7: Plymp 2C **138**
Bell Ct. EX4: Exe 4C **6** (6E **64**)
Belle Acre Cl. PL3: Plym 5A **136**
Belle Av. EX17: Cred 6G **39**
Belle Ct. EX17: Cred 6G **39**
Belle Cross Rd. TQ7: Kingsb 3H **157**
Belle Hill TQ7: Kingsb 3G **157**
Belle Isle Dr. EX2: Exe 1G **71**
Belle Mdw. Ct. *EX32: Barn 4E **18***
(off Albert La.)
Belle Mdw. Rd. EX32: Barn 5E **18**
Belle Pde. EX17: Cred 6H **39**
BELLEVER 3A **170**
Bellever Cl. PL20: Prin 6C **60**
Bellever Tor Dr. TQ5: Brixh 6B **122**
Belle Vue EX6: Kenton 6H **95**
EX22: Hols 2C **34**
PL11: Torp 1B **140**
Belle Vue Av. EX35: Lynt 2G **13**
PL9: Hooe 7C **142**
Belle Vue Cl. EX6: Kenn 3J **95**
Belle Vue Cross EX38: Gt T 1E **30**
Belle Vue Dr. PL9: Hooe 7C **142**
Belle Vue Ri. PL9: Hooe 7C **142**
Belle Vue Rd. EX4: Exe 2D **64**
EX8: Exmth 4C **76**
PL9: Hooe 7D **142**
TQ4: Paig 2J **119**
TQ7: Kingsb 4G **157**
Bellevue Sq. PL11: Torp 2A **140**
Belle Vue Ter. EX6: Kennf 2H **95**
EX15: Cull 3H **45**
EX39: Bide 3E **22**
Bellflower Cl. PL6: Robo 1D **132**
Bellingham Cres. PL7: Plymp 5E **138**
Belliver Ind. Est. PL6: Robo 1C **132**
Belliver Way PL6: Robo 1C **132**
Bell La. TQ3: Blag 7B **114**
Bell Pk. PL7: Plymp 2D **138**
Bellrock Cl. TQ2: Torq 2D **112**
Bell St. EX9: Ott'n 6H **83**
Belmont EX32: Barn 4F **19**
Belmont Av. EX34: Com M 6A **12**
EX34: Ilfra 3G **11**
Belmont Cl. EX16: Tiv 3D **40**
TQ12: Kingst 2H **105**
Belmont Ct. EX16: Tiv 3D **40**
Belmont Ho. EX4: Exe 1H **7** (5G **65**)
Belmont Pl. PL3: Plym 7F **135**
Belmont Rd. EX1: Exe 2H **7** (5G **65**)
EX16: Tiv 3D **40**
EX32: Barn 3F **19**
EX34: Ilfra 3G **11**
PL21: Ivy 5G **145**
TQ1: Torq 7D **112**
TQ5: Brixh 4E **122**
Belmont St. PL1: Plym 4B **8** (2H **141**)
Belmont Ter. EX8: Exmth 3E **76**
*EX12: Beer 7B **86***
(off Causeway)
TQ9: Tot 5E **102**
TQ10: S Bre 1C **100**
Belmont Vs. PL3: Plym 1F **141**
BELSFORD 2D **175**
BELSTONE 1A **170**
Belstone Cl. PL5: Plym 7F **131**
BELSTONE CORNER 1A **170**
Belvedere TQ3: Pres 6J **115**
Belvedere Cl. EX3: Top 7D **72**
Belvedere Ct. EX4: Exe 3B **6**
*EX7: Daw 4H **97***
(off High St.)
EX10: Sidm 6C **84**
Belvedere Rd. EX8: Exmth 5C **76**
EX34: Ilfra 3H **11**
PL4: Plym 2C **142**
TQ12: New A 6B **104**
Belvidere Rd. EX4: Exe 3D **64**
Belvoir Rd. EX39: Bide 3E **22**
Benbow St. PL2: Dev 7E **134**
Bench Tor Cl. TQ2: Torq 5H **111**
Bendarroch Rd.
EX11: W Hill 3G **79**
Bendle La. EX36: N Mol 2E **26**
Bendley Hill EX16: With 5J **33**
Benedict Cl. TQ14: Teignm 2J **107**
Benedicts Cl. TQ12: Live 4G **93**
Benedicts Rd. TQ12: Live 4G **93**
Benedict Way PL21: Modb 6G **147**
Ben Jonson Cl. TQ2: Torq 7K **111**
Benlears Acre TQ12: Live 4G **93**
BENNACOTT 1B **168**
BENNAH 2C **171**
Bennett Cl. EX2: Alph 5D **70**
Bennett Rd. TQ8: Salc 5B **158**
Bennetts Cl. EX12: Brans 6J **85**
Bennetts Hill EX10: Sidm 3A **84**
Bennett Sq. EX4: Whip 4K **65**
Bennett St. PL1: Dev 3D **140**
Benning Ct. EX31: Barn 3B **18**
Bens Cl. TQ7: Galm 2K **155**
Benson Cl. EX16: With 6H **33**
Benson Dr. EX39: N'ham 6F **21**
Benton Rd. EX32: Brat F 6J **13**
Ben Venue Cl. TQ1: Torq 1E **116**
Berachah Rd. TQ1: Torq 7D **112**
BERE ALSTON 2C **128** (1A **174**)
Bere Alston Station (Rail) 1A **128**
Berea Rd. TQ1: Torq 7E **112**
BERE FERRERS 7C **128** (1A **174**)
Bere Ferrers Station (Rail) 6B **128**
Beresford St. PL2: Plym 7F **135**
Berkeley Av. TQ2: Torq 4J **111**
Berkeley Cotts. PL1: Plym 1F **141**
Berkeley Pl. *EX34: Ilfra 3H **11***
(off Highfield Rd.)
Berkeley Ri. TQ2: Torq 4J **111**
Berkeley Way PL21: Ivy 5H **145**
Berkshire Cl. TQ12: E Ogw 4C **108**
Berkshire Dr. EX4: Exe 1B **70**
PL2: Plym 6E **134**
Berman Ct. *TQ12: New A 1E **108***
(off Clarendon Rd.)
Bernadette Cl. EX4: Whip 3B **66**
Bernice Cl. PL4: Plym 7C **136**
Bernice Ter. PL4: Plym 7B **136**
Berretts Way TQ12: Live 4H **93**
Berrow Pk. Rd. PL3: Plym 4J **135**
Berry Av. TQ3: Paig 1F **119**
Berryball Cl. EX20: Oke 2C **48**
Berrybrook Mdw. EX6: Exmin 3D **74**
Berry Cl. EX8: Exmth 4G **77**
TQ8: Salc 4B **158**
TQ12: A'well 6E **108**
BERRY CROSS 2C **163**
BERRY DOWN CROSS 2B **160**
Berry Dr. TQ3: Paig 1F **119**
Berry Head Country Pk. 3H **123**
Berry Head Fortifications 2J **123**
Berry Head Gdns. PL6: Plym 2K **135**
Berry Head National Nature Reserve 4H **123**
Berry Head Rd. TQ5: Brixh 3F **123**
Berry Hill EX12: Beer 6B **86**
EX12: Brans 6F **85**
TQ14: Bi'ton 3B **106**
Berry La. EX6: Dunsf 5B **62**
EX12: Beer 6B **86**
EX34: Berry 2E **12**
TQ12: Kingst 4H **105**
Berry Mdw. TQ12: Kingst 5H **105**
BERRYNARBOR 3C **12** (2B **160**)
Berry Pk. Cl. PL9: Plyms 6F **143**
Berry Pk. Rd. PL9: Plyms 5F **143**
BERRY POMEROY 4K **103** (1A **176**)
Berry Pomeroy Castle 1A **176**
Berry Rd. EX32: Barn 5H **19**
EX33: Brau 3K **15**
TQ3: Paig 1F **119**
Berry Sq. *TQ4: Paig 1J **119***
(off Beach Rd.)
Berrys Wood TQ12: New A 1C **108**
Berthon Rd. PL5: Plym 4A **134**
Berwick Av. PL5: Plym 7K **131**
Besigheim Way TQ12: New A 1H **109**
Besley Cl. EX16: Tiv 5F **41**
Besley Ct. EX2: Mar B 2E **70**
Best Pk. EX5: Cranb 3B **68**
Bestridge Mdw. EX32: Swim 2H **25**
Best's La. EX38: Gt T 1C **30**
Bethel Ter. *TQ1: Torq 1D **116***
(off Princes Rd.)
Betjeman Cl. EX10: Sidm 2A **84**
Betjeman Dr. EX8: Exmth 1E **76**
Betjeman Wlk. PL5: Plym 7H **131**
Betony Ri. EX2: Won 2B **72**
BETTISCOMBE 1D **173**
Betton Way TQ13: More 6H **61**
Bettysmead EX4: Whip 3K **65**
Bettysmead Ct. EX4: Whip 4K **65**
Beuvron Cl. EX39: Wools 2B **28**
Bevan Rd. EX32: Barn 5F **19**
Beverley Cl. EX2: Won 1A **72**
Beverley Gdns. TQ13: Ashb 2J **99**
Beverley Pk. TQ4: Good 6H **119**
Beverley Ri. TQ5: Brixh 4D **122**
Beverley Rd. PL3: Plym 7D **136**
Beverley Way TQ12: New A 2D **108**
Beverston Way PL6: Plym 2C **132**
Bevil Cl. EX39: Bide 4E **22**
Bevin Ct. EX17: Cred 6J **39**
Bewhay Gdns. TQ9: Darti 3B **102**
Bewsley Hill EX17: Cop 6D **38**
Bewsley La. EX17: Cop 5D **38**
Bexley La. TQ2: Torq 1B **116**
Beyrout Cotts. *PL1: Dev 1E **140***
(off Beyrout Pl.)
Beyrout Pl. PL1: Dev 1E **140**
Bhutan Cl. EX14: Hon 4G **55**
Bias La. *EX33: Brau 4J **15***
(off Chaloner's Rd.)
Bicclescombe *EX34: Ilfra 4H **11***
(off Bicclescombe Gdns.)
Bicclescombe Gdns. EX34: Ilfra 4H **11**
Bicclescombe Pk. Rd. EX34: Ilfra 4H **11**
Bicclescombe Watermill 4H **11**
BICKENHALL 2C **167**
Bickern Rd. PL11: Torp 1A **140**
Bickford La. TQ14: Teignm 5J **107**
Bickfords Grn. TQ12: Live 4G **93**
Bickham Pk. Rd. PL3: Plym 5J **135**
Bickham Rd. PL5: Plym 1C **134**
BICKINGTON
Barnstaple 6K **17** (3B **160**)
Newton Abbot 3C **171**
Bickington Hill EX31: Bick'n 6K **17**
Bickington Lodge EX31: Bick'n 5J **17**
Bickington Pk. EX31: Bick'n 6K **17**
Bickington Rd. EX31: Barn, Bick'n 5H **17**
Bickington Steam Railway 5H **93**
BICKLEIGH
Plymouth 1H **133** (1B **174**)
Tiverton 3D **165**
Bickleigh Cl. EX4: Pin 2C **66**
PL6: Plym 2B **136**
Bickleigh Down Bus. Pk.
PL6: Plym 2E **132**
Bickleigh Down Rd. PL6: Robo 2D **132**
BICKLETON 3B **160**
Bickley Rd. TQ12: Ipp, Ston 5B **110**
Bickwell Ho. La. EX10: Sidm 5A **84**
Bickwell La. EX10: Sidm 4A **84**
Bickwell Valley EX10: Sidm 6A **84**
BICTON 5F **83**
Bicton Cl. PL6: Plym 2E **136**
Bicton Park Botanical Gdns. 5F **83**
Bicton Pl. EX1: Heav 4K **7** (6J **65**)
EX8: Exmth 6C **76**
Bicton St. EX8: Exmth 6C **76**
EX32: Barn 3F **19**
Bicton Vs. EX8: Exmth 6D **76**
Bicton Woodland Railway 4F **83**
Biddamoor La. EX19: Bea 2G **31**
Bidder Cl. TQ13: More 7J **61**
Bidders Cl. TQ6: Sto F 2H **153**
Bidders Wlk. TQ6: Sto F 3H **153**
Biddiblack Way EX39: Bide 3H **23**
Biddick Dr. PL2: Plym 5E **134**

Biddington Way EX14: Hon 5D 54
BIDEFORD 3F 23 (1C 163)
Bideford Arts Cen. 3F 23 (off The Quay)
Bideford Bus. Pk. EX39: Bide 5K 23
Bideford Quay Fountain 3G 23
Bideford Railway Museum & Tarka Trail Vis. Cen. 4G 23
Bideford Wlk. PL6: Plym 3F 137
BIDLAKE 2D 169
Bidmead Cl. EX8: L'ham 5G 77
Bidna La. EX39: N'ham 4G 21
Bidwell Brook Dr. TQ4: Good 6H 119
Bidwell La. EX5: Thor 1C 50
Bidwell Wlk. TQ4: Good 6H 119
Biera Vw. TQ13: Chag 2H 61
Bigadon La. TQ11: B'leigh 6D 98
BIGBURY 3C 175
Bigbury Golf Course 1D 154
BIGBURY-ON-SEA 3B 154 (3C 175)
Bigbury Wlk. PL6: Plym 3F 137
Bigbury Way TQ2: Torq 3D 112
Biggin Hill PL5: Plym 5E 130
Big Sheep, The 4A 22
Bilbie Cl. EX15: Cull 4F 45
Bilbury St. PL4: Plym 4F 9 (2K 141)
BILLACOMBE 4G 143
Billacombe Rd. PL9: Plyms 3D 142
Billacombe Vs. PL9: Plyms 4G 143
Bill Douglas Centre, The 4E 64
Billing Cl. PL6: Plym 4J 131
Billington Cl. PL6: Plym 3C 136
Bilton Ter. EX39: Bide 4F 23 (off Buttgarden St.)
Biltor Rd. TQ12: Ipp 7G 101
Bimbom La. EX13: Kilm, Shute 4A 88
Bindon Rd. EX4: Pin 2D 66
Binford Cl. EX1: Whip 6A 66
Bingfield Cl. TQ1: Torq 1E 116
Bingham Cres. EX32: Barn 4G 19
Binkham Hill PL20: Yelv 5H 127
Bircham Valley Local Nature Reserve 7C 132
Bircham Vw. PL6: Plym 2D 136 (not continuous)
Birch Cl. PL6: Plym 3F 133
Birch End EX5: Rock 4F 69
Birchen La. EX16: Tiv 5C 40
Birches, The PL6: Plym 4E 132
Birchfield Av. PL2: Plym 5G 135
Birch Gro. EX11: W Hill 5H 79
BIRCHILL 3D 167
Birchland Rd. PL7: Spa 1K 139
Birchland Way PL7: Spa 1J 139
Birch La. EX17: Morc 2A 38
EX31: Roun 7B 18
Birchlea Cl. TQ13: Bov T 7B 92
Birch Pond Rd. PL9: Plyms 5E 142
Birch Rd. EX8: Lymp 6H 75
EX32: L'key 1B 24 (not continuous)
TQ12: New A 3J 109
Birch Wlk. TQ2: Torq 5J 111
BIRCHWOOD 2C 167
Birchwood Cl. PL19: Tavi 6J 59
TQ9: Tot 6D 102
Birchwood Gdns. PL7: Plymp 2D 138
Birchwood Rd. EX8: Exmth 2F 77
Birchy Barton Hill EX1: Heav 7A 66
Birdcage La. EX11: Ott M 1J 79
Bird Cl. EX1: Pin 3D 66
BIRDSMOORGATE 3D 167
Birdswell La. EX34: Berry 3B 12
Birdwood Ct. TQ9: Tot 6E 102
Birkbeck Cl. PL7: Plymp 2B 138
Birkett Cl. EX2: Won 1B 72
Birks Grange EX4: Exe 3D 64
BISH MILL 1B 164
Bishop Ct. EX24: Colyt 6C 88
Bishops Av. TQ14: Bi'ton 4B 106
Bishops Cl. EX6: Star 1E 96
PL21: Ivy 3J 145
TQ1: Torq 2H 117
BISHOPS CLYST 2F 73
Bishops Ct. PL8: New F 5H 149
TQ13: Chud 2C 94
TQ14: Bi'ton 3B 106
Bishops Ct. Ind. Est. EX2: Sow 1D 72
Bishop's Ct. La. EX5: Clyst M 1H 73
Bishop's Ct. Rd.
EX5: Clyst H, Clyst M 2F 73
Bishops Dr. EX17: Cop 6C 38
BISHOP'S HULL 1C 167
BISHOPS LYDEARD 1B 166
Bishops Mead TQ10: S Bre 1B 100
Bishops Mdw. EX17: Morc 1B 38
BISHOP'S NYMPTON 1B 164
Bishops Pl. PL1: Plym 7B 8 (4H 141)
TQ3: Paig 1H 119
Bishops Ri. EX15: Kent 6A 46
TQ1: Torq 2J 117
BISHOP'S TAWTON 6B 24 (3B 160)
Bishop's Tawton Rd.
EX32: Barn, Bish T 5A 24 & 7G 19
BISHOPSTEIGNTON 3B 106 (3D 171)
Bishopsteignton Ho.
TQ14: Bi'ton 3A 106
Bishopsteignton Museum of Rural Life 3C 106
Bishopsteignton Rd.
TQ14: Teignm 5E 106
Bishop's Wlk. TQ1: Torq 7H 113
BISHOPSWOOD 2C 167
Bishop Westall Ho. EX2: Exe 6E 6 (off Good Shepherd Dr.)
Bishop Westall Rd. EX2: Cou W 3K 71
Bishop Wilfrid Rd.
TQ14: Teignm 3F 107
Bitney La. TQ12: A'well 7F 109
BITTADON 2B 160
BITTAFORD 3C 146 (2C 175)
Bittaford Ter. PL21: Bitta 4C 146
Bittaford Wood PL21: Bitta 4C 146
Bittaford Wood Pk. Homes
PL21: Bitta 4C 146
Bittern Ind. Units EX2: Sow 7D 66
Bittern Rd. EX2: Sow 6D 66
Bitton Av. TQ14: Teignm 4H 107
Bitton Ct. TQ14: Teignm 4G 107
Bitton Pk. Rd. TQ14: Teignm 4G 107 (not continuous)
Blachford Cl. PL21: Corn 6J 129
Blachford Rd. PL21: Ivy 3F 145
Blackabrook Av. PL20: Prin 6C 60
Blackalder Ter. PL7: L Moor 1J 129
Blackall Gdns. PL6: Plym 4J 131
Blackall Rd. EX4: Exe 2E 6 (5F 65)
BLACKAWTON 3B 152 (2A 176)
Blackball La. TQ5: Brixh 2E 122
Blackberry Cl. PL9: Plyms 4E 142
TQ9: Tot 7G 103
Blackberry La. PL9: Plyms 4F 143
Blackberry Way TQ12: Kingst 2H 105
BLACKBOROUGH 3A 166
Blackboy Rd. EX4: Exe 1H 7 (5G 65)
Blackbrook Av. TQ4: Good 6H 119
Blackbrook Cl. PL20: Walk 2J 127
Blackbrook Wlk. TQ4: Good 6H 119
Blackbury Camp 1B 172
BLACK DOG 3C 165
BLACKDOWN
Mary Tavy 1B 60
Thorncombe 3D 167
Blackdown Pk. EX15: Will 3C 44
Blackdown Vw. EX15: Hemy 1G 47
EX16: Sam P 2A 42
Blackenway La. TQ12: Coff 5K 109
Blackett Cl. PL21: Ivy 4J 145
Blackeven Cl. PL6: Robo 1E 132
Blackeven Hill PL6: Robo 1E 132
Blackfriars La. PL1: Plym 6F 9
Blackfriars Ope PL1: Plym 6F 9
Blackhaven Cl. TQ4: Good 7H 119
BLACKHORSE 4H 67
Blackhorse La. EX5: Clyst H 4F 67
Black La. TA21: Holc R 1F 43
Black Lion Ct. EX14: Hon 3F 55
BLACKMOOR GATE 2C 161
Blackmore Ct. EX8: Exmth 3G 77
Blackmore Cres. PL6: Plym 4J 131
Blackmore Dr. EX10: Sidm 6C 84
Blackmore M. EX2: Won 1B 72
Blackmore Rd. EX16: Tiv 5F 41
Blackmore's Path EX35: Lynt 2G 13
Blackmore Theatre 6C 76
Blackmore Vw. EX10: Sidm 6C 84 (off May Ter.)
BLACKNEY 1D 173
BLACKPOOL
Chaddlewood 7G 139
Halford 5F 93
Stoke Fleming 4F 153 (3A 176)
BLACKPOOL CORNER 1D 173
Blackpool Gdns. 3F 153
Blackpool Hill TQ6: Blackp 4F 153
Blackpool Rd. EX17: Bow 6K 37
Blackpool Valley Rd.
TQ6: Blackp 2F 153
Blackpost La. TQ9: Tot 6H 103
Blacksmith La. TQ10: Wran 2E 146
Blackstone Cl. PL9: Elb 6J 143
Blackstone Rd. TQ12: Ipp 7H 101
Blackstone Rocks to Warren Point 3B 174
Blackthorn Av. EX16: Tiv 2F 41
Blackthorn Cl. EX10: Sidm 2A 84
EX14: Hon 5F 55
PL5: Plym 7G 131
PL6: Plym 2E 132
Blackthorn Cres. EX1: Whip 6B 66
Blackthorn Dr. PL21: Ivy 5J 145
Blackthorn Way TQ4: Paig 3D 118
BLACK TORRINGTON 3C 163
BLACKWATER 2C 167
Blackwater Rd. EX15: Culm 2B 46
BLACKWELL 1A 166
Blackwood Path TQ10: Wran 1B 146
Bladon Cl. TQ12: New A 3G 109
BLAGDON 1B 118 (1A 176)
Blagdon EX17: Cred 6J 39
Blagdon Cl. EX17: Cred 6J 39
BLAGDON HILL 2C 167
Blagdon Pl. EX17: Cred 6J 39 (off Exhibition Rd.)
Blagdon Ri. EX17: Cred 5J 39
Blagdon Rd. TQ3: Blag 7A 114
Blair Atholl EX8: Exmth 7E 76
Blairgowrie Rd. PL5: Plym 1B 134
Blair Rd. PL21: Ivy 5H 145
Blake Cl. TQ1: Torq 5D 112
Blake Gdns. PL5: Plym 7H 131
Blakeland Rd. EX31: Frem 6E 16
Blakes Hill Rd.
EX32: L'key, Swim 1B 24
Blakeslee Dr. EX2: Cou W 4C 72
Blakey Down La. TQ3: Paig 5E 114
Blanchard Pl. PL7: Plymp 2B 138
Blandford Rd. PL3: Plym 6B 136
Blangy Cl. EX20: N Taw 7C 36
Blatchcombe Dr. TQ3: Paig 7F 115
Blatchcombe Rd. TQ3: Paig 7F 115
Blatchford La. EX20: Bride 1J 57
Blatchfords Ct. EX20: Oke 3B 48
Blatchmore La. TQ6: Dartm 7D 124
Blaxton La.
PL5: Tam F 7E 128 & 1H 131
Blenheim Cl. TQ1: Torq 2G 117
TQ12: New A 7D 104
Blenheim Ct. EX2: Matf 4F 71
EX15: Will 3D 44
Blenheim Dr. EX15: Will 3D 44
Blenheim La. EX20: Exbo 6J 35
Blenheim Rd. EX2: Alph 3E 70
PL4: Plym 2F 9 (1K 141)
Blenheim Ter. PL19: Lam 5B 58
TQ13: Bov T 4B 92
Bligh Cl. TQ14: Teignm 1G 107
Blind La. EX5: Hux 7K 51
EX34: Berry 3B 12
BLINDMOOR 2C 167
Blindwell Av. TQ12: Kingst 4H 105
Blindwylle Rd. TQ2: Torq 1A 116
Blogishay La. TQ13: Ashb 4H 99
Bloomball Cl. PL3: Plym 5C 136
Blossom Cl. EX14: Dunk 7H 47
Blossom Hill EX14: Dunk 7H 47
Blue Ball Hill TQ9: Tot 6E 102
Bluebell Av. EX16: Tiv 2F 41
Bluebell Cl. EX12: Seat 3F 87
Bluebell Rd. EX14: Dunk 7H 47
Bluebell Way PL19: Tavi 5K 59
Blueberry Downs EX9: Bud S 6E 82
Blueboy La. EX1: Exe 3F 7 (off Dix's Field)
Blue Boy Sq. EX1: Exe 3F 7
Blue Cedar Ct. EX8: Exmth 6D 76
Bluehayes La. EX5: Broadc 3A 68
Blue Haze Cl. PL6: Plym 5E 132
Blue Ridge Rd. TQ13: Bov T 7B 92
Blue Waters Dr. DT7: Lym R 5G 91
TQ4: Broads 7J 119
Blue Waters Ind. Est.
TQ13: Bov T 6B 92
Blundell's Av. EX16: Tiv 4F 41
Blundell's Rd. EX16: Tiv 4D 40 (not continuous)
BLUNTS 1A 174
Blunts La. PL6: Plym 6D 132
Blyth Ct. EX39: West H 6A 20
Blythe Way TQ4: Paig 3D 118
Blythswood Cres. TQ1: Torq 6D 112
Boarden Barn EX8: Exmth 6D 76
Boards Ct. EX39: Bide 4G 23
BOASLEY CROSS 1D 169
Bockland Cl. EX15: Cull 4F 45
Boconnic La. PL20: Yelv 5G 127
Bodley Cl. EX1: Whip 6A 66
Bodley Ho. EX1: Whip 5A 66
Bodmin Rd. PL5: Plym 6G 131
Bodmin St. EX22: Hols 3B 34
Body Hayes Cl. TQ9: Sto G 4A 120
Bogmoor La. EX5: Whim 4F 53
Bohemia Vs. EX10: Sidm 5B 84
BOLBERRY 4K 155 (3C 175)
Bolberry Down 3C 175
Bolberry Ho. Farm Caravanning Pk.
TQ7: Bolb 4K 155
Bolberry Rd.
TQ7: Bolb, Hope 3G 155 & 4J 157
Boldventure PL8: Torr 3B 150
BOLHAM 1C 40 (2D 165)
Bolham La. EX16: Bolh 1C 40
Bolham Rd. EX16: Bolh, Tiv 1C 40
BOLHAM WATER 2B 166
Bolt Head TQ8: Salc 6A 158
Bolt Ho. Cl. PL19: Tavi 4G 59
Bolton Ct. TQ5: Brixh 4E 122 (off Windmill Hill)
Bolton St. TQ5: Brixh 4E 122
Bolt Tail Cliff Castle 3C 175
BOLVENTOR 3A 168
Bonair Cl. TQ5: Brixh 5E 122
Bonaventure Cl. TQ8: Salc 3C 158
Bonaventure Rd. TQ8: Salc 3C 158
BONDLEIGH 3A 164
Bond's La. EX5: Wood, Wood S 4A 78
Bonds Mdw. TQ13: Bov T 3B 92
Bond Spear Ct. PL1: Plym 7B 8
Bond St. EX19: Bea 2H 31
PL6: Plym 4K 131
PL21: Corn 6J 129
Bonehayne and Purlbridge Rd.
EX24: Colyt 5A 88
BONEHILL 3B 170
Bonfire Hill TQ8: Salc 3B 158
Bonfire La. EX5: Wood 5B 78
Bonhay Cl. EX6: Star 1E 96
Bonhay Ho. EX4: Exe 1B 6 (off Bonhay Rd.)
Bonhay Rd. EX4: Exe 2A 6 (5D 64)
EX6: Star 1E 96
Boniface Ct. EX17: Cred 6J 39
Boniface La. PL5: Plym 1K 135
Bonners C'way. EX13: Axmin 2K 89
Bonners Dr. EX13: Axmin 3K 89
Bonners Glen EX13: Axmin 3K 89
Bonnicott La. EX33: Croy 3B 14
Bonnington Gro. EX1: Heav 6J 65
Bonville Cl. EX1: Whip 5A 66
Bonville Cres. EX16: Tiv 5G 41
Bonville Rd. PL6: Plym 4J 131
BOOBERY 1B 42
Boobery EX16: Sam P 2A 42
Boode Rd. EX33: Boo, Brau 3K 15
BOOHAY 4K 125
Boon's La. TQ7: Kingsb 4F 157 (off Ropewalk)
Boon's Pl. PL1: Plym 2D 8 (1J 141)
Booth Way EX8: Exmth 2D 76
Border Rd. EX14: Hon 4D 54
BORESTON 2D 175
Boringdon Av. PL5: Plym 3C 134
Boringdon Cl. PL7: Plymp 2A 138
Boringdon Hill PL7: Plymp 2B 138
Boringdon Pk. PL21: Ivy 4E 144
Boringdon Park Golf Course 3J 137
Boringdon Rd. PL7: Plymp 3A 138
PL9: Hooe 5B 142
Boringdon Ter. PL7: Plymp 3A 138
PL9: Hooe 5B 142
PL9: Plyms 4G 143
Boringdon Vs. PL7: Plymp 3A 138
Borough, The PL8: Yeal 2B 150
Borough Cl. TQ4: Paig 4E 118
Borough Flds. EX5: Cranb 3B 68
Borough Pk. Rd. TQ3: Paig 2D 118
TQ9: Tot 5E 102
Borough Rd. EX34: Com M 5A 12
EX38: Gt T 2D 30
TQ1: Torq 4D 112
TQ4: Paig 3D 118
Borough Vw. EX38: Gt T 2D 30
Borrowdale Cl. PL6: Plym 5J 131
Borthay Orchard TQ12: A'well 6E 108
Boscastle Gdns. PL2: Plym 3H 135
Boscawen Pl. PL2: Dev 7D 134
TQ14: Teignm 4H 107
Boshill Hill EX12: Axmth 1H 87
EX24: Colyt 1H 87
Bossell Ho. TQ11: B'leigh 5C 98 (off Bossell Pk.)
Bossell Pk. TQ11: B'leigh 5C 98
Bossell Rd. TQ11: B'leigh 5C 98
Bossell Ter. TQ11: B'leigh 4C 98
Bosuns Point TQ4: Good 3J 119
Boswell Cl. PL5: Plym 1G 135
Boswell's La. EX20: N Taw 5D 36
Boswell Way EX12: Seat 4D 86
Bottle Bri. Hill TQ13: Chud 1D 94
Bottle Pk. PL21: L Mill 5A 144
Bottom La. EX13: Mus 5D 90
Bottompark La. TQ2: Torq 2B 112
Bottoms La. EX33: Georgeh 6D 14
TQ12: Dacc 1A 112
BOTTREAUX MILL 1C 165
BOTUS FLEMING 1A 174
Boucher Rd. EX9: Bud S 6D 82
BOUCHERS HILL 5B 36
Boucher Way EX9: Bud S 6D 82
Bouchiers Cl. EX20: N Taw 5B 36
Boughmore La. EX10: Sidm 6A 84
Boughmore Rd. EX10: Sidm 6A 84
Boughthayes PL19: Tavi 4G 59
Boughthayes Est. PL19: Tavi 5G 59
Boulden Cl. PL7: Plymp 4F 139
Boulter Cl. PL6: Robo 1D 132
Boundary Cl. TQ12: Kingsk 6J 109
Boundary Pk. EX12: Seat 3E 86

Boundary Pl. PL6: Plym 3D 132
Boundary Rd. PL20: Dous 4K 127
TQ2: Torq 1K 115
Bounds Pl. PL1: Plym 6B 8 (3H 141)
Bounsells La. EX20: Mer 5B 30
Bourchier Cl. EX16: Bam 1H 33
Bourchier Dr. EX16: Bam 1H 33
Bourne Cl. PL3: Plym 5E 136
Bourne Ct. TQ5: Brixh 6B 122
Bourne Rd. TQ12: Kingsk 7K 109
Bourn Ri. EX4: Pin 2C 66
Bournville Pl. EX16: Tiv 3E 40
Bourton La. TQ9: Tot 5F 103
Bourton Rd. TQ9: Tot 5G 103
Bourtons, The TQ9: Tot 4F 103
Boutport St. EX31: Barn 3E 18
Bovemoor's La. EX2: Won 7J 65
Bove Pk. Rd. TQ2: Torq 1C 112
Bovey La. EX12: Beer 6A 86
BOVEY TRACEY 4B 92 (3C 171)
Bovey Tracey Golf Course 2A 92
Bovey Tracey Heritage Cen. 4B 92
Bovey Tracey Rd. TQ12: New A 4B 104
Boville La. PL9: Elb 5K 143
BOVISAND 1B 148
Bovisand La.
PL9: Bovis, Down T 1A 148
PL9: Bovis, Stad 1B 148
Bovisand Lodge Est. PL9: Bovis . . .1B 148
Bovisand Rd. PL9: Stad 1D 148
BOW 5H 37 (3B 164)
Bowcombe Rd. TQ7: Kingsb 6J 157
BOWD 2B 172
BOWDEN 3A 176
Bowden Farm PL8: Yeal 2A 150
BOWDEN GREEN 5D 22
Bowden Grn. EX39: Bide 5D 22
Bowden Hill EX17: Cred 6J 39
PL8: Yeal 2B 150
TQ12: New A 2F 109
TQ13: Ashb 4F 99
Bowden Pk. Rd. PL6: Plym 2B 136
Bowden Rd. TQ12: Ipp 6J 101
BOWDENS 1D 167
Bowdens Cl. TQ13: Bov T 4B 92
Bowdens Pk. PL21: Ivy 5F 145
Bowe Ct. EX1: Exe 1J 7
Bowering Ct. EX32: Barn 6G 19
(off Cyprus Ter.)
Bowerland Av. TQ2: Torq 1B 112
Bowerman's Nose 2B 170
Bowers Pk. Dr. PL6: Plym 3F 133
Bowers Rd. PL2: Plym 6G 135
Bowhay La. EX4: Exe 7A 64
(not continuous)
EX34: Com M 7C 12
Bowhays Wlk. PL6: Plym 4D 136
Bowhill EX4: Exe 1C 70
EX5: Bradn 1D 52
BOWITHICK 2A 168
Bowland Cl. TQ4: Paig 5G 119
Bow La. TQ13: More 7H 61
Bowley Mdw. EX5: Bradn 2B 52
Bowling Grn. TQ13: Ashb 4H 99
(off Whistley Hill)
Bowling Grn. Chalets DT7: Lym R . . .6J 91
Bowling Grn. La. EX14: Hon 4F 55
EX20: Hath 2G 35
EX34: Com M 7C 12
Bowling Green Marsh Bird Sanctuary
. . . . .7C 74
Bowling Green Marsh Nature Reserve
. . . . .6C 74
Bowling Grn. Rd. EX3: Top 6C 74
Bowmans Mdw. EX20: Hath 1H 35
Bow Mill La. EX17: Bow 5G 37
Bowring Cl. EX1: Whip 5A 66
Bowring Mead TQ13: More 7J 61
Bowring Pk. TQ13: More 7J 61
Bowringsleigh Pl. TQ7: Kingsb 4E 156
Bow Rd. TQ9: H'ford 6C 100
Boxfield Rd. EX13: Axmin 4H 89
Boxhill Cl. PL5: Plym 7G 131
Boxhill Gdns. PL2: Plym 3H 135
BOX'S SHOP 3A 162
Boyce Ct. TQ2: Torq 5A 112
Boyce Pl. EX16: Tiv 4B 40
Boyds Dr. TQ14: Teignm 4J 107
Boyes Cl. EX16: Hal 6C 42
Boyland Rd. EX6: Dunsf 6A 62
Boyne Rd. EX9: Bud S 5C 82
BOYTON .1B 168
Bracken Cl. EX14: Hon 6C 54
PL6: Plym 2E 132
TQ12: New A 3J 109
Brackendale EX8: Exmth 1E 76
Brackendown EX11: W Hill 6H 79
Bracken Ri. TQ4: Broads 2J 121
Bracken Way EX7: Daw W 7D 96
(off Beechwood Cres.)
Brackenwood EX8: Exmth 3E 76
Bradden Cres. TQ5: Brixh 4C 122
Braddicks Holiday Cen.
EX39: West H 5A 20
Braddons Cliffe TQ1: Torq 2D 116
Braddons Hill PL7: Plymp 4J 137
Braddons Hill Rd. E. TQ1: Torq 2D 116
Braddons Hill Rd. W. TQ1: Torq . . .2D 116
Braddons St. TQ1: Torq 2D 116
Bradfield Cl. PL6: Plym 2F 137
Bradfield Rd. EX4: Pin 3C 66
BRADFORD 3C 163
BRADFORD BARTON 2C 165
Bradford Cl. EX8: Exmth 1E 76
PL6: Plym 4C 136
Bradford Ct. EX39: N'ham 6F 21
BRADFORD-ON-TONE 1B 166
Bradham Ct. EX8: Exmth 4F 77
Bradham La. EX8: Exmth 3E 76
BRADIFORD 2D 18 (3B 160)
Bradiford EX31: Barn 2D 18
BRADLEY .6E 92
Bradley 2C 108
Bradley Ct. TQ12: New A 1E 108
Bradley La. TQ12: New A 1D 108
Bradley Pk. Rd. TQ1: Torq 5C 112
Bradley Rd. PL4: Plym 7A 136
TQ12: New A 3D 108
TQ13: Bov T 3D 92
Bradman Way EX2: Mar B 3E 70
BRADNINCH 1C 52 (3A 166)
Bradninch Pl. EX4: Exe 3E 6
BRADSTONE 2B 168
Bradwell Rd. EX34: Ilfra 3G 11
BRADWORTHY 5B 28 (2B 162)
Braemar Cl. PL7: Plymp 5F 139
Braeside M. TQ4: Good 3J 119
Braeside Rd. TQ2: Torq 1C 112
TQ4: Good 3J 119
Braggs' Hill EX37: High B 3A 32
Brahms Way EX32: Barn 4H 19
Brakefield TQ10: S Bre 2C 100
Brakeridge Cl. TQ5: Chur F 2J 121
Brake Rd. PL5: Plym 1K 135
Brake Wood Cl. EX31: Frem 6E 16
Bramble Cl. EX9: Bud S 6D 82
EX10: Sidm 2C 84
PL3: Plym 4C 136
TQ2: Torq 1K 115
TQ9: Darti 3B 102
Bramble Hill Ind. Est. EX14: Hon . . .3E 54
Bramble La. EX14: Hon 4D 54
EX17: Cred 5K 39
Bramble Path EX32: L'key 2C 24
Bramble Wlk. EX31: Roun 6A 18
PL6: Plym 4D 136
Bramfield Pl. PL6: Plym 4E 136
Bramley Av. EX1: Heav 6B 66
Bramley Cl. EX6: Kenton 6J 95
EX15: Will 4D 44
EX16: Tiv 1D 40
Bramley Gdns. EX5: Whim 7G 53
Bramley Mdw. EX32: L'key 2D 24
Bramley Rd. PL3: Plym 7D 136
Bramleys, The EX14: Hon 2H 55
BRAMPFORD SPEKE 5F 51 (1D 171)
Brancker Rd. PL2: Plym 5H 135
Brand Cl. EX14: Hon 5F 55
BRANDIS CORNER 3C 163
Brandis Pk. TQ7: Slap 2H 159
Brandize Pk. EX20: Oke 5B 48
Brandon Rd. PL3: Plym 7D 136
Brandreth Rd. PL3: Plym 5A 136
Brand Rd. EX14: Hon 5F 55
Branksome Cl. TQ3: Pres 4J 115
Brannam Ct. EX31: Roun 7A 18
Brannam Cres. EX31: Roun 7K 17
Brannams Sq. EX32: Barn 5F 19
(off Kiln La.)
Brannams Wlk. EX32: Barn 5F 19
(off Litchdon St.)
BRANSCOMBE 6H 85 (2B 172)
Branscombe Cl. EX4: Exe 7B 64
EX24: Colyf 1F 87
TQ1: Torq 7F 113
Branscombe Forge 6H 85
Branscombe Gdns. PL5: Plym 7F 131
Branscombe La. EX7: Daw 6A 96
Branscombe Rd. EX16: Tiv 4F 41
Branson Ct. PL7: Plymp 4F 139
Brantwood Cl. TQ4: Good 3G 119
Brantwood Cres. TQ4: Good 4G 119
Brantwood Dr. TQ4: Good 3G 119
BRATTON CLOVELLY 1C 169
BRATTON FLEMING 6H 13 (3C 161)
BRAUNTON 4J 15 (3A 160)
Braunton & District Mus. 4J 15
Braunton Countryside Cen. 4J 15
(off Caen St.)
Braunton Gt. Fld. EX33: Brau 5G 15
Braunton Rd. EX31: Barn 2B 18
Braunton Wlk. PL6: Plym 3F 137
Bray Cl. PL19: Tavi 4G 59
BRAYFORD 3C 161
Brayford Cl. PL5: Plym 7G 131
Brayhams Ter. EX20: Oke 2C 48
Brays Cl. EX17: Cred 6H 39
BRAY SHOP 3B 168
BRAZACOTT 1A 168
Breakaway Sports Centre, The 3E 116
Breakneck Hill TQ14: Teignm 1H 107
Breakwater Ct. TQ5: Brixh 2G 123
Breakwater Hill
PL4: Plym 7J 9 (4B 142)
Breakwater Ind. Est.
PL9: Plyms 4D 142
Breakwater Rd. PL9: Plyms 4D 142
Brean Down Cl. PL3: Plym 5K 135
Brean Down Rd. PL3: Plym 4K 135
Brecon Cl. EX39: Bide 4J 23
PL3: Plym 4B 136
TQ4: Coll M 3D 118
Bredon Ct. EX2: Exe 5K 7
Bredon La. EX9: Ott'n 5J 83
BRENDON 2D 161
Brendon Hill EX17: Cop . . . .4E 38 & 5E 38
Brendons, The EX16: Sam P 1B 42
Brendons Av. TQ2: Torq 3J 115
Brennacott Pl. EX39: Bide 5C 22
(off Brennacott Rd.)
Brennacott Rd. EX39: Bide 5C 22
Brent Cl. EX5: Wood 5C 78
Brentford Av. PL5: Plym 5G 131
Brent Hill PL8: Holb 6C 150
Brent Knoll Rd. PL3: Plym 5K 135
Brent Mill Bus. Pk. TQ10: S Bre . . .2B 100
Brenton Rd. EX6: Kennf 1G 95
Brentor Cl. EX4: Exe 4C 64
Brentor Rd. PL4: Plym 2C 142
PL19: Mary T 1A 60
Brent Rd. TQ3: Paig 1G 119
Brentwood Gdns. EX34: Ilfra 3K 11
(off Channel Vw.)
Brest Rd. PL6: Plym 6B 132
Brest Way PL6: Plym 7B 132
Bretonside PL4: Plym 5F 9 (3K 141)
Breton Way EX8: Exmth 3G 77
Bretteville Cl. EX5: Wood 5C 78
TQ13: Chag 2H 61
Brett Wlk. PL7: Plymp 2C 138
Brewer Rd. EX32: Barn 5H 19
Brewers Ct. EX2: Exe 7C 6 (1E 70)
Brewery Ct. EX7: Daw 4H 97
(off High St.)
Brewery La. EX1: Heav 7J 65
(off North St.)
EX10: Sidm 5B 84
TQ5: Brixh 3E 122
(off Market St.)
Brewhouse PL1: Plym 4E 140
Brewin Rd. EX16: Tiv 5C 40
Briar Cl. EX8: Exmth 4F 77
EX14: Hon 6F 55
Briar Cres. EX2: Won 3J 71
Briardale Rd. PL2: Plym 5E 134
Briarleigh Cl. PL6: Plym 1G 137
Briar Rd. PL3: Plym 4A 136
Briar Tor PL20: Yelv 5G 127
Briary La. TQ1: Torq 1D 116
Briary M. TQ1: Torq 2F 117
Brickfields Cl. PL1: Dev 2E 140
Brickfields Recreation Ground 2E 140
Brickfields Sports Cen. 2E 140
Brickfields Stadium 2E 140
Brickfield Ter. EX16: Tiv 4D 40
(off Martins La.)
Brickhouse Dr. EX16: Tiv 2D 40
Brickhouse Hill EX16: Tiv 2D 40
(not continuous)
Brickyard La. EX6: Star 1D 96
Brickyard Rd. EX5: Rock, Whim 1F 79
Brid Cl. EX20: Bride 3H 57
Bridespring Rd. EX4: Exe 3J 65
Bridespring Wlk. EX4: Exe 3J 65
BRIDESTOWE 3H 57 (2D 169)
Bridewell Ct. EX16: Tiv 5C 40
BRIDFORD 1F 63 (2C 171)
Bridford Rd. EX2: Mar B 3F 71
EX6: Bridf, Chri 1H 63
BRIDGE .3D 167
Bridge, The PL1: Plym 7B 8
Bridge Bldgs. EX16: Tiv 4C 40
Bridge Chambers Bus. Cen.
EX31: Barn 4E 18
Bridge Cotts. EX4: Exe 1G 7 (4G 65)
EX9: E Bud 2D 82
EX9: Know 5A 82
Bridge Ct. EX4: Exe 3C 6
EX32: L'key 2B 24
Bridge Cft. TQ13: Ashb 3G 99
BRIDGE END 5J 81
Bridgefield EX11: Ott M 3D 80
(off Chineway Rd.)
Bridge Hill EX3: Top 5B 74
Bridgehill Gth. EX3: Top 5B 74
Bridgeland St. EX39: Bide 3F 23
Bridge La. EX39: Ins 3K 21
Bridge Mill La. PL21: Corn 7H 129
BRIDGEND 5K 149 (3B 174)
Bridgend Hill PL8: New F 5J 149
Bridge Pk. PL21: Ivy 4H 145
Bridge Plats Way EX39: Bide 3C 22
BRIDGE REEVE 2A 164
Bridge Retail Pk. TQ2: Torq 5A 112
Bridge Rd. EX2: Cou W, Exmin 6J 71
EX6: Exmin 6J 71
EX8: Exmth 4C 76
EX9: Bud S 5D 82
TQ2: Torq 1B 116
TQ5: Chur F 3K 121
TQ5: Hill 3G 125
TQ6: Kingsw 3G 125
TQ9: Tot 5B 102
TQ14: Shal 6G 107
BRIDGERULE 3A 162
Bridgeside TQ9: H'ford 6B 100
(off Woodland Rd.)
Bridge Site EX36: N Mol 2D 26
Bridge St. DT7: Lym R 5K 91
EX10: Sidb 2H 85
EX15: Uff 6H 43
EX16: Tiv 4C 40
EX20: Hath 2H 35
EX39: Bide 4F 23
TQ7: Kingsb 4G 157
TQ11: B'leigh 4C 98
TQ12: Ipp 6H 101
Bridge St. Ho. TQ12: New A 1E 108
(off Bank St.)
Bridge Ter. EX16: Bam 2H 33
EX16: Tiv 4C 40
BRIDGETOWN
Dulverstone 1D 165
Totnes 6G 103 (1A 176)
Bridgetown TQ9: Tot 6F 103
Bridgetown Ct. TQ9: Tot 6F 103
Bridgetown Hill TQ9: Tot 6F 103
Bridge Vw. EX5: Rock 3F 69
EX12: Brans 6H 85
PL5: Plym 3C 134
Bridgewater Gdns. TQ9: Tot 6G 103
Bridge Way EX4: Exe 4D 6
Bridgwater Cl. PL6: Plym 2C 136
Bridle Cl. PL7: Plymp 2E 138
TQ4: Good 7H 119
Bridle Path, The TQ9: Tot 7E 102
BRIDPORT 1D 173
Bridwell Av. EX15: Uff 7F 43
Bridwell Cl. PL5: Plym 3D 134
Bridwell La. Nth. PL5: Plym 3D 134
Bridwell Rd. PL5: Plym 3D 134
BRIGHTLEY 1A 170
Brightley Rd. EX20: Oke 1C 48
Bright Vw. EX20: Oke 4A 48
Brimacombe Rd. EX39: Hart 2H 27
Brim Brook Ct. TQ2: Torq 5H 111
(off Chinkwell Ri.)
Brimhay TQ9: Darti 3B 102
Brim Hill TQ1: Maid 1J 113
Brimhill Cl. PL7: Plymp 6E 138
Brimhill La. PL19: Horn 1E 60
Brimlands TQ5: Brixh 4D 122
Brimlands Ct. TQ5: Brixh 4D 122
(off New Rd.)
BRIMLEY 3C 171
Brimley Bus. Pk. TQ13: Bov T 6B 92
Brimley Ct. TQ13: Bov T 6A 92
Brimley Cross TQ13: Bov T 6A 92
Brimley Dr. TQ14: Teignm 4J 107
Brimley Gdns. TQ13: Bov T 6B 92
Brimley Grange TQ13: Bov T 6A 92
Brimley Halt TQ13: Bov T 6B 92
Brimley La. TQ13: Bov T 6A 92
Brimley Pk. TQ13: Bov T 6B 92
Brimley Rd. TQ13: Bov T 6A 92
Brimley Va. TQ13: Bov T 5B 92
Brimpenny Rd. EX8: Exmth 3E 76
Brinkburn Ct. EX10: Sidm 7B 84
Briseham Cl. TQ5: Brixh 5F 123
Briseham Rd. TQ5: Brixh 5F 123
Brismar Wlk. PL6: Plym 4D 136
Bristol Row PL20: Bere F 6C 128
Britannia Av. TQ6: Dartm 6C 124
Britannia Mus. 5E 124
Britannia Pl. PL4: Plym 2C 142
Britannia Row EX34: Ilfra 2J 11
(off Broad St.)
Britannia Way EX39: West H 5D 20
Briticheston Cl. PL9: Spri 7H 143
Briton St. EX16: Bam 2H 33
Briton St. La. EX6: Dunsf 6C 62
Brittany Rd. EX8: Exmth 1E 76
Brittany St. PL1: Plym 5A 8 (3G 141)
Britten Dr. EX2: Won 7A 66
EX32: Barn 4G 19
Britton Cl. EX16: Hal 6C 42
Brittons, The EX33: Brau 5K 15
Brittons Cl. EX33: Brau 5K 15

Briwere Rd. TQ1: Torq 6A **112**
BRIXHAM 3F 123 (2B **176**)
Brixham (Park & Ride) 3K **121**
Brixham Battery Heritage Cen. . . .2D **122**
Brixham Ent. Est. TQ5: Brixh 4F **123**
(off Windmill Hill)
Brixham Heritage Mus. 3E **122**
Brixham Holiday Pk. TQ5: Brixh . . .2D **122**
Brixham Leisure Cen. 4F **123**
Brixham Rd. TQ4: Good, Paig 3E **118**
TQ5: Brixh, Chur F 3K **121**
TQ6: Kingsw 6H **125**
Brixham Theatre 3E **122**
Brixham Wlk. PL6: Plym 3F **137**
Brixham Yacht Club 2F **123**
BRIXINGTON 2F **77**
Brixington Dr. EX8: Exmth 2F **77**
Brixington La. EX8: Exmth 3E **76**
(not continuous)
Brixington Pde. EX8: Exmth 2F **77**
BRIXTON 2H 149 (2B **174**)
Brixton Caravan & Camping Pk.
PL8: Brixt 3G **149**
Brixton Lodge Gdns. PL8: Brixt 2G **149**
Broadacre Dr. TQ5: Brixh 3F **123**
Broad Cl. EX17: Cred 6F **39**
EX36: N Mol 2D **26**
Broadclose Rd. EX31: Barn 6C **18**
BROADCLYST 5C 52 (1D **171**)
Broadclyst Rd. EX5: Whim 5F **53**
Broadclyst Sports Hall 7D **52**
BROADCLYST STATION 1K **67**
Broadfield Rd. EX32: Barn 5F **19**
Broadfields Rd. EX32: Won 7B **66**
Broadgate EX1: Exe 4D 6 (6E **64**)
Broadgate Cl. EX31: Barn 2D **18**
EX33: Brau 4J **15**
Broadgate Cres. TQ12: Kingsk . . .1F **111**
Broadgate La. EX17: Morc 2C **38**
Broadgate Rd. TQ12: Kingsk 7J **109**
BROADHEMBURY 3B **166**
BROADHEMPSTON 1A **176**
Broadland Gdns. PL9: Plyms 4H **143**
Broadland La. PL9: Plyms 4G **143**
BROADLANDS 1C **108**
Broadlands EX5: Thor 3A **50**
EX39: Bide 4J **23**
EX39: N'ham 4E **20**
TQ14: Shal 6G **107**
Broadlands Av. TQ12: New A 1D **108**
Broadlands Cl. PL7: Plymp 6D **138**
Broadlands Ct. TQ12: New A 1D **108**
Broadlands Rd. TQ4: Paig 3G **119**
Broad La. EX16: Tiv 5B **40**
EX33: Brau, Lobb 2F **15**
EX39: Apple 3G **21**
Broadleaf Cl. EX1: Pin 4D **66**
Broadley Dr. TQ2: Torq 3J **115**
Broadley Pk. Rd. PL6: Robo 1B **132**
Broadmead EX5: Wood 5B **78**
EX8: Exmth 2F **77**
Broadmead Bungs. EX32: Barn . . .7H **19**
Broadmeade Ct. TQ12: New A 2G **109**
Broadmeadow Av. EX4: Exe 1C **70**
Broadmeadow Ind. Est.
TQ14: Teignm 4F **107**
Broadmeadow La.
TQ14: Bi'ton, Teignm 3E **106**
Broadmeadow Sports Cen. 4F **107**
Broadmeadow Vw.
TQ14: Teignm 3F **107**
Broadmoor La. EX20: Oke 3A **48**
BROADOAK 1D **173**
BROAD OAK 5H 79 (4A **172**)
Broadoak Cl. EX11: W Hill 5H **79**
Broad Oak Cres. TQ9: Tot 6F **103**
Broadoaks PL7: L Moor 2H **129**
Broad Pk. PL9: Plyms 5D **142**
TQ6: Dartm 6D **124**
Broadpark EX5: Bram S 6F **51**
EX20: Oke 3D **48**
TQ13: Ashb 2H **99**
TQ13: Bov T 6A **92**
Broad Pk. Av. EX34: Ilfra 4G **11**
Broad Pk. Cl. EX33: Croy 2C **14**
EX34: Ilfra 4G **11**
Broad Pk. Cres. EX34: Ilfra 4G **11**
Broad Pk. Rd. PL3: Plym 5J **135**
PL20: Bere A 1B **128**
Broadpark Rd. EX8: Exmth 3E **76**
TQ2: Torq 3J **115**
TQ3: Paig 6F **115**
Broadparks Av. EX4: Pin 2D **66**
Broadparks Cl. EX4: Pin 2D **66**
Broad Pk. Ter. EX20: N Taw 6C **36**
Broadpath TQ9: Sto G 4B **120**
(not continuous)
Broad Reach TQ4: Broads 1J **121**
Broadridge Cl. TQ12: New A 7A **104**
Broad Rd. TQ6: Kingsw 3K **125**

BROADSANDS 1H **121**
Broadsands Av. TQ4: Broads 1J **121**
Broadsands Bend TQ4: Broads . . .7J **119**
Broadsands Ct. TQ4: Broads 1H **121**
Broadsands Pk. Rd.
TQ4: Broads 7J **119**
Broadsands Rd. TQ4: Broads 1H **121**
BROADSHARD 2D **167**
Broad Steps TQ5: Brixh 3E **122**
(off Higher St.)
Broadstone TQ6: Dartm . . .1A 124 (5F **125**)
Broadstone Pk. Rd. TQ2: Torq . . .3K **115**
Broad St. DT7: Lym R 5K **91**
EX11: Ott M 4C **80**
EX34: Ilfra 2J **11**
EX36: S Mol 6C **26**
PL16: Lift 6B **56**
PL21: Modb 6G **147**
Broad Vw. TQ9: Darti 3B **102**
Broadview EX5: Broadc 6C **52**
Broadwalk Ho. EX1: Exe 4F **7**
BROADWAY 2D **167**
Broadway EX2: Exe 2C **70**
EX5: Whim 6G **53**
EX5: Wood 6B **78**
EX10: Sidm 5A **84**
EX31: Frem 6G **17**
Broadway, The EX8: Exmth 4G **77**
PL9: Plyms 5F **143**
Broadway Av. TQ12: Kingst 3G **105**
Broadway Hill EX2: Exe 2B **70**
Broadway La. EX33: Croy 1B **14**
Broadway Rd. TQ12: Kingst 3F **105**
BROADWINDSOR 3D **167**
BROADWOODKELLY 3A **164**
BROADWOODWIDGER 2C **169**
Broady Strap EX31: Frem 6G **17**
Brockey Wlk. EX2: Sow 1C **72**
Brockhole La. PL7: Plymp 1B **138**
Brockhurst Pk. TQ3: Marl 4D **114**
Brockley Rd. PL3: Plym 7D **136**
Brocks La. TQ12: Teigng 1C **104**
Brockton Gdns. PL6: Plym 4C **132**
Brodick Cl. EX4: Exe 3G **65**
Bromhead Ct. PL6: Plym 3B **136**
Bromhill La. EX33: N Buck 5E **14**
Bromley Pl. PL2: Plym 7F **135**
Brompton Gdns. TQ1: Torq 1G **117**
BROMPTON RALPH 1A **166**
BROMPTON REGIS 1D **165**
Bronescombe Av. TQ14: Bi'ton . . .3C **106**
Bronshill M. TQ1: Torq 7D **112**
Bronshill Rd. TQ1: Torq 7D **112**
Bronte Ct. EX8: Exmth 5E **76**
Bronte Ho. EX2: Won 2J **71**
Bronte Pl. PL5: Plym 2J **135**
BROOK 7H **59**
Brook Cl. EX1: Whip 4A **66**
EX7: Holc 7F **97**
EX10: Sidf 1D **84**
PL7: Plymp 6D **138**
TQ13: Bov T 4B **92**
Brook Ct. EX31: Roun 6A **18**
TQ5: Brixh 4D **122**
Brookdale Av. EX34: Ilfra 3G **11**
Brookdale Cl. TQ5: Brixh 4D **122**
Brookdale Ct. TQ5: Brixh 4D **122**
Brookdale Pk. TQ5: Brixh 4D **122**
Brookdale Ter. EX7: Daw 4H **97**
EX32: Barn 5G **19**
(off Victoria St.)
BROOKEADOR 7J **109**
Brooke Av. EX2: Won 2J **71**
Brooke Cl. PL12: Salt 1A **134**
Brookedor TQ12: Kingsk 7J **109**
Brookedor Gdns. TQ12: Kingsk . . .7J **109**
Brooke Rd. EX16: With 6H **33**
Brookfield EX39: Bide 5D **22**
Brookfield Cl. EX33: Brau 5J **15**
PL7: Plymp 4E **138**
TQ3: Pres 6J **115**
TQ12: Kingst 3H **105**
Brookfield Ct. TQ13: Chud 1D **94**
(off New Exeter St.)
Brookfield Dr. EX24: Colyt 6D **88**
TQ14: Teignm 2J **107**
Brookfield Gdns. EX2: Alph 4E **70**
Brookfield M. EX4: Exe . . .1C 6 (5E **64**)
Brookfield Orchard TQ12: Kingst . . .4H **105**
Brookfield Pl. EX34: Ilfra 3H **11**
Brookfield Rd. EX9: E Bud 1D **82**
Brookfield St. EX39: Bide 4G **23**
Brook Gdns. PL21: Ugb 6E **147**
Brook Grn. Ter. EX4: Exe 1G 7 (5G **65**)
Brook Haven Cl. TQ12: Kingsk . . .7J **109**
Brookhayes Cl. EX8: Exmth 4D **76**
Brookhill TQ6: Kingsw 7H **125**
Brook Ho. EX7: Daw 4F **97**
(off Church St.)
Brooking Cl. PL6: Plym 2B **136**
Brookingfield Cl. PL7: Plymp 6K **137**

Brooklands EX7: Daw 4G **97**
(off Alexandra Rd.)
PL6: Plym 7K **131**
TQ9: Tot 6G **103**
Brooklands Farm Cl. EX13: Kilm . . .3C **88**
Brooklands La. TQ2: Torq 2E **116**
Brooklands Orchard EX11: Ott M . . .3D **80**
EX13: Kilm 3C **88**
Brooklands Rd. EX8: Exmth 3F **77**
Brookland Ter. EX11: Ott M 4D **80**
(off Brook St.)
Brook La. EX10: Sidf 1D **84**
PL19: Tavi 6H **59**
TQ14: Shal 6F **107**
Brookleigh Av. EX1: Heav 7A **66**
Brooklyn Pk. EX8: Exmth 3E **76**
Brook Mdw. EX8: Exmth 3E **76**
EX10: New P 5H **81**
EX36: S Mol 6D **26**
Brook Mdw. Ct. EX9: Bud S 6A **82**
Brook Orchard TQ12: Kingsk 7J **109**
Brook Rd. EX9: Bud S 7C **82**
EX15: Cull 5G **45**
EX19: Dol 6H **31**
EX21: Ivy 4H **145**
TQ12: Ipp 6H **101**
Brookside EX8: Lymp 6G **75**
EX10: Sidm 3B **84**
EX31: Bick'n 6K **17**
TQ7: Kingsb 5F **157**
Brookside Cl. EX13: Kilm 2B **88**
PL9: Hey B 4B **148**
TQ14: Teignm 4G **107**
Brookside Cres. EX4: Whip 2A **66**
Brookside Vs. EX34: Com M 7C **12**
Brook St. EX7: Daw 4G **97**
EX11: Ott M 4C **80**
EX16: Bam 2H **33**
PL19: Tavi 3J **59**
TQ7: Slap 1H **159**
Brooks Warren EX5: Cranb 3C **68**
Brook Ter. EX12: Axmth 3H **87**
Brookvale Cl. TQ14: Shal 7F **107**
Brookvale Orchard TQ14: Shal . . .7F **107**
Brook Vw. TQ9: Tot 5B **102**
Brook Way TQ12: Kingst 1G **105**
Brookway EX1: Whip 5A **66**
Brookwood Cl. TQ10: S Bre 1B **100**
Brookwood Rd. PL9: Elb 7K **143**
Broomborough Ct. TQ9: Tot 6D **102**
Broomborough Dr. TQ9: Tot 6C **102**
Broom Cl. EX2: Won 7K **65**
EX7: Daw 1J **97**
Broome Cl. EX13: Axmin 3J **89**
Broomfield Dr. PL9: Hooe 6C **142**
Broomhill EX6: Chri 1K **63**
EX16: Tiv 4B **40**
TQ13: Chag 2J **61**
Broomhill Way TQ2: Torq 4A **112**
Broomhouse Pk. EX16: With 6H **33**
Broom Pk. EX5: Cranb 3B **68**
PL9: Hooe 7E **142**
TQ2: Torq 2B **112**
TQ9: Darti 2A **102**
Broom Pk. Hill TQ9: Darti 1A **102**
Broughton Cl. PL3: Plym 4A **136**
Brow Hill TQ12: Heat 2K **93**
Brownhill La. PL9: Wem 6C **148**
Brownhills Rd. TQ12: New A 1D **108**
Browning Cl. EX2: Won 1K **71**
Browning Rd. PL2: Plym 6F **135**
Brownings End TQ12: E Ogw 3C **108**
Brownings Mead EX6: Dunsf 7C **62**
Brownings Wlk. TQ12: E Ogw 3C **108**
Brownlands Cl. EX10: Sidm 5D **84**
Brownlands Rd. EX10: Sidm 5D **84**
Brownlees EX6: Exmin 2C **74**
Brownlow St. PL1: Plym 3G **141**
Brown's Bri. La. EX15: Will 2A **44**
Browns Bri. Rd. TQ2: Torq 4K **111**
Brownscombe Cl. TQ3: Marl 4D **114**
Brownsham 1A **162**
Brown's Hill TQ6: Dartm 6B **124**
BROWNSTON 2C **175**
BROWNSTONE 3B **164**
Brownstone Rd. TQ6: Kingsw 7K **125**
Brownston St. PL21: Modb 6G **147**
Broxton Dr. PL9: Plyms 3F **143**
Brunel Av. PL2: Plym 6E **134**
TQ2: Torq 1D **112**
Brunel Cl. EX4: Exe 2A 6 (5D **64**)
TQ14: Teignm 3J **107**
Brunel Ct. EX7: Daw 4H **97**
(off Solsbro Rd.)
Brunel M. TQ2: Torq 2B **116**
(off Solsbro Rd.)
Brunel Rd. EX6: Star 1D **96**
TQ4: Broads 1J **121**
TQ9: Tot 1G **109**
Brunel Ter. PL2: Plym 6E **134**
Brunel Way PL1: Plym 6A 8 (3G **141**)
PL21: Ivy 3J **145**

Brunenburg Way EX13: Axmin 5H **89**
Brunswick Pl. EX7: Daw 4G **97**
PL2: Dev 7E **134**
Brunswick Rd. PL4: Plym 5J 9 (3A **142**)
(not continuous)
Brunswick Sq. TQ1: Torq 7B **112**
(off Teignmouth Rd.)
Brunswick St. EX4: Exe 6A 6 (7D **64**)
TQ14: Teignm 5J **107**
Brunswick Ter. TQ1: Torq 7B **112**
BRUSHFORD
Dulverton 1D **165**
Winkleigh 3A **164**
Brutus Cen. TQ9: Tot 6E **102**
(off Station Rd.)
Brymon St. TQ2: Torq 6C **132**
Brynmoor Cl. PL3: Plym 4B **136**
Brynmoor Pk. PL3: Plym 4B **136**
Brynmoor Wlk. PL3: Plym 5B **136**
Brynsworthy La.
EX31: Bick'n, Roun 7K **17**
Brynsworthy Pk. EX31: Roun 6A **18**
Buchanan Cl. EX14: Hon 5E **54**
BUCKERELL 3B **166**
Buckerell Av. EX2: Exe 2H **71**
Buckeridge Av. TQ14: Teignm 3H **107**
Buckeridge Rd. TQ14: Teignm 2H **107**
BUCKFAST 2C 98 (1D **175**)
Buckfast Abbey 2D **98**
Buckfast Butterflies &
Dartmoor Otter Sanctuary 4E **98**
Buckfast Cl. PL3: Plym 3E **134**
PL21: Ivy 5H **145**
TQ11: Buck 3D **98**
BUCKFASTLEIGH 4C 98 (1D **175**)
Buckfastleigh Miniature Railway . . .4E **98**
Buckfastleigh Station
South Devon Railway 4E **98**
Buckfastleigh Swimming Pool 5C **98**
Buckfast Rd. TQ11: Buck 2C **98**
Buckingham Cl. EX8: Exmth 5G **77**
EX36: S Mol 7C **26**
Buckingham Orchard
TQ13: Chud K 5B **94**
Buckingham Pl. PL5: Plym 1C **134**
Buckingham Rd. EX2: Sow 2C **72**
BUCKLAND 2J **109**
Buckland Abbey 7A **126**
Buckland Brake TQ12: New A 2H **109**
BUCKLAND BREWER 2H 29 (1C **163**)
Buckland Cl. EX39: Bide 5D **22**
PL7: Plymp 2A **138**
Buckland Ct. PL20: C'stone 6C **126**
Buckland Cross EX33: Brau 3H **15**
BUCKLAND FILLEIGH 3C **163**
Buckland Hgts. TQ12: New A 1J **109**
BUCKLAND IN THE MOOR 3B **170**
BUCKLAND MONACHORUM
. . . . .5A 126 (1A **174**)
Buckland Rd. EX33: Georgeh 5C **14**
EX39: Bide, L'ham 7B **22**
TQ12: New A 2H **109**
(Buckland Brake, not continuous)
TQ12: New A 1J **109**
(Haytor Rd.)
BUCKLAND ST MARY 2C **167**
Buckland St. PL1: Plym 5C 8 (3H **141**)
Buckland Ter. PL20: Yelv 5F **127**
BUCKLAND-TOUT-SAINTS 3D **175**
Buckland Vw. EX39: Buck B 2H **29**
TQ12: New A 7G **105**
Buckland Wlk. EX6: Exmin 1B **74**
BUCKLEIGH 6B 20 (1C **163**)
Buckleigh Grange EX39: West H . . .6B **20**
Buckleigh Rd. EX39: West H 6B **20**
Buckley Rd. EX10: Sidb 2J **85**
Buckley St. TQ8: Salc 3D **158**
Bucknall Cl. EX12: Brans 6H **85**
Bucknill Cl. EX6: Exmin 2C **74**
Bucknole Rd. PL9: Nomons 4C **92**
BUCK'S CROSS 1B **162**
Bucks La. TQ13: Bov T 7C **92**
(off Fore St.)
BUCK'S MILLS 1B **162**
Buckwell Cl. TQ7: Kingsb 3G **157**
Buckwell Rd. TQ7: Kingsb 3G **157**
Buckwell St. PL1: Plym 5F 9 (3K **141**)
Buctor Pk. PL19: Tavi 5F **59**
Buddle Cl. PL9: Plyms 7H **143**
PL19: Tavi 3H **59**
PL21: Ivy 4J **145**
Buddle La. EX4: Exe 7C **64**
EX20: Hath 2H **35**
BUDE 3A **162**
Bude Hill EX19: Wink 3E **36**
Bude St. EX1: Exe 3F 7 (6F **65**)
EX39: Apple 3H **21**
BUDLAKE 3D **165**
Budlake Old Post Office 3D **165**
Budlake Rd. EX2: Matf 4F **71**
Budleigh Cl. PL9: Plyms 7G **143**
TQ1: Torq 7F **113**

Budleigh Hill EX9: E Bud 2D 82
BUDLEIGH SALTERTON 7C 82 (2A 172)
Budshead Grn. PL5: Plym 6H 131
Budshead Rd. PL5: Plym 7E 130
PL6: Plym 7K 131
Budshead Way PL6: Plym 1K 135
Budshead Wood Local Nature Reserve 6F 131
Buena Vista Cl. PL6: Plym 4E 132
Buena Vista Dr. PL6: Plym 4D 132
Buena Vista Gdns. PL6: Plym 4D 132
Buena Vista Way PL6: Plym 4D 132
Bulgis Pk. EX36: S Mol 5B 26
BULKWORTHY 2B 162
Bullands Cl. TQ13: Bov T 3B 92
Bull Ct. EX31: Barn 4E 18
Bulleid Cl. PL2: Plym 4E 134
Bullens Cl. EX5: Thor 3A 50
Bullen St. EX5: Thor 2A 50
Buller Cl. PL7: Plymp 5C 138
PL11: Torp 1A 140
Buller Ct. EX2: Exe 7A 6 (1D 70)
Buller Rd. EX4: Exe 6A 6 (7D 64)
EX17: Cred 5G 39
EX32: Barn 4F 19
PL11: Torp 1A 140
TQ12: New A 2G 109
Bullfinch Cl. EX15: Cull 5F 45
Bull Hill EX31: Barn 2E 18
EX39: Bide 4F 23
Bull Mdw. Rd. EX2: Exe 6F 7 (7F 65)
Bullow Vw. EX19: Wink 3C 36
Bull Point Barracks PL5: Plym 3A 134
Bull Ring TQ13: Ashb 4H 99
Bulls Ct. EX24: Colyt 6D 88
Bulmer Cl. EX15: Cull 3H 45
Bulmer Rd. PL4: Plym 4K 9 (2B 142)
Bulteel Gdns. PL6: Plym 3K 131
BULVERTON 4A 84
Bulverton Pk. EX10: Sidm 4A 84
Bunclarks PL21: Lutt 7G 129
(off Old Rd.)
Bunkers Farm TQ9: E All 7D 152
Bunn Rd. EX8: Exmth 1F 77
Bunting Cl. TQ12: E Ogw 3D 108
TQ14: Teignm 3G 107
Buntings, The EX6: Exmin 2B 74
Bunts La. EX12: Seat 5C 86
Bunyan Cl. PL5: Plym 1H 135
Burch Cl. EX8: Exmth 2G 77
Burch Gdns. EX7: Daw 1H 97
Burdouns Way
TQ12: Kingst, New A 1H 105
Burgh Island Causeway
TQ7: Bigb S 3A 154
Burgh Island Causeway Leisure Cen. 3A 154
Burgmanns Hill EX8: Lymp 6F 75
Burke Rd. TQ9: Tot 5F 103
Burlands, The EX14: Fen 2G 53
Burleigh La. PL3: Plym 4J 135
Burleigh Mnr. PL3: Plym 4J 135
Burleigh Pk. Rd. PL3: Plym 5J 135
Burleigh Rd. TQ2: Torq 6J 111
BURLESCOMBE 2A 166
BURLESTONE 3A 176
Burlington Cl. EX32: Barn 7G 19
Burlington Gro. EX32: Barn 7G 19
Burnard Cl. PL6: Plym 3K 131
Burnards Cl. EX24: Colyt 6C 88
Burnards Fld. Rd. EX24: Colyt 6C 88
Burnet Cl. EX2: Won 2B 72
Burnett Rd. PL6: Plym 3A 136
Burnham Cl. EX12: Seat 2E 86
Burnham Ct. TQ12: Kingst 4H 105
(off Orchid Av.)
Burnham Pk. Rd. PL3: Plym 4J 135
Burniston Cl. PL7: Plymp 6D 138
Burnley Cl. TQ12: New A 7A 104
Burnley Rd. TQ12: New A 7A 104
Burn River Ri. TQ2: Torq 5H 111
Burns Av. EX2: Won 2J 71
PL5: Plym 1G 135
Burnside EX8: Exmth 3D 76
Burnside Rd. EX34: Ilfra 5G 11
Burns La. PL21: Modb 6G 147
Burnthouse Hill TQ12: N Whil 5E 110
Burnthouse La. EX2: Won 2J 71
Burnt Oak EX10: Sidb 3H 85
BURRATON 2A 174
Burrator Av. PL20: Prin 6C 60
Burrator Dr. EX4: Exe 5B 64
Burrator Rd. PL20: Dous 4K 127
BURRIDGE 3D 167
Burridge Av. TQ2: Torq 1K 115
Burridge La. TQ2: Torq 1C 116
Burridge Rd. EX5: Bram S 7F 51
TQ2: Torq 1K 115
BURRINGTON 2A 164
Burrington Ind. Est. PL5: Plym 2F 135
Burrington Rd. PL5: Plym 2F 135
Burrington Way PL5: Plym 2F 135
Burrough Lawn EX39: N'ham 6F 21
(off Burrough Rd.)
Burrough Rd. EX39: N'ham 6F 21
BURROW
Broadclyst 5E 52
Newton Poppleford 5F 81 (2A 172)
Burrow, The EX12: Seat 6F 87
BURROWBRIDGE 1D 167
Burrow Cl. EX10: New P 5F 81
Burrowe, The EX17: Cred 6H 39
Burrow Farm Gdns. 1C 173
Burrow Hill PL9: Plyms 6F 143
Burrow La. EX10: New P 5F 81
Burrow Rd. EX5: Broadc 5D 52
EX12: Seat 6F 87
EX34: Ilfra 3H 11
Burrows Centre 2D 20
Burrows Cl. EX33: Brau 5H 15
Burrows La. EX39: Apple 3F 21
Burrows Pk. EX33: Brau 5H 15
(not continuous)
Burrows Way EX39: N'ham 4E 20
Burscombe La. EX10: Sidb, Sidf 1B 84
BURSCOTT 6G 27
Bursledon Ct. EX7: Daw 4J 97
(off E. Cliff Rd.)
BURSTOCK 3D 167
BURSTON 3B 164
Burton Art Gallery & Museum 2G 23
Burton Cl. PL6: Plym 4C 132
Burton Pl. TQ5: Brixh 4E 122
Burton Rd. EX39: Bide 4D 22
Burton St. TQ5: Brixh 5E 122
Burton Villa Cl. TQ5: Brixh 4E 122
Burvill St. EX35: Lynt 2G 13
Burwell Cl. PL6: Plym 6F 133
Burwood La. EX38: Gt T 2D 30
Burwood M. EX38: Gt T 3E 30
Burwood Pl. TQ14: Teignm 3K 107
Burwood Rd. EX38: Gt T 2D 30
BURY 1D 165
Bury, The EX5: Thor 2A 50
Bury Rd. TQ12: New A 7E 104
BUSH 3A 162
Bushell Rd. TQ12: New A 7D 104
Bushens, The EX32: Bish T 6A 24
Bushes La. EX12: Axmth 3K 87
Bushmead Av. TQ12: Kingsk 7K 109
Bush Pk. PL6: Plym 7G 133
Butcher Pk. Hill PL19: Tavi 2H 59
Butchers La. TQ10: S Bre 1B 100
(off Stockbridge La.)
Butcher's Moor La. EX19: Wink 1B 36
Butchers Row EX31: Barn 4E 18
EX39: Bide 4F 23
(off Market Pl.)
Butcombe La. EX17: Morc 3E 38
Bute Rd. PL4: Plym 7B 136
Butland Av. TQ3: Pres 5J 115
Butland Rd. TQ12: Kingst 3G 105
Butler Cl. EX16: Tiv 5E 40
PL6: Plym 4C 132
Buttercombe Cl. TQ12: E Ogw 4C 108
Buttercup Cl. EX12: Seat 2F 87
Buttercup Rd. EX15: Will 3E 44
Butterdon Stone Row 2C 175
Butterdon Wlk. PL21: Ivy 4K 145
Butterlake TQ3: Marl 2D 114
BUTTERLEIGH 3D 165
Butterleigh Dr. EX16: Tiv 5E 40
Butterpark PL21: Ivy 4H 145
Buttery Cl. EX14: Hon 5F 55
Buttery Rd. EX14: Hon 5F 55
Buttgarden St. EX39: Bide 4F 23
Buttlands Ind. Est. TQ12: Ipp 6J 101
Button La. EX31: Brat F 4H 13
Butt Pk. PL20: Buck M 5A 126
TQ7: Stoke 6J 159
Butt Pk. Rd. PL5: Plym 1G 135
Butt Parks EX17: Cred 7J 39
Butt Pk. Ter. TQ7: Chur 1B 156
BUTTS 6B 62
Butts, The EX24: Colyt 6C 88
TQ7: Lodd 1G 151
Butts Cl. EX6: Bridf 1F 63
EX14: Hon 6E 54
EX16: With 6J 33
Butts Ct. EX2: Heav 7K 65
Buttsford Ter. PL21: L Mill 5A 144
(off New Pk. Rd.)
Butts Hill EX6: Kenton 6H 95
EX11: Ott M 3D 80
TQ3: Blag 6B 114
Butts La. EX6: Chri 4J 63
Buttsons Cl. TQ7: Stoke 6K 159
Butts Path EX33: Brau 4J 15
(not continuous)
Butts Rd. EX2: Heav 7K 65
EX11: Ott M 3D 80
Butts Way EX20: N Taw 6B 36
Buzzacott Cl. EX34: Com M 7D 12
Buzzacott La. EX34: Com M 7D 12
Buzzard Rd. PL19: Whitc 7K 59
Byard Cl. PL5: Plym 2D 134
Bydown EX32: Swim 4H 25
Byes, The EX10: Sidm 6C 84
Byes Cl. EX10: Sidf 2D 84
Byeside Rd. EX10: Sidm 2D 84
Byes La. EX10: Sidf 2E 84
Byeways Cl. EX31: Frem 6G 17
Bygones Mus.
Torquay 5E 112
Byland Rd. PL3: Plym 5B 136
Byron Av. PL5: Plym 1G 135
Byron Cl. EX31: Barn 2E 18
Byron Rd. EX2: Won 7B 66
TQ1: Torq 5C 112
Byron Way EX8: Exmth 7K 75
Byslades Intl. Touring Pk.
TQ4: Blag 2A 118
BYSTOCK 1H 77 (2A 172)
Bystock Cl. EX4: Exe 2C 6 (5E 64)
Bystock M. EX8: Exmth 1G 77
Bystock Rd. EX8: Exmth 1F 77
Bystock Ter. EX4: Exe 2C 6 (5E 64)
Byter Mill La. TQ9: Sto G 1A 120

C

Cabbage Hill TQ13: Ashb 5G 99
Cabourg Cl. TQ8: Salc 3C 158
CADBURY 3D 165
Cadbury Castle 3D 165
Cadbury Gdns. EX9: E Bud 1D 82
Caddsdown Ind. Pk. EX39: Bide 6C 22
Caddywell La. EX38: Gt T 2D 30
Caddywell Mdw. EX38: Gt T 2D 30
CADELEIGH 3D 165
Cadewell Cres. TQ2: Torq 4K 111
Cadewell La. TQ2: Torq 5J 111
Cadewell Pk. Rd. TQ2: Torq 4J 111
Cadhay 2A 80
Cadhay Cl. EX11: Ott M 4A 80
Cadhay La. EX11: Coom, Ott M 2A 80
Cad La. TQ13: Ashb 4H 99
(off Stapledon La.)
Cadleigh Cl. PL21: L Mill 5C 144
Cadleigh La. PL21: Ivy 4D 144
CADLEIGHPARK 5C 144
Cadover Cl. PL6: Plym 2B 136
Cadwell Rd. TQ3: Paig 7H 115
Caen Fld. EX33: Brau 5J 15
Caen Fld. Shop. Cen. EX33: Brau 4J 15
Caen Gdns. EX33: Brau 4J 15
Caen St. EX33: Brau 4J 15
Caen Vw. EX33: Brau 5H 15
Caernarvon Gdns. PL2: Plym 4G 135
Cairn Pleasure Ground &
Old Railway Reserve 5G 11
Cairn Rd. EX34: Ilfra 4H 11
Cairnside EX34: Ilfra 5H 11
Cake Down La. EX36: S Mol 6E 26
Calder Cl. PL3: Plym 5C 136
Caldicot Gdns. PL6: Plym 2C 132
Caledonia Cl. PL7: Plymp 4E 138
Calf St. EX38: Gt T 2C 30
California Cl. EX4: Exe 1G 65
California Cotts. PL20: Horr 1F 127
California Gdns. PL3: Plym 5C 136
Callards Combe La. EX18: Chul 5A 32
CALLINGTON 3B 168
Callington Rd. PL19: Tavi, Trew 6F 59
Calm La. EX10: N'town 7J 81
CALSTOCK 1A 174
Calthorpe Rd. EX4: Exe 4J 65
Calvados Cl. TQ13: Chud 2C 94
Calvados Ho. EX32: Barn 4F 19
(off Bevan Rd.)
Calvados Pk. TQ12: Kingst 4J 105
CALVERLEIGH 2D 165
Calvesford Cl. EX38: Gt T 1D 30
Calvesford Rd. EX38: Gt T 2D 30
Camber Rd. PL1: Plym 7A 8 (4G 141)
Camborne Cl. PL5: Plym 5F 131
Camborne Cres. TQ4: Good 7H 119
Cambrian Cl. TQ4: Coll M 3D 118
Cambridge Gro. EX34: Ilfra 3J 11
Cambridge La. W. PL1: Plym 3C 8
Cambridge Rd. PL2: Plym 6E 134
TQ1: Torq 4D 112
TQ5: Brixh 4C 122
Cambridge St. EX4: Exe 6A 6 (7D 64)
Cambridge Ter. EX4: Exe 2G 7
(off Well St.)
EX10: Sidm 6C 84
(off Salcombe Rd.)
Camden Ct. PL4: Plym 3G 9
Camden Pl. PL4: Plym 3G 9
Camden Rd. TQ1: Torq 1D 116
Camden St. PL4: Plym 3G 9 (2K 141)
Camellia Cl. EX16: Tiv 2F 41
TQ5: Chur F 2K 121
Camelot Cl. EX4: Whip 3K 65
CAMEL'S HEAD 4D 134
Cameron Cl. EX16: Tiv 5B 40
Cameron Dr. PL21: Ivy 4E 144
Cameron Way PL6: Plym 2C 136
Camfield Dr. EX16: Tiv 2F 41
Camilla Ct. EX4: Exe 2E 6
Camilla Ter. PL2: Plym 4J 135
Campbell Rd. PL9: Plyms 5G 143
Camperdown Rd. TQ8: Salc 4B 158
Camperdown St. PL2: Plym 7D 134
Camperdown St. La. Nth.
PL2: Plym 7D 134
(off Camperdown St.)
Camperdown Ter. EX8: Exmth 6A 76
Campion Cl. PL7: Plymp 4F 139
Campion Ct. EX15: Will 3D 44
Campion Dr. EX32: Barn 4K 19
Campion Gdns. EX2: Won 2A 72
Campion Ri. PL19: Tavi 3K 59
Campion Vw. PL6: Plym 2F 133
Campion Way EX14: Hon 6C 54
Camplehaye Cotts. PL19: Lam 6C 58
Cample Haye Vs. PL5: Plym 2A 134
(off Little Ash Rd.)
Camp Rd. EX20: Oke 5C 48
Canaan Way EX11: Ott M 4C 80
Canada Hill TQ12: E Ogw 3C 108
Canal Banks EX2: Exe 2F 71
Canal Hill EX16: Tiv 5E 40
Canal Rd. EX22: Hols 1D 34
PL19: Tavi 4H 59
Canal Way TQ12: Kingst 5G 105
Canberra Cl. EX4: Exe 2H 65
Candar, The EX34: Ilfra 2H 11
Candish Dr. PL9: Elb 7K 143
Candy's Path EX8: Lymp 6G 75
Canefields Av. PL7: Plymp 6E 138
Cane's Cotts. PL8: Brixt 2H 149
(off Elliotts Hill)
Canhaye Cl. PL7: Plymp 6D 138
Cann Cotts. PL5: Tam F 4H 131
Cann Gdns. PL6: Plym 4J 131
Cannington La. DT7: Uply 3F 91
Cannington Rd. EX16: With 6H 33
Cannon Rd. TQ12: Heat 2K 93
Cannon St. PL1: Dev 2C 140
Cannon St. Flats PL1: Dev 2C 140
(off Cannon St.)
Cann Wood Vw. PL6: Plym 3F 133
Canon Ho. EX1: Exe 4F 7
Canons Cl. TQ14: Bi'ton 3B 106
Canons Ga. PL19: Tavi 6G 59
Canons Way PL19: Tavi 6G 59
Canon Way EX2: Alph 5E 70
Canterbury Cl. EX14: Fen 2G 53
PL21: Ivy 5J 145
Canterbury Dr. PL5: Plym 6G 131
Canterbury Rd. EX4: Exe 5B 64
Canterbury Way EX8: Exmth 1G 77
CANWORTHY WATER 1A 168
Capel Cotts. EX8: L'ham 5H 77
Capel La. EX8: Exmth, L'ham 4H 77
Capern Cl. EX33: Wraf 6K 15
Capern Rd. EX39: Bide 4E 22
Capper Cl. EX10: New P 5G 81
Caprera Pl. PL4: Plym 2D 8
Caprera Ter. La.
PL4: Plym 2D 8 (1J 141)
Capstone Ct. EX34: Ilfra 3K 11
Capstone Cres. EX34: Ilfra 2J 11
Capstone Pde. EX34: Ilfra 1H 11
Capstone Pl. EX34: Ilfra 2J 11
(off Capstone Rd.)
Capstone Rd. EX34: Ilfra 2J 11
Captains Gdns. PL5: Plym 2K 135
Captains Rd. TQ12: Kingst 3G 105
CAPTON 2A 176
Caradon Cl. PL6: Plym 5B 132
Caradon Ct. PL20: Horr 2E 126
CARADON TOWN 3A 168
Carbeile Rd. PL11: Torp 2A 140
Carberry Av. EX8: Exmth 3C 76
Carders Ct. EX2: Exe 6C 6 (7E 64)
Cardiff Cl. PL7: Plymp 5E 138
Cardigan Rd. PL6: Plym 2D 136
Cardinal Av. PL5: Plym 3C 134
Careswell Av. PL2: Plym 3E 134
Carew Av. PL5: Plym 7G 131
Carew Gdns. PL5: Plym 7G 131
TQ12: New A 1J 109
Carew Gro. PL5: Plym 7G 131
Carew Rd. EX16: Tiv 2D 40
Carew Ter. PL11: Torp 2A 140
Carew Wharf PL11: Torp 2B 140
Carey Rd. TQ6: Dartm 6C 124
CARGREEN 1A 130 (1A 174)
Carhaix Way EX7: Daw 2J 97
Carisbrooke Rd. PL6: Plym 2D 136
CARKEEL 1A 174
Carlile Rd. EX2: Won 7K 65
TQ5: Brixh 3C 122

Carling Ct.—Chapelton

Carling Ct. TQ7: Kingsb 5F 157
Carlisle Rd. PL5: Plym 7H 131
Carlisle St. TQ12: New A 1F 109
Carlton Cl. PL3: Plym 6C 136
TQ3: Pres 4J 115
Carlton Ct. *TQ14: Teignm 5J 107*
(off Bank St.)
Carlton Dr. TQ3: Pres 4J 115
Carlton Hill EX8: Exmth 7C 76
Carlton Pl. TQ14: Teignm 5J 107
Carlton Rd. EX2: Won 1A 72
TQ1: Torq 7E 112
Carlton Ter. EX7: Daw 4H 97
EX32: Barn 5F 19
(off Barbican Rd.)
PL1: Plym 2G 141
PL4: Plym 3J 9 (2A 142)
PL5: Plym 3D 134
Carlton Theatre 5J 107
Carlyle Av. EX32: Barn 3F 19
Carlyon Cl. EX1: Heav 6K 65
Carlyon Gdns. EX1: Heav 6K 65
Carmarthen Rd. PL4: Plym 2C 142
Carmel Gdns. PL19: Tavi 4G 59
Carnegie Nth. *EX39: N'ham 6F 21*
(off Clevelands Pk.)
Carnegie Sth. *EX39: N'ham 6F 21*
(off Clevelands Pk.)
Carnegie Wlk. EX2: Cou W 4D 72
Carnock Rd. PL2: Plym 3J 135
Carolina Gdns. PL2: Plym 4E 134
Caroline Av. EX2: Cou W 4C 72
Caroline Cl. EX8: Exmth 3F 77
TQ12: Kingsk 2G 111
Caroline Pl. PL1: Plym 3F 141
Carousel Ct. EX4: Exe 7A 6 (1D 70)
Carpenter Cl. EX4: Exe 4C 6 (6E 64)
EX16: Tiv 5C 40
Carpenter Rd. PL9: Plyms 4G 143
Carpenters Ct. *TQ12: New A 2F 109*
(off Church Rd.)
Carradale Rd. PL6: Plym 4D 136
Carrington Pl. EX14: Hon 4G 55
Carrington Ter. *EX32: Barn 3F 19*
(off Yeo Vale Rd.)
Carrionpit La. EX19: Wink 2C 36
Carrions, The TQ9: Tot 6E 102
Carr La. TQ7: Slap 1H 159
Carroll Rd. PL5: Plym 7H 131
Carrolls Way PL9: Spri 7H 143
Carron La. PL6: Robo 1E 132
Carslake Cl. EX10: Sidm 3D 84
Carswells TQ12: Kingsk 7J 109
Carter Av. EX8: Exmth 4C 76
Carter Rd. PL21: Ivy 3H 145
Cartwright Cres.
TQ14: Teignm 3F 107
Cary Av. TQ1: Torq 6E 112
Cary Castle TQ1: Torq 5D 112
Cary Castle Dr. TQ1: Torq 5D 112
Cary Pde. TQ2: Torq 2D 116
Cary Pk. TQ1: Torq 6D 112
Cary Pk. Rd. TQ1: Torq 6E 112
Cary Rd. TQ2: Torq 2C 116
TQ3: Pres 5G 115
Caseberry La. EX5: Bradn 3A 52
Case Gdns. EX12: Seat 4F 87
Cassiobury Way TQ2: Torq 3A 112
Castle EX12: Brans 6J 85
Castle Acre Gdns. PL3: Plym 6C 136
Castle Bank Gdns. PL3: Plym 6C 136
Castle Barbican PL7: Plymp 5B 138
Castlebar Cl. EX16: Tiv 5E 40
Castle Carey Gdns. PL3: Plym 6C 136
Castle Cir. TQ1: Torq 1C 116
Castle Cir. Ct. TQ1: Torq 1C 116
Castle Ct. EX32: L'key 2C 24
TQ9: Tot 6D 102
Castle Drogo 1B 170
Castle Dyke La. PL1: Plym 6F 9
Castle Farm EX11: W Hill 4J 79
Castle Gate EX6: Kenton 6J 95
Castle Ham Lodge EX20: Oke 4B 48
Castlehayes Gdns. PL7: Plymp 5B 138
Castle Hgts. EX35: Lynt 2H 13
Castle Hill EX12: Seat 6E 86
EX13: Axmin 3H 89
EX34: Berry 3C 12
EX34: Ilfra 2J 11
EX35: Lynt 2H 13
Castle Hill Av. EX34: Ilfra 3J 11
Castle Hill Gdns. 1A 164
Castle Hill Gdns. EX38: Gt T 2C 30
Castle Hill Vw. EX10: Sidf 1D 84
Castle Hill Vis. Cen. 3B 30
Castle La. EX5: Wood 5C 78
EX8: L'ham 5H 77
EX20: Oke 5A 48
EX33: Brau 1J 15
PL7: Plymp 5B 138
TQ1: Torq 1D 116
(not continuous)
Castle La. TQ3: Comp 7C 110
TQ9: Blacka 2C 152
Castle Mdw. EX39: Buck B 1H 29
Castle M. EX13: Axmin 3H 89
Castle Mt. EX4: Exe 1D 6 (5E 64)
Castle Pk. EX15: Hemy 2G 47
Castle Pk. Rd. EX32: Barn 6K 19
Castle Quay EX31: Barn 4E 18
Castle Quay Ct. EX31: Barn 4D 18
Castle Ri. PL3: Plym 7C 136
Castle Rd. EX20: Oke 4B 48
TQ1: Torq 1C 116
TQ6: Dartm 7G 125
TQ6: Kingsw 7G 125
Castle Rock EX34: Mort 4A 10
Castle St. EX4: Exe 3E 6 (6F 65)
EX13: Axmin 3H 89
EX16: Bam 2H 33
EX16: Tiv 4D 40
EX19: Wink 2C 36
EX31: Barn 4E 18
EX34: Com M 7C 12
EX38: Gt T 2C 30
EX39: N'ham 6E 20
PL1: Plym 6F 9 (3K 141)
TQ9: Tot 5E 102
Castle Ter. EX34: Ilfra 3J 11
Castleton Cl. PL3: Plym 7B 136
Castle Vw. EX24: Colyt 6D 88
Castle Vw. Ter. *TQ9: Tot 5E 102*
(off Castle St.)
Castle Way TQ12: New A 7B 104
Castlewood Av. TQ12: New A 6B 104
Castor Cl. TQ5: Brixh 5F 123
Castor La. TQ4: Good 6H 119
Castor Rd. TQ5: Brixh 5E 122
Catacombs, The 4C 6
Catalina Cl. EX14: Dunk 7H 47
Catalina Vs. PL9: Hooe 6B 142
Cat & Fiddle Pk. EX5: Clyst M 2K 73
Cater Rd. EX32: Barn 5G 19
Catford Ct. EX15: Kent 6A 46
Cathcart Av. PL4: Plym 2C 142
Cathedral Cl. EX1: Exe 4E 6 (6F 65)
Cathedral St. PL1: Plym 3B 8 (2H 141)
Cathedral Yd. EX1: Exe 4D 6 (6F 65)
(not continuous)
Catherine Cl. EX16: Tiv 3E 40
Catherine Cres. TQ4: Paig 3F 119
Catherine Sq. EX1: Exe 4E 6
Catherine St. EX1: Exe 4E 6 (6F 65)
PL1: Plym 5E 8 (3J 141)
CATHERSTON LEWESTON 1D 173
Catnip Cl. EX13: Axmin 3J 89
CATON 3B 170
Cator TQ9: Sto G 3B 120
Catshole La. EX39: Bide 5E 22
CATTEDOWN 7K 9 (4B 142)
Cattedown Rd. PL4: Plym 5K 9 (3B 142)
(Embankment Rd.)
PL4: Plym 7K 9 (4B 142)
(Esso Wharf Rd.)
Cattedown Rdbt.
PL4: Plym 5J 9 (3A 142)
Catterick Cl. PL5: Plym 5D 130
Cattewater Rd. PL4: Plym 3C 142
Cauleston Cl. EX8: Exmth 2C 76
Caumont Cl. EX15: Uff 7F 43
Caunters Cl. TQ12: Ipp 6H 101
Causeway EX12: Beer 7B 86
Causeway Cl. EX39: N'ham 5F 21
Causeway Cotts. EX12: Beer 6B 86
Causeway Cross TQ12: Ipp 6J 101
Causey Gdns. EX1: Pin 3D 66
Causey La. EX1: Pin 3D 66
CAUTE 2C 163
Cavalier Rd. TQ12: Heat 1H 93
Cavalry Dr. TQ12: Heat 3J 93
Cavell Way EX20: Oke 2C 48
Cavendish Cl. EX7: Daw 3F 97
Cavendish Pl. EX35: Lynt 2G 13
Cavendish Rd.
EX1: Heav 3K 7 (6J 65)
PL4: Plym 3C 142
Cavern Rd. TQ1: Torq 1D 116
TQ5: Brixh 4E 122
Caversham Cl. EX6: Chri 3J 63
Cavie Cres. EX33: Brau 4G 15
Cavie Rd. EX33: Brau 4G 15
Cawley Av. EX13: Axmin 2K 89
CAWSAND 2A 174
Cawsand Vw. *EX20: Exbo 6J 35*
(off High St.)
Caxton Gdns. PL5: Plym 2H 135
Caxton Row EX16: Tiv 2D 40
Cayley Way PL5: Plym 1E 134
Cayman Cl. TQ2: Torq 2A 112
Cecil Av. PL4: Plym 2K 9 (1B 142)
TQ3: Pres 6H 115
Cecil Cotts. PL1: Plym 4A 8 (2G 141)
Cecilia Rd. TQ3: Pres 5H 115
Cecil M. TQ3: Paig 7H 115
Cecil Rd. EX2: Exe 7B 6 (1D 70)
TQ3: Paig 1G 119
Cecil St. PL1: Plym 3B 8 (2H 141)
(not continuous)
Cedar Av. PL9: Hooe 7D 142
Cedar Cl. EX8: Exmth 1F 77
EX12: Seat 3E 86
EX13: Axmin 4H 89
EX14: Hon 4E 54
TQ14: Teignm 2K 107
Cedar Ct. Rd. TQ1: Torq 6D 112
Cedarcroft Rd. PL2: Plym 4G 135
Cedar Gdns. EX13: Axmin 4H 89
Cedar Gro. EX31: Roun 7A 18
Cedar Rd. EX16: Tiv 3F 41
TQ3: Pres 5J 115
TQ12: New A 4J 109
Cedars, The EX14: Hon 2H 55
TQ9: Tot 5G 103
Cedars Pk. EX31: Barn 5A 18
Cedars Rd. EX2: Exe 7F 7 (7F 65)
TQ1: Torq 1E 116
Cedar Units TQ9: Darti 3B 102
Cedar Way EX39: Bide 5C 22
TQ5: Brixh 6C 122
Celandine Cl. EX12: Seat 3F 87
Celandine Gdns. PL7: Plymp 4F 139
Celandine Lawns EX15: Will 3D 44
Celia Cres. EX4: Whip 2K 65
Celtic Ct. *EX7: Daw 3H 97*
(off Celtic Flds.)
Celtic Flds. EX7: Daw 3H 97
Cembra Cl. EX14: Hon 4G 55
Cemetery La. EX5: Bradn 2C 52
Centenary Way TQ2: Torq 3J 111
Central Av. EX2: Cou W 6C 72
EX4: Whip 2A 66
EX22: Hols 2B 34
PL21: L Mill 4B 144
TQ3: Paig 7H 115
Central Cinema, The
Merlin Cinemas 2D 116
Scott Cinemas 4E 18
Central Park 1D 8 (7H 135)
Central Pk. Av.
PL4: Plym 1C 8 (1H 141)
Central Pk. Leisure Pool 6G 135
Central Pk. Towers
PL4: Plym 1D 8 (1J 141)
Central Rd. PL1: Plym 7C 8 (4H 141)
Centre Ct. PL21: Moor 2C 146
Centry Ct. TQ5: Brixh 4G 123
Centry Rd. TQ5: Brixh 4G 123
Century Dr. EX39: N'ham 6D 20
Century of Playtime Doll & Toy Mus.
. . . . .1H 119
Century Quay PL4: Plym 5G 9
Ceramic Ter. *EX32: Barn 5F 19*
(off Trinity St.)
Chaddiford La. EX31: Barn 2C 18
CHADDLEHANGER 3C 169
CHADDLEWOOD 4F 139
Chaddlewood Av.
PL4: Plym 2J 9 (1A 142)
Chaddlewood Cl. PL7: Plymp 4C 138
Chaddlewood District Cen.
PL7: Plymp 4F 139
Chad Rd. PL9: Hey B 3B 148
CHAFFCOMBE 2D 167
Chaffcombe La. EX17: Cop 6A 38
Chaffinch Dr. EX15: Cull 5F 45
CHAGFORD 2H 61 (2B 170)
Chagford Cross TQ13: More 6G 61
Chagford Swimming Pool 1J 61
Chagford Wlk. PL6: Plym 3F 137
Chains Rd. EX16: Sam P 2A 42
Chalfield Cl. TQ2: Torq 2B 112
CHALLABOROUGH 2B 154 (3C 175)
Challaborough Caravan Pk.
TQ7: Chal 1B 154
Challabrook La. TQ13: Bov T 5A 92
CHALLACOMBE 2C 161
Challacombe Cl. *EX32: L'key 2C 24*
(off Blakes Hill Rd.)
Challacombe Hill EX34: Woolc 7A 10
Challacombe Hill Rd.
EX34: Woolc 6A 10
Challgood Cl. PL9: Plyms 7G 143
Challgood Ri. PL9: Plyms 7G 143
Challock Cl. PL6: Plym 6E 132
Challowell La. EX33: Brau 2H 15
Challycroft Rd. TQ5: Brixh 7C 122
Chaloner's Rd. EX33: Brau 3J 15
CHAMBERCOMBE 3K 11
Chambercombe La. EX34: Ilfra 4K 11
Chambercombe Manor 4K 11
Chambercombe Pk. Rd.
EX34: Ilfra 3K 11
Chambercombe Rd. EX34: Ilfra 3K 11
Chambercombe Ter. EX34: Ilfra 3K 11
Chamberlain Rd. EX2: Exe . . .7D 6 (1E 70)
Chamberlayne Dr. PL7: Plymp 3B 138
Chambers Cl. EX10: Sidm 2B 84
Champernowne PL21: Modb 6G 147
Champernowne Cres. EX34: Ilfra . . .3K 11
Chancel Ct. EX4: Pin 3C 66
Chancel La. EX4: Pin 3C 66
Chancellor's Way EX4: Whip 2K 65
Chandlers Ct. EX39: Ins 3K 21
Chandlers Hgts. TQ8: Salc 3C 158
Chandlers La. EX10: Sidm 5C 84
Chandlers Wlk. EX2: Exe 7D 6 (1E 70)
Chandlers Way EX34: Ilfra 5H 11
Channel Pk. Av. PL3: Plym 6C 136
Channel Vw. EX34: Ilfra 4K 11
EX34: Mort 3B 10
TQ7: Hope 3G 155
Channel Vw. La. EX7: Holc 7F 97
Channel Vw. Ter.
PL4: Plym 2K 9 (1B 142)
Chanter Ct. EX2: Cou W 3K 71
Chanter's Hill EX32: Barn 4G 19
Chanters Rd. EX39: Bide 2F 23
(not continuous)
Chantry Av. EX39: Bide 2F 23
Chantry Cl. TQ14: Teignm 2K 107
Chantry Hill TQ7: Slap 2J 159
Chantry Mdw. EX2: Alph 5E 70
Chantry Orchard EX24: Colyt 5C 88
Chantry Pl. EX24: Colyt 5C 88
Chantry Rd. PL7: Plymp 6J 137
Chapel, The *TQ9: Tot 6F 103*
(off The Plains)
Chapel Cl. EX16: Hal 6D 42
EX33: Brau 4J 15
PL20: Horr 2E 126
Chapel Cotts. PL7: L Moor 1J 129
Chapel Ct. *EX2: Alph 4E 70*
(off Church Rd.)
EX32: Swim 3H 25
TQ1: Torq 6B 112
TQ9: Sto G 3B 120
Chapeldown Rd. PL11: Torp 2A 140
Chapel Downs Dr. EX17: Cred 5F 39
Chapel Downs Rd. EX17: Cred 5F 39
Chapel Flds. TQ10: S Bre 1B 100
Chapel Hgts. PL19: Tavi 3J 59
Chapel Hill EX3: Clyst G 7H 73
EX8: Exmth 6C 76
EX9: Bud S 6C 82
EX15: Uff 6H 43
EX17: Cher F 1K 39
TQ12: New A 1E 108
Chapel La. EX10: Col R 2G 83
EX11: Ott M 3D 80
EX34: Com M 6B 12
PL8: Yeal 2B 150
PL19: Mary T 1B 60
PL20: Horr 2E 126
PL21: Lutt 7G 129
TQ6: Dartm 2A 124
TQ6: Sto F 3H 153
TQ7: Malb 6G 155
TQ9: Tot 6F 103
TQ12: Live 4G 93
Chapel Mdw. PL20: Buck M 5A 126
Chapel Pk. Cl. EX39: Bide 3H 23
Chapel Pl. EX3: Top 5B 74
PL21: Erm 2H 147
PL21: Ivy 4H 145
Chapel Rd. EX2: Alph 4E 70
EX5: Bram S 5G 51
EX8: Lymp 6F 75
EX10: Sidm 7C 84
PL8: Torr 3C 150
TQ12: New A 1G 109
Chapel Row EX12: Brans 6F 85
PL11: Torp 1A 140
Chapel St. EX1: Exe 4E 6 (6F 65)
EX8: Exmth 6C 76
EX9: Bud S 7C 82
EX10: Sidb 3H 85
EX10: Sidm 7C 84
EX12: Axmth 3H 87
EX14: Hon 3F 55
EX16: Tiv 4D 40
EX17: Morc 1B 38
EX19: Dol 6H 31
EX22: Hols 2C 34
EX33: Brau 5J 15
EX33: Georgeh 5B 14
EX39: Bide 3F 23
EX39: Wools 2B 28
PL1: Dev 2D 140
PL4: Plym 3F 9 (2K 141)
PL8: Holb 6C 150
PL16: Lift 6B 56
PL19: Tavi 4H 59
PL20: Bere A 2C 128
PL21: Erm 2H 147
TQ9: Blacka 3C 152
TQ11: B'leigh 4C 98
Chapel St. Ope PL1: Dev 2D 140
CHAPELTON 1D 163

Chapel Vs.—Church La.

Chapel Vs. PL7: L Moor 1J 129
Chapel Way PL3: Plym 5B 136
CHAPMANS WELL 1B 168
Chapple Cl. EX6: Star 2E 96
Chapple Cross TQ13: Bov T 6A 92
Chapple Rd. EX16: With 6H 33
TQ13: Bov T 5A 92
CHARD 3D 167
Chard Av. EX5: Whim 6G 53
Chard Barton PL5: Plym 7G 131
CHARD JUNCTION 3D 167
Chard Rd. EX1: Heav 6K 65
EX13: Axmin, Wey 3J 89
PL5: Plym 1C 134
Chards Orchard EX6: Kennf 1G 95
CHARDSTOCK 3D 167
Chardstock Cl. EX1: Sow 6C 66
Chard St. EX13: Axmin 3H 89
Charfield Dr. PL6: Plym 2B 136
Charingthay Gate EX4: Exe 4H 65
Charlemont Rd. TQ14: Teignm 1H 107
CHARLES 3C 161
Charles Av. EX39: Bide 2F 23
Charles Church 4F 9
Charles Cross PL4: Plym . . . 4F 9 (2K 141)
Charles Dart Cres. EX32: Barn 3F 19
Charles Darwin Rd. PL1: Dev 3E 140
Charles Hankin Cl. PL21: Ivy 5J 145
Charles Hudson La. EX31: Barn 2F 19
Charles Rd. EX14: Hon 3F 55
TQ12: Kingsk 3G 111
Charles St. EX8: Exmth 5C 76
EX32: Barn 3E 18
PL1: Plym 3F 9 (2K 141)
TQ6: Dartm 1A 124 (6F 125)
Charles Ter. PL3: Plym 5B 136
Charleton Way TQ7: W Cha 7K 157
Charlotte Cl. TQ2: Torq 5B 112
Charlotte M. *EX2: Exe* *5F 7*
(off Pavilion Pl.)
Charlotte St. EX17: Cred 6J 39
PL2: Dev 7D 134
CHARLTON 1C 167
Charlton Cres. PL6: Plym 1B 136
Charlton Ho. *EX7: Daw* *4H 97*
(off E. Cliff Rd.)
Charlton Rd. PL6: Plym 7A 132
Charlton Ter. PL21: Ivy 4H 145
Charlwood Ct. TQ1: Torq 5E 112
CHARMOUTH 1D 173
Charmouth Cl. DT7: Lym R 4K 91
TQ1: Torq 7F 113
Charmouth Ho. *DT7: Lym R* *5H 91*
(off Portland Ct.)
Charmouth Rd. DT7: Lym R 3K 91
EX13: Ray H 2C 90
Charnhill Cl. PL9: Elb 6H 143
Charnhill Way PL9: Elb 6H 143
Charnley Av. EX4: Exe 7B 64
Charter Cl. EX16: Tiv 4A 40
Charter Ct. EX31: Roun 7K 17
Chartwell Cl. TQ3: Paig 7E 114
Chartwell Dr. TQ12: New A 7D 104
Charwell Mdw. EX5: Bradn 2C 52
Chase, The EX14: Hon 2G 55
EX20: Oke 2D 48
PL21: Ivy 5H 145
CHASTY 4C 34 (3B 162)
Chasty La. EX22: Hols 4C 34
Chatham Cl. EX8: Exmth 3F 77
Chatsworth Gdns. PL5: Plym 7E 130
Chatsworth Rd. TQ1: Torq 7D 112
Chatto Rd. TQ1: Torq 6C 112
Chatto Way TQ1: Torq 6C 112
Chatwell La. PL21: Modb 5G 147
Chaucer Av. EX2: Won 2J 71
Chaucer Gro. EX4: Whip 4J 65
Chaucer Ri. EX8: Exmth 7K 75
Chaucer Rd. PL19: Tavi 4K 59
Chaucer Way PL5: Plym 2G 135
Chaves Cl. EX16: Tiv 5F 41
CHAWLEIGH 2B 164
Chawleigh Hill EX18: Chaw, Chul . . . 7D 32
Chawleigh Week Hill EX18: Chaw . . . 7B 32
Chawleigh Week La. EX18: Chaw . . . 7A 32
Cheavestone Lea TQ9: Blacka 3B 152
CHEDDON FITZPAINE 1C 167
Chedworth St. PL4: Plym . . . 3G 9 (2K 141)
Cheeke St. EX1: Exe 3G 7 (6G 65)
Cheese La. EX10: Sidm 6A 84
CHEGLINCH 2B 160
CHELDON 2B 164
Chelmer Cl. PL7: Plymp 4D 138
Chelmsford Pl. PL5: Plym 6H 131
Chelmsford Rd. EX4: Exe 6A 64
Chelsea Pl. TQ14: Teignm 4H 107
Chelson Gdns. PL6: Plym 7F 133
CHELSTON
Torquay 2A 116
Wellington 1B 166
Chelston Rd. TQ2: Torq 3A 116
TQ12: New A 7E 104
Cheltenham Cl. EX4: Exe 5B 64
Cheltenham Pl.
PL4: Plym 1G 9 (1K 141)
Cheltenham Vs. PL4: Plym 1H 9
Chelwood Gro. PL7: Plymp 4C 138
Cheney's La. EX14: Hon 1H 55
Chepstow Av. PL6: Plym 2D 132
Chepstow Cl. EX2: Cou W 5A 72
Chercombe Bri. Rd.
TQ12: New A 1A 108
Chercombe Cl. TQ12: New A 7B 104
Chercombe Valley Rd.
TQ12: New A 7B 104
Cheristow Lavender 1G 27
Cheriswood Av. EX8: Exmth 3F 77
Cheriswood Cl. EX8: Exmth 3F 77
CHERITON 2D 161
CHERITON BISHOP 2C 62 (1B 170)
Cheriton Cl. PL5: Plym 7F 131
CHERITON CROSS 2C 62 (1B 170)
CHERITON FITZPAINE 2H 39 (3C 165)
Cherry Arbour EX32: Barn 6H 19
Cherry Brook Dr. TQ4: Good 7H 119
Cherry Brook Sq. TQ4: Good 7H 119
Cherry Brook Wlk. TQ4: Good 6H 119
Cherry Cl. EX8: Exmth 1E 76
EX14: Hon 5C 54
EX15: Will 4D 44
EX16: Tiv 3D 40
EX17: Cher F 2J 39
Cherry Cross TQ9: Tot 7E 102
Cherry Dr. EX12: Seat 5E 86
Cherry Gdns. EX2: Won 1K 71
EX17: Cred 6H 39
TQ3: Paig 7G 115
Cherry Gro. EX32: Barn 7H 19
Cherry Mdw. EX17: Cher F 2J 39
Cherry Pk. EX39: Apple 3G 21
PL7: Plymp 6D 138
Cherry Pk. Cl. TQ2: Torq 4K 115
Cherry Tree Cl. EX4: Exe 1D 64
Cherry Tree Dr. EX32: L'key 2B 24
PL8: Brixt 2H 149
Cherry Tree Farm Campsite
EX33: Croy 1B 14
Cherry Tree Gdns. EX16: Tiv 3E 40
Cherry Tree La. PL7: Plymp 5D 138
Cherry Tree Rd. EX13: Axmin 3J 89
Cherry Tree Way EX5: Rock 3E 68
Cherrywood Cl. TQ12: New A 7B 104
Cheshire Dr. PL6: Plym 4H 131
Cheshire Rd. EX8: Exmth 2G 77
Chester Cl. EX4: Exe 5B 64
Chester Ct. *EX8: Exmth* *5B 76*
(off Manchester Rd.)
Chesterfield Rd. PL3: Plym 7C 136
Chester Pl. PL4: Plym 1G 9 (7K 135)
Chester Ter. *EX32: Barn* *5F 19*
(off Barbican Rd.)
Chesterton Cl. PL5: Plym 7H 131
Chestnut Av. EX2: Won 2K 71
EX15: Cull 5H 45
PL9: Hooe 7D 142
TQ2: Torq 2B 116
TQ6: Dartm 5E 124
Chestnut Cl. EX6: Cher B 2C 62
EX8: Exmth 1E 76
EX12: Seat 3E 86
EX17: Cred 5J 39
EX33: Brau 4K 15
PL19: Lam 5C 58
PL19: Tavi 7K 59
PL20: Bere A 2B 128
Chestnut Ct. EX2: Alph 5E 70
Chestnut Cres. EX5: Sto C 7J 51
TQ13: Chud 1D 94
Chestnut Dr. EX15: Will 4C 44
EX39: Bide 5C 22
TQ5: Brixh 6C 122
TQ12: Kingst 5J 105
TQ12: New A 3K 109
Chestnut Gro. TQ6: Dartm 5C 124
Chestnut M. EX14: Fen 2J 53
Chestnut Rd. EX16: Tiv 3F 41
PL3: Plym 4J 135
Chestnut Ter. PL19: Lam 6C 58
Chestnut Wlk. EX7: Daw 5F 97
Chestnut Way EX10: New P 5H 81
EX14: Hon 5D 54
CHESTON 2C 175
CHESTWOOD 5A 24
Chestwood Av. EX31: Barn 6B 18
Chestwood Cl. EX31: Barn 6C 18
CHETTISCOMBE 1F 41 (2D 165)
CHEVITHORNE 2D 165
Cheyne Beach EX34: Ilfra 2J 11
Cheynegate La. EX4: Pin 1B 66
Cheyne Ri. EX4: Pin 2C 66
CHICHACOTT 1E 48 (1A 170)
Chichacott Rd. EX20: Chich, Oke . . . 2D 48
Chichester Cl. EX8: Exmth 5E 76
EX32: Barn 7G 19
Chichester Cl. EX34: Ilfra 4G 11
EX39: Ins 2K 21
TQ14: Teignm 1G 107
Chichester Ct. *EX32: Barn* *4H 19*
(off Valley Cl.)
PL20: Horr 2E 126
Chichester Cres. EX32: Barn 7G 19
Chichester Ho. EX2: Won 7A 66
PL1: Plym 6C 8 (3H 141)
Chichester M. EX1: Exe 4F 7 (6F 65)
Chichester Pk. EX34: Woolc 6B 10
Chichester Pl. EX16: Tiv 5G 41
Chichester Rd. EX32: Barn 7G 19
Chichester's Yd. *EX33: Brau* *5J 15*
(off Exeter Rd.)
Chichester Way EX9: E Bud 1D 82
EX39: West H 6B 20
TQ12: New A 1H 109
CHIDEOCK 1D 173
Chideock Ct. *DT7: Lym R* *5H 91*
(off Clappentail La.)
Chieftain Way EX2: Exe 7A 6 (1D 70)
Chilcote Cl. TQ1: Torq 5E 112
Chilcott Cl. EX16: Tiv 5G 41
Children's Adventure Land 6C 44
Childrey Gdns. PL6: Plym 2D 136
Childrey Wlk. PL6: Plym 2D 136
CHILLA 3C 163
CHILLATON 2C 169
CHILLINGTON
Ilminster 2D 167
Stokenham 6G 159 (3D 175)
Chilpark EX31: Frem 6E 16
CHILSWORTHY
Holsworthy 3B 162
Tavistock 3C 169
Chiltern Cl. TQ2: Torq 3K 115
CHILTON 3C 165
Chilton Av. TQ14: Teignm 3J 107
Chilton Cl. PL6: Plym 4C 136
China Blue 5E 102
Chineway Gdns. EX11: Ott M 3E 80
Chineway Rd. EX11: Ott M 3D 80
Chingswell St. EX39: Bide 3F 23
Chinkwell Ri. TQ2: Torq 5H 111
Chinon Ct. EX16: Tiv 2G 41
Chinon Pl. EX16: Tiv 2A 40
Chinston Cl. EX14: Awli 1A 54
CHIPLEY 1B 166
Chipmunk Wlk. EX32: Barn 4G 19
Chipple Pk. PL21: Lutt 7G 129
CHIPSTABLE 1A 166
Chircombe La. EX39: N'ham 7F 21
Chiseldon Farm TQ5: Brixh 6D 122
Chiseldon Hill TQ5: Brixh 6E 122
Chiseldon Ho. *EX4: Exe* *3D 64*
(off Copplestone Dr.)
Chiseldon La. TQ5: Brixh 7E 122
CHITTERLEY 3D 165
Chittleburn Bus. Pk. PL8: Brixt 2F 149
Chittleburn Hill PL8: Brixt 1F 149
CHITTLEHAMHOLT 1A 164
CHITTLEHAMPTON 5J 25 (1A 164)
CHIVELSTONE 3D 175
CHIVENOR 1E 16 (3B 160)
Chivenor Av. PL5: Plym 6C 130
Chivenor Caravan Pk. EX31: Chive . . . 1E 16
Chivenor Ind. Est. EX31: Chive 1E 16
Chiverstone La. EX6: Kenton 5G 95
Chiverstone Rd. EX6: Kenton 5G 95
Chockenhole La. EX9: Ott'n 5J 83
Chockland Rd. TQ12: Kingst 2G 105
Chollacott Cl. PL19: Tavi 6J 59
Chollacott La. PL19: Whitc 6K 59
Chope Rd. EX39: N'ham 6E 20
Chopes Cl. EX39: Bide 5J 23
Christcross La. EX5: Bradn 1A 52
Christian Mill Bus. Pk.
PL6: Plym 6K 131
Christina Pde. TQ9: Tot 6G 103
Christina Pk. TQ9: Tot 6G 103
CHRISTOW 3J 63 (2C 171)
Christow Rd. EX2: Mar B 3E 70
Chrystel Cl. EX10: Tip J 1J 81
Chubb Dr. PL3: Plym 7G 135
Chubb Rd. EX39: Bide 5H 23
Chubby Cft. Cl. EX39: Hart 3J 27
CHUDLEIGH 1C 94 (3C 171)
Chudleigh EX39: Bide 3G 23
Chudleigh Av. EX39: Bide 4G 23
Chudleigh Fort 4G 23
CHUDLEIGH KNIGHTON . . . 6B 94 (3C 171)
Chudleigh Knighton Heath Nature Reserve
. . . . 6A 94
Chudleigh Rd. EX2: Alph 5E 70
EX39: Bide 4G 23
PL4: Plym 7B 136
TQ12: Kingst 2F 105
Chudleigh Rocks 3B 94
Chudleigh Ter. EX39: Bide 4G 23
Chudley Cl. EX8: Exmth 3F 77
Chugg's Orchard EX33: Croy 2D 14
Chuley Hill TQ13: Ashb 5H 99
Chuley Rd. TQ13: Ashb 5H 99
CHULMLEIGH 6C 32 (2A 164)
Chulmleigh Golf Course 6C 32
Chulmleigh Hill EX18: Chul 6C 32
Chulmleigh Rd. EX17: Morc 1A 38
EX19: Wink 2C 36
Chulmleigh Sports Cen. 5C 32
Church Av. EX20: Oke 3A 48
PL19: Lam 6D 58
Church Cl. EX5: Broadc 5C 52
EX17: Lap 2K 37
EX18: Chul 6C 32
EX19: Dol 7H 31
EX31: Brat F 6H 13
PL7: Plymp 4J 137
PL8: Yeal 2B 150
TQ6: Dartm 1B 124 (6F 125)
TQ7: Kingsb 4G 157
TQ9: Tot 6E 102
Church Cotts. PL8: Brixt 2H 149
TQ3: Marl 2D 114
Church Ct. TQ12: Kingst 5H 105
TQ12: New A 1E 108
Church Cross Rd. TQ11: B'leigh 3C 98
Church Elm Rd. EX24: Colyf 1F 87
Church End Rd. TQ12: Kingsk 7J 109
Church Farm TQ7: Thur 6B 154
Churchfield EX39: Apple 2H 21
Churchfields TQ6: Dartm 6D 124
Churchfields Dr. TQ13: Bov T 4C 92
Churchfields W. TQ6: Dartm 6D 124
Churchford Rd. EX33: Know 1K 15
CHURCH GREEN 1B 172
Church Gro. EX32: Barn 6G 19
Church Hill EX4: Pin 1B 66
EX6: Ted M 5H 49
EX9: Ott'n 6G 83
EX12: Beer 7B 86
EX13: Mus 7C 90
EX14: Awli 1A 54
EX14: Hon 4G 55
EX19: Wink 2C 36
EX31: Frem 6F 17
EX34: Ilfra 3G 11
EX35: Lynt 2H 13
PL6: Plym 2C 136
PL7: Spa 1J 139
PL8: Holb 6B 150
PL19: Whitc 7K 59
TQ3: Marl 2D 114
TQ6: Kingsw 7G 125
TQ9: Blacka 2B 152
TQ11: B'leigh 3C 98
Church Hill Cl. TQ9: Blacka 2B 152
Church Hill Cotts. TQ3: Marl 3D 114
Church Hill E. TQ5: Brixh 3E 122
Church Hill La. EX33: Know 1K 15
Church Hill Rd. PL9: Hooe 6B 142
Church Hill W. TQ5: Brixh 3E 122
Church Ho. Cl. TQ13: Chud K 6B 94
Church House, The 3B 170
CHURCHILL
Axminster 3D 167
Barnstaple 2B 160
Churchill Av. EX7: Daw 5G 97
Churchill Cl. EX6: Kenton 6H 95
EX32: Barn 3G 19
Churchill Cotts. PL21: Ugb 6D 146
Churchill Ct. EX8: Lymp 5G 75
TQ5: Brixh *4E 122*
(off Bolton St.)
TQ6: Dartm 1A 124
Churchill Cres. EX36: S Mol 7C 26
Churchill Dr. EX17: Cred 5G 39
TQ14: Teignm 3J 107
Churchill Rd. EX2: Exe 7A 6 (1C 70)
EX8: Exmth 2F 77
EX16: Tiv 4A 40
EX39: Bide 5H 23
PL19: Whitc 7K 59
Churchills EX15: Hemy 2G 47
Churchills, The TQ12: New A 7D 104
Churchills Ri. EX15: Hemy 2G 47
Churchill Way
EX39: Apple, N'ham 6E 20
PL3: Plym 5K 135
CHURCHINFORD 2C 167
Church Lake EX32: L'key 2B 24
Churchlands EX17: Bow 5J 37
Churchlands Cl. PL6: Plym 3F 133
Churchlands Rd. PL6: Plym 2F 133
Church La. EX2: Exe 7B 6 (1D 70)
EX2: Won 6K 7 (7J 65)
EX4: Exe 2F 7 (5F 65)
EX4: Pin 2C 66
EX5: Broadc 5C 52
EX5: Clyst M 3G 73
EX6: Bridf 1F 63
EX6: Cher B 1C 62
EX6: Chri 4K 63
EX9: E Bud 1D 82

Church La. EX10: Sidm 7C 84
EX14: Fen 2J 53
EX17: Cred 6J 39
EX19: Wink 2C 36
(off High St.)
EX20: Hath 1H 35
EX22: Hols 2C 34
EX31: Barn 4E 18
(off High St.)
EX32: Swim 3H 25
EX38: Gt T 2B 30
PL8: Yeal 2B 150
PL12: Car 1A 130
PL19: Tavi 4J 59
PL21: Modb 6F 147
PL21: Moor 3C 146
TQ2: Torq 1B 116
TQ7: W Cha 7J 157
TQ8: Salc 3D 158
Church Lea PL19: Whitc 7K 59
Church Mdw. EX20: Oke 3A 48
EX32: L'key 2B 24
EX37: High B 2B 32
PL21: Ivy 5E 144
Church M. TQ12: Kingst 5H 105
Church Pk. PL8: New F 5J 149
PL20: Horr 2E 126
PL21: Corn 7H 129
Church Pk. Ct. PL6: Plym 2F 133
Church Pk. Rd. PL6: Plym 2F 133
PL8: New F 5J 149
PL8: Torr 3C 150
Church Path EX2: Exe 7B 6
EX3: Top 5B 74
EX4: Exe 2B 6 (5D 64)
EX8: Lymp 6G 75
EX16: Hal 6C 42
EX20: Oke 3A 48
EX31: Barn 2D 18
PL1: Dev 2F 141
TQ3: Paig 1H 119
TQ12: Ipp 6G 101
TQ12: New A 6D 104
TQ13: Ashb 4H 99
Church Path La. EX2: Heav 7K 65
Church Path Rd. EX2: Exe 2C 70
Church Path Ter. EX8: Lymp 7G 75
Church Quillet TQ9: Blacka 3B 152
Church Rd. EX2: Alph 3E 70
EX2: Exe 7B 6 (1D 70)
EX5: Silv 2H 51
EX5: Whim 6G 53
EX6: Cockw, Star 4C 96
EX8: Exmth 5C 76
EX8: Lymp 6G 75
EX10: Col R 3H 83
EX33: Georgeh 5B 14
EX34: Ilfra 3G 11
PL7: Plymp 5C 138
PL9: Plyms 5F 143
PL9: Wem 7B 148
TQ1: Torq 4D 112
TQ2: Torq 2C 112
TQ5: Chur F 3A 122
TQ6: Dartm 5D 124
TQ6: Sto F 3H 153
TQ12: E Ogw 3A 108
TQ12: New A 2F 109
TQ14: Bi'ton 3C 106
Church Row EX12: Brans 6G 85
PL21: Ugb 6E 146
Church Row La. PL5: Tam F 4H 131
Church Side EX5: Clyst H 5J 67
CHURCHSTANTON 2B 166
Church Steps *EX5: Wood 5B 78*
(off Church Stile La.)
Church Stile EX6: Exmin 2D 74
Church Stile La. EX5: Wood 5B 78
CHURCHSTOW 1B 156 (3D 175)
Churchstow Wlk. PL6: Plym 3F 137
Church St. DT7: Lym R 5K 91
DT7: Uply 3G 91
EX2: Heav 7J 65
EX5: Bradn 1C 52
EX6: Kenton 6H 95
EX6: Star 1E 96
EX7: Daw 4F 97
EX8: Exmth 6C 76
EX10: Sidb 2J 85
EX10: Sidf 1D 84
EX10: Sidm 7C 84
EX12: Axmth 3H 87
EX13: Axmin 4H 89
EX14: Hon 3F 55
EX15: Cull 4H 45
EX16: Tiv 4C 40
EX16: With 5H 33
EX17: Cred 6J 39
EX17: Morc 1C 38
EX18: Chul 6C 32
EX19: Dol 6H 31
EX20: Oke 3B 48
Church St. EX24: Colyt 5D 88
EX33: Brau 3J 15
EX34: Com M 7C 12
EX34: Ilfra 3H 11
EX36: S Mol 6C 26
PL3: Plym 7F 135
PL21: Erm 2H 147
PL21: Modb 6G 147
TQ2: Torq 1B 116
TQ3: Paig 1H 119
TQ5: Brixh 3E 122
TQ7: Kingsb 4G 157
TQ8: Salc 3C 158
TQ10: S Bre 1B 100
TQ11: B'leigh 4C 98
TQ12: Kingst 5H 105
Church Ter. EX2: Heav 5K 7 (7J 65)
EX16: Bam 2H 33
EX24: Colyt 5D 88
(off Lwr. Church St.)
CHURCHTOWN 2C 161
Churchtown PL21: Corn 7H 129
Churchtown Cl. PL21: Corn 7J 129
Church Vw. *EX6: Kenton 6J 95*
(off Kenton Hill)
EX7: Daw 4F 97
EX11: Ott M 4C 80
PL16: Lift 6B 56
PL20: Walk 2J 127
TQ12: Kingst 5H 105
(off Greenhill Rd.)
TQ13: Chud 1C 94
Church Wlk. EX38: Gt T 2B 30
EX39: Bide 4F 23
(off Buttgarden St.)
PL9: Wem 7A 148
PL21: Modb 6G 147
TQ9: Sto G 4B 120
Churchward Rd. TQ3: Paig 7H 115
Church Way PL8: Yeal 2B 150
TQ12: Coff 7K 109
TQ12: New A 3H 109
Churchway PL5: Plym 3D 134
TQ1: Torq 6E 112
Church Wells TQ7: Slap 2J 159
Churchwood Valley Holiday Cabins
PL9: Wem 6A 148
Church Yd. EX36: S Mol 6C 26
Churscombe Grn. TQ3: Marl 4E 114
Churscombe Pk. TQ3: Marl 4D 114
Churscombe Rd. TQ3: Marl 4D 114
Churston B'way. TQ4: Broads 1H 121
Churston Cl. TQ5: Galm 3J 121
CHURSTON FERRERS 3A 122 (2B 176)
Churston Go-Karts 3K 121
Churston Golf Course 2J 121
Churston Ri. EX12: Seat 4C 86
Churston Rd. TQ5: Chur F 4A 122
Churston Station
Dartmouth Steam Railway 3J 121
Churston Way TQ5: Brixh 4C 122
Chute St. EX1: Exe 2H 7 (5G 65)
Cinders La. TQ6: Sto F 2H 153
Cintra Ter. EX39: Bide 1F 23
Cistern Mdw. *TQ6: Dartm 6E 124*
(off Victoria Rd.)
Cistern St. TQ9: Tot 6D 102
Citadel Hill PL1: Plym 7E 8 (4J 141)
Citadel Ope PL1: Plym 6F 9
Citadel Rd. PL1: Plym 6B 8 (3H 141)
Citadel Rd. E. PL1: Plym 6E 8 (3K 141)
City Arc. EX4: Exe 5D 6
City Bank EX1: Exe 4D 6
City Bus. Pk. PL3: Plym 7F 135
City Ind. Est. EX2: Exe 7E 6 (1F 71)
City Market 4C 8 (2H 141)
Claddon La. TQ1: Maid 1C 112
Clampet La. *TQ14: Teignm 5J 107*
(off Fore St.)
Clampitt Cl. TQ12: Ipp 7H 101
Clampitt Rd. TQ12: Ipp 6H 101
Clampitts EX15: Cull 5G 45
Clanage Cross TQ14: Bi'ton 2A 106
Clanage St. TQ14: Bi'ton 3B 106
CLAPHAM 2C 171
Clappentail Ct. DT7: Lym R 4H 91
Clappentail La. DT7: Lym R 5H 91
Clappentail Pk. DT7: Lym R 5H 91
Clapperbrook La. EX2: Alph 4E 70
Clapper La. EX14: Com R, Hon 2F 55
Clapps La. EX11: Ott M 4C 80
EX12: Beer 7B 86
EX12: Seat 5F 87
CLAPTON 3D 167
CLAPWORTHY 1A 164
Claradon M. *TQ9: Tot 6E 102*
(off Leechwell St.)
Clara Pl. EX3: Top 5A 74
Claredale Rd. EX8: Exmth 6D 76
Clare Dr. EX16: Tiv 2F 41
Claremont Av. TQ12: Kingsk 1G 111
Claremont Fld. EX11: Ott M 5C 80
Claremont Gro. EX2: Exe 7G 7 (1G 71)
EX8: Exmth 5D 76
Claremont La. EX8: Exmth 5E 76
Claremont Pl. EX20: Hath 1H 35
Claremont St. PL1: Plym 2C 8 (1H 141)
(not continuous)
Clarence PL1: Plym 4E 140
Clarence Cotts. *EX34: Ilfra 2H 11*
(off Belvedere Rd.)
Clarence Ct. *EX8: Exmth 5C 76*
(off Meadow St.)
PL1: Plym 2G 141
Clarence Hill
TQ6: Dartm 1A 124 (6F 125)
Clarence Pl. EX4: Exe 1G 7 (5G 65)
PL1: Plym 4A 8 (2G 141)
PL2: Dev 7D 134
Clarence Rd. EX4: Exe 6A 6 (7D 64)
EX8: Exmth 5C 76
EX9: Bud S 5C 82
PL11: Torp 1A 140
Clarence St.
TQ6: Dartm 1B 124 (5F 125)
Clarendon Cl. TQ1: Torq 6B 112
Clarendon Ct. TQ1: Torq 2E 116
Clarendon La. PL2: Dev 1E 140
Clarendon Rd. TQ12: Ipp 6H 101
TQ12: New A 1E 108
Clarendon Ter. *PL2: Dev 1E 140*
(off Clarendon La.)
Clare Pl. PL4: Plym 6J 9 (3A 142)
Clare St. PL21: Ivy 5G 145
Clarke Cl. EX15: Uff 7F 43
Clarke Mead EX2: Won 1B 72
Clarkes La. EX20: Mer 7A 30
EX33: Brau 1H 15
Clarks Barn Rd. TQ7: Lodd 3G 151
Clark's Ct. EX15: Cull 4H 45
CLATWORTHY 1A 166
Claude Dix Cl. EX31: Barn 3F 19
CLAWTON 1B 168
CLAYHANGER 1A 166
CLAYHIDON 2B 166
Clay Ho. *TQ14: Teignm 4H 107*
(off Clay La.)
CLAYLAND CROSS 3E 118
Claylands Dr. TQ4: Paig 3F 119
Claylands Vw. EX14: Hon 5E 54
Clay La. EX8: Lymp 7G 75
EX15: Uff 4G 43
EX17: Cop 5B 38
EX24: Colyt 6C 88
TQ9: Darti 3C 102
TQ13: Chud, Chud K 7A 94
TQ14: Teignm 4H 107
Claymans Pathway PL21: Ivy 3E 144
Claypark Ter. TQ9: Sto G 1A 120
Claytonia Cl. PL6: Robo 1D 132
Clayton Pl. PL4: Plym 2C 142
Clayton Rd. EX4: Exe 2B 6 (5D 64)
PL4: Plym 2C 142
CLEARBROOK 1B 174
Clearbrook Av. PL5: Plym 2D 134
Cleatlands Cl. TQ4: Paig 3E 118
Cleave EX39: N'ham 7G 21
Cleaveanger La. EX17: Cold 4F 37
Cleave Cl. EX6: Ted M 7J 49
EX31: Barn 5C 18
Cleave Hill EX19: Dol 7G 31
Cleaveland Ri. TQ12: E Ogw 3C 108
Cleave Pk. EX31: Frem 6G 17
Cleave Point EX31: Barn 5D 18
Cleave Rd. EX31: Barn 5C 18
Cleaves Cl. EX5: Thor 2A 50
Cleavewood Dr. EX39: Bide 4J 23
Cleavewood Holiday Pk.
EX34: Woolc 7C 10
Cleeve, The EX15: Culm 2B 46
Cleeve Dr. PL21: Ivy 3F 145
Cleeve Gdns. PL2: Plym 3F 135
Cleland Ct. TQ14: Bi'ton 3B 106
Clementon Hill TQ7: Bigb S 3C 154
Clement Rd. PL7: Plymp 4E 138
Clennon Av. TQ4: Good 3H 119
Clennon Ct. TQ2: Torq 3C 112
Clennon Dr. TQ4: Good 3H 119
Clennon Gdns. TQ4: Good 3H 119
Clennon Hgts. TQ4: Good 3H 119
Clennon La. TQ2: Torq 3B 112
TQ4: Paig 3G 119
Clennon Pk. TQ4: Good 3H 119
Clennon Ri. TQ4: Good 3H 119
Clennon Summit TQ4: Good 3H 119
Clerk Cl. EX8: Exmth 2E 76
Cleve Ct. EX4: Exe 5B 64
Clevedon Cl. EX4: Exe 3G 65
Clevedon Pk. EX10: Sidm 5D 84
Clevedon Pk. Av. PL2: Plym 5G 135
Cleveland Ct. EX1: Exe 2H 7 (5G 65)
TQ4: Paig 2J 119
Cleveland Dr. TQ7: Bigb S 2B 154
Cleveland Gdns. EX1: Exe 2H 7
Cleveland Pl. *EX7: Daw 4H 97*
(off High St.)
EX8: Exmth 6B 76
Cleveland Rd. PL4: Plym 3K 9 (2B 142)
TQ2: Torq 7B 112
TQ4: Paig 2J 119
Clevelands Pk. EX39: N'ham 6E 20
Cleveland St. EX4: Exe 6A 6 (7D 64)
Cleveland Ter. *EX39: West H 5B 20*
(off Atlantic Way)
Cleve La. EX4: Exe 5B 64
Cleve Rd. EX4: Exe 6C 64
Cleve Ter. TQ1: Torq 1G 117
Cliff Bastin Cl. EX2: Won 1B 72
Cliff Ct. EX7: Daw 4H 97
Cliffden Cl. TQ14: Teignm 4J 107
Cliff Ho. TQ4: Paig 2K 119
Cliff M. TQ4: Paig 2K 119
Clifford Av. TQ12: Kingst 2G 105
Clifford Cl. EX1: Whip 5A 66
PL5: Plym 1D 134
TQ12: Kingst 4H 105
TQ13: Chud 1C 94
TQ14: Shal 6G 107
Clifford Dr. TQ12: Heat 2J 93
Clifford Gdns. EX17: Cred 5H 39
Clifford Rd. EX4: Exe 4J 65
Clifford St. TQ12: Kingst 4H 105
TQ13: Chud 1C 94
Cliff Pk. Av. TQ4: Good 4J 119
Cliff Pk. Ct. TQ4: Good 4J 119
Cliff Pk. Rd. TQ4: Good 5J 119
Cliff Path EX9: Bud S 7A 82
Cliff Rd. EX9: Bud S 7C 82
EX10: Sidm 7C 84
PL1: Plym 7B 8 (4H 141)
PL9: Wem 7B 148
TQ2: Torq 4A 116
TQ4: Paig 2K 119
TQ8: Salc 6A 158
TQ14: Teignm 2K 107
Cliffs, The EX7: Daw 6H 97
Cliffside Rd. TQ1: Torq 5E 112
Cliff Ter. EX9: Bud S 7C 82
CLIFTON 2C 161
Clifton Av. PL7: Plymp 2B 138
Clifton Bank TQ3: Paig 1G 119
Clifton Cl. PL7: Plymp 2B 138
TQ3: Paig 1F 119
Clifton Ct. EX1: Exe 2J 7
EX34: Ilfra 3H 11
(off High St.)
EX39: West H 6A 20
Clifton Cres. TQ3: Paig 1G 119
Clifton Gdns. TQ3: Paig 1G 119
Clifton Gro. TQ1: Torq 2F 117
TQ3: Paig 1G 119
Clifton Hill EX1: Exe 2J 7 (5H 65)
Clifton Hill Driving Range 3J 7
Clifton Hill Sports Centre & Ski Slope
3J 7 (5H 65)
Clifton Pl. EX7: Daw 4F 97
EX34: Ilfra 3H 11
(off Belvedere Rd.)
PL4: Plym 1G 9 (1K 141)
TQ8: Salc 3D 158
Clifton Ri. TQ3: Paig 1G 119
Clifton Rd. EX1: Exe 3H 7 (6G 65)
TQ3: Paig 1F 119
Clifton St. EX1: Exe 3H 7 (6G 65)
EX31: Barn 5E 18
EX39: Bide 4G 23
PL4: Plym 2G 9 (1K 141)
Clifton Ter. EX31: Barn 5D 18
EX39: N'ham 5F 21
(off Northcott Gdns.)
TQ1: Torq 2D 116
Climsland Rd. TQ4: Paig 2G 119
Clinton Av. EX4: Exe 1K 7 (4H 65)
PL4: Plym 1K 9 (1B 142)
Clinton Cl. EX9: Bud S 5B 82
Clinton Gdns. EX20: Mer 5B 30
Clinton Ri. EX12: Beer 6C 86
Clinton Rd. EX32: Barn 7G 19
Clinton Sq. EX8: Exmth 6B 76
Clinton St. EX4: Exe 6A 6 (7D 64)
Clinton Ter. EX9: Bud S 5C 82
EX20: Mer 5B 30
(off Clinton Gdns.)
EX32: Barn 6G 19
EX38: Gt T 2A 30
(off New St.)
Clipper Quay EX2: Exe 7E 6 (1F 71)
Clipper Wharf *EX8: Exmth 6A 76*
(off Shelly Rd.)
Cliston Av. EX8: Exmth 2F 77
Clittaford Rd. PL6: Plym 4K 131
Clittaford Vw. PL6: Plym 3K 131
Cliveden Rd. EX39: Bide 5J 23
Cloakham Lawn Sports Cen. 2J 89
Clobells TQ10: S Bre 2B 100
Cloister Rd. EX4: Exe 5J 65

Cloisters, The EX1: Exe 5E 6 (6F 65)
Clonway PL20: Yelv 5F 127
Clooneavin Path EX35: Lynm 2H 13
Close, The EX7: Holc 7G 97
EX12: Seat 5E 86
EX16: Tiv 2F 41
EX32: Barn 4H 19
PL20: Bere A 2C 128
TQ4: Broads 7J 119
TQ5: Brixh 3D 122
Cloutman's La. EX33: Croy 2C 14
CLOVELLY 5H 27 (1B 162)
Clovelly Apartments *EX34: Ilfra 3H 11*
(off Oxford Pk.)
Clovelly Cl. EX39: Bide 4D 22
Clovelly Court Garden 1B 162
Clovelly Court Gdns. 4G 27
Clovelly Donkeys 5H 27
Clovelly Dykes 7G 27
Clovelly Fisherman's Cottage 5H 27
Clovelly Gdns. Nth. EX39: Bide 4E 22
Clovelly Gdns. Sth. EX39: Bide 4E 22
Clovelly Ri. EX7: Daw 5G 97
TQ3: Paig 1E 118
Clovelly Rd. EX39: Bide 5A 22
PL4: Plym 7K 9 (4B 142)
Clovelly Rd. Ind. Est.
EX39: Bide 5B 22
Clovelly Vw. PL9: Hooe 5B 142
Clovelly Visitor Cen. 5G 27
Clover Av. EX4: Exe 4B 64
Cloverdale Ct. DT7: Lym R 4K 91
Clover Dr. EX15: Cull 5G 45
Clover Ri. PL6: Plym 2F 133
Clover Way EX32: Barn 5K 19
Clowance Cl. PL1: Dev 3E 140
Clowance La. PL1: Dev 3D 140
Clowance La. Flats *PL1: Dev 3D 140*
(off Clowance La.)
Clowance St. PL1: Dev 3D 140
(not continuous)
Cluden Rd. EX39: N'ham 6E 20
Cludens Cl. EX2: Alph 5E 70
Clumpit La. EX6: Kenton 4F 95
Clydesdale Ct. EX4: Exe 3D 64
Clydesdale Ho. *EX4: Exe 3D 64*
(off Clydesdale Rd.)
Clydesdale Ri. EX4: Exe 3D 64
Clydesdale Rd. EX4: Exe 3D 64
Clyde St. PL2: Plym 6E 134
Clyst Av. EX5: Broadc 2K 67
TQ5: Brixh 6C 122
Clyst Halt Av. EX2: Sow 2D 72
Clyst Hayes Ct. EX9: Bud S 6A 82
Clyst Hayes Gdns. EX9: Bud S 6A 82
Clyst Heath EX2: Sow 2C 72
CLYST HONITON 4J 67 (1D 171)
Clyst Honiton By-Pass
EX5: Clyst H 4K 67
CLYST HYDON 3A 166
Clyston Mill 5C 52
Clyst Rd. EX3: Top 7D 72
CLYST ST GEORGE 7H 73 (2D 171)
CLYST ST LAWRENCE 3A 166
CLYST ST MARY 2F 73 (1D 171)
Clystside EX5: Clyst H 4J 67
Clyst Valley Rd. EX5: Clyst M 3G 73
Coach Dr. EX39: Bide 6F 23
Coach House, The *TQ3: Paig 7J 115*
(off Steartfield Rd.)
Coach Ho. La. TQ2: Torq 2A 116
Coach Ho. M. PL9: Elb 6J 143
Coach Pl. TQ12: New A 2F 109
Coach Rd. EX5: Silv 2H 51
PL8: Noss M 7H 149
TQ12: New A 3E 108
Coach Road, The DT7: Harc B 1G 91
COAD'S GREEN 3A 168
Coastguard Cotts. EX7: Daw 4J 97
TQ1: Torq 4E 116
Coastguard Hill EX9: Bud S 7D 82
Coastguard Rd. EX9: Bud S 6D 82
Coast Vw. Holiday Pk.
TQ14: Shal 7G 107
COAT 1D 167
Coates Rd. EX2: Won 7A 66
Coaver Club 7H 7 (1G 71)
COBB 6J 91
COBBATON 1A 164
Cobbaton Combat Collection 1A 164
Cobbett Rd. PL5: Plym 2G 135
Cobb La. PL9: Plyms 6G 143
Cobblestone La. *PL1: Plym 3F 141*
(off Brownlow St.)
Cobb Rd. DT7: Lym R 6J 91
Cobb Ter. DT7: Lym R 6J 91
Cobham Cl. PL6: Plym 4D 132
Cob Mdw. EX20: Hath 2H 35
Cobourg St. PL1: Plym 3E 8 (2J 141)
COBURG 2B 94 (3C 171)
Coburg Field 7C 84
Coburg Grn. EX2: Sow 1C 72
Coburg Pl. EX15: Cull 1H 45
TQ2: Torq 2D 116
(off Warren Rd.)
Coburg Rd. EX10: Sidm 7B 84
Coburg Ter. EX10: Sidm 7B 84
EX34: Ilfra 2J 11
Cockhaven Cl. TQ14: Bi'ton 4B 106
Cockhaven Mead TQ14: Bi'ton 4B 106
Cockhaven Rd. TQ14: Bi'ton 4B 106
COCKINGTON 2J 115 (1B 176)
Cockington Cl. PL6: Plym 2F 137
Cockington Country Park 2J 115
Cockington Country Park Visitor Cen.
2J 115
Cockington Court Craft Cen. 2H 115
Cockington La. TQ2: Torq 7J 111
TQ3: Pres 5J 115
Cockington Rd. TQ3: Marl 3F 115
Cockington Wlk. PL6: Plym 2D 136
Cockles La. EX17: Cred 6J 39
Cockles Ri. EX17: Cred 6J 39
Cockpit Hill EX15: Cull 4H 45
COCKWOOD 3E 96 (2D 171)
CODDA 3A 168
CODDEN 6D 24
Coddiford Hill EX17: Cher F 1H 39
Coddiford La. EX17: Cher F 1J 39
Codrington Ct. EX1: Exe 3H 7
Codrington St. EX1: Exe 3H 7 (6G 65)
Coffins La. EX6: Exmin 3B 74
COFFINSWELL 1A 176
Coffinswell La. TQ12: Kingsk 1G 111
COFTON 4C 96
Cofton Cl. EX6: Cockw 4E 96
Cofton Hill EX6: Cockw 3E 96
Cofton Rd. EX2: Mar B 4G 71
Coftons Country Holidays
EX6: Star 4C 96
Coker Av. TQ2: Torq 1B 112
Colands Ct. EX2: Alph 5D 70
Colaton La. EX5: Thor 1B 50
COLATON RALEIGH 3J 83 (2A 172)
Colaton Ter. *EX10: Sidm 6A 84*
(off Cotmaton Rd.)
Colborne Rd. PL6: Plym 1B 136
Colcombe Rd. EX24: Colyt 4D 88
COLDEAST 3F 93 (3C 171)
Coldharbour EX15: Uff 7G 43
EX39: Bide 3F 23
TQ9: Tot 6G 103
Coldharbour Mill (Working Wool)
Industrial Mus. 7G 43
Coldharbour Rd. EX16: Tiv 5A 40
COLD NORTHCOTT 2A 168
Coldrenick St. PL5: Plym 2B 134
COLDRIDGE 3A 164
Coldstream Pl. *EX39: Bide 4E 22*
(off Clovelly Rd.)
Coldwell La. EX12: Axmth 4H 87
Coldwell La. Ter. EX12: Axmth 3H 87
COLEBROOK
Cullompton 3A 166
Plympton 3B 138
COLEBROOKE 3B 164
Colebrooke La. EX15: Cull 6F 45
Colebrook La. PL7: Plymp 2B 138
Colebrook Rd. PL5: Plym 2C 134
PL7: Plymp 3B 138
COLEFORD 3B 164
Cole La. PL21: Ivy 3H 145
(Carter Rd.)
PL21: Ivy 7F 145
(Keaton La.)
Coleman Av. TQ14: Teignm 3G 107
Coleman Cl. EX16: Tiv 3G 41
Coleman Dr. PL9: Plyms 7G 143
Cole Mdw. EX37: High B 3C 32
Cole Moore Mdw. PL19: Tavi 3H 59
Coleridge Av. PL6: Plym 1A 136
Coleridge Cl. EX8: Exmth 1E 76
Coleridge Ct. TQ2: Torq 3C 112
Coleridge Gdns.
PL4: Plym 1K 9 (1B 142)
Coleridge La. TQ7: Chil 4G 159
Coleridge Rd. EX2: Exe 1C 70
EX11: Ott M 3E 80
EX16: Tiv 4G 41
PL4: Plym 1J 9 (7A 136)
Coles Cotts. PL7: Plymp 3B 138
PL9: Down T 1C 148
Cole's Ct. TQ6: Dartm 2B 124 (6F 125)
Colesdown Hill PL9: Plyms 4H 143
Cole's La. TQ12: Kingsk 7J 109
Coles Mead EX16: Tiv 4F 41
Coles M. EX2: Exe 7A 6 (1D 70)
Coles Mill Cl. EX22: Hols 2C 34
COLESTOCKS 3A 166
Coleton Fishacre 2B 176
Colin Campbell Ct.
PL1: Plym 4C 8 (2H 141)
Colin Rd. TQ3: Pres 7J 115
Colin Tooze Sports Cen. 4A 80
Collabridge Hill EX6: Dunsf 5A 62
Collabridge La. EX6: Dunsf 6A 62
Collabridge Rd. EX6: Dunsf 5B 62
Collaford Cl. PL7: Plymp 6D 138
Collaford La. TQ6: Dartm 1A 124
Collapark TQ9: Tot 6C 102
COLLATON 7K 155 (3D 175)
Collaton Ct. TQ2: Torq 5J 111
Collaton Ho. *TQ1: Torq 2F 117*
(off Old Torwood Rd.)
Collaton M. TQ4: Coll M 3D 118
Collaton Rd. TQ2: Torq 4H 111
TQ7: Malb 6G 155
COLLATON ST MARY 3D 118 (1A 176)
Collatons Wlk. EX17: Bow 6H 37
College TQ13: Bov T 3D 92
College, The EX2: Ide 3A 70
EX11: Ott M 3C 80
College Av. EX2: Exe 5H 7 (7G 65)
PL4: Plym 6K 135
PL19: Tavi 3K 59
College Cl. EX39: West H 6B 20
College Ct. EX15: Uff 7G 43
EX31: Barn 6C 18
College Dean Cl. PL6: Plym 5D 132
College Grn. EX15: Uff 6G 43
EX39: Bide 3E 22
College La. EX2: Ide 3A 70
PL4: Plym 7K 135
College Pk. Pl. PL3: Plym 6K 135
College Rd. EX1: Exe 5H 7 (7G 65)
EX15: Cull 3H 45
EX21: Sheb 6K 29
PL2: Plym 6D 134
TQ12: New A 3E 108
College Vw. EX16: Tiv 2C 40
PL3: Plym 7K 135
College Way
TQ6: Dartm 1A 124 (5E 124)
Colleton Cl. EX8: Exmth 4E 76
Colleton Cres. EX2: Exe 6E 6 (7F 65)
Colleton Gro. EX2: Exe 7F 7 (1F 71)
Colleton Hill EX2: Exe 7E 6 (1F 71)
Colleton M. EX2: Exe 7F 7 (1F 71)
Colleton Row EX2: Exe 7F 7 (1F 71)
Colleton Way EX8: Exmth 4E 76
Collett Way TQ12: New A 1H 109
Colleybrook Cl.
TQ12: Kingst 1G 105
Colley Cres. TQ3: Paig 1G 119
Colley End Pk. TQ3: Paig 1G 119
Colley End Rd. TQ3: Paig 1E 118
Colley Pk. Rd. EX33: Brau 5J 15
Colliepriest Vw. EX16: Ashl 7B 40
Colliers Cl. PL9: Wem 6C 148
Colliers M. EX20: Oke 2B 48
Collin Cl. PL5: Plym 2C 134
Collingwood Av. PL4: Plym 3B 142
Collingwood Cl. TQ1: Torq 4E 116
TQ6: Dartm 6C 124
Collingwood Rd. PL1: Plym 1F 141
TQ4: Paig 2G 119
TQ6: Dartm 6C 124
Collingwood Vs. *PL1: Plym 1F 141*
(off Collingwood Rd.)
Collins Pk. EX9: E Bud 1D 82
Collins Rd. EX4: Exe 2G 65
TQ9: Tot 5D 102
COLLIPRIEST 7C 40
Collipriest Rd. EX16: Colli, Tiv 6C 40
COLLITON 3A 166
Colne Gdns. PL3: Plym 6C 136
Colombelles Cl. EX31: Frem 6F 17
Colonel R.H. Maclaren Memorial
2D 161
COLSCOTT 2B 162
Colston Cl. PL6: Plym 4C 132
Colston Rd. TQ11: B'leigh 5E 98
Coltishall Cl. PL5: Plym 6E 130
Coltness Rd. PL9: Elb 7J 143
Coltsfield Cl. PL6: Plym 3C 136
Columbus Cl. PL5: Plym 1B 134
Colvin Cl. EX8: Exmth 5F 77
Colway Cl. DT7: Lym R 3J 91
Colway La. DT7: Lym R 4J 91
TQ13: Chud 1D 94
COLWAY MEAD 4J 91
Colwill Rd. PL6: Plym 7F 133
Colwill Wlk. PL6: Plym 7G 133
Colwyn Ct. TQ1: Torq 1G 117
Colwyn Rd. PL11: Torp 1A 140
COLYFORD 1F 87 (1C 173)
Colyford Common Local Nature Reserve
1G 87
Colyford Rd. EX12: Seat 4F 87
Colyford Stop
Seaton Tramway 1G 87
Coly Rd. EX14: Hon 5F 55
EX24: Colyf, Colyt 6D 88 & 1G 87
COLYTON 5D 88 (1C 173)
Colyton Hill EX13: Whitf 6A 90
Colyton Sports Cen. 1E 86
Colyton Stop
Seaton Tramway 5E 88
Colyvale EX24: Colyt 7D 88
Combas La. EX33: Croy 2D 14
COMBE
Buckfastleigh 1D 175
Plymouth 2F 149
Combe Bank TQ5: Brixh 4D 122
COMBEBOW 2C 169
Combe Cl. EX13: Axmin 4H 89
Combe Down La. PL8: Noss M 6H 149
COMBE FISHACRE 1A 176
COMBE FLOREY 1B 166
COMBEINTEIGNHEAD 7A 106 (3D 171)
Combe La. PL8: Brixt 2F 149
TQ5: Galm 6H 121
COMBE MARTIN 6B 12 (2B 160)
Combe Martin Beach Holiday Pk.
EX34: Com M 5A 12
Combe Martin Mus. 5A 12
Combe Martin Wildlife & Dinosaur Pk.
2B 160
COMBE PAFFORD 4C 112
Combe Pk. EX34: Ilfra 3K 11
Combe Point 3A 176
COMBE RALEIGH 1E 54 (3B 166)
Combe Rd. TQ2: Torq 3D 112
COMBE ST NICHOLAS 2D 167
Combined Court Cen.
Exeter 5F 7 (7F 65)
Plymouth 5E 8 (3J 141)
Combley Dr. PL6: Plym 6E 132
Combourg Cl. EX8: Exmth 1H 77
COMBPYNE 1C 173
Combpyne Rd. EX13: Mus 7C 90
COMBREW 6H 17
Combrew La. EX31: Bick'n 6H 17
Comer Cl. *EX20: Exbo 6J 35*
(off High St.)
Comers La. EX34: Com M 7C 12
Comilla Cl. EX8: Exmth 1E 76
Commanders Cut *TQ6: Dartm 5E 124*
(off Chestnut Av.)
Commercial Ope PL4: Plym 6J 9
Commercial Pl. PL4: Plym 7J 9
Commercial Rd. EX2: Exe 6C 6 (7E 64)
EX7: Daw 4H 97
EX15: Uff 7G 43
EX17: Cred 6K 39
EX31: Barn 4E 18
PL4: Plym 6J 9 (3A 142)
PL20: Horr 2E 126
TQ4: Paig 1H 119
Commercial St.
PL4: Plym 6J 9 (3A 142)
Commin's Rd. EX1: Heav 1K 7 (5J 65)
Commodore Cl. EX39: West H 5D 20
Common Hill EX12: Beer 7B 86
Common La. EX12: Beer 7B 86
EX24: Colyf 2F 87
TQ12: N Whil 3D 110
Commonmarsh La. EX17: Cred 6K 39
COMMON MOOR 3A 168
Commons Hill EX6: Chri 4G 63
Commons La. EX7: Daw 3G 97
TQ14: Shal 6F 107
Commons Old Rd. TQ14: Shal 6G 107
(not continuous)
Compass Dr. PL7: Plymp 2D 138
Compass Quay EX2: Exe 7E 6 (1F 71)
Compass Sth. TQ1: Torq 3H 117
COMPTON 7D 110 (1A 176)
Compton Av. PL3: Plym 6A 136
Compton Castle 7D 110
Compton Ho. *TQ1: Torq 6E 112*
(off Palermo Rd.)
Compton Knoll Cl. PL3: Plym 5B 136
Compton Leigh PL3: Plym 5B 136
Compton Pk. Rd. PL3: Plym 6A 136
Compton Pl. TQ1: Torq 4D 112
Compton Va. PL3: Plym 6B 136
Comyn Hill EX34: Ilfra 4K 11
Concorde Dr. EX32: Barn 3H 19
Concorde Rd. EX8: Exmth 3G 77
Condor Dr. TQ2: Torq 3K 111
Condor Way TQ2: Torq 3K 111
Conduit La. *EX39: Bide 3F 23*
(off The Quay)
Conduit Sq. TQ13: Chud 1C 94
Coney Av. EX32: Barn 6G 19
Coney Ct. EX2: Exe 7D 6
Coney Pk. La. EX34: Com M 7C 12
CONGDON'S SHOP 3A 168
Congella Rd. TQ1: Torq 7E 112
Congram's Cl. EX32: Barn 6G 19
Congreve Gdns. PL5: Plym 2H 135
Conifer Cl. EX15: Cull 2H 45
Conifer M. EX2: Sow 2C 72
Conifers, The TQ2: Torq 2D 112
TQ13: Bov T 7B 92
Conigar Cl. EX15: Hemy 2F 47
Conigar La. EX15: Hemy 3F 47

Coniston Cl.—Coxs Steps

Coniston Cl. TQ5: Brixh 6C **122**
Coniston Ct. TQ4: Paig 3G **119**
Coniston Gdns. PL6: Plym 6A **132**
Coniston Rd. TQ12: E Ogw 4C **102**
Connaught Av. PL4: Plym 7K **135**
Connaught Cl. EX10: Sidm 6B **84**
Connaught La. PL4: Plym 7K **135**
Connaught Pl. *EX32: Barn 4E 18*
(off Silver St.)
Connaught Rd. EX10: Sidm 6B **84**
Conniford La. TQ12: Ipp 7H **101**
Conqueror Dr. PL5: Plym 2K **135**
Conrad Av. EX4: Whip 4A **66**
Conrad Rd. PL5: Plym 2H **135**
Consort Cl. PL3: Plym 4K **135**
Constable Cl. *PL5: Plym 1J 135*
(off Cowley Rd.)
Constance Pl. PL1: Plym . . .3A **8** (2G **141**)
Constantine Cl. EX12: Seat 4D **86**
Constantine Ho. EX4: Exe 2D **6**
Constantine St. PL4: Plym . . .4G **9** (2K **141**)
Constitution Hill EX32: Barn 4G **19**
Contour Hgts. TQ6: Kingsw 6G **125**
Convent Cl. EX32: Barn 7H **19**
Convent Flds. EX10: Sidm 6A **84**
Convent Rd. EX10: Sidm 5A **84**
Conway Ct. EX1: Exe 5G **7** (7G **65**)
Conway Cres. TQ4: Paig 2G **119**
Conway Gdns. PL2: Plym 4G **135**
Conway Rd. TQ4: Paig 2H **119**
Conybeare Cl. EX4: Exe 5A **66**
Conybeare Dr. EX39: N'ham 6D **20**
Conyngham Ct. PL6: Plym 3B **136**
Cooban Ct. PL6: Plym 3B **136**
COOKBURY 3C **163**
COOKBURY WICK 3B **162**
Cooke Dr. TQ12: Ipp 6J **101**
Cooks Cl. TQ12: Kingst 4J **105**
TQ13: Ashb 3J **99**
Cooks Ct. EX16: Tiv 4D **40**
Cooks Cross EX36: S Mol 7C **26**
Cooks La. EX13: Ray H 1A **90**
Cooks Mead DT7: Uply 2F **91**
Cooksons Rd. EX6: Star 1D **96**
Cookworthy Rd. PL2: Plym 5E **134**
TQ7: Kingsb 4F **157**
Coolings, The EX2: Exe 7E **6**
COOMBE
Bude 2A **162**
Sidmouth 1B **172**
Teignmouth 2G **107** (3D **171**)
Coombe, The TQ5: Galm 3H **121**
TQ6: Dartm 5F **125**
Coombe Av. TQ14: Teignm 4G **107**
Coombe Ball Hill EX16: With 6F **33**
Coombe Cl. EX14: Hon 5F **55**
TQ6: Dartm 1A **124** (5F **125**)
TQ13: Bov T 4D **92**
Coombe Cross TQ13: Bov T 4D **92**
Coombe Dean Sports Cen. 6H **143**
Coombe Dr. PL12: Car 1A **130**
Coombefield La. EX13: Axmin 4H **89**
Coombe Hayes EX10: Sidm 2C **84**
Coombe Ho. La. TQ9: Aish 5A **118**
COOMBELAKE 1A **80**
Coombe La. EX13: Axmin 4H **89**
PL5: Tam F 4H **131**
PL12: Car 1A **130**
TQ2: Torq 4C **112**
TQ13: Bov T 4D **92**
TQ14: Teignm 2G **107**
Coombe Mdw. TQ13: Bov T 4D **92**
Coombe Mdws. TQ7: Chil 6F **159**
Coombe Orchard EX12: Axmth 4J **87**
Coombe Pk. Cotts. TQ1: Torq 4C **112**
Coombe Pk. La. PL5: Plym 7F **131**
Coombe Pk. La. Sth. PL5: Plym . . .7F **131**
Coombe Pk. Rd. TQ14: Teignm 3G **107**
Coombe Rd. TQ3: Pres 5H **115**
TQ6: Dartm 5F **125**
TQ14: Shal 6D **106**
Coombes, The EX31: Roun 7K **17**
Coombesend Rd. TQ12: Kingst 4J **105**
(not continuous)
Coombesend Rd. E.
TQ12: Kingst 4K **105**
Coombeshead Rd. TQ12: New A . . .7C **104**
Coombe Shute TQ9: Sto G 4B **120**
Coombe St. DT7: Lym R 5K **91**
EX1: Exe 5E **6** (7F **65**)
Coombe Ter. EX12: Axmth 4J **87**
Coombe Va. EX10: Tip J 1K **81**
Coombe Va. Rd. TQ14: Teignm 3G **107**
Coombe Vw. *PL2: Plym 4D 134*
(off Ainslie Ter.)
TQ14: Teignm 2F **107**
Coombe Way PL5: Plym 2E **134**
TQ14: Bi'ton 2C **106**
Coopers Ct. EX16: Tiv 5D **40**
Coopers Dray EX5: Whim 5G **53**
Coopers Dr. EX31: Roun 7A **18**
Coopers Hill EX19: Wink 2C **36**
Cooper St. EX39: Bide 3F **23**
Coot Hide EX16: Sam P 2B **42**
Copland La. TQ9: Tot 4B **102**
Copland Mdws. TQ9: Tot 5C **102**
Copleston Rd. PL6: Plym 5J **131**
Copley Cl. TQ3: Paig 1F **119**
Copley Dr. EX31: Barn 6C **18**
Coppard Mdws. PL7: Plymp 5J **137**
COPPATHORNE 3A **162**
Copper Beech Way PL6: Plym 3D **132**
Copper Cl. EX39: Wools 2B **28**
Copperfield Cl. EX8: Exmth 3G **77**
Copperfields PL20: Horr 2D **126**
Coppers Pk. PL6: Plym 3F **133**
Copperwood Cl. TQ13: Ashb 4G **99**
Copp Hill La. EX9: Bud S 5C **82**
Coppice, The EX7: Daw 6G **97**
PL21: Ivy 5E **144**
Coppice Cl. EX13: Ray H 2B **90**
EX31: Frem 5F **17**
EX32: Barn 6K **19**
Coppice Gdns. PL5: Plym 1K **135**
Coppice Ga. EX32: Barn 6H **19**
Coppice Wood Dr. PL6: Plym 2D **132**
Coppledown Gdns. EX9: Bud S 5A **82**
COPPLESTONE 6D **38** (3B **164**)
Copplestone Dr. EX4: Exe 3D **64**
Copplestone La. EX10: Col R 2G **83**
Copplestone Rd. EX9: Bud S 6C **82**
Copplestone Station (Rail) 5C **38**
Copp Path *EX7: Daw 5F 97*
(off Taylor Cl.)
Copp's Cl. EX39: Bide 2E **22**
Copse, The EX2: Cou W 6B **72**
EX8: Exmth 2G **77**
EX10: New P 5H **81**
EX20: Oke 2D **48**
EX31: Roun 6A **18**
TQ7: Chil 6G **159**
TQ9: Tot 5A **102**
TQ12: New A 2K **109**
Copse Cl. PL7: Plymp 5A **138**
Copseclose La. EX5: Cranb 3B **68**
Copse Rd. PL7: Plymp 5A **138**
Copsey La. TQ12: Den 2J **101**
Copthorne Gdns. PL9: Plyms 7G **143**
Copythorne Cl. TQ5: Brixh 4C **122**
Copythorne Pk. TQ5: Brixh 4C **122**
Copythorne Rd.
TQ5: Brixh, Chur F 3A **122**
Coral Av. EX39: West H 5C **20**
Coram Av. DT7: Lym R 6J **91**
Coram Ct. DT7: Lym R 5J **91**
Cordery Rd. EX2: Exe 2C **70**
Corea Ter. PL1: Dev 2F **141**
Corefields EX10: Sidf 2C **84**
Core Hill Rd. EX10: Sidb, Stow 1A **84**
EX10: Sidm 3B **84**
Core Hill Wood Nature Reserve 1B **84**
Coreway EX10: Sidf 2C **84**
Coreway Cl. EX10: Sidf 2B **84**
CORFE .2C **167**
Corfe Av. PL3: Plym 4A **136**
Corfe Cl. PL21: Ivy 5H **145**
Corfe Cres. TQ2: Torq 5B **112**
Corilhead Rd. EX33: Brau 2J **15**
Coringdean Cl. PL6: Plym 4C **132**
Coriolis Way Nth. EX1: Sow 5C **66**
Coriolis Way Sth. EX1: Sow 6C **66**
Cormelles Ct. EX34: Com M 7C **12**
Cormorant Cl. TQ2: Torq 2K **111**
Cornacre Cl. TQ2: Torq 6J **111**
Cornacre Rd. TQ2: Torq 7J **111**
Cornborough Rd. EX39: West H 6A **20**
Corner Brake PL6: Plym 3E **132**
Corner Cl. EX17: Morc 1B **38**
Corner La. EX16: Hal 6D **42**
EX34: Com M 7C **12**
Cornerstone *TQ9: Tot 6E 102*
(off Warland)
Corn Exchange
Exeter . . . .**5D 6 (7E 64)**
Cornfield Gdns. PL7: Plymp 2E **138**
Cornfield Grn. *TQ2: Torq 3D 112*
(off Bellrock Cl.)
Cornflower Cl. EX15: Will 3E **44**
EX31: Roun 6A **18**
Cornflower Hill EX4: Exe 4A **64**
Cornhill EX11: Ott M 3C **80**
EX15: Hemy 3F **47**
Cornlands EX16: Sam P 1B **42**
Cornmarket St. EX38: Gt T 2C **30**
Cornmill Cres. EX2: Alph 4D **70**
Corn Pk. TQ10: S Bre 2B **100**
Corn Pk. Rd. TQ12: A'well 6D **108**
CORNTOWN 7H **129**
Cornwall Beach PL1: Dev 2C **140**
Cornwall St. EX4: Exe 6A **6** (7D **64**)
PL1: Dev 2C **140**
PL1: Plym 4C **8** (2H **141**)
(not continuous)
PL20: Bere A 2C **128**
Cornwall St. Flats *PL1: Dev 2C 140*
(off Cornwall St.)
CORNWOOD 6J **129** (2C **175**)
Cornwood Rd. PL7: Plymp 5E **138**
PL21: Ivy 4E **144**
CORNWORTHY 2A **176**
Cornworthy Cl. PL2: Plym 4F **135**
Coronation Av. EX7: Daw 5G **97**
Coronation Cotts. PL11: Torp 1A **140**
Coronation Cres. EX15: Uff 6G **43**
Coronation Pl. EX21: Sheb 6J **29**
PL5: Plym 3D **134**
Coronation Rd. EX2: Won 1K **71**
EX39: Bide 4E **22**
TQ7: Kingsb 4G **157**
TQ8: Salc 3C **158**
TQ9: Tot 5E **102**
TQ12: Kingst 4H **105**
TQ12: New A 1D **108**
Coronation St. EX32: Barn 3E **18**
TQ14: Shal 6G **107**
Coronation Ter. EX6: Star 1E **96**
EX34: Ilfra 2J **11**
Corondale Rd. PL2: Plym 4G **135**
Coronet Cl. EX2: Sow 2C **72**
Corporation Cres. *EX32: Barn 7G 19*
(off Corporation Ter.)
Corporation Rd. PL2: Plym 4J **135**
Corporation St. EX32: Barn 6G **19**
Corporation Ter. EX32: Barn 6G **19**
Corsham Cl. PL6: Plym 4C **132**
Corsham Rd. TQ4: Paig 2G **119**
Cory Ct. PL9: Wem 5D **148**
CORYTON 2C **169**
Coryton Cl. EX7: Daw 4G **97**
Coryton La. EX13: Kilm 1B **88**
Cosdon Pl. PL6: Plym 2A **136**
Costly St. PL21: Ivy 4H **145**
Cosway Rd. EX16: Tiv 3D **40**
Cotehele Av. PL2: Plym 6E **134**
PL4: Plym 5K **9** (3B **142**)
Cotehele Dr. TQ3: Paig 7D **114**
Cotfield Cl. EX14: Hon 2G **55**
Cotfield St. EX2: Exe 2F **71**
Cotford EX10: Sidb 1J **85**
Cotford Cl. EX10: Sidb 1J **85**
Cotford Rd. EX10: Sidb 2J **85**
COTFORD ST LUKE 1B **166**
COTHELSTONE 1B **166**
Cot Hill PL7: Plymp 6J **137**
Cot Hill Cl. PL7: Plymp 5H **137**
Cot Hill Dr. PL7: Plymp 6J **137**
Cot Hill Trad. Est. PL7: Plymp 5H **137**
Cotlands EX10: Sidm 7A **84**
COTLEIGH 3C **167**
Cot Mnr. *EX32: Barn 6G 19*
(off Landkey Rd.)
COTMATON 6A **84**
Cotmaton Rd. EX10: Sidm 7A **84**
Cotmore Cl. TQ5: Brixh 6C **122**
TQ7: Chil 6G **159**
Cotmore Way TQ7: Chil 6G **159**
Cotswold Cl. TQ2: Torq 3K **115**
COTT 3B **102** (1D **175**)
Cottage Cl. EX33: Know 1K **15**
Cottage Homes *EX36: S Mol 7D 26*
(off Alswear New Rd.)
Cottage M. PL7: Plymp 5B **138**
Cottage Rd. EX16: Tiv 3B **40**
Cotterell Rd. EX5: Broadc 2K **67**
Cotters Cl. EX15: Kent 6B **46**
Cottey Brook EX16: Tiv 5B **40**
Cottey Cres. EX4: Whip 2K **65**
COTTEYLANDS 5B **40** (2D **165**)
Cottey Mdw. TQ12: Kingst 5H **105**
Cottingham Cres. EX39: Bide 2E **22**
Cottington Ct. EX10: Sidm 6B **84**
Cottington Mead EX10: Sidm 6B **84**
Cottisbourne TQ13: Chag 2H **61**
Cott La. EX33: Croy 3C **14**
TQ9: Darti 3B **102**
Cottlass La. PL21: Modb 7F **147**
Cottles La. EX5: Wood 4C **78**
Cotton Cl. PL7: Plymp 5C **138**
Cott Rd. TQ9: Darti 2B **102**
COTTS .1A **174**
Couches La. EX5: Wood 6C **78**
COUCHILL 5C **86**
Couchill Dr. EX12: Seat 4D **86**
Couchill La. EX12: Seat 4D **86**
Coulsdon Rd. EX10: Sidm 4C **84**
Council La. EX5: Broadc . . .7E **52** & 2A **68**
Countess Pl. EX16: Tiv 3E **40**
COUNTESS WEAR 5A **72**
Countess Wear Rd. EX2: Cou W 4K **71**
Counties Cres. EX6: Star 2E **96**
COUNTISBURY 2D **161**
Countisbury 1D **161**
Countisbury Cliffs 1D **161**
Countisbury Hill EX35: Lynm 2H **13**
Countryside Mus. 5F **83**
County Cl. PL7: Plymp 4D **138**
County Court
Barnstaple **4D 18**
Torquay & Newton Abbot **4A 112**
Couper Mdws. EX2: Sow 2C **72**
Court, The EX6: Dunsf 6C **62**
PL6: Plym 3D **132**
Court Barton TQ7: S Hui 1K **155**
Court Barton Hill EX12: Beer 6B **86**
Court Barton La. EX5: New C 7D **50**
Court Barton M. PL19: Lam 5D **58**
Court Dr. EX15: Cull 2H **45**
Courtenay EX14: Hon 4D **54**
Courtenay Cl. EX6: Star 1D **96**
EX24: Colyt 7D **88**
Courtenay Dr. EX24: Colyt 7D **88**
Courtenay Gdns. EX2: Alph 5D **70**
TQ12: New A 2F **109**
Courtenay Mnr. *TQ1: Torq 2E 116*
(off Grafton Rd.)
Courtenay Pk. TQ10: S Bre 1C **100**
TQ12: New A 1G **109**
Courtenay Pl. *TQ14: Teignm 5J 107*
(off Den Promenade)
Courtenay Rd. EX2: Exe 2E **70**
EX20: Oke 4C **48**
PL19: Tavi 3H **59**
TQ4: Good 5J **119**
TQ12: New A 2E **108**
Courtenay St. PL1: Plym 5D **8** (2J **141**)
TQ8: Salc 3C **158**
TQ12: New A 1E **108**
Courtenay Ter. EX6: Star 1E **96**
TQ8: Salc 3C 158
(off Devon Rd.)
TQ13: More 7J **61**
Court Farm Barn TQ12: A'well 6E **108**
Courtfield TQ9: Tot 6H **103**
Courtfield Cl. EX11: W Hill 3H **79**
Courtfield Rd. PL3: Plym 6A **136**
Court Ga. Cl. TQ12: Ipp 7G **101**
Court Grange TQ12: A'well 6D **108**
Court Grange La. TQ12: A'well 6C **108**
Courthayes La. EX5: Thor 2B **50**
Courtis Gdns. EX17: Cred 7J **39**
Courtlage Wlk. TQ7: Kingsb 3F **157**
Courtland Cres. PL7: Plymp 2A **138**
Courtland Rd. TQ2: Torq 6H **111**
TQ3: Paig 7H **115**
Courtlands Cl. PL19: Tavi 3H **59**
Courtlands La. EX8: Exmth 7H **75**
Courtlands Rd. PL19: Tavi 3H **59**
TQ12: New A 2G **109**
Court La. EX12: Seat 4E **86**
Court M. *TQ12: New A 1E 108*
(off Wolborough St.)
Courtney Rd. EX16: Tiv 3E **40**
Court Orchard EX5: New C 6D **50**
Court Pk. TQ7: Thur 5C **154**
Court Pk. Rd. TQ7: Thur 5C **154**
Court Rd. PL8: New F 5F **149**
(not continuous)
TQ2: Torq 1J **115**
TQ12: A'well 6E **108**
Court St. TQ13: More 7G **61**
Court Vw. EX14: Dunk 7H **47**
PL8: Brixt 3G **149**
Court Wlk. EX19: Wink 2C **36**
COURTWAY 1C **167**
Court Way EX16: Sam P 2B **42**
Courtyard, The *TQ12: New A 1E 108*
(off Wolborough St.)
Cousens Cl. EX7: Daw 2J **97**
COVE 2D **165**
Coventry Cl. EX14: Fen 2G **53**
Coventry Farm Trad. Est.
TQ12: Kingsk 3G **111**
Coventry Rd. EX4: Exe 6C **64**
Coverdale Ct. *TQ3: Paig 1H 119*
(off Bishops Pl.)
Coverdale Pl. PL5: Plym 2G **135**
Coverdale Rd. EX2: Exe 2E **70**
TQ3: Paig 1H **119**
Covetts EX5: Wood 5C **78**
Cowick Ct. EX2: Exe 3D **70**
Cowick Hill EX2: Exe 2B **70**
Cowick La. EX2: Exe 1C **70**
Cowick Rd. EX2: Exe 7B **6** (1D **70**)
Cowick St. EX4: Exe 7A **6** (1C **70**)
Cow La. EX34: Ilfra 2H **11**
COWLEY 1C **64** (1D **171**)
Cowley Bri. Rd. EX4: Exe 1A **6** (1C **64**)
COWLEYMOOR 3E **40** (2D **165**)
Cowleymoor Rd. EX16: Tiv 3E **40**
Cowley Rd. PL5: Plym 7J **131**
Cownhayne La.
EX24: Colyt . . . . .5E **88** & 7E **88**
Cowpark Ter. EX39: N'ham 5E **20**
Cowper Av. EX2: Won 2H **71**
Cox's Cl. PL6: Plym 2C **136**
COXSIDE 6J **9** (4A **142**)
Coxs Steps *TQ6: Dartm 1A 124*
(off Clarence Hill)

Cox Tor Cl. PL20: Yelv 5F **127**
Cox Tor Rd. PL19: Tavi 4K **59**
Coypool (Park & Ride) 5H **137**
Coypool Rd. PL7: Plymp 5H **137**
Coysh Sq. EX3: Top 5A **74**
Crabb La. EX2: Exe 3C **70**
Crabbs Cl. PL15: St G 6C **34**
Crabshell Hgts. TQ7: Kingsb 6G **157**
CRABTREE 6E **136**
Crabtree Cl. PL3: Plym 6F **137**
Crabtree Vs. PL3: Plym 6F **137**
CRACKINGTON HAVEN 1A **168**
Crackston Cl. PL6: Plym 4C **136**
CRADDOCK 2A **166**
Craddock Cl. EX22: Hols 1C **34**
CRAFTHOLE 2A **174**
Craig Cotts. EX5: Clyst M 2G **73**
Craig Ct. EX10: Sidm 6D **84**
Craigie Dr. PL1: Plym 3A **8** (2G **141**)
Craigmore Av. PL2: Plym 6E **134**
Cramber Cl. PL6: Robo 1D **132**
    PL19: Tavi 5H **59**
Crampit La. EX39: Westl 7J **21**
Cranbourne Av.
    PL4: Plym 2K **9** (1B **142**)
CRANBROOK 3B **68** (1A **172**)
Cranbrook Castle 2B **170**
Cranbrook Rd. EX2: Won 7K **65**
Crandford Cl. EX20: Bride 3H **57**
Cranes La. EX3: E Bud 1D **82**
Cranfield PL7: Plymp 4K **137**
CRANFORD 1E **28**
Cranford EX10: Sidm 5C **84**
Cranford Av. EX8: Exmth 6E **76**
Cranford Cl. EX8: Exmth 6E **76**
Cranford Cross EX39: Cranf 1E **28**
Cranford Hill Ho. EX8: Exmth 5F **77**
Cranford Ho. EX8: Exmth 6F **77**
Cranford Rd. TQ3: Pres 5G **115**
Cranford Sports Club 6E **76**
Cranford Vw. EX8: Exmth 6E **76**
Cranishaies La. EX5: Bradn 7F **45**
Cranleigh Ter. EX34: Com M 6B **12**
                                            (off King St.)
Cranley Gdns. TQ13: Chag 2H **61**
Cranmere Ct. EX2: Matf 5G **71**
Cranmere Rd. EX20: Oke 2E **48**
    PL3: Plym 5B **136**
Cranmore Vw. EX16: Ashl 7B **40**
Crannafords Ind. Pk. TQ13: Chag 1K **61**
Crantock Ter. PL2: Plym 6F **135**
Craon Gdns. EX20: Oke 2D **48**
CRAPSTONE 6C **126** (1B **174**)
Crapstone Rd. PL20: Yelv 6E **126**
Crapstone Ter. PL20: C'stone 6C **126**
Crashaw Cl. PL5: Plym 7J **131**
Craven Av. PL4: Plym 2K **9** (1B **142**)
Crawford Gdns. EX2: Exe 2D **70**
Crawford Rd. PL1: Plym 1A **8** (1G **141**)
CRAWLEY .3C **167**
CRAZE LOWMAN 1J **41**
CREACOMBE 2C **165**
Creadly La. EX3: Top 7E **72**
Crealy Adventure Pk.
    Devon .3K **73**
Creamery Cl. PL8: Torr 3C **150**
Crease La. PL19: Tavi 5F **59**
CREDITON 6H **39** (3C **165**)
Crediton La. EX6: Cher B 1E **62**
Crediton Rd. EX5: Cow 1C **64**
    EX20: Oke 3C **48**
Crediton Station (Rail) 7K **39**
Crediton Wlk. PL6: Plym 3F **137**
CREECH HEATHFIELD 1C **167**
CREECH ST MICHAEL 1C **167**
Creedy Rd. EX17: Cred 6J **39**
    PL3: Plym 6D **136**
Creedy Vw. EX5: New C 4C **50**
Creek Rd. TQ6: Dartm 5D **124**
Creely Cl. EX5: Alph 5F **71**
Crelake Cl. PL19: Tavi 5J **59**
Crelake Ind. Est. PL19: Tavi 5H **59**
Crelake Pk. PL19: Tavi 5J **59**
Crelake Vs. PL19: Tavi 5J **59**
CREMYLL 5D **140** (2A **174**)
Cremyll Rd. PL11: Torp 2A **140**
Cremyll St. PL1: Plym 3F **141**
Crescent, The EX8: Exmth 4G **77**
    EX13: Kilm 2B **88**
    PL1: Plym 5C **8** (3H **141**)
    PL8: Brixt 2H **149**
    PL16: Lift 6B **56**
    PL20: C'stone 6C **126**
    TQ5: Brixh 5F **123**
Crescent Av. EX31: Barn 6C **18**
    PL1: Plym 6C **8** (3H **141**)
Crescent Av. M. PL1: Plym 6C **8**
Crescent Ct. TQ6: Dartm 6D **124**
                                        (off Townstal Cres.)
Crescent Gdns. PL21: Ivy 3G **145**
Crescent Mans. EX2: Exe 6G **7**
Crescent Rd. PL21: Ivy 3G **145**

Cressbrook Cl. PL6: Plym 1G **137**
Cressbrook Dr. PL6: Plym 1G **137**
Cressbrook Wlk. PL6: Plym 1F **137**
Cresswell Cl. TQ12: Kingsk 7K **109**
Crestas, The TQ1: Torq 7E **112**
Crestfield Ri. PL21: Ivy 4F **145**
Crestfields TQ6: Strete 6G **153**
                                            (off Crestway)
Crest Hill TQ11: B'leigh 4C **98**
Cresthill Rd. PL2: Plym 4G **135**
Crest Vw. TQ4: Paig 2J **119**
Crestway TQ6: Strete 6G **153**
CREWKERNE 3D **167**
Crewkerne Rd. EX13: Ray H 2B **90**
Cricket Cl. EX18: Chul 6D **32**
Cricketers, The EX13: Axmin 2H **89**
Cricketers Grn. TQ2: Torq 5A **112**
Cricketfield Cl. TQ2: Chud 1D **94**
Cricket Fld. Ct. EX9: Bud S 6C **82**
Cricket Fld. La. EX9: Bud S 6C **82**
Cricket Fld. Rd. TQ12: New A 7F **105**
Cricketfield Rd. TQ2: Torq 6A **112**
Cricket La. TQ11: B'leigh 3B **98**
CRICKET MALHERBIE 2D **167**
CRICKET ST THOMAS 3D **167**
Cricklepit La. EX1: Exe 6D **6**
                                        (off Commercial Rd.)
Cricklepit St. EX1: Exe 6D **6** (7E **64**)
Cridlake EX13: Axmin 4J **89**
CRIMCHARD 3D **167**
Crispin Rd. TQ7: Kingsb 4F **157**
Critchards EX5: Wood 6C **78**
Criterion Pl. EX8: Exmth 6C **76**
                                            (off Tower St.)
Crocken Tor Rd. EX20: Oke 3D **48**
Crocker Ct. EX2: Torq 2E **70**
Crockern Tor 3A **170**
CROCKERNWELL 1B **170**
Crockers Way PL15: St G 6C **34**
Crockwells Cl. EX6: Exmin 3C **74**
Crockwells Rd. EX6: Exmin 3D **74**
CROFORD .1B **166**
Croft, The EX20: S Zeal 3H **49**
    TQ12: E Ogw 3A **108**
Croft Chase EX4: Exe 1B **70**
Croft Cl. TQ12: E Ogw 3A **108**
Croft Ct. TQ2: Torq 5C **112**
                                            (off Abbey Rd.)
Crofters Cl. PL21: Fil 5K **145**
Croft Hill TQ2: Torq 1C **116**
Croft Ho. EX22: Hols 2C **34**
Croft Lea EX34: Berry 4C **12**
Croft Mdw. TQ12: Ipp 6H **101**
Croft Orchard TQ12: Ipp 6H **101**
Croft Pk. PL6: Plym 3D **132**
                                        (off Copper Beech Way)
Croft Rd. EX22: Hols 2C **34**
    TQ2: Torq 1C **116**
    TQ8: Salc 3C **158**
    TQ12: E Ogw 3A **108**
    TQ12: Ipp 6H **101**
Croftside EX34: Ilfra 3H **11**
Crofts Lea Pk. EX34: Ilfra 3K **11**
Croftswood Gdns. EX34: Ilfra 4K **11**
Croftswood Vs. EX34: Ilfra 3K **11**
Croftview Ter. TQ8: Salc 3C **158**
                                            (off Island St.)
Crogg La. DT7: Uply 3G **91**
Crocker's Mdw. TQ13: Bov T 3B **92**
Crokers Way TQ12: Ipp 6H **101**
Cromartie Point TQ2: Torq 4A **116**
                                        (off Livermead Hill)
Cromartie Rd. PL4: Plym 3C **142**
                                        (off Cavendish Rd.)
Cromer Cl. PL6: Plym 3B **132**
Cromer Wlk. PL6: Plym 3B **132**
Cromwell Cl. EX38: Gt T 1E **30**
Cromwell Ct. EX1: Heav 7K **65**
Cromwell Ga. PL6: Plym 3D **132**
Cromwell Pk. EX16: Tiv 6G **41**
    PL21: Modb 5J **147**
Cromwell Rd. PL4: Plym 5K **9** (3B **142**)
Cromwells Mdw. EX17: Cred 5K **39**
Cromwells Way TQ13: Bov T 3B **92**
Cromwell Ter. EX2: Won 7C **66**
                                        (off Sidmouth Rd.)
Crookeder Cl. PL9: Plyms 7H **143**
Crooklake Hill EX5: New C 7A **50**
Croppins Cl. TQ11: B'leigh 4D **98**
CROSS 2E **14**
Cross Cl. EX31: Frem 6E **16**
Crosscut Way EX14: Hon 4F **55**
Cross Farm Ct. EX32: Bish T 6B **24**
Cross Grange Trad. Est.
    TQ12: Heat 1J **93**
CROSS GREEN 2B **168**
Cross Hill PL2: Dev 7D **134**
    TQ12: C'head, Neth 7A **106**
Crossingfields Dr. EX8: Exmth 3H **77**
Crossings Cl. PL19: Mary T 1B **60**
Crosslands EX31: Barn 5B **18**
    TQ7: Thur 6C **154**

Cross La. EX10: Sidm 7C **84**
                                            (off Fore St.)
    EX34: Berry 3C **12**
    TQ8: E Port 4E **158**
Crossley Cl. TQ12: Kingst 3H **105**
Crossley Moor Rd. TQ12: Kingst 4H **105**
Crossmead EX35: Lynt 2G **13**
Cross Mdws. EX31: Roun 7K **17**
Crossmoor Vs. EX2: Exe 2A **70**
Cross Pk. EX20: S Zeal 2H **49**
    EX34: Ilfra 2H **11**
    EX37: High B 3C **32**
    PL8: Brixt 2J **149**
    PL20: Buck M 5A **126**
    TQ5: Brixh 5D **122**
Crosspark TQ9: Tot 5G **103**
Cross Pk. Av. PL6: Plym 2A **136**
Crosspark Av. TQ2: Torq 5J **111**
Crosspark Cl. EX31: Barn 2D **18**
Cross Pk. Rd. PL6: Plym 2A **136**
    PL9: Wem 6B **148**
Cross Parks EX15: Cull 5F **45**
Crossparks EX16: Ash T 7B **42**
    TQ6: Dartm 7C **124**
Cross Pk. Way PL6: Plym 2A **136**
CROSS ROADS 1C **56**
CROSS SIDE 1C **165**
Cross St. EX12: Seat 5E **86**
    EX31: Barn 4E **18**
    EX34: Com M 5A **12**
    EX35: Lynt 2G **13**
    EX39: N'ham 5E **20**
    TQ13: More 6H **61**
Cross Tree Cen. EX33: Brau 4J **15**
Cross Vw. EX2: Alph 4E **70**
    TQ11: Upp D 7B **98**
Cross Vw. Ter. EX2: Ide 3B **70**
Crossway PL7: Plymp 4K **137**
    TQ4: Good 5J **119**
Crossway Av. PL4: Plym 1C **142**
Crossway Country Caravan Pk.
    EX32: L'key 1F **25**
Crossways PL7: Spa 1J **139**
    PL9: Wem 6B **148**
    PL21: Corn 2J **129**
Crossways Shop. Cen., The
    TQ4: Paig 1H **119**
Crowbeare Mdw. EX38: Gt T 1D **30**
CROWBOROUGH 5C **14**
Crowborough La. EX33: Georgeh 5B **14**
Crowborough Rd. EX33: Georgeh 5C **14**
Crow Bri. EX15: Cull 4F **45**
                                        (not continuous)
Crowbridge Pk. EX15: Cull 5G **45**
CROWDEN 1C **169**
Crowden Cres. EX16: Tiv 5F **41**
Crowder Mdw. TQ10: S Bre 2C **100**
Crowder Pk. TQ10: S Bre 2C **100**
Crowder's Hill EX8: Exmth 1D **76**
Crow Grn. EX15: Cull 4G **45**
Crown & Anchor Way TQ3: Paig 1H **119**
Crowndale Av. PL3: Plym 5B **136**
Crowndale Rd. PL19: Tavi 7G **59**
Crown Gdns. PL6: Plym 2B **136**
CROWNHILL 2B **136**
Crown Hill EX16: Hal 5B **42**
Crownhill Ct. TQ2: Torq 7A **112**
Crownhill Cres. TQ5: Galm 3H **121**
Crownhill Fort 7A **132**
Crownhill Fort Rd. PL6: Plym 7A **132**
Crownhill Pk. TQ2: Torq 7A **112**
Crownhill Ri. TQ2: Torq 7A **112**
Crownhill Rd. PL5: Plym 7E **130**
    PL6: Plym 7H **131**
Crownley La. TQ9: Sto G 6A **118**
Crown Sq. TQ4: Shal 6G **107**
Crown Way EX2: Sow 2C **72**
Crow Pk. PL3: Plym 6A **136**
Crowther's Hill
    TQ6: Dartm 2A **124** (6F **125**)
Crow Vw. EX32: Barn 4H **19**
CROYDE 2D **14** (3A **160**)
CROYDE BAY 1B **14**
Croyde Bay Holiday Village
    EX33: Croy 3B **14**
Croyde Rd. EX33: Croy, Saun 4A **14**
Croydon Gdns. PL5: Plym 6D **130**
Crozier Rd. PL4: Plym 7A **136**
Crudges La. EX8: Exmth 5C **76**
Cruffen La. EX33: Lobb 1G **15**
CRUFT 1D **169**
CRUWYS MORCHARD 2C **165**
Crystal Cl. TQ4: Good 5J **119**
Cuckoo Down La. EX14: Hon 5H **55**
Cuckoo La. DT7: Uply 4F **91**
Cudhill Rd. TQ5: Brixh 4D **122**
CUDLIPPTOWN 2E **60** (3D **169**)
Cudmore Pk. EX16: Tiv 6G **41**
CUDWORTH 2D **167**
Cuffe Rd. PL3: Plym 7G **135**
Culbin Grn. PL6: Plym 3E **136**
Culdrose Cl. PL5: Plym 7D **130**

CULLOMPTON 4H **45** (3A **166**)
Cullompton Hill EX5: Bradn 1D **52**
CULLOMPTON SERVICE AREA 3H **45**
Culmbridge La. EX15: Hemy 3G **47**
Culm Cl. EX2: Sow 1C **72**
    EX39: Bide 3H **23**
    TQ2: Torq 5H **111**
CULM DAVY 2B **166**
Culme Cl. EX14: Dunk 7H **47**
Culme Rd. PL3: Plym 6B **136**
Culme Way EX14: Dunk 7G **47**
Culm Gro. EX2: Sow 1C **72**
Culm Haven EX15: Uff 6G **43**
Culm Lea EX15: Cull 4K **45**
CULMSTOCK 1B **46** (2B **166**)
Culmstock Rd. EX15: Hemy 2F **47**
Culm Valley Sports Cen. 5H **45**
Culm Valley Way EX15: Uff 7F **43**
CULVER 1C **171**
Culver Cl. EX5: Bradn 2D **52**
    EX16: Tiv 6F **41**
    PL6: Plym 3B **136**
Culverdale TQ9: Tot 7G **103**
Culver Gdns. EX10: Sidm 6C **84**
Culver Ho. TQ13: Chud 1C **94**
Culverland Cl. EX4: Exe 4G **65**
Culverland Rd. EX4: Exe 4G **65**
CULVERLANE 1D **175**
Culver La. TQ13: Chud 1D **94**
Culver Pk. Cl. TQ7: Kingsb 6H **157**
Culvert Rd. EX5: Sto C 6J **51**
Culver Way PL6: Plym 3A **136**
Culverwood Cl. PL7: Plymp 3F **139**
Culvery Cl. EX5: Wood 5C **78**
Culvery Grn. TQ2: Torq 5H **111**
Cumber Cl. TQ5: Brixh 3D **122**
    TQ7: Malb 6H **155**
Cumber Dr. TQ5: Brixh 3D **122**
Cumberland Cl. EX8: Exmth 3F **77**
Cumberland Dr. EX2: Sow 1C **72**
Cumberland Grn. TQ5: Brixh 3D **122**
Cumberland Rd. PL1: Dev 3E **140**
Cumberland St. PL1: Dev 2D **140**
Cumberland Way EX1: Pin 4D **66**
Cummings Cross TQ12: Live 3F **93**
Cundy Cl. PL7: Plymp 4H **137**
Cunliffe Av. PL9: Hooe 6B **142**
Cunningham Av.
    EX13: Axmin 2K **89**
Cunningham Rd. EX8: Exmth 2F **77**
    PL5: Tam F 2H **131**
Curie Mews EX2: Exe 1H **71**
CURLAND .2C **167**
CURLAND COMMON 2C **167**
Curledge St. TQ4: Paig 2H **119**
Curlew Cl. EX20: Oke 2A **48**
    TQ2: Torq 2J **111**
Curlew Dr. TQ7: W Cha 7J **157**
Curlew M. PL3: Plym 7D **136**
Curlew Way EX4: Exe 2F **65**
Currington Mdw. EX31: Bick'n 6K **17**
                                        (not continuous)
CURRY MALLET 1D **167**
CURRY RIVEL 1D **167**
Cursons Way PL21: Ivy 4E **144**
CURTISKNOWLE 2D **175**
Curtis St. PL1: Dev 3D **140**
Curve Acre EX33: Brau 5K **15**
Curwood Cres. EX16: Tiv 5C **40**
Custance Ho. EX14: Hon 3F **55**
                                            (off Queen St.)
Custom Ho. Hill TQ14: Teignm 5H **107**
Custom Ho. La.
    PL1: Plym 7B **8** (4H **141**)
Cuthbert Cl. TQ1: Torq 4C **112**
Cutliffe La. EX39: Hart 3G **27**
Cutterburrow La. EX33: Brau 5H **15**
Cutters Wharf EX8: Exmth 6A **76**
                                            (off Shelly Rd.)
CUTTIFORD'S DOOR 2D **167**
CUTTIVETT 1A **174**
Cuxton Mdws. PL20: Buck M 5A **126**
Cygnet Ind. Units EX2: Sow 7D **66**
Cygnet New Theatre 6G **7**
Cypress Cl. EX14: Hon 6C **54**
    PL7: Plymp 4F **139**
    TQ2: Torq 1C **116**
Cypress Ct. TQ4: Paig 2H **119**
                                            (off Fisher St.)
Cypress Dr. EX4: Exe 5C **64**
Cyprus Gdns. EX8: Exmth 6E **76**
                                        (not continuous)
Cyprus Rd. EX8: Exmth 6D **76**
Cyprus Ter. EX32: Barn 6G **19**

D

Dabby La. EX6: Cher B 1D **62**
Daccabridge Rd. TQ12: Kingsk 1F **111**
DACCOMBE 1A **112**
Daccombe Hill TQ12: Dacc 1A **112**

Daccombe Mill La.—Dewar Wlk.

Daccombe Mill La.
TQ12: Coff, Kingsk 1G **111**
Daddon Hill EX39: N'ham 6D **20**
Daddyhole Plain TQ1: Torq 4F **117**
Daddyhole Rd. TQ1: Torq 3E **116**
(not continuous)
Daggers Copse TQ12: New A 1C **108**
Dagmar Rd. EX8: Exmth 6C **76**
Dagmar St. TQ14: Shal 6G **107**
Dagra La. TQ14: Shal 7D **106**
Daimonds La. TQ14: Teignm 4H **107**
DAINTON 4A **110**
Dainton Ct. TQ4: Good 5J **119**
Dainton M. TQ4: Paig 2H **119**
Dainton Park Golf Course 5K **101**
Dairy Cl. EX6: Exmin 3D **74**
Dairy Est., The EX4: Pin 4C **66**
Dairy Hill TQ2: Torq 6J **111**
Dairy La. PL1: Plym 2A **8** (1G **141**)
PL21: Ivy 4H **145**
Daison Cotts. TQ1: Torq 6C **112**
Daison Cres. TQ1: Torq 5D **112**
Daisy Links EX4: Exe 4A **64**
Dalditch La. EX9: Know . . . .1K **77** & 4A **82**
Dale Av. PL6: Plym 4D **136**
Dale Gdns. PL4: Plym 1E **8** (7J **135**)
Dale Rd. PL4: Plym 1D **8** (7J **135**)
Daleside Rd. EX4: Exe 3H **65**
Daleswood Rd. PL19: Tavi 5G **59**
Dalton Gdns. PL5: Plym 7D **130**
Dalverton Ct. TQ5: Brixh 2E **122**
DALWOOD 3C **167**
Damage Barton Caravan & Camping Site
EX34: Mort 3D **10**
Damerel Cl. PL1: Dev 2E **140**
Damson Cl. EX15: Will 4D **44**
Danby Hgts. Cl. TQ1: Torq 2G **117**
Danby La. EX8: Exmth 5C **76**
Danby Ter. EX8: Exmth 5C **76**
Dane Ct. EX39: N'ham 6F **21**
Dane Heath Bus. Pk.
TQ12: Heat 1J **93**
Danes, The 1F **13**
Daneshay EX39: N'ham 5F **21**
Danes Mead EX15: Cull 1H **45**
Dane's Rd. EX4: Exe 1D **6** (5E **64**)
Danesway EX4: Pin 2D **66**
Danes Wood 1D **171**
Danum Dr. PL7: Plymp 6E **138**
Danvers Rd. TQ2: Torq 3B **112**
Daphne Cl. TQ1: Torq 2F **117**
D'arcy Ct. TQ12: New A 7F **105**
Dares Orchard EX24: Colyf 1F **87**
DARITE .3A **168**
Darkey La. EX20: Oke 4A **48**
PL16: Lift 6A **56**
Darklake Cl. PL6: Plym 5F **133**
Darklake La. PL6: Plym 2E **132**
Darklake Vw. PL6: Plym 5E **132**
Dark La. EX5: Thor 2A **50**
EX9: Bud S 6B **82**
EX10: Sidm 4A **84**
EX31: Barn 2E **18**
PL21: Modb 5G **147**
Dark St. La. PL7: Plymp 4B **138**
Darky La. EX18: Chaw 7C **32**
TQ7: Kingsb 1E **156**
Darnell Cl. EX10: Sidm 4C **84**
Darracombe Cres. TQ12: New A . . .6B **104**
DARRACOTT 6D **14** (3A **160**)
Darracott EX38: Gt T 1D **30**
Darracotts Ct. EX39: Apple 2H **21**
Darran Cl. TQ12: Kingst 4J **105**
Darran Rd. TQ12: Kingst 4J **105**
Dart Av. TQ2: Torq 5J **111**
Dartbridge Mnr. TQ11: B'leigh 3D **98**
Dart Bri. Rd. TQ11: B'leigh 4D **98**
Dart Bus. Cen. TQ9: Darti 2B **102**
Dart Cl. EX31: Chive 1D **16**
PL3: Plym 5E **136**
Dart Hill EX16: With 4G **33**
DARTINGTON 2A **102** (1D **175**)
Dartington 2B **102**
Dartington Cl. EX38: Gt T 1D **30**
Dartington Crystal Vis. Cen. 1B **30**
Dartington Flds. EX38: Gt T 1D **30**
Dartington Hall Gdns. 1D **102**
Dartington La. TQ9: Darti 4D **102**
Dartington Wlk. EX6: Exmin 1B **74**
PL6: Plym 3F **137**
Dart Marina TQ6: Dartm 4F **125**
DARTMEET 3A **170**
Dartmeet Av. PL3: Plym 5C **136**
DARTMOOR 2D **169**
Dartmoor Caravan Pk.
PL20: C'stone 7B **126**
Dartmoor Cotts. PL7: Wot 1F **129**
Dartmoor Country Holidays
PL20: Horr 1D **126**
Dartmoor Ct. *TQ13: Bov T 4B* ***92***
(off Station Rd.)
Dartmoor National Pk. 2D **169**
Dartmoor National Pk. Info. Cen.
Haytor 3B **170**
Postbridge 3A **170**
Dartmoor Prison Mus. 5B **60**
Dartmoor Railway
Okehampton Station 5C **48**
Dartmoor Vw. EX18: Chul 6C **32**
PL4: Plym 1D **142**
Dartmoor Zoo 2B **174**
DARTMOUTH 6F **125** (2A **176**)
Dartmouth (Park & Ride) 7C **124**
Dartmouth Caravan Site
TQ6: Sto F 1H **153**
Dartmouth Castle 7H **125**
Dartmouth Ct. *TQ6: Dartm 2B* ***124***
(off Oxford St.)
Dartmouth Hill TQ6: Sto F 2H **153**
Dartmouth Leisure Cen. 7C **124**
Dartmouth Mus. 1B **124** (6F **125**)
Dartmouth Outdoor Heated Pool
. . . . .7D **124**
Dartmouth Rd.
TQ4: Broads, Good, Paig 1H **119**
TQ5: Chur F 2H **121**
TQ6: Sto F 2H **153**
TQ9: E All 6D **152**
Dartmouth Steam Railway
Churston Station 3J **121**
Goodrington Station 3J **119**
Greenway Halt Station 5G **121**
Kingswear Station 6G **125**
Paignton Station 2H **119**
Dartmouth Wlk. PL6: Plym 3F **137**
(not continuous)
Dartmouth Yacht Club 2B **124**
Darton Gro. TQ9: Sto G 4B **120**
Dart Pk. EX36: S Mol 6D **26**
Dartridge La. EX18: Chul 6A **32**
Dart Rock 4E **98**
Darts Cl. PL15: St G 6C **34**
Darts Farm Shop. Village
EX3: Clyst G 5D **74**
Dartside TQ9: Tot 4D **102**
Dartside Ct. *TQ6: Dartm 5F* ***125***
(off Clarence St.)
Dartside Quay TQ5: Galm 4G **121**
Dart Vw. Rd. TQ5: Galm 2H **121**
Dart Vs. TQ9: Tot 7E **102**
Dart Wlk. EX2: Sow 1C **72**
Darwin Ct. EX2: Exe 6F **7** (7F **65**)
TQ2: Torq 2B **112**
Darwin Cres. PL3: Plym 6E **136**
TQ2: Torq 2B **112**
Dashpers TQ5: Brixh 5D **122**
Dathan Cl. PL19: Tavi 4J **59**
Daucus Cl. PL19: Tavi 5H **59**
Davenham Cl. PL6: Plym 4C **132**
David Cl. EX33: Brau 5J **15**
PL7: Plymp 3C **138**
David Rd. TQ3: Paig 7G **115**
Davids Cl. EX10: Sidb 1H **85**
David's Hill EX33: Georgeh 5B **14**
Davids La. PL21: Fil 5A **146**
David Southgate Ct. PL1: Plym 5A **8**
DAVIDSTOW 2A **168**
Davies Av. TQ4: Good 6H **119**
Davies Cl. EX5: Silv 1H **51**
Davis Av. TQ2: Torq 7K **111**
Davis Ct. TQ12: New A 7D **104**
Davis Rd. TQ6: Dartm 6C **124**
Davy Rd. PL6: Plym 6D **132**
Dawes Cl. TQ12: E Ogw 4C **108**
Dawes La. PL9: Elb 5K **143**
DAWLISH 4H **97** (3D **171**)
Dawlish Bus. Pk. EX7: Daw 7C **96**
Dawlish Leisure Cen. 2J **97**
Dawlish Mus. 4G **97**
Dawlish Pk. Ter. EX8: Exmth 7H **75**
Dawlish Rd. EX2: Alph, Matf 4E **70**
EX2: Matf 6H **71**
EX6: Exmin 6H **71**
TQ14: Teignm 4J **107**
Dawlish Sands Holiday Pk.
EX7: Daw W 6E **96**
Dawlish Station (Rail) 4H **97**
Dawlish St. TQ14: Teignm 4J **107**
Dawlish Wlk. PL6: Plym 4F **137**
DAWLISH WARREN 7E **96** (3D **171**)
Dawlish Warren Holiday Pk.
EX7: Daw W 7E **96**
Dawlish Warren Rd.
EX6: Cockw, E'don 3E **96**
EX7: Daw W, Star 3E **96**
Dawlish Warren Station (Rail) 7E **96**
Dawn Cl. EX1: Heav 6K **65**
DAW'S HOUSE 2B **168**
Daws Mdw. TQ12: Kingst 5H **105**
Dawson Cl. PL5: Plym 2D **134**
Daymond Rd. PL5: Plym 1C **134**
Days-Pottles La. EX6: Exmin 2A **74**
Dayton Cl. PL6: Plym 1K **135**
Deacon Cl. EX2: Alph 5E **70**
Deacons Grn. PL19: Tavi 5G **59**
Deadhorse La. EX13: Mus 7B **90**
DEAN
Combe Martin 2C **161**
Lynton 2D **161**
Dean Clarke Gdns. EX2: Exe 5F **7**
DEAN CROSS 2B **160**
Dean Cross PL9: Plyms 5F **143**
Dean Cross Rd. PL9: Plyms 5F **143**
Deane Cl. EX33: Know 1K **15**
Deanery Pl. EX1: Exe 5E **6**
Deanes, The EX16: Tiv 5B **40**
Dean Hill PL9: Plyms 5F **143**
Dean Hill Rd. EX15: Will 5B **44**
Dean Pk. Rd. PL9: Plyms 5E **142**
DEAN PRIOR 1D **175**
Dean Rd. PL7: Plymp 3A **138**
Deans Cl. EX39: N'ham 5E **20**
TQ14: Bi'ton 3B **106**
Deans La. EX36: S Mol 5D **26**
Deans Mead EX10: Sidm 5B **84**
Deans Pk. EX36: S Mol 5D **26**
Dean St. EX2: Exe 6F **7** (7F **65**)
EX17: Cred 6J **39**
Debden Cl. PL5: Plym 6C **130**
De Brionne Hgts. EX20: Oke 3C **48**
De Courcy Rd. TQ8: Salc 6A **158**
Decoy Country Pk. 3F **109**
Decoy Discovery Cen. 3G **109**
Decoy Ind. Est. TQ12: New A 4G **109**
Decoy Rd. TQ12: New A 2G **109**
Deeble Cl. PL7: Plymp 2B **138**
Deep Dene Cl. TQ5: Brixh 5C **122**
Deepdene Pk. EX2: Exe 7J **7** (1H **71**)
Deep La. EX17: Cred 5H **39**
EX31: Brat F 7G **13**
PL7: Plymp 7F **139**
Deepway EX10: Sidb 2H **85**
EX16: Tiv 4F **41**
Deepway Ct. EX6: Exmin 2C **74**
Deepway Gdns. EX6: Exmin 2B **74**
Deepway La. EX2: Matf 1A **74**
(not continuous)
EX6: Exmin 2A **74**
EX12: Brans 6G **85**
Deepways EX9: Bud S 5A **82**
Deer Combe *TQ6: Sto F 1H* ***153***
(off West Pk.)
Deerhill La. EX36: S Mol 4B **26**
Deer Leap PL19: Tavi 5K **59**
Deer Pk. PL21: Ivy 4J **145**
TQ6: Sto F 1H **153**
Deer Pk. Av. TQ14: Teignm 3G **107**
Deer Pk. Cl. PL19: Tavi 4J **59**
TQ14: Teignm 3G **107**
Deer Pk. Cres. PL19: Tavi 4J **59**
Deer Pk. Dr. PL3: Plym 4D **136**
TQ14: Teignm 3G **107**
Deer Pk. La. PL19: Tavi 4J **59**
Deer Pk. Rd. EX32: Barn 7H **19**
PL19: Tavi 4J **59**
TQ6: Sto F 1H **153**
TQ12: New A 3G **109**
Deers Leap Cl. TQ3: Pres 4H **115**
Deer Valley Rd. EX22: Hols 2B **34**
Deer Wood Vw. EX32: Bish T 6B **24**
Defoe Cl. PL5: Plym 1H **135**
Delacombe Cl. PL7: Plymp 2C **138**
De-la-Hay Av. PL3: Plym . . .1A **8** (1G **141**)
De-la-Hay Vs. PL3: Plym . . .1A **8** (1G **141**)
Delamere Rd. PL6: Plym 4D **136**
Delamore Cl. PL21: Ivy 4E **144**
De La Pole Ct. *EX12: Seat 5F* ***87***
(off Fore St.)
De La Rue Way EX4: Pin 3C **66**
Delaware Gdns. PL2: Plym 4E **134**
Delderfield Gdns. EX8: Exmth 6E **76**
Delgany Dr. PL6: Plym 5B **132**
Delgany Vw. PL6: Plym 5B **132**
Delgany Vs. PL6: Plym 5B **132**
Delia Gdns. EX5: Rock 4E **68**
Delius Cres. EX2: Won 7B **66**
Dell, The PL7: Plymp 5J **137**
PL19: Tavi 3H **59**
Den, The TQ14: Teignm 5J **107**
Denbeigh Ter. EX10: Sidm 5C **84**
Den Brook Cl. TQ1: Torq 7F **113**
DENBURY 2H **101** (1A **176**)
Denbury Ct. EX2: Mar B 5G **71**
Denbury Down La. TQ12: Den 2G **101**
Denbury Grn. TQ12: Den 2H **101**
Denbury Rd. TQ12: Den, E Ogw 2J **101**
Denby Ho. TQ4: Paig 2J **119**
Den Cres. TQ14: Teignm 5J **107**
Dendy Rd. TQ4: Paig 1H **119**
Dene Cl. EX8: Exmth 3F **77**
Denes Cl. EX32: L'key 2B **24**
Denes Rd. EX32: L'key 2B **24**
Dengie Cl. PL7: Plymp 4E **138**
Denham Cl. PL5: Plym 1H **135**
Dening Ct. EX8: Exmth 4D **76**
Denise Cl. EX2: Alph 5E **70**
Denmark Rd. EX1: Exe 5G **7** (7G **65**)
EX8: Exmth 4F **77**
Denners Way EX15: Uff 6H **43**
Dennesdene Cl. EX8: Exmth 1D **76**
Dennington Hill EX32: Swim 3G **25**
Dennis Cl. PL5: Plym 4B **134**
Dennysmead Ct. *EX4: Exe 3D* ***64***
(off Glenthorne Rd.)
Den Promenade TQ14: Teignm 5J **107**
Den Rd. TQ14: Teignm 5J **107**
Denver Cl. EX3: Top 7D **72**
Denver Rd. EX3: Top 7D **72**
Denys Rd. TQ1: Torq 7E **112**
TQ9: Tot 6E **102**
Deptford Pl. PL4: Plym 2G **9** (1K **141**)
Deptford Vs. EX31: Barn 6B **18**
Derby Rd. EX32: Barn 3F **19**
PL5: Plym 6H **131**
TQ7: Kingsb 5G **157**
Derick Rd. EX16: Tiv 3B **40**
Derncleugh Gdns. EX7: Holc 7G **97**
Derrell Rd. TQ4: Paig 3G **119**
DERRIFORD 6C **132**
Derriford Bus. Pk. PL6: Plym 7B **132**
Derriford Health & Leisure Cen. . . .7D **132**
Derriford Pk. PL6: Plym 7B **132**
Derriford Rd. PL6: Plym 6B **132**
DERRIL .3B **162**
DERRITON 3A **34** (3B **162**)
Derriton Rd. EX22: Derr, Pyw 3A **34**
Derry Av. PL4: Plym 1E **8** (1J **141**)
Derry's Cross PL1: Plym 5C **8** (3H **141**)
Derwent Av. PL3: Plym 6D **136**
Derwent Rd. TQ1: Torq 6D **112**
Desborough La.
PL4: Plym 4K **9** (2B **142**)
Desborough Rd.
PL4: Plym 4J **9** (2A **142**)
De Tracey Pk. TQ13: Bov T 4C **92**
Dettingen Path *EX2: Won 2H* ***71***
(off Barrack Rd.)
Deveron Cl. PL7: Plymp 4D **138**
Devil's Cauldron 6G **57**
Devington Pk. EX6: Exmin 1B **74**
Devon Bird of Prey Centre, The . . .4J **101**
Devon Bus. Pk. EX15: Cull 3J **45**
Devon Cliffs Holiday Pk.
EX8: San B 7J **77**
Devon County Showground 2J **73**
Devoncourt TQ5: Brixh 2G **123**
Devondale Ct. EX7: Daw W 7E **96**
Devon Heath TQ13: Chud K 6A **94**
Devon Ho. Dr. TQ13: Bov T 3D **92**
Devon Ho. Flats TQ13: Bov T 3D **92**
Devonia Cl. PL7: Plymp 2B **138**
Devon M. *TQ13: Chud K 6A* ***94***
(off Devon Heath)
Devon Pl. *TQ9: Tot 6F* ***103***
(off Bridgetown)
DEVONPORT 1E **140** (2A **174**)
Devonport Column 3D **140**
Devonport Hill PL1: Dev 3E **140**
Devonport Pk. 1D **140**
Devonport Pk. PL1: Dev 2E **140**
Devonport Playhouse *2D* ***140***
(off Fore St.)
Devonport Rd. PL1: Plym 2E **140**
PL3: Plym 7F **135**
Devonport Station (Rail) 1E **140**
Devon Railway Cen. 3D **165**
Devon Rd. EX4: Exe 1K **7** (4J **65**)
TQ8: Salc 5B **158**
Devonshire Ct. EX14: Hon 5C **54**
PL11: Torp 1A **140**
Devonshire Gdns. EX20: N Taw 6C **36**
Devonshire Health & Raquets Club
. . . . .6C **132**
Devonshire Ho. PL1: Plym 5B **8**
TQ1: Torq 5E **112**
Devonshire Pk. EX39: Bide 5F **23**
Devonshire Pl. EX4: Exe 1G **7** (4G **65**)
Devonshire Ri. EX16: Tiv 5E **40**
Devonshire Rd. EX14: Hon 5B **54**
Devonshire Row PL20: Prin 6C **60**
Devonshire St. PL4: Plym 3G **9**
Devonshire Traditional Breeds Cen.
. . . . .7K **39**
Devonshire Way EX14: Hon 5D **54**
Devon Sq. TQ7: Kingsb 4F **157**
TQ12: New A 1F **109**
Devons Rd. TQ1: Torq 6E **112**
Devon Ter. PL3: Plym 7K **135**
TQ9: Tot 6F **103**
Devon Tors PL20: Yelv 6G **127**
Devon Tors Rd. PL20: Yelv 5F **127**
Devon Valley Holiday Village
TQ14: Shal 6D **106**
Devon Vw. EX7: Daw W 7E **96**
Devon Wildlife Centre & Hospital
. . . . .5C **108**
Devon Windsurf & Canoe Cen. . . .3F **109**
Dewar Wlk. PL5: Plym 1E **134**

Dewberry Dr. EX31: Roun 6A **18**
DEXBEER 3A **162**
Deyman's Hill EX16: Tiv 5D **40**
Dial St. EX19: Wink 2C **36**
Diamond Av. PL4: Plym 2H **9** (1A **142**)
Diamond Rd.
　EX2: Exe 7D **6** (1E **70**)
Diamond St. EX32: Barn 5E **18**
Diane Cl. EX8: Exmth 1F **77**
Dickens Dr. EX2: Won 2J **71**
Dickens Rd. PL5: Plym 1G **135**
Dickers Ter. TQ12: Kingst 4H **105**
Dick Hills La. EX38: Gt T 2C **30**
Dickiemoor La. PL5: Plym 1H **135**
Dick Pym Cl. EX2: Won 1B **72**
Dicna Cl. PL15: St G 6C **34**
Diddywell Cl. EX39: N'ham 4F **21**
Diddywell Rd. EX39: N'ham 5E **20**
DIDWORTHY 1C **175**
Dieppe Cl. PL1: Dev 2E **140**
　(off St Nazaire App.)
Digby (Park & Ride) 2C **72**
Digby Dr. EX2: Sow 2C **72**
Digby Gro. PL5: Plym 5E **130**
Digby Ho. EX2: Sow 2C **72**
Digby Rd. EX2: Sow 2B **72**
Digby & Sowton Station (Rail) . .1D **72**
Diggerland 6C **44**
Diggories La. EX14: Hon 3E **54**
Dillons PL8: New F 5J **149**
Dinan Way EX8: Exmth 7K **75**
Dinan Way Trad. Est. EX8: Exmth . .3H **77**
Dince Hill Cl. EX5: Whim 6H **53**
Dingle Rd. PL2: Plym 5F **135**
　PL7: Plymp 5K **137**
Dingles Fairground Heritage Cen.
　. . . . . .2C **169**
Dingwall Av. PL5: Plym 7K **131**
Dinham Cres. EX4: Exe 4B **6** (6E **64**)
Dinham M. EX4: Exe 4C **6**
Dinham Rd. EX4: Exe 4C **6** (6E **64**)
Dinnaton Golf Course 2E **144**
Dinneford St. EX5: Thor 2A **50**
DINNINGTON 2D **167**
Dinnis Cl. EX6: Ted M 7J **49**
Dinosaurland Fossil Mus. 5K **91**
DINWORTHY 2B **162**
Dipper Dr. PL19: Whitc 7K **59**
DIPPERTOWN 2C **169**
DIPTFORD 2D **175**
Diptford Cl. TQ4: Paig 4E **118**
Discovery Quay PL1: Plym 3E **8**
Discovery Wharf PL4: Plym 5G **9**
　(off North Quay)
Distine Cl. PL3: Plym 4C **136**
DITTISHAM 5C **120** (2A **176**)
Dittisham Ct. TQ6: Ditt 5C **120**
Dittisham Sailing Club 5D **120**
Dittisham Wlk. PL6: Plym 3F **137**
Ditton Cl. PL6: Plym 3B **136**
Divett Dr. TQ12: Live 4F **93**
Dixon Cl. TQ3: Paig 5E **114**
Dixon Pl. PL2: Dev 7E **134**
Dixon Ter. PL8: Torr 3B **150**
Dix's Field EX1: Exe 3F **7** (6F **65**)
DIZZARD 1A **168**
Doatshayne Cl. EX13: Mus 7D **90**
　(not continuous)
Doatshayne La. EX13: Mus 7D **90**
　(not continuous)
Dobbin Arch TQ12: Kingsk 1F **111**
Dobles Cl. EX22: Hols 1C **34**
Dobles La. EX22: Hols 1C **34**
Dobles La. Ind. Est. EX22: Hols . . .1C **34**
DOCCOMBE 2B **170**
Dockray Cl. PL6: Plym 6E **132**
Dock Rd. EX8: Exmth 6B **76**
Dockyard Station (Rail) 7D **134**
Docton Mill Gdns. 1A **162**
Doctors Rd. TQ5: Brixh 5E **122**
Doctors Steps PL8: New F 6G **149**
　(off Yealm Rd.)
Doctors Wlk. EX2: Ide 2A **70**
　(not continuous)
DODBROOKE 4H **157** (3D **175**)
Dodbrooke Ct. TQ7: Kingsb 4G **157**
DODDISCOMBSLEIGH 2C **171**
Doddridge Cl. PL9: Plyms 7G **143**
Doe Ct. EX38: Gt T 2C **30**
Doggie La. EX34: Ilfra 5B **11**
DOG VILLAGE 7D **52** (1D **171**)
Doidges Farm Cl. PL6: Plym 3C **136**
Dokkum Rd. EX17: Cred 7J **39**
Dolbeare Rd. TQ13: Ashb 3J **99**
　(not continuous)
Dolforgan Ct. EX8: Exmth 6C **76**
Dolphin Bldg. PL4: Plym . .7H **9** (4A **142**)
　PL9: Plyms 6G **143**
Dolphin Cl. EX39: N'ham 5D **20**
　TQ5: Brixh 3E **122**
　TQ14: Shal 6G **107**
　(off Albion St.)

Dolphin Ct. Rd. PL9: Plyms 6G **143**
　TQ3: Pres 5F **115**
Dolphin Cres. TQ3: Pres 5F **115**
Dolphin Ho. PL4: Plym 5G **9**
Dolphin Rd. EX12: Beer 7B **86**
Dolphin Sq. PL9: Plyms 5G **143**
Dolphin St. EX24: Colyt 5D **88**
DOLTON 6H **31** (2D **163**)
Dolton Caravan Pk. EX19: Dol 7G **31**
Dolvin Rd. PL19: Tavi 4J **59**
Domehayes Ter. EX20: Oke 3B **48**
　(off Church St.)
Dommett Cl. EX13: Axmin 2J **89**
Donkey La. PL21: Ivy 4G **145**
　PL21: Ugb 6E **146**
Donkey Sanctuary, The 2B **172**
Donn Gdns. EX39: Bide 3H **23**
Donnington Dr. PL3: Plym 4C **136**
DONYATT 2D **167**
Doone Valley 2D **161**
Doone Way EX34: Ilfra 4H **11**
Dorchester Av. PL5: Plym 6J **131**
Dorchester Gro. TQ2: Torq 4B **112**
Dorchester Way EX8: Exmth 1F **77**
Doreena Rd. PL9: Elb 5K **143**
Doriam Cl. EX4: Exe 2F **65**
Dormy Av. PL3: Plym 6A **136**
Dornafield Cl. TQ12: Two O 7A **108**
Dornafield Cl. TQ12: Ipp 6H **101**
Dornafield Dr. E. TQ12: Ipp 6H **101**
Dornafield Dr. W. TQ12: Ipp 6H **101**
Dornafield La.
　TQ12: Ipp, Two O . . .5H **101** & 7B **108**
Dornafield Rd. TQ12: Ipp 6H **101**
Dorset Av. EX4: Exe 1B **70**
Dorset Pl. EX14: Hon 3F **55**
　(off New St.)
Dorsmouth Ter. PL7: Plymp 5B **138**
Dosson Gro. TQ1: Torq 6A **112**
DOTTERY 1D **173**
Dotton Cl. EX1: Sow 6C **66**
Dotton La. EX10: New P 1J **83**
Doughy La. TQ12: Den 1H **101**
Douglas Av. EX8: Exmth 7D **76**
　TQ5: Brixh 4G **123**
Douglas Ct. EX8: Exmth 6E **76**
Douglas Dr. PL9: Plyms 6H **143**
Douglas Ho. TQ14: Teignm 4H **107**
　(off Bitton Pk. Rd.)
Douglass Rd. PL3: Plym 5D **136**
Douro Ct. PL21: Ivy 4H **145**
DOUSLAND 4K **127** (1B **174**)
Dousland Rd. PL20: Dous, Yelv . . .6G **127**
Dousland Ter. PL20: Dous 4K **127**
Dove Cl. EX14: Hon 5E **54**
　EX15: Cull 5F **45**
Dovedale Rd. PL20: Plym 4F **135**
Dove Gdns. PL3: Plym 5E **136**
Dove La. EX10: Sidm 7C **84**
Dover Rd. PL6: Plym 7F **133**
Dove Way EX2: Exe 2A **70**
Dowell St. EX14: Hon 3E **54**
Dower Ct. TQ3: Pres 6J **115**
Dower Rd. TQ1: Torq 6C **112**
DOWLAND 2D **163**
DOWLANDS 1C **173**
DOWLISH WAKE 2D **167**
Down, The PL20: Bere A 2C **128**
Downaway La. TQ12: Dacc 1A **112**
Down Cl. EX10: New P 6F **81**
Down End EX33: Croy 3B **14**
Downes Crediton Golf Course 7K **39**
Downeshead La. EX17: Cred 6J **39**
Downfield Cl. TQ5: Brixh 5C **122**
Downfield Dr. PL7: Plymp 4C **138**
Downfield Wlk. PL7: Plymp 4C **138**
Downfield Way PL7: Plymp 4C **138**
DOWNGATE
　Kelly Bray 3B **168**
　Upton Cross 3A **168**
Downgate Gdns. PL2: Plym 3J **135**
Downham Gdns. PL5: Tam F 3H **131**
Downhorne Pk. PL9: Plyms 6G **143**
Downland PL2: Dev 7F **135**
　EX33: Croy 3D **14**
Downlea PL19: Tavi 5K **59**
Down Pk. Dr. PL19: Tavi 5K **59**
Down Rd. PL7: Plymp 4F **139**
　PL19: Tavi 5J **59**
Downs, The TQ7: Thur 5B **154**
DOWN ST MARY 3B **164**
Downshead La. EX17: Cred 6K **39**
Downside Av. PL6: Plym 4D **136**
Downs Rd. EX39: Ins 3K **21**
　TQ7: Thur 5C **154**
DOWN THOMAS 1C **148** (2B **174**)
Downton Cl. PL1: Plym 2A **8** (1G **141**)
Down Vw. Rd. TQ12: Den 2H **101**
Doyle Cen., The EX8: Exmth 4G **77**
Dracaena Av. EX31: Barn 5B **18**
Dragons Hill DT7: Lym R 3K **91**
Dragon's Mead EX13: Axmin 5G **89**

Dragoon Cl. TQ12: Heat 1H **93**
Drake Av. EX2: Won 7C **66**
　TQ2: Torq 7J **111**
　TQ14: Teignm 1G **107**
Drake Cir. PL1: Plym 4F **9** (2J **141**)
　PL4: Plym 3F **9** (2K **141**)
Drake Ct. PL4: Plym 3J **9** (2A **142**)
　PL5: Plym 6D **130**
Drake Dr. TQ4: Good 5G **119**
Drake Gdns. PL19: Tavi 5J **59**
Drake La. TQ13: Bov T 4D **92**
Drake Rd. PL19: Tavi 3H **59**
　TQ8: Salc 3B **158**
　TQ12: New A 1J **109**
　TQ13: Bov T 4D **92**
Drake's Av. EX8: Exmth 4F **77**
　EX10: Sidf 2D **84**
Drakes Cl. PL6: Plym 5A **132**
Drakes Farm EX2: Ide 3B **70**
Drakes Gdns. EX8: Exmth 4F **77**
Drakes Mdw. EX17: Cher F 2H **39**
Drakes Pk. PL20: Bere A 2C **128**
Drakes Rd. EX4: Exe 7A **6** (1D **70**)
　TQ4: Paig 3E **118**
Drake's Statue 7D **8** (4J **141**)
　(off Broad St.)
Drake Vs. PL19: Tavi 5H **59**
DRAKEWALLS 3C **169**
Drake Way PL9: Plyms 5F **143**
Drapers Cl. EX34: Com M 7D **12**
Drax Gdns. PL6: Plym 3K **135**
Draycott Cl. EX2: Won 1K **71**
Dray Ct. EX8: Exmth 6C **76**
　(off Rolle Rd.)
DRAYFORD 2B **164**
Drayford La. EX16: With 6G **33**
DRAYTON 1D **167**
Drayton Rd. PL5: Plym 2H **135**
Drew Cl. EX6: Star 1D **96**
Drew's Fld. La.
　TQ3: Comp 6D **110**
DREWSTEIGNTON 1B **170**
Drew St. TQ5: Brixh 5E **122**
Dreys Cl. EX1: Exe 4K **7** (6H **65**)
DRIMPTON 3D **167**
Drina La. PL5: Plym 1D **134**
Drive, The EX7: Daw 4H **97**
　EX9: Bic 5G **83**
　PL3: Plym 4K **135**
　PL8: Holb 6D **150**
　TQ5: Brixh 6E **122**
　TQ14: Bi'ton 3A **106**
Droridge TQ9: Darti 3B **102**
Droridge La. TQ9: Darti 3A **102**
Drovers Way EX12: Seat 2E **86**
　PL21: Ivy 3E **144**
Druid Rd. TQ13: Ashb 1F **99**
Drummond Cl. PL2: Plym 4E **134**
Drummond Pl. PL1: Dev 1E **140**
Drummond Way PL20: Bere F 7B **128**
Drum Way TQ12: Heat 2J **93**
Drunken Bri. Hill PL7: Plymp 1K **143**
Drupe Farm Ct. EX10: Col R 3H **83**
Dryburgh Cres. PL2: Plym 4F **135**
Dryden Av. PL5: Plym 2H **135**
Dryden Cl. EX8: Exmth 7K **75**
Dryden Rd. EX2: Won 7K **7** (1J **71**)
Dryfield EX6: Exmin 2D **74**
Dry La. EX6: Chri 3J **63**
Ducane Wlk. PL6: Plym 2C **136**
Duchy Av. TQ3: Pres 4G **115**
Duchy Dr. TQ3: Pres 4G **115**
Duchy Gdns. TQ3: Pres 3G **115**
Duchy Pk. TQ3: Pres 4G **115**
Duchy Rd. EX14: Hon 5D **54**
Duck La. EX20: Exbo 5J **35**
Duckpool Rd. EX31: Chive 1E **16**
Ducks Orchard EX6: Exmin 3D **74**
Duckspond Cl. TQ11: B'leigh 5B **98**
Duckspond Rd. TQ11: B'leigh 5B **98**
Duckworth Rd. EX2: Exe 1D **70**
Duckworth St. PL2: Dev 7F **135**
Dudley Gdns. PL6: Plym 3C **136**
Dudley Rd. PL7: Plymp 6J **137**
Dudley Vw. EX39: West H 6A **20**
Dudley Way EX39: West H 6A **20**
Duke of Cornwall Cl. EX8: Exmth . . .3G **77**
Dukes Cl. EX9: Ott'n 6H **83**
　TQ3: Paig 1E **118**
Dukes Cres. EX8: Exmth 5H **45**
Dukes Mead EX15: Cull 5H **45**
Dukes Orchard EX5: Bradn 2C **52**
Dukes Rd. EX9: Bud S 5B **82**
　TQ9: Tot 6H **103**
Dukes Ryde, The PL9: Plyms 5G **143**
Duke St. EX15: Cull 5H **45**
　EX36: S Mol 6C **26**
　PL1: Dev 2D **140**
　PL19: Tavi 4J **59**

Duke St. TQ6: Dartm 1A **124** (6F **125**)
　TQ7: Kingsb 4F **157**
Dukes Way EX13: Axmin 5G **89**
DULFORD 3A **166**
Dulings Mdw. EX17: Cop 6D **38**
Duloe Gdns. PL2: Plym 3H **135**
DULVERTON 1D **165**
Dulverton M. TQ3: Paig 6E **114**
Dumfries Av. PL5: Plym 7J **131**
DUMPINGHILL 7K **29**
Dunboyne Ct. TQ1: Torq 5D **112**
　(off St Marychurch Rd.)
Duncannon La. TQ9: Sto G 4A **120**
Duncannon Mead TQ9: Sto G 4B **120**
Duncan St. PL1: Dev 3D **140**
DUNCHIDEOCK 2C **171**
Dunchideock Rd. EX2: Ide 5A **70**
Dunclair Pk. PL3: Plym 6E **136**
Duncombe Av. PL5: Plym 7E **130**
Duncombe St. TQ7: Kingsb 3G **157**
Dundas St. PL2: Dev 7F **135**
Dundonald St. PL2: Dev 7E **134**
Dunes, The EX39: Ins 2K **21**
Dune Vw. EX39: West H 5C **20**
Dune Vw. (Mobile Home Pk.)
　EX33: Brau 3G **15**
Dune Vw. Rd. EX33: Brau 4G **15**
DUNKESWELL 5G **47** (3B **166**)
Dunkeswell Abbey (remains of) . . .2B **166**
Dunkeswell Airfield EX14: Dunk . . .5F **47**
Dunkeswell Bus. Pk. EX14: Dunk . . .5G **47**
Dunkeswell Cl. PL2: Plym 3E **134**
Dunkeswell Memorial Mus. 5H **47**
Dunley Wlk. PL6: Plym 2D **136**
Dunmere Rd. TQ1: Torq 7D **112**
Dunmore Cl. TQ14: Shal 7H **107**
Dunmore Dr. TQ14: Shal 7H **107**
Dunnard EX10: Sidm 6B **84**
　(off All Saint's Rd.)
Dunnet Rd. PL6: Plym 4J **131**
Dunning Ct. EX14: Hon 3E **54**
Dunning Grn. EX31: Barn 6B **18**
Dunning Rd. TQ14: Teignm 2G **107**
Dunning Wlk. TQ14: Teignm 2G **107**
　(off Lake Av.)
Dunn's Hill TA21: Holc R 1H **43**
Dun Point 3A **176**
Dunraven Dr. PL6: Plym 5A **132**
Dunrich Cl. EX2: Exe 5H **7** (7G **65**)
DUNSFORD 6C **62** (2C **171**)
Dunsford Cl. EX8: Exmth 6F **77**
Dunsford Gdns. EX4: Exe 2B **70**
Dunsford Rd. EX2: Sow 2A **70**
　EX4: Exe 2A **70**
Dunsford Way EX16: Tiv 5C **40**
　(off Narrow La.)
Dunsford Wood & Bridford Wood
　. . . . . .2B **170**
Dunsgreen La. EX15: Clay 1K **47**
Dunsland House 3C **163**
Dunster Cl. PL7: Plymp 5F **139**
Dunsterville Rd. PL21: Ivy 3J **145**
Dunster Wlk. EX6: Exmin 1B **74**
DUNSTONE 2E **150** (2B **174**)
Dunstone Av. PL9: Plyms 5H **143**
Dunstone Cl. PL9: Plyms 5G **143**
　TQ3: Paig 5E **114**
Dunstone Cotts. PL8: Dunst 2E **150**
Dunstone Dr. PL9: Plyms 5G **143**
Dunstone La. PL9: Elb 5J **143**
Dunstone Pk. Rd. TQ3: Paig 5E **114**
Dunstone Ri. TQ3: Paig 5E **114**
Dunstone Rd. PL5: Plym 7E **130**
　PL9: Plyms 5G **143**
Dunstone Vw. PL9: Elb, Plyms 5H **143**
DUNTERTON 3B **168**
Duntz Hill PL16: Lift 6B **56**
Dunvegan Cl. EX4: Exe 4D **64**
Durant Cl. EX20: N Taw 6B **36**
Durban Rd. PL3: Plym 6J **135**
Durbin Cl. EX14: Hon 4G **55**
Dure La. EX36: N Mol 2D **26**
Durham Av. PL4: Plym 2K **9** (1B **142**)
Durham Cl. EX1: Whip 5B **66**
　EX8: Exmth 1F **77**
　TQ3: Pres 5H **115**
Durham Cotts. PL1: Plym 2B **8**
Durham Way EX14: Hon 5D **54**
Durleigh Rd. TQ5: Brixh 4D **122**
Durley Rd. EX12: Seat 5D **86**
Durnford St. PL1: Plym 3F **141**
Durnford St. Ope PL1: Plym 3F **141**
Durrant Cl. EX39: N'ham 7F **21**
　PL1: Dev 1D **140**
Durrant La. EX39: N'ham 7F **21**
Durris Cl. PL6: Plym 6E **132**
Durris Gdns. PL6: Plym 6E **132**
Dursley Way EX39: Bide 3D **22**
DURSTON 1C **167**
Durwent Cl. PL9: Hooe 6B **142**
DURYARD 2E **64**
Duryard Halls EX4: Exe 2D **64**

Dutch Ct. EX3: Top 6B **74**
DUTSON 2B **168**
Duxford Cl. PL5: Plym 5D **130**
Dyers Cl. EX33: Brau 4J **15**
Dyers Ct. EX2: Exe 6C **6** (7E **64**)
Dyers Mdw. EX10: Sidf 2E **84**
Dyke Grn. Farm Camp Site
EX39: High C 7G **27**
Dymond Rd. EX39: Bide 4E **22**
Dynevor Cl. PL3: Plym 4A **136**

E

Eager Way EX6: Exmin 1B **74**
Eagle Cl. PL7: Plymp 5F **139**
TQ12: Kingst 1G **105**
Eagle Cotts. EX4: Exe 5B **6** (7D **64**)
Eagle Hurst Ct. *EX10: Sidm 6B **84***
(off Cotmaton Rd.)
Eagle Pl. TQ13: More 6H **61**
Eagle Rd. PL7: Plymp 4F **139**
Eagles Nest EX2: Exe 1A **70**
Eagle Way EX2: Sow 7E **66**
Eaglewood Cl. TQ2: Torq 3J **111**
Eagle Yd. EX4: Exe 5C **6**
Ealing Cl. TQ5: Brixh 5F **123**
Earl Richards Rd. Nth. EX2: Exe 2H **71**
Earl Richards Rd. Sth. EX2: Exe 3J **71**
Earl's Acre PL3: Plym 1B **8** (7H **135**)
Earls Ct. TQ1: Torq 7B **112**
Earls Mill Rd. PL7: Plymp 3B **138**
Earls Wood Cl. PL6: Plym 7G **133**
Earls Wood Dr. PL6: Plym 7G **133**
Earlswood Dr. TQ3: Paig 7D **114**
Easewell Farm Holiday Pk.
EX34: Mort 3B **10**
EASTACOMBE 1D **163**
EASTACOTT 1A **164**
Eastacott Cross 1A **164**
Eastacott La. EX34: Woolc 6D **10**
EAST ALLINGTON 6C **152** (3D **175**)
EAST ANSTEY 1C **165**
EAST ASHLEY 2A **164**
East Av. EX1: Heav 3K **7** (6H **65**)
East Ball Hill EX39: Hart 2J **27**
Eastbourne Ter. EX39: West H 4C **20**
EAST BUCKLAND
Barnstaple 3C **161**
Thurlestone 4C **154** (3C **175**)
EAST BUDLEIGH 1D **82** (2A **172**)
E. Budleigh Rd.
EX9: Bud S, E Bud 2D **82**
(not continuous)
Eastbury Av. PL5: Plym 1F **135**
EAST BUTTERLEIGH 3D **165**
E. Challacombe La.
EX34: Com M 5D **12**
EAST CHARLETON 3D **175**
East Cliff DT7: Lym R 5K **91**
E. Cliff Cl. EX7: Daw 3H **97**
Eastcliffe Ho. TQ14: Teignm 3K **107**
E. Cliff Gdns. EX7: Daw 3H **97**
E. Cliff Rd. EX7: Daw 3H **97**
Eastcliff Wlk. TQ14: Teignm 4K **107**
East Cl. EX16: With 6J **33**
EAST COMBE 1B **166**
EAST CORNWORTHY 5A **120** (2A **176**)
Eastcote Cl. PL6: Plym 4C **132**
EASTCOTT 2A **162**
East Devon Golf Course 7A **82**
East Devon Tennis Cen. 4D **76**
EASTDON 5E **96**
EAST DOWN 2C **161**
East Dr. EX8: Exmth 3C **76**
Eastella Rd. PL20: Yelv 6G **127**
East End PL9: Plyms 4D **142**
East End Ter. TQ13: Ashb 2K **99**
Easter Ct. EX31: Roun 7A **18**
Easterdown Cl. PL9: Plyms 5G **143**
Easterfield La. TQ1: Torq 3D **112**
Easter Hill La. EX6: Star 2C **96**
Easter La. EX34: Berry 3C **12**
Easterley Ter. *EX31: Barn 6B **18***
(off Bickington Rd.)
Eastern Av. EX2: Cou W 6B **72**
EX32: Barn 5G **19**
Eastern Backway *TQ7: Kingsb 4G **157***
(off Church St.)
Eastern Esplanade TQ3: Paig 2J **119**
TQ4: Paig 2J **119**
Eastern Rd. TQ13: Ashb 3J **99**
EASTERN TOWN 7C **84**
Easterntown PL8: Holb 6D **150**
Eastern Wood Rd. PL7: Plymp 4G **139**
Easter St. EX32: Bish T 6B **24**
Eastfield EX11: W Hill 4H **79**
Eastfield Av. PL9: Hooe 6D **142**
Eastfield Cres. PL3: Plym 4B **136**
Eastfield Orchard EX15: Uff 5H **43**
Eastgate EX1: Exe 3F **7** (6F **65**)
East Gro. Rd. EX2: Exe 7G **7** (1G **71**)
East Hill EX33: Brau 4J **15**
EASTINGTON 3B **164**
Eastington La. EX17: Lap 2K **37**
Eastington Rd. EX17: Lap 1K **37**
E. John Wlk. EX1: Exe 3J **7** (6H **65**)
EAST KNOWSTONE 1C **165**
Eastlake Ope PL1: Plym 4F **9** (2K **141**)
Eastlake St. PL1: Plym 3E **8** (2J **141**)
EAST LAMBROOK 2D **167**
Eastlands EX15: Hemy 2G **47**
EAST LEIGH
Crediton 3B **164**
Modbury 2C **175**
EASTLEIGH 1C **163**
Eastleigh Cl. EX13: Kilm 2C **88**
EAST LYNG 1D **167**
East Mead EX15: Hemy 2G **47**
East Mdw. Rd. EX33: Brau 3G **15**
EAST NYNEHEAD 1B **166**
EAST OGWELL 3A **108** (3C **171**)
EASTON 2B **170**
Easton La. EX16: Sam P 2C **42**
E. Pafford Av. TQ2: Torq 3D **112**
EAST PANSON 1B **168**
East Pk. EX19: Wink 2D **36**
EX39: Wools 2B **28**
East Pk. Av. PL4: Plym 1E **8** (1J **141**)
East Pk. Cl. EX19: Wink 2D **36**
East Pk. Rd. EX32: Barn 6J **19**
EAST PORTLEMOUTH 4E **158** (3D **175**)
EAST PRAWLE 3D **175**
EAST PUTFORD 2B **162**
E. Ridge Vw. EX39: Bide 4G **23**
EAST STOWFORD 1A **164**
East St. EX10: Sidm 7C **84**
EX15: Uff 6H **43**
EX17: Cred 6J **39**
EX18: Chul 6C **32**
EX20: Oke 3B **48**
EX32: Bish T 6B **24**
EX33: Brau 4J **15**
EX36: N Mol 2C **26**
EX36: S Mol 6D **26**
EX37: Chit 5J **25**
EX38: Gt T 2C **30**
PL1: Plym 5A **8** (3G **141**)
(not continuous)
TQ2: Torq 7B **112**
TQ12: Den 2H **101**
TQ12: Ipp 6H **101**
TQ12: New A 1E **108**
TQ13: Ashb 4H **99**
TQ13: Bov T 3C **92**
East Ter. EX1: Heav 6K **65**
EX9: Bud S 6C **82**
EAST-THE-WATER 4G **23** (1C **163**)
EAST TOWN 7J **39**
E. Town La. EX6: Kenton 6H **95**
East Vw. *PL3: Plym 7F **135***
(off Ann's Pl.)
East Vw. Pl. EX16: Tiv 3E **40**
East Vw. Ter. EX39: Bide 4F **23**
EAST VILLAGE 3C **165**
East Wlk. EX12: Seat 6F **87**
East Way PL21: L Mill 5B **144**
EAST WEEK 1A **170**
E. Wonford Hill EX1: Heav 7K **65**
Eastwood Cres. TQ12: New A 7B **104**
EAST WORLINGTON 2B **164**
EAST YOULSTONE 2A **162**
Eaton Ct. TQ14: Teignm 2H **107**
Eaton Dr. EX1: Exe 3G **7** (6G **65**)
Eaton Hill Dr. *TQ6: Dartm 5E **124***
(off Flagstaff Rd.)
Eaton Ho. EX1: Exe 3G **7**
Eaton Pl. TQ4: Paig 2H **119**
Eaton Villa *EX34: Ilfra 2J **11***
(off Montpelier Rd.)
EBBERLEY HILL 2D **163**
Ebberly Lawn EX32: Barn 4F **19**
Ebberly Ter. *EX32: Barn 4F **19***
(off Bear St.)
Ebdons Ct. *EX10: Sidm 7C **84***
(off Church St.)
Ebdon Way TQ1: Torq 7B **112**
Ebenezer Rd. TQ3: Paig 2G **119**
EBFORD 6E **74** (2D **171**)
Ebford La. EX3: Ebf 5E **74**
Ebrington Rd. EX2: Exe 2E **70**
Ebrington St. PL4: Plym 4G **9** (2K **141**)
TQ7: Kingsb 4G **157**
Echo Cres. PL5: Plym 1J **135**
Eddy's La. EX32: Barn 6G **19**
Eddystone Cl. PL3: Plym 5D **136**
PL9: Hey B 4B **148**
Eddystone Ri. TQ7: Galm 2J **155**
Eddystone Rd. PL9: Down T 1C **148**
TQ7: Thur 6B **154**
Eddystone Ter. PL1: Plym 4H **141**
Eddy Thomas Wlk. PL5: Plym 6H **131**
Eden Cl. TQ5: Brixh 5E **122**
Eden Cotts. PL21: Ivy 4H **145**
Eden Gro. TQ3: Paig 7F **115**
Edenhurst Ct. *TQ1: Torq 3D **116***
(off Parkhill Rd.)
Eden Pk. TQ5: Brixh 5E **122**
Edens Ct. *TQ14: Teignm 4J **107***
(off Heywoods Rd.)
Eden Vale Rd. TQ3: Paig 6F **115**
Eden Way EX10: Col R 3J **83**
Edgar Ter. PL4: Plym 7B **136**
Edgbaston Mead EX2: Won 1B **72**
EDGCOTT 3D **161**
Edgcumbe Av. PL1: Plym 2G **141**
Edgcumbe Dr. PL19: Tavi 3H **59**
Edgcumbe Pk. Rd. PL3: Plym 5J **135**
Edgcumbe St. PL1: Plym 3F **141**
Edgcumbe Ter. PL19: Mil A 2B **58**
PL20: Bere A 2C **128**
Edgecumbe Ho. PL1: Plym 5A **8**
Edgehill Theatre 2D **22**
Edgelands La. TQ12: Ipp 7G **101**
Edgeley Rd. TQ2: Torq 3C **112**
Edgerton Pk. Rd. EX4: Exe 1F **7** (4G **65**)
EDGINSWELL 5J **111**
Edginswell Cl. TQ2: Torq 4J **111**
Edginswell La. TQ2: Torq 4H **111**
TQ12: Kingsk 2F **111**
Edinburgh Cres. EX8: Lymp 5G **75**
Edinburgh Dr. EX4: Exe 6B **64**
Edinburgh Rd. TQ5: Brixh 5F **123**
Edinburgh St. PL1: Dev 3D **140**
Edinburgh Vs. TQ1: Torq 7B **112**
EDISTONE 1A **162**
Edith Av. PL4: Plym 1B **142**
Edith St. PL5: Plym 2C **134**
Edmonds Wlk. TQ1: Torq 7B **112**
Edmonton Cl. EX4: Exe 4K **65**
Edmund St. EX2: Exe 6C **6** (7E **64**)
Edna Ter. PL4: Plym 2C **142**
Edwards Cl. PL7: Plymp 5E **138**
TQ7: Thur 6C **154**
Edwards Ct. EX2: Sow 1C **72**
Edwards Dr. EX39: West H 5D **20**
PL7: Plymp 4E **138**
Edwards Rd. PL15: St G 6C **34**
Edwin Rd. EX2: Exe 2E **70**
Effingham Cres. PL3: Plym 4J **135**
EFFORD
Crediton 3C **165**
Lower Compton 6D **136**
Efford Crematorium PL3: Plym 5D **136**
Efford Cres. PL3: Plym 5C **136**
Efford La. PL3: Plym 7C **136**
Efford Marshes Local Nature Reserve
5F **137**
Efford Pathway PL3: Plym 5D **136**
(not continuous)
Efford Rd. PL3: Plym 5C **136**
Efford Wlk. PL3: Plym 5C **136**
Egerton Cres. PL4: Plym 3K **9** (2B **142**)
Egerton Pl. PL4: Plym 3K **9** (2B **142**)
Egerton Rd. PL4: Plym 4J **9** (2A **142**)
TQ1: Torq 7E **112**
EGGBUCKLAND 3C **136** (2A **174**)
Eggbuckland Rd. PL3: Plym 5A **136**
PL6: Plym 3C **136**
EGGESFORD 2A **164**
Eggesford Rd. EX19: Wink 3C **36**
Egham Av. EX2: Exe 2G **71**
EGLOSKERRY 2A **168**
Egremont Rd. EX8: Exmth 4C **76**
Egypt La. EX1: Exe 4E **6**
EX18: Chul 6C **32**
Eight Acres Cl. PL7: Plymp 4F **139**
Elaine Cl. EX4: Whip 2K **65**
PL7: Plymp 6J **137**
Elba Cl. TQ4: Good 6J **119**
Elberry La. TQ4: Broads 1K **121**
TQ5: Chur F 4K **121**
Elbow La. PL19: Tavi 3J **59**
Elbridge Cotts. PL8: Brixt 2H **149**
ELBURTON 5K **143** (2B **174**)
Elburton Rd. PL9: Elb, Plyms 4H **143**
Elbury Cl. EX5: Broadc 6E **52**
Eldad Hill PL1: Plym 3A **8** (2G **141**)
Elderberry Way EX15: Will 3E **44**
Elder Cl. PL7: Plymp 4E **138**
Elder Gro. EX17: Cred 5K **39**
Eldern Point to Chapman Rock 1A **162**
Eldertree Gdns. EX4: Exe 1B **6** (5D **64**)
Elford Cres. PL7: Plymp 2B **138**
Elford Dr. PL9: Plyms 5D **142**
Elfordleigh Golf Course 1C **138**
Elford Pk. PL20: Yelv 6G **127**
Elgar Cl. EX2: Won 7B **66**
EX32: Barn 4H **19**
Elgin Cres. PL5: Plym 7K **131**
Elim Cl. EX10: Sidm 5C **84**
Elim Ter. PL3: Plym 6K **135**
Eliot St. PL5: Plym 3D **134**
Elizabethan Ct. *EX2: Exe 6F **7***
(off Roberts Rd.)
Elizabethan House 6F **9**
Elizabeth Av. EX4: Exe 4H **65**
TQ5: Brixh 7C **122**
Elizabeth Cl. DT7: Lym R 4K **91**
EX5: Whim 6G **53**
EX31: Barn 7C **18**
PL21: Ivy 4K **145**
Elizabeth Ct. TQ2: Torq 1B **116**
TQ9: Tot 6H **103**
Elizabeth Dr. EX31: Barn 6C **18**
Elizabeth Lea Cl. EX22: Bradw 5B **28**
Elizabeth Pl. PL4: Plym 2F **9** (1K **141**)
Elizabeth Rd. EX8: Exmth 2E **76**
EX12: Seat 3E **86**
Elizabeth Sq. TQ12: New A 2J **109**
Elizabeth Way EX12: Seat 4E **86**
Elkins Hill TQ5: Brixh 3F **123**
ELLACOMBE 7D **112**
Ellacombe Chu. Rd. TQ1: Torq 7D **112**
Ellacombe Rd. TQ1: Torq 7D **112**
Ellards Cl. EX2: Exe 2H **71**
ELLBRIDGE 1A **174**
ELLERHAYES 3D **165**
Ellerslie Ho. *TQ14: Shal 6H **107***
(off Marine Pde.)
Ellerslie Rd. EX31: Barn 6A **18**
Ellesmere TQ1: Torq 2E **116**
Ellesmere Rd. TQ1: Torq 1G **117**
Ellimore Rd. TQ13: Lust 6G **63**
Elliot Cl. EX11: Ott M 4B **80**
EX32: Barn 5H **19**
Elliot Sq. PL11: Torp 1A **140**
Elliot St. PL1: Plym 7C **8** (4H **141**)
Elliott Cl. EX4: Exe 2H **65**
Elliott Ct. TQ12: Ipp 6H **101**
Elliot Ter. PL1: Plym 7D **8**
Elliot Ter. La. PL1: Plym 7D **8** (4J **141**)
Elliott Gallery, The 1K **15**
Elliott Gro. TQ5: Brixh 4C **122**
Elliott Plain TQ11: B'leigh 4D **98**
Elliott Rd. PL4: Plym 3B **142**
Elliotts Hill EX17: Morc 1E **38**
PL8: Brixt 3H **149**
Elliott Way EX2: Sow 7C **66**
Ellwood Rd. EX8: Exmth 2F **77**
Elm Bank TQ11: B'leigh 5B **98**
Elmbank Gdns. TQ4: Paig 2G **119**
Elmbank Rd. TQ4: Paig 2G **119**
Elmbridge Gdns. EX4: Exe 4D **64**
Elmbrook EX4: Exe 1B **6** (5E **64**)
Elm Cl. EX5: Broadc 6C **52**
PL19: Tavi 6J **59**
Elm Ct. EX6: Star 1E **96**
Elm Cres. PL3: Plym 7B **136**
Elm Cft. *PL6: Plym 4E **132***
(off Elm Rd.)
Elmcroft PL2: Plym 4G **135**
Elmdale Rd. EX39: Bide 2F **23**
Elmdon Cl. EX4: Exe 3G **65**
Elm Dr. TQ12: Kingst 4H **105**
Elm Farm La. EX24: Colyf 1F **87**
Elmfield Cres. EX8: Exmth 2C **76**
Elmfield Rd. EX12: Seat 3E **86**
EX31: Bick'n 6J **17**
Elmfield Ter. *EX39: N'ham 5F **21***
(off Oxmans La.)
Elm Gro. EX8: Exmth 6B **76**
EX39: Bide 3E **22**
PL6: Plym 3C **136**
PL7: Plymp 4B **138**
TQ14: Teignm 1H **107**
Elm Gro. Av. EX3: Top 5B **74**
Elm Gro. Cl. EX7: Daw 3H **97**
Elm Gro. Dr. EX7: Daw 3H **97**
Elm Gro. Gdns. EX3: Top 5B **74**
Elm Gro. Rd. EX3: Top 7E **72**
EX4: Exe 1C **6** (5E **64**)
EX7: Daw 2H **97**
Elm Gro. Ter. EX24: Colyt 5D **88**
Elmhirst Dr. TQ9: Tot 6G **103**
Elmhurst Ct. TQ14: Teignm 4H **107**
Elm La. EX8: L'ham 5H **77**
Elmlea Av. EX31: Frem 6E **16**
El Monte Cl. TQ14: Teignm 3H **107**
Elm Orchard *EX12: Axmth 3H **87***
(off Kemp's La.)
Elmore Way EX16: Tiv 3E **40**
Elm Pk. PL10: Mill 5A **140**
TQ3: Paig 1F **119**
Elm Rd. EX8: Exmth 5E **76**
PL4: Plym 6A **136**
PL6: Plym 4E **132**
TQ5: Brixh 6C **122**
TQ12: New A 1F **109**
Elms, The EX24: Colyf 1F **87**
PL3: Plym 1F **141**
TQ13: Chud 1C **94**
ELMSCOTT 1A **162**
Elmscott Ter. *EX39: Bide 3F **23***
(off Pitt La.)
Elmside EX4: Exe 1J **7** (5H **65**)
EX9: Bud S 6C **82**
EX15: Will 5D **44**

Elmside Cl. EX4: Exe 1J **7** (5H **65**)
Elmsleigh Ct. TQ4: Paig 2H **119**
(off Elmsleigh Rd.)
Elmsleigh Pk. TQ4: Paig 2H **119**
Elmsleigh Rd. TQ4: Paig 2H **119**
Elms Mdw. EX19: Wink 3C **36**
Elm Ter. EX14: Hon 3G **55**
  EX16: Tiv 4B **40**
  EX39: Ins 4K **21**
  PL4: Plym 6A **136**
(off Elm Rd.)
Elm Tree Cl. PL8: Yeal 2B **150**
Elm Tree Pk. PL8: Yeal 2B **150**
Elm Wlk. TQ9: Tot 6G **103**
Elm Way EX10: Sidf 1C **84**
Elmwood Av. TQ12: New A 7B **104**
Elmwood Cl. PL6: Plym 5E **132**
Elmwood Cres. 3H **57** TQ7: Daw 3H **57**
Elmwood Gdns. EX24: Colyf 1F **87**
Elmwood Pk. TQ7: Lodd 2G **151**
Elphinstone Rd. PL2: Plym 4H **135**
Elsdale Rd. TQ4: Paig 3G **119**
Elsdon EX11: W Hill 4J **79**
Elsdon La. EX11: W Hill 4J **79**
ELSTON 3B **164**
ELSTONE 2A **164**
Elston La. EX17: Cop 7E **38**
Elston Mdw. EX17: Cred 6F **39**
Elston Pk. TQ7: Chur 2A **156**
Elton Rd. EX4: Exe 1K **7** (4H **65**)
Elvestone EX9: Bud S 7D **82**
(off Fore Street Hill)
Elvis Rd. EX8: Exmth 5F **77**
Elwick Gdns. PL3: Plym 6C **136**
Elwyn Rd. EX8: Exmth 5E **76**
Ely Cl. EX4: Exe 6A **64**
  EX14: Fen 1G **53**
Elysian Ct. EX36: S Mol 6D **26**
Elysian Flds. EX10: Sidm 6B **84**
Embankment, The TQ14: Shal . . .6F **107**
Embankment La. PL4: Plym 2C **142**
Embankment Rd.
  PL4: Plym 5K **9** (3B **142**)
  TQ7: Kingsb 5G **157**
Embankment Rd. La. Nth.
  PL4: Plym 2C **142**
(off Grenville Rd.)
Embassy Cinema, The
  Merlin Cinemas 2H **11**
Ember Rd. TQ8: Salc 3B **158**
Embleford Cres. TQ13: More 6H **61**
Emblett Dr. TQ12: New A 7B **104**
Emblett Hill Vw. TQ12: E Ogw . . .3C **108**
Embridge Hill TQ6: Blackp 2F **153**
Embury Cl. TQ12: Kingsk 1G **111**
Emily Gdns. PL4: Plym 1J **9** (1A **142**)
Emlyn Pl. TQ13: Bov T 4C **92**
Emmanuel Cl. EX4: Exe 5A **6** (7D **64**)
Emmanuel Rd. EX4: Exe 5A **6** (7D **64**)
Emma Pl. PL1: Plym 3F **141**
Emma Pl. Ope PL1: Plym 3F **141**
Emmasfield EX8: Exmth 5F **77**
Emmetts Pk. TQ13: Ashb 3J **99**
Emmetts Pl. TQ12: A'well 6E **108**
Emperor Way EX1: Sow 6D **66**
Empire Ct. TQ1: Torq 6C **112**
Empire Rd. TQ1: Torq 6C **112**
Empsons Cl. EX7: Daw 4F **97**
Empsons Hill EX7: Daw 4F **97**
Endeavour Ct. PL1: Plym 1F **141**
Endfield Cl. EX1: Heav 6A **66**
Endsleigh EX5: Broadc 5C **52**
Endsleigh Cres. EX5: Clyst H 5G **67**
Endsleigh Gdns.
  PL4: Plym 2F **9** (1K **141**)
Endsleigh Pk. Rd. PL3: Plym 5J **135**
Endsleigh Pl. PL4: Plym . . .2F **9** (1K **141**)
Endsleigh Pl. PL9: Plyms 5D **142**
Endsleigh Vw. PL21: Ivy 4E **144**
Energic Ter. EX15: Cull 3H **45**
Enfield Cl. EX17: Cred 6F **39**
Enfield Rd. TQ1: Torq 6E **112**
England's Cl. EX10: Sidf 1E **84**
Eningdale Rd. PL19: Tavi 5G **59**
Ennerdale Gdns. PL6: Plym 6K **131**
Ennerdale Way EX4: Exe 6C **64**
Ennisfarne Rd. EX39: West H 5A **20**
Ensign Ct. EX39: West H 5D **20**
ENSIS 1D **163**
Enterprise Cen. EX22: Bradw 5C **28**
Enterprise Ct. PL11: Torp 2B **140**
Epping Cres. PL6: Plym 4E **136**
Epworth Ter. PL2: Plym 6E **134**
Erica Dr. TQ2: Torq 2B **112**
Eric Rd. PL4: Plym 4K **9** (2B **142**)
Erith Av. PL2: Plym 4E **134**
Erle Gdns. PL7: Plymp 6C **138**
Erlstoke Cl. PL6: Plym 2E **136**
Erme Ct. PL21: Ivy 4H **145**
Erme Dr. PL21: Ivy 4G **145**
Erme Gdns. PL3: Plym 6D **136**
Erme M. PL21: Ivy 5G **145**

Erme Pk. PL21: Erm 3H **147**
Erme Rd. PL21: Ivy 4H **145**
Erme Ter. PL21: Ivy 4H **145**
ERMINGTON 2H **147** (2C **175**)
Ermington Rd. PL21: Ivy 5F **145**
Ermington Ter. PL4: Plym 7K **135**
  PL21: Erm 2H **147**
Ermington Workshops
  PL21: Erm 2J **147**
ERNESETTLE 6D **130** (2A **174**)
Ernesettle Cres. PL5: Plym 7D **130**
Ernesettle Grn. PL5: Plym 6D **130**
Ernesettle La. PL5: Plym 5C **130**
Ernesettle Rd. PL5: Plym 7D **130**
Ernesettle Ter. PL5: Plym 7D **130**
(off Ernesettle Rd.)
Ernsborough Ct. EX2: Exe 6G **7**
Ernsborough Gdns. EX14: Hon . . .4E **54**
Erril Retail Pk. PL7: Plymp 6J **137**
Escot .1A **172**
Eskil Pl. EX38: Gt T 1B **30**
Esmonde Gdns. PL5: Plym 3A **134**
Esplanade EX8: Exmth 6B **76**
  EX12: Seat 6F **87**
  TQ14: Teignm 5J **107**
Esplanade, The EX10: Sidm 7B **84**
  EX34: Woolc 5A **10**
  EX35: Lynm 1G **13**
  PL1: Plym 7D **8** (4J **141**)
  TQ4: Paig 2J **119**
  TQ6: Dartm 4E **124**
Esplanade Rd. TQ3: Paig 2J **119**
  TQ4: Paig 2J **119**
Essex Cl. EX4: Exe 2B **70**
Essex St. PL1: Plym 2B **8** (1H **141**)
ESSINGTON 6C **36**
Essington Cl. EX8: Exmth 1D **76**
Essington Ct. EX8: Exmth 1D **76**
  EX20: N Taw 6C **36**
Essington La. EX20: N Taw 6C **36**
Essington Rd. EX20: N Taw 6C **36**
Esso Wharf Rd.
  PL4: Plym 7K **9** (4B **142**)
ESTOVER 7F **133** (2B **174**)
Estover Cl. PL6: Plym 6G **133**
Estover Ind. Est. PL6: Plym 6G **133**
Estover Rd. PL6: Plym 6F **133**
Estover Sports Cen. 1E **136**
Estuary Cl. EX8: Exmth 6A **76**
Estuary Vw. EX9: Bud S 6D **82**
  EX39: N'ham 4F **21**
Estuary Way PL5: Plym 3B **134**
Ethelston's Cl. DT7: Uply 3F **91**
Ethelwynne Brown Cl. EX39: Bide . . .3G **23**
Ethmar Ct. EX15: Will 3D **44**
Eton Av. PL1: Plym 2D **8** (1J **141**)
Eton Cl. EX39: Bide 2E **22**
Etonhurst Cl. EX2: Sow 2C **72**
Eton Pl. PL1: Plym 2D **8** (1J **141**)
Eton St. PL1: Plym 3D **8** (1J **141**)
Eton Ter. PL1: Plym 3C **8** (2H **141**)
Eton Wlk. EX4: Exe 1A **70**
Eugene Rd. TQ3: Pres 6J **115**
Eureka Ter. EX14: Hon 4F **55**
(off Jerrard Cl.)
  TQ13: Bov T 3C **92**
Europa Pk. EX34: Woolc 6D **10**
Evans Pl. PL2: Plym 6G **135**
Eveleigh Cl. TQ5: Brixh 5E **122**
Eveleighs Ct. EX4: Exe 2F **7**
Evelyn Pl. PL4: Plym 1F **9** (1K **141**)
Evelyn St. PL5: Plym 2C **134**
Evenden Ct. PL11: Torp 1A **140**
Everest Dr. EX12: Seat 3E **86**
Everett Pl. EX16: Tiv 2E **40**
Evergreen Cl. EX8: Exmth 1F **77**
Evett Cl. EX8: Exmth 4G **77**
Evil La. EX13: Axmin 3K **89**
Evran Dr. EX8: Exmth 1G **77**
EWORTHY 1C **169**
EXBOURNE 5J **35** (3A **164**)
Excalibur Cl. EX4: Whip 3K **65**
Exchange St. PL4: Plym 6F **9**
EXEBRIDGE 1D **165**
Exe Bri. Nth. EX2: Exe 6C **6** (7E **64**)
Exebridge Retail Pk.
  EX4: Exe 7C **6** (1E **70**)
Exe Bri. Sth. EX2: Exe 6C **6** (7E **64**)
Exe Cl. EX31: Chive 1D **16**
Exe Estuary Local Nature Reserve
  . . . . .7A **76**
Exe Estuary Nature Reserve 7A **74**
Exe Gdns. PL3: Plym 4D **136**
Exe Hill TQ2: Torq 5B **112**
EXE ISLAND 5C **6** (7E **64**)
Exe Reed Beds Nature Reserve . . .7C **72**
Exe Sailing Club 6A **76**
Exe St. EX3: Top 5B **74**
  EX4: Exe 4C **6** (6E **64**)
EXETER 4E **8** (1D **171**)
Exeter Airport Bus. Pk.
  EX5: Clyst H 7B **68**

Exeter Airport Ind. Est.
  EX5: Clyst H 7B **68**
Exeter & Devon Crematorium
  EX2: Exe 3J **71**
Exeter Arena Athletics Stadium . . .3A **66**
Exeter Av. TQ2: Torq 4B **112**
Exeter Bus. Pk. EX1: Sow 5D **66**
Exeter Castle 3E **6** (6F **65**)
Exeter Cathedral
  (The Cathedral Church of St Peter)
  . . . . .4E **6** (6F **65**)
Exeter Central Station (Rail)
  . . . . .2D **6** (5E **64**)
Exeter Chiefs RUFC 3D **72**
Exeter City FC 1G **7** (5G **65**)
Exeter Cl. EX14: Fen 2G **53**
  PL5: Plym 6C **130**
Exeter Cross TQ12: Live 4H **93**
Exeter Foyer EX1: Exe 6D **6**
Exeter Ga. EX36: S Mol 7C **26**
Exeter Golf Course 4B **72**
Exeter Hill EX6: Kenton 5H **95**
  EX15: Cull 5G **45**
  EX16: Tiv 5E **40**
EXETER INTERNATIONAL AIRPORT
  . . . . .7B **68** (1A **172**)
Exeter Phoenix 3E **6** (6F **65**)
Exeter Picture House 5C **6**
Exeter Racecourse 2D **171**
Exeter Rd. EX2: Cou W 6C **72**
  EX3: Top 6C **72**
  EX5: Silv 3G **51**
  EX5: Stre R 1F **79**
  EX6: Kennf 1H **95**
  EX6: Star 5B **96**
  EX7: Daw 5B **96**
  EX8: Exmth . . . . . . .1C **76** & 4H **75**
  EX10: New P 5F **81**
  EX11: Ott M . . . . . . .1G **79** & 4A **80**
  EX14: Hon 4C **54**
  EX15: Cull 5G **45**
  EX16: Ashl, Tiv 7B **40**
  EX17: Cred 7J **39**
  EX19: Wink 3C **36**
  EX20: Oke 3C **48**
  EX32: Bish T 5A **24**
  EX33: Brau, Wraf 5J **15**
  PL21: Fil, Ivy 4H **145**
  TQ10: S Bre 2B **100**
  TQ12: Kingst 1G **105**
  TQ12: Kingst, New A 5E **104**
  TQ12: New A 6C **104**
  TQ13: Chud 1D **94**
  TQ14: Teignm 2G **107**
Exeter Rd. Ind. Est. EX20: Oke 2E **48**
EXETER SERVICE AREA 1E **72**
Exeter St David's Station (Rail)
  . . . . .1A **6** (5D **64**)
Exeter St. EX20: N Taw 6B **36**
  PL4: Plym 5F **9** (2K **141**)
  TQ14: Teignm 1H **107**
Exeter Tennis Cen. 5B **64**
Exeter Tenpin 7E **6** (1F **71**)
Exeter Trade Cen. EX2: Mar B 5H **71**
Exeter Underground Passages 3F **7**
Exe Vale Rd. EX2: Cou W 4K **71**
Exe Vale Ter. EX16: Tiv 5C **40**
Exe Valley Leisure Cen. 3C **40**
Exc Vw. EX6: Exmin 2C **74**
Exe Vw. Cotts. EX4: Exe 1A **6** (4C **64**)
Exe View Rd. EX8: Lymp 4K **75**
EXFORD 3D **161**
Exhibition Rd. EX17: Cred 6J **39**
Exhibition Way EX4: Pin 3B **66**
EXMINSTER 2D **74** (2D **171**)
Exminster Hill EX6: Exmin 4D **74**
EXMOOR 3D **161**
Exmoor Cl. EX16: Tiv 2E **40**
Exmoor National Pk. 3H **13**
Exmoor National Pk. Vis. Cen. . . .1H **13**
Exmoor Vw. EX36: S Mol 5C **26**
Exmoor Zoo 2C **161**
EXMOUTH 6C **76** (2A **172**)
Exmouth Ct. EX8: Exmth 6D **76**
Exmouth Express Miniature Railway
  . . . . .7C **76**
(off Queen's Dr.)
Exmouth Leisure Cen. 6B **76**
Exmouth Lifeboat Station 7C **76**
Exmouth Mus. 5C **76**
Exmouth Pavilion 7C **76**
Exmouth Quay 6A **76**
Exmouth Rd.
  EX3: Clyst G, Ebf, Exton 5A **74**
  EX5: Clyst M 3F **73**
  EX8: Exmth, Lymp 5E **74**
  EX9: Bud S, Know 6A **82**
  EX10: Col R, New P 3H **83**
  PL1: Dev 1E **140**
(not continuous)
Exmouth Sports Cen. 5B **76**
Exmouth Station (Rail) 5B **76**

Exon Bldgs. EX15: Cull 5G **45**
Exonia Pk. EX2: Exe 2A **70**
Explorer Cl. PL2: Plym 6G **135**
Explorer Wlk. TQ2: Torq 2B **112**
(off Kingsley Av.)
EXTON
  Dulverton 1D **165**
  Exmouth 1G **75** (2D **171**)
Exton La. EX3: Exton 1G **75**
Exton Rd. EX2: Mar B 2F **71**
Exton Station (Rail) 2G **75**
EXWICK 5B **64** (1D **171**)
Exwick Ct. EX4: Exe 4C **64**
Exwick Hill EX4: Exe 4C **64**
Exwick La. EX4: Exe 5A **64**
Exwick Rd. EX4: Exe 4C **64**
Exwick Vs. EX4: Exe 5C **64**
Eyewell Grn. EX12: Seat 4E **86**
Eymore Dr. EX11: W Hill 5G **79**
Eyrecourt Rd. EX12: Seat 6E **86**

F

Factory Ope EX39: Apple 3J **21**
(off The Quay)
Factory Row TQ2: Torq 1C **116**
Fairacre Av. EX32: Barn 6H **19**
Fairby Cl. EX16: Tiv 2E **40**
Fairfax Dr. EX15: Cull 3H **45**
Fairfax Gdns. EX2: Alph 3E **70**
Fairfax Pl. TQ6: Dartm . . .2B **124** (6F **125**)
Fairfax Rd. TQ12: Heat 1H **93**
Fairfax Ter. PL2: Plym 7E **134**
Fairfax Way EX38: Gt T 1E **30**
Fair Fld. TQ10: S Bre 2C **100**
Fairfield EX16: Sam P 2B **42**
  EX31: Brat F 7H **13**
  EX34: Ilfra 3J **11**
  PL7: Plymp 2B **138**
Fairfield Av. EX4: Whip 4B **66**
  PL2: Plym 4H **135**
Fairfield Cl. EX8: Exmth 6D **76**
  EX13: Axmin 4H **89**
  TQ7: Kingsb 5G **157**
  TQ13: Bov T 4B **92**
Fairfield Gdns. EX14: Hon 4F **55**
Fairfield Pk. DT7: Lym R 4K **91**
Fairfield Rd. EX2: Alph 5E **70**
  EX8: Exmth 6D **76**
  EX17: Cred 5H **39**
  TQ2: Torq 5B **112**
  TQ12: Kingsk 2G **111**
Fairfield Ter. EX2: Exe 7B **6** (1D **70**)
  TQ12: New A 1F **109**
Fairfield Way TQ7: Chil 6H **159**
Fairhazel Dr. EX34: Exe 5C **64**
Fairholme Rd. EX34: Woolc 6A **10**
Fairies Hill TQ11: B'leigh 3D **98**
Fair Isle Cl. TQ2: Torq 3A **112**
Fairlands Av. EX6: Chri 4J **63**
Fairlawn Ct. EX10: Sidm 5C **84**
Fairlawns Pk. TQ4: Good 5H **119**
Fairlea Cl. EX7: Daw 1J **97**
Fairlea Cres. EX39: N'ham 6D **20**
Fairlea Gdns. EX39: N'ham 6D **20**
Fairlea Rd. TQ7: Daw 2H **97**
Fairleigh EX10: New P 5G **81**
Fairlynch Cl. EX33: Brau 3C **15**
Fairlynch Gro. EX33: Brau 3C **15**
Fairlynch La. EX33: Brau 3G **15**
Fairlynch Mus. 7D **82**
Fairmead EX10: Sidm 2A **84**
Fairmead Ct. EX1: Pin 3D **66**
FAIRMILE 1A **80** (1A **172**)
FAIR OAK 2A **166**
Fair Oak Cl. EX5: Clyst H 7C **68**
Fair Oak Ct. EX5: Clyst H 7B **68**
Fair Oaks TQ14: Teignm 3G **107**
Fairpark Cl. EX2: Exe 6G **7** (7G **65**)
Fairpark Rd. EX2: Exe 6F **7** (7F **65**)
Fairplace EX20: Oke 3B **48**
(off Mill Rd.)
Fairplace Ter. EX20: Oke 3B **48**
(off St James St.)
Fairseat Cl. TQ9: Tot 6F **103**
Fair Vw. EX31: Barn 3D **18**
Fairview EX22: Bradw 6B **28**
Fairview Av. EX5: Clyst M 3J **73**
  PL3: Plym 6E **136**
Fair Vw. La. EX24: Colyf . . . .7C **88** & 1F **87**
Fair Vw. Rd. EX14: Hon 4F **55**
Fairview Rd.
  TQ6: Dartm 1A **124** (6E **124**)
  TQ12: Den 1H **101**
Fairview Ter. EX1: Pin 3E **66**
  EX8: Exmth 5D **76**
Fairview Way PL3: Plym 6F **137**
Fairwater Cl. TQ12: Kingst 4J **105**
Fairwaters TQ12: Kingst 3H **105**
Fairway EX16: Tiv 3K **41**
  EX39: Apple 3G **21**

Fairway, The EX4: Exe 3H 65
EX33: Brau 4F 15
PL8: New F 5H 149
Fairway Av. PL21: Ivy 4F 145
Fairway Cl. EX33: Brau 4G 15
TQ5: Chur F 3K 121
Fairways, The EX39: West H 5C 20
FAIRY CROSS 1C 163
Fairy La. TQ11: B'leigh 5B 98
Falcon Rd. EX2: Sow 1D 72
PL1: Dev 3E 140
Falcon Way EX16: Tiv 2E 40
Falkland Cl. EX4: Exe 2H 65
Falkland Dr. TQ12: Kingst 3J 105
Falkland Rd. TQ2: Torq 2B 116
Falkland Way TQ14: Teignm 2G 107
Fallapit Cotts. TQ9: E All 5B 152
Fallapit Est., The TQ9: E All 6B 152
Fallapit Turn TQ9: E All 5A 152
Falloway Cl. TQ2: Torq 3C 112
Fallowfield Cl. TQ12: New A 1J 109
Fallow Flds. EX32: Barn 7H 19
Fallowfields TQ9: Tot 6C 102
Falmouth Cl. TQ2: Torq 5H 111
Fanshawe Way PL9: Hooe 6D 142
Faraday Ho. EX1: Exe 4K 7 (6H 65)
Faraday Mill Bus. Pk.
PL4: Plym 3C 142
Faraday Mill Trade Pk.
PL4: Plym 3C 142
Faraday Rd. PL4: Plym 3C 142
Faringdon Rd. PL4: Plym 1C 142
Farleigh Mdws. EX16: Tiv 2A 40
Farleys Ct. EX3: Top 5A 74
Farm, The EX5: Whim 6F 53
Farm Cl. EX2: Won 1B 72
PL7: Plymp 5K 137
TQ12: Kingsk 6J 109
Farmer Frank's La. EX19: Wink 3C 36
Farm Hill EX4: Exe 4A 64
Farmhouse Av. EX1: Pin 4E 66
Farm Ho. Ri. EX6: Exmin 2B 74
Farm La. PL5: Plym 1G 135
PL6: Plym 3C 136
Farm Pk. EX5: Cranb 3B 68
Farm Rd. EX39: Bide 6B 22
Farm Way EX14: Fen 2F 53
Farmyard La. TQ3: Comp 7D 110
Farnley Cl. PL6: Plym 4C 132
Farriers, The PL19: Lam 6C 58
Farriers Cotts. PL7: Plymp 3B 138
FARRINGDON 1A 172
Farthing La. TQ3: Marl 4C 114
Farthings La. EX10: New P 6F 81
Far Vw. Rd. EX20: Oke 3C 48
FARWAY 1B 172
Farwell Rd. TQ9: Tot 6D 102
Fast Rabbit Farm 2A 176
Fatherford Rd. EX20: Oke 3D 48
Faulkner Cl. TQ6: Dartm 6C 124
Fawns Cl. PL21: Erm 2H 147
FAWTON 3A 168
Fay Rd. EX7: Daw 4H 97
Featherbed La. EX8: Exmth 2C 76
Featherstone Rd. EX8: Exmth 2C 76
Federation Rd. PL3: Plym 7D 136
Fegen Rd. PL5: Plym 2A 134
Felixwell Ct. EX4: Exe 5A 6
Fellowes La. PL1: Plym 1G 141
Fellowes Pl. PL1: Plym 2F 141
Fellowes Pl. La. Sth. *PL1: Plym 2G 141*
(off Edgcumbe Av.)
Feltrim Av. EX2: Exe 2G 71
FENITON 2G 53 (1A 172)
Feniton Gdns. EX14: Fen 2G 53
Feniton Station (Rail) 2F 53
FENNY BRIDGES 3K 53 (1B 172)
Ferguson Cl. EX11: Ott M 4A 80
Fern Bank TQ7: W Alv 5D 156
Fernbank Av. PL21: Ivy 3E 144
Fern Cl. EX20: Oke 2C 48
PL7: Plymp 4E 138
TQ5: Brixh 4F 123
Ferncombe Cl. TQ12: Kingst 1H 105
Ferncombe Dr. TQ12: Kingst 1H 105
Ferndale TQ6: Dartm 2A 124 (6E 124)
Ferndale Av. PL2: Plym 4D 134
Ferndale Cl. EX14: Hon 6C 54
PL6: Plym 2E 132
Ferndale Gdns. EX2: Exe 1D 70
Ferndale M. TQ2: Torq 6H 111
Ferndale Rd. EX2: Exe 7B 6 (1D 70)
PL2: Plym 4D 134
TQ2: Torq 6H 111
TQ14: Teignm 3H 107
Ferndown Cl. EX39: Bide 3D 22
Ferndown Rd. DT7: Lym R 5K 91
Fernham Ter. TQ3: Paig 7H 115
Fernhill Cl. PL21: Ivy 4F 145
Fernicombe Cl. TQ3: Paig 7E 114
Fernicombe Rd. TQ3: Paig 7E 114
Fernleigh Ct. EX20: N Taw 6B 36
Fernleigh Rd. PL3: Plym 6A 136
Fern Mdw. EX20: Oke 2C 48
PL19: Tavi 3K 59
Fern Pk. EX34: Ilfra 3H 11
Fernpark Cl. EX2: Exe 3H 71
Fern Rd. TQ12: New A 4J 109
Fern Ter. *PL20: Prin 6C 60*
(off Heather Ter.)
Fern Way EX34: Ilfra 3H 11
Fernworthy Cl. EX17: Cop 6D 38
TQ2: Torq 6G 111
Fernworthy Gdns. EX17: Cop 6D 38
Fernworthy Pk. EX17: Cop 6D 38
Ferrers Grn. TQ5: Chur F 4A 122
Ferrers Rd. PL5: Plym 2D 134
Ferrymans TQ5: Hill 6J 123
Ferrymans Reach *TQ14: Shal 6H 107*
(off Marine Pde.)
Ferry Rd. EX3: Top 5A 74
PL1: Dev 1C 140
Ferry St. PL11: Torp 1B 140
Feversham Cl. PL7: Plymp 3E 138
Field Cl. EX33: Brau 5H 15
TQ3: Pres 4H 115
Field End EX13: Axmin 4J 89
EX39: Bide 3D 22
Fieldings, The EX37: Chit 6H 25
Field La. EX33: Brau 5H 15
FILFORD 1D 173
FILHAM 5K 145
Filham Ind. Est. *PL21: Ivy 4H 145*
(off Blair Rd.)
Filham Moor Cl. PL21: Ivy 5J 145
Fillablack Rd. EX39: Bide 3H 23
Fillace La. PL20: Horr 2E 126
Fillace Pk. PL20: Horr 2E 126
FILLEIGH
Crediton 2B 164
South Molton 1A 164
Fillham Moor La. PL21: Ivy 4H 145
Filmer Way EX2: Mar B 2E 70
Fincer Dr. PL21: Ivy 3E 144
Finch Cl. PL3: Plym 7E 136
Finches Cl. PL9: Elb 5K 143
Finch Foundry 1G 49
Findon Gdns. PL6: Plym 6E 132
Finewell St. PL1: Plym 5E 8 (3J 141)
Fingle Cl. EX4: Exe 4B 64
Finnigan Rd. PL4: Plym 4C 142
Finnimore Ind. Est. EX11: Ott M 4B 80
Firbank Rd. EX7: Daw 1J 97
Fir Cl. EX14: Hon 4E 54
EX15: Will 3D 44
Fircroft Rd. PL2: Plym 4G 135
Firestone Cl. PL6: Plym 2F 137
Firestone La. TQ12: A'well 5D 108
Firlands TQ14: Teignm 2H 107
Firlands Rd. TQ2: Torq 3C 112
Firleigh Rd. TQ12: Kingst 2G 105
Firs, The EX2: Exe 2A 70
EX6: Kennf 1G 95
EX8: Exmth 5F 77
Firs Gro. EX32: Barn 6G 19
First Av. EX1: Heav 3K 7 (6J 65)
EX2: Cou W 6B 72
EX7: Daw 5F 97
EX13: Axmin 2K 89
PL1: Dev 2F 141
PL9: Plyms 4G 143
TQ1: Torq 5C 112
TQ14: Teignm 4G 107
First Dr. TQ14: Teignm 4H 107
(Second Dr.)
TQ14: Teignm 3K 107
(The Rowdens)
First Raleigh EX39: Bide 2D 22
Fir Ter. EX36: S Mol 6D 26
Fir Tree Cl. EX8: Exmth 2H 77
Firtree Ri. PL21: Ivy 4H 145
Firtree Rd. *PL6: Plym 4F 133*
(off Glenfield Way)
Fir Wlk. TQ2: Torq 5J 111
Fishacre Cl. TQ3: Paig 6E 114
Fishchowter's La. TQ9: Tot 7E 102
Fishcombe Rd. TQ5: Brixh 2D 122
Fishermans Ct. *EX8: Exmth 6A 76*
(off Victoria Rd.)
Fisher Rd. PL2: Plym 6F 135
TQ12: New A 1E 108
Fisher's Sq. EX4: Exe 7A 6 (1D 70)
Fisher St. TQ4: Paig 2H 119
Fishers Way EX16: Hal 6C 42
Fishleigh Ct. EX31: Roun 7A 18
Fishleigh Rd. EX31: Roun 7A 18
FISHPOND BOTTOM 1D 173
Fish Quay PL4: Plym 6H 9
Fitness First
Exeter 5B 6
Fitzford Cotts. PL19: Tavi 5G 59
FITZHEAD 1B 166
Fitzroy Rd. EX1: Sow 6D 66
PL1: Plym 1F 141
Fitzroy Ter. PL1: Plym 1F 141
Five Acres TQ13: Bov T 7B 92
Five Elms La. EX5: New C 7A 50
FIVEHEAD 1D 167
FIVELANES 2A 168
Five Lanes Rd. TQ3: Marl 4D 114
Five Turnings EX34: Com M 5B 12
Flagstaff Rd. TQ6: Dartm 5E 124
Flamborough Rd. PL6: Plym 3B 132
Flamborough Way PL6: Plym 4B 132
Flamsteed Cres. PL5: Plym 2D 134
Flat Point 2B 160
Flats, The EX7: Daw 7B 96
Flavel Arts Centre, The *1A 124*
(off Mayor's Av.)
Flavel Pl. TQ6: Dartm 1A 124
Flavel St. TQ6: Dartm 1A 124
Flax Meadow La. EX13: Axmin 3J 89
Flayes Almshouses EX4: Whip 4B 66
Fleet Ct. EX12: Seat 5F 87
TQ1: Torq 2D 116
Fleet St. PL2: Plym 5D 134
TQ1: Torq 2D 116
TQ2: Torq 2D 116
Fleet Wlk. *TQ2: Torq 2D 116*
(off Fleet St.)
Fleet Wlk. Shop. Cen.
TQ2: Torq 2D 116
Fleetwood Gdns. PL6: Plym 3B 132
Fleming Av. EX10: Sidm 2D 84
Fleming Way EX2: Exe 7J 7 (1H 71)
Flemons Ct. *TQ4: Paig 2G 119*
(off St Michael's Rd.)
Fletcher Cl. TQ2: Torq 6A 112
Fletcher Cres. PL9: Plyms 6H 143
Fletcher Ind. Est. EX39: Bide 5D 22
Fletcher Way PL9: Plyms 6H 143
Flete Av. TQ12: New A 2J 109
Flete Cl. TQ12: New A 2J 109
Fletemoor Rd. PL5: Plym 2C 134
Flete Vw. Ter. PL21: Bitta 3C 146
Flexa Pk. EX34: Com M 6B 12
FLEXBURY 3A 162
Flexton, The *EX11: Ott M 3C 80*
(off Silver St.)
Flightway EX14: Dunk 4G 47
Flood's La. EX15: Cull 4G 45
Flood St. TQ9: Sto G 3A 120
Flora Cotts. PL1: Plym 5B 8 (3H 141)
Flora Ct. PL1: Plym 4B 8 (2H 141)
(not continuous)
Flora St. PL1: Plym 5B 8 (3H 141)
Florence Pl. PL4: Plym 2B 142
TQ12: New A 2G 109
Florence St. PL5: Plym 2C 134
Florida Dr. EX4: Exe 2F 65
Florida Gdns. PL3: Plym 5D 136
Florida Rd. TQ1: Torq 1E 116
Flowerpot La. EX4: Exe 5A 6 (7D 64)
Flowers Mdw. *TQ12: Live 4F 93*
(off Divett Dr.)
Flower St. EX5: Wood 5C 78
Flow La. TQ14: Bi'ton 4B 106
(not continuous)
Floyd Cl. PL2: Plym 4E 134
Floyers-Hay Ct. EX2: Exe 7D 6
Fluder Cres. TQ12: Kingsk 2H 111
Fluder Hill TQ12: Kingsk 1G 111
Fluder Ri. TQ12: Kingsk 2H 111
FLUXTON 7A 80 (1A 172)
Foales Ct. *TQ13: Ashb 4H 99*
(off North St.)
Foliot Av. PL2: Plym 5F 135
Foliot Rd. PL2: Plym 4E 134
Follafield Pk. TQ5: Brixh 6D 122
Follaton TQ9: Darti 5A 102
Follaton Bungs. TQ9: Tot 6B 102
Follett Rd. EX3: Top 5A 74
EX16: Tiv 5H 41
FOLLY CROSS 3C 163
Folly Farm Cl. EX33: Brau 4H 15
FOLLY GATE 1D 169
Folly Hill TQ7: Bigb S 3C 154
Folly La. *TQ8: Salc 3D 158*
(off Fore St.)
Fonthill TQ1: Torq 2F 117
Football La. TQ12: Kingst 3H 105
Footland La. TQ12: Dacc 1A 112
Forbes Cl. TQ12: Heat 2J 93
Forcefield Rd. EX15: Cull 5G 45
Forches Av. EX32: Barn 5G 19
FORCHES CROSS 4B 104
Forches Cross TQ12: New A 7K 93
Forches Gdns. EX32: Barn 5G 19
FORD
Bideford 1C 163
Holbeton 5C 150 (2C 175)
Holcombe Rogus 3F 43
Plymouth 6F 135 (2A 174)
Salcombe 3D 175
Taunton 1A 166
Ford TQ6: Dartm 6E 124
FORDA 6A 14 (3A 160)
FORD BARTON 2D 165
Fordbrook La. PL9: Brixt, Spri 2F 149
Ford Cl. PL21: Ivy 4E 144
Ford Cres. EX22: Bradw 6C 28
Ford Down La. EX36: S Mol 6A 26
Forde Cl. TQ12: A'well 5D 108
TQ12: New A 1G 109
Fordens La. EX7: Holc 7F 97
Forde Pk. TQ12: New A 2G 109
Forde Pl. TQ12: New A 2G 109
FORDER GREEN 1D 175
Forder Hgts. PL6: Plym 2C 136
Forder La. PL21: Bitta, Ugb 3E 146
TQ9: Darti 3A 102
TQ10: S Bre 1C 100
TQ13: Bov T 1A 92
TQ14: Bi'ton 4A 106
(not continuous)
Forder Mdw. TQ13: More 6H 61
Forde Rd. TQ12: New A 1G 109
Forder Valley Nature Reserve 3E 136
Forder Valley Rd. PL6: Plym 2C 136
Forde Vs. TQ12: New A 2G 109
Ford Farm Ct. EX6: Kenton 6H 95
Ford Hill EX5: Thor 1B 50
EX39: Hart 3J 27
PL2: Plym 6F 135
Fordishaies La. EX5: Bradn 1B 52
Fordlands Cres. EX39: Bide 1E 22
Fordlands Rd. TQ13: More 6H 61
Ford La. EX11: W Hill 5H 79
Ford Orchard EX16: Sam P 2B 42
FORD PARK 6J 135
Ford Pk. PL4: Plym 7K 135
TQ13: Chud K 6B 94
Ford Pk. La. PL4: Plym 7K 135
Ford Pk. Rd. PL4: Plym 7J 135
Ford Plain EX5: Thor 1A 50
Ford Ri. EX39: Bide 5F 23
Ford Rd. EX16: Bam 2J 33
EX16: Tiv 4F 41
PL8: Torr 3C 150
PL9: Wem 6A 148
TQ9: Tot 5F 103
TQ12: A'well 5E 108
Fords Rd. EX2: Exe 7D 6 (1E 70)
FORD STREET 2B 166
Ford St. PL19: Tavi 4H 59
TQ13: More 6H 61
FORDTON 7K 39 (1C 171)
Fordton Ind. Est. EX17: Cred 7K 39
Fordton Plain EX17: Cred 7J 39
Fordton Ter. EX17: Cred 7J 39
Ford Valley TQ6: Dartm 6E 124
Foredown La. TQ12: Kingsk 1E 110
Foreland Vw. EX34: Ilfra 4H 11
Forest Av. PL2: Plym 4H 135
Foresters Rd. EX22: Hols 1C 34
PL9: Plyms 5E 142
Foresters Ter. TQ14: Teignm 5H 107
Forest Hill EX39: Bide 6F 23
Fore St. EX1: Heav 5K 7 (7J 65)
EX2: Ide 3B 70
EX3: Top 5B 74
EX4: Exe 5C 6 (7E 64)
EX5: Bradn 1C 52
EX5: Silv 2H 51
EX6: Kenton 6H 95
EX8: Exmth 6C 76
EX9: Bud S 7C 82
EX9: Ott'n 6G 83
EX10: Sidb 2H 85
EX10: Sidm 7C 84
EX12: Beer 7B 86
EX12: Seat 5F 87
EX15: Cull 4H 45
EX15: Culm 2B 46
EX15: Hemy 2G 47
EX15: Kent 6B 46
EX15: Uff 6H 43
EX16: Bam 2H 33
EX16: Tiv 5C 40
EX16: With 6J 33
EX17: Morc 1B 38
EX18: Chul 6C 32
EX19: Dol 6G 31
EX19: Wink 2C 36
EX20: Bride 3H 57
EX20: Exbo 5J 35
EX20: N Taw 6A 36
EX20: Oke 3B 48
EX20: S Taw 1J 49
EX22: Hols 2C 34
EX34: Ilfra 2J 11
EX36: N Mol 2B 26
EX38: Gt T 2C 30
EX39: Hart 3H 27
EX39: N'ham 6E 20
PL1: Dev 2D 140
PL5: Tam F 4G 131

Fore St. PL7: Plymp 5B 138
PL8: Holb 7C 150
PL8: Yeal 2B 150
PL11: Torp 1A 140
PL12: Car 1A 130
PL16: Lift 6A 56
PL19: Mil A 2A 58
PL20: Bere A 2C 128
PL20: Bere F 6C 128
PL21: Corn 6J 129
PL21: Ivy 4G 145
PL21: Ugb 6E 146
TA21: Holc R 2G 43
TQ1: Torq 5D 112
TQ2: Torq 2B 112
TQ5: Brixh 3E 122
TQ6: Kingsw 6G 125
TQ7: Ave G 7H 151
TQ7: Kingsb 4F 157
TQ7: Lodd 2G 151
TQ8: Salc 3D 158
TQ9: Tot 6E 102
TQ10: S Bre 1B 100
TQ11: B'leigh 4C 98
TQ12: Ipp 6H 101
TQ12: Kingsk 1F 111
TQ12: Kingst 4H 105
TQ13: Bov T 4C 92
TQ13: Chud 2C 94
TQ13: More 6H 61
TQ14: Bi'ton 3B 106
TQ14: Shal 6G 107
TQ14: Teignm 4H 107
(not continuous)
Fore St. Hill EX9: Bud S 6D 82
EX18: Chul 6C 32
Fore St. M. *EX4: Exe 5D 6*
(off Friernhay St.)
Forest Ridge Rd. TQ3: Pres 5F 115
Forest Rd. TQ1: Torq 7C 112
Forest Vw. PL6: Plym 3E 132
Forge Cl. EX9: Bud S 5B 82
PL6: Robo 1D 132
Forge End EX19: Wink 3C 36
Forge Pl. TQ13: Bov T 4B 92
Forge Way EX15: Cull 4H 45
Forgeway Cl. TQ2: Torq 2K 115
Forresters Dr. PL6: Plym 3E 132
Forster Rd. TQ8: Salc 3C 158
Fort Austin Av. PL6: Plym 1A 136
Fort Bovisand 1A 148
FORTESCUE 3C 84
Fortescue Cl. EX33: Brau 5K 15
Fortescue Pl. PL3: Plym 5B 136
Fortescue Rd. EX2: Exe 2E 70
EX10: Sidm 3E 84
EX32: Barn 7G 19
EX34: Ilfra 2H 11
TQ3: Pres 5J 115
TQ8: Salc 4B 158
Fortescue Ter. PL19: Tavi 3G 59
Fortfield EX12: Seat 5F 87
Fortfield Gdns. EX10: Sidm 7B 84
Fortfield Lawn EX10: Sidm 7B 84
Fortfield Pl. EX10: Sidm 7B 84
Fortfield Ter. EX10: Sidm 7B 84
Fort Flats EX10: Sidm 7B 84
Forth Gdns. PL3: Plym 5E 136
FORT HILL 4G 19
Fort Hill Dr. EX32: Barn 4G 19
Fortmead Cl. EX32: Barn 4F 19
FORTON 3D 167
Forton Rd. EX8: Exmth 3E 76
Fort Stamford Country Club 6B 142
Fort Stamford The Ramparts
PL9: Hooe 6B 142
Fort St. EX32: Barn 4F 19
Fort Ter. *EX32: Barn 4F 19*
(off Alexabdra Rd.)
EX39: Bide 4G 23
PL6: Plym 7A 132
Fortune Way TQ1: Torq 6D 112
Fosbrooke Ct. PL3: Plym 5A 136
Fosketh Hill EX39: West H 6B 20
Fosketh Ter. EX39: West H 6B 20
Fosse Rd. TQ7: Kingsb 3G 157
Fosseway Cl. EX13: Axmin 4H 89
Fosse Way Ct. EX12: Seat 6F 87
Foss Slip TQ6: Dartm 1A 124
Foss St. TQ6: Dartm 1A 124 (6F 125)
Fosterlea EX15: Cull 4G 45
Foulston Av. PL5: Plym 3A 134
Foundry Ct. TQ13: Chud 2B 94
Foundry La. PL8: Noss M 7H 149
Foundry M. PL19: Tavi 3K 59
Foundry Yd. *EX10: Sidm 6C 84*
(off Salcombe Rd.)
Fountain Ct. EX4: Exe 3C 6
TQ13: Bov T 4C 92
(off Fore St.)
TQ14: Teignm 5J 107
(off Triangle Pl.)
Fountain Flds. EX37: High B 2B 32
Fountain Hill EX9: Bud S 7B 82
Fountain Ho. EX1: Exe 2G 7
Fountains Cres. PL2: Plym 3G 135
Fouracre Cl. EX4: Whip 3K 65
Four Acres EX39: Bide 3C 22
Fouracre Way TQ12: Kingst 3J 105
Four Cross Av. EX15: Will 3D 44
Fourcross Hill EX13: Axmin 2F 89
Fourcross Units TQ9: Sto G 7A 118
Four Elms Hill EX10: Harp 5J 81
Four Mills La. EX17: Cred 7J 39
Four Oaks Cl. EX32: L'key 1B 24
Four Oaks Rd. EX6: Ted M 7J 49
Four Seasons Village EX19: Wink 1A 36
Fourth Av. TQ14: Teignm 3G 107
Fourview Cl. TQ5: Brixh 4G 123
Four Ways Dr. EX18: Chul 5B 32
Fowey Av. TQ2: Torq 5H 111
Fowey Cl. EX1: Heav 1K 7 (5J 65)
Fowey Gdns. PL3: Plym 5E 136
Fowey Rd. EX31: Chive 1E 16
Fowler Cl. EX6: Exmin 2C 74
Foxbeare Rd. EX34: Ilfra 3K 11
Fox Cl. EX20: Oke 2D 48
Foxes Lair *EX20: Oke 3A 48*
(off Oaklands Pk.)
Fox Fld. Cl. PL3: Plym 6D 136
Foxglove Chase EX15: Will 3D 44
Foxglove Cl. EX14: Dunk 7H 47
EX16: Tiv 2F 41
EX32: Barn 5K 19
Foxglove End PL20: C'stone 6B 126
Foxglove Ri. EX4: Exe 4A 64
Foxglove Rd. EX12: Seat 3F 87
FOXHAYES 6B 64
Foxhayes Rd. EX4: Exe 6C 64
Foxhill EX13: Axmin 4H 89
EX39: N'ham 6E 20
Foxhole Hill EX6: Chri 2J 63
Foxhole La. EX39: N'ham 6E 20
Foxhole Rd. TQ2: Torq 2K 115
TQ3: Paig 1F 119
Foxholes Hill EX8: Exmth 7E 76
Foxhollows TQ12: New A 2K 109
Foxlands TQ1: Torq 6E 112
Foxlands Wlk. *TQ1: Torq 5E 112*
(off Fore St.)
Foxley Cres. TQ12: New A 1C 108
Fox Rd. EX4: Whip 2A 66
Fox Tor Cl. TQ4: Good 1H 121
Foxtor Cl. PL5: Plym 7G 131
Foxtor Rd. EX4: Exe 4B 64
Foxwell La. TQ12: New A 7D 104
Foxwood Gdns. PL6: Plym 5K 131
PL9: Plyms 7F 143
Foyle Cl. PL7: Plymp 4D 138
Frances Gdns. EX1: Exe 3H 7
Francis Cl. EX4: Exe 7A 6 (1C 70)
Francis Ct. EX2: Exe 5K 7 (7H 65)
EX17: Cred 6H 39
(off The Burrowe)
Francis Cres. EX16: Tiv 5G 41
Francis Dr. EX39: West H 6A 20
Francis Pl. PL1: Plym 3A 8 (2G 141)
Francis St. PL1: Plym 4A 8 (2G 141)
Francis Way EX24: Colyf 1G 87
Franeth Cl. TQ12: Kingst 3G 105
Frankford La. EX6: Ted M 5J 49
Frankfort Ga. PL1: Plym 4C 8 (2H 141)
Franklea Cl. EX11: Ott M 4C 80
Franklin St. EX2: Exe 6F 7 (7F 65)
Franklyn Av. EX33: Brau 5K 15
Franklyn Cl. EX2: Exe 2C 70
Franklyn Dr. EX2: Exe 2C 70
Franklyns PL6: Plym 6B 132
Franklyns Cl. PL6: Plym 6B 132
Frankmarsh Pk. EX32: Barn 3G 19
Frankmarsh Rd. EX32: Barn 3G 19
Fraser Ct. TQ3: Paig 2F 119
Fraser Dr. TQ14: Teignm 3G 107
Fraser Pl. PL5: Tam F 3H 131
Fraser Rd. EX8: Exmth 2F 77
PL5: Tam F 3H 131
Fraser Sq. PL5: Tam F 2H 131
FREATHY 2A 174
Frederick St. E.
PL1: Plym 4B 8 (2H 141)
Frederick St. W.
PL1: Plym 4B 8 (2H 141)
Frederick Ter. *EX7: Daw 4G 97*
(off Stockton Rd.)
Fredington Gro. PL2: Plym 5G 135
Freedom Sq. PL4: Plym 1H 9
Freelands Cl. EX8: Exmth 4F 77
Freeman's Wharf PL1: Plym 4F 141
Freemantle Gdns. PL2: Plym 7E 134
Freestone Rd. TQ12: Kingst 3G 105
Fremantle Pl. PL2: Plym 7E 134
FREMINGTON 6F 17 (3B 160)
Fremington Quay EX31: Frem 4G 17
Fremington Quay Heritage Cen. 4G 17
Fremington Rd. EX12: Seat 5D 86
FRENCHBEER 2A 170
French Cl. EX5: Silv 1H 51
French St. TQ14: Teignm 4J 107
Frensham Av. PL6: Plym 4D 132
Frensham Gdns. PL6: Plym 3D 132
Freshford Cl. PL6: Plym 2D 136
Freshford Wlk. PL6: Plym 2D 136
Freshwater Dr. TQ4: Good 7G 119
Frewin Gdns. PL6: Plym 4C 132
Frewins EX9: Bud S 5B 82
Friars Ga. EX2: Exe 6E 6 (7F 65)
FRIARS GREEN 6D 6 (7E 64)
Friars Grn. *EX2: Exe 6E 6*
(off Southgate)
Friars La. PL1: Plym 6F 9
Friars' Wlk. EX2: Exe 6E 6 (7F 65)
Friary Ct. EX1: Exe 4E 6
Friary Pk. PL4: Plym 4J 9 (2A 142)
Friary St. PL4: Plym 5H 9 (3A 142)
Friendship La. *EX34: Ilfra 2H 11*
(off High St.)
Friernhay Ct. EX4: Exe 5C 6
Friernhay St. EX4: Exe 5C 6 (7E 64)
FRITHELSTOCK 2C 163
Frithelstock Priory (remains of) 2C 163
FRITHELSTOCK STONE 2C 163
FRITTISCOMBE 3A 176
Frobisher App. PL5: Plym 1J 135
Frobisher Cl. TQ14: Teignm 1G 107
Frobisher Grn. TQ2: Torq 7J 111
Frobisher La. TQ8: Salc 3B 158
Frobisher Rd. EX8: Exmth 2E 76
TQ12: New A 7J 105
Frobisher Way PL19: Tavi 4H 59
TQ4: Good 5H 119
Frog La. EX5: Clyst M 2F 73
EX33: Brau 4J 15
EX36: S Mol 5B 26
TA21: Holc R 2G 43
FROGMORE 3D 175
Frogmore Av. PL6: Plym 3C 136
Frogmore Ct. PL6: Plym 4C 136
Frogmore Rd. EX9: E Bud 2E 82
Frogmore Ter. TQ7: Kingsb 5F 157
Frog St. EX1: Exe 6C 6 (7E 64)
EX4: Exe 6C 6 (7E 64)
EX16: Bam 1H 33
EX34: Woolc 6A 10
Frogstreet Hill
EX33: Forda, Georgeh 6A 14
FROGWELL 3B 168
Frome Cl. PL7: Plymp 5D 138
Frontfield Cres. PL6: Plym 5K 131
FROST 3C 38
Froude Av. TQ2: Torq 1D 112
Froude Rd. TQ8: Salc 6A 158
Fry's La. EX10: Sidf 1D 84
Fry St. EX22: Hols 2C 34
Fulda Cres. EX17: Cred 7J 39
FULFORD 1C 167
Fulford Cl. EX6: Ted M 7J 49
EX39: Bide 5H 23
Fulford Dr. EX15: Cull 5G 45
Fulford La. EX6: Dunsf 4B 62
Fulford Rd. EX1: Heav 5J 65
Fulford Way EX5: Wood 5C 78
Fullaford Pk. TQ11: B'leigh 5B 98
Fullers Ct. EX2: Exe 6D 6 (7E 64)
Fullerton Rd. PL2: Plym 6F 135
Fulton Cl. TQ12: Ipp 6H 101
FULWOOD 2C 167
Funder Zone 6J 19
Furland Cl. PL9: Hooe 7D 142
FURLEY 3C 167
Furlong Cl. TQ11: Buck 2C 98
Furneaux Av. PL2: Plym 6G 135
Furneaux Rd. PL2: Plym 6G 135
Furness Cl. TQ4: Paig 5G 119
Furrough Ct. TQ1: Torq 5E 112
Furrough Cross TQ1: Torq 5E 112
Fursdon 3D 165
Fursdon Cl. PL9: Elb 6K 143
Furse Hill Rd. EX34: Ilfra 3H 11
Furse Pk. PL5: Plym 4B 134
Furzeacre Cl. PL7: Plymp 2D 138
Furzebeam Row EX38: Gt T 2A 30
Furzebeam Ter. *EX39: Bide 4G 23*
(off Torrington La.)
Furzebrook EX11: Ott M 3D 80
Furze Cap TQ12: Kingst 1G 105
Furze Ct. EX4: Exe 2B 70
Furzedown Rd. TQ12: Kingsk 7K 109
Furze Gdns. TQ9: Tot 6G 103
Furzegood TQ3: Marl 4D 114
Furzeham Ct. TQ5: Brixh 3D 122
Furzeham Pk. TQ5: Brixh 3E 122
Furzehatt Av. PL9: Plyms 6H 143
Furzehatt Pk. Rd. PL9: Plyms 6H 143
Furzehatt Ri. PL9: Plyms 6H 143
Furzehatt Rd. PL9: Plyms 6G 143
Furzehatt Vs. PL9: Plyms 6G 143
Furzehatt Way PL9: Plyms 6H 143
FURZEHILL 2D 161
Furzehill EX10: Sidb 3H 85
(not continuous)
Furzehill Rd. PL4: Plym 1H 9 (7A 136)
PL9: Hey B 4B 148
TQ1: Torq 7C 112
Furze La. TQ5: Brixh 3F 123
Furzeleigh La. TQ13: Bov T 3B 92
Furze Pk. EX34: Com M 6A 12
Furzepark La. EX39: Hart 2K 27
Furze Pk. Rd. EX31: Brat F 6H 13
Furze Rd. EX5: Wood 5C 78
TQ9: Tot 6H 103

G

Gabber La. PL9: Down T 2D 148
Gables, The EX8: Exmth 6F 77
Gables Ct. *EX15: Will 4C 44*
(off Gables Lea)
Gables Lea EX15: Will 4C 44
Gables Rd. EX15: Will 4C 44
Gabriel Ct. EX2: Exe 6D 6
Gabriels Wharf EX2: Exe 2F 71
Gabwell Hill TQ1: S'head 1J 113
Gabwell La. TQ12: S'head 1H 113
Gainsborough Cl. TQ1: Torq 2F 117
Gainsborough Dr. EX39: West H 6A 20
Gala Bingo
Plymouth, Derry's Cross 5C 8
Torquay 1C 116
Galahad Cl. EX4: Whip 3K 65
Gales Crest TQ13: Chud K 6A 94
Galileo Cl. PL7: Plymp 3B 138
Gallants Bower Fort 7G 125
Galleon Way EX39: West H 5D 20
Gallery, The *TQ2: Torq 2D 116*
(off Fleet St.)
Gallery Cl. EX14: Hon 3E 54
Galloway Dr. TQ14: Teignm 2F 107
GALMINGTON 1C 167
GALMPTON
Brixham 3H 121 (2A 176)
Malborough 2K 155 (3C 175)
Galmpton Ct. *TQ5: Galm 3H 121*
(off Galmpton Farm Cl.)
Galmpton Farm Cl. TQ5: Galm 3H 121
Galmpton Glade TQ5: Galm 3H 121
Galmpton Ri. EX4: Exe 3H 65
Galmpton Touring Pk.
TQ5: Galm 4H 121
GALMPTON WARBOROUGH
1H 121 (2A 176)
Galpin St. PL21: Modb 6G 147
Galsworthy Cl. PL5: Plym 1H 135
Galva Rd. PL7: Drak, Hem 1F 139
Gamberlake EX13: Axmin 5G 89
GAMMATON 1C 163
Gammaton Rd. EX39: Bide 4H 23
Gammons Hill EX13: Kilm 2C 88
Gammon Wlk. EX31: Barn 4E 18
Ganders Pk. TQ2: Torq 4G 111
Gandy St. EX4: Exe 3D 6 (6F 65)
GANG 3B 168
Ganges Rd. PL2: Plym 6F 135
Ganna Pk. Rd. PL3: Plym 5J 135
GAPPAH 5E 94 (3C 171)
Gara Cl. PL9: Elb 6J 143
Gara Point & Blackstone Point 3B 174
Gard Cl. TQ2: Torq 2C 112
Garden Cl. EX2: Won 1B 72
EX33: Brau 4G 15
PL7: Plymp 4G 139
PL8: Holb 7C 150
Garden Ct. EX9: Bud S 6C 82
Garden Cres. PL1: Plym 7B 8 (4H 141)
Garden House, The 5B 126
Gardenia Dr. EX16: Tiv 1E 40
Garden La. PL19: Tavi 4H 59
Garden Mill Ind. Est.
TQ7: Kingsb 5G 157
Garden Pk. Cl. PL9: Elb 5J 143
Garden Rd. TQ1: Torq 7D 112
Gardens, The EX10: New P 5G 81
EX31: Barn 2E 18
(off Higher Raleigh Rd.)
TQ13: Chud 1C 94
Garden Spot La. TQ13: Chud 2D 94
Garden St. PL2: Dev 7D 134
Garden Ter. EX15: Cull 3H 45
Garden Village PL9: Plyms 4G 143
Gardiner Cl. EX5: Sto C 6K 51
Gards La. PL5: Plym 1D 134
Gareth Cres. EX4: Whip 2J 65
Garfield Rd. TQ4: Paig 1J 119
Garfield Ter. PL1: Plym 1E 140
Garland Cl. EX4: Exe 4A 64
Garlic Rea TQ5: Brixh 3F 123
(not continuous)
Garners Cl. TQ12: E Ogw 3A 108

Garners La. TQ12: E Ogw 3A 108
Garratt Cl. EX8: Exmth 1E 76
Garrett Cl. EX12: Seat 4F 87
Garrick Cl. PL5: Plym 1H 135
Garrison Cl. PL1: Dev 3D 140
Garrison Grn. PL1: Plym 6F 9
Garrow Cl. TQ5: Brixh 5E 122
Garston Av. TQ12: New A 7E 104
Garston Cl. PL9: Plyms 4H 143
Garth Rd. TQ2: Torq 3C 112
Gascoyne Cl. PL4: Plym ...4G 9 (2K 141)
Gascoyne Pl. PL4: Plym ...4G 9 (2K 141)
Gashouse La. PL4: Plym ...6J 9 (3A 142)
Gasking St. PL4: Plym 4G 9 (2K 141)
Gas La. EX38: Gt T 2C 30
Gatcombe La. EX12: Beer, Seat ... 3A 86
Gate Fld. Rd. EX39: Bide 3C 22
Gatehouse Barns EX7: Daw 2H 97
Gatehouse Cl. EX7: Daw 3G 97
EX15: Cull 4G 45
Gatehouse Hill EX7: Daw 3H 97
Gatehouse Ri. EX7: Daw 3H 97
Gater La. EX1: Exe 5E 6 (7F 65)
Gate Tree Cl. TQ12: Kingst ...4J 105
Gattery La. TQ5: Brixh 7B 122
Gavel, The EX36: S Mol 6D 26
Gaydon St. EX32: Barn 4F 19
Gaze Hill TQ12: New A 6C 104
Gdynia Way PL4: Plym ...5K 9 (3B 142)
Geasons La. PL7: Plymp 4B 138
Gees La. PL21: Modb 6H 147
Generals Cl. EX6: Star 2D 96
Generals La. EX6: Star 2D 96
Genesis La. EX34: Com M 6B 12
Geneva Cl. EX2: Exe 7K 7 (1H 71)
Geneva Ct. EX2: Exe 7K 7
EX39: Bide 4E 22
Geneva Pl. EX39: Bide 4E 22
Gentian Cl. TQ3: Marl 4D 114
George Arc. EX36: S Mol 6D 26
George Av. PL7: Plymp 3B 138
GEORGEHAM 5B 14 (3A 160)
Georgeham Rd.
EX33: Croy, Forda 2D 14
EX34: Woolc 7D 10
George Hill EX17: Cred 5F 39
George Junction (Park & Ride) ...4D 132
George La. EX13: Kilm 1B 72
PL7: Plymp 4C 138
(not continuous)
GEORGE NYMPTON 1B 164
George Nympton Rd.
EX36: S Mol 7C 26
George Pl. PL1: Plym ...5A 8 (3G 141)
George Rd. TQ3: Pres 5H 115
Georges Cl. EX1: Whip 6A 66
George Sq. PL1: Dev 3E 140
(off Theatre Ope)
George's Sq. DT7: Lym R 5K 91
(off Monmouth St.)
George St. EX1: Exe 5D 6 (7E 64)
EX8: Exmth 5C 76
EX13: Axmin 3H 89
EX14: Hon 3F 55
EX20: Oke 3B 48
EX32: Barn 3E 18
PL1: Dev 3E 140
TQ12: New A 1E 108
TQ13: More 6H 61
TQ14: Teignm 5J 107
George St. La. E. PL1: Dev 3E 140
Georgia Cres. PL3: Plym 5D 136
Georgian Cl. TQ1: Torq 7G 113
Gerald Dinnis Units EX2: Mar B ...4G 71
GERMANSWEEK 1C 169
Gerston La. TQ7: Kingsb 7F 157
Gerston Pl. TQ3: Paig 1H 119
Gerston Rd. TQ4: Paig 1H 119
Gerstons, The TQ3: Paig 1H 119
Gervase Av. EX2: Exe 7C 6 (7E 64)
Gerway La. EX11: Ott M 5D 80
Gestridge Rd. TQ12: Kingst ...3G 105
Gibb PL8: Holb 6D 150
Gibb Hill PL21: Lutt 6F 129
Gibbon La. PL4: Plym 3F 9 (2K 141)
Gibbon St. PL4: Plym 3F 9 (2K 141)
Gibbs La. EX39: Apple 2H 21
(off Market St.)
Giblands Pk. EX20: Oke 3D 48
Gibraltar Rd. EX8: Lymp 5G 75
Gibson Cl. EX8: Exmth 3G 77
Gibson Ct. TQ4: Good 6G 119
Gibson Dr. TQ4: Good 6G 119
Gibson Gdns. TQ4: Good 6G 119
Gibson Rd. TQ4: Good 6G 119
GIDLEIGH 2A 170
Gidleys Mdw. TQ9: Darti 3A 102
Gifford Cl. EX39: Hart 3J 27
Gifford Pl. PL3: Plym 7J 135
Gifford Ter. Rd. PL3: Plym 6J 135
Gilbert Av. EX2: Won 1B 72
TQ14: Teignm 2G 107

Gilbert Cl. TQ2: Torq 7K 111
Gilbert Ct. PL7: Plymp 3E 138
Gilbert Gro. EX34: Ilfra 2J 11
Gilbert La. PL2: Plym 6H 135
Gilbert Way TQ4: Good 5G 119
Gilbrook Cl. EX5: Wood 6B 78
Gilchrist Way EX10: Sidm 5D 84
Gillard Rd. TQ5: Brixh 4G 123
Gillard Way PL21: L Mill 4C 144
Gill Pk. PL3: Plym 6C 136
Gills Nursery TQ9: Tot 6E 102
(off South St.)
Gilpin Cl. EX7: Daw 2J 97
Gilwell Av. PL9: Plyms 5H 143
Gilwell Hall PL4: Plym 3F 9
Gilwell Pl. PL4: Plym 3F 9 (2K 141)
Gilwell St. PL4: Plym 3G 9 (2K 141)
Gimbletts Ct. EX22: Hols 2C 34
Gin Distillery 6F 9 (3K 141)
Gipsy Hill La. EX1: Pin 4E 66
Gipsy La. EX1: Pin 4E 66
EX8: Exmth 4E 66
EX34: Ilfra 3K 11
PL21: Ivy 4D 144
Girt Down & Hangman Point 2B 160
Girt La. EX34: Com M 5E 12
Gissage Vw. EX14: Hon 3E 54
Gissons EX6: Exmin 2D 74
Gissons La. EX6: Kenn, Kennf ...2G 95
GITTISHAM 7A 54 (1B 172)
Gittisham Cl. EX1: Sow 6C 66
Glade, The PL20: C'stone 6C 126
Glade Cl. PL6: Plym 6B 132
Glades, The EX16: Tiv 4E 40
Glade Wlk. EX5: Clyst M 3K 73
Gladstone Pl. TQ12: New A 1F 109
Gladstone Rd. EX1: Exe ...4J 7 (6H 65)
Gladstone Ter. TQ12: Teignm ...4J 107
Glanville Rd. EX14: Offw 7K 55
PL19: Tavi 4H 59
Glanvilles Mill PL21: Ivy 4G 145
Glanvilles Rd. PL21: Ivy 4H 145
Glanville St. PL4: Plym ...3E 8 (2J 141)
Glanvill Way EX14: Hon 5D 54
Glascott Cl. EX20: Hath 3F 35
Glasshouse La. EX2: Cou W 5K 71
Glastonbury Cl. EX4: Whip 2K 65
Glave Saunders Av. EX2: Won ...1B 72
Glazon Way EX39: N'ham 4F 21
Glebe, The EX5: Thor 3A 50
EX31: Brat F 6H 13
TQ12: Ipp 6G 101
EX8: Lymp 5G 75
EX9: Ott'n 6H 83
EX20: Nath 1H 35
TQ12: New A 1C 108
Glebe Cl. EX39: N'ham 5E 20
Glebe Fld. EX33: Georgeh 5C 14
TQ7: Thur 5C 154
Glebefields EX39: N'ham 6E 20
Glebe Land TQ7: Ave G 6H 151
Glebeland TQ7: Chur 1B 156
Glebelands Rd. EX16: Tiv 4G 41
Glebeland Way TQ2: Torq 5H 111
Glebelands DT7: Uply 3G 91
EX6: Cher B 2C 62
EX6: Exmin 2C 74
EX8: Lymp 5G 75
EX10: New P 5H 81
EX10: Sidm 6B 84
EX22: Hols 2B 34
EX33: Wraf 6K 15
TQ11: B'leigh 3B 98
TQ13: Chud 2C 58
Glebelands, The TQ13: More ...7H 61
Glebe Mdw. EX22: Hols 2B 34
Glebe Pk. EX20: Bride 3J 57
TQ6: Sto F 2H 153
Glen, The DT7: Uply 3G 91
EX20: Oke 4B 48
TQ12: New A 2J 109
Glenarm Ter. TQ9: Tot 5E 102
(off Castle St.)
Glenavon Rd. PL3: Plym 6K 135
Glenburn Cl. PL3: Plym 4K 135
Glenburnie Rd. EX39: Bide 2F 23
Glencarnock Cl. TQ1: Torq 6A 112
Glen Cl. EX5: Clyst M 3K 73
Glencoe EX2: Exe 6J 7 (7H 65)
Glen Creedy Cl. EX17: Cred 6J 39
Glen Creedy Ter. EX17: Cred ...6J 39
(off Mill St.)
Glendale Rd. EX20: Oke 2J 48
Glendale Ter. EX39: Bide 2F 23
TQ9: Tot 5E 102
(off Castle St.)
Glendaragh Rd. TQ14: Teignm ...4J 107
Glendower Rd. PL3: Plym 6J 135

Gleneagle Av. PL3: Plym 5A 136
Gleneagle Rd. PL3: Plym 5A 136
Gleneagle Vs. PL3: Plym 5A 136
(off Gleneagle Av.)
Glen Farm Cres. EX14: Hon 4G 55
Glenfield Cl. PL6: Plym 4E 132
Glenfield Rd. EX39: Bide 1F 23
PL6: Plym 5D 132
Glenfield Way PL6: Plym 4E 132
Glen Gdns. EX39: Bide 1E 22
Glengarth Cl. PL9: N'ham 3F 139
Glenhaven Cl. PL7: Plymp 3F 139
GLENHOLT 4E 132
Glenholt Cl. PL6: Plym 4E 132
Glenholt Pk. PL6: Plym 4E 132
Glenholt Rd. PL6: Plym 4D 132
Glenhurst Rd. PL3: Plym 5K 135
Glenisla Ter. EX10: Sidm 7C 84
(off Riverside Rd.)
Glen Lyn Gorge 2H 13
Glenmore Av. PL2: Plym 6E 134
Glenmore Rd. EX2: Won 7K 65
TQ5: Brixh 4E 122
Glenorchy Cl. EX8: Exmth 5C 76
(off Exeter Rd.)
Glen Pk. Av. PL4: Plym ...1E 8 (1J 141)
Glen Rd. EX10: Sidm 7H 84
PL3: Plym 6A 136
PL7: Plymp 3A 138
TQ3: Paig 7H 115
Glenside PL5: Plym 1K 135
(off Whitleigh Av.)
Glenside Cl. TQ14: Teignm 3H 107
Glenside Ri. PL7: Plymp 3B 138
Glenthorne Cl. TQ1: Torq 2F 117
Glenthorne Pinetum 2D 161
Glenthorne Rd. EX4: Exe 3D 64
Glentor Rd. PL3: Plym 4K 135
Glentorr Rd. EX39: Bide 2F 23
Glenview EX14: Hon 4G 55
Glen Wlk. EX4: Exe 2G 65
Glenwater Cl. EX12: Axmth 4H 87
Glenwood Ri. EX2: Exe 1H 71
Glenwood Rd. PL3: Plym 5K 135
Globefield EX3: Top 5B 74
Globe Hill EX5: Wood 5B 78
Globe La. EX3: Top 5B 74
Globe Ley EX3: Top 5B 74
(off Globefield)
Globe Theatre 3F 141
Gloster Rd. EX32: Barn 5F 19
Gloucester Cl. EX14: Hon 4D 54
TQ2: Torq 4B 112
Gloucester Ct. PL1: Plym 2D 8
Gloucester Cres. EX14: Hon 5C 54
Gloucester Pl. PL1: Plym ...2D 8 (1J 141)
Gloucester Rd. EX4: Exe 5B 64
EX8: Exmth 1F 77
TQ12: New A 2F 109
TQ14: Teignm 4H 107
Glove Ct. EX38: Gt T 2B 30
Glovers Cl. EX22: Hols 2C 34
Gnome Reserve & Wild Flower Garden
.... 2B 162
Goad Av. PL4: Plym 3B 142
Goaman Pk. EX39: Hart 3K 27
Goaman Rd. EX39: Hart 3K 27
Goats Hill Rd. EX39: N'ham 6F 21
Goat Wlk. EX3: Top 7B 74
Goblin La. EX15: Cull 4H 45
Godborough Vw. EX39: Bide 3C 22
Godding Gdns. PL6: Plym 3K 131
GODFORD CROSS 3B 166
Godfrey Av. TQ3: Pres 4H 115
Godfrey Cl. EX11: Ott M 4E 80
Godfreys Gdns. EX17: Bow 5G 37
Godolphin Cl. EX5: New C 6D 50
Godwell La. PL21: Ivy 6H 145
Gogwell La. EX16: Tiv 7F 41
GOLBERDON 3B 168
Golden Bay Ct. EX39: West H ...5A 20
Golden Bay Holiday Village
EX39: West H 5A 20
Golden Cl. TQ5: Brixh 6D 122
Golden Coast Holiday Village
EX34: Woolc 7C 10
Golden Coast Holiday Village
Ten Pin Bowling 7C 10
Golden Hind 4C 102
Golden Joy EX17: Cred 5J 39
Golden Lion Ct. TQ13: Ashb ...4H 99
Golden Pk. EX15: Kent 4H 45
Golden Pk. Av. TQ12: New A ...2B 112
Golden Sands Holiday Pk.
EX7: Daw W 7D 96
Golden Sq. PL7: Plymp 3B 138
Golden Ter. EX7: Daw 4E 97
Goldfinch Gdns. PL19: Whitc ...7K 59
Goldfinch Grn. EX15: Cull 5F 45
Golds Cross Hill EX6: Ted M ...7F 49
Golds La. EX6: Ted M 7F 49
Goldsmith Gdns. PL5: Plym 7J 131

Goldsmith St. EX1: Heav 6J 65
EX4: Exe 4D 6 (6E 64)
EX16: Tiv 4D 40
GOLDWORTHY 1B 162
Golf Links Rd.
EX39: N'ham, West H 5B 20
PL20: Yelv 7F 127
TQ10: Wran 1D 146
Gollands TQ5: Brixh 3D 122
Gollands Cl. TQ5: Brixh 3C 122
Gollands La. EX17: Morc 4C 38
(off Oldborough La.)
Golvers Hill Cl. TQ12: Kingst ...4H 105
Golvers Hill Rd. TQ12: Kingst ...4H 105
Goodeve Cl. PL9: Plyms 6F 143
Goodgates Cl. EX33: Brau 4H 15
Goodgates Cres. EX33: Brau ...4G 15
Goodgates Gro. EX33: Brau 4H 15
Goodgates Pk. EX33: Brau 4H 15
Goodgates Rd. EX33: Brau 4G 15
Gooding Ri. EX16: Tiv 4B 40
GOODLEIGH 3C 161
Goodleigh La. EX19: Wink 2B 36
Goodleigh Rd. EX32: Barn 4G 19
Goodridge Cl. EX7: Daw 2H 97
GOODRINGTON 6G 119 (2A 176)
Goodrington Holiday Cen.
TQ4: Good 3J 119
Goodrington Orchard TQ4: Good ...5J 119
(off Hookhills Rd.)
Goodrington Rd. TQ4: Good 6G 119
Goodrington Station
Dartmouth Steam Railway ...3J 119
Good Shepherd Dr.
EX2: Exe 6E 6 (7F 65)
GOODSTONE 3B 170
Goodstone Way TQ4: Paig 4F 119
Goodwin Av. PL6: Plym 4B 132
Goodwin Cres. PL2: Plym 4G 135
Goodwood Pk. Rd. EX39: N'ham ...7F 21
Gooseberry La.
PL1: Plym 6C 8 (3H 141)
Goose Grn. EX38: Gt T 2D 30
(off Calf St.)
GOOSEHAM 2A 162
GOOSEWELL
Ilfracombe 2A 12
Plymouth 7G 143 (2B 174)
Goosewell Hill PL6: Plym 3C 136
Goosewell Pk. Rd. PL9: Plyms ...6G 143
Goosewell Rd. PL9: Plyms 6G 143
Goosewell Ter. PL9: Plyms 6G 143
Gora La. EX34: Woolc 6B 10
Gordon Rd. EX1: Exe 2J 7 (5H 65)
EX3: Top 7D 72
Gordon's Pl. EX1: Heav 7J 65
Gordon Ter. EX12: Beer 7B 86
PL4: Plym 1F 9 (7K 135)
Gore La. DT7: Uply 5F 91
EX8: Exmth, San B 7G 77
EX13: Kilm 3B 88
Gorfin Cl. EX8: Exmth 4G 77
Gornhay Orchard EX16: Tiv 3G 41
Gorse Ho. EX4: Exe 4B 64
Gorse La. EX8: Exmth 1F 77
Gorse Way PL21: Ivy 5H 145
Gorseway EX10: Sidm 6A 84
Gorsey Cl. PL5: Plym 1K 135
Gorway TQ14: Teignm 3J 107
Gorwell Rd. EX32: Barn 3G 19
Gorwood Rd. EX39: Buck B 4G 29
Gorwyn La. EX6: Cher B 1E 62
Gosceline Wlk. EX14: Hon 5F 55
GOSFORD 1C 80
Gosford La. EX11: Tale 1B 80
Gosford Rd. EX11: Gos, Ott M ...1C 80
Goshen Rd. TQ2: Torq 1A 116
Goslings, The TQ7: Chil 6G 159
Goss Mdw. EX20: N Taw 5H 37
Gostwyck Cl. EX20: N Taw 6B 36
Goswela Cl. PL9: Plyms 7G 143
Goswela Gdns. PL9: Plyms 7G 143
Gothic Rd. TQ12: New A 2E 108
Gould Cl. EX32: Barn 5G 19
Gould Rd. EX32: Barn 5G 19
TQ8: Salc 3C 158
Gourders La. TQ12: Kingsk 3F 111
Govers Mdw. EX24: Colyt 5D 88
GOVETON 3D 175
Gower Ridge Rd. PL9: Plyms ...6E 142
Gowman's Ter. EX20: N Taw 6A 36
Grace Gdns. TQ14: Teignm 3G 107
Grace Rd. Central EX2: Mar B ...3F 71
Grace Rd. Sth. EX2: Mar B 4G 71
Grace Rd. W. EX2: Mar B 3E 70
Grafton Cl. TQ1: Torq 2D 116
(off Grafton Rd.)
Grafton Hgts. TQ1: Torq 1E 116
Grafton Rd. EX4: Exe 3D 64
(not continuous)
PL4: Plym 7K 135

Grafton Rd. TQ1: Torq 2D 116
TQ12: New A 1E 108
Grafton Ter. TQ1: Torq 2D 116
Graham Cl. EX16: Tiv 3D 40
Graham Rd. TQ3: Pres 5G 115
Grainger Cl. EX2: Won 7B 66
Grainge Rd. PL6: Plym 2B 136
Gramercy Flds. TQ5: Brixh 6D 122
Grampian Cl. TQ4: Coll M 3D 118
Granary Ct. EX15: Cull 3K 45
Granary La. EX9: Bud S 5D 82
Granby Ct. PL1: Dev 2D 140
Granby Grn. PL1: Dev 2D 140
Granby Pl. PL1: Dev 2D 140
Granby St. PL1: Dev 1D 140
Granby Way PL1: Dev 2D 140
Grand Hotel Rd.
PL1: Plym 7C 8 (4H 141)
Grandison Av. TQ14: Bi'ton 3C 106
Grandisson Ct. EX2: Cou W 3K 71
Grandisson Dr. EX11: Ott M 4E 80
Grand Pde. PL1: Plym 7C 8 (4H 141)
Grand Pier, The 5J 107
Grand Prix Go Karts
Paignton 4J 119
Grand Vw. Rd. TQ7: Hope 2G 155
Grand Western Canal Country Pk.
4A 42
Grand Western Canal Country Pk.
Visitor Cen. 5E 40
Grange, The EX2: Exe 7K 7 (1H 71)
EX33: Brau 5K 15
Grange Av. EX8: Exmth 3D 76
EX31: Barn 7B 18
TQ4: Good 5H 119
Grange Cl. EX8: Exmth 4D 76
EX8: Lymp 6H 75
EX32: Brat F 6J 13
TQ12: New A 3G 109
Grange Cotts EX5: Rock 3G 69
Grange Ct. *EX32: Barn 3F 19*
(off Yeo Vale Rd.)
Grange Ct. Holiday Cen.
TQ4: Good 4H 119
Grange Dr. TQ14: Teignm 3H 107
Grange Hgts. TQ4: Good 5G 119
Grange Hgts. Cl. TQ4: Good 5G 119
Grange Hill EX31: Brat F 6J 13
Grange Hill Ind. Est. EX31: Brat F 5J 13
Grange La. EX20: Mer 5A 30
Grange Pk. TQ14: Bi'ton 3A 106
Grange Pk. Caravan Pk.
TQ12: A'well 6D 108
Grange Rd. EX39: Bide 4G 23
PL7: Plymp 5C 138
PL20: Yelv 5F 127
TQ1: Torq 1E 116
TQ4: Good 6G 119
TQ11: Buck 2B 98
TQ12: A'well 6E 108
Grange Vw. TQ4: Good 5G 119
TQ12: A'well 6E 108
Grantham Cl. PL7: Plymp 7J 137
Grantlands EX15: Uff 7G 43
Grantley Gdns. PL3: Plym 7B 136
Granville Av. EX32: Barn 3E 18
Granville Pl. *EX15: Will 3C 44*
(off Station Rd.)
Granville Point EX34: Ilfra 2H 11
Granville Rd. EX34: Ilfra 2G 11
Gras Lawn EX2: Exe 7J 7 (1H 71)
Grasmere Cl. PL6: Plym 5K 131
TQ2: Torq 3D 112
Grasmere Ct. *EX4: Exe 7C 64*
(off Lakelands Dr.)
Grassendale Av. PL2: Plym 4E 134
Grasslands Dr. EX1: Pin 4E 66
Grass La. PL2: Plym 5H 135
Grattans Way EX17: Bow 6H 37
GRATTON 2B 162
Gratton Cl. TQ6: Sto F 2H 153
Gratton Ct. EX31: Roun 7B 18
Gratton Dr. TQ7: Chil 6H 159
Gratton La. PL20: Yelv 7G 127
Gratton Pk. EX5: Cranb 3C 68
Gratton Pl. PL6: Plym 2B 136
Grattons Dr. EX35: Lynt 2G 13
Grattons La. TQ9: L'ton 2F 103
Gratton Way EX31: Roun 7B 18
Gravel La. EX12: Seat 3F 87
Gravel Wlk. EX15: Cull 4H 45
Gravesend PL11: Torp 1A 140
Gravesend Gdns. PL11: Torp 1A 140
Gravesend Wlk. PL5: Plym 6C 130
Graybridge Rd. PL20: Horr 2E 126
Gray Cres. PL5: Plym 3B 134
Graynfylde Dr. EX39: Bide 3G 23
Gray's Hill EX15: Hemy 1J 47
Grays Mdw. TQ13: More 6H 61
Gt. Berry Rd. PL6: Plym 2A 136
Great Bridge TQ13: Ashb 3G 99
Gt. Burrow Ri. EX39: N'ham 4E 20
Great Churchway PL9: Plyms 5H 143
Great Cliff EX7: Daw 5H 97
Great Cl. EX15: Culm 1B 46
Great Exmouth 00 Model Railway, The
7D 76
Great Fellingfield PL19: Mary T 2B 60
Great Fld. Gdns. EX33: Brau 5H 15
Greatfield Rd. PL3: Plym 4C 136
Great Furlong TQ14: Bi'ton 3A 106
Great Gate La. *TQ3: Paig 1H 119*
(off Littlegate Rd.)
Gt. Headland Cres.
TQ3: Pres 5J 115
Gt. Headland Rd. TQ3: Pres 5J 115
Great Hill TQ13: Chud 2C 94
Great Hill Rd. TQ2: Torq 1B 112
Great Hill Vw. EX4: Exe 2H 65
Greatlands Cres. PL2: Plym 5F 135
Greatlands Pl. PL2: Plym 5F 135
Great La. TQ7: Malb 6G 155
Gt. Links Tor Rd. EX20: Oke 3D 48
Great Mead EX6: Dunsf 7C 62
Gt. Mis Tor Cl. PL20: Yelv 5F 127
Gt. Oak Mdw. EX22: Hols 1C 34
Gt. Orchard Cl. PL9: Plyms 7F 143
Grea Tor Cl. TQ3: Pres 5F 115
Great Pk. TQ7: Malb 6G 155
Great Pk. Cl. PL7: Plymp 4F 139
TQ14: Bi'ton 4B 106
Greatpark La. TQ3: Paig 1D 118
Gt. Parks Rd. TQ3: Paig 2E 118
GREAT POTHERIDGE 2D 163
GREAT TORR 3C 175
GREAT TORRINGTON 2C 30 (2C 163)
GREAT WEEKE 3K 61
Gt. Western Bus. Pk. EX14: Hon 5C 54
Gt. Western Cl. TQ4: Good 3H 119
Gt. Western Ind. Est. EX32: Barn 6G 19
Gt. Western Rd.
PL1: Plym 7B 8 (4H 141)
TQ4: Paig 1H 119
Gt. Western Way EX16: Tiv 5D 40
Gt. Woodford Dr. PL7: Plymp 5J 137
Greatwood Ter. EX3: Top 5A 74
Grebe Cl. PL7: Plymp 4C 138
Grecian Way EX2: Won 1B 72
Greebys, The TQ3: Paig 1G 119
Green, The EX2: Ide 4A 70
EX5: Whim 6G 53
EX8: L'ham 5H 77
EX9: Ott'n 6H 83
EX15: Cull 4H 45
(off Fore St.)
EX17: Morc 1B 38
EX18: Chul 6C 32
EX31: Frem 6E 16
PL5: Plym 7D 130
PL8: New F 5J 149
PL9: Hooe 6C 142
PL20: Horr 2E 126
(off Jordan La.)
PL20: Meavy 7K 127
TQ13: Ashb 4H 99
(off St Andrews Cl.)
TQ14: Shal 6G 107
Green Acre EX16: Hal 6E 42
Greenacre EX5: Rock 3F 69
EX33: Brau 4H 15
Greenacre Cl. EX20: N Taw 6A 36
EX22: Bradw 6B 28
EX39: N'ham 5F 21
Greenacres EX4: Exe 1D 64
PL9: Plyms 4G 143
Greenacres Cl. EX14: Fen 2G 53
Greenaway EX17: Morc 1B 38
Greenaway Rd. TQ12: New A 7D 104
Greenbank EX10: New P 5G 81
EX38: Gt T 1D 30
PL4: Plym 1H 9
TQ8: Bat 2C 158
Greenbank Av. PL4: Plym 2J 9 (1A 142)
TQ12: Kingst 3G 105
Greenbank Cl. EX38: Gt T 1E 30
Greenbank Cotts. PL4: Plym 1H 9
PL7: Plymp 5A 138
(off Underwood Rd.)
Greenbank Ct. PL4: Plym 2H 9
Greenbank Rd. EX32: Barn 5H 19
PL4: Plym 1G 9 (1A 142)
TQ5: Brixh 4D 122
Greenbanks Cl. TQ7: Slap 2H 159
Greenbank Ter.
PL4: Plym 2H 9 (1A 142)
PL20: Yelv 6G 127
TQ10: S Bre 1C 100
Green Cl. EX8: Exmth 4E 76
EX9: Ott'n 6H 83
(off Maunder's Hill)
TQ7: Kingsb 3G 157
Greenclose Ct. EX24: Colyt 6C 88
Greenclose Rd. EX34: Ilfra 2H 11
Greendale Bus. Pk. EX5: Wood S 1D 78
(not continuous)
Greendale La. EX5: Clyst M 1A 78
Greendale Rd. PL2: Plym 4F 135
Greenfield Cl. EX39: Bide 3D 22
Greenfield Cotts. PL19: Lam 6B 58
Greenfield Dr. PL21: Ivy 5H 145
TQ10: S Bre 3B 100
Greenfield Rd. TQ3: Pres 4G 115
Greenford Vs.
EX2: Exe 7D 6 (1E 70)
Green Gdns. EX39: N'ham 6D 20
GREENHAM
Crewkerne 3D 167
Wellington 1A 166
Greenhaven EX9: Bud S 5B 82
Greenhayes TQ9: Darti 3A 102
Greenhead EX10: Sidb 2F 85
Green Hill PL19: Tavi 3K 59
Greenhill PL19: Lam 6C 58
TQ9: E All 6C 152
TQ12: Kingst 5H 105
Greenhill Av. EX8: Exmth 5E 76
EX8: Lymp 6G 75
Greenhill Cl. PL9: Plyms 7G 143
Greenhill Gdns. TQ12: Kingsk 1F 111
Greenhill La. TQ12: Den 2H 101
Greenhill Rd. PL9: Spri 7H 143
TQ12: Kingsk 1F 111
TQ12: Kingst 5H 105
Greenhill Way TQ12: Kingst 5G 105
Greenings Rd. EX39: Buck B 2J 29
Greenlands Av. TQ3: Paig 1F 119
Greenlands Est. PL19: Tavi 4K 59
Green La. EX3: Exton 1F 75
EX4: Exe 7B 64
EX10: Sidb 2K 85
EX11: Ven O 1G 81
EX12: Axmth 3K 87
EX13: Ray H 2D 90
EX14: Fen 3G 53
EX19: Bea 3H 31
EX20: Hath 1K 35
EX24: Colyf 7C 88 & 1E 86
EX31: Barn 4E 18
(off High St.)
EX33: Brau 4K 15
EX39: Apple 2H 21
PL19: Tavi 4K 59
PL20: Yelv 7D 126
TQ5: Chur F 3A 122
TQ9: E All 5B 152
TQ9: Tot 7B 102
TQ10: Wran 1E 146
Green Lanes Shop. Cen.
EX31: Barn 4E 18
Greenlees Dr. PL7: Plymp 6E 138
Greenmeadow Dr. EX31: Barn 3F 19
Green M. EX9: Bud S 6C 82
Green Mt. EX10: Sidm 5D 84
Greenover Cl. TQ5: Brixh 5D 122
Greenover Rd. TQ5: Brixh 5D 122
Green Pk. Av. PL4: Plym 1E 8 (7J 135)
Greenpark Av. EX1: Pin 5C 66
Green Pk. Rd. PL9: Plyms 6E 142
TQ3: Pres 5F 115
Greenpark Rd. EX8: Exmth 2F 77
Green Pk. Wlk. TQ3: Pres 5F 115
Green Pk. Way TQ7: Chil 6G 159
Greenslade Rd. EX16: With 6H 33
TQ9: Blacka 3C 152
GREENSLINCH 1K 51
Greenslinch La. EX5: Silv 1K 51
Green St. PL4: Plym 4G 9 (2K 141)
Greensway Rd. PL19: Tavi 5G 59
Greenswood Rd. TQ5: Brixh 5E 122
Green Tree La. EX5: Broadc 6D 52
Greenway 6E 120
Greenway DT7: Lym R 5H 91
EX2: Exe 2B 70
EX5: Wood 5B 78
EX12: Seat 5D 86
EX16: Hal 5D 42
EX17: Cred 6G 39
Greenway Av. PL7: Plymp 5J 137
Greenway Cl. PL20: Horr 1E 126
PL21: Ivy 4H 145
TQ2: Torq 4C 112
Greenway Gdns. *EX16: Tiv 4C 40*
(off Wellbrook St.)
TQ2: Torq 3C 112
Greenway Halt Station
Dartmouth Steam Railway 5G 121
Greenway La. EX9: Bud S 5B 82
EX10: Stow 6K 81 & 2A 84
EX14: Awli 1A 54
TQ1: Torq 5D 112
Greenway Pk. TQ5: Galm 4H 121
Greenway Rd. TQ1: Torq 5D 112
TQ2: Torq 2K 115
TQ5: Galm 6E 120
Greenways EX34: Ilfra 3G 11
Greenways Valley Holiday Pk.
EX38: Gt T 4D 30
Greenwood EX15: Will 3E 44
Greenwood Cl. PL21: Ivy 4G 145
TQ7: Ave G 6H 151
Greenwood Dr. EX2: Sow 7C 66
Greenwood Pk. Cl. PL7: Plymp 3E 138
Greenwood Pk. Rd.
PL7: Plymp 3E 138
Greenwoods, The EX39: Hart 2J 27
Gregory Cl. EX16: Tiv 4F 41
EX17: Bow 6H 37
Gregorys Ct. TQ13: Chag 2G 61
Gregory Ter. EX39: Hart 3J 27
Grenadier Rd. EX1: Sow 5D 66
Grenadine Cl. TQ2: Torq 2A 112
Grendon Almshouses EX1: Exe 4J 7
Grendon Bldgs. EX1: Exe 5D 6
Grendon Ct. TQ14: Teignm 4G 107
Grendon Rd. EX1: Exe 4K 7 (6H 65)
GRENOFEN 3C 169
Grenville Av. EX4: Whip 4C 66
TQ2: Torq 7K 111
TQ14: Teignm 2G 107
Grenville Cl. TQ6: Dartm 6D 124
TQ7: Stoke 6K 159
TQ12: New A 1H 109
Grenville Ct. PL7: Plymp 3F 139
Grenville Dr. PL19: Tavi 6H 59
Grenville Est. *EX39: Bide 5D 22*
(off Clovelly Rd.)
Grenville Est. Cres. EX39: Bide 5D 22
Grenville Mdw. PL19: Tavi 6H 59
Grenville Pk. PL20: Yelv 6G 127
Grenville Rd. EX8: Exmth 2E 76
PL4: Plym 4J 9 (2A 142)
TQ8: Salc 4C 158
Grenville Rd. La. Sth.
PL4: Plym 2C 142
(off Greville Rd.)
Grenville St. EX39: Bide 3F 23
Grenville Ter. *EX39: Bide 4G 23*
(off Torrington La.)
EX39: N'ham 5F 21
Grenville Way EX15: Cull 3H 45
TQ4: Good 5H 119
Gresham Cl. PL5: Tam F 3H 131
Greycoat La. TQ12: New A 4B 104
Greyfriars Rd. EX4: Exe 4J 65
GREYLAKE 1D 167
Greysand Cres. EX39: Apple 2H 21
Greystoke Av. PL6: Plym 4D 136
Greystone Way TQ1: Torq 6D 112
Grey Wethers Stone Circles 2A 170
Gribble Cl. EX32: Barn 5H 19
Gribble La. EX5: Rock 2G 69
Gribble Mead EX24: Colyt 6D 88
Grieg Dr. EX32: Barn 4G 19
Griffin Way PL9: Elb 6K 143
Griggs Cl. EX39: N'ham 6F 21
PL7: Plymp 5E 138
Griggs Gdn. EX31: Frem 6E 16
Grigg's La. EX10: Sidm 3E 84
GRIMSCOTT 3A 162
Grimspound 2B 170
Grimspound Cl. PL6: Plym 3F 137
Grimstone Ter. PL20: C'stone 6C 126
GRINACOMBE MOOR 1C 169
GRINDHILL 1C 169
Grindle Way EX5: Clyst M 3G 73
Grizedale Rd. PL6: Plym 4E 136
Gronau Cl. EX14: Hon 5F 55
Grooms, The *EX10: Sidm 7C 84*
(off Russell St.)
Groper's La. TQ3: Comp 5A 110
TQ12: Ipp 5A 110
Grosvenor Av. TQ2: Torq 4J 111
Grosvenor Cl. TQ2: Torq 4J 111
Grosvenor Cotts. *PL4: Plym 7A 136*
(off Belgrave La.)
Grosvenor Ct. PL21: Ivy 4G 145
Grosvenor Mans. *EX10: Sidm 7C 84*
(off Church St.)
Grosvenor Pl. EX1: Exe 2H 7 (5G 65)
Grosvenor Rd. PL6: Plym 1A 136
TQ4: Paig 2H 119
Grosvenor St. EX32: Barn 4F 19
Grosvenor Ter. *EX32: Barn 4F 19*
(off Bear St.)
TQ4: Paig 2H 119
TQ14: Teignm 3H 107
Grove, The EX4: Pin 2D 66
EX10: Sidm 6C 84
EX34: Woolc 6A 10
PL3: Plym 7F 135
PL9: Plyms 4E 142
PL21: Moor 3C 146
TQ4: Paig 4E 118
TQ9: Blacka 3B 152
TQ9: Tot 6E 102
Grove Av. TQ14: Teignm 4H 107
Grove Cl. TQ9: Tot 6E 102

Grove Ct.—Hawkerland Rd.

Grove Ct. EX7: Daw . . . 4J 97
TQ14: Teignm . . . 3J 107
Grove Cres. TQ14: Teignm . . . 4H 107
Grove Hill EX3: Top . . . 5B 74
EX24: Colyt . . . 6D 88
Grove Mdw. EX20: Stic . . . 1F 49
Grove M. TQ9: Tot . . . 6E 102
(off Grove Cl.)
Grove Pk. PL19: Tavi . . . 4K 59
Grove Rd. EX5: Whim . . . 6H 53
Groves, The PL21: Ivy . . . 3G 145
Grove Ter. TQ14: Teignm . . . 4H 107
Growen La. EX15: Cull . . . 2F 45
Guardhouse Visitor Centre, The . . . 3J 123
Guardian Rd. EX1: Sow . . . 6D 66
Gubbin's La. EX33: Brau . . . 5J 15
Guestland Rd. TQ1: Torq . . . 6E 112
Guildford Cl. EX4: Exe . . . 5B 64
PL5: Plym . . . 7K 131
Guildford St. PL4: Plym . . . 3G 9 (2K 141)
Guildhall Shop. Cen.
EX4: Exe . . . 4D 6
Guildhall Sq. PL1: Plym . . . 5E 8 (3J 141)
Guildhall Yd. TQ9: Tot . . . 6E 102
GUINEAFORD . . . 3B 160
Guinea St. EX1: Exe . . . 5D 6 (7E 64)
Guinevere Way EX4: Whip . . . 3K 65
Guinness La. EX4: Exe . . . 4B 64
Gully Shoot EX24: Colyf . . . 1E 86
Gun La. PL1: Dev . . . 2D 140
GUNN . . . 3C 161
GUNNISLAKE . . . 3C 169
Gunswell La. EX36: S Mol . . . 5A 26
Gurnard Wlk. PL3: Plym . . . 5E 136
Gurneys, The TQ3: Paig . . . 2G 119
Gussiford La. EX8: Exmth . . . 6C 76
Guy Miles Way PL5: Plym . . . 7G 131
Guys Rd. EX4: Exe . . . 6C 64
Gwyn Rd. PL4: Plym . . . 1K 9 (1B 142)
Gwythers EX36: S Mol . . . 6D 26

H

Hacche La. EX36: S Mol . . . 4C 26
Haccombe Cl. EX4: Exe . . . 7B 64
Haccombe Path TQ12: New A . . . 2J 109
Hacker Cl. EX10: New P . . . 6H 81
Hackney La. TQ12: Kingst . . . 5J 105
(not continuous)
TQ12: Neth . . . 6K 105
Hackney Marshes Local Nature Reserve . . . 6H 105
Hackworthy Cross La.
EX6: Ted M . . . 6G 49
Hackworthy La. EX6: Ted M . . . 7F 49
Haddeo Dr. EX2: Sow . . . 1C 72
Haddington Rd. PL2: Dev . . . 7D 134
Haddon Ct. TQ3: Paig . . . 7H 115
(off Cecil Rd.)
Haddon Rd. EX13: Shute . . . 4A 88
Hadfield Ct. TQ13: Chud K . . . 6A 94
Hadrian Dr. EX4: Exe . . . 6B 64
Hadrians Way EX8: Exmth . . . 3F 77
HAGGINTON HILL . . . 3B 12
HALBERTON . . . 6D 42 (2A 166)
Halberton Rd. EX15: Will . . . 1A 44
Halcyon Ct. PL2: Plym . . . 5F 135
Halcyon Rd. PL2: Plym . . . 5F 135
TQ12: New A . . . 1E 108
Haldene Ter. EX32: Barn . . . 3E 18
Haldon Av. TQ14: Teignm . . . 3J 107
Haldon Belvedere (Lawrence Castle) . . . 2C 171
Haldon Cl. EX3: Top . . . 7D 72
TQ1: Torq . . . 2G 117
TQ12: New A . . . 2J 109
Haldon Ct. EX8: Exmth . . . 2C 76
Haldon Ho. TQ1: Torq . . . 4D 112
(off Teignmouth Rd.)
Haldon Pl. PL5: Plym . . . 7F 131
Haldon Ri. TQ12: New A . . . 2J 109
Haldon Rd. EX4: Exe . . . 3B 6 (6D 64)
TQ1: Torq . . . 2F 117
Haldon Ter. EX7: Daw . . . 4G 97
(off High St.)
Haldon Vw. TQ13: Chud . . . 2D 94
Haldon Vw. Ter. EX2: Won . . . 6K 7 (7J 65)
Hale La. EX14: Hon . . . 3H 55
Haley Cl. EX8: Exmth . . . 2E 76
Halfmoon Ct. TQ11: B'leigh . . . 6B 98
HALFORD . . . 4F 93
Hallamore La. PL21: Corn . . . 5G 129
Hallerton Cl. PL6: Plym . . . 2F 137
Hallett Ct. DT7: Lym R . . . 4J 91
Halletts Way EX13: Axmin . . . 3J 89
Halley Gdns. PL5: Plym . . . 2D 134
Hall La. EX7: Holc . . . 7F 97
EX17: Morc . . . 2A 38
HALLSANDS . . . 3A 176
HALLSANNERY . . . 7G 23
Hallsannery Field Cen. . . . 7G 23
Hall's La. TQ12: Kingsk . . . 1F 111
Hall's Mill La. EX31: Cher B . . . 1D 18
HALLSPILL . . . 1C 163
HALLWORTHY . . . 2A 168
Halsbury Rd. EX16: Tiv . . . 4F 41
Halscombe La. EX2: Ide . . . 4A 70
Halsdon Av. EX8: Exmth . . . 3C 76
Halsdon La. EX8: Exmth . . . 3C 76
Halsdon Rd. EX8: Exmth . . . 5C 76
Halsdon Ter. EX38: Gt T . . . 2B 30
Halsdown Gdns. EX8: Exmth . . . 2C 76
HALSE . . . 1B 166
Halse Hill EX9: Bud S . . . 6B 82
Halse La. EX20: N Taw . . . 6D 36
Halses Cl. EX4: Exe . . . 4A 64
Halse's La. EX10: N'town . . . 3K 83
HALSINGER . . . 3B 160
Halsteads Rd. TQ2: Torq . . . 3C 112
Halt, The EX2: Alph . . . 4E 70
HALWELL . . . 2D 175
HALWILL . . . 1C 169
HALWILL JUNCTION . . . 1C 169
Halyards EX3: Top . . . 5A 74
EX8: Exmth . . . 6A 76
HAM
Ilminster . . . 2C 167
Plymouth . . . 3F 135 (2A 174)
Taunton . . . 1C 167
Wellington . . . 1B 166
Wilmington . . . 3C 167
Hambeer La. EX2: Exe . . . 2B 70
Hamble Cl. PL3: Plym . . . 4E 136
Hambleton Way TQ4: Paig . . . 5G 119
HAMBRIDGE . . . 1D 167
Ham Cl. PL2: Plym . . . 3G 135
Ham Dr. PL2: Plym . . . 4F 135
Hameldown Cl. TQ2: Torq . . . 6H 111
Hameldown Rd. EX20: Oke . . . 3E 48
Hameldown Way TQ12: New A . . . 7G 105
Hamelin Way TQ2: Torq . . . 6F 111
TQ3: Marl . . . 6F 111
Ham Grn. PL2: Plym . . . 4F 135
Ham Grn. Ct. PL2: Plym . . . 4F 135
Ham Grn. La. PL2: Plym . . . 4F 135
Hamilton Av. EX2: Won . . . 3J 71
Hamilton Cl. EX10: Sidf . . . 1E 84
EX39: Bide . . . 5D 22
Hamilton Ct. EX8: Exmth . . . 6D 76
Hamilton Dr. EX2: Sow . . . 7C 66
TQ12: New A . . . 7E 104
Hamilton Gdns.
PL4: Plym . . . 1E 8 (7J 135)
Hamilton Gro. EX6: Star . . . 2E 96
Hamilton La. EX8: Exmth . . . 5D 76
Hamilton Rd. EX3: Top . . . 7D 72
EX8: Exmth . . . 5F 77
Hamiltons, The TQ14: Shal . . . 6G 107
Ham La. EX10: Sidm . . . 7C 84
EX24: Colyt . . . 6D 88
EX36: S Mol . . . 6E 26
PL2: Plym . . . 2E 134
PL5: Plym . . . 2E 134
TQ6: Ditt . . . 5C 120
TQ14: Shal . . . 7F 107
HAMLET . . . 5C 54
Hamlin Cl. EX16: Tiv . . . 5D 40
Hamlin Gdns. EX1: Heav . . . 5K 65
Hamlin La. EX1: Heav . . . 5K 65
Hamlyns La. EX4: Exe . . . 3A 64
Hamlyns Way TQ11: B'leigh . . . 4C 98
Hammett Rd. EX15: Cull . . . 4G 45
Hammetts La. EX32: Bish T . . . 4B 24
Hammett Sq. EX16: Tiv . . . 5D 40
(off Phoenix La.)
Hammond Cft. Way EX2: Alph . . . 5E 70
Hamoaze Av. PL5: Plym . . . 3C 134
Hamoaze Ct. PL1: Dev . . . 3D 140
Hamoaze Pl. PL1: Dev . . . 2C 140
Hamoaze Rd. PL11: Torp . . . 2A 140
Hampden Pl. EX2: Exe . . . 7C 6
Ham Pl. EX16: Tiv . . . 5C 40
PL2: Plym . . . 3F 135
Hampshire Cl. EX4: Exe . . . 1B 70
Hampson La. EX17: Bow . . . 6F 37
Hampstead La. EX3: Exton . . . 7D 74
HAMPTON . . . 1C 173
Hampton Av. TQ1: Torq . . . 5E 112
Hampton Bldgs. EX4: Exe . . . 1H 7 (5G 65)
Hampton Cl. TQ1: Torq . . . 5E 112
Hampton Ct. EX13: Whitf . . . 5A 90
Hampton La.
EX13: Shute, Whitf . . . 5A 90 & 3B 88
TQ1: Torq . . . 5E 112
Hampton Pk. EX39: Bide . . . 1D 22
Hampton Rd. TQ12: New A . . . 1F 109
Hampton St. PL4: Plym . . . 4F 9 (2K 141)
Hams, The EX2: Ide . . . 4A 70
Hams La. EX34: Com M . . . 5B 12
Hams Pl. EX34: Com M . . . 6B 12
Hancock Cl. PL6: Plym . . . 4J 131
HAND AND PEN . . . 2K 69 (1A 172)
Hand and Pen Cotts. EX5: Whim . . . 2K 69
Handley Ct. EX7: Holc . . . 7G 97
Handsford Way EX11: Ott M . . . 4B 80
Handy Cross EX39: Bide . . . 5D 22
Hangman Path EX34: Com M . . . 5A 12
HANNABOROUGH . . . 3D 163
Hannaburrow La.
EX33: Forda, Saun . . . 7A 14
HANNAFORD . . . 1A 164
Hannaford La. EX32: Swim . . . 3F 25
Hannaford Rd. PL8: Noss M . . . 7H 149
PL16: Lift . . . 7B 56
Hanover Cl. EX1: Heav . . . 6J 65
PL3: Plym . . . 6D 136
TQ5: Brixh . . . 5E 122
Hanover Ct. EX2: Matf . . . 5F 71
Hanover Gdns. EX15: Cull . . . 2H 45
Hanover Ho. TQ1: Torq . . . 3F 117
Hanover Rd. EX1: Heav . . . 6J 65
PL3: Plym . . . 6C 136
Hansford Ct. EX14: Hon . . . 4F 55
Hanson Pk. EX39: N'ham . . . 1E 22
Happaway Cl. TQ2: Torq . . . 3C 112
Happaway Rd. TQ2: Torq . . . 3B 112
HARBERTON . . . 2D 175
Harberton Cl. TQ4: Paig . . . 4E 118
HARBERTONFORD . . . 6B 100 (2D 175)
Harbour, The EX12: Seat . . . 5G 87
TQ4: Paig . . . 2J 119
(off Roundham Rd.)
Harbour Av. PL4: Plym . . . 5G 9 (3K 141)
PL5: Plym . . . 3D 134
Harbour Ct. EX8: Exmth . . . 6B 76
EX12: Seat . . . 5F 87
Harbourne Av. TQ4: Paig . . . 4E 118
HARBOURNEFORD . . . 1D 175
Harbour Rd. EX12: Seat . . . 6F 87
Harbourside Ct. PL4: Plym . . . 5G 9
Harbour St. PL11: Torp . . . 1A 140
Harbour Vw. PL9: Hooe . . . 5B 142
Harbour Vw. Cl. TQ5: Brixh . . . 3E 122
Harbour Vw. Rd. PL5: Plym . . . 3D 134
Harbour Way EX6: Cockw . . . 3E 96
(off Cofton Hill)
HARCOMBE . . . 1B 172
HARCOMBE BOTTOM . . . 4D 90 (1D 173)
Harcombe Flds. EX10: Sidf . . . 2E 84
Harcombe La. EX10: Sidf . . . 2E 84
Harcombe Rd.
DT7: Harc B . . . 1H 91 & 2C 90
EX13: Ray H . . . 2C 90
Hardaway Head EX32: Barn . . . 4F 19
Harding Cres. EX16: Tiv . . . 2E 40
Hardwick Wood Nature Reserve . . . 7J 137
Hardy Cl. TQ1: Torq . . . 4F 117
Hardy Cres. PL5: Plym . . . 2K 135
Hardy Rd. EX2: Won . . . 7C 66
Hardy's Ct. EX10: Col R . . . 2H 83
HARE . . . 2C 167
Harebell Copse EX4: Exe . . . 4A 64
Harebell Dr. EX15: Will . . . 3E 44
HAREFIELD . . . 5J 75
Harefield Cl. EX4: Exe . . . 4D 64
Harefield Cotts. EX8: Lymp . . . 6F 75
Harefield Dr. EX8: Lymp . . . 6H 75
TQ6: Sto F . . . 2H 153
Harefield Rd. EX8: Lymp . . . 5H 75
Harepath Hill EX12: Seat . . . 2C 86
Harepath Rd. EX12: Seat . . . 3E 86
Hares Grn. EX36: S Mol . . . 6C 26
Hares La. TQ13: Ashb . . . 4H 99
Hareston Cl. PL7: Plymp . . . 6E 138
Hare Tor Cl. EX20: Oke . . . 3E 48
Harewood TQ1: Torq . . . 6E 112
(off Cary Pk.)
Harewood Cl. PL7: Plymp . . . 4A 138
Harewood Cres. PL5: Plym . . . 1F 135
HARFORD
Ivybridge . . . 2C 175
Landkey . . . 1D 24
Harford Rd. EX32: L'key . . . 1C 24
PL21: Harf, Ivy . . . 4H 145
Hargood Ter. PL2: Dev, Plym . . . 7E 134
Hargreaves Cl. PL5: Plym . . . 1E 134
Harlech Cl. PL3: Plym . . . 4B 136
Harlequins Shop. Cen. EX4: Exe . . . 3D 6
HARLESTON . . . 3D 175
Harlington Ct. TQ12: New A . . . 7F 105
Harlseywood EX39: Bide . . . 3D 22
Harman Wlk. EX32: Barn . . . 4H 19
Harnorlen Rd. PL2: Plym . . . 4J 135
Haroldsleigh Av. PL5: Plym . . . 1K 135
Harper's Hill TQ9: Tot . . . 7C 102
HARPFORD . . . 4J 81 (1A 172)
Harpins Ct. TQ12: Kingsk . . . 6K 109
Harpitt Cl. EX15: Will . . . 5C 44
HARRACOTT . . . 1D 163
Harrier Ct. EX5: Clyst H . . . 7D 68
Harriers Cl. EX12: Seat . . . 4E 86
Harrier Way EX2: Sow . . . 1D 72
Harriet Gdns. PL7: Plymp . . . 5J 137
Harringcourt Rd. EX4: Pin . . . 2D 66
Harrington Dr. EX4: Pin . . . 2D 66
Harrington Gdns. EX4: Pin . . . 3D 66
Harrington La. EX4: Pin . . . 2B 66
Harris Ct. PL9: Hooe . . . 6C 142
Harrison St. PL2: Dev . . . 7E 134
Harrisons Way EX5: Sto C . . . 7J 51
Harris Way PL21: L Mill . . . 5A 144
HARROWBARROW . . . 3B 168
Harrowbeer La. PL20: Yelv . . . 4F 127
Harrowby Cl. EX16: Tiv . . . 4E 40
HARTFORD . . . 1D 165
HARTLAND . . . 3J 27 (1A 162)
Hartland Abbey & Gardens . . . 1A 162
Hartland Cl. PL6: Plym . . . 3B 132
Hartland Pottery . . . 3H 27
HARTLAND QUAY . . . 1A 162
Hartland Quay Mus. . . . 1A 162
Hartland Tor Cl. TQ5: Brixh . . . 6C 122
Hartland Vw. Rd. EX34: Woolc . . . 7C 10
HARTLEY . . . 4K 135
Hartley Av. PL3: Plym . . . 5A 136
Hartley Ct. PL3: Plym . . . 5B 136
PL21: Ivy . . . 4G 145
Hartley Pk. Gdns. PL3: Plym . . . 5A 136
Hartley Rd. EX8: Exmth . . . 6C 76
PL3: Plym . . . 5K 135
TQ4: Paig . . . 2G 119
HARTLEY VALE . . . 3B 136
Hart Mnr. EX33: Wraf . . . 7K 15
Harton Cross EX39: Hart . . . 3J 27
Harton Way EX39: Hart . . . 3K 27
Harton Way Ind. Est. EX39: Hart . . . 3K 27
Hartopp Rd. EX8: Exmth . . . 4C 76
Hartop Rd. TQ1: Torq . . . 4D 112
Harts Cl. EX1: Pin . . . 4D 66
TQ14: Teignm . . . 3G 107
Harts La. EX1: Pin, Whip . . . 4B 66
(not continuous)
TQ7: Chur . . . 2B 156
Hart St. EX39: Bide . . . 3F 23
HARTSWELL . . . 1A 166
Hartwell Av. PL9: Elb . . . 7K 143
Harvest La. EX39: Bide . . . 2C 22
Harvey Av. PL4: Plym . . . 3C 142
Harvey Cl. EX16: With . . . 6H 33
Harveys Cl. TQ13: Chud K . . . 6B 94
Harvey St. PL11: Torp . . . 1A 140
Harwell Ct. PL1: Plym . . . 4C 8 (2H 141)
Harwell La. TQ10: S Bre . . . 1C 100
Harwell St. PL1: Plym . . . 3C 8 (2H 141)
Harwin Apartments TQ4: Good . . . 3J 119
Harwood Av. PL5: Tam F . . . 3H 131
Harwood Cl. EX8: Exmth . . . 3F 77
Haslam Ct. TQ1: Torq . . . 6C 112
Haslam Rd. TQ1: Torq . . . 6C 112
Hastings St. PL1: Plym . . . 3C 8 (2H 141)
Hastings Ter. PL1: Plym . . . 3C 8 (2H 141)
Haswell Cl. PL6: Plym . . . 3B 136
HATCH BEAUCHAMP . . . 1D 167
Hatchcombe La. TQ2: Torq . . . 3B 112
Hatcher Cl. EX14: Hon . . . 6F 55
Hatcher St. EX7: Daw . . . 4G 97
HATCH GREEN . . . 2D 167
Hatchland Rd. EX4: Polt . . . 6A 52
Hatchmoor Comn. La. EX38: Gt T . . . 1E 30
Hatchmoor Est. EX38: Gt T . . . 2D 30
Hatchmoor Ind. Est. EX20: Hath . . . 3G 35
EX38: Gt T . . . 1E 30
Hatchmoor Rd. EX38: Gt T . . . 2D 30
Hatfield TQ1: Torq . . . 7D 112
Hatfield Rd. TQ1: Torq . . . 7D 112
HATHERLEIGH . . . 2H 35 (3D 163)
Hatherleigh La. TQ13: Bov T . . . 7K 63
Hatherleigh Pl. EX16: Tiv . . . 4D 40
Hatherleigh Rd. EX2: Exe . . . 3D 70
EX19: Wink . . . 3A 36
EX20: Oke . . . 2A 48
Hatshill Cl. PL6: Plym . . . 7H 133
Hatshill Farm Cl. PL6: Bickl . . . 1H 133
HATT . . . 1A 174
Hatway Hill EX10: Sidb . . . 2J 85
Hauley Rd. TQ6: Dartm . . . 2B 124 (6F 125)
Havelock Rd. TQ1: Torq . . . 4D 112
Havelock Ter. PL2: Dev . . . 1E 140
PL21: Lutt . . . 7F 129
Haven, The TQ14: Bi'ton . . . 3B 106
HAVEN BANKS . . . 7E 6 (1F 71)
Haven Banks EX2: Exe . . . 7D 6 (1E 70)
Haven Banks Outdoor Education Cen. . . . 7E 6 (1F 71)
Haven Banks Retail Pk.
EX2: Exe . . . 7D 6 (1E 70)
Haven Cl. EX2: Exe . . . 7D 6 (1E 70)
Haven Ct. EX12: Seat . . . 6F 87
(off Harbour Rd.)
Haven Rd. EX2: Exe . . . 7C 6 (1E 70)
Havenview Rd. EX12: Seat . . . 5E 86
Hawarden Cotts. PL4: Plym . . . 3C 142
(off Cavendish Rd.)
Haweswater Cl. PL6: Plym . . . 6K 131
HAWKCHURCH . . . 3D 167
HAWKERLAND . . . 2A 172
Hawkerland Rd. EX10: Col R . . . 2F 83

Hawkers Av.—Hickory Cl.

Hawkers Av. PL4: Plym 5G 9 (3K 141)
Hawkers La. PL3: Plym 6K 135
Hawkesdown Cl. EX12: Axmth 3H 87
Hawkes Way TQ9: Tot 6E 102
Hawkinge Gdns. PL5: Plym 6D 130
Hawkins Av. TQ2: Torq 6J 111
Hawkins Cl. PL6: Plym 5B 132
Hawkins Dr. TQ14: Teignm 3H 107
Hawkins La. EX11: W Hill 5H 79
Hawkins Pl. EX15: Cull 3H 45 (off Grenville Way)
Hawkins Rd. TQ12: New A 1J 109
Hawkins Wlk. EX20: Oke 3D 48
Hawkins Way EX17: Cred 6K 39
HAWKRIDGE 1C 165
Hawkridge Rd. EX31: Chive 1D 16
Hawksdown Vw. EX12: Seat 3E 86
Hawks Dr. EX16: Tiv 3E 40
Hawley Cl. EX32: Barn 4G 19
Hawley Mnr. EX32: Barn 4G 19
Hawthorn Av. EX34: Ilfra 3K 11
Hawthorn Cl. EX14: Hon 4E 54
– EX15: Cull 5G 45
– PL6: Plym 3E 132
– PL9: Hooe 7D 142
– TQ7: Kingsb 5F 157
– TQ12: New A 4J 109
Hawthorn Dr. EX10: Sidm 2A 84
– PL9: Wem 7B 148
Hawthorne Rd. EX16: Tiv 2F 41
Hawthorne Wlk. PL21: L Mill 5A 144 (off Holly Berry Rd.)
Hawthorn Gro. EX8: Exmth 3G 77
– PL2: Plym 4H 135
Hawthorn Pk. EX20: Lyd 5H 57
– EX39: Bide 4D 22
Hawthorn Pk. Cl. TQ2: Torq 3K 115
Hawthorn Pk. Rd. PL9: Wem 7B 148
Hawthorn Rd. EX2: Won 2J 71
– EX17: Cred 6H 39
– EX32: Barn 5K 19
– PL19: Tavi 7J 59
Hawthorn Row TQ9: Tot 7G 103
Hawthorn Way EX2: Alph 5D 70
– PL3: Plym 4C 136
Haxter Cl. PL6: Robo 1C 132
Haxton Down La. EX31: Brat F 7J 13
– EX32: Brat F 7J 13
Haxton La. EX31: Brat F 6H 13
Haycock La. TQ5: Brixh 3G 123
Haycross Hill EX21: Sheb 6H 29
Haydn Cl. EX32: Barn 4H 19
HAYDON 1C 167
Haydon Gro. PL5: Plym 2B 134
Haydon Rd. EX16: Tiv 3B 40
Haydons Pk. EX14: Hon 4F 55
HAYE 3B 168
Haye Cl. DT7: Lym R 4H 91
Haye La. DT7: Lym R 3H 91
Haye Rd. PL9: Elb 2J 143
Haye Rd. Sth. PL9: Elb 5K 143
Hayes, The TQ5: Chur F 3A 122
Hayes Barton Ct. EX4: Exe 5B 6 (7D 64)
Hayes Cl. EX9: Bud S 5C 82
– EX9: Ott'n 6H 83
– TQ9: Tot 7G 103
Hayes Ct. DT7: Lym R 5J 91
– TQ4: Paig 2F 119
Hayes Gdns. TQ4: Paig 3G 119
Hayes La. EX9: E Bud 1A 82
Hayes Pl. PL6: Plym 3C 136
Hayes Rd. PL9: Plyms 5D 142
– TQ4: Paig 3F 119
Hayes Sq. EX5: Cranb 3B 68
Hayeswood La. EX9: E Bud 2A 82
Hayfield Rd. EX20: Exbo 5J 35
Hay La. TQ7: Malb 6G 155
Hayle Av. TQ4: Good 7H 119
Hayley Pk. TQ12: Kingsk 2F 111
Haymans Cl. EX15: Cull 5G 45
Haymans Grn. EX15: Cull 5G 45
Haymans Orchard
– EX5: Wood 5C 78
HAYNE 3C 165
Hayne Cl. EX4: Exe 5K 65
– EX10: Tip J 1J 81
Hayne Ct. EX16: Tiv 1E 40
Hayne Hill EX10: Harp, Tip J 4J 81
Hayne La. EX5: Silv 3J 51
– EX14: Gitt 5B 54
Hayne Pk. EX10: Tip J 1J 81
– EX32: Barn 5G 19
Haystone Pl. PL1: Plym 2B 8 (1H 141)
Haytor Av. TQ4: Paig 5F 119
Haytor Cl. PL5: Plym 7G 131
– TQ14: Teignm 3F 107
Haytor Dr. EX4: Exe 5B 64
– PL21: Ivy 5H 145
– TQ12: New A 1J 109
Haytor Granite Tramway 3B 170
Haytor Gro. TQ12: New A 1K 109
Haytor Pk. TQ12: Kingst 4H 105
Haytor Rd. TQ1: Torq 6D 112
– TQ13: Bov T 4A 92
Haytor Rocks 3B 170
Haytor Ter. TQ12: New A 1E 108
HAYTOR VALE 3B 170
Haytor Vw. TQ12: Heat 1K 93
HAYTOWN 2B 162
Haywain Cl. TQ2: Torq 4H 111
Hazel Av. EX33: Brau 3K 15
Hazelbank Ct. PL5: Plym 2A 134
Hazel Cl. EX10: New P 5H 81
– EX12: Seat 3E 86
– PL6: Plym 4C 132
– TQ7: Kingsb 5F 157
– TQ12: New A 3K 109
– TQ14: Teignm 1H 107
Hazeldene Gdns. EX8: Exmth 3C 76
Hazeldown Rd. TQ14: Teignm 2H 107
Hazel Dr. PL9: Elb 5K 143
Hazel Gro. EX5: Rock 4F 69
– EX31: Roun 7B 18
– PL9: Elb 5K 143
– PL20: Yelv 5G 127
Hazelmead Rd. EX5: Clyst M 3J 73
Hazel Rd. EX2: Won 3J 71
– PL19: Tavi 7J 59
Hazelwood TQ1: Torq 1F 117 (off Lwr. Warberry Rd.)
Hazelwood Cl. EX14: Hon 5F 55
– TQ5: Brixh 4F 123
Hazelwood Cres. PL9: Elb 7K 143
Hazelwood Dr. EX7: Daw W 7D 96
– PL6: Plym 2E 132
Headborough Rd. TQ13: Ashb 3F 99
Headingley Cl. EX2: Won 1B 72
Headland Cl. EX1: Whip 5B 66
Headland Cres. EX1: Whip 5B 66
Headland Gro. TQ3: Pres 5J 115
Headland Pk. PL4: Plym 1G 9 (1K 141)
Headland Pk. Rd. TQ3: Pres 5J 115
Headland Rd. TQ2: Torq 4A 116
Headlands, The TQ2: Torq 4A 116
Headlands Vw. Av. EX34: Woolc 5E 10
Headon Gdns. EX2: Cou W 4K 71
Headway Cl. TQ14: Teignm 4F 107
Headway Cross Rd.
– TQ14: Teignm 3F 107
Headway Ri. TQ14: Teignm 3F 107
Head Weir Rd. EX15: Cull 2H 45
HEALE 2C 161
Heal Pk. Cres. EX31: Frem 6E 16
Heal's Fld. EX13: Axmin 2K 89
Healy Pl. PL2: Dev 1D 140
Heanton Hill La. EX31: Chive 1D 16
Heanton Lea EX31: Chive 1D 16
HEANTON PUNCHARDON 3B 160
Heanton St. EX33: Brau 5J 15
Heard Av. EX8: Exmth 4G 77
Heard Cl. EX39: Hart 3J 27
Hearts of Oak EX2: Sow 7D 66
HEASLEY MILL 3D 161
Heath Cl. EX14: Hon 5C 54
– TQ12: Heat 2K 93
Heathcoat Sq. EX16: Tiv 4C 40
Heathcoat Way EX16: Tiv 4E 40
Heath Ct. TQ5: Brixh 2G 123
– TQ9: Tot 6E 102
HEATH CROSS 1B 170
Heather Cl. EX1: Whip 6A 66
– EX12: Seat 3F 87
– EX14: Hon 6C 54
– EX16: Tiv 2F 41
– EX20: Oke 3B 48
– PL19: Tavi 5K 59
– TQ12: New A 7C 104
– TQ14: Teignm 2H 107
Heatherdale EX8: Exmth 6E 76
Heatherdene TQ13: Bov T 4B 92
Heather Est. TQ12: Heat 1J 93
Heather Grange EX11: W Hill 5H 79
Heather M. PL21: Ivy 4G 145
Heather Pk. TQ10: S Bre 1C 100
Heathers, The EX8: Exmth 5F 77
– EX20: Oke 2D 48
– PL6: Plym 3E 132
Heather Ter. PL20: Prin 6C 60
Heather Wlk. PL21: Ivy 5H 145
Heather Way TQ5: Brixh 4C 122
HEATHFIELD
– Chudleigh Knighton 2J 93 (3C 171)
– Norton Fitzwarren 1B 166
Heathfield Bus. Pk. TQ12: Heat 1J 93
Heathfield Cl. TQ13: Bov T 6B 92
Heathfield Cotts. TQ12: Heat 1K 93
Heathfield Ho. TQ13: Bov T 5B 92 (off Ashburton Rd.)
Heathfield Mdw. TQ13: Bov T 6B 92
Heathfield Pk. PL20: Dous 4H 127
Heathfield Rd. EX39: Bide 4H 23
– PL4: Plym 1C 142
– PL21: Corn 6H 129
– TQ12: Den 2H 101
Heathfield Ter. TQ13: Bov T 5B 92
Heath Hill TQ12: Heat 2K 93
Heathlands Ct. TQ14: Teignm 1G 107 (off Heathlands Ri.)
Heathlands Ri. TQ14: Teignm 1G 107
Heath Pk. TQ5: Brixh 3G 123
– TQ12: New A 3K 109
Heathpark Ind. Est. EX14: Hon 5C 54
Heathpark Way EX14: Hon 4C 54
Heath Ri. TQ5: Brixh 3G 123
Heath Rd. EX2: Won 1A 72
– EX6: Bridf 7D 62
– TQ5: Brixh 3F 123
HEATHSTOCK 3C 167
Heath Way TQ9: Tot 6E 102 (not continuous)
Heaton Hill EX33: Wraf 6K 15
Heatree Cl. TQ14: Teignm 1H 107
Heaviside Cl. TQ2: Torq 2D 112
HEAVITREE 6K 65 (1D 171)
Heavitree Pk. EX1: Heav 7K 65
Heavitree Rd. EX1: Exe 3G 7 (6G 65)
Hector Cl. EX19: Dol 6H 31
HEDDON 1A 164
Heddon Valley Shop Information Cen. 2C 161
Hederman Cl. EX5: Silv 2H 51
Hedge Row Cl. EX17: Cop 6C 38 (off Wright Dr.)
Hedgerow Cl. EX17: Cred 5K 39
– PL6: Plym 2F 133
HEDGING 1D 167
Hedingham Cl. PL7: Plymp 5F 139
Hedingham Gdns. PL6: Plym 3C 132
Heggadon Cl. EX5: Bradn 1D 52
Heights, The PL19: Tavi 3G 59
HELE
– Ashburton 3F 99
– Exeter 3D 165
– Holsworthy 1B 168
– Ilfracombe 2B 160
– Torquay 4B 112 (1B 176)
Hele Cl. EX31: Roun 6K 17
– PL6: Bickl 1H 133
– TQ2: Torq 4B 112
Hele Corn Mill 2B 160
Hele Gdns. PL7: Plymp 5C 138
Hele La. EX31: Roun 6K 17
Helena Pl. EX8: Exmth 6C 76
Helens Mead Cl. TQ2: Torq 1C 112
Helens Mead Rd. TQ2: Torq 1C 112
Hele Park Golf Course 6A 104
Hele Ri. EX31: Roun 6K 17
Hele Rd. EX4: Exe 2B 6 (5D 64)
– EX5: Bradn 4B 52
– TQ2: Torq 4A 112
– TQ12: Kingst 2G 105
Heles Ter. PL4: Plym 2C 142
Hele Valley Holiday Pk.
– EX34: Ilfra 3K 11
Helford Dr. TQ4: Good 7H 119
Helford Wlk. TQ4: Good 7H 119
Heligan Dr. TQ3: Paig 6E 114
HELLAND 1D 167
Hellevoetsluis Way
– TQ3: Marl 3E 114
Hellier Cl. EX14: Hon 5D 54
Hellings Gdns. EX5: Broadc 5C 52
Hellings Pk. La.
– EX5: Broadc 1K 67 & 7E 52
Helmdon Ri. TQ2: Torq 5H 111
Helmers Way TQ7: Chil 6G 159
Helston Cl. TQ3: Paig 7F 115
Heltor Bus. Pk. TQ12: Heat 7E 92
Hembury 3B 166
Hembury Castle 1D 175
Hembury Cock Hill TQ11: B'leigh 2B 98
Hembury Pk. TQ11: Buck 2C 98
HEMERDON 2F 139 (2B 174)
Hemerdon Hgts. PL7: Plymp 3D 138
Hemerdon La. PL7: Hem, Plymp 1E 138
Hemerdon Vs. PL7: Plymp 3B 138 (off Colebrook Rd.)
Hemerdon Way PL7: Plymp 3A 138
Hems Brook Ct. TQ2: Torq 5H 111
HEMYOCK 2G 47 (2B 166)
Hemyock Rd. EX15: Culm 3B 46
Henacre La. TQ7: Kingsb 4H 157
Henacre Rd. TQ7: Kingsb 4G 157
Henbury Cl. TQ1: Torq 7D 112
Henderson Pl. PL2: Plym 5E 134
Hendwell Cl. PL6: Plym 4K 131
Heneaton Sq. EX2: Cou W 5A 72
HENFORD 1B 168
HENLADE 1C 167
Henlake Cl. PL21: Ivy 3F 145
HENLEY 1D 167
Henley Dr. PL5: Tam F 3H 131
Henley Rd. EX8: Exmth 5E 76
Hennapyn Rd. TQ2: Torq 3A 116
Hennis, The EX4: Exe 2F 7
HENNOCK 2C 171
Hennock Ct. EX2: Mar B 4G 71
Hennock Rd. TQ4: Paig 5F 119
Hennock Rd. Central EX2: Mar B 4F 71
Hennock Rd. E. EX2: Mar B 4G 71
Hennock Rd. Nth. EX2: Mar B 3F 71
Henrietta Pl. EX4: Exe 3C 6
– EX8: Exmth 5C 76 (off Clarence Rd.)
Henrietta Rd. EX8: Exmth 5C 76
Henry Cl. PL21: L Mill 5A 144
Henry Lewis Cl. EX5: Whim 6G 53
Henrys Run EX5: Cranb 3B 68
Henry's Way DT7: Lym R 4K 91
Hensbury La. PL20: Bere F 6C 128
Hensford M. EX7: Daw 7A 96
Hensford Rd. EX7: Daw 1F 97
Hensleigh Dr. EX2: Exe 5J 7 (7H 65)
Hensleigh Rd. EX16: Tiv 4A 40
Hen St. EX5: Bradn 1C 52
Henty Av. EX7: Daw 3J 97
Henty Cl. EX7: Daw 2J 97
HENWOOD 3A 168
Heppenstall Rd. EX32: Barn 3F 19
Heraldry Row EX2: Sow 1C 72 (off Heraldry Way)
Heraldry Wlk. EX2: Sow 1C 72 (off Heraldry Way)
Heraldry Way EX2: Sow 1C 72
Herbert Pl. PL2: Dev 7D 134
Herbert Rd. EX1: Heav 5J 65
– TQ2: Torq 2K 115
– TQ8: Salc 4B 158
Herbert St. PL2: Dev 7D 134
Hereford Cl. EX8: Exmth 1F 77
Hereford Rd. EX4: Exe 6A 64
– PL5: Plym 5G 131
Heritage Ct. EX14: Hon 3F 55
Heritage Grange EX8: Exmth 5E 76
Heritage Pk. PL19: Tavi 3K 59
Heritage Way EX10: Sidm 2C 84
Hermes Av. EX16: Tiv 5E 40
Hermitage, The EX34: Ilfra 3H 11 (off Hermitage Rd.)
Hermitage Ct. PL4: Plym 7K 135
Hermitage Rd. EX34: Ilfra 2H 11
– PL3: Plym 6K 135
– TQ6: Dartm 5D 124
Hermosa Gdns. TQ14: Teignm 4H 107
Hermosa Rd. TQ14: Teignm 4H 107
Hernaford Rd. TQ9: H'ford 7B 100
HERNER 1D 163
Hern La. PL8: Yeal 2B 150
Heron Ct. EX8: Exmth 6E 76
– EX32: Barn 5K 19
Heron Rd. EX2: Exe 2A 70
– EX2: Sow 7D 66
– EX14: Hon 5E 54
Herons Brook EX20: Oke 2A 48
Herons Reach TQ7: W Cha 7K 157
Heron Way EX15: Cull 5G 45 (off Ploudal Rd.)
– TQ2: Torq 2J 111
Herschel Gdns. PL5: Plym 2D 134
Herschell Rd. EX4: Exe 1J 7 (4H 65)
HERSHAM 3A 162
Hertland Wlk. PL2: Plym 4F 135
Hescane Pk. EX6: Cher B 2C 62
Hesketh Cres. TQ1: Torq 3F 117
Hesketh M. TQ1: Torq 3F 117
Hesketh Rd. TQ1: Torq 3F 117
Hessary Dr. PL6: Robo 2D 132
Hessary Ter. PL20: Prin 6C 60
Hessary Vw. PL19: Tavi 3H 59
– PL20: Prin 6C 60
Hestow Rd. TQ12: Kingst 1H 105
Hetling Cl. PL1: Plym 3B 8 (2H 141)
Hewers Row PL4: Plym 4G 9 (2K 141)
Hewett Cl. TQ12: New A 1K 109
HEWISH 3D 167
HEWOOD 3D 167
Hexham Pl. PL2: Plym 3F 135
HEXTON 6D 142
Hexton Hill Rd. PL9: Hooe 6C 142
Hexton Quay 6C 142
HEXWORTHY 3A 170
Hexworthy Av. EX4: Exe 4B 64
Heybrook Av. PL5: Plym 2C 134
HEYBROOK BAY 3B 148 (3A 174)
Heybrook Dr. PL9: Hey B 4B 148
Heydon's La. EX10: Sidm 6B 84
Heyridge Mdw. EX15: Cull 6G 45
Heyswood Av. EX32: Barn 7H 19
Heywood Cl. EX39: Hart 3J 27
– TQ2: Torq 6K 111
Heywood Dr. EX6: Star 1D 96
Heywood Est. TQ12: Kingst 6G 105
Heywood Rd. EX39: Bide, N'ham 6E 20
Heywoods Cl. TQ14: Teignm 4J 107 (off Heywoods Rd.)
Heywoods Rd. TQ14: Teignm 4J 107
Hibernia Ter. PL5: Plym 3D 134
Hickory Cl. EX14: Hon 4H 55

Hickory Dr.—Hillsborough

Hickory Dr. PL7: Plymp 4E 138
Hicks La. PL4: Plym 5F 9 (3K 141)
Hides Rd. EX10: Sidm 2D 84
Hierns La. EX34: Ilfra 2J 11
High Acre Dr. PL21: Ivy 3E 144
HIGHAMPTON 3C 163
High Bank EX11: W Hill 5H 79
Highbank Cl. PL19: Tavi 5G 59
HIGH BICKINGTON 2C 32 (1A 164)
HIGH BRAY 3C 161
Highbridge Ct. *PL7: Plymp 4B 138*
(off Ridgeway)
HIGH BULLEN 1D 163
High Bullen EX5: Silv 1H 51
Highbury Cres. PL7: Plymp 2A 138
Highbury Hill EX39: N'ham 4F 21
Highbury Pk. EX8: Exmth 3C 76
Highbury Rd. EX32: Barn 6H 19
TQ1: Torq 7D 112
Highclere Gdns. PL6: Plym 2C 132
Highcliff Ct. *EX7: Daw 4H 97*
(off E. Cliff Rd.)
Highcliffe Cl. EX8: Lymp 7F 75
EX12: Seat 6D 86
Highcliffe Ct. EX8: Lymp 7F 75
Highcliffe Cres. EX12: Seat 6D 86
Highcliffe M. TQ4: Good 3J 119
Highcliff Rd. DT7: Lym R 5H 91
High Cl. TQ13: Bov T 4D 92
High Cft. EX4: Exe 3D 64
Highcroft Ct. EX4: Exe 3D 64
High Cross *EX32: Swim 3H 25*
(off High St.)
Highcross Rd. EX4: Exe 1E 6 (4F 65)
Higher Aboveway EX6: Exmin 3D 74
Higher Aller La. TQ13: Bov T 1A 92
HIGHER ASHTON 2C 171
Higher Audley Av. TQ2: Torq 5B 112
Higher Axmouth EX12: Axmth 4K 87
Higher Barley Mt. EX4: Exe 6B 64
Higher Bedlands EX9: Bud S 5B 82
Higher Bibbery TQ13: Bov T 4D 92
Higher Brand La. EX14: Hon 6F 55
Higher Brimley TQ14: Teignm 3H 107
Higher Brimley Rd.
TQ14: Teignm 4H 107
HIGHER BRIXHAM 5E 122
Higher Broad Oak Rd.
EX11: High M, W Hill 7G 79
Higher Broad Pk. TQ6: Dartm 6D 124
Higher Brook Mdw. EX10: Sidf 1D 84
Higher Brook Pk. PL21: Ivy 4E 144
Higher Brook St. TQ14: Teignm . . . 4H 107
Higher Buckeridge Rd.
TQ14: Teignm 2H 107
Higher Budleigh Mdw.
TQ12: New A 1C 108
Higher Buzzacott La.
EX34: Com M 7E 12
Higher Cadewell La. TQ2: Torq . . . 4H 111
HIGHER CHERITON 3B 166
Higher Church St. EX32: Barn 5F 19
Higher Churchway PL9: Plyms . . . 5H 143
Higher Clevelands *EX39: N'ham 6E 20*
(off Churchill Way)
HIGHER CLOVELLY 6F 27 (1B 162)
HIGHER COMPTON 5B 136 (2A 174)
Higher Compton Barton
TQ3: Comp 7E 110
Higher Compton Rd. PL3: Plym . . 5A 136
Higher Contour Rd.
TQ6: Kingsw 5H 125
Higher Coombe Dr.
TQ14: Teignm 2G 107
Higher Copythorne TQ5: Brixh 4C 122
Higher Cotteylands EX16: Tiv 5A 40
Higher Cross Mdw. EX16: Sam P . . 2B 42
Higher Cross Orchard
EX16: Sam P 2A 42
(off Higher Cross Mdw.)
Higher Cross Rd. EX31: Bick'n 5A 18
HIGHER DEAN 7A 98 (1D 175)
Higher Dean La. EX34: Com M 7D 12
Higher Doatshayne La.
EX13: Mus 7D 90
Higher Down EX6: Kenton 6H 95
Higher Downs Rd. TQ1: Torq 5E 112
Higher Dr. EX7: Daw 2J 97
HIGHER DUNSTONE 3B 170
Higher Duryard EX4: Exe 1F 65
Higher Edginswell La.
TQ2: Torq 6G 111
Higher Efford Rd. PL3: Plym 6C 136
Higher Elmwood EX31: Roun 6B 18
Higher Erith Rd. TQ1: Torq 2F 117
Higher Exeter Rd. TQ14: Teignm . . 1G 107
Higher Exwick Hill EX4: Exe 5B 64
Higher Fortescue EX10: Sidm 3E 84
Higher French Pk. TQ12: New A . . . 1C 108
Higher Furzeham Rd. TQ5: Brixh . . 2E 122
HIGHER GABWELL 1J 113 (1B 176)
Higher Grn. TQ10: S Bre 2C 100
Higher Greenhead EX10: Sidb 2G 85
Higher Greenway La.
EX10: Sidm, Stow 3A 84
Higher Gunstone EX39: Bide 3F 23
Higher Hill Vw. EX10: Sidm 5B 84
Higher Holcombe Cl.
TQ14: Teignm 2J 107
Higher Holcombe Dr.
TQ14: Teignm 1J 107
Higher Holcombe Rd.
TQ14: Teignm 1J 107
Higher Hoopern La. EX4: Exe 3F 65
(not continuous)
Higher Island TQ9: Blacka 2C 152
HIGHER KEATON . . . . . . 7H 145 & 1H 147
Higher King's Av. EX4: Exe 3G 65
Higher Kingsdown Rd.
TQ14: Teignm 4F 107
Higher Kinsman's Dale
TQ13: More 6H 61
Higher La. EX12: Axmth 3H 87
PL1: Plym 5E 8
Higher La. Cl. EX12: Axmth 3H 87
Higher Ley EX17: Nym R 2F 37
Higher Lincombe Rd. TQ1: Torq . . . 3F 117
Higher Loughborough EX16: Tiv . . . 3B 40
Higher Mnr. Rd. TQ5: Brixh 3E 122
Higher Mnr. Ter. *TQ3: Paig 2G 119*
(off Manor Ter.)
Higher Maudlin St. EX32: Barn 3F 19
Higher Maunders Hill EX9: Ott'n . . . 7H 83
Higher Mead EX15: Hemy 2G 47
Higher Mdw. EX5: Cranb 4B 68
EX37: High B 2B 32
Higher Mdws. EX12: Beer 7B 86
HIGHER METCOMBE 7H 79
Higher Millhayes EX15: Hemy 1G 47
Higher Mill La. EX15: Cull 4H 45
TQ11: Buck 2C 98
(not continuous)
Higher Moor Sq. EX16: Tiv 2F 41
Higher Mowles PL3: Plym 5C 136
Higher New Cl. La. EX31: Ashf 1A 18
Higher Orchard EX15: Cull 3G 45
Higher Pk. Cl. PL7: Plymp 6E 138
Higher Pk. Rd. EX33: Brau 4K 15
Higher Penn TQ5: Brixh 5F 123
Higher Polsham Rd. TQ3: Paig 7H 115
Higher Queen's Ter. TQ1: Torq 1D 116
Higher Raleigh Rd. EX31: Barn 2E 18
Higher Ramshill La.
TQ3: Blag, Paig 6B 114
Higher Ranscombe Rd.
TQ5: Brixh 4F 123
Higher Redgate EX16: Tiv 3D 40
Higher Rews Cl. EX34: Com M 5A 12
Higher Ridgeway EX11: Ott M 3D 80
Higher Ringmore Rd.
TQ14: Shal 6E 106
Higher Rd. EX5: Wood S 1A 78
EX17: Cred 4F 39
EX31: Frem 6F 17
Higher Roborough TQ13: Ashb 3J 99
Higher Rydons TQ5: Brixh 4C 122
Higher Sackery TQ12: C'head 7A 106
Higher Sandygate TQ12: Kingst . . . 1G 105
Higher Shapter Cl. EX3: Top 6B 74
Higher Shapter St. EX3: Top 6B 74
Higherside TQ6: Dartm 2A 124
HIGHER SLADE 5F 11 (2B 160)
Higher Slade Rd. EX34: Ilfra 5F 11
Higher Spring Gdns. EX11: Ott M . . . 4D 80
Higher Steps *TQ5: Brixh 3E 122*
(off Higher St.)
Higher Stert Ter.
PL4: Plym 4K 9 (2B 142)
Higher St. EX15: Cull 3H 45
EX20: Hath 2H 35
TQ5: Brixh 3E 122
TQ6: Dartm 1B 124 (6F 125)
TQ6: Ditt 6B 120
TQ6: Kingsw 6G 125
Higher Summerlands
EX1: Exe 3H 7 (6G 65)
HIGHER TALE 3A 166
Higher Ter. *EX22: Bradw 5B 28*
(off North Rd.)
HIGHER TOWN
Buckfastleigh 4B 98
Sampford Peverell 2A 42
Higher Town EX16: Sam P 2A 42
TQ7: Malb 6G 155
Highertown PL20: Horr 1E 126
Higher Tuckers Pk. EX22: Bradw . . . 5B 28
Higher Union La. TQ2: Torq 1C 116
Higher Union Rd. TQ7: Kingsb 4F 157
Higher Warberry Rd. TQ1: Torq 1E 116
Higher Warborough Rd.
TQ5: Galm 2H 121
HIGHER WARCOMBE 2E 10
Higher Warren Rd. TQ7: Kingsb . . . 6H 157
Higher Way EX10: Harp 4J 81
HIGHER WEAR 4J 71
Higher Wear Rd. EX2: Cou W 6B 72
Higher Wellbrook St. EX16: Tiv 4B 40
Higher Well Farm Holiday Pk.
TQ9: Sto G 7B 118
Higher Westlake Rd. EX31: Roun . . . 7K 17
Higher Westonfields TQ9: Tot 6G 103
HIGHER WHITELEIGH 1A 168
HIGHER WINSFORD 4B 22
Higher Woodfield Rd. TQ1: Torq . . . 3E 116
Higher Woodford La.
PL7: Plymp 4K 137
Higher Woodway Cl.
TQ14: Teignm 2J 107
Higher Woodway Rd.
TQ14: Teignm 1H 107
HIGHER WOOLBROOK 3A 84
Higher Woolbrook Pk.
EX10: Sidm 3A 84
HIGHER YALBERTON 4D 118 (2A 176)
Higher Yalberton Rd. TQ4: Paig . . . 4D 118
Higher Yannon Dr.
TQ14: Teignm 3G 107
Highfield EX3: Top 6E 72
EX10: Sidm 5B 84
(off Brewery La.)
EX14: Hon 4E 54
EX17: Lap 2K 37
EX39: N'ham 6D 20
Highfield Cl. EX32: Barn 5G 19
EX37: High B 2B 32
PL3: Plym 6D 136
TQ5: Brixh 4C 122
Highfield Cres. TQ3: Paig 1E 118
Highfield Dr. PL9: Wem 6B 148
TQ7: Kingsb 5G 157
Highfield Gdns. EX34: Com M 6B 12
Highfield La. EX8: Exmth 6D 76
Highfield Rd. EX14: Dunk 7G 47
EX34: Ilfra 3H 11
Highfield Ter. EX12: Beer 7B 86
EX32: Bish T 5A 24
EX34: Ilfra 3J 11
PL21: Bitta 4C 146
Highfield Vineyards 4A 40
Highglen Dr. PL7: Plymp 2E 138
Highgrove Pk. TQ14: Teignm 2J 107
HIGH HAM 1D 167
High Ho. Cl. EX7: Daw 3H 97
High Ho. La. TQ7: Kingsb 5G 157
Highland Cl. TQ2: Torq 7J 111
Highland Pk. EX15: Uff 6G 43
Highland Rd. TQ2: Torq 7J 111
Highlands EX11: Ott M 4C 80
PL8: Yeal 2B 150
Highlands Pk. TQ13: Chud 1C 94
Highland St. PL21: Ivy 4G 145
Highland Ter. EX15: Uff 6G 43
EX16: Tiv 4D 40
Highland Vw. EX20: Oke 5C 48
High Mdw. EX10: Sidm 3C 84
High Mdws. EX4: Exe 7B 64
High Moorland (Dartmoor National Park)
Visitor Cen. 7C 60
Highmount Ct. EX15: Will 2D 44
High Pk. Cl. EX39: Bide 5C 22
High Rd. PL9: Wem 6A 148
High St. EX2: Ide 4A 70
EX3: Top 7D 72
EX4: Exe 4D 6 (6E 64)
EX5: Bradn 2C 52
EX5: Silv 1H 51
EX5: Sto C 7J 51
EX6: Kenton 6H 95
EX7: Daw 4G 97
EX8: Exmth 6C 76
EX9: Bud S 7C 82
EX9: E Bud 1D 82
EX10: New P 5F 81
EX10: Sidm 6C 84
EX14: Hon 4E 54
EX15: Cull 4H 45
EX15: Hemy 2G 47
EX15: Kent 6B 46
EX15: Uff 6H 43
EX16: Bam 2G 33
EX16: Hal 5D 42
EX17: Cred 6G 39
EX19: Wink 2C 36
EX20: Exbo 6J 35
EX20: Hath 2H 35
EX20: N Taw 6B 36
EX20: Oke 4B 48
EX22: Hols 2C 34
EX31: Barn 4E 18
(not continuous)
EX32: Swim 2H 25
EX34: Com M 6B 12
EX34: Ilfra 3H 11
EX37: High B 2C 32
EX38: Gt T 2C 30
EX39: Bide 3F 23
High St. EX39: Clov 5H 27
PL1: Plym 5F 9
(Buckwell St.)
PL1: Plym 3F 141
(Edgcumbe St.)
TQ9: Tot 6D 102
TQ13: Chag 3H 61
High Vw. EX14: Fen 1G 53
EX39: Bide 4D 22
High Vw. Gdns. EX8: Exmth 5D 76
High Vw. Ter. EX39: West H 6B 20
High Wall EX31: Barn 5D 18
HIGHWEEK 6C 104 (3C 171)
Highweek Cl. TQ12: New A 6C 104
Highweek Rd. TQ12: New A 7D 104
(not continuous)
Highweek St. TQ12: New A 1E 108
Highweek Village TQ12: New A 6C 104
Highweek Way TQ12: New A 1E 108
Highwell Rd. EX12: Seat 5E 86
High Willhays 621 m (2,038 ft) . . . 2D 169
Highwood Grange TQ12: New A . . . 2E 108
(not continuous)
Hilary Cl. EX13: Axmin 3J 89
Hilary Gdns. EX13: Axmin 3J 89
Hill, The EX13: Kilm 2B 88
Hill Barton Cl. EX1: Whip 5B 66
Hill Barton La. EX1: Whip 5B 66
(not continuous)
Hill Barton Rd. EX1: Sow, Whip 4C 66
EX2: Sow 7C 66
Hillborough EX5: Wood 5C 78
Hillbrook Ri. TQ9: Tot 6G 103
Hillbrook Rd. TQ9: Tot 6G 103
Hillcliff Ter. *EX39: Apple 2H 21*
(off Irsha St.)
Hill Cl. EX4: Exe 3G 65
PL7: Plymp 5A 138
HILLCOMMON 1B 166
Hill Cres. EX14: Hon 3G 55
Hill Crest EX6: Exmin 2C 74
EX13: Kilm 2B 88
EX16: Tiv 3D 40
PL3: Plym 6K 135
PL21: Erm 2H 147
Hillcrest EX11: Ott M 4C 80
EX15: Cull 3H 45
EX20: S Taw 1J 49
Hillcrest Cl. PL7: Plymp 4D 138
PL9: Wem 7B 148
Hillcrest Dr. PL7: Plymp 5D 138
Hillcrest Pk. EX4: Exe 2F 65
Hillcrest Rd. EX5: Silv 1H 51
EX32: Barn 7G 19
EX39: Bide 5J 23
Hillcroft Ter. EX39: Bide 3F 23
Hilldale Rd. PL9: Plyms 6F 143
Hilldean Cl. PL5: Tam F 3H 131
Hilldown TQ9: Tot 6G 103
Hilldown Rd. EX17: Bow 7J 37
Hill Dr. EX8: Exmth 1D 76
Hilldrop Ter. TQ1: Torq 1D 116
Hiller La. TQ12: Neth 2K 109
HILLERTON 1B 170
Hillesdon Rd. TQ1: Torq 1D 116
HILLFARRANCE 1B 166
Hillfield EX20: S Zeal 3H 49
TQ9: Sto G 4B 120
Hill Gdn. Cl. EX39: Bide 3F 23
Hill Gdns. PL12: Car 1A 130
HILLHEAD 6K 123 (2B 176)
Hill Head *EX16: Hal 6D 42*
(off Pond Hill)
EX37: Chit 5J 25
Hillhead EX24: Colyt 7C 88
Hillhead Holiday Pk. TQ5: Hill 7J 123
Hillhead Pk. TQ5: Hill 6J 123
Hillhead Ter. EX13: Axmin 4H 89
Hill House Gdns. 1D 175
Hilliers EX19: Dol 6H 31
Hillington EX34: Ilfra 4G 11
Hill La. EX1: Whip 4A 66
(not continuous)
PL3: Plym 4A 136
Hillmans Rd. TQ12: New A 2F 109
HILLMOOR 3C 46
Hill Pk. PL21: Lutt 7G 129
Hill Pk. Cl. TQ5: Brixh 4G 123
Hill Pk. Cotts. PL21: Lutt 6G 129
Hill Pk. Cres. PL4: Plym . . . 1G 9 (1K 141)
Hill Pk. M. PL4: Plym 1H 9 (1A 142)
Hill Pk. Rd. TQ1: Torq 6C 112
TQ5: Brixh 4G 123
TQ12: New A 7C 104
Hill Pk. Ter. TQ4: Paig 2J 119
Hill Path PL5: Plym 5E 130
Hill Ri. EX1: Whip 5B 66
Hillrise TQ5: Galm 3H 121
Hill Ri. Rd. DT7: Lym R 5J 91
Hill Rd. DT7: Lym R 5J 91
TQ12: New A 2E 108
HILLSBOROUGH 3K 11

Hillsborough—Horsdon Rd.

Hillsborough PL4: Plym 7A 136
TQ1: Torq 2D 116
(off Hillesdon Rd.)
Hillsborough Av. EX4: Exe 1F 7 (5F 65)
Hillsborough Pk. Rd. EX34: Ilfra 3K 11
Hillsborough Rd. EX34: Ilfra 2J 11
Hillsborough Ter. EX34: Ilfra 2J 11
Hillsdunne Rd. PL3: Plym 5K 135
HILLSIDE 1C 100 (1D 175)
Hill Side EX10: Sidb 3H 85
Hillside EX10: New P 5F 81
EX11: W Hill 3J 79
EX12: Brans 5F 85
EX24: Colyt 6C 88
EX32: L'key 2A 24
PL21: Bitta 3C 146
TQ10: S Bre 1B 100
Hillside Av. EX4: Exe 1E 6 (5F 65)
PL4: Plym 7J 135
Hillside Camp TQ4: Good 6H 119
Hillside Cl. PL20: Buck M 5A 126
TQ10: S Bre 1C 100
TQ14: Teignm 2F 107
Hillside Cotts. PL8: Noss M 7H 149
PL21: Lutt 7G 129
TQ12: A'well 6D 108
Hillside Ct. PL7: Plymp 3B 138
PL20: Bere A 2C 128
TQ6: Dartm 6E 124
Hillside Cres. PL9: Plyms 4G 143
Hillside Dr. PL8: Torr 3B 150
TQ7: Kingsb 5G 157
Hillside Rd. EX10: Sidm 6C 84
EX34: Ilfra 3K 11
TQ3: Paig 7F 115
TQ5: Brixh 4E 122
Hillside Ter. EX39: Bide 3F 23
(off Pitt La.)
TQ3: Paig 1G 119
(off Colley End Pk.)
Hillside Vw. EX34: Com M 6B 12
Hillside Way PL8: Torr 3C 150
Hill St. PL4: Plym 4G 9 (2K 141)
Hills Vw. EX32: Barn 4F 19
EX33: Brau 4J 15
Hill Top EX31: Frem 5F 17
Hilltop Cotts. PL8: Brixt 2G 149
Hill Top Crest PL5: Plym 1D 134
Hilltop Rd. EX39: Bide 1D 22
Hill Vw. EX7: Holc 7F 97
EX10: Sidm 5C 84
EX11: Ott M 4C 80
PL20: Buck M 5A 126
Hill Vw. Ter. TQ1: Torq 6C 112
Hillway La. EX10: N'town 6J 81
Hillyfield Rd. EX1: Whip 5B 66
Hilly Gdns. Rd. TQ1: Torq 4D 112
Hillymead EX12: Seat 4F 87
Hilton Av. PL5: Plym 2H 135
Hilton Cres. TQ3: Pres 4J 115
Hilton Dr. TQ3: Pres 5J 115
Hilton Pk. Homes EX33: Brau 5J 15
Hilton Rd. TQ12: New A 2F 109
Hindharton La. EX39: Hart 2J 27
Hind St. EX11: Ott M 4C 80
TQ13: Bov T 3C 92
Hingston Ct. PL6: Plym 3B 136
Hingston Rd. TQ1: Torq 6E 112
Hinton Ct. PL6: Plym 2D 136
HINTON ST GEORGE 2D 167
Hirmandale Rd. PL5: Plym 7E 130
Hirscombe La. EX17: Morc 1A 38
HISCOTT 1D 163
HITTISLEIGH 1B 170
HITTISLEIGH BARTON 1B 170
HM Dockyard PL1: Dev 2C 140
HM Dockyard Nth. PL2: Dev 5B 134
HM Dockyard Sth. PL1: Dev 3C 140
HMP Channings Wood
TQ12: Den 1J 101
HMP Dartmoor PL20: Prin 5C 60
HMP Exeter EX4: Exe 2D 6 (5E 64)
Hobart St. PL1: Plym 5A 8 (3G 141)
Hobb's Hill EX33: Croy 3C 14
Hobbs Way EX17: Bow 5G 37
Hobby Dr., The EX39: Clov 5H 27
Hockmoor Hill TQ11: B'leigh 1A 98
HOCKWORTHY 2A 166
Hodder's La. DT7: Harc B 1H 91
Hodders Way PL12: Car 1A 130
Hodges Wlk. EX38: Gt T 2D 30
Hodson Cl. TQ3: Paig 7F 115
HOE, THE 4J 141 (2A 174)
Hoe App. PL1: Plym 6E 8 (3J 141)
Hoe Ct. PL1: Plym 6D 8
Hoe Gdns. PL1: Plym 6E 8
Hoegate Ct. PL1: Plym 6E 8
Hoegate Pl. PL1: Plym 6E 8
Hoegate St. PL1: Plym 6F 9 (3K 141)
Hoe Park 6D 8 (4J 141)
Hoe Rd. PL1: Plym 7C 8 (4H 141)
Hoe St. PL1: Plym 6E 8 (3J 141)
Hofheim Dr. EX16: Tiv 2A 40
Hogarth Cl. PL9: Elb 6J 143
Hogarth Ho. PL19: Tavi 3J 59
(off Taylor Sq.)
Hogarth Wlk. PL9: Elb 6J 143
Hoile La. TQ9: Sto G 3A 120
Hoker Rd. EX2: Won 7K 65
Holbeam Cl. TQ12: New A 7B 104
HOLBETON 6C 150 (2C 175)
Holborn Pl. PL7: Plymp 3B 138
Holborn Rd. TQ5: Brixh 2E 122
Holborn St. PL4: Plym 5J 9 (3A 142)
Holbrook Ter. TQ7: Stoke 6J 159
HOLCOMBE 7F 97 (3D 171)
Holcombe Court 1G 43
Holcombe Down Rd.
TQ14: Teignm 1H 107
Holcombe Dr. EX7: Holc 7G 97
PL9: Plyms 7G 143
Holcombe La. EX11: Ott M 1E 80
Holcombe Rd. EX7: Holc 7F 97
TQ14: Teignm 2K 107
HOLCOMBE ROGUS 2G 43 (2A 166)
Holcombe Village EX7: Holc 7F 97
HOLDITCH 3D 167
Holdridge La. EX36: N Mol 2C 26
Holdstone Down 2C 161
Holdstone Way EX34: Com M 7D 12
Holdsworth Ho. TQ6: Dartm 2A 124
Holdsworth St.
PL4: Plym 1C 8 (1H 141)
Holebay Cl. PL9: Plyms 7H 143
Holebrook La. EX20: Exbo 5J 35
Hole Cleave Rd.
EX33: Forda, Lobb 6A 14
Hole Ct. EX20: Hath 1H 35
Hole Hill EX16: With 4K 33
EX20: Exbo 6K 35
Hole La. EX33: Forda 7A 14
HOLEMOOR 3C 163
Holestone La. EX9: Ott'n 4K 83
HOLLACOMBE 3B 162
Hollacombe La. TQ3: Pres 5K 115
Hollamoor Vw. EX31: Bick'n 6A 18
Hollam Way TQ12: Kingst 3J 105
Holland Cl. EX31: Bick'n 5K 17
Holland Hall EX4: Exe 3D 64
Holland Rd. EX2: Exe 1C 70
EX8: Exmth 3F 77
PL3: Plym 5K 135
PL7: Plymp 4F 139
PL9: Plyms 6G 143
Hollands Pk. Av. EX34: Com M 6C 12
Hollands Rd. TQ14: Teignm 5J 107
Holland St. EX31: Barn 4E 18
Holland Wlk. EX31: Barn 4E 18
(off Holland St.)
Hollerday Dr. EX35: Lynt 1G 13
Holley Cl. EX6: Exmin 2C 74
Holley Pk. EX20: Oke 2D 48
HOLLICOMBE 4K 115
Hollies, The EX31: Roun 6A 18
Hollingarth Way EX15: Hemy 1G 47
Hollington Ho. TQ1: Torq 2F 117
Hollis Cl. EX11: Ott M 3D 80
HOLLOCOMBE 2A 164
Holloway Gdns. PL9: Plyms 7H 143
Holloway St. EX2: Exe 6E 6 (7F 65)
Hollow Hayes PL6: Plym 3C 136
(off Goosewell Hill)
Hollow La. EX1: Pin 5C 66
Hollowpits Ct. EX2: Alph 5E 70
Hollows, The EX8: Exmth 5D 76
PL9: Elb 4J 143
Hollowtree Ct. EX32: Barn 6G 19
Hollowtree Rd. EX32: Barn 6G 19
Holly Ball La. EX5: Whim 5J 53
Holly Berry Rd. PL21: L Mill 5A 144
Holly Cl. EX5: Broadc 5C 52
EX14: Hon 5F 55
EX16: Tiv 3E 40
TQ13: Chud 1D 94
Holly Ct. PL6: Plym 4F 137
Hollycroft Rd. PL3: Plym 4B 136
Hollyhead Rd. EX12: Beer 4A 86
Hollymount Cl. EX8: Exmth 1E 76
Holly Pk. Cl. PL5: Plym 5F 131
Holly Pk. Dr. PL5: Plym 5F 131
Holly Rd. EX2: Won 2J 71
EX16: Tiv 3E 40
Holly Wlk. EX8: Exmth 1F 77
Hollywater Cl. TQ1: Torq 1F 117
Holly Water Rd. EX17: Cher F 2F 39
Holly Way EX15: Cull 2H 45
Hollywood Ter. PL1: Plym 3A 8
HOLMACOTT 1D 163
Holman Cl. EX7: Daw 2J 97
Holman Ct. PL2: Plym 3H 135
Holman Hill TQ12: A'well 4A 110
Holmans Bldgs. PL1: Dev 2C 140
Holman Way EX3: Top 6B 74
PL21: Ivy 3E 144
Holmbush Way PL8: Brixt 3H 149
Holmdale EX10: Sidm 6C 84
Holme Ct. TQ1: Torq 1F 117
Holmer Down PL6: Plym 3E 132
Holmes Av. PL3: Plym 6C 136
Holmes Field EX20: Stic 1G 49
Holmes Rd. TQ12: Heat 2J 93
Holmwood Av. PL9: Plyms 7F 143
HOLNE 1D 175
Holne Chase PL6: Plym 3C 132
Holne Ct. EX4: Exe 4B 64
Holne Cross TQ13: Ashb 3F 99
Holne Moor Cl. TQ3: Paig 7E 114
Holne Ri. EX2: Won 7A 66
Holne Rd. TQ11: B'leigh 2A 98
HOLSWORTHY 2C 34 (3B 162)
HOLSWORTHY BEACON 3B 162
Holsworthy Leisure Cen. 1C 34
Holsworthy Mus. 2C 34
Holsworthy Rd. EX20: Hath 3F 35
Holsworthy Rural Life History Mus.
2C 34
Holsworthy Theatre 2C 34
Holt, The EX14: Hon 2H 55
Holtwood Dr. PL21: Ivy 4E 144
Holtwood Rd. PL6: Plym 4E 132
Holwell Cl. PL9: Plyms 7H 143
Holwell La. EX16: Colli 7C 40
Holwell Rd. TQ5: Brixh 4D 122
Holwill Dr. EX38: Gt T 2C 30
Holwill Tor Wlk. TQ4: Paig 4F 119
HOLY CITY 3D 167
Holyford La. EX12: Seat 1D 86
EX24: Colyf 1D 86
Holyford Woods Local Nature Reserve
1B 86
Holyrood Pl. PL1: Plym 7D 8 (4J 141)
Holyshute Gdns. EX14: Hon 2G 55
(off Monkton Rd.)
HOLYWELL LAKE 1B 166
Homebaye Ho. EX12: Seat 6F 87
(off Harbour Rd.)
Homebourne Ho. TQ4: Paig 2J 119
(off Belle Vue Rd.)
Home Cl. TQ5: Brixh 5E 122
TQ7: Chil 6H 159
Homeclyst Ho. EX2: Exe 7C 6
Homecombe Ho. TQ1: Torq 5E 112
(off St Albans Rd.)
Homecourt Ho. EX4: Exe 5C 6
Home Farm Cl. EX33: Croy 2D 14
Home Farm Rd. EX31: Frem 6E 16
PL9: Plyms 4F 143
Homefield TQ7: Thur 6C 154
Homefield Cl. EX11: Ott M 4D 80
Homefield Rd. EX1: Heav 6J 65
Homelace Ho. EX14: Hon 4F 55
Homelands Pl. TQ7: Kingsb 3F 157
Homelands Rd. TQ7: Kingsb 3F 157
Home Mdw. TQ9: Tot 6E 102
Home Orchard EX16: Sam P 2B 42
Homepalms Ho. TQ1: Torq 7B 112
(off Teignmouth Rd.)
Home Park 6H 135
Home Pk. PL2: Dev 7E 134
TQ13: Ashb 3H 99
Home Pk. Av. PL3: Plym 5K 135
Homer Cl. EX31: Brat F 6H 13
Homer Ct. EX33: Brau 3G 15
Homer Cres. EX33: Brau 3G 15
Homer Dr. EX33: Brau 3G 15
Homer La. EX12: Seat 4D 86
(not continuous)
Homer Pk. PL9: Hooe 7D 142
Homer Pk. La. Sth. PL9: Hooe 7D 142
Homer Ri. PL9: Elb 5J 143
Homer Rd. EX33: Brau 3G 15
Homers Cl. TQ12: Kingst 5G 105
Homers Cres. TQ12: Kingst 5G 105
Homers La. TQ12: Kingst 5G 105
Homestead Rd. TQ1: Torq 5C 112
Homestead Ter. TQ1: Torq 5C 112
Home Sweet Home Ter.
PL4: Plym 6K 9 (3B 142)
Hometeign Ho. TQ12: New A 7G 105
(off Salisbury Rd.)
Hometor Ct. EX8: Exmth 4C 76
Homeyards, The TQ14: Shal 6G 107
(off Commons Old Rd.)
Homeyards Botanical Gdns. 6G 107
Honcray PL9: Plyms 4E 142
Honestone St. EX39: Bide 4F 23
HONEYCHURCH 3A 164
Honey Cl. EX39: Bide 3J 23
Honey Ditches Dr. EX12: Seat 4D 86
Honeylands Dr. EX4: Exe 5K 65
Honeylands Way EX4: Exe 5K 65
Honey La. EX1: Pin 2E 66
EX5: Wood S 1C 78
Honeymeadows EX22: Hols 2C 34
Honey Pk. Rd. EX9: Bud S 5D 82
Honey St. EX39: N'ham 5F 21
Honeysuckle Cl. EX16: Tiv 2F 41
EX31: Roun 6A 18
PL6: Plym 3F 133
TQ3: Paig 6E 114
Honeysuckle Ct. EX4: Exe 4A 64
Honeysuckle Dr. EX14: Hon 5C 54
Honeywell TQ12: Kingst 5H 105
Honeywell Cl. EX32: Barn 7G 19
Honeywell Rd. TQ12: Kingst 5H 105
Honeywill Ct. EX2: Heav 7K 65
HONICKNOWLE 1H 135
Honicknowle Grn. PL5: Plym 7G 131
Honicknowle La. PL2: Plym 2G 135
PL5: Plym 2G 135
HONITON 3F 55 (3B 166)
Honiton Bottom Rd. EX14: Hon 5F 55
Honiton Bus. Pk. EX14: Hon 3E 54
Honiton Caravan and Camping Club
EX14: Hon 2H 55
Honiton Cl. PL5: Plym 7G 131
Honiton Golf Course 6H 55
Honiton Rd. EX1: Heav 7A 66
EX5: Clyst H 5F 67
EX15: Cull 3J 45
Honiton Road (Park & Ride) 6D 66
Honiton Sports Cen. 3E 54
Honiton Station (Rail) 4F 55
Honiton Swimming Pool 2F 55
Honiton Wlk. PL5: Plym 6G 131
Honors Farm EX5: Sto C 7J 51
Hooda Cl. EX32: Swim 2H 25
Hoodown La. TQ6: Kingsw 5G 125
HOOE 6C 142 (2B 174)
Hooe Hill PL9: Hooe 7D 142
Hooe Lake PL10: Mill 7A 140
Hooe Rd. PL9: Hooe 6C 142
Hooker Cl. EX9: Bud S 5B 82
Hook Farm Camping and Caravan Pk.
DT7: Uply 3F 91
Hookhills Dr. TQ4: Good 6J 119
Hookhills Gdns. TQ4: Good 7H 119
Hookhills Gro. TQ4: Good 6J 119
Hookhills Rd. TQ4: Good 7H 119
Hook La. TQ5: Galm 5G 121
Hooksbury Av. PL7: Plymp 6E 138
HOOKWAY 1C 171
Hooper Cl. EX20: Hath 2G 35
Hoopern Av. EX4: Exe 3F 65
Hoopern La. EX4: Exe 1F 7 (4F 65)
Hoopern M. EX4: Exe 1E 6 (4E 64)
Hoopern St. EX4: Exe 1E 6 (5F 65)
Hoopern Ter. EX7: Daw 4G 97
(off Stockton Rd.)
Hoopers Ct. EX5: Rock 3E 68
Hooper St. PL11: Torp 1B 140
Hoopers Way EX38: Gt T 2E 30
Hope Barton Barns TQ7: Hope 4H 155
Hope By-Pass TQ7: Hope 2G 155
Hope Cl. TQ9: Tot 6H 103
Hope Ct. EX4: Exe 4F 65
(off Prince of Wales Rd.)
HOPE COVE 3G 155
Hope Hall EX4: Exe 4F 65
Hope Pl. EX2: Won 7K 65
Hope Rd. EX2: Won 7K 65
Hope's Cl. TQ14: Teignm 3G 107
Hope Wlk. TQ9: Tot 6H 103
Hopkins Ct. TQ12: New A 1F 109
(off Hopkins La.)
Hopkins La. TQ12: New A 1F 109
Hopperstyle EX31: Bick'n 6A 18
Hopton Cl. PL6: Plym 3A 136
Hopton Dr. EX38: Gt T 2E 30
Horace Rd. TQ2: Torq 3B 112
Horizon Vw. EX39: West H 5B 20
Hornapark Cl. PL16: Lift 7B 56
HORN ASH 3D 167
Hornbeam Cl. EX14: Hon 5D 54
EX16: Tiv 3F 41
Hornbeam Gdns. EX5: Bradn 1D 52
Hornbeam Hollow EX31: Roun 6B 18
Hornbrook Gdns. PL6: Plym 4J 131
Hornby St. PL2: Plym 7E 134
Hornchurch La. PL5: Plym 6D 130
Hornchurch Rd. PL5: Plym 5D 130
Horn Cross Rd. PL9: Plyms 5F 143
HORNDON 1E 60 (2D 169)
Hornebrook Av. EX34: Ilfra 3H 11
(off Horne Rd.)
Horne Pk. Av. EX34: Ilfra 3H 11
(off Horne Pk. Rd.)
Horne Pk. Rd. EX34: Ilfra 3H 11
Horne Rd. EX34: Ilfra 3H 11
Horn Hill TQ6: Dartm 1A 124
Horn La. PL8: Brixt 2H 149
PL9: Plyms 5F 143
Horn La. Flats PL9: Plyms 5G 143
HORNSBURY 2D 167
HORNS CROSS 1B 162
Horns Pk. TQ14: Bi'ton 3A 106
HORRABRIDGE 2E 126 (1B 174)
Horsdon Rd. EX16: Tiv 4F 41

Horsdon Ter.—Joy St.

Horsdon Ter. EX16: Tiv 4F 41
HORSEBRIDGE 3C 169
Horseguards EX4: Exe 1E 6 (5F 65)
Horse La. TQ14: Shal 6H 107
Horsepond Mdw. EX36: S Mol 7C 26
Horsepool St. TQ5: Brixh 5D 122
Horseshoe Bend TQ4: Good 5J 119
Horseshoe Cl. TQ13: Chud 2C 94
Horseshoe Dr. PL7: Plymp 4A 138
Horsham La. PL5: Plym 1H 135
PL5: Tam F 2G 131
Horslears EX13: Axmin 5G 89
Horswell Cl. PL7: Plymp 4E 138
HORTON 2D 167
HORTON CROSS 2D 167
HORWOOD 1D 163
Hosegood Way TQ12: Kingst 4G 105
Hosford Cl. PL9: Plyms 7G 143
Hoskings Ct. TQ11: B'leigh 4C 98
Hospital Hill EX7: Daw 4G 97
Hospital La. EX1: Whip 4B 66
TQ13: Ashb 3J 99
(not continuous)
Hospital Rd. PL4: Plym 2H 9 (1A 142)
Hostle Pk. EX34: Ilfra 2J 11
Hostle Pk. Gdns. *EX34: Ilfra* *2H 11*
(off Hostle Pk. Rd.)
Hostle Pk. Rd. EX34: Ilfra 2J 11
Hotel Endsleigh Gdns. 3B 168
Hotham Pl. PL1: Plym 2A 8 (1G 141)
Houghton La. EX10: N'town 1K 83
Houldsworth Rd. PL9: Plyms 5D 142
Houndbeare La. EX5: Ayle, Mar G . . . 7K 69
Houndiscombe Rd.
PL4: Plym 1F 9 (1K 141)
HOUNDSMOOR 1B 166
Hound Tor Cl. TQ4: Good 1H 121
Hound Tor Deserted Medieval Village
. . . . 3B 170
House of Marbles & Teign Valley Glass
. . . . 6B 92
Housman Cl. PL5: Plym 7J 131
Howard Av. EX32: Barn 5G 19
Howard Cl. EX4: Exe 4B 64
EX7: Daw 4G 97
(Brook St.)
EX7: Daw 4F 97
(off Penfield Gdns.)
EX20: Oke 2D 48
PL5: Plym 1E 134
PL19: Tavi 4G 59
TQ2: Torq 7K 111
TQ14: Teignm 2G 107
Howard Ct. PL1: Plym 7B 8
TQ14: Teignm 2G 107
Howard Rd. PL9: Plyms 4F 143
Howards Cl. EX36: S Mol 7C 26
Howards Way PL21: Ivy 3E 144
TQ12: New A 7J 105
Howarth Cl. EX10: Sidm 2B 84
Howden Ind. Est. EX16: Tiv 6B 40
Howden La. EX16: Tiv 5B 40
Howden Rd. EX16: Tiv 5B 40
Howell Rd. EX4: Exe 1B 6 (5D 64)
Howeson La. PL6: Plym 6B 132
HOWLEIGH 2C 167
HOWLEY 3C 167
How St. PL4: Plym 5F 9 (3K 141)
Howton La. TQ12: New A 7J 93
Howton Rd.
TQ12: New A . . . . 7J 93 & 5A 104
Hoxton Rd. TQ1: Torq 1D 116
Hoyles Ct. TQ3: Paig 6E 114
Hoyle's Rd. TQ3: Paig 6E 114
Hubbastone Rd. EX39: Apple 3H 21
Huccaby Cl. TQ5: Brixh 6B 122
Hughes Av. EX32: Barn 6G 19
Hugh Squier Av. EX36: S Mol 5D 26
HUISH 7C 30 (2D 163)
HUISH CHAMPFLOWER 1A 166
HUISH EPISCOPI 1D 167
Huishlane End EX6: Ted M 6H 49
HULHAM 1D 76 (2A 172)
Hulham Rd. EX8: Exmth 3D 76
Hulham Va. EX8: Exmth 2E 76
Hulk La. EX5: Thor 4C 50
HUMBER 1A 106 (3D 171)
Humber Cl. PL3: Plym 5E 136
Humber La. TQ12: Kingst 3J 105
TQ14: Teignm . . . . . . 1A 106 & 3J 105
Hume Av. EX35: Lynt 2F 13
Hummingbird Cl. EX1: Pin 3D 66
Humphries Pk. EX8: Exmth 3F 77
Humpy, The EX7: Daw 3F 97
Hungerford Rd. PL2: Plym 5G 135
Hungry Fox Est. EX5: Broadc 1K 67
Huniver's La. EX17: Cred 7H 39
Hunivers Pl. EX17: Cred 7J 39
Hunsdon Rd. PL21: Ivy 6D 144
TQ1: Torq 2E 116
Huntacott Way TQ2: Torq 5H 111
Hunter Cl. PL6: Plym 1A 136
Hunter La. *EX34: Woolc 6A 10*
(off Mill La.)
Hunters Cl. PL21: Ivy 4F 145
Hunters Ga. EX20: Oke 2D 48
Hunters Hill EX15: Culm 1B 46
Hunters Moon *TQ1: Torq 2F 117*
(off Babbacombe Rd.)
TQ9: Darti 4B 102
Hunters Tor Dr. TQ4: Good 1H 121
Hunters Way EX15: Culm 1B 46
(not continuous)
Hunterswell Rd. TQ12: New A 1D 108
Hunterswood EX38: Gt T 2E 30
Hunter Wlk. *EX32: Barn 4H 19*
(off Martin Rd.)
HUNTHAM 1D 167
Hunthay La. EX13: Axmin 2E 88
Huntingdon Gdns. PL5: Plym 6J 131
Huntland Wood 2D 165
Huntley Cl. EX13: Axmin 2K 89
Huntley Pl. PL3: Plym 7D 136
Huntley Vs. PL3: Plym 7D 136
Hunton Cl. EX8: Lymp 6G 75
HUNTSHAM 1A 166
HUNTSHAW 1D 163
HUNTSTILE 1C 167
HURCOTT 2D 167
Hurdwick Rd. PL19: Tavi 4G 59
Hurrabrook Cl. PL6: Plym 1F 137
Hurrabrook Gdns. PL6: Plym 1F 137
Hurrell Cl. PL6: Plym 4J 131
Hurrell Ct. PL3: Plym 6D 136
TQ7: Kingsb 4F 157
Hurrell Rd. TQ7: Kingsb 4F 157
HURSEY 3D 167
Hursley Bus. Pk. PL6: Robo 1F 133
Hurst Av. EX2: Won 1A 72
Hurst Cl. PL9: Plyms 7G 143
Hurst's Almshouses EX2: Exe 5F 7
HUTCHERLEIGH 2D 175
Hutchings Cl. PL6: Plym 4J 131
Hutchings Mead EX1: Pin 4E 66
Hutchings Way TQ14: Teignm 3F 107
Hutgate Rd. EX14: Hon 3K 55
Hutton Rd. TQ3: Pres 5G 115
HUXHAM 7K 51 (1D 171)
Huxham Cl. PL6: Plym 3B 136
Huxhams Cross TQ9: Darti 1A 102
Huxley Cl. PL7: Plymp 2C 138
Huxley Va. TQ12: Kingsk 2F 111
Huxnor Rd. TQ12: Kingsk 2F 111
Huxtable Hill TQ2: Torq 2K 115
Hyde Pk. Rd. PL3: Plym 6K 135
Hyde Rd. TQ4: Paig 1H 119
Hyfield Gdns. *TQ1: Torq 2D 116*
(off Grafton Rd.)
Hyfield Pl. EX39: Bide 4F 23
Hylands Cl. EX11: W Hill 5H 79
Hylton Gdns. EX4: Exe 6C 64
Hyne Town TQ6: Strete 5G 153
Hynetown Est. TQ6: Strete 5G 153
Hynetown Rd. TQ6: Strete 6G 153
Hyperion TQ2: Torq 4A 116

I

Ian Hay Cl. EX39: Bide 4H 23
Ibex Ct. EX39: Apple 2H 21
Ice Ho. La. EX10: Sidm 4A 84
Icy Pk. TQ7: Ave G 6H 151
IDDESLEIGH 3D 163
Iddesleigh Rd. EX4: Exe 1J 7 (4H 65)
Iddesleigh Ter. EX3: Exton 2G 75
EX7: Daw 4H 97
IDE 4A 70 (1C 171)
IDEFORD 3C 171
Ide La. EX2: Exe, Ide, Alph 2A 70
(not continuous)
Idestone La. EX2: Ide 6A 70
Idewell Rd. TQ2: Torq 3D 112
IE Theatre 3H 89
Ilbert Rd. TQ7: Kingsb 4F 157
TQ7: Thur 6A 154
Ilbert St. PL1: Plym 2C 8 (1H 141)
Ilex Cl. EX4: Whip 2A 66
ILFORD 2D 167
Ilford Pk. TQ12: New A 4J 93
ILFRACOMBE 2H 11 (2B 160)
Ilfracombe Aquarium 2K 11
Ilfracombe Lifeboat Station 2J 11
Ilfracombe Mus. 2H 11
Ilfracombe Rd. EX33: Brau 2J 15
Ilfracombe Swimming Pool 2K 11
Ilfracombe Yacht Club 2J 11
ILLAND 3A 168
ILMINSTER 2D 167
Ilsham Cl. TQ1: Torq 1H 117
Ilsham Cres. TQ1: Torq 2H 117
Ilsham Ho. TQ1: Torq 1G 117
Ilsham Marine Dr. TQ1: Torq 1H 117
Ilsham M. TQ1: Torq 1G 117
Ilsham Rd. TQ1: Torq 1G 117
ILSINGTON 3B 170
ILTON 2D 167
Ilton Way TQ7: Kingsb 4G 157
Imperial Ct. EX35: Lynt 2H 13
TQ1: Torq 6E 112
Imperial M. *TQ12: New A 1F 109*
(off Lemon Rd.)
Imperial Rd. EX8: Exmth 5B 76
Imperial Road Athletics Track 5B 76
Imperial St. EX4: Exe 7C 64
Inchcoulter Apartments
EX8: Exmth 7E 76
Inchkeith Rd. PL6: Plym 4A 132
Incledon Hill EX33: Georgeh 4C 14
Independent St. *EX39: Clov 5H 27*
(off High St.)
Indio Rd. TQ13: Bov T 5B 92
INGLEIGH GREEN 3A 164
Ingleside EX13: Axmin 3J 89
Ingleside Ct. EX9: Bud S 6C 82
Inglewood Ho. EX4: Exe 1G 7
Ingra Rd. PL3: Plym 5B 136
Ingra Tor PL20: Yelv 5F 127
Ingra Wlk. PL6: Robo 2C 132
Innerbrook Rd. TQ2: Torq 1A 116
INNER HOPE 3G 155 (3C 175)
Inner Ting Tong EX9: Know 1K 77
INSTOW 3K 21 (3A 160)
Instow Signal Box 3K 21
Instow Wlk. PL5: Plym 7F 131
Inswell Ct. PL19: Tavi 3G 59
Inverdene PL3: Plym 6J 135
Inverteign Dr. TQ14: Teignm 4F 107
Inverteign Hgts. TQ14: Teignm 3F 107
INWARDLEIGH 1D 169
Iolanthe Dr. EX4: Whip 2K 65
Iona Av. EX8: Exmth 2C 76
IPPLEPEN 6H 101 (1A 176)
Ipplepen Cross TQ12: Den 2K 101
Ipplepen Rd. TQ3: Marl 7B 110
TQ12: Ipp 7B 110
Ipswich Cl. PL5: Plym 6H 131
Irene Way EX16: Tiv 2F 41
Iris Av. EX2: Exe 7C 6 (1E 70)
Iron Bri. EX4: Exe 3C 6 (6E 64)
Iron Mine La. PL20: Dous 5K 127
Irsha Ct. EX39: Apple 2H 21
Irsha St. EX39: Apple 2H 21
Irving Cl. EX33: Brau 4G 15
Isaac Cl. EX9: Ott'n 6H 83
Isaac Gro. TQ2: Torq 2B 112
Isaacs Rd. TQ2: Torq 2B 112
Isabella Rd. EX16: Tiv 3D 40
Isambard Ct. TQ2: Torq 2D 112
Isambard Pde. EX4: Exe 1A 6 (5D 64)
Isca Bowls & Bridge Cen. 3B 66
Isca Lofts EX4: Exe 2F 7
Isca Rd. EX2: Exe 7D 6 (1E 70)
EX8: Exmth 7E 76
Isigny Rd. TQ7: Kingsb 4F 157
Isis Cl. EX14: Hon 2H 55
Island Quay TQ8: Salc 3D 158
Island St. TQ8: Salc 3C 158
Island Ter. TQ8: Salc 3D 158
Island Vw. TQ7: Thur 5C 154
ISLE ABBOTTS 1D 167
ISLE BREWERS 1D 167
Isleworth Rd. EX4: Exe 7B 64
Isley Marshes Bird Sanctuary 5A 16
Isley Marsh Nature Reserve 5A 16
Iter Ct. EX17: Bow 5J 37
Iter Pk. EX17: Bow 5J 37
ITTON 1A 170
Ivanhoe Rd. PL5: Plym 1C 134
Ivatt Rd. TQ6: Dartm 6C 124
Iveagh Ct. EX4: Exe 4C 64
IVYBRIDGE 4H 145 (2C 175)
Ivybridge (Park & Ride) 3K 145
Ivybridge La. PL20: Prin 7D 60
Ivybridge Leisure Centre & Outdoor Pool
. . . . 5H 145
Ivybridge Rd. PL21: Erm 1J 147
Ivybridge Station (Rail) 3K 145
Ivybridge Viaduct 2H 145
Ivy Cl. EX2: Won 1K 71
EX10: Sidm 3C 84
Ivy Ct. EX39: Apple 2H 21
Ivydale EX8: Exmth 1F 77
Ivydale Rd. PL4: Plym 7A 136
Ivydene Rd. PL21: Ivy 4F 145
Ivy Ho. *TQ14: Teignm 5H 107*
(off Ivy La.)
Ivy La. TQ6: Dartm 1A 124
TQ14: Teignm 5H 107

J

Jackets La. EX39: N'ham 5E 20
Jacketts EX9: Ott'n 6H 83
JACK-IN-THE-GREEN 3D 68
Jackmans Cl. TQ9: Tot 5A 102
Jackman's La. TQ9: Harb 5A 102
Jack Sadler Way EX2: Cou W 4D 72
Jack's La. TQ2: Torq 2B 112
Jackson Cl. PL5: Plym 3D 134
Jackson Mdw. EX8: Lymp 6G 75
Jackson Pl. PL2: Dev 7E 134
Jacob's Pool EX20: Oke 3B 48
JACOBSTOW 1A 168
JACOBSTOWE 6F 35 (3D 163)
Jacolind Wlk. TQ5: Brixh 4F 123
Jacqueline Ho. *TQ9: Tot 6E 102*
(off Ticklemore St.)
Jago Av. PL11: Torp 1A 140
James Av. TQ3: Paig 5E 114
James Cl. PL9: Elb 5J 143
James Ct. EX1: Exe 5E 6 (7F 65)
James Owen Ct. EX4: Exe 1G 7
James Rd. PL19: Whitc 7K 59
James St. PL1: Dev 3D 140
PL4: Plym 3E 8 (2J 141)
Janes Ct. EX16: Tiv 4C 40
Jarvis Bungs. EX8: Exmth 5G 77
Jarvis Cl. EX8: Exmth 5G 77
Jasmine Cl. EX16: Tiv 2F 41
Jasmine Gdns. PL6: Plym 4F 133
PL7: Plymp 4E 138
Jasmine Gro. TQ3: Paig 6E 114
Jawbones Hill
TQ6: Dartm 2A 124 (6F 125)
Jaycroft EX15: Will 4D 44
Jean Cres. PL3: Plym 5C 136
Jedburgh Cres. PL2: Plym 3F 135
Jefferson Wlk. PL3: Plym . . . 1C 8 (1H 141)
Jeffery Cl. EX39: Hart 3J 27
PL6: Plym 4J 131
Jefford Ho. EX4: Exe 3D 64
Jeffs Way EX13: Axmin 3J 89
Jellicoe Rd. PL5: Plym 2K 135
TQ12: New A 1J 109
Jellicoe Vs. TQ9: Tot 6D 102
Jenker's Hill EX33: Georgeh 6C 14
Jenkins Cl. PL9: Plyms 7H 143
Jennifer Cl. EX2: Exe 2H 71
EX17: Cred 6G 39
Jennycliff La. PL9: Hooe 7B 142
Jennyscombe Cl. PL9: Plyms 7G 143
Jenwood Rd. EX14: Dunk 7G 47
Jephson Rd. PL4: Plym 1C 142
Jericho St. EX5: Thor 2B 50
Jerrard Cl. EX14: Hon 4F 55
Jerrard Cres. EX14: Hon 4F 55
Jesmond Rd. EX1: Exe 1J 7 (5H 65)
Jessops PL7: Plymp 2A 138
Jesu St. EX11: Ott M 4C 80
Jetty Marsh Local Nature Reserve
. . . . 6F 105
Jetty Marsh Rd. TQ12: New A 6E 104
Jewell Cres. EX32: Barn 3G 19
J H Taylor Dr. EX39: N'ham 5F 21
Jingles La. EX32: Barn 5F 19
Jinkin Av. PL4: Plym 1J 9 (1A 142)
Joan Spry Cl. EX16: With 6H 33
Jocelyn Mead EX17: Cred 5G 39
Jocelyn Rd. EX9: Bud S 5C 82
Jockey Hill EX17: Cred 5H 39
John Fowler Holiday Pk.
EX34: Ilfra 4J 11
John Gay Cl. EX32: Barn 5H 19
John Gaynor Homes PL4: Plym 4G 9
John Gay Rd. EX32: Barn 5G 19
John Greenway Cl. *EX16: Tiv 4D 40*
(off Gold St.)
John Hannam Ho. EX1: Exe 3G 7
John Howe Cl. EX38: Gt T 2C 30
John Hudson Way EX8: Exmth 5G 77
John Levers Way EX4: Exe . . . 4A 6 (7C 64)
John Nash Dr. EX7: Daw 5F 97
John Penrose Rd. EX31: Roun 7A 18
John's Av. TQ2: Torq 5B 112
John Smale Rd. EX31: Barn 5B 18
Johnson Cl. PL20: Bere A 2B 128
Johns Ter. EX16: Tiv 4B 40
Johnstone Dr. EX16: Tiv 3B 40
Johnston Ter. Ope PL2: Plym 5D 134
John St. EX1: Exe 5D 6 (7E 64)
EX16: Tiv 4B 40
Johns Way EX16: Tiv 3C 40
Jones's Hill EX33: Croy 2C 14
Jonida Cl. TQ1: Torq 6C 112
Jordan Cl. EX32: Barn 6H 19
Jordan Dr. TQ14: Teignm 3F 107
Jordan La. PL20: Horr 2E 126
Jordan Mdw. TQ13: Ashb 3J 99
Jordan Orchard *TQ11: B'leigh 4B 98*
(off Jordan St.)
Jordan St. TQ11: B'leigh 4B 98
Jordons Brook TQ9: Tot 5A 102
Joseph Lock Way EX17: Cred 7K 39
Joslin Ct. TQ12: Kingst 3G 105
Joslin Rd. EX14: Hon 5D 54
Joy St. EX31: Barn 4E 18

Jubilee Cl. EX6: Exmin 2D 74
EX20: Oke 3B 48
EX34: Ilfra 2H 11
PL21: Ivy 3K 145
TQ1: Torq 1D 116
TQ6: Dartm 6C 124
Jubilee Cotts. PL6: Plym 3C 136
(off Church Hill)
Jubilee Ct. EX4: Exe 3C 6
EX35: Lynt 2G 13
(off Burvill St.)
Jubilee Dr. EX8: Exmth 1E 76
EX15: Hemy 2G 47
Jubilee Gdns. EX10: Sidm 2D 84
EX15: Cull 5H 45
EX36: N Mol 2C 26
Jubilee Gro. EX8: Lymp 6H 75
Jubilee Lodge EX12: Seat 5F 87
(off The Underfleet)
Jubilee Path EX22: Hols 1C 34
Jubilee Pl. EX16: Tiv 5C 40
(off Orchard Leigh)
PL3: Plym 7D 136
(off Huntley Pl.)
Jubilee Rd. EX1: Heav 1K 7 (5H 65)
EX5: Bradn 2C 52
EX39: Apple 2G 21
PL5: Plym 7E 130
TQ7: Malb 6H 155
TQ9: Tot 5G 103
TQ12: New A 1E 108
Jubilee Sq. EX3: Top 6B 74
EX39: Bide 3F 23
Jubilee St. TQ7: Ave G 6H 151
Jubilee Ter. EX17: Cop 6D 38
PL4: Plym 2C 142
(off Brentor Rd.)
PL21: Bitta 4B 146
TQ3: Paig 1G 119
Julian Pl. PL2: Plym 6E 134
Julian Rd. PL21: Ivy 4F 145
Julian St. PL4: Plym 6K 9 (3B 142)
Julian Wlk. PL6: Plym 4F 133
Julius Ho. EX4: Exe 2D 6
Jump Cl. PL6: Robo 1D 132
Junction Gdns. PL4: Plym 2B 142
Junction Rd. EX17: Bow 5J 37
Jungleland 6H 19
Juniper Cl. EX4: Whip 2A 66
EX14: Hon 5D 54
EX16: Tiv 2F 41
Juniper Ct. EX31: Roun 6B 18
Juniper Way PL7: Plymp 4E 138
Junket St. EX37: High B 3B 32
Jupes Cl. EX6: Exmin 3D 74
Juries La. EX38: Gt T 1C 30
Jury Pk. EX36: S Mol 6B 26
Jurys Cnr. Cl. TQ12: Kingsk 1G 111
Jutland Way EX2: Cou W 4C 72

K

Kabale Cl. EX16: Tiv 2A 40
Kala Fair EX39: West H 5D 20
Kalendarhay La. EX1: Exe . . .4D 6 (6E 64)
Karageen Caravan & Camping Pk.
TQ7: Bolb 4J 155
Karen Cl. EX39: Bide 4J 23
Katherines La. EX11: Ott M 3D 80
Kathleaven St. PL5: Plym 2C 134
Kay Cl. EX8: Exmth 4E 76
PL7: Plymp 2C 138
Keals Cft. EX35: Lynt 2G 13
KEASON .3B 168
Keatings La. TQ14: Teignm 4G 107
Keaton La.
PL21: Erm, Ivy . . . . .6H 145 & 1G 147
Keaton Rd. PL21: Ivy 5G 145
Keats Cl. EX8: Exmth 7K 75
TQ14: Teignm 2F 107
Keat St. PL2: Dev 7D 134
Kedlestone Av. PL5: Plym 7F 131
Keegan Cl. EX11: Ott M 4A 80
Keep Gdns., The TQ6: Dartm 6E 124
Keep La. TQ6: Dartm 1A 124 (5E 124)
KELLACOTT 2C 169
Kelland Cl. TQ3: Paig 1F 119
Kelland Hill EX17: Lap 4J 37
Kellands La. EX20: Oke 2D 48
KELLATON 3A 176
Kellett Cl. TQ13: Ashb 3J 99
Kellock Dr. TQ9: Tot 6D 102
KELLY 2B 168
KELLY BRAY 3B 168
Kelly Cl. PL5: Plym 4B 134
TQ1: Torq 4E 116
Kelly Cross TQ13: Lust 5K 63
Kelvin Av. PL4: Plym 1K 9 (1B 142)
Kelvin Ct. TQ1: Torq 4E 112
TQ5: Brixh 3F 123
Kemmings Cl. TQ4: Paig 6F 119
Kempe Cl. PL2: Plym 5E 134
Kempley Rd. EX20: Oke 3B 48
Kemp M. TQ13: Ashb 4H 99
(off Bull Ring)
Kemps Fld. EX5: Cranb 3B 68
Kemp's La. EX12: Axmth 3H 87
Kempton Ter. PL11: Torp 1A 140
Kemyell Pl. PL2: Dev 7D 134
Kenandy EX10: Sidm 7B 84
Kenbury Cres. EX6: Cockw 3E 96
Kenbury Dr. EX2: Alph 5F 71
Kendall Cl. EX4: Exe 1H 7 (5G 65)
Kendal Pl. PL5: Plym 6K 131
Kendlewood Cl. TQ4: Paig 4F 119
Kenilworth TQ1: Torq 3F 117
Kenilworth Rd. PL2: Plym 4G 135
Kenley Gdns. PL5: Plym 6E 130
Kenmare Dr. PL7: Plymp 4D 138
KENN 3H 95 (2D 171)
Kennaway Rd. EX11: Ott M 3D 80
Kenn Cl. PL5: Plym 7G 131
Kennedy Way EX14: Dunk 6H 47
EX16: Tiv 3C 40
Kennel Hill PL7: Plymp 5A 138
Kennel Hill Cl. PL7: Plymp 7K 137
Kennel La. EX33: Georgeh 5C 14
PL21: Ivy 4E 144
Kennels, The PL21: Ivy 3F 145
Kennels Rd. TQ5: Chur F 5J 121
KENNERLEIGH 3C 165
Kennerley Av. EX4: Whip 4A 66
Kennet Cl. PL3: Plym 5C 136
Kenneth Ct. TQ2: Torq 5J 111
Kenneth Ter. TQ2: Torq 5J 111
(off Kenneth Ct.)
KENNFORD 1H 95 (2D 171)
Kennford Intl. Caravan Pk.
EX6: Kennf 2G 95
Kennford Rd. EX2: Mar B 2E 70
Kenn La. EX6: Exmin 4C 74
Kensey Cl. TQ1: Torq 7G 113
Kensham Av. EX5: Bradn 2D 52
Kensham Cl. EX5: Bradn 2C 52
Kensington Pl. PL4: Plym 7A 136
Kensington Rd.
PL4: Plym 1H 9 (7A 136)
Kenson Hill EX5: Silv 4G 51
Kent Cl. EX2: Won 1K 71
KENTISBEARE 6B 46 (3A 166)
KENTISBURY 2C 161
KENTISBURY FORD 2C 161
KENTON 6H 95 (2D 171)
Kenton Brook Ct. TQ2: Torq 5H 111
Kenton Hill EX6: Kenton 6J 95
Kenton M. EX6: Kenton 6H 95
(off Fore St.)
Kenton Pl. EX2: Mar B 3F 71
Kenton Vineyard 7F 95
Kent Rd. PL2: Plym 6E 134
Kent's Cavern & Visitor Cen. 1G 117
Kents Cl. EX15: Uff 6H 43
Kent's La. TQ1: Torq 1G 117
Kent's Rd. TQ1: Torq 1G 117
Kenwith Dr. TQ7: Kingsb 4G 157
Kenwith Rd. EX39: Bide 1E 22
Kenwith Ter. EX39: Bide 2E 22
Kenwith Valley Nature Reserve 2E 22
Kenwith Vw. EX39: Bide 3C 22
Kenwyn Rd. TQ1: Torq 7C 112
Keppel Pl. PL2: Dev 7E 134
Keppel St. PL2: Dev 7E 134
Keppel Ter. PL2: Dev 7E 134
(off Keppel St.)
Kernou Rd. TQ4: Paig 1J 119
Kerria Cl. TQ3: Paig 6E 114
Kerries La. TQ10: S Bre 2C 100
Kerries Rd. TQ10: S Bre 2C 100
KERSBROOK 5C 82 (2A 172)
Kersbrook Gdns. DT7: Lym R 5J 91
Kersbrook La. EX9: Bud S 4C 82
KERSCOTT 4K 25
Kerscott Hill EX32: Swim 4H 25
Kerse La. TQ7: Thur 5D 154
Kerslake's Ct. EX14: Hon 3F 55
Ker St. PL1: Dev 3D 140
Ker St. Ope PL1: Dev 2D 140
KERSWELL 3A 166
Kerswell La. TQ12: Coff 7K 109
Kerswill Rd. EX4: Exe 1C 70
Kestell Rd. EX10: Sidm 6D 84
Kes Tor Cl. EX20: Oke 3D 48
Kestor Dr. EX4: Exe 4B 64
TQ3: Pres 5G 115
Kestral Pk. PL5: Plym 2F 135
Kestrel Bus. Pk. EX2: Sow 7E 66
Kestrel Cl. EX16: Tiv 2E 40
EX20: Oke 2B 48
Kestrel Ct. TQ1: Torq 5E 112
Kestrel Pk. PL19: Whitc 7K 59
Kestrel Way EX2: Sow 7D 66
EX32: Barn 5K 19
PL6: Plym 2E 132
Keswick Cres. PL6: Plym 1E 136
Keverel Rd. EX8: Exmth 3C 76
Keyberry Cl. TQ12: New A 3G 109
Keyberry Mill TQ12: New A 3G 109
Keyberry Pk. TQ12: New A 3G 109
Keyberry Rd. TQ12: New A 3G 109
Keyes Cl. PL1: Dev 2E 140
KEYHAM .5D 134
Keyham Rd. PL2: Dev 7D 134
Keyham Station (Rail) 5D 134
Keyham St. PL5: Plym 3D 134
Keysfield Rd. TQ4: Paig 2J 119
Kiddicott EX17: Cred 6G 39
(off Buller Rd.)
Kidwelly Cl. PL7: Plymp 5F 139
Kiel Pl. PL3: Plym 6E 136
Kiel Pl. La. PL3: Plym 6E 136
Kilbarran Ri. EX4: Exe 4D 64
KILKHAMPTON 2A 162
Killerton 3D 165
Killerton Cl. TQ3: Paig 7H 115
Killerton Wlk. EX6: Exmin 1B 74
(off Devington Pk.)
KILMINGTON 2B 88 (1C 173)
Kilmorie TQ1: Torq 3H 117
Kilmorie Cl. TQ1: Torq 3H 117
Kilmorie Hall EX4: Exe 4F 65
Kiln Cl. EX39: Ins 2K 21
PL5: Plym 3B 134
TQ13: Bov T 6B 92
Kiln Cl. La. EX39: Ins 2K 21
Kilnford Rd. TQ12: Kingst 4J 105
Kiln Forehead La. TQ12: Kingst 4J 105
Kiln Ho. TQ7: Kingsb 5G 157
Kiln La. EX12: Brans 6F 85
EX32: Barn 5F 19
EX34: Com M 7D 12
TQ7: Stoke 6J 159
Kiln Orchard TQ12: New A 1C 108
Kiln Path TQ5: Brixh 4E 122
Kiln Rd. TQ3: Marl 3C 114
TQ5: Galm 4G 121
TQ13: Bov T 6B 92
Kilnwood Pk. EX31: Roun 6K 17
Kilworthy TQ1: Torq 5D 112
Kilworthy Hill PL19: Tavi 3J 59
Kilworthy Pk. PL19: Tavi 3J 59
Kilworthy Rd. PL19: Tavi 1J 59
Kimberley Pk. EX39: N'ham 5F 21
Kimberley Rd. EX2: Exe 6F 7 (7F 65)
Kimberley Ter. EX39: N'ham 4F 21
Kimberly Dr. PL6: Plym 2C 136
Kinevor Cl. EX34: Mort 3A 10
King Alfred Cres. EX39: N'ham 6F 21
King Alfred Way EX10: New P 5G 81
King Arthur's Rd. EX4: Whip 2J 65
King Charles Bus. Pk. TQ12: Heat . . .7E 92
King Charles Way EX10: Sidm 2C 84
Kingcome Ct. TQ11: B'leigh 4D 98
Kingdom M. EX4: Exe 2A 6 (5D 64)
Kingdon Av. EX36: S Mol 5B 26
Kingdon Ent. Pk. EX39: Bide 5B 22
King Edward Rd. EX13: Axmin 3H 89
(Victoria Pl.)
EX13: Axmin 4G 89
(Widepost La.)
King Edward St. EX4: Exe 3D 64
EX32: Barn 3E 18
King Edward Studios EX4: Exe 3D 64
King Edwards Vw. EX16: Tiv 4D 40
(off Maple Gro.)
Kingfisher Av. EX2: Exe 1A 70
Kingfisher Cl. PL6: Plym 4F 133
PL19: Whitc 7J 59
TQ2: Torq 3K 111
Kingfisher Ct. EX4: Pin 3C 66
Kingfisher Dr. EX4: Exe 2G 65
EX20: Oke 2A 48
EX32: Barn 5K 19
Kingfisher Gallery & Watermill 3H 85
Kingfisher Way EX2: Sow 7D 66
PL9: Plyms 5D 142
King Gdns. PL1: Plym 3C 8
King Henrys Rd. EX2: Exe 2H 71
Kingsacre EX33: Brau 4H 15
King St Bus. Pk. EX1: Exe 5D 6
Kingsale Rd. TQ8: Salc 4B 158
KINGSAND 2A 174
Kings Arms Pas. TQ7: Kingsb 4F 157
(off Fore St.)
King's Ash Rd. TQ3: Paig 5E 114
Kings Av. EX11: Ott M 3E 80
TQ3: Paig 7J 115
KINGSBRIDGE 4F 157 (3D 175)
Kingsbridge Cookworthy Mus. 3F 157
Kingsbridge Hill TQ9: Tot 7E 102
Kingsbridge La. TQ13: Ashb 4H 99
Kingsbridge La. M. TQ13: Ashb 4G 99
(off Kingsbridge La.)
KINGSBURY EPISCOPI 1D 167
Kings Cl. EX32: Barn 7H 19
PL6: Plym 4F 133
Kings Coombe Dr. TQ12: Kingst . . .2H 105
KINGSCOTT 2D 163
Kings Cotts. TQ12: New A 1F 109
Kings Ct. EX12: Seat 5F 87
EX14: Hon 3F 55
(off New St.)
PL1: Dev 1F 141
PL1: Plym 4A 8
TQ12: Kingsk 1F 111
TQ12: Kingst 5H 105
King's Cres. EX16: Tiv 4E 40
Kingsdale Ct. TQ2: Torq 2D 116
KINGSDON 5E 88
Kingsdon Hill
EX24: Colyt . . . . .5E 88 & 7A 90
Kingsdown Cl. EX7: Daw 3H 97
TQ14: Teignm 4F 107
Kingsdown Cres. EX7: Daw 3H 97
Kingsdown Rd. TQ14: Teignm 4F 107
King's Dr. TQ5: Brixh 4F 123
King's Dr., The TQ2: Torq 2B 116
Kings Dwellings EX1: Exe 7E 64
(off King St.)
Kings Farm La. EX19: Wink 2C 36
Kings Gdns. EX14: Hon 3F 55
(off Kerslakes Ct.)
Kingsgate EX4: Exe 4F 65
Kingsgate Bus. Cen. EX14: Hon 5D 54
(off Devonshire Way)
Kingsgate Cl. TQ2: Torq 1D 112
KINGSHEANTON 3B 160
Kingsholme EX24: Colyf 1G 87
Kingshurst Dr. TQ3: Paig 6H 115
KINGSKERSWELL 1F 111 (1A 176)
Kingskerswell Rd. TQ2: Torq 2J 111
TQ12: Kingsk 4J 111
TQ12: New A 3G 109
Kingslake Ct. EX8: Exmth 4C 76
Kingslake Ri. EX8: Exmth 4C 76
Kingsland Dr. TQ4: Paig 3E 118
Kingsland Gdn. Cl. PL3: Plym 5K 135
Kings La. EX10: Sidm 7C 84
Kingsleigh Mnr. TQ1: Torq 1E 116
(off Lwr. Warberry Rd.)
Kingsley Av. EX4: Whip 4A 66
EX32: Barn 3E 18
EX34: Ilfra 5H 11
(not continuous)
EX39: Apple 3H 21
PL11: Torp 2A 140
TQ2: Torq 2B 112
Kingsley Cl. PL21: L Mill 5C 144
Kingsley Ct. EX39: West H 6B 20
TQ2: Torq 2B 112
(off Kingsley Av.)
Kingsley Mus. 5H 27
Kingsley Pk. EX39: West H 5D 20
Kingsley Rd. EX39: Bide 1E 22
EX39: West H 6B 20
PL4: Plym 7K 135
TQ7: Kingsb 5F 157
Kingsley Sq. TQ2: Torq 2B 112
Kingsley St. EX39: Bide 3F 23
Kingsley Ter. EX34: Com M 6B 12
(off High St.)
EX39: Bide 4F 23
King's Mkt. TQ7: Kingsb 4F 157
Kingsmead Dr. EX38: Gt T 1D 30
Kings Mdw. TQ12: Kingsk 1F 111
Kings Mdw. Dr. EX19: Wink 2C 36
Kings M. EX14: Hon 4E 54
Kingsmill Ind. Est. EX15: Cull 2K 45
King's Mill Rd. EX15: Cull 3J 45
KING'S NYMPTON 2A 164
Kings Orchard TQ9: Tot 6G 103
Kings Pk. EX14: Hon 3F 55
(off King St.)
EX18: Chul 6C 32
Kings Quay TQ6: Dartm . . .1B 124 (5F 125)
Kings Rd. EX4: Exe 1K 7 (4H 65)
EX14: Hon 3G 55
EX32: Barn 3G 19
PL1: Dev 2E 140
PL5: Plym 7E 130
TQ3: Paig 7J 115
Kings Rydon Cl. TQ9: Sto G 3B 120
KING'S TAMERTON 2E 134
King's Tamerton Rd. PL5: Plym . . .1D 134
KINGSTEIGNTON 4H 105 (3C 171)
Kingsteignton Rd. TQ12: New A . . .1F 109
TQ13: Chud, Chud K 7C 94
Kingsteignton Swimming Pool . . .2G 105
King Stephen Cl. EX4: Exe . . .1E 6 (5F 65)
King's Ter. EX14: Hon 3F 55
KINGSTON 3C 175
Kingston Av. EX34: Com M 6B 12
Kingston Cl. PL7: Plymp 4D 138
TQ12: Kingsk 7K 109
Kingston Dr. PL7: Plymp 3D 138
KINGSTONE 2D 167
Kingston La. TQ6: Dartm 6D 124
Kingston Rd. EX8: Exmth 5E 76

KINGSTON ST MARY 1C 167
Kings Tor PL20: Walk 2J 127
King St. EX1: Exe 5D 6 (7E 64)
EX5: Silv 1G 51
EX7: Daw 4G 97
EX8: Exmth 6C 76
EX14: Hon 4E 54
EX16: Tiv 4C 40
EX24: Colyt 5C 88
EX34: Com M 5B 12
EX36: S Mol 6C 26
EX39: Bide 3F 23
PL1: Plym 4A 8 (2G 141)
PL11: Torp 1B 140
PL19: Tavi 3H 59
TQ5: Brixh 3F 123
TQ12: New A 1F 109
King's Wlk. EX7: Daw 5H 97
Kingswater Ct. TQ5: Brixh 3E 122
Kings Way DT7: Lym R 4K 91
EX20: Lew 1A 56
Kingsway EX2: Heav 7J 65
EX36: S Mol 7C 26
PL7: Plymp 4H 139
TQ14: Teignm 4F 107
Kingsway Av. TQ4: Good 6G 119
Kingsway Cl. TQ4: Good 6G 119
TQ7: Kingsb 5F 157
Kingsway Ct. TQ4: Good 6G 119
Kingsway Dr. TQ4: Good 6G 119
Kingsway Gdns. PL6: Plym 7A 132
Kingsway Pk. TQ7: Kingsb 5F 157
KINGSWEAR 6G 125 (2A 176)
Kingswear Cres. PL6: Plym 2C 136
Kingswear Rd. TQ5: Brixh, Hill 6J 123
Kingswear Station
Dartmouth Steam Railway . . . 6G 125
King's Wharf EX2: Exe 6E 6
Kingswood Cl. EX4: Exe 4B 64
Kingswood Ct. TQ4: Paig 2J 119
(off Cleveland Rd.)
Kingswood Ho. EX34: Ilfra 3G 11
Kingswood Mdw. EX22: Hols 1D 34
Kingswood Pk. Av. PL3: Plym 5J 135
King William St. EX4: Exe 2F 7 (6F 65)
Kiniver Ct. TQ14: Teignm 2J 107
Kinlacey Ct. TQ1: Torq 2E 116
Kinnaird Cres. PL6: Plym 3K 131
Kinnerton Ct. EX4: Exe 4C 64
Kinnerton Way EX4: Exe 4A 64
Kinross Av. PL4: Plym 1K 9 (7B 136)
Kinsale Rd. PL5: Plym 7E 130
Kinterbury Rd. PL5: Plym 3A 134
Kinterbury St. PL1: Plym . . . 5F 9 (3K 141)
Kinterbury Ter. PL5: Plym 3A 134
Kintyre Cl. TQ2: Torq 3A 112
Kinver Cl. PL6: Plym 6E 132
Kipling Cl. EX8: Exmth 1E 76
Kipling Ct. EX39: West H 6C 20
Kipling Dr. EX2: Won 1J 71
Kipling Gdns. PL5: Plym 1J 135
Kipling Ter. EX39: West H 6B 20
Kipling Tors 6A 20
Kirby Cl. EX13: Axmin 4H 89
Kirkby Pl. PL4: Plym 2E 8 (1J 141)
Kirkby Ter. PL4: Plym 2E 8
Kirkdale Gdns. PL2: Plym 4G 135
Kirkella Rd. PL20: Yelv 6G 127
Kirkham Ct. TQ3: Paig 1G 119
(off Colley End Rd.)
Kirkham House 1G 119
(off Cecil Rd.)
Kirkham St. TQ3: Paig 1H 119
Kirkland Cl. PL6: Plym 3D 132
Kirkstall Cl. PL2: Plym 4E 134
Kirkstead Cl. TQ2: Torq 5A 112
Kirkwall Rd. PL5: Plym 7K 131
(not continuous)
Kirton Dr. EX17: Cred 7J 39
Kirton Pl. PL3: Plym 6C 136
Kirtons Rd. TQ12: S'head 1H 113
Kistor Gdns. TQ9: Tot 5E 102
(off Castle St.)
Kit Hill Cres. PL5: Plym 3B 134
Kitley Vw. PL8: Brixt 2J 149
Kitley Way PL5: Plym 2D 134
Kits Cl. TQ13: Chud 2D 94
Kitter Dr. PL9: Plyms 7G 143
Kittersley Dr. TQ12: Live 4G 93
KITTISFORD 1A 166
Kittiwake Dr. TQ2: Torq 2J 111
Kitts La. EX10: N'town 6J 81
Kitwell St. EX15: Uff 6H 43
Klondyke Rd. EX20: Oke 5C 48
Knackershole La. EX17: Morc 2C 38
Knap Down La. EX34: Com M 5D 12
KNAPP 1D 167
Knapp Hill EX10: Sidm 5B 84
Knapp House Activity Cen. 5G 21
Knapp Pk. Rd. TQ4: Good 5J 119
Knapps Cl. PL9: Elb 6K 143
Knapp's La. EX10: Harp 4J 81
Knebworth Ct. TQ1: Torq 4E 112
Kneele Gdns. PL3: Plym 3K 135
Kneller Cl. EX34: Ilfra 4J 11
Knick Knack La. TQ5: Brixh 5E 122
KNIGHTACOTT 3C 161
Knighthayes Wlk. EX6: Exmin 2B 74
Knightley Rd. EX2: Exe 2H 71
KNIGHTON 5C 148 (3B 174)
Knighton Hill PL9: Wem 5D 148
Knighton Hill Bus. Cen.
PL9: Wem 5D 148
Knighton Rd. PL4: Plym . . . 4J 9 (2A 142)
PL9: Wem 5C 148
Knightons Units
PL20: Buck M 5B 126
Knighton Ter. PL20: Horr 1E 126
Knights Ct. EX20: Hath 2H 35
Knights Cres. EX2: Sow 2C 72
Knights Fld. Ri. EX39: N'ham 4F 21
Knightshayes Court 2D 165
Knights Mead TQ13: Chud K 6B 94
Knights Pl. EX4: Whip 3J 65
Knightstone EX11: Ott M 6E 80
Knightstone La. EX11: Ott M 6E 80
Knightstone Rd. EX11: Ott M 6D 80
Knightswood EX15: Cull 6G 45
Knoll, The PL7: Plymp 5J 137
Knowland Cl. PL1: Dev 2E 140
KNOWLE
Braunton 1K 15 (3A 160)
Budleigh Salterton . . . 5A 82 (2A 172)
Crediton 3B 164
Knowle Av. PL2: Plym 5D 134
Knowle Bus. Units EX2: Mar B 4G 71
Knowle Cl. EX14: Hon 3F 55
EX15: Cull 4F 45
EX32: L'key 2B 24
TQ13: Ashb 5F 99
Knowle Dr. EX4: Exe 5B 64
EX10: Sidm 6A 84
Knowle Gdns. EX10: Sidm 6A 84
EX34: Com M 7C 12
TQ7: Kingsb 3F 157
Knowle Hill EX9: Know 2K 77
Knowle Ho. Cl. TQ7: Kingsb 3G 157
Knowle La. EX15: Cull 4F 45
Knowle M. EX9: Know 4A 82
Knowle Rd. EX9: Bud S, Know 5A 82
TQ8: Salc 3C 158
TQ13: Lust 6J 63
KNOWLE ST GILES 2D 167
Knowles Dr. EX24: Colyt 7D 88
KNOWLES HILL 7E 104
Knowles Hill Rd. TQ12: New A 7E 104
Knowle Ter. PL20: Walk 2J 127
Knowle Vw. EX20: Oke 2D 48
Knowle Village EX9: Know 6A 82
Knowle Wlk. PL2: Plym 5E 134
KNOWSTONE 1C 165
Kynock Ind. Est. EX39: Bide 5G 23

L

Labatt Cl. PL6: Plym 7E 132
Laburnum PL19: Tavi 3J 59
Laburnum Cl. EX8: Exmth 1F 77
EX14: Hon 5C 54
Laburnum Ct. TQ12: A'well 6E 108
Laburnum Dr. EX32: Barn 6K 19
PL9: Wem 6B 148
Laburnum Gro. PL6: Plym 5E 132
(off Beech Ct.)
TQ9: Darti 4C 102
Laburnum Rd. EX2: Won 2J 71
TQ12: New A 3H 109
Laburnum Row TQ2: Torq 7B 112
Laburnum St. TQ2: Torq 1B 116
Laburnum Ter. TQ12: A'well 5E 108
Laburnum Way EX20: Oke 3C 48
TQ9: E All 6D 152
Lace Wlk. EX14: Hon 3F 55
Lackaborough Ct. EX2: Alph 5D 70
Lacy Rd. TQ3: Pres 5G 115
Ladder La. EX34: Com M 7D 12
Ladies Mile EX7: Daw 3K 97
EX32: Barn 7F 19
Ladram Bay 7K 83
Ladram Bay Holiday Cen.
EX9: Ott'n 5K 83
Ladram Rd. EX9: Ott'n 6J 83
LADYCROSS 2B 168
Lady Fern Rd. PL6: Robo 1D 132
Ladymead EX10: Sidm 2A 84
Lady Pk. Rd. TQ2: Torq 3K 115
Ladysmead 3C 40
Lady's Mile Touring & Caravan Pk.
EX7: Daw 1J 97
Ladysmith Ct. PL4: Plym . . . 1K 9 (1B 142)
Ladysmith La. EX1: Heav 6J 65
Ladysmith Rd. EX1: Heav 2K 7 (5J 65)
PL4: Plym 1K 9 (1B 142)
Ladywell EX31: Barn 2E 18
(off Under Minnow Rd.)
Ladywell Av. PL4: Plym 3G 9
Ladywell La. EX18: Chul 6B 32
Ladywell Path EX35: Lynt 2F 13
Ladywell Pl.
PL4: Plym 3G 9 (2A 142)
Lafrowda EX4: Exe 4F 65
Lag Hill EX17: Cher F 2J 39
Lagoon Vw. EX31: Yell 7B 16
LAIRA 7D 136
Laira Av. PL3: Plym 7E 136
Laira Bridge 3D 142
Laira Bri. Rd. PL4: Plym 2C 142
Laira Gdns. PL3: Plym 7D 136
Laira Pk. Cres. PL4: Plym 7C 136
Laira Pk. Pl. PL4: Plym 7C 136
Laira Pk. Rd. PL4: Plym 7C 136
Laira Pl. PL4: Plym 4K 9 (2B 142)
Laira St. PL4: Plym 4K 9 (2B 142)
Laity Wlk. PL6: Plym 4J 131
LAKE
Barnstaple 7D 18 (3B 160)
Yelverton 5J 127
Lake Av. TQ14: Teignm 2G 107
Lake Cl. EX14: Hon 4G 55
Lake Ind. Est. EX21: Sheb 6K 29
Lakeland TQ12: A'well 6E 108
Lakelands Cl. EX16: With 6J 33
Lakelands Dr. EX4: Exe 6C 64
Lake La. EX5: New C 4C 50
PL20: Dous 5H 127
Lakenham Hill EX39: N'ham 5D 20
Lake Rd. PL9: Hooe 6C 142
Lakes Cl. TQ5: Brixh 3C 122
Lakeside EX7: Daw W 7D 96
EX34: Woolc 7C 10
PL19: Tavi 3H 59
TQ8: Salc 3C 158
Lakeside Av. EX2: Cou W 5A 72
Lakeside Cl. TQ13: Bov T 7B 92
Lakeside Dr. PL5: Plym 5C 130
Lakes Rd. TQ5: Brixh 4C 122
Lake St. TQ6: Dartm 1A 124 (6F 125)
Lake Vw. EX17: Cred 5K 39
Lake Vw. Cl. PL5: Plym 4G 131
Lake Vw. Dri PL5: Plym 4F 131
Lake Vw. Dr. PL5: Plym 5F 131
Lalebrick Rd. PL9: Hooe 7B 142
Lamacraft Cl. EX7: Daw 2J 97
Lamacraft Dr. EX4: Exe 5K 65
Lamaton Pk. EX36: S Mol 7D 26
Lamb, The TQ9: Tot 6D 102
Lamb All. EX1: Exe 4E 6
Lambert Cl. EX7: Daw 2J 97
Lambert Rd. PL5: Tam F 4G 131
(off Station Rd.)
Lambert's La. TQ14: Shal 7F 107
Lambhay Hill PL1: Plym 6F 9 (3K 141)
Lambhay St. PL1: Plym 7F 9 (4K 141)
Lamb Pk. EX34: Ilfra 4G 11
TQ13: Chag 2H 61
Lamb Pk. Cl. TQ12: Kingst 1H 105
LAMBROOK 1C 167
Lambs Cl. TQ7: Thur 5C 154
Lame Johns Fld. EX17: Cred 5J 39
LAMERTON 6C 58 (3C 169)
Lamerton Cl. PL5: Plym 7G 131
LAMERTON GREEN 6B 58
Lamerton Vs. PL19: Lam 6B 58
Lammas La. TQ3: Pres 6F 115
Lamplough Rd. EX8: Exmth 1C 76
LANA
Ashwater 1B 168
Holsworthy 3B 162
Lancaster Cl. EX2: Won 7A 66
EX15: Cull 2H 45
Lancaster Ct. EX5: Clyst H 7B 68
Lancaster Dr. TQ4: Paig 5F 119
Lancaster Gdns. PL5: Plym 6J 131
Lancaster Ho. TQ4: Paig 2J 119
(off Belle Vue Rd.)
Lancelot Rd. EX4: Whip 2K 65
Landboat Vw. EX17: Cher F 2J 39
Landcombe La. TQ6: Strete 5J 153
LANDCROSS 1C 163
Landhayes Rd. EX4: Exe 7C 64
LANDKEY 2B 24 (3B 160)
LANDKEY NEWLAND 2C 24 (3B 160)
Landkey Rd.
EX32: Barn, L'key . . . . 6G 19 & 1A 24
Landmark Rd. TQ8: Salc 4A 158
Landmark Theatre 2H 11
Land Pk. EX18: Chul 5B 32
LAND PART 5B 84
Landpath TQ7: Thur 5C 154
LANDRAKE 1A 174
Landrake Cl. PL5: Plym 3B 134
Landreath Gdns. PL2: Plym 3J 135
Landscore EX17: Cred 6F 39
Landscore Cl. EX17: Cred 6G 39
TQ14: Teignm 4H 107
Landscore Rd. EX4: Exe 5A 6 (7C 64)
TQ14: Teignm 4G 107
LANDSCOVE 1D 175
Landscove Holiday Village
TQ5: Brixh 4H 123
Lands Pk. PL9: Plyms 5G 143
Lands Rd. EX4: Pin 3C 66
TQ5: Brixh 2H 123
LANDULPH 1A 174
Landulph Gdns. PL5: Plym 3B 134
Landunvez Pl. EX5: Bradn 3C 52
Lane, The PL7: Plymp 3A 138
PL21: Lutt 7F 129
TQ6: Ditt 6C 120
LANEAST 2A 168
Lane End EX39: Ins 2K 21
Lane End Cl. EX39: Ins 2K 21
Lane End Pk. EX32: Barn 5J 19
Lane Fld. Rd. EX39: Bide 3C 22
LANE HEAD 3B 60
Lanehead EX12: Beer 7B 86
Lane Head Cl. EX33: Croy 2C 14
Lanehead Rd. EX12: Beer 7B 86
LANGAGE 5F 139
Langage Bus. Pk. PL7: Plymp 4G 139
Langage Energy Cen.
PL7: Plymp 4H 139
Langage Ind. Est. PL7: Plymp 4G 139
Langage Pk. PL7: Plymp 5G 139
Langage Pk. Office Campus
PL7: Plymp 5F 139
Langaller Cl. TQ13: Bov T 6A 92
Langaller La. TQ13: Bov T 7A 92
Langarron Pk. EX32: Barn 4G 19
Langaton Gdns. EX1: Pin 3E 66
Langaton La. EX1: Pin 3E 66
Langdale Cl. PL6: Plym 2E 136
Langdale Gdns. PL6: Plym 2E 136
LANGDON 1A 168
Langdon Bus. Pk. EX5: Clyst M 3J 73
Langdon Ct. PL9: Elb 6J 143
LANGDON CROSS 2B 168
Langdon Flds. TQ5: Galm 2H 121
Langdon La. EX7: Daw 1F 97
TQ5: Galm 3H 121
Langdon Rd. EX7: Daw 1F 97
EX22: Bradw 5B 28
TQ3: Pres 5J 115
Langerwehe Way EX8: Exmth 6B 76
LANGFORD
Plymtree 3A 166
Taunton 1C 167
Langford Av. EX14: Hon 3G 55
LANGFORD BUDVILLE 1B 166
Langford Cres. TQ2: Torq 2B 112
Langford Rd. EX14: Hon 2G 55
(not continuous)
Lang Gro. PL9: Elb 5J 143
PL19: Tavi 4K 59
Langham Levels PL21: Ivy 3F 145
Langham Pl. PL4: Plym 2B 142
Langham Way PL21: Ivy 4F 145
Langhill Rd. PL3: Plym 6J 135
Langlands Cl. TQ4: Paig 3E 118
Langlands Mdw. PL21: Ivy 5K 145
Langlands Rd. EX15: Cull 4F 45
Langleigh EX34: Ilfra 4G 11
Langleigh La. EX34: Ilfra 4F 11
Langleigh Pk. EX34: Ilfra 4F 11
Langleigh Rd. EX34: Ilfra 3G 11
Langleigh Ter. EX34: Ilfra 3G 11
LANGLEY 1A 166
Langley EX18: Chul 5C 32
Langley Av. TQ5: Brixh 4E 122
Langley Cl. PL6: Plym 3B 132
TQ5: Brixh 4E 122
Langley Cres. PL6: Plym 3A 132
Langley Gdns. EX18: Chul 6C 32
Langley La. EX18: Chul 5C 32
LANGLEY MARSH 1A 166
Langmead EX39: Westl 7K 21
Langmead Cl. PL6: Plym 3D 136
Langmead Rd. PL6: Plym 3D 136
Langmoor Cl. DT7: Lym R 5J 91
(off Pound St.)
Langmore Cl. PL6: Plym 3B 136
LANGORE 2B 168
LANGPORT 1D 167
LANGRIDGEFORD 1D 163
Langridge Rd. TQ3: Paig 6E 114
Langs Fld. EX33: Croy 3B 14
Langs Rd. TQ3: Pres 6J 115
Langstone Cl. TQ1: Torq 6F 113
TQ12: Heat 2J 93
Langstone Dr. EX8: Exmth 2E 76
Langstone Rd. PL2: Plym 4H 135
Langstone Ter. PL2: Plym 4H 135
Langton Rd. PL20: Yelv 5F 127
LANGTREE 2C 163
Lang Way TQ12: Ipp 6J 101
Langwells Ct. TQ9: Blacka 3C 152
Lanherne EX7: Daw 4H 97

Lanhydrock Cl.—Linketty La. W.

Lanhydrock Cl. TQ3: Paig 6D 114
Lanhydrock Rd. PL4: Plym . . .3J 9 (2A 142)
(not continuous)
Lansdowne EX2: Won 1A 72
Lansdowne Ct. TQ2: Torq 1B 116
Lansdowne La. TQ2: Torq 7B 112
Lansdowne Pk. EX39: N'ham 4E 20
TQ9: Tot 7G 103
Lansdowne Rd. EX9: Know 6A 82
PL6: Plym 1A 136
TQ2: Torq 7B 112
Lansdowne Ter. EX2: Exe 6F 7 (7F 65)
EX39: Bide 4E 22
Lansdown Ter. *EX32: Barn 3F 19*
(off St George's Rd.)
Lansport La. EX7: Daw 6A 96
Lanteglos Cl. PL21: Bitta 4C 146
LAPFORD 2K 37 (3B 164)
LAPFORD CROSS 3J 37 (3B 164)
Lapford Mill 3K 37
Lapford Station (Rail) 3J 37
Lapthorn Cl. PL9: Plyms 5D 142
Lapthorne Ind. Est. TQ12: Ipp 5K 101
Lapwing Cl. EX15: Cull 5F 45
Larch Cl. EX8: Exmth 1F 77
EX12: Seat 2E 86
TQ14: Teignm 1H 107
Larch Dr. PL6: Plym 3F 133
Larch Rd. EX2: Exe 2C 70
Larch Wlk. TQ2: Torq 5J 111
LARKBEARE 7F 7 (1F 71)
Larkbeare Rd. EX2: Exe 7F 7 (1F 71)
Lark Cl. EX4: Exe 3G 65
Larkhall Ri. PL3: Plym 6C 136
Larkham Cl. PL7: Plymp 5K 137
Larkham La. PL7: Plymp 5J 137
Lark Hill PL2: Plym 5F 135
Lark Ri. EX10: New P 5G 81
EX31: Roun 7K 17
Larks Cl. TQ14: Shal 7F 107
Larksmead Cl. TQ12: E Ogw 3D 108
Larksmead Way TQ12: E Ogw 3C 108
Larkspur Gdns. EX32: Barn 5K 19
Larks Ri. EX15: Cull 5F 45
Larkstone Cres. EX34: Ilfra 3K 11
Larkstone Gdns. EX34: Ilfra 3K 11
Larkstone La. EX34: Ilfra 2K 11
Larkstone Ter. EX34: Ilfra 2K 11
Laskeys Heath TQ12: Live 3F 93
Laskeys La. EX10: Sidm 6D 84
Latches Wlk. EX13: Axmin 3H 89
LATCHLEY 3C 169
Latchmount Gdns. EX13: Axmin 3H 89
Latham Cl. PL6: Plym 4B 136
Latimer Cl. PL7: Plymp 4E 138
Latimer Rd. EX4: Whip 4K 65
Latimer Wlk. PL6: Plym 3K 131
Lauderdale Dr. EX32: Barn 5G 19
Lauder La. EX31: Roun 7B 18
LAUNCELLS 3A 162
LAUNCESTON 2B 168
Launceston Cl. PL6: Plym 3C 132
Launceston Rd. EX20: Bride 4G 57
Launchycroft DT7: Uply 3G 91
Laundry La. EX10: Sidf 1D 84
Laura Av. TQ3: Paig 6H 115
Laura Gro. TQ3: Pres 6F 115
Laura Pl. *TQ3: Paig 1G 119*
(off Well St.)
Laurel Av. EX39: Bide 4C 22
Laurel Cotts. *PL5: Plym 2C 134*
(off Trelawny Pl.)
Laurel Ct. PL2: Plym 4F 135
Laurel Dene PL2: Plym 4F 135
Laurel Dr. PL6: Plym 5F 133
Laurel La. TQ14: Shal 6F 107
Laurel Ri. EX8: Exmth 4F 77
Laurel Rd. EX2: Won 2J 71
EX14: Hon 5C 54
PL2: Plym 4F 135
Laurels, The EX10: Sidm 5B 84
EX31: Roun 7A 18
Laureston Rd. TQ12: New A 2F 109
Laurie Av. TQ12: New A 7C 104
Lauriston Cl. TQ2: Torq 1B 116
Lavender Cl. TQ5: Brixh 4C 122
Lavender Rd. EX4: Exe 4B 64
Lavington Cl. PL7: Plymp 4E 138
Lavinia Dr. PL7: Plymp 6K 137
LAWHITTON 2B 168
Law Memorial Ho's. *EX32: Bish T . . .6B 24*
(off Bishop's Tawton Rd.)
Lawn, The EX9: Bud S 7C 82
PL19: Tavi 3J 59
Lawn Cl. PL7: Plymp 4F 139
TQ2: Torq 2B 112
Lawn Dr. TQ13: Chud 2C 94
Lawn Gdns. TQ13: Chud 2C 94
Lawn Hill EX7: Daw 4H 97
Lawn Rd. EX8: Exmth 5C 76
Lawns, The PL5: Plym 2K 135
PL11: Torp 7A 134
Lawns End TQ14: Bi'ton 3A 106
Lawn Ter. EX7: Daw 4H 97
Lawn Vista EX10: Sidm 5C 84
Lawrence Av. EX4: Exe 6A 6 (1D 70)
Lawrence Rd. PL9: Hooe 5A 142
Lawrence Wlk. EX6: Exmin 1B 74
Lawson Gro. PL9: Plyms 5D 142
Law Wlk. PL6: Plym 4J 131
Laxton Av. EX1: Heav 6B 66
LAYMORE 3D 167
Layne Cl. EX6: Chri 3J 63
Layne Flds. EX6: Chri 3J 63
Laywell Cl. TQ5: Brixh 6D 122
Laywell Rd. TQ5: Brixh 5C 122
Lazenby EX4: Exe 4F 65
Lazenby Rd. EX16: Tiv 5F 41
Lea, The TQ14: Bi'ton, Teignm 3C 106
(not continuous)
Lea Cliff Pk. EX7: Daw W 7E 96
Lea Combe EX13: Axmin 4H 89
Leacroft Touring Pk. EX24: Colyt 1A 86
Leadengate Cl. EX33: Croy 3B 14
Leadengate Flds. EX33: Croy 3B 14
Leader La. TQ3: Marl 4D 114
Leadstone Camping EX7: Daw 1K 97
Leaholes Av. EX20: Oke 3C 48
Lealands TQ13: Bov T 5B 92
Lea La. EX9: Ott'n 6H 83
(not continuous)
Lea Mt. TQ14: Bi'ton 3C 106
Lea Mt. Cl. EX7: Daw 5H 97
Lea Mt. Dr. EX7: Daw 5G 97
Lea Mt. Rd. EX7: Daw 5H 97
Leander Ct. TQ14: Teignm 5H 107
Leander Way PL5: Plym 1J 135
Lear La. EX13: Axmin 5G 89
Lea Rd. EX9: Ott'n 6H 83
EX16: Tiv 2D 40
TQ2: Torq 2D 112
Lears La. TQ13: Chud 2D 94
Leas, The EX34: Ilfra 5G 11
Leaside EX6: Dunsf 6B 62
Leas Rd. EX9: Bud S 6C 82
LEAT 7C 56
Leat, The PL20: Walk 2J 127
Leat Cl. PL20: Dous 4K 127
TQ12: Kingst 4H 105
Lea Ter. EX39: Apple 3H 21
Leatfield Dr. PL6: Plym 5K 131
Leatherby Cl. PL6: Plym 3K 131
Leather Tor Cl. PL20: Yelv 5F 127
Leat Mdw. EX16: Tiv 3B 40
TQ12: Live 4G 93
Leat Rd. EX16: Tiv 3B 40
PL16: Lift 6B 56
Leatside *EX1: Exe 6D 6*
(off Commercial Rd.)
PL6: Robo 1D 132
Leat St. EX16: Tiv 4B 40
Leat Ter. TQ12: Kingst 4H 105
Leat Wlk. PL3: Plym 5K 135
PL6: Robo 1D 132
Leatway Gdns. EX15: Cull 4G 45
Lea Va. Rd. TQ12: New A 1D 108
Leaves Yd. PL3: Plym 5C 136
Lea Vw. EX15: Will 3D 44
Leaze Rd. TQ12: Kingst 3G 105
Lebanon Cl. EX4: Exe 3H 65
Ledgate La. PL7: Plymp, Spa 1J 139
Ledsgrove TQ12: Ipp 6J 101
LEDSTONE 3D 175
LEE
Ilfracombe 2A 160
South Molton 1C 165
Leechwell Ct. *TQ9: Tot 6E 102*
(off The Lamb)
Leechwell La. TQ9: Tot 6E 102
(not continuous)
Leechwell St. TQ9: Tot 6E 102
(not continuous)
Lee Cl. EX14: Hon 3E 54
Lee Ct. TQ5: Brixh 4G 123
Lee La. EX6: Dunsf 7B 62
LEE MILL 5A 144 (2B 174)
Lee Mill Ind. Est. PL21: L Mill 5B 144
LEE MOOR 1J 129 (1B 174)
Lee Pl. *EX34: Ilfra 2J 11*
(off Ropery Rd.)
Lee Rd. EX35: Lynt 2G 13
Leeward Ct. EX8: Exmth 6A 76
Leeward La. TQ2: Torq 2A 112
Leeze Pk. EX20: Oke 5B 48
Legion La. PL8: Brixt 2H 149
Legion Way EX2: Alph 4E 70
Legis Wlk. PL6: Robo 2C 132
Leg O Mutton Cnr. PL20: Yelv 6F 127
Leicester Mead EX4: Exe 5B 64
LEIGHAM 2F 137 (2B 174)
Leigham Bus. Units EX2: Mar B 5G 71
Leigham Ct. EX7: Daw 4H 97
Leigham Mnr. Dr. PL6: Plym 4G 137
Leigham St. PL1: Plym 7C 8 (4H 141)
Leigham Ter. *TQ7: Kingsb 4F 157*
(off Fore St.)
Leigham Ter. La.
PL1: Plym 6C 8 (3H 141)
Leigh Cl. PL21: Bitta 3C 146
Leigh Ct. PL6: Plym 3B 136
Leighdene Cl. EX2: Exe 7J 7 (1H 71)
Leigh La. PL6: Robo 1E 132
PL21: Bitta 2C 146
Leighon Rd. TQ3: Paig 1J 119
Leigh Rd. EX18: Chul 6A 32
EX39: Bide 4D 22
Leighton Rd. PL3: Plym 3K 135
Leighton Ter. EX4: Exe 2F 7 (5F 65)
Leigh Vs. EX18: Chul 6B 32
Leland Gro. PL21: Ivy 5H 145
Le Locle Cl. EX10: Sidm 2A 84
Le Marchant Cl. EX14: Dunk 7G 47
Lembury Rd. TQ9: Sto G 6A 118
Le Molay-Littry Way TQ13: Bov T . . .4C 92
Lemon Ct. *TQ12: New A 1F 109*
(off Marsh Rd.)
Lemon M. *TQ12: New A 1F 109*
(off The Avenue)
Lemon Pl. TQ12: New A 1F 109
Lemon Rd. TQ12: New A 1F 109
Lenards Rd. EX39: N'ham 6E 20
Lendon Way EX19: Wink 3C 36
Lennard Rd. EX17: Cred 6H 39
Lennox Av. EX10: Sidm 6C 84
Lentney Cl. PL9: Hey B 3B 148
Lenwood Pk. EX39: Bide 1D 22
Lenwood Rd. EX39: Bide, N'ham 1D 22
(not continuous)
Leofric Rd. EX16: Tiv 2D 40
LEONARD MOOR 3E 42
Leonard's Cl. TQ7: Thur 6C 154
Leonards Cove Holiday Pk.
TQ6: Sto F 3H 153
Leonards Rd. PL21: Ivy 4H 145
Leper's Well 5K 91
(off Mill La.)
Leslie Rd. EX8: Exmth 4C 76
Lester Cl. PL3: Plym 5C 136
Lester Point EX34: Com M 5A 12
Lestock Cl. EX8: L'ham 5G 77
Lethaby Rd. EX32: Barn 3F 19
Lethbridge Ct. *TQ12: New A 1F 109*
(off Courtenay Pk. Rd.)
Lethbridge Rd. EX2: Won 7A 66
Letheren's La. EX20: N Taw 5B 36
Let's Go 3C 18
LETTAFORD 2B 170
LEUSDON 3B 170
Level, The TQ6: Ditt 6C 120
Lever Cl. EX39: N'ham 4E 20
Leverlake Cl. EX16: Tiv 2F 41
Leverlake La. EX16: Chet, Tiv 1F 41
LEWANNICK 2A 168
LEWDOWN 1A 56 (2C 169)
Lewesdon Ct. DT7: Lym R 5J 91
Lewes Gdns. PL5: Plym 6H 131
Lewhaven Cl. EX20: Lew 1A 56
Lewis Av. EX16: Tiv 4E 40
Lewis Ct. *EX34: Ilfra 3H 11*
(off Victoria Rd.)
Lewis Cres. EX2: Sow 2C 72
Lewis's Pas. *EX34: Ilfra 3H 11*
(off Victoria Rd.)
LEWORTHY
Bratton Fleming 3C 161
Holsworthy 3B 162
LEWTHORN CROSS 3B 170
LEWTRENCHARD 2C 56 (2C 169)
LEY 3A 168
Leyburn Gro. TQ4: Paig 3G 119
Ley Cl. TQ12: Live 7G 93
Ley Cres. TQ12: Live 7G 93
Leyfield Wlk. EX7: Daw 3H 97
Leyford Cl. PL9: Wem 6C 148
Ley La. PL20: Bere F 5A 128
TQ12: Kingst 3G 105
Ley Mdw. Dr. EX31: Roun 6K 17
Leypark Cl. EX1: Whip 5B 66
Leypark Cres. EX1: Whip 6B 66
Leypark Dr. PL6: Plym 1E 136
Leypark Rd. EX1: Whip 5B 66
Leypark Wlk. PL6: Plym 7F 133
Leys Rd. TQ2: Torq 1K 115
LEZANT .3B 168
Libbaton Golf Course 4B 32
Liberator Way EX14: Dunk 7H 47
Liberty Ct. EX31: Roun 7A 18
Liberty Rd. EX31: Roun 7A 18
Liberty Way EX2: Cou W 4C 72
Libra Gdns. EX34: Com M 5A 12
Lichfield Av. TQ2: Torq 3C 112
Lichfield Cl. TQ5: Brixh 4C 122
Lichfield Dr. TQ5: Brixh 4C 122
Lichfield Rd. EX4: Exe 6A 64
Lichgate Rd. EX2: Alph 5E 70
Lidburn Hill EX6: Ted M 5G 49
LIDDATON 2C 169
Liddle Way PL7: Plymp 3E 138
Lidford Tor Av. TQ4: Paig 4E 118
Lifeboat Station
Ilfracombe 2J 11
Teignmouth 6H 107
Life Centre, Plymouth 6H 135
Liffey Ri. EX4: Exe 4B 64
LIFTON 6B 56 (2B 168)
LIFTONDOWN 2B 168
Lifton Rd. PL4: Plym 5J 9
Light La. TQ5: Galm 4H 121
Lilac Cl. PL9: Hooe 7D 142
Lilac Rd. EX2: Won 2J 71
EX16: Tiv 3F 41
Lilac Ter. *EX16: Tiv 4D 40*
(off Martins La.)
Lilian Cl. EX17: Bow 5G 37
Lillage La. EX9: E Bud 1C 82
LILLESDON 1D 167
Lilley Wlk. EX14: Hon 4G 55
LILLY 4K 19
Lillybrook La. EX6: Ted M 4K 49
Lilly La. EX5: New C 7D 50
Lilybridge EX39: N'ham 5F 21
Lily Cl. EX39: N'ham 4F 21
Lily Mt. EX4: Exe 4A 64
Lilypond La. EX5: Whim 6J 53
Lime Av. TQ2: Torq 1B 116
Lime Cl. EX5: Broadc 6C 52
EX16: Tiv 3E 40
Lime Cres. EX15: Will 4C 44
Lime Gro. EX6: Exmin 1C 74
EX8: Exmth 1E 76
EX39: Bide 3E 22
EX39: Ins 4K 21
TQ7: Kingsb 4F 157
Limegrove Rd. EX4: Exe 7C 64
Limehayes Rd. EX20: Oke 2C 48
Lime Kiln La. DT7: Uply 2F 91
EX2: Cou W 4K 71
Limekiln La. EX8: Exmth 7E 76
EX31: Ashf 1H 17
Lime Kiln Rd. EX16: Tiv 5F 41
Limerick Pl. PL4: Plym 4K 9 (2B 142)
Lime Rd. EX16: Tiv 3F 41
Limers Hill EX38: Gt T 2A 30
Limers La. EX20: Mer 4A 30
EX36: S Mol 7A 26
EX39: N'ham 7F 21
Limes, The PL6: Plym 1A 136
Limes La. PL19: Tavi 3G 59
Lime St. TQ13: More 6H 61
Lime Tree Cl. EX2: Won 2B 72
Limetree Gro. EX33: Brau 4H 15
Lime Tree Mead EX16: Tiv 5G 41
Limetree Rd. PL3: Plym 4J 135
Lime Tree Wlk. TQ12: New A 3H 109
Lime Way EX12: Seat 3E 86
Linacre Rd. TQ2: Torq 2B 112
Lincoln Av. PL4: Plym 1K 9 (1B 142)
Lincoln Cl. EX8: Exmth 1G 77
EX14: Fen 2G 53
Lincoln Grn. TQ2: Torq 4C 112
Lincoln Rd. EX4: Exe 6B 64
Lincombe Dr. TQ1: Torq 2G 117
Lincombe Hill Rd. TQ1: Torq 2G 117
Linda Cl. EX1: Heav 7A 66
Lindemann Cl. EX10: Sidm 2B 84
Linden Cl. EX8: Exmth 2F 77
EX31: Barn 6B 18
EX33: Brau 4J 15
EX38: Gt T 1B 30
Linden Gdns. EX31: Barn 6B 18
Linden Rd. EX7: Daw 5F 97
EX15: Cull 3H 45
Linden Ter. PL4: Plym 2B 142
TQ12: New A 1D 108
Linden Va. EX4: Exe 1C 6 (5E 64)
Lindfield Cl. TQ2: Torq 5B 112
Lindisfarne Way TQ2: Torq 3A 112
Lindridge Cl. TQ12: Kingst 1G 105
Lindridge Hill TQ12: Kingst 1H 105
Lindridge La. TQ12: Kingst 1G 105
(not continuous)
Lindridge Rd. TQ1: Torq 5E 112
TQ14: Bi'ton, Teignm 2A 106
Lindsay Rd. TQ3: Pres 4G 115
Lindthorpe Way TQ5: Brixh 4D 122
Linfield Gdns. EX4: Exe 1C 70
Linhay Bus. Pk. TQ13: Ashb 2K 99
Linhay Cl. EX14: Hon 6E 54
EX15: Culm 2B 46
TQ5: Hill 6K 123
Linhay Dr. EX31: Frem 5G 17
Linhey Cl. TQ7: Kingsb 5G 157
Linkadells PL7: Plymp 3A 138
Linkadell Vs. PL7: Plymp 3A 138
Linketty La. PL7: Plymp 6K 137
Linketty La. E. PL6: Plym 2B 136
Linketty La. W. PL3: Plym 4K 135
PL6: Plym 3A 136

Link Ho. Cl. EX39: West H 5B 20
LINKINHORNE 3B 168
Link Rd. EX20: Oke 2C 48
Links, The EX39: N'ham 5D 20
TQ1: Torq 4E 112
Links Cl. EX8: Exmth 5E 76
TQ5: Chur F 2A 122
Links Ct. TQ7: Thur 7C 154
Links Rd. EX9: Bud S 7A 82
Linnet Cl. EX4: Exe 2G 65
Linnet Dene EX15: Cull 5F 45
Linscott Cres. EX31: Yell 7B 16
Linton Cl. PL5: Tam F 2H 131
Linton Rd. PL5: Tam F 2H 131
Linton Sq. PL5: Tam F 2H 131
Linton Wlk. PL5: Tam F 2H 131
Lion Cl. TQ7: Kingsb 4F 157
Lion's Cl. Hill EX24: Colyt 4C 88
Lions Mill EX31: Cher B 2D 18
Lippell Dr. PL9: Plyms 6E 142
LIPSON 1J 9 (7B 136)
Lipson Av. PL4: Plym 2K 9 (1B 142)
Lipson Ct. PL4: Plym 2H 9 (2A 142)
Lipson Hill PL4: Plym 1K 9 (1B 142)
Lipson Rd. PL4: Plym 4G 9 (2A 142)
(Beaumont Pl.)
PL4: Plym 1K 9 (7B 136)
(Mostyn Av.)
Lipson Sports Cen. 7C 136
Lipson Ter. PL4: Plym 1K 9 (1B 142)
LIPSON VALE 7B 136
Lipson Va. PL4: Plym 7B 136
Lipstone Cres. PL4: Plym . . .1K 9 (1B 142)
Lisa Cl. EX2: Won 1K 71
Lisburne Cres. TQ1: Torq 2F 117
Lisburne Pl. *TQ1: Torq 2F 117*
(off Lisburne Sq.)
Lisburne Sq. TQ1: Torq 2F 117
Liscawn Ter. PL11: Torp 1A 140
LISCOMBE 1C 165
Lisham's Drain EX24: Colyt 5D 88
Lisson Gro. PL4: Plym 7K 135
Lister Cl. EX2: Exe 7K 7 (1H 71)
PL7: Plymp 3C 138
Lister Way TQ9: E All 6D 152
Litchaton Cres. PL7: Plymp 4J 137
Litchaton Way PL7: Plymp 4J 137
Litchdon La. EX32: Barn 5E 18
Litchdon St. EX32: Barn 5E 18
Litchfield Cl. PL7: Plymp 3E 138
Litelbury Rd. EX16: Tiv 5H 41
Littabourne EX31: Barn 2E 18
Little Ash Gdns. PL5: Plym 2A 134
Little Ash Rd. PL5: Plym 2A 134
Little Barley EX4: Exe 7C 64
Little Barton TQ12: Kingst 2H 105
Lit. Bicton Ct. *EX8: Exmth 6C 76*
(off Lit. Bicton Pl.)
Lit. Bicton Pl. EX8: Exmth 6C 76
LITTLEBOROUGH 2C 165
Lit. Bossell La. TQ11: B'leigh 5C 98
Littlebourne EX16: With 5H 33
Little Bradley Ponds Nature Reserve
. . . . .5E 92
Little Bri. Bus. Pk. EX5: Clyst M 4J 73
Little Butts PL9: Plyms 6F 143
Lit. Castle St. EX4: Exe 3E 6 (6F 65)
Lit. Chockenhole La. EX9: Ott'n 5K 83
Little Cl. EX11: Ott M 4C 80
TQ12: Kingst 2H 105
Lit. Cotton Caravan Pk.
TQ6: Dartm 7B 124
LITTLE DARTMOUTH 1K 153
Lit. Dock La. PL5: Plym 1F 135
Littledown Cl. EX8: L'ham 5H 77
Lit. Down La. EX9: E Bud 2C 82
PL6: Robo 1G 133
Littledown La. EX10: New P 6F 81
Lit. Down Orchard EX10: New P 6F 81
Lit. Fancy Cl. PL6: Plym 3D 132
Little Fld. EX39: Bide 3C 22
Littlefield TQ14: Bi'ton 3A 106
Littlefield Cl. EX32: Barn 5J 19
TQ2: Torq 4K 111
Lit. Field Ct. PL19: Tavi 4K 59
Littlefields EX12: Seat 3E 86
Little Gate TQ7: Lodd 3H 151
Littlegate Rd. TQ3: Paig 1H 119
Lit. Gornhay La. EX16: Tiv 2G 41
LITTLEHAM
Bideford 1C 163
Exmouth 5H 77 (2A 172)
Littleham Chu. Path EX8: L'ham . . .4K 77
EX9: Bud S 7A 82
Littleham Leisure Cen. 5H 77
Littleham Rd. EX8: Exmth, L'ham . . .5F 77
EX39: Bide 7F 23
Littleham Village EX8: L'ham 5H 77
Little Hayes TQ12: Kingst 2H 105
LITTLEHEMPSTON 1F 103 (1A 176)
Little Hill TQ8: Salc 3B 158
Lit. John's Cross Hill EX2: Exe 2B 70
Lit. John's Wlk. TQ13: Bov T 1B 92
Littlejoy Rd. TQ12: New A 7A 104
LITTLE KNOWLE 6B 82
Little Knowle EX9: Bud S 6B 82
Lit. Knowle Ct. EX9: Bud S 6B 82
Little La. EX12: Beer 7B 86
Littlemead La. EX8: Exmth 1C 76
Little Mdw. EX8: Exmth 1F 77
Lit. Meadow Campsite
EX34: Berry 1A 12
Lit. Meadow Way EX39: Bide 3D 22
Littlemoor Cl. EX31: Yell 7B 16
Little Park PL20: Bere F 7C 128
Lit. Park Rd. TQ3: Paig 1G 119
LITTLE POTHERIDGE 2D 163
Lit. Queen St. EX4: Exe 4E 6 (6F 65)
Lit. Rack St. EX1: Exe 5D 6 (7E 64)
Little Roborough TQ13: Ashb 3H 99
Little Silver EX4: Exe 3C 6 (5E 64)
EX16: Tiv 5C 40
Little Theatre, The
Torquay 3F 117
Little Toms EX15: Cull 3F 45
Littleton Pl. PL2: Dev 7E 134
LITTLE TORRINGTON 2C 163
LITTLETOWN 5E 54
Littletown Rd. EX14: Hon 5E 54
Littletown Vs. *EX14: Hon 5F 55*
(off Manor Cres.)
Little Triangle *TQ14: Teignm 5J 107*
(off Triangle Pl.)
Littleway EX2: Exe 2C 70
Lit. Week Cl. EX7: Daw 1J 97
Lit. Week Gdns. EX7: Daw 1J 97
Lit. Week La. EX7: Daw 1J 97
Lit. Week Rd. EX7: Daw 1J 97
LITTLEWINDSOR 3D 167
Littlewood Cl. PL7: Plymp 5D 138
Livarot Wlk. EX36: S Mol 6B 26
LIVERMEAD 4A 116
Livermead Hill TQ2: Torq 4A 116
Livermore Rd. EX14: Hon 4F 55
Liverpool Hill EX4: Exe 5B 64
LIVERTON 4G 93 (3C 171)
Liverton Bus. Pk. EX8: Exmth 3H 77
Liverton Cl. EX8: Exmth 4G 77
Liverton Copse Nature Reserve 3G 77
Liverton Dr. EX32: Swim 3G 25
Livery Dole Almshouses
EX2: Exe 5K 7 (7H 65)
Living Coasts 3D 116
Livingshayes Rd. EX5: Silv 1J 51
Livingstone Rd. TQ14: Teignm 3J 107
Livonia Rd. EX10: Sidm 4C 84
Lizard Cl. PL6: Plym 3A 132
Lizard Wlk. PL6: Plym 3B 132
Llantillio Dr. PL2: Plym 3G 135
Lloyd Av. TQ2: Torq 5K 111
Lloyd Maunder Rd. EX15: Will 4C 44
Lloyds Ct. EX1: Whip 4B 66
Lloyds Cres. EX1: Whip 5B 66
LOBB 2F 15 (3A 160)
Lobb Flds. Caravan & Camping Pk.
EX33: Brau 3F 15
LOBHILLCROSS 1D 56 (2C 169)
Locarno Av. TQ3: Pres 5K 115
Locarno Rd. EX4: Exe 1C 70
Lock Cl. EX10: Sidm 2B 84
Lockeridge Rd. PL20: Bere A 2A 128
Lockfield Ct. EX2: Alph 4E 70
Lockington Av. PL3: Plym 4A 136
Locks Cl. EX33: Brau 5J 15
TQ1: Torq 6F 113
Locksey's La. EX12: Brans 4G 85
Locks Hill TQ1: Torq 6F 113
Locksley Cl. EX2: Cou W 5K 71
TQ1: Torq 6D 112
Locksley Grange TQ1: Torq 6C 112
Locks Wlk. PL1: Dev 3D 140
Lockyer Av. EX10: Sidm 2D 84
Lockyer Ct. PL1: Plym 6D 8
Lockyer Cres. EX16: Tiv 2A 40
Lockyer Rd. PL3: Plym 6K 135
Lockyers Quay PL4: Plym . . .6H 9 (3A 142)
Lockyer St. PL1: Plym 5D 8 (3J 141)
(not continuous)
LODDISWELL 2G 151 (3D 175)
Lodge Gdns. PL6: Plym 7K 131
Lodge Hill EX4: Exe 4D 64
EX20: Oke 3A 48
Lodge La. EX13: Wey 1K 89
EX18: Chul 6E 32
PL8: Brixt 2G 149
Lodge Rd. EX16: Tiv 4E 40
Lodge Trad. Est. EX5: Broadc 1K 67
Lofoten Cl. PL1: Dev 2D 140
Loftus Gdns. PL5: Plym 1B 134
Logan Rd. TQ3: Paig 7J 115
Logan Way EX15: Hemy 2F 47
Lombard Cl. EX39: Bide 5C 22
London Ct. PL21: Ivy 4H 145
London Inn Sq. EX4: Exe 3F 7 (6F 65)
London Rd. EX5: Rock 3D 68
EX5: Whim 2J 69
Longacre PL7: Plymp 4J 137
Longacres EX2: Exe 6H 7 (7G 65)
Long Barton TQ12: Kingst 2H 105
Long Barton Av. EX20: Oke 2E 48
LONGBRIDGE 4F 137
Long Bri. EX31: Barn 5E 18
Longbridge Av. PL6: Plym 5G 137
Longbridge Cl. PL6: Plym 5G 137
Longbridge Mdw. EX15: Cull 4H 45
Longbridge Mdw. Trad. Est.
EX15: Cull 4H 45
Longbridge Rd. PL6: Plym 4F 137
Longbrook TQ7: Chil 6H 159
Longbrook Barton PL7: Plymp 4A 138
Longbrook Cl. PL21: Ivy 4E 144
Longbrook La. EX8: Lymp 7G 75
Longbrook Rd. PL21: Ivy 4F 145
Longbrook St. EX4: Exe 3F 7 (5F 65)
PL7: Plymp 6C 138
Longbrook Ter. EX4: Exe 2E 6 (5F 65)
Longcause PL7: Plymp 5C 138
Long Causeway EX8: Exmth 6D 76
Long Copp EX9: Bud S 5C 82
Longcroft Av. TQ5: Brixh 5D 122
Longcroft Dr. TQ5: Brixh 5D 122
Longdogs Cl. EX11: Ott M 4D 80
Longdogs La. EX11: Ott M 4D 80
LONGDOWN 1C 171
Long Down Gdns. PL6: Plym 7F 133
Long Drag EX15: Will 7E 44
Longdrag Hill EX16: Tiv 4A 40
Long Entry DT7: Lym R 5K 91
Longfield EX39: Apple 3H 21
PL21: Lutt 7F 129
Longfield Av. TQ12: Kingst 4J 105
Longfield Cl. EX33: Brau 5K 15
PL21: Lutt 7F 129
Longfield Dr. TQ8: Salc 3B 158
Longfield Est. EX6: Star 1D 96
Longfield Pl. PL4: Plym 1H 9 (1A 142)
Longfield Rd. EX6: Star 1D 96
Longfields TQ7: W Alv 5D 156
Longfield Ter. *EX34: Ilfra 3J 11*
(off Highfield Rd.)
Longfield Vs. PL9: Plyms 4E 142
Longford La. TQ12: Kingst 3H 105
Longford Pk. TQ12: Kingst 3H 105
Long Hill EX12: Beer 7B 86
Longland La. EX33: Georgeh 5C 14
Longlands EX7: Daw 4G 97
Longlands Brake Nature Reserve
. . . . .3C 148
Longlands Dr. PL9: Hey B 3B 148
Longlands Rd. PL9: Plyms 4E 142
Long La. EX7: Daw 2F 97
EX8: Exmth 6E 76
EX16: Wash 1A 40
EX31: Ashf 1K 17
(not continuous)
EX33: Forda, Lobb 7A 14
EX39: Apple, N'ham 4F 21
TQ12: Hacc 3K 109
TQ14: Shal 7E 106
Long Ley PL3: Plym 5C 136
Longmead EX15: Hemy 1G 47
EX35: Lynt 2F 13
Long Meadow PL7: Plymp 2A 138
TQ10: S Bre 2A 100
Longmeadow EX5: Clyst M 2F 73
EX5: Wood 5C 78
EX16: Tiv 3D 40
Long Mdw. Cl. PL7: Plymp 2B 138
Long Meadow Dr. EX32: Barn 3G 19
Longmeadow Rd. EX8: Lymp 6H 75
Longmeadows EX17: Cred 5H 39
Longmead Rd. TQ3: Pres 5F 115
Longmead Wlk. TQ3: Pres 5F 115
Long Moor EX15: Cull, Will 7D 44
Long Orchard EX5: Cranb 3B 68
PL20: Bere A 2B 128
Long Pk. EX5: Wood 5C 78
PL21: Modb 5G 147
TQ13: Ashb 2J 99
TQ13: Chag 3H 61
Long Pk. Cl. PL9: Plyms 7G 143
Long Pk. Dr. PL6: Plym 3E 132
Longpark Hill TQ1: Maid 1J 113
Long Rd. TQ4: Paig 5B 118
Longroom PL1: Plym 7A 8 (4G 141)
Long Rowden PL3: Plym 5K 135
Long Rydon TQ9: Sto G 3B 120
Long Sands & Southdown Cliff . . .2B 176
Longstone Av. PL6: Plym 4B 132
Longstone Rd. TQ4: Paig 3E 118
Long Ter. Cl. PL7: Plymp 4F 139
Longtimber & Pithill Woods
Woodland Walks 2H 145
Longview Ter. PL3: Plym 5C 136
Longwood Cl. PL7: Plymp 5D 138
Longwood La. EX16: Burl 4K 43
Long Wools TQ4: Broads 1K 121
Lonsdale Rd. EX1: Heav 7K 65
TQ12: New A 2G 109
Lonsdale Vs. *PL4: Plym 7A 136*
(off Pearson Av.)
Lonsee Gdns. TQ12: Kingsk 7J 109
Looe Rd. EX4: Exe 2B 6 (5D 64)
Looe St. PL4: Plym 5F 9 (3K 141)
Looseleigh Cl. PL6: Plym 6B 132
Looseleigh La. PL6: Plym 5K 131
Looseleigh Pk. PL6: Plym 5K 131
LOPEN 2D 167
Lopes Cres. EX20: Oke 3C 48
Lopes Dr. PL6: Robo 1D 132
Lopes Hall EX4: Exe 3F 65
Lopes Rd. PL2: Plym 5G 135
PL20: Dous 4K 127
Lopwell Cl. PL6: Plym 5A 132
Loram Way EX2: Alph 5F 71
Lord Louis Cres. PL9: Hooe 6A 142
Lord Nelson Dr. TQ6: Dartm 6C 124
Lord Robarts Ct. PL4: Plym 4J 9
Lords Mdw. Ind. Est. EX17: Cred . . .6K 39
Lords Mdw. La. EX16: Bam 2H 33
Lords Meadow Leisure Cen. 6K 39
Lord's Pl. TQ1: Torq 7D 112
Lords Way EX2: Won 2B 72
Loretto Gdns. EX13: Axmin 4J 89
Loretto Rd. EX13: Axmin 4J 89
Loring Rd. TQ8: Salc 4C 158
Lorrimore Av. PL2: Plym 6E 134
Lorris Dr. TQ14: Teignm 3G 107
Lotherton Cl. PL7: Plymp 6E 138
Loughboro Rd. PL5: Plym 2B 134
Louisa Pl. EX8: Exmth 6C 76
Louisa Ter. EX8: Exmth 7C 76
Louise Ter. EX38: Gt T 2B 30
Louis Way EX14: Dunk 7H 47
Loup Ct. EX13: Axmin 4K 89
Louvigny Cl. EX14: Fen 2G 53
Louville Camp TQ5: Brixh 3H 123
Louville Cl. TQ4: Good 5J 119
Lovelace Cres. EX8: Exmth 4E 76
Lovelace Gdns. EX2: Alph 5E 70
Love La. EX24: Colyt 7C 88
EX39: Bide 4D 22
TQ3: Marl 2D 114
(not continuous)
TQ13: Ashb 4H 99
TQ14: Teignm 2K 107
Love La. Cl. TQ3: Marl 2D 114
Lovelane Cotts. TQ3: Marl 2D 114
Lovell Cl. EX8: Exmth 1E 76
Lovell Rd. PL3: Plym 5A 136
Loventor Cres. TQ3: Marl 4D 114
Loventor La. TQ9: Berr P 4A 114
Lovering Cl. EX8: Exmth 1E 76
Loverings Ct. EX31: Barn 4E 18
Lover's La. EX39: Apple 2G 21
Lovers' Wlk. EX32: Barn 7F 19
Lowbrook EX5: Rock 4F 69
Lowena La. EX11: W Hill 3H 79
Lwr. Albert St. EX1: Exe 3H 7 (6G 65)
Lwr. Aller La. TQ13: Bov T 1A 92
Lower Anderton PL10: Mill 7B 140
Lwr. Argyll Rd. EX4: Exe 3D 64
LOWER ASHTON 2C 171
Lwr. Audley Rd. TQ2: Torq 5B 112
Lower Av. EX1: Heav 3K 7 (6J 65)
Lower Barton EX5: Cranb 3C 68
Lwr. Blagdon La. TQ3: Blag 1B 118
Lwr. Brand La. EX14: Hon 5F 55
Lwr. Brimley Cl. TQ14: Teignm 4J 107
Lwr. Brimley Rd. TQ14: Teignm 3J 107
Lwr. Broad Oak Rd. EX11: W Hill 6J 79
Lwr. Broad Pk. TQ6: Dartm 6D 124
Lwr. Broad Path TQ9: Sto G 1A 120
Lwr. Brookfield Ter. TQ13: Lust 6J 63
Lwr. Brook Mdw. EX10: Sidf 1D 84
Lwr. Brook Pk. PL21: Ivy 4E 144
Lwr. Brook St. TQ14: Teignm 5J 107
Lower Budleigh EX9: E Bud 2D 82
Lwr. Budleigh Mdw.
TQ12: New A 1C 108
Lwr. Bull Ring *EX15: Cull 4H 45*
(off Fore St.)
Lwr. Burwood Rd. EX38: Gt T 2D 30
Lwr. Cannon Rd. TQ12: Heat 2J 93
LOWER CHERITON 3B 166
Lwr. Church St. EX24: Colyt 5D 88
EX32: Barn 5F 19
(off Trinity St.)
Lwr. Clay Pk. EX34: Mort 4A 10
Lower Cleave EX39: N'ham 7G 21
Lower Cleve EX33: Brau 3H 15
Lwr. Cloister Wlk. *EX6: Exmin 1B 74*
(off Devington Pk.)
Lower Cl. EX16: Hal 6C 42
Lower Collapark TQ9: Tot 5D 102
Lwr. Collins Rd. TQ9: Tot 5D 102
LOWER COMPTON 6B 136
Lwr. Compton Rd. PL3: Plym 5A 136

Lwr. Congella Rd. TQ1: Torq 7E 112
Lwr. Contour Rd. TQ6: Kingsw 6H 125
Lwr. Coombe Rd. TQ12: Kingst 4J 105
Lwr. Coombe St. EX1: Exe . . .6D 6 (7E 64)
Lower Cotteylands EX16: Tiv 5B 40
Lower Ct. Rd. PL8: New F 5F 149
Lwr. Crooked Mdw. EX20: Oke 3C 48
Lwr. Cross Rd. EX31: Bick'n 5K 17
LOWER DEAN 7B 98 (1D 175)
Lower Dean EX12: Brans 6F 85
Lwr. Dean La. EX34: Com M 7D 12
LOWER DITTISHAM 6C 120
Lower Dr. EX7: Daw 2J 97
Lwr. Duck St. EX6: Exmin 3D 74
Lwr. Ellacombe Chu. Rd.
TQ1: Torq 7E 112
Lwr. Erith Rd. TQ1: Torq 2F 117
LOWER ERNESETTLE 5C 130
LOWER EYPE 1D 173
Lwr. Fairview Rd. TQ6: Dartm 6E 124
Lwr. Farm Rd. PL7: Plymp 5D 138
Lower Farthings EX10: New P 6G 81
Lwr. Fern Rd. TQ12: New A 4J 109
Lwr. Fore St. EX8: Exmth 6C 76
PL12: Salt 1A 134
Lower Fowden TQ4: Broads 2K 121
Lwr. French Pk. TQ12: New A 1C 108
LOWER GABWELL 1B 176
Lwr. Gaydon St. *EX32: Barn 4F 19*
(off Richmond St.)
Lower Griggs EX10: Sidm 3E 84
Lower Gunstone EX39: Bide 3F 23
Lwr. Halsdon La. EX8: Exmth 3B 76
Lwr. Harrington La. EX4: Pin 3D 66
Lwr. Hill Barton Rd.
EX1: Heav, Sow 6B 66
LOWER HOLDITCH 3D 167
Lwr. King's Av. EX4: Exe 4G 65
Lwr. Kingsdown Rd.
TQ14: Teignm 4F 107
Lwr. Kinsman's Dale TQ13: More . . .6H 61
Lower Knoll EX8: Exmth 6F 77
Lwr. Knowle Rd. TQ13: Lust 6J 63
Lwr. Ladram La. EX9: Ott'n 6K 83
Lower La. EX3: Ebf 6E 74
Lwr. Long Cl. EX34: Com M 3E 12
Lower Loughborough EX16: Tiv 3B 40
LOWER LOVACOTT 1D 163
LOWER LOXHORE 3C 161
Lwr. Manor Rd. TQ5: Brixh 3E 122
Lwr. Marlpits Hill EX14: Hon 5G 55
Lwr. Meadow Ri. EX7: Daw 4F 97
Lwr. Meddon St. EX39: Bide 4F 23
Lower Millhayes EX15: Hemy 1G 47
Lwr. Mill La. EX15: Cull 4H 45
Lower Moor EX32: Barn 5J 19
Lwr. Moor Way EX16: Tiv 2G 41
Lwr. Northcote Rd. EX14: Hon 2H 55
Lwr. North St. EX4: Exe 3C 6 (6E 64)
Lower Pk. TQ3: Paig 7G 115
Lwr. Park Dr. PL9: Plyms 7G 143
Lwr. Park Rd. EX33: Brau 5K 15
Lwr. Penns Rd. TQ3: Pres 5J 115
Lwr. Polsham Rd. TQ3: Paig 7H 115
Lwr. Rackclose La. *EX1: Exe 5C 6*
(off West St.)
Lwr. Raleigh Rd. EX31: Barn 3F 19
Lwr. Rea Rd. TQ5: Brixh 3F 123
Lower Redgate *EX16: Tiv 4D 40*
(off Bartows C'way.)
Lower Ridings PL7: Plymp 2E 138
Lower Rd. EX5: Wood S 1A 78
Lwr. St German's Rd. EX4: Exe 4F 65
Lower Saltram PL9: Plyms 5D 142
LOWER SANDYGATE 1G 105
Lower Sandygate TQ12: Kingst 1G 105
Lwr. Shapter St. EX3: Top 6B 74
Lower Shillingford EX2: Shil A 7D 70
Lwr. Shirburn Rd. TQ1: Torq 6C 112
Lowerside PL2: Plym 3E 134
LOWER SLADE 5G 11 (2B 160)
Lower St. PL4: Plym 5G 9 (3K 141)
TQ6: Dartm 2B 124 (6F 125)
TQ6: Ditt 5B 120
TQ7: W Alv 5D 156
TQ13: Chag 2H 61
Lower Summerlands
EX1: Exe 3H 7 (6G 65)
LOWER TALE 3A 166
Lower Ter. EX22: Bradw 5B 28
Lwr. Thurlow Rd. TQ1: Torq 7C 112
LOWER TOWN
Buckfastleigh 4D 98
Halberton 6C 42
Sampford Peverell 2B 42
Lower Town EX16: Hal 7C 42
EX16: Sam P 2B 42
EX19: Wink 3C 36
EX39: Wools 3B 28
TQ7: Malb 6G 155
Lwr. Trindle Cl. TQ13: Chud 2B 94
Lwr. Union La. TQ2: Torq 1C 116
Lwr. Union Rd. TQ7: Kingsb 4F 157
Lwr. Warberry Rd. TQ1: Torq 1D 116
Lwr. Warren Rd. TQ7: Kingsb 6G 157
Lower Way EX10: Harp 4J 81
LOWER WEAR 6A 72 (2D 171)
Lwr. Wear Rd. EX2: Cou W 5K 71
Lwr. Westlake Rd. EX31: Roun 7K 17
Lower Wheathill EX10: Sidm 2C 84
(not continuous)
Lwr. Woodfield Rd. TQ1: Torq 3E 116
Lwr. Woodhayes Ct. EX5: Whim 7H 53
LOWER WOOLBROOK 4B 84
Lwr. Yalberton Holiday Pk.
TQ4: Paig 6D 118
Lwr. Yalberton Rd. TQ4: Paig 5C 118
LOW HAM 1D 167
Lowley Brook Ct. TQ2: Torq 5H 111
Lowman Grn. *EX16: Tiv 4D 40*
(off Station Rd.)
Lowman Units EX16: Tiv 3G 41
Lowman Way EX16: Tiv 3F 41
Low Rd. PL9: Wem 6B 148
LOWTON
North Towton 3A 164
Pitminster 2B 166
LOXBEARE 2D 165
Loxbury Ri. TQ2: Torq 2K 115
Loxbury Rd. TQ2: Torq 1K 115
LOXHORE 3C 161
Lucas Av. EX4: Exe 1H 7 (4G 65)
Lucas La. PL7: Plymp 3A 138
Lucas Ter. PL4: Plym 2C 142
Luccombe La. *EX2: Exe 2D 70*
(off Alphington Rd.)
Lucerne TQ1: Torq 2F 117
Lucius St. TQ2: Torq 1B 116
LUCKETT 3B 168
Luckhams La. TQ7: Malb 6G 155
Lucky La. EX2: Exe 6E 6 (7F 65)
Lucombe Ct. EX4: Exe 1H 7
Ludlow Rd. PL3: Plym 5K 135
Ludwell La. EX2: Won 1K 71
LUFFINCOTT 1B 168
Lukesland Gdns. 1J 145
Luke St. EX16: Bam 2H 33
Lulworth Cl. TQ4: Paig 5F 119
Lulworth Dr. PL6: Plym 3C 132
Lumley Cl. EX6: Kenton 6J 95
Lummaton Cross TQ2: Torq 3C 112
Lummaton Pl. TQ2: Torq 4D 112
Lundy Cl. EX32: Barn 4H 19
PL6: Plym 3A 132
Lundy Flds. EX34: Woolc 7C 10
Lundy Island 1A 160
Lundy Vw. EX39: N'ham 5D 20
Lupin Way EX15: Will 3E 44
LUPPITT 3B 166
LUPRIDGE 2D 175
Lupton House 5A 122
LURLEY .2D 165
LUSCOMBE 4E 100 (2D 175)
Luscombe Cl. PL21: Ivy 4E 144
TQ12: Ipp 7H 101
Luscombe Cres. TQ3: Paig 1E 118
Luscombe La. TQ3: Paig 6D 114
Luscombe Rd. TQ3: Paig 7D 114
Luscombe Ter. EX7: Daw 4G 97
LUSON 6A 150 (3C 175)
LUSTLEIGH 6H 63 (2B 170)
Lustleigh Cleave 2B 170
Lustleigh Cl. EX2: Matf 5F 71
Lusways EX10: Sidm 6D 84
Lutehouse La. EX19: Wink 2A 36
LUTON
Honiton 3A 166
Teignmouth 3D 171
Lutterburn St. PL21: Ugb 6E 146
LUTTON
Ivybridge 7G 129 (2B 174)
South Brent 1C 175
LUTWORTHY 2B 164
Lutyens Dr. TQ3: Paig 7D 114
Lutyens Fold PL19: Mil A 2B 58
Luxmoore Way EX20: Oke 2D 48
Luxmore Cl. PL6: Plym 2F 137
Luxton Ct. EX15: Cull 4H 45
Luxton Rd. TQ12: E Ogw 4C 108
Luxtons Pk. EX11: Ott M 4B 80
Lych Cl. PL9: Hooe 6B 142
Lychgate Pk. EX17: Cop 6C 38
LYDCOTT 3C 161
Lydcot Wlk. PL6: Plym 3B 136
Lyddicleave EX31: Bick'n 6K 17
LYDEARD ST LAWRENCE 1B 166
LYDFORD 6H 57 (2D 169)
Lydford Castle 6G 57
Lydford Cl. PL21: Ivy 5H 145
Lydford Gorge 6G 57
Lydford Ho. *TQ12: New A 7G 105*
(off Hameldown Way)
Lydford Pk. Rd. PL3: Plym 6J 135
Lyd Gdns. PL19: Tavi 4K 59
Lydgates Rd. EX12: Seat 4D 86
Lydia Cl. EX10: New P 5F 81
Lydiate La. EX35: Lynt 3F 13
Lydia Way PL4: Plym 1H 9 (1A 142)
LYDMARSH 3D 167
Lydwell Pk. Rd. TQ1: Torq 7F 113
Lydwell Rd. TQ1: Torq 7F 113
Lym Cl. DT7: Lym R 5K 91
Lyme Bay Rd. TQ14: Teignm 2J 107
Lymeborne Av. EX1: Heav 6K 65
Lymebourne Av. EX10: Sidm 4C 84
Lymebourne La. EX10: Sidm 4C 84
Lymebourne Pk. EX10: Sidm 4C 84
Lyme Cl. EX13: Axmin 4H 89
Lyme M. EX12: Seat 6F 87
LYME REGIS 5K 91 (1D 173)
Lyme Regis Golf Course 2K 91
Lyme Regis Ind. Est. DT7: Lym R . . .4H 91
Lyme Regis Lifeboat Station 6J 91
Lyme Regis Marine Aquarium
(& Cobb History) 6K 91
Lyme Regis Mus. 5K 91
Lyme Regis Sailing Club 6J 91
Lyme Rd. DT7: Uply 2F 91
EX13: Axmin 4J 89
EX13: Ray H 4B 90
Lyme St. EX13: Axmin 3H 89
Lyme Vw. Cl. TQ1: Torq 6F 113
Lyme Vw. Rd. TQ1: Torq 6E 112
Lymington Rd. TQ1: Torq 6B 112
Lympne Av. PL5: Plym 5E 130
LYMPSTONE 6G 75 (2D 171)
Lympstone Commando Station (Rail)
. . . . .3G 75
Lympstone Village Station (Rail) . . .6F 75
Lyn & Exmoor Mus. 2H 13
LYNBRIDGE 3H 13 (2D 161)
Lynbridge Rd. EX35: Lynt 4G 13
Lynbro Rd. EX31: Barn 2E 18
Lynch Cl. EX5: Thor 2A 50
EX13: Axmin 2H 89
Lynch Head EX11: S'ton, Ven O 2F 81
Lyncombe Cl. EX4: Exe 3H 65
Lyncombe Cres. TQ1: Torq 3G 117
Lyncourt TQ1: Torq 3F 117
Lyndale Rd. TQ12: Kingst 3G 105
Lyndhurst Av. TQ12: Kingsk 7K 109
Lyndhurst Cl. PL2: Plym 5H 135
TQ12: Kingsk 7K 109
Lyndhurst Rd. EX2: Exe 6J 7 (7H 65)
EX8: Exmth 4C 76
PL2: Plym 5H 135
Lyndrick Rd. PL3: Plym 4K 135
Lyn Gro. TQ12: Kingsk 6J 109
Lyngrove Ct. *TQ12: Kingsk 6J 109*
(off Moor Pk. Rd.)
Lynhayes EX13: Kilm 2B 88
Lynher St. PL5: Plym 1C 134
Lyn Hill EX35: Lynt 3H 13
Lynhurst Av. EX31: Barn 5A 18
LYNMOUTH 2H 13 (2D 161)
Lynmouth Av. TQ4: Paig 5F 119
Lynmouth Cl. PL7: Plymp 4K 137
Lynmouth Hill EX35: Lynm 2H 13
Lynmouth St. EX35: Lynm 1H 13
LYNSTONE 3A 162
LYNTON 2G 13 (2D 161)
Lynton & Barnstaple Railway 2C 161
Lynton & Lynmouth Cliff Railway . . .1G 13
Lynton Cinema 1G 13
Lynton Rd. EX34: Com M 7D 12
Lynway EX35: Lynt 2H 13
Lynway Ct. TQ1: Torq 7D 112
Lynwood TQ12: E Ogw 3C 108
Lynwood Av. EX4: Exe 5A 6 (7D 64)
PL7: Plymp 5H 137
Lynwood Ho. EX32: Barn 7G 19
Lyte Hill Ct. *TQ2: Torq 2B 112*
(off Lyte Hill La.)
Lyte Hill La. TQ2: Torq 2B 112
Lyte La. TQ7: W Cha 7K 157
Lyte's Rd. TQ5: Brixh 4F 123
Lytton Ho. *TQ2: Torq 2C 116*
(off St Luke's Rd. Sth.)

M

Mabel Pl. TQ4: Paig 2H 119
Macadam Rd. PL4: Plym . . .7K 9 (4B 142)
Macandrew Wlk. PL21: Ivy 3J 145
Macaulay Cres. PL5: Plym 2H 135
Macauley Cl. EX14: Hon 3H 55
McCaulay's Health Club
Ivybridge 2D 144
Plymouth 5C 8 (3H 141)
McCoys Arc. EX4: Exe 5C 6
Macey's Ter. EX20: Oke 2C 48
Macey St. PL11: Torp 1A 140
McKay Av. TQ1: Torq 7B 112
Mackenzie Pl. PL5: Plym 1B 134
Mackenzie Way EX16: Tiv 4F 41
Mackrells Ter. TQ12: New A 2D 108
Maclins Cl. EX36: S Mol 6C 26
Macwood Dr. EX12: Seat 4E 86
Madagascar Cl. EX8: Exmth 4G 77
Maddacombe Rd. TQ12: Kingsk . . .2D 110
Maddacombe Ter. TQ12: A'well 2C 110
Madden Rd. PL1: Dev 2E 140
Maddicks Orchard TQ9: Sto G 4B 120
Maddock Cl. PL7: Plymp 6D 138
Maddock Dr. PL7: Plymp 5D 138
Maddocks Row EX4: Exe . . .3D 6 (6E 64)
Madeira Ct. EX8: Exmth 7D 76
Madeira Pl. TQ2: Torq 1C 116
Madeira Rd. PL1: Plym 7E 8 (4J 141)
Madeira Vs. EX8: Exmth 5C 76
Madeira Wlk. EX8: Exmth 7D 76
EX9: Bud S 7D 82
MADFORD 2B 166
Madge Ct. *PL19: Tavi 3H 59*
(off King St.)
Madge La. PL19: Tavi 4H 59
Madison Av. EX1: Heav 6K 65
Madison Cl. EX5: Sto C 7J 51
Madison Wharf EX8: Exmth 6A 76
Madrepore Pl. *TQ1: Torq 1D 116*
(off Pimlico)
Madrepore Rd. TQ1: Torq 2D 116
Maer Bay Ct. EX8: Exmth 7D 76
Maer La. EX8: Exmth, L'ham 7E 76
Maer Rd. EX8: Exmth 7E 76
Maer Top Way EX31: Barn 2F 19
Maer Va. EX8: Exmth 6E 76
Magdala Rd. EX31: Bick'n 6J 17
Magdalen Bri. Ct. EX2: Exe 5F 7
Magdalen Cotts.
EX1: Exe 5G 7 (7G 65)
Magdalene Cl. TQ9: Tot 6E 102
Magdalene Lawn EX32: Barn 4F 19
Magdalene Rd. TQ1: Torq 7B 112
Magdalen Gdns. EX2: Exe . . .5J 7 (7H 65)
PL7: Plymp 6C 138
Magdalen Rd. EX2: Exe 5G 7 (7G 65)
Magdalen St. EX2: Exe 5E 6 (7F 65)
Magistrates' Court
Barnstaple 4D 18
Exeter 4J 7 (6H 65)
Newton Abbot 1E 108
Plymouth 5E 8 (3J 141)
Torquay 1C 116
Magnolia Av. EX2: Won 2K 71
EX8: Exmth 4G 77
Magnolia Cen. *EX8: Exmth 6C 76*
(off Chapel St.)
Magnolia Cl. EX32: Barn 5K 19
PL7: Plymp 4E 138
Magnolia Ct. EX16: Tiv 1E 40
PL9: Plyms 5G 143
(off Horn Cross Rd.)
Magnolia Dr. TQ13: Chud 1D 94
Magnolia Wlk. EX8: Exmth 6C 76
Magpie Cres. EX2: Exe 1A 70
Magpie La. EX14: Hon 6G 55
Magpie Leisure Pk. PL20: Horr . . .1D 126
Maida Vale Ter.
PL4: Plym 1H 9 (7A 136)
MAIDENCOMBE 1J 113 (1B 176)
Maidencombe Ho. TQ1: Torq 1E 112
MAIDENHAYNE 6C 90 (1C 173)
Maidenhayne La. EX13: Mus 6B 90
Maiden St. EX31: Barn 4E 18
Maidenway La. TQ3: Paig 6F 115
Maidenway Rd. TQ3: Paig 6F 115
MAIDENWELL 3A 168
Maidenwell Rd. PL7: Plymp 6K 137
Maidstone Pl. PL5: Plym 6D 130
Main Av. TQ1: Torq 5C 112
Maine Cl. EX39: Bide 3C 22
Maine Gdns. PL2: Plym 4E 134
Main Rd. EX4: Pin 3D 66
EX5: Sto C 6K 51
EX6: Exmin 7K 71
(Sannerville Way)
EX6: Exmin 3E 74
(Station Rd.)
TQ8: Salc 4B 158
MAINSTONE 7G 133
Mainstone Av. PL4: Plym . . .6K 9 (3B 142)
Main St. TQ9: Blacka 3C 152
Maitland Dr. PL3: Plym 3A 136
Majorfield Rd. EX3: Top 5B 74
Majors Mdw. EX20: Oke 3C 48
Major Ter. EX12: Seat 5E 86
Maker Rd. PL11: Torp 2A 140
Maker Vw. PL3: Plym 1A 8 (7G 135)
MALBOROUGH 6G 155 (3D 175)
Malborough Grn. TQ7: Malb 6F 155
Malborough Pk. TQ7: Malb 7H 155
Malden Cl. EX10: Sidm 3C 84
Malden La. EX10: Sidm 2C 84
Malden Rd. EX10: Sidm 2C 84
Malderek Av. TQ3: Pres 5J 115
Mallands Mdw. TQ12: A'well 5D 108

Mallard Cl.—Marshall Rd.

Mallard Cl. PL7: Plymp 4C **138**
TQ2: Torq 2K **111**
Mallard Rd. EX2: Sow 7D **66**
Mallet Rd. PL21: Ivy 3E **144**
Malletts La. EX32: Barn 4F **19**
Mallison Cl. EX4: Exe 4C **64**
Mallock Rd. TQ2: Torq 1A **116**
Mallocks Cl. EX10: Tip J 1J **81**
Mallow Ct. EX15: Will 3D **44**
Malmesbury Cl. PL2: Plym 3G **135**
MALMSMEAD **2D 161**
Malory Cl. PL5: Plym 1J **135**
Malt Field EX8: Lymp 6H **75**
Malt Ho., The TQ9: Tot 6F **103**
Maltings, The EX2: Heav 7J **65**
EX17: Cred 6J **39**
Malt Mill La. TQ9: Tot 5D **102**
Malvern Gdns. EX2: Won 1K **71**
Malvernleigh *TQ1: Torq 5D 112*
(off St Marychurch Rd.)
Malvern Rd. EX10: Sidm 4B **84**
Malvern Way EX39: Bide 3C **22**
Mamhead Bus. Units EX2: Mar B . . .5G **71**
Mamhead Obelisk **2D 171**
Mamhead Rd. EX2: Won 1B **72**
EX6: Kenton 7G **95**
Mamhead Vw. EX8: Exmth 6A **76**
MANADON **2J 135**
Manadon Cl. PL5: Plym 2K **135**
Manadon Dr. PL5: Plym 2K **135**
Manadon Football Development Cen.
. . . . **1J 135**
MANATON **2B 170**
Manaton Cl. EX2: Matf 5F **71**
Manaton Ct. EX2: Matf 5F **71**
Manaton Tor Rd. TQ3: Pres 5F **115**
Manby Gdns. PL5: Plym 6E **130**
Manchester Rd. EX8: Exmth 6B **76**
Manchester St. EX8: Exmth 5B **76**
Mandrake Cl. EX2: Alph 4E **70**
Mandrake Rd. EX2: Alph 4D **70**
Manifold Gdns. PL3: Plym 6E **136**
Manitoba Gdns. EX15: Cull 4G **45**
Manleigh Holiday Pk.
EX34: Com M 7C **12**
Manley Cl. EX5: Whim 6G **53**
Manley La. EX16: Tiv 6K **41**
Manleys La. EX14: Dunk 5G **47**
Manna Ash Ct. EX2: Exe 7H **7**
MANNAMEAD **6A 136**
Mannamead Av. PL3: Plym 6A **136**
Mannamead Ct. *PL3: Plym 5A 136*
(off Lwr. Compton Rd.)
Mannamead Rd. PL3: Plym 3K **135**
PL4: Plym 6K **135**
Manning Av. EX15: Cull 5F **45**
Mannings Mdw. TQ13: Bov T 4C **92**
Mannings Way EX31: Barn 2E **18**
Manor Av. DT7: Lym R 4J **91**
TQ3: Pres 6J **115**
Manor Bend TQ5: Galm 3J **121**
MANOR BOURNE **2B 148**
Mnr. Bourne Rd. PL9: Down T 2A **148**
Manor Cl. EX7: Daw 4G **97**
EX10: Sidm 5B **84**
EX12: Seat 5E **86**
EX14: Westo 4B **54**
EX15: Kent 6B **46**
EX15: Uff 5J **43**
EX31: Barn 6B **18**
EX31: Frem 5F **17**
EX33: Wraf 6K **15**
PL19: Tavi 3G **59**
PL21: Ivy 4G **145**
TQ12: A'well 5D **108**
TQ12: Kingsk 2G **111**
Manor Cotts. *TQ12: New A 1E 108*
(off Wolborough St.)
Manor Ct. EX12: Seat 5E **86**
EX32: L'key 2B **24**
PL3: Plym 5D **136**
TQ6: Sto F 3H **153**
TQ10: S Bre 1B **100**
TQ12: Kingsk 2G 111
(off Torquay Rd.)
Manor Cres. EX14: Hon 5F **55**
TQ3: Pres 6J **115**
Manor Dr. PL21: Ivy 4G **145**
TQ12: Kingsk 2G **111**
TQ13: Chag 3G **61**
Manor Est. PL20: Horr 2D **126**
Manor Farm PL20: Dous 4K **127**
Mnr. Farm Camp Site
TQ12: Dacc 1A **112**
Mnr. Farm Caravan Site
EX12: Seat 3D **86**
Manor Gdns. *EX6: Kenton 5H 95*
(off Slittercombe La.)
EX12: Seat 5F **87**
EX20: Exbo 5J **35**
PL1: Plym 5A **8** (3G **141**)
PL20: Horr 2D **126**
Manor Gdns. TQ1: Torq 3G **117**
TQ3: Pres 6J **115**
TQ7: Kingsb 3G **157**
TQ12: A'well 6E **108**
TQ12: Kingsk 2G **111**
Manorglade Ct. TQ1: Torq 1F **117**
Mnr. Hall, The EX20: Hath 2H **35**
Manor Ho. TQ1: Torq 3G **117**
Manor House, The TQ9: Tot 5E **102**
Manor Ho. Apartments, The
TQ2: Torq 3A 116
(off Seaway La.)
Manor La. PL3: Plym 6E **136**
Mnr. Mill Rd. EX33: Know 1K **15**
Manor Orchard *TQ12: E Ogw 3A 108*
(off Garners La.)
Manor Pk. EX5: Clyst M 2F **73**
EX22: Bradw 6C **28**
EX31: Barn 6B **18**
EX39: Wools 2B **28**
PL20: Dous 4K **127**
TQ7: Kingsb 3G **157**
Manor Pk. Cl. PL7: Plymp 4C **138**
Manor Pk. Dr. PL7: Plymp 5C **138**
Manor Pavilion Theatre **7B 84**
Manor Rd. EX4: Exe 6A **6** (7D **64**)
EX10: Sidm 7B **84**
EX12: Seat 5E **86**
EX32: L'key 2B **24**
PL9: Plyms 4F **143**
PL19: Tavi 3H **59**
TQ1: Torq 5D **112**
TQ3: Pres 6J **115**
TQ5: Brixh 3E **122**
TQ12: A'well 5D **108**
TQ12: New A 1C **108**
TQ13: Chag 3F **61**
TQ14: Bi'ton 3B **106**
Manor Row *EX7: Daw 4G 97*
(off Brook St.)
Manor Steps TQ5: Brixh 3E **122**
Manor St. PL1: Plym 4A **8** (2G **141**)
TQ6: Ditt 6C **120**
Manor Ter. *EX12: Seat 5E 86*
(off Manor Rd.)
TQ3: Paig 2G **119**
TQ5: Brixh 3E **122**
Manor Va. Rd. TQ5: Galm 3J **121**
Manor Vw. TQ12: New A 1D **108**
Manor Way PL19: Tavi 3H **59**
PL21: Ivy 4G **145**
TQ9: Tot 6E **102**
Mansbridge Rd. TQ9: Tot 6G **103**
Manscombe Cl. TQ2: Torq 3K **115**
Manscombe Rd. TQ2: Torq 4K **115**
Mansell Copse Wlk. EX2: Won 1J **71**
Mansfield Rd. EX4: Exe 4H **65**
Mansfield Ter. EX9: Bud S 5D **82**
Mansion, The PL21: Moor 3C **146**
Mansion Ho., The EX6: Exmin 1B **74**
Mansion Ho. St. TQ6: Dartm 2B **124**
Manston Cl. PL5: Plym 5D **130**
Manstone Av. EX10: Sidm 3B **84**
(not continuous)
Manstone Cl. EX10: Sidm 2C **84**
(not continuous)
Manstone La. EX10: Sidm 4C **84**
Manstone Mead EX10: Sidm 2C **84**
Manston Rd. EX1: Heav 1K **7** (5H **65**)
Manston Ter. EX2: Exe 5K **7** (7H **65**)
Manteo Way EX39: Bide 3H **23**
Mantle Gdns. PL5: Plym 3C **134**
Maple Av. TQ13: Bov T 7B **92**
Maple Cl. EX12: Seat 3E **86**
EX14: Hon 6C **54**
EX15: Will 4C **44**
PL6: Plym 4F **133**
PL19: Tavi 6J **59**
TQ5: Brixh 6C **122**
TQ12: Kingst 5H **105**
TQ13: Chud K 6B **94**
Maple Ct. PL9: Plyms 5G **143**
Mapledene Cl. TQ9: Sto G 3B **120**
Maple Dr. EX8: Exmth 1F **77**
Maple Gro. EX16: Tiv 4D **40**
EX31: Roun 6B **18**
PL4: Plym 1E **8** (7J **135**)
PL7: Plymp 6J **137**
TQ4: Good 5H **119**
Maple Rd. EX4: Exe 6A **6** (7C **64**)
EX5: Broadc 6D **52**
TQ5: Brixh 6C **122**
(not continuous)
Mapleton Cl. TQ12: New A 7C **104**
Maple Wlk. PL21: L Mill 5A **144**
TQ2: Torq 5J **111**
Maple Way PL6: Plym 3F **133**
Mapstone Hill TQ13: Lust 4G **63**
Marble Ct. TQ1: Torq 6B **112**
Marcent Ho. TQ5: Brixh 5F **123**
March Ct. EX20: Oke 3B **48**
Marcombe Rd. TQ2: Torq 1A **116**
Marcom Cl. EX8: Exmth 1F **77**
Marcus Ho. EX4: Exe 2D **6**
Marcus Rd. EX8: Exmth 3F **77**
EX14: Dunk 5G **47**
Mardle Way TQ11: B'leigh 4C **98**
Mardle Way Ind. Est.
TQ11: B'leigh 4C **98**
Mardon Cl. PL6: Plym 6E **132**
Mardon Hall EX4: Exe 3E **64**
Mardon Hill EX4: Exe 3E **64**
Mare La. EX12: Beer 7A **86**
Marett Rd. PL5: Plym 7E **130**
Margaret Cl. TQ12: E Ogw 3C **108**
TQ12: Kingst 4H **105**
Margaret Ct. EX4: Whip 3B **66**
Margaret Gdns. TQ12: New A 2J **109**
Margaret Pk. PL3: Plym 3K **135**
Margaret Rd. EX4: Exe 3H **65**
TQ12: E Ogw 3C **108**
TQ12: Kingst 4H **105**
Margaret St. *EX8: Exmth 6C 76*
(off Chapel St.)
Margrove Ter. *EX32: Barn 3E 18*
(off Yeo Vale Rd.)
Marguerite Cl. TQ12: New A 7C **104**
Marguerite Rd. EX16: Tiv 2F **41**
Marguerite Way TQ12: Kingsk 1G **111**
MARHAMCHURCH **3A 162**
MARIANSLEIGH **1B 164**
Marina Cl. TQ5: Brixh 3G **123**
Marina Ct. EX8: Exmth 7D **76**
TQ4: Paig 2J 119
(off Roundham Rd.)
Marina Dr. TQ5: Brixh 3G **123**
Marina Rd. PL5: Plym 7E **130**
TQ5: Brixh 4G **123**
Marina Ter. PL4: Plym 1H **9** (7A **136**)
Marina Way EX16: Tiv 5G **41**
Marine Cotts. PL4: Plym 7J **9** (4A **142**)
Marine Ct. EX9: Bud S 7D **82**
EX39: Ins 3K **21**
PL11: Torp 2A **140**
TQ3: Pres 6J **115**
Marine Cres. *EX12: Seat 6E 86*
(off Marine Pl.)
Marine Dr. EX34: Woolc 7A **10**
PL11: Torp 2A **140**
TQ3: Pres 7J **115**
TQ7: Bigb S 2B **154**
Marine Gdns. *EX39: Bide 4F 23*
(off New Rd.)
TQ3: Pres 6J **115**
Marine House at Beer Arts & Pottery
. . . . **7C 86**
Marine Mt. TQ1: Torq 3J **117**
Marine Palms TQ2: Torq 2C **116**
Marine Pde. DT7: Lym R 6J **91**
EX7: Daw 5H **97**
EX9: Bud S 7D **82**
EX39: Apple 3H **21**
EX39: Ins 3K **21**
TQ3: Pres 6K **115**
TQ14: Shal 6H **107**
Marine Pk. TQ3: Pres 7J **115**
Marine Pk. Holiday Cen.
TQ4: Good 5H **119**
Marine Pl. EX12: Seat 6E **86**
EX34: Ilfra 2H 11
(off Wilder Rd.)
PL4: Plym 7J **9** (4A **142**)
Marine Rd. PL9: Plyms 5C **142**
Mariners Cl. EX33: Brau 5J **15**
Mariners Ct. PL1: Plym 3F **141**
PL4: Plym 5G **9**
TQ14: Shal 6G 107
(off Commons Old Rd.)
Mariners Way EX39: Apple 2H **21**
TQ3: Pres 5F **115**
Marine Ter. *TQ14: Teignm 5H 107*
(off Foresters Ter.)
Marine Theatre, The **5K 91**
Marine Wlk. TQ5: Brixh 2E **122**
Marine Way EX8: Exmth 5C **76**
Marino, The EX10: Sidm 7A **84**
Marions Way EX8: Exmth 2F **77**
Maristow Av. EX8: Exmth 2D **76**
PL2: Plym 6E **134**
Maristow Cl. PL6: Plym 5A **132**
Marist Way EX32: Barn 7H **19**
Maritime Ct. EX2: Exe 7E **6** (1F **71**)
Marjon Sports & Leisure **6C 132**
Marjorie Kelly Way PL21: Ivy 5G **145**
Marjory Wlk. PL8: Yeal 3A **150**
Marker Cl. EX14: Gitt 7A **54**
Markers EX15: Uff 6H **43**
Marker's Cottage **5D 52**
Markers Rd. EX15: Uff 6H **43**
Marker Way EX14: Hon 5F **55**
Market, The TQ1: Torq 1D **116**
TQ6: Dartm 1A 124
(off Market St.)
Market Av. PL1: Plym 4C **8** (2H **141**)
Market Cl. EX16: Bam 2G **33**
PL1: Plym 3F **141**
TQ11: B'leigh 4B **98**
Market Pl. EX10: Sidm 7C **84**
EX15: Will 3C **44**
EX24: Colyt 5D **88**
EX39: Bide 3F **23**
Market Place, The EX20: Lew 1B **56**
Market Rd. PL7: Plymp 4A **138**
PL19: Tavi 4J **59**
Market Sq. EX4: Exe 4D **6**
EX13: Axmin 3H **89**
EX34: Ilfra 2H **11**
PL1: Plym 4C **8** (2J **141**)
TQ6: Dartm 1A **124** (6F **125**)
TQ12: New A 1E **108**
Market Stalls PL1: Plym 4C **8** (2H **141**)
Market St. EX1: Exe 5D **6** (7E **64**)
EX8: Exmth 6C **76**
EX17: Cred 6H **39**
EX20: Hath 1H **35**
EX20: N Taw 6B **36**
EX20: Oke 3B **48**
EX31: Barn 4E **18**
EX34: Ilfra 2H **11**
EX35: Lynt 2H **13**
EX36: S Mol 6C **26**
EX39: Apple 3H **21**
PL1: Plym 3F **141**
(not continuous)
PL8: Yeal 2B **150**
PL19: Tavi 3J **59**
TQ1: Torq 1D **116**
TQ5: Brixh 3E **122**
TQ6: Dartm 1A **124** (6F **125**)
TQ8: Salc 3D **158**
TQ11: B'leigh 4C **98**
TQ12: New A 1E **108**
Market Ter. EX16: Tiv 4D **40**
Market Wlk. EX16: Tiv 4D **40**
TQ12: New A 1E **108**
Market Way PL1: Plym 4C **8** (2H **141**)
TQ13: Chud 1C **94**
Markham Ct. *TQ4: Paig 2H 119*
(off Dartmouth Rd.)
Markham La. EX2: Alph 6D **70**
EX2: Ide, Shil A 6A **70**
MARKWELL **2A 174**
Marland Ter. EX39: Bide 4E **22**
Marlborough Av. TQ1: Torq 1F **117**
Marlborough Cl. EX8: Exmth 2G **77**
EX13: Mus 7C **90**
EX34: Ilfra 3H **11**
Marlborough Ct. EX2: Matf 5F **71**
EX39: Bide 2F **23**
Marlborough Dr. EX2: Won 7C **66**
Marlborough Pk. EX34: Ilfra 3H **11**
Marlborough Pl. TQ12: New A 7D **104**
Marlborough Rd. EX2: Exe . . .6H **7** (7G **65**)
EX13: Mus 7C **90**
EX34: Ilfra 3H **11**
PL4: Plym 2F **9** (1K **141**)
Marlborough Row PL1: Dev 2D **140**
Marlborough St. PL1: Dev 2D **140**
Marlborough Ter. TQ13: Bov T 4A **92**
Marlborough Way EX34: Ilfra 4J **11**
MARLDON . . . . **4D 114 (1A 176)**
Marldon Av. TQ3: Paig 1G **119**
Marldon Cl. PL5: Plym 7G **131**
Marldon Cross Hill TQ3: Marl 3D **114**
Marldon Gro. TQ3: Marl 3C **114**
Marldon La. TQ3: Marl 2B **114**
Marldon Rd. TQ2: Torq 6F **111**
TQ3: Paig 5E **114**
TQ12: Ipp 6K **101**
Marldon Way TQ3: Marl 4E **114**
Marlen Ct. EX39: Bide 5F **23**
Marles, The EX8: Exmth 2E **76**
Marles Cl. EX14: Awli 2A **54**
Marley Cl. EX16: Tiv 2E **40**
Marley Rd. EX8: Exmth 2D **76**
Marlow Ct. EX39: West H 5C **20**
Marlowe Cl. TQ2: Torq 6K **111**
Marlow Gdns. PL9: Plyms 7G **143**
Marl Pk. TQ9: H'ford 6C **100**
Marlpit Cl. EX12: Seat 5D **86**
Marlpit La. EX12: Seat 5D **86**
Marlpits La. EX14: Hon 4F **55**
Marmora Ter. *EX12: Beer 7B 86*
(off Clapp's La.)
Marnham Rd. TQ1: Torq 6D **112**
Marpool Cres. EX8: Exmth 4E **76**
Marpool Hill EX8: Exmth 5D **76**
Marrowbone Slip
PL4: Plym 5H **9** (3A **142**)
Marryat Gdns. PL5: Plym 2K **135**
MARSH **2C 167**
Marshall Cl. EX16: Tiv 5F **41**
PL19: Whitc 7K **59**
Marshall Dr. PL21: Ivy 5G **145**
Marshall Rd. PL7: Plymp 6H **137**
PL19: Whitc 7K **59**

Marshalls Mead EX19: Bea 3H **31**
MARSHALSEA 3D **167**
Marshals Fld. PL21: Ivy 4J **145**
MARSH BARTON 4G **71**
Marsh Barton Rd. EX2: Mar B 2E **70**
Marsh Barton Trad. Est.
EX2: Mar B 5H **71**
(Exeter Trade Cen.)
EX2: Mar B 3F **71**
(Marsh Grn. Rd. E.)
Marsh Cl. PL6: Plym 5G **137**
Marsh End EX17: Cred 6K **39**
MARSHGATE 1A **168**
MARSH GREEN 6K **69** (1A **172**)
Marsh Grn. Hill EX5: Mar G 6K **69**
Marsh Grn. La. EX5: Mar G 6K **69**
Marsh Grn. Rd. E. EX2: Mar B 3F **71**
Marsh Grn. Rd. Nth. EX2: Mar B 2F **71**
Marsh Grn. Rd. W. EX2: Mar B 3E **70**
Mars Hill Way EX35: Lynm 1H **13**
Marsh La. EX3: Clyst G 7F **73**
EX5: New C 7C **50**
EX12: Seat 3F **87**
EX17: Bow 4F **37**
EX17: Cred 6K **39**
EX39: Ins 3K **21**
TQ7: Slap 2H **159**
TQ7: W Cha 7K **157**
TQ13: Bov T 5B **92**
MARSH MILLS 5H **137**
Marsh Mills Junc. PL3: Plym 5G **137**
Marsh Mills Pk. PL6: Plym 5G **137**
Marsh Mills Retail Pk.
PL6: Plym 5G **137**
Marsh Path TQ13: Bov T 4B **92**
Marsh Rd. EX12: Seat 5F **87**
EX17: Cred 6K **39**
TQ12: New A 1F **109**
MARSHWOOD 1D **173**
Marston Cl. EX7: Daw 3J **97**
Mart, The EX20: Oke 3B **48**
MARTINHOE 2C **161**
MARTINHOE CROSS 2C **161**
Martinique Gro. TQ2: Torq 2B **112**
Martin La. PL1: Plym 5B **8**
PL4: Plym 5G **9**
Martin Rd. EX32: Barn 4G **19**
Martins Cl. EX20: Hath 1H **35**
EX38: Gt T 2E **30**
Martins La. EX1: Exe 4E **6** (6F **65**)
EX16: Tiv 4D **40**
Martins Rd. EX8: Exmth 2G **77**
Martin St. PL1: Plym 5A **8** (3H **141**)
Martlesham Pl. PL5: Plym 6E **130**
Marven Ct. DT7: Uply 2G **91**
MARWOOD 3B **160**
Marwood Ct. EX38: Gt T 2C **30**
Marwood Hill Gdns. 3B **160**
Marwood La. EX5: Ayle 7D **68**
Marwood Pl. *EX14: Hon 3G 55*
(off Monkton Rd.)
Mary Arches St. EX4: Exe 4C **6** (6E **64**)
Mary Dean Av. PL5: Tam F 3H **131**
Mary Dean Cl. PL5: Tam F 3H **131**
MARYFIELD 2A **174**
Maryfield Av. EX4: Exe 4G **65**
Maryland Gdns. PL2: Plym 4E **134**
Mary La. EX16: Bam 2H **33**
Marypole Rd. EX4: Exe 3J **66**
Marypole Wlk. EX4: Exe 3J **65**
Mary Seacole Rd.
PL1: Plym 4A **8** (2G **141**)
MARYSTOW 2C **169**
Mary St. TQ13: Bov T 3B **92**
MARY TAVY 2B **60** (3D **169**)
Marythorne Rd. PL20: Bere A 2C **128**
Masefield Av. EX31: Barn 2E **18**
Masefield Gdns. PL5: Plym 2G **135**
Masefield Rd. EX4: Whip 4B **66**
Masey Rd. EX8: Exmth 4F **77**
Mashford Av. TQ6: Dartm 5C **124**
Masons Yd. PL8: Holb 6C **150**
Massey Rd. EX16: Tiv 2E **40**
Masterman Rd. PL2: Dev 7E **134**
Masterson St. EX2: Won 2J **71**
MATFORD 6G **71**
Matford (Park & Ride) 6G **71**
Matford Av. EX2: Exe 7H **7** (1G **71**)
Matford Bus. Pk. EX2: Mar B 5G **71**
Matford Cen., The EX2: Matf 5G **71**
Matford La. EX2: Exe 7G **7** (1G **71**)
Matford M. EX2: Matf 6H **71**
Matford Pk. Rd. EX2: Matf 4F **71**
Matford Rd. EX2: Exe 7H **7** (1G **71**)
Mathews Cl. EX14: Hon 5E **54**
Mathill Cl. TQ5: Brixh 5D **122**
Mathill Rd. TQ5: Brixh 5D **122**
Matlock Ter. *TQ2: Torq 1C 116*
(off St Luke's Rd.)
Maton Cl. PL21: Ivy 5H **145**
Matthews Ct. EX4: Pin 2C **66**
EX15: Cull 4H **45**
Maudlin Dr. TQ14: Teignm 1H **107**
Maudlin Rd. TQ9: Tot 6E **102**
Maudlins La. PL19: Tavi 4G **59**
Maudlins Pk. PL19: Tavi 4G **59**
Maunder's Hill EX9: Ott'n 6H **83**
Maunders Pl. EX9: Ott'n 6H **83**
Maunsell Cl. PL2: Plym 4E **134**
Mavisdale PL2: Plym 5E **134**
Maxstoke Ct. TQ1: Torq 1F **117**
Maxwell Ct. *TQ1: Torq 7B 112*
(off McKay Av.)
TQ12: New A 2G **109**
Maxwell Rd. PL4: Plym 4C **142**
MAXWORTHY 1A **168**
Maybank Rd. PL4: Plym 3K **9** (2B **142**)
Mayers Way PL9: Hooe 6E **142**
Mayfair EX16: Tiv 3K **41**
Mayfair Cres. PL6: Plym 2C **136**
Mayfair Ho. PL4: Plym 3G **9**
Mayfair Rd. TQ12: Ipp 6H **101**
Mayfield PL21: Ivy 5E **144**
Mayfield Cres. TQ12: New A 1C **108**
Mayfield Dr. EX8: Exmth 6F **77**
Mayfield Rd. EX2: Won 7K **65**
EX4: Pin .3D **66**
Mayfield Way EX5: Cranb 3B **68**
Mayflower Av. EX4: Exe 2G **65**
TQ12: New A 2J **109**
Mayflower Cl. EX7: Daw 4H **97**
EX37: Chit 5H **25**
PL9: Plyms 5G **143**
PL20: Bere A 2B **128**
TQ6: Dartm 5C **124**
Mayflower Dr. PL2: Plym 6G **135**
TQ5: Brixh 5E **122**
Mayflower Intl. Marina
PL1: Dev 4E **140**
Mayflower Leisure Cen. 6H **135**
Mayflower Sailing Club 6G **9**
Mayflower Stone & Steps
. . . . .7G **9** (4K **141**)
Mayflower St. PL1: Plym 3D **8** (2J **141**)
Mayflower Vis. Cen. 6F **9** (3K **141**)
May Hilder Way *EX39: West H 6B 20*
(off Atlantic Way)
Maynarde Cl. PL7: Plymp 4E **138**
Maynard Pk. PL20: Bere A 2B **128**
Mayne Cl. EX20: Hath 2G **35**
Mayor's Av. TQ6: Dartm . . .1B **124** (6F **125**)
May St. EX4: Exe 1H **7** (5G **65**)
May Ter. EX10: Sidm 6C **84**
PL4: Plym 3H **9** (2A **142**)
Mazzard Cl. EX32: L'key 2B **24**
MEAD 2A **162**
Mead, The EX5: Silv 1H **51**
PL7: Plymp 4K **137**
Mead Cl. EX15: Cull 5G **45**
PL21: Ivy 3E **144**
TQ3: Paig 7H **115**
Meadcombe Rd. TQ7: Thur 6C **154**
Mead Cotts. EX8: L'ham 5H **77**
Mead Cross EX5: Cranb 3B **68**
Mead Dr. TQ7: Thur 6C **154**
Meadfoot TQ7: Thur 6C **154**
Meadfoot Cl. TQ1: Torq 2H **117**
Meadfoot Ct. TQ1: Torq 3E **116**
Meadfoot Cross *TQ1: Torq 3E 116*
(off Parkhill Rd.)
Meadfoot Grange TQ1: Torq 3E **116**
Meadfoot La. TQ1: Torq 3E **116**
Meadfoot Rd. TQ1: Torq 3E **116**
Meadfoot Sea Rd. TQ1: Torq 3F **117**
Meadfoot Ter. PL4: Plym 6A **136**
Meadhurst Ct. EX10: Sidm 6B **84**
Mead La. TQ3: Paig 7H **115**
TQ7: Thur 6C **154**
Meadow Av. EX12: Seat 4E **86**
Meadow Bank EX13: Kilm 2C **88**
Meadowbank TQ13: Chud K 6B **94**
Meadow Brook EX31: Roun 6A **18**
PL19: Tavi 5G **59**
TQ9: Tot 6F **103**
Meadowbrook Cl. EX4: Exe 4B **64**
Meadow Bus. Pk. EX17: Cred 6K **39**
Meadow Cl. EX5: Clyst M 2K **73**
EX8: Lymp 6H **75**
EX9: Bud S 6B **82**
EX11: Ott M 3D **80**
EX31: Brat F 6H **13**
EX32: L'key 3D **24**
EX34: Ilfra 4H **11**
PL7: Plymp 5G **139**
PL8: New F 4J **149**
TQ9: Tot 6H **103**
TQ12: Kingsk 6J **109**
Meadow Ct. EX39: Wools 3B **28**
Meadow Ct. Barns
TQ7: Stoke 6K **159**
Meadow Cres. EX8: San B 6J **77**
Meadowcroft Dr. TQ12: Kingst 2G **105**
Meadow Dr. EX10: New P 5H **81**
PL8: Brixt 3H **149**
Meadowfield Pl. PL7: Plymp 6E **138**
Meadow Gdns. EX17: Cred 6J **39**
Meadow Halt TQ12: E Ogw 2D **108**
Meadowlands EX5: New C 7C **50**
PL6: Plym 3E **132**
Meadowlands Leisure Pool 4H **59**
Meadow La. EX5: Cranb 3B **68**
EX9: Bud S 6C **82**
EX15: Cull 5H **45**
EX33: Croy, Puts 1D **14**
EX39: Ins 3K **21**
Meadow Lea EX5: Silv 1H **51**
Meadow Pk. EX7: Daw 3F **97**
EX15: Will 4C **44**
EX21: Sheb 6J **29**
EX31: Roun 7A **18**
EX36: S Mol 7C **26**
EX39: Bide 5C **22**
PL9: Hooe 7D **142**
TQ3: Marl 3D **114**
TQ5: Brixh 3D **122**
TQ11: B'leigh 3E **98**
TQ12: Ipp 6J **101**
Meadow Rise EX7: Daw 3F **97**
PL7: Plymp 5D **138**
TQ14: Teignm 2F **107**
Meadow Rd. EX9: Bud S 6B **82**
EX12: Seat 5E **86**
EX31: Barn 2C **18**
EX32: Barn 5F **19**
TQ2: Torq 3A **116**
Meadows, The EX12: Beer 7B **86**
TQ12: Kingst 5J **105**
Meadows Cres. EX14: Hon 4F **55**
Meadows Edge EX6: Cher B 2C **62**
Meadow Side TQ12: New A 1D **108**
Meadowside EX31: Ashf 1K **17**
PL9: Plyms 5G **143**
TQ7: Chil 6G **159**
Meadowside Ct. EX17: Cop 6C **38**
Meadowside Holiday Cen.
TQ4: Good 6H **119**
Meadow St. EX8: Exmth 5C **76**
Meadowsweet La. EX31: Roun 6A **18**
Meadow Va. EX20: Mer 5B **30**
Meadow Vw. EX8: Lymp 6H **75**
EX15: Uff 6H **43**
EX16: Bam 2G **33**
EX22: Hols 1C **34**
EX39: Hart 2J **27**
PL8: Brixt 3F **149**
TQ12: E Ogw 3C **108**
Meadow Vw. Cl. EX10: Sidm 5D **84**
Meadow Vw. Rd. EX8: Exmth 2G **77**
PL7: Plymp 6K **137**
Meadowville Rd. EX39: Bide 2F **23**
Meadow Way EX2: Heav 7J **65**
EX10: Col R 3H **83**
PL7: Plymp 2A **138**
Mead Pk. EX31: Bick'n 5J **17**
Mead Pk. Cl. EX31: Bick'n 5J **17**
Mead Rd. TQ2: Torq 4K **115**
Mead Vw. Rd. EX14: Hon 4F **55**
Mead Way EX12: Seat 4E **86**
TQ12: New A 4G **109**
Meadway EX10: Sidm 4C **84**
MEADWELL 2C **169**
Meadwood TQ1: Torq 3F **117**
MEARE GREEN
Curry Mallet 1C **167**
Stoke St Gregory 1D **167**
Mear Top EX31: Barn 2E **18**
Meatherel Cl. PL21: Ivy 5F **145**
MEAVY 7K **127** (1B **174**)
Meavy Av. PL5: Plym 1K **135**
TQ2: Torq 6H **111**
Meavy Bourne PL20: Yelv 6H **127**
Meavy La. PL20: Yelv 6G **127**
Meavy Vw. PL20: Prin 6C **60**
Meavy Vs. PL20: Yelv 6G **127**
Meavy Way PL5: Plym 1K **135**
PL19: Tavi 4K **59**
Mecca Bingo
Devonport *. 2D 140*
(off Fore St.)
Exeter .4D **6**
Medard Ho. EX32: Barn 4F **19**
MEDDON .2A **162**
Meddon St. EX39: Bide 4E **22**
Mede, The EX3: Top 5A **74**
EX4: Whip 4A **66**
Medland Cres. PL6: Plym 4J **131**
Medley Ct. EX4: Exe 4B **64**
Medway Pl. PL3: Plym 5E **136**
Medway Rd. TQ2: Torq 3D **112**
MEETH 3D **163**
Meeting La. EX8: Lymp 5G **75**
Meeting St. EX8: Exmth 5C **76**
EX39: Apple 2H **21**
Meetways La. EX8: Exmth 6F **77**
Megabowl
Plymouth 6J **137**
Melbourne Cotts.
PL1: Plym 3B **8** (2H **141**)
TQ6: Dartm 2A **124**
Melbourne Ct. EX2: Exe 6F **7**
Melbourne Pl. EX2: Exe 6F **7** (7F **65**)
PL1: Plym 2B **8**
Melbourne St. EX2: Exe 7F **7** (1F **71**)
EX16: Tiv 4B **40**
PL1: Plym 2B **8** (1H **141**)
Melcot Cl. TQ12: Kingst 4H **105**
MELDON 1D **169**
Meldon Ct. EX9: Bud S 6D **82**
Meldon Rd. TQ13: Chag 4H **61**
Meldrum Cl. EX7: Daw 4H **97**
Melhuish Cl. EX16: With 6H **33**
Mellons Cl. TQ12: New A 7A **104**
Mellons Wlk. *TQ12: New A 7A 104*
(off Mellons Cl.)
Mellowes Ct. EX13: Axmin 3G **89**
Mellows Mdw. TQ12: New A 1C **108**
Melrose Av. PL2: Plym 3G **135**
Melville La. TQ2: Torq 2D **116**
Melville Pl. *PL2: Plym 6F 135*
(off Melville Rd.)
TQ2: Torq 2D 116
(off Melville St.)
Melville Rd. PL2: Plym 6F **135**
Melville St. TQ2: Torq 2D **116**
Melville Ter. La. PL2: Plym 6F **135**
MEMBURY 3C **167**
Membury Castle 3C **167**
Membury Cl. EX1: Sow 6C **66**
Membury Rd. EX13: Axmin 1F **89**
Memory La. PL9: Plyms 5F **143**
Mena Pk. Cl. PL9: Elb 5J **143**
TQ4: Paig 5F **119**
Mena Pk. Rd. PL9: Elb 5J **143**
Mendip Rd. TQ2: Torq 3J **115**
Menors Pl. EX22: Hols 1C **34**
Merafield Cl. PL7: Plymp 6J **137**
Merafield Dr. PL7: Plymp 7K **137**
Merafield Farm Cotts.
PL7: Plymp 7J 137
(off Merafield Rd.)
Merafield Ri. PL7: Plymp 7K **137**
Merafield Rd. PL7: Plymp 7H **137**
Mercer Ct. EX2: Cou W 3K **71**
Mercers Cl. EX16: Tiv 2E **40**
Merchants Cnr. *TQ12: New A 1G 109*
(off Quay Rd.)
Merchant's House Mus. 5E **8**
Meredith Rd. PL2: Plym 4H **135**
Mere La. TQ14: Teignm 4J **107**
Meresyke EX8: Exmth 6E **76**
Meridian Pl. EX34: Ilfra 2H **11**
Merivale Cl. TQ14: Teignm 2J **107**
Merley Rd. EX39: West H 5A **20**
Merlin Bus. Pk. EX5: Clyst H 7C **68**
Merlin Cinemas
The Central Cinema 2D **116**
The New Carlton Cinema 3B **48**
The Tivoli Cinema 5D **40**
Merlin Cl. PL6: Plym 2E **132**
Merlin Cres. EX4: Whip 3K **65**
Merlin Way TQ2: Torq 3K **111**
Mermaid Ct. EX1: Exe 5D **6**
Mermaid Wlk. *EX31: Barn 4E 18*
(off Boutport St.)
Mermaid Yd. EX1: Exe 5D **6** (7E **64**)
Merrifield PL21: Fil 4K **145**
Merrifield Rd. TQ11: B'leigh 3A **98**
Merrion Av. EX8: Exmth 6F **77**
MERRIOTT 2D **167**
Merritt Flats *TQ3: Paig 2G 119*
(off Merritt Rd.)
Merritt Rd. TQ3: Paig 2G **119**
MERRIVALE 3D **169**
Merrivale Cl. TQ2: Torq 1D **112**
Merrivale Prehistoric Settlement
. . . . .3D **169**
Merrivale Rd. EX4: Exe 1C **70**
EX20: Oke 2E **48**
PL2: Plym 4F **135**
PL5: Plym 7G **131**
Merrivale Vw. Rd. PL20: Dous 4K **127**
Merrow Down Dr. EX12: Seat 4D **86**
Merryfield Rd. EX39: Bide 4H **23**
Merryland Cl. TQ3: Pres 4H **115**
Merryland Gdns. TQ3: Pres 4H **115**
Merrylees Dr. EX32: Barn 6H **19**
MERRYMEET 3A **168**
Merrythorn Rd. EX31: Frem 6D **16**
Merrywood TQ12: E Ogw 3C **108**
Mersey Cl. PL3: Plym 5E **136**
MERTON 5B **30** (2D **163**)
MESHAW 2B **164**
METCOMBE 1G **81** (1A **172**)
Metcombe Ri. EX11: Metc 1H **81**
Metcombe Va. EX11: Metc 1H **81**
Meteorological Office 5C **66**
Meteor Wlk. *EX32: Barn 4G 19*
(off Oliver Rd.)

METHERELL 1A 174
Metherell Av. TQ5: Brixh 5E 122
Metherell Av. Ind. Est.
TQ5: Brixh 5E 122
Metherell Rd. EX39: Bide 4E 22
Mews, The EX7: Daw 4H 97
PL1: Plym 1E 140
PL21: Moor 3C 146
Mews Gdns. TQ6: Dartm 1A 124
Mewstone Av. PL9: Wem 7B 148
Meyer Ct. EX2: Heav 7K 65
Meyrick Rd. TQ1: Torq 6E 112
Michael Browning Way
EX2: Exe 7E 6 (1F 71)
Michael Foot Av. PL1: Dev 3D 140
Michael Rd. PL3: Plym 6B 136
MICHELCOMBE 1C 175
Michigan Way EX4: Exe 2F 65
PL3: Plym 5D 136
Mid Churchway PL9: Plyms 5H 143
Middle Blagdon La. TQ3: Blag 1B 118
Middleborough La. EX33: Croy 1A 14
Middle Budleigh Mdw.
TQ12: New A 1C 108
Middle Combe Dr. EX31: Roun 7K 17
Middlecombe La. PL8: Noss M 7H 149
MIDDLECOTT 2B 170
Middlecott La. EX17: Morc 2A 38
Middle Cross EX31: Bick'n 5A 18
Middle Down Cl. PL9: Plyms 7H 143
Middlefield Rd. PL6: Plym 4J 131
Middle Gunstone EX39: Bide 3F 23
(off Lower Gunstone)
Middlehill La. EX33: Croy 1A 14
Middle Leigh PL8: New F 5G 149
Middle Lincombe Rd. TQ1: Torq 3F 117
MIDDLE MARWOOD 3B 160
Middlemead Rd. EX16: Tiv 3D 40
Middle Mill La. EX15: Cull 4H 45
MIDDLEMOOR 3C 169
MIDDLE MOOR 1C 72
Middle Pk. Ter. TQ7: S Mil 6E 154
Middle Ramshill La. TQ3: Paig 7C 114
Middle Rd. PL9: Wem 6A 148
Middle St. EX9: E Bud 1D 82
TQ5: Brixh 3E 122
TQ14: Shal 6G 107
Middleton Rd. EX39: Bide 3E 22
Middleton Wlk. PL5: Plym 6C 130
Middletown La. EX9: E Bud 1D 82
Middle Warberry Rd. TQ1: Torq 1E 116
MIDDLEWOOD
North Hill 3A 168
Starcross 3D 96
Middlewood Hill EX6: Cockw 4D 96
MIDDLE WOOLBROOK 3B 84
MIDDLEZOY 1D 167
Midella Rd. PL20: Yelv 6G 127
MIDELNEY 1D 167
MID LAMBROOK 2D 167
Midland Holiday Pk.
EX31: Ashf 1K 17
Midvale Rd. TQ4: Paig 2H 119
Midway EX8: Exmth 4G 77
TQ12: Kingsk 6J 109
Midway Cl. EX2: Alph 4D 70
Midway Ter. EX2: Alph 4D 70
Miers Cl. PL5: Plym 3B 134
Miglo Ind. Est. TQ4: Paig 4E 118
Mignonette Wlk. EX39: Bide 2F 23
(off Stella Maris Ct.)
MILBER 3H 109
Milber La. TQ12: Coff, New A 5K 109
TQ12: New A 2K 109
Milber Trad. Est. TQ12: New A 2K 109
Milbury Cl. EX6: Exmin 1C 74
Milbury La. EX6: Exmin 2D 74
Mildmay Cl. EX4: Exe 5C 64
Mildmay St. PL4: Plym 2G 9 (1K 141)
Mildren Way PL1: Dev 2D 140
MILE END 6B 104
Mile End Rd. TQ12: New A 6B 104
Mile Gdns. EX4: Whip 2J 65
MILEHOUSE 7F 135
Milehouse (Park & Ride) 6H 135
Milehouse Rd. PL3: Plym 7F 135
Mile La. EX4: Whip 1J 65
(not continuous)
Miles Mitchell Av. PL6: Plym 2B 136
MILFORD 1A 162
Milford Cl. TQ14: Teignm 4G 107
Milford La. EX5: Thor 2B 50
PL5: Plym 5F 131
Military Rd. PL1: Dev 2E 140
(off Raglan Rd.)
PL3: Plym 5E 136
PL6: Plym 4D 136
Milizac Cl. PL8: Yeal 2A 150
Milkaway La. EX33: Croy 2D 14
Milky Way Adventure Pk. 1B 162
Mill, The EX2: Exe 7G 7 (1G 71)
TQ12: New A 7F 105
Millards Hill EX39: Ins 2K 21
Mill Av. EX17: Cop 5C 38
MILLBAY 7B 8 (3G 141)
Millbay Docks PL1: Plym 7A 8 (4G 141)
Millbay Marina Village
PL1: Plym 7B 8 (4H 141)
Millbay Pk. 6B 8 (3H 141)
Millbay Rd. PL1: Plym 6A 8 (3G 141)
Mill Bottom La. TQ14: Shal 7C 106
Mill Bri. PL1: Plym 3A 8 (1G 141)
MILLBROOK 2A 174
Millbrook Dale EX13: Axmin 2J 89
Millbrook La. EX2: Exe 3H 71
Millbrook Pk. Rd. TQ2: Torq 1A 116
Millbrook Rd. TQ3: Paig 1H 119
Mill Cl. PL21: L Mill 5C 144
TQ12: New A 7B 104
Millcombe Cnr. TQ9: Blacka 3B 152
Mill Ct. EX7: Daw 4F 97
EX32: Swim 2H 25
Mill Cres. TQ6: Dartm 5D 124
Millcroft EX11: Ott M 4C 80
Milldale Cres. EX14: Hon 4E 54
Mill Dr. EX2: Cou W 4J 71
Mill End TQ12: Kingst 1H 105
Millennium Pl. EX16: Tiv 3G 41
Millennium Way EX15: Cull 2H 45
EX39: West H 5D 20
Miller Cl. EX2: Won 1B 72
Miller Ct. PL1: Plym 5A 8 (3G 141)
Miller Cres. EX32: Barn 4F 19
Millers Brook EX33: Croy 2D 14
Millers La. TQ9: Sto G 4A 120
Millers Way EX6: Ted M 7J 49
EX14: Hon 4E 54
Miller Way EX6: Exmin 1B 74
PL6: Plym 6D 132
Milletts Cl. EX6: Exmin 2C 74
MILLFIELDS, THE 2G 141
Millford Av. EX10: Sidm 6C 84
Millford Rd. EX10: Sidm 6C 84
Mill Grn. DT7: Lym R 5K 91
Millgreen Ct. DT7: Lym R 5K 91
Millgreen La. EX13: Kilm 1B 88
MILLHAYES
Honiton 3C 167
Wellington 1G 47 (2B 166)
Millhayes Farm EX15: Hemy 1G 47
Mill Head EX16: Bam 2J 33
EX34: Ilfra 2J 11
Millhead Rd. EX14: Hon 4E 54
Mill Hill EX31: Frem 6F 17
TQ9: Sto G 4B 120
Mill Hill Ct. TQ9: Sto G 4B 120
Mill Hill La. PL19: Tavi 3F 59
Millin Way EX7: Daw W 7D 96
Mill La. DT7: Lym R 5K 91
DT7: Uply 3G 91
EX2: Alph 4E 70
EX2: Cou W 4J 71
(not continuous)
EX3: Exton 1G 75
EX5: Broadc 3H 67
EX10: New P 7G 81
EX12: Brans 6H 85
EX17: Bow 5G 37
EX17: Cher F 1F 39
EX20: N Taw 6A 36
EX31: Barn 3D 18
EX31: Brat F 6F 13
EX33: Croy 2D 14
EX33: Wraf 6K 15
EX34: Berry 3B 12
EX34: Woolc 6A 10
TQ2: Torq 1B 116
TQ3: Comp 5C 110
TQ3: Paig 7H 115
TQ5: Brixh 7C 122
TQ5: Galm 4F 121
TQ6: Sto F 3F 153
TQ7: Ave G 7H 151
TQ9: Tot 6F 103
TQ12: E Ogw 3A 108
TQ12: N Whil 4C 110
(not continuous)
TQ13: Ashb 3G 99
TQ14: Teignm 3F 107
Mill Leat EX15: Hemy 1G 47
Mill Leat Cl. PL8: Yeal 2C 150
Mill-Leat Gdns. EX32: L'key 2B 24
Millmans Rd. TQ3: Marl 3D 114
Mill Mdw. EX34: Com M 6B 12
PL21: Ivy 4H 145
TQ13: Ashb 3G 99
MILLMOOR 2B 46
Millmoor La. EX10: New P 5H 81
Millmoor Va. EX10: New P 5H 81
Mill on the Mole Res. Pk.
EX36: S Mol 6E 26
Mill Pk. Ind. Est. EX5: Wood S 1E 78
Mill Pk. Touring Caravan & Camping Site
EX34: Berry 2B 12
Mill Path TQ13: Ashb 4H 99
(off St Andrews Cl.)
Mill Rd. EX2: Cou W 4J 71
EX19: Bea 4F 31
EX20: Oke 3B 48
EX22: Bradw 5B 28
EX31: Barn 4D 18
EX31: Frem 6F 17
EX32: L'key 3C 24
EX37: High B 2A 32
TQ9: Darti 3A 102
TQ13: Lust 6H 63
Mill Row EX39: Westl 7K 21
Mills Rd. PL1: Dev 2E 140
Mill Stile EX33: Brau 5H 15
Mill Stream Ct. EX11: Ott M 4B 80
Mill Stream Gdns. EX16: Hal 6D 42
Millstream Mdw. TQ13: Chud 1D 94
Mill St. EX10: Sidm 6C 84
EX11: Ott M 4C 80
EX14: Hon 4E 54
EX15: Uff 6H 43
EX17: Cred 6J 39
EX36: S Mol 6C 26
EX38: Gt T 3A 30
EX39: Bide 3F 23
PL1: Dev 2D 140
TQ7: Kingsb 4F 157
TQ13: Chag 2G 61
Mill St. Comn. EX38: Gt T 2A 30
Mills Way EX31: Barn 3E 18
Mill Tail TQ9: Tot 6E 102
MILLTOWN 3B 160
Milltown La. EX10: Sidm 4D 84
Millway EX5: Bradn 2C 52
TQ13: Chud 2C 94
Millway Gdns. EX5: Bradn 2C 52
Millway Pl. PL9: Plyms 4E 142
Millwey Av. EX13: Axmin 3K 89
Millwey Ct. EX13: Axmin 2K 89
Millwey Ri. Ind. Est.
EX13: Axmin 1K 89
Millwood TQ13: Bov T 7B 92
Millwood Bus. Pk.
TQ12: New A 7H 105
Millwood Dr. PL6: Plym 2F 137
Mill Yd. EX2: Cou W 4J 71
Milne Pl. PL1: Dev 1E 140
MILTON ABBOT 2B 58 (3C 169)
Milton Cl. EX8: Exmth 7K 75
PL5: Plym 1H 135
TQ5: Brixh 6D 122
MILTON COMBE 1A 174
Milton Ct. PL4: Plym 3B 142
(not continuous)
Milton Cres. PL19: Tavi 4K 59
TQ5: Brixh 6D 122
MILTON DAMEREL 2B 162
Milton Flds. TQ5: Brixh 6C 122
MILTON GREEN 3B 58
MILTON HILL 3D 171
Milton Ho. TQ12: New A 2F 109
Milton La. TQ6: Dartm 7C 124
Milton Pk. TQ5: Brixh 6D 122
Milton Pl. EX39: Bide 4E 22
Milton Rd. EX2: Won 2J 71
TQ12: New A 7E 104
Milton St. TQ5: Brixh 7C 122
Miltons Yd. EX13: Axmin 3H 89
Milton Ter. EX34: Com M 6B 12
MILVERTON 1B 166
Mimosa Cl. EX16: Tiv 2E 40
Minacre La. TQ12: N Whil 5E 110
Mincent Cl. TQ2: Torq 2C 112
Mincent Hill TQ2: Torq 2C 112
Mincinglake Rd. EX4: Exe 3H 65
Minden Rd. TQ14: Teignm 4H 107
Miners Cl. TQ13: Ashb 3J 99
Minerva Bus. Pk. TQ12: New A 1G 109
Minerva Cl. PL7: Plymp 3D 138
Minerva Way TQ12: New A 1H 109
Mines Rd. EX39: Bide 4H 23
(not continuous)
Miniature Pony Cen. 2B 170
Minifie Rd. EX14: Hon 3E 54
MINIONS 3A 168
Minnows Camping & Caravan Site
EX16: Sam P 1D 42
Minses Cl. PL9: Elb 5K 143
Minster Ct. EX13: Axmin 4G 89
Minster Rd. EX6: Exmin 1D 74
Mint, The EX4: Exe 4C 6 (7E 64)
Mint Casino
Torquay 1C 116
Mint Pk. Rd. EX33: Brau 3G 15
Mirador Pl. PL4: Plym 1C 142
Miranda Rd. TQ3: Pres 6F 115
Mirey La. EX5: Wood 5C 78
Miry La. EX15: Kent 7C 46
Mission Ct. EX4: Exe 6C 6
Misterton Cl. PL9: Elb 4J 143
Mitchell Cl. PL9: Hooe, Plyms 7E 142
Mitchell Gdns. EX13: Axmin 4H 89
Mitchum's Beach Campsite
EX33: Croy 1A 14
Mitchum's Village Campsite
EX33: Croy 2C 14
Mitre Cl. PL19: Tavi 6G 59
TQ14: Bi'ton 3A 106
(not continuous)
Mitre La. EX4: Exe 4C 6 (6E 64)
Mizzen Rd. PL1: Dev 3E 140
Moat Hill TQ9: Tot 7E 102
Moat Pk. PL6: Plym 2D 136
(off Bircham Vw.)
MODBURY 6G 147 (2C 175)
Modbury Cl. PL5: Plym 7G 131
Model Ter. EX39: Bide 4F 23
Modred Cl. EX4: Whip 3K 65
Modyford Wlk. PL20: Buck M 5A 126
MOGWORTHY 2C 165
Mohun's Cl. PL19: Tavi 5J 59
Mohun's Pk. PL19: Tavi 6J 59
Mole Bri. La. EX36: S Mol 6E 26
Mole Ridge Way EX36: S Mol 5C 26
Moles La. TQ3: Marl 5E 110
TQ12: Kingst, N Whil 5E 110
Molesworth Cotts. PL3: Plym 7F 135
(off Molesworth Rd.)
Molesworth Rd. PL1: Plym 7F 135
PL3: Plym 7F 135
PL7: Plymp 5J 137
Molesworth Way EX22: Hols 2A 34
MOLLAND 1C 165
Mollison Rd. PL5: Plym 1D 134
Molyneaux Pl. PL1: Dev 1E 140
Monastery Rd. TQ3: Paig 1G 119
Mondeville Way EX39: N'ham 6E 20
Moneycentre Precinct, The
PL1: Plym 3E 8
Monica Wlk. PL4: Plym 1H 9 (1A 142)
Monitor Cl. EX2: Exe 7D 6 (1E 70)
MONKERTON 4D 66
Monkerton Ct. EX1: Pin 4D 66
Monkerton Dr. EX1: Pin 4D 66
Monkey La. EX10: New P 7F 81
Monkey Puzzle Dr. EX20: Oke 3E 48
MONKLEIGH 1C 163
Monkleigh Mill La. EX39: Buck B 1J 29
MONKOKEHAMPTON 3D 163
Monksbridge Rd. TQ5: Brixh 5D 122
Monks Cl. EX17: Cred 5G 39
EX39: Bide 5J 23
Monksmead PL19: Tavi 5G 59
Monks Orchard TQ12: A'well 6D 108
Monk's Rd. EX4: Exe 1K 7 (5H 65)
Monkstone Gdns. EX13: Axmin 4J 89
(off Cridlake)
Monks Way TQ13: Bov T 2A 92
Monkswell Rd. EX4: Exe 1K 7 (4H 65)
MONKTON 3B 166
MONKTON HEATHFIELD 1C 167
Monkton Rd. EX14: Hon, Monk 3G 55
MONKTON WYLD 1D 173
Monkton Wyld Camping Site
DT6: Monk W 1D 90
MONKWOOD 1D 173
Monmouth Av. EX3: Top 6B 74
Monmouth Beach Chalets
DT7: Lym R 6H 91
Monmouth Gdns. PL5: Plym 6G 131
Monmouth Hill EX3: Top 6B 74
Monmouth St. DT7: Lym R 5K 91
EX3: Top 6B 74
Monmouth Way EX14: Hon 4G 55
Monroe Gdns. PL3: Plym 1C 8
Monro Mead TQ12: Live 4F 93
Montacute Av. PL5: Plym 1F 135
Montagu Cl. TQ7: Kingsb 3G 157
Montague Gdns. EX9: Bud S 6A 82
Montague Pl. EX39: Bide 4E 22
Montague Ri. EX4: Exe 1E 6 (5F 65)
Montague Ter. PL7: L Moor 1J 129
Montagu M. TQ7: Kingsb 3G 157
(off Montagu Cl.)
Montagu Rd. TQ7: Kingsb 4F 157
Monterey EX8: Exmth 7E 76
TQ4: Good 6J 119
(off Hookhills Rd.)
Monterey Cl. TQ2: Torq 3A 116
Monterey Gdns. EX4: Exe 3H 65
Monterey Pk. TQ12: New A 3J 109
Montesson Cl. TQ3: Paig 7D 114
Montesson Rd. TQ3: Paig 7D 114
Montgomery Cl. PL21: Ivy 3J 145
Montgomery Dr. PL19: Tavi 3H 59
Montgomery Rd. EX2: Won 7C 66
(off Sidmouth Rd.)
Mont Le Grand EX1: Heav 4K 7 (6H 65)
Montpelier Ct. EX4: Exe 2B 6 (5D 64)
TQ3: Pres 5H 115
Montpelier La. EX34: Ilfra 2J 11
Montpelier M. EX34: Ilfra 2J 11
(off Montpelier Rd.)

Montpelier Rd. EX34: Ilfra 2J 11
PL2: Plym 4H 135
Montpelier Ter. *EX34: Ilfra 2J 11*
(off Montpelier Rd.)
Montpellier Ct. *EX8: Exmth 6D 76*
(off Montpellier Rd.)
Montpellier Rd. EX8: Exmth 6C 76
TQ1: Torq 2D 116
Montpellier Ter. *TQ1: Torq 2D 116*
(off Montpellier Rd.)
Montserrat Ri. TQ2: Torq 2A 112
Monument St. PL1: Dev 3D 140
Moonhill Cl. EX2: Alph 5F 71
Moon La. PL21: Modb 6G 147
Moon Ridge EX2: Cou W 6B 72
Moon St. PL4: Plym 4G 9 (2K 141)
MOOR .2D 167
Moorashes *TQ9: Tot 6E 102*
(off Grove Cl.)
MOORBATH 1D 173
Moor Cl. TQ14: Teignm 2J 107
Moorcourt Cl. EX10: Sidm 7A 84
Moor Cres. PL20: Prin 6C 60
Moorcroft Cl. EX20: Oke 3E 48
PL9: Plyms 5H 143
Moorcroft Ct. EX20: Oke 3E 48
MOOR CROSS 2C 175
Moore Cl. TQ12: New A 4J 109
Moore Cres. EX22: Hols 2A 34
Moorfield EX24: Colyt 6D 88
PL16: Lift 6B 56
Moorfield Av. PL6: Plym 4D 136
Moorfield Cl. EX8: Exmth 4E 76
Moorfield Rd. EX8: Exmth 4D 76
PL15: St G 6C 34
Moorfields PL21: Moor 3D 146
Moorhaven EX9: Bud S 5B 82
Moorhaven Cl. TQ1: Torq 6A 112
MOORHAVEN VILLAGE 3C 146
Moorhayes TQ13: Bov T 4C 92
Moorings, The
EX8: Exmth 6A 76
EX33: Brau 4J 15
TQ4: Paig 2J 119
(off Belle Vue Rd.)
TQ7: Kingsb 6G 157
Moorings Reach TQ5: Brixh 3F 123
MOORLAND 1D 167
Moorland Av. PL7: Plymp 3B 138
TQ12: Den 1H 101
Moorland Cl. PL21: Bitta 3C 146
Moorland Ct. PL20: Yelv 7E 126
Moorland Dr. PL7: Plymp 3B 138
Moorland Gdns. PL7: Plymp 3C 138
Moorland Ga. TQ12: Heat 2K 93
Moorland Pk. TQ10: S Bre 1B 100
Moorland Pk. Caravan Pk.
TQ13: Bov T 7C 92
Moorland Ri. EX36: S Mol 6C 26
Moorland Rd. PL7: Plymp 4B 138
Moorlands EX11: W Hill 3H 79
EX16: Tiv 2E 40
Moorlands Cl. TQ12: New A 2J 109
Moorlands Rd. EX9: Bud S 6A 82
Moorland Ter. EX38: Gt T 2A 30
Moorland Vw. EX17: Lap 2K 37
PL6: Plym 5B 132
PL9: Elb 5J 143
PL20: Prin 6C 60
(not continuous)
TQ11: B'leigh 4B 98
TQ12: New A 2J 109
Moorland Way EX4: Exe 4B 64
Moor La. EX2: Sow 6D 66
EX5: Clyst M, Wood S
. . . . .3A 78 & 7K 73
EX9: Bud S 5B 82
EX11: S'ton 3G 81
EX20: Hath 1J 35
EX33: Brau 5F 15
EX33: Croy 1A 14
PL5: Plym 2D 134
TQ2: Torq 2C 112
TQ13: Bov T 6B 92
Moor La. Cl. TQ2: Torq 2C 112
Moor Lea EX33: Brau 5K 15
Moormead EX9: Bud S 6B 82
Moor Pk. EX8: Exmth 6E 76
EX14: Hon 6E 54
PL21: Moor 3C 146
TQ12: Kingsk 6J 109
TQ13: Chag 2H 61
Moor Pk. Cl. EX33: Croy 1B 14
Moor Pk. La. EX10: Sidm 4A 84
Moor Pk. Rd. TQ12: Kingsk 6J 109
Moor Rd. TQ12: Ipp 4F 101
Moors End TQ12: Kingst 4G 105
Moorsend TQ12: New A 7B 104
Moorside TQ7: Malb 6G 155
Moors Pk. TQ14: Bi'ton 4B 106
Moorstone Leat TQ4: Good 6J 119
MOORTOWN 1B 168
Moor Vw. EX20: Hath 3G 35
EX20: N Taw 7B 36
PL2: Plym 6E 134
PL3: Plym 7D 136
PL9: Plyms 5E 142
PL11: Torp 1A 140
PL19: Mary T 2B 60
PL21: Bitta 3C 146
TQ13: Bov T 6B 92
(off Brimley Rd.)
TQ13: Chud 2B 94
Moorview TQ3: Marl 4D 114
Moor Vw. Cl. EX10: Sidm 3A 84
Moorview Cl. EX4: Exe 3G 65
Moorview Ct. PL6: Plym 5G 133
Moor Vw. Dr. TQ14: Teignm 2F 107
Moorview End TQ3: Marl 4D 114
Moor Vw. Ter. PL4: Plym . . .1G 9 (7K 135)
PL20: Yelv 6G 127
Moory Mdw. EX34: Com M 5A 12
MORCHARD BISHOP 1B 38 (3B 164)
MORCOMBELAKE 1D 173
MOREBATH 1D 165
MORELEIGH 2D 175
Moreleigh Rd. TQ9: H'ford 7A 100
Moreton Av. EX39: Bide 4D 22
PL6: Plym 2A 136
Moreton Dr. EX39: Bide 3D 22
MORETONHAMPSTEAD . . .6H 61 (2B 170)
Moretonhampstead Almshouses . . .6J 61
Moretonhampstead Rd.
TQ13: Bov T 2B 92
Moreton Pk. Rd. EX39: Bide 5C 22
Moreton Ter. EX6: Bridf 1F 63
Morgan Av. TQ2: Torq 1C 116
Morgan Ct. *EX8: Exmth 6C 76*
(off Rolle Rd.)
Morgan Rd. PL6: Plym 4D 132
Morgans Quay TQ14: Teignm 6H 107
Morice Sq. PL1: Dev 2D 140
Morice St. PL1: Dev 2D 140
MORICE TOWN 7E 134
Morin Rd. TQ3: Pres 6J 115
Morlaix Dr. PL6: Plym 6B 132
Morley Cl. PL7: Plymp 6H 137
Morley Ct. PL1: Plym 4C 8 (2H 141)
Morley Dr. PL20: C'stone 6B 126
Morley Rd. EX4: Exe 1K 7 (4H 65)
Morley Vw. Rd. PL7: Plymp 5K 137
Morningside EX7: Daw 6F 97
TQ1: Torq 1G 117
(off Barrington Rd.)
Morris Cl. EX20: Hath 2G 35
Morrish Pk. PL9: Plyms 6G 143
Morshead Rd. PL6: Plym 1A 136
MORTEHOE 3A 10 (2A 160)
Mortehoe Heritage Cen. 3A 10
Mortehoe Sta. Rd.
EX34: Mort, Woolc 3A 10
Mortimer Av. TQ3: Pres 6H 115
Mortimer Ct. EX2: Cou W 3K 71
(not continuous)
Morton Cres. EX8: Exmth 6B 76
Morton Cres. M. EX8: Exmth 6B 76
Morton Dr. EX38: Gt T 2C 30
Morton Rd. EX8: Exmth 6B 76
Morton Way EX13: Axmin 5H 89
Morven Dr. EX8: Exmth 2C 76
Morville Pl. *EX16: Tiv 4D 40*
(off Water La.)
Morwell Gdns. PL2: Plym 5F 135
Morwellham Cl. PL5: Plym 3B 134
Morwellham Quay 1A 174
Morwenna Pk. Rd. EX39: N'ham 5E 20
Morwenna Ter. *EX39: N'ham 5E 20*
(off Diddywell Rd.)
MORWENSTOW 2A 162
Moses Cl. PL6: Plym 3K 131
Moses Ct. *PL6: Plym 3K 131*
(off Moses Cl.)
Mosshayne La. EX1: W Cly 1F 67
EX5: Clyst H 2H 67
Mossop Cl. EX11: Ott M 4C 80
Mostyn Av. PL4: Plym 1K 9 (7B 136)
Motehole Rd. TQ12: Ipp 6H 101
MOTHECOMBE 3C 175
Mothecombe Wlk. PL6: Plym 2F 137
Motoring Memories Motor Mus. . . .1G 87
Moult Hill TQ8: Salc 6A 158
Moulton Cl. PL7: Plymp 4E 138
Moulton Wlk. PL7: Plymp 5E 138
Moult Rd. TQ8: Salc 6A 158
MOUNT 3A 168
Mount, The EX39: Apple 2H 21
TQ2: Torq 1B 112
TQ5: Brixh 2E 122
TQ14: Teignm 3H 107
Mountain Cl. EX8: Exmth 4H 77
Mount Batten Centre, The 5A 142
Mt. Batten Cl. PL9: Plyms 6E 142
Mountbatten Cl. EX8: Exmth 2F 77
Mountbatten Rd. EX16: Tiv 3C 40
Mt. Batten Way PL9: Plyms 6E 142
Mt. Boone TQ6: Dartm . . .1A 124 (5E 124)
Mt. Boone Hill
TQ6: Dartm 1A 124 (5F 125)
Mt. Boone La.
TQ6: Dartm 1A 124 (5F 125)
Mt. Boone Way TQ6: Dartm 5E 124
Mt. Braddons M. TQ1: Torq 2E 116
Mount Cl. EX14: Hon 4E 54
MOUNT DINHAM 4C 6 (6E 64)
Mt. Dinham Ct. EX4: Exe 3C 6 (6E 64)
Mount Edgcumbe Country Park . . .6E 140
Mount Edgcumbe Country Park
Formal Gdns. 5D 140
Mount Edgcumbe House 6D 140
Mt. Flagon Steps TQ6: Dartm 1A 124
Mount Ford PL19: Tavi 4G 59
Mt. Galpine
TQ6: Dartm 1A 124 (5F 125)
MOUNT GOULD 1C 142
Mt. Gould Av. PL4: Plym 2C 142
Mt. Gould Cres. PL4: Plym 1C 142
Mt. Gould Rd. PL4: Plym . . .1K 9 (1B 142)
Mt. Gould Way PL4: Plym 1C 142
Mt. Hermon Rd. TQ1: Torq 7D 112
Mount Hill *EX12: Beer 7B 86*
(off Long Hill)
Mounthill La. EX13: Mus 7D 90
Mount Howe EX3: Top 6C 74
Mt. Pleasant EX13: Axmin 4H 89
EX14: Offw 4K 55
EX32: Bish T 5B 24
EX39: Bide 2H 23
PL5: Plym 1G 135
TQ13: Chud 2D 94
TQ13: More 7H 61
Mt. Pleasant Av. EX8: Exmth 1D 76
Mt. Pleasant Cl. TQ7: Kingsb 3G 157
TQ12: Kingsk 2G 111
Mt. Pleasant Ct. EX8: Exmth 2D 76
Mt. Pleasant La. TQ14: Shal 6G 107
Mt. Pleasant M. TQ5: Brixh 4E 122
Mt. Pleasant Rd. EX4: Exe . . .1J 7 (4H 65)
EX7: Daw W 1K 97
TQ1: Torq 7D 112
TQ5: Brixh 4E 122
TQ12: Kingsk 2G 111
TQ12: New A 2F 109
Mt. Pleasant Ter. *PL2: Dev 7F 135*
(off Masterman Rd.)
MOUNT RADFORD 5G 7 (7G 65)
Mt. Radford Cres.
EX2: Exe 6G 7 (7G 65)
Mt. Radford Sq. EX2: Exe 6G 7
Mt. Raleigh Av. EX39: Bide 1D 22
Mt. Raleigh Dr. EX39: Bide 2D 22
Mt. Ridley Rd. TQ6: Kingsw 6H 125
Mount Ri. EX6: Kenn 3J 95
Mount Rd. TQ5: Brixh 4F 123
MOUNTS, THE 6A 152
Mounts, The TQ9: E All 5A 152
Mounts Farm Touring Pk.
TQ9: E All 6A 152
Mt. Stone Rd. PL1: Plym 4F 141
Mount St. PL1: Dev 3D 140
PL4: Plym 3G 9 (1K 141)
Mt. Tamar Cl. PL5: Plym 1D 134
Mt. Tavy Rd. PL19: Tavi 3K 59
Mount Vw. EX14: Fen 1G 53
EX24: Colyt 6D 88
EX34: Ilfra 3J 11
Mountview Home Pk. EX32: Barn . . .7K 19
Mount Vw. Ter. *TQ9: Tot 6E 102*
(off Heath Way)
Mt. Wear Sq. EX2: Cou W 5A 72
MOUNT WISE 4E 140
Mt. Wise Cres. PL1: Dev 3E 140
Mount Wise Outdoor Pools 4D 140
Mowbray Av. EX4: Exe 2F 7 (5F 65)
Mowbray Ct. EX2: Won 7K 65
Mowhay PL5: Plym 2E 134
Mowhay, The EX22: Hols 2C 34
Mowhay Rd. PL5: Plym 3E 134
(not continuous)
Mowstead Pk. EX33: Brau 3G 15
Mowstead Rd. EX33: Brau 3G 15
Moxeys Cl. EX17: Cher F 2H 39
Moyses La. EX20: Oke 4A 48
Moyses Mdw. EX20: Oke 4A 48
MUCHELNEY 1D 167
MUCHELNEY HAM 1D 167
Mucky La. EX19: Dol 7F 31
Mudbank La. EX8: Exmth 3B 76
MUDDIFORD 3B 160
MUDDLEBRIDGE 6H 17
Mudge Way PL7: Plymp 4B 138
Mudstone La. TQ5: Brixh 5F 123
Mulberry Cl. EX1: Whip 6A 66
EX15: Will 4D 44
PL6: Plym 3F 133
TQ3: Paig 7E 114
Mulberry Gro. PL19: Tavi 7J 59
Mulberry St. TQ14: Teignm 4H 107
Mulberry Way EX31: Roun 7A 18
Mulgrave St. PL1: Plym 6D 8 (3J 141)
MULLACOTT 7G 11 (2B 160)
Mullacott Farm EX34: Ilfra 7G 11
Mullet Av. PL3: Plym 7D 136
Mullet Cl. PL3: Plym 7D 136
Mullet Rd. PL3: Plym 7D 136
MURCHINGTON 2A 170
Murley Cl. EX17: Cred 5G 39
Murley Cres. TQ14: Bi'ton 3A 106
Murley Grange TQ14: Bi'ton 3A 106
MUSBURY 7C 90 (1C 173)
Musbury Rd. EX13: Axmin 6G 89
Museum Ct. TQ7: Kingsb 3F 157
Museum of Barnstaple & North Devon, The
. . . . .5E 18
Museum of Dartmoor Life 3B 48
Museum Rd. TQ1: Torq 2E 116
Musgrave Ho. *EX4: Exe 3E 6*
(off Musgrave Row)
Musgrave Row EX4: Exe 3E 6 (6F 65)
Musket Rd. TQ12: Heat 2J 93
MUTLEY 7K 135
Mutley Plain PL4: Plym 1G 9 (7K 135)
Mutley Plain La. PL4: Plym 7K 135
Mutley Rd. PL3: Plym 6K 135
Muttersmoor Rd. EX10: Sidm 5A 84
MUTTERTON 3A 166
Mutton La. EX2: Alph 5F 71
EX38: Lit T 4B 30
Muxey La. EX38: Gt T 3B 30
Mylor Cl. PL2: Plym 3J 135
Myra Ct. EX39: Apple 2H 21
Myrtleberry La. EX35: Lynt 4K 13
Myrtle Cl. EX2: Alph 4E 70
EX15: Will 3E 44
PL20: Dous 4K 127
Myrtle Cott. Rd. EX39: Apple 4G 21
Myrtle Farm Vw. EX33: Croy 2C 14
Myrtle Gdns. EX39: Bide 3F 23
Myrtle Gro. EX39: Bide 3F 23
Myrtle Hill TQ14: Teignm 4J 107
Myrtle Rd. EX4: Exe 1B 70
Myrtle Row EX8: Exmth 6C 76
Myrtle St. EX39: Apple 3H 21
Myrtleville PL2: Plym 4F 135

N

Nadder La. EX36: S Mol 6A 26
Nadder Mdw. EX36: S Mol 6B 26
Nadder Pk. Rd. EX4: Exe 7A 64
Naida Va. TQ6: Dartm 4F 125
NAILSBOURNE 1C 167
Napier St. PL1: Dev 1E 140
Napier Ter. EX4: Exe 4C 6 (6E 64)
PL4: Plym 1F 9 (7K 135)
Napps Touring Holidays
EX34: Berry 1C 12
Naps La. EX10: Col R 1F 83
Nap Vw. EX14: Awli 1A 54
Narracott La. EX36: S Mol 7A 26
Narrow La. EX16: Tiv 5C 40
Naseby Dr. TQ12: Heat 2J 93
Nash Cl. PL7: Plymp 4D 138
Nash Gdns. EX7: Daw 6G 97
Nash Gro. EX4: Exe 3D 64
Nasmith Cl. EX8: Exmth 3F 77
Nassau Ct. EX39: West H 5A 20
NATCOTT 1A 162
Natcott La. EX39: Hart 3K 27
National Marine Aquarium
. . . . .6G 9 (3K 141)
Nats La. PL21: Corn, Ivy 1B 144
Natson Mill La. EX17: Bow 6G 37
Nattadon Rd. TQ13: Chag 4H 61
Neadon La. EX6: Bridf 1F 63
Neal Cl. PL7: Plymp 5E 138
Neardale Ter. PL19: Lam 7C 58
Neath Rd. PL4: Plym 1B 142
Needlewood Cl. EX11: W Hill 5G 79
Nelson Av. PL1: Plym 1E 140
Nelson Cl. EX3: Top 5A 74
TQ1: Torq 4F 117
TQ14: Teignm 3G 107
Nelson Dr. EX8: Exmth 4G 77
EX39: West H 5B 20
Nelson Gdns. PL1: Plym 1E 140
Nelson M. EX39: West H 5B 20
Nelson Pl. TQ12: New A 6E 104
Nelson Rd. EX4: Exe 7A 6 (1D 70)
EX39: West H 5B 20
TQ5: Brixh 3E 122
TQ6: Dartm 7B 124
Nelson Rd. Ind. Est. *TQ6: Dartm . . .5C 124*
(off Nelson Rd.)
Nelson St. PL4: Plym 2G 9 (1K 141)
Nelson Ter. EX39: West H 5B 20
PL6: Plym 4F 133
Nelson Way EX2: Won 7B 66

Nepean St. PL2: Plym 6E 134
Neptune Pk. PL4: Plym 4C 142
Ness Dr. TQ14: Shal 6H 107
Ness Vw. Rd. TQ14: Teignm 1J 107
Neswick St. PL1: Plym 4A 8 (2G 141)
Neswick St. Ope
    PL1: Plym 4A 8 (2G 141)
NETHERCOTT 3A 160
Nethercott Rd. EX33: Brau 6E 14
NETHER EXE 3D 165
Netherhams Hill EX33: Georgeh . . .5B 14
Netherleigh Rd. TQ1: Torq 6D 112
Nether Mdw. TQ3: Marl 3D 114
NETHERTON 3C 171
Netherton Est. PL20: Buck M 4A 126
Netherton La. EX34: Com M 5C 12
Netley Rd. TQ12: New A 7E 104
Nettlehayes PL9: Elb 7K 143
NETTON 3B 174
Netton Cl. PL9: Elb 6J 143
Nevada Cl. PL3: Plym 5E 136
Nevada Ct. EX12: Seat 5E 86
Neville Rd. EX20: Oke 3C 48
    TQ12: New A 7D 104
New Barn Hill PL7: Plymp 6B 138
New Barnstaple Rd.
    EX34: Ilfra 3K 11
Newberry Cl. EX34: Berry 2D 12
Newberry Cotts. EX33: Georgeh . . .5C 14
Newberry Hill EX34: Berry 2E 12
Newberry La. EX34: Com M 2E 12
Newberry Rd. EX33: Georgeh 5C 14
    EX34: Com M 2E 12
Newberry Valley Touring & Camping Pk.
    EX34: Berry 3E 12
Newbery Cl. EX13: Axmin 3J 89
    EX24: Colyt 7D 88
Newbery Commercial Cen.
    EX5: Clyst H 7C 68
Newbridge Cl. EX39: Bide 1F 23
New Bridge Gdns. TQ7: Lodd 3G 151
    (off Town's La.)
Newbridge Hill EX16: With 5G 33
New Bridge St. EX4: Exe 5C 6 (7E 64)
NEWBUILDINGS 3B 164
New Bldgs. EX4: Exe 1G 7
    EX5: Broadc 5C 52
    EX16: Bam 2H 33
    EX31: Frem 6F 17
    EX34: Barn 4F 19
Newbury Cl. PL5: Plym 6G 131
Newbury Dr. TQ13: Bov T 4D 92
New Carlton Cinema, The
    Merlin Cinemas 3B 48
Newcastle Gdns. PL5: Plym 5G 131
Newcause TQ11: B'leigh 4C 98
    (off Jordan St.)
New Causeway EX39: N'ham 5E 20
    (off Diddywell Rd.)
Newcombe Cl. EX20: Oke 3D 48
Newcombes EX17: Cred 6H 39
Newcombe St. EX1: Heav 6K 65
Newcombe St. Gdns. EX1: Heav . . .6K 65
Newcombe Ter. EX1: Heav 6J 65
    (off Newcombe St.)
Newcomen Engine House
    . . . . .1B 124 (6F 125)
Newcomen Rd.
    TQ6: Dartm 2B 124 (6F 125)
NEWCOTT 3C 167
Newcourt Rd. EX3: Top 5D 72
    EX5: Silv 2H 51
Newcourt Way EX2: Cou W 3C 72
NEW CROSS 2D 167
Newcross Pk. TQ12: Kingst 2F 105
New Cut EX12: Beer 7B 86
    EX17: Cred 6G 39
    (off High St.)
New Cut, The EX15: Cull 4G 45
New England Hill PL7: Plymp 7A 144
New Esplanade Ct. TQ3: Paig 1J 119
New Est. EX5: New C 5D 50
New Exeter St. TQ13: Chud 1C 94
Newfoundland Cl. EX4: Exe 2H 65
Newfoundland Way
    TQ12: New A 1E 108
New George St.
    PL1: Plym 4C 8 (2H 141)
Newhaven EX5: Bradn 1C 52
Newhay, The EX7: Daw 4F 97
Newhay Cl. EX7: Daw 4F 97
Newhayes TQ12: Ipp 7G 101
Newhayes Cl. EX2: Exe 3D 70
Newhouse Hill EX16: With 4H 33
New Inn Ct. EX15: Cull 4G 45
    EX22: Hols 2C 34
NEWLAND 3D 161
Newland Cotts. EX32: L'key 3D 24
Newland Pk. Rd. EX32: L'key 3C 24
Newlands Av. EX8: Exmth 4F 77

Newlands Cl. EX2: Exe 3D 70
    EX10: Sidm 2C 84
    EX32: L'key 7D 24
Newlands Dr. TQ13: Bov T 7B 92
Newlands Pk. EX12: Seat 4D 86
Newlands Rd. EX10: Sidm 2C 84
New La. EX11: Ott M 3D 80
    EX33: Brau 1K 15
    EX33: Croy 1B 14
New Launceston Rd. PL19: Tavi . . .3G 59
New London PL20: Prin 6D 60
Newman Ct. EX4: Exe 7B 64
Newman Cres. TQ9: Darti 3B 102
Newman Rd. EX4: Exe 1B 70
    PL5: Plym 1D 134
Newmarket Cl. PL19: Tavi 4J 59
    (off Duke St.)
New Meadow PL21: Ivy 3E 145
New Mills Ind. Est. PL21: Modb . . .6F 147
Newnham Cl. PL7: Plymp 2D 138
Newnham Ind. Est. PL7: Plymp . . .2C 138
Newnham Rd. PL7: Plymp 3B 138
Newnham Way PL7: Plymp 3C 138
New North Rd. EX4: Exe 1B 6 (4D 64)
    EX8: Exmth 5C 76
New Orchard TQ10: S Bre 2B 100
New Pk. PL20: Horr 2F 127
    (not continuous)
    TQ13: Bov T 7B 92
New Pk. Cl. TQ5: Brixh 4F 123
New Pk. Cres. TQ12: Kingst 3G 105
New Pk. Est. EX6: Bridf 1F 63
New Pk. Rd. PL7: Plymp 5D 138
    PL21: L Mill 5A 144
    TQ3: Paig 7F 115
    TQ12: Kingst 3G 105
New Passage Hill PL1: Dev 1D 140
New Pl. EX16: Tiv 4B 40
NEWPORT
    Barnstaple 6G 19 (3B 160)
    Launceston 2B 168
    North Curry 1D 167
Newport Pk. EX2: Cou W 6B 72
Newport Rd. EX2: Cou W 6B 72
    EX32: Barn 5F 19
Newport St. EX16: Tiv 4C 40
    PL1: Plym 3F 141
    TQ6: Dartm 1A 124 (6F 125)
Newport Ter. EX32: Barn 5F 19
    EX39: Bide 4G 23
New Quay La. TQ5: Brixh 3F 123
New Quay St. EX39: Apple 3H 21
    TQ14: Teignm 5H 107
New Rd. EX5: Rock 2F 79
    EX6: Star 2D 96
    EX12: Beer 6B 86
    EX17: Morc 1D 38
    EX20: Huish, Mer 6B 30
    EX20: Oke 5A 48
    EX32: Barn 5F 19
    EX32: Bish T 6B 24
    EX36: S Mol 6D 26
    EX38: Gt T 2C 30
    EX39: Bide 5F 23
    EX39: Ins 3K 21
    PL6: Bickl 1H 133
    PL6: Robo 1D 132
    PL8: Yeal 2B 150
    PL16: Lift, Tin 6B 56
    PL20: Bere A 1B 128
    PL21: Lutt 7G 129
    PL21: Modb 6G 147
    TQ5: Brixh 4D 122
    TQ6: Sto F 4H 153
    TQ7: Lodd 3H 151
    TQ9: Sto G 4B 102
    TQ9: Tot 5F 103
    TQ11: B'leigh 4C 98
    TQ14: Teignm 3H 107
New Row EX39: Bide 3F 23
New Sidmouth Rd. EX24: Colyt . . .7A 88
New St. EX8: Exmth 5C 76
    EX10: Sidm 7C 84
    EX11: Ott M 3D 80
    EX14: Hon 3F 55
    EX15: Cull 4G 45
    EX18: Chul 6C 32
    EX38: Gt T 2A 30
    (not continuous)
    EX39: Apple 3H 21
    EX39: Bide 3F 23
    PL1: Plym 6F 9 (3K 141)
    (not continuous)
    TQ3: Paig 1H 119
    TQ13: Chag 3H 61
    TQ13: More 6H 61
New St. Flats EX39: Bide 3F 23
    (off New St.)
NEWTAKE 3J 109
Newtake Ho. TQ2: Torq 4B 112
Newtake Mt. TQ12: New A 2J 109
Newtake Ri. TQ12: New A 3J 109

Newtake Rd. PL19: Whitc 7K 59
Newte's Hill EX16: Tiv 6G 41
NEWTON ABBOT 1G 109 (3C 171)
Newton Abbot Leisure Cen. 7D 104
Newton Abbot Racecourse 6G 105
Newton Abbot Rd. TQ12: Tor 6F 103
Newton Abbot Sailing Club 3F 109
Newton Abbot Station (Rail) 1G 109
Newton Abbot Town &
    Great Western Railway Mus.
    . . . . .1F 109
Newton Av. PL5: Plym 1D 134
Newton Cen. EX2: Mar B 5H 71
Newton Cl. PL8: New F 5J 149
Newton Ct. EX16: Bam 2H 33
NEWTON FERRERS 5J 149 (3B 174)
Newton Gdns. PL5: Plym 1E 134
Newton Hall TQ12: New A 2F 109
Newton Hill PL8: New F 5H 149
Newton Ho. EX5: New C 6C 50
NEWTON POPPLEFORD . .5H 81 (2A 172)
Newton Rd. EX39: Bide 2F 23
    TQ2: Torq 4J 111
    TQ8: Salc 4C 158
    TQ9: L'ton, Tot 5F 103
    TQ12: Heat 6C 92
    TQ12: Kingsk 7K 109
    TQ12: Kingst, New A 7F 105
    TQ13: Bov T 4B 92
    TQ14: Bi'ton 4A 106
Newton Rd. Retail Pk.
    TQ12: Kingst 5G 105
NEWTON ST CYRES 6D 50 (1C 171)
NEWTON ST PETROCK 2C 163
Newtons Orchard EX13: Kilm 2B 88
Newton Sq. EX16: Bam 2H 33
NEWTON TRACEY 1D 163
NEWTOWN
    Combe St Nicholas 2C 167
    Exeter .6H 65
    Lezant .3A 168
    South Molton 1B 164
NEW TOWN 6C 84
Newtown EX10: Sidm 6C 84
    PL21: Corn 6J 129
Newtown Cl. EX1: Exe 3H 7
New Valley Rd. EX4: Exe 5C 64
New Wlk. TQ9: Tot 6F 103
New Way PL5: Wood S 2C 78
New Way Bldgs. EX8: Exmth 5C 76
New Way Est. EX14: Dunk 5G 47
New Wood Cl. PL6: Plym 2C 136
New Zealand Ho.
    PL3: Plym 1A 8 (7G 135)
Nicholas Cen. EX1: Exe 1J 7 (5H 65)
NICHOLASHAYNE 2B 166
Nicholas Rd. EX1: Heav 6K 65
Nicholson Rd. PL5: Plym 1K 135
    TQ2: Torq 3K 111
Nichols Way EX1: Exe 1J 7 (5H 65)
NIGHTCOTT 1C 165
Nightingale Cl. PL9: Elb 5K 143
    TQ2: Torq 3A 112
Nightingale Lawns EX15: Cull 5F 45
Nightjar Cl. TQ2: Torq 3A 112
Nilgala Cl. EX39: Bide 1D 22
NIMMER 2D 167
Nine Oaks PL20: Dous 5K 127
Nineteen Steps EX9: Bud S 7D 82
    (off Madeira Wlk.)
Nirvana Cl. PL21: Ivy 4G 145
Noelle Dr. TQ12: New A 7D 104
Noland Pk. TQ10: S Bre 2C 100
NOMANSLAND 2C 165
Nook, The PL19: Tavi 3J 59
    TQ7: Thur 5C 154
Norah Bellot Ct. EX32: Barn 4E 18
    (off Vicarage St.)
Norcombe Ct. EX12: Seat 6F 87
    (off Harbour Rd.)
Norden La. TQ7: Kingsb 4E 156
Norfolk Cl. PL3: Plym 6D 136
Norfolk Rd. PL3: Plym 7D 136
Norfolk Ter. EX32: Barn 5F 19
Norley Rd. EX33: Know 1K 15
Norman Cl. EX8: Exmth 2F 77
    TQ12: New A 6B 104
Norman Ct. EX2: Matf 4F 71
Norman Cres. EX9: Bud S 5B 82
Norman Dr. EX15: Cull 2H 45
Normandy Cl. EX8: Exmth 3G 77
Normandy Hill PL5: Plym 1A 134
Normandy Ho. EX32: Barn 5F 19
Normandy Pl. EX20: Hath 2H 35
Normandy Rd. EX1: Heav 6J 65
Normandy Way EX36: S Mol 6B 26
Norman Lockyer Observatory 5E 84
Norman M. EX2: Sow 1C 72

Norman Pl. EX2: Sow 1C 72
Norman Rd. TQ3: Paig 7J 115
Normans Cleave EX35: Lynt 2G 13
NORMAN'S GREEN 3A 166
Norman Stevens Cl. EX8: Exmth . . .6E 76
Normans Way EX34: Ilfra 3J 11
    (off Worth Rd.)
Norman Ter. EX39: N'ham 5F 21
Norns La. TQ6: Blackp 4F 153
NORTHAM 5E 20 (1C 163)
Northam Burrows Country Pk. 2D 20
Northampton Cl. PL5: Plym 5G 131
Northam Rd. EX39: Bide 2E 22
Northams Mdw. EX20: Oke 4A 48
North Av. DT7: Lym R 4J 91
    EX1: Heav 3K 7 (6H 65)
    EX39: Bide 4J 23
NORTHAY .2C 167
Nth. Boundary Rd. TQ5: Brixh 3C 122
NORTH BOVEY 2B 170
Nth. Bovey Rd. TQ13: More 7G 61
NORTH BOWOOD 1D 173
NORTH BRENTOR 2C 169
North Bri. Pl. EX4: Exe 3C 6 (6E 64)
Northbrook Cl. EX4: Whip 3K 65
Northbrook Golf Course 3J 71
NORTH BUCKLAND 4E 14 (2A 160)
NORTH CHIDEOCK 1D 173
Northcliffe EX32: Bish T 7B 24
    (off New Rd.)
NORTH COOMBE 2C 165
NORTHCOTE 2H 55
Northcote Hill EX14: Hon 2H 55
Northcote La. EX14: Hon 3E 54
Northcote Rd. EX14: Hon 2H 55
NORTHCOTT
    Boyton .1B 168
    Culmstock 2A 166
Northcott Gdns. EX39: N'ham 5F 21
Northcott Ter. EX22: Hols 2C 34
Northcott Theatre 3E 64
North Cross PL1: Plym 2D 8 (1J 141)
NORTH CURRY 1D 167
Northdene EX39: Bide 1D 22
North Devon EX16: Tiv 3B 40
North Devon Athletics Track 5K 15
Nth. Devon Crematorium
    EX31: Barn 7B 18
North Devon Karting Cen. 2B 18
North Devon Leisure Cen. 5E 18
North Devon Maritime Mus. 3H 21
North Devon Yacht Club 3K 21
Nth. Down Cres. PL2: Plym 5E 134
Northdown Dr. EX39: Bide 2E 22
Nth. Down Gdns. PL2: Plym 5E 134
Nth. Down Rd. EX33: Brau 4K 15
    PL2: Plym 5G 135
Northdown Rd. EX5: Thor 1B 50
    EX39: Bide 3D 22
North East Quay
    PL4: Plym 5H 9 (3K 141)
North End St. EX39: N'ham 5F 21
North Embankment
    TQ6: Dartm 1B 124 (5F 125)
North End Cl. TQ12: Ipp 6G 101
Northernhay EX16: Tiv 2F 109
Northernhay Gdns. 2E 6 (5E 64)
Northernhay Ga. EX4: Exe . . .3D 6 (6E 64)
Northernhay Pl. EX4: Exe . . .3E 6 (6F 65)
Northernhay Sq. EX4: Exe . . .3D 6 (6E 64)
Northernhay St. EX4: Exe . . .4D 6 (6E 64)
Northern La. EX12: Brans 5F 85
Northesk St. PL2: Plym 7F 135
Northfield EX4: Exe 1B 6 (4D 64)
    EX13: Mus 7D 90
Northfield La. EX31: Barn 2E 18
Northfield Ri. EX31: Barn 2E 18
Northfield Rd. EX20: Oke 3B 48
    EX33: Georgeh 4D 14
    EX34: Ilfra 2H 11
    EX39: Bide 4H 23
Northfields Ind. Est. TQ5: Brixh . . .3D 122
Northfields La. TQ5: Brixh 3D 122
Northfield Ter. EX34: Ilfra 2H 11
NORTH FILHAM 4K 145
Northford Rd.
    TQ6: Dartm 1A 124 (6E 124)
Nth. Furzeham Rd. TQ5: Brixh 2E 122
Northgate EX39: Hart 2H 27
    TQ9: Tot 5E 102
    (off Castle St.)
North Ga. Ho. EX4: Exe 3D 6
Northgate La. EX14: Hon 3K 55
North Grange EX2: Sow 2C 72
North Grn. EX32: Barn 5G 19
Northground La. EX10: Harc 4K 85
NORTH HEASLEY 3D 161
NORTH HILL 3A 168
North Hill EX39: Clov 5K 27
    (off High St.)
    PL4: Plym 2F 9 (1K 141)
North Hill Cl. TQ5: Brixh 3D 122

NORTH HUISH 2D 175
North Jaycroft EX15: Will 3D 44
North La. EX31: Bick'n 5K 17
Nth. Lawn Ct. EX1: Heav 6J 65
Northleat Av. TQ3: Paig 2E 118
NORTHLEIGH
 Barnstaple 3C 161
 Honiton 1B 172
Northleigh Hill Rd.
 EX14: Hon, Offw 6H 55
NORTHLEW 1D 169
NORTH LOBB 1F 15
Nth. Lodge Cl. EX7: Daw 1F 7
NORTH MOLTON 2C 26 (1B 164)
NORTHMOOR GREEN 1D 167
NORTH MORTE 3A 10
Nth. Morte Farm Caravan & Camping Pk.
 EX34: Mort 2B 10
Nth. Morte Rd. EX34: Mort 3A 10
NORTHMOSTOWN 6J 81
NORTH NEWTON 1C 167
Northolt Av. PL5: Plym 6C 130
North Pk. EX20: N Taw 6A 36
North Pk. Almshouses EX1: Exe 5G 7
North Pk. Rd. EX4: Exe 3E 64
 EX6: Ted M 7H 49
NORTH PETHERTON 1C 167
NORTH PETHERWIN 2A 168
NORTH PROSPECT 5G 135
Nth. Prospect Pl. PL2: Plym 3E 134
North Quay PL4: Plym 5G 9 (3K 141)
NORTH RADWORTHY 3D 161
North Rd. EX20: Oke 2B 48
 EX22: Bradw 4B 28
 EX22: Hols 1C 34
 EX31: Barn 1F 19
 EX36: S Mol 5C 26
 EX37: High B 2B 32
 EX39: Bide 3F 23
 EX39: Hart 2H 27
 PL11: Torp 2A 140
 PL16: Lift 6B 56
 PL20: Yelv 4E 126
 PL21: L Mill 4B 144
North Rd. E. PL4: Plym 2D 8 (1J 141)
North Rd. Ind. Est. EX20: Oke 2C 48
North Rd. W. PL1: Plym 3A 8 (2G 141)
Nth. Rocks Rd. TQ4: Broads 1H 121
North St. EX1: Heav 6J 65
 EX3: Top 6B 74
 EX4: Exe 4D 6 (6E 64)
 EX8: Exmth 5C 76
 EX11: Ott M 3D 80
 EX13: Axmin 3H 89
 EX16: With 6J 33
 EX17: Cred 6H 39
 EX19: Dol 6H 31
 EX20: N Taw 6B 36
 EX20: Oke 3B 48
 EX33: Brau 4J 15
 EX36: S Mol 6C 26
 EX39: Hart 3H 27
 EX39: N'ham 5E 20
 PL4: Plym 4G 9 (2K 141)
 (not continuous)
 PL19: Tavi 4J 59
 TQ9: Tot 5E 102
 TQ12: Den 1H 101
 TQ12: Ipp 6C 101
 TQ13: Ashb 3G 99
 TQ13: Chag 2H 61
NORTH TAMERTON 1B 168
NORTH TAWTON 6B 36 (3A 164)
North Ter. EX31: Bick'n 5K 17
NORTH TOWN 3D 163
Northumberland Pl.
 TQ14: Teignm 5H 107
Northumberland St. PL5: Plym 3D 134
Northumberland Ter. PL1: Plym 7C 8
North Vw. EX21: Sheb 6J 29
 TQ14: Shal 6G 107
 (off Commons Old Rd.)
North Vw. Av. EX39: Bide 2E 22
North Vw. Hill EX39: Bide 2E 22
North Vw. Rd. TQ5: Brixh 3F 123
Northview Rd. EX9: Bud S 7B 82
Northville Pk. TQ7: Kingsb 3F 157
Northville Rd. TQ7: Kingsb 3F 157
North Wlk. EX31: Barn 4E 18
 EX32: Barn 4E 18
 EX35: Lynt 1F 13
North Wlk. Hill EX35: Lynt 1H 13
Northways La. PL21: Ugb 5C 146
Nth. Weald Gdns. PL5: Plym 5D 130
NORTH WHILBOROUGH
 . . . . .5E 110 (1A 176)
Northwood La. EX39: Buck B 2H 29
 TQ11: Buck 1C 98
Northwoods TQ13: Bov T 7F 92
NORTON 6A 124 (2A 176)
Norton Av. PL4: Plym 1K 9 (1B 142)
NORTON FITZWARREN 1C 167

Norton Pk. TQ6: Norton 6A 124
Norton Pl. EX8: Exmth 4G 77
Norton Vw. TQ6: Dartm 6C 124
Nortonwood La. EX5: New C 5E 50
Norwich Av. PL5: Plym 5F 131
Norwich Cl. EX8: Exmth 1F 77
Norwich Rd. EX4: Exe 6B 64
Norwood Av. EX2: Exe 7H 7 (1G 71)
Norwood Ho. EX4: Exe 1F 7 (5F 65)
Norwood Rd. EX16: Tiv 2D 40
NOSS MAYO 6H 149 (3B 174)
Notre Dame Cl. PL6: Plym 5A 132
Notre Dame Ho. PL1: Plym 3B 8
Notte St. PL1: Plym 6D 8 (3J 141)
Nottingham Gdns. PL4: Plym 1G 9
Novorossiysk Rd. PL6: Plym 2E 136
Nuffield Health Club
 Plymouth 6K 9 (3B 142)
Nunnery Wlk. EX39: Bide 4F 23
 (off Lwr. Meddon St.)
Nurseries Cl. EX3: Exton 2E 18
 EX3: Top 7D 72
Nursery Cl. EX8: Exmth 4E 76
 PL5: Tam F 3G 131
 TQ3: Paig 2G 119
Nursery End EX31: Barn 2E 18
Nursery M. EX8: Exmth 4E 76
Nursery Rd. TQ12: Kingst 4H 105
Nutaberry Hill EX39: Bide 4G 23
Nutaberry Works EX39: Bide 4G 23
Nutaberry Yd. EX39: Bide 4G 23
Nutbrook EX8: Exmth 3D 76
Nut Bush La. TQ2: Torq 6H 111
Nuthatch Dr. TQ2: Torq 3A 112
Nut Tree Cl. TQ5: Brixh 6D 122
Nut Tree Orchard TQ5: Brixh 6D 122
Nutwell Rd. EX8: Lymp . . . .5G 75 & 3J 75
Nymet Av. EX17: Bow 6H 37
Nymet Hayes EX17: Bow 5H 37
NYMET ROWLAND 2F 37 (3B 164)
NYMET TRACEY 7J 37 (3B 164)
NYNEHEAD 1B 166

O

Oakapple Cl. PL7: Plymp 4J 137
Oakbank TQ13: Bov T 7B 92
Oakbeer Orchard EX5: Cranb 3B 68
Oak Bri. EX10: Sidb 2H 85
Oak Bus. Units EX2: Mar B 5H 71
Oak Cliff Chalet Pk. EX7: Daw W . . .7E 96
Oak Cliff Holiday Pk. EX7: Daw W . .7E 96
Oak Cl. EX2: Shil A 7D 70
 EX4: Pin 3D 66
 EX5: Silv 1H 51
 EX6: Exmin 2C 74
 EX11: Ott M 5C 80
 EX16: Tiv 3D 40
 TQ12: Kingst 5J 105
Oak Ct. EX22: Hols 1C 34
Oak Cres. EX15: Will 4C 44
Oakcroft Rd. PL2: Plym 5G 135
Oakdale Av. EX32: Swim 2H 25
Oakdene Ri. PL9: Plyms 6G 143
Oak Dr. EX15: Cull 2H 45
 PL6: Plym 7K 131
OAKE 1B 166
Oak End Ct. TQ3: Marl 4D 114
Oakery Cres. EX20: Prin 6D 60
Oakfield EX15: Will 3E 44
Oakfield Cl. PL7: Plymp 3F 139
Oakfield Pl. PL4: Plym 3C 142
Oakfield Rd. EX4: Exe 6A 6 (7D 64)
 EX20: Hath 1H 35
 PL7: Plymp 5K 137
Oakfields EX16: Tiv 2D 40
Oakfield St. EX1: Heav 7J 65
Oakfield Ter. EX39: N'ham 5F 21
 (off Diddywell Rd.)
Oakfield Ter. Rd. PL4: Plym 3B 142
OAKFORD 1D 165
Oakford TQ12: Kingst 4G 105
OAKFORDBRIDGE 1D 165
Oakford Cl. EX36: N Mol 2B 26
Oakford Vs. EX36: N Mol 2B 26
Oak Gdns. PL21: Ivy 4J 145
Oakham Rd. PL5: Plym 5G 131
Oakhayes Rd. EX5: Wood 5B 78
Oakhays EX36: S Mol 7D 26
Oak Hill EX7: Daw 6F 97
 EX9: E Bud 1E 82
Oakhill Cl. EX9: E Bud 1D 82
Oak Hill Cross Rd.
 EX7: Holc . . . . . . .6F 97 & 2K 107
 TQ14: Teignm 2K 107
Oakhill Ri. EX31: Roun 6B 18
Oak Hill Rd. TQ1: Torq 7B 112
Oakland Av. EX31: Barn 6B 18
Oakland Dr. EX7: Daw 5G 97
Oakland Pk. EX31: Barn 6C 18
Oakland Pk. Sth. EX31: Barn 5A 18

Oakland Pl. EX36: S Mol 6C 26
 (off South St.)
Oakland Rd. TQ12: New A 2H 109
OAKLANDS 2B 48
Oaklands EX39: Bide 5C 22
 PL19: Whitc 7K 59
Oaklands Cl. EX12: Seat 2E 86
 EX18: Chul 6C 32
 PL6: Plym 3D 132
 TQ11: B'leigh 4B 98
Oaklands Ct. EX16: Tiv 3F 41
Oaklands Dr. EX20: Oke 3B 48
 (not continuous)
Oaklands Gdns. EX31: Barn 5C 18
Oaklands Pk. EX20: Oke 3A 48
 TQ11: B'leigh 3B 98
Oaklands Res. Pk. EX20: Oke 2B 48
Oaklands Rd. TQ11: B'leigh 2A 98
Oakland Wlk. EX7: Daw 5G 97
Oak Lawn TQ12: New A 2F 109
Oaklawn Ct. TQ1: Torq 6B 112
 (off Barton Rd.)
Oaklawn Ter. TQ1: Torq 6B 112
 (off St Vincent's Rd.)
Oaklea EX14: Hon 3E 54
 EX16: Tiv 2D 40
Oaklea Cl. TQ7: Kingsb 5F 157
Oaklea Cres. EX31: Frem 6E 16
Oaklea Pk. TQ12: Live 4H 93
Oakleigh Rd. EX8: Exmth 5D 76
 EX32: Barn 5F 19
Oakley Cl. EX1: Pin 3D 66
 TQ14: Teignm 2H 107
Oakley Wlk. EX5: Clyst M 2K 73
Oak Mdw. EX36: S Mol 6B 26
Oak Meadow Golf Course 2D 96
Oak Pk. Av. TQ2: Torq 5K 111
Oak Pk. Cl. TQ2: Torq 5K 111
Oak Pk. Rd. TQ12: New A 7C 104
Oak Pk. Vs. EX7: Daw 4J 97
Oak Pl. TQ12: New A 1F 109
 (not continuous)
Oak Ridge EX2: Alph 5D 70
 PL16: Lift 6A 56
Oak Rd. EX4: Exe 1C 70
 EX5: Ayle 6F 79
 EX11: High M 6F 79
 EX20: Oke 2C 48
 PL19: Tavi 6J 59
Oaks, The EX15: Hemy 1G 47
 PL19: Mary T 2B 60
 TQ12: New A 4J 109
 TQ13: Bov T 4D 92
Oak Tree Cl. EX5: Broadc 6D 52
Oaktree Ct. EX8: Exmth 1G 77
 PL21: Ivy 4E 144
Oak Tree Dr. EX32: Barn 5K 19
 TQ12: New A 4J 109
Oak Tree Gdns. EX34: Ilfra 3K 11
Oak Tree Gro. TQ14: Shal 6G 107
Oak Tree La. PL19: Tavi 6J 59
Oak Tree Pk. PL6: Plym 4E 132
Oaktree Pk. EX20: Stic 1G 49
Oak Tree Pl. EX2: Matf 5F 71
Oak Tree Sq. EX10: Sidm 3B 84
Oaktree Vs. EX10: New P 5H 81
Oak Vw. EX14: Hon 5D 54
Oak Vw. Cl. TQ2: Torq 4H 111
Oakwell Cl. EX38: Gt T 2D 30
Oakwood Cl. EX31: Roun 7B 18
 PL6: Plym 2E 132
 TQ6: Dartm 6C 124
Oakwood Ct. EX36: S Mol 6D 26
Oakwood Dr. PL21: Modb 5G 147
Oakwood Pk. TQ7: Lodd 2G 151
Oakwood Rd. EX8: Exmth 1G 77
Oakymead Pk. TQ12: Kingst 5G 105
OARE 2D 161
OAREFORD 2D 161
Oates Rd. PL2: Plym 6G 135
OATH 1D 167
Oatlands Av. EX32: Bish T 7F 19
Oatlands Dr. TQ4: Paig 3G 119
Oberon Rd. EX1: Sow 5D 66
Occombe Farm 3E 114
Occombe Valley Rd. TQ3: Pres 4G 115
Ocean Ct. PL1: Dev 4E 140
Ocean Pk. EX39: West H 4G 21
Ocean St. PL2: Plym 5D 134
Ocean Vw. Cres. TQ5: Brixh 7C 122
Ocean Vw. Dr. TQ5: Brixh 7C 122
Ochil Cl. EX39: Bide 5J 23
Ochre Ct. TQ5: Brixh 4F 123
Ockington Cl. EX20: Oke 3D 48
Ockment Ct. EX20: Oke 3B 48
Octagon, The PL1: Plym 5B 8 (3H 141)
Octagon St. PL1: Plym 4B 8 (2H 141)
Octon Gro. TQ1: Torq 6A 112
Oddicombe Beach Hill TQ1: Torq . .5E 112
Odeon Cinema
 Exeter 2G 7 (5G 65)

Odhams Wharf EX3: Ebf 5D 74
Odle Hill TQ12: A'well 5D 108
Odlehill Gro. TQ12: A'well 6D 108
Odun Pl. EX39: Apple 3H 21
Odun Rd. EX39: Apple 3H 21
Odun Ter. EX39: Apple 3H 21
Offields PL8: Holb 6C 150
OFFWELL 1B 172
Ogwell End Dr. TQ12: E Ogw 2C 108
Ogwell Grn. TQ12: E Ogw 3B 108
Ogwell Mill Rd. TQ12: New A 2B 108
Ogwell Rd. TQ12: E Ogw 3B 108
Oil Mill La. EX5: Clyst M 3H 73
Oil Mill Rd. EX5: Clyst M 3H 73
Okefield Av. EX17: Cred 5H 39
Okefield Ridge EX17: Cred 5G 39
Okefield Rd. EX17: Cred 5G 39
OKEHAMPTON 3B 48 (1D 169)
OKEHAMPTON CAMP 7B 48 (1D 169)
Okehampton Castle 5A 48
Okehampton Pl. PL7: Plymp 5E 138
Okehampton Golf Course 6A 48
Okehampton Pl. EX4: Exe . .6B 6 (7D 64)
Okehampton Rd. EX4: Exe . . .5A 6 (7C 64)
Okehampton Station
 Dartmoor Railway 5C 48
Okehampton Station (Rail) 5C 48
Okehampton Station Vis. Cen. 4C 48
Okehampton St. EX4: Exe . . .6B 6 (7D 64)
Okehampton Way PL21: Ivy 5H 145
Oke Tor Cl. EX20: Oke 3D 48
 TQ3: Pres 4G 115
Okewood Cl. EX8: Exmth 6D 76
Old Abbey Ct. EX2: Exe 2H 71
Old Bakery, The 6H 85
Old Bakery Cl. EX4: Exe 1A 6 (5C 64)
 EX19: Wink 3B 36
Old Barn Cl. EX5: Sto C 7J 51
Old Barnstaple Rd.
 EX34: Ilfra, Two P 4K 11
 EX39: Bide, Westl 3G 23
OLD BARTON 6D 148
Old Beer Rd. EX12: Seat 6C 86
Old Bideford Cl. EX31: Roun 7A 18
Old Bideford Rd.
 EX31: Barn, Roun 7A 18
 (not continuous)
Old Blundell's EX16: Tiv 4D 40
OLDBOROUGH 4C 38 (3B 164)
Oldborough La. EX17: Morc 4C 38
Old Brewery, The TQ2: Torq 4D 112
 (off Lummaton Pl.)
Old Butterleigh Rd. EX5: Silv 1H 51
Old Bystock Dr. EX8: Exmth 1G 77
Old Chapel Gdns. EX19: Wink 2C 36
Old Cider Works La.
 TQ12: A'well 5D 108
Old Coach La. EX1: Heav 4K 7 (6H 65)
Old Coach Rd. EX5: Broadc 6C 52
Old Coast Rd. EX34: Berry 2D 12
Old Court House, The EX5: Wood . . .5B 78
Old Dawlish Rd. EX6: Kennf 1J 95
Old Ebford La. EX3: Ebf 6E 74
Old Elm Rd. EX14: Hon 5C 54
Oldenburg Pk. TQ3: Paig 7J 115
Old English Ind. Est. PL20: Dous . . .5J 127
 TQ12: New A 7E 104
 TQ13: Ashb 2K 99
Old Exeter Rd. PL19: Tavi 3J 59
Old Exeter St. TQ13: Chud 1C 94
Old Farm Bungs. EX10: Sidm 3C 84
Old Farm Rd. PL5: Plym 3B 134
Old Farm Way EX7: Daw 6G 97
Oldfields EX8: Exmth 6E 76
Old Fore St. EX10: Sidm 7C 84
Old Garden Pasture EX5: Cranb 3B 68
Old Gatehouse Rd. EX7: Daw 3K 97
Old George St. PL1: Plym . . .5D 8 (3J 141)
Oldham Rd. EX20: Hath 2G 35
Old Hill EX15: Cull 5J 45
Old Ide Cl. EX2: Ide 3B 70
Old Ide La. EX2: Ide 3B 70
Olditch Holiday Pk. EX20: Stic 3G 49
Old Jaycroft EX15: Will 5D 44
Old Laira Rd. PL3: Plym 7C 136
Oldlands Cl. PL6: Plym 4C 132
Old Launceston Rd. PL19: Tavi 3G 59
Old Laundry, The
 PL1: Plym 3A 8 (2G 141)
Old Liverton Rd. TQ12: Live 7G 93
Old Manor Cl. TQ13: Ashb 2F 99
Old Manor Gdns. EX24: Colyf 1G 87
Old Market, The EX15: Hemy 2G 47
 TQ6: Dartm 1A 124
 (off Market St.)
Old Market Cl. EX2: Exe 2E 70
Old Market Dr. EX39: Wools 2A 28
Old Market Fld. Ind. Est.
 EX16: With 5G 33
Old Matford La. EX2: Matf 6G 71
OLD MILL 3B 168
Old Mill, The 7A 148

Old Mill, The EX15: Culm 2B **46**
Old Mill Cl. EX2: Exe 7F **7** (1G **71**)
EX16: Tiv 5C **40**
Old Mill Ct. PL7: Plymp 4B **138**
Old Mill La. TQ6: Dartm 5C **124**
Old Mill Rd. TQ2: Torq 4A **116**
(not continuous)
Old Newton Rd. TQ12: Heat 6C **92**
TQ12: Kingsk 6H **109**
TQ13: Bov T 6C **92**
Old Nursery Dr. EX4: Whip 4A **66**
Old Okehampton Rd.
EX4: Nad, White 5A **64**
Old Orchard TQ13: Bov T 4C **92**
Old Paignton Rd. TQ2: Torq 4K **115**
(Roundhill Rd.)
TQ2: Torq 3K **115**
(Stoneleigh Dr.)
Old Park Rd. EX4: Exe 2F **7** (5F **65**)
PL3: Plym 5J **135**
Old Pavilion Cl. EX2: Won 1B **72**
Old Pinn La. EX1: Pin 3D **66**
Old Plymouth Rd. TQ7: Kingsb 3F **157**
Old Priory PL7: Plymp 4A **138**
Old Quarry Rd. PL20: Buck M 5A **126**
Old Quay TQ14: Teignm 5H **107**
Old Quay La. EX39: Ins 3K **21**
Old Quay St. TQ14: Teignm 5H **107**
Old Rectory Cl. EX39: Ins 7A **16**
Old Rectory Gdns. EX17: Morc 1C **38**
TQ7: Thur 5C **154**
Old Rectory La. EX31: Brat F 6H **13**
Old Rice Mill, The PL16: Tin 6D **56**
OLDRIDGE 1C **171**
Oldridge Vw. EX6: Ted M 6J **49**
Old Rd. EX16: Tiv 4E **40**
EX20: Oke 4A **48**
PL8: Brixt 2H **149**
PL21: Lutt 7G **129**
TQ5: Galm 3H **121**
TQ6: Sto F 3G **153**
TQ9: H'ford 6B **100**
Old Rydon Cl. EX2: Cou W 3D **72**
Old Rydon La. EX2: Cou W 4B **72**
Old Rydon Ley EX2: Cou W 3C **72**
Old Saddlery, The *EX14: Hon 3F 55*
(off Queen St.)
Old Sawmills, The EX10: Col R 2G **83**
Old School Cl. EX16: Tiv 4B **40**
Old School Ct. *EX3: Top 5B 74*
(off Majorfield Rd.)
EX14: Hon 3F **55**
EX15: Hemy 2G 47
(off Station Rd.)
Old School La. EX31: Frem 6F **17**
Old School M. *EX7: Daw 4G 97*
(off School Hill)
Old School Rd. EX32: Barn 7H **19**
PL5: Plym 3B **134**
Old Sidmouth Rd. EX24: Colyt 7A **88**
Old Sludge Beds Nature Reserve ...**7B 72**
Old Station, The PL20: Horr 3D **126**
Old Station Rd. EX32: Barn 5G **19**
PL20: Horr 3E **126**
Old Station Yd. TQ7: Kingsb 4F **157**
Old Sticklepath Hill EX31: Barn 6C **18**
Old Stone Cl. EX39: West H 6A **20**
Old's Vw. EX4: Exe 1A **6** (5D **64**)
Old Tannery M. TQ13: Chud 1C **94**
Old Teignmouth Rd. EX7: Daw 6G **97**
Old Tinhay PL16: Tin 6C **56**
Old Tiverton Rd. EX4: Exe ...1H **7** (5G **65**)
EX16: Bam 2J **33**
EX17: Cred 6J **39**
Old Torquay Rd. TQ3: Pres 6J **115**
Old Torrington Rd. EX31: Barn 7B **18**
Old Torwood Rd. TQ1: Torq 2E **116**
Old Totnes Rd. TQ11: B'leigh 4D **98**
TQ12: New A 2D **108**
(not continuous)
TQ13: Ashb 5G **99**
Old Town EX39: Bide 4E **22**
Old Town St. EX7: Daw 4F **97**
PL1: Plym 4E **8** (2J **141**)
Old Vicarage Cl. EX2: Ide 4A **70**
Old Vicarage Gdn. DT7: Lym R 5J **91**
Old Vicarage Rd. EX2: Exe ...7A **6** (1D **70**)
Old Walls Hill
TQ14: Bi'ton, Teignm 2C **106**
Old Warleigh La. PL5: Tam F 2E **130**
(not continuous)
OLDWAY **7H 115**
Oldway TQ13: Chud 3A **94**
Oldway Mansion **6H 115**
Oldway Rd. TQ3: Paig, Pres 7H **115**
OLDWAYS END **1C 165**
Old Wharf, The PL9: Plyms 5C **142**
Old Widdicombe La. TQ3: Blag 6A **114**
TQ3: Paig 7C **114**
Old Woodlands Rd. PL5: Plym 7H **131**
Old Woods Hill TQ2: Torq 6A **112**
Old Woods Trad. Est. TQ2: Torq ...5A **112**
Olga Ter. EX8: Lymp 6H **75**
Olive Gdns. EX7: Daw W 7E **96**
Olive Gro. EX7: Daw W 7E **96**
Oliver Pl. TQ12: Heat 2K **93**
Oliver Rd. EX32: Barn 3G **19**
Olivia Ct. PL4: Plym 1H **9**
Omaha Dr. EX2: Cou W 4C **72**
Omega Cen., The EX2: Sow 6D **66**
One End St. EX39: Apple 3H **21**
Onslow Rd. PL2: Plym 4H **135**
TQ8: Salc 3B **158**
Opie La. PL4: Plym 2H **9** (1A **142**)
Ora Cl. EX33: Croy 2C **14**
Ora La. EX33: Croy 2C **14**
Orange Gro. TQ2: Torq 3C **112**
Orangery, The *EX6: Exmin 1B 74*
(off Devington Pk.)
Ora Stone Pk. EX33: Croy 3B **14**
Orbec Av. TQ12: Kingst 4J **105**
Orchard, The EX6: Dunsf 7C **62**
EX7: Holc 7F **97**
EX10: Tip J 1J **81**
EX12: Seat 5E **86**
EX13: Kilm 2B **88**
EX14: Hon 4E **54**
(Mill St.)
EX14: Hon 2J **55**
(Tunnel La.)
EX31: Bick'n 6K **17**
EX34: Woolc 7C **10**
PL7: Spa 1J **139**
PL8: Torr 3B **150**
PL21: Modb 7H **147**
TQ9: Tot 6F 103
(off Shute Rd.)
TQ11: B'leigh 4D **98**
TQ12: A'well 6E **108**
TQ14: Bi'ton 3B **106**
Orchard Av. PL6: Plym 4C **136**
Orchard Cl. EX1: Pin 3E **66**
EX5: Wood 5C **78**
EX7: Daw 4G **97**
EX8: Exmth 3D **76**
EX8: Lymp 6G **75**
EX8: San B 6J 77
(off Gore La.)
EX9: E Bud 1D **82**
EX10: New P 5F **81**
EX10: Sidf 2D **84**
EX10: Sidm 7A **84**
EX11: Ott M 4D **80**
EX13: Whitf 5A **90**
EX15: Uff 6H **43**
EX20: Oke 4B **48**
EX24: Colyf 1G **87**
EX31: Barn 6B **18**
EX33: Brau 4H **15**
EX34: Com M 6B **12**
PL7: Plymp 4F **139**
PL8: Torr 3B **150**
PL15: St G 6C **34**
PL19: Tavi 5F **59**
TQ5: Brixh 5E **122**
TQ5: Galm 3J **121**
TQ9: Sto G 4B 120
(off Paignton Rd.)
TQ12: Den 2H **101**
TQ12: E Ogw 3A **108**
TQ12: Kingst 4J **105**
(Ware Cl.)
TQ12: Kingst 1G **105**
(Woodlands Copse)
TQ13: Chud 2D **94**
TQ14: Shal 6F **107**
Orchard Cotts. PL8: Holb 6D **150**
PL19: Lam 7D **58**
Orchard Ct. EX2: Sow 6D **66**
EX5: Whim 6G **53**
EX17: Cred 5H **39**
EX20: N Taw 6B **36**
PL19: Lam 5C **58**
PL21: Ivy 4F **145**
TQ8: Salc 3C 158
(off Island St.)
TQ12: New A 1E 108
(off Bradley La.)
Orchard Cres. PL9: Plyms 5D **142**
Orchard Dr. EX9: Ott'n 6H **83**
TQ12: Ipp 6H **101**
TQ12: Kingsk 1F **111**
Orchard Gdns. EX4: Exe 1C **70**
EX5: Broadc 6D **52**
EX7: Daw 4G **97**
EX39: Bide 1F **23**
TQ6: Dartm 6E **124**
TQ12: Kingst 4H 105
(off Crossley Moor Rd.)
TQ14: Teignm 5J **107**
Orchard Ga. EX19: Dol 6J **31**
Orchard Gro. EX33: Croy 2C **14**
TQ5: Brixh 6E **122**
ORCHARD HILL **2F 23** (**1C 163**)
Orchard Hill EX2: Exe 2B **70**
EX39: Bide 1E **22**
PL8: Wors 1E **150**
Orchard Ho. TQ13: Chud 1C **94**
Orchard Ind. Est. (North)
TQ7: Kingsb 4F **157**
Orchard Ind. Est. (South)
TQ7: Kingsb 4F **157**
Orchard La. EX5: Silv 1H **51**
EX6: E'don 5D **96**
PL7: Plymp 3A **138**
Orchard Leigh EX16: Tiv 5C **40**
Orchard Mdw. EX17: Cop 6C **38**
TQ13: Chag 2H **61**
Orchardon La. EX33: Brau 7D **14**
Orchard Pk. PL21: Ivy 5G **145**
TQ9: Darti 2B **102**
Orchard Pl. EX32: Barn 5J **19**
TQ1: Torq 3F **117**
ORCHARD PORTMAN **1C 167**
Orchard Ri. EX39: Bide 1F **23**
Orchard Rd. EX32: Barn 5G **19**
EX33: Know 1K **15**
EX33: Wraf 7K **15**
EX34: Ilfra 3J 11
(off Cambridge Gro.)
PL2: Plym 4F **135**
TQ1: Torq 7D **112**
TQ2: Torq 4B **112**
TQ13: Ashb 4H **99**
Orchards, The EX32: L'key 2C **24**
EX32: Swim 3H **25**
TQ5: Galm 3H **121**
Orchardside EX10: Sidm 3C **84**
Orchard Ter. EX6: Ted M 6H **49**
EX32: Barn 7G **19**
EX35: Lynt 2G 13
(off Lydiate La.)
TQ9: Tot 6E **102**
TQ11: B'leigh 4C **98**
TQ12: A'well 5E **108**
TQ12: Kingsk 7J **109**
TQ13: Bov T 3C **92**
TQ13: Chag 2H **61**
Orchardton Ter. PL9: Plyms 7G **143**
Orchard Vw. EX1: Heav 7J **65**
EX16: Hal 6E **42**
TQ7: Chil 6G 159
(off Helmers Way)
Orchard Way EX3: Top 5A **74**
EX6: Kenton 6H **95**
EX14: Hon 3G **55**
(not continuous)
EX15: Cull 5G **45**
EX15: Uff 6H **43**
EX15: Will 4D **44**
EX16: Tiv 5B **40**
EX17: Lap 2J **37**
TQ2: Torq 4H **111**
TQ7: Chil 6G **159**
TQ9: Sto G 3B **120**
TQ13: Bov T 3C **92**
Orchard Waye TQ9: Tot 6D **102**
Orchid Av. PL21: Ivy 3E **144**
TQ12: Kingst 4H **105**
Orchid Cl. EX16: Tiv 2F **41**
Orchid Paradise **4B 104**
Orchid Vale TQ12: Kingst 2H **105**
Orcombe Ct. EX8: Exmth 4F **77**
Ordnance St. PL1: Dev 2C **140**
Ordulf Rd. PL19: Tavi 4G **59**
Oregon Way PL3: Plym 5D **136**
ORESTON **5D 142**
Orestone Dr. TQ1: Maid 2J **113**
Orestone La. TQ12: Dacc 2K **111**
Oreston Quay PL9: Plyms 5C **142**
Oreston Rd. PL9: Plyms 5D **142**
Orient Rd. TQ3: Pres 5K **115**
Oriole Dr. EX4: Exe 3G **65**
Orkney Cl. TQ2: Torq 3A **112**
Orkney M. EX16: Tiv 2D **40**
Orleigh Av. TQ12: New A 6E **104**
Orleigh Cl. EX39: Buck B 2J **29**
Orleigh Cross TQ12: New A 6E **104**
Orleigh Mill Ct. EX31: Barn 3E **18**
Orleigh Pk. TQ12: New A 6E **104**
Orley Rd. TQ12: Ipp 6F **101**
Ormidale Sq. EX16: Tiv 2G **41**
Ormond Lodge TQ4: Paig 2J **119**
Orpington Ct. EX16: Hal 6E **42**
Orwell Gth. EX4: Whip 4B **66**
Osbern Rd. TQ3: Pres 4G **115**
Osborn Cl. TQ12: Ipp 6H **101**
Osborne Cl. EX39: Bide 3C **22**
Osborne Gdns. EX32: Bish T 6A **24**
Osborne La. EX39: Bide 3C **22**
Osborne Pl. PL1: Plym 7D **8** (4J **141**)
Osborne Rd. EX34: Ilfra 3G **11**
PL3: Plym 1F **141**
Osborne St. TQ12: New A 1G **109**
Osbourne Ter. EX31: Barn 5E **18**
Osmand Gdns. PL7: Plymp 4A **138**
Osmonds La. TQ14: Teignm 5H **107**
Osney Av. TQ4: Good 3H **119**
Osney Cres. TQ4: Good 2H **119**
Osney Gdns. TQ4: Good 3H **119**
Osprey Dr. TQ2: Torq 2K **111**
Osprey Gdns. PL9: Elb 5K **143**
Osprey Ho. *TQ1: Torq 6F 113*
(off Babbacombe Rd.)
Osprey Rd. EX2: Sow 6E **66**
OSSABOROUGH **7C 10**
Ossaborough La. EX34: Woolc 7C **10**
Oswald Browning Way
EX31: Barn 2F **19**
Otago Cotts. EX2: Exe 2H **71**
OTHERY **1D 167**
Otterbourne Ct. *EX9: Bud S 7D 82*
(off Coastguard Rd.)
Otter Cl. EX10: Tip J 1J **81**
EX11: W Hill 4H **79**
EX20: Oke 2D **48**
TQ2: Torq 6J **111**
Otter Ct. EX2: Matf 5F **71**
EX9: Bud S 6E **82**
Otter Estuary Nature Reserve **6E 82**
OTTERFORD **2C 167**
OTTERHAM **1A 168**
Otter Reach EX10: New P 5H **81**
Otter Rd. TQ2: Torq 6J **111**
Otters Reach EX9: Bud S 5D **82**
OTTERTON **6H 83** (**2A 172**)
Otterton Mill **6G 83**
Ottervale Rd. EX9: Bud S 6E **82**
Otter Valley Pk. EX14: Hon 1J **55**
Otter Vw. *EX11: Ott M 4C 80*
(off St Saviours Rd.)
Otter Way EX32: Barn 5J **19**
Ottery La.
EX10: Sidb, Sidm .....3F **85** & 1D **84**
Ottery Moor EX14: Hon 3E **54**
Ottery Moor La. EX14: Hon 3D **54**
Ottery Rd. EX14: Fen 2G **53**
OTTERY ST MARY **4C 80** (**1B 172**)
Ottery St. EX9: Ott'n 6H **83**
Quicks Fld. TQ10: S Bre 2B **100**
Outer Down PL19: Lam 6C **58**
OUTER HOPE **2G 155** (**3C 175**)
Outer Ting Tong EX9: Know 1K **77**
Outland Rd. PL2: Plym 6G **135**
PL3: Plym 3K **135**
Outlook Ct. *EX7: Daw 4H 97*
(off E. Cliff Rd.)
Oval Grn. *EX2: Won 2B 72*
(off Woodwater La.)
Overbeck's **7A 158**
Overbrook EX7: Daw 4F **97**
Overcliff Ct. EX7: Daw 3H **97**
Overclose TQ3: Paig 6E **114**
Overdale EX6: Ted M 6J **49**
Overdale Cl. TQ2: Torq 1B **112**
Overdale Rd. PL2: Plym 4E **134**
Overgang TQ5: Brixh 3F **123**
Overgang Rd. TQ5: Brixh 2E **122**
Overseas Est. TQ6: Sto F 4H **153**
OVER STRATTON **2D 167**
OVERTON **7C 24**
Overton Cl. DT7: Lym R 3K **91**
Overton Gdns. PL3: Plym 6A **136**
Owen Dr. PL7: Plymp 4K **137**
Oxenham Grn. TQ2: Torq 7K **111**
Oxenpark Ga. EX6: Bridf 1F **63**
Oxford Av. PL3: Plym 6K **135**
Oxford Cl. EX8: Exmth 1G **77**
Oxford Ct. TQ2: Torq 4B **112**
Oxford Gdns. PL3: Plym 6K **135**
Oxford Gro. EX34: Ilfra 2H **11**
Oxford La. TQ5: Brixh 4C **122**
Oxford Pk. EX34: Ilfra 3H **11**
Oxford Pl. PL1: Plym 3D **8** (2J **141**)
Oxford Rd. EX4: Exe 2G **7** (5G **65**)
Oxford St. EX2: Exe 7B **6** (1D **70**)
PL1: Plym 3C **8** (2J **141**)
TQ6: Dartm 2B **124** (6F **125**)
Oxford Ter. EX17: Cred 6J **39**
PL1: Plym 3C **8**
Ox Hill La. EX24: Colyt 6B **88**
Oxlea Cl. TQ1: Torq 2G **117**
Oxlea Rd. TQ1: Torq 2G **117**
Oxmans La. EX39: N'ham 5F **21**
Oyster Bend TQ4: Good 5J **119**
Oystercatcher Ct. TQ14: Shal 6F **107**
Oyster Cl. TQ4: Good 5J **119**
Ozone Ter. DT7: Lym R 6J **91**

P

Packhall La. TQ5: Brixh 6C **122**
(not continuous)
Packhorse Cl. EX10: Sidf 2E **84**
Packington St. PL2: Plym 7F **135**
Pack O'Cards Inn Mus. **6B 12**
Packs Cl. TQ9: H'ford 6B **100**

Padacre Rd.—Pearson Cl.

Padacre Rd. TQ2: Torq 1C 112
Padbrook Park Golf Course 6G 45
Paddock, The EX7: Daw 3G 97
Paddock Cl. EX12: Seat 5D 86
PL9: Plyms 7F 143
Paddock Dr. PL21: Ivy 5H 145
Paddocks, The EX14: Hon 7D 54
EX19: Dol 6H 31
TQ9: Tot 5F 103
TQ12: A'well 5E 108
Paddons Coombe TQ12: Kingst 2H 105
Paddons La. TQ14: Teignm 2G 107
Paddons Row *PL19: Tavi 3J 59*
(off Brook St.)
Padshall Pk. EX39: N'ham 1E 22
PADSON 1D 169
Pafford Av. TQ2: Torq 3D 112
Pafford Cl. TQ2: Torq 3C 112
Paige Adams Rd. TQ9: Tot 5D 102
Paiges Farm PL9: Down T 1C 148
Paiges La. EX31: Barn 4E 18
PAIGNTON 1H 119 (1A 176)
Paignton & Dartmouth Steam Railway Visitors Cen. 6G 125
Paignton Holiday Pk. TQ4: Blag 2A 118
Paignton Pier 1K 119
Paignton Rd. TQ4: Paig 3B 120
TQ9: Sto G 3B 120
Paignton Sailing Club *2K 119*
(off South Quay)
Paignton Station
Dartmouth Steam Railway 2H 119
Paignton Station (Rail) 1H 119
Paignton Zoo 3F 119
Pail Pk. EX33: Know 1K 15
Painters Ct. EX2: Exe 7D 6 (1E 70)
Paizen La. EX12: Beer 6A 86
Palace Av. TQ3: Paig 1H 119
Palace Cotts. *EX8: Exmth 5C 76*
(off Parade)
Palace Gdns. TQ13: Chud 2C 94
Palace Ga. EX1: Exe 4E 6 (7F 65)
Palace La. PL21: Fil 4K 145
Palace Mdw. TQ13: Chud 3C 94
Palace Pl. TQ3: Paig 1H 119
Palace St. PL1: Plym 5E 8 (3K 141)
Palace Theatre
Paignton 1H 119
Palatine Cl. TQ1: Torq 1D 116
Pale Ga. Cl. EX14: Hon 2G 55
Palermo TQ1: Torq 2F 117
Palermo Rd. TQ1: Torq 6E 112
Palk Cl. TQ14: Shal 6F 107
Palk Pl. *TQ1: Torq 4D 112*
(off Teignmouth Rd.)
Palk St. TQ2: Torq 2D 116
Palm Cl. EX8: Exmth 1F 77
Palm Ct. EX7: Daw W 7D 96
Palm Cross PL21: Modb 6G 147
Palmer Ct. EX9: Bud S 6C 82
Palmer M. *EX9: Bud S 7C 82*
(off Victoria Pl.)
Palmers Cl. EX33: Brau 5J 15
Palmers Ct. EX38: Gt T 2D 30
Palmer's La. EX5: Mar G 5K 69
Palmerston Dr. EX4: Exe 5B 64
Palmerston Pk. EX16: Tiv 6B 40
Palmerston St. PL1: Plym 2A 8 (1G 141)
Palm Rd. TQ2: Torq 1C 116
Palms, The TQ1: Torq 2F 117
Palstone La. TQ10: S Bre 1C 100
Palstone Lodges TQ10: S Bre 2D 100
Pamela Rd. EX1: Heav 5J 65
Pancras Sq. EX4: Exe 4D 6
PANCRASWEEK 3A 162
Pankhurst Cl. EX8: L'ham 5G 77
Panney, The EX4: Exe 5K 65
Pannier Market *4J 59*
(off Market Rd.)
Pannier Mkt. EX31: Barn 4E 18
EX38: Gt T 2C 30
Pannier M. *EX39: Bide 4F 23*
(off Silver St.)
Pannier St. EX17: Cred 6H 39
Panorama *TQ2: Torq 4A 116*
(off Livermead Hill)
Paper Makers La. PL21: Ivy 3J 145
Parade EX8: Exmth 5C 76
PL1: Plym 6F 9 (3K 141)
TQ13: Chud 2C 94
Parade, The PL19: Mil A 2B 58
Parade Bus. Pk. PL19: Tavi 5J 59
Parade Ope PL1: Plym 6F 9
Parade Rd. PL5: Plym 7F 131
Parade Ter. *EX34: Ilfra 2J 11*
(off Capstone Rd.)
Paradise Glen TQ14: Teignm 3H 107
Paradise Lawn EX36: S Mol 6D 26
Paradise Pl. PL1: Dev 2F 141
TQ5: Brixh 3E 122
Paradise Rd. PL1: Dev 2E 140
TQ14: Teignm 3H 107
Paradise Wlk. TQ4: Good 3J 119
Paragon *EX34: Ilfra 2H 11*
(off Granville Rd.)
Paramore Way EX36: S Mol 6C 26
Parely Hill TQ13: Chag 2G 71
Paris Rd. TQ3: Pres 6J 115
Paris St. EX1: Exe 3F 7 (6F 65)
Park, The PL8: Brixt 2H 149
Park & Ride
Barnstaple 7F 19
Brixham 3K 121
Coypool 5H 137
Dartmouth 7C 124
Digby 2C 72
George Junction 4D 132
Honiton Road 6D 66
Ivybridge 3K 145
Matford 6G 71
Milehouse 6H 135
Salcombe 3B 158
Sowton 1D 72
Park Av. EX31: Barn 5B 18
EX39: Bide 2F 23
EX39: West H 5B 20
PL1: Dev 1D 140
PL9: Plyms 5E 142
TQ5: Brixh 5D 122
Park Cl. EX5: Silv 2H 51
EX5: Wood 6C 78
EX16: Tiv 3D 40
EX22: Hols 1C 34
EX31: Frem 6F 17
PL7: Plymp 4J 137
PL21: Ivy 4G 145
Park Ct. EX14: Hon 5C 54
EX34: Ilfra 4H 11
TQ5: Brixh 3G 123
Park Cres. EX34: Com M 7C 12
PL9: Plyms 5D 142
Parkelands TQ13: Bov T 4B 92
Parker Cl. PL7: Plymp 6J 137
Parker Rd. PL2: Plym 5G 135
TQ7: Bigb S 3B 154
Parkers Cl. TQ9: Tot 7F 103
Parkers Cross La. EX1: Pin 2E 66
Parkers Hollow EX31: Roun 6A 18
Parker's Rd. EX6: Star 2D 96
Parkers Way TQ9: Tot 7F 103
Parkes Rd. EX38: Gt T 2D 30
PARKFIELD 3B 168
Parkfield 7J 115
Parkfield TQ7: Thur 6B 154
Parkfield Cl. TQ3: Marl 3D 114
TQ9: Tot 6H 103
Parkfield Dr. PL6: Plym 1G 137
Parkfield Rd. EX3: Top 5B 74
TQ1: Torq 6B 112
Parkfield Ter. EX12: Brans 6H 85
Parkfield Wlk. TQ7: Thur 6B 154
Parkfield Way EX3: Top 5B 74
Park Five Bus. Cen. EX2: Sow 1D 72
Park Gdns. EX35: Lynt 2G 13
Park Hall TQ1: Torq 3E 116
PARKHAM 1B 162
PARKHAM ASH 1B 162
Parkham Glade TQ5: Brixh 4E 122
Parkham La. TQ5: Brixh 4E 122
Parkham Rd. TQ5: Brixh 4E 122
Parkham Towers *TQ5: Brixh 4E 122*
(off Wren Hill)
Parkhayes EX5: Wood S 1C 78
Park Hill EX16: Tiv 3C 40
TQ12: Ipp 6K 101
TQ14: Teignm 5H 107
Park Hill Rd. EX34: Ilfra 3H 11
Parkhill Rd. TQ1: Torq 3D 116
Park Hills Ind. Units
EX34: Com M 7B 12
Park Ho. PL4: Plym 2H 9 (1A 142)
Parkhouse Rd. EX2: Exe 2C 70
Parkhurst Rd. TQ1: Torq 6B 112
Parkland Caravan & Camping Site
TQ7: Kingsb 1E 156
Parkland Caravan Pk.
TQ4: Good 6G 119
Parkland Dr. EX2: Won 2B 72
Parklands EX12: Seat 5E 86
EX15: Hemy 2F 47
EX20: Oke 5B 48
EX31: Roun 6B 18
EX36: S Mol 7B 26
TQ9: Tot 5E 102
Parklands Cl. EX36: S Mol 7B 26
Parklands Leisure Cen. 4C 48
Parklands Way TQ13: Bov T 7B 92
Park La. EX4: Pin 1C 66
EX8: Exmth 4C 76
EX9: Bud S 6B 82
EX9: Ott'n 7H 83
EX13: Whitf 5A 90
EX17: Morc 1B 38
EX32: Barn 6F 19
Park La. EX34: Com M 6B 12
EX39: Bide 2F 23
PL7: Plymp 1C 138
PL9: Plyms 5D 142
PL20: Bere A 1C 128
TQ1: Torq 3D 116
TQ9: Blacka 3B 152
Park La. Steps *TQ1: Torq 3E 116*
(off Park La.)
Park Mdw. Cl. EX17: Lap 1K 37
Park M. TQ5: Brixh 3G 123
Park Mill La. EX18: Chul 6C 32
Park Pl. EX1: Heav 6J 65
EX2: Exe 6H 7 (7G 65)
EX19: Wink 2C 36
Park Pl. La. PL3: Plym 7F 135
Park Ri. EX7: Daw 5G 97
TQ8: Salc 4B 158
Park Rd. EX1: Heav 2K 7 (5H 65)
EX5: Silv 2H 51
EX7: Daw 4G 97
EX8: Exmth 4C 76
EX12: Beer 7A 86
EX16: Tiv 3D 40
EX17: Cred 7J 39
EX17: Lap 1K 37
EX20: Hath 1H 35
PL3: Plym 5B 136
PL11: Torp 1A 140
PL16: Lift 7B 56
TQ1: Torq 4D 112
TQ9: Darti 1D 102
TQ12: Kingsk 7J 109
Park Row EX20: Oke 3B 48
Parks Dr. PL9: Spri 7H 143
Parkside PL2: Plym 6D 134
PL21: Ivy 4J 145
TQ8: Salc 3C 158
Parkside Ct. EX2: Exe 5F 7
Parkside Cres. EX1: W Cly 1E 66
Parkside Dr. EX8: Exmth 2F 77
Parkside Rd. EX1: W Cly 1E 66
TQ4: Paig 1J 119
Parkside Vs. *TQ1: Torq 6E 112*
(off Palermo Rd.)
Parks La. EX9: Bud S 7D 82
Parkstone La. PL7: Plymp 3C 138
Park St. EX15: Will 3C 44
EX16: Tiv 4D 40
EX17: Cred 6J 39
EX35: Lynt 2G 13
PL3: Plym 7F 135
PL21: Ivy 5G 145
Park St. M. PL21: Ivy 5G 145
Park St. Ope PL3: Plym 7F 135
Park Ter. EX16: Tiv 3D 40
EX32: Barn 5F 19
PL4: Plym 4G 9
PL21: Ivy 5G 145
(off Park St.)
Park Vw. EX4: Exe 7A 6 (1D 70)
EX6: Kenton 6K 95
EX8: Lymp 6J 75
EX19: Bea 3H 31
EX24: Colyt 6C 88
EX32: Barn 3E 18
(off Pilton C'way.)
PL4: Plym 4K 9
PL16: Lift 6D 56
TQ12: New A 4J 109
Park Vw. Caravan Site
EX32: Barn 3F 19
Park Vw. Cl. EX34: Com M 7C 12
Park Vw. Rd. EX32: Barn 3F 19
Park Vw. Ter. EX20: Oke 5C 48
EX39: West H 5B 20
Park Vw. Way EX32: Barn 3F 19
Park Vs. EX32: Bish T 7B 24
Park Way EX8: Exmth 4E 76
(not continuous)
Parkway EX2: Exe 2C 70
EX5: Wood 6C 78
EX34: Ilfra 5H 11
Parkway, The PL5: Plym 1C 134
PL6: Plym 3A 136
Parkway Ct. PL6: Plym 4F 137
Parkway Ind. Est., The
PL6: Plym 4F 137
Parkway M. TQ13: Chud 2C 94
Parkway Rd. TQ13: Chud 3C 94
Parkwood Cl. PL6: Robo 1C 132
Parkwood Ct. PL19: Tavi 3K 59
Park Wood Ri. PL16: Lift 7A 56
Parkwood Rd. PL19: Tavi 3J 59
Parliament Ct. *EX34: Ilfra 2J 11*
(off Hierns La.)
Parliament St. EX4: Exe 4D 6 (6E 64)
EX17: Cred 6H 39
Parnell Cl. PL6: Plym 3B 136
PARRACOMBE 2C 161
Parr Cl. EX1: Exe 2H 7 (5G 65)
Parr La. PL4: Plym 6J 9 (3A 142)
Parrots Cl. *TQ7: Malb 6G 155*
(off Higher Town)
Parr's La. TQ13: Chud 1B 94
Parr St. EX1: Exe 2H 7 (5G 65)
PL4: Plym 6J 9 (3A 142)
Parrys Farm Cl. EX8: Exmth 2E 76
Parsonage Ct. PL16: Lift 6B 56
Parsonage La. EX5: Silv 1H 51
EX14: Gitt 7A 54
EX14: Hon 4G 55
EX36: S Mol 5C 26
PL21: Ugb 6E 146
Parsonage Rd. PL8: New F 5J 149
Parsonage St. EX5: Bradn 1D 52
Parsonage Way EX5: Wood 5C 78
PL4: Plym 6H 9 (3A 142)
Parson Cl. EX8: Exmth 2E 76
Parsons Cl. EX10: New P 6F 81
EX15: Kent 6A 46
EX22: Hols 2C 34
PL9: Plyms 7H 143
Parsons La. EX5: Rock 4C 68
EX12: Brans 6J 85
Parsons Mdw. EX15: Kent 6A 46
Parsons Path *EX3: Top 5B 74*
(off Monmouth Av.)
Parson St. TQ14: Teignm 4H 107
Parthia Pl. EX8: Exmth 3G 77
Partridge Rd. EX8: Exmth 1E 76
Partwayes PL19: Lam 6C 58
Pasley St. PL2: Plym 7D 134
Pasley St. E. PL2: Plym 7E 134
Passaford La. EX10: N'town 2K 83
EX20: Hath 3G 35
Passage Rd. PL8: Noss M 6G 149
Passmore Rd. EX5: Bradn 2B 52
PATCHACOTT 1C 169
Patches Rd. EX16: Tiv 3B 40
PATCHOLE 2C 161
Paternoster La. TQ12: Ipp 6G 101
Paternoster Row EX11: Ott M 3C 80
EX31: Barn 4E 18
(off High St.)
Path, The EX39: Apple 2H 21
Pathdown La. EX33: Croy 3D 14
(not continuous)
PATHE 1D 167
Pathfield EX38: Gt T 2E 30
Pathfield Cl. EX31: Roun 6K 17
Pathfield Lawn EX31: Barn 3D 18
Pathfields EX15: Uff 6G 43
EX16: Tiv 5C 40
(off King St.)
EX33: Croy 1C 14
TQ9: Tot 6F 103
Pathfields Cl. TQ9: Tot 6F 103
PATHFINDER VILLAGE 1C 171
Pathwhorlands EX10: Sidm 4B 84
Patna Pl. PL1: Plym 2C 8 (1H 141)
Paton Watson Quadrate PL1: Plym 7F 9
Pato Point PL11: Wilc 5A 134
Patricia Cl. EX4: Exe 2F 65
Patterdale Cl. PL6: Plym 7E 132
Patterdale Wlk. PL6: Plym 7E 132
Patteson Dr. EX11: Ott M 3E 80
Pattinson Cl. PL6: Plym 1F 137
Pattinson Ct. PL6: Plym 1F 137
Pattinson Dr. PL6: Plym 1F 137
Paullet EX16: Sam P 2A 42
Paul St. EX4: Exe 4D 6 (6E 64)
Pauntley Gdns. EX10: Sidm 7A 84
Paviland Grange PL1: Plym 1F 141
Pavilion, The TQ2: Torq 3D 116
Pavilion Pl. EX2: Exe 5F 7 (7F 65)
Pavilions Cl. TQ5: Brixh 3D 122
Pavor Rd. TQ2: Torq 3D 112
Paws Rd. EX37: High B 3A 32
Paxford Ho. Sq. EX11: Ott M 3C 80
PAYHEMBURY 3A 166
Paynes Ct. EX4: Whip 4A 66
Paynsford M. TQ12: New A 7E 104
Paynsford Rd. TQ12: New A 7E 104
Paynter Wlk. PL7: Plymp 4E 138
PAYTON 1B 166
Peacock Av. PL11: Torp 1A 140
Peacock Cl. PL7: Plymp 2C 138
Peacock La. PL4: Plym 5F 9
Peacock Pl. EX6: Star 1E 96
Peadhill La. EX16: Chev 1H 41
Peak Hill Rd. EX10: Sidm 7A 84
Peak Tor Av. TQ1: Torq 4E 116
Pear Dr. EX15: Will 4D 44
Peard Rd. EX16: Tiv 5G 41
Peards Down Cl. EX32: Barn 5J 19
Pearmain Cl. EX15: Will 4D 44
Pearn Cotts. PL3: Plym 5A 136
Pearn Gdns. PL3: Plym 4B 136
Pearn Ridge PL3: Plym 4B 136
Pearn Rd. PL3: Plym 4B 136
Pearse Cl. EX20: Hath 2G 35
Pearson Av. PL4: Plym 7A 136
Pearson Cl. EX22: Hols 1C 34

Pearson Rd.—Plover Ri.

Pearson Rd. PL4: Plym 7A 136
Pear Tree Cl. EX6: Kenton 6J 95
Pear Tree Way EX32: L'key 2C 24
Peaseditch TQ5: Brixh 5F 123
Peasland Rd. TQ2: Torq 1C 112
Peaslands Rd. EX10: Sidm 5B 84
PEASMARSH 2D 167
Peazen Flats EX12: Beer 6A 86
Pebble Cl. EX39: West H 5C 20
Pebble Ct. TQ4: Good 3H 119
Pebble La. EX9: Bud S 7C 82
Pebbleridge Rd. EX39: West H 5C 20
Pecorama 7A 86
Pedlerspool La. EX17: Cred 4J 39
Peek La. PL21: Bitta 3B 146
Peeks Av. PL9: Plyms 5G 143
Peel Row EX4: Whip 4B 66
Peel St. PL1: Plym 3F 141
Peel St. Flats PL1: Plym 2F 141
Peep La. EX4: Exe 3B 6 (6D 64)
EX17: Cred 6J 39
Pegasus Ct. EX1: Heav 6J 65
TQ3: Paig 6H 115
Pegwell La. TQ14: Shal 7D 106
Pelican Cl. EX39: West H 6A 20
Pellew Arc. *TQ14: Teignm* *5H 107*
(off Teign St.)
Pellew Ho. *TQ14: Teignm* *5H 107*
(off Teign St.)
Pellew Pl. PL2: Dev 7E 134
Pellew Way TQ14: Teignm 2G 107
Pellinore Rd. EX4: Whip 3K 65
Pembrey Wlk. PL5: Plym 6D 130
(not continuous)
Pembroke La. PL1: Dev 3D 140
Pembroke Pk. TQ3: Marl 3E 114
Pembroke Rd. TQ1: Torq 1D 116
TQ3: Paig 7E 114
Pembroke St. PL1: Dev 3D 140
(not continuous)
Pemros Rd. PL5: Plym 1A 134
Pencarwick Ho. EX8: Exmth 7C 76
Pencorse Rd. TQ2: Torq 5B 112
Pencreber Rd. PL20: Horr 2E 126
Pencross Vw. EX15: Hemy 1G 47
Pendeen Cl. PL6: Plym 4A 132
Pendeen Ct. EX8: Exmth 5F 77
Pendeen Cres. PL6: Plym 4A 132
Pendeen Pk. TQ7: Chil 6G 159
Pendennis Cl. PL3: Plym 3A 136
Pendennis Rd. TQ2: Torq 5B 112
Pendragon Rd. EX4: Whip 2J 65
Penfield Gdns. EX7: Daw 4G 97
Pengelly Way TQ2: Torq 2A 112
Pengilly Way EX39: Hart 3J 27
Penhale Dr. EX22: Hols 1B 34
Penhayes Cl. EX6: Kenton 6J 95
Penhayes Rd. EX6: Kenton 6J 95
PENHILL 4G 17
Penhill Chalets TQ6: Sto F 3J 153
Penhill La. TQ5: Hill 6J 123
Peninsula Pk. EX2: Won 1B 72
Penitentiary Ct. EX2: Exe 6E 6 (7F 65)
Penlee EX9: Bud S 7C 82
Penlee Gdns. PL3: Plym 7F 135
Penlee Pl. PL4: Plym 7A 136
Penlee Rd. PL3: Plym 7F 135
Penlee Way PL3: Plym 1A 8 (7F 135)
Penleonard Cl. EX2: Exe 6J 7 (7H 65)
PENN 1D 173
Pennant Ho. *EX8: Exmth* *6A 76*
(off Shelly Rd.)
Pennant Way PL21: L Mill 5C 144
Penn Ct. TQ5: Brixh 5F 123
Pennine Dr. TQ4: Coll M 3D 118
Pennington Cl. EX17: Cop 6C 38
PENNINN 3G 109
Penn Inn Cl. TQ12: New A 2H 109
Penn La. TQ5: Brixh 5E 122
Penn Mdws. TQ5: Brixh 5F 123
Penn Mdws. Cl. TQ5: Brixh 5F 123
PENNSYLVANIA 3G 65 (1D 171)
Pennsylvania Cl. EX4: Exe 4G 65
Pennsylvania Ct. EX4: Exe 4G 65
Pennsylvania Cres. EX4: Exe 4F 65
Pennsylvania Pk. EX4: Exe 3G 65
Pennsylvania Rd. EX4: Exe . . . 1F 7 (1F 65)
TQ1: Torq 1D 116
PENNTORR 1A 140
Pennyacre Rd. TQ14: Teignm 3J 107
Penny Cl. EX6: Exmin 2C 74
PENNYCOMEQUICK 1C 8 (1H 141)
Pennycomequick Hill
PL3: Plym 1C 8 (1H 141)
Pennycomequick Vs. PL4: Plym 1C 8
PENNYCROSS 3J 135 (2A 174)
Pennycross Cl. PL2: Plym 3J 135
Pennycross Pk. Rd. PL2: Plym 4H 135
Penny Hill EX33: Croy 1C 14
PENNYMOOR 2C 165
Penny Pk. EX16: Tiv 4B 40
Penny Plot DT7: Lym R 4H 91
Penny's Hill TQ1: Torq 6B 112
Penny's La. PL9: Elb 6K 143
Pennys Terrace *EX13: Axmin* *4H 89*
(off Musbury Rd.)
Pennywell Farm & Wildlife Cen.
. . . . . 1D 175
Penpethy Cl. TQ5: Brixh 4D 122
Penpethy Ct. TQ5: Brixh 4D 122
Penpethy Rd. TQ5: Brixh 3D 122
Penpont Ct. EX39: Bide 3E 22
PENQUIT . . . . . 7K 145 & 1K 147 (2C 175)
Penrhyn Pl. TQ14: Shal 6G 107
Penrith Cl. PL6: Plym 7E 132
Penrith Gdns. PL6: Plym 7E 132
Penrith Wlk. PL6: Plym 7E 132
Penrose Gdns. EX22: Hols 2C 34
Penrose Sq. *EX32: Barn* *5F 19*
(off Litchdon St.)
Penrose St. PL1: Plym 2C 8 (2H 141)
Penrose St. W. PL1: Plym 3C 8
Penrose Ter. EX22: Hols 2C 34
Penrose Vs. PL4: Plym 7A 136
Penshurst Rd. TQ12: New A 3E 108
PENSILVA 3A 168
Pensilva Pk. TQ5: Brixh 5E 122
Pens La. EX15: Hemy 3G 47
PENSTONE 3B 164
Pentamar St. PL2: Dev 7D 134
Pentgrove Ct. EX8: Exmth 5F 77
Pentice La. EX34: Com M 5C 12
Pentillie Cl. PL20: Bere A 3C 128
Pentillie Cres. PL4: Plym 7J 135
Pentillie Rd. PL4: Plym 7K 135
PL20: Bere A 3C 128
Pentillie Vw. PL20: Bere A 2C 128
Pentland Cl. PL6: Plym 3A 132
Penton Cl. EX17: Cred 5J 39
Penton La. EX17: Cred 6J 39
Penton Ri. EX17: Cred 5J 39
Pentridge Av. TQ2: Torq 4J 115
Pentyre Ter. PL4: Plym 2J 9 (1A 142)
Penwill Way TQ4: Good, Paig 3F 119
Pen-y-Dre EX15: Cull 3H 45
Peoples Pk. Rd. EX17: Cred 5G 39
Pepper La. PL9: Elb 7K 143
Peppermint Pk. Holiday Pk.
EX7: Daw W 7D 96
Pepper St. PL19: Tavi 3J 59
Peppery La. TQ14: Shal 6F 107
Pepys Pl. PL5: Plym 2J 135
Perceval Rd. EX4: Whip 3K 65
Percy Rd. EX2: Exe 2E 70
Percy St. PL5: Plym 2C 134
Percy Ter. PL4: Plym 7B 136
Peregrine Cl. TQ2: Torq 2K 111
Perinville Cl. TQ1: Torq 7G 113
Perinville Rd. TQ1: Torq 6F 113
Periwinkle Dr. EX31: Roun 6A 18
PL7: Plymp 4F 139
Perranporth Cl. PL5: Plym 7D 130
Perriam's Pl. EX9: Bud S 6C 82
Perridge Cl. EX2: Exe 2B 70
Perriman's Row EX8: Exmth 5C 76
Perrin Way EX4: Pin 3C 66
Perros Cl. TQ14: Teignm 3F 107
Perry Cl. PL19: Tavi 3H 59
Perry Hill EX17: Cher F 4H 39
Perry La. TQ12: New A . . . 7K 93 & 5A 104
Perryman Cl. PL7: Plymp 2B 138
Perry Rd. EX4: Exe 4E 64
Perrys Gdns. EX11: W Hill 4H 79
PERRY STREET 3D 167
Perth Cl. EX4: Exe 2H 65
Peryam Cres. EX2: Won 1K 71
Peryn Rd. PL19: Tavi 4G 59
Peterborough Rd. EX4: Exe 5B 64
Peterclose Rd. EX16: Tiv 5F 41
Peter's Cl. PL9: Elb 5J 143
Peters Cres. TQ3: Marl 3D 114
Petersfield Cl. PL3: Plym 5C 136
PETERS MARLAND 2C 163
Peters Pk. Cl. PL5: Plym 2D 134
Peter's Pk. La. PL5: Plym 1C 134
Peter St. EX5: Bradn 1C 52
PETER TAVY 3D 169
Pethertons EX16: Hal 6C 42
PETHERWIN GATE 2A 168
Pethick Cl. PL6: Plym 4J 131
Pethill Cl. PL6: Plym 1G 137
PETHYBRIDGE 6G 63
Petitor M. TQ1: Torq 4D 112
Petitor Rd. TQ1: Torq 4D 112
Petitwell La. TQ1: Torq 4D 112
Petrel Cl. TQ2: Torq 2J 111
Petroc Dr. TQ12: New A 7F 105
PETROCKSTOWE 3D 163
Petticoat La. EX13: Axmin 1E 88
PETTON 1A 166
PEVERELL 4J 135
Peverell Pk. Rd. PL3: Plym 4J 135
Peverell Ter. PL3: Plym 6J 135
Pew Tor Cl. PL20: Yelv 5F 127
Phear Av. EX8: Exmth 5D 76
Phear Park 4D 76
Phelps Rd. PL1: Dev 2D 140
PHILHAM 1A 162
Philip Av. EX31: Barn 7C 18
Philip Cl. PL9: Plyms 6H 143
Philip Gdns. PL9: Plyms 6G 143
Philip Ho. EX2: Sow 6D 66
Philip Rd. EX4: Exe 4J 65
Philips La. EX33: Brau 5J 15
Phillimore St. PL2: Plym 7E 134
Phillipps Av. EX8: Exmth 3D 76
Phillips Ct. EX13: Axmin 4H 89
Phillips Sq. EX14: Hon 3E 54
Philpott La. PL19: Tavi 7H 59
Phoenix Cl. PL20: Horr 2E 126
Phoenix La. EX16: Tiv 5D 40
Phoenix Pl. TQ7: W Alv 5D 156
Phoenix St. PL1: Plym 5A 8 (3G 141)
Piazza Terracina EX2: Exe 7E 6
PIBSBURY 1D 167
Piccadilly La. *EX11: Ott M* *4C 80*
(off Mill St.)
Picket Head Hill TQ14: Shal 7G 107
Picklecombe Dr. PL5: Plym 6K 131
Pick Pie Dr. PL6: Plym 2F 133
PICKWELL 2A 160
Pickwick Arc. EX4: Exe 5D 6
PICT'S HILL 1D 167
Pidgeon's La. EX13: Ray H 1B 90
Pidgley Rd. EX7: Daw 1J 97
Piece Hill EX6: Ted M 7F 49
Pier Head EX8: Exmth 6A 76
Piermont Pl. EX7: Daw 4H 97
Pier St. PL1: Plym 7B 8 (4H 141)
Piggy La. EX39: N'ham 5E 20
(not continuous)
Pig La. EX13: Axmin 3H 89
Pike Rd. PL3: Plym 6E 136
Pikes Mead EX20: Oke 4B 48
Pilgrim Cl. PL2: Plym 5G 135
Pilgrim Dr. PL20: Bere A 2C 128
Pilgrim Hall PL4: Plym 3F 9
Pilgrim Ho. EX4: Exe 4J 65
Pilland Way EX31: Barn 3C 18
Pillar Av. TQ5: Brixh 3D 122
Pillar Cl. TQ5: Brixh 3D 122
Pillar Cres. TQ5: Brixh 3D 122
Pillar Wlk. PL6: Plym 4K 131
PILLATON 1A 174
Pill Gdns. EX33: Brau 6J 15
Pill La.
EX32: Barn, Bish T . . . 4A 24 & 7F 19
Pill Lawn EX32: Barn 7F 19
Pillman Dr. EX39: Hart 3K 27
Pillory Hill PL8: Noss M 6H 149
Pill Rd. EX39: Bide 3F 23
Pilmuir Av. TQ2: Torq 1A 116
Pilot Wharf *EX8: Exmth* *6A 76*
(off Pier Head)
PILSDON 1D 173
PILTON 2D 18
Pilton C'way. EX32: Barn 3E 18
Pilton La. EX1: Pin 4C 66
Pilton Lawn EX31: Barn 3E 18
Pilton Quay EX31: Barn 3E 18
Pilton St. EX31: Barn 2E 18
Pimlico TQ1: Torq 1D 116
Pimm Rd. TQ3: Paig 7E 114
Pinaster Cl. EX14: Hon 4H 55
Pinbridge Ct. *EX1: Pin* *4D 66*
(off Old Pinn La.)
Pinbridge M. EX4: Pin 3C 66
Pinbrook Ind. Est. EX4: Pin 3C 66
Pinbrook M. EX4: Pin 2B 66
Pinbrook Rd. EX4: Pin 3C 66
Pinbrook Units EX4: Pin 3C 66
Pinces Cotts. EX2: Exe 2D 70
Pinces Gdns. EX2: Exe 2D 70
Pinces Rd. EX2: Exe 2D 70
Pinder Ct. PL19: Tavi 4H 59
Pine Av. EX4: Exe 5C 64
Pine Cl. EX16: Tiv 4B 40
EX34: Ilfra 4K 11
TQ5: Brixh 6D 122
TQ14: Teignm 2K 107
Pine Cones EX34: Woolc 7C 10
Pine Ct. TQ1: Torq 1F 117
Pinefields Cl. EX11: W Hill 5J 79
Pine Gdns. EX14: Hon 3G 55
Pine Gro. EX14: Hon 3G 55
Pinehurst Way PL21: Ivy 3E 144
Pine Pk. Rd. EX14: Hon 4G 55
Pine Ridge DT7: Lym R 3K 91
Pineridge Cl. EX4: Exe 1C 70
Pines, The EX4: Exe 5C 64
EX14: Hon 4G 55
Pines Cl. EX39: Hart 3J 27
Pines Rd. EX8: Exmth 1E 76
TQ3: Paig 6E 114
Pine Tree Cl. EX7: Daw W 7E 96
Pine Vw. Av. TQ1: Torq 7E 112
Pine Vw. Cl. EX8: Exmth 2H 77
Pine Vw. Gdns. TQ1: Torq 7E 112
Pine Vw. Rd. TQ1: Torq 7E 112
Pine Wlk. DT7: Lym R 6J 91
Pinewood Cl. EX7: Daw 2K 97
PL7: Plymp 3C 138
Pinewood Dr. PL6: Plym 3F 133
Pinewood Rd. TQ12: New A 2H 109
PINHOE 2D 66 (1D 171)
Pinhoe Rd.
EX4: Exe, Pin, Whip 1K 7 (5H 65)
Pinhoe Station (Rail) 3D 66
Pinhoe Trad. Est. EX4: Pin 3C 66
Pink Ho. Cnr. EX8: Lymp 3J 75
Pin La. PL1: Plym 6F 9 (3K 141)
Pinnacle Quay *PL4: Plym* *4H 9*
(off Harbour Av.)
Pinncourt La. EX1: Pin 2E 66
Pinn Ct. Rd. EX1: Pin 2E 66
Pinnex Moor Rd. EX16: Tiv 2D 40
Pinn Hill EX1: Pin 2E 66
Pinn La. EX1: Pin 3D 66
Pinn Valley Rd. EX1: Pin 3E 66
Pinslow Cross PL15: St G 7B 34
Pins Pk. EX22: Hols 1B 34
Pinwood La. EX4: Whip 2A 66
(not continuous)
Pinwood Mdw. Dr. EX4: Whip 2A 66
Pioneer Cotts. *EX12: Beer* *7B 86*
(off New Cut)
Pioneer Ter. TQ11: B'leigh 4B 98
Pipehouse La. TQ13: Chud K 6B 94
PIPERS POOL 2A 168
Piper St. PL6: Plym 6C 132
PIPPACOTT 3B 160
Pippin Cl. EX1: Heav 6B 66
Pippins, The PL21: Ivy 4E 144
Pippins Ct. EX12: Beer 7B 86
Pippins Fld. EX15: Uff 7G 43
Pippins M. *TQ13: Ashb* *3J 99*
(off Eastern Rd.)
Piscombe La. EX9: Ott'n 6J 83
Pissleton La. EX17: Morc 4A 38
Pitcairn Cres. TQ2: Torq 2A 112
Pitfield Cl. EX15: Will 5D 44
Pitham La. EX11: Ott M 1D 80
Pit Hill EX34: Berry 2A 12
Pitley Rd. TQ13: Ashb 3K 99
Pitman's La. PL21: Corn 7H 129
PITMINSTER 2C 167
PITNEY 1D 167
PITSFORD HILL 1B 166
Pitson La. EX10: N'town 7J 81
Pitt Av. EX39: Apple 3H 21
Pitt Ct. EX17: Nym R 2F 37
EX39: Apple 3H 21
TQ7: Lodd 2H 151
Pitt Cres. TQ9: Berr P 4K 103
Pitt Hill EX6: Kenton 6H 95
EX17: Cred 6F 39
EX21: Sheb 6H 29
EX39: Apple 4G 21
Pitt Hill Rd. TQ12: New A 6C 104
Pitt La. EX17: Bow 4F 37
EX39: Bide 3F 23
Pitt Pk. EX5: Cranb 3C 68
Pitts Ct. EX2: Exe 7F 7 (1G 71)
Pixie Dell EX33: Brau 3G 15
Pixie La. EX33: Brau 3G 15
Pixon La. PL19: Tavi 5H 59
Pixon Trad. Cen. PL19: Tavi 5H 59
Place La. TQ13: Ashb 2J 99
PLAINMOOR 6D 112
Plainmoor 6D 112
Plainmoor Rd. TQ1: Torq 6D 112
Plains, The TQ9: Tot 6F 103
Plaistow Cl. PL5: Plym 1D 134
Plaistow Cres. PL5: Plym 1D 134
Plantagenet Dr. EX15: Cull 1H 45
Plantagenet Wlk. *EX2: Sow* *1C 72*
(off Heraldry Way)
Plantation Cl. TQ12: New A 3J 109
Plantation Ter. EX7: Daw 4G 97
Plantation Way TQ2: Torq 3J 111
TQ9: Tot 5B 102
Plant World Gdns. 1A 176
Plassey Cl. EX4: Exe 2G 65
Plat, The TQ6: Strete 6G 153
Platt Cl. TQ8: Salc 4A 158
Platway La. TQ14: Shal 6F 107
Play Hut, The *2H 11*
(off Bath Pl.)
Playmoor Dr. EX1: Pin 3E 66
Pleasant Ter. TQ3: Paig 1G 119
Pleasaunce, The PL8: New F 5J 149
Pleasure Hill Cl. PL9: Plyms 4E 142
Plintona Vw. PL7: Plymp 2B 138
Ploudal Rd. EX15: Cull 5G 45
Plough Arts Centre, The *2C 30*
(off Fore St.)
Ploughman Way PL8: Torr 3C 150
Plover Ri. PL21: Ivy 4F 145

Plume of Feathers Cl.—Princes St.

Plume of Feathers Cl.
EX11: Ott M 3D 80
Plume of Feathers Inn, The
PL20: Prin 7D 60
Plumer Rd. PL6: Plym 1A 136
Plumtree Dr. EX2: Won 1A 72
Plumtree La. EX5: Whim 7H 53
Plum Way EX15: Will 4D 44
PLUSHABRIDGE 3B 168
Plymbridge Gdns. PL7: Plymp 4K 137
Plymbridge La. PL6: Plym 6C 132
Plym Bridge Riverside & Woodland Walks 1H 137
Plymbridge Rd. PL6: Plym 2D 136 (Freshford Wlk.)
PL6: Plym 4D 132 (Glenholt Rd.)
PL7: Plymp 1H 137
Plym Cl. TQ2: Torq 6H 111
Plym Cres. PL19: Tavi 4K 59
PLYMOUTH 4F 9 (2A 174)
Plymouth Albion RFC 2E 140
Plymouth & West Devon Record Office 6J 9
Plymouth Argyle FC 6H 135
Plymouth Arts Cen. 5F 9
Plymouth Athenaeum Theatre, The 5C 8 (3H 141)
Plymouth City Museum & Art Gallery 3F 9 (2K 141)
Plymouth Hill PL20: Prin 7C 60
Plymouth Intl. Bus. Pk.
PL6: Plym 7A 132
Plymouth Life Cen. 6H 135
Plymouth Pavilions 5B 8 (3H 141)
Plymouth RC Cathedral 3B 8 (2H 141)
Plymouth Rd. PL3: Plym 6F 137
PL6: Plym 5G 137
PL7: Plymp 5H 137
PL19: Tavi, Whitc 5H 59
PL20: Horr 2E 126
TQ7: Kingsb 1D 156
TQ9: Tot 5A 102
TQ10: S Bre 1B 100
TQ11: B'leigh, Lwr D 7B 98 (not continuous)
TQ13: Chud K 6B 94
Plymouth Rd. Ind. Est. PL19: Tavi 6J 59
Plymouth Ski & Snowboarding Cen. 4F 137
Plymouth Station (Rail) 1D 8 (1J 141)
Plymouth Swallows School of Gymnastics 6D 132
Plymouth Yacht Haven
PL4: Plym 2D 142
PLYMPTON 4B 138 (2B 174)
Plympton By-Pass PL7: Plymp 6H 137
Plympton Castle 5B 138
Plympton Hill PL7: Plymp 6C 138
PLYMPTON ST MAURICE 5C 138
Plympton Swimming Pool 4A 138
PLYMSTOCK 5F 143 (2B 174)
Plymstock Rd. PL9: Plyms 5D 142
Plymstock Sports Cen. 4G 143
Plym St. PL4: Plym 3G 9 (2K 141)
PLYMTREE 3A 166
Plymtree Dr. PL7: Plymp 4K 137
Plym Valley Mdws. PL6: Plym 3G 137
Plym Valley Railway 4H 137
Poachers Paddock EX34: Woolc 7C 10
Pocklington Ri. PL7: Plymp 4B 138
POCOMBE BRIDGE 2A 70
Pocombe Hill EX2: Exe 2A 70
Pode Dr. PL7: Plymp 5E 138
Point Cotts. PL9: Hooe 5C 142
Point Exe EX4: Exe 2A 6 (5D 64)
Point Ter. EX8: Exmth 6A 76
POLBATHIC 2A 174
Polehouse La. EX2: Ide 5B 70
Poles Hill EX31: Cher B 2D 18
Poleshill La. EX31: Cher B 1C 18
Polhearne La. TQ5: Brixh 5D 122
Polhearne Way TQ5: Brixh 5D 122
Policeman's Hill EX32: Bish T 7B 24 (off Village St.)
Pollard Cl. PL9: Hooe 7C 142
Pollards, The EX32: Barn 6H 19
Pollards Pl. EX39: Bide 3H 23
Pollyblank Rd. TQ12: New A 1E 108
Polruan Ter. PL1: Plym 3A 8 (2G 141)
Polsham Pk. TQ3: Paig 7H 115
POLSLOE BRIDGE 5K 65
Polsloe Bridge Station (Rail) 5K 65
POLSLOE PARK 2J 7 (5H 65)
POLSLOE PRIORY 1K 7 (4J 65)
Polsloe Rd. EX1: Exe 1J 7 (5H 65)
Polson Hill EX17: Morc 2B 38
Polston Pk. PL9: Spri 7H 143
POLTIMORE 1D 171
Poltimore Cl. EX36: S Mol 6D 26
Poltimore Lawn EX32: Barn 3G 19
Poltimore Rd. EX36: S Mol 6D 26
Poltimore Sq. EX4: Exe 2F 7 (5F 65)
Polwhele Rd. EX16: Tiv 5H 41
POLYPHANT 2A 168
Polywell EX39: Apple 2G 21
Polzeath Gdns. PL2: Plym 3J 135
Pomeroy Av. TQ5: Brixh 3C 122
Pomeroy Pl. TQ12: Live 4F 93
Pomeroy Rd. EX16: Tiv 3J 41
TQ12: New A 1E 108
Pomeroy Vs. TQ9: Tot 5F 103
POMPHLETT 4E 142
Pomphlett Cl. PL9: Plyms 4E 142 (not continuous)
Pomphlett Farm Ind. Est.
PL9: Plyms 3F 143
Pomphlett Gdns. PL9: Plyms 4E 142
Pomphlett Rd. PL9: Plyms 4E 142
Pond Hill EX16: Hal 6D 42
Ponsford La. EX15: Cull 3F 45
Ponsonby Rd. PL3: Plym 1A 8 (7G 135)
PONSWORTHY 3B 170
Pook La. TQ13: Ashb 3H 99
Pool Anthony Dr. EX16: Tiv 3J 41
POOLE 1B 166
Poole La. EX34: Woolc 5D 10
Poole Pk. Rd. PL5: Plym 3B 134
Poole's Ct. DT7: Lym R 5K 91
Pool Hill EX20: Bride 3H 57
Pool Pk. TQ10: S Bre 1C 100
Popes Cl. EX17: Cred 5H 39
Popes La. EX17: Lap 2J 37 (not continuous)
EX24: Colyf 1F 87
Popham Cl. EX16: Tiv 4F 41
Poplar Cl. EX2: Exe 2D 70
EX8: Exmth 1F 77
PL7: Plymp 4E 138
TQ5: Brixh 7B 122
TQ12: New A 4K 109
Poplar Dr. TQ7: Kingsb 4F 157
Poplar Mt. EX13: Axmin 3H 89
Poplar Row EX9: Bud S 7D 82
Poplars, The EX4: Pin 2D 66
TQ13: Chud K 5B 94
Poplars Dr. TQ3: Marl 4D 114
Poplars Wlk. EX5: Clyst M 3J 73 (off Hazelmead Rd.)
Poplar Ter. EX37: High B 3C 32
TQ12: Ipp 6H 101
Poplar Tree Dr. EX12: Seat 3E 86
Popplestone Pk. PL8: Brixt 2G 149
Poppy Cl. EX4: Exe 4A 64
EX15: Will 4E 44
Porchester Hgts. EX4: Exe 2G 7 (off Acland Rd.)
Porlock Way TQ4: Paig 5F 119
Porsham Cl. PL6: Robo 1C 132
Porsham La. PL5: Tam F 3J 131
Portal Pl. PL21: Ivy 4F 145
PORT BRIDGE 7B 118
Porteous Cl. PL1: Dev 1E 140
Porter's La. EX8: Lymp 3J 75
PORTFIELD 1D 167
Portford La. TQ10: S Bre 2C 100
PORTGATE 2C 169
Portland Av. EX8: Exmth 6D 76
TQ14: Teignm 2J 107
Portland Bldgs. EX32: Barn 3F 19
Portland Ct. DT7: Lym R 5H 91
EX32: Barn 5F 19 (off Victoria Rd.)
PL1: Dev 1E 140
TQ1: Torq 6F 113 (off Portland Rd.)
Portland Head La. EX34: Com M 6D 12
Portland Pk. EX34: Ilfra 2J 11
Portland Pl. E. PL4: Plym 2F 9 (1K 141)
Portland Rd. PL1: Dev 1E 140
TQ1: Torq 6F 113
Portland Sq. PL4: Plym 3E 8 (1J 141) (not continuous)
Portland Sq. La. Nth.
PL4: Plym 2E 8 (1J 141)
Portland St. EX1: Exe 2H 7 (6H 65)
EX32: Barn 6G 19
EX34: Ilfra 2J 11
Portland Vs. PL4: Plym 2E 8 (1J 141)
Port La. TQ7: Chil 6F 159
Port La. Cl. TQ7: Chil 6F 159
Portlemore Cl. TQ7: Malb 6G 155
Portlemore Gdns. TQ7: Malb 6G 155
Portmarsh La. EX32: Barn 5F 19
Port Mer Cl. EX8: Exmth 1G 77
Port Mill Ct. EX31: Barn 3E 18
Portmore Golf Course 7K 19
Portreath Gdns. PL2: Plym 3J 135
Port Rd. EX7: Daw 5A 96
Portugal Way EX20: Oke 3D 48
Portway EX15: Ashill 7K 43
Portway Cl. PL9: Elb 7K 143
PORTWRINKLE 2A 174
POSTBRIDGE 3A 170
Post Coach Way EX5: Cranb 3C 68
Post Cross Bus. Pk. EX15: Kent 7A 46
Post Hill EX16: Tiv 3J 41
Post Office La. EX17: Cher F 2J 39
Potacre St. EX38: Gt T 2C 30 (off Calf St.)
Potters Cl. EX11: W Hill 3H 79
Potters Hill TQ1: Torq 1D 116
Potters Stile EX14: Dunk 7H 47
Potters Way PL7: Plymp 4A 138
Potterswell EX31: Roun 6K 17
Pottery, The TQ6: Dartm 7G 125 (off Warfleet Creek Rd.)
Pottery Cl. EX14: Hon 3G 55
TQ13: Bov T 6B 92
Pottery Cotts. TQ6: Dartm 7G 125 (off Warfleet Creek Rd.)
Pottery Ct. TQ6: Dartm 6D 124
Pottery La. EX31: Yell 6B 16
Pottery Rd. PL1: Dev 1C 140
TQ12: Kingst 5G 105
TQ13: Bov T 6B 92
Pottery Rd. Flats PL1: Dev 1C 140
Pottery Yd. TQ12: Live 7G 93
Pottington Bus. Pk. EX31: Barn 3B 18
Pottington Dr. EX31: Barn 3D 18
Pottington Ind. Est. EX31: Barn 3C 18
Pottington Rd. EX31: Barn 3D 18
Pottles Cl. EX6: Exmin 3C 74
POUGHILL
Stratton 3A 162
Woolfardisworthy 3C 165
Poultney Cl. PL7: Plymp 4D 138
Pouncel La. EX5: Cranb 3C 68
Pound Cl. EX3: Top 7D 72
EX8: Exmth 3E 76
EX10: Sidb 2H 85
Pound Fld. TQ9: Sto G 3B 120
Poundfield Cl. EX31: Frem 6G 17
Pound Hill EX12: Axmth 3H 87
TA21: Holc R 2G 43
Pound La. DT7: Uply 2F 91
EX3: Top 7D 72
EX5: Wood 5C 78
EX6: Bridf 1F 63
EX8: Exmth 2D 76
EX10: Col R 1G 83
EX34: Com M 7C 12
EX37: High B 2C 32
TQ12: Kingsk 1F 111
TQ12: Shal 6E 106
TQ14: Teignm 5J 107
Pound La. Trad. Est. EX8: Exmth 3E 76
Pound Mdw. EX20: Hath 2H 35
Pound Pk. EX20: Oke 2D 48
Pound Pl. TQ12: New A 1E 108 (off Jubilee Rd.)
TQ13: Bov T 3C 92
Pound Rd. DT7: Lym R 5J 91
PL20: Buck M 5B 126
POUNDSGATE 3B 170
Poundsgate Cl. TQ5: Brixh 4G 123
Pounds Hill EX17: Cred 5J 39
Poundsland EX5: Broadc 6C 52
Pounds Pk. Rd. PL3: Plym 4J 135
PL20: Bere A 2B 128
Pound Sq. EX15: Cull 4H 45 (off Cockpit Hill)
POUNDSTOCK 1A 168
Poundstone Ct. TQ8: Salc 4C 158
Pound St. DT7: Lym R 5J 91
EX8: Exmth 6C 76
PL1: Plym 4F 141
TQ13: More 7H 61
Poundwell Mdw. PL21: Modb 6G 147
Poundwell St. PL21: Modb 6G 147
POWDERHAM 2D 171
Powderham Castle 5K 95
Powderham Cl. EX3: Top 7D 72
TQ12: New A 2E 108
Powderham Ct. TQ12: New A 1E 108 (off Powderham Rd.)
Powderham Cres.
EX4: Exe 1F 7 (4G 65)
Powderham Rd. EX2: Exe 7A 6 (1D 70)
PL3: Plym 4A 136
TQ2: Torq 4B 112
TQ12: New A 1E 108
Powderham Ter. TQ12: New A 2E 108
TQ14: Teignm 5J 107
Powderham Wlk. EX6: Exmin 1B 74
Powell Cl. EX12: Seat 4E 86
Powells Way EX14: Dunk 5K 47
Power of Water Exhibition 2H 13
Powhay Mills EX4: Exe 5B 6 (7E 64)
Powis Gdns. PL5: Plym 1G 135
Powisland Dr. PL6: Plym 5A 132
Powlesland Rd. EX2: Alph 4E 70
Powys Ho. EX10: Sidm 6B 84
Poyers EX33: Wraf 6K 15
Precinct, The TQ7: Kingsb 3G 157
Premier Pl. EX2: Exe 6H 7 (7G 65)
Prescot Rd. EX4: Exe 7B 64
PRESCOTT 2A 166
Prescott Pinetum 1D 173
Prescott Rd. EX15: Culm 1A 46
PRESTON
Sandygate 1E 104 (3C 171)
Torbay 5J 115
PRESTON BOWYER 1B 166
Prestonbury Castle 1B 170
Prestonbury Cl. PL6: Plym 3C 132
Preston Down Av. TQ3: Pres 4H 115
Preston Down Rd. TQ3: Pres 3E 114
Preston Mnr. Clay Works
TQ12: Kingst 1E 104
Preston St. EX1: Exe 5D 6 (7E 64)
Prestor EX13: Axmin 4J 89
Pretoria Rd. EX1: Heav 2K 7 (5H 65)
Pretoria Ter. EX34: Ilfra 5G 11
Priddis Cl. EX8: Exmth 1E 76
Prideaux Cres. EX16: Tiv 2D 40
Prideaux La. TQ6: Strete 5G 153
Prideaux Mdw. EX38: Gt T 2E 30
Prideaux Rd. PL21: Ivy 4J 145
Pridham La. PL2: Plym 4J 135
Pridhams Way EX6: Exmin 2C 74
Priest Hill EX15: Kent 6B 46
Priestley Av. EX4: Whip 4A 66
PL5: Plym 1D 134
Prigg Mdw. TQ13: Ashb 4H 99
Primley Ct. TQ3: Paig 2E 118
PRIMLEY CROSS 2F 119
Primley Gdns. EX10: Sidm 3D 84
Primley Mead EX10: Sidm 3D 84
Primley Paddock EX10: Sidm 3C 84
Primley Pk. TQ3: Paig 2F 119
Primley Pk. E. TQ3: Paig 2G 119
Primley Rd. EX10: Sidm 3C 84 (not continuous)
Primrose Av. EX32: Barn 5K 19
Primrose Cl. EX16: Tiv 2F 41
PL21: Ivy 4H 145
TQ7: Chil 6F 159
TQ12: Kingst 4H 105
Primrose Gdns. PL19: Tavi 5K 59
Primrose La. EX39: N'ham 4G 21
Primrose Lawn EX4: Exe 4A 64
Primrose Mdw. PL21: Ivy 3E 144
Primrose Way EX12: Seat 2F 87
EX17: Cred 5K 39
TQ12: Kingsk 6J 109
Prince Albert Pl. EX7: Daw 4G 97 (off Brook St.)
Prince Charles Cl. EX8: Exmth 3G 77
Prince Charles Ct. TQ2: Torq 2C 112
Prince Charles Rd. EX4: Exe 4H 65
Prince Charles Ter. EX20: Lyd 5H 57
Prince Charles Way EX12: Seat 3E 86
Prince Maurice Ct.
PL4: Plym 4H 9 (2A 142)
Prince Maurice Rd.
PL4: Plym 1J 9 (1A 142)
Prince of Wales Dr. EX8: Exmth 4F 77
TQ6: Dartm 5F 125
Prince of Wales Rd.
EX4: Exe 1C 6 (4E 64)
EX17: Cred 5H 39
TQ7: Kingsb 4F 157
Prince Rupert Way TQ12: Heat 2K 93
Prince's Point TQ1: Torq 3E 116
Princes Rd. PL6: Plym 4F 133 (off Sycamore Way)
TQ1: Torq 1D 116
Princes Rd. E. TQ1: Torq 1E 116
Princes Rd. W. TQ1: Torq 1D 116
Princess Av. EX34: Ilfra 3H 11
PL5: Plym 7F 131
PL9: Plyms 6F 143
Princess Cres. PL9: Plyms 6F 143
Princess Elizabeth Ter.
EX20: Bride 2J 57
Princess Gdns. 3D 116 (off Princess Pde.)
Princesshay EX1: Exe 4E 6 (6F 65)
Princesshay Garden Apartments
EX1: Exe 3F 7 (off Dix's Field)
Princesshay La. EX1: Exe 3F 7
Princesshay Sq. EX1: Exe 4E 6
Princess Pde. TQ2: Torq 3D 116
Prince's Sq. EX2: Exe 1D 70
Princess Rd. TQ12: Kingsk 1G 111
TQ12: Kingst 3G 105
Princess St. EX32: Barn 3F 19
PL1: Plym 5D 8 (3J 141)
Princess Ter. Ope
PL1: Plym 5E 8 (3J 141)
Princess Theatre 3C 116
Princes St. EX7: Daw 4G 97
EX8: Exmth 6C 76
PL1: Dev 2D 140
TQ1: Torq 6F 113
TQ3: Paig 1H 119

Prince's St. E. EX2: Exe 2D **70**
Prince's St. Nth. EX2: Exe 1D **70**
Prince's St. Sth. EX2: Exe 2D **70**
Prince's St. W. EX2: Exe 1D **70**
Princess Way PL1: Plym 5D **8** (3J **141**)
Prince St. TQ12: New A 1F **109**
PRINCETOWN 6C **60** (3D **169**)
Princetown Rd. PL20: Dous 5H **127**
Prince William Ct. TQ5: Brixh 4E **122**
Prings Ct. *TQ5: Brixh 3E **122***
(off Market St.)
Priors Pk. PL9: Plyms 3H **143**
Priory TQ13: Bov T 3B **92**
Priory, The *EX6: Exmin 1B **74***
(off Devington Pk.)
PL21: Modb 6G **147**
TQ12: A'well 5F **109**
Priory Av. TQ9: Tot 5E **102**
TQ12: Kingsk 7K **109**
Priory Cl. EX9: E Bud 1D **82**
EX31: Barn 2E **18**
PL19: Whitc 6K **59**
PL21: Ivy 4F **145**
Priory Ct. TQ9: Tot 6E **102**
Priory Dr. PL7: Plymp 4A **138**
TQ9: Tot 5E **102**
Priory Gdns. EX4: Exe 5C **6**
EX7: Daw 4H **97**
EX31: Barn 2E **18**
PL19: Whitc 7K **59**
TQ9: Tot 5E **102**
Priory Ga. TQ9: Tot 5E **102**
Priory Hill EX7: Daw 4H **97**
TQ9: Tot 5E **102**
Priory La. EX6: Chri 2J **63**
Priory Lawn Ter. PL3: Plym 5B **136**
Priory Mill PL7: Plymp 4A **138**
Priory Pk. Rd. EX7: Daw 4G **97**
Priory Ridge PL7: Plymp 4A **138**
Priory Rd. EX4: Exe 1J **7** (4H **65**)
EX7: Daw 4H **97**
EX16: Tiv 2F **41**
EX31: Barn 2E **18**
PL3: Plym 5B **136**
TQ1: Torq 5D **112**
TQ12: A'well 5E **108**
Priory St. TQ6: Kingsw 7G **125**
Priory Ter. *TQ9: Tot 5E **102***
(off Priory Hill)
Priory Vw. EX4: Whip 4K **65**
Priscott Way TQ12: Kingst 5H **105**
Prison La. EX4: Exe 1E **6** (5F **65**)
Prispen Dr. EX5: Silv 1H **51**
Prispen Ho. EX5: Silv 1H **51**
Prispen Vw. EX5: Silv 1H **51**
PRIXFORD 3B **160**
Promenade EX39: West H 5A **20**
TQ3: Pres 6K **115**
TQ4: Broads 1K **121**
TQ4: Good 3J **119**
(not continuous)
TQ7: Kingsb 4G **157**
TQ14: Teignm 5J **107**
Promenade, The EX34: Ilfra 2H **11**
PL1: Plym 7C **8** (4H **141**)
Prospect Cres. EX15: Uff 6H **43**
Prospect Gdns. EX4: Exe 1J **7** (5H **65**)
Prospect Hill EX20: Oke 4B **48**
TQ7: Slap 1H **159**
Prospect Pk. EX4: Exe 4G **65**
Prospect Pl. EX4: Exe 7A **6** (1D **70**)
*EX10: Sidm 7C **84***
(off Kings La.)
EX11: Ott M 4C **80**
EX15: Uff 6H **43**
*EX16: Tiv 4B **40***
(off Wellbrook St.)
EX32: Barn 6G **19**
PL1: Plym 6B **8** (3H **141**)
TQ10: S Bre 1B **100**
Prospect Rd. TQ5: Brixh 3E **122**
Prospect Row PL1: Dev 3D **140**
Prospect Row Flats *PL1: Dev 3D **140***
(off Prospect Row)
Prospect Steps *TQ5: Brixh 3E **122***
(off Sth. Furzeham Rd.)
Prospect St. PL4: Plym 3G **9** (2K **141**)
Prospect Ter. EX24: Colyt 6C **88**
TQ12: New A 1F **109**
Prospect Way EX17: Lap 2J **37**
Prouse Cres. PL2: Plym 3H **135**
Providence Pl. DT7: Lym R 5J **91**
PL1: Plym 1F **141**
Providence Row EX39: Bide 3F **23**
Providence St.
PL4: Plym 2G **9** (1K **141**)
Prowse La. EX17: Lap 2K **37**
Prowses EX15: Hemy 2G **47**
Prynne Cl. PL1: Plym 3C **8** (2H **141**)
Prysten House 5E **8**
PUCKINGTON 2D **167**
Puckridge Rd. EX4: Pin 2C **66**
Puddavine Ter. TQ9: Darti 3D **102**
PUDDINGTON 2C **165**
Pudleylake Rd. EX13: Abb G 7F **89**
Puffin Cl. TQ2: Torq 3J **111**
Puffin Way EX2: Exe 2A **70**
Pugsley Rd. EX16: Tiv 4G **41**
Pulborough Farm Caravan Pk.
EX20: Lyd 5G **57**
Pulchrass St. EX32: Barn 5F **19**
Pullen's Row EX16: With 6H **33**
Pulleys Cl. TQ7: Ave G 6H **151**
Pulling Rd. EX4: Pin 2C **66**
Pullins Ter. TQ13: Chud 1C **94**
Pulpit Wlk. EX2: Alph 6F **71**
Pump La. EX39: A'sham 3A **22**
Pump St. EX5: New C 7D **50**
TQ5: Brixh 3F **123**
Punchards Down TQ9: Tot 5A **102**
Purbeck Av. TQ2: Torq 4J **115**
Purcell Cl. EX2: Won 7B **66**
PURTINGTON 3D **167**
Purzebrook Cl. EX13: Axmin 4H **89**
PUSEHILL 7A **20**
Pusehill Rd. EX39: West H 6A **20**
PUTSBOROUGH 1D **14** (2A **160**)
Putsborough Cl. EX33: Georgeh 5B **14**
Putsborough Rd.
EX33: Georgeh, Puts 1D **14**
Pye Cnr. EX6: Kennf 1H **95**
EX15: Cull 4H **45**
Pykes Down PL21: Ivy 5K **145**
Pym St. PL1: Dev 1D **140**
PL19: Tavi 3J **59**
Pynes Cl. EX9: E Bud 1D **82**
EX17: Cher F 2H **39**
Pynes Hill EX2: Cou W 3A **72**
Pynes Hill Bus. Pk. EX2: Cou W 3B **72**
Pynes La. EX39: Bide 4D **22**
Pynes Wlk. EX39: Bide 4D **22**
Pyne Vs. PL9: Hooe 6C **142**
Pynsant Ct. TQ13: Chud 2C **94**
Pyramids Swimming and
Leisure Centre, The 3G **7** (6G **65**)
Pytte Gdns. EX3: Clyst G 6H **73**
PYWORTHY 3B **162**

Q

Quadrangle, The EX4: Exe 1E **6** (5F **65**)
Quadrant, The EX2: Exe 6G **7** (7G **65**)
Quaker La. PL3: Plym 6K **135**
Quantocks EX33: Brau 4G **15**
Quantocks Rd. TQ2: Torq 3J **115**
Quant Pk. PL19: Tavi 3J **59**
Quarries, The EX4: Exe 1A **70**
Quarries La. EX37: High B 3B **32**
Quarry Cl. EX39: Bide 3D **22**
TQ9: Tot 5B **102**
Quarry Cotts. PL5: Plym 1G **135**
Quarry Flds. EX20: Oke 2C **48**
Quarry Gdns. TQ3: Paig 7G **115**
Quarry La. EX2: Sow, Won 7A **66**
EX5: Silv 4F **51**
EX12: Beer 4K **85** & 7A **86**
EX17: Cop 5A **38**
Quarry Pk. Av. PL9: Plyms 5E **142**
Quarry Pk. Rd. EX2: Won 1B **72**
PL3: Plym 6J **135**
PL9: Plyms 5E **142**
Quarry Rd. EX37: High B 3B **32**
Quarry St. PL11: Torp 1A **140**
Quarterdeck, The PL1: Plym 4F **141**
Quarter Mile La. EX5: Mar G 7J **69**
Quay, The EX2: Exe 6E **6** (7F **65**)
EX34: Ilfra 2J **11**
EX39: Apple 2J **21**
EX39: Bide 3F **23**
PL9: Plyms 4D **142**
PL19: Tavi 4H **59**
TQ5: Brixh 3F **123**
TQ6: Ditt 1B **124** (6D **120**)
*TQ7: Kingsb 4F **157***
(off Prince of Wales Rd.)
TQ8: Bat 2B **158**
Quayfield Path EX34: Ilfra 2J **11**
Quayfield Rd. EX34: Ilfra 2J **11**
Quay Hill EX2: Exe 6D **6** (7E **64**)
Quay House Vis. Cen. 6E **6** (7E **64**)
Quay La. EX2: Exe 6E **6** (7F **65**)
EX8: Lymp 7F **75**
EX39: Ins 3K **21**
TQ7: Kingsb 4G **157**
Quay Rd. PL1: Plym 6F **9** (3K **141**)
TQ12: New A 1G **109**
(not continuous)
TQ14: Teignm 5H **107**
Quayside PL19: Tavi 4H **59**
Quayside Leisure Cen. 5G **157**
Quay Steps EX2: Exe 6E **6**
Quay Ter. TQ12: New A 1G **109**
Quaywest Waterpark 4J **119**
Queen Alexandra Sq.
PL1: Plym 3A **8** (2G **141**)
Queen Annes EX39: Bide 3F **23**
Queen Anne's Battery 7J **9** (4A **142**)
Queen Annes Copse
TQ12: E Ogw 3C **108**
Queen Anne's Ct. *EX31: Barn 4E **18***
(off Commercial Rd.)
Queen Anne's Wlk. *EX31: Barn 4E **18***
(off The Strand)
Queen Anne Ter. PL4: Plym 2F **9**
QUEEN DART 2C **165**
Queen Elizabeth Av.
TQ6: Dartm 5E **124**
Queen Elizabeth Ct.
EX39: West H 6B **20**
Queen Elizabeth Dr. EX17: Cred 5F **39**
TQ3: Paig 1E **118**
Queen La. EX7: Daw 4G **97**
Queen's Av. EX34: Ilfra 3J **11**
Queens Cl. PL6: Plym 4F **133**
TQ12: Kingst 3J **105**
Queens Ct. *EX8: Exmth 6C **76***
(off Queen St.)
EX24: Colyt 6C **88**
Queen's Cres. EX4: Exe 2F **7** (5F **65**)
TQ5: Brixh 5F **123**
Queen's Dr. EX8: Exmth 7D **76**
Queens Dr., The EX4: Exe 4E **64**
Queen's Ga. PL1: Plym 2A **8** (1G **141**)
PL4: Plym 1J **9** (1A **142**)
Queen's Gate M.
PL4: Plym 1J **9** (1A **142**)
Queen's Gate Vs. PL4: Plym 1J **9**
Queen's Gate Vs. Rd.
PL4: Plym 1J **9** (1A **142**)
Queen's Ho. *EX32: Barn 4F **19***
(off Queen St.)
Queensland Dr. EX4: Exe 2H **65**
Queen's Pk. Rd. TQ4: Paig 1J **119**
Queen Sq. EX15: Cull 4H **45**
Queens Rd. EX2: Exe 7C **6** (2D **70**)
EX9: Bud S 5B **82**
PL4: Plym 1J **9** (1A **142**)
PL5: Plym 7E **130**
TQ4: Paig 1J **119**
TQ5: Brixh 2E **122**
TQ13: More 6H **61**
Queens Sq. EX5: Broadc 5C **52**
EX24: Colyt 5C **88**
Queens Steps *TQ5: Brixh 3F **123***
(off King St.)
Queens Ter. EX4: Exe 2C **6** (5E **64**)
EX5: Sto C 6J **51**
EX38: Gt T 2A **30**
TQ9: Tot 5E **102**
Queen's Theatre 4E **18**
Queen St. EX4: Exe 2D **6** (5E **64**)
EX7: Daw 4G **97**
EX8: Exmth 6C **76**
EX9: Bud S 7C **82**
EX12: Seat 5E **86**
EX14: Hon 3F **55**
EX16: Tiv 5C **40**
EX19: Wink 2C **36**
EX24: Colyt 6D **88**
EX32: Barn 4E **18**
EX35: Lynt 2H **13**
EX36: S Mol 6C **26**
EX39: Bide 3F **23**
PL1: Dev 2C **140**
(not continuous)
TQ1: Torq 1D **116**
TQ12: New A 1F **109**
TQ14: Teignm 5H **107**
Queens Wlk. DT7: Lym R 4J **91**
EX4: Exe 3D **6**
Queensway EX16: Tiv 3F **41**
TQ2: Torq 7K **111**
TQ12: New A 2H **109**
Queensway Cl. TQ2: Torq 6A **112**
Queensway Cres. TQ2: Torq 6A **112**
Queensway Ho. TQ12: New A 2H **109**
Quentin Av. TQ5: Brixh 6D **122**
Questant La. EX10: Sidm 4D **84**
Quicks Wlk. EX38: Gt T 2E **30**
Quilletts, The TQ7: Malb 6G **155**
Quince Honey Farm 5C **26**
Quinnell Ho. *TQ14: Teignm 4G **107***
(off Coombe Va. Rd.)
Quinta Cl. TQ1: Torq 7E **112**
Quinta Ct. TQ1: Torq 6E **112**
Quinta Rd. TQ1: Torq 7E **112**
Quintet Cl. EX1: Heav 7B **66**
QUODITCH 1C **169**

R

Raceworld 1D **78**
Rackclose La. EX4: Exe 5C **6** (7E **64**)
RACKENFORD 2C **165**
Rackenford Rd. EX16: Calv, Tiv 2A **40**
EX16: With 5J **33**
Rackfield EX16: Tiv 5C **40**
EX31: Barn 3E **18**
Rackfield Cotts. EX4: Exe 4C **64**
Rackfield Ct. *EX31: Barn 3E **18***
(off Rackfield)
Rackfield Dr. EX15: Hemy 1H **47**
Rackmead EX37: Chit 5H **25**
Rackmead Ter. *EX37: Chit 6H **25***
(off South Vw.)
Rack Pk. EX38: Gt T 2A **30**
Rack Pk. Cl. EX38: Gt T 2B **30**
Rack Pk. Rd. TQ7: Kingsb 4G **157**
Rack St. EX1: Exe 5D **6** (7E **64**)
Radcliffe Cl. PL6: Plym 4K **131**
Raddenstile Ct. EX8: Exmth 6D **76**
Raddenstile La. EX8: Exmth 6D **76**
Raddicombe Cl. TQ5: Hill 6K **123**
Raddicombe Dr. TQ5: Hill 6K **123**
Radford Av. PL4: Plym 3B **142**
Radford Pk. Dr. PL9: Plyms 6E **142**
Radford Pk. Rd. PL9: Plyms 6E **142**
Radford Rd. EX2: Exe 6F **7** (7F **65**)
PL1: Plym 7B **8** (4H **141**)
Radford Vw. PL9: Plyms 6E **142**
Radford Way EX20: Oke 2E **48**
Radnor Hall PL4: Plym 3G **9**
Radnor Pl. EX2: Exe 5G **7** (7G **65**)
PL4: Plym 3G **9** (2K **141**)
Radnor St. PL4: Plym 3G **9** (2K **141**)
Radnor Ter. TQ9: Tot 5E **102**
Radway EX10: Sidm 6C **84**
Radway Cinema, The
Scott Cinemas 6C **84**
Radway Ct. TQ14: Bi'ton 3C **106**
Radway Gdns. TQ14: Bi'ton 3C **106**
Radway Hill TQ14: Bi'ton 3C **106**
Radway La. EX9: Ott'n 4K **83**
Radway Pl. EX10: Sidm 6C **84**
Radway St. TQ14: Bi'ton 3C **106**
RAF Memorial 7E **8** (4J **141**)
Ragg La. EX9: Bud S 7C **82**
Raglan Ct. *PL1: Dev 2E **140***
(off Damerel Cl.)
Rag La. EX5: Rock 7H **69**
(not continuous)
Raglan Gdns. PL1: Dev 2E **140**
Raglan Rd. PL1: Dev 2E **140**
Raglans EX2: Alph 5F **71**
Railway Cotts. EX1: Whip 6B **66**
PL2: Plym 6E **134**
PL19: Tavi 3J **59**
Railway Ter. EX39: Bide 4G **23**
Railway Vw. PL8: Brixt 3F **149**
Rainbow Ct. TQ2: Torq 6A **112**
Raleigh Av. TQ2: Torq 7K **111**
Raleigh Cl. EX10: Sidm 3C **84**
EX36: S Mol 6C **26**
TQ2: Torq 7K **111**
TQ6: Dartm 6C **124**
Raleigh Cotts. EX31: Barn 2F **19**
Raleigh Ct. EX9: Bud S 5D **82**
PL7: Plymp 3E **138**
Raleigh Dr. EX15: Cull 3H **45**
TQ4: Good 5H **119**
Raleigh Hgts. EX31: Barn 2E **18**
Raleigh Hill EX39: Bide, N'ham 7C **20**
(not continuous)
Raleigh Ho. EX2: Exe 5H **7**
*EX10: Sidm 3C **84***
(off Raleigh Cl.)
Raleigh Lawn EX31: Barn 2E **18**
Raleigh Mead EX36: S Mol 6C **26**
Raleigh Mdw. EX31: Barn 3F **19**
Raleigh Pk. EX31: Barn 1F **19**
EX36: S Mol 6B **26**
Raleigh Rd. EX1: Exe 4H **7** (7G **65**)
EX8: Exmth 6C **76**
EX9: Bud S 5D **82**
EX11: Ott M 3D **80**
EX31: Barn 3E **18**
PL21: Ivy 3E **144**
TQ6: Dartm 5E **124**
TQ8: Salc 4B **158**
TQ12: New A 1J **109**
TQ14: Teignm 2G **107**
Raleigh St. PL1: Plym 4C **8** (2H **141**)
TQ6: Dartm 1B **124** (6F **125**)
Raleigh Vw. *EX39: Bide 2F **23***
(off Kingsley Rd.)
Ralph Cl. EX33: Brau 4G **15**
Ralph Rd. EX33: Brau 4G **15**
Ralph's Ct. PL19: Tavi 4H **59**
Ramage Cl. PL6: Plym 7G **133**
RAME 3A **174**
Ramillies Av. PL5: Plym 6F **131**
Ramparts Wlk. *TQ9: Tot 6E **102***
(off High St.)
Ramsey Gdns. PL5: Plym 2J **135**
Ramshill Rd. TQ3: Paig 6E **114**
Ramslade Touring Pk. TQ9: Aish 6A **118**

Ramsley—Riverside Mill

RAMSLEY . . . 3H 49 (1A 170)
Rance Dr. EX8: Exmth . . . 1G 77
Randell's Grn. EX8: Exmth . . . 6G 77
Randolph Cl. PL5: Plym . . . 7K 131
Randolph Ct. TQ12: New A . . . 7D 104
Randwick Pk. Rd. PL9: Plyms . . . 5E 142
Ranelagh Rd. EX20: Oke . . . 3A 48
Rangers Cl. TQ11: B'leigh . . . 5C 98
Ranscombe Cl. TQ5: Brixh . . . 3G 123
Ranscombe Rd. TQ5: Brixh . . . 3F 123
Ransom Pickard EX4: Exe . . . 4F 65
Ransum Way PL19: Tavi . . . 5H 59
Raphael Cl. PL9: Elb . . . 6H 143
Raphael Dr. PL9: Elb . . . 6H 143
RAPPS . . . 2D 167
Rashleigh Av. PL7: Plymp . . . 2B 138
Rathlin *TQ1: Torq . . . 6E 112*
(off Palermo Rd.)
Rathmore Rd. TQ2: Torq . . . 2A 116
(not continuous)
Ratsash La. EX15: Crad . . . 6K 43
RATTERY . . . 1D 175
Ravelin Gdns. EX32: Barn . . . 4G 19
Ravelin Mnr. Rd. EX32: Barn . . . 4G 19
Raven Cl. EX4: Exe . . . 3F 65
Ravensbourne La. TQ6: Sto F . . . 2H 153
Ravensbury Dr. TQ6: Dartm . . . 7G 125
Rawlin Cl. PL6: Plym . . . 3D 136
Rawlin Homes *PL4: Plym . . . 4G 9*
(off Green St.)
Rawlyn Rd. TQ2: Torq . . . 2K 115
Rawnsley La. EX34: Woolc . . . 6A 10
RAWRIDGE . . . 3C 167
Rayer Rd. EX16: Tiv . . . 5H 41
RAYMOND'S HILL . . . 2C 90 (1D 173)
Raymond Way PL7: Plymp . . . 3A 138
Rayners EX6: Kennf . . . 1G 95
Raynham Rd. PL3: Plym . . . 1A 8 (1G 141)
Rea Barn Cl. TQ5: Brixh . . . 4F 123
Rea Barn Rd. TQ5: Brixh . . . 4F 123
Read Cl. EX8: Exmth . . . 3E 76
Reading Wlk. PL5: Plym . . . 6H 131
Rea Dr. TQ5: Brixh . . . 3F 123
Rear Dunmere Rd. *TQ1: Torq . . . 7D 112*
(off Dunmere Rd.)
Rear Hyde Pk. Rd. *PL3: Plym . . . 6K 135*
(off Gifford Ter. Rd.)
Recreation Rd. PL2: Plym . . . 4H 135
Recreation Way PL7: L Moor . . . 1J 129
Rectory Cl. EX5: Whim . . . 6G 53
EX15: Will . . . 4D 44
EX33: Wraf . . . 6K 15
(not continuous)
Rectory Dr. EX2: Alph . . . 5E 70
Rectory Gdns. EX3: Clyst G . . . 7H 73
Rectory Hill EX17: Cher F . . . 2H 39
EX34: Berry . . . 3B 12
Rectory La. EX34: Com M . . . 7B 12
TQ6: Sto F . . . 3H 153
Rectory Pk. EX39: Bide . . . 3E 22
Rectory Rd. EX17: Morc . . . 1B 38
EX19: Dol . . . 6H 31
EX20: Bride . . . 3H 57
EX34: Com M . . . 7B 12
PL1: Dev . . . 2F 141
TQ12: E Ogw . . . 3B 108
Redavon Ri. TQ2: Torq . . . 5H 111
Red Brook Cl. TQ4: Good . . . 6J 119
Redburn Cl. TQ3: Paig . . . 7G 115
Redburn Rd. TQ3: Paig . . . 7G 115
Redcliff Ct. EX9: Bud S . . . 7C 82
Redcliffe Ct. TQ3: Pres . . . 7K 115
Redcliffe Rd. TQ1: Torq . . . 4E 112
Red Cow Village EX4: Exe . . . 1A 6 (4D 64)
Reddaway Dr. EX6: Exmin . . . 1B 74
Reddenhill Rd. TQ1: Torq . . . 7E 112
Red Devon Ct. *PL21: Modb . . . 6G 147*
(off New Rd.)
Reddicliff Cl. PL9: Hooe . . . 7E 142
Reddicliffe M. EX20: Lew . . . 1A 56
Reddicliff Rd. PL9: Hooe . . . 7D 142
Reddington Rd. PL3: Plym . . . 4B 136
Redford Mdw. TQ7: Kingsb . . . 4F 157
Redford Way TQ7: Kingsb . . . 4F 157
REDGATE . . . 3A 168
Redgate Cl. TQ1: Torq . . . 7F 113
REDHILL . . . 1A 38
Redhill Cl. PL5: Plym . . . 6D 130
REDHILLS . . . 6B 64
Redhills EX4: Exe . . . 5A 64
EX9: Bud S . . . 7C 82
Redhills Cl. EX4: Exe . . . 6B 64
Red Ho. Cl. TQ13: Chud K . . . 6B 94
Redlake TQ9: Darti . . . 3B 102
Redlake Trad. Est. PL21: Bitta . . . 4A 146
Redlands EX16: Tiv . . . 4F 41
Redlands, The EX10: Sidm . . . 7B 84
Redlands Cl. EX4: Whip . . . 4K 65
Redlands Ct. TQ3: Paig . . . 7F 115
Redlands Rd. EX31: Frem . . . 6G 17
Red La. EX13: Ray H . . . 3C 90
EX20: Hath . . . 1H 35
Redlap La. TQ6: Dartm, Sto F . . . 2H 153
Redlap Rd. TQ6: Dartm . . . 1J 153
Red Lion Hill PL8: Brixt . . . 2H 149
Red Lion La. EX1: Exe . . . 2G 7 (5G 65)
Red Lion Yd. EX20: Oke . . . 3B 48
Redmoor Cl. PL19: Tavi . . . 2G 59
Redoubt Hill TQ6: Kingsw . . . 6G 125
RED POST . . . 3A 162
Red Rock Rd. EX5: Bram S . . . 5F 51
Redruth Cl. PL5: Plym . . . 5F 131
Redstart Cl. TQ12: E Ogw . . . 3C 108
Redvers Gro. PL7: Plymp . . . 5B 138
Redvers Rd. EX4: Exe . . . 6A 6 (7D 64)
Redvers Way EX16: Tiv . . . 2E 40
Redwalls Mdw. TQ6: Dartm . . . 5E 124
Redwell La. TQ3: Paig . . . 6F 115
Redwell Rd. TQ3: Paig . . . 6F 115
Redwing Dr. PL6: Plym . . . 2E 132
Redwood Cl. EX8: Exmth . . . 1F 77
EX14: Hon . . . 5C 54
EX15: Hemy . . . 2G 47
TQ13: Bov T . . . 7B 92
Redwood Ct. EX7: Daw . . . 4H 97
Redwood Dr. PL7: Plymp . . . 4E 138
Redwood Rd. EX10: Sidm . . . 5C 84
Redwoods TQ13: Bov T . . . 6B 92
Redworth Ct. *TQ9: Tot . . . 5D 102*
(off Station Rd.)
Redworth Ter. TQ9: Tot . . . 5E 102
Reed Mdw. EX20: Hath . . . 2H 35
Reeds Pl. EX15: Cull . . . 4G 45
Reed Va. TQ14: Teignm . . . 4G 107
REEDY . . . 6E 62
Reedy Hill EX6: Dunsf . . . 6D 62
Reel Cinema, The
Kingsbridge . . . 4F 157
Plymouth . . . 5D 8
Reeves EX17: Bow . . . 5G 37
Reeves Cl. *TQ9: Tot . . . 6F 103*
(off New Wlk.)
Reeves Rd., The TQ2: Torq . . . 1K 115
Reform St. EX31: Barn . . . 3E 18
Regatta Ct. EX8: Exmth . . . 6A 76
Regency Ct. *EX34: Ilfra . . . 3H 11*
(off Church St.)
Regency Cres. EX8: Exmth . . . 6E 76
Regency Ga. EX10: Sidm . . . 5D 84
Regent Cinema, The
Scott Cinemas . . . 5J 91
Regent Cl. EX31: Barn . . . 7B 18
EX31: Frem . . . 6G 17
TQ2: Torq . . . 5A 112
Regent Gdns. *TQ14: Teignm . . . 5J 107*
(off Regent St.)
Regent Pl. EX34: Ilfra . . . 2H 11
Regents Ct. TQ4: Paig . . . 2J 119
Regents Ga. EX8: Exmth . . . 6D 76
Regent's Pk. EX1: Heav . . . 3K 7 (6H 65)
(not continuous)
Regent Sq. EX1: Heav . . . 7J 65
Regent St. EX2: Exe . . . 7B 6 (2D 70)
EX7: Daw . . . 4G 97
PL4: Plym . . . 3F 9 (2K 141)
TQ14: Teignm . . . 5J 107
Reigate Rd. PL9: Plyms . . . 4F 143
Reme Dr. EX14: Hon . . . 5C 54
Rena Hobson Ct. EX16: Tiv . . . 5F 41
Renaissance Gdns. PL2: Plym . . . 4H 135
Rendells Mdw. TQ13: Bov T . . . 4D 92
Rendlesham Gdns. PL6: Plym . . . 7F 133
Rendlesham Rd. PL6: Plym . . . 7F 133
Rendle St. PL1: Plym . . . 4A 8 (2G 141)
Rennes Dr. EX4: Exe . . . 3F 65
Rennes Ho. EX1: Whip . . . 5A 66
Renney Rd. PL9: Down T . . . 1C 148
Rennie Av. PL5: Plym . . . 2B 134
Rennie Rd. EX16: Tiv . . . 5G 41
Renoir Cl. PL9: Elb . . . 6H 143
Renown St. PL2: Plym . . . 5D 134
Rensey La. EX17: Lap . . . 1J 37
Renslade Ho. EX4: Exe . . . 6C 6
Research Way PL6: Plym . . . 6D 132
Reservoir Cres. PL9: Elb . . . 5J 143
Reservoir La. PL3: Plym . . . 5A 136
Reservoir Rd. PL3: Plym . . . 5A 136
PL9: Elb . . . 6J 143
Reservoir Way PL9: Elb . . . 5J 143
Resolution Ho. PL4: Plym . . . 4H 9
Resolution Rd. EX2: Cou W . . . 4C 72
Restarick Cl. EX39: Bide . . . 5H 23
Restormel Rd. PL4: Plym . . . 1E 8 (1J 141)
Restormel Ter. PL4: Plym . . . 1E 8
Retail Pk. Cl. EX2: Mar B . . . 2E 70
Retreat, The EX8: Exmth . . . 5F 77
EX16: Tiv . . . 4D 40
PL3: Plym . . . 4C 136
Retreat Cl. TQ7: Kingsb . . . 4F 157
Retreat Dr., The EX3: Top . . . 7C 72
Retreat Pl. *EX39: Apple . . . 2H 21*
(off Vernon's La.)
Retreat Rd. EX3: Top . . . 7D 72
Revell Pk. Rd. PL7: Plymp . . . 3A 138
Revel Rd. PL3: Plym . . . 5B 136
Revelstoke Rd. PL8: Noss M . . . 6H 149
REW
Ashburton . . . 2H 99
Salcombe . . . 3D 175
REWE . . . 1D 171
Rewe La. EX5: Rock, Whim . . . 3H 69
Rewlea Cotts. TQ13: Ashb . . . 2H 99
Rew Rd. TQ13: Ashb . . . 1H 99
Rew's Cl. EX34: Com M . . . 5A 12
Rews Mdw. EX1: Pin . . . 3E 66
Rews Pk. Dr. EX1: Pin . . . 3E 66
REXON . . . 2C 169
Rexona Cl. EX2: Exe . . . 3D 70
Reynell Av. TQ12: New A . . . 1J 109
Reynell Rd. TQ12: E Ogw . . . 4C 108
Reynolds Cl. EX4: Pin . . . 3C 66
Reynolds Gro. PL5: Plym . . . 3B 134
Reynolds Rd. PL7: Plymp . . . 5K 137
REZARE . . . 3B 168
Rheola Gdns. PL6: Plym . . . 7E 132
Rhine Vs. TQ9: Tot . . . 6F 103
Rhodanthe Rd. TQ3: Pres . . . 5H 115
Rhode Island Dr. EX2: Cou W . . . 4D 72
Rhode La. DT7: Uply . . . 2G 91
Rhodes Cl. PL7: Plymp . . . 2B 138
Rhododendron Av. EX14: Dunk . . . 7G 47
EX31: Barn . . . 6C 18
RHS Garden Rosemoor . . . 2D 163
Ribble Gdns. PL3: Plym . . . 4E 136
Ribston Av. EX1: Heav . . . 6B 66
Ribston Cl. EX1: Heav . . . 6B 66
Rice Bldgs. EX16: Tiv . . . 4C 40
Rices M. EX2: Exe . . . 1D 70
Richard Cl. EX39: Bide . . . 5D 22
Richards Cl. EX7: Daw . . . 5G 97
EX8: Exmth . . . 2F 77
EX20: Oke . . . 3D 48
Richardson Wlk. *TQ1: Torq . . . 7B 112*
(off Barton Rd.)
Richards Row PL3: Plym . . . 4A 136
Richina Dr. EX20: N Taw . . . 6A 36
Richmond Av. EX34: Ilfra . . . 3G 11
Richmond Cl. EX16: Sam P . . . 1B 42
TQ1: Torq . . . 1J 117
Richmond Ct. EX4: Exe . . . 3C 6 (6E 64)
EX7: Daw . . . 4H 97
(off Richmond Pl.)
TQ3: Paig . . . 7H 115
Richmond Gdns. EX24: Colyt . . . 5C 88
Richmond Grn. EX39: Apple . . . 3G 21
Richmond Hill TQ12: Kingsk . . . 7K 109
Richmond Pk. EX39: N'ham . . . 5E 20
Richmond Pl. EX7: Daw . . . 4H 97
Richmond Rd. EX4: Exe . . . 3C 6 (6E 64)
EX8: Exmth . . . 5F 77
EX34: Ilfra . . . 4G 11
EX39: Apple . . . 3H 21
PL6: Plym . . . 1B 136
Richmond St. EX32: Barn . . . 4F 19
Richmond Ter. *EX12: Beer . . . 7B 86*
(off Causeway)
EX24: Colyt . . . 5C 88
EX32: Barn . . . 4F 19
(off Bear St.)
EX39: Apple . . . 3H 21
PL20: Buck M . . . 5A 126
(off The Village)
Richmond Vs. *EX34: Ilfra . . . 3G 11*
(off Station Rd.)
Richmond Wlk. EX32: Barn . . . 3F 19
PL1: Dev . . . 4D 140
RICKARD'S DOWN . . . 2A 22
Rickards Grn. EX39: A'sham . . . 3A 22
RICKHAM . . . 6E 158 (3D 175)
Riddell Av. EX32: Barn . . . 3E 18
RIDDLECOMBE . . . 2A 164
Ride, The PL9: Plyms . . . 3D 142
Rider's Rings Enclosures . . . 1C 175
Ridge Hill EX34: Berry . . . 3C 12
EX34: Com M . . . 7A 12
TQ6: Dartm . . . 1A 124 (5F 125)
Ridge La. EX16: Calv . . . 2A 40
TQ3: Marl . . . 5F 111
Ridgemark Cl. TQ5: Brixh . . . 3G 123
Ridgemonte *EX24: Colyt . . . 6C 88*
(off The Butts)
Ridge Pk. PL7: Plymp . . . 4B 138
Ridge Pk. Av. PL4: Plym . . . 1E 8 (7J 135)
Ridge Pk. Rd. PL7: Plymp . . . 4B 138
Ridge Rd. PL7: Plymp . . . 1K 143
PL21: Erm . . . 4J 147
PL21: Ugb . . . 6D 146
TQ1: Maid . . . 1H 113
TQ12: S'head . . . 1H 113
Ridges, The TQ6: Dartm . . . 7D 124
Ridge Way EX6: Kenton . . . 7J 95
Ridgeway EX4: Exe . . . 1D 64
EX10: Sidb . . . 1H 85
EX11: Ott M . . . 3D 80
EX14: Hon . . . 5E 54
PL7: Plymp . . . 4A 138
Ridgeway Av. EX39: West H . . . 5D 20
Ridgeway Cl. EX10: Sidb . . . 2H 85
EX39: West H . . . 5C 20
TQ12: New A . . . 3J 109
Ridgeway Community Sports Cen. . . . 4B 138
Ridgeway Ct. EX1: Exe . . . 2J 7 (5H 65)
EX39: West H . . . 5C 20
Ridgeway Dr. EX39: West H . . . 5C 20
Ridgeway Gdns.
EX11: Ott M . . . 3D 80
Ridgeway Grn. EX37: High B . . . 3C 32
Ridgeway Hgts. TQ1: Torq . . . 2F 117
Ridgeway Hill TQ3: Comp . . . 7D 110
Ridgeway La. EX24: Colyt . . . 6B 88
Ridgeway Mead EX10: Sidm . . . 3A 84
Ridgeway Rd. TQ1: Torq . . . 3F 117
TQ12: New A . . . 3J 109
Ridgeway Ter. *EX39: Bide . . . 1G 23*
(off Orchard Hill)
Ridgway Ct. EX13: Axmin . . . 4H 89
Ridings, The EX3: Ebf . . . 6E 74
Ridley Hill TQ6: Kingsw . . . 7G 125
Rifford Rd. EX2: Won . . . 1K 71
Rifleman Wlk. PL6: Plym . . . 3C 132
Riga Ter. PL3: Plym . . . 7D 136
Rigdale Cl. PL6: Plym . . . 4B 136
Rillage La. TQ2: Torq . . . 7B 112
RILLA MILL . . . 3A 168
RINGMORE
Kingsbridge . . . 3C 175
Teignmouth . . . 6F 107 (3D 171)
Ringmore Cl. TQ14: Shal . . . 6F 107
Ringmore Dr. TQ7: Bigb S . . . 2B 154
Ringmore Rd. TQ14: Shal . . . 6E 106
Ringmore Way PL5: Plym . . . 6F 131
Ringrone TQ8: Salc . . . 6A 158
Ringslade Cl. TQ12: New A . . . 6C 104
Ringslade Rd. TQ12: New A . . . 5C 104
Ringswell Av. EX1: Heav . . . 6B 66
Ringswell Pk. EX2: Won . . . 7B 66
Ripon Cl. EX4: Exe . . . 6B 64
Rippon Cl. EX16: Tiv . . . 5A 74
TQ5: Brixh . . . 6B 122
Riscombe Hill EX5: New C . . . 7A 50
Risdon Av. PL4: Plym . . . 3C 142
Riverbank Cotts. EX39: Bide . . . 1G 23
River Cl. EX5: Sto C . . . 7J 51
TQ12: Kingst . . . 6J 105
River Ct. EX10: Sidb . . . 2J 85
PL19: Tavi . . . 3K 59
Riverdale EX12: Seat . . . 3F 87
TQ9: H'ford . . . 6C 100
Riverdale Cl. EX12: Seat . . . 3F 87
Riverdale Orchard EX12: Seat . . . 3F 87
River Dart Adventures . . . 1D 175
River Dart Country Pk. . . . 3B 170
River Dr. EX15: Cull . . . 4J 45
River Exe Country Pk. . . . 4H 71
Riverford Cl. PL6: Plym . . . 3E 132
Riverford Organic Farm . . . 1D 175
River Front EX3: Exton . . . 1F 75
Rivermead EX15: Cull . . . 5H 45
Rivermead Av. EX8: Exmth . . . 2C 76
Rivermead Ct. EX8: Exmth . . . 1C 76
Rivermead Rd. EX2: Exe . . . 2G 71
River Pk. PL20: Horr . . . 2F 127
PL21: Erm . . . 2J 147
River Plate Rd. EX2: Cou W . . . 4C 72
Rivers Cl. PL21: Ivy . . . 4J 145
Riversdale EX34: Ilfra . . . 2G 11
River's Edge Ct. EX20: Oke . . . 2B 48
RIVERSIDE . . . 1A 134
Riverside EX7: Daw W . . . 7D 96
EX10: Sidm . . . 6C 84
(off York St.)
EX15: Hemy . . . 1H 47
EX36: N Mol . . . 2D 26
TQ9: Tot . . . 4D 102
TQ14: Shal . . . 6G 107
Riverside 2 TQ12: New A . . . 7G 105
Riverside Apartments
EX36: S Mol . . . 6E 26
Riverside Bus. Pk. PL1: Dev . . . 1D 140
Riverside Caravan Pk.
PL6: Plym . . . 3G 137
Riverside Cl. EX14: Hon . . . 3E 54
EX39: Bide . . . 1F 23
PL20: Horr . . . 2E 126
Riverside Ct. EX2: Exe . . . 6E 6
EX16: Tiv . . . 4D 40
EX31: Barn . . . 4E 18
(off Castle St.)
EX39: Bide . . . 1G 23
(not continuous)
TQ6: Dartm . . . 1B 124
(off South Embankment)
TQ12: New A . . . 7G 105
Riverside Leisure Cen. . . . 7C 6 (1E 70)
Riverside Mill
(The Devon Guild of Craftsmen) . . . 4C 92

Riverside Pl.—Royal Navy Av.

Riverside Pl. *PL1: Dev* *2C 140*
(off Cannon St.)
Riverside Rd. EX3: Top 7D 72
EX10: Sidm 6C 84
EX31: Barn 3B 18
EX35: Lynm 1H 13
TQ6: Ditt 5C 120
Riverside Rd. E. PL8: New F 6H 149
Riverside Rd. W. PL8: New F 6H 149
Riverside Ter. *EX10: Sidm* *6C 84*
(off York St.)
Riverside Units EX31: Barn 3A 18
Riverside Vw. EX11: Ott M 4C 80
Riverside Wlk. PL5: Tam F 4G 131
PL8: Torr 2C 150
Riverside Way EX12: Seat 5G 87
Riverside Workshops EX12: Seat . . .5G 87
Riversleigh PL3: Plym 6F 137
Riversmeet EX3: Top 7C 74
EX39: Apple 2H 21
Rivers Wlk. EX2: Cou W 6B 72
Rivervale Cl. TQ13: Chag 2G 61
River Valley Rd. TQ13: Chud K 6B 94
River Vw. EX32: Barn 7H 19
PL4: Plym 3C 142
Riverview TQ12: New A 2J 109
River Vw. Cl. EX24: Colyt 7D 88
TQ13: Chud K 6B 94
River Vw. Commercial Cen.
EX31: Barn 3C 18
River Vw. Dr. EX24: Colyt 7D 88
Riverview Dr. EX4: Exe 4C 64
River Vw. La. PL4: Plym 3B 142
Riverview Pl. *TQ7: Kingsb* *4F 157*
(off Fore St.)
River Vw. Ter. EX6: Exmin 3D 74
Riviera, The *TQ1: Torq* *3D 116*
(off Parkhill Rd.)
TQ4: Paig 2H 119
Riviera Ct. TQ1: Torq 2E 116
Riviera International Cen. 2B 116
Riviera Ter. EX6: Exmin 3D 74
EX7: Daw 3J 97
Riviera Way TQ2: Torq 4H 111
Rixey La. EX17: Morc 3C 38
Rixey Pk. TQ13: Chud 7C 94
RIXHILL .7H 59
RMB Chivenor EX31: Chive 1C 16
ROACHILL 1C 165
Roach La. EX5: Silv 1H 51
Roadford Lake Country Pk. 1C 169
ROAD GREEN 5D 88
Robbins Hall PL4: Plym 3F 9
Robers Rd. TQ12: Kingst 3G 105
Robert Adams Cl. PL7: Plymp 6H 137
Robert Davy Dr. EX2: Cou W 4C 72
Roberts Av. PL11: Torp 1A 140
Roberts Cl. EX15: Cull 5G 45
TQ2: Torq 3D 112
Roberts Rd. EX2: Exe 6F 7 (7F 65)
PL5: Plym 3B 134
Roberts Way TQ12: New A 7C 104
Robert Way EX10: New P 5H 81
Robin Cl. EX15: Cull 5G 45
Robins Fld. TQ7: Chil 6F 159
Robins Hill EX39: Bide 1D 22
Robinsons Row *TQ8: Salc* *4D 158*
(off Fore St.)
Robins Pk. TQ7: Lodd 1G 151
Robins Way PL9: Plyms 4F 143
Robin Wlk. EX16: Tiv 2E 40
ROBOROUGH
Barnstaple 1G 19
Great Torrington 2D 163
Plymouth 1D 132 (1B 174)
Roborough Av. PL6: Plym 5C 132
Roborough Cl. PL6: Plym 5C 132
Roborough Gdns. TQ13: Ashb 2J 99
Roborough La. PL5: Tam F 2H 131
(Allern La.)
PL5: Tam F 1A 132
(Soper's Hill)
PL6: Robo 2H 131
TQ13: Ashb 3H 99
Roborough Rd. EX31: Barn, Shir 1F 19
Roborough Ter. TQ13: Ashb 3H 99
Robyns Cl. PL7: Plymp 4E 138
Roche Gdn. EX2: Cou W 5K 71
Rochester Rd. PL4: Plym 1G 9
Rochford Cres. PL5: Plym 5E 130
Rock, The EX31: Barn 2E 18
Rock Av. EX32: Barn 6F 19
EX35: Lynt 2F 13
ROCKBEARE 3F 69 (1A 172)
Rockbeare Hill EX5: Rock 3F 79
Rockcliffe Ct. EX34: Ilfra 2J 11
Rock Cl. TQ4: Broads 1J 121
Rockdale Rd. PL8: Torr 3C 150
Rock End Av. TQ1: Torq 4E 116
Rockfield Av. PL6: Plym 4A 132
Rockfield Cl. TQ14: Teignm 2K 107
Rockfield Ho. EX4: Exe 2F 7
Rockfield Rd. EX34: Woolc 5A 10
Rock Gardens, The 3B 94
Rock Gdns. EX32: Barn 6F 19
PL9: Plyms 3E 142
Rock Hill EX18: Chul 7B 32
EX33: Brau 4J 15
EX33: Georgeh 5C 14
EX34: Berry 4B 12
PL5: Tam F 3H 131
TQ7: Ave G 7H 151
Rock Ho. La. TQ1: Maid 1E 112
Rockingham Rd. PL3: Plym 6B 136
Rocklands TQ13: Chud 3A 94
Rock La. *EX34: Com M* *7C 12*
(off Castle St.)
Rock Lodge Pk. EX35: Lynt 2G 13
Rockmount Ter. *EX39: Bide* *3F 23*
(off Myrtle Gro.)
Rock Pk. TQ6: Dartm 5D 124
TQ13: Ashb 2J 99
Rock Pk. Ter. *EX32: Barn* *5F 19*
(off Park Ter.)
Rock Rd. TQ2: Torq 2D 116
TQ13: Chud 2C 94
Rockside EX4: Exe 4B 6 (6D 64)
Rockside Vs. EX4: Exe 3B 6 (6D 64)
Rockstone, The EX7: Daw 3K 97
Rock Ter. PL7: Plymp 5A 138
Rock Vw. EX16: Hal 6E 42
Rockville Pk. PL9: Plyms 4F 143
Rock Wlk. TQ2: Torq 2C 116
ROCKWELL GREEN 2B 166
Rockwood Rd. PL6: Plym 2F 133
Rocky Hill PL19: Tavi 4H 59
Rocky La. EX34: Com M 5B 12
TQ11: B'leigh 6B 98
TQ14: Teignm 3G 107
(not continuous)
Rocky Pk. Av. PL9: Plyms 4F 143
Rocky Pk. Rd. PL9: Plyms 5F 143
Rocombe Cl. TQ2: Torq 1B 112
Roddick Way PL7: Plymp 4F 139
Rodgemont's La. EX18: Chaw 7E 32
Rodgers Ind. Est. TQ4: Paig 4D 118
Rodney Cl. EX8: L'ham 5J 77
TQ6: Dartm 6D 124
Rodney La. *EX34: Ilfra* *2J 11*
(off Quayfield Rd.)
Rodney St. PL5: Plym 3C 134
Rods La. PL19: Mary T 1B 60
Roeselare Av. PL11: Torp 1A 140
Roeselare Cl. PL11: Torp 1A 140
Rogada Ct. TQ5: Brixh 6F 123
Rogate Dr. PL6: Plym 6E 132
Rogate Wlk. PL6: Plym 6E 132
Rogers Cl. EX16: Tiv 2E 40
Rogers Cres. EX39: Bide 3J 23
Rohaise Ct. DT7: Uply 3G 91
Roland Bailey Gdns. PL19: Tavi 3G 59
Roland Matthews Ct. *PL2: Dev* *7D 134*
(off Boscawen Pl.)
Rolle, The EX9: Bud S 7C 82
Rolle Barton EX9: Ott'n 6G 83
Rolle Cotts. EX9: E Bud 2D 82
EX9: Know 5A 82
Rolle Ct. EX12: Seat 1E 86
EX38: Gt T *2B 30*
(off New St.)
Rolle Quay EX31: Barn 4D 18
Rolle Rd. EX8: Exmth 6C 76
EX9: Bud S 7C 82
EX38: Gt T 2A 30
Rolles Ter. EX39: Buck B 2H 29
Rollestone Cres. EX4: Exe 2H 65
Rolle St. EX8: Exmth 6C 76
EX31: Barn 3D 18
Rolle Studios *EX8: Exmth* *6C 76*
(off Rolle St.)
Rolle Ter. EX38: Gt T 2A 30
Rolle Vs. EX8: Exmth 6C 76
Rollis Pk. Cl. PL9: Plyms 4D 142
Rollis Pk. Rd. PL9: Plyms 4D 142
Rolston Cl. PL6: Plym 4J 131
Roly Poly Hill EX2: Exe 3B 70
Romaleyn Gdns. TQ4: Good 3H 119
Roman Rd. DT7: Lym R 4H 91
PL5: Plym 2D 134
ROMANSLEIGH 1B 164
Romans Way EX16: Tiv 2F 41
Roman Wlk. EX1: Exe 4F 7
Roman Way EX5: Cranb 4B 68
EX12: Seat 4D 86
EX14: Hon 2G 55
PL5: Plym 1D 134
Romilly Gdns. PL7: Plymp 6J 137
Romney Cl. PL5: Plym 2G 135
Romsey Dr. EX2: Exe 6J 7 (7H 65)
Ronald Ter. PL2: Plym 6E 134
Roncombe La. EX10: Sidb 1J 85
Ronsdale Cl. PL9: Plyms 4E 142
Rookery Cotts. TQ3: Marl 2D 114
Rookery La. DT7: Harc B 1H 91
Rooklands Av. TQ1: Torq 6B 112
Rook La. PL21: Corn 4J 129
Rooks Cl. EX31: Roun 6A 18
Rooks Farm Rd. EX31: Yell 7B 16
ROOK'S NEST 1A 166
Rooks Nest EX31: Frem 6F 17
Rooks Way EX16: Tiv 2E 40
Rookswood La. EX5: Rock 4F 69
Rookwood Cl. EX14: Hon 3E 54
Roope Cl. PL5: Plym 4B 134
Roper Av. PL9: Plyms 4E 142
Ropers Ct. EX9: Ott'n 6H 83
Roper's La. EX9: Ott'n 6H 83
Ropery Rd. EX34: Ilfra 2J 11
Rope Wlk. EX39: Bide 3F 23
PL4: Plym 6G 9 (3A 142)
TQ14: Teignm 4H 107
Ropewalk TQ7: Kingsb 5F 157
Ropewalk Hill TQ5: Brixh 3E 122
Ropewalk Ho. *EX8: Exmth* *6A 76*
(off Shelly Rd.)
Rorkes Cl. PL5: Plym 1D 134
Rosalie Ter. *EX34: Woolc* *6A 10*
(off Arlington Rd.)
Roscoff Cl. EX38: Gt T 2D 30
Rosea Bri. La. EX34: Com M 5A 12
Rose Acre Ter. TQ5: Brixh 4F 123
ROSE ASH 1B 164
Rosebank Cres. EX4: Exe 3G 65
Rosebarn Av. EX4: Exe 3G 65
Rosebarn La. EX4: Exe 2G 65
Rosebery Av. PL4: Plym 2K 9 (1B 142)
Rosebery La. PL4: Plym 1K 9 (1B 142)
Rosebery Rd. EX4: Exe 1J 7 (4H 65)
EX8: Exmth 4C 76
PL4: Plym 2K 9 (1B 142)
Roseclave Cl. PL7: Plymp 3F 139
Rose Cl. EX16: Tiv 2F 41
Rose Cotts. PL6: Plym 3C 136
Rosedale Av. PL2: Plym 4J 135
Rosedale Ter. EX12: Seat 3F 87
Rose Dene TQ2: Torq 3B 112
Rosedown Av. PL2: Plym 4F 135
Rose Gdns. PL6: Plym 4E 132
TQ12: Ipp 6J 101
Rose Hill PL9: Wem 7B 148
TQ12: Kingsk 1F 111
Rose Hill Cl. TQ12: Kingsk 1F 111
Rosehill Cl. TQ1: Torq 1E 116
Rosehill Gdns. TQ12: Kingsk 1F 111
Rosehill Rd. TQ1: Torq 1D 116
Rosehip Cl. PL6: Plym 3F 133
Roseland Av. EX1: Heav 6K 65
Roseland Cres. EX1: Heav 6K 65
Roseland Dr. EX1: Heav 7K 65
Roselands EX10: Sidm 6B 84
Roselands Dr. TQ4: Paig 4E 118
Roseland Sq. TQ12: Kingst 4H 105
Roselands Rd. TQ4: Good, Paig 4F 119
TQ4: Paig 4E 118
Rose La. EX32: Barn 6H 19
Rose Lawn EX32: Swim 3G 25
Roselyn Ter. EX31: Barn 3D 18
Rosemary Av. TQ12: New A 7C 104
Rosemary Cl. PL7: Wot 1F 129
Rosemary Ct. TQ3: Pres 6H 115
Rosemary Gdns. TQ3: Paig 6F 115
Rose Mary Ho. *EX15: Hemy* *2G 47*
(off Jubilee Dr.)
ROSEMARY LANE 2B 166
Rosemary La. EX13: Mus 7C 90
EX24: Colyt 5D 88
Rosemary St. EX4: Exe 7C 64
Rosemont TQ1: Torq 2F 117
Rosemont Ct. EX2: Alph 4E 70
Rosemoor Rd. EX38: Gt T 2D 30
Rosemount *TQ4: Good* *3J 119*
(off Roundham Rd.)
Rosemount Cl. EX14: Hon 4E 54
Rosemount Ct. *TQ8: Salc* *3C 158*
(off Church St.)
Rosemount La. EX14: Hon 4D 54
Rosemullion, The EX9: Bud S 7C 82
Rosemullion Ct. EX9: Bud S 7C 82
Rosery Rd. TQ2: Torq 1A 116
Rosevale Ter. *EX16: Tiv* *5C 40*
(off Howden Rd.)
Rosevean Ct. PL3: Plym 5A 136
Rosevean Gdns. PL3: Plym 5A 136
Roseveare Cl. PL9: Plyms 4H 143
Rose Vs. PL21: Bitta 3B 146
Roseville St.
TQ6: Dartm 1A 124 (6F 125)
Rosewarne Av. TQ12: New A 2J 109
Roseway EX8: Exmth 4H 77
Rosewell Cl. EX14: Hon 2G 55
Rosewood Cl. PL9: Plyms 7G 143
Rosewood Cres. EX5: Clyst M 3K 73
Rosewood Gro. EX31: Roun 6B 18
Rosewood Ter. EX4: Exe 1G 7 (4G 65)
Rospeath Cres. PL2: Plym 3J 135
Rossall Dr. TQ3: Paig 2G 119
Ross Cl. EX1: Pin 3E 66
Rosse Rd. EX16: Tiv 2D 40
Rosslyn Pk. Rd. PL3: Plym 6J 135
Ross Pk. Caravan Pk. TQ12: Ipp . . .5J 101
Ross St. PL2: Dev 7D 134
(not continuous)
Roswell Ct. EX8: Exmth 7D 76
Rosyl Av. EX7: Holc 7F 97
Rothbury Cl. PL6: Plym 6F 133
Rothbury Gdns. PL6: Plym 6E 132
Rotherfold TQ9: Tot 6D 102
Rothesay Gdns. PL5: Plym 7H 131
Rougemont Av. TQ2: Torq 4J 111
Rougemont Cl. PL3: Plym 4C 136
Rougemont Ct. EX6: Exmin 2B 74
Rougemont Ter. EX13: Axmin 5H 89
Roundball Cl. EX14: Hon 5F 55
Roundball La. EX14: Hon 7E 54
Round Berry Dr. TQ8: Salc 4B 158
ROUNDHAM 3D 167
Roundham Av. TQ4: Good 3K 119
Roundham Cres. TQ4: Good 2K 119
Roundham Gdns. TQ4: Good 3J 119
Roundham Ho. *TQ4: Paig* *2J 119*
(off Belle Vue Rd.)
Roundham Rd. TQ4: Paig 2J 119
Roundhead Rd. TQ12: Heat 1J 93
ROUND HILL 4J 115 (1B 176)
Roundhill EX16: Tiv 5B 40
Roundhill Cl. EX4: Exe 1D 64
Roundhill Rd. TQ2: Torq 4K 115
Roundhouse La. EX8: Exmth 2D 76
Roundings, The TQ5: Galm 3H 121
Roundmoors Cl. TQ12: Kingsk 2G 111
Roundsleys La. PL19: Mary T 2C 60
Rounds Nest 3B 150
ROUNDSWELL 7A 18
Roundswell Bus. Pk. EX31: Roun . . .7A 18
Roundtable Meet EX4: Whip 3A 66
Roundway, The TQ12: Kingsk 6J 109
ROUSDON 1C 173
Rousdown Rd. TQ2: Torq 2A 116
Rowan Cl. EX14: Hon 5C 54
EX16: Tiv 3F 41
PL7: Plymp 4E 138
PL19: Tavi 6J 59
TQ12: E Ogw 3C 108
Rowancroft EX1: Heav 4K 7 (6J 65)
Rowan Dr. EX12: Seat 2E 86
Rowan Pk. EX31: Roun 7B 18
Rowans, The PL16: Lift 6B 56
Rowantree Rd. TQ12: New A 3H 109
Rowan Way EX4: Exe 5C 64
PL6: Plym 3F 133
TQ5: Brixh 6B 122
Rowbrook Cl. TQ4: Paig 4E 118
Rowcroft Cl. EX14: Hon 4E 54
Rowcroft Rd. TQ3: Pres 6J 115
ROWDEN 1A 170
Rowdens, The *TQ2: Torq* *1B 116*
(off Belgrave Rd.)
TQ14: Teignm 3K 107
Rowdens Rd. TQ2: Torq 1B 116
Rowden St. PL3: Plym 6K 135
Row Down Cl. PL7: Plymp 5G 139
Rowe Cl. EX39: Bide 5E 22
Rowe Ho. EX4: Exe 4F 65
Rowells Mead TQ12: Live 4G 93
Rowes Farm Barns TQ9: Sto G 3B 120
Rowes Orchard EX15: Will 5C 44
Rowe St. PL11: Torp 1A 140
Rowhorne Rd. EX4: Nad 5A 64
Rowland Cl. PL9: Hooe 7F 143
Row La. PL5: Plym 1D 134
Rowley Rd. TQ1: Torq 5E 112
Rowlstone Cl. EX8: Exmth 1E 76
Rowsell's La. TQ9: Tot 6F 103
Rows La. EX34: Com M 7C 12
Row Tor Cl. EX20: Oke 3D 48
Royal Albert Memorial Museum &
Art Gallery . . : 3D 6
Royal Av. EX8: Exmth 5B 76
Royal Charter Pk. EX18: Chul 6C 32
Royal Citadel, The 7F 9 (4K 141)
Royal Clarence Apartments
EX12: Seat *6F 87*
(off Harbour Rd.)
EX34: Ilfra *2H 11*
(off Regent Pl.)
Royal Cl. EX2: Alph 6E 70
Royal Corinthian Yacht Club
. . . . .7F 9 (4K 141)
Royal Ct. *TQ1: Torq* *6F 113*
(off Bedford Rd.)
TQ12: New A 1F 109
TQ14: Teignm *5J 107*
(off Den Cres.)
Royal Cres. EX2: Sow 2C 72
Royal Dart Yacht Club 7G 125
Royal Naval War Memorial
. . . . .7D 8 (4J 141)
Royal Navy Av. PL2: Plym 6D 134

Royal North Devon Golf Course 4D 20
Royal Observer Way
  EX12: Seat 5F 87
Royal Pde. PL1: Plym 5D 8 (3J 141)
Royal Pines TQ1: Torq 3F 117
Royal Terrace Gdns. 2C 116
Royal Torbay Yacht Club 3D 116
Royal Way EX6: Star 1E 96
Royal William Rd. PL1: Plym 4F 141
Royal William Yd. PL1: Plym 5F 141
Royston Ct. EX1: Whip 4B 66
Royston Rd. EX39: Bide 4E 22
ROYSTON WATER 2C 167
Rozel TQ1: Torq 3F 117
Ruckamore Rd. TQ2: Torq 1A 116
Ruda Holiday Pk. EX33: Croy 1B 14
  (not continuous)
Rudds Bldgs. EX16: Tiv 4B 40
  (off Melbourne St.)
Rudyard Way EX39: West H 6A 20
Rudyerd Wlk. PL3: Plym 5D 136
Rue St Pierre PL21: Ivy 4J 145
Rufford Cl. PL2: Plym 4F 135
Rugby Rd. EX4: Exe 7A 6 (1D 70)
Ruggaton La. EX34: Berry 4B 12
RUGWELL .4F 155
RUISHTON 1C 167
Rull La. EX15: Cull 1G 45
  (not continuous)
Rumbelow Rd. EX16: Tiv 2E 40
RUMSAM 7G 19
Rumsam Cl. EX32: Barn 7G 19
Rumsam Gdns. EX32: Barn 7G 19
Rumsam Mdws. EX32: Barn 7G 19
Rumsam Rd. EX32: Barn 7G 19
RUMWELL .1B 166
Runaway La. PL21: Modb 7F 147
Rundle Rd. TQ12: New A 7F 105
RUNDLESTONE 3D 169
Runnacleave Cres. EX34: Ilfra 2H 11
  (off Runnacleave Rd.)
Runnacleave Rd. EX34: Ilfra 2H 11
RUNNINGTON 1B 166
Runnymede Ct. PL6: Plym 1F 137
Rupertswood Ter. EX34: Ilfra 2J 11
  (off Hillsborough Rd.)
Rushcott Cl. EX31: Yell 7B 16
RUSHFORD 7C 58 (3C 169)
Rushforth Pl. EX4: Exe 4B 64
Rushlade Cl. TQ4: Paig 5F 119
Rush Way TQ9: Tot 6H 103
Ruskin Cres. PL5: Plym 1J 135
Russell Av. PL3: Plym 4A 136
Russell Cl. EX9: E Bud 1D 82
  EX32: L'key 2D 24
  PL9: Plyms 5J 143
Russell Ct. PL19: Tavi 3H 59
  TQ8: Salc 3D 158
  (off Fore St.)
  TQ9: Tot 6E 102
Russell Ct. Gdns. PL19: Tavi 3H 59
Russell Dr. EX9: E Bud 1D 82
Russell Pl. PL4: Plym 1D 8 (1J 141)
Russell St. EX1: Exe 3G 7 (6G 65)
  EX10: Sidm 7C 84
  PL19: Tavi 4J 59
Russell Ter. EX4: Exe 2C 6
  (off Little Silver)
Russell Wlk. EX2: Sow 2B 72
Russell Way EX2: Cou W, Sow 2B 72
  EX2: Sow 2D 72
Russel's Pk. La. EX5: Bradn 7F 45
Russet Av. EX1: Heav 6B 66
Russet Cl. EX1: Heav 6B 66
Russets La. TQ11: B'leigh 4D 98
Russett Cl. EX15: Uff 7G 43
Russet Wood PL5: Plym 6E 130
Rutger Pl. PL1: Plym 1G 141
Rutherford St. EX2: Won 1K 71
Ruthven Cl. PL6: Plym 3A 136
Rutland Rd. PL4: Plym 7A 136
Rutt La. PL21: Ivy 3K 145
RYALL 1D 173
Ryalls Ct. EX12: Seat 5E 86
RYBHAY 5G 49
Rydal Cl. PL6: Plym 1E 136
Rydal M. EX4: Exe 7C 64
  (off Windermere Cl.)
Ryde Cl. TQ2: Torq 3C 112
Ryder Cl. EX16: Tiv 5H 41
Ryder Rd. PL2: Dev, Plym 6E 134
  (not continuous)
Ryders Bank TQ11: B'leigh 5B 98
RYDON 3H 105
Rydon Acres TQ9: Sto G 3B 120
  TQ12: Kingst 3H 105
Rydon Av. TQ12: Kingst 3H 105
Rydon Est. TQ12: Kingst 3H 105
Rydon Ind. Est. TQ12: Kingst 5G 105
Rydon La. EX2: Cou W, Sow 4A 72
  EX3: Exton 1H 75
  EX5: Sow 1H 75

Rydon La. EX9: Ott'n 5H 83
  TQ12: A'well 6F 109
Rydon La. Retail Pk. EX2: Sow 2B 72
Rydon Pk. EX2: Sow 1C 72
Rydon Path TQ12: Kingst 2H 105
Rydon Rd. EX22: Hols 1B 34
  TQ12: Kingst 2H 105
Rydons TQ5: Brixh 4C 122
Ryeland Cl. PL9: Wem 6C 148
Rye Pk. EX19: Bea 3H 31
Rye Pk. Cl. EX19: Bea 3H 31
Ryll Cl. EX8: Exmth 5D 76
Ryll Ct. Dr. EX8: Exmth 5D 76
Ryll Gro. EX8: Exmth 5D 76
Ryll La. EX9: Bud S 7D 82

Sabre Cl. TQ12: Heat 1H 93
Sabre Wlk. EX32: Barn 3G 19
  (off Oliver Rd.)
Sackery TQ12: C'head 7A 106
Saddle, The TQ4: Good 5J 119
Saddlers La. EX11: Ott M 4C 80
Saddlers Way EX20: Oke 2D 48
Sadler Cl. EX8: Exmth 4G 77
Saffron Cl. TQ7: Kingsb 4G 157
Saffron Pk. TQ7: Kingsb 4G 157
Sage Gro. EX16: Tiv 4F 41
Sage Pk. Rd. EX33: Brau 3G 15
Sages Lea EX5: Wood S 2E 72
Sailmakers Ct. EX8: Exmth 6A 76
St Agnes La. TQ2: Torq 3A 116
St Albans Cl. EX4: Exe 6B 64
St Albans La. TQ1: Torq 6E 112
St Albans Pk. PL20: Yelv 6G 127
St Albans Rd. TQ1: Torq 6E 112
St Andrews Cl. EX6: Kenn 3J 95
  EX14: Fen 2G 53
  EX15: Cull 4G 45
  EX24: Colyt 5D 88
  (off Dolphin St.)
  PL20: Bere A 2C 128
  TQ13: Ashb 4H 99
St Andrews Ct. EX16: Tiv 2F 41
  (off Rooks Way)
St Andrews Cross
  PL1: Plym 5E 8 (3J 141)
St Andrews Dr. EX13: Axmin 2K 89
St Andrew's Est. EX15: Cull 3G 45
St Andrews Ho. EX8: Exmth 6B 76
  (off St Andrew's Rd.)
St Andrews Mdw. DT7: Lym R 4J 91
St Andrews Orchard EX24: Colyt . .5D 88
St Andrews Rd. EX4: Exe 1C 64
  EX5: Cow 4A 62
  EX8: Exmth 6B 76
  EX15: Cull 3G 45
  EX31: Frem 5E 16
  PL19: Whitc 7K 59
  TQ4: Paig 2J 119
St Andrews Sq. EX24: Colyt 5D 88
  (off Rosemary La.)
St Andrews Ter. EX24: Colyt 5D 88
St Andrew St. EX16: Tiv 5C 40
  (not continuous)
  PL1: Plym 5E 8 (3J 141)
St Annes EX6: Kenton 6H 95
St Anne's Chapel 4E 18
  (off Butchers Row)
St Anne's Chapel EX4: Exe 1H 7
St Annes Ct. TQ12: New A 1D 108
St Annes Pl. EX5: Silv 2A 62
St Annes Rd. EX1: Heav 1K 7 (5H 65)
  PL6: Plym 4E 132
  TQ1: Torq 6E 112
ST ANN'S CHAPEL
  Aveton Gifford 3C 175
  Gunnislake 3D 80
St Anthony's Cl. EX11: Ott M 3D 80
St Aubyn Av. PL2: Plym 6E 134
St Aubyn Rd. PL1: Dev 2D 140
St Aubyn's Pk. EX16: Tiv 5F 41
St Aubyn St. PL1: Dev 2D 140
St Aubyn's Vs. EX16: Tiv 5F 41
St Aubyn Ter. PL7: L Moor 1J 129
St Augustine's Cl. TQ2: Torq 2C 112
St Austin Cl. PL21: Ivy 4G 145
St Barnabas Ct.
  PL1: Plym 2B 8 (1H 141)
St Barnabas Ter.
  PL1: Plym 2A 8 (1G 141)
St Bartholomews Rd.
  TQ12: E Ogw 4C 108
St Bartholomew Way
  TQ12: E Ogw 4A 108
St Bernard's Cl. EX2: Exe 1G 71
  TQ11: Buck 2C 98
  (not continuous)
St Boniface Cl. PL2: Plym 4H 135
St Boniface Dr. PL2: Plym 4H 135

St Boniface Rd. EX17: Cred 6F 39
St Brannock's Hill EX33: Brau 3J 15
St Brannock's Pk. Rd. EX34: Ilfra . .3H 11
St Brannock's Rd. EX34: Ilfra 3H 11
St Brannock's Well Cl. EX33: Brau . .3J 15
St Briac Way EX8: Exmth 1G 77
St Bridget Av. PL6: Plym 2A 136
ST BUDEAUX 2C 134 (2A 174)
St Budeaux By-Pass PL5: Plym 3D 134
St Budeaux Cl. EX11: Ott M 4D 80
St Budeaux (Ferry Road) Station (Rail)
  . . . . .3C 134
St Budeaux Orchard EX11: Ott M . .4D 80
St Budeaux (Victoria Road) Station (Rail)
  . . . . .2C 134
St Catherine's Chapel & Almshouse (ruins)
  . . . . .4E 6
  (off Bedford St.)
St Catherines Pk. PL8: New F 5J 149
St Catherine's Rd. TQ1: Torq 5D 112
St Chad Cl. PL5: Plym 6H 131
St Clares Cl. EX12: Seat 5E 86
ST CLEER .3A 168
St Clements Ct. TQ6: Dartm 5E 124
  (off Church Rd.)
St Clements La. EX4: Exe 1B 6 (5D 64)
ST CLETHER 2A 168
St Columba Cl. TQ12: Kingst 3H 105
St Cyres Rd. EX14: Hon 3E 54
ST DAVID'S 1B 6 (5D 64)
St David's Cl. EX13: Axmin 2K 89
St David's Dr. EX13: Axmin 2K 89
St David's Hill EX4: Exe 1B 6 (5D 64)
St David's Pk. TQ4: Coll M 3B 118
St Davids Pl. EX4: Exe 1A 6
  (not continuous)
St Davids Rd. PL19: Tavi 5K 59
  TQ14: Teignm 1H 107
St Davids Ter. EX4: Exe 3C 6 (6E 64)
ST DOMINICK 3B 168
St Dominics Cl. TQ1: Torq 5D 112
St Dunstan's Abbey The Plymouth College
  Junior School Sports Hall
  . . . . .4A 8 (2G 141)
St Dunstans Rd. TQ8: Salc 4B 158
St Dunstan's Ter.
  PL4: Plym 3K 9 (2B 142)
St Edmonds Ct. EX4: Exe 5C 6
St Edmunds TQ7: Kingsb 3F 157
St Edmund's Rd. TQ1: Torq 6D 112
  (not continuous)
St Edmunds Wlk. TQ7: Kingsb 4F 157
St Edward Gdns. PL6: Plym 2C 136
St Efride's Rd. TQ2: Torq 1B 116
Sainte Honorine Du Fay Cl.
  EX32: Swim 3H 25
St Elizabeth Cl. PL7: Plymp 5C 138
St Elmo Ct. TQ8: Salc 5A 158
ST ERNEY .2A 174
St Erth Rd. PL2: Plym 4J 135
St Eval Pl. PL5: Plym 4D 130
St Francis Ct. PL5: Plym 7F 131
St Gabriel's Av. PL3: Plym 6J 135
ST GENNYS 1A 168
St Georges EX13: Axmin 3H 89
  (off Chard St.)
St Georges Av. EX13: Axmin 2K 89
  PL2: Plym 4H 135
St Georges Cl. PL21: Modb 7G 147
St George's Ct. TQ2: Torq 2D 112
St Georges Cres. TQ1: Torq 6E 112
St George's Hill DT7: Lym R 4H 91
St George's Rd. EX32: Barn 3E 18
  TQ1: Torq 6E 112
St Georges Sq. TQ6: Dartm 2B 124
  (off Newcomen Rd.)
St George's Ter. EX32: Barn 3E 18
  PL2: Plym 7E 134
St George's Vw. EX15: Cull 3G 45
St George's Way EX16: Tiv 5C 40
St George's Well EX15: Cull 2G 45
  (not continuous)
St George's Well Av. EX15: Cull . . .3G 45
ST GERMANS 2A 174
St German's EX4: Exe 4F 65
St German's Rd. EX4: Exe 4F 65
ST GILES IN THE WOOD 2D 163
ST GILES ON THE HEATH
  . . . . .6C 34 (1B 168)
St Gregorys Ct. EX12: Seat 4E 86
St Helen's Cl. EX39: A'sham 3A 22
St Helen's Cl. EX33: Croy 2C 14
St Helens Ct. PL10: Sidm 7A 84
St Helen's Wlk. PL5: Plym 5H 131
St Hilarian EX8: Exmth 7D 76
St Hilary Ter. PL4: Plym 3K 9 (2B 142)
SAINT HILL 3A 166
St Hill Cl. EX2: Ide 3D 70
St Ida's Cl. EX2: Ide 4A 70
ST IVE 3B 168
St Ive's Ct. TQ1: Torq 7C 112
ST JAMES' 4G 65

St Boniface Rd. EX17: Cred 6F 39
St James Cl. EX4: Exe 1G 7 (5G 65)
  EX32: L'key 3D 24
St James Cl. EX20: Oke 3B 48
  (off St James St.)
  PL11: Torp 1A 140
St James' Park 1G 7
St James' Park Station (Rail)
  .1G 7 (5G 65)
St James Pl. EX34: Ilfra 2J 11
  TQ1: Torq 6F 113
St James Pl. E.
  PL1: Plym 6C 8 (3H 141)
St James Pl. W.
  PL1: Plym 6C 8 (3H 141)
St James Rd. EX4: Exe 1G 7 (5G 65)
  PL11: Torp 2A 140
  TQ1: Torq 6C 112
St James's Ho. TQ14: Teignm 4H 107
  (off Fore St.)
St James's Pl. EX6: Chri 3J 63
St James's Pct. TQ14: Teignm 4H 107
  (off Bitton Pk. Rd.)
St James St. EX20: Oke 3B 48
St James Ter. EX4: Exe 1G 7 (5G 65)
St James Way EX16: Tiv 2E 40
ST JOHN 2A 174
St John Cl. EX14: Hon 3F 55
St Johns PL19: Tavi 4J 59
St Johns Av. PL19: Tavi 4J 59
St John's Bri. Rd.
  PL4: Plym 6J 9 (3A 142)
ST JOHN'S CHAPEL 1D 163
St Johns Cl. EX16: Tiv 2E 40
  EX24: Colyt 6C 88
  EX32: Barn 6H 19
  PL6: Plym 6E 132
  PL21: Ivy 4F 145
  TQ13: Bov T 5B 92
  TQ14: Bi'ton 4B 106
St Johns Ct. PL19: Tavi 5H 59
  TQ3: Paig 1H 119
  (off Littlegate Rd.)
  TQ9: Tot 6F 103
  (off Weston Rd.)
St John's Dr. EX22: Bradw 6B 28
  PL9: Hooe 6C 142
St John's Farm M. EX8: Exmth 1H 77
St Johns La. EX32: Barn 7H 19
  TQ13: Bov T 4B 92
St Johns Pl. EX1: Exe 4E 6
  TQ1: Torq 2D 116
  (off Braddons Hill Rd. W.)
St John's Rd. EX1: Heav 1K 7 (5H 65)
  EX8: Exmth 3F 77
  (not continuous)
  PL4: Plym 5J 9 (3A 142)
  (not continuous)
  PL9: Hooe 6B 142
  PL20: Horr 2E 126
  PL21: Ivy 4F 145
St Johns Rd. PL4: Plym 5J 9 (3A 142)
  TQ12: New A 7F 105
St John's Ter. TQ9: Tot 5D 102
St Johns Vs. EX2: Heav 7J 65
St Johns Yd. PL4: Plym 5H 9 (3A 142)
St Joseph's Cl. PL6: Plym 2A 136
St Josephs Ct. TQ14: Teignm 5J 107
  (off Carlton Pl.)
ST JUDE'S .2C 142
St Judes Cl. PL4: Plym 5J 9 (3A 142)
St Julian Cres. PL10: Crem 5D 140
St Katherine's Cl. EX31: Yell 6B 16
St Katherine's M. TQ9: Tot 6E 102
  (off St Kathcrine's Way)
St Katherine's Rd. EX4: Whip 4K 65
  TQ1: Torq 7A 112
St Katherine's Way TQ9: Tot 6E 102
St Keverne Pl. PL2: Plym 3J 135
St Keyes Cl. EX32: L'key 2B 24
St Kitts Cl. TQ2: Torq 3B 112
St Lawrence Cl. EX16: Tiv 5G 41
St Lawrence Cres. EX1: Heav 6C 66
St Lawrence Dr. EX17: Cred 5G 39
St Lawrence La. TQ13: Ashb 4H 99
St Lawrence M. PL4: Plym 1F 9
St Lawrence Rd.
  PL4: Plym 1F 9 (1K 141)
St Lawrence's Grn. EX17: Cred 6G 39
ST LEONARD'S 6J 7 (7H 65)
St Leonard's Av. EX2: Exe 7F 7 (1F 71)
St Leonard's Cl. TQ12: New A 2E 108
St Leonards Pl. EX2: Exe 6G 7 (7G 65)
  EX5: Clyst M 2F 73
St Leonards Rd. EX2: Exe 7G 7 (1G 71)
  EX14: Hon 4D 54
  PL4: Plym 5K 9 (3B 142)
  TQ12: New A 2E 108
St Leonard's Ter. EX24: Colyt 6C 88
  (off The Butts)
St Leonard's Tower 1E 108
St Levan Rd. PL2: Plym 6D 134

ST LOYE'S 1K 71
St Loyes Gdns. EX2: Won 7A 66
St Loyes Rd. EX2: Won 7K 65
St Loyes Ter. EX2: Won 1K 71
St Luke's Cl. TQ14: Teignm 3J 109
St Lukes Dr. TQ14: Teignm 3G 107
St Luke's Pk. TQ2: Torq 2C 116
St Luke's Rd. TQ2: Torq 1C 116
  TQ12: New A 3H 109
St Luke's Rd. Nth. TQ2: Torq 2C 116
St Luke's Rd. Sth. TQ2: Torq 2C 116
St Luke's Sports Cen. 4J 7 (6H 65)
St Lukes Vw. EX2: Cou W 4J 71
St Malo Cl. EX8: Exmth 1G 77
St Marco Gdns. TQ7: Kingsb 3G 157
St Margaret's Av. TQ1: Torq 6D 112
St Margarets Cl. EX15: Hemy 1G 47
  TQ1: Torq 5D 112
St Margarets Gdn. EX31: Barn 3E 18
St Margaret's M. TQ1: Torq 5D 112
St Margarets Rd. PL7: Plymp 4J 137
  TQ1: Torq 5D 112
St Margarets Ter. EX3: Top 5B 74
        (off Fore St.)
St Margaret's Vw. EX8: L'ham 5J 77
St Market St. PL1: Plym 3F 141
St Marks Av. EX1: Heav 1K 7 (5J 65)
St Mark's Dr. TQ1: Torq 3F 117
       (off St Mark's Rd.)
St Marks Rd. EX14: Hon 5D 54
  PL6: Plym 5E 132
  TQ1: Torq 3F 117
St Martin's Av. PL3: Plym 4J 135
St Martins Cl. EX10: Sidm 3C 84
  EX17: Bow 5J 37
St Martins Ct. EX10: Sidm 4C 84
      (off St Martins Cl.)
  TQ2: Torq 4B 112
St Martins La. EX17: Cred 5G 39
St Martin's M. TQ1: Torq 5E 112
       (off Fore St.)
ST MARYCHURCH 4E 112 (1B 176)
St Marychurch Rd. TQ1: Torq 4D 112
    (not continuous)
  TQ12: Coff, Dacc, New A, S'head
  . . . . .2H 109 & 1B 112
St Maryhaye TQ19: Tavi 4G 59
St Mary Magdalen Cl.
  TQ14: Bi'ton 4B 106
St Marys EX13: Ray H 4A 90
St Mary's Arches EX4: Exe . . .4D 6 (6E 64)
St Mary's Bay Holiday Cen.
  TQ5: Brixh 5G 123
St Marys Cl. EX6: Ted M 6J 49
  EX13: Axmin 4K 89
  EX38: Gt T 3A 30
  PL7: Plymp 4A 138
  TQ5: Brixh 6D 122
  TQ12: A'well 6D 108
  TQ13: Chud 2C 94
St Marys Ct. PL7: Plymp 4A 138
  TQ3: Paig 1G 119
  TQ12: New A 1E 108
     (off Highweek St.)
St Mary's Dr. TQ5: Brixh 5F 123
St Mary's Flats EX39: Bide 4F 23
     (off Buttgarden St.)
St Mary's Hill TQ5: Brixh 5F 123
St Mary's La. DT7: Uply 4A 90
St Marys Pk. EX11: Ott M 4D 80
  TQ4: Coll M 3C 118
St Mary's Rd. EX32: Barn 3F 19
  EX33: Croy 2D 14
  PL7: Plymp 5K 137
  TQ5: Brixh 6E 122
  TQ12: New A 2E 108
  TQ14: Teignm 2G 107
St Mary's Sq. TQ5: Brixh 5D 122
St Mary Steps Ter. EX1: Exe 5B 6
St Mary St. PL1: Plym 2G 141
St Marys Vw. EX5: Silv 2H 51
  EX11: W Hill 3J 79
St Matthews Cl. EX1: Exe 3J 7 (6G 65)
St Matthews Ct. EX1: Exe 3H 7
St Matthew's Rd. TQ2: Torq 2K 115
St Matthews Wlk. EX1: Exe . .3H 7 (6G 65)
St Matthias Chu. Rd. TQ1: Torq . .1G 117
St Maurice M. PL7: Plymp 5B 138
St Maurice Rd. PL7: Plymp 6C 138
St Maurice Vw. PL7: Plymp 5E 138
St Mawes Dr. TQ4: Good 7H 119
St Mawes Ter. PL2: Plym 6E 134
ST MELLION 1A 174
St Michael Av. PL2: Plym 6E 134
ST MICHAELS 2H 119 (2A 176)
St Michaels DT7: Lym R 4K 91
St Michaels Cl. EX2: Alph 4E 70
  EX5: Clyst H 4J 67
  EX9: Ott'n 6H 83
  PL1: Dev 3D 140
  TQ1: Torq 7A 112
  TQ10: S Bre 2B 100

St Michael's Ct. PL1: Dev 1E 140
     (off Stopford Pl.)
  TQ4: Paig 3G 119
     (off Derrell Rd.)
St Michaels Hill EX5: Clyst H 4J 67
St Michael's M. EX4: Exe 3C 6
  TQ4: Paig 2G 119
  TQ12: Kingst 5G 105
  TQ12: New A 3G 109
  TQ14: Teignm 2J 107
St Michaels Ter. PL1: Dev 1E 140
  TQ1: Torq 1D 116
  TQ10: S Bre 3B 100
St Michael's Ter. La.
  PL4: Plym 2D 8 (1J 141)
St Michaels Vw. EX21: Sheb 6J 29
St Michaels Way EX5: Cranb 3C 68
St Modwen Rd. PL6: Plym 4F 137
St Nazaire App. PL1: Dev 2E 140
St Nazaire Cl. PL1: Dev 2E 140
     (off St Nazaire App.)
ST NEOT 3A 168
St Nicholas Priory 5C 6
St Olaves Cl. EX4: Exe 5D 6 (6E 64)
St Olaves M. EX4: Exe 4C 6
St Pails Ct. TQ1: Torq 6D 112
     (off St Edmunds Rd.)
St Pancras Av. PL2: Plym 2H 135
St Patricks Ct. TQ14: Teignm 3G 107
St Pauls Cl. EX2: Won 2J 71
  PL3: Plym 6A 136
  TQ13: Bov T 4C 92
St Paul's Cres. TQ1: Torq 6D 112
St Pauls Dr. EX22: Hols 1B 34
St Paul's Rd. EX14: Hon 5D 54
  TQ1: Torq 6D 112
  TQ3: Pres 5K 115
  TQ12: New A 1F 109
St Paul's Sq. EX16: Tiv 5C 40
     (not continuous)
St Paul St. EX16: Tiv 4C 40
  PL1: Plym 4F 141
St Peters Cl. PL7: Plymp 5C 138
  TQ2: Torq 7K 111
  TQ13: Bov T 3D 92
St Peters Ct. EX10: Sidm 6D 84
     (off Church St.)
  EX16: Tiv 4C 40
St Peter's Hill TQ5: Brixh 3F 123
St Peters Ho. EX2: Exe 6E 6
St Peters Mt. EX4: Exe 5A 64
St Peter's Quay TQ9: Tot 7F 103
St Peter's Rd. EX14: Hon 4D 54
  EX22: Hols 1B 34
  EX31: Frem 6E 16
  PL5: Plym 1H 135
St Peters Ter. EX31: Barn 4E 18
     (off Butchers Row)
  EX34: Ilfra 3J 11
     (off Highfield Rd.)
  TQ5: Brixh 3F 123
     (off Elkins Hill)
St Peter St. EX16: Tiv 4C 40
St Peter's Way PL21: Ivy 5J 145
St Peter's Well La. EX22: Bradw . . .5C 28
St Petrock's Cl. EX2: Exe . . .6H 7 (7G 65)
St Saviours Rd. EX11: Ott M 4C 80
St Saviour's Way EX17: Cred 6G 39
St Scholasticas TQ14: Teignm 2K 107
St Sevan Way EX8: Exmth 1G 77
St Sidwell's Av. EX4: Exe 1G 7 (5F 65)
ST STEPHENS
  Launceston 2B 168
  Saltash 2A 174
St Stephen's Pl. PL7: Plymp 4B 138
St Stephen's Rd. PL7: Plymp 6C 138
St Stephen St. PL1: Dev 3E 140
St Teresa Ho. PL4: Plym 4B 8
St Teresa's Cl. EX39: N'ham 5E 20
St Teresa's M. EX39: N'ham 5E 20
     (off St Teresa's Cl.)
St Theresa's Ct. PL1: Dev 2E 140
     (off Raglan Rd.)
ST THOMAS 1D 70 (1D 171)
St Thomas Cl. PL7: Plymp 6C 138
  TQ13: Bov T 4D 92
St Thomas Ct. EX4: Exe 7B 6 (1D 70)
  EX16: Tiv 2E 40
  PL4: Plym 4G 9
St Thomas M. EX2: Exe 1D 70
St Thomas Shop. Cen.
  EX4: Exe 6B 6 (1D 70)
St Thomas Station (Rail) 7B 6 (1D 70)
St Vincent's Cl. TQ1: Torq 7B 112
St Vincent's Rd. TQ1: Torq 6B 112
St Vincent St. PL2: Plym 7D 134
St Werburgh Cl. PL9: Wem 7B 148
ST WINNOLLS 2A 174
Salamanca St. PL11: Torp 1A 140
SALCOMBE 3D 158 (3D 175)
Salcombe (Park & Ride) 3B 158

Salcombe Ct. EX10: Sidm 6D 84
Salcombe Hgts. Cl. TQ8: Salc 3B 158
Salcombe Hill EX10: Sidm 6D 84
Salcombe Hill Cl. EX10: Sidm 6C 84
Salcombe Hill Rd. EX10: Sidm 6C 84
Salcombe Lawn EX10: Sidm 6C 84
Salcombe Maritime & Local History Mus.
  . . . . .3D 158
SALCOMBE REGIS 2B 172
Salcombe RNLI Mus. 3D 158
Salcombe Rd. EX10: Sidm 6C 84
  PL4: Plym 1J 9 (7A 136)
  TQ7: Malb 6H 155
Salcombe Yacht Club 4C 158
Salem Chapel 4A 8
Salem Pl. EX4: Exe 1H 7 (5G 65)
  TQ12: New A 1E 108
Salem Sq. EX32: Barn 5F 19
     (off Trinity St.)
Salem St. EX32: Barn 5F 19
Salisbury Av. EX14: Fen 2G 53
  TQ2: Torq 3B 112
Salisbury Cl. EX14: Fen 2G 53
Salisbury Ope PL3: Plym 6G 135
Salisbury Rd. EX4: Exe 1J 7 (4H 65)
  EX8: Exmth 5C 76
  PL4: Plym 3H 9 (2A 142)
  TQ2: New A 7G 105
Salisbury Ter. EX13: Kilm 2B 88
Salmon Leap Cl. TQ11: B'leigh 4D 98
Salmon Pool La. EX2: Exe 2H 71
Salston Barton EX11: Ott M 5B 80
Salston Ride EX11: Ott M 5A 80
SALTASH 2A 174
Saltash Rd. PL2: Plym 6C 134
  PL3: Plym 1C 8 (1J 141)
Saltash Sailing Club 1A 134
Saltburn Rd. PL5: Plym 1H 135
Salterne Mdws. EX9: Bud S 5C 82
Salterns Ter. EX39: Bide 3G 23
Salters Bldgs. EX16: Tiv 4D 40
     (off Barrington St.)
Salter's Ct. EX2: Won 1K 71
Salter's La. EX24: Colyf 7C 88
Salters Mdw. EX10: Sidm 5C 84
Salter's Rd. EX2: Won 1K 71
Salterton Ct. EX8: Exmth 1E 77
Salterton Rd. EX8: Exmth 6D 76
Salting Hill EX9: Bud S 7E 82
Saltings, The EX12: Seat 3F 87
  TQ14: Shal 6F 107
Saltmer Cl. EX34: Ilfra 6G 11
Saltpill Duck Pond (Nature Reserve)
  . . . . .4E 16
Salt Quay Moorings TQ7: Kingsb . .5G 157
     (off Embankment Rd.)
Saltram 7G 137
Saltram Ter. PL7: L Moor 1J 129
  PL7: Plymp 4A 138
SALTRENS 1C 163
Salt Wood La. EX34: Com M 3E 12
     (not continuous)
Salty La. TQ14: Shal 6F 107
Salutary Mt. EX1: Heav 5K 7 (7J 65)
SALWAYASH 1D 173
Salway Cl. EX15: Cull 4G 45
Salway Gdns. EX13: Axmin 4K 89
Samara Bus. Pk. TQ12: Heat 1J 93
SAMPFORD ARUNDEL 2B 166
SAMPFORD COURTENAY 3A 164
Sampford Gdns. PL20: Horr 1G 127
SAMPFORD PEVERELL . .2A 42 (2A 166)
SAMPFORD SPINEY 3D 169
Sampford Ter. PL20: Horr 1F 127
Sampson Cl. EX10: Sidm 2B 84
Sampsons La. EX1: Heav . . .2K 7 (5H 65)
Sampson's Plantation
  EX31: Frem 7D 16
Samuel Bassett Av. PL6: Plym 3C 132
Sanctuary Cl. EX32: Bish T 6B 24
  PL2: Plym 6E 134
Sanctuary La. EX20: Hath 1H 35
Sanctuary Rd. EX22: Hols 2C 34
Sand 1K 85
Sandalwood EX7: Daw W 7E 96
  EX34: Berry 2E 12
Sandaway La. EX34: Berry 2E 12
Sand Down La. EX5: New C 7D 50
Sanderling Ct. TQ2: Sow 6E 66
Sanders Cl. EX5: Broadc 1C 68
Sanders La. EX22: Hols 1C 34
  EX32: Bish T 6B 24
Sanderspool Cross TQ10: S Bre . .2C 100
Sanders Rd. EX4: Exe 3C 66
  EX17: Bow 4G 37
  TQ5: Brixh 3C 122
SANDFORD 3C 165
Sandford Cl. EX32: Barn 7J 19
Sandford Orleigh TQ12: New A 6E 104

Sandford Rd. PL9: Plyms 4G 143
Sandfords EX6: Kennf 1H 95
Sandfords Gdns. EX38: Gt T 3A 30
Sandford Vw. TQ12: New A 7E 104
Sandford Wlk. EX1: Exe 3H 7 (6G 65)
     (not continuous)
Sandgate La. EX11: Wigg 7B 80
Sandhills EX39: Ins 1K 21
Sandhills Rd. TQ8: Salc 5B 158
Sandhill St. EX11: Ott M 3C 80
Sand La. TQ9: L'ton 3H 103
Sand Martins, The TQ12: New A . . .2H 109
     (off St Marychurch Rd.)
Sandon Wlk. PL6: Plym 3B 136
Sandown Rd. TQ4: Paig 5F 119
Sandpath Rd. TQ12: Kingst 5H 105
Sandpiper Cl. EX4: Pin 3C 66
  EX34: Woolc 6C 10
Sandpiper Dr. EX3: Exton 2G 75
Sandpiper Grn. EX2: Exe 1A 70
Sandpiper Way TQ2: Torq 3J 111
Sand Pit Hill La. EX24: Colyt 7A 88
Sandquay Rd. TQ6: Dartm 4F 125
Sandringham Dr. TQ3: Pres 4G 115
Sandringham Gdns. TQ3: Pres 4H 115
Sandringham Rd. TQ12: New A 1H 109
Sands Beach Wlk. TQ4: Good 5J 119
Sands Cl. EX12: Seat 5D 86
  TQ4: Paig 2H 119
Sands Rd. TQ4: Paig 2H 119
  TQ7: Slap 2J 159
SANDYGATE
  Clyst St Mary 3E 72
  Kingsteignton 2G 105 (3C 171)
Sandygate TQ12: Kingst 2F 105
Sandygate Bus. Pk.
  TQ12: Kingst 2F 105
Sandygate M. TQ12: Kingst 1G 105
    (off Lower Sandygate)
Sandygate Mill TQ12: Kingst 1G 105
Sandy La. EX5: Bram S 6F 51
  EX5: Broadc 7D 52
  EX5: Rewe 4K 51
  EX7: Daw 2J 97
  EX33: Croy 2B 14
  EX34: Woolc 6A 10
  PL21: Ivy 4H 145
  TQ7: Gov, Kingsb 1J 157
Sandymere Rd. EX39: N'ham 4D 20
Sandy Park Stadium 3D 72
Sandy Pk. Way EX2: Cou W 2D 72
Sandy Rd. PL7: Plymp 5F 139
Sandy Way EX33: Croy 3C 14
Sanford Pl. EX2: Exe 7A 6 (1D 70)
Sanford Rd. TQ2: Torq 1A 116
Sannerville Way EX6: Exmin 7K 71
San Remo Ter. EX7: Daw 4J 97
Sanson Cl. EX5: Sto C 7J 51
Sarah Cl. PL20: Bere A 2B 128
Sargent Cl. EX1: Heav 6B 66
Sarlsdown Rd. EX8: Exmth 5F 77
Sarum Cl. PL3: Plym 4A 136
SATTERLEIGH 1A 164
Saturday's La. TQ2: N Whil 4F 111
Saundercroft Rd. EX5: Broadc 1C 68
Saunders Wlk. PL6: Plym 4J 131
Saunders Way EX15: Cull 3J 45
  TQ7: W Cha 7K 157
SAUNTON 3A 160
Saunton Cl. EX33: Brau 4H 15
Saunton Rd. EX33: Brau, Saun 3F 15
Savage Rd. PL5: Plym 3B 134
Savery Cl. PL21: Ivy 3J 145
Savery Ter. PL4: Plym 7B 136
Savile Rd. EX4: Exe 7C 64
Savoy Cinema, The
  Scott Cinemas 6C 76
     (off Rolle St.)
Savoy Hill EX4: Whip 2K 65
Savoy Mews, The EX36: S Mol 6D 26
Saw Mill Ct. EX31: Barn 3E 18
     (off Mills Way)
Sawmill La. EX9: E Bud 1B 82
Sawmills Way EX14: Hon 4F 55
Sawpit La. TQ9: Darti 4B 102
Sawrey St. PL1: Plym 5A 8 (3G 141)
Sawyer Dr. TQ14: Teignm 2F 107
Sawyers Cl. TQ13: More 6G 61
Saxon Av. EX4: Pin 2D 66
Saxon Cl. EX17: Cred 7J 39
Saxon Hgts. TQ5: Brixh 4E 122
Saxon Mdw. TQ4: Coll M 2C 118
Saxon Rd. EX1: Heav 6J 65
  PL19: Tavi 3G 59
Saxons Cft. EX32: Barn 6H 19
Saxon Way EX15: Cull 2H 45
Scalders La. PL21: Modb 7G 147
Scalwell La. EX12: Seat 3E 86
Scalwell Mead EX12: Seat 3E 86
Scalwell Pk. EX12: Seat 3E 86
Scanniclift Copse Nature Reserve
  . . . . .2K 63

Scarborough Pl. TQ2: Torq 1B 116
Scarborough Rd. TQ2: Torq 1B 116
Scarsdale EX8: Exmth 7E 76
Scattor Vw. EX6: Bridf 1F 63
Scholars Wlk. TQ7: Kingsb 3G 157
School Cl. EX16: Bam 2G 33
(not continuous)
EX31: Frem 6F 17
PL7: Plymp 2A 138
PL19: Tavi 4K 59
School Cotts. TQ12: Teigng 3D 104
School Ct. TQ6: Dartm 6D 124
School Dr. PL6: Plym 3E 132
School Gdns. TQ10: S Bre 1B 100
School Hill EX5: Whim 6G 53
EX6: Cockw 3E 96
EX7: Daw 4G 97
EX8: Lymp 6G 75
TQ9: Sto G 4B 120
School Hill Cotts. *TQ9: Sto G* *4B 120*
(off School Hill)
School Ho. Gdns. TQ7: Lodd 2G 151
School La. EX2: Cou W 4K 71
EX5: Broadc 5C 52
EX5: Thor 2B 50
EX6: Ted M 6J 49
EX8: Exmth 3D 76
EX10: New P 5H 81
EX11: W Hill 3H 79
EX14: Hon 3F 55
EX24: Colyt 6C 88
EX32: Bish T 6B 24
EX38: Gt T 1B 30
EX39: Hart 3J 27
PL7: Plymp 5B 138
PL21: Corn 6J 129
TQ9: Blacka 2B 152
TQ14: Shal 6G 107
School Rd. EX2: Exe 7B 6 (1D 70)
EX5: Silv 2H 51
EX20: Lyd 5H 57
PL19: Whitc 7K 59
PL21: Erm 2H 147
TQ6: Sto F 2F 153
TQ12: Kingsk 7J 109
TQ12: New A 1F 109
TQ12: Teigng 3C 104
School Steps TQ6: Dartm 2A 124
School St. EX10: Sidf 1D 84
School Ter. *EX7: Daw* *4G 97*
(off School Hill)
School Way EX20: Oke 3B 48
Schooner's Ct. EX8: Exmth 6A 76
Scoldens Cl. PL21: Modb 7G 147
Sconner Rd. PL11: Torp 1A 140
Scoresby Cl. TQ2: Torq 1D 112
Score Vw. EX34: Ilfra 5J 11
Scorhill Stone Circle 2A 170
SCORRITON 1D 175
Scott Av. EX2: Won 2J 71
EX39: Apple 3H 21
PL5: Plym 3B 134
Scott Bus. Pk. PL2: Plym 5F 135
Scott Cinemas
The Alexandra Cinema 1E 108
The Central Cinema 4E 18
The Radway Cinema 6C 84
The Regent Cinema 5J 91
The Savoy Cinema *6C 76*
(off Rolle St.)
Scott Dr. EX8: Exmth 2D 76
Scott Memorial 3E 140
Scott Rd. PL2: Plym 6G 135
(Bowers Rd.)
PL2: Plym 5F 135
(Scott Bus. Pk.)
Scotts EX16: Bam 3G 33
Scotts Cl. TQ7: Chur 1B 156
Scotts Cotts. *PL9: Plyms* *4E 142*
(off Millway Pl.)
Scott's La. DT6: Monk W 1D 90
Scratch Face La. EX2: Ide 3A 70
Scratchface La. EX39: Bide 6B 22
Scratton Path *TQ12: E Ogw* *4C 108*
(off Reynell Rd.)
Screechers Hill TQ13: Ashb 3G 99
Scurfield Cl. EX33: Brau 3J 15
SEA 2D 167
Seabee Pl. EX14: Dunk 4G 47
SEABOROUGH 3D 167
Seabourne Ct. *TQ4: Good* *3J 119*
(off Alta Vista Rd.)
Seabrook Av. EX2: Cou W 6B 72
Seabrook M. EX2: Cou W 6B 72
Seacliff TQ14: Teignm 3K 107
Seacroft Rd. PL5: Plym 1B 134
Seafield Av. EX8: Exmth 2C 76
Seafield Gdns. 6E 86
Seafield La. EX10: Sidm 7B 84
Seafield Pk. EX39: West H 5A 20
Seafield Rd. EX10: Sidm 6B 84
EX12: Seat 6E 86
Seafields TQ4: Good 5J 119
Sea Front TQ2: Torq 4A 116
Sea Haven *EX12: Seat* *6F 87*
(off Harbour Rd.)
Sea Hill EX12: Beer 7C 86
EX12: Seat 5E 86
Sea La. TQ5: Brixh 4G 123
Sea Lawn Ter. EX7: Daw 3J 97
Seale Cl. TQ6: Dartm 5D 124
Seale Hayne 7J 93
Seapoint *TQ14: Teignm* *5H 107*
(off Strand)
Searle St. EX17: Cred 5H 39
Searle Ter. EX39: N'ham 5F 21
Seascape TQ2: Torq 3B 116
Seashore Centre, The 3J 119
Seaside EX34: Com M 5A 12
Seasons, The *EX4: Whip* *4B 66*
(off Summerway)
SEATON 5E 86 (1C 173)
Seaton Av. PL4: Plym 7K 135
Seaton Bus. Pk. PL6: Plym 7C 132
Seaton Cl. TQ1: Torq 6F 113
Seaton Down Cl. EX12: Seat 4D 86
Seaton Down Hill EX12: Seat 3C 86
Seaton Down Rd. EX12: Seat 5D 86
SEATON JUNCTION 1C 173
Seaton La. PL4: Plym 7K 135
Seaton Marshes Local Nature Reserve
4F 87
Seaton Orchard PL7: Spa 1K 139
Seaton Pl. PL2: Plym 6E 134
Seaton Rd. EX13: Mus 7C 90
EX24: Colyf 2F 87
Seaton Stop
Seaton Tramway 5F 87
Seaton Tramway
Colyford Stop 1G 87
Colyton Stop 5E 88
Seaton Stop 5F 87
Seaton Way PL20: C'stone 6B 126
SEATOWN 1D 173
Sea Vw. EX34: Ilfra 4K 11
Seaview EX39: A'sham 4A 22
Sea Vw. Av. PL4: Plym 1K 9 (1B 142)
Seaview Cres. TQ3: Pres 5J 115
Sea Vw. Dr. PL9: Wem 6B 148
Sea Vw. Gdns. TQ7: Hope 2G 155
Sea Vw. Pl. *EX39: Apple* *3H 21*
(off New Quay St.)
Sea Vw. Rd. EX39: N'ham 5E 20
Seaview Rd. TQ7: Thur 5C 154
Sea Vw. Ter. EX10: Sidm 5B 84
EX12: Beer 7B 86
PL4: Plym 2J 9 (1A 142)
TQ5: Brixh *2E 122*
(off Overgang Rd.)
TQ7: Thur 5C 154
SEAVINGTON ST MARY 2D 167
SEAVINGTON ST MICHAEL 2D 167
Seaward Cl. EX12: Brans 6J 85
Seaway Cl. TQ2: Torq 3A 116
Seaway Ct. TQ2: Torq 3B 116
TQ5: Brixh 4D 122
Seaway Cres. TQ3: Pres 6K 115
Seaway Gdns. TQ3: Pres 6K 115
Seaway Head EX24: Colyt 7C 88
Seaway La. EX10: Tip J 2J 81
TQ2: Torq 2K 115
Seaway Rd. TQ3: Pres 6J 115
Seckington Hamlet EX19: Wink 1A 36
Secmaton La. EX7: Daw 2H 97
Secmaton Ri. EX7: Daw 1H 97
Second Av. EX1: Heav 3K 7 (6J 65)
EX2: Cou W 6B 72
EX7: Daw 5F 97
EX13: Axmin 2K 89
PL1: Dev 2F 141
PL2: Plym 4D 134
PL9: Plyms 3H 143
TQ1: Torq 5C 112
TQ14: Teignm 4G 107
Second Dr. TQ14: Teignm 3K 107
(Burwood Pl.)
TQ14: Teignm 4H 107
(Third Dr.)
Second Fld. La. EX33: Brau 5H 15
Sector La. EX13: Axmin 4J 89
Sedemuda Cl. EX10: Sidm 2B 84
Sedemuda Rd. EX10: Sidm 2A 84
Sedgeclaire Cl. EX1: Pin 3E 66
Sedge Cl. PL21: Ivy 5H 145
Sedley Way PL5: Plym 7J 131
Sefton Av. PL4: Plym 1K 9 (7B 136)
Sefton Cl. PL4: Plym 1B 142
Sefton Ct. EX7: Daw 4G 97
TQ1: Torq 6F 113
Segrave Rd. PL2: Plym 6G 135
Selborne Cl. *EX33: Brau* *5J 15*
(off Barton La.)
Seldons Cl. PL21: Ugb 6E 146
Selkirk Pl. PL5: Plym 1K 135
Sellers Cl. EX24: Colyf 1G 87
Seller's Wood Hill EX12: Brans 4J 85
Sellick Av. TQ5: Brixh 5F 123
SELLICK'S GREEN 2C 167
Sellon Ct. PL1: Plym 4C 8 (2H 141)
Selsden Cl. PL9: Elb 6K 143
Senate Ct. *EX8: Exmth* *3G 77*
(off Senate Way)
Senate Way EX8: Exmth 3F 77
Sendall's Way PL6: Plym 7A 132
Sennen Pl. PL2: Dev 7D 134
Sentry Cnr. EX39: Bide 4H 23
Sentry La. EX32: Bish T 6B 24
Sentrys Orchard EX6: Exmin 3D 74
Sercombes Gdns. EX6: Star 1E 96
Serge Ct. EX2: Exe 6D 6
Serpell Cl. PL6: Plym 4K 131
Sett Cl. TQ13: Bov T 4C 92
Seven Acre La. EX33: Brau 5K 15
Seven Acres EX5: Cranb 4B 68
Seven Acres Pk. EX33: Brau 5K 15
SEVEN ASH 1B 166
Seven Brethren Bank EX31: Barn 5E 18
Seven Crosses Rd. EX16: Tiv 6A 40
Seven Hills Ho. *TQ2: Torq* *1C 116*
(off Burridge La.)
Seven Stars La. PL5: Tam F 4G 131
Seventh St. *EX32: Barn* *3E 18*
(off King Edward St.)
Seven Trees Ct.
PL4: Plym 1G 9 (1A 142)
Severn Brethren Ind. Est.
EX31: Barn 6E 18
Severn Pl. PL3: Plym 6D 136
Severn Rd. TQ2: Torq 6H 111
Sexton's Cottage Info. Cen. 3B 170
Seymour Av. PL4: Plym 2J 9 (1A 142)
Seymour Caravan Pk. *TQ12: Live* *4H 93*
(off Old Liverton Rd.)
Seymour Ct. EX8: Exmth 2D 76
Seymour Dr. PL3: Plym 6A 136
TQ2: Torq 1C 112
TQ6: Dartm 6C 124
Seymour Ho. PL1: Dev 3E 140
Seymour M. PL4: Plym 2K 9 (1B 142)
Seymour Pk. PL3: Plym 6B 136
Seymour Pl. PL1: Plym 2A 8 (1G 141)
TQ9: Tot 6F 103
Seymour Rd. EX8: Exmth 2D 76
PL3: Plym 6A 136
PL7: Plymp 5J 137
TQ9: Tot 6F 103
TQ12: New A 7E 104
Seymour St. PL4: Plym 3G 9 (2K 141)
Seymour Ter. EX16: Tiv 4C 40
TQ9: Tot *6F 103*
(off Bridgetown)
Seymour Vs. EX34: Woolc 5C 10
Shackhayes EX34: Com M 5B 12
Shackleton Cl. EX8: Exmth 2D 76
Shackleton Ct. PL5: Plym 2J 135
Shackleton Wlk. TQ14: Teignm 1G 107
SHADYCOMBE 3C 158
Shadycombe Ct. TQ8: Salc 3C 158
Shadycombe Rd. TQ8: Salc 2B 158
Shady La. TQ6: Sto F 3H 153
Shady Nook Caravan Site
TQ12: Kingst 4H 105
Shaftesbury Cl. *EX7: Daw* *4H 97*
(off Brunswick Pl.)
Shaftesbury Cotts.
PL4: Plym 1G 9 (1K 141)
Shaftesbury Ct.
PL4: Plym 2G 9 (1K 141)
Shaftesbury Pl. *PL4: Plym* *2G 9*
(off Shaftesbury Cotts.)
TQ9: Tot *6E 102*
(off Maudlin Rd.)
Shaftesbury Rd. EX2: Exe 1D 70
EX34: Ilfra 3J 11
Shaftesbury Theatre
Dawlish 4G 97
Shakespeare Cl. EX16: Tiv 2D 40
TQ2: Torq 7K 111
Shakespeare Rd. EX2: Won 2J 71
PL5: Plym 1G 135
Shakespeare Way EX8: Exmth 7K 75
SHALDON 6G 107 (3D 171)
Shaldon Approach Golf Course 7H 107
Shaldon Bri. TQ14: Shal 5G 107
Shaldon Cres. PL5: Plym 7G 131
Shaldon Rd. TQ12: C'head 7A 106
TQ12: New A 2H 109
TQ14: Shal 7A 106
(not continuous)
Shaldon Wildlife Trust 7H 107
Shalford Ter. EX13: Whitf 5A 90
SHALLOWFORD 2D 161
Shallowford Cl. PL6: Plym 3D 136
Shallowford Rd. PL6: Plym 4D 136
Shambles Dr. EX17: Cop 5C 38
Shamwickshire Cl. EX39: Bide 4H 23
Shand Pk. EX13: Axmin 4G 89
Shapland Pl. EX16: Tiv 6B 40
Shapleys Gdns. PL9: Plyms 7H 143
Shapley Tor Cl. TQ5: Brixh 6C 122
Shapley Way TQ12: Live 4F 93
Shapter Ct. EX8: L'ham 5H 77
Shapters Rd. PL4: Plym 6K 9 (3B 142)
Shaptor & Furzeleigh Woods
Nature Reserve 1B 92
Shaptor Vw. TQ13: Bov T 6A 92
Sharkham Ct. TQ5: Brixh 5F 123
Sharkham Dr. TQ5: Brixh 5F 123
Sharkham Ho. TQ5: Brixh 5F 123
Sharkham Point Caravan Pk.
TQ5: Brixh 6F 123
Sharland's Ct. *EX16: Tiv* *4D 40*
(off Gold St.)
Sharland's La. EX33: Brau 4H 15
Sharon Way PL6: Plym 5B 132
Sharper La. TQ14: Shal 7E 106
Sharpham Dr. TQ9: Tot 7F 103
Sharpham Wines & Cheeses 2A 176
Sharp Hill EX20: Oke 4B 48
Sharpitor TQ8: Salc 7A 158
Sharpitor Cl. TQ3: Pres 5F 115
Sharpitor Row PL20: Dous 3K 127
Sharpland La. EX33: Puts 1D 14
Sharp Rock EX34: Mort 4A 10
Sharp's Cl. TQ12: Heat 2K 93
Sharps Ct. EX8: Exmth 6A 76
Sharp's Crest TQ12: Heat 2K 93
Sharrose Rd. PL9: Hooe 7C 142
SHAUGH PRIOR 1B 174
Shauls Ct. EX1: Exe 2G 7
Shaw Way PL9: Hooe 5A 142
Shearers Way TQ13: Chud 1D 94
Shearford La. EX31: Barn 1E 18
Shearman Ct. EX2: Exe 6D 6 (7E 64)
SHEARSTON 1C 167
Shearwater Dr. TQ2: Torq 2K 111
Shearwood Cl. PL7: Plymp 5K 137
SHEBBEAR 6J 29 (3C 163)
Shedden Hill TQ2: Torq 2C 116
SHEEPSTOR 1B 174
Sheepstor Rd. PL6: Plym 2E 136
SHEEPWASH 3C 163
SHELDON 3B 166
Sheldon La. EX6: Dodd 1K 63
Shell Cl. PL6: Plym 2F 137
Shelley Av. PL19: Tavi 4K 59
TQ1: Torq 5C 112
Shelley Cl. EX2: Exe 3D 70
Shelley Way PL5: Plym 2C 134
Shells La. EX24: Colyf 7D 88
Shelly Ct. EX8: Exmth 6A 76
EX20: S Zeal 2J 49
Shelly Reach EX8: Exmth 6B 76
Shelly Rd. EX8: Exmth 6A 76
EX20: S Zeal 3J 49
Shelston Tor Dr. TQ4: Paig 4F 119
Shelton Pl. EX1: Heav 6J 65
Shepherd Cl. TQ3: Paig 2E 118
Shepherds Hill *EX2: Cou W* *4K 71*
(off Countess Wear Rd.)
Shepherds La. EX10: Col R 1J 83
PL4: Plym 5H 9 (3A 142)
TQ14: Teignm 1E 106
Shepherds Mdw. EX19: Bea 3J 31
EX39: A'sham 3A 22
Sheppard Rd. EX4: Exe 2G 65
Sheppards Row EX8: Exmth 5C 76
SHEPTON BEAUCHAMP 2D 167
Sherborne Cl. PL9: Elb 6K 143
Sherborne La. DT7: Lym R 5K 91
Sherborne Rd. TQ12: New A 1E 108
Sherbrook Cl. EX9: Bud S 7B 82
Sherbrook Hill EX9: Bud S 7B 82
Shercroft Cl. EX5: Broadc 2K 67
SHERFORD 3D 175
Sherford Cres. PL5: Plym 7F 131
PL9: Elb 5K 143
Sherford Proposed Development
7D 138
Sherford Rd. PL9: Elb 5K 143
Sherford Wlk. PL9: Elb 7K 143
Sheridan Rd. EX4: Whip 4B 66
PL5: Plym 2H 135
Sherman Tank Memorial 3A 176
Sherratt's Oak EX31: Barn 2G 19
Sherrell Pk. PL20: Bere A 2B 128
Sherril Cl. PL9: Plyms 7G 143
Sherwell Arc. PL4: Plym 2F 9
Sherwell Hill TQ2: Torq 1K 115
Sherwell La. PL4: Plym 2F 9 (1K 141)
TQ2: Torq 1K 115
Sherwell Pk. Rd. TQ2: Torq 1K 115
Sherwell Ri. Sth. TQ2: Torq 1K 115
Sherwells Cl. EX7: Daw W 7D 96
Sherwell Valley Rd. TQ2: Torq 7J 111
Sherwill Cl. PL21: Ivy 3E 144
Sherwood Cl. EX2: Won 7J 65
Sherwood Dr. EX8: Exmth 1F 77

Sherwood Green—Southdowns Rd.

SHERWOOD GREEN ... 1D 163
Shetland Cl. TQ2: Torq ... 3A 112
SHEVIOCK ... 2A 174
Shields, The EX34: Ilfra ... 4H 11
(not continuous)
Shieling Rd. EX31: Bick'n ... 6J 17
Shillands EX16: Tiv ... 3B 40
Shillingate Cl. EX7: Daw ... 6F 97
SHILLINGFORD ... 1D 165
SHILLINGFORD ABBOT ... 7D 70
Shillingford Rd. EX2: Alph ... 6D 70
EX2: Alph, Shil A ... 6D 70
SHILLINGFORD ST GEORGE ... 2D 171
Shindle Pk. TQ7: Chil ... 6F 159
SHINNER'S BRIDGE ... 2B 102 (1D 175)
Shinners Bri. TQ9: Darti ... 2B 102
Shinners Bri. Cen. TQ9: Darti ... 2B 102
SHIPHAY ... 6J 111 (1A 176)
Shiphay Av. TQ2: Torq ... 6J 111
Shiphay La. TQ2: Torq ... 5J 111
Shiphay Mnr. Dr. TQ2: Torq ... 6K 111
Shiphay Pk. Rd. TQ2: Torq ... 6K 111
Ship La. EX5: Clyst H ... 4J 67
Shipley Cl. TQ10: S Bre ... 1C 100
Shipley Rd. EX14: Hon ... 3G 55
Shipley Wlk. PL6: Plym ... 2B 136
Shirburn Rd. PL6: Plym ... 2C 136
TQ1: Torq ... 6C 112
Shire Cl. TQ4: Good ... 7G 119
Shirehampton Ho. EX4: Exe ... 3B 6
Shire La. DT7: Lym R ... 5G 91
Shirley Cl. EX8: Exmth ... 1F 77
Shirley Ct. *TQ1: Torq* ... *2F 117*
(off Torwood Gdns. Rd.)
Shirley Gdns. PL5: Plym ... 2H 135
Shirley Towers TQ1: Torq ... 3D 116
SHIRWELL ... 3B 160
Shirwell Rd. EX31: Barn, Shir ... 1F 19
Shoalstone Pool ... 2G 123
Shobbrook Hill TQ12: New A ... 7B 104
SHOBROOKE ... 3C 165
Shooting Marsh Stile
EX2: Exe ... 7C 6 (1E 70)
SHOP
Abbots Bickington ... 2B 162
Bude ... 2A 162
SHOREDITCH ... 1C 167
Shorelands Rd. EX31: Barn ... 6C 18
Shorelands Way EX31: Barn ... 6C 18
Shoreland Way EX39: West H ... 5D 20
Shore Line, The EX12: Seat ... 6G 87
Shoreside TQ14: Shal ... 6G 107
Shorland Cl. EX7: Daw ... 2J 97
Shorneywell TQ7: Chil ... 6G 159
SHORTACOMBE ... 2D 169
Shortacombe Dr. EX33: Brau ... 3G 15
Short Cl. EX39: Bide ... 3C 22
Short Cotts. PL11: Torp ... 1A 140
Short Furlong EX12: Beer ... 7A 86
Shortlands La. EX15: Cull ... 4G 45
Shortlands Rd. EX15: Cull ... 4G 45
Short La. TQ14: Shal ... 7E 106
SHORTON ... 5G 115 (1A 176)
Shorton Rd. TQ3: Paig, Pres ... 6G 115
TQ3: Pres ... 5G 115
Shorton Valley Rd. TQ3: Pres ... 5G 115
Short Pk. Rd. PL3: Plym ... 6J 135
Shortridge Cl. EX14: Hon ... 5F 55
EX16: With ... 6H 33
Shortridge Mead EX16: Tiv ... 4B 40
Shorts Way TQ9: Tot ... 5B 102
Shortwood Cl. EX9: Bud S ... 5B 82
Shortwood Cres. PL9: Plyms ... 5H 143
Shortwood La. EX9: Know ... 3A 82
Shoulsbury Castle ... 3D 161
Shovel Down Stone Rows ... 2A 170
Shrewsbury Av. TQ2: Torq ... 4C 112
Shrewsbury Rd. PL5: Plym ... 6G 131
Shrinkhill La. EX16: Tiv ... 5D 40
Shrubbery, The EX3: Top ... 5B 74
EX20: Exbo ... 5J 35
Shrubbery Cl. EX32: Barn ... 6H 19
SHUTE
Axminster ... 1C 173
Crediton ... 3C 165
Shute TQ7: Malb ... 6G 155
Shute Barton ... 1C 173
Shutecombe Ter. PL20: Bere F ... 6D 128
Shute Ct. TQ14: Bi'ton ... 3C 106
Shute Hill TQ7: Malb ... 6G 155
TQ14: Bi'ton ... 3C 106
TQ14: Teignm ... 4J 107
Shute Hill Cres. TQ14: Teignm ... 4J 107
Shute La. EX19: Wink ... 3C 36
(not continuous)
EX34: Com M ... 6B 12
TQ12: Den ... 2H 101
TQ13: More ... 6J 61
Shute Mdw. St. *EX8: Exmth* ... *5C 76*
(off Meadow St.)
Shute Pk. TQ7: Malb ... 6G 155
Shute Pk. Rd. PL9: Plyms ... 7G 143
Shute Rd. EX13: Kilm ... 2A 88
EX13: Whitf ... 5A 90
TQ9: Tot ... 6F 103
Shutes Mead EX11: Ott M ... 3D 80
Shuttern Cl. EX5: New C ... 7D 50
Shutterton La. EX7: Daw, Daw W ... 7C 96
Sicklemans Cl. TQ7: W Cha ... 7K 157
SID ... 5D 84 (2B 172)
Sidborough Hill EX17: Morc ... 4C 38
SIDBURY ... 2H 85 (1B 172)
Sidcliffe EX10: Sidm ... 4D 84
Siddalls Gdns. EX16: Tiv ... 4E 40
Sideling Flds. EX16: Tiv ... 6F 41
SIDFORD ... 1D 84 (1B 172)
Sidford High St. EX10: Sidf, Stow ... 2A 84
Sidford Rd. EX10: Sidm ... 4C 84
Sidgard Rd. EX10: Sidm ... 4D 84
Siding Rd. PL4: Plym ... 1D 8 (1J 141)
Sidlands EX10: Sidm ... 6B 84
Sid La. EX10: Sidm ... 4C 84
Sidleigh EX10: Sidm ... 5D 84
Sidmount Gdns. EX10: Sidm ... 5B 84
SIDMOUTH ... 7C 84 (2B 172)
Sidmouth Cotts. PL4: Plym ... 1J 9
Sidmouth Golf Course ... 7A 84
Sidmouth Mus. ... *7C 84*
(within Sid Vale Heritage Cen.)
Sidmouth Rd. DT7: Lym R ... 5G 91
EX2: Sow ... 2E 72
EX2: Sow, Won ... 7B 66
EX5: Clyst M ... 3G 73
EX11: Ott M, Wigg ... 4D 80
EX14: Hon ... 5D 54
EX24: Colyt ... 6C 88
Sidmouth Sports Cen. ... 3D 84
Sidmouth Swimming Pool ... 7C 84
Sidney Ct. *EX7: Daw* ... *4G 97*
(off Old Town St.)
Sidney Wlk. TQ4: Good ... 6H 119
Sid Pk. Rd. EX10: Sidm ... 5C 84
Sid Rd. EX10: Sidm ... 6C 84
Sid Vale Cl. EX10: Sidf ... 1D 84
Sid Vale Heritage Cen. ... 7C 84
Sid Vale M. *EX10: Sidf* ... *1D 84*
(off Sid Vale Cl.)
Sidwell Ho. EX1: Exe ... 3F 7
Sidwell St. EX4: Exe ... 3F 7 (6F 65)
SIGFORD ... 3B 170
Sigford Rd. EX2: Mar B ... 5G 71
Signal Ct. EX33: Brau ... 5J 15
Signals, The EX14: Fen ... 2G 53
Signal Ter. EX31: Barn ... 5D 18
Silbury Pl. EX17: Cred ... 6H 39
Silford Cross EX39: West H ... 7B 20
Silford Rd. EX39: N'ham ... 7D 20
Silvan Dr. EX33: Brau ... 3K 15
Silver Birch Cl. EX2: Won ... 2K 71
PL6: Plym ... 3D 132
Silver Birch Ct. EX31: Roun ... 7B 18
Silver Bri. Cl. TQ4: Good ... 7J 119
Silverdale EX5: Silv ... 1H 51
(not continuous)
EX8: Exmth ... 1G 77
Silverdown Office Pk.
EX5: Clyst H ... 7C 68
Silverhill TQ7: Malb ... 6G 155
Silverhills Rd. TQ12: New A ... 4G 109
Silveridge La. TQ7: Lodd ... 1H 151
Silver La. EX4: Exe ... 1H 7 (5G 65)
EX5: Rock ... 4F 69
Silver Lea EX13: Kilm ... 2B 88
Silvers, The EX3: Top ... 3E 72
Silver Stream Way PL8: Brixt ... 2J 149
Silver St. DT7: Lym R ... 5H 91
EX5: Thor ... 2B 50
EX11: Ott M ... 3C 80
EX13: Axmin ... 4H 89
EX13: Kilm ... 2B 88
EX14: Hon ... 3F 55
EX15: Culm ... 3A 46
EX15: Kent ... 6B 46
EX15: Will ... 4D 44
EX16: Bam ... 2H 33
EX16: Tiv ... 4D 40
EX20: Lyd ... 6H 57
EX24: Colyt ... 5D 88
EX32: Barn ... 4E 18
EX33: Brau ... 3J 15
EX34: Berry ... 3C 12
EX39: Apple ... 3H 21
EX39: Bide ... 4F 23
PL20: Bere F ... 7C 128
TQ11: B'leigh ... 4C 98
TQ12: Ipp ... 7G 101
Silver Ter. EX4: Exe ... 3C 6 (6E 64)
PL10: Mill ... 6A 140
SILVERTON ... 1H 51 (3D 165)
Silverton Rd. EX2: Mar B ... 5G 71
Silverwell Pk. PL21: Modb ... 6G 147
Silverwood Av. TQ12: New A ... 3H 109
Silverwood Hgts. EX32: Barn ... 3G 19
Simcoe Pl. EX15: Hemy ... 2F 47
Simcoe Way EX14: Dunk ... 7G 47
Simey Cl. EX4: Exe ... 5C 64
Simmonds Pl. EX15: Cull ... 3K 45
Simmons Cl. EX20: Oke ... 3C 48
Simmons Way EX20: Oke ... 4C 48
Simon Cl. PL9: Plyms ... 6F 143
SIMONSBATH ... 3D 161
Sinai Hill EX35: Lynt ... 2G 13
Singer Cl. TQ3: Paig ... 2G 119
Singmore Rd. TQ3: Marl ... 4E 114
Sings La. EX33: Brau ... 5J 15
Sir Alex Wlk. EX3: Top ... 7C 72
Sir Christopher Ondaatje
Indoor Cricket Centre, The ... 3E 64
Sir John Hunt Sports Cen. ... 6J 131
Siskin Chase EX15: Cull ... 5F 45
Sisna Pk. Rd. PL6: Plym ... 6F 133
Sithney St. PL5: Plym ... 2B 134
Sivell Ct. *EX2: Heav* ... *7J 65*
(off Sivell Pl.)
Sivell M. *EX2: Heav* ... *7J 65*
(off Sivell Pl.)
Sivell Pl. EX2: Heav ... 7J 65
Six Mile Hill EX6: Ted M ... 6J 49
Sixmile Hill EX6: Dunsf ... 6E 62
Six O'Clock La. PL7: Plymp ... 5B 138
Skardale Gdns. PL6: Plym ... 3E 136
Skardon Pl. PL4: Plym ... 2F 9 (1K 141)
Skelmersdale Cl.
TQ7: Kingsb ... 4G 157
Skern Cl. EX39: N'ham ... 4E 20
Skern Lodge Activity Cen. ... 2G 21
Skern Way EX39: N'ham ... 4E 20
Skerries Rd. PL6: Plym ... 3A 132
SKILGATE ... 1D 165
Skinner Cl. *EX16: Tiv* ... *4B 40*
(off Shortridge Mead)
Skinners Cl. EX10: Sidm ... 6A 84
Skirhead La. EX34: Com M ... 7D 12
Skye Cl. TQ2: Torq ... 3A 112
Skylark Ri. PL6: Plym ... 2F 133
PL19: Whitc ... 7K 59
Skylark Spinney EX31: Roun ... 7K 17
Skyways Bus. Pk. EX5: Clyst H ... 7C 68
Slade EX39: Bide ... 3D 22
Slade Cl. EX11: Ott M ... 3E 80
PL9: Plyms ... 7H 143
Slade La. TQ5: Galm ... 3H 121
TQ12: A'well ... 6D 108
(not continuous)
Slade Rd. EX11: Ott M ... 4D 80
EX34: Ilfra ... 5G 11
Slade Valley Rd. EX34: Ilfra ... 4G 11
Sladnor Pk. Rd. TQ1: Maid ... 2J 113
Slanns Mdw. TQ12: Kingst ... 5G 105
Slapper's Hill TQ5: Hill ... 3K 125
SLAPTON ... 2J 159 (3A 176)
Slapton Ley Field Cen. ... 2J 159
Slapton Ley National Nature Reserve
... 4J 159
Slapton Monument ... 3K 159
Slatelands Cl. PL7: Plymp ... 6E 138
Slate La. PL1: Plym ... 3G 141
Sleap Hill EX9: E Bud ... 6F 83
Sleepy Hollow *EX2: Cou W* ... *6B 72*
(off Moon Ridge)
Sleepy La. TQ3: Pres ... 5G 115
Slewton Cres. EX5: Whim ... 5G 53
Slipperstone Dr. PL21: Ivy ... 3E 144
Slittercombe La. EX6: Kenton ... 5J 95
Sloe La. EX32: L'key ... 2C 24
SLONCOMBE ... 2B 170
SLOUGH GREEN ... 1C 167
Smallack Cl. PL6: Plym ... 1A 136
Smallack Dr. PL6: Plym ... 1A 136
Smallacombe Rd. EX16: Tiv ... 4B 40
SMALLBROOK ... 5A 50 (1C 171)
Smallcombe Rd. TQ3: Paig ... 6E 114
Smalldon La. TQ1: Torq ... 2D 112
Small La. EX5: Broadc ... 5C 52
SMALLRIDGE ... 3D 167
Smallridge Cl. PL9: Plyms ... 7G 143
Smallwell La. TQ3: Marl ... 3B 114
Smardon Av. TQ5: Brixh ... 3C 122
Smardon Cl. TQ5: Brixh ... 3C 122
SMEATHARPE ... 2C 167
Smeaton Sq. PL3: Plym ... 5E 136
Smeaton's Tower ... 7D 8 (4J 141)
SMITHALEIGH ... 6K 139
Smithaleigh Caravan & Camping Pk.
PL7: Smit ... 6K 139
Smithay Mdws. EX6: Chri ... 3J 63
Smith Ct. TQ1: Torq ... 7B 112
Smith Fld. Rd. EX2: Alph ... 5D 70
Smithfields TQ9: Tot ... 6C 102
Smith Hill TQ14: Bi'ton ... 3B 106
SMITHINCOTT ... 2A 166
Smiths Ct. EX2: Exe ... 1E 70
Smith St. TQ6: Dartm ... 1B 124 (6F 125)
Smithys Way EX16: Sam P ... 2B 42
Smockpark La. PL9: Wem ... 4C 148
Smokey Ho. Caravans TQ3: Marl ... 4E 114
Smoky Ho. La. EX31: Barn ... 1G 19
EX32: Snap ... 1G 19
Smugglers Caravan Pk. EX7: Holc ... 7F 97
Smugglers Cl. EX12: Brans ... 6J 85
Smugglers La. EX7: Holc ... 7G 97
Smythen St. EX1: Exe ... 5D 6 (7E 64)
SNAPPER ... 3B 160
Snowberry Cl. TQ1: Torq ... 6B 112
Snowdonia Cl. TQ4: Coll M ... 3D 118
Snowdrop Cl. EX14: Hon ... 5D 54
Snowdrop M. EX4: Exe ... 4A 64
Sog's La. EX11: Ven O ... 2H 81
Solar Cres. EX4: Exe ... 1C 70
SOLDON CROSS ... 2B 162
Soloman Dr. EX39: Bide ... 4F 23
Solsbro M. TQ2: Torq ... 2A 116
Solsbro Rd. TQ2: Torq ... 2A 116
Somer Flds. DT7: Lym R ... 5G 91
Somerlea EX15: Will ... 3D 44
Somerset Av. EX4: Exe ... 1B 70
Somerset Cotts. PL3: Plym ... 7F 135
Somerset Ct. *TQ5: Brixh* ... *3F 123*
(off Mt. Pleasant Rd.)
Somerset Pl. *EX31: Barn* ... *4E 18*
(off Wells St.)
PL3: Plym ... 7F 135
TQ9: Tot ... 6F 103
TQ14: Teignm ... 5H 107
Somerset Pl. La. PL3: Plym ... 7F 135
Somers Rd. DT7: Lym R ... 5H 91
Something La. EX33: Croy ... 3C 14
Somerville Cl. EX8: Exmth ... 3F 77
EX15: Will ... 3C 44
Somerville Pk. EX15: Will ... 3C 44
Somerville Rd. EX15: Will ... 4C 44
Somerwell La. EX16: With ... 7G 33
Sommers' Cres. EX34: Ilfra ... 2J 11
Soper Rd. TQ14: Teignm ... 2G 107
Soper's Hill PL5: Tam F ... 1K 131
Soper Wlk. TQ14: Teignm ... 2G 107
Sophia Way TQ12: New A ... 2D 108
Sorrell Ct. TQ12: Kingst ... 4G 105
Sorrento TQ1: Torq ... 1E 116
Sortridge Pk. PL20: Horr ... 1D 126
SOURTON ... 1D 169
Sourton Quarry (Conservation Area)
... 2K 57
SOUTH ALLINGTON ... 3D 175
South Av. DT7: Lym R ... 4J 91
EX1: Heav ... 3K 7 (6H 65)
EX39: Bide ... 4J 23
Sth. Bank Dr. EX39: Bide ... 3E 22
Sth. Bay Holiday Camp
TQ5: Brixh ... 6F 123
SOUTH BOWOOD ... 1D 173
SOUTH BRENT ... 1B 100 (1D 175)
Sth. Brent Rd. TQ7: Lodd ... 2G 151
SOUTHBROOK ... 2A 92
Southbrook Cl. TQ13: Bov T ... 3B 92
Southbrook La. EX5: Whim ... 1F 69
TQ13: Bov T ... 3A 92
(not continuous)
Southbrook Rd. EX2: Cou W ... 3K 71
TQ13: Bov T ... 3B 92
Sth. Burrow Rd. EX34: Ilfra ... 3H 11
SOUTH CHARD ... 3D 167
Sth. Church La. EX20: Oke ... 4A 48
Southcliffe EX32: Bish T ... 7B 24
South Cl. *EX33: Brau* ... *5J 15*
(off South St.)
Southcombe St. TQ13: Chag ... 2H 61
Southcombe Ter. EX12: Axmth ... 3J 87
SOUTH COMMON ... 3D 167
Southcote Orchard TQ9: Tot ... 6G 103
SOUTHCOTT
East-the-Water ... 1J 23
Great Torrington ... 2C 163
Okehampton ... 1D 169
Southcott Rd. EX39: Bide ... 1E 22
Sth. Devon Coast Path
TQ14: Shal ... 6H 107
Sth. Devon M. TQ12: New A ... 1G 109
South Devon Railway
Buckfastleigh Station ... 4E 98
Totnes
(Littlehempston Riverside) Station
... 4E 102
South Devon Railway Mus. ... 4E 98
South Devon Railway (Primrose Line)
... 1D 175
South Devon Tennis Cen. ... 5G 145
SOUTHDOWN ... 6A 140
Southdown Av. TQ5: Brixh ... 6D 122
Southdown Cl. EX12: Beer ... 7B 86
TQ5: Brixh ... 6D 122
Southdown Hill TQ5: Brixh ... 6D 122
Southdown Quay ... 6A 140
Sth. Down Rd. PL2: Plym ... 5G 135
Southdown Rd. EX12: Beer ... 7B 86
PL10: Mill ... 6A 140
TQ5: Brixh ... 7D 122
Southdowns Rd. EX7: Daw ... 6G 97

South Dr.—Stanbury Copse

South Dr. EX38: Gt T 2A 30
Southella Rd. PL20: Yelv 6G 127
South Embankment
TQ6: Dartm 2B 124 (6F 125)
South End Cl. EX33: Brau 5J 15
SOUTHERLY 2D 169
Southern Cl. PL2: Plym 4E 134
TQ2: Torq 1C 112
Southern Gdns. *EX34: Com M 6B 12*
(off Valley La.)
Southernhay EX19: Wink 3C 36
TQ12: New A 2F 109
Southernhay E. EX1: Exe 5E 6 (7F 65)
(not continuous)
Southernhay Gdns.
EX1: Exe 4F 7 (6F 65)
(not continuous)
Southernhay W. EX1: Exe . . . 5F 7 (7F 65)
(not continuous)
Southern Rd. EX8: Exmth 4C 76
Southern Ter. PL4: Plym 1H 9 (7A 136)
Southernway PL9: Plyms 5H 143
Southern Wood EX8: Exmth 2G 77
SOUTHERTON 4F 81 (1A 172)
Southey Cres. TQ12: Kingsk 2G 111
Southey Dr. TQ12: Kingsk 2G 111
Southey La. TQ12: Kingsk 1G 111
Sth. Farm Rd. EX9: Bud S 5D 82
Southfield *TQ7: W Alv 5D 156*
(off Longfields)
TQ9: Berr P 5K 103
Southfield Av. TQ3: Pres 5F 115
Southfield Cl. TQ3: Pres 6F 115
Southfield Dr. EX17: Cred 5G 39
Southfield Ri. TQ3: Paig 7G 115
Southfield Rd. EX39: Bide 4H 23
TQ3: Paig 7G 115
Southfield Way EX16: Tiv 4A 40
Sth. Ford Rd.
TQ6: Dartm 1A 124 (6E 124)
Sth. Furzeham Rd. TQ5: Brixh 3E 122
Southgate EX2: Exe 6E 6 (7F 65)
Southgate Av. PL9: Plyms 7F 143
Southgate Cl. PL9: Plyms 7F 143
Southgate Ct. *EX2: Exe 7F 65*
(off Holloway St.)
South Grange EX2: Sow 2C 72
South Grn. EX32: Barn 5G 19
South Hams Bingo 4G 157
Sth. Hams Bus. Pk. TQ7: Chur 1C 156
South Hayes *PL21: Modb 6G 147*
(off Church St.)
Sth. Hayes Copse EX32: L'key 2C 24
Sth. Hayes Mdw. EX5: Cranb 4B 68
SOUTH HILL 3B 168
South Hill PL1: Plym 1F 141
PL9: Hooe 7D 142
South Hill Rd. TQ1: Torq 2E 116
SOUTH HOLE 1A 162
SOUTH HUISH 1K 155 (3C 175)
SOUTH KNIGHTON 3C 171
Southland Pk. Cres. PL9: Wem 6B 148
Southland Pk. Rd. PL9: Wem 7B 148
Southlands EX1: Heav 4K 7 (6H 65)
EX33: Brau 5J 15
(off Exeter Rd.)
EX33: Wraf 6K 15
Southlands Rd. TQ2: Torq 1B 116
South La. EX39: Hart 3J 27
South Lawn EX2: Exe 5G 7
EX10: Sidm 2D 84
Sth. Lawn Ter. EX1: Heav 6J 65
Southlea EX39: N'ham 6D 20
South Lea Cl. EX33: Brau 5K 15
SOUTHLEIGH 1C 173
Southleigh Rd. EX24: Colyt 5A 88
Southley Rd. EX36: S Mol 6C 26
SOUTH MILTON 7A 156 (3D 175)
Sth. Milton St. PL4: Plym . . 6K 9 (3B 142)
SOUTH MOLTON 6C 26 (1B 164)
South Molton & District Mus. 6C 26
Sth. Molton Rd. EX16: Bam 2F 33
Sth. Molton St. EX18: Chul 5C 32
South Molton Swimming Pool 6D 26
Southolme Ter. EX39: Bide 3G 23
South Pde. EX9: Bud S 7D 82
South Pk. EX32: Barn 6G 19
EX33: Brau 5K 15
EX39: Wools 3B 28
South Parks Rd. TQ2: Torq 3B 112
SOUTH PETHERTON 2D 167
SOUTH PETHERWIN 2B 168
SOUTH POOL 3D 175
Southport Av. EX4: Exe 7B 64
South Quay TQ4: Paig 2J 119
SOUTH RADWORTHY 3D 161
South Rd. EX39: Apple 3H 21
TQ12: New A 2E 108
SOUTH SANDS 6A 158
South Sands TQ8: Salc 6A 158
South Sands Sailing 6A 158
Southside Ope PL1: Plym 6F 9
Southside St. PL1: Plym 6F 9 (3K 141)
South Sq. EX24: Colyt 6D 88
South St. EX1: Exe 4D 6 (6E 64)
EX8: Exmth 6C 76
EX13: Axmin 4H 89
EX19: Dol 6H 31
EX19: Wink 2C 36
EX20: Hath 2H 35
EX24: Colyt 6D 88
EX32: Barn 7G 19
(not continuous)
EX33: Brau 6J 15
EX34: Woolc 6A 10
EX36: S Mol 6C 26
EX38: Gt T 2B 30
TA21: Holc R 2G 43
TQ2: Torq 1B 116
TQ9: Tot 6E 102
TQ12: Den 2H 101
SOUTH TAWTON 1J 49 (1A 170)
South Ter. EX8: Lymp 6H 75
SOUTH TOWN 7K 95 (2D 171)
South Town EX6: Kenton 6K 95
TQ6: Dartm 7F 125
South Vw. EX15: Hemy 2G 47
EX16: Tiv 4D 40
EX20: Lyd 6H 57
EX31: Barn 2C 18
EX31: Brat F 6J 13
EX32: Bish T 5A 24
EX33: Brau 6J 15
EX34: Ilfra 4F 11
EX37: Chit 6H 25
PL5: Plym 1K 135
PL7: Hem 2F 139
PL8: Brixt 2H 149
PL9: Elb 6J 143
PL19: Mary T 2B 60
PL20: Horr 2E 126
PL21: Lutt 7G 129
TQ12: A'well 6E 108
TQ13: Bov T 4C 92
(off Old Orchard)
TQ14: Teignm 5H 107
Southview TA21: Holc R 1G 43
South Vw. Cl. EX15: Will 3D 44
EX33: Brau 6J 15
PL7: Plymp 2A 138
South Vw. Est. EX15: Will 3C 44
South Vw. Pk. PL7: Plymp 2A 138
South Vw. Pasture EX5: Cranb 4B 68
South Vw. Rd. EX15: Will 3D 44
Southview Rd. TQ3: Paig 7G 115
South Vw. Ter. EX4: Exe 1G 7 (4G 65)
EX6: Exmin 2D 74
EX15: Will 3D 44
EX39: Bide 3E 22
PL4: Plym 3K 9 (2B 142)
Southville Gdns. TQ7: Kingsb 6G 157
South Wlk. EX32: Barn 5F 19
Southwater Ct. TQ7: Kingsb 5G 157
SOUTHWAY 3B 132
Southway EX6: Ted M 7J 49
EX10: Sidm 6D 84
Southway Av. TQ2: Torq 4B 112
Southway Dr. PL6: Plym 5J 131
Southway La. PL6: Plym 4H 131
(Coombe La.)
PL6: Plym 3C 132
(Lulworth Dr.)
Southwell Rd. PL6: Plym 3K 135
SOUTH WHEATLEY 1A 168
Southwood Ct. TQ1: Torq 1E 116
Southwood Dr. EX39: Bide 2F 23
Southwood Mdws. EX39: Buck B . . . 2H 29
Southyard Way PL1: Dev 2D 140
SOUTH ZEAL 2J 49 (1A 170)
Sovereign Cl. EX8: Exmth 3G 77
Sovereign Ct. EX2: Sow 2C 72
PL7: Plymp 6K 137
Sovereign M. TQ1: Torq 3D 112
Sovereign Ter. *TQ1: Torq 2D 116*
(off The Terrace)
Sowden La. EX8: Lymp 7F 75
EX32: Barn 4G 19
(not continuous)
Sowden Pk. EX32: Barn 5H 19
SOWTON 6G 67 (1D 171)
Sowton (Park & Ride) 1D 72
Sowton Ind. Est. EX2: Sow 7D 66
(not continuous)
Sowton La. EX5: Sow 5F 67
Spacex Gallery 5D 6
Spa Ct. TQ1: Torq 2E 116
Sparkatown La. PL20: Dous 5K 127
Sparke Cl. PL7: Plymp 5E 138
Sparks Barn Rd. TQ4: Paig 3H 119
SPARKWELL 1J 139 (2B 174)
Sparkwell Golf Course 1K 139
Sparrow Pk. TQ7: Malb 6H 155
Sparrow Rd. TQ9: Tot 6D 102
Sparrows Row EX20: Oke 3B 48
Speakers Rd. PL21: Ivy 4J 145
Spearfield Cl. EX36: S Mol 6D 26
Speculation Cotts. PL8: Yeal 2A 150
Speedwell Cl. EX32: Barn 6K 19
EX39: Bide 5E 22
TQ5: Brixh 5E 122
Speedwell Cres. PL6: Plym 4B 136
Speedwell Units TQ6: Dartm 6C 124
Speedwell Wlk. PL6: Plym 4C 136
Spencer Cl. EX8: Exmth 2G 77
Spencer Ct. *EX11: Ott M 4C 80*
(off St Saviours Rd.)
Spencer Dr. EX16: Tiv 6F 41
Spencer Rd. PL9: Plyms 4F 143
TQ3: Paig 1E 118
TQ12: New A 2F 109
Spenser Av. EX2: Won 2J 71
Speranza Gro. TQ14: Teignm 4H 107
Spicer Cl. EX15: Cull 5G 45
Spicer Rd. EX1: Exe 5G 7 (7G 65)
Spider's La. EX8: Exmth 1E 76
Spindlebury EX15: Cull 5F 45
Spindlewood Cl. EX14: Hon 6F 55
Spinnaker Quay PL9: Hooe 5A 142
Spinnakers *EX8: Exmth 6A 76*
(off Shelly Rd.)
Spinney, The EX15: Uff 5H 43
PL7: Plymp 5D 138
PL21: Ivy 4E 144
Spinney Cl. EX2: Won 1B 72
Spinning Path EX4: Exe 1H 7
Spinning Path Gdns. EX17: Cred . . . 7H 39
Spinster's Rock Burial Chamber . . . 1B 170
Spion Kop Steps *TQ8: Salc 4C 158*
(off Bennett Rd.)
Spire Ct. PL3: Plym 5C 136
Spitfire Wlk. *EX32: Barn 4H 19*
(off Valley Cl.)
Spithead TQ6: Dartm 1B 124 (6F 125)
Spittis Pk. *TQ6: Kingsw 6H 125*
(off Lwr. Contour Rd.)
Spittles La. DT7: Lym R 4K 91
Spitup La. EX10: Sidm 3A 84
Splatford Dr. EX15: Cull 2H 45
SPLATT 2A 168
SPREYTON 1B 170
Spring Cl. EX39: N'ham 6D 20
TQ12: New A 7B 104
Spring Cotts. *TQ9: Tot 6F 103*
(off Weston La.)
Springdale Cl. TQ5: Brixh 6E 122
Spring Fld. EX39: Hart 3H 27
Springfield EX14: Dunk 5H 47
EX19: Wink 1A 36
PL20: Horr 2F 127
TQ12: Ipp 7H 101
Springfield Av. EX32: Barn 6G 19
PL9: Elb 6J 143
Springfield Cl. PL9: Elb 6J 143
Springfield Cres. EX31: Frem 5G 17
EX39: N'ham 5E 20
Springfield Dr. EX16: Tiv 4B 40
PL3: Plym 7F 135
TQ7: Kingsb 5F 157
Springfield Gdns. EX7: Daw 1J 97
Springfield La. PL9: Elb 5J 143
Springfield Pk. EX20: Bride 3J 57
TQ11: B'leigh 4E 98
Springfield Ri. PL9: Elb 5J 143
Springfield Rd. EX4: Exe 4G 65
EX8: Exmth 3D 76
EX14: Hon 4H 55
EX31: Bick'n 6A 18
EX34: Ilfra 3H 11
EX34: Woolc 6A 10
PL9: Elb 6H 143
TQ1: Torq 6D 112
TQ10: S Bre 1B 100
Springfields EX24: Colyf 1F 87
Springfield Ter. EX34: Com M 7B 12
EX39: Bide 4G 23
(off Grange Rd.)
EX39: N'ham 5E 20
(off Diddywell Rd.)
EX39: West H 5B 20
Spring Gdns. EX11: Ott M 4D 80
Springhead DT7: Uply 3G 91
Springhead La. EX13: Kilm 2A 88
Spring Head Rd. DT7: Uply 1G 91
Spring Hill PL19: Tavi 4H 59
Springhill PL2: Plym 3H 135
Springhill Gdns. DT7: Lym R 4J 91
Springhill Grn. PL2: Plym 3H 135
Spring Hill Rd. TQ9: Tot 6G 103
Spring Pk. PL6: Plym 3F 133
Spring Rd. PL9: Down T, Wem 4D 148
Springwood Cl. PL7: Plymp 6D 138
PL21: Ivy 4J 145
Spruce Cl. EX4: Whip 2A 66
EX8: Exmth 1F 77
Spruce Gdns. PL7: Plymp 4E 138
Spruce Pk. EX17: Cred 7H 39
Spruce Way TQ3: Paig 6E 114
Spry La. PL16: Lift 6D 56
Sprys Tenements PL20: Horr 1E 126
Spurway Gdns. EX34: Com M 7D 12
Spurway Hill EX6: Exmin 3B 74
Spurway Rd. EX16: Tiv 5F 41
Square, The EX4: Exe 4C 64
EX5: Rock 4F 69
EX5: Whim 6G 53
EX10: Sidm 3A 84
EX12: Beer 7B 86
(off Fore St.)
EX12: Seat 5E 86
EX15: Uff 6H 43
EX16: With 6H 33
EX18: Chul 6C 32
EX19: Dol 6G 31
EX19: Wink 2C 36
EX20: Mer 5B 30
EX20: N Taw 6B 36
EX21: Sheb 6H 29
EX22: Bradw 5B 28
EX22: Hols 2C 34
EX31: Frem 6F 17
EX32: Barn 5E 18
EX32: Bish T 6B 24
EX32: Swim 2G 25
EX33: Brau 4J 15
EX36: N Mol 2C 26
EX36: S Mol 6C 26
(off Broad St.)
EX37: Chit 5J 25
EX39: Hart 3H 27
EX39: N'ham 5E 20
PL1: Plym 2F 141
PL8: Holb 6C 150
(off Brent Hill)
PL20: Bere A 2C 128
PL21: Erm 2H 147
PL21: Lutt 7F 129
PL21: Ugb 6E 146
TQ6: Kingsw 6G 125
TQ7: Hope 3G 155
TQ13: Chag 2H 61
TQ13: More 6H 61
Square's Quay TQ7: Kingsb 5G 157
Squires Cl. EX32: Barn 7G 19
Squire's La. EX12: Axmth 5G 87
Squirrel Cl. PL5: Plym 6K 131
Stabb Cl. TQ4: Good 6G 119
Stabb Dr. TQ4: Good 6G 119
Stable Cotts. PL7: Plymp 4B 138
Stable La. *TQ1: Torq 4D 112*
(off Havelock Rd.)
Stables, The TQ9: Tot 5F 103
STADDISCOMBE 2B 174
Staddiscombe Rd.
PL9: Plyms, Stad 7H 143
STADDON 3B 162
Staddon Cl. EX4: Exe 5A 66
EX33: Brau 4H 15
Staddon Ct. Cotts. PL9: Down T . . 2C 148
Staddon Cres. PL9: Plyms 6F 143
Staddon Gdns. TQ2: Torq 3D 112
Staddon Grn. PL9: Plyms 6E 142
Staddon Heights Golf Course 7B 142
Staddon Pk. Rd. PL9: Plyms 7F 143
Staddon Rd. EX22: Hols 3E 34
EX39: Apple 3G 21
Staddons Lea La. TQ2: Torq 7J 111
Staddons Vw. TQ13: Bov T 3B 92
Staddon Ter. La.
PL1: Plym 2C 8 (1H 141)
Stadium Dr. TQ12: Kingsk 3G 111
Stadium Way EX4: Exe 1H 7 (5G 65)
Stadway Mdw. EX10: Sidm 5A 84
Staffick Cl. EX6: Kenton 6J 95
Stafford Ct. TQ9: Tot 6G 103
Stafford La. EX24: Colyf . . . 7C 88 & 1E 86
Stafford Rd. EX4: Exe 7C 64
EX19: Dol 6H 31
TQ4: Paig 2J 119
Stafford Way EX19: Dol 6H 31
Staggers La. EX33: Wraf 7K 15
Stag La. PL9: Elb 4J 143
STAG'S HEAD 1A 164
Stakes Hill TQ7: Bigb 7F 151
Stallards EX33: Brau 3H 15
Stall Moor Stone Row 1C 175
Stamford Cl. PL9: Hooe 6B 142
Stamford Fort Cotts. *PL9: Hooe . . . 6B 142*
(off Stamford Rd.)
Stamford La. PL9: Hooe 7B 142
Stamford Rd. PL9: Hooe 6B 142
Stamps Hill PL8: Brixt 1H 149
Stanborough Cross PL9: Elb 5K 143
Stanborough Rd.
PL9: Elb, Plyms 5G 143
Stanbridge Pk. EX39: Bide 3C 22
Stanbury Av. PL6: Plym 2A 136
Stanbury Cl. PL15: St G 6C 34
Stanbury Copse EX34: Ilfra 4G 11

Stanbury Ct. EX17: Cred 6H 39
Stanbury Rd. EX33: Know 1K 15
TQ2: Torq 6J 111
Standard Ct. PL19: Mary T 1B 60
Standarhay Cl. PL9: Elb 5K 143
Standarhay Vs. PL9: Elb 5K 143
Stanfield *TQ1: Torq 1G 117*
(off Barrington Rd.)
Stanford Rd. EX2: Won 7B 66
Stangray Av. PL4: Plym 7J 135
Stanhope Cl. EX22: Hols 1C 34
Stanhope Dr. EX10: Sidm 4C 84
Stanhope Gdns. EX22: Hols 2C 34
Stanhope Rd. PL5: Plym 1B 134
Stanhope Sq. EX22: Hols 2C 34
Stanhope Ter. EX39: Bide 2F 23
Staniforth Dr. PL21: Ivy 5H 145
Stanley Ct. TQ1: Torq 5E 112
Stanley Gdns. TQ3: Paig 7F 115
Stanley M. EX9: Bud S 6C 82
Stanley Pl. PL4: Plym 2C 142
Stanley Rd. TQ1: Torq 5E 112
Stanley Sq. EX3: Top 6B 74
Stanley St. TQ14: Teignm 5H 107
Stanley Wlk. EX8: Exmth 1F 77
Stanmore Ri. EX7: Daw 3H 97
Stanmore Tor TQ3: Paig 2G 119
Stannary Bri. Rd. PL19: Tavi 3K 59
Stannary Cl. PL21: Ivy 4J 145
Stannary Ct. EX20: Oke 3D 48
PL19: Tavi 4H 59
(off Garden La.)
Stannary Pl. TQ13: Chag 3H 61
Stansfeld Av. TQ3: Paig 1G 119
Stantaway Hill *TQ1: Torq 6B 112*
(off Stantaway Pk.)
Stantaway Pk. TQ1: Torq 6B 112
Stantor La. TQ3: Marl 7F 111
Stantyway Rd. EX9: Ott'n 7J 83
Stanwell Dr. EX39: West H 6B 20
Stanwell Hill EX39: West H 6A 20
Stanwey EX1: Heav 7K 65
Staplake La. EX6: Star 2C 96
Staplake Ri. EX6: Star 1D 96
Staplake Rd. EX6: Star 1E 96
Staple Cl. PL6: Robo 1D 132
STAPLE CROSS 1A 166
Stapledon La. TQ13: Ashb 3H 99
STAPLE FITZPAINE 2C 167
Stapleford Dr. TQ14: Teignm 2H 107
Stapleford Gdns. PL5: Plym 5E 130
STAPLEGROVE 1C 167
STAPLEHAY 1C 167
Staple Hill TQ9: Darti 3B 102
Staplehill Rd. TQ12: Live, New A 6F 93
Staple Orchard TQ9: Darti 3B 102
Staple's Bldgs. *EX8: Exmth 5C 76*
(off Crudges La.)
Staples M. *EX8: Exmth 5C 76*
(off Exeter Rd.)
Staples Ter. DT7: Lym R 4K 91
(not continuous)
Stapleton Cl. TQ4: Paig 4E 118
STAPLEY 2B 166
Star Barton La. EX5: Cow 1A 64
STARCROSS 1E 96 (2D 171)
Starcross Station (Rail) 1E 96
Starkey Cl. EX16: Tiv 5G 41
Starlings Roost EX15: Cull 5F 45
Starpitten Gro. TQ2: Torq 2D 112
Starpitten La. W. TQ2: Torq 3C 112
Starre Cl. EX12: Seat 3F 87
START 1F 159 (3A 176)
Start Av. TQ7: Chil 6G 159
TQ14: Teignm 2J 107
Start Bay Caravan Pk.
TQ6: Strete 5G 153
Start Bay Pk. TQ6: Strete 5G 153
STATHE 1D 167
Station App. EX17: Cred 7J 39
TQ10: S Bre 1B 100
Station Bus. Pk. *TQ14: Teignm 4J 107*
(off Lwr. Brimley Rd.)
Station Cl. EX22: Hols 2C 34
EX33: Brau 5J 15
Station Ct. TQ13: Bov T 4B 92
Station Hill EX31: Brat F 4H 13
EX32: Swim 2H 25
EX35: Lynt 2G 13
EX38: Gt T 2A 30
EX39: Bide 4G 23
TQ5: Brixh 3E 122
TQ13: Chud 3A 94
Station La. TQ4: Paig 2H 119
Station Rd. EX1: Pin 3D 66
EX2: Ide 4A 70
EX3: Exton 2G 75
EX3: Top 5B 74
EX4: Exe 1A 6 (4C 64)
EX5: Broadc 7D 52 & 1J 67
EX5: New C 5D 50
EX6: Exmin 3E 74 & 7A 74
Station Rd. EX7: Daw 4H 97
EX9: Bud S 6C 82
EX10: Harp, New P 5H 81
EX10: Sidm 5B 84
EX14: Fen 2G 53
EX15: Cull 3H 45
EX15: Hemy 2G 47
EX15: Will 3C 44
EX16: Bam 2H 33
EX16: Tiv 4D 40
EX17: Bow 7G 37
EX17: Cop 5C 38
EX17: Cred 7J 39
EX20: Bride 4H 57
EX20: Oke 4B 48
EX22: Hols 2C 34
EX24: Colyt 5D 88
EX31: Barn 5E 18
EX31: Brat F 6H 13
EX33: Brau 5J 15
EX34: Ilfra 3G 11
EX34: Woolc 6C 10
EX36: S Mol 5D 26
PL2: Plym 6D 134
PL5: Tam F 4D 130
PL7: Plymp 3B 138
PL9: Elb 5K 143
PL16: Lift, Tin 6C 56
PL19: Mary T 3A 60
PL20: Bere A 1A 128
PL20: Bere F 6B 128
PL20: Horr 2E 126
PL20: Prin 7C 60
(not continuous)
PL21: Ivy 3H 145
TQ7: Lodd 2H 151
TQ9: Tot 5E 102
TQ10: S Bre 1B 100
TQ11: B'leigh 4D 98
TQ12: New A 1G 109
TQ13: Bov T 4B 92
TQ13: More 7H 61
TQ14: Teignm 5J 107
Station Rd. Ind. Est. EX15: Hemy 1G 47
Station Yd. EX4: Exe 2C 6 (5E 64)
EX10: Sidm 4B 84
EX13: Axmin 4G 89
EX14: Hon 4F 55
TQ9: Tot 5E 102
(off Station Rd.)
TQ13: Ashb 4H 99
(off Prigg Mdw.)
Station Yd. Ind. Est. TQ7: Kingsb 4F 157
STAVERTON 1D 175
STAWLEY 1A 166
Steamer Quay Caravan Pk.
TQ9: Tot 6F 103
Steamer Quay Rd. TQ9: Tot 6F 103
Steam Gallery at Beer *7B 86*
(off Fore St.)
Steartfield Rd. TQ3: Paig 7J 115
Steed Cl. TQ4: Good 7G 119
Steel Cl. EX14: Hon 3G 55
Steeperton Cl. EX20: Oke 3D 48
Steep Hill TQ1: Maid 1J 113
Steeple Dr. EX2: Alph 6E 70
Steer Pk. Rd. PL7: Plymp 4F 139
Steer Point Rd. PL8: Brixt 3H 149
Stefan Cl. PL9: Hooe 7C 142
Stella Maris Ct. EX39: Bide 2F 23
Stella Rd. TQ3: Pres 5G 115
STEMBRIDGE 1D 167
STENHILL 2A 166
Stenlake Pl. *PL4: Plym 2C 142*
(off Stenlake Ter.)
Stenlake Ter. PL4: Plym 2C 142
Stentaway Cl. PL9: Plyms 4G 143
Stentaway Dr. PL9: Plyms 4G 143
Stentaway La. EX33: Croy, Puts 1C 14
Stentaway Rd. PL9: Plyms 5G 143
Stentiford Hill TQ7: Kingsb 2F 157
Stentiford Hill Rd. TQ1: Torq 1D 116
Stepcote Hill EX1: Exe 5D 6 (7E 64)
Stephenson Way PL5: Plym 1E 134
Stephen St. EX4: Exe 4E 6 (6F 65)
Steppes Mdw. TQ12: New A 2D 108
Stepps La. EX12: Axmth 4J 87
Steps Cl. EX1: Pin 3E 66
Steps La. TQ2: Torq 2D 112
(not continuous)
Stepstone La. EX33: Know 1K 15
Sterlings Way EX20: Oke 2D 48
Stevens La. EX10: Sidm 3B 84
STEVENSTONE 2D 163
Stevenstone Rd. EX8: Exmth 5F 77
Stewart Cl. EX8: Exmth 3G 77
Stewart Ct. EX13: Axmin 2J 89
Stewart Gdns. EX7: Daw 3H 97
Stewart Ho. *EX7: Daw 3H 97*
(off Old Gatehouse Rd.)
STEWLEY 2D 167
STIBB 2A 162
STIBB CROSS 2C 163
Stibb La. PL21: Ivy 3D 144
STICKLEPATH
Barnstaple 6C 18
South Zeal 1G 49 (1A 170)
Sticklepath Ct. EX31: Taw 6D 18
Sticklepath Hill EX31: Barn 6C 18
Sticklepath Ter. EX31: Barn 5E 18
Stidston La. TQ10: S Bre 1C 100
Stile La. DT7: Lym R 5J 91
Stile Orchard TQ7: Lodd 2H 151
Stillman Ct. PL4: Plym 5F 9
Stillman St. PL4: Plym 5F 9 (3K 141)
Stintway La. EX10: Sidm 5A 84
Stirling Ct. PL5: Plym 2B 134
Stirling Rd. PL5: Plym 2B 134
Stitchill Rd. TQ1: Torq 2E 116
Stoat Pk. EX32: Barn 5J 19
Stoats Cl. EX36: S Mol 7C 26
Stockbridge La. TQ10: S Bre 2B 100
Stocker Rd. EX4: Exe 3E 64
STOCKLAND 3C 167
Stock La. EX12: Seat 5E 86
STOCKLEIGH ENGLISH 3C 165
STOCKLEIGH POMEROY 3C 165
STOCKLINCH 2D 167
Stockmeadow Gdns.
TQ14: Bi'ton 4C 106
Stockton Av. EX7: Daw 4G 97
Stockton Hill EX7: Daw 4G 97
Stockton La. *EX7: Daw 4G 97*
(off Stockton Rd.)
Stockton Rd. EX7: Daw 4G 97
Stoggy La. PL7: Plymp 3C 138
STOKE
Philham 1A 162
Plymouth 1G 141
STOKE ABBOTT 3D 167
STOKE CANON 7J 51 (1D 171)
STOKE CLIMSLAND 3B 168
Stoke Damerel Community Sports Cen.
7G 135
STOKE FLEMING 2H 153 (3A 176)
STOKE GABRIEL 4B 120 (2A 176)
Stoke Gabriel Rd.
TQ5: Galm, Wadd 2E 120
STOKE HILL 3H 65
Stoke Hill EX4: Exe 3H 65
EX5: Sto C 7J 51
TQ9: Sto G 4B 120
Stoke Hill Cres. EX4: Exe 3H 65
Stoke Hill La. PL20: C'stone, Yelv 7C 126
Stoke Ho. Gdns. *TQ6: Sto F 3H 153*
(off Dartmouth Hill)
STOKEINTEIGNHEAD 3D 171
Stokelake TQ13: Chud 4A 94
Stoke Lyne EX8: Exmth 3E 76
Stoke Mdw. Cl. EX4: Exe 2H 65
STOKENHAM 6K 159 (3A 176)
STOKE RIVERS 3C 161
Stoke Rd. EX4: Exe 1C 64
EX5: Sto C 7J 51
PL1: Plym 3A 8 (2G 141)
PL8: Noss M 6H 149
TQ1: Maid 1J 113
TQ4: Coll M, Paig 5B 118
STOKE ST GREGORY 1D 167
STOKE ST MARY 1C 167
Stokesay Av. PL6: Plym 5A 132
Stokes La. *EX16: Tiv 4D 40*
(off Barrington St.)
PL1: Plym 6F 9
Stokes Mead EX5: Wood 5C 78
Stoke Valley Rd. EX4: Exe 1F 65
Stokingway Cl. PL9: Plyms 7F 143
Stoneacre Cl. TQ5: Brixh 5E 122
Stone Ash La. EX17: Morc 1E 38
Stone Barton Cl. PL7: Plymp 5K 137
Stone Barton Rd. PL7: Plymp 5K 137
Stoneborough Ct. EX9: Bud S 6D 82
Stoneborough La. EX9: Bud S 6D 82
Stone Cl. EX14: Hon 5E 54
Stone Ct. TQ2: Torq 4K 111
Stonehall Flats PL1: Plym 3F 141
Stonehedge Cl. PL21: Ivy 5H 145
STONEHOUSE 3F 141
Stonehouse Bri. PL1: Plym 3F 141
Stonehouse St. PL1: Plym 3F 141
Stonelands M. EX7: Daw 4F 97
Stonelands Pk. EX7: Daw 4F 97
Stonelands Ter. *EX7: Daw 4F 97*
(off Stonelands Pk.)
Stone La. EX2: Exe 2D 70
EX8: Lymp 6G 75
Stone Lane Gdns. 1B 170
Stone La. Retail Pk. EX2: Mar B 2E 70
Stoneleigh Cl. TQ12: New A 7C 104
Stoneleigh Dr. TQ2: Torq 3K 115
Stoneman's Hill TQ12: A'well 4E 108
Stoneman's La. EX38: Gt T 1B 30
Stone Pk. TQ4: Broads 2K 121
Stonepark TQ13: Ashb 5G 99
Stonepark Cres. TQ13: Ashb 5G 99
Stonepark Ter. TQ13: Ashb 5G 99
Stones Cl. PL21: Modb 6H 147
TQ12: Kingst 2H 105
Stone's Pl. EX15: Cull 3H 45
Stonewall La. EX17: Cred 5H 39
Stoneycliffe Pl. PL20: Prin 6D 60
STONEYCOMBE 3C 110
STONEYFORD 3J 45 (3A 166)
Stoneyford Pk. EX9: Bud S 6D 82
Stoneyhill TQ12: A'well 3A 110
Stoneylands EX5: Rock 4E 68
Stoney La. EX5: Bradn 1C 52
EX13: Axmin 3J 89
EX14: Hon 7F 55
Stoney Pk. La. EX20: Oke 4A 48
Stoneywell EX39: Ins 2K 21
Stonybridge Hill EX36: S Mol 2A 26
Stony Cl. La. EX12: Axmth 5J 87
STONY CROSS 1D 163
Stony La. EX5: Wood S 2C 78
EX8: Lymp 3K 75
EX16: Bam 3J 33
EX32: L'key 4C 24
EX39: Apple 3G 21
Stonypark La. EX17: Cred 6G 39
STOODLEIGH
Barnstaple 3C 161
Tiverton 2D 165
Stooks Cl. EX5: Bram S 6G 51
Stopford Pl. PL1: Dev 1E 140
Storrs Cl. TQ13: Bov T 3B 92
Stott Cl. PL3: Plym 6E 136
Stour Cl. PL3: Plym 5E 136
Stovar Long La. EX12: Beer 5A 86
Stover Country Pk. 3K 93
Stover Country Pk. Interpretation Cen.
3K 93
Stover Ct. EX1: Exe 2G 7 (5G 65)
Stover Golf Course 4K 93
Stowbrook EX10: Sidm 2A 84
Stowe Gdns. PL5: Plym 1G 135
Stowe La. EX20: Exbo 6J 35
STOWFORD
Combe Martin 2C 161
Exmouth 2A 172
Sidmouth 2A 84
Tavistock 2C 169
Stowford Bus. Pk. *PL21: Ivy 5H 145*
(off Blair Rd.)
Stowford Cl. PL20: Dous 4K 127
Stowford Hgts. EX12: Seat 4D 86
Stowford Ri. EX10: Sidm 3A 84
STOWFORD WATER 6E 46
Strand EX3: Top 6B 74
EX8: Exmth 6C 76
TQ1: Torq 2D 116
TQ14: Shal 6G 107
TQ14: Teignm 6H 107
Strand, The EX6: Star 1E 96
EX7: Daw 4H 97
EX8: Lymp 6F 75
EX15: Culm 2B 46
EX31: Barn 4E 18
EX34: Ilfra 2J 11
(off Hierns La.)
EX39: Bide 3F 23
TQ5: Brixh 3F 123
TQ14: Shal 6E 106
Strand Cl. EX31: Ashf 1K 17
Strand Ct. EX3: Top 6B 74
EX39: Bide 2F 23
Strand Hill EX7: Daw 4H 97
Strand La. EX31: Ashf 1J 17
Strand St. PL1: Plym 4F 141
Strand Vw. EX3: Top 6B 74
Strap La. TQ12: Kingst 1G 105
Strashleigh Vw. PL21: L Mill 5C 144
Stratford Av. EX4: Whip 4B 66
Strathbrook Ter. *PL2: Plym 6E 134*
(off St Levan Rd.)
Stratheden Ct. *TQ1: Torq 1D 116*
(off Market St.)
STRATTON 3A 162
Stratton Wlk. PL2: Plym 3J 135
Strawberry Av. EX2: Alph 5F 71
Strawberry Flds. EX20: N Taw 7C 36
Strawberry Hill EX8: Lymp 6G 75
Strawberry La. EX5: Bradn 1E 52
EX7: Holc 7F 97
EX11: Ott M 5A 80
Strawberry Ter. TQ12: Kingst 3H 105
Stray Pk. PL8: Yeal 2A 150
Stream Ct. EX2: Exe 7D 6 (1E 70)
Streamers Mdws. EX14: Hon 4F 55
Streatham Dr. EX4: Exe 1B 6 (4D 64)
Streatham Ri. EX4: Exe 1B 6 (4D 64)
Streatham Sports Pk. 3E 64
STREET
Branscombe 6F 85
Chard 1A 168
Whitstone 3D 167

Street, The EX13: Kilm 2B 88
EX13: Mus 7C 90
STREET ASH 2C 167
STRETCH DOWN 7K 33
STRETE 6G 153 (3A 176)
Stringland La. TQ3: Marl 1D 114
Strode Rd. PL7: Plymp 3C 138
TQ11: B'leigh 5C 98
Stroma Cl. PL6: Plym 3A 132
Stroud Pk. Rd. PL2: Plym 4H 135
Stuart Ct. EX7: Daw 6G 97
Stuart Cres. EX15: Cull 1H 45
Stuart Rd. EX1: Heav 6J 65
PL1: Plym 1A 8 (1G 141)
PL3: Plym 1A 8 (1G 141)
Stucley Rd. EX39: Bide 4D 22
Studhayes Rd. EX13: Kilm 1A 88
Studley Rd. TQ1: Torq 6C 112
Sturcombe Av. TQ4: Paig 4E 118
Sturdee Rd. PL2: Plym 6F 135
Sturges Rd. EX8: Exmth 4F 77
Style Cl. EX32: Barn 7G 19
Subway App. EX15: Will 3C 44
Sugar Loaf Hill & Saltern Cove Nature Reserve 6J 119
Sugar Mill Bus. Pk. PL9: Plyms 3D 142
Sullivan Rd. EX2: Won 7B 66
Summer Cl. EX4: Whip 4A 66
EX8: Exmth 4G 77
EX15: Hemy 2F 47
Summercourt Way TQ5: Brixh 6B 122
Summerfield EX5: Wood 4C 78
EX10: Sidm 2C 84
Summerfield Ct. PL21: Ivy 4E 144
Summerfield Rd. TQ2: Torq 5A 112
Summerhayes EX7: Daw 6F 97
Summerhill TQ12: Live 4G 93
Summerhill Cl. TQ12: Live 4G 93
Summerhill Cres. TQ12: Live 4G 93
Summerhill Ho. DT7: Lym R 4K 91 (off Charmouth Rd.)
Summerhill Rd. DT7: Lym R 4K 91
TQ12: Live 4G 93
Summerhill Ter. PL10: Mill 6A 140
Summer Ho. Hill Path EX35: Lynt 4H 13
Summerhouse Path EX35: Lynm 2H 13
Summerland EX14: Hon 4F 55
Summerland Av. EX7: Daw 3G 97
Summerland Cl. EX7: Daw 4G 97
Summerland Cotts. TQ12: New A 1F 109 (off Carlisle St.)
Summerland Ct. TQ12: New A 1F 109
Summerland Ga. EX1: Exe 3G 7
Summerland Pl. EX32: Barn 5F 19 (off Summerland St.)
Summerlands Cl. PL7: Plymp 4F 139
TQ5: Brixh 6C 122
Summerlands Ct. TQ5: Brixh 6C 122
TQ12: Live 4H 93
Summerlands Gdns. PL7: Plymp 4F 139
Summerland St. EX1: Exe 2G 7 (5G 65)
EX32: Barn 4F 19
Summerland Ter. EX32: Barn 4F 19 (off Summerland St.)
EX34: Com M 6B 12
Summer La. EX4: Whip 3A 66
EX8: Exmth 1C 76
TQ5: Brixh 5C 122
TQ12: Teign 1B 104
Summer Mdw. EX5: Cranb 3B 68
Summersby Cl. EX12: Seat 4E 86
Summers Cl. PL6: Plym 4C 136
Summersfield Ct. TQ4: Paig 2J 119
Summerway EX4: Whip 4A 66
Sumner Rd. PL21: Bitta 4C 146
Sunbury Hill TQ1: Torq 7C 112
Sunbury Rd. TQ4: Paig 2H 119
Sun Ct. TQ12: New A 1E 108
Suncrest Caravan Site TQ2: Torq 2B 112
Suncrest Cl. TQ2: Torq 3B 112
Sunderland Cl. PL9: Hooe 6B 142
Sunflower Rd. EX32: Barn 4F 19
Sunhill Av. EX3: Top 7E 72
Sunhill La. EX3: Top 7E 72
Sun La. TQ14: Teignm 5H 107 (off Somerset Pl.)
Sunningbrook Rd. EX16: Tiv 3E 40
Sunningdale Ter. EX39: Bide 2F 23 (off Northam Rd.)
Sunny Bank EX32: Barn 5G 19 (not continuous)
Sunnybank EX6: Kenton 6J 95
TQ12: A'well 6E 108
TQ12: New A 6E 104
Sunny Cl. TQ12: New A 1J 109
Sunny Dene PL5: Plym 2C 134
Sunnyfield EX5: Broadc 5C 52
Sunnyhill EX11: Ott M 3D 80
Sunny Hollow TQ12: E Ogw 4A 108
Sunny Lands Way EX7: Holc 7G 97
Sunny Lyn Holiday Pk. EX35: Lynt 4G 13
Sunnymead EX17: Cop 6C 38
Sunnymead Ter. TQ9: Tot 6E 102 (off Maudlin Rd.)
Sunnymoor Cl. EX1: Pin 3E 66
Sunny Side EX33: Brau 5J 15 (off South St.)
Sunnyside EX10: New P 4H 81
EX14: Awli 2B 54
EX15: Cull 5H 45
EX34: Com M 7C 12
EX34: Woolc 7C 10
EX39: Bide 4G 23
PL8: Yeal 2B 150
Sunnyside Cotts. PL9: Plyms 4E 142 (off Roper Av.)
Sunnyside Rd. EX34: Woolc 6A 10
PL4: Plym 2C 142
TQ12: Kingsk 2G 111
Sunnyside Ter. EX35: Lynt 2G 13
Sunny Vw. EX19: Wink 2C 36
Sunset Hgts. EX21: Sheb 6J 29
EX32: Barn 4F 19
Sunset Ho. EX12: Seat 6D 86
Sunshine Ter. PL19: Tavi 3K 59
Sun Ter. PL21: Modb 6G 147
Sun Valley Cl. TQ5: Brixh 3E 122
Sunway Cl. PL19: Tavi 3G 59
Sunwine Pl. EX8: Exmth 6D 76
Surbiton Cres. EX4: Exe 1C 70
Surf Bay Caravan Pk. EX39: West H 4C 20
Sussex Cl. EX4: Exe 1B 70
TQ2: Torq 2C 112
Sussex Pl. PL1: Plym 6E 8 (3J 141)
Sussex Rd. PL2: Plym 6E 134
Sussex St. PL1: Plym 6E 8 (3J 141)
Sussex Ter. PL2: Plym 6E 134
Sutcliffe Cl. TQ9: Darti 4B 102
SUTCOMBE 2B 162
Suter Dr. EX16: Tiv 2E 40
Sutherlake Gdns. EX5: Broadc 6E 52
Sutherland Cl. TQ12: New A 4J 109
Sutherland Dr. TQ2: Torq 3D 112
Sutherland Rd. PL4: Plym 1E 8 (1K 141)
TQ1: Torq 1E 116
Sutton Cl. EX7: Daw 3G 97
TQ2: Torq 1B 112
Sutton Ct. PL1: Dev 3E 140
Sutton Harbour 6G 9 (3K 141)
Sutton M. TQ2: Torq 1B 112
Sutton Pl. PL4: Plym 6J 9 (3A 142)
Sutton Rd. PL4: Plym 5H 9 (3A 142)
Sutton Vw. EX17: Bow 5H 37
PL4: Plym 4G 9
Sutton Wharf PL4: Plym 5G 9 (3K 141)
Swain Cl. EX13: Axmin 5H 89
Swaindale Rd. PL3: Plym 5K 135
Swains Ct. EX3: Top 5A 74
Swains Rd. EX9: Bud S 5D 82
Swale Cl. PL3: Plym 5C 136
TQ2: Torq 2C 112
Swallow Cl. EX32: Barn 5K 19
Swallow Ct. EX4: Exe 4C 64
EX12: Seat 6G 87 (off Harbour Rd.)
Swallow Dr. EX2: Exe 2A 70
Swallow Fld. EX31: Roun 7K 17
Swallowfield Ri. TQ2: Torq 3J 111
Swallowfield Rd. EX2: Cou W 3K 71
SWALLOWFIELDS 4D 102
Swallowfields TQ9: Tot 4D 102
Swallows Acre EX7: Daw 3H 97
Swallows End PL9: Plyms 4F 143
Swallow Way EX15: Cull 5F 45
Swanaford Rd. EX6: Bridf 7D 62 & 7E 62
Swan Av. EX16: Tiv 2E 40
Swanborough Rd. TQ12: New A 3J 109
Swan Ct. EX2: Exe 7G 7 (1G 71)
TQ6: Dartm 6E 124 (off Victoria Rd.)
Swan Gdns. PL7: Plymp 4C 138
Swan Hill Rd. EX24: Colyf 1F 87
Swannaton Rd. TQ6: Dartm 7F 125
Swanpool Marsh Nature Reserve 4F 15
Swan Rd. EX6: Star 2D 96
EX12: Seat 5F 87
Swan St. TQ2: Torq 2D 116 (off Fleet St.)
Swanswood Gdns. EX39: West H 5C 20
Swan Units EX2: Sow 7D 66
Swan Yd. EX4: Exe 6B 6 (7D 64)
Swedwell La. TQ2: Torq 1C 112
Swedwell Rd. TQ2: Torq 1C 112
Sweetbriar Cl. EX7: Holc 7F 97
Sweetbriar La. EX7: Holc 7F 97
Sweetbrier La. EX1: Heav 6K 65
SWEETHAM 4D 50 (1C 171)
SWEETS 1A 168
SWELL 1D 167
Swift Gdns. PL5: Plym 1H 135
Swift Ind. Est. TQ12: Kingst 5G 105
SWIMBRIDGE 3H 25 (1A 164)
Swimbridge Ct. EX32: Swim 1H 25
SWIMBRIDGE NEWLAND 3D 24 (3C 161)
Swim Torquay 6D 112
Swinburne Gdns. PL5: Plym 2G 135
Swincombe Dr. TQ3: Paig 1F 119
Swiss Cl. EX8: Exmth 1D 76
Swiss Lake Ice Rink 5B 8 (3H 141)
Sycamore Av. EX7: Daw W 7D 96
PL4: Plym 3B 142
PL19: Tavi 7J 59
Sycamore Cl. EX1: Heav 7A 66
EX5: Broadc 6D 52
EX8: Exmth 2G 77
EX14: Hon 5D 54
EX15: Will 4C 44
EX39: Ins 2K 21 (off Marine Pde.)
TQ4: Broads 1K 121
Sycamore Dr. PL6: Plym 3D 132
Sycamore Rd. EX16: Tiv 3E 40
Sycamore Wlk. PL21: L Mill 5A 144
Sycamore Way PL6: Plym 5F 133
TQ5: Brixh 6C 122
TQ13: Chud 1D 94
SYDENHAM DAMEREL 3C 169
Sydenham Ho. EX1: Exe 1J 7
Sydney Cl. PL7: Plymp 5B 138
Sydney Pl. EX2: Exe 7C 6
Sydney Rd. EX2: Exe 7B 6 (1D 70)
PL11: Torp 1A 140
Sydney St. PL1: Plym 2C 8 (1H 141)
Sylvan Av. EX4: Exe 3G 65
Sylvan Cl. EX8: Exmth 2C 76
Sylvan Ct. EX8: Exmth 2C 76 (off Exeter Rd.)
PL1: Plym 1F 141
Sylvania Dr. EX4: Exe 2H 65
Sylvan Rd. EX4: Exe 3G 65
SYMONDSBURY 1D 173
Symons Pas. TQ9: Tot 6F 103
Synagogue Pl. EX4: Exe 4D 6 (6E 64)

T

Tabernacle Ct. EX1: Exe 6D 6
Tacket Ct. TQ7: Kingsb 5F 157
Taddiforde Rd. EX4: Exe 1B 6 (5D 64)
TADDIPORT 3A 30 (2C 163)
Taddyforde Ct. EX4: Exe 1A 6
Taddyforde Ct. Mans. EX4: Exe 4D 64 (off Taddyforde Est.)
Taddyforde Est. EX4: Exe 1B 6 (4D 64)
Tadworthy Rd. EX39: N'ham 5D 20
Tailyour Rd. PL6: Plym 1A 136
TALATON 1A 172
Talaton Rd. EX5: Whim 6H 53
Talbot Ct. TQ14: Teignm 4G 107 (off Bitton Pk. Rd.)
Talbot Gdns. PL5: Plym 4C 134
Talbot Rd. DT7: Lym R 4J 91
TALEFORD 1A 80 (1A 172)
Taleford Vs. EX11: Tale 1B 80
Tallow Wood Cl. TQ3: Paig 1E 118
Tamar Av. PL2: Plym 6D 134
PL19: Tavi 4K 59
TQ2: Torq 6H 111
Tamar Bri. PL12: Salt 1A 134
Tamar Bri. Rd. PL5: Plym 1B 134
Tamar Cl. PL20: Bere A 2C 128
Tamar Ho. PL1: Dev 3D 140
Tamarind EX15: Will 4C 44
Tamarisk Cl. EX4: Whip 2A 66
Tamar River Sailing Club 2A 134
Tamar Rd. EX31: Chive 1E 16
Tamar Science Pk. PL6: Plym 6D 132
Tamar's Dr. EX15: Will 4C 44
Tamarside Sports Complex 1D 134
Tamar St. PL1: Dev 1D 140
PL11: Torp 1B 140
PL12: Salt 1A 134
Tamar Vw. PL19: Mil A 2B 58
Tamar Vs. PL9: Plyms 5E 142
Tamar Way PL5: Plym 1F 135
Tamar Wharf PL1: Dev 1C 140
Tamerton Av. PL5: Plym 2C 134
Tamerton Cl. PL5: Plym 4F 131
TAMERTON FOLIOT 4G 131 (1A 174)
Tamerton Foliot Rd. PL5: Plym, Tam F 4H 131
PL6: Plym 4H 131
Tamerton Rd. PL6: Robo 1D 132
Tamworth Cl. TQ12: E Ogw 4C 108
Tamwyn Cl. TQ3: Pres 6J 115
Tangmere Av. PL5: Plym 5D 130
Tan La. EX2: Exe 2E 70
Tanners Cl. EX15: Cull 5G 45
Tanners M. EX15: Will 3E 44
Tanners Rd. EX32: L'key 2D 24
TQ4: Good 3J 119
Tanpits La. TQ7: Chil 6G 159
Tanpits Mdw. TQ7: Chil 6G 159
TANTON'S PLAIN 1A 30
Tanyards Ct. EX12: Seat 5E 86 (off Beer Rd.)
Tape La. EX14: Awli 3A 54
Tapley Gdns. TQ14: Bi'ton 3C 106
Tappers Cl. EX3: Top 5B 74
Tappers Knapp DT7: Uply 3G 91
Tappers Mdw. EX20: Oke 3D 48
Tapp's La. PL8: Brixt 2J 149
Taps Cl. EX6: Exmin 2D 74
Tapson Dr. PL9: Hooe 6B 142
Tarbet Av. EX1: Heav 5J 65
Tarka Cl. EX20: Oke 2D 48
Tarka La. EX34: Woolc 7C 10
Tarka Tennis Cen. 6E 18
Tarka Trail, The 3C 163
TARR 1B 166
Tarraway Rd. TQ3: Pres 5K 115
Tarr's Av. TQ12: Kingst 4H 105
Tarrs End TQ12: Kingst 4H 105
Tarr's La. TQ12: Kingst 4H 105
Tarry La. EX34: Ilfra 3H 11 (off Belvedere Rd.)
TATWORTH 3D 167
TAUNTON 1C 167
Taunton Av. PL5: Plym 5G 131
Taunton Cl. EX2: Exe 2D 70
Taunton Ct. TQ9: Tot 6F 103 (off New Wlk.)
Taunton Pl. PL5: Plym 5G 131
Tavern M. EX38: Gt T 2B 30
Tavis Rd. TQ3: Paig 6F 115
TAVISTOCK 4J 59 (3C 169)
Tavistock College Sports Cen. 5G 59
Tavistock Golf Course 5K 59
Tavistock Mus. 4J 59
Tavistock Pl. PL4: Plym 3F 9 (2K 141)
TQ4: Good 7H 119
Tavistock Rd. EX4: Exe 2A 6 (5D 64)
PL2: Plym 3K 135
PL5: Plym 3K 135
PL6: Plym 3K 135
PL6: Robo 1D 132
PL20: Horr, Yelv 1D 126
PL20: Prin 5B 60
Tavy Av. TQ2: Torq 5H 111
Tavy Cleave 2D 169
Tavy Pl. PL4: Plym 7A 136
Tavy Rd. PL19: Tavi 4K 59
Taw Cl. PL3: Plym 5E 136
Taw Ct. EX32: Barn 5F 19
Taw Cres. EX31: Chive 2E 16
TAW GREEN 1A 170
Taw Mdw. Cres. EX31: Frem 5G 17
Taw Rd. EX31: Chive 1E 16
TAWSTOCK 7A 24 (1D 163)
Tawton La. EX20: S Zeal 2J 49
Taw Trade Pk. EX31: Barn 3D 18
Taw Vale EX32: Barn 5E 18
Taw Va. Av. EX20: N Taw 6A 36
Taw Va. Cl. EX20: N Taw 6A 36
Taw Vale Pde. EX32: Barn 5E 18 (off Taw Vale)
Taw Vw. EX31: Frem 5G 17
Taw Vw. Ter. EX32: Bish T 5A 24
Tay Gdns. PL3: Plym 4E 136
Taylor Cl. EX7: Daw 5F 97
EX11: Ott M 3A 80
Taylors Ct. EX16: Tiv 1E 40
Taylors Fld. EX20: N Taw 6C 36
Taylor's La. EX37: High B 4E 32
Taylors Newtake TQ12: Live 4F 93
Taylor Sq. PL19: Tavi 3H 59
Teachers Cl. PL9: Plyms 6G 143
Teal Cl. TQ2: Torq 3J 111
Teats Hill Flats PL4: Plym 7J 9 (4A 142)
Teats Hill Rd. PL4: Plym 6H 9 (3A 142)
Teazle Ct. EX2: Exe 6D 6
Tedburn Rd. EX4: Exe, White 1A 70
TEDBURN ST MARY 6J 49 (1C 171)
Tedders Cl. EX15: Hemy 1G 47
Tedstone La. EX8: Lymp 5J 75
Ted's Way EX20: Oke 3C 48
Tees Cl. PL3: Plym 4D 136
Teignbridge Bus. Cen. TQ12: Heat 1J 93
Teignbridge Indoor Bowls Cen. 6H 105
Teign Cl. TQ14: Bi'ton 3A 106
TEIGNCOMBE 2A 170
Teign Corinthian Yacht Club 4K 107
Teign Ct. TQ14: Bi'ton 3C 106
Teignfield Caravan Site TQ14: Shal 6D 106
TEIGNGRACE 3C 104 (3C 171)

Teigngrace Rd. TQ12: New A 4D 104
Teignharvey Rd. TQ14: Shal 6C 106
Teign Heritage Cen. 4J 107
TEIGNMOUTH 5J 107 (3D 171)
Teignmouth Golf Course 1D 106
Teignmouth Hill EX7: Daw 5H 97
Teignmouth Lifeboat Station 6H 107
Teignmouth Rd. EX7: Daw, Holc 7G 97
TQ1: Maid, Torq 6B 112
TQ12: Kingst 4J 105
TQ14: Bi'ton 4C 106
TQ14: Teignm 2K 107
Teignmouth Station (Rail) 4J 107
Teign Rd. PL3: Plym 5C 136
TQ12: New A 1G 109
Teign St. TQ14: Teignm 5H 107
Teign Valley Rd. EX6: Chri 1K 63
Teign Vw. TQ13: Chud K 5B 94
Teign Vw. Pl. TQ14: Teignm 5H 107
Teign Vw. Rd. TQ14: Bi'ton 2A 106
Telegraph La. EX5: Rock 2F 79
Telegraph Wharf PL1: Plym 4F 141
Telford Cres. PL5: Plym 1E 134
Telford Rd. EX4: Exe 1B 6 (5D 64)
Tembani Ct. TQ3: Pres 7J 115
Temeraire Rd. PL5: Plym 1J 135
Temperance Pl. TQ5: Brixh 3F 123
Temperance St. TQ2: Torq 1C 116
TEMPLE 3A 168
Temple Cres. EX16: Tiv 4F 41
Temple Gdns. EX10: Sidm 5C 84
Temple Rd. EX2: Exe 6F 7 (7F 65)
Templer Rd. TQ3: Pres 3G 115
Templer's Rd. TQ12: New A 7G 105
Templer's Way TQ12: Kingst 2G 105
Templer Way TQ12: New A 7H 105
TQ12: Teigng 1C 104
Temple St. EX10: Sidm 5C 84
TEMPLETON 2C 165
Tenby Rd. PL5: Plym 2B 134
Tencery Orchard EX14: Dunk 5H 47
Ten Commandments Stone 3B 170
Teneriffe *TQ1: Torq 1E 116*
(off Middle Warberry Rd.)
Tennacott Hgts. EX39: Bide 5J 23
Tennacott La. EX39: Bide 5K 23
Tennyson Av. EX2: Won 2J 71
Tennyson Cl. TQ1: Torq 5C 112
Tennyson Gdns. PL5: Plym 2G 135
Tennyson Way EX8: Exmth 7K 75
Tenpin
Plymouth 6J 9 (3B 142)
TERHILL 1B 166
Tern Gdns. PL7: Plymp 4C 138
Terrace, The EX33: Brau 4J 15
PL1: Dev 2C 140
TQ1: Torq 2D 116
Terrace Wlk. TQ13: Ashb 3G 99
Terracina Ct. EX2: Exe 7E 6
Terra Nova Grn. PL2: Plym 6G 135
TETCOTT 1B 168
Tewkesbury Cl. PL2: Plym 3F 135
Tews La. EX31: Bick'n, Roun 6K 17
Tewsley Cl. EX31: Bick'n 6K 17
Thackeray Gdns. PL5: Plym 2G 135
Thackeray Rd. EX4: Whip 4B 66
Thames Gdns. PL3: Plym 6E 136
Thanckes Cl. PL11: Torp 1A 140
Thanckes Dr. PL11: Torp 1A 140
Thatcher Av. TQ1: Torq 3H 117
Thatcher Dr. TQ14: Teignm 1J 107
Thatcher Hgts. TQ1: Torq 3H 117
Thatcher's La. EX5: Thor 1A 50
The
Names prefixed with 'The' for example 'The Acre' are indexed under the main name such as 'Acre, The'
Theatre La. *EX31: Barn 4E 18*
(off The Strand)
Theatre Ope PL1: Dev 3E 140
Theatre Royal
Plymouth 5D 8 (3J 141)
THELBRIDGE BARTON 2B 164
Thelma Hulbert Gallery, The 3E 54
Therlow Rd. PL3: Plym 5C 136
Thetford Gdns. PL6: Plym 3E 136
Third Av. EX1: Heav 3K 7 (6J 65)
EX2: Cou W 6B 72
EX2: Won 7C 66
EX7: Daw 5G 97
PL1: Dev 2F 141
PL2: Plym 4D 134
PL9: Plyms 3H 143
TQ1: Torq 5C 112
TQ14: Teignm 4G 107
Third Dr. TQ14: Teignm 4H 107
Thirlmere Gdns. PL6: Plym 6K 131
Thistle Cl. PL6: Plym 3F 133
Thomas Bassett Dr.
EX24: Colyf 1F 87
Thomas Cl. EX8: Exmth 7K 75
Thomas La. *EX4: Exe 4D 64*
(off Harefield Cl.)
Thomas Newcomen Ct.
TQ6: Dartm 6C 124
(off Ivatt Rd.)
Thompson Cl. EX7: Daw 3J 97
Thompson Rd. EX1: Heav 5K 65
Thongsleigh Wood 2D 165
THORN 6E 148
Thornberry Av. EX1: Whip 6A 66
THORNBURY 3C 163
Thornbury Pk. Av. PL3: Plym 5J 135
Thornbury Rd. PL6: Plym 6F 133
Thorncliff Cl. TQ1: Torq 1G 117
Thorn Cl. EX1: Whip 6A 66
TQ12: New A 7B 104
THORNCOMBE 3D 167
Thorn Cross TQ13: Bov T 6B 92
Thorndale Courts EX4: Exe 4A 64
THORNDON CROSS 1D 169
Thorne Farm Way EX11: Ott M 3B 80
THORNEHILLHEAD 2C 163
Thorne La. EX17: Bow 7K 37
Thorne Pk. EX17: Cred 6K 39
Thorne Pk. Rd. TQ2: Torq 1K 115
THORNE ST MARGARET 1A 166
Thornes Ter. EX36: S Mol 6C 26
THORNEY 1D 167
THORNFALCON 1C 167
Thornfield Cl. EX8: Exmth 2C 76
EX12: Seat 3E 86
THORNGROVE 1D 167
Thornhill Rd. PL3: Plym 5K 135
Thornhill Way PL3: Plym 5K 135
Thorning St. TQ8: Salc 3D 158
Thornlea Av. EX31: Frem 6E 16
Thornley Dr. TQ14: Teignm 4G 107
Thornley Way EX39: Hart 3J 27
Thorn Orchard TQ12: Ipp 6J 101
Thorn Pk. PL3: Plym 6K 135
Thornpark Ri. EX1: Whip 6A 66
Thornton Av. PL4: Plym 2J 9 (1A 142)
Thornton Cl. EX9: Bud S 7C 82
EX39: Bide 3D 22
Thornton Hill EX4: Exe 1E 6 (4F 65)
Thornton Pearn Ri. DT7: Lym R 4H 91
Thorntree Bus. Units EX8: Exmth 3H 77
Thornville Ter. PL9: Plyms 5D 142
Thornyville Cl. PL9: Plyms 4D 142
Thornyville Dr. PL9: Plyms 5D 142
Thornyville Vs. PL9: Plyms 5D 142
Thorpe Av. EX8: Exmth 1D 76
THORVERTON 2B 50 (3D 165)
Thorverton Rd. EX2: Mar B 5G 71
Threadneedle St. *EX15: Culm 2B 46*
(off Hemyock Rd.)
Three Corner Fld. EX5: Cranb 4B 68
Three Corner Pl. EX2: Alph 5F 71
Three Corners TQ12: Kingst 3J 105
Three Ways EX31: Brat F 6H 13
Threshers EX17: Cred 6F 39
Threwstones Cl. EX16: Tiv 3E 40
Throgmorton Ho. TQ9: Tot 6F 103
THROWLEIGH 1A 170
Thrushel Cl. TQ5: Brixh 6C 122
THRUSHELTON 2C 169
THURDON 2A 162
THURLBEAR 1C 167
THURLESTONE 6C 154 (3C 175)
Thurlestone Ct. *TQ6: Dartm 6E 124*
(off Victoria Rd.)
Thurlestone Gdns. TQ6: Dartm 6E 124
Thurlestone Golf Course 7B 154
Thurlestone Rd. TQ12: New A 7E 104
Thurlestone Wlk. PL6: Plym 2E 136
(not continuous)
Thurlow Cl. EX17: Cred 6F 39
Thurlow Hill TQ1: Torq 7C 112
Thurlow Pk. TQ1: Torq 7C 112
Thurlow Rd. EX4: Exe 1J 7 (4H 65)
TQ1: Torq 7C 112
THURLOXTON 1C 167
Thursby Wlk. EX4: Pin 3C 66
Tichfield Gdns. TQ3: Paig 7F 115
Ticklemore St. TQ9: Tot 6F 103
Tidal Vw. Cl. TQ7: Ave G 7H 151
Tidcombe Cl. EX16: Tiv 5G 41
Tidcombe La. EX16: Tiv 4G 41
Tidcombe Wlk. EX16: Tiv 4G 41
Tiddy Brook Rd. PL19: Whitc 7K 59
Tiddy Cl. PL19: Tavi 6H 59
TIDEFORD 2A 174
TIDEFORD CROSS 1A 174
Tidwell Cl. EX9: Bud S 5C 82
Tidwell La. EX9: E Bud 3C 82
Tidwell Rd. EX9: Bud S 5C 82
TIGLEY 1D 175
Tillard Cl. PL7: Plymp 4F 139
Tilly Cl. PL9: Plyms 7G 143
Timber Hill DT7: Lym R 3K 91
Timbers Cl. TQ11: B'leigh 6B 98
Timbers Rd. TQ11: B'leigh 6B 98
Timber Ter. TQ12: Kingsk 1F 111
Timber Vale Caravan Pk.
DT7: Lym R 3K 91
Times M. TQ9: Tot 6E 102
TINHAY 6C 56 (2B 168)
Tinhay Ct. *PL16: Tin 6C 56*
(off Station Rd.)
Tinhay Mill Ind. Est. PL16: Tin 7C 56
Tin La. EX2: Exe 7A 6 (1D 70)
PL4: Plym 5G 9 (3K 141)
Tinside Lido 7D 8 (4J 141)
Tintagel Cl. EX4: Whip 2K 65
TQ2: Torq 5B 112
Tintagel Cres. PL2: Plym 3H 135
Tintern Av. PL4: Plym 5K 9 (3B 142)
Tip Hill EX11: Ott M 4C 80
TIPPACOTT 2D 161
Tipton La. EX11: W Hill 1J 79
TIPTON ST JOHN 1J 81 (1A 172)
Tipton Va. EX11: Metc 1H 81
TITCHBERRY 1A 162
Tithebarn Copse EX1: Pin 4E 66
Tithebarn La. EX1: Pin 4E 66
Tithe Rd. PL7: Plymp 4H 137
TITSON 3A 162
TIVERTON 4D 40 (2D 165)
Tiverton Bus. Pk. EX16: Tiv 2G 41
Tiverton Castle 4C 40
Tiverton Cl. PL6: Plym 2C 132
Tiverton Golf Course 3K 41
Tiverton Museum of Mid Devon Life 5C 40
Tiverton Parkway Golf Driving Range 2C 42
Tiverton Parkway Station (Rail) 3D 42
Tiverton Rd. EX5: Silv 1F 51
EX15: Cull 3F 45
EX16: Bam 4G 33
Tiverton Town FC 3C 40
Tiverton Way EX16: Tiv 3F 41
Tivoli Cinema, The
Merlin Cinemas 5D 40
Toadpit La. EX11: W Hill 2J 79
Toby La. EX5: Wood S 3D 78
Tolchers TQ9: Darti 3B 102
TOLLAND 1B 166
Tollards Rd. EX2: Cou W 4K 71
Tollbar Cl. PL21: Ivy 4K 145
Tollit Gdns. *TQ9: Tot 6F 103*
(off Weston Rd.)
Tollox Pl. PL3: Plym 7C 136
Tolman Cres. EX12: Seat 4F 87
Tom Maddock Gdns. PL21: Ivy 5J 145
Tomouth Cres. EX39: Apple 3H 21
Tomouth Rd. EX39: Apple 3H 21
Tomouth Sq. EX39: Apple 3H 21
Tomouth Ter. EX39: Apple 3H 21
Tom Sanders Cl. EX34: Com M 7C 12
Tom's Fld. EX33: Croy 1C 14
TONEDALE 1B 166
Topcliff Rd. TQ14: Shal 6F 107
(not continuous)
TOPSHAM 5B 74 (2D 171)
Topsham Mus. 6B 74
Topsham Pool 5B 74
Topsham Rd.
EX2: Cou W, Exe 7F 7 (1G 71)
Topsham Station (Rail) 5B 74
TORBAY 6J 115 (1B 155)
Torbay Bus. Pk. TQ4: Paig 6E 118
Torbay Ct. TQ5: Brixh 3G 123
Torbay Holiday Chalets
TQ5: Brixh 2D 122
Torbay Leisure Cen. 4H 119
Torbay Lifeboat Station 2G 123
Torbay Rd. TQ2: Torq 5K 115
TQ4: Paig 1J 119
Torbay Trad. Est. TQ5: Brixh 4E 122
Torbridge Rd. PL7: Plymp 3B 138
PL20: Horr 2E 126
TORBRYAN 1A 176
Torbryan Cl. PL6: Plym 3F 137
Tor Chu. Rd. TQ2: Torq 1B 116
Tor Cl. EX4: Whip 3K 65
PL3: Plym 4K 135
TQ4: Broads 1H 121
Tor Cres. PL3: Plym 4K 135
TORCROSS 3A 176
Tor Dale TQ1: Torq 7C 112
Tor Gdns. TQ12: E Ogw 3A 108
Tor Haven *TQ2: Torq 2D 116*
(off Abbey Rd.)
Tor Hill Rd. TQ2: Torq 1C 116
Toriana Pl. *PL7: Plymp 3A 138*
(off Boringdon Rd.)
Torland Rd. PL3: Plym 4K 135
Toronto Ho. EX4: Exe 4H 65
Toronto Rd. EX4: Exe 1H 7 (5G 65)
Tor Pk. Rd. TQ2: Torq 7B 112
TQ4: Paig 4C 118
TORPOINT 1A 140 (2A 174)
Torpoint Mosquito Sailing Club 2B 140
TORQUAY 1C 116 (1B 176)
Torquay Crematorium TQ2: Torq 4A 112
Torquay Golf Course 4E 112
Torquay Holiday Village
TQ2: Torq 2K 111
Torquay Mus. 2E 116
Torquay Rd. TQ2: Torq 1G 111
TQ3: Paig, Pres 1H 119
TQ12: Kingsk 1G 111
TQ12: New A 1F 109
TQ14: Shal 6G 107
Torquay Station (Rail) 3B 116
Torquay United FC 6D 112
TORR 3C 150 (2B 174)
Torr Bri. Pk. PL8: Yeal 2C 150
TORRE 1B 116 (1A 176)
Torre Abbey 2B 116
Torre Cl. PL21: Ivy 4K 145
Torre Station (Rail) 7A 112
Torr Hill PL8: Yeal 2B 150
Torridge Av. TQ2: Torq 6H 111
Torridge Bri. EX39: N'ham 1G 23
Torridge Cl. *EX39: Bide 4G 23*
(off Torrington La.)
PL7: Plymp 3D 138
Torridge Hill EX39: Bide 4F 23
Torridge Mt. EX39: Bide 4G 23
Torridge Pl. EX39: Bide 4G 23
Torridge Pool 5F 21
Torridge Rd. EX31: Chive 1E 16
EX39: Apple 2G 21
PL7: Plymp 3C 138
Torridge St. EX39: Bide 4G 23
Torridge Vw. EX38: Gt T 2A 30
EX39: Bide 4F 23
Torridge Way PL3: Plym 6D 136
Torrington 1646 3B 30
Torrington La. EX39: Bide 4G 23
Torrington Mus. 2C 30
Torrington Pl. *EX6: Kenton 6H 95*
(off Chiverstone Rd.)
Torrington Pool 2C 30
Torrington Rd. EX19: Wink 1B 36
Torrington Sports Hall 2D 30
Torrington St. EX39: Bide 4G 23
Torr La. PL3: Plym 4J 135
PL8: Torr 3C 150
Tor Rd. PL3: Plym 4K 135
Tor Royal La. PL20: Prin 7D 60
Torrs Pk. EX34: Ilfra 4G 11
Torrs Wlk. Av. EX34: Ilfra 2G 11
Torr Vw. Av. PL3: Plym 4J 135
Tors, The TQ12: Kingsk 1F 111
Tor Sands *TQ4: Paig 2J 119*
(off Sands Rd.)
Tors Pk. EX35: Lynm 2J 13
Tor Sq. Ho. *TQ2: Torq 7B 112*
(off South St.)
Tors Rd. EX20: Oke 5B 48
EX35: Lynm 2J 13
Tors Vw. EX39: West H 6A 20
Tor Va. TQ1: Torq 7B 112
Torver Cl. PL6: Plym 1E 136
Tor Vw. EX20: Lew 1A 56
PL20: Horr 2E 126
PL20: Prin 5B 60
TQ11: B'leigh 5B 98
Tor Vw. Av. TQ12: New A 2J 109
Tor Vw. Gdns. TQ3: Paig 1G 119
Torville Pk. EX39: West H 5C 20
Torwood Cl. TQ1: Torq 3E 116
Torwood Ct. TQ1: Torq 2F 117
Torwood Gdns. Rd. TQ1: Torq 3E 116
Torwood Mt. TQ1: Torq 2E 116
Tor Woods 3D 175
Torwood St. TQ1: Torq 2E 116
Tory Brook Av. PL7: Plymp 3B 138
Tory Brook Ct. *PL7: Plymp 3B 138*
(off Chamberlayne Dr.)
Tory Way PL7: Plymp 3A 138
Tothill Av. PL4: Plym 3H 9 (2A 142)
Tothill Ct. TQ14: Shal 6G 107
Tothill Rd. PL4: Plym 4J 9 (2A 142)
TOTNES 6E 102 (1A 176)
Totnes Castle (remains) 5D 102
Totnes Cl. PL7: Plymp 5E 138
Totnes Costume Mus. 6E 102
Totnes Down Hill TQ9: Tot 7E 102
Totnes Elizabethan House Mus. 6E 102
Totnes Guildhall 6E 102
Totnes Image Bank & Rural Archive
6F 103
(within Tourist Info. Cen.)
Totnes Ind. Est. TQ9: Tot 5E 102
Totnes (Littlehempston Riverside) Station
South Devon Railway 4E 102
Totnes Pavilion Leisure Cen. 5E 102
Totnes Rare Breeds Farm 3E 102
Totnes Rd. PL21: Erm 3H 147
TQ2: Torq 3G 115
TQ3: Marl 7A 114
TQ3: Paig 2A 118

Totnes Rd. TQ4: Coll M, Paig 2A 118
  TQ6: Strete 6H 153
  TQ10: S Bre 1B 100
  TQ11: B'leigh 4E 98
  TQ12: A'well, Ipp, New A, Two O
  . . . . .7H 101 & 7C 108
Totnes Station (Rail) 5E 102
Totnes Town Mill 6F 103
  (within Tourist Info. Cen.)
Tottons Ct. EX2: Alph 5D 70
Tourist Info. Cen.
  Ashburton 4G 99
  Axminster 4H 89
  Bampton 2H 33
  Barnstaple 5E 18
  Bideford 2G 23
  Bovey Tracey 4B 92
  Braunton 4J 15
  Brixham 3F 123
  Buckfastleigh 4D 98
  Budleigh Salterton 7C 82
  Combe Martin 5A 12
  Crediton 6H 39
  Dartmouth 1B 124 (6F 125)
  Dawlish .4H 97
  Exeter 3F 7 (6F 65)
  Exmouth 6C 76
  Great Torrington 3C 30
  Holsworthy 2C 34
  Honiton .3F 55
  Ilfracombe 2H 11
  Ivybridge 4H 145
  Kingsbridge 4G 157
  Lyme Regis 5K 91
  Lynton 1G 13
  Modbury 6G 147
  Morehampstead 6H 61
  Newton Abbot 1E 108
  Okehampton 3B 48
  Ottery St Mary 4C 80
  Paignton 1J 119
  Plymouth, The Barbican
  . . . . .6G 9 (3K 141)
  Salcombe 3D 158
  Seaton 5F 87
  Shaldon 7H 107
  Sidmouth 7C 84
  South Molton 6C 26
  Tavistock 4J 59
  Teignmouth 5J 107
  Tiverton .5D 40
  Torquay 3D 116
  Totnes 6F 103
  Woolacombe 6A 10
Touts Ct. EX36: S Mol 6D 26
  (off East St.)
Tovey Cres. PL5: Plym 1J 135
Tovey M. EX14: Hon 3F 55
  (off King St.)
Towell La. EX19: Bea 2J 31
Towerfield EX3: Top 6D 72
Towerfield Dr. PL6: Plym 2D 132
Tower Gdns. EX17: Cred 5H 39
Tower Hill EX17: Cher F 1H 39
Tower Hill Rd. PL15: St G 5E 34
Tower La. PL21: Moor 3C 146
Tower Pk. EX36: S Mol 7C 26
  TQ13: More 7H 61
Tower Rd. EX14: Hon 6J 55
  TQ3: Paig 1H 119
Towers Cl. PL6: Plym 1G 137
Tower St. EX8: Exmth 6C 76
  EX39: Bide 4F 23
  (off Buttgarden St.)
  EX39: N'ham 5E 20
Tower Vw. EX5: Broadc 7C 52
Tower Wlk. EX2: Alph 5F 71
Tower Way EX14: Dunk 7G 47
TOWN BARTON 6G 49
Town Cl. TQ6: Dartm 1A 124 (6E 124)
Town Cotts. TQ12: A'well 6E 108
Town End EX5: Broadc 5D 52
Town Farm Cl. EX14: Hon 3E 54
  PL20: Horr 2E 126
Town Farm Cotts. TQ9: Blacka 3C 152
Town Farm Ct. EX33: Brau 4H 15
Townfield EX6: Exmin 2C 74
Town Hall Pl. TQ13: Bov T 3C 92
Town Hill EX5: Broadc 5C 52
  EX15: Culm 2B 46
  PL21: Erm 3H 147
Townlands EX5: Bradn 2B 52
  EX15: Will 5D 44
Town La. EX5: Wood 5C 78
Town Mdw. EX20: Bride 3H 57
Town Mdws. EX39: Wools 2A 28
Town Mill, The 5K 91
Town Mill Ct. EX31: Barn 3E 18
  (off Mills Way)
Town Mill Gdns. PL19: Tavi 3J 59
Town Pk. EX17: Cred 6G 39
  EX38: Gt T 2B 30

Town Pk. TQ7: Lodd 3G 151
  TQ7: W Alv 5E 156
Town Quay TQ9: Tot 6F 103
  (off The Plains)
TOWNSEND 6H 25
Towns End EX33: Brau 4H 15
Townsend EX12: Beer 6A 86
  TQ12: Den 2H 101
Townsend Av. EX12: Seat 4E 86
Townsend Cl. TQ7: W Alv 5D 156
Townsend Hill TQ12: Ipp 6G 101
Townsend Rd. EX12: Seat 5E 86
  TQ7: W Alv 5D 156
Townsend Ter. TQ9: E All 6D 152
Townshend Av. PL2: Plym 6D 134
Town's La. TQ7: Lodd 3G 151
Town Sq. EX17: Cred 6H 39
  (off Parliament St.)
TOWNSTAL 6D 124
Townstal Cres. TQ6: Dartm 6D 124
Townstal Hill
  TQ6: Dartm 1A 124 (6E 124)
Townstal Pathfields TQ6: Dartm . . .6D 124
Townstal Rd. TQ6: Dartm 6C 124
Town Tree Hill EX7: Daw 4G 97
Town Vw. EX17: Cred 6H 39
Town Wlk. EX32: Barn 5G 19
Towsington La. EX6: Exmin 4B 74
Tracey Ct. PL1: Plym 3C 8
Tracey Grn. EX16: With 6H 33
Traceys Av. EX12: Seat 4D 86
Tracey Va. TQ13: Bov T 5B 92
Tracey Vw. EX14: Hon 3E 54
  (off Northcote La.)
Trafalgar Cl. PL5: Plym 3C 134
  TQ12: New A 6E 104
Trafalgar Ct. EX3: Top 5A 74
  (off High St.)
  EX15: Uff .6H 43
Trafalgar Dr. EX38: Gt T 1B 30
Trafalgar Gdns. EX32: Barn 6F 19
Trafalgar Lawn EX32: Barn 6F 19
Trafalgar Pl. EX4: Exe 1G 7 (5G 65)
Trafalgar Pl. La. PL1: Dev 1E 140
Trafalgar Rd. EX8: Lymp 5G 75
Trafalgar St. PL4: Plym 4G 9 (2K 141)
Trafalgar Ter. EX12: Brans 6H 85
  TQ5: Brixh 2E 122
  (off Higher Furzeham Rd.)
Trafalgar Way, The
  EX13: Axmin, Kilm 2E 88
Trafford M. EX2: Won 2B 72
  (off Lords Way)
Trago Mills .5H 93
Traine Rd. PL9: Wem 4C 148
Traine Ter. PL21: Modb 7H 147
Traine Vs. PL21: Modb 5H 147
Tramway Rd. PL6: Plym 8E 132
Tramways TQ1: Torq 6D 112
Transit Way PL5: Plym 7H 131
Travershes Cl. EX8: Exmth 3D 76
Trayes Ter. La. PL4: Plym 2C 142
Treacle Hill TQ12: Kingst 4H 105
  (off Fore St.)
Treago Gdns. PL6: Plym 2D 132
TREBARTHA 3A 168
Trebblepark Rd. TQ7: Kingsb 3F 157
Trebblepark Wlk. TQ7: Kingsb 3F 157
TREBULLETT 3B 168
TREBURLEY 3B 168
Treby Rd. PL7: Plymp 5C 138
TRECOTT 2A 168
TREDAULE .2A 168
TREDINNICK 3A 168
Treefield EX32: Brat F 6J 13
Treefields TQ5: Brixh 4D 122
Treefield Wlk. EX32: Barn 5H 19
  (off Barton Rd.)
Treesdale Cl. TQ3: Paig 1F 119
Trefusis Gdns. PL3: Plym 7B 136
Trefusis Pl. EX8: Exmth 7C 76
Trefusis Ter. EX8: Exmth 7C 76
  EX20: Mer 5B 30
Trefusis Way EX9: E Bud 1D 82
TREGADA .2B 168
TREGADILLETT 2B 168
TREGEARE .2A 168
Tregenna Cl. PL7: Plymp 5F 139
TREGOLE 1A 168
TREGONHAWKE 2A 174
TREHAN 2A 174
Trehill Rd. PL21: Ivy 4H 145
TREKENNER 3B 168
TRELASH 1A 168
Trelawney Av. PL5: Plym 2C 134
Trelawney Ct. EX39: N'ham 5F 21
  (off Diddywell Rd.)
Trelawney La. PL3: Plym 6J 135
Trelawney Pl. PL5: Plym 6J 135
Trelawney Rd. PL3: Plym 6J 135
Trelawney Rd. PL7: Plymp 4K 137
  PL19: Tavi .3J 59

Trelissick Cl. TQ3: Paig 7D 114
Trelissick Rd. TQ3: Paig 7D 114
Trelivan Cl. EX8: Exmth 1G 77
Trelorrin Gdns. PL3: Plym 6K 135
Treloweth Cl. PL2: Plym 3J 135
TREMAIL 2A 168
TREMAINE .2A 168
Tremaine Cl. EX14: Hon 3G 55
TREMAR 3A 168
TREMATON 2A 174
Trematon Av. TQ1: Torq 1C 116
Trematon Dr. PL21: Ivy 4J 145
Trematon Ter. PL4: Plym 7K 135
Tremayne Ri. PL19: Tavi 4H 59
Tremford Ct. EX9: Bud S 6B 82
Tremlett Gro. TQ12: Ipp 6H 101
Tremletts Cl. EX6: Ted M 6H 49
Trenance Dr. PL19: Lam 6C 58
Trendlewood Pk. PL6: Plym 3E 132
TRENEGLOS 1A 168
TRENGUNE .1A 168
Trenode Av. EX34: Com M 6A 12
Trentbridge Sq. EX2: Won 1B 72
Trent Cl. EX39: Bide 5J 23
  PL3: Plym 5C 136
Trentham Cl. PL6: Plym 4C 132
  TQ3: Paig .6E 114
TRENTISHOE 2C 161
Trentishoe Down 2C 161
Trescote Way EX20: Bride 1J 57
Tresillian Cotts. EX3: Top 7B 74
Tresillian Gdns. EX3: Top 6B 74
  EX4: Exe 4H 65
Tresillian St. PL4: Plym 6K 9 (3B 142)
TRESKINNICK CROSS 1A 168
Tresluggan Rd. PL5: Plym 2C 134
TRESMEER .2A 168
TRESPARRETT 1A 168
TRESPARRETT POSTS 1A 168
Treston Cl. EX7: Daw 3J 97
Trethewey Gdns. PL7: Wot 1F 129
Tretower Cl. PL6: Plym 5A 132
TREVADLOCK 3A 168
Trevanna Rd. TQ7: Kingsb 5F 157
Trevannion Cl. PL6: Plym 3B 136
Trevelyan Rd. EX12: Seat 6G 87
Trevena EX5: Clyst M 2F 73
Treveneague Gdns. PL2: Plym 3J 135
Trevenn Dr. TQ12: Kingsk 2G 111
Treveor Gdns. PL21: Modb 5H 147
Treverbyn Cl. PL7: Plymp 3A 138
Treverbyn Rd. PL7: Plymp 3A 138
Trevessa Cl. PL2: Plym 3J 135
Trevethan Pk. PL20: Bere F 6C 128
TREVIGRO 3B 168
Trevithick Rd. PL5: Plym 2D 134
TREVIVIAN .2A 168
Trevol Rd. PL11: Torp 1A 140
Trevone Gdns. PL2: Plym 3J 135
Trevose Way PL3: Plym 5D 136
TREWARLETT 2B 168
TREWASSA .2A 168
TREWEEN 2A 168
TREWEN 2A 168
TREWINT 1A 168
Trewithy Ct. PL6: Plym 2A 136
Trewithy Dr. PL6: Plym 1A 136
Trews Weir Ct. EX2: Exe 7G 7 (1G 71)
Trews Weir Reach EX2: Exe . . .7G 7 (1G 71)
Trewyn Pk. EX22: Hols 1B 34
Trewyn Rd. EX22: Hols 1B 34
Triangle, The EX6: Kenton 6H 95
  (off Exeter Hill)
  EX10: Sidm 7B 84
  TQ14: Teignm 5J 107
Triangle Pl. TQ14: Teignm 5J 107
Trickey Cl. EX16: Tiv 3F 41
Trickhay St. EX4: Exe 4D 6 (6E 64)
Trick's Ter. EX19: Bea 2H 31
Trigger's Hill EX19: Bea, Robo 1G 31
Trigley La. EX36: S Mol 7C 26
Trill La. EX13: Abb G 6E 90
  EX13: Mus .6E 90
TRIMSTONE .2B 160
Trinfield Av. EX8: Exmth 3D 76
Trinity Apartments EX1: Exe 4F 7
Trinity Cl. PL20: Bere A 2C 128
  TQ14: Teignm 3H 107
Trinity Ct. EX1: Exe 5F 7 (7F 65)
  EX10: Sidm 7C 84
  EX39: West H 6A 20
  (off Atlantic Way)
Trinity Gdns. EX34: Ilfra 3G 11
Trinity Hill TQ1: Torq 3E 116
Trinity Hill Local Nature Reserve 3A 90
Trinity Hill Rd. EX13: Ray H 2A 90
Trinity M. TQ14: Teignm 2H 107
  (off Maudlin Dr.)
Trinity Pl. EX32: Barn 5E 19
  PL1: Plym 7C 8 (4H 141)
Trinity Rd. EX8: Exmth 6A 76
Trinity Sq. EX13: Axmin 3H 89

Trinity St. EX32: Barn 5F 19
Trinity Ter. EX13: Axmin 3H 89
  (off Castle St.)
Trinity Way PL19: Tavi 5G 59
Trinnaman Cl. PL21: Ivy 5H 145
Trinnicks Orchard PL21: Ugb 6E 146
Tristan Cl. EX4: Whip 2K 65
Triumphal Cres. PL7: Plymp 4H 137
Troarn Way TQ13: Chud 3C 94
Trojan Ind. Pk. TQ4: Paig 3E 118
Trood La. EX2: Matf 7G 71
Trough La. TQ13: Bov T 3C 92
Trouville EX32: Barn 4F 19
  (off Bevan Rd.)
Trowbridge Cl. PL5: Plym 6H 131
Trow Hill EX10: Sidf 2E 84
TRULL 1C 167
Trumans Cl. EX4: Exe 6C 6
Trumans Pl. EX7: Daw 4H 97
  (off High St.)
Trumlands Rd. TQ1: Torq 4C 112
Trumpers Cl. PL21: Ivy 3E 144
Trumps Ct. EX10: Sidm 7C 84
  (off East St.)
Trumps Orchard EX15: Cull 3F 45
Truro Av. TQ2: Torq 4C 112
Truro Dr. EX4: Exe 5B 64
  EX8: Exmth 1F 77
  PL5: Plym 5F 131
TRUSHAM 2C 111
Trusham Rd. EX2: Mar B 3F 71
TUCKENHAY 2A 176
Tucker Cl. PL5: Plym 3E 134
Tucker Ct. EX14: Hon 3F 55
TUCKERMARSH 1C 128
Tuckers Brook PL21: Modb 6G 147
Tuckers Cl. EX17: Cred 6F 39
  PL8: Torr .2C 150
Tuckers Hall 5C 6 (7E 64)
Tucker's Hill PL21: Corn 7H 129
Tuckers Maltings 7G 105
Tuckers Mdw. EX17: Cred 6F 39
Tuckers Pk. EX22: Bradw 5B 28
  EX39: Buck B 2H 29
Tuckfield Cl. EX2: Exe 1K 71
Tucking Mill La. EX36: S Mol 6D 26
Tudor Cl. EX39: N'ham 6E 20
  PL9: Plyms 7F 143
  PL16: Lift .6B 56
  (off Darkey La.)
  TQ4: Paig .5G 119
  TQ12: New A 1E 108
Tudor Ct. EX4: Exe 5C 6 (7E 64)
  TQ13: Ashb 4H 99
  (off North St.)
Tudor Dr. EX31: Barn 7B 18
Tudor Gro. EX15: Cull 2H 45
Tudor Rd. TQ12: New A 1E 108
Tudor St. EX4: Exe 5C 6 (7E 64)
Tuffery Cl. EX4: Exe 1K 7 (4J 65)
Tugela Ter. EX5: Clyst M 2F 73
Tully Gdns. EX10: Sidm 3C 84
Tuly St. EX31: Barn 4E 18
Tumbles, The EX20: Exbo 5J 35
Tumbling Fld. La. EX16: Tiv 5D 40
Tumbling Flds. EX16: Tiv 5D 40
Tumbling Weir 3B 80
Tumbly Hill TQ7: Kingsb 5G 157
Tunnel La. EX14: Hon 2J 55
Tunnels Beaches 2G 11
Tuns La. EX5: Silv 2G 51
Tunworth Ct. EX1: Exe 5D 6
Tuplins TQ12: Kingst 3H 105
Turbill Gdns. PL7: Plymp 4E 138
TURFMOOR 3C 167
Turkey La. EX5: Rock, Whim 3K 69
  (not continuous)
Turk's Head La. EX14: Hon 4D 54
TURNCHAPEL 6B 142 (2A 174)
Turner Av. EX8: Exmth 3D 76
Turner Cl. EX10: New P 6H 81
Turners Cres. EX39: Hart 2H 27
Turnpike EX14: Hon 3G 55
  EX16: Sam P 3A 42
Turnpike Cl. EX39: High C 6G 27
Turnquay PL9: Plyms 5C 142
Turpins Plot EX20: Oke 3D 48
Turret Gro. PL4: Plym 7A 136
Tute's La. EX34: Com M 5C 12
TUTWELL 3B 168
Tuxton Cl. PL7: Plymp 6E 138
Tweed Cl. EX14: Hon 5E 55
TWEENAWAYS 2E 118
Tweenaways TQ11: B'leigh 5B 98
Tweenways TQ12: Kingst 4G 105
Twelve Oaks Farm Caravan Pk.
  TQ12: Teigng 3D 104
Twickenham Rd. TQ12: New A 2J 109
Twindle Beer TQ13: Chud 2B 94
TWITCHEN 3G 43 (3D 161)
Twitchen Ho. Holiday Pk.
  EX34: Woolc 4C 10

Two Acre Cl. TQ3: Paig 1E 118
Two Acre Ct. EX2: Alph 5D 70
TWO BRIDGES 3A 170
Two Bridges Rd. EX10: Sidf 1D 84
　PL20: Prin 6D 60
TWO MILE OAK 7B 108 (1A 176)
TWO POTTS 7K 11
Two Rivers Ind. Est. EX31: Barn . . .3C 18
Two Trees Rd. EX31: Frem 6E 16
Twyford Pl. EX16: Tiv 4D 40
Tylney Cl. PL6: Plym 4C 132
Tyndale Cl. PL5: Plym 2G 135
Tyrrell Mead EX10: Sidm 3C 84
Tyrrell Rd. EX16: Tiv 4B 40
TYTHECOTT 2C 163
Tytheing Cl. EX5: New C 7D 50
TYTHERLEIGH 3D 167
Tything Wlk. PL3: Plym 5K 135

U

UFFCULME 6H 43 (2A 166)
Uffculme Ct. EX15: Uff 6H 43
　(off Ashley Rd.)
Uffculme Rd. EX15: Culm 3A 46
　EX15: Uff, Will . . . . . . .3E 44 & 7F 43
UGBOROUGH 6E 146 (2C 175)
Ugborough Rd. PL21: Bitta 4C 146
Ugbrooke 3C 171
Ullswater Ct. EX4: Exe 7C 64
Ullswater Cres. PL6: Plym 5K 131
Ultimate Adventure Cen. 3A 22
Ulysses Pk. EX2: Sow 7D 66
Umber Cl. EX34: Com M 5A 12
UMBERLEIGH 1A 164
Undercliffe TQ6: Dartm 1B 124
Undercliff Rd. PL9: Hooe 5C 142
Underfleet EX12: Seat 6F 87
　(not continuous)
Underfleet, The EX12: Seat 5F 87
Underhay PL8: Yeal 2A 150
Underheath TQ1: Torq 1F 117
　(off Middle Warberry Rd.)
Underhill EX8: Lymp 6F 75
Underhill Cl. EX8: Lymp 7G 75
Underhill Cres. EX8: Lymp 7G 75
Underhill Pk. EX16: Tiv 3C 40
　(off Johns Way)
Underhill Rd. PL3: Plym 7F 135
　TQ2: Torq 3A 116
Underhill Ter. EX3: Top 5B 74
Underhill Vs. PL3: Plym 1F 141
Underidge Cl. TQ3: Paig 1E 118
Underidge Dr. TQ3: Paig 1E 118
Underidge Rd. TQ3: Paig 1E 118
Underlane EX22: Hols 3C 34
　PL7: Plymp 6J 137
　PL9: Plyms 6E 142
Underleat Cl. TQ13: Chud 1D 94
Underleys EX12: Beer 7A 86
Under Minnow Rd. EX31: Barn . . .2D 18
Undertown PL21: Ugb 6E 146
Under Way TQ12: Coff 6K 109
Underways PL20: Bere A 2C 128
UNDERWOOD 4A 138 (2B 174)
Underwood Cl. EX7: Daw 6G 97
Underwood Rd. PL7: Plymp 4A 138
Unicorn Cl. PL7: Plymp 5J 137
Unicorn St. EX2: Sow 1C 72
Union Cl. EX39: Bide 4E 22
Union La. TQ5: Brixh 5C 148
Union Pl. PL1: Plym 5A 8 (3G 141)
　EX4: Exe 4G 65
　EX17: Cred 6H 39
Union Sq. Shop. Cen. TQ1: Torq . . .1D 116
Union St. EX2: Exe 7B 6 (1D 70)
　EX8: Exmth 6C 76
　PL1: Plym 5A 8 (3G 141)
　TQ1: Torq 1C 116
　TQ2: Torq 7B 112
　TQ6: Dartm 1A 124
　TQ8: Salc 3D 158
　TQ12: New A 1E 108
Union Ter. EX17: Cred 6H 39
　EX31: Bick'n 5K 17
　EX32: Barn 5F 19
　(off Litchdon St.)
Unity Cl. PL6: Plym 5E 132
University of Exeter
　Knightley 4E 64
　(off Streatham Dr.)
　New North Rd. 1C 6 (5E 64)
　Redcot 4E 64
　(off Streatham Dr.)
　St Lukes Campus 4H 7 (6G 65)
　Streatham Campus 3E 64
University of Plymouth
　Constantine TQ12: Kingsk 4G 9
　Diving & Marine Cen.
　　. . . . . .7H 9 (4A 142)
　Exeter Campus 2H 71

University of Plymouth
　Gibbon St. 3F 9
　Portland Sq. 3F 9 (1J 141)
University of Plymouth Squash &
　Fitness Complex 2F 9
UPCOTT
　Bideford 6E 22
　Meeth 3D 163
Upcott Av. EX31: Barn 3B 18
Upcott Hill EX20: Oke 2A 48
　EX31: Ashf, Cher B 1C 18
　EX39: Bide 6F 23
Upcott La. EX5: Thor 1B 50
Upcottmead Rd. EX16: Tiv 4B 40
Upcott Valley EX20: Oke 2A 48
UP EXE 2E 50 (3D 165)
Upexe La. EX5: Silv 2F 51
UPHAM 3C 165
Uphay La. EX13: Axmin 2F 89
Uphill Cl. PL21: Ivy 4J 145
Upland Chase EX14: Hon 6E 54
Upland Dr. PL6: Plym 5A 132
Upland Gdns. PL9: Wem 5C 148
Uplands PL19: Tavi 5G 59
Uplands Dr. EX4: Exe 3K 65
Uplands Rd. TQ3: Pres 4G 115
Uplands Ter. EX22: Hols 3C 34
UPLOWMAN 2F 91 (1D 173)
Uplowman Rd. EX16: Tiv, U'man . . .3J 41
UPLYME 2F 91 (1D 173)
Uplyme Rd. DT7: Lym R 4H 91
Uplyme Rd. Ind. Est. DT7: Lym R . . .4H 91
UPOTTERY 3C 167
Uppaton La. PL21: Ivy 1C 144
Upper Barton Rd. EX5: Cranb 3B 68
Up. Braddons Hill Rd. TQ1: Torq . . .2E 116
UPPER CHEDDON 1C 167
Up. Church St. EX8: Exmth 6C 76
Up. Churston Ri. EX12: Seat 4C 86
Upper Claypark EX34: Mort 4A 10
Up. Cloister Wlk. EX6: Exmin 1B 74
　(off Devington Pk.)
Up. Cockington La. TQ2: Torq 7J 111
Up. Crooked Mdw. EX20: Oke 3C 48
Up. Headland Pk. Rd. TQ3: Pres . . .5J 115
Up. Hermosa Rd. TQ14: Teignm . . .4H 107
Upper Highfield EX10: Sidm 5B 84
Up. Knollys Ter. La.
　PL3: Plym 1B 8 (7H 135)
Upper Longlands EX7: Daw 3F 97
Up. Manor Rd. TQ3: Pres 6H 115
Up. Morin Rd. TQ3: Pres 6H 115
Up. Paul St. EX4: Exe 3D 6 (6E 64)
Up. Penns Rd. TQ3: Pres 5J 115
Upper Plym Valley Prehistoric Sites
　. . . . . .1B 174
Upper Ridings PL7: Plymp 2E 138
Up. Stoneborough La.
　EX9: Bud S 6C 82
Upperton Rd. EX6: Dunsf 4A 62
Upper Torrs EX34: Ilfra 3F 11
Up. Westhill Rd. DT7: Lym R 5H 91
Up. West Ter. EX9: Bud S 6C 82
Up. Wood La. TQ6: Kingsw 6H 125
UPPINCOTT 3C 165
UPTON
　Bude 3A 162
　Honiton 3A 166
　Kingsbridge 3D 175
　Liskeard 3A 168
　Torquay 7C 112
　Wiveliscombe 1D 165
Upton Cl. PL3: Plym 4C 136
UPTON CROSS 3A 168
UPTON HELLIONS 3C 165
Upton Hill TQ1: Torq 7C 112
Upton Hill Rd. TQ5: Brixh 6E 122
Upton Mnr. Pk. TQ5: Brixh 6E 122
Upton Mnr. Rd. TQ5: Brixh 6D 122
UPTON PYNE 1D 171
Upton Rd. EX39: Bide 4G 23
　(off Nutaberry Hill)
　TQ1: Torq 7B 112
Usticke La. EX34: Com M 7D 12
UTON 1C 171
Uxbridge Dr. PL5: Plym 6D 130

V

Vaagso Cl. PL1: Dev 2D 140
Vachell Cres. EX2: Sow 7C 66
　(off Elliott Way)
Vale Cl. EX32: Barn 3F 19
　TQ5: Galm 3H 121
Vale La. EX31: Ashf, Land 3H 89
Valenia Ter. TQ13: Ashb 4H 99
Vale Rd. EX8: Exmth 5F 77
　TQ12: Kingsk 7K 109
　TQ12: New A 3G 109
Vales Rd. EX9: Bud S 6D 82
Valiant Av. PL5: Plym 6F 131

Valiant Soldier Museum &
　Heritage Centre, The 4D 98
Valletort Cotts. PL1: Plym 1F 141
Valletort Flats PL1: Plym 2F 141
　(off Valletort Pl.)
Valletort Ho. PL1: Plym 1F 141
　(Sydney St.)
　PL1: Plym 5A 8 (3G 141)
　(Union Pl.)
Valletort La. PL1: Plym 1F 141
Valletort Pk. TQ5: Brixh 4C 122
Valletort Pl. PL1: Plym 2F 141
Valletort Rd. PL1: Plym 1F 141
Valletort Ter. PL1: Plym 1G 141
　(off Wilton Rd.)
Valley Cl. EX32: Barn 4G 19
Valley Dr. PL9: Wem 6B 148
Valley La. EX34: Com M 6B 12
Valley of Rocks, The 1F 13
Valley Pk. Cl. EX4: Exe 2G 65
Valley Path TQ12: New A 7B 104
Valley Rd. EX4: Exe 5C 64
　EX5: Clyst M 2K 73
　PL7: Plymp 6J 137
Valley Vw. EX5: Rock 3E 68
　EX12: Seat 4E 86
　EX13: Axmin 4J 89
　EX21: Sheb 6J 29
　EX32: L'key 3D 24
　EX39: Bide 3C 22
　PL6: Plym 3E 132
　TQ13: Chag 2H 61
Valley Vw. Cl. EX12: Seat 4F 87
　PL3: Plym 4C 136
　TQ1: Torq 6B 112
Valley Vw. Rd. EX12: Seat 4E 86
　(off Valley Vw.)
　PL3: Plym 4C 136
Valley Wlk. PL6: Plym 4E 132
Valley Way EX8: Exmth 1G 77
Van Buren Pl. EX2: Sow 2C 72
Vane Hill Rd. TQ1: Torq 3E 116
Vanguard Cl. PL5: Plym 2J 135
Vansittart Dr. EX8: Exmth 1E 76
Vansittart Rd. TQ2: Torq 7B 112
Vapron Rd. PL3: Plym 5K 135
Varco Sq. EX2: Won 1B 72
Varian Ct. TQ9: Tot 6G 103
Vauban Pl. PL2: Dev 7E 134
Vaughan Cl. PL2: Plym 4H 135
Vaughan Pde. TQ2: Torq 3D 116
Vaughan Ri. EX1: Whip 6A 66
Vaughan Rd. EX1: Whip 6A 66
　TQ2: Torq 3D 116
Vauxhall Cl. PL4: Plym 5G 9
Vauxhall Quay PL4: Plym . .5G 9 (3K 141)
Vauxhall St. PL4: Plym 6F 9 (3K 141)
Vauxhall St. Flats PL4: Plym 5G 9
Vavasours Slip TQ6: Dartm 5F 125
Veale Cl. EX20: Hath 3G 35
Veale Dr. EX2: Won 2H 71
Veales Rd. TQ7: Kingsb 5F 157
Veasy Pk. PL9: Wem 6C 148
Veille La. TQ2: Torq 5J 111
　(not continuous)
Veitch Cl. EX2: Exe 7J 7 (1H 71)
Veitch Gdns. EX2: Alph 5E 70
VELATOR 6J 15
Velator Cl. EX33: Brau 6J 15
Velator Dr. EX33: Vela 6J 15
Velator Ind. Est. EX33: Vela 6J 15
Velator La. Av. EX33: Brau 5J 15
Velator Rd. EX33: Vela, Wraf 6J 15
Vellacott La. EX34: Com M 6E 12
Velland Av. TQ2: Torq 1B 112
Vellator Way EX33: Brau 6J 15
VELLY 1A 162
Velwell Rd. EX4: Exe 1C 6 (5E 64)
Venborough Cl. EX12: Seat 4D 86
Venbridge Hill EX6: Cher B 1C 62
Venford Cl. TQ4: Good 7H 119
VENHAY 2B 164
Venlake DT7: Uply 3F 91
Venlake Cl. DT7: Uply 3F 91
Venlake End DT7: Uply 3F 91
Venlake La. DT7: Uply 3G 91
Venlake Mdw. DT7: Uply 3F 91
Venlock Cl. EX32: Barn 5J 19
VENN
　Avaton Gifford 7K 151 (3D 175)
　Bishop's Tawton 5E 24
Venn Cl. PL3: Plym 5K 135
　TQ6: Sto F 2H 153
Venn Ct. PL3: Plym 5K 135
　PL8: Brixt 3H 149
Venn Cres. PL3: Plym 5K 135
Venn Dr. PL8: Brixt 3H 149
Venn Gdns. PL3: Plym 4K 135
VENNGREEN 2B 162
Venn Gro. PL3: Plym 4K 135

Venn Hill PL19: Mil A 2B 58
Venn La. PL2: Plym 5H 135
　PL3: Plym 5H 135
　TQ6: Dartm, Sto F
　　. . . . . .7A 124 & 1H 153
VENN OTTERY 2F 81 (1A 172)
Venn Ottery Nature Reserve 7G 79
Venn Ottery Rd. EX10: New P 5F 81
　EX11: S'ton 5F 81
Venn Pk. TQ6: Sto F 1H 153
Venn Rd.
　EX32: Barn, L'key . . . . .7H 19 & 4D 24
Venn Way PL3: Plym 4K 135
　TQ6: Sto F 2H 153
Venny Bri. EX4: Pin 3C 66
VENNY TEDBURN 1C 171
VENTERDON 3B 168
Vention La. EX33: Puts 1D 14
Venton Dr. EX39: West H 5C 20
　(not continuous)
Venture Ct. TQ12: New A 1D 108
Verbena Ter. TQ14: Shal 6F 107
Verden Cl. PL3: Plym 6K 135
Vermont Gdns. PL2: Plym 4E 134
Verna Pl. PL5: Plym 1C 134
Verna Rd. PL5: Plym 1C 134
Verney St. EX1: Exe 2G 7 (5G 65)
Vernon Cl. TQ1: Torq 4E 116
Vernon Rd. EX8: Exmth 2F 77
Vernon's La. EX39: Apple 2H 21
Verona Cl. EX32: Barn 3F 19
Veryan Cl. EX7: Daw 1H 97
Vestry Dr. PL2: Alph 5E 70
Viaduct Vw. EX22: Hols 2C 34
VICARAGE 6K 85 (2C 173)
Vicarage Cl. EX39: Hart 3H 27
　TQ5: Brixh 3E 122
　TQ9: Sto G 4B 120
Vicarage Gdns. EX2: Exe 1D 70
　(off Old Vicarage Rd.)
　EX7: Daw 4F 97
　PL5: Plym 1A 134
　PL19: Mil A 2B 58
Vicarage Gro. TQ9: Sto G 3B 120
Vicarage Hill PL8: Holb 6C 150
　PL21: Corn 5K 129
　TQ2: Torq 2J 115
　TQ3: Marl 2D 114
　(Church Hill)
　TQ3: Marl 2D 114
　(Nether Mdw.)
　TQ5: Brixh 5E 122
　TQ6: Dartm 1A 124 (6E 124)
　TQ12: Kingst 4H 105
Vicarage La. EX4: Pin 2D 66
　EX20: S Taw 1J 49
　TQ6: Strete 6H 153
　TQ13: Chud 2C 94
Vicarage Lawn EX32: Barn 4E 18
Vicarage Rd. EX6: Cockw 3E 96
　EX9: E Bud 1D 82
　EX10: Sidm 6C 84
　EX20: Oke 3A 48
　EX32: L'key 2B 24
　PL7: Plymp 6K 137
　PL11: Torp 2A 140
　TQ2: Torq 2K 115
　TQ3: Marl 4E 114
　TQ5: Brixh 5E 122
　TQ9: Blacka 3B 152
　TQ9: Sto G 3A 120
　TQ10: S Bre 1B 100
　TQ12: A'well 6E 108
Vicarage St. EX24: Colyt 5D 88
　EX32: Barn 4E 18
Vicary Cl. TQ12: New A 1D 108
Vickers Ground EX39: N'ham 4E 20
Vickery Cl. EX15: Cull 4G 45
Vicks Mdw. EX20: Hath 2H 35
Victor Cl. EX1: Heav 7K 65
Victoria Av. PL1: Plym 2A 8 (1G 141)
Victoria Cl. EX6: Kenton 6H 95
　EX15: Will 4D 44
　EX32: Barn 5G 19
Victoria Cotts. PL6: Plym 3C 136
Victoria Ct. EX4: Exe 5B 6 (7D 64)
　EX8: Exmth 6A 76
　(off Victoria Rd.)
　TQ9: Tot 6E 102
Victoria Cres. EX17: Cred 5J 39
　EX39: Apple 2H 21
Victoria Gdns. EX39: Bide 4F 23
Victoria Gro. EX39: Bide 4F 23
Victoria Hgts. TQ6: Dartm 6E 124
Victoria Hill EX22: Hols 1C 34
Victoria Lawn EX32: Barn 5G 19
Victoria Pde. TQ1: Torq 3D 116
Victoria Pk. 2A 8 (1G 141)
Victoria Pk. Rd. EX2: Exe 7J 7 (1H 71)
　TQ1: Torq 6D 112
Victoria Pl. EX8: Exmth 6C 76
　EX9: Bud S 6C 82

Victoria Pl. EX13: Axmin 3H **89**
EX35: Lynt 2G **13**
(off Lydiate La.)
EX36: S Mol 5C **26**
PL1: Plym 3G **141**
(off Millbay Rd.)
PL2: Dev 7E **134**
TQ5: Brixh 2E **122**
(off Higher Furzeham Rd.)
TQ6: Dartm 1A **124** (6F **125**)
TQ8: Salc 3D **158**
TQ12: New A 1F **109**
Victoria Quay TQ8: Salc 3D **158**
Victoria Rd. EX3: Top 5B **74**
EX4: Exe 1G **7** (4G **65**)
EX8: Exmth 6B **76**
EX20: Hath 2H **35**
EX32: Barn 5F **19**
EX34: Ilfra 3H **11**
PL5: Plym 2C **134**
TQ1: Torq 7D **112**
TQ5: Brixh 2H **123**
TQ6: Dartm 1A **124** (6D **124**)
Victoria Shop. Cen. TQ4: Paig 1J **119**
Victoria Sq. EX22: Hols 2C **34**
(off Victoria Hill)
TQ4: Paig 1J **119**
(off Parkside Rd.)
Victoria St. EX4: Exe 1G **7** (4G **65**)
EX20: Oke 3C **48**
EX22: Hols 2C **34**
EX32: Barn 5G **19**
EX34: Com M 7C **12**
PL11: Torp 1A **140**
TQ4: Paig 1H **119**
TQ9: Tot 6E **102**
Victoria Ter. EX6: Kennf 1H **95**
(off Exeter Rd.)
EX11: Ott M 4B **80**
EX14: Hon 3E **54**
(off Dowell St.)
EX15: Cull 4H **45**
(off Exeter Hill)
EX32: Barn 5F **19**
EX39: Bide 3F **23**
(off Honestone St.)
EX39: Ins 3K **21**
PL4: Plym 1E **8** (1K **141**)
TQ5: Brixh 4E **122**
(off Mt. Pleasant Rd.)
TQ12: Kingst 4H **105**
(off Oakford)
TQ13: Bov T 3C **92**
(off Marty St.)
TQ14: Shal 6G **107**
(off Bridge Rd.)
Victoria Way EX8: Exmth 6B **76**
Victoria Wharf PL4: Plym 7J **9**
Victoria Yd. EX4: Exe 3D **6** (6E **64**)
Victor La. EX1: Heav 7K **65**
Victor St. EX1: Heav 7K **65**
Victory Cl. TQ12: New A 6E **104**
Victory Ho. EX2: Exe 5F **7**
TQ6: Dartm 2A **124**
Victory Rd. TQ6: Dartm 6D **124**
Victory St. PL2: Plym 5D **134**
Victory Way EX38: Gt T 1B **30**
Vieux Cl. EX9: Ott'n 6H **83**
View Rd. DT7: Lym R 5J **91**
Vigo Bri. Rd. PL19: Tavi 3J **59**
Vigo M. PL19: Tavi 3J **59**
Villa Cl. EX32: Barn 7G **19**
Village, The EX5: Clyst M 2F **73**
EX5: Rock 4F **69**
PL20: Buck M 5A **126**
Village Cl. EX8: L'ham 5H **77**
Village Cross Rd. TQ7: Lodd 3G **151**
Village Dr. PL6: Robo 1D **132**
Village Rd. EX5: Wood S 1C **78**
EX6: Chri 4J **63**
TQ3: Marl 3D **114**
Village St. EX32: Bish T 6B **24**
Villa Rd. EX38: Gt T 2B **30**
Villas, The TQ12: Kingst 1G **105**
Villiers Av. TQ12: New A 2J **109**
Villiers Cl. PL9: Plyms 5E **142**
Vincents Rd. TQ7: Kingsb 4G **157**
Vine Cl. EX2: Exe 6G **7** (7G **65**)
Vine Cres. PL2: Plym 5G **135**
Vine Gdns. PL2: Plym 5G **135**
Vinegar Hill EX39: Bide 3G **23**
Vine Ho. EX9: Bud S 6D **82**
Vine Pas. EX14: Hon 3F **55**
(off Northcote La.)
Vine Rd. TQ2: Torq 7B **112**
Vinery, The TQ1: Torq 2D **116**
(off Montpellier Rd.)
Vinery La. PL7: Plymp 7B **138**
PL9: Elb 7K **143** & 7B **138**
Vine St. EX19: Wink 3C **36**
Vine Ter. TQ7: Kingsb 3F **157**
TQ7: Lodd 3G **151**
Vineyard Hill TQ9: Darti 3B **102**
Vineyard La. EX13: Axmin 2G **89**
Vineyards, The EX22: Hols 1C **34**
Vineyard Ter. TQ9: E All 6C **152**
(off Addlehole)
Vinnicombes Rd. EX5: Sto C 6J **51**
Vinstone Way PL5: Plym 2C **134**
Violet Dr. PL6: Plym 2F **133**
Violet La. PL19: Tavi 4K **59**
Virginia Cl. EX39: Bide 4F **23**
Virginia Gdns. PL2: Plym 4E **134**
Virginia Lodge TQ1: Torq 2F **117**
(off Lwr. Erith Rd.)
VIRGINSTOW 1B **168**
Vision Hill Rd. EX9: Bud S 5D **82**
Vista Cl. DT7: Lym R 5H **91**
Vittery Cl. TQ5: Brixh 3D **122**
Vixen Tor Cl. EX20: Oke 3E **48**
PL20: Yelv 5F **127**
Voisey Cl. TQ13: Chud K 5B **94**
Vomero TQ1: Torq 2E **116**
Voysey Hill EX17: Cher F 1J **39**
Vue Cinema
Exeter 3G **7** (6G **65**)
Plymouth 6J **9** (3A **142**)
Vuefield Hill EX2: Exe 2B **70**
Vyvyan Ct. EX1: Heav 7K **65**
(off Fore St.)

W

WADBROOK 3D **167**
WADDETON 2E **120** (2A **176**)
Waddeton Cl. TQ4: Paig 6F **119**
Waddeton Cotts. TQ5: Wadd 2E **120**
Waddeton Rd. TQ4: Paig 1E **120**
TQ5: Wadd 1E **120**
TQ9: Sto G 7A **118**
WADDON 3C **171**
Waddon Cl. PL7: Plymp 2B **138**
Wade Cl. EX8: Exmth 4G **77**
WADEFORD 2D **167**
Wadham Ho. EX4: Exe 3D **64**
Wadham Ter. PL2: Plym 6F **135**
Wadlands Mdw. EX20: Oke 3D **48**
WADLEY HILL 3F **91**
Waggoners Way EX4: Exe 1A **6** (4D **64**)
Waggon Hill PL7: Plymp 5D **138**
Wagon Hill Way EX2: Won 1J **71**
WAINHOUSE CORNER 1A **168**
Wain La. TQ12: New A 7D **104**
(not continuous)
Wain Pk. PL7: Plymp 5C **138**
Wakefield Av. PL5: Plym 2D **134**
Wakeham Ct. EX33: Brau 6K **15**
(off Exeter Rd.)
Wakehams Cl. PL21: Modb 7H **147**
Wake St. PL4: Plym 1C **8** (1H **141**)
Walcot Cl. PL6: Plym 7F **133**
Walcott Way EX14: Dunk 7H **47**
Walden Rd. EX14: Dunk 7H **47**
Waldon Cl. PL7: Plymp 3E **138**
Waldon Ct. TQ2: Torq 2D **116**
(off St Luke's Rd. Sth.)
Waldon Ho. TQ2: Torq 2D **116**
(off St Luke's Rd. Sth.)
Waldon Point TQ2: Torq 2D **116**
(off St Luke's Rd. Sth.)
Waldron's Almshouses EX16: Tiv 4C **40**
(off King St.)
Walkers Chocolate Emporium 2H **11**
Walker Ter. PL1: Plym 7B **8** (4H **141**)
Walkham Bus. Pk. PL5: Plym 2G **135**
Walkham Cl. PL19: Tavi 4K **59**
Walkham Mdws. PL20: Horr 2F **127**
WALKHAMPTON 2J **127** (1B **174**)
Walkhampton Rd. PL20: Horr 2E **126**
Walkhampton Wlk. PL6: Plym 2F **137**
Walkham Ri. TQ2: Torq 5H **111**
Walkham Ter. PL20: Horr 1E **126**
Walkham Vw. PL20: Horr 2E **126**
Wallace Av. EX4: Whip 4A **66**
EX7: Daw 3H **97**
TQ2: Torq 5J **111**
Wallace Rd. PL7: Plymp 5D **138**
Wallaford Rd. TQ11: B'leigh 5A **98**
Walled Garden, The EX2: Cou W 6B **72**
Wallfield Rd. TQ13: Bov T 6A **92**
Wallingford Rd. TQ7: Kingsb 3G **157**
Wallis Gro. TQ14: Bi'ton 3C **106**
Wall Pk. TQ9: Tot 5B **102**
Wall Pk. Cl. PL7: Plymp 2C **138**
TQ5: Brixh 3G **123**
Wall Pk. Rd. TQ5: Brixh 3G **123**
Walls Cl. EX8: Exmth 2F **77**
Walls Hill Rd. TQ1: Torq 6F **113**
Wall St. PL1: Dev 2D **140**
Walnut Cl. EX6: Exmin 2C **74**
PL7: Plymp 4E **138**
TQ9: Tot 5D **102**
TQ13: Chud 1C **94**
Walnut Ct. TQ5: Brixh 4F **123**
(off Higher Ranscombe Rd.)
Walnut Dr. EX16: Tiv 3F **41**
EX17: Cred 5J **39**
PL7: Plymp 4F **139**
Walnut Gdns. EX4: Exe 2B **6** (5D **64**)
PL7: Plymp 4F **139**
Walnut Gro. EX8: Exmth 5E **76**
Walnut La. TQ2: Torq 2A **116**
Walnut Rd. EX2: Won 3J **71**
EX14: Hon 5D **54**
TQ2: Torq 2A **116**
Walnut Way EX32: Barn 5J **19**
Walpole Cl. EX4: Whip 3B **66**
Walreddon Cl. PL19: Tavi 5H **59**
Walronds, The EX16: Tiv 6C **40**
Walsingham Ct. PL7: Plymp 3E **138**
Walsingham Pl. EX2: Sow 1C **72**
Walsingham Rd. EX2: Sow 1C **72**
Walson Rd. EX17: Bow 7J **37**
Waltacre PL8: Torr 3B **150**
Walters Orchard EX15: Cull 4H **45**
Walters Rd. PL5: Plym 1B **134**
Waltham Pl. PL2: Plym 3F **135**
Waltham Rd. TQ12: New A 1D **108**
Waltham Way PL21: Ivy 5J **145**
Walton Cres. PL5: Plym 2H **135**
Walton Rd. EX2: Won 7B **66**
Walton Way EX32: Barn 4G **19**
WAMBROOK 3C **167**
Wandle Pl. PL3: Plym 6E **136**
Wanstead Gro. PL5: Plym 7F **131**
Wantage Gdns.
PL1: Plym 3A **8** (2G **141**)
Warberry Rd. W. TQ1: Torq 1D **116**
Warberry Va. TQ1: Torq 7D **112**
Warboro Ter. EX6: Star 1E **96**
Warborough Hill EX6: Kenton 6J **95**
Warborough Rd. TQ5: Chur F 2J **121**
Warbro Ct. TQ1: Torq 6D **112**
(off St Marychurch Rd.)
Warbro Rd. TQ1: Torq 6D **112**
WARBSTOW 1A **168**
Warburton Gdns. PL5: Plym 2B **134**
Warcombe Farm Camping Pk.
EX34: Mort 4E **10**
Warcombe La. EX34: Mort 5E **10**
Wardens Cl. EX37: High B 2B **32**
Ward La. EX19: Wink 3E **36**
Wardlow Cl. PL6: Plym 3A **136**
Wardlow Gdns. PL6: Plym 3A **136**
Wardour Wlk. PL6: Plym 3C **132**
(not continuous)
Ward Pl. PL3: Plym 6C **136**
Wardrew Rd. EX4: Exe 7A **6** (7C **64**)
WARE 6G **91**
Ware Barton Caravan Site
TQ12: Kingst 5K **105**
Ware Cliff Chalets DT7: Lym R 6J **91**
Ware Cl. TQ12: Kingst 4J **105**
Ware Ct. EX14: Hon 5D **54**
Warecroft Rd. TQ12: Kingst 4J **105**
Ware Cross TQ12: Kingst 4J **105**
Ware Cross Gdns. TQ12: Kingst 4J **105**
Warefield Rd. TQ3: Paig 7J **115**
Ware Hill PL21: Ugb 6E **146**
Ware La. DT7: Lym R, Ware 6F **91**
Waresfoot Dr. EX17: Cred 5G **39**
Warfield Vs. EX34: Ilfra 3J **11**
WARFLEET 7G **125** (2A **176**)
Warfleet Creek Rd. TQ6: Dartm 7G **125**
Warfleet (Gallants Bower) 3A **176**
Warfleet Rd. TQ6: Dartm 7G **125**
Waring Bowen Ct. EX2: Cou W 4J **71**
Waring Rd. PL6: Plym 3J **131**
WARKLEIGH 1A **164**
Warland TQ9: Tot 6E **102**
WARLEGGAN 3A **168**
Warleigh Av. PL2: Plym 6D **134**
Warleigh Cres. PL6: Plym 5A **132**
Warleigh La. PL2: Plym 6D **134**
Warleigh Point Nature Reserve 4C **130**
Warleigh Rd. PL4: Plym 7K **135**
Warleigh Vw. PL20: Bere F 7B **128**
Warleigh Wood Nature Reserve
3D **130**
Warmwell Rd. PL5: Plym 6D **130**
Warneford Gdns. EX8: Exmth 2G **77**
Warne La. PL19: Mary T 2B **60**
Warnicombe La. EX16: Tiv 6H **41**
Warran La. PL19: Tavi 6J **59**
Warren, The TQ12: New A 1C **108**
Warren Beach Holiday Camp
EX7: Daw W 7D **96**
Warren Cl. EX11: W Hill 4H **79**
EX38: Gt T 2A **30**
PL9: Wem 7B **148**
Warren Dr. EX9: Bud S 5D **82**
Warren Hill TQ2: Torq 2D **116**
Warren La. EX4: Exe 2F **7** (5F **65**)
EX38: Gt T 2A **30**
PL5: Tam F 2E **130**
Warren La. PL9: Wem 6D **148**
PL21: Ivy 6B **144**
TQ9: Darti 1D **102**
Warren Pk. EX11: W Hill 4H **79**
PL6: Plym 3E **132**
Warren Rd. EX7: Daw 2K **97**
PL19: Mary T 1B **60**
TQ2: Torq 2C **116**
TQ7: Bigb S 3B **154**
TQ7: Kingsb 6H **157**
TQ7: Thur 6B **154**
Warrens Mead EX10: Sidf 2E **84**
Warren St. PL2: Dev 7D **134**
Warren, The 3D **175**
Warren Vw. EX39: Bide 3D **22**
Warspite Gdns. PL5: Plym 1J **135**
Warton Cl. PL5: Plym 1J **135**
Warwick Av. EX1: Heav 7B **66**
PL5: Plym 6J **131**
Warwick Cl. EX14: Fen 2H **53**
TQ1: Torq 6G **113**
Warwick Orchard Cl. PL5: Plym 7G **131**
Warwick Rd. EX1: Heav 6B **66**
Warwick Ter. EX32: Barn 3E **18**
Warwick Way EX4: Whip 4B **66**
Wasdale Cl. PL6: Plym 1E **136**
Wasdale Gdns. PL6: Plym 1E **136**
Washabrook La. TQ7: Kingsb 3H **157**
Washabrook Way TQ7: Kingsb 4H **157**
WASHBOURNE 2A **176**
Washbourne Cl. PL1: Dev 1D **140**
TQ5: Brixh 3G **123**
Washbrook Vw. EX11: Ott M 3D **80**
WASHFIELD 2D **165**
Washfield La. EX16: Tiv, Wash 2A **40**
WASHFORD PYNE 2C **165**
Washington Cl. TQ3: Pres 5H **115**
WATCOMBE 2D **112** (1B **176**)
Watcombe Beach Rd. TQ1: Torq 2E **112**
Watcombe Hgts. Rd. TQ1: Torq 1D **112**
WATER 2B **170**
Waterbeer St. EX4: Exe 4D **6** (6E **64**)
Waterbridge Ct. EX2: Matf 5G **71**
Waterbridge Golf Course 4A **38**
Waterdale Mobile Home Pk.
TQ12: Kingsk 1G **111**
(off Waterdale Pk.)
Waterdale Pk. TQ12: Kingsk 1G **111**
Waterford La. EX13: Mus 7B **90**
Waterfront Sports Cen. 7C **76**
Watergate EX2: Exe 6E **6** (7F **65**)
Watergate Path EX2: Exe 6E **6**
(off Watergate)
WATERHEAD 6G **151**
Waterhead Cl. TQ6: Kingsw 5H **125**
Waterhead Ter. TQ6: Kingsw 5H **125**
Watering Ct. EX9: Ott'n 6H **83**
Watering La. EX9: Ott'n 5J **83**
Waterlands EX34: Ilfra 2J **11**
(off Quayfield Rd.)
Water La. EX1: Heav 7K **65**
(off Victor La.)
EX2: Exe 7D **6** (1E **70**)
EX10: Sidm 5C **84**
EX16: Tiv 4D **40**
EX17: Bow 5H **37**
EX32: Barn 6G **19**
EX34: Com M 6B **12**
TQ2: Torq 5J **111**
TQ12: Kingsk 1G **111**
TQ12: New A 7C **104**
Water La. Cl. EX32: Barn 6G **19**
(off Water La.)
Waterleat Av. EX14: Hon 4G **55**
TQ3: Paig 2E **118**
Waterleat Cl. TQ3: Paig 2F **119**
Waterleat Ct. TQ3: Paig 2F **119**
Waterleat Dr. TQ3: Paig 2F **119**
Waterleat Rd. TQ3: Paig 2E **118**
Waterloo Cl. PL1: Plym 2F **141**
Waterloo Ct. PL1: Plym 2F **141**
Waterloo Rd. EX2: Exe 2D **70**
EX22: Hols 1D **34**
TQ1: Torq 7D **112**
TQ7: Kingsb 3G **157**
Waterloo St. PL1: Plym 1E **140**
PL4: Plym 2G **9** (1K **141**)
TQ14: Teignm 5J **107**
Waterloo Ter. EX39: Bide 4E **22**
Waterloo Yd. Flats PL1: Plym 2F **141**
Watermark, The 4H **145**
Water Mdw. EX15: Cull 5H **45**
Watermill Ct. TQ5: Brixh 4E **122**
(off Bolton St.)
Watermore Ct. EX4: Exe 1K **7**
WATERMOUTH 1B **12**
Watermouth Castle 1A **12**
Watermouth Cove Holiday Pk.
EX34: Berry 1B **12**
Watermouth Lodges EX34: Berry 1B **12**
Watermouth Valley Camping Pk.
EX34: Berry 1B **12**

Watermouth Yacht Club 1A 12
Water Pk. Rd. EX39: Bide 3C 22
Waterpool Rd.
TQ6: Dartm 2A 124 (7D 124)
WATERROW 1A 166
Waters Edge PL19: Tavi 3K 59
Waterside EX2: Exe 7D 6 (1E 70)
TQ7: Kingsb 5G 157
TQ9: Tot 6F 103
TQ13: Bov T 4C 92
Waterside Holiday Camp
TQ4: Broads 6J 119
Waterside Ho. PL21: Ivy 5G 145
TQ9: Tot 6F 103
(off The Plains)
Waterside M. PL1: Dev 1C 140
Waterside Rd. TQ4: Broads 6J 119
Waterside Row PL21: Ivy 5G 145
(off Keaton Rd.)
Waterslade Dr. PL21: Ivy 5J 145
Waterslade La. EX5: Clyst H 4J 67
Watersmeet 2D 161
Watersmeet Rd. EX35: Lynm 2J 13
Waterstream Sq.
TQ13: Chud 1D 94
Water Ter. EX34: Com M 6B 12
WATERTOWN 3F 21
Waterwell La. EX6: Chri 4K 63
Waterworks La.
TQ14: Shal 7F 107
Watery La. EX5: Wood 4B 78
EX13: Smal 1J 89
EX16: Tiv 3E 40
EX33: Croy 2D 14
EX34: Com M 6C 12
EX38: Gt T 2D 30
(Roscoff Cl.)
EX38: Gt T 3A 30
(St Mary's Cl.)
Watkins Way EX39: Bide 3H 23
TQ3: Paig 7D 114
Watson Gdns. PL4: Plym 4J 9 (2A 142)
Watson Pl. EX2: Exe 7K 7 (1H 71)
PL4: Plym 4K 9 (2B 142)
WATTON 1D 173
Watts Pk. Rd. PL2: Plym 4H 135
Watts Rd. PL4: Plym 3K 9 (2B 142)
PL19: Tavi 4H 59
Waveney Gdns. PL5: Plym 7H 131
Waverley Av. EX4: Exe 1E 6 (5F 65)
Waverley Rd. EX8: Exmth 4C 76
PL5: Plym 1C 134
TQ7: Kingsb 5F 157
TQ12: New A 7E 104
Waverley Ter. EX35: Lynt 2G 13
(off Lydiate La.)
Waves Leisure Pool 2B 116
Waybrook Cotts. EX2: Matf 6E 70
Waybrook Cres. EX2: Alph 5E 70
Waybrook La. EX2: Shil A 7D 70
Waycott Wlk. PL6: Plym 4H 131
Wayfaring EX32: Barn 6J 19
WAYFORD 3D 167
Wayland Av. EX2: Exe 7H 7 (1G 71)
Waylands Cnr. EX16: Tiv 1D 40
Waylands Rd. EX16: Tiv 2D 40
Wayside PL21: Ivy 4G 145
TQ5: Brixh 4C 122
Wayside Cl. TQ5: Brixh 4C 122
Wayside Cres. EX1: Whip 5A 66
Way's La. EX15: Cull 5H 45
WAY VILLAGE 2C 165
Wear Barton Rd. EX2: Cou W 5A 72
Wear Cl. EX2: Cou W 6B 72
WEARE GIFFARD 1C 163
WEARNE 1D 167
Weatherdon Dr.
PL21: Ivy 4K 145
Weatherill Rd. EX14: Hon 6F 55
Weaver Ct. TQ2: Torq 5H 111
Weavers Ct. EX2: Exe 6D 6
Weavers Wlk. EX15: Cull 5G 45
Weavers Way TQ12: Kingsk 1F 111
Webber Cl. TQ12: E Ogw 4C 108
Webbers Caravan & Camping Pk.
EX5: Wood 5D 78
Webbers Cl. EX5: Whim 6G 53
Webbers Est. TQ9: Darti 3B 102
Webbers Way EX15: Will 4D 44
EX16: Tiv 2E 40
TQ9: Darti 3A 102
Webbs Orchard
EX20: N Taw 6C 36
Webland Farm Holiday Pk.
TQ10: Avon 3E 100
Webley Rd. EX2: Exe 2C 70
Wedgwood Ct. TQ14: Teignm 5H 107
(off Somerset Pl.)
Wedlake M. EX7: Daw 4G 97
(off Brook St.)
Weech Cl. EX7: Daw 4F 97
Weech Rd. EX7: Daw 4F 97
WEEK
Barnstaple 1D 163
Bridgetown 1D 165
Okehampton 6A 36 (3A 164)
South Molton 2B 164
Totnes 2A 102 (1D 175)
Weekaborough Dr. TQ3: Marl 4D 114
WEEKE 3B 164
Weeke Hill
TQ6: Dartm, Sto F 1J 153 & 7G 125
WEEK GREEN 1A 168
Week La. EX7: Daw, Daw W 1J 97
WEEK ST MARY 1A 168
Weeksland Rd. TQ2: Torq 7J 111
Weir Cl. PL6: Plym 1G 137
Weirfield Ho. EX2: Exe 7F 7
Weirfield Path EX2: Exe 2G 71
Weirfield Rd. EX2: Exe 7F 7 (1F 71)
Weirfields TQ9: Tot 5E 102
Weir Gdns. PL6: Plym 1G 137
Weir Rd. PL6: Plym 7F 133
Weirside Pl. EX2: Exe 7F 7 (1F 71)
Weirside Way EX32: Barn 3G 19
Welbeck Av. PL4: Plym 1E 8 (1J 141)
Welch's La. EX31: Yell 7A 16
WELCOMBE 2A 162
Welcome Family Holiday Pk.
EX7: Daw W 7E 96
Welcome St. EX2: Exe 1E 70
Weld Pk. Av. EX34: Ilfra 3K 11
Welland Gdns. PL3: Plym 6D 136
Wellands Cl. EX15: Uff 7J 43
Wellbrook Grn. EX16: Tiv 4B 40
Wellbrook St. EX16: Tiv 4B 40
Wellbrook Ter. EX16: Tiv 4B 40
(off Wellbrook St.)
EX39: Bide 4F 23
Well Cl. TQ12: Kingst 4H 105
Wellclose Rd. EX33: Brau 5J 15
Welle Ho. Gdns. TQ7: Kingsb 3G 157
Weller Rd. EX13: Axmin 5H 89
Wellesley Rd. TQ1: Torq 7D 112
Wellfield Cl. PL7: Plymp 4F 139
Well Gdns. PL1: Plym 3C 8 (2H 141)
Wellhay Cl. PL9: Elb 6K 143
Well Hill TQ7: Malb 6G 155
Well Hill Cl. TQ7: Malb 6G 155
WELLINGTON 1B 166
Wellington Cl. EX2: Won 7C 66
Wellington Pl. TQ1: Torq 7D 112
Wellington Rd. EX2: Exe 2D 70
TQ1: Torq 1D 116
Wellington Sq. TQ10: S Bre 1B 100
Wellington St. PL1: Plym 1F 141
PL4: Plym 2G 9 (1K 141)
PL11: Torp 1A 140
TQ14: Teignm 5J 107
Well Mead EX13: Kilm 2B 88
Well Oak Pk. EX2: Won 1J 71
Well Pk. EX22: Hols 1C 34
Wellpark Cl. EX4: Exe 7C 64
Well Pk. Rd. EX38: Gt T 2C 30
PL11: Torp 1A 140
Wells Av. EX14: Fen 2G 53
Wellsbourne Pk. PL3: Plym 5B 136
Wells Cl. EX8: Exmth 1G 77
Well Spring Cl. EX39: Hart 3J 27
Wells St. EX32: Barn 4E 18
Wells Ter. EX17: Cher F 2H 39
Wellstones Cl. PL21: Ivy 5J 145
Well St. EX4: Exe 2G 7 (5G 65)
EX6: Star 1E 96
EX38: Gt T 2C 30
TQ3: Paig 1G 119
WELLSWOOD 1F 117 (1B 176)
Wellswood Av. TQ1: Torq 1F 117
(not continuous)
Wellswood Gdns. EX4: Exe 7B 64
TQ1: Torq 1G 117
Wellswood Mnr. TQ1: Torq 1F 117
Wellswood Pk. TQ1: Torq 1F 117
Wellswood Path TQ1: Torq 1F 117
(off Cedars Rd.)
TQ1: Torq 2E 116
(Clarendon Ct.)
TQ1: Torq 1F 117
(Marlborough Av.)
WELLTOWN 1K 127
WELSFORD 1A 162
Welsford Av. PL2: Plym 6E 134
WEMBURY 6C 148 (3B 174)
Wembury Dr. TQ2: Torq 3D 112
Wembury Marine Cen. 7A 148
Wembury Mdw. PL9: Wem 5C 148
Wembury Pk. Rd. PL3: Plym 5J 135
Wembury Rd.
PL9: Elb, Spri, Wem
7H 143 & 4D 148
WEMBWORTHY 3A 164
Wendover Way EX2: Cou W 3A 72
Wenlock Gdns. PL2: Plym 3G 135
Wensum Cl. PL7: Plymp 5D 138
Wentwood Gdns. PL6: Plym 7F 133
Wentwood Pl. PL6: Plym 7F 133
Wentworth Gdns. EX4: Exe 1B 70
Wentworth Pl. PL4: Plym 2C 142
Wentworth Rd. TQ12: Heat 2J 93
WERRINGTON 2B 168
Wesley Av. PL3: Plym 6K 135
Wesley Cl. EX2: Exe 2D 70
EX16: Tiv 5G 41
TQ2: Torq 2C 112
Wesley Ct. PL1: Plym 6C 8
PL11: Torp 1B 140
(off Tamar St.)
TQ2: Torq 2C 112
TQ6: Dartm 1A 124
Wesley M. TQ2: Torq 3C 112
(off Starpitten La. W.)
Wesley Pl. PL2: Dev 7F 135
PL3: Plym 6K 135
Wesley Rd. EX22: Hols 1B 34
Wesley Ter. EX39: Hart 3H 27
Wesley Vw. TQ12: Ipp 6H 101
(off Croft Rd.)
Wesley Way EX2: Alph 5E 70
Wessex Cl. EX3: Top 7C 72
Wessex Est. EX4: Exe 1A 6 (4D 64)
Wessex Way
TQ6: Dartm 7C 124
Wessiters EX12: Seat 5D 86
Westabrook Av. TQ13: Ashb 3G 99
Westabrook Cl. TQ13: Ashb 3G 99
Westabrook Dr. TQ13: Ashb 3G 99
WESTACOTT 5K 19
Westacott Mdw. EX32: Barn 6K 19
Westacott Rd. EX32: Barn 6J 19
West Acres EX12: Seat 5D 86
WEST ALVINGTON 5D 156 (3D 175)
W. Alvington Hill TQ7: Kingsb 5E 156
WEST ANSTEY 1C 165
WEST APPLEDORE 2H 21
West Av. EX4: Exe 1F 7 (4F 65)
EX31: Barn 6C 18
PL19: Tavi 4H 59
Westaway EX31: Frem 6F 17
Westaway Cl. EX31: Barn 2F 19
Westaway Hgts. EX31: Barn 1F 19
Westaway Plain EX31: Barn 2E 18
Westaway Rd. EX24: Colyt 6C 88
WEST BAGBOROUGH 1B 166
West Ball Hill EX39: Hart 2H 27
Westbourne Gro. EX34: Ilfra 3G 11
Westbourne Rd. PL3: Plym 6J 135
TQ1: Torq 6C 112
Westbourne Ter. EX9: Bud S 7B 82
EX34: Com M 6C 12
EX39: West H 5B 20
Westbridge Cl. EX20: Oke 3B 48
Westbridge Cotts. PL19: Tavi 5H 59
Westbridge Ind. Est. PL19: Tavi 5H 59
Westbrook Av. TQ14: Teignm 4G 107
Westbrook Cl. EX4: Whip 4A 66
Westbrook Ct. EX4: Whip 4A 66
Westbrook Pl. EX16: Tiv 4E 40
(off Chapel St.)
West Buckeridge TQ14: Teignm 3H 107
WEST BUCKLAND
Barnstaple 3C 161
Taunton 1B 166
Thurlestone 4B 154 (3C 175)
Westbury Cl. PL5: Plym 6G 131
W. Challacombe La.
EX34: Com M 5B 12
WEST CHARLETON 7K 157 (3D 175)
W. Charleton Ct. TQ7: W Cha 7K 157
West Cliff EX7: Daw 4H 97
(off The Mews)
Westcliff TQ14: Teignm 5H 107
(off Mulberry St.)
West Cliff Cl. EX7: Daw 5G 97
Westcliffe EX32: Bish T 7B 24
Westcliffe Ter. EX12: Seat 6E 86
TQ5: Brixh 3F 123
(off Nth. Furzeham Rd.)
West Cliff Pk. Dr. EX7: Daw 5G 97
West Cliff Rd. EX7: Daw 4F 97
West Cl. EX13: Axmin 4G 89
WEST CLYST 1F 67
W. Clyst Barnyard EX1: W Cly 1G 67
Westcombe EX2: Alph 5E 70
Westcombe Cres. PL9: Hooe 7E 142
Westcombe La. EX39: Bide 3E 22
Westcots Dr. EX19: Wink 3C 36
WESTCOTT 3A 166
Westcott Cl. PL6: Plym 3B 136
Westcott La. EX5: Mar G, Rock 7H 69
Westcott Rd. EX16: Tiv 5H 41
Westcott Way EX14: Hon 3G 55
Westcountry Cl. PL2: Plym 4E 134
Westcroft Ct. EX39: Bide 4F 23
Westcroft Rd. EX22: Hols 2B 34
PL5: Plym 2C 134
Westcroft Ter. EX39: Apple 2H 21
West Cross EX33: Brau 4J 15
(off Caen St.)
West Croyde EX33: Croy 3B 14
WEST CURRY 1A 168
W. Devon Bus. Pk. PL19: Tavi 6H 59
WEST DOWN 2B 160
W. Down Ct. EX5: Cranb 3C 68
W. Down La. EX8: L'ham, San B 5H 77
W. Down Rd. PL2: Plym 5G 135
Westella Rd. PL20: Yelv 6G 127
West End EX14: Hon 4E 54
(off High St.)
EX31: Barn 3D 18
West End Rd. EX5: Bradn 3B 52
TQ11: B'leigh 5B 98
West End Ter. EX36: S Mol 6C 26
TQ12: Den 2H 101
TQ13: Ashb 5G 99
Westeria Ter. PL2: Plym 4H 135
Westerland TQ6: Kingsw 6H 125
Westerland La. TQ3: Marl 4D 114
Wester-Moor Cl. EX31: Roun 7K 17
(off Wester-Moor Way)
Wester-Moor Dr. EX31: Roun 7K 17
Wester-Moor Way EX31: Roun 7K 17
Western App. PL1: Plym 4C 8 (2H 141)
Western Av. EX2: Cou W 6C 72
(off Central Av.)
EX39: Apple 2H 21
Western Backway TQ7: Kingsb 4F 157
(off Fore St.)
Western Bus. Pk. TQ4: Paig 5F 119
Western By-Pass TQ9: Tot 7D 102
Western College Rd. PL4: Plym 6A 136
Western Common 493 m (1,617 ft)
3D 161
Western Ct. EX10: Sidm 7B 84
(off Bedford Sq.)
Western Dr. EX6: Star 1E 96
PL3: Plym 7C 136
TQ12: New A 7C 104
Western Gdns. EX34: Com M 6B 12
Westernlea EX17: Cred 6F 39
Western Pl. EX24: Colyt 6C 88
Western Ri. EX34: Woolc 6C 10
Western Rd. EX4: Exe 5A 6 (7D 64)
EX17: Cred 5F 39
EX22: Hols 2C 34
PL21: Ivy 5G 145
TQ1: Torq 4D 112
TQ12: New A 2F 109
TQ13: Ashb 5G 99
Western Ter. EX31: Barn 4D 18
EX34: Ilfra 4G 11
TQ9: Tot 6D 102
(off Lwr. Collins Rd.)
WESTERN TOWN 7B 84
Western Vs. TQ9: Tot 6D 102
(off Lwr. Collins Rd.)
Western Way EX1: Exe 6C 6 (7E 64)
(Edmund St.)
EX1: Exe 5F 7 (7F 65)
(Magdalen St.)
Western Wood Way PL7: Plymp 4G 139
Wester Way EX35: Lynm 1H 13
West Exe Nth. EX16: Tiv 4C 40
West Exe Sth. EX16: Tiv 5C 40
West Exe Sports Cen. 3D 70
Westfield EX5: Bradn 3B 52
EX6: Exmin 3D 74
PL7: Plymp 3C 138
Westfield Av. EX31: Barn 5C 18
PL9: Hooe 6D 142
Westfield Bus. Pk. TQ4: Paig 6D 118
Westfield Cl. EX9: Bud S 6C 82
TQ5: Brixh 5D 122
Westfield Gdns. EX9: Bud S 6C 82
Westfield Rd. EX9: Bud S 6C 82
EX16: Tiv 5C 40
Westfield Ter. EX16: Tiv 5C 40
(off Exeter Rd.)
WESTFORD 2B 166
West Gth. Ct. EX4: Exe 2C 64
West Gth. Rd. EX4: Exe 2D 64
Westgate EX17: Lap 2K 37
W. Golds Rd. TQ12: New A 6E 104
W. Golds Way TQ12: New A 6E 104
West Gro. Rd. EX2: Exe 7G 7 (7G 65)
Westhampnett Pl. PL5: Plym 5E 130
West Hartley TQ9: Blacka 1B 152
WEST HATCH 1C 167
Westhays Cl. PL9: Plyms 7G 143
WEST HILL 4H 79 (1A 172)
West Hill EX9: Bud S 6B 82
PL9: Hey B 4B 148
Westhill Av. TQ1: Torq 5D 112
Westhill Av. Cl. TQ1: Torq 6D 112
West Hill Ct. EX9: Bud S 7B 82
Westhill Cres. TQ3: Paig 7H 115
West Hill Gdns. EX9: Bud S 7B 82
West Hill La. EX9: Bud S 6B 82
EX33: Brau 4J 15

West Hill Rd. DT7: Lym R 5J 91
EX11: Ott M, W Hill . . .5G 79 & 5A 80
PL4: Plym 1J 9 (7A 136)
Westhill Rd. TQ1: Torq 5C 112
TQ3: Paig 7G 115
Westhill Ter. TQ12: Kingsk 1G 111
West Hoe Park 7C 8
W. Hoe Rd. PL1: Plym 6B 8 (3H 141)
Westholme TQ1: Torq 1E 116
(off Middle Warberry Rd.)
WESTLAKE 2C 175
Westlake Ri. PL9: Hey B 3B 148
Westlake Rd. PL9: Down T 3A 148
WEST LAMBROOK 2D 167
Westlands EX8: Exmth 6E 76
EX33: Wraf 6K 15
Westlands La. TQ1: Torq 6D 112
West La. EX17: Lap 1J 37
EX19: Dol 7F 31
TQ3: Blag 7A 114
TQ3: Marl 1C 114
Westleat Av. TQ3: Paig 1E 118
WESTLEIGH
Bideford 6K 21 (1C 163)
Tiverton 2A 166
WEST LEIGH 3A 164
WEST LYN 4J 13
WEST LYNG 1D 167
W. Malling Av. PL5: Plym 5D 130
W. Manley La. EX16: Tiv 3H 41
Westmead Cl. EX33: Brau 4H 15
West Mdw. Cl. EX33: Brau 3G 15
West Mdw. Rd. EX33: Brau 4F 15
Westminster Cl.
EX8: Exmth 1F 77
EX14: Fen 2G 53
Westminster Rd. EX4: Exe 6A 64
WEST MONKTON 1C 167
W. Moor Cl. EX39: N'ham 4E 20
Westmoor Cl. PL7: Plymp 3F 139
Westmoor Pk. PL19: Tavi 5J 59
W. Moor Way EX39: N'ham 4E 20
West Mt. TQ12: New A 3G 109
WEST NEWTON 1C 167
WEST OGWELL 1A 176
WESTON
Honiton 4B 54 (3B 166)
Sidmouth 2B 172
Weston Cl. TQ5: Brixh 5E 122
Westonfields TQ9: Tot 6G 103
Weston Ho. TQ9: Berr P 6J 103
Weston La. EX14: Awli 2A 54
TQ9: Tot 6G 103
WESTON MILL 4E 134
Weston Mill Crematorium
PL2: Plym 4E 134
Weston Mill Dr. PL5: Plym 4D 134
Weston Mill Hill PL5: Plym 2D 134
Weston Mill La. PL5: Plym 2F 135
Weston Mill Rd. PL5: Plym 2D 134
Weston Pk. Rd. PL3: Plym 4J 135
Weston Rd. TQ9: Tot 6F 103
Weston Ter. EX11: Ott M 3D 80
(off Sandhill St.)
Westover Cl. PL21: Ivy 4F 145
TQ5: Brixh 4F 123
Westover Ind. Est. PL21: Ivy 5F 145
Westover La. PL21: Ivy 5F 145
WESTOWN 3E 46
Westown Rd. EX2: Ide 4A 70
W. Pafford Av. TQ2: Torq 3C 112
WEST PANSON 1B 168
WEST PARK 7F 131
West Pk. EX33: Brau 4H 15
EX36: S Mol 5B 26
TQ6: Sto F 1H 153
West Pk. Dr. PL7: Plymp 4F 139
West Pk. Hill PL7: Plymp 2E 138
West Pk. M. TQ7: Hope 2H 155
West Pk. Rd. EX10: Sidm 5B 84
Westpark Vs. PL20: Horr 1E 126
Westpoint (Devon County Showground)
. . . . .2J 73
WESTPORT 2D 167
WEST PUTFORD 2B 162
West Rd. EX34: Woolc 6A 10
WEST SANDFORD 3C 165
West St. EX1: Exe 5C 6 (7E 64)
EX13: Axmin 4G 89
EX16: Bam 2G 33
EX16: With 6H 33
EX20: Oke 3B 48
EX36: S Mol 6C 26
EX39: Hart 3H 27
PL19: Tavi 4H 59
TQ12: Den 2H 101
TQ13: Ashb 4G 99
TQ14: Bi'ton 3B 106
West St. M. EX1: Exe 5C 6
West Ter. EX1: Heav 6J 65
EX9: Bud S 6C 82
EX38: Gt T 2A 30
WEST TOWN
Crediton 6G 39
Newton St Cyres 7C 50
Woolsery / Woolfardisworthy
. . . . .2A 28
West Town TQ14: Bi'ton 3A 106
W. Town Mdw. TQ14: Bi'ton 3A 106
W. Town Rd. EX5: New C 7C 50
West Underleys EX12: Beer 7A 86
West Vw. EX12: Beer 7B 86
EX22: Hols 1C 34
EX24: Colyf 1F 87
EX31: Barn 5D 18
PL19: Whitc 7K 59
West Vw. Av. EX39: Bide 3G 23
West Vw. Cl. TQ12: E Ogw 3C 108
Westview Cl. EX5: Whim 6H 53
West Vw. Rd. EX20: Oke 3C 48
PL20: Bere A 1C 128
TQ3: Marl 3D 114
West Vw. Ter. EX4: Exe 5C 6 (7E 64)
EX14: Hon 3E 54
(off Dowell St.)
TQ8: Salc 4B 158
Westville Hill TQ7: Kingsb 5F 157
(off Frogmore Ter.)
West Wlk. EX12: Seat 6E 86
Westward Cl. TQ9: Tot 6E 102
Westward Dr. EX8: Exmth 5D 76
WESTWARD HO! 5B 20 (1C 163)
Westward Vw. TQ12: New A 2K 109
Westwater Hill EX6: Ted M 6G 49
Westway PL9: Hooe 7C 142
WEST WEMBURY 5C 148
WESTWOOD
Broadclyst 1A 172
Crediton 6F 39
Starcross 3D 96
Westwood Av. PL6: Plym 4D 132
Westwood Cleave TQ12: E Ogw . . .4C 108
Westwood Cl. EX17: Cred 6F 39
Westwood Hill EX6: Cockw 3D 96
Westwood Rd. EX17: Cred 6F 39
TQ12: E Ogw 4D 108
Westwood Way EX12: Seat 3F 87
WEST WORLINGTON 2B 164
WEST YELLAND 7A 16
West Yelland EX31: Yell 7A 16
WEST YOULSTONE 2A 162
Wethered Cl. EX16: Tiv 5C 40
Wet La. EX6: Chri 3J 63
EX34: Com M 7C 12
WEYCROFT 2K 89 (1D 173)
Weycroft Av. EX13: Axmin 1K 89
Weycroft Cl. EX1: Sow 6C 66
Weymouth Pk. TQ7: Hope 2G 155
Whalley La. DT7: Uply 4F 91
Wharf, The PL19: Tavi 4J 59
Wharf Rd. TQ12: New A 7G 105
WHATLEY 3D 167
Wheal Betsy 2D 169
Wheal Rd. PL19: Mary T 1C 60
Wheatfield Cl. EX15: Cull 5G 45
Wheat Field La. EX5: Cranb 3B 68
Wheatlands Rd. TQ4: Good 3G 119
WHEATLEY 2A 70 (1C 171)
Wheatley Cl. EX4: Exe 7B 64
Wheatley Ct. EX1: Exe 5D 6
Wheatridge PL7: Plymp 4J 137
Wheatridge La. TQ2: Torq 4A 116
Wheatsheaf EX5: Cranb 3C 68
Wheatsheaf Way EX2: Alph 4D 70
Wheelbarrow La. EX15: Hemy 1J 47
Wheelwright Ct. PL20: Walk 2J 127
Whickham Lodge EX7: Daw 3H 97
Whidborne Av. TQ1: Torq 2H 117
Whidborne Cl. TQ1: Torq 2H 117
Whidborne M. TQ14: Bi'ton 2C 106
WHIDDON
Northlew 3C 163
Rumsam 7J 19
WHIDDON DOWN 1A 170
Whiddon Dr. EX32: Barn 6J 19
Whiddon Rd.
TQ12: A'well, Two O
. . . . .7C 108 & 1A 110
Whiddon Valley EX32: Barn 6J 19
Whiddon Valley Ind. Est.
EX32: Barn 6J 19
Whidley La. EX6: Dunsf 7A 62
Whilborough Rd.
TQ12: Kingst, N Whil 5D 110
WHIMBLE 3E 34 (3B 162)
Whimble Hill EX22: Hols 3D 34
Whimbrels Edge TQ7: Thur 6C 154
WHIMPLE 6G 53 (1A 172)
Whimple Station (Rail) 6H 53
Whimple St. PL1: Plym 5E 8 (3K 141)
Whin Bank Rd. PL5: Plym 1J 135
WHIPCOTT 2J 43
WHIPTON 4A 66 (1D 171)
Whipton Barton Rd. EX1: Whip 5A 66
Whipton La. EX1: Heav 7K 65
Whipton Rd. EX4: Whip 4K 65
Whipton Village Rd. EX4: Whip 4A 66
Whistley Down PL20: Yelv 6D 126
Whistley Hill TQ13: Ashb 4H 99
Whitby Cres. PL6: Plym 2B 136
Whitby Rd. PL6: Plym 2B 136
WHITCHURCH 7K 59 (3C 169)
Whitchurch Av. EX2: Won 1A 72
WHITCHURCH CANONICORUM . . .1D 173
Whitchurch Rd. PL19: Tavi, Whitc . . .4J 59
PL20: Horr 1E 126
Whitear Cl. TQ14: Teignm 2F 107
Whitears Way TQ12: Kingst 4H 105
Whitebeam Cl. EX4: Whip 2A 66
TQ3: Paig 7E 114
Whitebeam Gro. EX14: Dunk 7G 47
Whitebridges EX14: Hon 5E 54
Whitebrook Ter. TA21: Holc R 3F 43
White Cl. TQ3: Pres 4H 115
White Cross Ct. PL4: Plym 3G 9
Whitecross Gdns. EX12: Seat 3F 87
White Cross Hill EX17: Cher F 1K 39
White Cross Rd. EX5: Wood S 2D 78
White Down Copse & Paradise Copse
. . . . .3A 166
White Farm La. EX11: W Hill 5H 79
WHITEFIELD 1A 166
Whitefield Ter.
PL4: Plym 2H 9 (1A 142)
Whiteford Rd. PL3: Plym 5K 135
Whiteford Rd. La. Sth.
PL3: Plym 6K 135
White Friars La.
PL4: Plym 4H 9 (2A 142)
Whitefriars Wlk. EX4: Exe 4J 65
White Gables TQ2: Torq 2A 116
Whitegates EX34: Com M 6A 12
WHITEHALL 2B 166
Whitehall Cl. EX36: S Mol 7C 26
Whitehall Dr. PL9: Elb 5J 143
PL20: Bere A 1C 128
Whitehall Mnr. TQ7: Chur 1B 156
Whitehaven Way PL6: Plym 3B 132
Whitehayes Cl. EX13: Kilm 2B 88
White Heather Ter. TQ13: Bov T 3C 92
Whitehill Cl. TQ12: New A 6E 104
Whitehill Cotts. TQ12: New A 6C 104
Whitehill Country Pk. 5B 118
Whitehill Gdns. PL7: L Moor 1J 129
Whitehill La. EX3: Top 5D 72
TQ4: Paig 6C 118
TQ9: Sto G 7B 118
Whitehill Rd. TQ12: New A 6C 104
Whitehorse La. EX39: Apple 3F 21
White Ho. Cl. EX39: Ins 2K 21
WHITELACKINGTON 2D 167
White Lady Rd.
PL9: Hooe, Plyms 7E 142
White La. PL1: Plym 6F 9
Whiteley Av. TQ9: Tot 5A 102
White Lodge EX9: Bud S 7D 82
(off Coastguard Rd.)
Whitemoor Hill EX32: Bish T 6B 24
Whiteside Cl. EX2: Won 1B 72
Whites La. EX31: Barn 2E 18
EX38: Gt T 2B 30
WHITESTAUNTON 2C 167
WHITESTONE 1C 171
Whitestone Dr. EX16: Tiv 2C 40
White Stones EX8: Exmth 6E 76
White St. EX3: Top 6B 74
Whitethorn Cl. EX10: Sidm 2A 84
EX14: Hon 5F 55
Whitethorn Pk. EX4: Exe 1F 65
White Tor Cl. EX20: Oke 3D 48
Whitewater Ct. PL7: Plymp 3A 138
Whiteway Cl. EX5: Whim 6H 53
Whiteway Dr. EX1: Heav 6A 66
Whiteway Rd. TQ12: Kingst 4G 105
WHITEWORKS 3A 170
WHITFORD 5A 90 (1C 173)
Whitford Rd. EX13: Kilm 4C 88
EX13: Mus, Whitf 6A 90
Whitham Pk. PL19: Tavi 5J 59
WHITLEIGH 6H 131 (2A 174)
Whitleigh Av. PL5: Plym 1K 135
Whitleigh Cotts. PL5: Plym 1K 135
(off Whitleigh Av.)
Whitleigh Ct. PL5: Plym 6J 131
Whitleigh Grn. PL5: Plym 6H 131
Whitleigh Vs. PL5: Plym 1K 135
Whitleigh Way PL5: Plym 7H 131
Whitleigh Wood Nature Reserve . . .5J 131
Whitley Rd. TQ4: Paig 3G 119
Whitlow Copse EX2: Won 1B 72
Whitman Cl. EX8: Exmth 7K 75
Whitmore Way EX14: Hon 5D 54
WHITNAGE 2A 166
Whitnage Rd. EX16: Sam P 1B 42
(not continuous)
Whitsoncross La. PL5: Tam F 3H 131
WHITSTONE
Bovey Tracey 2B 92
Week St Mary 1A 168
Whitstone La. TQ13: Bov T 2B 92
Whitstone Rd. TQ4: Paig 2H 119
Whittingham Rd. EX34: Ilfra 3J 11
Whittington St.
PL3: Plym 1A 8 (1G 141)
Whitton Ct. EX10: Sidm 3A 84
Whitton Way EX15: Cull 3H 45
Whitwell La.
EX24: Colyf . . . . .7B 88 & 1D 86
Whitycombe Way EX4: Exe 4A 64
WICK
Honiton 3B 166
Somerton 1D 167
Wickham Cl. EX39: Bide 4H 23
Widdicombe Dr. PL21: Ivy 5H 145
Widdicombe Farm Touring Pk.
TQ3: Marl 1E 114
WIDECOMBE IN THE MOOR 3B 170
Widecombe Way EX4: Exe 3H 65
Widemoor La. TQ5: Chur F 4J 121
WIDEMOUTH BAY 3A 162
Widend Touring Pk. TQ3: Marl 6A 114
Widepost La. EX13: Axmin 4G 89
WIDEWELL 3C 132
Widewell La. PL6: Plym 3D 132
Widewell Rd. PL6: Plym 4C 132
Widey Ct. PL6: Plym 2A 136
Widey Hill PL8: New F 5K 149
Widey La. PL6: Plym 2A 136
Widey Vw. PL3: Plym 5A 136
Widgery Dr. EX36: S Mol 6C 26
Widgery Rd. EX4: Whip 4K 65
WIDWORTHY 1C 173
WIGBOROUGH 2D 167
WIGGATON 7D 80 (1B 172)
Wilbarn Rd. TQ3: Paig 7J 115
Wilbraham Ct. TQ14: Teignm 2J 107
(off Higher Woodway Rd.)
Wilbury Way EX7: Daw 3H 97
Wilcocks Rd. EX4: Pin 3C 66
WILCOVE 2A 174
Wilderness Rd. PL3: Plym 6K 135
Wilder Pk. EX34: Ilfra 3H 11
Wilder Rd. EX34: Ilfra 2G 11
Wildersmouth Ct. EX34: Ilfra 2H 11
Wildwoods Cres.
TQ12: New A 7J 105
Wildwoods La. TQ3: Marl 5A 114
Wilford Rd. EX2: Won 7A 66
Wilkey Cl. EX32: Barn 5G 19
Wilkinson Rd. PL5: Plym 3B 134
Willake Rd. TQ12: Kingsk 7K 109
WILLAND 5D 44 (2A 166)
Willand Ind. Est. EX15: Will 3C 44
Willand Moor M. EX15: Will 3E 44
(off Willand Moor Rd.)
Willand Moor Rd. EX15: Will 3D 44
Willand Old Village EX15: Will 5C 44
Willand Rd. EX15: Cull 3H 45
EX15: Will 1A 44
EX16: Hal . . . . .6E 42 & 1A 44
EX33: Brau 4H 15
Willas Rd. PL16: Lift 6A 56
Willet St. EX39: Bide 3F 23
WILLETT 1B 166
Willey La. EX20: Stic 1G 49
Willey's Av. EX2: Exe 7C 6 (1E 70)
Willeys Ct. EX2: Exe 1E 70
Willhayes Pk. EX13: Axmin 3H 89
Willhay La. EX13: Axmin 2H 89
Willhayne La. EX24: Colyt 4B 88
Willhays Cl. TQ12: Kingst 2H 105
William Crossing Memorial 1C 175
William Evans Cl. PL6: Plym 5J 131
William Prance Rd. PL6: Plym 7B 132
Williams Av. EX2: Exe 7C 6 (1E 70)
PL4: Plym 3C 142
Williams Cl. EX7: Daw 5F 97
EX33: Wraf 6K 15
Williams Ct. EX31: Roun 7B 18
TQ11: B'leigh 4C 98
Williamson Cl. EX33: Georgeh 5B 14
Williamson Way EX36: S Mol 6C 26
William St. EX16: Tiv 4D 40
Willicombe Rd. TQ3: Paig 2G 119
Willis Ct. TQ1: Torq 6C 112
Willoughby Cl. EX8: Exmth 1E 76
Willoughby Rd. TQ1: Torq 7E 112
Willow Av. EX8: Exmth 1D 76
TQ2: Torq 2C 112
Willoway Cl. EX33: Brau 4H 15
Willoway Gro. EX33: Brau 4H 15
Willoway La. EX33: Brau 2G 15
Willowbrook Av. EX4: Whip 4B 66
Willowby Gdns. PL20: Yelv 6G 127
Willowby Pk. PL20: Yelv 6G 127
Willow Cl. EX5: Sto C 7J 51
EX12: Seat 2E 86
EX34: Ilfra 3K 11

Willow Cl.—Woodwater La.

Willow Cl. PL3: Plym 6F 137
TQ12: New A 4J 109
Willow Cotts. PL7: Plymp 4A 138
Willow Ct. EX2: Won 1K 71
PL6: Plym 4F 137
Willowdale Cl. EX14: Hon 3E 54
Willowfield EX33: Brau 3H 15
Willow Gdns. EX5: Broadc 6C 52
Willow Gro. EX39: Bide 5C 22
Willowpark La. TQ12: Coff 1J 111
Willow Rd. PL19: Tavi 6J 59
Willows, The EX31: Frem 6D 16
TQ2: Torq 3K 111
Willow St. TQ14: Teignm 4H 107
Willow Tree Cl. EX20: Oke 3C 48
Willow Tree Ct. EX31: Roun 7A 18
Willow Tree Rd. EX32: Barn 7G 19
Willow Wlk. EX4: Exe 1G 7 (4G 65)
EX14: Hon 5E 54
EX17: Cred 5K 39
PL6: Plym 5E 132
Willow Way EX4: Whip 4B 66
EX7: Daw W 7D 96
Wills Av. TQ3: Pres 5J 115
Wills Cl. PL6: Plym 3K 131
Willsdown Rd. EX2: Alph 5F 71
Willshere Rd. EX32: Barn 5H 19
Willsland Cl. EX6: Kenton 6H 95
Wills Rd. TQ9: Tot 5F 103
WILMINGTON 1C 173
Wilminstone Ind. Est. PL19: Tavi . . .2K 59
Wilmot Cl. EX8: Exmth 3G 77
Wilmot Gdns. PL5: Plym 1J 135
Wilnecote Lodge *TQ1: Torq 7C 112*
(off Furzehill Rd.)
Wilson Cres. PL2: Plym 6G 135
Wilson Ter. TQ1: Torq 7B 112
Wilton Cl. TQ12: A'well 6E 108
Wilton Rd. PL1: Plym 1F 141
TQ3: Pres 4H 115
Wilton St. PL1: Plym 2A 8 (1G 141)
Wilton Way EX1: Sow 6C 66
TQ12: A'well 6D 108
Wiltshier Cl. EX5: Broadc 5C 52
Wiltshire Cl. EX4: Exe 1B 70
PL4: Plym 7A 136
Wimborne Ter. *EX32: Barn 3F 19*
(off Yeo Vale Rd.)
Winchester Av. EX4: Exe 5B 64
TQ2: Torq 4B 112
Winchester Cl. EX14: Fen 2G 53
Winchester Dr. EX8: Exmth 1F 77
Winchester Gdns. PL5: Plym 5F 131
Windbury Point 1A 162
Windeatt Sq. *TQ9: Tot 6F 103*
(off Warland)
Windermere Cl. EX4: Exe 6C 64
Windermere Cres. PL6: Plym 6A 132
Windermere Rd. TQ1: Torq 7E 112
Winding Wlk. TQ6: Dartm 5F 125
Windjammer Ct. EX8: Exmth 6A 76
Windmill Av. TQ3: Pres 5G 115
Windmill Cl. TQ5: Brixh 4F 123
Windmill Ct. TQ5: Brixh 4F 123
Windmill Gdns. TQ3: Pres 5G 115
WINDMILL HILL 2D 167
Windmill Hill TQ5: Brixh 4E 122
Windmill La. EX11: W Hill 3H 79
EX39: N'ham 5F 21
TQ3: Pres 5F 115
TQ12: N Whil 5D 110
Windmill Rd. EX22: Hols 3D 34
TQ3: Pres 5G 115
TQ5: Brixh 4F 123
Windrush Ri. EX11: Ott M 4C 80
Windsor Av. TQ12: New A 1J 109
Windsor Cl. EX4: Exe 1B 6 (5D 64)
EX15: Cull 1H 45
PL21: Ivy 5H 145
TQ1: Torq 7D 112
TQ12: New A 2F 109
Windsor Ct. EX34: Ilfra 3H 11
TQ7: Kingsb 4G 157
Windsor Dr. EX7: Daw 7B 96
Windsor Gdns. EX31: Roun 7B 18
Windsor Mead EX10: Sidf 1C 84
Windsor Pl. PL1: Plym 6D 8 (3J 141)
Windsor Rd. EX31: Barn 2D 18
EX39: N'ham 5E 20
PL3: Plym 5C 136
TQ1: Torq 7D 112
TQ6: Dartm 6C 124
TQ7: Kingsb 4G 157
Windsor Sq. EX8: Exmth 5C 76
Windsor Ter. DT7: Lym R 4J 91
EX6: Kennf 1H 95
(off Exeter Rd.)
PL11: Torp 1B 140
Windsor Vs. PL1: Plym 6D 8
Windthorn La. TQ3: Comp 6B 110
TQ12: Ipp 6B 110
Windward Ct. EX8: Exmth 6A 76
Windward La. EX7: Holc 7G 97
Windward Ri. EX7: Holc 7G 97
Windward Rd. TQ2: Torq 2A 112
Windwhistle La. EX16: Bam 4G 33
Windy Ash Hill
EX32: Barn . . . . .7H 19 & 5C 24
Windys Way EX8: Exmth 5F 77
Wingate La. EX20: Hath 1J 35
Wingfield TQ7: Thur 6C 154
Wingfield Cl. EX16: Tiv 5C 40
Wingfield Rd. PL3: Plym . . .1A 8 (1F 141)
Wingfield Way PL3: Plym . . .1A 8 (1G 141)
Winifred Baker Ct. PL4: Plym 2F 9
Winifred Cliff Ct. *EX16: Bam 2G 33*
(off School Cl.)
WINKLEIGH 2C 36 (3A 164)
Winkleigh Cl. EX2: Exe 3D 70
Winneford La. EX14: Awli, Westo . . .4B 54
Winner Hill Rd. TQ3: Paig 1G 119
Winner St. TQ3: Paig 1G 119
Winner St. (Rear) *TQ3: Paig 1G 119*
(off Winner St.)
Winnicott Cl. PL6: Plym 3K 131
Winnings Way *TQ1: Torq 6F 113*
(off Princes St.)
Winnow Cl. PL9: Plyms 7G 143
Winsbury Ct. PL6: Plym 2B 136
Winsford Rd. TQ2: Torq 3J 115
Winsford Walled Garden 3C 163
WINSHAM
Braunton 3B 160
Chard 3D 167
Winsham Rd. EX33: Know, Wins 1K 15
Winslade Pk. EX5: Clyst M 4G 73
Winslade Pk. Av. EX5: Clyst M 3F 73
Winslade Rd. EX10: Sidm 4B 84
Winsland Av. TQ9: Tot 5A 102
Winstanley Wlk. PL3: Plym 5E 136
Winston Av. PL4: Plym 1E 8 (1J 141)
Winston Cl. TQ12: Kingst 4H 105
Winston Ct. TQ14: Teignm 3J 107
Winstone Av. TQ2: Torq 4C 112
Winstone La. PL8: Brixt 2J 149
Winston Pk. EX36: S Mol 5C 26
Winston Rd. EX8: Exmth 1G 77
Winsu Av. TQ3: Pres 6G 115
WINSWELL 2C 163
Winswood EX17: Cred 7J 39
Winsworthy EX39: High C 6G 27
Winterbourne Rd. TQ14: Teignm . . .4H 107
Winter Gdn. TQ2: Torq 2D 116
WINTERHAY GREEN 2D 167
Winterland La. EX22: Hols 4C 34
Winter's La. EX11: Ott M 4C 80
Wiriga Way EX16: With 6H 33
Wishcroft Ter. EX15: Cull 3H 45
Wishings Rd. TQ5: Brixh 5F 123
Wish Mdw. La. EX5: Broadc 1J 67
Wisteria Cl. *TQ7: Kingsb 4G 157*
(off Windsor Rd.)
Witcombe La. EX6: Kenton 6H 95
Withalls Gdns. EX8: Lymp 6G 75
Witham Gdns. PL3: Plym 6D 136
Witheby EX10: Sidm 7A 84
WITHERIDGE 6H 33 (2C 165)
Withey, The EX5: Whim 6H 53
WITHIEL FLOREY 1D 165
WITHLEIGH 2D 165
Withy Bed La. EX5: Mar G 7J 69
Withy Cl. EX16: Tiv 5E 40
Withycombe Pk. Dr. EX8: Exmth 2G 77
WITHYCOMBE RALEIGH
. . . . .3F 77 (2A 172)
Withycombe Rd. EX8: Exmth 4C 76
Withycombe Village Rd.
EX8: Exmth 4D 76
Withy La. EX15: Hemy 1F 47
WITHYPOOL 3D 161
Withywell La. EX33: Croy 3B 14
Witten Gdns. EX39: N'ham 7F 21
WIVELISCOMBE 1A 166
Wixenford Ct. PL9: Plyms 4G 143
Wixenford Farm Ind. Est.
PL9: Plyms 3H 143
Wizz-Kidz 3D 122
Woburn Cl. TQ3: Paig 7D 114
Woburn Ter. PL9: Plyms 5D 142
WOLBOROUGH 3C 108 (3C 171)
Wolborough Chu. Path
TQ12: New A 2D 108
Wolborough Cl. TQ12: New A 2F 109
Wolborough Gdns. TQ5: Brixh 2G 123
TQ12: New A 2F 109
Wolborough Ga. *TQ12: New A 2F 109*
(off Wolborough Cl.)
Wolborough St. TQ12: New A 2D 108
Wollaton Gro. PL5: Plym 7E 130
Wolrige Av. PL7: Plymp 4D 138
Wolrige Way PL7: Plymp 4D 138
Wolsdon Pl. PL1: Plym 3A 8
Wolsdon St. PL1: Plym 3A 8 (2G 141)
Wolseley Cl. PL2: Plym 6F 135
Wolseley Rd. PL2: Plym 4D 134
PL5: Plym 1A 134
(Normandy Hill)
PL5: Plym 2C 134
(Trelawney Av.)
Wolseley Rd. Flats
PL2: Plym 5E 134
Wolston Cl. TQ5: Brixh 2D 122
Wolverton Dr. TQ12: Kingst 4G 105
Wolverwood Cl. PL7: Plymp 6F 139
Wolverwood La. PL7: Plymp 6C 138
Wombwell Cres. PL2: Plym 4D 134
WONFORD 1K 71
Wonford Rd. EX2: Exe 6G 7 (7G 65)
Wonford Sports Cen. 2K 71
Wonford St. EX2: Won 1K 71
Wonnacott's Rd. EX20: Oke 3C 48
WONSON 2A 170
WOODACOTT 3B 162
Woodah Rd. EX4: Exe 7C 64
Wooda Rd. EX39: N'ham 4G 21
Woodberry Down 3K 91
Woodbine Pl. EX12: Seat 5E 86
Woodbine Ter. EX4: Exe 2C 6 (5E 64)
WOODBRIDGE 1B 172
Woodbrook Rd. TQ9: Tot 6G 103
Woodburn Cl. PL21: Ivy 4F 145
WOODBURY 5C 78 (2A 172)
Woodbury Castle 2A 172
Woodbury Ct. EX8: Exmth 6E 76
Woodbury Gdns. PL5: Plym 7F 131
Woodbury La. EX13: Axmin 5H 89
Woodbury Pk. EX13: Axmin 5G 89
Woodbury Rd.
EX3: Clyst G . . . . .6H 73 & 7H 73
EX5: Wood 4A 78
WOODBURY SALTERTON
. . . . .1C 78 (2A 172)
Woodbury Vw. EX2: Exe 3D 70
EX5: Broadc 6C 52
Woodbury Wlk. *EX6: Exmin 1B 74*
(off Devington Pk.)
Woodbury Way EX13: Axmin 5H 89
Woodchurch PL20: C'stone 5C 126
Wood Cl. EX6: Chri 3K 63
Woodcote Ct. *EX5: Wood 5C 78*
(off Culvery Cl.)
Woodcourt Rd. TQ9: H'ford 7A 100
Woodcroft PL20: C'stone 6C 126
Woodend Rd. PL6: Plym 3E 132
TQ1: Torq 2F 117
Woodfield Cl. EX8: Exmth 2G 77
Woodfield Ct. TQ1: Torq 3F 117
Woodfield Cres. PL21: Ivy 5J 145
Woodfields EX12: Seat 3E 86
WOODFORD
Blackawton 3A 152 (2D 175)
Morwenstow 2A 162
Plymouth 5J 137 (2B 174)
Woodford Av. PL7: Plymp 5H 137
Woodford Cl. PL7: Plymp 4H 137
Woodford Cres. PL7: Plymp 5H 137
Woodford Gdns. EX32: Barn 7H 19
Woodford Grn. PL7: Plymp 5J 137
Woodford Rd. PL6: Plym 4E 132
Woodhaye Cl. TQ10: S Bre 2B 100
Woodhayes La. EX5: Whim 7H 53
Woodhey Rd. PL2: Plym 4F 135
WOODHILL 1D 167
Woodhill Vw. EX14: Hon 6E 54
Woodhouse Cl. TQ7: Kingsb 5F 157
Woodhouse La. DT7: Uply 3F 91
WOODHUISH 2B 176
WOODLAND 1D 175
Woodland Av. PL9: Plyms 4H 143
TQ12: Kingsk 7J 109
TQ14: Teignm 2K 107
Woodland Bus. Pk. TQ2: Torq 5A 112
Woodland Cl. EX16: Bam 3G 33
EX32: Barn 5K 19
PL21: Ivy 4F 145
TQ2: Torq 5A 112
TQ12: Den 2G 101
Woodland Ct. *EX32: Barn 5F 19*
(off Summerland St.)
PL21: Ivy 4E 144
Woodland Dr. PL7: Plymp 7J 137
PL8: Brixt 2J 149
Woodland Gdns.
TQ14: Teignm 4J 107
(off Lwr. Brimley Rd.)
WOODLAND HEAD 1B 170
Woodland M. *EX5: Broadc 6D 52*
(off Woodland Rd.)
Woodland Pk. EX39: N'ham 1F 23
TQ3: Paig 7H 115
Woodland Rd. EX1: Pin 5C 66
EX5: Broadc 6C 52
PL7: Plymp 5K 137
PL21: Ivy 4D 144
(not continuous)
TQ2: Torq 5A 112
Woodland Rd. TQ9: H'ford 6B 100
TQ12: Den 2G 101
TQ13: Ashb 4H 99
Woodlands EX5: New C 7C 50
EX9: Bud S 7A 82
EX10: Sidm 6B 84
EX34: Com M 2E 12
PL9: Plyms 6G 143
PL20: Dous 4K 127
TQ7: Chur 1B 156
TQ12: Kingst 1G 105
Woodlands Caravan Pk.
TQ9: Blacka 1D 152
Woodlands Cl. EX33: Know 1K 15
TQ7: Chur 1B 156
TQ14: Teignm 4J 107
Woodlands Copse TQ12: Kingst . . .1G 105
Woodlands Ct. EX8: Exmth 1D 76
PL5: Plym 7F 131
Woodlands Dr. EX8: Exmth 1D 76
Woodlands End PL6: Plym 5E 132
Woodlands Gdns. TQ12: New A 2J 109
Woodlands La. PL6: Plym 2G 137
Woodlands Leisure Pk. 1D 152
Woodlands Rd. TQ12: New A 2J 109
Woodlands Wlk. TQ13: Bov T 7B 92
Woodlands Way EX5: Clyst M 2J 73
Woodland Ter. *EX39: Bide 3F 23*
(off North Rd.)
PL4: Plym 2H 9 (1A 142)
PL21: Ivy 5F 145
TQ6: Kingsw 6G 125
Woodland Ter. La.
PL4: Plym 2H 9 (1A 142)
Woodland Vw. EX22: Hols 3C 34
EX35: Lynt 3H 13
Woodland Wood Nature Reserve
. . . . .6G 131
Wood La. EX6: Chri 3J 63
EX8: Exmth 3F 77
EX17: Morc 1B 38
EX34: Com M 7D 12
TQ6: Kingsw 6G 125
TQ7: Slap 2J 159
TQ12: A'well, Two O 6D 108
Woodlark La. EX31: Roun 7K 17
WOODLEIGH 3D 175
Woodleigh Cl. EX4: Exe 1D 64
Woodleigh Pk. TQ14: Shal 7H 107
Woodleigh Rd. TQ12: New A 1C 108
Woodley La. EX5: New C 7A 50
Woodleys Dr. EX10: New P 5F 81
Woodleys Mdw. TQ2: Torq 4A 116
Woodmans Cres. EX14: Hon 4F 55
WOODMANTON 7C 78 (2A 172)
Woodmead Rd. DT7: Lym R 5J 91
EX13: Axmin 4G 89
Woodmere Way TQ12: Kingst 5H 105
Wood Pk. PL6: Plym 7H 133
PL21: Ivy 3H 145
Wood Pk. La. EX34: Berry 4B 12
Woodpark La. TQ3: Marl 5E 110
Woodpecker Way EX6: Cher B 2C 62
PL19: Whitc 7K 59
Woodroffe Mdw. DT7: Lym R 4H 91
Woodroffe Vs. DT7: Lym R 4H 91
Woods, The TQ1: Torq 2G 117
Woodside PL4: Plym 2J 9 (1A 142)
Woodside Av. PL9: Hooe 6D 142
Woodside Cl. EX13: Ray H 1D 90
PL21: Ivy 5H 145
Woodside Ct. EX31: Roun 7A 18
EX35: Lynm 2J 13
PL7: Plymp 5A 138
Woodside Dr. TQ1: Torq 2E 116
Woodside La. PL4: Plym 2J 9 (1A 142)
Woodside Ter. PL20: C'stone 6C 126
Woodside Wlk. *EX14: Hon 3G 55*
(off Langford Av.)
Woods La. EX5: Up E 1E 50
Woods Pasture EX5: Cranb 3C 68
Woodstock Gdns. PL5: Plym 2C 134
Woodstock Rd. EX2: Won 7K 65
WOODTOWN
Buckland Brewer 1C 163
East-the-Water 1C 163
Woodvale Ct. *TQ12: New A 1E 108*
(off East St.)
Wood Vw. TQ12: New A 1D 108
Woodview Pk. PL9: Elb 6H 143
Woodview Rd. TQ4: Paig 6E 118
Wood Vw. Ter. PL21: Erm 3H 147
Woodville EX31: Barn 5B 18
Woodville Av. PL20: Prin 6C 60
Woodville Cl. EX31: Barn 5B 18
PL2: Plym 4E 134
Woodville Rd. EX2: Exe 2E 70
EX8: Exmth 4C 76
PL2: Plym 5E 134
TQ1: Torq 7D 112
Woodward Rd. EX16: Tiv 6B 40
Woodwater La. EX2: Won 1K 71

Woodway PL9: Plyms 5H **143**
Woodway Cl. TQ14: Teignm 2J **107**
Woodway Dr. TQ14: Teignm 3J **107**
Woodway Rd. TQ14: Teignm 2J **107**
Woodway St. TQ13: Chud 1C **94**
WOODY BAY 2C **161**
Woody La. EX35: Lynt 4J **13**
WOOLACOMBE 6A **10** (2A **160**)
Woolacombe & Mortehoe Golf Course
. . . . .3C **10**
Woolacombe Bay Holiday Village
EX34: Woolc 5C **10**
Woolacombe Ct. EX34: Woolc 6B **10**
Woolacombe Down 2A **160**
Woolacombe Ri. EX34: Woolc 6D **10**
Woolacombe Rd. PL20: Bere A 2D **128**
Woolacombe Sands Holiday Pk.
EX34: Woolc 6C **10**
Woolacombe Sta. Rd.
EX34: Woolc 6D **10**
Woolaway Av. EX6: Exmin 2D **74**
Woolbarn Lawn EX32: Barn 5J **19**
Woolbrook Cl. EX10: Sidm 4B **84**
Woolbrook Mead EX10: Sidm 3A **84**
Woolbrook Mdws. EX10: Sidm 3B **84**
Woolbrook Pk. EX10: Sidm 3B **84**
Woolbrook Ri. EX10: Sidm 3B **84**
Woolbrook Rd. EX10: Sidm, Stow . . .2A **84**
Woolcombe La. EX10: Sidm 5C **84**
PL21: Ivy 5H **145**
WOOLCOTTS 1D **165**
Woolcott Way EX15: Cull 5G **45**
WOOLFARDISWORTHY
Bideford 2B **28** (1B **162**)
Crediton 3C **165**
Woolhanger's La. EX34: Berry 4D **12**
Woollcombe Av. PL7: Plymp 5C **138**
WOOLLEY 2A **162**
WOOLMINSTONE 3D **167**
Woolms Mdw. PL21: Ivy 5F **9**
WOOLSERY 2B **28** (1B **162**)
Woolsery Av. EX4: Whip 4A **66**
Woolsery Cl. EX4: Whip 4A **66**
Woolsery Gro. EX4: Whip 4K **65**
Woolster Ct. PL4: Plym 5F **9**
WOOLSTON 3D **175**
WOOLSTON GREEN 3D **175**
WOOLWELL 2E **132** (1B **174**)
Woolwell Cres. PL6: Plym 2D **132**
Woolwell Dr. PL6: Plym 3D **132**
Woolwell Rd. PL6: Plym 3D **132**
Woolwell Shop. Cen. PL6: Plym 2E **132**
WOOTTON FITZPAINE 1D **173**
Worcester Cres. EX15: Will 4D **44**
Wordland Cross EX17: Cher F 3J **39**
Wordsworth Av. EX31: Barn 2E **18**
Wordsworth Cl. EX8: Exmth 7K **75**
TQ2: Torq 7A **112**
Wordsworth Cres. PL2: Plym 4E **134**
Wordsworth Rd. PL2: Plym 4E **134**
Works, The EX16: Tiv 4C **40**
World of Country Life, The 6J **77**
Worthele Cl. PL21: Ivy 4E **144**
Worth Rd. EX34: Ilfra 3J **11**
WOTTER 1F **129** (1B **174**)
Wotton Cotts. EX4: Pin 2B **66**
Wotton La. EX8: Lymp 6J **75**
WRAFTON 6K **15** (3A **160**)
Wrafton Rd. EX33: Brau, Wraf 5J **15**
WRANGATON 1E **146**

Wrangaton Golf Course 1D **146**
Wrangaton La. TQ10: Wran 2D **146**
Wrangaton Rd. PL21: Bitta 3C **146**
WRANGWAY 2B **166**
WRANTAGE 1D **167**
Wreford's Cl. EX4: Exe 1C **64**
Wreford's Dr. EX4: Exe 1D **64**
Wreford's La. EX4: Exe 1C **64**
Wreford's Link EX4: Exe 1D **64**
(not continuous)
Wren Cl. EX14: Hon 5E **54**
EX39: N'ham 6F **21**
Wren Ct. TQ5: Brixh 4E **122**
Wren Gdns. PL7: Plymp 5K **137**
Wren Hill TQ5: Brixh 4E **122**
Wren Pk. TQ2: Torq 3K **111**
Wrens Ga. PL9: Plyms 4F **143**
Wrentham Est. EX4: Exe 4G **65**
Wressing Vw. EX15: Kent 6A **46**
Wrey Av. EX31: Barn 5C **18**
WREYLAND 6J **63** (2B **170**)
Wright Cl. PL1: Dev 1D **140**
Wright Dr. EX17: Cop 6C **38**
Wrights La. PL8: New F 5H **149**
TQ1: Torq 6C **112**
Wrigwell La. TQ12: Ipp 7J **101**
Wrinkleberry La. EX39: High C 6G **27**
Wroxall Grange TQ1: Torq 2E **116**
(off Grafton Rd.)
Wulphere Cl. EX14: Dunk 7G **47**
Wyatts La. PL19: Tavi 3H **59**
Wychall Orchard EX12: Seat 4E **86**
Wychall Pk. EX12: Seat 3D **86**
Wychwood Cl. EX7: Daw 3H **97**
Wycliffe Rd. PL3: Plym 7C **136**
Wye Gdns. PL3: Plym 4E **136**
WYKE 1C **171**
WYKE GREEN 7H **89**
Wykeham Dr. PL2: Plym 4E **134**
Wyke La. EX13: Wyke G 7H **89**
Wyke Rd. EX13: Axmin, Wyke G . . .6H **89**
Wykes Rd. EX1: Heav 5J **65**
Wymering Ct. TQ14: Teignm 2J **107**
Wynards EX2: Exe 5F **7**
Wynards Cl. EX9: E Bud 1D **82**
Wynards La. EX2: Exe 5F **7** (7F **65**)
Wynards Rd. EX9: E Bud 1D **82**
Wyndham Av. EX1: Heav 6J **65**
Wyndham La. PL1: Plym . . .3A **8** (2G **141**)
Wyndham M. PL1: Plym 3A **8**
Wyndham Pl. PL1: Plym 3A **8**
Wyndham Rd. EX5: Silv 2D **82**
Wyndham Sq. PL1: Plym . . .3A **8** (2G **141**)
Wyndham St. E.
PL1: Plym 3B **8** (2H **141**)
Wyndham St. W.
PL1: Plym 3A **8** (2G **141**)
Wyndthorpe Gdns. EX34: Ilfra 2J **11**
(off Castle Hill)
Wynford Rd. EX4: Exe 3J **65**
Wyoming Cl. PL3: Plym 5D **136**
Wyre Cl. TQ4: Paig 5G **119**
Wythburn Gdns. PL6: Plym 7E **132**

Y

Yalberton Ind. Est. TQ4: Paig 4D **118**
(not continuous)
Yalberton Rd. TQ4: Paig 4C **118**

Yalberton Tor Ind. Est.
TQ4: Paig 4D **118**
Yallop Way EX14: Hon 5E **54**
Yannon Dr. TQ14: Teignm 3G **107**
Yannon La. TQ12: Kingsk 7H **109**
(not continuous)
Yannons, The TQ14: Teignm 3H **107**
Yannon Ter. TQ14: Teignm 3H **107**
YARCOMBE 3C **167**
Yarda Wlk. PL8: Brixt 3H **149**
(off Steer Point Rd.)
Yarde Cl. EX10: Sidm 3C **84**
Yarde Hill Orchard
EX10: Sidm 3C **84**
Yardelands EX10: Sidm 3C **84**
Yardelands Cl. EX10: Sidm 3C **84**
Yarde Mead EX10: Sidm 3C **84**
Yardley Gdns. PL6: Plym 7F **133**
Yards La. TQ5: Brixh 7D **122**
YARNACOTT 1H **25**
YARNSCOMBE 1D **163**
Yarrow Mead PL9: Elb 7K **143**
YAWL 1D **173**
Yawl Hill La. DT7: Uply 4C **90**
YEALMBRIDGE 1D **150**
Yealmbury Hill PL8: Yeal 2B **150**
Yealmbury Vs. PL8: Yeal 2B **150**
Yealm Gro. TQ2: Torq 6J **111**
Yealm Pk. PL8: Yeal 2A **150**
Yealmpstone Cl.
PL7: Plymp 5D **138**
Yealmpstone Dr. PL7: Plymp 5E **138**
YEALMPTON 2B **150** (2B **174**)
Yealm Rd. PL8: New F 5G **149**
Yealm Vw. Rd. PL8: New F 6J **149**
Yeats Cl. PL5: Plym 1H **135**
Yellaford Way EX31: Bick'n 6A **18**
YELLAND 7B **16** (3A **160**)
Yelland Rd.
EX31: Frem, Yell 5E **16**
YELVERTON 6G **127** (1B **174**)
Yelverton Bus. Pk.
PL20: C'stone 6D **126**
Yelverton Cl. PL5: Plym 7D **130**
Yelverton Golf Driving Range 7C **126**
Yelverton Paperweight Cen. 6F **127**
Yelverton Ter. PL19: Tavi 3K **59**
PL20: Yelv 6G **127**
(off Meavy La.)
Yeo Cl. PL3: Plym 6D **136**
Yeo Dr. EX39: Apple 3H **21**
YEOFORD .1B **170**
Yeoford Way EX2: Mar B 5G **71**
Yeoland La. EX32: Swim 2H **25**
Yeolands, The
TQ9: Sto G 3B **120**
Yeo La. EX20: N Taw 4A **36**
Yeolland La. PL21: Ivy 4H **145**
Yeolland Pk. PL21: Ivy 4H **145**
YEOLMBRIDGE 2B **168**
Yeomans Way PL7: Plymp 5D **138**
YEO MILL .1C **165**
Yeo Pk. PL8: Yeal 1D **150**
Yeo Rd. EX31: Chive 1E **16**
Yeo Vale Cross Ind. Est.
EX17: Lap 3J **37**
Yeo Vale Rd. EX32: Barn 3E **18**
Yerris Rd. EX15: Kent 7A **46**
YETTINGTON 2A **172**
Yettington Rd. EX9: E Bud 1C **82**

Yew Cl. EX14: Hon 5C **54**
TQ5: Brixh 6B **122**
Yewdale Gdns. PL6: Plym 1E **136**
Yews, The PL6: Robo 1D **132**
Yew Tree Cl. EX4: Exe 3H **65**
EX8: Exmth 1E **76**
Yew Tree Dr. TQ12: Kingst 5H **105**
Yolhey La. TQ12: A'well 7F **109**
Yonder Cl. EX11: Ott M 4D **80**
Yonder Cnr. EX11: Ott M 4D **80**
(off Chapel La.)
Yonder Mdw. TQ9: Sto G 3B **120**
Yonder Mt. EX13: Mus 7D **90**
Yonder St. EX11: Ott M 4D **80**
PL9: Hooe 6C **142**
YONDERTOWN 7F **129**
Yon St. TQ12: Kingsk 1F **111**
York Cl. EX8: Exmth 2G **77**
EX13: Axmin 3J **89**
EX14: Fen 2G **53**
York Cres. EX14: Fen 2G **53**
TQ1: Torq 5E **112**
Yorke Rd. TQ6: Dartm 7D **124**
York Gdns. TQ4: Paig 3H **119**
York Ho. EX4: Exe 1F **7** (5F **65**)
York Pl. EX15: Cull 2H **45**
EX39: Bide 2F **23**
PL2: Dev 7E **134**
York Rd. EX4: Exe 1F **7** (5F **65**)
EX12: Seat 5E **86**
PL5: Plym 3D **134**
PL11: Torp 1A **140**
TQ1: Torq 5E **112**
TQ4: Paig 3G **119**
York St. EX10: Sidm 7C **84**
(not continuous)
PL1: Dev 2D **140**
York Ter. EX4: Exe 1G **7** (5G **65**)
PL2: Plym 6E **134**
York Vs. TQ1: Torq 5E **112**
(off Babbacombe Rd.)
Youings Dr. EX31: Barn 1F **19**
Youldons Cl. TQ9: H'ford 6C **100**
Youldon Way PL20: Horr 3E **126**
Youngaton Rd.
EX39: West H 5B **20**
Younghayes Rd. EX5: Cranb 4B **68**
Young's Pk. La. TQ4: Good 3J **119**
Young's Pk. Rd. TQ4: Good 3J **119**

Z

ZEAL MONACHORUM 3B **164**
Zeal Rd. EX6: Dunsf 5C **62**
Zephyr Cres. EX32: Barn 4G **19**
Zeth Hill La. PL21: Ivy 2D **144**
Zig Zag Path
EX9: Bud S 7B **82**
Zion Pl. PL21: Ivy 4G **145**
TQ6: Dartm 1A **124** (5F **125**)
Zion Rd. TQ2: Torq 1B **116**
Zion's Pl. EX32: Barn 5E **18**
(off Litchdon St.)
Zion St. PL1: Plym 6E **8** (3J **141**)

HOSPITALS, HOSPICES and selected HEALTHCARE FACILITIES covered by this atlas.

N.B. Where it is not possible to name these facilities on the map,
the reference given is for the road in which they are situated.

ASHBURTON & BUCKFASTLEIGH COMMUNITY HOSPITAL
....3J **99**
9-15 Eastern Road
Ashburton
NEWTON ABBOT
TQ13 7AP
Tel: 01364 652203

AXMINSTER HOSPITAL 3H **89**
Chard Road
AXMINSTER
EX13 5DU
Tel: 01297 630400

BIDEFORD COMMUNITY HOSPITAL 3E **22**
Abbotsham Road
BIDEFORD
EX39 3AG
Tel: 01271 322577

BOVEY TRACEY HOSPITAL 3C **92**
Furzeleigh Lane
Bovey Tracey
NEWTON ABBOT
TQ13 9HJ
Tel: 01626 832279

BRIXHAM HOSPITAL 5E **122**
Greenswood Road
BRIXHAM
TQ5 9HW
Tel: 01803 881399

BRUNEL LODGE 3D **108**
Old Totnes Road
NEWTON ABBOT
TQ12 6AA
Tel: 01626 356101

BUDLEIGH SALTERTON HOSPITAL 6D **82**
East Budleigh Road
BUDLEIGH SALTERTON
EX9 6HF
Tel: 01395 442020

CHILDREN'S HOSPICE S.W. LITTLE BRIDGE HOUSE
....6G **17**
Redlands Road
Fremington
BARNSTAPLE
EX31 2PZ
Tel: 01271 325270

CREDITON HOSPITAL 6F **39**
Western Road
CREDITON
EX17 3NH
Tel: 01363 775588

CUMBERLAND CENTRE 3E **140**
Damerel Close
PLYMOUTH
PL1 4JZ
Tel: 0845 155 8003

DARTMOUTH & KINGSWEAR HOSPITAL
.................................2B **124** (6F **125**)
Mansion House Street
DARTMOUTH
TQ6 9BD
Tel: 01803 832255

DAWLISH COMMUNITY HOSPITAL 4G **97**
Barton Terrace
DAWLISH
EX7 9DH
Tel: 01626 868500

DERRIFORD HOSPITAL 6C **132**
Derriford Road
PLYMOUTH
PL6 8DH
Tel: 0845 1558155

EXETER COMMUNITY HOSPITAL (WHIPTON) 5B **66**
Hospital Lane
EXETER
EX1 3RB
Tel: 01392 208333

EXETER NUFFIELD HEALTH HOSPITAL 1H **71**
Wonford Road
EXETER
EX2 4UG
Tel: 01392 262110

EXMOUTH HOSPITAL 5D **76**
Claremont Grove
EXMOUTH
EX8 2JN
Tel: 01395 279684

FRANKLYN HOSPITAL 2C **70**
Franklyn Drive
EXETER
EX2 9HS
Tel: 01392 208400

GLENBOURNE UNIT 7C **132**
Morlaix Drive
Derriford
PLYMOUTH
PL6 5AF
Tel: 08451 558 018

HOLSWORTHY HOSPITAL 1D **34**
Dobles Lane
HOLSWORTHY
EX22 6JQ
Tel: 01409 253424

HONITON HOSPITAL 4F **55**
Marlpits Lane
HONITON
EX14 2DE
Tel: 01404 540540

HOSPISCARE 7K **7** (1J **71**)
Dryden Road
EXETER
EX2 5JJ
Tel: 01392 688000

ILFRACOMBE & DISTRICT TYRRELL HOSPITAL ...3H **11**
St Brannock's Park Road
ILFRACOMBE
EX34 8JF
Tel: 01271 863448

LANGDON HOSPITAL 7B **96**
Exeter Road
DAWLISH
EX7 0NR
Tel: 01626 888372

LEE MILL UNIT 4B **144**
Beech Road
IVYBRIDGE
PL21 9HL
Tel: 01752 314800

LYNTON RESOURCE CENTRE 2G **13**
Lee Road
LYNTON
EX35 6BP
Tel: 01598 753226

MORETONHAMPSTEAD HOSPITAL 6H **61**
Ford Street
Moretonhampstead
NEWTON ABBOT
TQ13 8LN
Tel: 01647 440217

MOUNT GOULD HOSPITAL 1C **142**
Mount Gould Road
PLYMOUTH
PL4 7QD
Tel: 01752 268011

MOUNT STUART PRIVATE HOSPITAL 6B **112**
St Vincent's Road
TORQUAY
TQ1 4UP
Tel: 01803 313881

NEWTON ABBOT COMMUNITY HOSPITAL 6E **104**
West Golds Road
NEWTON ABBOT
TQ12 2TS
Tel: 01626 324500

NHS WALK-IN CENTRE (EXETER- SIDWELL STREET)
....3F **7**
Unit 4
31 Sidwell Street
EXETER
EX4 6NN
Tel: 01392 276892

NHS WALK-IN CENTRE (EXETER- WONFORD) 1J **71**
Within Royal Devon & Exeter Hospital
Barrack Road
EXETER
EX2 5DW
Tel: 01392 406304

NORTH DEVON DISTRICT HOSPITAL 2G **19**
Raleigh Park
BARNSTAPLE
EX31 4JB
Tel: 01271 322577

NORTH DEVON HOSPICE 7G **19**
Deer Park Road
Barnstaple
BARNSTAPLE
EX32 0HU
Tel: 01271 344248

OKEHAMPTON COMMUNITY HOSPITAL 3C **48**
Cavell Way
OKEHAMPTON
EX20 1PN
Tel: 01837 658000

OTTERY ST MARY HOSPITAL 4A **80**
Keegan Close
OTTERY ST. MARY
EX11 1DN
Tel: 01404 816000

PAIGNTON HOSPITAL 1H **119**
Church Street
PAIGNTON
TQ3 3AG
Tel: 01803 557425

PENINSULA NHS TREATMENT CENTRE 7C **132**
20 Brest Road
PLYMOUTH
PL6 5XP
Tel: 01752 506070

PLYMOUTH NUFFIELD HEALTH HOSPITAL 6C **132**
Derriford Road
PLYMOUTH
PL6 8BG
Tel: 01752 548823

ROWCROFT HOSPICE 7A **112**
Avenue Road
TORQUAY
TQ2 5LS
Tel: 01803 210800

ROYAL DEVON & EXETER HOSPITAL (HEAVITREE)
.............................4J **7** (6H **65**)
Gladstone Road
EXETER
EX1 2ED
Tel: 01392 411611

ROYAL DEVON & EXETER HOSPITAL (WONFORD)
.............................7K **7** (1J **71**)
Barrack Road
EXETER
EX2 5DW
Tel: 01392 411611

ROYAL EYE INFIRMARY 1F **9** (7K **135**)
Apsley Road
PLYMOUTH
PL4 6PL
Tel: 0845 1558094

ST LUKE'S HOSPICE PLYMOUTH 6B **142**
Stamford Road
PLYMOUTH
PL9 9XA
Tel: 01752 401172

SCOTT HOSPITAL, PLYMOUTH
CHILD DEVELOPMENT CENTRE 5F **135**
Scott Business Park, Beacon Park Road
PLYMOUTH
PL2 2PQ
Tel: 0845 1558174

SEATON & DISTRICT COMMUNITY HOSPITAL
...............................4E **86**
Valley View
SEATON
EX12 2UU
Tel: 01297 23901

SIDMOUTH VICTORIA HOSPITAL 6B **84**
All Saint's Road
SIDMOUTH
EX10 8EW
Tel: 01395 512482

SOUTH HAMS HOSPITAL 3F **157**
Plymouth Road
KINGSBRIDGE
TQ7 1AT
Tel: 01548 852349

SOUTH MOLTON COMMUNITY HOSPITAL
...............................6C **26**
Widgery Drive
SOUTH MOLTON
EX36 4DP
Tel: 01769 572164

TAVISTOCK HOSPITAL 4H **59**
Spring Hill
TAVISTOCK
PL19 8LD
Tel: 01822 612233

TEIGNMOUTH HOSPITAL 4G **107**
Mill Lane
TEIGNMOUTH
TQ14 9BQ
Tel: 01626 772161

TIVERTON & DISTRICT HOSPITAL 3C **40**
Kennedy Way
TIVERTON
EX16 6NT
Tel: 01884 235400

TORBAY HOSPITAL 5K **111**
Newton Road
TORQUAY
TQ2 7AA
Tel: 01803 614567

TORBAY HOSPITAL (ANNEXE) 4K **111**
Newton Road
TORQUAY
TQ2 7BA
Tel: 01803 614567

TORRINGTON COMMUNITY HOSPITAL 2C **30**
Calf Street
TORRINGTON
EX38 7BJ
Tel: 01805 622208

TOTNES COMMUNITY HOSPITAL 5E **102**
Coronation Road
TOTNES
TQ9 5GH
Tel: 01803 862622

WONFORD HOUSE HOSPITAL 1J **71**
Dryden Road
EXETER
EX2 5AF
Tel: 01392 208866

The representation on the maps of a road, track or footpath is no evidence of the existence of a right of way.

The Grid on this map is the National Grid taken from Ordnance Survey® mapping with the permission of the Controller of Her Majesty's Stationery Office.

Copyright of Geographers' A-Z Map Company Ltd.

SAFETY CAMERA INFORMATION

PocketGPSWorld.com's CamerAlert is a self-contained speed and red light camera warning system for SatNavs and Android or Apple iOS smartphones/tablets. Visit www.cameralert.co.uk to download.

Safety camera locations are publicised by the Safer Roads Partnership which operates them in order to encourage drivers to comply with speed limits at these sites. It is the driver's absolute responsibility to be aware of and to adhere to speed limits at all times.

By showing this safety camera information it is the intention of Geographers' A-Z Map Company Ltd., to encourage safe driving and greater awareness of speed limits and vehicle speed. Data accurate at time of printing.

Printed and bound in the United Kingdom by Polestar Wheatons Ltd., Exeter